INTRODUCTION TO

MANAGEMENT SCIENCE

WITH SPREADSHEETS

CANADIAN EDITION

William J. Stevenson
Rochester Institute of Technology

Ceyhun Ozgur
Valparaiso University

Aaron L. Nsakanda
Carleton University

Toronto Montréal Boston Burr Ridge, IL Dubuque, IA Madison, WI New York
San Francisco St. Louis Bangkok Bogotá Caracas Kuala Lumpur Lisbon London
Madrid Mexico City Milan New Delhi Santiago Seoul Singapore Sydney Taipei

The McGraw·Hill Companies

Introduction to Management Science with Spreadsheets
Canadian Edition

ISBN-13: 978-0-07-081380-9
ISBN-10: 0-07-081380-9

1 2 3 4 5 6 7 8 9 10 TCP 0 9

Printed and bound in Canada

Vice-President and Editor-in-Chief: *Joanna Cotton*
Sponsoring Editor: *Kim Redhead*
Executive Marketing Manager: *Joy Armitage Taylor*
iLearning Sales Specialist: *Jeremy Guimond*
Managing Editor, Development: *Kelly Dickson*
Editorial Associate: *Stephanie Hess*
Permissions Editor: *Shelley Wickabrod*
Manager, Editorial Services: *Margaret Henderson*
Supervising Editor: *Cathy Biribauer*
Copy Editor: *Cat Haggert*
Team Lead, Production: *Paula Brown*
Inside Design: *Greg Devitt Design*
Compositor: *Laserwords Private Limited*
Cover Design: *Greg Devitt Design*
Cover Photos: *Michael Rosenfeld/Photographer's Choice/Getty and Salih Guler/iStockphoto*
Printer: *Transcontinental Printing Group*

Library and Archives Canada Cataloguing in Publication Data

Stevenson, William J.
Introduction to management science with spreadsheets / William J. Stevenson, Ceyhun Ozgur, Aaron Nsakanda. — 1st Canadian ed.
Includes index.
ISBN 978-0-07-081380-9
1. Management science—Textbooks. I. Ozgur, Ceyhun II. Nsakanda, Aaron Luntala III. Title.
T56.S74 2009 658 C2008-907248-0

Dedication

To Linda ALN, Ann Marie and John
WJS

To Jan Ozgur
CO

To my late father Gaston Tadibote Nsakanda,
for his unconditional love and the invaluable seeds
implanted during my childhood and beyond.
ALN

About the Authors

William J. Stevenson is an associate professor of Decision Sciences in the College of Business at Rochester Institute of Technology. He teaches graduate and undergraduate courses in operations management and management science. Dr. Stevenson is the author of textbooks in management science, statistics, and operations managment. His articles have appeared in *Management Science, Decision Sciences, Quality Progress,* and other journals. He received a bachelor's degree in industrial engineering, an MBA, and a PHD in production/operations management, from Syracuse University.

Ceyhun Ozgur, CPIM, is a professor of information and decision sciences in the College of Business Administration at Valparaiso University. He earned a BS in Industrial Management and a MS in Management from the University of Akron and a PhD in business administration (Operations Management/Operations Research) from Kent State University. Among others, Dr. Ozgur has published in *Decision Sciences Journal of Innovative Education, Interfaces, OMEGA, Quality Management Journal, Mid-American Journal of Business, Production Planning and Control, International Journal of Operations and Quantitative Management, International Journal of Quality and Reliability Management, International Journal of Business Disciplines, Industrial Mathematics and Teaching Statistics.* He has written study guides, test banks and instructors' manuals for business statistics, operations management and managment science textbooks. He is a member of the Decision Sciences Institute, INFORMS and APICS and serves as a member of the editorial review board for *Decision Sciences Journal of Innovative Education and International Journal of Operations and Quantitative Management.*

Aaron L. Nsakanda is Associate Professor of Management Science and Operations Management at the Sprott School of Business, Carleton University. He received a BS in Forest Engineering, an MBA in Operations Management, and a PhD in Management Science, all degrees from Laval University. His research interests are in the areas of modelling and analysis of advanced manufacturing systems, operations management in the airline industry, modelling and analysis of loyalty/incentive programs, global supply chain management in the digital economy, and pricing and revenue management. Over the years, he has taught courses on topics such as business forecasting, management science, simulation, and supply chain management. Before joining Carleton University, Dr. Nsakanda worked as a Senior Operations Research Consultant in the airline industry. He worked extensively in various projects involving the application of management science techniques to a wide range of practical problems, such as cargo operations, airport resources management, manpower planning and scheduling, and loyalty program management. His papers have appeared in various journals, including the *European Journal of Operational Research,* the *Journal of the Operational Research Society,* and the *International Journal of Production Research.* Dr. Nsakanda's research has been funded by the Canadian National Science and Engineering Research Council (NSERC). He is a member of the following professional societies: the Institute for Operations Research and the Management Sciences (INFORMS) and the Canadian Operations Research Society (CORS).

Contents in Brief

Contents

The following chapters can be found on the text OLC at www.mcgrawhill.ca/olc/stevensonmgmtsci:

Answers to Most Odd-Numbered Problems can be found on the text OLC at www.mcgrawhill.ca/olc/stevensonmgmtsci.

Preface

The material covered in the first Canadian edition of *Introduction to Management Science with Spreadsheets* is intended as an introduction to the field of management science. The subject matter covers the mainstream management science topics, along with the many practical applications of management science concepts in accordance with the Canadian perspective. We include discussion and explanation of the concepts, formulation of problems, and their associated manual and spreadsheet solutions. We have incorporated Canadian and international content in examples, case studies, real-world applications, end-of-chapter problems, and review questions. Vignettes have been added to illustrate the successful implementation of some of the management science techniques by a number of Canadian organizations to improve performance and results. We have provided a sample of Canadian-based management science solution providers. The goal of the first Canadian edition is to engage students and emphasize the relevance and importance of Management Science.

The book describes both manual and computer solutions for a variety of management science tools. The purpose of manual solutions is to foster a conceptual understanding of each technique while presenting computer solutions to provide a practical approach to solving real-world problems. The key areas of application for each topic are described, and appropriate techniques are explained in simple terms, with step-by-step procedures for both manual and computer solutions. There are ample discussions of how to interpret solutions.

Every effort has been made to develop a textbook that is readable and interesting. The writing style is light and informal and assumes that readers have no prior knowledge of the subject matter. The concepts are developed in a logical format, usually beginning with an overview so that readers can immediately see what the discussion will be. Explanations are clear and simple and often intuitive and examples are sprinkled liberally throughout the text.

Solved problems are provided at the end of all chapters. Students can use them as a guide for solving the end-of-chapter problems. Answers are given to most odd-numbered problems in an appendix, located on the text's Online Learning Centre.

Prerequisites for being able to understand the material in this book are basic algebra and introductory statistics.

Pedagogical Features

Much attention has been devoted to pedagogy. This book has a number of features designed to enhance learning, including:

1. Every chapter begins with a chapter outline and a list of behavioural objectives. These provide the reader with a topical overview of the chapter and a guide as to what to expect from the chapter. Every chapter includes a summary.
2. There are numerous examples throughout the chapter and a set of solved problems at the end of each chapter that serves as a resource guide for solving problems.
3. The end-of-chapter problems are plentiful, and answers to most odd-numbered problems are located on the text's Online Learning Centre.
4. The writing style is a key feature of this book. It is light and informal and concentrates primarily on key concepts and ideas; it does not spend a lot of time with fine points and minor details. Every effort has been made to present an interesting, readable book.
5. A glossary of key terms is provided at the end of every chapter.

New Features in the Canadian Edition

The first Canadian edition addresses a number of issues raised by Canadian instructors and reviewers, while retaining the best pedagogical material of the U.S. edition. It includes the following enhancements.

New modern management science applications. A total of 28 application vignettes are included in the textbook, including 21 new ones. These applications describe successful applications of management science techniques by mainly Canadian organizations. The vignettes are tied to the material covered in the chapter where they are discussed.

New cases and problems. This edition features a total of 13 new cases and 65 new problems of a higher difficulty level. This brings the total number of cases and problems throughout the textbook to 26 and 442, respectively. Whenever possible, a number of existing problems or cases have been revised to reflect Canadian units of measurement and/or locations.

Additional coverage of methods and models of management science. We have added a new chapter in project management as well as depth to the coverage of applications of linear programming, sensitivity analysis in linear programming, integer programming, distribution and network flow models, decision analysis, and simulation.

A new chapter on Distribution and Network Flow Models is the result of a merger of two chapters. We focus the presentation on problem formulation, solving with Excel Solver, and solution interpretation. Therefore, we have moved all special procedures for solving network models to the Online Learning Center (OLC).

A slight reorganization of the book. The chapter on forecasting has been moved to the Online Learning Centre. To streamline the flow, the order of some chapters (Applications of Linear Programming and Linear Programming: Sensitivity Analysis and Computer Solution Interpretation) has been altered. We have also changed the titles of some chapters to reflect the changes that were carried out. All chapters were reviewed to improve the flow, to eliminate redundancies, and to bring the topics closer to the Canadian experience.

An integration of Excel 2007. All Excel outputs have been updated to be in conformity with Microsoft Excel 2007.

Changes in Individual Chapters

Chapter 1, Introduction to Management Science. The section on "Getting Started with Excel" has been extended to include discussion on spreadsheet engineering. Table 1-2 has been updated to include more Canadian companies. The section on "Break-Even Analysis" has been extended to include "Sensitivity Analysis."

Chapter 2, Linear Programming: Basic Concepts, Graphical Solution, and Computer Solution. We updated the introduction and provided an alternative solution method to solve simultaneous equations (substitution method). We also included a new section on solving LP problems with a spreadsheet, specifically with Excel Solver.

Chapter 3, Linear Programming: Sensitivity Analysis and Computer Solution Interpretation. The section on duality has been deleted. However, a brief discussion has been added to refer to this concept and its importance. The chapter has been expanded to interpret sensitivity analysis from a management perspective. We introduce examples with more than two decision variables and discuss them in the context of the problem formulation process, computer solution with Excel Solver, and managerial interpretation of the optimal solution as well as of the sensitivity analysis information.

Chapter 4, Applications of Linear Programming. We expanded the discussion to include examples and problems on multiple-stage models and multiple-period models (e.g., multi-stage financial planning problems), as well as on sensitivity analysis.

Chapter 5, Distribution and Network Flow Models. Chapters 6 and 8 in the current U.S. edition have been merged into this new chapter. We expanded the various models to include how to handle unbalanced cases. All special algorithms have been moved to the Online Learning Centre, including the section on the minimum spanning tree.

Chapter 6, Integer Programming Methods. We illustrated the types of integer programming problems through an example, expanded the discussion on graphical solution methods for pure-integer IP to illustrate the effect of rounding a solution, and reorganized and expanded the modelling examples to a variety of management applications, taking into account the formulation process.

Chapter 7, Nonlinear Programming. No major changes were made to this chapter other than streamlining the flow of the text.

Chapter 8, Project Scheduling: PERT/CPM. This is a *new chapter in the textbook*. A managerial perspective was taken to address questions such as how to display a project graphically, what types of information are required, what approaches are available to schedule project activities, and how to accelerate a project to meet a targeted completion date.

Chapter 9, Multicriteria Decision-Making Models. No major changes were made to this chapter other than streamlining the flow of the text.

Chapter 10, Decision Analysis. We expanded the topic on computing revised probabilities and utility.

Chapter 11, Markov Analysis. No major changes were made to this chapter other than streamlining the flow of the text.

Chapter 12, Waiting-Line Models. We made the mathematical notation uniform within the chapter. We also moved certain tables to the appendix to facilitate their use.

Chapter 13, Simulation. We reorganized and expanded the modelling examples to the context of management applications and we expanded computer simulation to include simulation using Crystal Ball.

Pedagogical Features

Introduction to Management Science with Spreadsheets, Canadian Edition, offers an introduction to the field of management science using a modern spreadsheet approach. The text presumes a basic background in introductory statistics and some exposure to Excel. The presentation is straightforward and written in a readable, step-by-step procedural style that will help students develop a conceptual understanding of the concepts. The benefit is accessibility for undergraduate students and success in the course.

The Text

Within each chapter, you will find the following elements developed to help organize and facilitate the learning process.

Chapter Learning Objectives

Each chapter includes a list of learning objectives students should be able to attain upon reading and studying the chapter material. This gives students an overview of what is expected and identifies the goals for learning and understanding the material.

Chapter Outline

Each chapter begins with a list of section topics that are covered in the chapter.

Project Scheduling: PERT/CPM

CHAPTER 8

LEARNING OBJECTIVES

After completing this chapter, you should be able to:

1. Describe the role and application of PERT/CPM for project scheduling.
2. Define a project in terms of activities such that a network representation can be developed.
3. Develop a complete project schedule.
4. Compute the critical path, the project completion time and its variance.
5. Convert optimistic, most likely, and pessimistic time estimates into expected activity time estimates.
6. Compute the probability of the project being completed by a specific time.
7. Compute the project completion time given a certain level of probability.
8. Find the least expensive way to shorten the duration of a project to meet a target completion date.
9. Formulate the crashing problem as a linear programming model.
10. Formulate project scheduling as a linear programming model.
11. Know some of the specialised software available in the market for scheduling and tracking project activities.

CHAPTER OUTLINE

Figures, Tables, and Exhibits

In every chapter, there are many visual elements, including charts, graphs, tables, and spreadsheets to illustrate concepts being applied. These visuals help stimulate student interest and clarify the text explanations.

FIGURE 10-1 Decision Tree Format

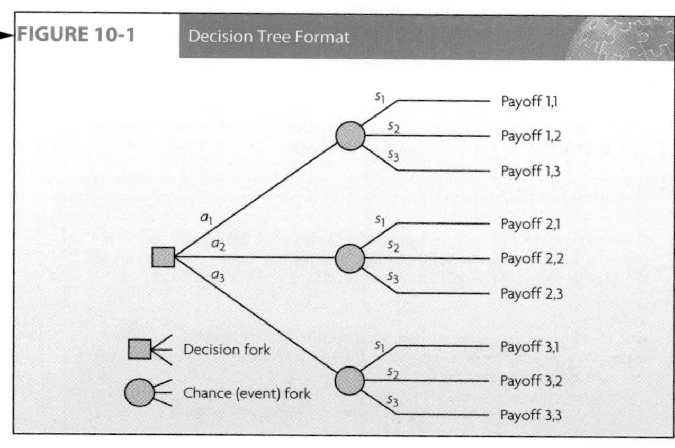

EXHIBIT 10-8 Modified Decision Tree with Three Branches and the Added Event Node with Three Nodes

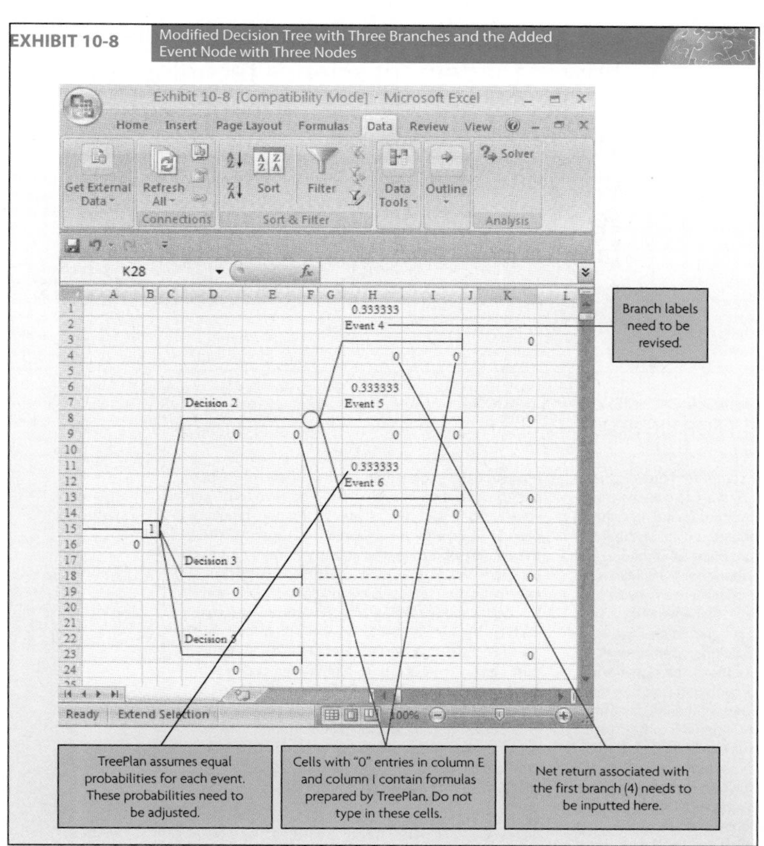

EXAMPLE 3-1

In Chapter 2, the optimal values for the decision variables and the objective function for the server problem were determined. They were

$x_1 = 9$
$x_2 = 4$
$Z = 740$

In this chapter, we just found the range of optimality for each coefficient of the objective function for the server problem. They were

For the x_1 coefficient, 50 to 100
For the x_2 coefficient, 30 to 60

Given this information, analyze the impact of a change in the x_1 coefficient of the objective function from 60 to 82.50. Specifically, what impact will there be on the optimal values of the decision variables and the objective function?

Solution
First, check to see if the new value of the x_1 coefficient is within the range of optimality. We can see that 82.50 is within the range of 50 to 100. Consequently, there will be no change in the optimal values of x_1 and x_2.

However, the optimal value of Z will change. To find its new value, we must substitute the new coefficient into the objective function with the optimal values of the decision variables and solve. Thus:

$Z = 82.50(9) + 50(4) = 942.50$

Examples

Examples use applications to illustrate the concepts in the chapter. Students learn a concept more easily when they are able to walk through the application and the solution.

Management Science Applications

Most chapters include "A Modern Management Science Application," which is a short summary of management science applications. These describe the company issue and how management science techniques were applied to improve performance and results. This feature provides students with an opportunity to learn how management science is applied in companies they are familiar with and how useful it is to have management science knowledge and tools.

A MODERN MANAGEMENT SCIENCE APPLICATION:
BIG BENEFITS FOR BIG BLUE

IBM is the world's largest computer hardware, software, and services company with operations worldwide in more than 164 countries including Canada. IBM Canada Ltd. is headquartered in Markham. It operates a semi-conductor plant in Bromont and software development laboratories in Markham, Ottawa, Montreal, and Victoria. There are a variety of projects undertaken where management science techniques such as linear programming have been successfully applied, providing opportunities to answer "what if . . . ?" questions through the use of sensitivity analysis and computer solution interpretation. One project addresses the needs of managers in semi-conductor manufacturing for a decision support system that would assist in identifying the optimal product mix, optimally allocating products to tools, identifying gating tools, and determining a minimum set of tools required to produce for a given demand. IBM Research developed a linear programming model in which the decision variables represent the production volume of each product and the allocation of each product to each tool. The constraints reflect production limits, the required process steps, and the available tool capacity, while the primary objective is to maximize profit. Another project is aimed at solving the allocation of scarce raw materials and capacity in IBM's supply chain through a multi-echelon bill of materials. The core problem was solved using linear programming and greedy heuristics. A key indicator of the decision support system is its ability to identify the production bottlenecks and to indicate how to fix them. It includes modelling constructs to address multi-plant enterprises, semiconductor planning, and component aggregation, as well as a suite of algorithms that provide sensitivity analysis beyond the standard shadow pricing of linear programming.

Source: B. Dietrich, N. Donofrio, G. Lin, and J. Snowdon. "Big Benefits for Big Blue," *OR/MS Today Vol.* 27, no. 3 (June 2000), pp. 52–56. Reprinted with permission.

Excel Screenshots and Programs

Throughout the text, Excel screenshots are included. Where applicable, dialogue and input boxes are shown. In many cases, the text provides both an Excel screenshot along with a grid listing the specific cells and the formulae and functions used to create that screen.

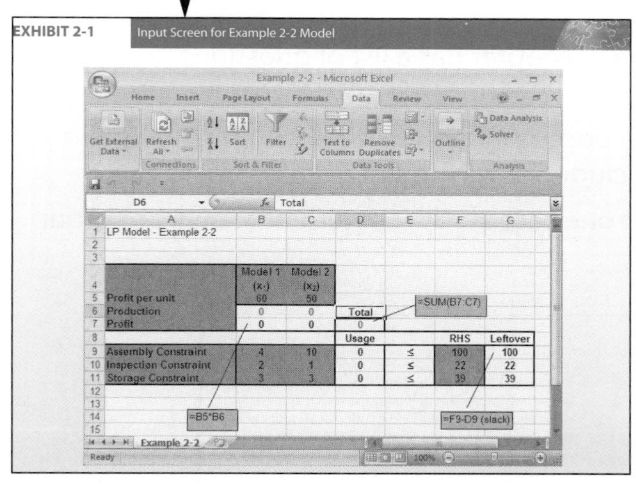

EXHIBIT 2-1 Input Screen for Example 2-2 Model

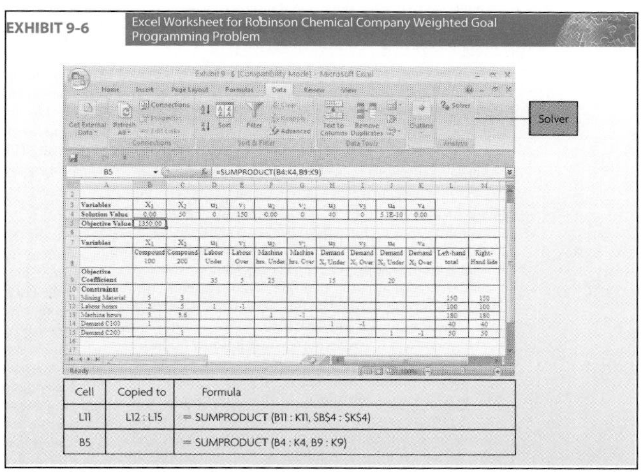

EXHIBIT 9-6 Excel Worksheet for Robinson Chemical Company Weighted Goal Programming Problem

Cell	Copied to	Formula
L11	L12 : L15	= SUMPRODUCT (B11 : K11, $B$4 : $K$4)
B5		= SUMPRODUCT (B4 : K4, B9 : K9)

End-of-Chapter Resources

For student study and review, the following items are included at the end of each chapter.

- **Summary** The summaries provide an overview of the material covered.
- **Glossary** Key terms are highlighted in the text, and are listed and defined at the end of each chapter to aid in reviewing.
- **Solved Problems** A number of representative problems are included with step-by-step solutions, including graphics.
- **Discussion and Review Questions** Each chapter has a list of questions for student self-review or for discussion.
- **Problems** Problems give students an opportunity to test their understanding of the chapter material. Problems are included at the end of each chapter.
- **Cases** Every chapter includes at least one case study for student analysis or group work and discussion in class.

Case 1: Fantasy Products

Company Background

The Fantasy Products Company (disguised name) is a manufacturer of high-quality small appliances intended for home use. Their current product line includes irons, a small hand-held vacuum, and a number of kitchen appliances such as toasters, blenders, waffle irons, and coffeemakers. Fantasy Products has a strong R&D department that continually searches for ways to improve existing products as well as developing new products.

Currently, the R&D department is working on the development of a new kitchen appliance that will chill foods quickly much as a microwave oven heats them quickly, although the technology involved is quite different. Tentatively named The Big Chill, the product will initially carry a price tag of around $125, and the target market consists of upper-income consumers. At this price, it is expected to be a very profitable item. R&D engineers now have a working prototype and are satisfied that, with the cooperation from the production and marketing people, the product can be ready in time for the all-important Christmas buying season. A target date has been set for product introduction that is 24 weeks away.

Current Problem

Fantasy Products' Marketing Vice-President Vera Sloan has recently learned from reliable sources that a competitor is also in the process of developing a similar product, which it intends to bring out at almost the same time. In addition, her source indicated that the competitor plans to sell its product, which will be smaller than The Big Chill, for $99 in the hope of appealing to more customers. Vera, with the help of several of her key people who are to be involved in marketing The Big Chill, has decided that to compete, the selling price for The Big Chill will have to be lowered to within $10 of the competitor's price. At this price level it will still be profitable, although not nearly as profitable as originally anticipated.

However, Vera is wondering whether it would be possible to expedite the usual product introduction process to beat the competition to the market. If possible, she would like to get a six-week jump on the competition; this would put the product introduction date only 18 weeks away. During this initial period, Fantasy Products could sell The Big Chill for $125, reducing the selling price to $109 when the competitor's product actually enters the market. Since forecasts based on market research show that sales during the first six weeks will be about 400 per week, there is an opportunity for $25 per unit profit if the early introduction can be accomplished. In addition, there is a certain amount of prestige involved in being first to the market. This should help enhance The Big Chill's image during the anticipated battle for market share.

Data Collection

Since Fantasy Products has been through the product-introduction process a number of times, Vera has developed a list of the tasks that must be accomplished and the order in which they must be completed. Although the duration and costs vary depending on the particular product, the basic process does not. The list of activities involved and their precedence relationships are presented in Table 8-17. Duration and cost estimates for the introduction of The Big Chill are presented in Table 8-18. Note that some of the activities can be completed on a crash basis, with an associated increase in cost. For example, activity B can be crashed from 8 weeks to 6 weeks at an additional cost of $3000 (i.e., $12 000–$9000). Assume that if B is crashed to 7 weeks, the additional cost will be $1500 (i.e., $3000/2).

Comprehensive Teaching and Learning Package

For Instructors

All of the Instructor supplements described below can be found on the text's password-protected Online Learning Centre at www.mcgrawhill.ca/olc/stevensonmgmtsci.

***Instructor's Solutions Manual* prepared by Aaron L. Nsakanda and Yuheng Cao, Carleton University.** Co-written by the textbook author, the Instructor's Solutions Manual includes detailed solutions to all problems and questions at the end of each chapter.

***Computerized Test Bank* prepared by Ron Craig, Wilfrid Laurier University.** Available for Macintosh or Windows users, the computerized test bank using EZ Test—a flexible and easy-to-use electronic testing program—allows instructors to create tests from book-specific items. EZ Test accommodates a wide range of question types and allows instructors to add their own questions. Test items are also available in Word format (Rich Text Format). For secure online testing, exams created in EZ Test can be exported to WebCT, Blackboard, and EZ Test Online. EZ Test comes with a Quick Start Guide, and once the program is installed, users have access to a User's Manual and Flash tutorials. Additional help is available online at www.mhhe.com/eztest.

***Microsoft® PowerPoint® Presentations* prepared by Bill McConkey, University of Toronto.** The PowerPoint package contains relevant figures and tables from the text, lecture outlines, and additional examples that you can customize for your lectures.

Instructor's Online Learning Centre (www.mcgrawhill.ca/olc/stevensonmgmtsci)

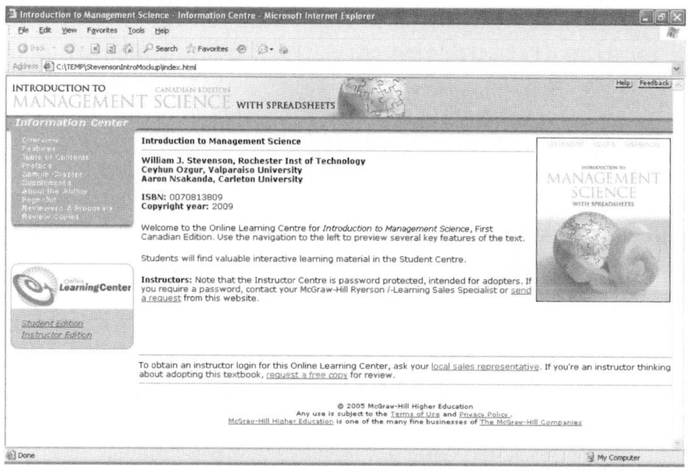

For Students

Student Online Learning Centre (www.mcgrawhill.ca/olc/stevensonmgmtsci). The Student Online Learning Centre includes a number of resources for student self-study and tools for working the problems in the text. These resources include self-quizzes, Excel templates, Excel screencam tutorials, Excel text spreadsheet files, PowerPoint slides, the answers to most odd-numbered problems, and software—Premium Solver, Treeplan, Crystal Ball, and Risksim. Five chapter supplements are also included to extend student learning. These are Forecasting, Linear Programming: The Simplex Method; Procedures for Solving Network Methods of Solving Integer Programming Problems, and Mini Review of Differiential Arithmetic.

Crystal Ball Software

Students will have access to Crystal Ball Software to solve some of the problems in the Simulation chapter. The software will show students how to use data in decision making and risk analysis.

Superior Service

Service takes on a whole new meaning with McGraw-Hill Ryerson and *Introduction to Management Science with Spreadsheets*, Canadian Edition. More than just bringing you the textbook, we have consistently raised the bar in terms of innovation and educational research. These investments in learning and the academic community have helped us to understand the needs of students and educators across the country, and allowed us to foster the growth of truly innovative, integrated learning.

*i*Learning Sales Specialist

Your Integrated Learning Sales Specialist is a McGraw-Hill Ryerson representative who has the experience, product knowledge, training, and support to help you assess and integrate any of the following products, technology and services into your course for optimum teaching and learning performance. Whether it's helping your students improve their grades, or putting your entire course online, your *i*Learning Sales Specialist is there to help you. Contact your local *i*Learning Sales Specialist today to learn how to maximize all of McGraw-Hill Ryerson's resources!

*i*Learning Services Program

McGraw-Hill Ryerson offers a unique *i*Learning Services package designed for Canadian faculty. Our mission is to equip providers of higher education with the superior tools and resources required for excellence in teaching. For additional information, visit www.mcgrawhill.ca/highereducation/iservices/.

Teaching, Technology & Learning Conference Series

The educational environment has changed tremendously in recent years, and McGraw-Hill Ryerson continues to be committed to helping you acquire the skills you need to succeed in this new milieu. Our innovative Teaching, Learning, & Technology Conference Series brings faculty together from across Canada with 3M Teaching Excellence award winners to share teaching and learning best practices in a collaborative and stimulating environment. Pre-conference workshops on general topics, such as teaching large classes and technology integration, will be offered. We will also work with you at your own institution to customize workshops that best suit the needs of your faculty.

CourseSmart

CourseSmart brings together thousands of textbooks across hundreds of courses in an eTextbook format, providing unique benefits to students and faculty. By purchasing an eTextbook, students can save up to 50 percent off the cost of a print textbook, reduce their impact on the environment, and gain access to powerful Web tools for learning including full text search, notes and highlighting, and e-mail tools for sharing notes between classmates. For faculty, CourseSmart provides instant access to review and compare textbooks and course materials in their discipline area without the time, cost, and environmental impact of mailing print examination copies. For further details contact your iLearning Sales Specialist or go to www.coursesmart.com.

Course Management Systems

WebCT and Blackboard. Content cartridges are available for course management systems such as WebCT and Blackboard. These platforms provide instructors with user-friendly, flexible teaching tools. Please contact your McGraw-Hill Ryerson *i*Learning Sales Specialist for details.

Acknowledgments

I want to thank many contributors to this first Canadian edition. I appreciate the contributions and the valuable input of the reviewers for this edition, who contributed many important suggestions. While the number of suggestions exceeded the space available, many of them were directly incorporated. The following reviewers provided invaluable assistance:

Igor Averbakh, University of Toronto at Scarborough
Romulus Cismaru, University of Regina
Ron Craig, Wilfrid Laurier University
Sapna Isotupa, Wilfrid Laurier University
Halina Kaminski, University of Western Ontario
Kevin Li, University of Windsor
Jim Mason, University of Regina
Bill McConkey, University of Toronto at Scarborough
Abdur Rahim, University of New Brunswick
Earl Rosenbloom, University of Manitoba
Mahesh Sharma, Concordia University
Trent Tucker, Wilfrid Laurier University
David Tullett, Memorial University

I would like to extend a special thanks to Dr. Kevin W. Li (University of Windsor), the Technical Reviewer, and Cat Haggert, the Copy Editor, for their insightful comments, arduous efforts, and diligence to make this book a much better final product, free of errors and accessible to readers. Yuheng Cao provided assistance in developing some of the new problems included in this first Canadian edition as well as in the preparation of the solution manual. Shelley Wickabrod helped obtain the permissions needed to use a number of materials incorporated in the textbook. I am grateful to them. I am also indebted to the following outstanding colleagues and friends, who have inspired me over years and who have played an incommensurable role as mentors or role models in my scholarly life so far: Dr. Moustapha Diaby (University of Connecticut), Dr. Louise Heslop (Carleton University), Dr. Moses Kiggundu (Carleton University), Dr. Vinod Kumar (Carleton University), Dr. Jean-Marie Nkongolo-Bakenda (University of Regina), and Dr. Nicolas Papadopoulos (Carleton University).

Several people from McGraw-Hill Ryerson deserve my thanks for providing the guidance, collaboration, and the support to successfully complete this book. I am grateful to Cathy Biribauer (Supervising Editor), Kelly Dickson (Managing Editor), and Kimberley Redhead (Sponsoring Editor). I also acknowledge the contributions of the following people, who worked hard at various stages during the development process to advance this project: Jennifer Bastarache (Developmental Editor), Jennifer DiDomenico (Managing Editor), Stahl Kara (Associate Developmental Editor), Lynn Fisher (Publisher), Sarah Fulton (Developmental Editor), and Bruce McIntosh (Sponsoring Editor). It was a pleasure to work with such a competent group of people, and many others who contributed directly or indirectly.

Finally, I owe a debt and express my gratitude to my wife Sylvie Chouinard and sons Raphaël Nsakanda and Alexandre Nsakanda for their patience, attention, understanding, and collaboration, during the many long hours and days devoted to the writing of this book.

Dr. Aaron Luntala Nsakanda
Associate Professor
Sprott School of Business
Carleton University

PART 1

Introduction to Management Science

PART OUTLINE

Part I begins with an introduction to the field of management science. Chapter 1 discusses the importance of models, the use of the management science approach, which focuses on model development, and then presents the use of break-even analysis, and an introduction on how to use basic Excel functions. The chapter also sets forth the layout of the book, which includes definitions of what is to be covered in each chapter.

CHAPTER 1

Introduction to Management Science

LEARNING OBJECTIVES

After completing this chapter, you should be able to:

1. Describe the importance of management science.
2. Describe the advantages of a quantitative approach to problem solving.
3. List some of the applications and use of management science models.
4. Discuss the types of models most useful in management science.
5. Demonstrate the basic building blocks and components of Excel.
6. Describe the basic nature and usefulness of break-even analysis.
7. List and briefly explain each of the components of break-even analysis.
8. Solve typical break-even problems manually and with Excel.
9. Realize how the use of management science has impacted various organizations.

CHAPTER OUTLINE

Management science is the discipline of applying advanced analytical methods to help make better decisions. It is a discipline devoted to solving managerial-type problems using quantitative models. This quantitative approach is widely employed in business. Areas of application include forecasting, capital budgeting, portfolio analysis, capacity planning, scheduling, marketing, inventory management, project management, and production planning. The Modern Management Science Application vignette on Canadian Pacific Railway describes how the use of management science techniques saved the company millions of dollars and transformed it into a more agile, profitable, highly cost-effective, and competitive railway.

In this first chapter, some of the basics of management science are covered, including the answers to such questions as: What is management science? Who uses it? Why use a quantitative approach? What are models, and why are they used? What are the different types of models? How are models used? Why are computers important in management science?

A MODERN MANAGEMENT SCIENCE APPLICATION: CANADIAN PACIFIC RAILWAY

Canadian Pacific Railway (CPR) is one of Canada's oldest corporations and was North America's first coast-to-coast transcontinental railway. CPR transports rail freight over a 14 000-mile network extending from Montreal to Vancouver and throughout the U.S. Northeast and Midwest. Alliances with other carriers extend CPR's market reach beyond its own network and into the major business centres of Mexico. In the mid-'90s, CPR was struggling with high costs, low profitability, and rising customer-service requirements. CPR thought its traditional operating strategies would not be adequate for dealing with these issues. Every day CPR receives approximately 7000 new shipments from its customers going to destinations across North America and for export. It must route and move these shipments safely and efficiently over its 14 000-mile network of track. It must coordinate the shipments with its operational plans for 1600 locomotives, 65 000 railcars, and over 5000 train crew members and take into account the capacity and storage space at 250 yards. In planning, it must also account for track-maintenance windows and connections with other railways. These vital connections account for 40 percent of CPR's business. The railway must manage and integrate a complex set of issues and assets efficiently, seven days a week, 24 hours a day. To meet rising customer expectations and to make a return on capital investment, CPR decided to make a wholesale change in its operating philosophy. Like most large North American railways, CPR used a tonnage-based approach in dispatching trains, running trains only when they had enough freight. Although this approach attempts to minimize the total number of trains needed by maximizing their size, in practice it disrupts the efficient utilization of crews, locomotives, and equipment. It also yields inconsistent transit times, making delivery service less reliable at a time when shippers need better service to compete in their own markets. The alternative to the tonnage-based approach is a more disciplined, schedule-based approach. In 1997, CPR began exploring the concept of running a scheduled railway. It was one of the first railways to adopt a true schedule-based approach that allowed the company to adjust quickly to changing traffic demands. Shifting to a schedule-based model from a tonnage approach was a huge challenge. CPR turned to management science tools and techniques to tackle the challenges involved and develop its operating plans. The proposed solutions were imbedded within a decision support system and included heuristic algorithms, forecasting methods (Chapter 14), optimization techniques (Chapters 2 and 6), network flow models (Chapter 5), and simulation (Chapter 13). This implementation has saved C$300 million from mid-1999 through autumn 2000. It is also estimated that it has saved at least an additional C$210 million during 2001 and 2002 in fuel and labour costs alone.

Source: Reprinted by permission, P. Ireland, R. Case, J. Fallis, C. Van Dyke, J. Kuehn, M. Meketon, "The Canadian Pacific Railways Transforms Operations by Using Models to Develop Its Operating Plans," *Interfaces* 34, no. 1, January–February 2004, pp. 5–14. Copyright 2004, the Institute for Operations Research and the Management Sciences (INFORMS), 7240 Parkway Drive, Suite 310, Hanover, MD 21076 USA.

1.1 INTRODUCTION

Management science uses a logical approach to problem solving. The problem is viewed as the focal point of analysis, and quantitative models are the vehicles by which solutions are obtained.

A Problem Focus

By adopting a problem focus, a decision maker has the advantage of directing attention to the essence of an analysis: to solve a specific problem. The problem in question may pertain to a current condition or it may relate more to the future. An example of a current condition would be customers complaining to the manager of a bank about the amount of time they have to wait in line for a teller. It is hoped that these kinds of problems can be kept to a minimum; a manager cannot be productive if he or she spends much time putting out fires.

Often, problems result from inadequate planning. Hence, an ideal use of a manager's time, and of management science models, is to plan for the future. An example of that kind of problem would be deciding where to locate a warehouse to minimize future shipping costs. Another example would be choosing a plan for assigning jobs to machines that will minimize the total time needed to complete the jobs. Still other examples include predicting future demand so that intelligent decisions can be made about production levels, work-force levels, capacity, and inventory; selecting the combination of product output quantities that will maximize profits; and identifying appropriate levels of inventory.

Use of a Quantitative Approach

Problem solving can be either qualitative or quantitative. In qualitative problem solving, intuition and subjective judgment are used. Past experience with similar problems is often an important factor in choosing a qualitative approach, as are the complexity and importance of a problem. Managers tend to use a qualitative approach to problem solving when:

1. The problem is fairly simple
2. The problem is familiar
3. The costs involved are not great

Conversely, managers tend to use a quantitative approach when one or more of the following conditions exist:

1. The problem is complex
2. The problem is not familiar
3. The costs involved are substantial
4. Enough time is available to analyze the problem

Generally speaking, decisions based on quantitative analysis tend to be more objective than those based on a purely qualitative analysis. On the other hand, a purely quantitative analysis will include only information that can be quantified. Therefore, the results of models should be followed routinely only for the simplest and best-understood cases; otherwise, the results should be questioned and analyzed. As a general rule, the results of a mathematical analysis should be reviewed by management for reasonableness and feasibility.

The use of quantitative analysis is not new. Quantitative methods of problem solving can be traced back to ancient times. Who would doubt that the great pyramids of Egypt were designed and built using quantitative methods? In similar fashion, the movements and supply requirements of Roman armies, the construction of ancient canals and waterways, and the ancient shipbuilding processes undoubtedly benefited from the use of quantitative methods.

Many of the early uses involved engineering applications. However, there were very few *managerial* applications of mathematical analysis before the Industrial Revolution, particularly with respect to problem solving. Even then, management science as we now know it did not exist.

A key period in the development of the use of the quantitative approach to problem solving came during World War II when teams of scientists were brought together to help solve complex military problems on deploying troops, searching the seas, supplying troops, and so on. These developments were given the name of operations research (OR) because scientists were doing research on managing military operations. The abbreviation for operations research is often used in conjunction with the abbreviation for management science, referring to the discipline as OR/MS. The following societies publish journals and newsletters dealing with news and the state-of-the-art research and applications of operations research and management science techniques: the Canadian Operational Research Society (**CORS**), http://www.cors.ca; the Institute for Operations Research and the Management Sciences **(INFORMS),** http://www.informs.org; and Decision Sciences Institute **(DSI),** http://www.decisionsciences.org. After the war, many of the techniques used by the operations researchers were adapted to business applications, and management science began to emerge as a discipline. Previously developed quantitative techniques were added along with newly developed techniques to form an expanding body of knowledge that had important business applications.

One difficulty that early practitioners faced was the burdensome computational requirements that often were required to solve even fairly simple problems. It is not surprising, then, that increasing use of management science has accompanied advances in computer technology, both in hardware and software. Today, access to computers, both mainframe and personal, puts the power of management science within the reach of virtually all managers.

The combination of access to computers and computer codes for solving management problems, continuing developments in management science models, and successful applications have contributed to the respectability of management science as a discipline. Successful applications of management science and new developments in this field are reported regularly in such journals as *Management Science, Decision Sciences, Interfaces, Infor,* and *Operations Research.*

Finally, it should be noted that although the field of management science is not entirely quantitative, the preponderance of management science applications fall under the heading of quantitative analysis. For that reason, this book emphasizes applications involving quantitative models.

1.2 MODELS

A **model** is an abstraction of reality. It is a simplified, and often idealized, representation of reality. An equation, an outline, a diagram, and a map are each an example of a model. By its very nature a model is incomplete: A good model will capture the important details of reality without including innumerable minor details that would obscure rather than illuminate. You could think of a model as a selective abstraction because only those details that are considered to be important for the problem at hand are included in the model. For example, suppose the problem involved aerodynamic properties of a new automotive design. Important details that come to mind are weight, shape, size, and height. Unimportant details include colour, interior design, type of radio, and so on. Thus, it is important to carefully decide which aspects of reality to include in a model.

Models provide a manager or analyst with an alternative to working directly with reality. This allows the person using the model greater freedom in terms of experimenting with different ideas, controlling certain aspects of the situation, and investigating alternative solutions. It also reduces the cost of mistakes if they can be corrected within the realm of the model.

In practice, models are employed in a variety of ways. For example, **iconic models** are used, mainly in engineering, to physically represent a scaled down or miniature version of real objects. Examples of such models are a miniature airplane, train, or material handling system. Their shape is similar to real objects but differs in terms of scale and material used. **Analog models** are used to physically represent an analogy for reality. A graph representing the yearly sales of a product, a blueprint of a plant layout, or a thermometer representing temperature are examples of analog models. **Symbolic** or **mathematical models,** primarily the focus of study in this textbook, incorporate numbers and algebraic symbols to represent important aspects of the problem, often in equation form. These numbers and symbols are then manipulated to solve for unknown values of key variables. Moreover, mathematical models lend themselves to the computational power inherent in calculators and computers.

Consider this simple mathematical model:

$$\text{Profit} = 5x$$

where

$$x = \text{pounds of material sold}$$

The number 5 represents the profit per unit of material, and the symbol x represents the quantity of a certain material; profit is the product of the profit per unit and the number of units sold. Thus, if 15 units are sold, the profit is $5(15) = \$75$.

A slightly more complex version of this model is the following:

$$\text{Profit} = 5x_1 + 8x_2 + 4x_3$$

where

$$x_1 = \text{pounds of material 1 sold}$$
$$x_2 = \text{pounds of material 2 sold}$$
$$x_3 = \text{pounds of material 3 sold}$$

Thus, if $x_1 = 10$, $x_2 = 20$, and $x_3 = 30$, the total profit would be

$$5(10) + 8(20) + 4(30) = \$330$$

Mathematical models are made up of constants (**parameters**) and variables; constants are fixed or known quantities not subject to variation, whereas **variables** can take on different values and can be either probabilistic or deterministic. Constants generally are represented by numbers and variables by letters.

Thus, in the model Profit $= 5x_1 + 8x_2 + 4x_3$, the unit profits (5, 8, and 4) are the constants and the quantities of materials 1, 2, and 3 (i.e., x_1, x_2, and x_3) are the variables. In this example, the variables are **decision variables.** The manager or analyst would want to know what values to set these at (i.e., how much of each material to produce) to obtain the highest profit. Decision variables, therefore, are under the control of a decision maker and can be set at a desired level. Another kind of variable that is often encountered is an **uncontrollable variable.** An example would be the weather: Although it is beyond the control of a manager, weather sometimes is a factor that can have some bearing on profits. For instance, a mild, rainy winter can substantially reduce profits at ski resorts. Similarly, rainy weather and flooding can slow down a construction project. Other examples of uncontrollable variables include government decisions (for example, revision of the tax code, pollution regulations), competitors' decisions (e.g., product design, advertising, pricing), and consumer decisions.

Thus, models that are used for problem solving include constants, decision variables, and uncontrollable variables. The challenge for the manager or analyst who is developing a model is to determine the levels of the decision variables that will best serve the goals of the manager, given the constants and uncontrollable variables.

The models used in this book will be a blend of graphical, mathematical, and spreadsheet models. The graphical models will help to illustrate important concepts and help you to develop an intuitive understanding of various models, whereas the mathematical models will enable you to determine solutions for a wide range of problems. The spreadsheet models translate mathematical models to a spreadsheet.

Benefits and Risks of Using Models

Models have numerous benefits for problem solvers, but there are also certain risks for the users. Obviously, the benefits generally must tend to outweigh the risks, or models would not be used.

An important benefit of using a model is that it allows an analyst to strip away many unimportant details of reality and thereby focus attention on a small number of important aspects of a problem. The risk in doing this is that one or more of the important aspects of a problem may be inadvertently left out. If this happens, it is highly unlikely that the analyst will be able to successfully solve the real-world problem using the model.

Another benefit of using quantitative models is that they force the analyst to quantify information. The risk is that non-quantitative information may be down-played or ignored because it is difficult or impossible to include that type of information in a quantitative model.

The third benefit of models is the structure they provide for analyzing a problem in terms of what information is needed and how to organize information. One risk is that an inexperienced analyst may attempt to force a problem to fit the model. In effect, chances of obtaining a good solution would be diminished.

The process of developing a model can generate tremendous insight about reality. However, care must be taken, so that modelling does not become an end in itself. In fact, it is easy to get carried away with modelling and to end up with a model that is more complex and powerful than what is needed to solve the problem.

Another benefit of models is that they compress time. They usually are also less costly than a real-life situation would be, and they permit users the luxury of experimentation without dangers that would be inherent in a real-life setting. However, due to their abstract nature, models sometimes do not adequately portray relationships that exist in reality.

A consequence of this kind of error is that solutions obtained from the model fail under the harsh light of reality. One way to reduce this risk is to give careful consideration to the assumptions on which the model is based.

Assumptions of Models

All models are based on assumptions (that is, conditions that are assumed to exist). Some of these will be technical, such as "the relationship is linear"; others will be operational, such as "the budget is $25 000"; and still others may be political, such as "Marketing will support the proposal."

It is usually wise to write out the assumptions that can be identified before developing the model. This will increase the chances of developing a workable and acceptable model. Moreover, those who are in a position to approve or reject a solution (e.g., manager, customer, potential investor) may want to know what assumptions were made, why they were made, how realistic they are, and so on.

In terms of studying management science, assumptions in the technical category will be most relevant. As each new model is introduced, make note of the assumptions and what impact they have on the model. Recognize that many assumptions simplify; they reduce the complexity that would be inherent in reality. Using simplifying assumptions in practice always involves evaluating the trade-offs: The simpler the model, the easier it will be to understand and use it to obtain solutions, but the greater the risk will be that the solutions based on the model will not apply to reality.

Deterministic Versus Probabilistic Models

Some models can be used to determine an optimal, or best, solution to a problem, whereas other models are used to predict approximate, or average, future outcomes. The choice between these two kinds of models depends primarily on the *degree of certainty* that can be assigned to the information available to the analyst. **Deterministic models** are used for problems in which information is known with a high degree of certainty. For instance, in a problem involving production times, if the production times are known and are constant (that is, the same time is required for every repetition of the process), a deterministic model could be used to determine an optimal solution to the problem. Conversely, when it cannot be determined precisely what value will occur (usually in the future) a **probabilistic model** that incorporates *probabilities* is appropriate. For example, choosing the size of a warehouse to build depends on how large future demand will be. If, because of contractual commitments from a buyer, a manager knows what demand to plan for, an optimal-size warehouse could be determined. However, such cases are quite rare. Instead, managers usually are faced with situations in which future demand is subject to variability (i.e., it cannot be predicted exactly, but only approximately). Then the goal is to minimize the error in predictions; without complete knowledge, it is virtually impossible to specify an optimal solution.

It should be noted that an optimal solution is generally optimal only in the context of a model and not necessarily in the larger context of reality. This is because all models are simplified versions of reality; that is, they do not and cannot incorporate all of the details and factors that comprise reality. Consequently, it is debatable whether any solution is truly optimal in the purest sense of the word. Therefore, when the term *optimal* is employed in this text, and in management science in general, it refers to the conditions contained in a mathematical model. This is not to say that optimal solutions are unacceptable in reality or that they are not good solutions. On the contrary, such solutions may not only be very good, they also may be much better than solutions generated in less scientific ways. Nonetheless, it would be incorrect to believe that optimal solutions obtained from models will be truly optimal when applied to reality. Because of this, a manager should review all but the most routine solutions before implementing them, and should decide whether to implement the solution as it stands or to first modify it because of some other subjective considerations. In addition, some deterministic models do not result in optimal solutions.

1.3 THE MANAGEMENT SCIENCE APPROACH

Although management science incorporates quantitative analysis in its approach to problem solving, it would be a mistake to regard management science as merely a collection of techniques. It is as much a *philosophy* of problem solving as it is the use of quantitative methods.

The management science approach is quite similar to the **scientific approach** commonly used in the physical sciences. Both involve a logical sequence that includes careful definition of the problem, use of models, and analysis leading to solution of the problem. The management science approach is outlined in Figure 1-1.

Problem Definition

The first step in problem solving is *careful* problem definition. It is important to resist the temptation to rush through this stage to begin working on the model and the solution. Unfortunately, exactly the opposite occurs in many cases. When that happens, the solution

FIGURE 1-1 The Management Science Approach

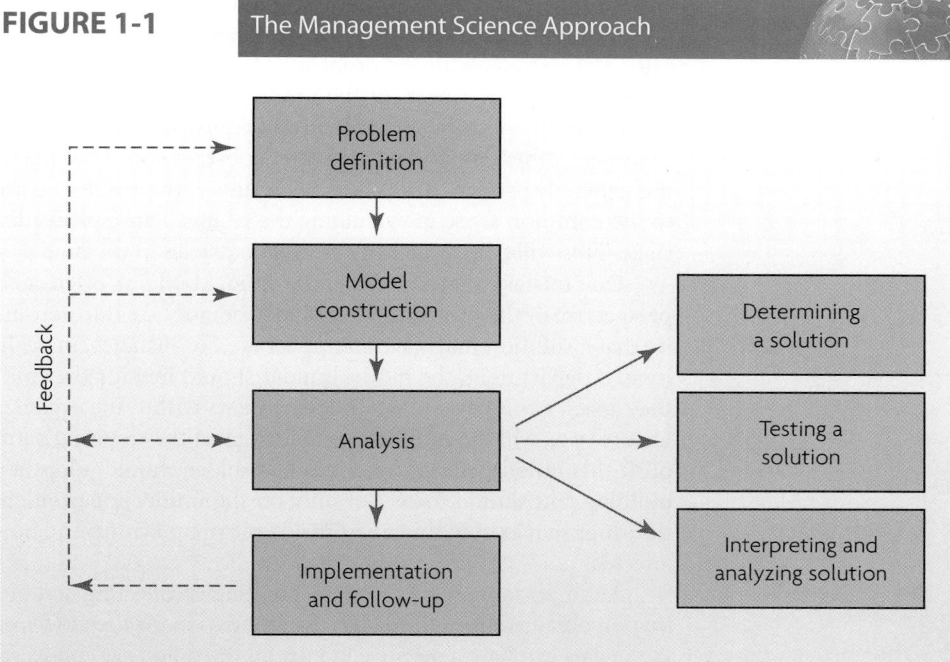

is less likely to solve the problem, and it may create additional problems. Furthermore, senior managers may become disillusioned in the process, and they may turn to other, less objective, methods for handling problems.

Good problem definition may involve observing a current situation or process to better understand it. Almost always, it is highly desirable to talk with the people who are closely involved (e.g., workers, supervisors, salespeople, staff). Not only do such people usually possess considerable knowledge and insight that enable them to suggest potential solutions, they also are the ones who must live with the solution. By including them in the process, they are less likely to resist the solution because they will feel that they contributed to it.

Once the problem has been reasonably defined, it is time to construct a model. However, it is wise to leave room for possible future redefinition of the problem. It is quite common to gain new insights and raise additional questions as modelling progresses. These often lead to refining, or even modifying, the initial problem definition.

Model Construction

The goal of modelling should be to achieve an accurate, yet relatively simple, representation of reality. Hence, the model should reflect the major aspects of the problem as simply as possible. Often, this requires trade-offs because simplicity and accuracy rarely go hand in hand. Therefore, the model builder must decide on an appropriate balance between a model that is highly accurate in its portrayal of reality (and, consequently, complex) and one that is relatively simple. Usually, the more complex the model, the more costly and time-consuming it is to build and the more difficult it is to understand. Conversely, a model that is too simple may not provide an adequate portrayal of reality, thereby decreasing the chances of finding a reasonable solution to the problem. Ideally, a model will enable the analyst or manager to study a problem in a quasi-laboratory environment that will lead to a clearer understanding of the problem and its solution.

Although model building requires abstraction of reality, it is important to obtain accurate information about the problem. This may relate to production times, machine times, or other technical aspects of the problem. In many instances, this information will come from three main sources: the accounting department, those directly involved (for example, managers, other employees), and direct observation. After the model has been constructed, it is generally prudent to confirm the results with people who are more closely involved and to use common sense in evaluating the results before proceeding very far into the analysis stage. This will help to identify any inadequacies in the model.

One mistake that inexperienced model builders often make is failing to take a broad perspective of the problem. That is, they do not take into account other dimensions of reality that a solution may have an impact on. For instance, in dealing with the optimal capacity of a department, the model builder should include the ability to assess the impact that the capacity will have on *other* departments within the organization as well as on external factors (e.g., will the suppliers be able to meet the resulting demands on them?). To accomplish this broad perspective, a model builder should adopt a *systems approach* to model building and should focus not only on the immediate problem but also on the interrelationships that exist within and outside the organization and how these relationships will be affected.

An important aspect of model building is collecting and preparing data. Because information obtained from the data is the foundation for the model, errors or missed information in the data can have a negative impact on the validity of model results.

Model Analysis

The nature of the analysis will depend on the type of model that is used. For instance, models that portray a situation that has a high degree of certainty lend themselves to *algorithms* (a series of steps that are repeated until the best solution is found) that generally help to identify optimal solutions. However, in some instances, no algorithms exist for identifying optimal solutions. Instead, *search techniques* may be used to identify acceptable solutions. In less certain situations, models may be used to identify approximate solutions.

In order to identify optimal or acceptable solutions, the analyst uses a **measure of effectiveness** such as profit, revenue, time, or cost to evaluate alternative solutions. Thus, if profit is the measure of effectiveness, the solution chosen will be the one that is projected to yield the highest profit. The measure of effectiveness that is used usually will come from the objective of the manager who is responsible for solving the problem. If the objective is not obvious or known, it will be necessary to solicit it from the manager or other appropriate person.

After the model is solved successfully, the solution must be tested to make sure that it is logical and the model is appropriate. The use of additional data may be necessary to compare the results obtained with the original data against the results obtained with the new data. At this point, the solution should be reviewed with the managers. In reviewing the solution, the analyst must go over all the assumptions that are used in the model.

Very often, the size of a problem and its computational requirements necessitate using a computer. Consequently, the user of a management science model usually will become involved with examining and interpreting computer output. Therefore, to be successful, the manager or other analyst must understand the basics of such techniques as well as how to interpret computer output.

An important part of model analysis, whether done manually or by using a computer, is determining how sensitive a particular solution is to changes in one or more of the constants in the model. This is referred to as **sensitivity analysis.** A manager can use sensitivity analysis to learn if changes in the values of certain constants used in the model will have any effect on the solution and, if so, what that effect would be. One reason for examining possible changes is that the manager has acquired new information indicating that the value of a constant may be different than that used in the model, and the manager wants to know if that will change the results. Another reason for using sensitivity analysis is to answer "What if . . .?" type questions. For example, a manager may be able to purchase an additional amount of some raw material used in a production process. The question is, would it be profitable to obtain additional amounts of the raw material, and, if so, how much?

Implementation and Follow-Up

Once an appropriate solution has been identified, it must be implemented. This may involve reporting the recommended solution to the appropriate manager (e.g., the manager who requested the analysis) or it may mean making a presentation to senior managers (i.e., selling it to them). Presentations of results based on quantitative models to senior managers can seem more difficult than the analysis itself. One reason is that these people often ask probing questions. Another is that they have the power to approve or reject the solution. One obstacle that can be encountered is that senior managers may lack quantitative skills. This means that the presenter must explain the model and the results in layman's terms, a feat some find difficult. For these reasons, it is wise to carefully prepare the presentation lest all the work that preceded it be in vain.

Not all solutions will be implemented. Some, of course, will be judged as not solving the problem. Others may be judged as too costly or they may be unacceptable for other reasons. One other reason might be that the goals of management have changed during the problem-solving interval. For instance, a new manager who has different experiences, priorities, and perspectives may have replaced the previous manager. Then too, certain aspects of the problem may have changed (for example, there may be new or different constraints, different legal requirements, new technology, and so on). In some cases, the problem may have corrected itself, or the organization may have decided to abandon that phase of the operation.

If a solution is implemented, it is important to carefully monitor that implementation. One reason for this is to make sure that the recommended solution is applied correctly. Consider the advice of a physician: "Take two every four hours." Unfortunately, the patient takes *four* every *two* hours and ends up in the emergency room. Also, the solution could be implemented correctly but the desired results may not be realized. A reasonable checklist would include questions such as: Were there mistakes in the implementation? Did the analysis support the solution? Was the analysis correct? Were there errors in the model? Was the problem correctly and completely defined?

In some cases, only minor corrections will be needed to achieve the desired results, whereas in other cases, major reworking will be called for. The chances of needing major re-working will be less if each step of the management science process is given careful attention. Continuing feedback at every phase of the process can help uncover inadequacies that can then be corrected, thereby avoiding such pitfalls as working on the wrong problem, working with an incorrect model, using misleading data, and so on. Feedback allows for continual evaluation and corrective action throughout the process.

1.4 THE UTILIZATION OF DECISION SUPPORT SYSTEMS (DSS) IN THE CONTEXT OF MANAGEMENT SCIENCE

A decision support system involves a collection of computerized technologies used to support decision making. DSS is the marriage of the information technology and information systems (IT/IS) field with operations research and management science (OR/MS). The greatest benefit is realized in the context of DSS when IT and OR work together. The DSS framework is described in Figure 1-2. In the data management domain, we organize the information into databases and manage it by software called *database management system* (DBMS). The DBMS interacts with model management systems, which include software packages to solve financial, statistical, and management science problems. These two systems interact and contribute to the intelligence and decision-making capabilities of the entire system. Data management and the model management components contribute to knowledge management, which consists of an expert system that enhances DSS when decision making is rather complex. The knowledge-based subsystem component consists of an intelligence system or systems; it is generally connected with the organizational knowledge base. Knowledge also may be provided through Web servers using a Web development program such as Java. Knowledge-based systems provide the necessary execution of the DSS. Finally, the user communicates with the system through a user interface. It is a good idea to provide graphics in the user interface to make it more effective. The interaction between the user and DSS is crucial to the development of user-friendly and user-oriented DSS models.

FIGURE 1-2 DSS Framework

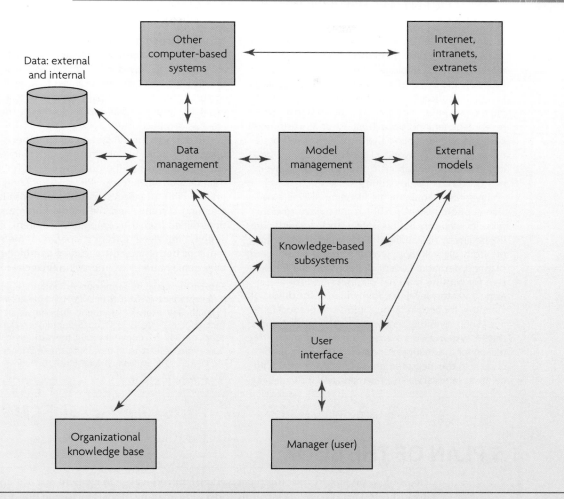

Source: E. Turban, Jay Aronson, and Ting-Peng Liang, *Decision Support Systems and Intelligence Systems,* 7th ed. (Upper Saddle River, NJ: Prentice Hall, 2005), p. 109.

A DSS provides an interactive, computer-based environment that enables managers not only to get answers to various questions and make decisions, but also to perform what-if scenarios and sensitivity analyses. The Modern Management Science Application, "Lucent Technologies," describes how the company uses a decision support system to manage inventories for its many product lines.

Excel is a desirable modelling tool to set up DSS. Excel is not only readily available in both the classroom and the workplace, but it is also relatively easy to learn and use. It is highly functional and extendable and can be integrated with other systems such as Access (Microsoft's database language that has the capability to use information from a variety of formats with a common user interface).

A MODERN MANAGEMENT SCIENCE APPLICATION: LUCENT TECHNOLOGIES

Lucent Technologies is in the business of designing software that drives modern communications networks. Lucent Technologies is supported by Bell Labs Research and Development. Lucent provides services in mobile, optical, software, data, and voice networking technologies. The mission of Lucent is to find new revenue-generating opportunities for its customers, particularly by enabling them to deploy and better manage their networks. Lucent's customer base includes communications service providers, governments, and companies around the world.

Inventory Requirements Planning (IRP) is a decision support system (DSS) Lucent utilizes to determine its inventory buffers (safety stock) for parts. The IRP begins by measuring the deviation of actual supply from planned supply and actual demand from planned demand. Lucent depends on the IRP system for routine material planning and for associating inventory levels recommended to the drivers of inventory for both individual items and product families. When inventory requirements change over time, the IRP system assists managers in understanding the reason for the change. For example, there might be a change in the measurement of forecast accuracy. IRP computes the variability of demand and the variability of supply. Based on these variabilities, IRP is able to distinguish between common causes (variation not attributable to any special cause) and assignable causes (variation that can be linked to a specific reason or event). As the company can then decrease the variability in demand as supply decreases, they also are able to reduce safety stock.

Lucent uses the IRP system at a number of manufacturing plants to determine inventory levels and inform managers of the possible causes of higher-than-desired inventory. IRP is completely integrated with the firm's material and production planning systems, and the model parameters are determined from the company ERP system. The IRP system improved Lucent's operation metrics in terms of better forecast accuracy and higher supplier quality as well as improving financial metrics.

Source: Reprinted by permission, A. Bangash, R. Bollapragada, R. Klein, N. Raman, H. Schulman, and D. Smith, "Inventory Requirements Planning at Lucent Technologies," *Interfaces* 34, no. 5 (September–October 2004), pp. 342–52. Copyright 2004, the Institute for Operations Research and the Management Sciences (INFORMS), 7240 Parkway Drive, Suite 310, Hanover, MD 21076 USA.

1.5 PLAN OF THE BOOK

The book is organized into three parts. Part I introduces management science and use of spreadsheets. Part II covers deterministic decision-making models including linear programming, sensitivity analysis with linear programming, distribution and network flow models, integer programming, nonlinear, and multicriteria models. Part III introduces probabilistic decision models including decision theory, Markov analysis, waiting line, and simulation models. Project scheduling covers both deterministic and probabilistic models. The Modern Management Science Application box on Hongkong International Terminals reports the use of some of these techniques, such as linear programming (Chapters 2–4), integer programming (Chapter 6), transportation model (Chapter 5), and simulation (Chapter 13).

Table 1-1 provides a brief overview of the parts and chapters.

1.6 ROLE OF COMPUTERS AND SPREADSHEETS IN MANAGEMENT SCIENCE

Computers are an important tool in management science. The use of quantitative models lends itself to computerized solutions. Moreover, the nature of many management science models is such that substantial calculations are required to solve everyday problems.

TABLE 1-1 Overview of the book

Chapter or Part	Title	Brief description
Part 1	**Introduction to Management Science**	
Chapter 1	Introduction to Management Science	Provides an introduction to management science, modelling, and the use of Excel
Part II	**Deterministic Decision Models**	
Chapter 2	Linear Programming: Basic Concepts, Graphical Solution, and Computer Solution	Basic background about LP and how to solve simple LP problems graphically and with Excel Solver
Chapter 3	Linear Programming: Sensitivity Analysis and Computer Solution Interpretation	Extension of problem formulation, discussion of sensitivity analysis and how to interpret computer output
Chapter 4	Applications of Linear Programming	Extension of problem formulation and problem solution are explained and realistic application examples are provided
Chapter 5	Distribution and Network Flow Models	Provides coverage of special-purpose linear programming models for transportation, transshipment, assignment, shortest path, and maximum flow problems
Chapter 6	Integer Programming Methods	How to formulate and obtain optimal solutions when the variables are restricted to being integer
Chapter 7	Nonlinear Programming	Optimization of nonlinear models
Chapter 8	Project Scheduling: PERT/CPM	Introduce techniques used for project analysis (CPM and PERT)
Chapter 9	Multicriteria Decision-Making Models	How to handle problems with multiple objectives
Part III	**Probabilistic Decision Models**	
Chapter 10	Decision Analysis	A general approach for handling problems that have multiple alternatives and a discrete set of possible outcomes
Chapter 11	Markov Analysis	Studying the evolution of systems over repeated time periods
Chapter 12	Waiting-Line Models	Analysis of waiting lines
Chapter 13	Simulation	Describes a class of problems used to learn about a real system by experimenting with a model that represents the system
OLC Modules		
Chapter 14	Forecasting	Provides the decision makers with an improved picture of future occurrences of events
Chapter 15	Linear Programming: The Simplex Method	
Chapter 16	Procedures for Solving Network Models	Solution procedures for transportation, assignment, shortest path, maximum flow, and minimal amount of cost to connect all points
Chapter 17	Methods of Solving Integer Programming Problems	
Chapter 18	Mini Review of Differential Arithmetic	

A MODERN MANAGEMENT SCIENCE APPLICATION: HONGKONG INTERNATIONAL TERMINALS

Hongkong International Terminals (HIT) is the busiest container terminal on the planet. The facility is operated by Hutchison Port Holdings (HPH) and in 2003, HIT handled 20 million 20-foot-equivalent units. HIT receives over 10 000 trucks and 15 vessels every day.

HIT's terminal management system uses Productivity Plus Program (3P), which optimizes the use of resources at the terminal using operations research and management science techniques for such decisions as to how to route container trucks, where to store arriving containers, and when to schedule incoming trucks for container pickup.

In the early 1990s, China's manufacturing expansion created a very high demand for HIT. At the time, HIT also faced tough competition in southern China where labour costs are much cheaper, making the situation difficult. HIT decided to take on the competition on the basis of efficiency and productivity. The terminal initiated 3P, which is a decision support system for optimizing daily operations. It is designed to monitor the movement of containers within the terminal and to organize the movements in an effective, optimized way. There were many implementation issues to overcome for HIT, but 3P quickly resulted in a large number of benefits for HIT, including adding additional capacity at low cost. Because of the improved efficiency, HIT began to develop a reputation of being a "catch-up" port. In other words, companies came to rely on HIT to regain time they had lost elsewhere in their schedules. Another benefit that resulted from the 3P innovation was environmental. HIT was able to reduce the number of diesel-burning trucks within their transfer business by one-half. In addition, HIT experienced a 30 percent improvement in vessel turnaround time, a 47 percent improvement in vessel operating rate, a 35 percent reduction of material-handling cost, a 15 percent increase in yard crane productivity, and, overall, a 50 percent increase in throughput.

By utilizing a number of management science techniques within 3P such as linear programming, integer programming, transportation model, and simulation, Hongkong International Terminals was able to exceed expected results. HIT has not only created an additional value to the customers, but also differentiated the company from the competitors in terms of the speed and services that it offers.

Source: Reprinted by permission, K. T. Murty, Y. Wan, J. Liu, M. Tseng, E. Leung, K. Lai, and H. Chiu, "Hongkong International Terminals Gains Elastic Capacity Using a Data-Intensive Decision-Support System," *Interfaces* 35, no. 1 (January–February 2005), pp. 61–75. Copyright 2005, the Institute for Operations Research and the Management Sciences (INFORMS), 7240 Parkway Drive, Suite 310, Hanover, MD 21076 USA.

Until recently, the modelling techniques that will be covered in the remaining chapters of this book were solved using specialized software packages. Even though these packages were effective in solving various management science problems, the students that learned to solve problems with these packages did not own them. Therefore, after completing the course, they did not have the ability to use the packages unless they purchased them. Excel is an application program for Microsoft Office®. After many revisions, Microsoft Excel is now capable of solving many of the basic management science problems. Since it is readily available to most students, Excel has become a popular and practical means of solving these problems. Therefore, many colleges have begun to offer spreadsheet-based courses. The use of spreadsheets, and specifically Microsoft Excel, has become an important tool in teaching the decision modelling techniques. In this book, we will utilize Excel to teach these modelling techniques. This approach will be beneficial to students by allowing them to improve their proficiency in using Excel while gaining an understanding of the management science techniques in the context of a commonly used program. We will introduce the basic commands and structure of Excel in the next section. In addition, we will discuss various Excel functions and procedures when they are used with respect to a specific decision model. Consequently, illustration and discussion of computer output using Excel will be covered throughout the book.

It is important to recognize that for instructional purposes, manual solutions are demonstrated in each chapter. These will provide you with a basic understanding of the important concepts related to the various models that are discussed and insights on how the models can be used to generate solutions. Both are important parts to the learning process. Hence, it is important to devote a reasonable amount of time and energy to manual solutions. Once you have mastered the important concepts of a model, you will be in a better position to use and *understand* computer (Excel) input and output.

Getting Started with Excel

This section of the chapter contains an explanation of some basic information about the commands and procedures of Excel. It also provides an explanation of how add-ins such as *Solver* and *Data Analysis* can be installed. Spreadsheets provide a relatively easy means of analyzing data and using management science techniques for a wide variety of management problems. A *spreadsheet* allows the analyst to prepare hidden equations that perform calculations on a given data set. The main document in Excel used to store and analyze data is called a *workbook.* A workbook can consist of multiple *worksheets.* The worksheets can be used to analyze and manipulate data. Excel provides the means for the analyst to work with multiple worksheets simultaneously.

Once Excel has been installed, the user can start the program by clicking on **Start | Programs | Microsoft Excel,** by clicking on the Microsoft Excel icon on the Office toolbar, or by double-clicking on any Excel workbook that already exists on the computer. If the user starts Excel without opening an existing workbook, Excel will automatically create an empty workbook.

Description of a Worksheet A worksheet consists of rows and columns, as shown in Exhibit 1-1. Columns are labelled with letters A, B, C, and so forth, and rows are identified with numbers 1, 2, 3, and so on. The intersection of a row and a column is defined as a *cell,* which provides the basic means of data storage for Excel. Each cell's reference, based on the column and row numbers, is displayed in the cell reference towards the upper left corner of the worksheet. Different types of data can be stored, including numbers, labels, text, formulas, dates, and times. Not only can the user make use of the vertical and horizontal scroll bars and the mouse to navigate between cells, but the user can also use **Home | Editing | Find & Select | Go To** to allow more flexibility of movement between cells.

The Microsoft Office button (MOB) and the tab list provide shortcuts to various Excel commands and features. Each of the seven tabs (**Home, Insert, Page Layout, Formulas, Data, Review,** and **View**) is divided into groups of related commands and features. For instance, the Home tab contains the clipboard, formatting, style commands, editing commands in addition to commands to insert and delete rows or columns. An arrow at the bottom right corner of each group provides additional features within the group. The MOB provides commands to create a new workbook, open an existing workbook, save and save as, print, send, or close a workbook. It also provides access to a number of customizable options that can be used to set up the Excel's working environment.

Using Worksheets To enter data or information into a worksheet, simply click on the cell and then enter the data. By pressing Enter, the data will be inserted into the cell and the next cell (row) will be selected automatically. The user can select *adjacent cells* by clicking on the first cell in the sequence of cells. Then, by holding the Shift key and clicking on the last cell to be selected, all cells between these two cells will be selected. The same task also can be performed by clicking the first cell, holding the left mouse button down, and

EXHIBIT 1-1 Excel Worksheet

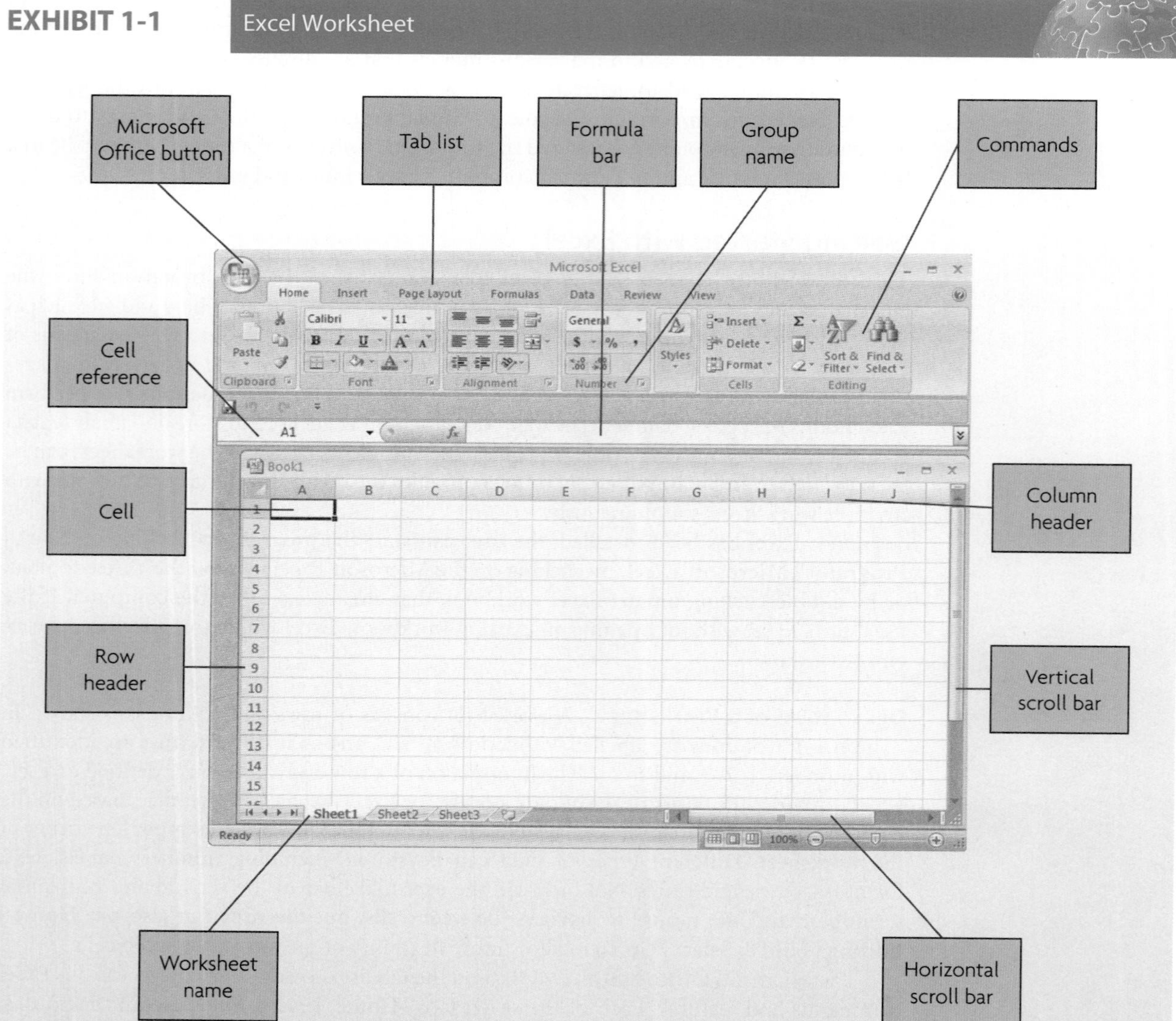

dragging it until all of the desired cells have been selected. Clicking on the row or column header will enable the user to select an *entire row or column.* If you want to select more than one row or column, then simply click on the row or column to start the rows or columns to be selected and hold the left mouse button down. Drag it until all of the desired rows or columns have been selected.

If you want to edit or modify existing data that have already been entered, double-click on the cell to be edited. To clear data, first select the cells that need to be cleared, then press the Delete button. If you want to insert a new row, right-click with the mouse on the row header and hit **Insert** and a new row will be added above the chosen row. If you want to insert a new column, right click with the mouse on the column header and select **Insert.** A new column will then be added to the left of the selected column. To delete rows and columns, you simply select the row(s) or column(s) to be deleted, right-click with the mouse in the highlighted area, and then select **Delete.**

Changing the width of a column can be accomplished by placing the cursor on the right edge of the column header (the cursor will change to a cross with arrows to the right and to the left) and dragging the mouse until a desired width is achieved. By placing the cursor on the right edge of the column header, the user can double-click to adjust the width of the column to the largest entry in the column.

Changing the row height can be accomplished by placing the cursor on the bottom edge of the row header (the cursor will change to a cross with arrows pointing up and down) and dragging the mouse until a desired height is achieved. The user can place the cursor on the right edge of the row header and double-click, which will automatically adjust the row height to the highest entry in a given row.

Excel can hide and unhide rows and columns. To hide a row or set of rows, first select the rows to be hidden, right-click with the mouse, and then click **Hide.** Likewise, to hide a column, select the columns to be hidden, right-click with the mouse, and then click **Hide.** To unhide a hidden row, first select the rows before and after the hidden row, right-click with the mouse, and then click **Unhide.** A similar process is used to unhide a column or columns by selecting the columns before and after the hidden columns and clicking on **Unhide.**

Using Formulas and Functions Formulas will allow you to perform calculations on the worksheet data. A formula must start with an "equal to" (=) sign. When entering a formula, first click on the cell where you want the formula to take effect, and then type = followed by the formula. A formula can consist of mathematical operations involving cell numbers or references. After typing in a formula, press enter to perform the calculations.

There are functions or formulas automatically built in to Excel. Using these functions will save the user time from preparing formulas. If you click **Formula | Insert Function,** it will bring up a menu window as shown Exhibit 1-2, which shows a list of functions available in Excel. The various subset categories can be viewed by clicking the down arrow on the "Or select a category" box (second box in Exhibit 1-2). When a function is selected, a syntax for that function is provided at the bottom of the window. For example, Exhibit 1-2 shows the syntax for the AVERAGE function.

There are many errors that could occur with the use of functions and formulas. The user should use the Help command in case of an error to determine why an error occurred and consequently to remedy the problem.

Printing Worksheets If you wish to print the entire worksheet, then click on the Microsoft Office Button and select the Print icon. However, if you only wish to print a certain portion of the output, first select the desired section of the worksheet, then click **Page Layout | Print Area | Set Print Area.** Before printing a worksheet or output from a worksheet, you may want to ensure that the printed document will look as desired by utilizing the print preview option found by clicking on the **Microsoft Office Button | Print | Print Preview.**

Installing and Enabling Excel Add-ins Excel add-ins are special programs designed to perform specific tasks. Throughout the textbook we will utilize two of these add-ins: **Solver** and **Data Analysis.** In recent versions of Excel, both Solver and Data Analysis are available options. To check to see if both Solver and Data Analysis have been activated, you will need to click on **Data Tab | Analysis.** If you see both Solver and Data Analysis as options, then both add-ins have been enabled. However, if you don't see an active add-in for Solver or Data Analysis, then you need to enable them by clicking on **Microsoft Office Button | Excel Options | Add-ins | Manage | Excel Add-ins.** Doing this will bring up a display menu with a list of all add-ins. If the add-in is enabled, there will be a check by its name. If there is no check mark by Solver or Data Analysis ToolPak and Analysis ToolPak-VBA, then they will need to be checked. After checking the Solver or Data Analysis, you need to go

EXHIBIT 1-2 Functions Screen

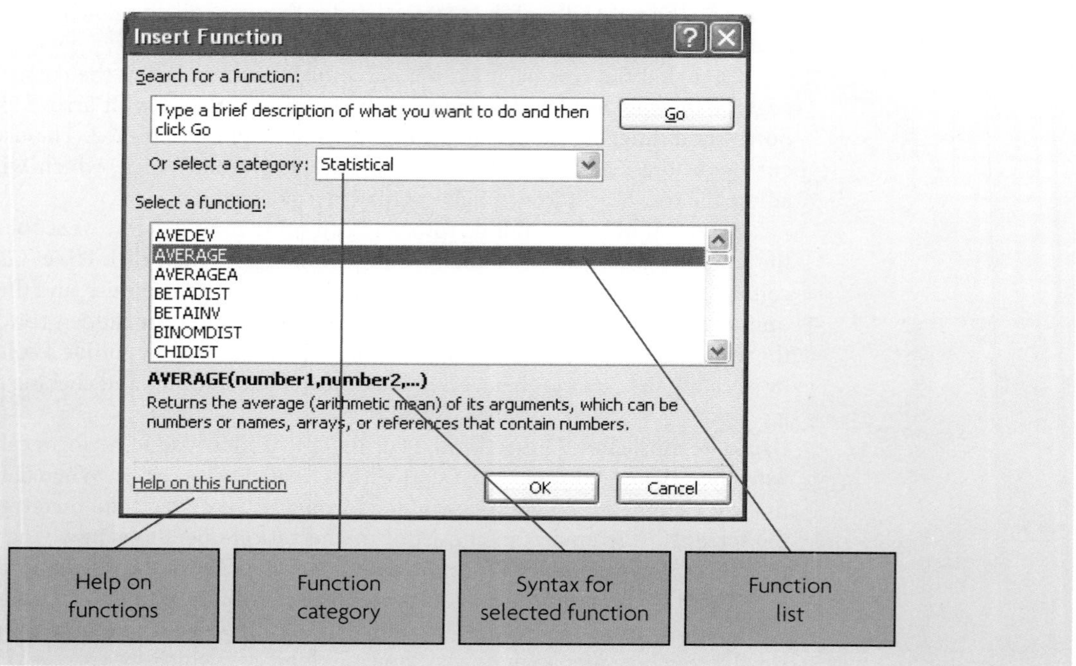

back and click on **Data Tab | Analysis** to make sure the two add-ins have been activated. However, once these add-ins are activated, then you do not need to check them as they will be available each time you start Excel. See Exhibit 1-3 for the menu of available add-ins.

As we go through the various chapters, we will explain how to utilize different options with Excel. We recommend obtaining the following book to learn details and intricacies about Excel: *Excel 2007 Bible* by John Walkenbach published by Wiley Publishing Inc, 2007.

Spreadsheet Engineering

Creating a spreadsheet model involves entering the problem's input data and the expressions defining the model statement by means of formulas into a spreadsheet to obtain outputs and business insights about the problem under study. This process may become tedious if not carefully undertaken. Therefore, the use of best practices, based on software engineering principles, are strongly recommended to build efficient (i.e., with minimal waste of effort, rework, and debugging) as well as effective (i.e., models that capture the essence of a business problem, achieve results that meet requirements, and are understood and reproducible by other people) spreadsheet models. This has led to the concept of **spreadsheet engineering.** Powel and Baker offer helpful guidelines for devising **efficient** and **effective spreadsheet models**, centred on the three stages involved in spreadsheet modelling: designing, building, and testing.[1]

---

[1]Stephen G. Powell, Kenneth R. Baker, "Chapter 5," *Management Science: the Art of Modeling with Spreadsheets,* 2nd ed., (Hoboken, NJ: John Wiley & Sons, 2007), p.121.

EXHIBIT 1-3 Add-in Options

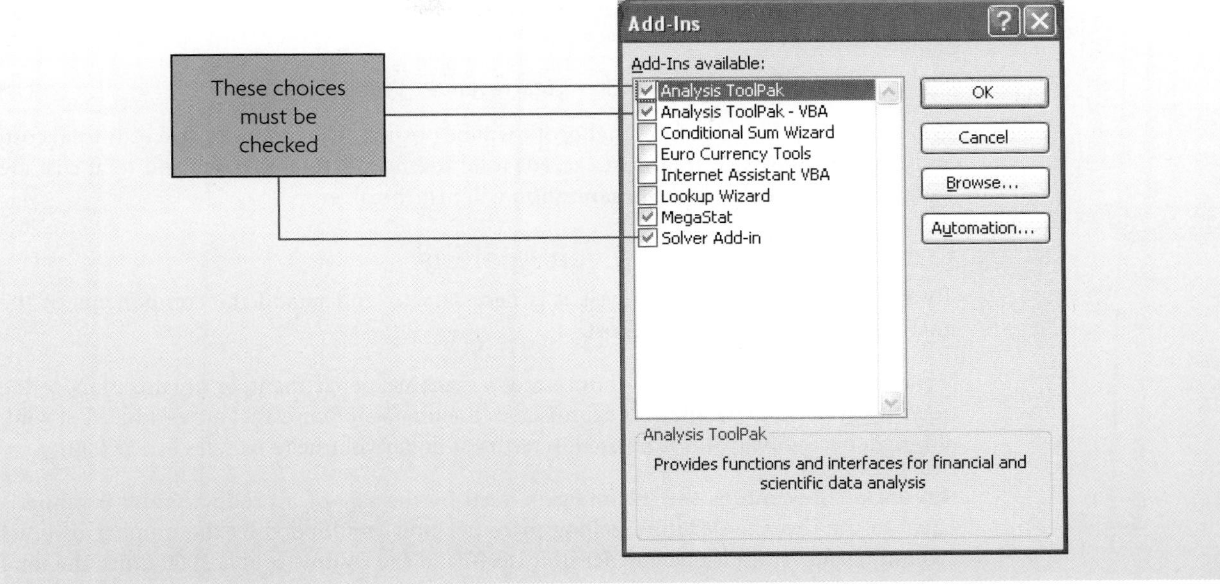

At the designing stage, good practices involve developing a sketch of the spreadsheet, organizing the spreadsheet into modules or groups of similar items, and isolating the input parameters by placing them in a single location and separating them from calculations. It is also recommended to start small instead of building a complex model all at once, to keep the model simple, and to document its important data and formulas.

In building a spreadsheet model, good practices involve following a plan, building a single module at a time; predicting the expected outcome of each formula; copying and pasting formulas carefully; using relative and absolute addressing to simplify copying; using the function Wizard to ensure correct syntax; and using range names to make formulas easy to read.

In testing a workbook, good practices involve checking that numerical results look plausible; formulas are correct; and model performance is plausible.

These good practices are followed in all examples built throughout this textbook.

1.7 BREAK-EVEN ANALYSIS

Introduction to Break-Even Analysis

One of the simplest quantitative models used by managers is the break-even model. Break-even analysis, which is sometimes referred to as cost-volume analysis, is concerned with the interrelationship of costs, volume (quantity of output or sales), and profit. Break-even analysis provides managers with answers to questions such as

1. What profit can be expected if sales are 6000 units this month?
2. Would it be profitable to produce this product if annual demand is 50 000 units?

3. How many units must be sold to cover costs?
4. What costs will result if 3000 units are made?

The basic relationship that underlies break-even analysis is summarized by the following formula:

$$\textbf{Profit} = \textbf{Total revenue} - \textbf{Total cost} \tag{1-1}$$

We can see from this equation that profit will be positive if total revenue exceeds total cost, and negative (a loss) if total cost exceeds total revenue. If total revenue and total cost are equal, profit will be zero; the organization will just "break even."

Components of Break-Even Analysis

To understand break-even analysis it is necessary to understand the components of the analysis: volume, revenue, and cost.

Volume **Volume** is the level of output of a machine, department, or organization, or the quantity of sales. Generally, it is expressed as the *number of units* that are produced or sold, although occasionally it is expressed in terms of dollar volume (e.g., sales of $32 000).

Revenue **Revenue** is the income generated by the sale of a product. **Total revenue** is equal to the revenue per unit (selling price per unit) multiplied by the number of units (volume) sold. Thus, if revenue per unit is $10 and the volume sold is 2000 units, the total revenue is $10(2000) = $20 000.

If the selling price per unit remains the same regardless of the number sold (i.e., there are no quantity discounts), then total revenue will increase linearly as volume increases. A graph of total revenue is illustrated in Figure 1-3.

Costs There are usually a number of different costs that must be taken into account to determine profit. A useful way of thinking about them is by classifying them either as *fixed* or *variable.* **Fixed costs** are costs that are not related (at least within reasonable limits) to

FIGURE 1-3 Total Revenue Increases Linearly as Volume Increases

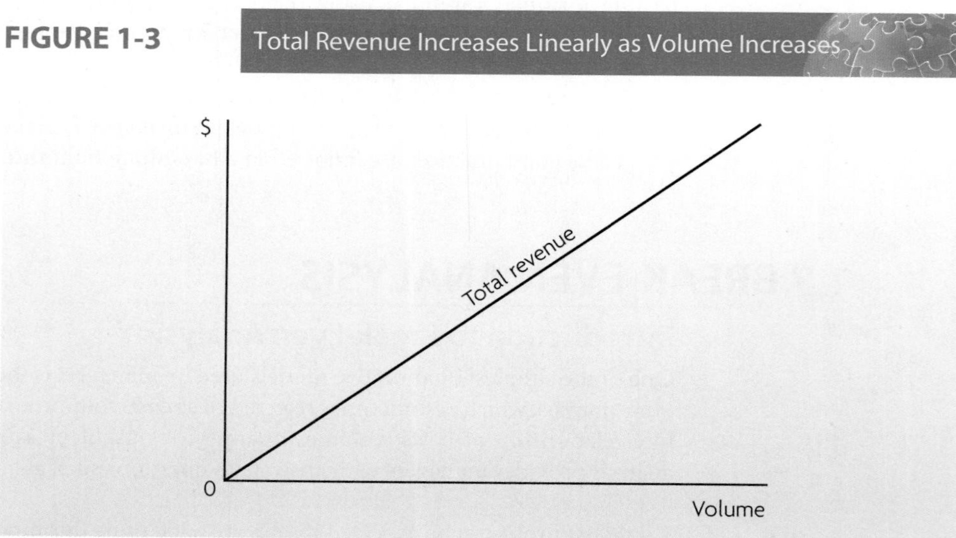

the volume of output. Consequently, fixed costs remain the same regardless of volume. Examples of fixed costs include such expenses as

- rent/leasing costs for plant and equipment;
- administrative costs;
- heat, light, and air conditioning;
- maintenance;
- janitorial services;
- insurance;
- depreciation on plant and equipment.

Fixed costs are the sum of these and other costs that do not vary with level of output. Figure 1-4 illustrates fixed costs.

Variable costs are expenses that vary with volume; each unit produced requires certain inputs (e.g., material) that add to the cost. Typical examples of variable costs include such expenses as

- raw materials and purchased parts;
- direct labour;
- packaging and shipping costs.

Total variable cost is equal to the product of variable cost per unit and the volume that is produced. Thus, if the variable cost per unit is \$5 and the volume is 2000 units, the total variable cost is \$5(2000) = \$10 000. Total variable cost is illustrated in Figure 1-5.

Total cost is the sum of fixed cost and total variable cost. Thus, if fixed cost *for the period during which the 2000 units were produced* was \$7000, then total cost (*TC*) would be

$$TC = \$7000 + \$5(2000) = \$17\,000$$

The computation of total cost is summarized by the following formula:

$$TC = F + VQ \tag{1-2}$$

FIGURE 1-4 Fixed Costs

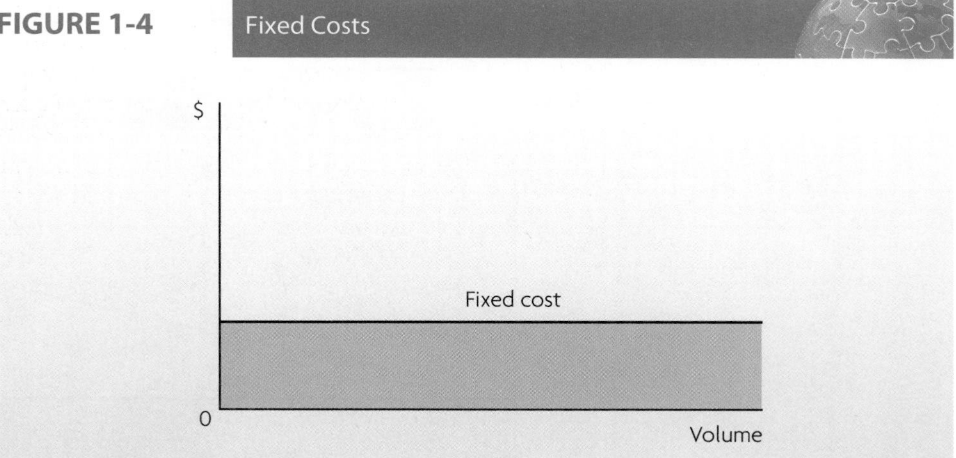

FIGURE 1-5 Total Variable Cost

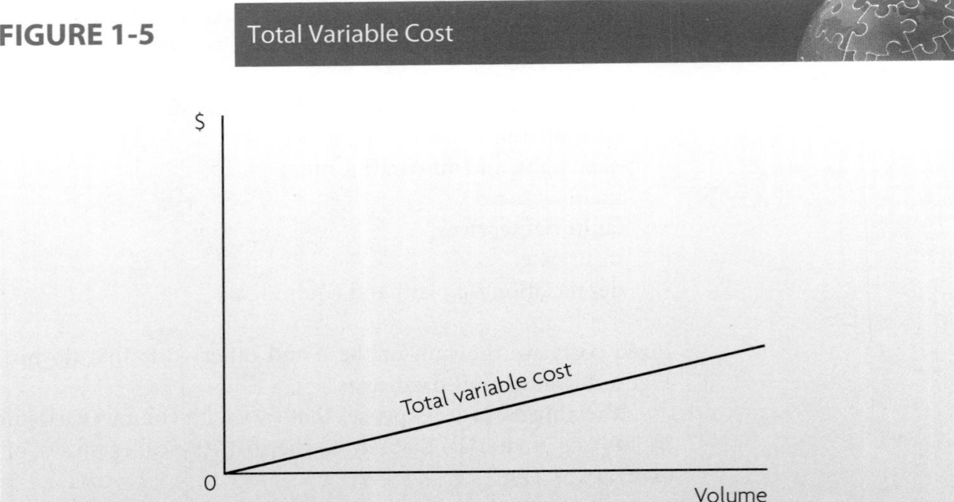

where

$$F = \text{fixed cost assigned}$$
$$V = \text{variable cost per unit}$$
$$Q = \text{volume or quantity}$$

Total cost is illustrated in Figure 1-6.

Profit Recall that profit is the difference between total revenue and total cost. Using the preceding illustrations where

$$\begin{aligned} \text{Fixed cost} &= \$7000 \\ \text{Total variable cost} &= \$10\,000 \\ \text{Total revenue} &= \$20\,000 \end{aligned}$$

we can determine that profit is $3000:

$$\begin{aligned} \text{Profit} &= \text{Total revenue} - (\text{Fixed cost} + \text{Total variable cost}) \\ &= \$20\,000 - (\$7000 + \$10\,000) \\ &= \$3000 \end{aligned} \tag{1-3}$$

FIGURE 1-6 Total Cost

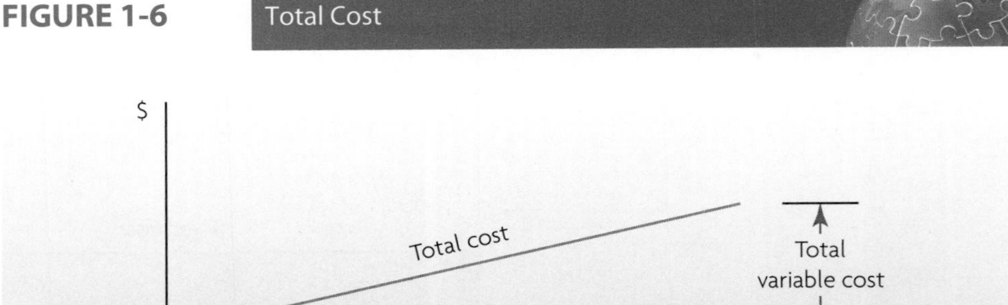

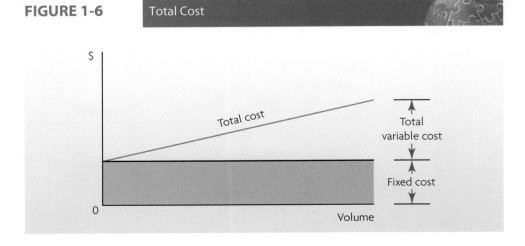

We can write Equation 1-3 in a slightly different form to clearly indicate how each of the components is included in the computation of profit:

$$\text{Profit} = RQ - (F + VQ) \tag{1-4}$$

where

R = revenue per unit
Q = quantity or volume
V = variable cost per unit
F = fixed cost assigned

Figure 1-7 incorporates total revenue and total cost on the same graph. Note that profit is the vertical difference between the total revenue line and the total cost line for any given volume. Moreover, notice that if total cost exceeds total revenue, there is a loss (negative profit). If total cost and total revenue are equal, profit is zero. The volume or quantity at which that occurs is called the break-even point (BEP).

The Break-Even Point

The **break-even point (BEP)** is the volume for which total revenue and total cost are equal. Knowledge of that volume is useful because it reveals to management where the dividing line is between profit and loss; a volume of sales that is higher than the break-even point will result in a profit, while a volume of sales that is lower than the break-even point will result in a loss.

We can obtain an expression that will enable us to calculate the break-even quantity by turning to Equation 1-4. If we set profit equal to zero and then solve for Q, we have an expression for the break-even point:

$$RQ = F + VQ$$
$$RQ - VQ = F$$
$$Q(R - V) = F$$
$$Q_{BEP} = \frac{F}{R - V} \tag{1-5}$$

FIGURE 1-7 Profit and the Break-Even Point

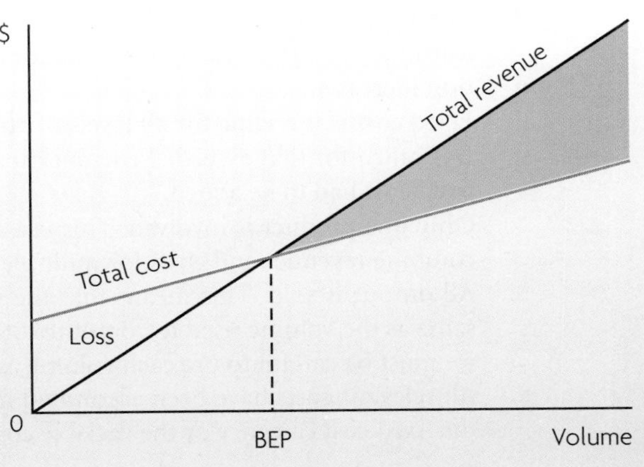

EXAMPLE 1-1

Given this information on costs and revenue:

$F = \$60\,000$
$V = \$20$ per unit
$R = \$30$ per unit

determine each of the following:

a. Profit (loss) at a volume of 5000 units.
b. Profit (loss) at a volume of 10 000 units.
c. The break-even point.

Solution

Profit $= RQ - (F + VQ)$

a. $Q = 5\,000$ units.

$$\text{Profit} = \$30(5000) - [\$60\,000 + \$20(5000)] = -\$10\,000$$

Hence, there is a loss of \$10 000; total cost exceeds total revenue by that amount.

b. $Q = 10\,000$ units.

$$\text{Profit} = \$30(10\,000) - [\$60\,000 + \$20(10\,000)] = \$40\,000$$

c. $$Q_{BEP} = \frac{F}{R - V} = \frac{\$60\,000}{\$30 \text{ per unit} - \$20 \text{ per unit}} = 6000 \text{ units}$$

Hence, if 6000 units are sold, revenues will just cover costs; if a smaller quantity is sold, there will be a loss, but if a larger quantity is sold, there will be a profit.

Assumptions of Break-Even Analysis

The appropriateness of any model in a given situation depends on how well the assumptions of the model are satisfied by the situation. In the case of the break-even model, the key assumptions made for solving the problems presented in this book are

1. The revenue per unit is the same for all volumes. This would not be the case if quantity discounts caused revenue per unit to decrease as the quantity sold increased.
2. The variable cost per unit is the same for all volumes. This would not be the case if learning was a factor, so that the labour cost per unit decreased as the level of production increased.
3. Fixed cost is the same for all levels of volume. This would not be the case if a volume was called for that exceeded current capacity, so that additional capacity at a different fixed cost had to be added.
4. Only one product is involved. This is a simplifying assumption that avoids having to combine revenues and costs for multiple items.
5. All output is sold. This means that the volume used to compute total revenue is the same as the volume used to compute total variable cost. If this assumption is not met, we must be careful to use each volume as appropriate in computing profit.
6. All relevant costs have been accounted for, and have been correctly assigned to either the fixed cost category or the variable cost category.

Sensitivity Analysis

The break-even analysis model discussed above assumes that all input parameters (selling unit price, unit variable cost, and fixed cost) are correctly estimated and remain constant. This is far from the case in real life, and sensitivity analysis is used to examine the impact on the model results, if any, if the estimates change, as well as to answer "What if . . . ?" type questions. It provides managers with answers to questions such as

1. What profit can be expected if units sold decreases by 15 percent from the original estimates?
2. What profit can be expected if variable cost per unit increases by 20 percent?
3. How many units must be sold if changes occurred in price, fixed costs, and variables costs?

From Example 1-1, the company involved is considering upgrading its products. What is the impact on the break-even point if the upgrade results on the increase of the selling price from \$30 to \$35?

If the selling price increases, all other parameters held constant, the total revenue will increase, resulting on the reduction of break-even point from 6000 units to 4000 units. That is,

$$Q_{BEP} = \frac{F}{R - V} = \frac{\$60\,000}{\$35 \text{ per unit} - \$20 \text{ per unit}} = 4000 \text{ units}$$

In general, an increase in price will result in a higher profit and a reduction of the break-even point, assuming all other parameters are held constant. However, in practice this is not always feasible, especially in an open market, unless some other actions are taken such as, the upgrade of the product (e.g., enhanced quality). This generally results not only in the increase of the unit variable cost price but also in fixed cost (e.g., advertising expenditures). If it is now assumed that the variable cost increases to \$22.50, in addition to the changes of the selling price, what is the impact on the break-even point?

The additional change of the variable cost will result in break-even point of 4800 units, that is,

$$Q_{BEP} = \frac{F}{R - V} = \frac{\$60\,000}{\$35 \text{ per unit} - \$22.5 \text{ per unit}} = 4800 \text{ units}$$

In general, an increase in unit variable cost results in an increase of the break-even point, assuming all other parameters are held constant.

If the fixed costs increase to \$80 000, in addition to the previous changes, what is the impact on the break-even point? These changes yield a break-even point of 6400 units.

$$Q_{BEP} = \frac{F}{R - V} = \frac{\$80\,000}{\$35 \text{ per unit} - \$22.5 \text{ per unit}} = 6400 \text{ units}$$

In general, an increase in fixed costs results in the increase of the break-even point, assuming all other parameters are held constant.

Figure 1-8 illustrates the changes in the break-even point when changes occurred, independently or simultaneously, in the selling price and costs.

Using Excel to Solve the Break-Even Model

In this section, we will resolve Example 1-1 by utilizing Excel. To solve the break-even model, first we must prepare a spreadsheet with headings that identify model parameters and variables. Once the model variables and parameters are identified, then the

FIGURE 1-8 Break-Even Point with Changes in Selling Price and Costs

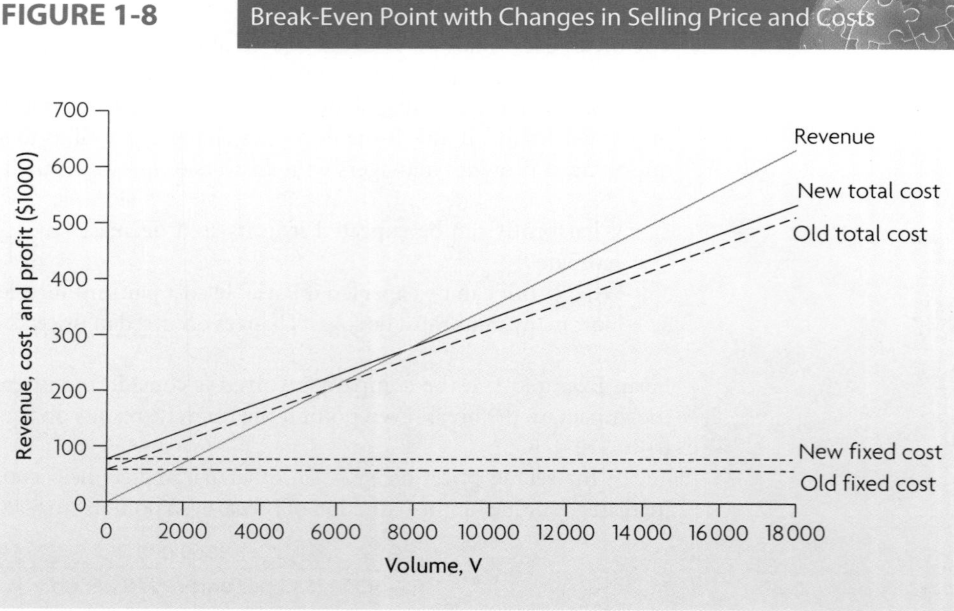

appropriate mathematical formulas are entered into appropriate cells. Exhibit 1-4 shows the spreadsheet for the Example 1-1. Note that cell C10 contains the formula for the break-even volume while cell C12 contains the total cost formula and cell C14 contains the formula for total profit or total loss. This is a simple demonstration of modelling using Excel. As we cover more complicated models in the upcoming chapters, we will have the opportunity to demonstrate other aspects and features of Excel in the context of modelling management science techniques.

Using Excel's Goal Seek to Compute the Break-Even Point

Even though the previous analysis of the break-even point with Excel is very simple, we can utilize Excel to automatically calculate the break-even point by using Excel's **Goal Seek** feature. Using this feature allows us to state a goal or target for a certain cell and also specify the cell that must be automatically changed to achieve this goal. In the case of break-even analysis, we indicate the number of units necessary so that the profit is zero. The results of **Goal Seek** are displayed in Exhibits 1-5 and 1-6.

Exhibit 1-5 shows how the **Goal Seek** function is implemented with Excel. First, we activate the Goal Seek feature in Excel by clicking on **Data | Data Tools | What-If-Analysis | Goal Seek** from the Excel menu. This brings up the Excel **Goal Seek** input window displayed in Exhibit 1-5. On this screen, we first specify cell C16 in Exhibit 1-4 (total profit) as the "set value" cell. In doing the Goal Seek, we simply need to eliminate the formula in cell C10 and instead indicate a value of 0. In the "To value" box, we specify a value of zero, indicating the break-even point or zero profit. In the "By changing cells" box we indicate cell C10, which contains the number of units made. When we click OK, it brings up the **Goal Seek** Status window (output screen) shown in Exhibit 1-6. This screen indicates that the goal of 0 profit (break-even) has been achieved. We also can indicate different profit values in the "To value" box to see the number of units needed to achieve that level of profit. For example, if we indicate a total profit of $2000 in the "To value" box and run the Goal Seek program again, it will give an answer that we need to sell 6200 units in cell C10 to achieve a profit of $2000 in cell C16.

EXHIBIT 1-4 Break-Even Analysis

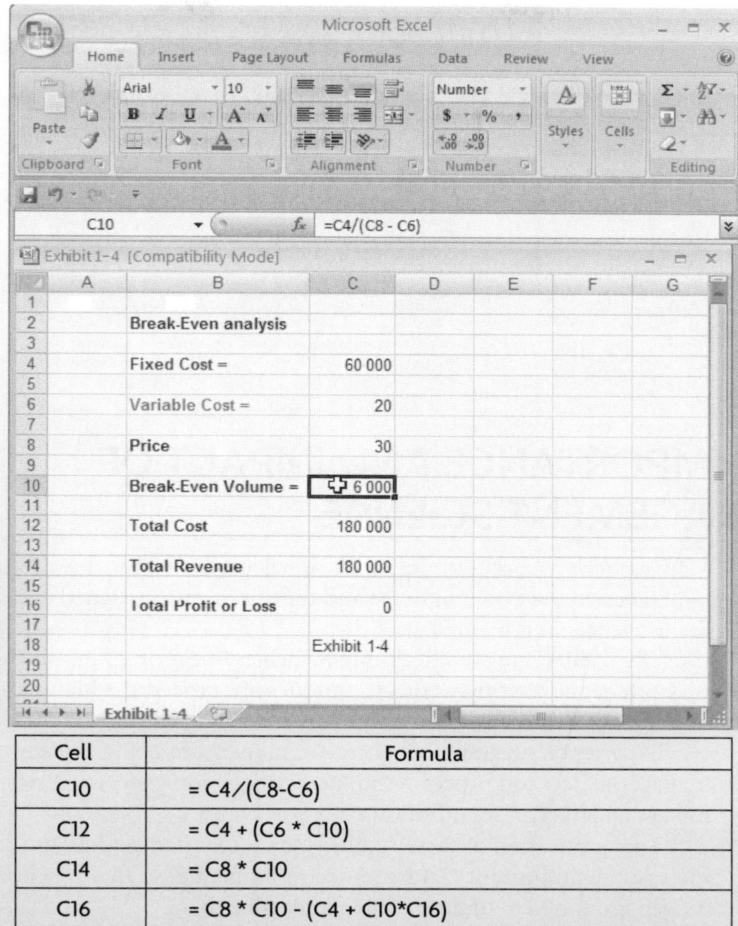

Cell	Formula
C10	= C4/(C8-C6)
C12	= C4 + (C6 * C10)
C14	= C8 * C10
C16	= C8 * C10 - (C4 + C10*C16)

EXHIBIT 1-5 Goal Seek Input Screen

Goal Seek

Set cell: $C$16

To value: 0

By changing cell: $C$10

OK Cancel

EXHIBIT 1-6 Goal Seek Output Screen

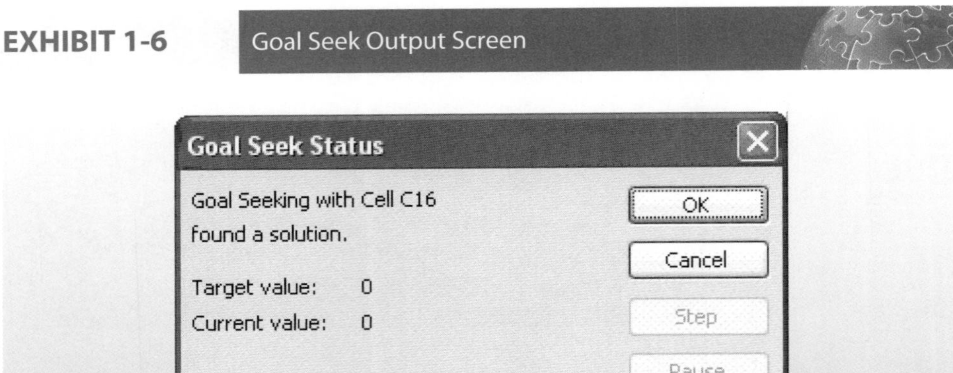

1.8 THE IMPORTANCE AND IMPACT OF MANAGEMENT SCIENCE

Management science techniques are widely used in today's businesses. A number of surveys have revealed the extent of usage and the importance assigned to the usefulness of management science tools by managers.

The results show that techniques such as linear programming and simulation are used very often, and that these two techniques are ranked the highest in terms of their usefulness. Moreover, most of the techniques are widely used.

Experience suggests that these techniques are being increasingly integrated into the managerial decision process. And increasingly, computers and statistical analysis are being used at all levels of organizations.

The implication of these results is that quantitative tools and computers are becoming increasingly important factors in decision making, so that it behooves decision makers to be well grounded in understanding and using them.

Management science has made a profound difference in many organizations around the globe. Table 1-2 summarizes some of the successful applications of management science. These have been selected from numerous applications published in *Interfaces* journal.

Canadian Management-Science-Based Solution Providers

In Canada, a number of Canadian-owned companies or subsidiaries provide management-science-based solutions to various organizations worldwide. The following sample of companies have developed products that are recognized as leaders in their core markets. A brief introduction of each is given, as reported in the company's website.

Giro Inc. (www.giro.ca). Founded in 1979, this privately owned, Canadian company develops and implements integrated solutions for planning and managing public transit and postal operations. Established in Montreal, the company serves customers in South America, North America, Australia, and Asia. Their core products include *HASTUS* (for

TABLE 1-2 Successful Applications of Management Science

Organization	Explanation of the Application	Literature Citation	Savings or Added Revenue
Air Transat	Optimization of aircraft routing, crew pairing, and work assignment	*Interfaces*, March–April 2000	12% of operating cost the first year and over $1 million during the second year
American Airlines	Developing a crew scheduling system to maximize service and minimize cost	*Interfaces*, January–February 1992	$500 million additional revenue per year
ATT	Developing a computerized system for business customer call centres	*Interfaces*, January–February 1993	$750 million per year
Bombardier Flexjet	Improving fractional aircraft ownership operations	*Interfaces*, January–February 2005	$27 million per year
Canadian Pacific Railway	Optimization of the routing and classification plan for railcar scheduling	*Interfaces*, January–February 2003	$170 million per year
Chipita International Inc.	Systems analysis speeds up Chipita's food-processing line	*Interfaces*, May–June 2002	$1 million per year
Continental Airlines	Developing crew scheduling and crew recovery decision support system	*Interfaces*, January–February 2003	$40 million per year
Delta Airlines	Assignment of airplanes to flights	*Interfaces*, January–February 1994	$100 million per year
General Electric	GE's energy rentals business automates its credit assessment process	*Interfaces*, September–October 2003	Savings of 60% of the cost per credit decision
Hewlett-Packard	Designing an assembly line to improve production methods	*Interfaces*, January–February 1998	$280 million additional revenue per year

Organization	Explanation of the Application	Literature Citation	Savings or Added Revenue
Hewlett-Packard	Optimization of supply chain network analysis, including inventory optimization	*Interfaces*, January–February 2002	$130 million per year
Hutchison Port Holdings	Optimize resources throughout the container yard	*Interfaces*, January–February 2005	$100 million per year
IBM	Inventory management of spare parts	*Interfaces*, January–February 1990	$250 million less in inventory per year
Merrill Lynch	Pricing analysis for Merrill Lynch Integrated Choice	*Interfaces*, January–February 2002	$40 million per year
Procter & Gamble	Designing production and distribution systems	*Interfaces*, January–February 1997	$200 million per year
Quebec Liquor Board (SAQ)	Developing an automated employees scheduling system	*Interfaces*, September–October 2005	$1 million per year
STCUM	Vehicle and manpower scheduling	*Interfaces*, January–February 1990	$4 million per year
Taco Bell	Scheduling of employees to improve customer service and minimize cost	*Interfaces*, January–February 1997	$750 million per year
Texas Children's Hospital	Developing contract optimization	*Interfaces*, January–February 2004	$6 million per year
UPS	Design of service networks for delivering express packages	*Interfaces*, January–February 2004	$87 million per year
Workers' Compensation of British Columbia	Early detection of high-risk claims at the Workers' Compensation Board of British Columbia	*Interfaces*, July–August 2003	$4.7 million per year

transit scheduling, daily operations, and customer information), *GeoRoute* (a routing software for postal operations and municipal services such as waste collection and meter reading), and *GIRO/ACCES* (for managing and scheduling transit for the disabled). *HASTUS* is used by transit authorities in over 250 customer sites in 21 countries, including installations in Montreal, Los Angeles, Chicago, New York, Barcelona, Brussels, Geneva, Stockholm, Vienna, Hamburg, Singapore, and Sydney. *GeoRoute* is the most widely used routing software in the postal sector with installations at Deutsche Post in Germany, Royal Mail in United Kingdom, La Poste in Belgium, An Post in Ireland, Norway Post, P&T Luxembourg, Canada Post, and CTT Correios in Portugal.

INRO (www.inro.ca). Founded in 1976, this company designs and develops products to model urban, metropolitan, and regional transportation systems. The company core products include Emme (a travel forecasting software), Dynameq (for modelling and evaluating dynamic traffic conditions on large, congested networks), and STAN (for strategic planning and analysis of regional or national multiproduct, multimode freight transportation systems). These products are used by transport planners in over 900 organizations in more than 70 countries, including half of the world's 25 largest cities. Headquartered in the city of Montreal, the company has business partners acting as representatives around the world.

Kronos Canadian Systems Inc. (www.kronos.com/canada) provides workforce management solutions for manufacturing, retail, hospitality, health care, government, and education sectors. It is a wholly owned subsidiary of Kronos Inc., headquartered in Mississauga with offices in Montreal, Ottawa, Calgary, Kelowna, and Vancouver. Over 1200 Canadian companies use their products, which include *Workforce Central* (to create and manage optimized schedules that balance the needs of employees, customers, and business); *Altitude* (to automate crew planning, management, and optimization in the airline industry); and *Kronos for Health Care* (to optimize complex staff scheduling needs in health care organizations).

Jeppesen (www.jeppesen.com) is a subsidiary of Boeing Company, headquartered in Englewood, Colorado, with offices in many other countries including Canada. The company serves primarily the transportation industry (aviation, rail and logistics, marine) with information solutions that make it possible for people around the globe to safely and efficiently reach their destinations. In the aviation market, one of their products is the resource optimization software, CARMEN, which provides airlines with flight planning, scheduling, and operations management solutions. CARMEN is used by most of the world's largest airlines.

In the rail and logistics market the company provides software and services to passenger and freight railway operators worldwide that allow them to optimize their equipment allocation, crew scheduling and rostering, as well as to ensure day-of-operation management and administration. The company also provides integrated planning and decision support solutions to transportation and logistic providers worldwide (e.g., postal and courier companies, logistics integrators, forwarders, and urban transport companies and authorities). In the maritime market, the company provides, for example, integrated scheduling of staff and equipment at maritime terminals.

Summary

Management science is the discipline devoted to the solution of management problems using a scientific approach. The focus is on problem solving using quantitative models. The approach is to define the problem, construct a model that reflects the important aspects of the problem, analyze the model to identify an appropriate solution to the problem, implement the solution, and check to see that the problem has been solved.

The core of management science is the scientific approach to problem solving. An important part of this is the use of quantitative models. Models are abstractions of reality: Ideally, a model will capture the important aspects of a situation without including all of the minor details that would increase complexity and thereby reduce the chances of finding a solution to the problem.

There are a variety of model types that are employed in decision-making environments; management science models fall under the heading of symbolic models (that is, numbers and symbols are used to form mathematical models). Using these models tends to be a more objective approach than using qualitative models, although in symbolic models the more important qualitative aspects of a problem may be ignored. Furthermore, quantitative models enable users to take advantage of the tremendous computational abilities of computers and calculators.

Glossary

Analog Model A physical representation of a real object, but in the appearance other than the object being modelled.
Break-Even Point (BEP) The volume of sales for which total revenue equals total cost; profit is zero at the break-even point.
CORS The Canadian Operational Research Society (www.cors.ca).
Decision Variable A variable whose value can be set by a decision maker; the purpose of modelling is to determine appropriate values for decision variables.
Deterministic Model A model in which all numerical values are known with certainty.
DSI Decision Sciences Institute (http://www.decisionsciences.org) .
Effective Spreadsheet Model A model that captures the essence of a business problem, achieves results that meets requirements, and is understood and reproducible by other people.
Efficient Spreadsheet Model A model built with minimum waste of effort, rework, and debugging.
Fixed Costs Costs that do not vary with the level of output or sales. An example would be monthly rent on a facility.
Iconic Model A physical, scaled-down representation of a real object.
INFORMS Institute for Operations Research and the Management Science (http://www.informs.org).
Management Science A discipline devoted to the use of quantitative models for solving managerial-type problems.
Mathematical Model A symbolic model; uses numbers and symbols.
Measure of Effectiveness A basis for evaluating the desirability of a particular solution. Common measures include profits, costs, and revenues.
Model A selective abstraction of reality.
Parameter A constant in a mathematical model.
Probabilistic Model A model that incorporates probability to reflect inherent randomness in certain variables.
Revenue Income received from sale of a product or service.
Scientific Approach A logical approach to problem solving that includes defining the problem, constructing a model, analyzing the model, solving, and implementing the solution.
Sensitivity Analysis Determining the degree to which possible changes in various model dimensions will affect the result of model analysis.

Spreadsheet Engineering Application of best practices to the development of spreadsheet-based models, based on software engineering principles.

Symbolic Model A model that uses numbers and algebraic symbols to represent selected aspects of reality.

Total Revenue Revenue per unit multiplied by number of units sold.

Total Variable Cost Variable cost per unit multiplied by the number of units produced.

Uncontrollable Variable A variable that influences the results of a model but cannot be controlled by the analyst.

Variable A portion of a model that can take on different values (e.g., the speed of a vehicle, the number of newspapers sold per day).

Variable Costs Costs associated with producing units of a product (e.g., typewriters) that are related to the number of units produced. Typical examples are labour and material costs.

Volume The quantity of units produced and/or sold.

Discussion and Review Questions

1. Explain what is meant by the term *management science.*
2. Suppose you have just been hired by a small firm. After being on the job for a few weeks, you realize that most problem solving is done on an informal basis—quantitative models are not being used. You share your reservations about this with your manager, and after a certain amount of discussion, your manager asks you to outline your reasoning on why the firm should adopt a more quantitative approach to problem solving. What would the main points of your response be?
3. Suppose that senior management has asked you to give a presentation that will enlighten them on the use of models for problem solving. Specifically, they want to know what a model is, what types of models there are, how models can lead to good solutions, and any potential pitfalls to be aware of. Outline your presentation.
4. You are faced with making a choice between two models. One is a fairly simple model that will provide an approximate answer to the problem; the other is a much more complex model that can be expected to provide a much more precise answer to the problem.
   a. Under what circumstances would you choose the simple model?
   b. Under what circumstances would the more sophisticated model be your choice?
5. Briefly describe the management science approach to problem solving.
6. Briefly describe the symbolic model type and give an example.
7. Contrast deterministic and probabilistic models, and indicate the conditions under which each type would be appropriate.
8. How would you respond to a student who says, "Why should I have to study management science? My major is marketing."
9. Suppose that after a considerable amount of time and effort, the solution obtained from a model is not implemented.
   a. List some possible reasons for this.
   b. Would you say that the time and effort was, therefore, probably wasted? Explain your answer.
10. What does the phrase "modelling can become an end in itself" mean? Is this necessarily bad?
11. Why might a solution that is optimal in a model not be optimal in reality? How might the gap be closed? What risks might there be in attempting to close the gap?
12. How and why are computers an integral part of management science?

Problems

1. Consider the following mathematical model, which represents the total number of potential buying customers reached by XYZ company with the use of five advertising mediums (1-radio, 2-TV, 3-newspaper, 4-direct mail, and 5-email, respectively):

$$Z = 7000x_1 + 50\,000x_2 + 18\,000x_3 + 34\,000x_4 + 90\,000x_5$$

   a. What are the model decision variables and the meaning of each of them?
   b. What are the model parameters (constants) and the meaning of each of them?

2. The Exxoff Corporation produces an automotive lubricant that is sold to wholesale distributors for $25 a case. Fixed costs are $80 000 and variable costs are $15 per case.
   a. What profit or loss would result if 4000 cases are sold?
   b. What profit or loss would result if 10 000 cases are sold?
   c. What is the break-even volume in cases?
   d. If the Exxoff Corporation has to offer a 15% discount on the selling price per case, what effect will the change has on the break-even volume in cases?
   e. If the Exxoff Corporation reduces the fixed costs to $60 000 through technology innovation, what effect will the change have on the break-even volume in cases if no discount is offered on the selling price per case?

3. The Greene Daisy Company offers a spring tune-up service for power lawn mowers at a price of $24.95. Labour and supplies cost an average of $10 per tune-up, and overhead charged to the operation is $5000 a month. Determine:
   a. The monthly volume needed to break even.
   b. The profit that would result if 375 tune-ups are performed per month.
   c. The monthly volume needed to break even, if the company estimates that the costs of labour and supplies will increase to $15 per tune-up.
   d. The break-even monthly volume, if with an increase on the costs of labour and supplies to $15 per tune-up, the company believes that the selling price will also increase by 5 percent? What are the changes on total costs and profit if the selling volume remains 375?

4. A company that produces cleaning products is considering a proposal to begin production of a new detergent that would cost $1 a bottle to make and distribute, and retail for $2.19 a bottle. Fixed cost for the operation would be $3000 a week. Assume that all output can be sold.
   a. What would the total cost, total revenue, and profit (or loss) be for a weekly volume of 10 000 bottles?
   b. What is the break-even volume?

5. Fast-Lube operates a chain of shops that offer a 20-minute oil change and lubrication service for passenger cars and light trucks. The shops have an overhead of $1000 per day. Labour and materials cost $5 per job, and customers are charged $19.95 for the service. Determine:
   a. The number of jobs per day that a shop needs to cover all of its costs.
   b. The profit or loss that would result if 35 cars were serviced in a day.
   c. Suppose two workers work together in a shop and each receives $20 a day in pay and benefits plus $1 per job, customers are still charged 19.95, and material costs $3 per job. What is the break-even volume for the shop? (Hint: $20 per employee is a fixed cost.)

6. Schmaltz, Ltd., produces a variety of specialty beverages. One of its products is made in a separate facility for which monthly rent, administrative costs, and equipment leasing is $80 000. The facility has a monthly capacity of 50 000 cases of the specialty beverage. Eight workers handle production and shipping. Each receives salary and fringe benefits of $2500 per month. Packaging and distribution costs are $0.30 per case, and ingredients cost $1.10 per case. The product is sold for $5.89 a case. Determine the following:
   a. The profit or loss on sales of 40 000 cases.
   b. The break-even volume. Hint: note carefully which costs are truly variable.
   c. The profit or loss that would result from sales of 60 000 cases. Discuss your answer.

7. Lamb, Stew is a fledgling catering firm that serves the meat-and-potato segment of the market. The co-owners want to expand their successful operations to include a neighbouring town. After investigating their options, they have narrowed their choices to two. One option is to have a capacity of 10 events per month. This would result in a cost of $1600 a month plus a cost of $250 per event. The other option would

have a capacity of 20 events per month, a cost of \$3200 a month, and a cost of \$200 per event. The firm would charge \$450 for each event.

a. Determine the break-even volume for each option.
b. What profit (or loss) would each option produce if monthly demand is 10 events?
c. If monthly demand is 14 events, which option would yield the greater profit?

8. The construction firm of Smagglewhetsy & Kid must decide whether to continue to perform payroll functions in-house or to subcontract those services. In-house costs are \$2000 a month plus \$30 per employee. The same services can be performed by a contractor for \$50 per employee plus a monthly service fee of \$1200.

a. If the construction firm has 30 employees, which option would provide the lower cost?
b. Suppose the firm is undergoing an expansion, adding two new employees to its payroll each month. At this rate, in how many months should the firm consider doing its own payroll?

9. The law firm of Smith, Jones, and Greene provides accounting services for some of its clients. The person who handles this service and her secretary cost the firm an average of \$80 000 a year in salary and benefits. Clients are charged a fixed rate of \$300 a year for these services, and the firm is billed \$50 per client for computer time, postage, and supplies. Now, a local accounting firm has offered to provide comparable service for a fee of \$600 per client.

a. What profit or loss would the firm realize if 354 clients use its accounting service each year?
b. Assuming 300 clients a year, would the law firm be better off using its own staff, or using the outside accounting firm?
c. At what level of client usage would the two alternatives produce the same profit or loss?

10. A firm plans to begin production of a new appliance. The manager must decide whether to purchase the motors for the appliance from a vendor to be sold at \$7 each or to produce them in-house. Either of the two processes could be used for production. Purchasing the motor from a vendor would have an annual fixed cost of \$160 000 and variable cost of \$5 per unit, while the in-house production would have an annual fixed cost of \$190 000 and a variable cost of \$4 per unit.

a. What is the break-even point if an outside vendor is used?
b. What is the break-even point if the motor is produced in-house?
c. Determine the range of annual volume for which each alternative would be the best.
d. Determine the range of annual volume for which each alternative would be the best if the firm can increase the selling price by 15%.
e. Determine the range of annual volume for which each alternative would be the best if the firm can reduce the variable cost of in-house production from \$4 per unit to \$3 per unit, assuming no changes in the selling price.

11. A manager must decide how many machines of a certain type to purchase. Each machine can process 100 customers per day. Purchasing one machine will result in a fixed cost of \$2000 per day while purchasing two machines will result in a fixed cost of \$3800 per day. Variable cost will be \$20 per customer and revenue will be \$45 per customer.

a. Determine the break-even point for one machine.
b. Determine the break-even point for two machines.
c. If estimated demand is 90 to 120 customers per day, how many machines should be purchased?

12. A firm has to decide whether to set up an in-house production line to launch a new appliance in the market. Management wishes to make a decision that will maximize the firm's profit. If the firm goes ahead, it would incur an annual fixed cost of \$190 000 and a variable cost of \$4 per unit. The appliance would need to be sold for \$7 each. Let y be a variable defining the sales forecast of the number of appliances that can be sold.

a. Write a mathematical model that can be used by the firm to determine the production level, x, of the new appliance that maximizes the total profit without exceeding the sales forecast, y.
b. Use break-even analysis to recommend whether the appliance should be introduced in the market, taking into account the sales forecast.

13. The Professional division at one Canadian business school provides over 100 development programs that have been tailored to the specific training needs of both the public and private sectors. The program director is planning to offer a one-full-day course in risk management to be sold at \$2250 plus GST (5%) per participant. The division incurs a cost of \$14 700 for promotion, classroom space, staff and instructor's salary, as well as a cost of \$285 per participant for refreshments, lunch, course material, a gift package, and a framed certificate of completion. Let x represent the number of participants who register in the course.

a. Develop a model for the total cost to put on the course.

b. Develop a model for the total profit to put on the course.
c. How much profit will be earned if an enrolment of 15 participants has been forecast?
d. How many participants need to register in the course for it to be worthwhile to offer it?

14. A publisher located in Kingston is considering publishing a novel that will be sold for $45 each. The fixed project costs are estimated to be $65 000 and include the manuscript preparation, the cover design, and the setup cost of the production line. The production cost for each novel is estimated to be $8.50. Determine:
    a. The break-even volume.
    b. The profit or loss that would result with a demand of 3500 copies.
    c. The minimum price per copy that the publisher must charge to break-even with a demand of 3500 copies.

Case 1: Green Daisy Company

The manager of Green Daisy Inc. is in the process of deciding whether to make or buy carburetors for its power lawn mowers. If Green Daisy decides to manufacture the carburetor, it could utilize one of two manufacturing processes. The first process would entail a variable cost of $17 per unit and an annual fixed cost of $200 000, while the second process would entail variable cost of $14 per unit and an annual fixed cost of $240 000. The manager knows of three vendors who are capable and willing to provide the carburetor. Vendor A charges $20 per unit for any volume up to 30 000 units and cannot supply Green Daisy's need for volume above 30 000 units due to its capacity restrictions. Vendor B offers a price of $22 per unit for a demand of 1000 units or less and $18 per unit for each unit above the 1000 units. Vendor C's price is $21 per unit for the first 1000 units and $19 per unit for any additional units. The manager is unsure about what the demand is going to be for power lawnmowers. (a) If the demand is forecasted to be 10 000, 20 000, 28 000, or 60 000 units, which alternative would be best from a cost standpoint? (b) What is the break-even volume of internal process 1, if we use the price of the best external alternative found in part *a*? What is the break-even volume of internal process 2 if we use the same best price? (c) Determine the range for which each alternative is best.

Case 2: Wood Made Company

Wood Made Co. is a family-run manufacturing company of solid wood chairs, located in a small town in Eastern Ontario. The company is seeking a break-even analysis for the month of December. During this same month last year 570 chairs were sold. The company has registered a moderate growth over the last year, so it is assumed that a 10 percent increase can be expected to be sold in the month of December. The company incurs the following monthly expenses, which are based upon such expected increase in volume of sales. The building rent and property tax cost $14 000. The cost for utilities, telephone, depreciation, insurance, and advertising are estimated at $13 250 monthly. The office salaries run another $7000. The general maintenance costs $2000, of which 35 percent is incurred regardless of how many chairs are made. The remaining 65 percent is due to the direct use of the machinery to make chairs. The direct costs for raw materials are estimated at $28 900, and the company evaluates the direct labour and overtime costs at $27 500. The costs for customer invoice preparation, processing, and management are estimated as $2.07 per chair, whereas the selling price per chair is estimated at $350.

Perform the break-even analysis and prepare a report to the senior management that provides answers to the following questions.

1. What is the break-even point in units and in sales dollars?
2. What would be the impact to the break-even point if the selling price is lowered to $325?
3. What would be the impact to the break-even point if the company contracts with the machinery manufacturer to provide maintenance on a contract basis for a monthly cost of $2000, assuming that the selling price remains at $350?
4. How many chairs must be sold if the company targets a profit of $55 000?
5. What price would the company charge to make a profit of $55 000 if physical capabilities limit the monthly production volume to 90 percent of the quantity obtained in question 4?
6. How many chairs must be sold to meet the targeted profit of $55 000 if the company expands its warehouse facility by renting an additional space in another building at the monthly cost of $5500, assuming nothing else changes?

PART 2

DETERMINISTIC DECISION MODELS

PART OUTLINE

The chapters in Part II cover deterministic models. In such models the inputs or variables not controlled by the decision maker are assumed to be known with certainty and not able to vary, in contrast to probabilistic models where variable values must be estimated.

Chapters 2, 3, and 4 focus on one of the most widely used and most powerful tools of management science: *linear programming*. The coverage includes formulation of problems, the use of the simplex method, sensitivity analysis, and discussion of business applications and Excel solutions.

Chapter 5 covers distribution and network flow models. These optimization models are applied in a wide range of businesses to solve shipping, transportation, and logistics problems. They take into account such things as allocating or assigning tasks or jobs, analyzing multiple transportation options to maximize results or revenue as well as minimizing costs. In Chapter 5, linear programming formulations as well as the Excel Solution of these problems are shown. Chapter 16 on the OLC explains the special purpose algorithms used to solve transportation, assignment, shortest route, maximal flow, and minimum spanning tree problems.

Chapter 6 and Chapter 17 on the OLC cover integer programming, a special case of linear programming in which only integer values are used. Chapter 6 covers the formulation of the problem and the Excel solution, while Chapter 17 demonstrates solution of an integer programming problem using a popular technique called branch and bound.

In Chapter 7, we investigate situations in which the objective function and/or one or more constraints are nonlinear. (Chapters 2–6 assumes the solution is "linear.") The chapter shows not only the importance and relevance of nonlinear programming to business applications, but also provides Excel solutions to numerous applied business problems.

Chapter 9 discusses multi-criteria models, which should be utilized whenever more than one criterion needs to be considered in order to arrive at the best decision. Three different multi-criteria models are discussed in Chapter 9, Goal Programming, the Analytical Hierarchy Process, and Scoring Models.

Linear Programming: Basic Concepts, Graphical Solution, and Computer Solution

CHAPTER 2

LEARNING OBJECTIVES

After completing this chapter, you should be able to:

1. Explain what is meant by the terms *constrained optimization* and *linear programming.*
2. List the components and the assumptions of linear programming and briefly explain each.
3. Identify the type of problems that can be solved using linear programming.
4. Formulate simple linear programming models.
5. Identify LP problems that are amenable to graphical solutions.
6. Explain these terms: *optimal solution, feasible solution space, corner point, redundant constraint slack,* and *surplus.*
7. Solve two-variable LP problems graphically and interpret your answers.
8. Identify problems that have multiple solutions, problems that have no feasible solutions, unbounded problems, and problems with redundant constraints.
9. Use Excel to solve a linear programming model.

CHAPTER OUTLINE

2.1 INTRODUCTION

Linear programming is at the heart of many extensive optimization systems that have been used to solve thousands of problems in industries as wide ranging as transportation, telecommunications, banking, manufacturing, health care, retailing, and natural resources; in both the private or public sectors; for large or small corporations; and for profit or not-for-profit organizations. The fundamental question these optimization systems can answer is "how do we get the most out" when we only have limited resources to put in. For example, major airlines have to decide what flight schedules yield the highest revenue and keep the costs the lowest. These airlines have thousands of costs to consider, and thousands of decisions that "constrain" their total return. They must have enough planes at each location to start the daily flight schedule, they all must be fueled, crewed up, and ready to fly. At the same time, even for the most popular and profitable routes, they are "constrained" from just sending their whole fleet of planes to service that particularly high-profit route. Carriers such as Air Canada, American, United, and others have optimization software built into their scheduling systems that use linear programming. Similarly, networks such as the global telephone network, utility providers, and private firms with widespread logistics needs also utilize optimization techniques such as linear programming to allocate resources to maximize output subject to the limitations and constraints of their system. On the next page, a Modern Management Science Application vignette, "Scotiabank Canada," reports how the company has benefited from the use of linear programming.

The purpose of this chapter is to provide you with an introduction to linear programming models. Emphasis is placed on familiarization with terminology, problem recognition, model formulation, and examples of applications of linear programming. The chapter is designed to help you to develop four very important skills:

1. The ability to *recognize* problems that can be solved using LP models.
2. The ability to set up, or *formulate,* an LP model in mathematical terms.
3. The ability to *solve* LP problems using the graphical method.
4. The ability to *set up* and *solve* LP problems using an Excel spreadsheet.

Constrained Optimization

A commonly encountered form of decision making involves situations in which the set of acceptable solutions is somehow restricted. The restrictions may be imposed internally or externally. For example, an internal restriction might be the amount of raw material that a department has available to produce its products. This would impose a limit on the amount of product that could be produced. Other internal restrictions can include availability of labour time, machine time, technical requirements (for example, drying times, curing times), and budgets. An external restriction might be labour regulations (e.g., safety equipment, training requirements, overtime) that *limit* the options open to decision makers.

The restrictions are referred to as *constraints* for purposes of linear programming. The goal in linear programming is to find the best solution given the constraints imposed by the problem; hence, the term **constrained optimization.**

Linear Programming

In 1947, George Dantzig developed the use of linear algebra for determining solutions to problems that involved the optimal allocation of scarce resources. In spite of numerous potential applications in business, response to this new technique was low, primarily because of the substantial computational burden it required. Subsequent advances that were made during the last five decades in computer technology and related computer

A MODERN MANAGEMENT SCIENCE APPLICATION: SCOTIABANK CANADA

Scotiabank® has set out to be the best and most successful Canadian-based international financial services group. The company offers a diverse range of financial products and services to customers in more than 50 countries around the world. Like most financial service companies, Scotiabank regularly mounts multi-channel campaigns that offer new products and services to existing and potential customers. The problem consists of determining, for any given mix of campaigns, which products should be marketed to each individual customer and through which channel, in a way that maximizes the marketing return on investment while taking account various business constraints. The company was using standard database marketing models, which allowed it to determine the best recipients for each specific campaign. While helpful for many years, these models no longer allowed Scotiabank to fully realize the most efficient use of channel resources and marketing dollars. The increase in the number and frequency of campaigns, competition, and executive expectations for results from marketing campaigns forced the company to seek alternative methods. Scotiabank turned to SAS®, a leader in business analytics and the largest independent vendor in the business intelligence market, to create the best multi-channel offer selection and targeting solution in the industry. By combining SAS predictive modelling with SAS Marketing Optimization, and through the use of linear programming, a solution was developed to evaluate multiple campaigns simultaneously and determine the optimal assignment of offers to customers for each campaign, while taking into account several types of business constraints. Typically, there are restrictions on the minimum and the maximum number of product offers that can be made in a campaign, requirements on the minimum expected profit from product offers, limits on funding available for the campaign, limits of channel capacity, requirements on the campaign return-on-investment hurdle rates that must be met, etc. The implementation of a linear programming-based approach provides significant improvements over standard approaches, including more incremental profit and more control over the direct marketing process. Moreover, the SAS solution allows Scotiabank to conduct sensitivity analysis on business constraints (e.g., effects of making different budget allocations, effects of changing channel capacity, effects of changing product offerings, etc.) and gain insights on how to make future campaigns even more successful.

Source: "Scotiabank takes CRM to the next level with SAS®," (www.sas.com/success/scotiabank.html).

software have removed the computational burden. This has led to widespread use of linear programming in business.

Although computers are often used to solve linear programming problems, computer programming is not required to obtain computer solutions: Preprogrammed packages are used to input the problem. The *programming* aspect of linear programming refers to the use of *algorithms*. An **algorithm** is a well-defined sequence of steps that will lead to a solution. The term *linear* refers to straight-line relationships. **Linear programming** (LP) models are based on linear relationships. Taken as a whole, the term linear programming refers to a family of mathematical techniques that can be used to find solutions to constrained optimization problems. LP problems can be solved using different techniques. These techniques include the **graphical method** (demonstrated later in this chapter, but limited to two variables), the **simplex method** (explained and demonstrated in Chapter 14 available on the OLC), and **Karmarkar's method** (see details in "Karmarkar's Linear Algorithm," *Interfaces* 16:4, 75–90, July–August 1986).

A Simple Example

To see the framework of LP models, consider Example 2-1. When formulating a model, it can be helpful to think of the problem in words before attempting to describe it in mathematical terms.

EXAMPLE 2-1

Suppose a manager wants to know how much of each of three products (call them product A, product B, and product C) he should tell his production department to produce to maximize the profit obtained from those products. He knows that he must take into account the fact that the department has limited amounts of labour time, material, and machine time available to produce these items. The manager wants at least 40 units of product B to be produced, and exactly 30 units of product C. He also recognizes that the resulting quantities cannot be less than zero. The manager estimates that 200 labour hours, 80 pounds of material, and 50 minutes of machine times will be available. The profit contribution is estimated to \$8, \$3, and \$4 per unit, for each product, respectively. The unit production of product A will require 1 labour hour, 2 pounds of material, and 4 minutes of machine time. The unit production of product B will require 1 labour hour, 1 pound of material, and 2 minutes of machine time. Finally, the unit production of product C will require 1 labour hour, 2 pounds of material, and 2 minutes of machine time.

A verbal model of this would be:

Maximize profit on products A, B, and C.

subject to (i.e., satisfying) the following requirements:

The labour hours used cannot exceed the available labour hours.
The amount of materials used cannot exceed the amount of materials available.
The machine time used cannot exceed the available machine time.
Produce at least 40 units of product B.
Produce exactly 30 units of product C.
The quantities produced cannot be less than zero.

The mathematical model of this problem would look something like this:

x_1 = the number of units of product A to produce
x_2 = the number of units of product B to produce
x_3 = the number of units of product C to produce

maximize $8x_1 + 3x_2 + 4x_3$
subject to

Labour	$1x_1 + 1x_2 + 1x_3 \leq 200$ **hours**
Material	$2x_1 + 1x_2 + 2x_3 \leq 80$ **lbs.**
Machine	$4x_1 + 2x_2 + 2x_3 \leq 50$ **minutes**
Product B	$x_2 \geq 40$ **units**
Product C	$x_3 = 30$ **units**
	$x_1, x_2, x_3 \geq 0$

This is the general form of a linear programming model. Once such a model has been formulated, it can be solved to determine the optimal quantities of each product (i.e., the quantities to produce to maximize profit). For now, we are only concerned with understanding and formulating linear programming models. Solution techniques are described in the following sections of this chapter.

Now, before we turn our attention to model formulation, let us first consider two very important aspects of linear programming models: Their structure and the assumptions they are based on.

2.2 COMPONENTS AND ASSUMPTIONS OF LP MODELS

A linear programming model is a mathematical statement of a problem, written in a form that lends itself to a solution using standard solution techniques. The components of linear programming models provide the *structure* of the models. The assumptions of linear programming models relate to model validity; they prescribe the conditions under which the models are valid. A list of the components and assumptions of LP models is given in Table 2-1. These are explained in detail in the following two sections. Knowledge of the components and the assumptions of LP models is essential to the formulation of valid models.

Components of LP Models

The *objective* in problem solving is the criterion by which all decisions are evaluated. As such, it provides the focus for problem solving. In linear programming models, a single, *quantifiable* objective must be specified by the decision maker. For example, the objective might relate to profits, *or* costs, *or* market share, but to only *one* of these. Moreover, because we are dealing with optimization, the objective will be either maximization or minimization. Hence, every LP problem will be either a maximization (max) problem or a minimization (min) problem. Maximization problems often involve profit, revenue, market share, or return on investment, whereas minimization problems often involve cost, time, or distance. Once the objective is specified, it becomes the measure of effectiveness against which alternate solutions are judged. For example, the optimal solution will be the one that yields the highest profit or the one that provides the lowest cost. In Example 2-1 the problem involves maximizing the profit.

The decision maker can control the value of the objective, which is achieved through choices in the levels of **decision variables.** Decision variables represent choices available to a decision maker, usually with respect to the amount or *quantity* of either an input to a process or an output from a process. For instance, the problem facing the decision maker in

TABLE 2-1 Characteristics of LP Models

Components		
1.	Objective	Model structure
2.	Decision variables	
3.	Constraints	
4.	Parameters	
5.	Nonnegativity	
Assumptions		
1.	Proportionality	Model validity
2.	Additivity	
3	Divisibility	
4.	Certainty	

Example 2-1 is to determine how much of each of the three products to produce to obtain the greatest profit, assuming that all the output can be sold. In terms of the LP model, the decision variables represent those unknown quantities and will be expressed in alphanumerical symbols such as x_1, x_2, and x_3 where:

x_1 = **the number of units of product A to produce**
x_2 = **the number of units of product B to produce**
x_3 = **the number of units of product C to produce**

The ability of a decision maker to select values of the decision variables in LP is subject to certain restrictions or limits. These can come from a variety of sources. The restrictions may reflect availabilities of resources (e.g., raw materials, labour time, machine time, work space, or storage space), legal or contractual requirements (e.g., product or work standards) or technological requirements (e.g., necessary compressive strength or tensile strength), or they may reflect other limits based on forecasts, customer orders, company policies, and so on. In an LP model, the restrictions are referred to as **constraints.** Only solutions that satisfy all constraints in a model are acceptable. These are referred to as **feasible solutions.** The **optimal solution** is the feasible solution that yields the best value of the objective (e.g., the maximum profit, the minimum cost). The constraints in Example 2-1 reflect availability of resources as well as limits on customers demand.

Therefore an LP model consists of a mathematical statement of the objective, called the **objective function,** and a set of mathematical statements of the restrictions (the *constraints*). The objective function and the constraints consist of symbols that represent the decision variables (for example, x_1, x_2, x_3) and numerical values called **parameters.** The parameters are fixed values that specify the impact that one unit of each decision variable will have on the objective and on any constraint it pertains to. For example, if the profit per unit on product 1 is \$8, the 8 is a parameter. Similarly, if each unit of product 1 requires 1 hour of labour, the 1 is a parameter. And, if there are 200 hours of labour available, the 200 is also a parameter.

The **nonnegativity constraint** requirement is that negative values of variables are unrealistic and, therefore, will not be considered in any potential solutions; only positive values and zero will be allowed. For instance, in a problem involving the number of houses to construct, an answer of −2 would imply that two houses that have already been constructed should be torn down! Consider another negative solution that requires preparing −3 apple pies. Neither of these makes sense. For that reason, the nonnegativity requirement is inherent in LP models.[1]

Assumptions of LP Models

Table 2-1 lists four basic assumptions of LP models:

1. Proportionality (linearity)
2. Additivity
3. Divisibility
4. Certainty

[1]In the strictest sense, nonnegativity is not a theoretical requirement, although certain LP algorithms do require it. However, such unrestricted variables ordinarily would not be found in business applications. For that reason, the discussion here treats nonnegativity as a requirement of LP models.

The **proportionality** (Linearity) assumption is that each decision variable have a *linear* impact in the objective function and in each constraint in which it appears. This means, for example, that if the profit of x_1 is \$8 per unit, that same figure must hold regardless of the quantity of x_1: It must be true over the entire range of possible values of x_1. This also applies to each of the constraints: It is required that the same coefficient (for example, 2 lb. per unit) apply over the entire range of possible values of the decision variable.

In terms of a mathematical model, a function or equation is linear when the variables included are all to the power 1 (that is, not squared, cubed, square root, etc.) and no products (e.g., x_1x_2) appear. Thus, this constraint is linear:

$$2x_1 + x_2 = 40$$

These constraints are not linear:

$$2x_1^2 + x_2 \leq 40 \quad (x_1 \text{ is squared})$$
$$2x_1 + x_1x_2 \leq 40 \quad (\text{the second term is a product of variables})$$

The **additivity** assumption requires that terms of the objective function be additive (e.g., the total profit must equal the sum of the profits from each decision variable) and the terms of each constraint be additive (e.g., the total amount of resource used must equal the sum of the resources used by each of the decision variables).

The **divisibility** assumption pertains to potential values of decision variables. It is assumed that noninteger values are acceptable. For instance, $x_1 = 3.5$ is presumed to be an acceptable value. If a problem concerns the quantity of sugar to mix in a recipe, 3.5 pounds would be acceptable. However, if the problem concerns the optimal number of houses to construct, 3.5 does not appear to be acceptable. Instead, that type of problem would seem to require strictly integer solutions. In such cases, *integer programming* methods should be used, which are discussed in a later chapter. It should be noted, however, that some obvious integer-type situations can be handled under the assumption of divisibility. For instance, suppose 3.5 is determined to be the optimal number of television sets to produce per hour. This would result in 7 sets every two hours, which would be acceptable. Another possibility exists when the items are relatively inexpensive (e.g., nuts, bolts, nails, or small pieces of plastic). For example, a model might yield an optimal solution of 210.33 units to be produced. That quantity could easily be rounded to 210 units, and it would still result in a solution that probably is within a few pennies of equalling the (unattainable) optimal value of the objective function.

Thus, the divisibility assumption allows noninteger values to be acceptable. We have seen that in the strictest sense this holds only if the variables are measured on a continuous scale (such as time, distance, weight, volume, etc.), but that in certain cases, little harm is done if the items are measured on a discrete basis (i.e., by counting, such as number of cars, number of television sets, and number of tables).

The **certainty** assumption involves two aspects of LP models. One aspect relates to the model parameters (i.e., the numerical values). It is assumed that these values are known and constant. For instance, if $2x_1$ appears in a labour constraint with hours as the unit of measure, it is assumed that each unit of x_1 will require exactly 2 hours of labour. If the right-hand side of the constraint is 200 labour hours, it is assumed that this quantity will remain at 200. In practice, production times and other parameters may not be truly constant. Therefore, the model builder must make an assessment as to the degree to which the certainty requirement is met. Small departures may not have a significant effect on the model; large departures almost surely will.

Certainty has another aspect in LP models. It is the assumption that all relevant constraints have been identified and represented in the model. For example, if there is a limit on the demand for some item, that limit should be recorded as a constraint (e.g., $x_2 \geq 40$).

2.3 FORMULATING LP MODELS

Consider the problem defined in Example 2-2. Although simplified, it represents the type of problems to which linear programming can be applied and provides an opportunity to illustrate the components as well as the assumptions of LP models in Table 2-1. Just as it is important to carefully define a problem, it is important to carefully formulate the model that will be used to solve the problem. Linear programming algorithms (solution techniques) are widely used and understood, and computer software packages such as Excel are readily available for solving LP problems. Consequently, *obtaining* solutions is not the real issue. In fact, the ease with which solutions can be obtained may tempt an analyst or decision maker to rush through the formulation phase to get a quick idea of what the solution will look like. Too often, though, the analyst fails to check that all constraints have been accounted for and have been correctly formulated. This is unfortunate because if a model is ill-structured, it can easily lead to poor decisions.

Problem formulation is the process of developing a mathematical statement of the business problem under study and it involves the following steps:

1. Define the decision variables.
2. Determine the objective function.
3. Identify the constraints.
4. Determine appropriate values for parameters and determine whether an upper limit, lower limit, or equality is called for.
5. Use this information to build a model.
6. Validate the model.

In practice, the first step is usually straightforward. In many cases, the decision variables are obvious; in others, a brief discussion with the appropriate manager is necessary. However, identifying the constraints and then determining appropriate values for the parameters can require considerable time and effort on the part of the analyst. Potential sources of information include historical records, interviews with managers and staff, and data collection. Obtaining parameters for the objective function is usually not difficult; accounting records or personnel can generally provide that information. Once the information about constraints and parameters has been obtained, constructing an appropriate mathematical model becomes the focus. At this stage, the objective and the problem constraints are translated into a set of mathematical expressions. This can be both demanding and time-consuming, especially for large problems. Validating the model will involve a critical review of the output, perhaps under a variety of inputs, to decide if the results are reasonable. This typically involves checking with people who are familiar with the situation (managers and staff) about the reasonableness of the results.

EXAMPLE 2-2

The Server Problem

General description A firm that assembles computers and computer equipment is about to start production of two new Web server models. Each type of model will require assembly time, inspection time, and storage space. The amounts of each of these resources that can be devoted to the production of the servers is limited. The manager of the firm would like to determine the quantity of each model to produce to maximize the profit generated by sales of these servers.

Additional information To develop a suitable model of the problem, the manager has met with design and manufacturing personnel. As a result of those meetings, the manager has obtained the following information:

	Type 1	**Type 2**
Profit per unit	\$60	\$50
Assembly time per unit	4 hours	10 hours
Inspection time per unit	2 hours	1 hour
Storage space per unit	3 cubic feet	3 cubic feet

The manager also has acquired information on the availability of company resources. These (daily) amounts are:

Resource	**Amount Available**
Assembly time	100 hours
Inspection time	22 hours
Storage space	39 cubic feet

The manager also met with the firm's marketing manager and learned that demand for the servers was such that whatever combination of these two models of servers is produced, all of the output can be sold.

In determining whether the problem can be solved using linear programming, we can first note that there are *restrictions* on assembly time, inspection time, and storage space. We also can note that the manager has an *objective,* which is to maximize profit. Thus, it would appear that this is a *constrained optimization* problem.

In terms of meeting the assumptions, it would appear that the relationships are *linear:* The contribution to profit per unit of each server and the time and storage space per unit of each are the same regardless of the quantity produced. Therefore, the total impact of each server on the profit and each constraint is a linear function of the quantity of that variable. There may be a question of *divisibility* because, presumably, only whole servers will be sold. However, because this is a recurring process (i.e., the servers will be produced daily: therefore, a noninteger solution such as 3.5 servers per day will result in 7 servers every other day), this does not seem to pose a problem. The question of *certainty* cannot be explored here; in practice, the manager could be questioned to determine if there are any other possible constraints and whether the values shown for assembly times, and so forth, are known with certainty. For the purposes of discussion, we will assume certainty. Lastly, the assumption of *nonnegativity* seems justified; negative values for production quantities would not make sense.

Because we have concluded that linear programming is appropriate, let us now turn our attention to constructing a model of the server problem. First, we must define the decision variables. Based on the statement, "The manager . . . would like to determine the quantity of each server to produce," the decision variables are the quantities of each type of server. Thus:

x_1 = **quantity of server model 1 to produce**
x_2 = **quantity of server model 2 to produce**

Next, we can formulate the objective function. The profit per unit of server model 1 is listed as \$60, and the profit per unit of server model 2 is listed as \$50, so the appropriate objective function is

$$\text{maximize} \quad Z = 60x_1 + 50x_2$$

where Z is the value of the objective-function, given values of x_1 and x_2.

Second, we must define the constraints. There are three resources with limited availability: assembly time, inspection time, and storage space. The fact that availability is limited means that these constraints will all be $\leq$ constraints. Suppose we begin with the assembly constraint. The server model 1 requires 4 hours of assembly time per unit, whereas the server model 2 requires 10 hours of assembly time per unit. Therefore, with a limit of 100 hours available, the assembly constraint is

$$4x_1 + 10x_2 \leq 100 \text{ hours}$$

This constraint states that the number of hours of assembly time used cannot exceed the total amount of assembly time available.

Similarly, each unit of server model 1 requires 2 hours of inspection time, and each unit of server model 2 requires 1 hour of inspection time. With 22 hours available, the inspection constraint is

$$2x_1 + x_2 \leq 22$$

This constraint states that the number of hours of inspection time used cannot exceed the total amount of inspection time available.

The storage constraint is determined in a similar manner. It is

$$3x_1 + 3x_2 \leq 39$$

This constraint states that the number of cubic feet of storage space used cannot exceed the total number of cubic feet of storage space available.

There are no other system or individual constraints. The nonnegativity constraints are

$$x_1, x_2 \geq 0$$

This constraint specifies that negative quantities for the decision variables are not acceptable.

In summary, the mathematical model of the microcomputer problem is

x_1 = **quantity of server model 1 to produce**
x_2 = **quantity of server model 2 to produce**

$$\text{maximize} \quad Z = 60x_1 + 50x_2$$

subject to

Assembly	$4x_1 + 10x_2 \leq 100$ hours
Inspection	$2x_1 + 1x_2 \leq 22$ hours
Storage	$3x_1 + 3x_2 \leq 39$ cubic feet
	$x_1, x_2 \geq 0$

Generally, in formulating a problem, a constraint has four elements:

1. A right-hand side (RHS) quantity that specifies the limit for that constraint. It is usually a constant, not a variable. For instance, 100 hours of assembly time is available.
2. An algebraic sign that indicates whether the limit is an upper bound ($\leq$), a lower bound ($\geq$), or an equality ($=$) that must be met exactly. The $\geq$ type of constraint imposes a minimum limit that is acceptable. Examples include "employees must work a minimum of six hours per shift," and "the cottage cheese must contain at least 4 percent butterfat." The $\leq$ type of constraint sets an upper limit that is not to be exceeded. Often such limits pertain to the amount of some resource that will be available. Other examples include an upper limit on demand, technological limits, and managerial preferences. The $=$ type of constraint is the most specific of the three types. Whereas the other two types can be satisfied by a *range* of values (for example, ≤ 30 can be satisfied by any value from 0 to 30), an equality constraint must be met *exactly*. Therefore, the constraint $x_1 = 30$ means that the only acceptable value of x_1 is 30.
3. The decision variables to which the constraint applies.
4. The impact that one unit of each decision variable will have on the right-hand-side quantity of the constraint.

It is a common practice to write constraints in such a way that the variables are on the left side of the expression while a numerical value is placed on the right side of the expression. For example, the expression $x_1 \geq x_2$, would be written as $x_1 - x_2 \geq 0$.

Moreover, a separate expression is used to address each constraint of the problem taking into account the units of measurement rule which stipulates that both the left-hand-side (LHS) and the right-hand-side (RHS) of the constraint must be expressed in the same units of measurements. In our example, in the assembly time constraint the LHS as well as the RHS represent the number of hours. For the storage space constraint, the LHS and the RHS refer each to the number of cubic feet.

Finally, the objective function and the constraints are the expressions in the mathematical model and should be defined only in terms of the decision variables and the parameters. However, without loss of generality, it is not necessary that every single decision variable must appear in each expression.

After covering the basic concepts associated with LP and learning about formulating basic LP problems, we can discuss how to solve simple problems with two variables using the graphical method.

2.4 GRAPHICAL METHOD

Graphical linear programming is a relatively straightforward method for determining the optimal solution to certain linear programming problems. In practical terms, this method can be used only to solve problems that involve two decision variables. However, most linear programming applications involve situations that have more than two decision variables, so graphical linear programming methods cannot be used to solve them. Even so, much can be gained from studying the graphical approach, particularly in terms of the insight it generates about important concepts of models and solutions. Graphical methods provide a visual portrayal of many important concepts. Moreover, they provide a framework for intuitive explanations of other LP techniques that are covered in later chapters. Viewed from this perspective, graphical LP is a valuable learning tool.

To demonstrate the graphical method, the server problem that was formulated earlier in the chapter in Example 2-2 will be solved. The model is

$$x_1 = \text{quantity of server model 1 to produce per day}$$
$$x_2 = \text{quantity of server model 2 to produce per day}$$

$$\text{maximize} \quad Z = 60x_1 + 50x_2$$

subject to

$$\begin{array}{ll} \text{Assembly} & 4x_1 + 10x_2 \leq 100 \text{ hours} \\ \text{Inspection} & 2x_1 + \ \ 1x_2 \leq 22 \text{ hours} \\ \text{Storage} & 3x_1 + \ \ 3x_2 \leq 39 \text{ cubic feet} \\ & \qquad x_1, x_2 \geq 0 \end{array}$$

The graphical approach consists of the following steps:

1. Plot each of the constraints.
2. Determine the feasible region or area that contains all of the points that satisfy the entire *set* of constraints.
3. Determine the optimal solution.

Let's examine these steps as we solve the server problem.

Plotting the Constraints and Determining the Feasible Region

We begin by plotting the nonnegativity constraints, as shown in Figure 2-1. For purposes of illustration, the area of feasibility for these two constraints (i.e., the area that satisfies both constraints) has been shaded in. However, as a general rule, the shading would be done after all constraints have been plotted.

The procedure for graphing each of the remaining constraints relies on the fact that a straight line can be plotted if any two points on that line can be identified. Of course, the constraints in this problem are all inequalities rather than lines. As such, they describe a region or area that will satisfy them. However, the boundary of that area of feasibility is represented by the equal portion of the less-than-or-equal-to constraint. Recognizing this,

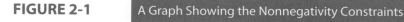

FIGURE 2-1 A Graph Showing the Nonnegativity Constraints

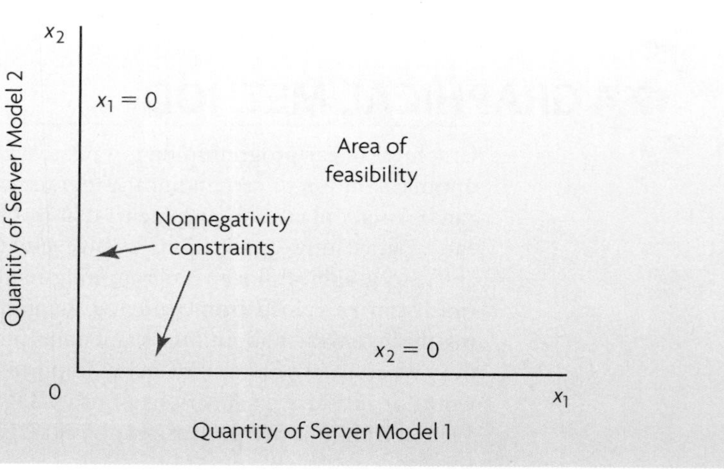

we can deal with the task of graphing a constraint in two parts. First, treat the constraint as an equality and plot the straight line that is the boundary of the feasible region; then, shade in the feasible region.

Consider the assembly time constraint:

$$4x_1 + 10x_2 \leq 100$$

Removing the inequality portion of the constraint produces this straight line:

$$4x_1 + 10x_2 = 100$$

There are a number of different ways to determine the coordinates of two points on the line. Perhaps the easiest two points to identify and work with are the points where the line intersects each axis (i.e., where $x_1 = 0$ and where $x_2 = 0$). We can solve for those points, first by setting $x_2 = 0$ and solving for x_1, and then setting $x_1 = 0$ and solving for x_2. Thus with $x_2 = 0$, we find

$$4x_1 + 10(0) = 100$$

Solving, we find that $4x_1 = 100$, so $x_1 = 25$ when $x_2 = 0$. Similarly, we can solve the equation for x_2 when $x_1 = 0$:

$$4(0) + 10x_2 = 100$$

Solving for x_2, we find $x_2 = 10$ when $x_2 = 0$.

Thus, we have two points: $x_1 = 0, x_2 = 10$, and $x_1 = 25, x_2 = 0$. We can now add this line to our graph of the nonnegativity constraints by connecting these two points (see Figure 2-2).

Next we must determine which side of the line represents points that are less than 100. To do this, we can select a test point that is not on the line, and we can substitute the x_1 and x_2 values of that point into the left side of the equation of the line. If the result is less than 100, this tells us that all points on that side of the line are less than the value of the line (e.g., 100). Conversely, if the result is greater than 100, this indicates that the other side of the line represents the set of points that will yield values that are less than 100. A relatively simple test point to use is the origin (i.e., $x_1 = 0, x_2 = 0$) if both constraint coefficients are positive. Substituting these values into the equation yields:

$$4(0) + 10(0) = 0$$

FIGURE 2-2 Feasible Region Based on a Plot of the First Constraint (assembly time) and the Nonnegativity Constraint

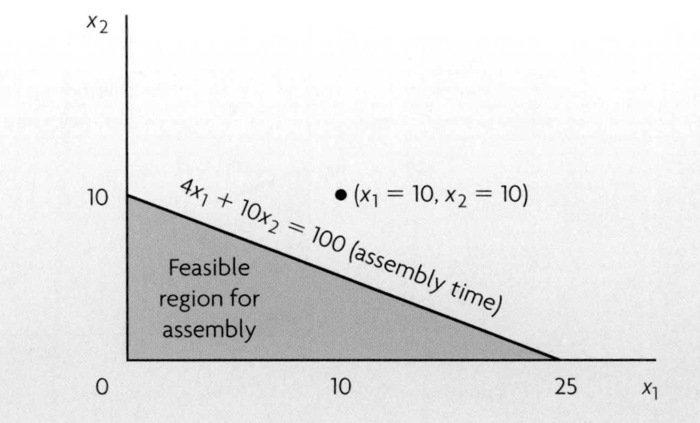

Obviously this is less than 100. Hence, the side of the line closest to the origin represents the "less than" area.

The feasible region for this constraint and the nonnegativity constraints then becomes the shaded portion shown in Figure 2-2.

For the sake of illustration, suppose we try one other point, say $x_1 = 10$, $x_{2} = 10$. Substituting these values into the assembly constraint yields

$$4(10) + 10(10) = 140$$

Clearly this is greater than 100. Therefore, all points on this side of the line are greater than 100 (see Figure 2-2). However, if one of the constraint coefficients is negative, then we would substitute a value of x_1 slightly larger and slightly smaller than its value of the x_1 axis and determine which one is less than the right-hand-side value of the constraint.

Continuing with the problem, we can add the two remaining constraints to the graph in a similar manner. Figure 2-3 shows the feasible region after graphing the inspection constraint. Figure 2-4 shows the feasible region after graphing the storage constraint. The region that satisfies all constraints is called **feasible solution space** or **feasible region.**

Once the constraints have been graphed and the area of feasibility has been identified, it is possible to obtain the optimal solution to the problem. Two different approaches to obtaining the solution will be demonstrated. One involves examining points at the edge of the feasible solution space where constraints meet, and the other involves graphing the objective function. The extreme point approach will be demonstrated first.

Finding the Optimal Solution: The Extreme Point Approach

The **extreme point** approach involves finding the coordinates of each corner point that borders the feasible solution space and then determining which corner point provides the best value of the objective function (i.e., the highest value for a maximization problem or the lowest value for a minimization problem). An important mathematical theorem provides the rationale for this approach: The **extreme point theorem** states that if a problem has an optimal solution, at least one optimal solution will occur at a corner point of the

FIGURE 2-3 A Completed Graph of the Server Problem Showing the Assembly and Inspection Constraints and the Feasible Solution Space

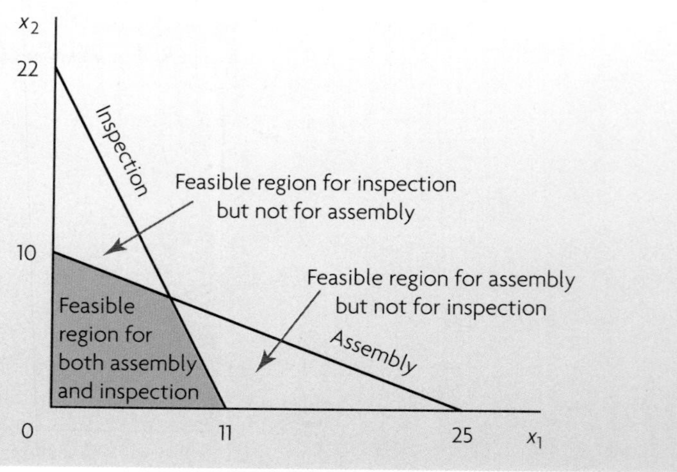

FIGURE 2-4 Completed Graph of the Server Problem Showing All of the Constraints and the Feasible Solution Space

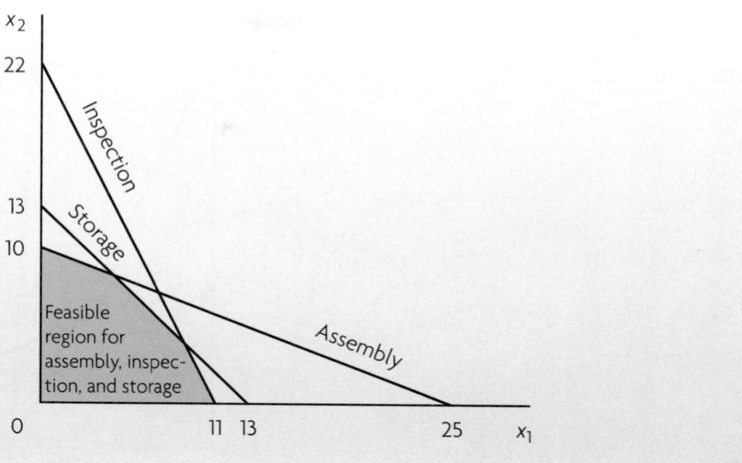

feasible solution space. Note that not every problem has an optimal solution; for example, some do not have a feasible solution space. Also note that the extreme point theorem does not exclude the occurrence of an optimal solution somewhere else on the border of the feasible solution space (solutions will *only* occur on the border, never at an internal point of the feasible solution space). In fact, problems that have *multiple* optimal solutions will have solutions that occur at points along a border of the feasible solution space *as well as* at a corner point. In other words, an optimal solution to *every* LP problem that has an optimal solution will occur at a corner point. Therefore, an approach that examines every corner point of the feasible solution space will be able to identify the optimal solution. Note, too, that corner points represent *intersections* of constraints; so finding the corner points involves finding the coordinates of intersections of constraints. Let us now see how this approach works.

The necessary steps are

1. Graph the problem and identify the feasible solution space.
2. Determine the values of the decision variables at each corner point of the feasible solution space. The values of some points can be identified by inspection; others require the use of simultaneous equations.
3. Substitute the values of the decision variables at each corner point into the objective function to obtain its value at each corner point.
4. After all corner points have been evaluated in a similar fashion, select the one with the highest value of the objective function (for a maximization problem) or lowest value (for a minimization problem) as the optimal solution.

The extreme point solution can be obtained by following the steps outlined above. Figure 2-5 repeats the graph of the problem that was constructed previously in Figure 2-4, with each of the extreme points now labelled for discussion purposes as A, B, C, D, and E. Note that 0,0 is included as an extreme point, even though it will not yield any profit because both decision variables are equal to zero.

FIGURE 2-5 Graph of Server Problem with Extreme Points of the Feasible Solution Space Indicated

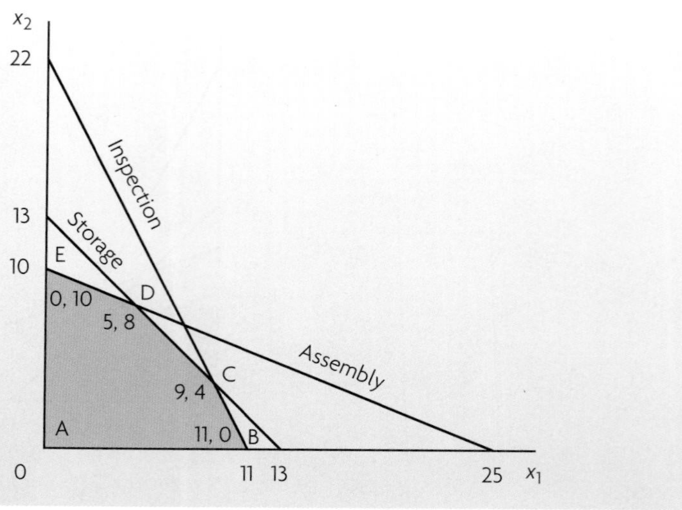

Table 2-2 summarizes the approach used to obtain each point and its profit.

Note that the coordinates of points A, B, and E were determined by inspection. The coordinates of the origin are obvious. In addition, the x_1 intercept of the inspection constraint and the x_2 intercept of the assembly constraint were known by having determined them in the course of plotting the constraints. The coordinates of point C and point D can be determined by the solution of simultaneous equations. Using point D to illustrate, we can solve simultaneously for the intersection of the assembly and storage lines because the assembly constraint intersects the inspection constraint at point D (see Figure 2-5)

Assembly	$4x_1 + 10x_2 = 100$
Storage	$3x_1 + 3x_2 = 39$

TABLE 2-2 Extreme Point Solutions for the Server Problem

	Coordinates			
Point	x_1	x_2	**How Determined**	**Value of the Objective Function**
A	0	0	Inspection	\$60(0) + \$50(0) = \$0
B	11	0	Inspection	\$60(11) + \$50(0) = \$660
C	9	4	Simultaneous equations	\$60(9) + \$50(4) = \$740 (largest)
D	5	8	Simultaneous equations	\$60(5) + \$50(8) = \$700
E	0	10	Inspection	\$60(0) + \$50(10) = \$500

As usual, there are a number of ways for obtaining a common solution to this set of equations. One way would be to multiply each coefficient of the assembly constraint by 3/4 thereby resulting in a new x_1 coefficient of 3, which would lead to the elimination of x_1. Thus:

$$\frac{3}{4}(4x_1 + 10x_2 = 100) = 3x_1 + 7.5x_2 = 75$$

Subtracting the storage line from this new line results in one equation with x_2 the only variable:

$$\begin{array}{lr} \textbf{New} & 3x_1 + 7.5x_2 = 75 \\ \textbf{Storage} & -(3x_1 + \quad 3x_2 = 39) \\ \hline & 4.5x_2 = 36 \end{array} \qquad \textbf{Solving, } x_2 = 8$$

By substituting $x_2 = 8$ into either of the original lines, or the new line, the value of x_1 at intersection D can be determined. If the original assembly equation is used, we find

$$4x_1 + 10(8) = 100$$

Solving, $x_1 = 5$. Hence, the coordinates of point D are $x_1 = 5$ and $x_2 = 8$.

Alternatively, a solution to this set of equations can be obtained by first "solving" one equation to get an expression for one variable. Then substitute this expression into the other equation to get a second expression and solve it to get the value of the other variable. Once this value is known, use it in the first expression to get the value of the remaining unknown variable. For example, assuming the expression defined by the storage constraint is used and solving for x_1 gives

$$x_1 = 39/3 - 3x_2/3 \text{ or } x_1 = 13 - x_2 \tag{2-1}$$

Substituting out this expression into the assembly constraint expression yields the following:

$$\begin{aligned} 4(13 - x_2) + 10x_2 &= 100 \\ 52 - 4x_2 + 10x_2 &= 100 \\ 6x_2 &= 48 \\ x_2 &= 8 \end{aligned}$$

Replacing the value of x_2 in expression (2-1) and solving provides $x_1 = 13 - 8$ or $x_1 = 5$.

At point C, the values of x_1 and x_2, are calculated by simultaneously solving the inspection and storage equations.

The profit at each corner point can be computed by substituting the coordinates of the point into the objective function. Point C ($x_1 = 9, x_2 = 4$) represents the optimal solution because it yields the largest profit for the extreme points (see Table 2-2).

Finding the Optimal Solution: The Objective Function Approach

The objective function approach avoids the need to determine the coordinates of all of the corner points of the feasible solution space. Instead, this approach directly identifies the optimal corner point, so only the coordinates of the optimal point need to be determined. It accomplishes this by adding the objective function to the graph and then using it to determine which point is optimal. Let's see how the objective function approach works.

The first step is to plot the objective function. Plotting an objective function line involves the same logic as plotting a constraint line: Determine where the line intersects each axis. Recall that the objective function for the server problem is

$$60x_1 + 50x_2$$

Now, this is not an equation because it does not include an equal sign. We can get around this by simply setting it equal to some quantity. Any quantity will do, although one that is evenly divisible by both coefficients and one that falls in the feasible region is desirable.

Suppose we decide to set the objective function equal to 300. That is,

$$60x_1 + 50x_2 = 300$$

We can now plot the line of our graph. As before, we can determine the x_1 and x_2 intercepts of the line by setting one of the two variables equal to zero, solving for the other, and then reversing the process. Thus, with $x_1 = 0$, we have

$$60(0) + 50x_2 = 300$$

Solving, we find $x_2 = 6$. Similarly, with $x_2 = 0$, we have

$$60x_1 + 50(0) = 300$$

Solving, we find $x_1 = 5$. This line is plotted in Figure 2-6.

The profit line can be interpreted in the following way. Every point on the line (i.e., every combination of x_1 and x_2 that lies on the line) will provide a profit of \$300. We can see from the graph many combinations that are both on the \$300 profit line and within the feasible solution space. In fact, considering noninteger as well as integer solutions, the possibilities are infinite.

Suppose we now consider another line, say the \$600 line. To do this, we set the objective function equal to this amount. Thus,

$$60x_1 + 50x_2 = 600$$

Solving for the x_1 and x_2 intercepts yields these two points:

x_1 Intercept	x_2 Intercept
$x_1 = 10$	$x_1 = 0$
$x_2 = 0$	$x_2 = 12$

This line is also plotted in Figure 2-6, along with the previous \$300 line for purposes of comparison.

FIGURE 2-6 The Server Problem with Profit Lines of \$300, \$600, and \$900

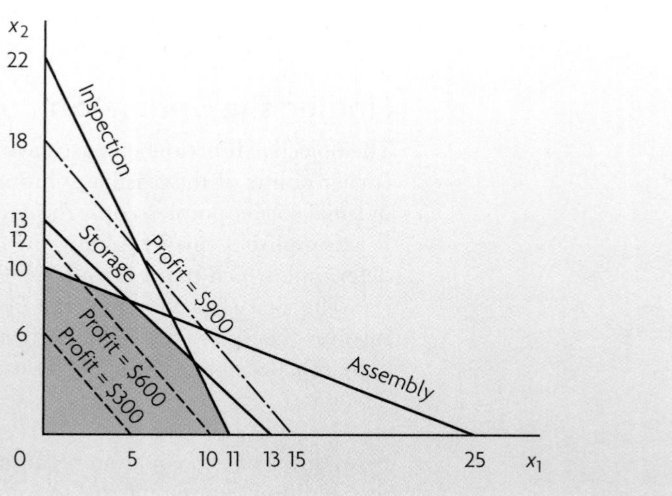

Two things are evident in Figure 2-6 regarding the profit lines. One is that the $600 line is *farther* from the origin than the $300 line; the other is that the two lines are *parallel.* These parallel lines are referred to as *iso-profit lines* (or *iso-cost lines* for a minimization problem). The lines are parallel because they both have the same slope. The slope is not affected by the right side of the equation. Rather, it is determined solely by the coefficients 60 and 50. It would be correct to conclude that regardless of the quantity we select for the value of the objective function, the resulting line will be parallel to these two lines. Moreover, if the amount is greater than 600, the line will be even farther away from the origin than the $600 line. If the value is less than 300, the line will be closer to the origin than the $300 line. And if the value is between 300 and 600, the line will fall between the $300 and $600 lines.

Also in Figure 2-6 a third profit line, one with the profit equal to $900, is shown along with the previous two profit lines. As expected, it is parallel to the other two, and even farther away from the origin. However, the line does not touch the feasible solution space at all. Consequently, there is no feasible combination of x_1 and x_2 that will yield that amount of profit. Evidently, the maximum possible profit is an amount between $600 and $900, which we can see by referring to Figure 2-6. We could continue to select profit lines in this manner, and, eventually, we could determine an amount that would yield the greatest profit. However, there is a much simpler alternative. We can plot just one line, say the $300 line. We know that all other lines will be parallel to it. Consequently, by moving this one line parallel to itself we can represent other profit lines. We also know that as we move away from the origin, the profits get larger. What we want to know is how far the line can be moved out from the origin and still be touching the feasible solution space, and the values of the decision variables at that point of greatest profit (i.e., the optimal solution). We can locate this point on the graph by placing a straight edge along the $300 line (or any other convenient line) and sliding it away from the origin, being careful to keep it parallel to the $300 line. This approach is also illustrated in Figure 2-7.

FIGURE 2-7

Finding the Optimal Solution to the Server Problem

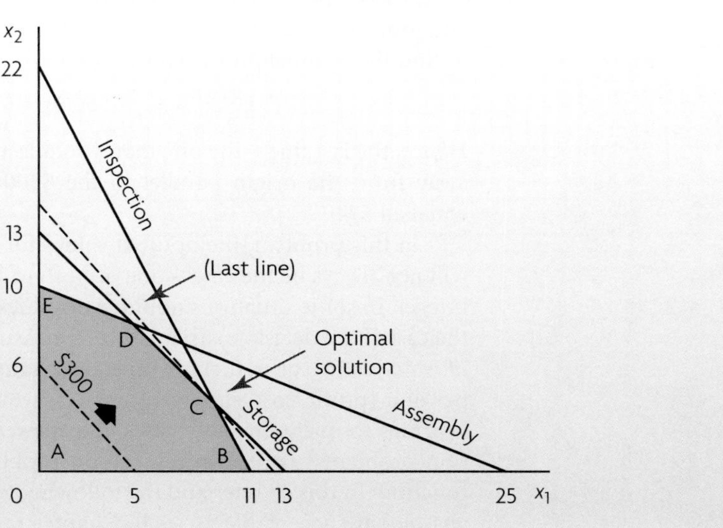

Once we have determined where the optimal solution is in the feasible solution space, we must determine what the values of the decision variables are at that point. Then, we can use that information to compute the profit for that combination.

Note that the optimal solution is at the intersection of the inspection boundary and the storage boundary (see Figure 2-7). The last point touched in the feasible region as we move the profit line parallel to itself is given by point C. In other words, the optimal combination of x_1 and x_2 must satisfy both boundary (equality) conditions. We can determine those values by solving the two equations *simultaneously.* The equations are

$$\text{Inspection} \qquad 2x_1 + 1x_2 = 22$$
$$\text{Storage} \qquad 3x_1 + 3x_2 = 39$$

The idea behind solving two **simultaneous equations** is to algebraically eliminate one of the unknown variables (i.e., to obtain an equation with a single unknown). This can be accomplished by multiplying the constants of one of the equations by a fixed amount and then adding (or subtracting) the modified equation from the other. (Occasionally, it is easier to multiply each equation by a fixed quantity.) For example, we can eliminate x_2 by multiplying the inspection equation by 3 and then subtracting the storage equation from the modified inspection equation. Thus,

$$3(2x_1 + 1x_2 = 22) \qquad \text{becomes} \qquad 6x_1 + 3x_2 = 66$$

Subtracting the storage equation from this produces

$$\begin{array}{r} 6x_1 + 3x_2 = 66 \\ -(3x_1 + 3x_2 = 39) \\ \hline 3x_1 + 0x_2 = 27 \end{array}$$

Solving the resulting equation yields $x_1 = 9$. The value of x_2 can be found by substituting $x_1 = 9$ into either of the original equations or the modified inspection equation. Suppose we use the original inspection equation. We have

$$2(9) + 1x_2 = 22$$

Solving, we find $x_2 = 4$.

Hence, the optimal solution to the server problem is to produce nine model 1 servers and four model 2 servers per day. We can substitute these values into the objective function to find the optimal profit. Thus,

$$\$60(9) + \$50(4) = \$740$$

Hence, the last line—the one that would last touch the feasible solution space as we moved away from the origin parallel to the $300 profit line—would be the line where profit equalled $740.

In this problem, the optimal values for both decision variables are integers. Now this will not always be the case—one or both of the decision variables may turn out to be noninteger. In some situations noninteger values would be of little consequence. This would be the case if the decision variables were measured on a continuous scale, such as the amount of water, sand, sugar, fuel oil, time, or distance needed for optimality, or if the contribution per unit (profit, cost, etc.) were small, as would be the case with the number of nails or ball bearings to make. In some cases, the answer would simply be rounded down (maximization problems) or up (minimization problems) with very little impact on the objective function. In this chapter and the following two chapters, it will be assumed that noninteger answers are acceptable as such. Chapter 6 on integer programming will discuss how to obtain optimal integer solutions.

Note that the solution to this problem occurred where two constraint lines intersected. These intersections are called **corner points,** or *extreme points,* of the feasible solution space. The optimal solution to an LP problem will always occur at a corner point because as the objective function line is moved in the direction that will improve its value (e.g., away from the origin in a maximization problem), it will last touch one of these intersections of constraints. This is the **fundamental theorem of LP.** (In fact, this is the basis for the extreme point approach to finding the optimal solution that was demonstrated in the previous section.)

Let's review the procedure for finding the optimal solution using the objective function approach, which is also referred to as the **iso-profit line** approach in the case of a maximization problem.

1. Graph the constraints.
2. Identify the feasible solution space.
3. Set the objective function equal to some amount that is divisible by each of the objective function coefficients. This will yield integer values for the x_1 and x_2 intercepts and, thereby, simplify plotting the line. Often, the product of the two objective function coefficients will provide a satisfactory line. Ideally, the line selected will cross the feasible solution space close to the optimal point, in which case it would not be necessary to slide a straight edge: The optimal solution can be readily identified visually. In some cases, sliding the ruler or straight edge parallel to itself will not provide a clear answer as to which point in the feasible region in the last point touched as we move the profit line parallel to itself. Then we need to determine the value of the objective function (Z) for all the competing extreme points and select the one with the highest value of Z for a maximization problem. However, the process described above can only be utilized for relatively small two-variable problems. It is highly inefficient to try to utilize it for large problems (problems with more than six constraints).
4. After identifying the optimal point, determine which two constraints intersect there. Solve their equations simultaneously to obtain the values of the decision variables at the optimum.
5. Substitute the values obtained in the previous step into the objective function to determine the value of the objective function at the optimum.

2.5 SOLVING LP MODELS WITH A SPREADSHEET

Various software packages are available for solving larger LP models (for example, LINDO, GAMS, CPLEX, XPRESS-MP, etc.). However, most of them are intended for a particular market, and they are not available everywhere. For a number of years, Microsoft Office, a widely used business application in virtually every organization, has included the capability to solve practical LP problems in Microsoft Excel by using Excel **Solver,** a built-in problem-solving tool. This inclusion is attractive since Excel is not only accessible in universities, but its commands are also already familiar to many students, and it provides convenient features for data entry, editing, and processing that allow students to gain an understanding of linear programs construction. We focus in this section on how to use Excel Solver to solve LP problems and we centre our presentation on Example 2-2 formulated earlier in this chapter. The corresponding LP model is:

x_1 = **quantity of server model 1 to produce per day**
x_2 = **quantity of server model 2 to produce per day**

maximize $Z = 60x_1 + 50x_2$

subject to

Assembly	$4x_1 + 10x_2 \leq 100$ **hours**
Inspection	$2x_1 + 1x_2 \leq 22$ **hours**
Storage	$3x_1 + 3x_2 \leq 39$ **cubic feet**
	$x_1, x_2 \geq 0$

Generally, a LP model on Excel may be developed in many ways depending on the user's preference. However, common steps involve

1. setting up the spreadsheet model;
2. invoke Excel Solver;
3. discussion of the solution.

We will apply these steps to Example 2-2. For reasons of convenience and uniformity, we will use the approach described here for all problems in the textbook.

Setting up the Spreadsheet Model

This stage consists of entering, in a consistent manner, the problem's input data (objective function coefficients, constraints coefficients, and RHS) and the expressions defining the model statement (function objective and constraints). Exhibit 2-1 shows the Excel

EXHIBIT 2-1 Input Screen for Example 2-2 Model

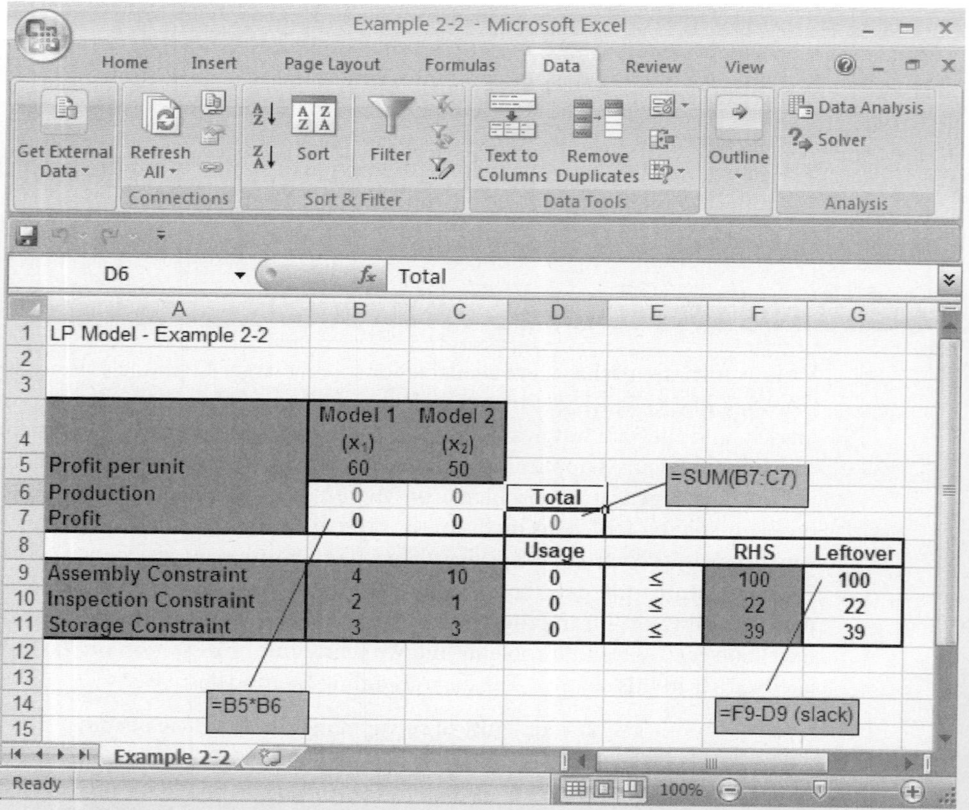

spreadsheet associated with Example 2-2's model. The following steps are involved in this model development stage:

1. When the Excel spreadsheet is first made available, we should start by setting up the *headings* and *labels.* Column A is designated as the column that contains all of the labels for each of the constraints and the objective function coefficients. Columns B and C are earmarked for each decision variable (server model 1 and server model 2), respectively. The labels for decision variables are in cells B4 and C4. Immediately below these labels, we have three rows (5, 6, and 7) designated by profit per unit, production quantity, and profit, respectively. The unit profit values in row 5 are coming from the objective function, while the quantities, called the *output cells,* are the decision variable values that Solver will provide after solving the model.
2. The profit values are obtained by multiplying the unit profit values in row 5 by the quantity values (output cells) in row 6. For example, cell B7 contains the equation B5*B6, which is the multiplication of the unit profit (B5) by the quantity of the decision variable (B6). The formula for cell C7 is similar to the formula for cell B7. Rows 9 through 11 list the constraints of the model. The signs of the constraints can be ignored but for information we show them in column E. The nonnegativity constraints are not explicitly stated.
3. In listing the model constraints, we need an extra column that will show the value of the left-hand side of each constraint once Solver has determined the values of the decision variables. This column is designated as column D and is labelled as "Usage." In the usage column, we utilize the SUMPRODUCT function, which will sum up the product of each of the individual terms in two different ranges provided that the two ranges have the same number of rows or columns included. For example, for cell D9, we have the equation SUMPRODUCT ($B$6:$C$6, B9:C9). To determine the value of cell D9, this function will multiply the value in cell B6 by the value in cell B9 and multiply the value in cell C6 by the value in cell C9. Once both terms are multiplied, then all product terms are summed to obtain the value of cell D9. The values in column F indicate the right-hand-side (RHS) values of each of the constraints. The values in column G represent the difference between the left-hand side and the right-hand side of the inequality or equality sign. For a less-than-or-equal-to resource constraint, column G values are a convenient way of showing the unused resources. Since D9 provides the total for the left-hand side of the equation and F9 is the value of the right-hand side of the constraint equation, F9 – D9 is the correct formula for cell G9.
4. The overall performance of the model measured by the total profit is stated in cell D7. This total profit value is calculated by summing the values in rows B7 through C7; therefore, the equation in cell D7 is SUM(B7:C7). Since cell B7 represents the portion of the profit attributable to server model 1 and cell C7 represents the portion of the profit attributable to server model 2, summing these profit values will yield the total profit for the linear programming model given in cell D7.

Once we complete the data entry and the equations for various cells discussed above, we are ready to execute the Solver.

Using Solver

When we start executing the Solver, among other things, we need to specify the signs of the constraints. We click on **Data|Analysis|Solver,** and the Solver dialogue box given in Exhibit 2-2 appears.

In executing Solver, we need to specify exactly where each component of the model is located on the spreadsheet. We have two options: (1) manually enter the appropriate

EXHIBIT 2-2 Solver Dialogue Box

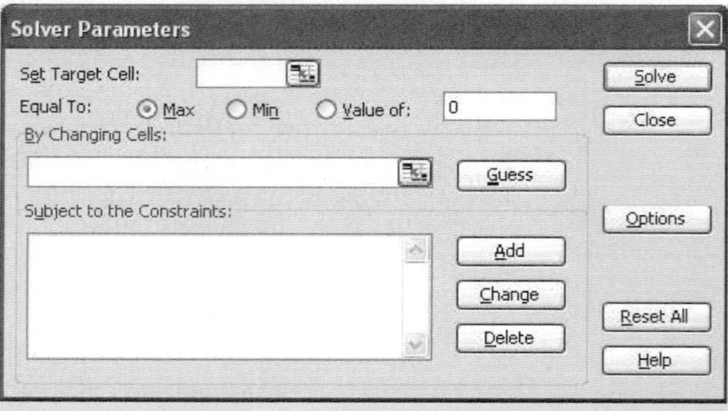

information in the Solver dialogue box, or (2) click on the appropriate cells, which in turn will automatically identify the specific components of the model in the Solver dialogue box. We would recommend the clicking option because it is faster and will save time, especially in solving large problems.

The following steps describe what needs to be done.

1. The first information requested by the Solver dialogue box is to complete the "Set Target Cell" box. The *target cell* contains the value of the objective function, which measures the overall performance of the model. In our spreadsheet, given in Exhibit 2-1, this particular value is specified in cell D7.
2. The objective is to either minimize or maximize the target cell. Therefore, in the second line of the dialogue box, we have the option of choosing "Max," "Min," or "Value of." In this problem we choose "Max."
3. The dialogue box next requests that we specify the decision variables in the text box labelled "By Changing Cells." Since the output cells (decision variables) are located in cells B6 and C6, click on cell B6 and drag it through cell C6.
4. Since the cells associated with the decision variables, the objective function, and the total profit have been specified, next we specify the constraints by clicking on the "Add" button of the Solver dialogue box. After clicking the "Add" button, the "Add Constraint" dialogue box given in Exhibit 2-3 will appear. In the "Add Constraint" dialogue box, we

EXHIBIT 2-3 Add Constraint Dialogue Box

Change Constraint

Cell Reference: $D$9:$D$11 <= Constraint: =$F$9:$F$11

OK Cancel Add Help

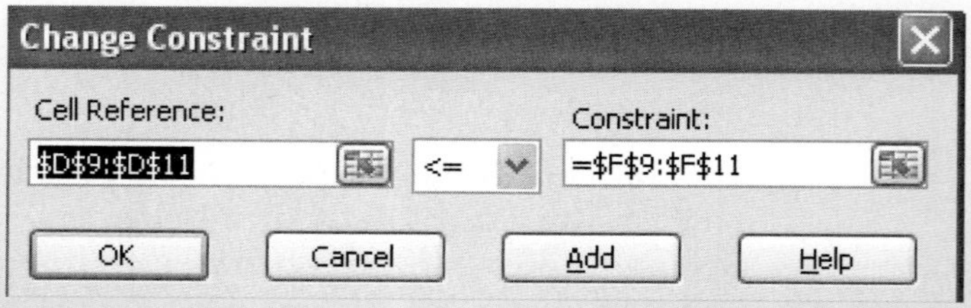

click on the "Cell Reference" box and then click cell D9 and drag it through cell D11. For the sign box, we choose the less-than-or-equal-to sign (≤). Similar to what we did with the "Cell Reference" box, we click in the "Constraint box" and then click cell F9 and drag it through F11. The "Add" button can be used to specify all the greater-than-or-equal-to types of constraints and all equal-to types of constraints as well.

We have now completed the specification of the problem in the Solver dialogue box (see Exhibit 2-4).

5. However, before asking Solver to solve a linear programming problem, we need to check to make sure that the right options have been specified. Clicking on the "Options" button will bring up the Options dialogue box shown in Exhibit 2-5. This box allows the user to specify a number of options about how the problem will be solved. As shown in Exhibit 2-5, make sure that the options "Assume Linear Model" and "Assume Non-Negative" are checked. Checking these boxes will ensure that the problem solved is a linear programming problem, as opposed to nonlinear programming, with all decision variables being subject to nonnegativity constraints. Therefore, $x_1, x_2 \geq 0$ (nonnegativity constraints) do not have to be specified as Excel will automatically take them into account if "Assume Non-Negative" is checked. With respect to the remaining options presented in the Solver Options dialogue box, simply choose the default options. Clicking on the "OK" button will return you to the Solver Parameters dialogue box. At this point we are ready to solve the problem.
6. Clicking on the "Solve" button will solve the problem and bring up the Solver Results dialogue box shown in Exhibit 2-6. If the Solver Results dialogue box, as shown in Exhibit 2-6, has the message "Solver found a solution. All constraints and optimality conditions are satisfied" an optimal solution has been found. However, if the formulation does not lead to an optimal or feasible solution, then the Solver Results dialogue box will state: "Solver could not find a feasible solution" or "The Set Cell values do not converge."
7. After solving the problem, Solver will change the values of the decision variables (quantities) from blanks to the optimal values, as shown in Exhibit 2-7. According to Exhibit 2-7, the company should produce the following: 9 units of server model 1 and 4 units of server model 2 for a total profit of $740. Column G, labelled Leftover, shows the difference between the left and right-hand side of each constraint. It indicates that not all the assembly time hours are used.

EXHIBIT 2-4 Completed Solver Dialogue Box

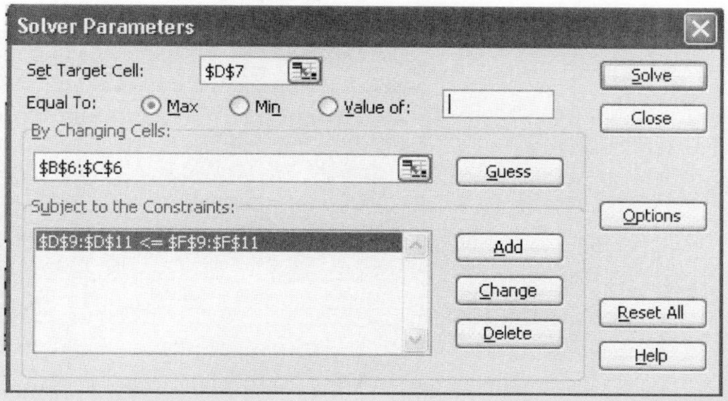

EXHIBIT 2-5 Solver Options Dialogue Box

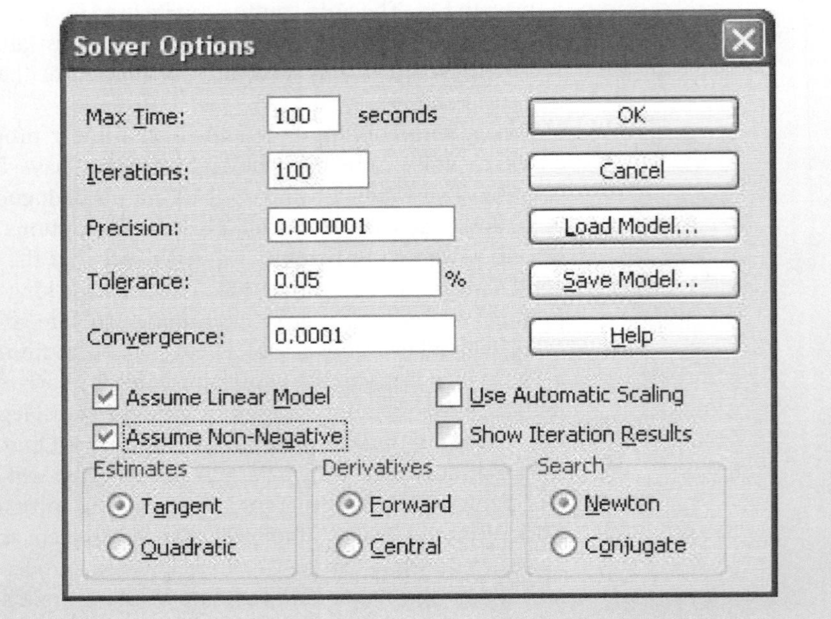

In summarizing Solver usage, there are three types of cells:

Target cell. This cell shows the overall performance measure (i.e., the maximum profit or the minimum cost).
Output cells. As the name suggests, these cells show the output or quantity of the decision variables based on the changing cells.
Data cells. These cells simply show the data of the problem (constraint coefficients, objective function coefficients, and right-hand-side constraints).

EXHIBIT 2-6 Solver Results Dialogue Box

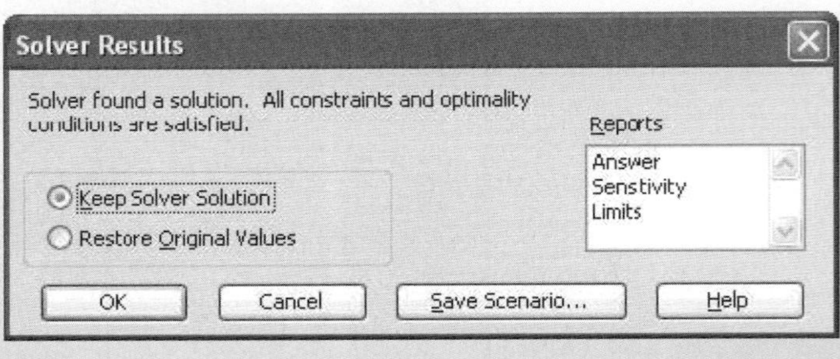

EXHIBIT 2-7 Output Screen for Example 2-2 Model

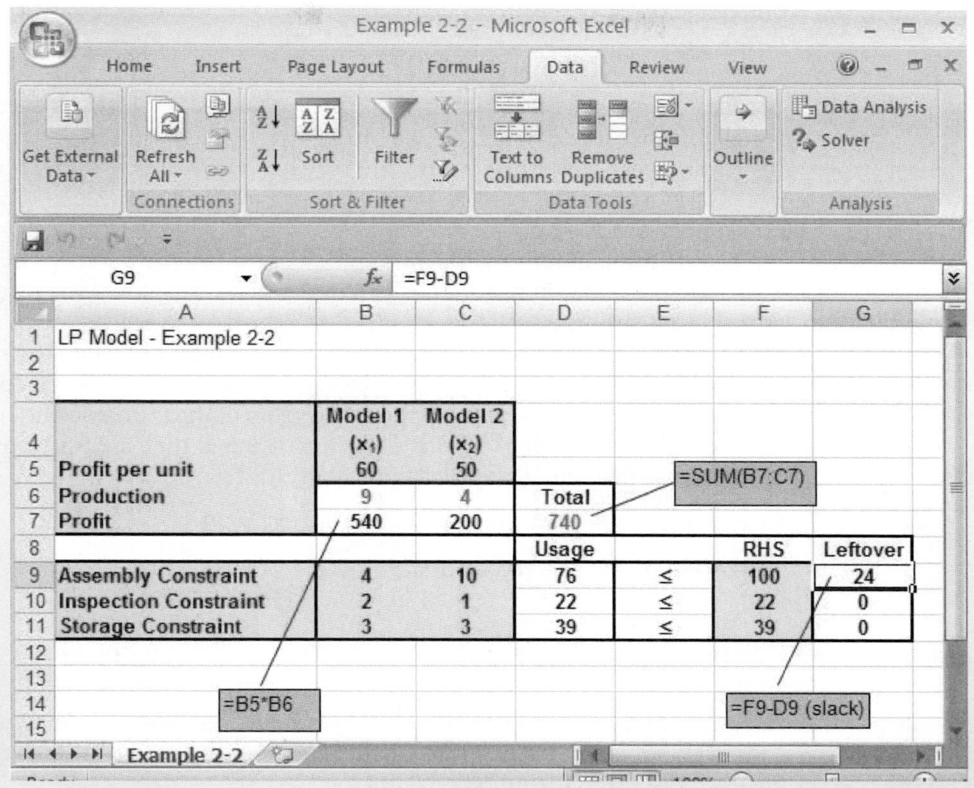

2.6 A MINIMIZATION EXAMPLE

Graphical solutions to minimization problems are very similar to maximization problems. There are few differences that will be highlighted in this section. The main difference is that the optimum is the point that has the smallest possible value of the objective function, instead of the largest. Also, at least one of the constraints must be a $\geq$ constraint. In some instance, all constraints will be greater-than-or-equal-to constraints.

EXAMPLE 2-3

Determine the values of decision variables x_1 and x_2 that will yield the minimum cost in the following problem. Solve using the objective function approach.

minimize $\quad Z = .10x_1 + .07x_2$

subject to

Constraint 1	$6x_1 + 2x_2 \geq 18$
Constraint 2	$8x_1 + 10x_2 \geq 40$
Constraint 3	$x_2 \geq 1$
	x_1 and $x_2 \geq 0$

The feasible region is obtained as shown in the shaded area in Figure 2-8. Let the initial objective function line be $.10x_1 + .07x_2 = .7$, then x_1 intercept would now be 7 and the x_2 intercept would be 10. This line is much more acceptable because it crosses the feasible solution space in the region close to what we now perceive as the optimal solution.

Because the solution is at the intersection of constraints 1 and 2, we can solve these two equations simultaneously to determine the optimal values of x_1 and x_2. As before, the approach is to multiply the constants in one equation by some amount that will cause one of the two variables to drop out when the modified equation is added to, or subtracted from, the other. In this case, the coefficient of x_2 in the second constraint is 5 times the value of the x_2 coefficient in the first constraint, so multiplying the first equation by 5 and then subtracting the second from the first equation will eliminate x_2. Thus,

$$5(6x_1 + 2x_2 = 18) \qquad \text{becomes} \qquad 30x_1 + 10x_2 = 90$$

Subtracting the second constraint equation from this yields

$$\begin{array}{l} 30x_1 + 10x_2 = 90 \\ \underline{-(8x_1 + 10x_2 = 40)} \\ 22x_1 \qquad\quad = 50 \end{array}$$

Solving, we find $x_1 = 2.27$. Substituting this value into either of the two original constraint equations or the modified first equation will yield a value of $x_2 = 2.19$. For example, using the modified equation, we find

$$30(2.27) + 10x_2 = 90$$

Then, $10x_2 = 90 - 30(2.27)$, or $10x_2 = 21.9$. Solving, $x_2 = 21.9/10 = 2.19$.

The optimum value of the objective function (i.e., the minimum cost) is determined by substituting these values into the objective function:

$$Z = .10(2.27) + .07(2.19) = .38$$

The objective function approach to solve an LP model graphically is also referred to as the **iso-cost line** approach in the case of the minimization problem.

EXAMPLE 2-4

Solve the preceding problem using the extreme point approach.

Solution

The extreme points can be determined either by inspection of Figure 2-8 or from simultaneous equations. The results are summarized in Table 2-3.

The minimum value of the objective function is .38, which occurs when $x_1 = 2.27$ and $x_2 = 2.19$. This agrees with the solution found in Example 2-3 using the objective function approach.

FIGURE 2-8 Graphing the Feasible Region and Using the Objective Function to Find the Optimum for Example 2-3

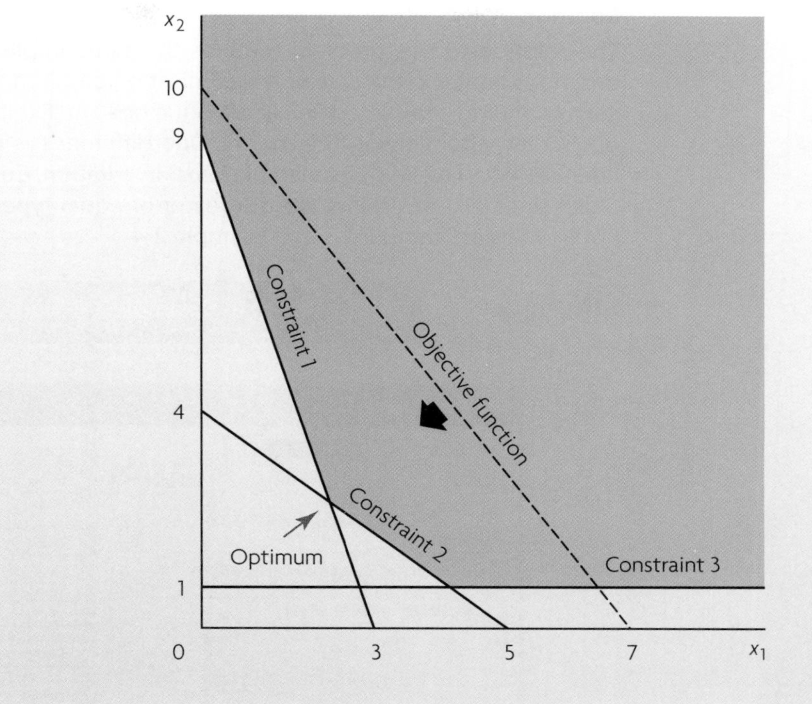

TABLE 2-3 Summary of Extreme Point Analysis for Example 2-4

Extreme Point		How Determined	Value of the Objective Function
x_1	x_2		
0	9	Inspection (see Figure 2-8)	$.10(0) + .07(9) = .63$
3.75	1	Inspection (see Figure 2-8)	$.10(3.75) + .07(1) = .445$
2.27	2.19	Simultaneous equations (see Example 2-3)	$.10(2.27) + .07(2.19) = .38$

EXAMPLE 2-5

Solving the preceding problem using Excel Solver.

Solution

The solution to this problem requires the same implementation steps as we described earlier in the case of a maximization problem. Exhibit 2-8 presents the corresponding completed Solver dialogue box and Exhibit 2-9 presents the output screen after solving the model. One difference is that the target cell has been set equal to "Min" instead of "Max." In addition, Column G is labelled "Surplus," since all constraints are of greater-or-equal types. The same solution is obtained as in Example 2-3 and Example 2-4.

EXHIBIT 2-8 Output Screen for Example 2-5 Model

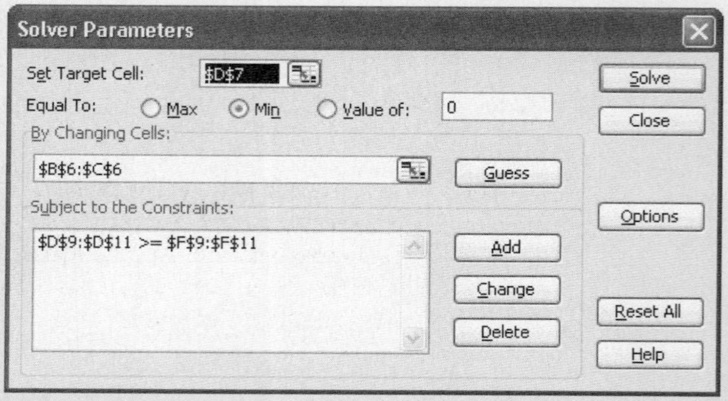

Solver Parameters

Set Target Cell: $D$7

Equal To: ○ Max ◉ Min ○ Value of: 0

By Changing Cells:

$B$6:$C$6

Subject to the Constraints:

$D$9:$D$11 >= $F$9:$F$11

Solve | Close | Guess | Options | Add | Change | Reset All | Delete | Help

2.7 SLACK AND SURPLUS

The primary goal of a decision maker who is using linear programming is to determine the optimal solution to a problem. However, it also can be useful for the decision maker to know of any *slack* or *surplus* that will occur when the optimal solution is achieved.

Slack relates to a $\leq$ constraint; it is the amount of a constraint that is *unused* by a solution. For example, if one constraint in a problem is that labour $\leq$ 100 hours, and the solution requires the use of 90 hours of labour, then we can say that the labour constraint has a slack of 10 hours. Thus, slack is the amount by which the left-hand side of a $\leq$ constraint is less than the right-hand side of the constraint.

Surplus relates to a $\geq$ constraint; it is the amount by which a constraint is *exceeded* by a solution. For example, if a constraint requires that the number of units of product A that are made be $\geq$ 10, and a solution results in 12 units being produced, we can say that there is a surplus of 2 units. Thus, surplus is the amount by which the left-hand side of a $\geq$ constraint exceeds the right-hand side.

Determination of slack and surplus is straightforward. First, note whether the constraint in the question is a $\leq$ constraint or a $\geq$ constraint. (By definition, = constraints never have slack or surplus because the left side of these constraints must always be equal to the right side.) Next, substitute the optimal values of the decision variables into the left-hand side of the constraint and solve. Then, compare the resulting value to the right-hand side of the constraint. The difference between the two is the amount of slack (for a $\leq$ constraint) or surplus (for a $\geq$ constraint).

EXHIBIT 2-9 Output Screen for Example 2-5 Model

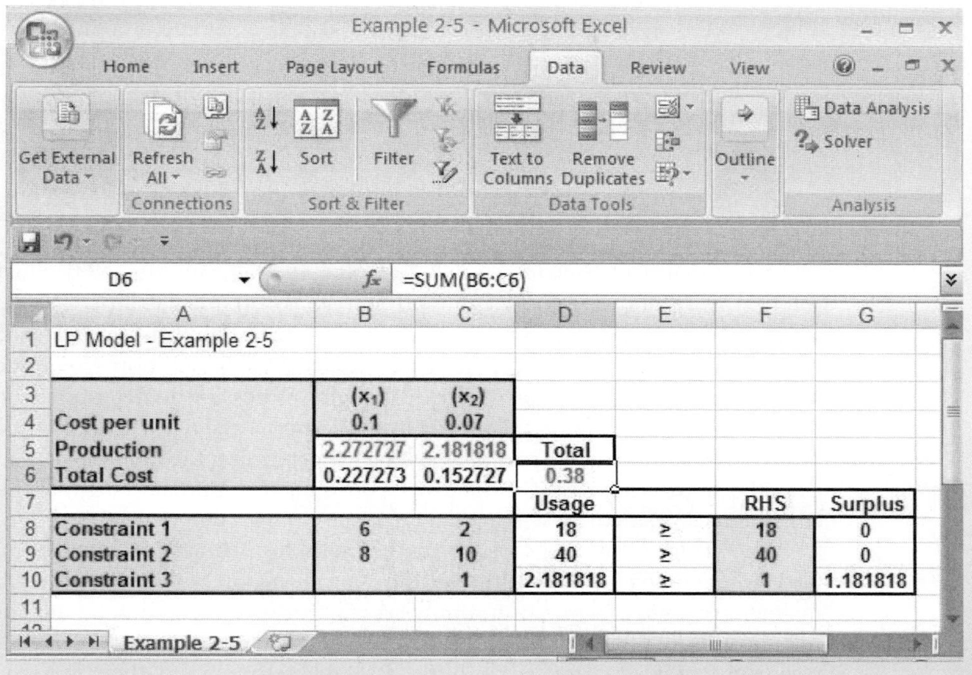

	A	B	C	D	E	F	G
1	LP Model - Example 2-5						
2							
3		(x_1)	(x_2)				
4	Cost per unit	0.1	0.07				
5	Production	2.272727	2.181818	Total			
6	Total Cost	0.227273	0.152727	0.38			
7				Usage		RHS	Surplus
8	Constraint 1	6	2	18	≥	18	0
9	Constraint 2	8	10	40	≥	40	0
10	Constraint 3		1	2.181818	≥	1	1.181818
11							

For example, suppose that we have the constraint $2x_1 + 3x_2 \leq 50$, and that $x_1 = 4$ and $x_2 = 5$. Because this is a $\leq$ constraint, we know that slack rather than surplus is relevant. Substituting the values of x_1 and x_1 into the left side of the constraint, we obtain

$$2(4) + 3(5) = 23.$$

This is 27 less than the right-hand-side value. Hence, slack = 27.

Now, suppose we have the constraint $4x_1 + 2x_2 \geq 10$, and $x_1 = 3$ and $x_2 = 1$. Because this is a $\geq$ constraint, we know that surplus is involved. Substituting the values of x_1 and x_2 into the left-hand side, we obtain

$$4(3) + 2(1) = 14.$$

This exceeds the right-hand-side value of 10 by 4. Hence, surplus = 4.

Table 2-4 illustrates the computations for the server problem. Because every constraint was of the $\leq$ variety, only slack is relevant.

Notice that slack is equal to zero for two of the constraints. This is not unexpected. In fact, in *every* problem, at least one, and usually two, of the constraints will have slack or surplus equal to zero. This is because the solution is *on* those constraint lines. (Recall that the solution to an LP model is at one of the corner points, which is an intersection of constraints, meaning the solution is on those constraints.) A constraint that the optimal solution is on is referred to as a **binding constraint,** meaning that it limits, or binds, the solution. And because the solution is on a binding constraint, it will have slack = 0 (if it is a $\leq$ constraint) or surplus = 0 (if it is a $\geq$ constraint). Moreover, it isn't necessary to calculate slack or surplus for the binding constraints; once they have been identified, it follows that slack or surplus (whichever is appropriate) is equal to zero.

TABLE 2-4 Computing the Amount of Slack for the Optimal Solution to the Server Problem

Constraint	Amount Used with $x_1 = 9$ and $x_2 = 4$	Originally Available	Amount of Slack (Available − Used)
Assembly	4(9) + 10(4) = 76	100	100 − 76 = 24 hours
Inspection	2(9) + 1(4) = 22	22	22 − 22 = 0 hours
Storage	3(9) + 3(4) = 39	39	39 − 39 = 0 cubic feet

For instance, go back to Figure 2-7. Point C (9,4) is optimum. Notice that the optimal solution is on both the Inspection and Storage constraints. That is why they both have slack = 0. Conversely, the optimal solution is less than (beneath) the Assembly constraint, meaning that some of the assembly time is unused by the solution. Consequently, there is some slack for assembly time. (Note: Although it is possible to determine constraints that have zero slack or zero surplus directly from the graph, and to identify constraints that have nonzero slack or surplus, it is *not* possible to determine the amount of slack or surplus from the graph. That has to be done by substituting the optimal values into the nonbinding constraints and solving).

Knowledge of unused capacity can be useful for planning. A manager may be able to use the remaining assembly time for other products, or, perhaps, to schedule equipment maintenance, safety seminars, training sessions, or other activities. In still another vein, it may be profitable to consider the acquisition of additional amounts of the two other resources to allow for greater use of the assembly resource and, thereby, to increase profits by increasing the size of the feasible solution space.

Slack can potentially exist in a ≤ constraint. Moreover, it can be useful to represent slack in a constraint. This is accomplished using a *slack variable, s,* which carries a subscript that denotes which constraint it applies to. For instance, s_1 refers to the amount of slack in the first constraint, s_2 to the amount of slack in the second constraint, and so on. When slack variables are added to the constraints, they are no longer inequalities because the slack variable accounts for any difference between the left- and right-hand sides of the expression. Hence, once slack variables are added to the constraints, they become *equalities.* Furthermore, every variable in a model must be represented in the objective function. However, since slack does not provide any real contribution to the objective, each slack variable is assigned a coefficient of zero in the objective function. With slack variables included, the server problem would appear as follows:

$$\text{maximize} \quad 60x_1 + 50x_2 + 0s_1 + 0s_2 + 0s_3$$

subject to

$$\begin{aligned}
&\text{Assembly} && 4x_1 + 10x_2 + s_1 = 100\\
&\text{Inspection} && 2x_1 + 1x_2 + s_2 = 22\\
&\text{Storage} && 3x_1 + 3x_2 + s_3 = 39\\
& && \text{All variables} \geq 0
\end{aligned}$$

Note that all variables, including slack variables, must be nonnegative.

When all of the constraints are written as equalities, the linear program is said to be in **standard form.**

Since surplus is defined as the amount by which the left-hand side of a constraint exceeds the right-hand side, subtracting the difference between the left-hand side and the right-hand side of the constraint can represent surplus in a constraint. Also, surplus variables must be accounted for in the objective function. As with slack variables, this is done by using a coefficient of zero for each surplus variable. For the problem illustrated in Example 2-3, the addition of surplus variables produced the following standard form of the linear programming problem.

$$\text{Min} \quad Z = .10x_1 + .07x_2 + 0s_1 + 0s_2 + 0s_3$$

subject to

$$\begin{aligned} 6x_1 + 2x_2 - s_1 \qquad\qquad &= 18 \\ 8x_1 + 10x_2 \qquad - s_2 \qquad &= 40 \\ x_2 \qquad\qquad - s_3 &= 1 \\ \text{All variables} &\geq 0 \end{aligned}$$

The reader should be advised that in real applications of LP, we do not convert LP problems to standard form because virtually all commercial software accept $\leq$, $=$, and $\geq$ constraints and do not require the analyst to convert LP problems into standard form.

2.8 SOME SPECIAL ISSUES

This section points out some special issues that may arise during the formulation or solution of LP problems. These issues are

1. problems that have no feasible solutions;
2. unbounded problems;
3. redundancy in constraints;
4. problems that have multiple optimal solutions.

No Feasible Solutions

It is possible to formulate a problem for which it is impossible to satisfy the set of all constraints. This situation sometimes occurs in problems that have a mix of greater-than-or-equal-to constraints and less-than-or-equal-to constraints, where in order to satisfy one of the constraints, another constraint must be violated. Consider the graph in Figure 2-9, where constraint A places an upper bound on feasible solutions and constraint B places a lower bound on feasible solutions. Since the two constraints do not touch or overlap, there is no combination of decision variable values that can satisfy both constraints at the same time.

Sometimes it happens that the problem has been formulated incorrectly (e.g., a constraint coefficient is incorrect, an inequality has the wrong direction). Therefore, when this situation occurs, the first step is to check for one of those errors. If it turns out that the formulation is correct, the manager or analyst might decide to revise some constraint(s), say, by obtaining additional scarce resources, or loosening restrictions. The manager might decide that some constraints are more important than others and might focus on the important ones. Chapter 9 includes a discussion of *goal programming*, which might be of some use in such instances.

Note that if Excel Solver is used and the problem has no solution, the message in Exhibit 2-10 will be obtained, indicating that the problem is infeasible.

Unbounded Problems

An unbounded problem exists when the value of the objective function can be increased without limit. A graphical example of this is shown in Figure 2-10. This difficulty is usually

FIGURE 2-9 Infeasible Solution: No Combination of x_1 and x_2 Can Simultaneously Satisfy Both Constraints

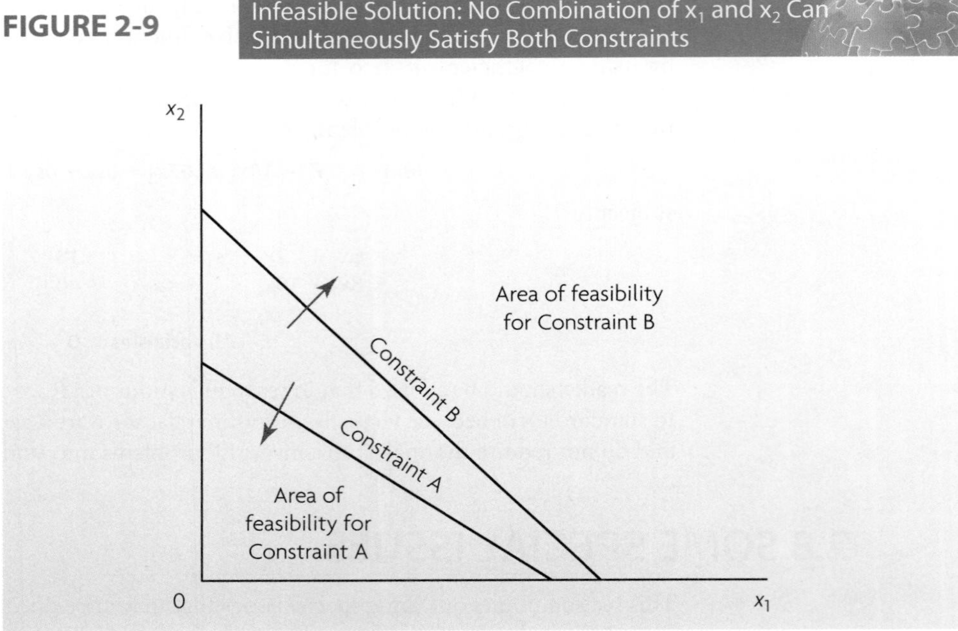

due to either incorrectly maximizing when the real goal is to minimize an objective function or using greater-than-or-equal-to constraints when less-than-or-equal-to constraints are called for. Although the latter error also may occur in a minimization problem, the problem will not be unbounded because of the nonnegativity constraints (i.e., the resulting solution will be 0, 0). Again, checking equalities or rethinking the problem statement may resolve the problem. The latter case may uncover another constraint that should have been included in the original statement of the problem.

Note that if Excel Solver is used and the problem has an unbounded solution, the message in Exhibit 2-11 will be obtained, indicating that the target cell value does not converge.

Redundant Constraints

In some cases, a constraint does not form a unique boundary of the feasible solution space. Such a constraint is called a **redundant constraint.** This constraint is illustrated in Figure 2-11. Note that a constraint is redundant if its removal would not alter the feasible solution space.

EXHIBIT 2-10 Solver Dialogue Box Indicating No Feasible Solution

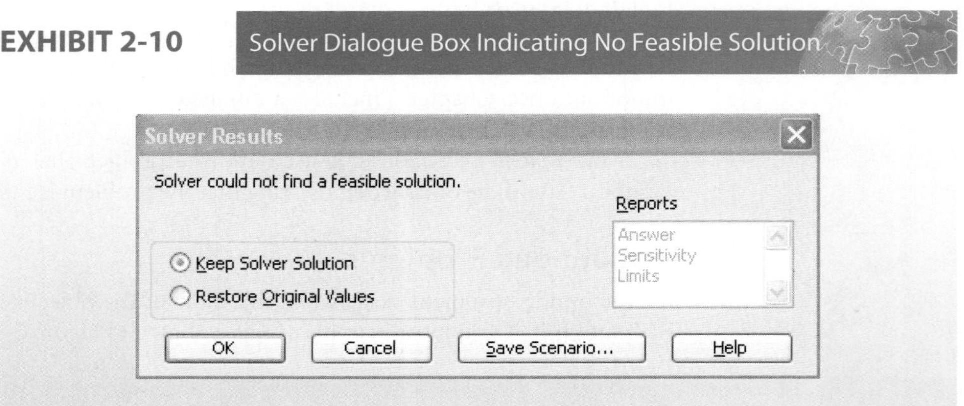

FIGURE 2-10

An Unbounded Solution Space

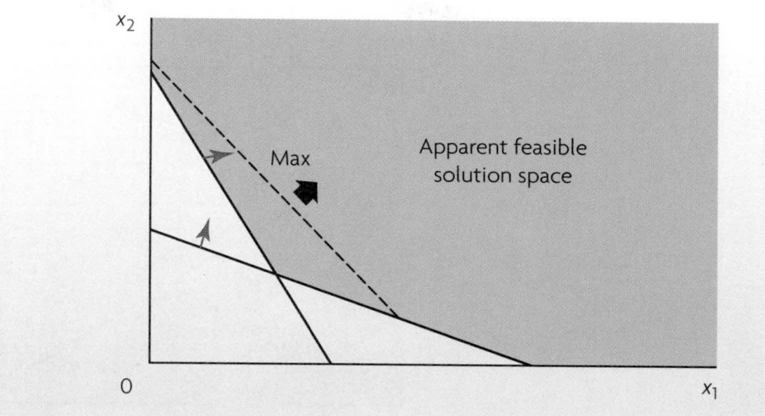

When a problem has a redundant constraint, at least one of the other constraints in the problem is more restrictive than the redundant constraint.

Multiple Optimal Solutions

Most linear programming problems have a single optimal solution. However, in some instances, a problem will have multiple optimal solutions, which is to say that different combinations of values of the decision variables will yield the same optimal value for the objective function.

Figure 2-12 illustrates how this happens in a two-variable problem. We can see that the objective function is parallel to a portion of the boundary of the feasible solution space. Because of this, it ends up last touching an entire segment of the boundary (constraint line). Hence, every combination of x_1 and x_2 on this line will yield the same (optimal) solution. Note, however, that this does not refute the earlier statement that the solution will always be at a corner point. In fact, we can see that there are two corner points that are optimal, one at either end of the line segment.

One benefit of having multiple optimal solutions in that for other (perhaps qualitative) reasons, a manager may prefer one of these solutions over the others, even though each would achieve the same value of the objective function. Furthermore, if noninteger solutions are acceptable, the manager has infinite optimal solutions to choose from. In practical terms, one of the two corner points is usually chosen because of ease in identifying those values.

EXHIBIT 2-11 Solver Dialogue Box Indicating an Unbounded Solution

Solver Results

The Set Cell values do not converge.

Reports

Answer
Sensitivity
Limits

Keep Solver Solution

Restore Original Values

OK | Cancel | Save Scenario... | Help

FIGURE 2-11 Examples of Redundant Constraints

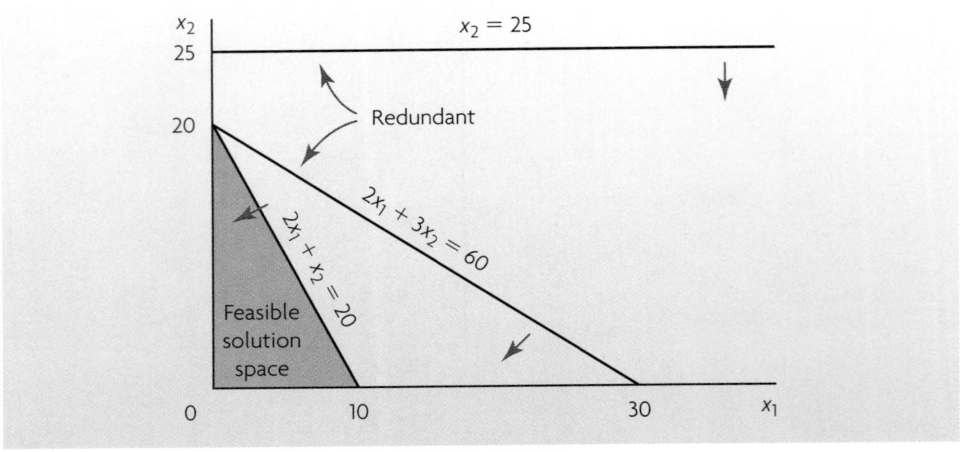

FIGURE 2-12 Multiple Optimal Solutions

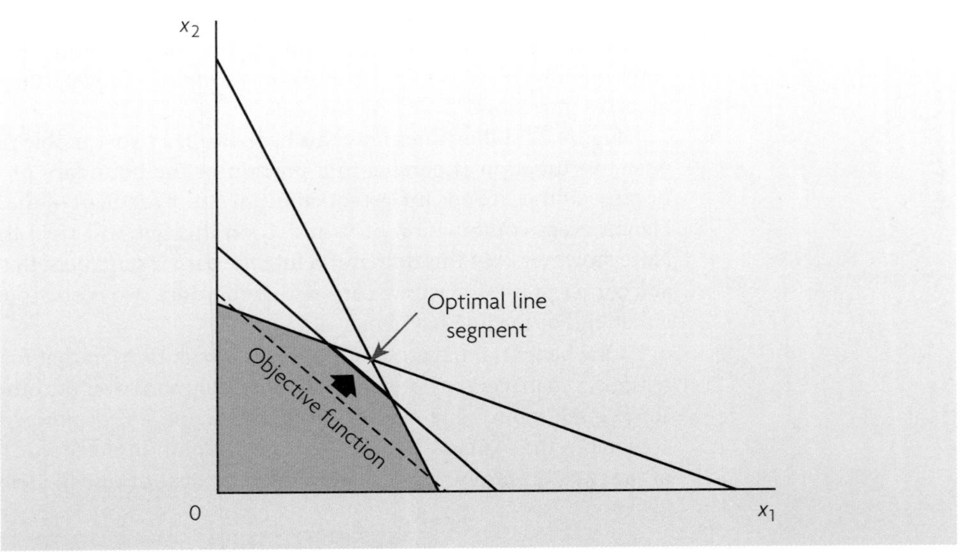

2.9 COMMENTS ABOUT THE USE OF EXCEL SOLVER

Throughout this book, Excel solutions will be provided for only certain problems. The reason for not providing the Excel solution to all of the problems is that the principal ideas for setting up and using Excel to solve various problems are essentially the same for each problem. Therefore, if we had solved each problem using Excel, we would have wasted valuable space in the book that could be utilized to cover other important topics or concepts. However, the Excel solutions to all of the problems are available on the Online Learning Centre.

Summary

Linear programming models are used to find optimal solutions to constrained optimization problems. For linear programming models to be used, the problems must involve a single objective, a linear objective function, and linear constraints and have known and constant numerical values.

Linear programming models are composed of decision variables and numerical values that are arranged into an objective function and a set of constraints. The constraints are restrictions that can pertain to any decision variable or to a combination of decision variables. In general, variables are not allowed to have negative values. These restrictions are referred to as nonnegativity constraints.

This chapter illustrates how to formulate LP problems. This chapter also shows how two-variable linear programming problems can be approached using graphical techniques. Sometimes, the solution can be read directly from the graph, but usually it must be found algebraically using simultaneous equations.

The graphical technique can only handle problems involving two variables; therefore, its value as a general tool for solving LP models is rather limited. Nonetheless, as a vehicle for illustrating important concepts related to LP models and solutions, it is invaluable.

The chapter illustrates how to set up and solve LP models in Excel. Although an example with two decision variables is used, the process can be easily adapted to handle larger sized problems.

The chapter illustrates the solution of both maximization and minimization problems. In addition, the calculating of slack and surplus is demonstrated. Also, certain special issues that sometimes arise, including problems that have no feasible solutions, unbounded problems, problems with multiple optimal solutions, and redundant constraints, are discussed.

We close this chapter with a brief description of another Modern Management Science Application at the Quebec Ministry of Natural Resources.

A MODERN MANAGEMENT SCIENCE APPLICATION: QUEBEC MINISTRY OF NATURAL RESOURCES

The fibre market, where wood chips and wood shavings are traded, constitutes an important link between the lumber industry and the pulp-and-paper industry. Two to three times a year, Quebec's provincial government organizes a round table on the wood-fibre market. The gathering provides an opportunity for various actors in the lumber industry and the pulp-and-paper industry to meet with representatives of the Ministry of Natural Resources (MNR) and discuss the state of the fibre market. Wood fibre is a free market, in which prices are set by demand, availability, and the willingness of various actors to trade. Therefore, the round table is not a mechanism to set prices, but industry representatives have regularly attended in the hopes of smoothing demand and avoiding long periods of overproduction or shortage as well as roller-coaster prices. Discussion topics include prices, stocks, availability, and long-term trading contracts between paper producers and sawmills, as well as acquisitions of sawmills by paper producers. The ministry has been under pressure to provide help and understanding in this erratic market, one in which stocks went from high to zero and back in a few months. Data was not a problem. The MNR regularly commissions province-wide comprehensive studies on the state of forests, sawmills, paper mills, technologies, lumber, paper prices, and so forth. Still, these did not turn into reliable insights into the price of fibre. To obtain some insights, Quebec's Ministry of Natural Resources began using modelling and optimization to support various negotiations in the wood-fibre market. A set of linear programming models was developed and implemented to solve an economic-equilibrium program, allowing the representative of the ministry to come to industry roundtables with accurate scenario analyses for the wood-fibre market. These models helped to foresee and explain the general economic trends facing both lumber and paper producers as well as to develop an unprecedented understanding of the wood-fibre market. The ministry incorporated these insights into subsequent government policies aimed at improving sawmill yield and stabilizing market behaviour.

Source: Reprinted by permission, A. Gautier, B. F. Lamond, D. Pare, and F. Rouleau, "Quebec Ministry of Natural Resources Uses Linear Programming to Understand the Wood-Fiber Market," *Interfaces* 30, no. 6, (November–December 2000), pp. 32–48. Copyright 2000, the Institute for Operations Research and the Management Sciences (INFORMS), 7240 Parkway Drive, Suite 310, Hanover, MD 21076 USA.

Glossary

Additivity A requirement of LP models that both the terms of the objective function and the terms of the constraints be additive.

Algorithm A solution technique; a sequence of steps that will lead to a solution.

Binding Constraints Constraints whose intersection determines the optimal solution to a problem.

Certainty A requirement that LP model parameters are known and constant.

Constrained Optimization Finding the optimal solution to a problem given that certain constraints must be satisfied by the solution.

Constraint A restriction that must be satisfied by a solution.

Corner Point An extreme point of the feasible solution space; an intersection of two or more constraints that touches the feasible solution space.

Data cells. The cells in a spreadsheet that show the data of the problem (constraint coefficients, objective function coefficients, and right-hand-side constraints).

Decision Variable A variable that is under the control of the decision maker.

Divisibility The assumption of LP models that noninteger values are acceptable solutions for decision variables.

Extreme Point See Corner Point.

Extreme Point Theorem If an LP problem has an optimal solution, at least one optimal solution will occur at a corner point of the feasible solution space.

Feasible Region See Feasible Solution Space.

Feasible Solution Any solution that satisfies all of a problem's constraints.

Feasible Solution Space Determined by the set of constraints of a problem, it contains all feasible solutions to an LP problem, including the optimal solutions.

Fundamental Theorem of LP If there is a solution to an LP problem, at least one optimal solution will occur at a corner point of the feasible solution space.

Graphical Method Method for determining the optimal solution to LP problems with two decision variables that involve visual portrayal of the LP concepts.

Iso-Cost Line A line on a graph in which all points have the same objective function value (minimization problem).

Iso-Profit Line A line on a graph in which all points have the same objective function value (maximization problem).

Karmakar's Method Interior method of solution to LP problems where the optimal solution is obtained by moving through the interior of the feasible solution space.

Linear Programming A family of mathematical techniques that can be used for constrained optimization problems with linear relationships.

Nonnegativity Constraints Variables are not allowed to have negative values.

Objective Function A mathematical expression that incorporates the contribution per unit of each variable.

Optimal Solution A combination of decision variable amounts that yields the best possible value of the objective function and satisfies all constraints. There may be multiple combinations of decision variables that yield that same best value of the objective function.

Output Cells The cells in a spreadsheet that show the output or quantity of the decision variables based on the changing cells.

Parameters Numerical values that appear in the objective function and constraints; assumed known and constant in LP models.

Proportionality A requirement of LP models that the impact or contribution of every decision variable in the objective function, and each constraint in which it appears, be linear.
Redundant Constraint A constraint that does not form a unique part of the boundary of the feasible solution space.
Simplex Method An exterior, algebraic method for solving any size (i.e. large number of decision variables) LP problem where the optimal solution is obtained by moving from corner point to another corner point.
Simultaneous Equations Solving a set of two equations *simultaneously* for the values of the decision variables that will satisfy both equations.
Slack The amount of scarce resource of capacity that will be unused by a given feasible solution to an LP problem.
Solver A Microsoft Office Excel add-in program used to solve optimization problems.
Standard Form A linear program in which all constraints are written as equalities, including slack and surplus variables.
Surplus The amount by which a ≥ constraint is exceeded by a given solution to an LP problem.
Target Cell The cell in a spreadsheet that shows the overall performance measure (i.e., the maximum profit or the minimum cost).

Solved Problems

Problem 1

A toy manufacturer makes three versions of a toy robot. The first version requires 10 minutes each for fabrication and packaging and 2 pounds of plastic, the second version requires 12 minutes for fabrication and packaging and 3 pounds of plastic, and the third version requires 15 minutes for fabrication and packaging and 4 pounds of plastic. There are 8 hours of fabrication and packaging time available and 200 pounds of plastic available for the next production cycle. The unit profits are $1 for each version 1, $5 for each version 2, and $6 for each version 3. A minimum of 10 units of each version of robot must be made to fill previous orders.

Formulate an LP model that will determine the optimal production quantities for profit maximization.

Solution

a. Identify the decision variables:

x_1 = number of version 1 robots
x_2 = number of version 2 robots
x_3 = number of version 3 robots

b. Identify the constraints by name:

Fabrication and packaging time
Quantity of plastic
Quantity of version 1 robots (minimum of 10)
Quantity of version 2 robots (minimum of 10)
Quantity of version 3 robots (minimum of 10)

c. Write the objective function:

$$\text{maximize} \quad 1x_1 + 5x_2 + 6x_3$$

d. Write the constraints:

Note that fabrication and packaging times are given in minutes per unit but that available time is given in hours. It is necessary that both sides of a constraint have the same units. This can be accomplished by converting 8 hours to 480 minutes.

The constraints are:

Fabrication and packaging	$10x_1 + 12x_2 + 15x_3 \leq 480$ minutes
Plastic	$2x_1 + 3x_2 + 4x_3 \leq 200$ pounds
Version 1	$x_1 \geq 10$ robots
Version 2	$x_2 \geq 10$ robots
Version 3	$x_3 \geq 10$ robots
	$x_1, x_2, \text{and } x_3 \geq 0$

Problem 2

Given this LP model:

$$\text{maximize} \quad 10x_1 + x_2$$

subject to

A	$3x_1 + 4x_2 \leq 12$
B	$2x_1 + 2x_2 \leq 16$
C	$x_1 - x_2 \leq 2$
	$x_1, x_2 \geq 0$

a. Graph the model.
b. Find the optimal point on the graph using the objective function method.
c. Use simultaneous equations to determine the optimal values of x_1 and x_2.
d. Determine the amount of slack for each constraint.

Solution

a. Plot each constraint by first setting one variable equal to zero and solving for the other, and then setting the other variable equal to zero and solving for the first. Then, connect those two points with a straight line. The last constraint is a bit different than the majority of constraints you will encounter in this chapter due to the negative value. Even so, we still follow the same procedure in determining the x_1 and x_2 intercept: The result is that the x_2 intercept is -2, and the x_1 intercept is $+2$.

After all of the constraints have been plotted, shade in the feasible solution space. To determine which side of the third constraint represents less than 2, substitute 0,0 into the constraint.

The plot is shown in Figure 2-13.

b. The objective function can be plotted by first setting it equal to the product of the x_1 and x_2 coefficients (10) and solving for the x_1 and x_2 intercepts. The objective function is shown in Figure 2-13 with the dotted line. It is apparent that the optimum point occurs at the intersection of constraint lines A and C.

c. The intersection of A and C is found as follows:

A	$3x_1 + x_2 = 12$	
C	$x_1 - x_2 = 2$	
	$4x_1 \quad = 14$	subracting

Solving, $x_1 = 3.5$.

Substituting $x_1 = 3.5$ into either of the constraints and solving for x_2 yields $x_2 = 1.5$. Then the optimal value of the objective function is found by substituting these values into the objective function: $10(3.5) + 1.5 = 36.5$.

d. There is no slack for the two constraints whose intersection determines the optimal solution because any point *on* the line means the left and right sides of the constraint expression are *equal.* For constraint B, we

FIGURE 2-13 Constraints and Feasible Solution Space for Solved Problem 2

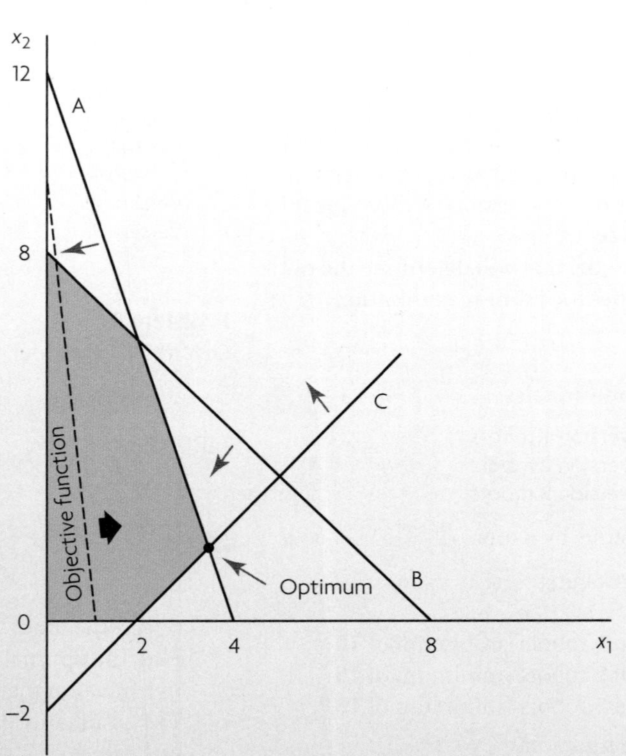

can determine the amount of slack by substituting in the optimal values of x_1 and x_2 and solving:

$$2(3.5) + 2(1.5) = 10$$

The slack is the original value minus this amount. Thus, slack equals $16 - 10 = 6$.

Problem 3

Given this LP model:

$$\text{minimize} \quad 3x_1 + 4x_2$$

subject to

$$\begin{aligned} &\text{A} \quad 6x_1 + 1x_2 \geq 120 \\ &\text{B} \quad 4x_1 + 4x_2 \geq 320 \\ &\text{C} \quad 3x_1 + 5x_2 \geq 300 \\ &\qquad x_1, x_2 \geq 0 \end{aligned}$$

a. Graph the model.
b. Determine the optimal point on the graph using the objective function method.
c. Use simultaneous equations to determine the optimal values of x_1 and x_2, and then find the minimum cost.
d. Determine the amount of slack or surplus for each constraint.

Solution

a. To plot the model, for each constraint:
(1) Make the constraint an equality.
(2) Alternately set one of the variables equal to zero and solve for the other. For example, for the first constraint, setting $x_1 = 0$ and solving for x_2, we find $x_2 = 120$; setting $x_2 = 0$ and solving for x_1, we find $x_1 = 20$. Thus, we have two points: $x_1 = 0, x_2 = 120$, and $x_1 = 20, x_2 = 0$.
(3) Mark the points on the graph and connect with a straight line. Label the line (i.e., A).
(4) After all constraints have been plotted, identify and shade in the feasible solution space. (See Figure 2-14.)

b. To plot the objective function, set it equal to any value, usually some multiple of the product of the x_1 and x_2 coefficients (e.g., 12), and then solve for the x_1 and x_2 intercepts in the same way as with a constraint. Connect the intercepts with a straight (dashed) line (see Figure 2-14). The objective function line was plotted using $3x_1 + 4x_2 = 360$.

c. The optimal solution is at the intersection of lines B and C. Solving these simultaneously, we find

FIGURE 2-14 A Graph of Solved Problem 3

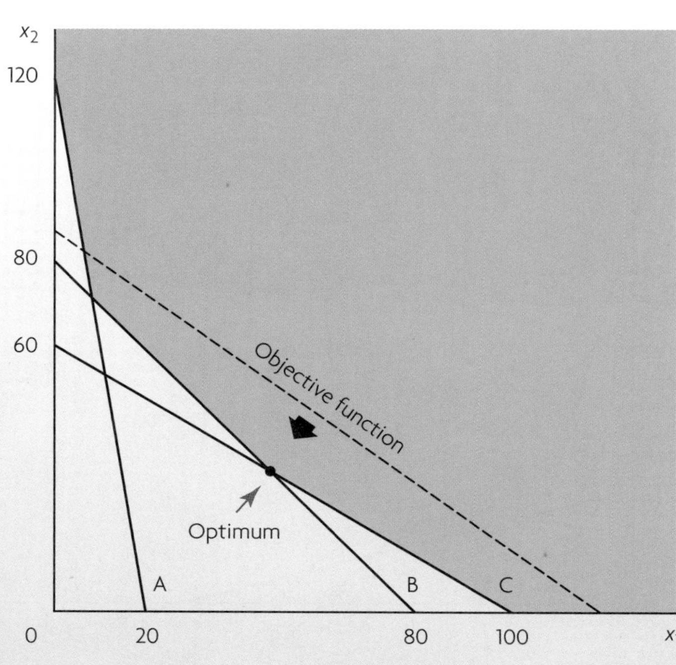

B $4x_1 + 4x_2 = 320$
C $3x_1 + 5x_2 = 300$

Multiplying the B equation by 5 and the C equation by 4 and then subtracting the modified C equation from the modified B equation will cause the x_2 term to drop out:

$$\begin{array}{lrcl} B' & 20x_1 + 20x_2 & = & 1600 \\ C' & 12x_1 + 20x_2 & = & 1200 \\ \hline & 8x_1 & = & 400 \end{array}$$

Solving, $x_1 = 50$. Substituting $x_1 = 50$ into either of the original equations or the modified equations will permit determination of x_2. For instance, using the original B:

$$4(50) + 4x_2 = 320$$

Multiplying and rearranging terms, we have

$$4x_2 = 120.$$

Thus, $x_2 = 30$. The minimum cost is found by substituting the optimal values into the objective function: $3(50) + 4(30) = 270$.

d. The term *slack* pertains to ≤ constraints; *surplus* pertains to ≥ constraints. Because the constraints in this problem are of the ≥ variety, *surplus* is the appropriate term.

Because the intersection of constraints B and C determines the optimal solution (i.e., they are binding constraints), they have no surplus. (You can verify this by substituting the optimal values into these two constraints.) For constraint A, substitution yields

$$6(50) + 1(30) = 330$$

Because this *exceeds* the minimum requirement of 120 by 210 (i.e., $330 - 120 = 210$), the surplus is 210.

Problem 4

Solve the following problem for the optimal values of the decision variables and the objective function. Then answer the questions about slack and surplus.

$$\text{maximize} \quad 5x_1 + 8x_2$$

FIGURE 2-15 Graph for Solved Problem 4

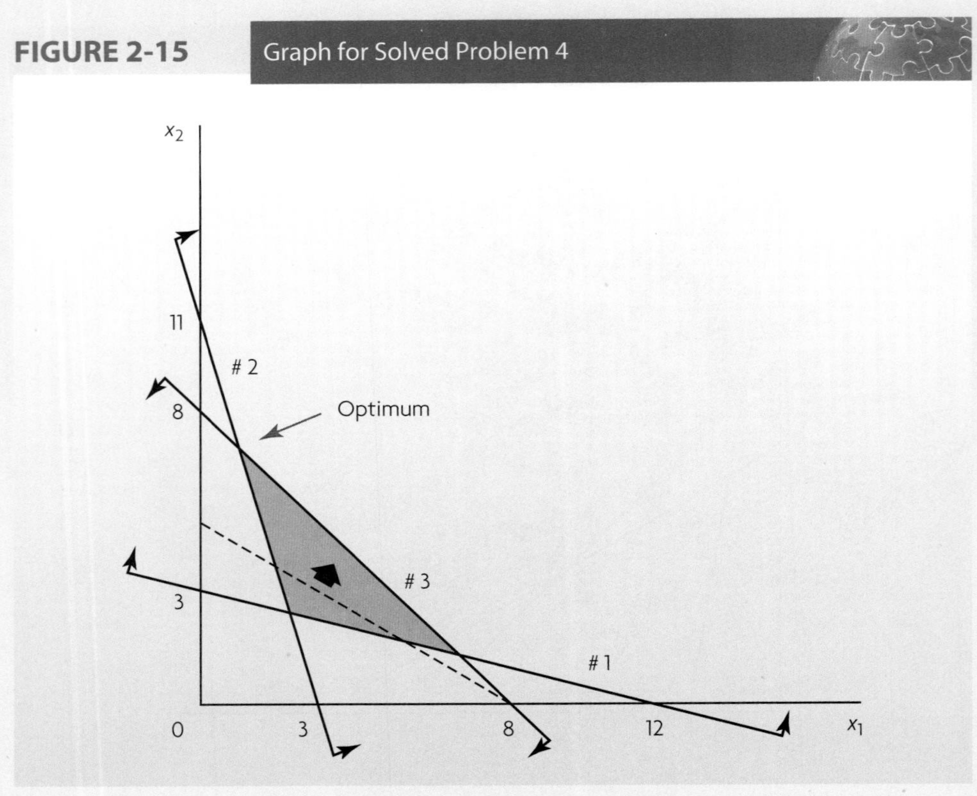

subject to

#1	$3x_1 + 12x_2 \geq 36$
#2	$11x_1 + 3x_2 \geq 33$
#3	$2x_1 + 2x_2 \leq 16$
	$x_1, x_2 \geq 0$

a. Do any of the constraints have surplus? If so, which one(s) and how much surplus?
b. Do any of the constraints have slack? If so, which one(s), and how much slack?

Solution

Notice that this problem involves *mixed constraints.* That is, the first two constraints are greater-than-or-equal-to constraints and the third is a less-than-or-equal-to constraint. This can lead to incorrectly identifying the feasible solution space if we are not careful. To avoid this possibility, it can be helpful to place arrows at the ends of the constraint lines on the graph to show which direction is feasible. (See Figure 2-15.)

Adding the objective function line to the graph reveals the optimal solution is at the point where constraints #2 and #3 intersect. Using simultaneous equations, we can determine that the optimal values are $x_1 = 1.1$ and $x_2 = 6.9$. Substituting these values into the objective function and solving yields an optimal profit value of 60.7.

a. The only type of constraint that can have surplus is a $\geq$ constraint. Constraints #1 and #2 are this type. However, the optimal solution is at the intersection of #2 and #3. Because the solution point is on #2, its surplus is zero. The solution is not on #1, so it has surplus. We can determine the amount by substituting the optimal values of x_1 and x_2 into the left side of that constraint and comparing the result to the right side. The difference is the amount of surplus. Thus,

#1: $3(1.1) + 12(6.9) = 86.10$

The right-hand-side value is 36. The difference (surplus) is

$86.10 - 36 = 50.1$

b. Only $\leq$ constraints can have slack. Constraint #3 is such a constraint. However, the optimal point is on this constraint, so its slack equals zero. We can also determine this by substituting the optimal values of x_1 and x_2 into the left-hand side of constraint #3 and comparing the result to the right-hand-side value of this constraint. Thus,

#3: $2(1.1) + 2(6.8) = 16$

This equals the right-hand-side value, indicating that slack is zero.

Discussion and Review Questions

1. What are the key advantages of using linear programming as a decision-making tool?
2. In using Excel, explain target cells, output cells, and data cells.
3. In using Excel to solve a linear programming problem, briefly explain the following:
    a. Input screen.
    b. Solver dialogue box.
    c. Add constraint dialogue box.
    d. Solver options dialogue box.
    e. Solver results dialogue box.
    f. Output screen.
    g. Excel answer report.
4. Explain the SUMPRODUCT command. How is it used in solving linear programming problems? Why is it useful?
5. What are the assumptions of linear programming problems? Briefly explain each assumption.
6. What are the components of LP models? Briefly discuss each component.
7. What are the three signs for constraints in formulating a linear programming problem?
8. List the steps in formulating a linear programming problem.
9. Describe how an LP problem formulation can be converted into standard form.
10. List the steps in using the graphical approach to obtain an optimal solution to a linear programming problem.
11. In using the graphical approach, the optimal solution can be found by using two methods. Describe the methods in finding the optimal solution using the graphical approach. What are the differences between the two approaches?
12. Describe slack and surplus and explain how they can be determined.
13. Explain how an infeasible solution can be identified on an LP graph.
14. Explain how an unbounded solution can be identified on an LP graph.

15. Does having an unbounded solution space always result in an unbounded solution for a maximization problem? Explain.
16. Using the graphical approach, under what condition is it possible for an LP problem to have more than one optimal solution?
17. Develop two less-than-or-equal-to constraints such that one of them is a redundant constraint.
18. Explain what is meant by the term *binding constraint?*
19. In solving a linear programming problem, the condition of infeasibility occurred. What are some of the factors we should check to resolve this problem?
20. What is the impact of removing a nonredundant constraint from a linear programming problem on the graphical solution?
21. Discuss the similarities and differences in using the graphical approach to solving LP between maximization and minimization problems.

Problems

1. A furniture company produces a variety of products. One department specializes in wood tables, chairs, and bookcases. These are made using three resources: labour, wood, and machine time. The department has 60 hours of labour available each day, 16 hours of machine time, and 400 board feet of wood. A consultant has developed a linear programming model for the department:

   x_1 = quantity of tables
   x_2 = quantity of chairs
   x_3 = quantity of bookcases

   maximize $40x_1 + 30x_2 + 45x_3$ (profit)

   subject to

Labour	$2x_1 + 1x_2 + 2.5x_3 \leq$	60 hours
Machine	$.8x_1 + .6x_2 + 1.0x_3 \leq$	16 hours
Wood	$30x_1 + 20x_2 + 30x_3 \leq$	400 board-feet
Tables	$x_1 \geq$	10 tables

   $$x_1, x_2, x_3 \geq 0$$

   Answer these questions posed by department manager Barbara Brady:
   a. What is the main purpose of the model?
   b. What are the decision variables?
   c. What are the system constraints (name them)?
   d. What is the meaning of the number 2.5 in the labour constraint?
   e. Explain what is meant by $x_1 \geq 10$.
   f. What does the term $40x_1$ in the objective function represent?

2. The Stone Company produces three sizes of window fans: small, medium, and large. The manager has formulated an LP model for fan production:

   maximize $6x_1 + 8x_2 + 5x_3$ (profit)

   subject to

Labour	$3x_1 + 4x_2 + 5x_3 \leq$	160 hours
Metal	$1x_1 + 2x_2 + 3x_3 \leq$	100 pounds
Plastic	$2x_1 + 2x_2 + 2x_3 \leq$	110 pounds
Large fan	$x_3 \geq$	18

   $$x_1, x_2, x_3 \geq 0$$

   Briefly explain or define each of these parts of the model:
   a. x_1, x_2, and x_3.
   b. The 6 in the objective function.
   c. The product of the 8 and x_2 in the objective function.
   d. The terms *labour, metal,* and *plastic.*
   e. The 5 in the labour constraint.
   f. The 160 hours.
   g. $x_3 \geq 18$.
   h. The product of 5 and x_3 in the labour constraint.
   i. $x_1, x_2, x_3 \geq 0$.
   j. What two key questions can be answered using this model?

3. A confectionary company produces two sizes of its popular dark chocolate bars: a 3.5-ounce size and a 6-ounce size. The 3.5-ounce bar costs \$0.22 to make and sells for \$0.35, whereas the 6-ounce bar costs \$0.40 to make and sells for \$0.55. The company has 15 000 ounces of chocolate in stock, and the manager wants to use it all on the next production run. In addition, the manager has specified that a minimum of 1000 of the 3.5-ounce bars and 1200 of the 6-ounce bars should be made.
   a. What are the decision variables in this problem?
   b. What are the constraints?
   c. Formulate a linear programming model that will enable the manager to determine how many

of each size bar to produce to satisfy the conditions specified with maximum profit.

4. The Mantell Company makes softballs and baseballs. To make each type of ball, leather, nylon, wood chips, and machine time and labour are needed. The requirements for each item and the resources available are shown in the following table:

Item	Softball	Baseball	Available
Leather	6	4	6000 ounces
Nylon	8	3	5000 yards
Wood chips	10	2	5000 ounces
Labour	3	2	3600 minutes
Machine	1	1	2000 minutes

Softballs sell for \$17 each, and baseballs sell for \$15 each. Formulate a linear programming model that can be used to determine the number of each type of ball to produce to maximize revenue.

5. Given this linear programming model:

maximize $Z = 10x_1 + 16x_2$ (profit)

subject to

A $8x_1 + 20x_2 \leq 120$
B $25x_1 + 20x_2 \leq 200$
$x_1, x_2 \geq 0$

a. Graph the constraints.
b. Shade in the feasible solution space.
c. Plot the objective function and determine the optimal point on the graph.
d. Use simultaneous equations to determine the optimal values of the decision variables and the maximum value of the objective function.
e. What would the optimal values be if the objective function had been $6x_1 + 3x_2$?

6. For the preceding problem, determine the coordinates of each feasible corner point using the original objective function. Then, determine the profit at each of those corner points. Use that information to identify the optimal solution.

7. The manager of a construction project has formulated this LP model:

maximize $Z = 25x_1 + 30x_2$ (profit)

subject to

Time $20x_1 + 15x_2 \leq 1100$ hours
Materials $8x_1 + 12x_2 \leq 600$ tons
$x_1, x_2 \geq 0$

a. Graph the model.
b. Determine the optimal values of the decision variables using the objective function approach. What is the maximum profit?

8. For the previous problem, use the extreme point approach to determine the optimal solution.

9. The manager of a warehouse has developed this LP model:

maximize $Z = 50x_1 + 30x_2$ (revenue)

subject to

Time $15x_1 + 12x_2 \leq 900$ minutes
Space $8x_1 + 16x_2 \leq 800$ square feet
$x_1 \geq 40$ units
$x_1, x_2 \geq 0$

a. Graph the constraints and shade in the feasible solution space.
b. Determine the optimal solution and maximum revenue.

10. Answer the questions of the previous problem with this modification: Assume the objective function is $30x_1 + 50x_2$. (The manager had the coefficients of the objective function reversed.)

11. The owner of a telephone subscription service specializes in taking orders for two magazines, x_1 and x_2. She has formulated the following model that describes the unit contributions to profits and the use of scarce resources involved:

maximize $Z = .60x_1 + .90x_2$

subject to

Telephone $8x_1 + 12x_2 \leq 480$ minutes per day
Paperwork $10x_1 + 6x_2 \leq 480$ minutes per day
$x_1 \geq 20$
$x_1, x_2 \geq 0$

a. Is there a unique optimal solution?
b. What is the maximum profit?
c. Can you find an optimal solution for which both decision variables are integer?

12. The manager of a food processing plant that specializes in potato chips has developed an LP model to reflect processing times.

x_1 = boxes of regular chips
x_2 = boxes of crinkle cut chips

maximize $Z = .40x_1 + .30x_2$ (profit)

subject to

Cutting	$3.6x_1 + .8x_2 \leq 144$ minutes
Frying	$3.2x_1 + 1.6x_2 \leq 160$ minutes
Packing	$4.8x_1 + 7.2x_2 \leq 576$ seconds
Crinkle	$x_2 \leq 80$ boxes
Crinkle	$x_2 \geq 20$ boxes
	$x_1, x_2 \geq 0$

a. Determine the combination of boxes of the two types of chips that will maximize profits.
b. Is any constraint redundant? Explain briefly.

13. For the previous problem, determine each of the following:
a. The amount of each resource that will be used.
b. The amount of slack for each resource.
c. The special situation that would exist if the profit for crinkle cut chips dropped to \$0.20 per box. (Hint: Plot the revised objective function on your graph.)

14. A manager of an automobile dealership must decide how many cars to order for the end of the model year. Midsize cars yield an average profit of \$500 each, and compact cars yield an average of \$400 each. Either type of car will cost the dealership \$8000 each and no more than \$720 000 can be invested. The manager wants at least 10 of each type of car but no more than 50 of the midsized cars and no more than 60 of the compact cars.
a. Formulate the linear programming model of this problem.
b. Solve for the optimal quantities of each type of car and the optimal value of the objective function.

15. Given this model:

minimize $Z = 4x_1 + 2x_2$ (cost)

subject to

A	$16x_1 + 5x_2 \geq 80$
B	$18x_1 + 15x_2 \geq 180$
C	$24x_1 + 45x_2 \geq 360$
	$x_1 \geq 0, x_2 \geq 0$

a. Solve for the values of x_1 and x_2 that will minimize cost.
b. Which restriction is exceeded by the optimal solution to the model? By how much?

16. Given this model:

minimize $Z = 20x_1 + 30x_2$ (cost)

subject to

Town	$6x_1 + x_2 \geq 12$
Country	$7x_1 + 7x_2 \geq 49$
Province	$3x_1 + 11x_2 \geq 33$
	$x_1, x_2 \geq 0$

a. Find the optimal values of x_1 and x_2 and the minimum cost.
b. Determine the amount of surplus associated with each constraint.

17. The manager of a health-food store has formulated the following LP model, which describes parameters for a new product:

minimize $Z = 2.40x_1 + 1.50x_2$ (cost)

subject to

Vitamin A	$10x_1 + 6x_2 \geq 1200$ mg
Vitamin B_1	$10x_1 + 30x_2 \geq 1800$ mg
	$x_1, x_1 \geq 0$

a. Determine the optimal solution.
b. What is the minimum cost at the optimum?

18. The new manager of a food processing plant hopes to reduce costs by using linear programming to determine the optimal amounts of two ingredients it uses, x_1 and x_2. The manager has constructed this model:

minimize $Z = .40x_1 + .40x_2$

subject to

Protein	$3x_1 + 5x_2 \geq 30$ grams
Carbohydrates	$6x_1 + 4x_2 \geq 48$ grams
	$x_1, x_2 \geq 0$

a. Determine the optimal solution.
b. Compute the minimum cost for the optimal solution.

19. There is a single optimal solution to Problem 18. However, if the objective function had been parallel to one of the constraints, there would have been two equally optimal solutions. If the cost of x_2 remains at \$0.40, what cost of x_1 would cause the objective function to be parallel to the carbohydrate constraint? Explain how you determined this.

20. Graph this problem and briefly explain why it cannot be solved:

maximize $Z = 2.20x_1 + 2.35x_2$

subject to

A	$6x_1 + 9x_2 \geq 108$
B	$3x_1 + 5x_2 \leq 45$
	$x_1, x_2 \geq 0$

21. Given this linear programming problem:

maximize $Z = 5x_1 + 3x_2$

subject to

1 $7x_1 + 4x_2 \geq 84$
2 $5x_1 + 8x_2 \geq 80$
$x_1, x_2 \geq 0$

a. Graph the problem.
b. Why is it impossible to obtain an optimal solution for the problem?
c. Can you suggest two different possible errors that might have occurred in formulating the problem that prevent a solution?

22. Explain why the following linear programming problem cannot be solved for an optimal solution.

minimize $Z = 7x_1 + 3x_2$

subject to

1 $6x_1 + 8x_2 \leq 48$
2 $4x_1 + 3x_2 \geq 24$
3 $x_2 \geq 5$
$x_1, x_2 \geq 0$

23. Explain why the following linear programming formulation is probably in error:

minimize $Z = 30x_1 + 33x_2$

subject to

1 $15x_1 + 18x_2 \leq 90$
2 $20x_1 + 12x_2 \leq 120$
$x_1, x_2 \geq 0$

24. A wood products firm uses leftover time at the end of each week to make goods for stock. Currently, there are two products on the list of items that are produced for stock: a chopping board and a knife holder. Both items require three operations: cutting, gluing, and finishing. The manager of the firm has collected the following data on these products:

	Profit	Time per Unit (minutes)		
Item	per Unit	Cutting	Gluing	Finishing
Chopping board	$2	1.4	5	12
Knife holder	$6	.8	13	3

The manager has also determined that during each week 56 minutes are available for cutting, 650 minutes are available for gluing, and 360 minutes are available for finishing.

a. Formulate this problem as a linear programming model.
b. Determine the optimal quantities of the decision variables.
c. Which resources are not completely used by your solution? How much of each resource is unused?

25. The manager of an inspection department has been asked to help reduce a backlog of safety devices that must be inspected. There are two types of safety devices: one for construction workers and one for window washers. The manager will be permitted to select any combination of items because new testing equipment will soon be available that will handle the remaining items. However, in the short run, the manager has been asked to help generate revenue. The revenue for inspecting each construction device is $60, and the revenue for inspecting each windowwashing device is $40. The manager has obtained data on the necessary inspection operations, which are

	Time per Unit(minutes)		Total Time
		Window	Available
Operation	Construction	Washing	(minutes)
Test #1	3/4	1/3	75
Test #2	1/4	1/2	50
Test #3	1/2	1/4	40

a. Formulate this problem as a linear programming model.
b. Determine the optimum values of the decision variables and the revenue that will result.
c. Which testing operations will have slack time? How much?
d. Is any constraint redundant? Which one? Why?

26. A dietician has been asked by the athletic director of a university to develop a snack that athletes can use in their training programs. The dietician intends to mix two separate products together to make the snack. The following information has been obtained by the dietician:

	Minimum Amount Required	Contribution per Ounce (grams)	
Nutrient	(grams)	Product A	Product B
Carbohydrates	20	2	5
Protein	12	6	1
Calories	450	90	50

Product A costs $0.20 per ounce and Product B costs $0.10 per ounce

a. Formulate this problem as a linear programming model.
b. Determine the optimal quantities of the two products for cost minimization. What is the cost per snack?

c. Are any requirements exceeded? If so, which ones, and by how much?

27. The manager of the deli section of a grocery superstore has just learned that the department has 112 pounds of mayonnaise, of which 70 pounds is approaching its expiration date and must be used. To use up the mayonnaise, the manager has decided to prepare two items: a ham spread and a deli spread. Each pan of the ham spread will require 1.4 pounds of the mayonnaise and each pan of the deli spread will require 1.0 pound. The manager has received an order for 10 pans of ham spread and 8 pans of the deli spread. In addition, the manager has decided to have at least 10 pans of each spread available for sale. Both spreads will cost \$3 per pan to make, but ham spread yields revenue of \$5 per pan and deli spread yields \$7 per pan.
   a. Formulate this problem as a linear programming model.
   b. Determine the solution that will minimize cost.
   c. Determine the solution that will maximize profit.

28. A production manager is faced with the question of how to allocate the manufacturing of a microwave oven between his own company and a subcontractor because neither firm can handle the demand alone. Fabrication costs are \$10 per unit within the company and \$20 per unit from the subcontractor; assembly costs are \$8 per unit within the company and \$5 from the subcontractor; and inspection costs are \$3 per unit within the company and \$1 per unit from the subcontractor. The company has a budget of \$120 000 for fabrication, \$40 000 for assembly, and \$12 000 for inspection. The contribution to profits is \$60 per unit regardless of which firm does the work.
   a. Formulate this problem as a linear programming model.
   b. What is the optimal solution? How much profit will it yield?
   c. How much of the total budget will be unused by the optimal solution?

29. Determine the optimal solution and value of the objective function for Problem 3.

30. (Refer to Problem 4.)
   a. What are the optimal values of the decision variables and the objective function?
   b. What is the amount of slack for each resource?
   c. Which constraints are redundant?

31. An accountant has developed the following LP model:

$$\text{maximize} \quad Z = 4.0A + 3.6B \quad \text{(revenue)}$$

subject to

$$\begin{aligned} &1 \quad 11A + 5B \geq 55 \\ &2 \quad 3A + 4B \leq 36 \\ &3 \quad 4A - 9B \leq 0 \\ &\qquad A, B \geq 0 \end{aligned}$$

   a. Determine the optimal quantities of variables A and B and the maximum revenue.
   b. For the optimal solution, determine the slack or surplus that would result for each constraint.
   c. Are any constraints redundant? Explain.

32. Given this LP model:

$$\text{maximize} \quad Z = x_1 + 5x_2$$

subject to

$$\begin{aligned} x_1 + 3x_2 &\leq 12 \\ 3x_1 + 4x_2 &= 24 \\ x_1 &\leq 6 \\ x_1, x_2 &\geq 0 \end{aligned}$$

   a. Determine the optimal values of the decision variables.
   b. Compute the optimal value of the objective function.
   c. Is any constraint redundant? If so, which one?

33. Tom Smith is the manager of a discount store. He wants to maximize the total revenue from two furniture items; a bedroom set and a living room set. It is important that the showroom space of 40 000 square feet be *completely* filled with these sets, some of which will be in crates. Nonetheless, the manager wants to give the impression that the store is overstocked on these items. The bedroom sets will occupy an average of 400 square feet each, and the living room sets will occupy an average of 500 square feet each. The manager estimates that it requires approximately 14 minutes to unload a bedroom set and 7 minutes to unload a living room set. There are 980 minutes available for the unloading. The living room sets will produce a revenue of \$500 each, and the bedroom sets will produce a revenue of \$1000 each. The manager also has decided that a minimum of 20 living room sets should be ordered.
   a. What question is to be answered by linear programming?

b. Formulate the problem in a linear programming format.
c. Determine the optimal solution.

34. A real estate broker is responsible for selling homes in a new development. There will be two types of floor plans: Model I and Model II. Each Model I will require .6 acre of land, and each Model II will require 1.0 acre of land. Twelve acres of land are available. The broker already has orders for three Model I and three Model II homes, and the contractor has requested that no more than 10 Model I homes be sold because of other circumstances. The broker also operates a tree nursery and wants to use at least 81 maple trees to landscape the development. Each Model I and Model II home will receive nine maple trees. The broker receives commissions of \$9000 to sell each Model I home and \$12 000 to sell each Model II home.
   a. What question can be answered using linear programming?
   b. Formulate this problem in an LP format.
   c. Determine the optimal solution graphically.
   d. If the broker had estimated a cost of \$2500 to sell each Model I and \$1800 to sell each Model II, what solution would be optimal?

35. Consider the following LP model:

maximize $Z = 450x_1 + 200x_2$

subject to

$$10x_1 + 7x_2 \leq 70\,000$$
$$x_1 + x_2 \leq 10\,000$$
$$x_1 \leq 7000$$
$$x_2 \leq 7000$$
$$x_1, x_2 \geq 0$$

   a. Write the LP model in standard form
   b. Solve with the graphical method
   c. Are any constraints redundant? If so, which one?
   d. Are any constraints binding? If so, which one?
   e. Suppose the second constraint is now stated as $x_1 + x_2 = 10\,000$, what happens to the problem solution?

36. Given this linear programming problem:

maximize $Z = x_1 + 2x_2$

subject to

$$x_1 + x_2 \leq 6$$
$$x_1 - x_2 \geq 0$$
$$x_1 + x_2 \geq 3$$
$$x_1, x_2 \geq 0$$

   a. Solve with the graphical method.
   b. Are any constraints binding? If so, which one?

37. Given this linear programming problem:

minimize $Z = 6x_1 + 8x_2$

subject to

$$2x_1 + 3x_2 \leq 9$$
$$3x_1 + 2x_2 \geq 6$$
$$x_1, x_2 \geq 0$$

   a. Write the LP model in standard form.
   b. Solve with the graphical method.
   c. For the optimal solution, determine the slack or surplus that would result for each constraint.

Determine if each of the following five problems involves infeasibility, unboundedness, multiple optimal solutions, or a single optimal solution. Explain why.

38. Maximize $Z = 4x_1 - 2x_2$ subject to

$$2x_1 - x_2 \leq 1$$
$$x_1 + x_2 \geq 6$$
$$x_1, x_2 \geq 0$$

39. Maximize $Z = 3x_1 + 5x_2$ subject to

$$2x_1 + 2x_2 \leq 8$$
$$2x_1 - 2x_2 \geq 10$$
$$x_1, x_2 \geq 0$$

40. Maximize $Z = 8x_1 + 2x_2$ subject to

$$16x_1 + 2x_2 \leq 8$$
$$2x_1 - 2x_2 \geq 10$$
$$x_1, x_2 \geq 0$$

41. Maximize $Z = 2x_1 + 6x_2$ subject to

$$2x_1 - 2x_2 \leq 8$$
$$2x_1 + 4x_2 \geq 8$$
$$x_1, x_2 \geq 0$$

42. Maximize $Z = x_1 + 2x_2$ subject to

$$x_1 \leq 9$$
$$2x_2 \leq 6$$
$$1.5x_1 + 3x_2 \leq 15$$
$$x_1, x_2 \geq 0$$

43. The Canadian Association of University Teachers has retained two mutual funds (TDMF and RBCMF) to

invest a generous donation of $750 000 received recently from a previous member who is now a successful entrepreneur. The TDMF fund has a projected annual return of 11.5 percent, while the RBCMF fund has a projected annual return of 8.5 percent. Because of the risk associated with each option, it has been decided that no more than 40 percent of the donation should be placed on the TDMF fund and no more than 70 percent of the investment should be placed on the RBCMF fund. Moreover, to maintain a balanced mix, it has also been decided to set the amount invested in the TDMF fund to at least half of the amount invested in the RBCMF fund. Conversely, the amount invested in the RBCMF fund must be at least half of the amount invested in the TDMF fund. Assume a processing cost of 2.5 percent and 1.5 percent per $100 of investment in the TDMF fund and the RBCMF fund, respectively.

a. Formulate a LP model that can be used to determine the amount to allocate in each of the possible investment alternatives to maximize the return for the investment while meeting all constraints.
b. Determine the optimal solution graphically.

44. For Problem 43, assume a third mutual fund (SBKMF) is also retained with a projected return of 12.5 percent and a processing cost of 2.75 percent per $100 of investment. Because of the risk associated with this option, it has been decided that no more than 25 percent of the donation should be placed in this fund. However, the amount to invest in this fund must be at least 30 percent of the total amount invested in the other two mutual funds.
    a. Reformulate the problem with two decision variables and solve it using the graphical approach.
    b. What is the amount invested in each mutual fund and what is the expected return with each investment option?

45. An investor is considering investing a maximum amount of $45 000 in the shares of two companies, A and B, that are likely candidates for a takeover in the future. Company A is currently trading for $30 per share, but this price is estimated to increase by 30 percent if the takeover occurs. Company B is trading for $45, but the price is estimated to increase by 25 percent if the takeover occurs. Company B presents a higher risk investment than company A. According to a risk measurement system provided by a talented financial advisor, each unit invested in shares of company B has a risk index of 9, whereas each unit invested in shares of company A has a risk index of 4. The investor wants to minimize risk subject to the requirement that the annual income from the investment be at least $8500. The investor wants to invest at least $10 000 in company B shares.
    a. Formulate a linear programming model that can be used to determine the number of shares to purchase from each company while meeting the investment constraints.
    b. Determine the coordinates of each extreme point.
    c. Find the optimal solution.

46. A local cable TV company would like to spend a monthly advertising budget of $20 000 on a new multicultural TV program. The management has determined two approaches to promote the program: phone promotion and newspaper advertising. Management decided that the total budget spent on phone promotion advertising cannot exceed twice the amount of budget spent on newspaper advertising. In addition, it has also decided that at least 25 percent of the budget must be spent on each type of media. The marketing department has developed an index to measure new customer exposure per dollar of advertising on a scale from 0 to 100, with higher values implying a greater exposure. If the value of the index for the newspaper advertising is 50 and the value of the index for phone promotion is 80, how should the company allocate its advertising budget to maximize the new customer exposure while still meeting all the management constraints?

47. A hotel chain owns a reward loyalty program which is used to reward customers for repeat business. For the coming summer, the hotel chain is seeking how to split the promotion budget among current customers already enrolled in the program and new customers not enrolled yet. The management estimates that about 30 percent of existing customers reached will inquire about the promotion campaign and 25 percent will result in a booking. These estimates are 30 percent for new customers. The cost is $4.50 for each promotion sent to a current customer and $7.50 for each promotion sent to a new customer. The management expectation is that a minimum of 3000 current customers will make hotel bookings and a minimum of 1000 new customers will make hotel bookings. The marketing promotional budget is $199 000, excluding the cost of the reward loyalty program itself.
    a. Formulate a linear programming model that can be used to determine how many promotions

should be sent to each group of customers to maximize the total booking sales while meeting the management requirement.

b. Solve the model using the graphical method.

48. A consulting company is seeking to hire nonpermanent employees to complete a short-term project for a period of six months. Two types of employees are targeted: experienced and inexperienced. Each newly hired employee is required to complete a three-day basic training program. In addition, each inexperienced employee is required to complete another two-day advanced training program. The cost of the basic program is $1200 per employee and the cost of the advanced program is $800 per employee. The company has requested that at least 10 experienced employees and at least 8 inexperienced employees be hired and trained. However, the total number of employees hired and trained should not exceed 25.
    a. Formulate a linear programming model that can be used to determine the number of employees of each group to hire and train to minimize total cost.
    b. Solve for the model using the graphical method.

49. For Problem 48, if the monthly salary is $2500 and $2000 for respectively for an experienced and an inexperienced employee, reformulate a linear programming model that can be used to determine the number of hires in each group to minimize the monthly salary cost, considering a training budget limitation of $28 000.

50. A supermarket sells two types of eggs, Omega-3 eggs and regular eggs. The Omega-3 eggs cost $1.70 per dozen, but 9 percent of them are defective and can not be sold. The regular eggs cost only $0.90 per dozen, but they have a 12 percent defective rate. The manager of the supermarket has decided to order at least 10 000 dozen of each type, but at least 10 percent of the order should be Omega-3 eggs and at most 70 percent of the order should be regular eggs. The manager needs to know how many Omega-3 eggs and regular eggs should be ordered to minimize the overall cost.
    a. Formulate a linear programming model for this problem.
    b. Find the optimal solution.
    c. If the demand of Omega-3 eggs increases by 5 percent, but overall demand does not change, how many Omega-3 eggs and regular eggs should be ordered to minimize the overall cost? Solve the problem again and find out the changes on optimal solution.

51. In Problem 50, the profit margin of Omega-3 eggs is $1.00 per dozen, which is two times the profit margin of regular eggs. How many Omega-3 eggs and regular eggs should be ordered to maximize the overall profit? Formulate a linear programming model for this problem and find out the optimal solution.

52. Carleton University Bookstore (CUB) purchases bags with logos from two suppliers and makes them available for sale during the spring convocation period. Bags from supplier A cost $6.50 each but 2 percent of them are defective, whereas bags from supplier B cost only $4.50 each but 5 percent of them are defective. For the coming convocation period, at least 1500 non-defective bags are needed. Because there may be differences in the delivery time, management wants to order at least 250 bags from each supplier. Formulate a linear programming model that can be used to determine the number of bags to order from each supplier such that the ordering cost is minimized and solve it by using graphical analysis.

53. For Problem 53, assume that management wants to minimize the number of bags that cannot be sold and has set a total ordering budget of $10 000. Reformulate the problem and determine how many bags should be ordered from each supplier. How does the percentage of defective items compare to the model in Problem 53?

Case 1: Son, Ltd.

Son, Ltd. manufactures a variety of chemical products used by photoprocessors. Son was recently bought out by a conglomerate, and managers of the two organizations have been working together to improve the efficiency of Son's operations.

Managers have been asked to adhere to weekly operating budgets and to develop operating plans using quantitative methods whenever possible. The manager of one department has been given a weekly operating budget of $11 980 for production of three chemical products, which for convenience shall be referred to as Q, R, and W. The budget is intended to pay for direct labour and materials. Processing requirements for the three products, on a per unit basis, are

Product	Labour (hours)	Material A (pounds)	Material B (pounds)
Q	5	2	1
R	4	2	—
W	2	1/2	2

The company has a contractual obligation for 85 units of Product R per week.

Material A costs $4 per pounds, as does material B. Labour costs $8 an hour.

Product Q sells for $122 a unit, product R sells for $115 a unit, and product W sells for $76 a unit.

The manager is considering a number of different proposals regarding the quantity of each product to produce. The manager is primarily interested in maximizing contribution. Moreover, the manager wants to know how much labour will be needed, as well as the amount of each material to purchase.

Required

Prepare a report that addresses the following issues:

1. The optimal quantities of products and the necessary quantities of labour and materials.
2. One proposal is to make equal amounts of the products. What amount of each will maximize contribution, and what quantities of labour and materials will be needed? How much less will total contribution be if this proposal is adopted?
3. How would you formulate the constraint for material A if it was determined that there is a 5 percent waste factor for material A and equal quantities of each product are required?

Case 2: ABC Company

ABC Company has a sales department, two production departments, and produces two products, X and Y. Both products require processing in each of the two production departments. The company's budgeting covers a period of one year at a time. The marketing manager has control over the selling prices and the sales mix during the budget period, and aims to maximize the operating profit. However, the manager cannot change the demands for the two products. At the beginning of each budget period, ABC needs to develop its plan of operations, that is, the production volume based on the sales forecasts and the production information. No end inventory is assumed since the company operates on a just-in-time production principle. Therefore, the total production for each of the two products is entirely sold. During the budget period the company revises its production plan at the end of each month based on the latest firm sales orders and other relevant changes in market and production conditions. These monthly revised solutions act as new targets for operational managers to modify their affected operations. ABC has a 30-day lead-time from receiving a customer order to manufacturing and shipping it. A final revision is done at the beginning of the last period and an *ex post* budget is developed accordingly to reflect what should have been the production quantities for the budget period. A comprehensive variance analysis is performed at the end of the budget period. The following information is drawn from the accounting records at three different periods of time during a budget period (at the beginning, or *ex ante* period, at the mid-period, and the end, or *ex post* period).

	Ex ante period		Mid-period		*Ex post* period	
	X	Y	X	Y	X	Y
Unit selling price ($)	38	34	36	35	36	35
Unit material cost ($)	16	14	15.99	13.65	16.40	14.35
Unit material usage (lbs)	4	3.5	4.1	3.5	4	3.5
Unit material price (lbs)	4	4	3.9	3.9	4.10	4.10
Unit processing time in:						
Department 1 (hours)	1	0.25	0.8	0.2	1	0.25
Department 2 (hours)	0.25	1	0.28	1.12	0.25	1
Total operating expenses						
Department 1 ($)		80 000		78 000		80 000
Department 2 ($)		120 000		125 000		120 000
Department 1 (hours)		10 000		7057		7750
Department 2 (hours)		7750		10 000		10 000

The production departments have a maximum capacity of 10 000 hours each. The total (combined) demand for the two products over the budget period is 14 200 units.

Managerial Report

Prepare a report presenting your findings and recommendations and to answer the following questions:

1. Formulate a LP model to determine at the beginning of the planning period (*ex ante* period) the number of units of each product to make to maximize the total contribution to profit. What is the operating profit (net income) at this optimal solution?
2. Reformulate the LP model to determine what the quantities in Question 1 would be if the mid-period review information were available at the beginning of the budget period.
3. What if the *ex post* period information were available? What would the operating profit be in each case?
4. What would be the impact of the changes in the market prices of the products and materials on the capacity of each department between the *ex ante* and *ex post* periods?

Source: Based on Massood Yahya-Zahed, "A linear programming framework for flexible budgeting and its application to classroom teaching," *Issues in Accounting Education* 17 no. 1, 2002, pp. 69–93.

Case 3: ALN Motorcycles Canada

ALN Canada manufactures and sells motorcycles in a variety of engines and configurations. The company products are classified in five families: Off-road, Sports, Classic, Touring, and All-around motorcycles. Within each family, various models are manufactured from a variety of engines, performance/fuel consumptions, electrical systems, power transmissions, chassis, brake systems, and dimensions. The company has an assembly plant located in Whitby, where all models are assembled, tested, and packaged. Parts used for the assembly of motorcycles are shipped to the assembly plant from other plants of the company located in the United States and Germany. The assembly plant is flexible and can be re-configured on a monthly basis either in one production line or two production lines: regular and dedicated. The latter is used for assembling, testing, and packaging the most popular models. The company has recently launched two new models in the All-around family: AR1250 and AR1350. The retail suggested selling price is $16 500 for AR1250 and $20 500 for AR1350. The number of already committed and anticipated orders has far exceeded the management forecast. As a result, the plant manager has decided to re-configure the assembly line and dedicate one line to the assembly of the two models. It takes five labour-hours to assemble each AR1250 model. In addition, one labour-hour is spent in the testing department and forty-five labour-minutes in the packaging department. Each AR1350 model requires six labour-hours in the assembly department, one-half labour-hour in the testing department, and one labour-hour in the packaging department. For the next two months, the plant manager can dedicate up to 35 000 labour-hours for assembly, up to 10 000 labour-hours for testing, and up to 7500 labour-hours for packaging. The hourly labour costs are $35 for assembly time, $32.50 for testing time, and $20 for packaging time. The costs for parts used for assembling of each product are $6500 and $7700 for the AR1250 model and AR1350 model, respectively.

Managerial Report

Prepare a report to the plant manager presenting your findings and recommendations to the following questions:

1. Formulate an LP model to determine the number of units of each model to make to maximize the total contribution to profit. What is the operating profit at this optimal solution? How many unused hours are available at each department?
2. Determine the maximum overtime labour costs the company should be willing to pay if the labour-hours available at the packaging department can be increased by 30 percent by using overtime. How many units of each model should the company assemble?
3. If management decides that the number of the AR1250 models produced must be at least 30 percent of the total production, how does this decision impact the profit and the unused labour-hours available found in Question 1?

Linear Programming: Sensitivity Analysis and Computer Solution Interpretation

CHAPTER 3

LEARNING OBJECTIVES

After completing this chapter, you should be able to:

1. Explain how sensitivity analysis can be used by a decision maker.
2. Explain why it can be useful for a decision maker to extend the analysis of a linear programming problem beyond determination of the optimal solution.
3. Explain how to analyze graphically and interpret the impact of a change in the value of the objective function coefficient.
4. Explain how to graphically analyze and interpret the impact of a change in the right-hand-side value of a constraint.
5. Interpret and understand the managerial use of the information provided in the computer solution of a linear programming model.

CHAPTER OUTLINE

3.1 INTRODUCTION TO SENSITIVITY ANALYSIS

This chapter describes **sensitivity (postoptimality) analysis** of LP models, analysis that *begins* with the optimal solution to gain additional insights into how potential changes to the model would impact the optimal solution.

The purpose of sensitivity analysis is to explore the effects of potential changes in parameters of LP models on the optimal solution. It is designed to give a decision maker the ability to answer "what if . . .?" questions about an LP model that involve changing the value of a model parameter, such as changing the right-hand-side (RHS) value of a constraint, or changing the value of an objective function coefficient. For example, the decision maker may be considering a price change that will cause a change in a profit coefficient. Two obvious questions come to mind: Will the optimal values of the decision variables change? Will the optimal value of the objective function change? Sensitivity analysis enables the decision maker to easily answer these and similar questions concerning potential changes in values of parameters without having to re-solve an entire problem.

The Modern Management Science Application vignette about Scotiabank Canada in the previous chapter pointed out how the company answers a number of questions by conducting sensitivity analysis. The Modern Management Science Application vignette below, "Financial Reporting Improvement at Nestlé," reports the use of sensitivity analysis within an integrated framework scheme aimed at evaluating the economic profitability of the company's investment projects.

There are three categories of model parameters that might be subject to potential changes:

1. A change in the value of an objective function coefficient
2. A change in the right-hand-side (RHS) value of a constraint
3. A change in a coefficient of a constraint

The discussion here will be limited to the first two of these; it will not cover changes to coefficients of constraints. And unless otherwise noted; the discussion will assume that only *one* parameter is being changed, while all other parameters remain unchanged.

Sensitivity analysis involves identification of ranges of change for various parameters. A central concept in sensitivity analysis is that changes to parameters that fall within prescribed ranges either have no effect or have an easily determinable effect on the optimal solution. There are three aspects of these ranges that are important for understanding sensitivity analysis:

1. Which range pertains to a given situation? For example, which range relates to a change in the RHS value of a constraint?
2. How can the range be determined?
3. What impact on the optimal solution does a change that is within the range have?

A decision maker's interest in analyzing the impact of a change in the value of a parameter can come from a variety of sources. For example, changes in either costs or revenues can cause a change in the value of an objective function coefficient. Or a decision maker might wonder what the impact would be if a change in cost or revenue *could* be made (i.e., would it be worth the time, cost, etc.?). Another example would be an opportunity to obtain additional amounts of a scarce resource (e.g., raw material). It could be very useful to know if acquiring additional amounts would be profitable, and how much more could be profitably used, given other constraints of the problem.

A MODERN MANAGEMENT SCIENCE APPLICATION: FINANCIAL REPORTING IMPROVEMENT AT NESTLÉ

Nestlé is the largest food and beverage company in the world. The company is headquartered in Switzerland with corporate offices worldwide, including Canada, where it has been established since 1918. Nestlé Canada Inc. employs approximately 3600 people in 25 manufacturing sites, sales offices, and distribution centres across the country. To assess the profitability of new projects and develop coherent strategies, Nestlé Canada Inc. and other branches of the company rely on an integrated financial valuation framework that incorporates four modules based on management science techniques: the sensitivity analysis module, the forecasting module, the simulation module, and the optimization module. The latter uses inputs from the previous modules to solve a mathematical model that maximizes the value added by a new investment project while respecting different constraints. It also provides the managerial information required for further computer solution interpretation and sensitivity analysis. For instance, the payback of the new investment project can be evaluated under various conditions, such as changes to the production capacity, storage capacity, or changes in demand.

Source: Reprinted by permission, C. Oggier, E. Fragnière, J. Stuby, "Nestle Improves Its Financial Reporting With Management Science," *Interfaces* 35, no. 4 (July–August 2005), pp. 271–280. Copyright 2005, the Institute for Operations Research and the Management Sciences (INFORMS), 7240 Parkway Drive, Suite 310, Hanover, MD 21076 USA.

This chapter begins by describing how graphical methods can be used for sensitivity analysis, determining the impact that a change in one of the parameters (numerical values) of an LP model will have on the optimal solution and on the optimal value of the objective function. Then, we extend the discussion to elaborate on how the sensitivity analysis can be performed using a computer package such as Excel or simple computations with the information contained in the optimal solution to the linear programming.

3.2. GRAPHICAL APPROACH TO SENSITIVITY ANALYSIS

Sensitivity analysis is useful because it enables a decision maker to quickly assess the impact of a change. Graphical sensitivity analysis provides a visual portrayal of the process and the results, but can only be performed on a linear programming model with two decision variables. Sensitivity analysis pertains to a change in the value of one parameter *while all other parameters are held constant.* Thus, the procedure and interpretations described here do not apply to situations that involve changes to more than one parameter.

For purposes of illustration, the Web server problem from Chapter 2 will be used. That problem is repeated here for easy reference:

x_1 = quantity of the server model 1 to produce
x_2 = quantity of the server model 2 to produce

$$\text{maximize } Z = 60x_1 + 50x_2 \text{ (profit)}$$

subject to

Assembly	$4x_1 + 10x_2 \le 100$ hours
Inspection	$2x_1 + 1x_2 \le 22$ hours
Storage	$3x_1 + 3x_2 \le 39$ cubic feet
	$x_1, x_2 \ge 0$

The graph of this problem and optimal solution are repeated in Figure 3-1.

Let us begin with an analysis of changes in an objective function coefficient.

FIGURE 3-1 A Graph of the Server Problem

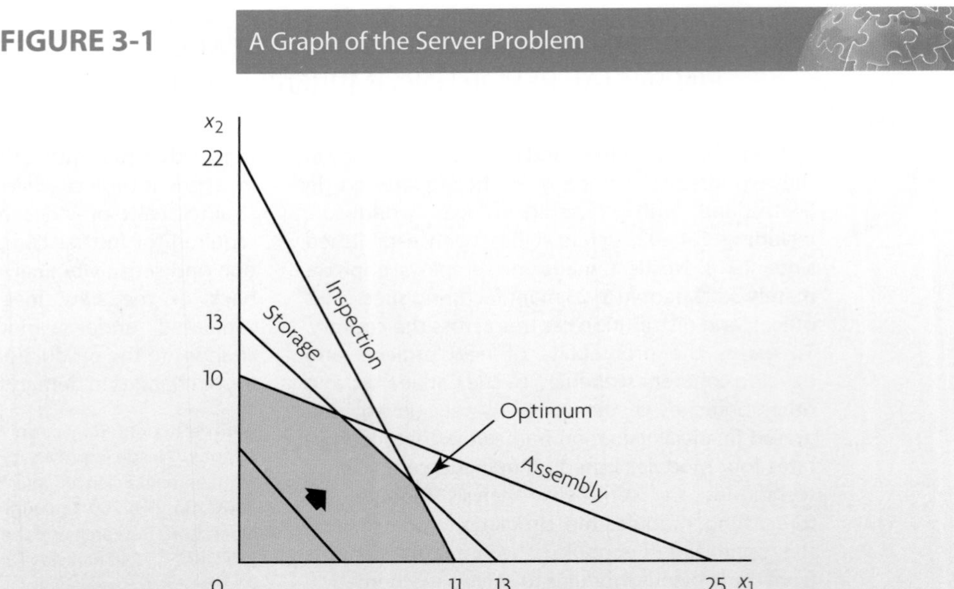

A Change in the Value of an Objective Function Coefficient

If there is a change in the value of one of the objective function coefficients (while the other one remains fixed), this will cause the slope of the objective function line to change. However, if the change in slope is relatively small, the optimal corner point of the feasible solution space will not change. Of particular interest is the amount by which a coefficient can be changed without changing the optimal solution point. This is known as the **range of optimality.**

We can see graphically in Figure 3-2 how much the slope of the objective function line can change and not change the optimal solution point. If the direction of change causes the slope to become less steep (see Figure 3-2a), the same solution point (intersection of inspection and storage constraints) will be optimal as long as the revised objective function line does not go beyond being parallel to the storage constraint. If it is just parallel to the storage constraint line, multiple solutions are optimal, *including* the original solution point. But beyond that, the next intersection (storage and assembly constraints) will become optimal.

Similarly, if changing the coefficient results in a *steeper* slope (see Figure 3-2b), the same solution will hold as long as the objective function line does not go beyond being parallel to the inspection constraint. If it does, the optimal solution will move to the intersection of the inspection constraint and the x_1 axis.

Thus, as long as a change in the coefficient does not cause the slope of the objective function line to exceed either of those parallel conditions, the same solution will be optimal.

A change in either of the objective function coefficients can cause its slope to change in either direction. In either case, a coefficient change in one direction will cause the slope to increase, while a change in the opposite direction will cause the slope to decrease. Let's take one of the coefficients at a time and see how we can determine its range of optimality.

Suppose we begin with the objective function coefficient of x_1, which is 60. Let's determine what its value would have to be for the objective function line to be parallel to the storage constraint line. Note that the two lines will be parallel if the ratio of the

FIGURE 3-2 Graphical Representation of a Change in the Objective Function Coefficients

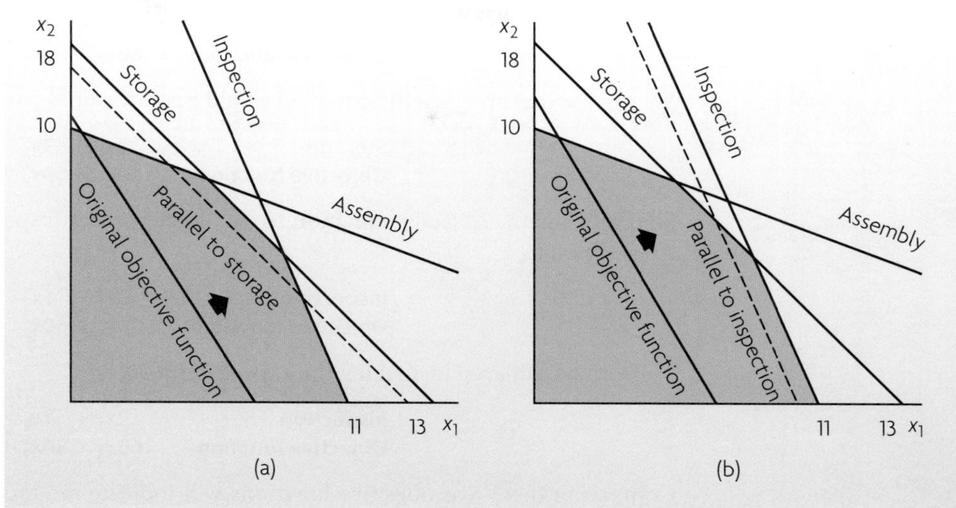

x_1 coefficient to the x_2 coefficient is the same for both lines. As they currently exist, the two sets of coefficients are

Storage	$3x_1 + 3x_2$
Objective function	$60x_1 + 50x_2$

As you can see, the storage constraint coefficient ratio (x_1 to x_2) is 3 to 3. Consequently, for the objective function line to be parallel to storage constraint line, its coefficients would have to be equal. If we are changing the x_1 coefficient while holding the x_2 coefficient constant at 50, this would mean the x_1 coefficient would also have to be equal to 50. Hence, the objective function would be $50x_1 + 50x_2$.

Similarly, to be parallel to the inspection line, the coefficients of the objective function would have to be such that the x_1 coefficient was double the x_2 coefficient, as you can see by comparing the two sets of coefficients as they are in the original problem:

Inspection	$2x_1 + 1x_2$
Objective function	$60x_1 + 50x_2$

To achieve the 2 to 1 ratio of the inspection constraint line, the x_1 coefficient must be 100. Hence, the objective function would be $100x_1 + 50x_2$.

Thus, our analysis shows:

Parallel to storage	$50x_1 + 50x_2$
Parallel to inspection	$100x_1 + 50x_2$

Therefore, we can say that the range of optimality for the x_1 coefficient of the objective function is 50 to 100. (Note that the x_2 coefficient remained at 50.) This means that for *any* value of the x_1 coefficient in this range, including the end-points, the same values of x_1 and x_2 will be optimal, which is $x_1 = 9$ and $x_2 = 4$. Formally, let c_1 be the objective function coefficient for variable x_1. Therefore, $c_1/50 = 3/3$ for the storage constraint, which implies that $c_1 = 50$. Similarly, $c_1/50 = 2/1$ for the inspection constraint which implies that $c_1 = 100$.

We can determine the range of optimality for the x_2 coefficient of the objective function in the same manner. First, determine what x_2 coefficient is needed to achieve parallelism with the storage constraint line, with the x_1 objective function coefficient held at 60.

Storage	$3x_1 + 3x_2$
Objective function	$60x_1 + 50x_2$

We can see that an x_2 coefficient of 60 would make the lines parallel:

Storage	$3x_1 + 3x_2$
Objective function	$60x_1 + 60x_2$

Similarly, for the objective function to be parallel to the inspection line, the ratio would have to be 2 to 1:

Inspection	$2x_1 + 1x_2$
Objective function	$60x_1 + 50x_2$

This can be achieved by making the x_2 coefficient 30:

Inspection	$2x_1 + 1x_2$
Objective function	$60x_1 + 30x_2$

Comparing these two objective functions will indicate the range of optimality for the x_2 coefficient of the objective function:

Parallel to storage	$60x_1 + 60x_2$
Parallel to inspection	$60x_1 + 30x_2$

Hence, the range of optimality for the x_2 coefficient is 30 to 60. Again, for any value of the x_2 coefficient in this range, the optimal solution will remain the same. Alternatively, let c_2 be the objective function coefficient for variable x_2. Therefore, $60/c_2 = 3/3$ for the storage constraint which implies that $c_2 = 60$. For the inspection constraint, $60/c_2 = 2/1$ which implies that $c_2 = 30$.

We have just seen that the optimal values of decision variables do not change if a change in the value of an objective function coefficient is within that coefficient's range of optimality. But what about the optimal value of the objective function? Does it change? The answer is yes, it does. The reason is that its value is determined by *both* the values of the decision variables and the values of the objective function coefficients. Hence, if one of the coefficients changes, while everything remains the same, its value must change.

EXAMPLE 3-1

In Chapter 2, the optimal values for the decision variables and the objective function for the server problem were determined. They were

$x_1 = 9$
$x_2 = 4$
$Z = 740$

In this chapter, we just found the range of optimality for each coefficient of the objective function for the server problem. They were

For the x_1 coefficient, 50 to 100
For the x_2 coefficient, 30 to 60

Given this information, analyze the impact of a change in the x_1 coefficient of the objective function from 60 to 82.50. Specifically, what impact will there be on the optimal values of the decision variables and the objective function?

Solution

First, check to see if the new value of the x_1 coefficient is within the range of optimality. We can see that 82.50 is within the range of 50 to 100. Consequently, there will be no change in the optimal values of x_1 and x_2.

However, the optimal value of Z will change. To find its new value, we must substitute the new coefficient into the objective function with the optimal values of the decision variables and solve. Thus:

$$Z = 82.50(9) + 50(4) = 942.50$$

An interesting situation occurs when a decision variable has a value of zero in the optimal solution. For example, suppose in the server problem that the x_2 coefficient in the objective function had been 20 instead of 50, so the objective would have been

$$\text{maximize} \quad Z = 60x_1 + 20x_2$$

If we assume an arbitrary profit of \$360, we get the following coordinate points for the objective function: (0, 18) and (6, 0).

The optimal solution would have been $x_1 = 11, x_2 = 0$ (20 is outside the range of optimality for x_2). This is illustrated in Figure 3-3. The slope of the objective function in this case is such that the lower right-hand corner of the feasible solution space is now optimal.

The reason that x_2 is zero is that it is not profitable enough relative to x_1. The question of interest then becomes, "What would the profit per unit (objective function coefficient) of

FIGURE 3-3 Solution for Revised Server Problem

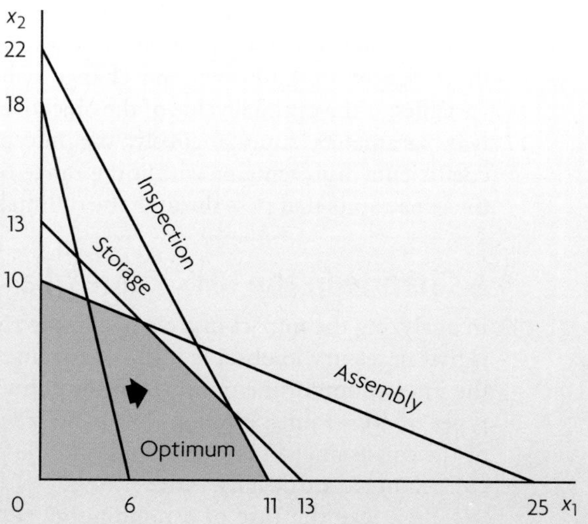

x_2 have to be for it to have a nonzero optimal value?" The answer depends on the value of the x_2 coefficient of the objective function that would make the objective function just parallel to the inspection constraint, because then the solution would include a nonzero value of x_2.

The objective function would be parallel to the inspection constraint if its coefficients were in the ratio of 2 to 1. With the x_1 objective function coefficient held at 60, this would mean an x_2 objective function coefficient of 30. Hence, we can say that the value of the x_2 coefficient must be at least 30 for x_2 to "come into" the solution. This is a special case of the range of optimality; it is sometimes referred to as the **range of insignificance,** meaning the range of values for which a decision variable will be zero. In this example, the range of insignificance for the x_2 coefficient of the objective function is less than 30: any value less than 30 will be too small to cause x_2 to have a nonzero value in the optimal solution.

As stated earlier, the interpretation described above pertains only to the situation when a change involves a value of one parameter at a time. When changes involve more parameters simultaneously, further analysis is generally required. However, in the case of a two-decision-variables problem, the same interpretation as above will hold if the new c_1 to c_2 objective function coefficients ratio remains within the range defined by the a_1 and a_2 constraint coefficients ratio of each of the constraints that cross the optimal solution (a_1 is the coefficient of the decision variable, x_1, in the constraint, and a_2 is the coefficient of the decision variable, x_2). If this is not satisfied, the problem will have to be re-solved with the new parameter values. For example, in the web server problem suppose the unit profit of model 1 increases to \$82 and the unit profit of model 2 decreases to \$40. This would result in a new optimal solution even if each change taken independently would not result in a new solution (since each is within the range of optimality). In effect, the objective function coefficient ratio ($82/40 = 2.05$) is outside the range defined by the storage constraint coefficients ratio ($3/3 = 1$) and the inspection constraint coefficients ratio ($2/1 = 2$). This sets the principle of the 100 percent rule discussed later in this chapter.

In summary, in performing sensitivity analysis on objective function coefficients, we can determine the range of optimality for variables that are nonzero in the optimal solution, and we can determine the range of insignificance for variables that are zero in the optimal solution. For a change in the value of an objective function that is within its range of optimality, the optimal values of the decision variables will not change although the value of the objective function will change. For a variable that has a value of zero in the optimal solution, if a change in its objective function coefficient occurs that is within the range of insignificance, no change will occur in either optimal values of decision variables or the optimal value of the objective function. In the case of a change that involves two parameters simultaneously, the interpretation above holds only if the objective coefficients ratio remains within the range of the constraint coefficients ratios defined by the constraints that pass through the optimal solution.

A Change in the RHS Value of a Constraint

In analyzing the impact of a change in the **right-hand-side (RHS) value** of a constraint, it is first necessary to observe if the constraint in question is a *binding constraint* (i.e., forms the intersection of the optimal corner point of the feasible solution space). There are two types of constraints, binding (left-hand side of the constraint equals the right-hand side of the constraint) and nonbinding, and the procedure differs depending on which type of constraint we are dealing with.

Let's take the case of a nonbinding constraint first. The assembly constraint in the server problem is nonbinding on the optimal solution because it does not pass through the optimal corner point (the left-hand side of the constraint is less than the right-hand side of the constraint) (see Figure 3-1). The constraint is

$$4x_1 + 10x_2 \leq 100 \text{ hours}$$

Because it is nonbinding, and a less-than-or-equal-to constraint, it will have a certain amount of slack in the optimal solution. By substituting the optimal values of the decision variables into the left-hand side of the constraint and then subtracting the result from the right-hand side, we can determine the amount of slack. Recall that the optimal values in the server problem were $x_1 = 9$, $x_2 = 4$. Substituting into the assembly constraint gives us

$$4(9) + 10(4) = 76$$

Subtracting 76 from the RHS value of 100 hours, we get

$$100 - 76 = 24 \text{ hours}$$

Thus, in the optimal solution, there are 24 hours of assembly time that are unused. Consequently, if additional hours of assembly time became available (say, by scheduling overtime in the assembly department), that would simply increase the amount of slack. So if an additional 10 hours of assembly time were scheduled, the amount of slack would increase by 10 to 34 hours. It would not make sense to schedule additional hours because the department already has excess capacity of 24 hours. Conversely, if there were fewer hours available (say, because of absenteeism), as long as the decrease did not exceed the 24 hours of slack, this would have no impact on the solution. Hence, no amount of increase would affect the optimal values of the decision variables, nor would a decrease that left at least 76 hours (i.e., $100 - 24 = 76$). This range, from 76 to infinity (or 76 to no upper limit) is known as the **range of feasibility** for the assembly constraint. Because the assembly constraint is a nonbinding constraint, any change within this range will have no effect on the solution quantities or on the optimal value of the objective function.

Let us now consider how to determine the range of feasibility for a binding constraint. For the optimal solution in the server problem, both the storage and the inspection constraints were binding; the optimal corner point occurred at their intersection (see Figure 3-1). Because each is a binding constraint, even a slight change in the RHS value of either constraint will cause the optimal corner point to shift, and consequently, cause the optimal values of the decision variables and the optimal value of the objective function to change. However, an interesting phenomenon occurs as long as the change in the RHS value of a binding constraint is within its range of feasibility: The change in the optimal value of the objective function is linearly related to the amount of change. For example, we will be able to determine that the value of the objective function will change by \$10 for each one-unit change in the RHS value of the inspection constraint, increasing \$10 for each additional hour of inspection time and decreasing \$10 for each hour the inspection constraint is decreased from its original amount of 22 hours, as long as the increase or decrease is within the range of feasibility. A \$10 change per additional inspection hour in the objective function will be explained in the next few paragraphs. At the end of this section, the issue of changes that go beyond the range of feasibility will be addressed.

For binding constraints, there are two pieces of information that are of interest. One relates to the procedure for determining the range of feasibility for the RHS value of the constraint, and the other relates to determining the amount by which the optimal value of the objective function will change for each one-unit change in the RHS value of the constraint within the range of feasibility. This amount is referred to as the **shadow price** of a constraint. We begin with the change in the optimal value of the objective function for a one-unit change in the RHS of a constraint.

We can determine the impact of a one-unit change in the RHS value of a constraint on the optimal value of the objective function by increasing (or decreasing) the RHS value of the constraint in question by one unit and solving this revised problem. For instance, for the inspection constraint, this would yield the following:

$$2x_1 + 1x_2 = 22 + 1 \text{ (i.e., } 2x_1 + 1x_2 = 23)$$

Although we could graph the problem again using this revised inspection constraint, we would find that the new graph would appear almost identical to the former graph; the solution point would move only slightly. It would still be at the intersection of the storage and inspection constraints. Therefore, we can simply avoid replotting the graph and instead proceed to using a simultaneous solution of the two constraints to determine the new optimal values of x_1 and x_2:

$$\begin{array}{ll} \textbf{Inspection} & 2x_1 + 1x_2 = 23 \\ \textbf{Storage} & 3x_1 + 3x_2 = 39 \end{array}$$

One way to solve this is to multiply the entire inspection constraint by 3 and then subtract the storage constraint from it. Thus:

$$\begin{array}{lr} \textbf{Inspection} \times 3 & 6x_1 + 3x_2 = 69 \\ \textbf{Storage} & \underline{-(3x_1 + 3x_2 = 39)} \\ & 3x_1 \qquad = 30 \end{array}$$

Solving, we find that $x_1 = 10$. Then, substituting this value into either the storage or the inspection constraint and solving, we can determine the new optimal value of x_2. For instance, using the inspection constraint, we find

$$2(10) + 1x_2 = 23$$

Solving, $x_2 = 3$.

Now, if we substitute these new optimal values into the objective function, we obtain

$$60(10) + 50(3) = 750$$

previously, with $x_1 = 9$ and $x_2 = 4$, we found

$$60(9) + 50(4) = 740$$

Thus, we see that the one-unit increase in inspection time produced an increase in the objective function of 10. Hence, the shadow price of the inspection constraint is 10, and for *each* one-unit increase or decrease that is within the range of feasibility for the RHS of the inspection constraint, the optimal value of the objective function will increase or decrease by 10. For example, an increase of 2 in the RHS of the inspection constraint will cause an increase of 20 in the optimal value of the objective function. This relationship holds as long as the amount of change in the RHS is within the range of feasibility for that particular constraint.

We can determine the shadow price of the storage constraint in the same manner. Adding one unit to its RHS changes it to 40. Solving using simultaneous equations yields:

$$\begin{array}{lr} \textbf{Inspection} \times 3 & 6x_1 + 3x_2 = 66 \\ \textbf{Storage} + 1 & \underline{-(3x_1 + 3x_2 = 40)} \\ & 3x_1 \qquad = 26 \end{array}$$

Solving, $x_1 = 8.67$. Substituting into the inspection constraint and solving for x_2, we find $x_2 = 4.67$. Using these new values in the objective function, we obtain the following (note that rounding will give a slightly larger value):

$$60(8.67) + 50(4.67) = 753.33$$

Compared to the original value of 740 for the objective function, we can see that an increase in one unit in the RHS of the storage constraint caused an increase of 13.33. Hence, the shadow price for the storage constraint is 13.33. This tells us that for a change in the amount of storage space that is within the range of feasibility, the value of the objective function will change by 13.33 times the amount of change in storage space. This shows the importance of knowing what the range of feasibility is: "Over what range of values is the shadow price valid?" That is our next topic.

The shadow price that is in effect at the optimal solution will remain in effect (i.e., it will not change) as long as the same constraints that are binding continue to be binding. Thus, as long as the optimal solution is at the point where the same constraints intersect, the shadow price will be the same.

A key factor in understanding analysis of the range of feasibility is recognizing that when the RHS value of a constraint is changed, the resulting graph of the revised constraint line will be *parallel* to the original line. The new line will be closer to the origin if the RHS has been decreased or farther from the origin if the RHS value has been increased. Moreover, the larger the change, the farther apart the revised line and the original line will be.

To determine the range of feasibility for binding constraints using the graphical approach, we follow this procedure:

1. Place a straight edge along the constraint.
2. Slide it away from the origin, making sure to keep it parallel to the constraint. Continue until you come to the last point where your straight edge intersects the other binding constraint. Note that point on the graph.
3. Return the straight edge to the original line. Now move it parallel to the constraint but in the direction of the origin until you get to the last point where the two binding constraints intersect. Note this point.
4. Determine the coordinates of the two points you identified. Substitute each set of values into the left-hand side of the constraint and solve. The resulting two values are the endpoints of the range of feasibility.

EXAMPLE 3-2

Determine the range of feasibility for each of these binding constraints in the server problem:

1. The inspection constraint.
2. The storage constraint.

Solution

1. Following the above procedure, we determine the last point where the storage constraint intersects with the line that is parallel to the inspection constraint line, moving away from the origin. See Figure 3-4.

   Next, we repeat the procedure moving toward the origin. See Figure 3-5.

   The coordinates of the upper limit, the point where the storage constraint intersects with the line parallel to the inspection constraint line, are easy to obtain directly from the graph: $x_1 = 13, x_2 = 0$. For the lower limit, note that at that last point, the storage and assembly lines intersect. Hence, we can determine the coordinates of that point by solving the equations of the storage and assembly lines simultaneously. This will yield $x_1 = 5$ and $x_2 = 8$.

FIGURE 3-4 The Upper Limit on Using Additional Inspection Time

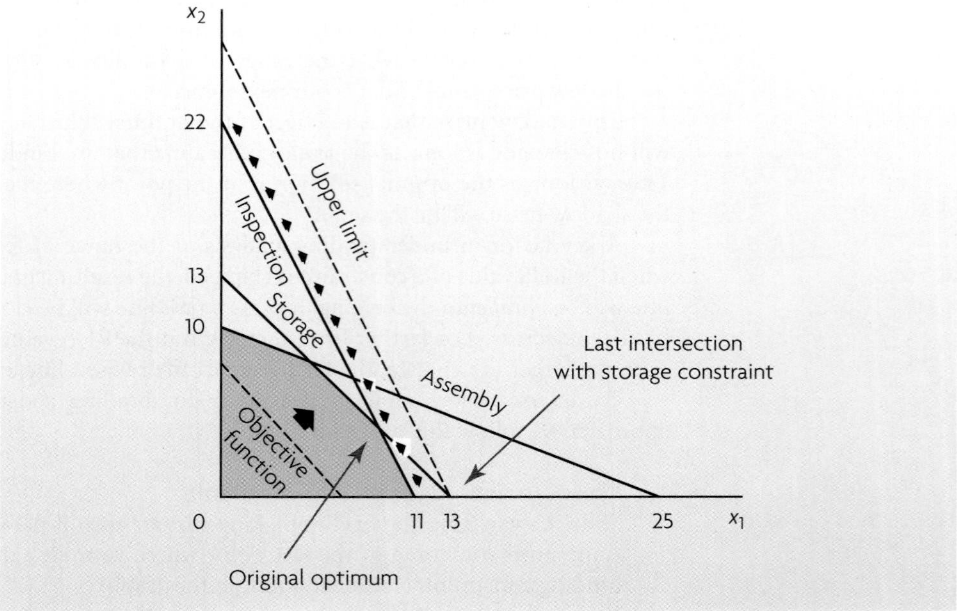

x_2
22
13
10
0
11
13
25
x_1
Upper limit
Inspection
Storage
Assembly
Objective function
Last intersection with storage constraint
Original optimum

FIGURE 3-5 The Lower Limit on Inspection Time

x_2
22
13
10
0
11
13
25
x_1
Inspection
Lower limit
Storage
Assembly
Objective function
Last intersection with storage constraint
Original optimum

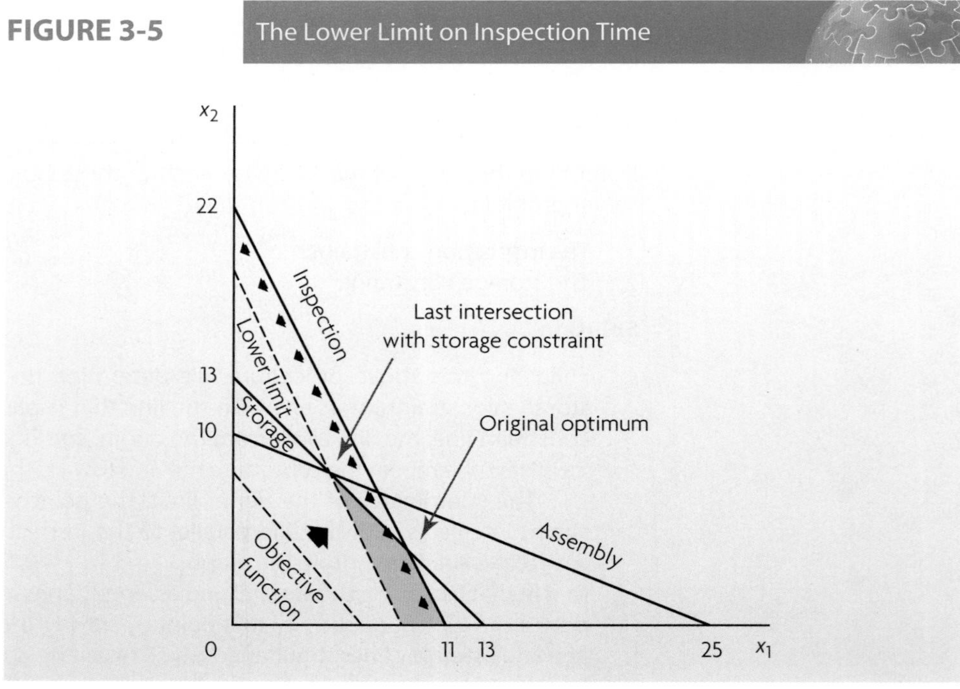

FIGURE 3-6 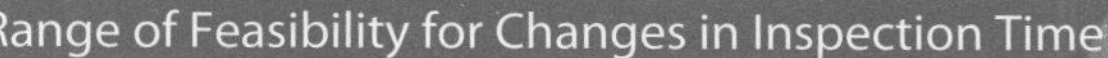 Range of Feasibility for Changes in Inspection Time

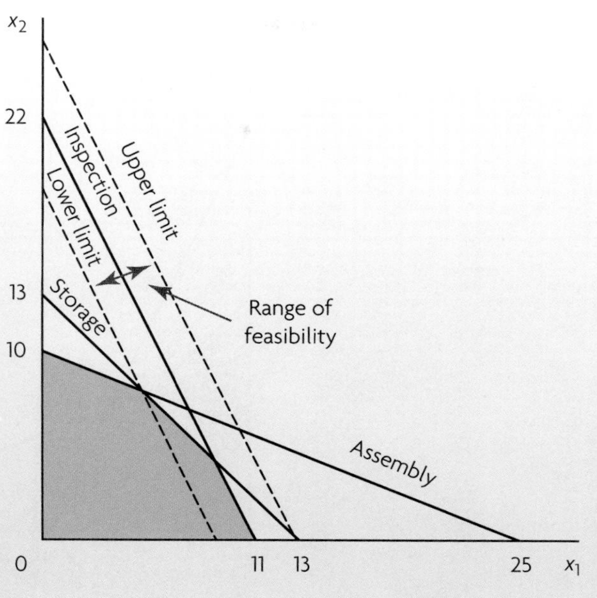

By substituting these two sets of coordinates into the left-hand side of the inspection constraint, we obtain the upper and lower ends of the range of feasibility for the inspection constraint. For $x_1 = 13, x_2 = 0$, we get

$2(13) + 1(0) = 26$ (upper limit)

For $x_1 = 5, x_2 = 8$, we get

$2(5) + 1(8) = 18$ (lower limit)

Hence, the range of feasibility for the RHS of the inspection constraint is 18 to 26.

The range of feasibility is bordered by these two limits, as illustrated in Figure 3-6.

2. Repeating the process for the storage constraint, we determine the last points (upper limit and lower limit) for which the line parallel to *storage* constraint intersects the *inspection* constraint (see Figure 3-7).

We can see on the graph in Figure 3–7 that the lower limit intersects at $x_1 = 11, x_2 = 0$, and at the upper limit the inspection and assembly lines cross. Solving those two equations simultaneously yields $x_1 = 7.5$ and $x_2 = 7$.

Substituting these two sets of values into the storage constraint gives us

$3(7.5) + 3(7) = 43.5$ (upper limit)
$3(11) + 3(0) = 33$ (lower limit)

Hence, the range of feasibility for the RHS of the storage constraint is 33 cubic feet to 43.5 cubic feet.

FIGURE 3-7 Range of Feasibility for the Storage Constraint

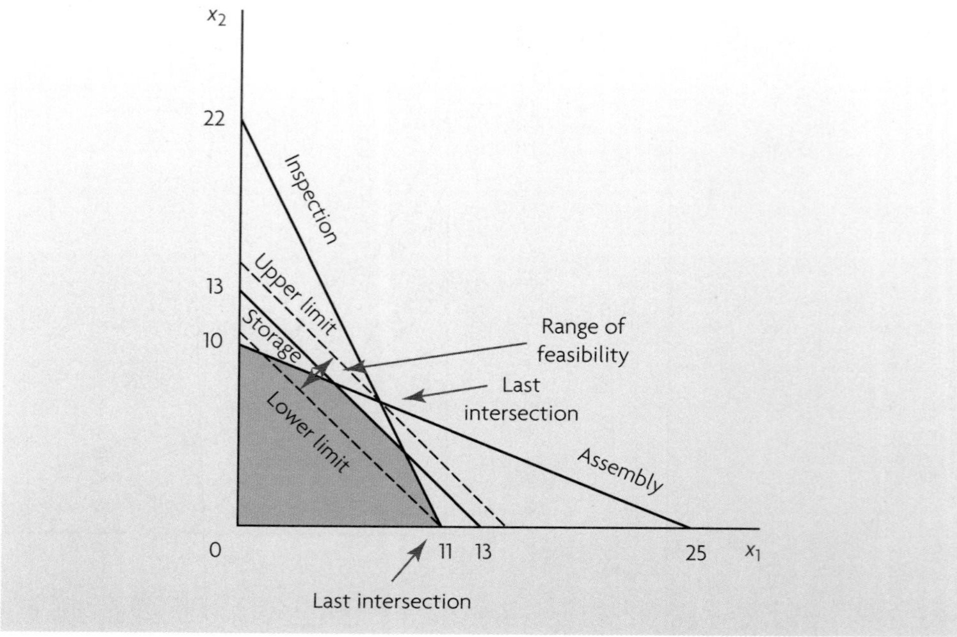

As a final note, let us consider what happens if a change in the RHS value of a constraint takes it beyond its range of feasibility. There are two cases. One is a decrease that results in a RHS that is below the lower limit of the range of feasibility. Should this occur, it would be necessary to solve the modified problem to find the new optimal solution and find the new shadow prices. The other case occurs when the upper limit of the range of feasibility is exceeded. In such instances, the excess beyond the upper limit becomes slack and the shadow price for that constraint becomes zero. For example, suppose analysis indicates that the upper limit of the range of feasibility of a constraint is 200. If the RHS of this constraint is changed to, say, 210, the excess of 10 will become slack.

Minimization Problems

Minimization problems are handled in exactly the same way that maximization problems are, except that in finding the range of feasibility, *subtract* 1 from the RHS instead of adding 1 to the RHS. Note, too, that for the range of insignificance, the value will be *lower* than the current value, instead of higher.

3.3 SENSITIVITY ANALYSIS WITH EXCEL

Excel has the capability of performing sensitivity analysis of the objective function coefficients and the right-hand-side values. The Excel input screen along with the necessary formulas for the server problem is given in Exhibit 3-1. Once the necessary formulas and the

EXHIBIT 3-1 Excel Input Screen for the Server Problem

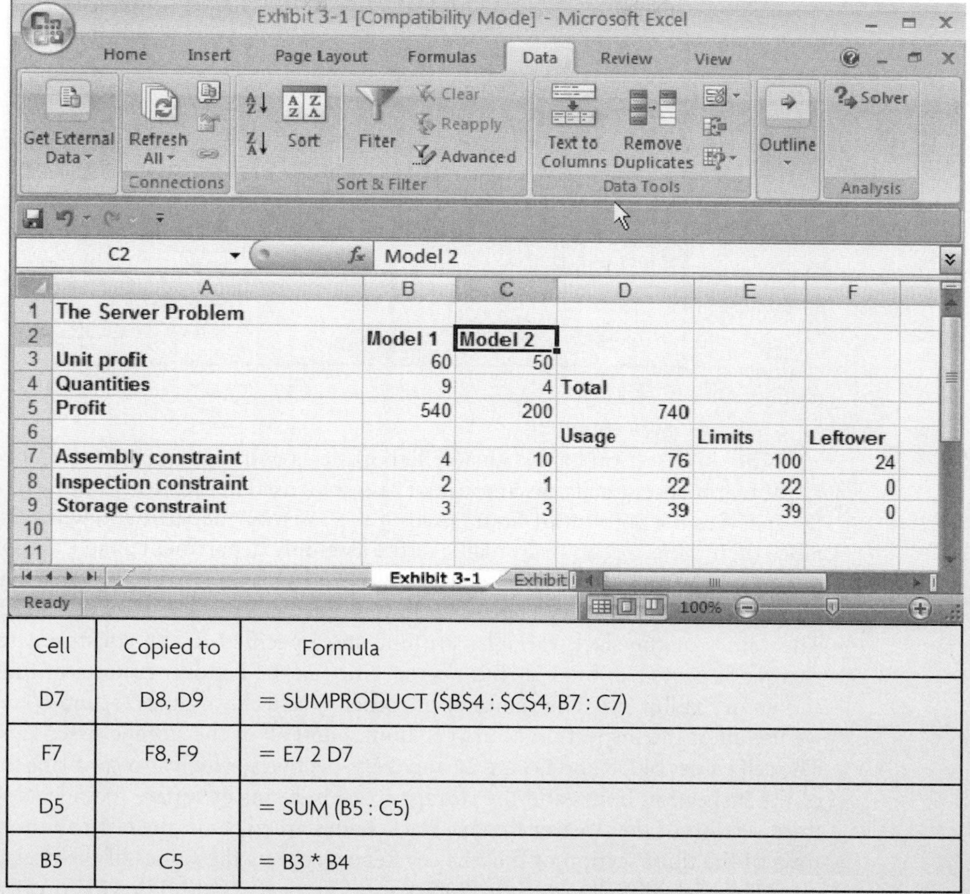

	A	B	C	D	E	F
1	The Server Problem					
2		Model 1	Model 2			
3	Unit profit	60	50			
4	Quantities	9	4	Total		
5	Profit	540	200	740		
6				Usage	Limits	Leftover
7	Assembly constraint	4	10	76	100	24
8	Inspection constraint	2	1	22	22	0
9	Storage constraint	3	3	39	39	0
10						
11						

Cell	Copied to	Formula
D7	D8, D9	= SUMPRODUCT ($B$4 : $C$4, B7 : C7)
F7	F8, F9	= E7 2 D7
D5		= SUM (B5 : C5)
B5	C5	= B3 * B4

data have been entered as shown in Exhibit 3-1, we choose **Data | Analysis | Solver** and specify the input parameters the same way as we specified the input parameters in solving Example 3-1. Once the Solver input specification screen is completed as shown in Exhibit 3-2, we click on Solve, and Solver will show the optimization output screen given in Exhibit 3-3. The optimization output screen states that Solver has found an optimal solution. On the right-hand side of this screen is the specification of output reports made available by Solver. Clicking on these will generate the following reports. The first report is the Answer Report, as shown in Exhibit 3-4. This report begins with the Target Cell, which is cell D5 in the server data input screen. The target cell specifies the total profit as $740. The next portion of the Answer Report states the optimal values of the decision variables. These optimal values are given in cells B4 and C4 as specified in the Answer Report under the heading of Adjustable Cells. As can be observed in Exhibit 3-4, the optimal value of server model 1 is 9 and of server model 2 is 4.

EXHIBIT 3-2 Solver Input Specification (parameter) Screen

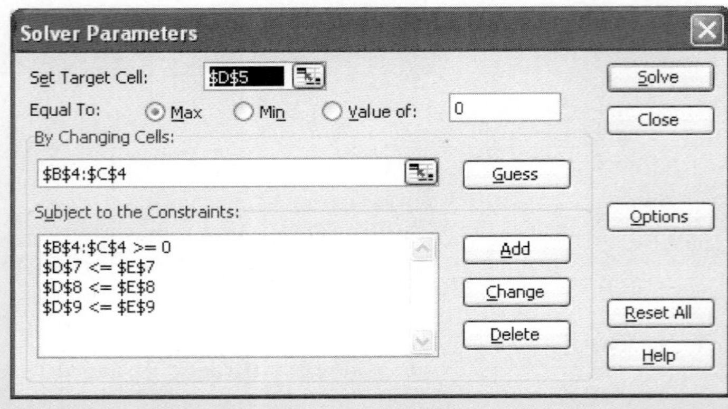

The third section of the Answer Report deals with the constraints. Cells D7, D8, and D9 of Exhibit 3-1 specify the amount of resources used in each constraint. For example, cell D7 specifies the amount of hours used in the assembly department, which is equal to 76. Since there were 100 hours available in the assembly department as specified in cell E7, the difference between cell E7 and cell D7 indicates the amount of slack available in the assembly department, which is 24 hours. The 24 hours is also the value of the slack variable 1 (s_1). The values of the slack variables are not only specified in the constraint section of the Answer Report (Exhibit 3-4), but also specified in the Leftover column of the input screen shown in Exhibit 3-1. The values of the other two slack variables (s_2 and s_3) are zeros since we use all of the inspection hours (22 hours) and all of the storage space (39 square feet). The cell values of D8 and D9 are 22 and 39 respectively, which also confirms the usage of all of the inspection hours and the storage space in terms of square footage. Note that in the third section of the Answer Report, slack values are given in the last column. The last two rows of the third section of the Answer Report repeats the values of the decision variables.

When labelling constraints, Solver scans the Left Hand Side (LHS) cell of each constraint to the left until a label is encountered and above the LHS cell's column until a label

EXHIBIT 3-3 Optimization Output Screen

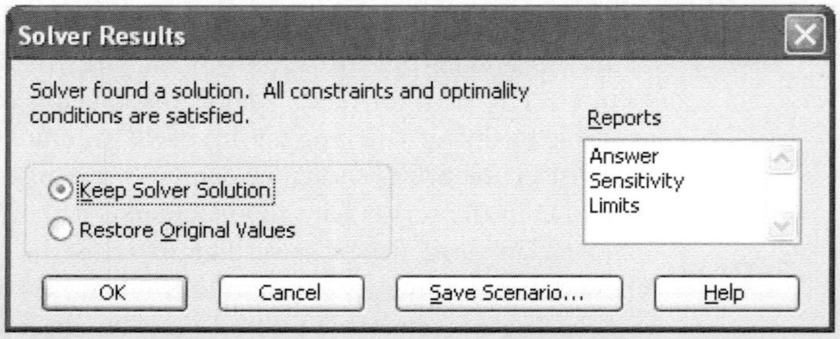

Solver Results

Solver found a solution. All constraints and optimality conditions are satisfied.

Reports: Answer, Sensitivity, Limits

Keep Solver Solution

Restore Original Values

OK | Cancel | Save Scenario... | Help

EXHIBIT 3-4 Excel Basic Output (Answer) Report for the Server Problem

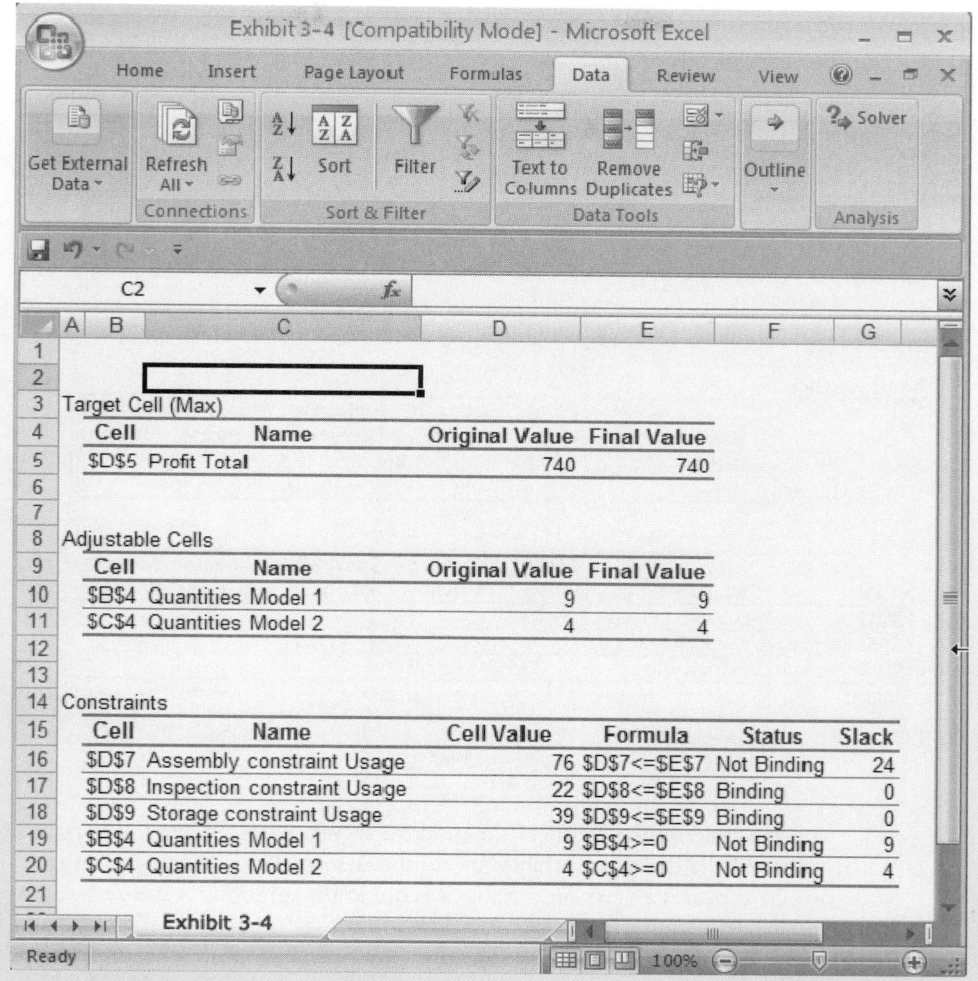

Target Cell (Max)

Cell	Name	Original Value	Final Value
$D$5	Profit Total	740	740

Adjustable Cells

Cell	Name	Original Value	Final Value
$B$4	Quantities Model 1	9	9
$C$4	Quantities Model 2	4	4

Constraints

Cell	Name	Cell Value	Formula	Status	Slack
$D$7	Assembly constraint Usage	76	$D$7<=$E$7	Not Binding	24
$D$8	Inspection constraint Usage	22	$D$8<=$E$8	Binding	0
$D$9	Storage constraint Usage	39	$D$9<=$E$9	Binding	0
$B$4	Quantities Model 1	9	$B$4>=0	Not Binding	9
$C$4	Quantities Model 2	4	$C$4>=0	Not Binding	4

is found, if any. The two labels found, if present, are concatenated to form the constraint's label in the sensitivity report. Similarly, Solver scans each decision variable cell to the left until a label is found and above the cell's column until a label is encountered. Both labels, if present, are concatenated to form the decision variable's label in the sensitivity report. Therefore, a self-documenting sensitivity report can be produced with an appropriate selection and location of labels in the Excel spreadsheet model.

The second report generated by Solver is entitled Sensitivity Report and is shown in Exhibit 3-5. The first part of this report is the statement of the optimal values of the decision variables. The first row of this report indicates the cell in which the optimal values of the decision variables appear in the input sheet of the server problem (Exhibit 3-1). In the input sheet, cell B4 provides the optimal value of the model 1 server (9 units) and cell C4

EXHIBIT 3-5 Excel Sensitivity Analysis Report for the Server Problem

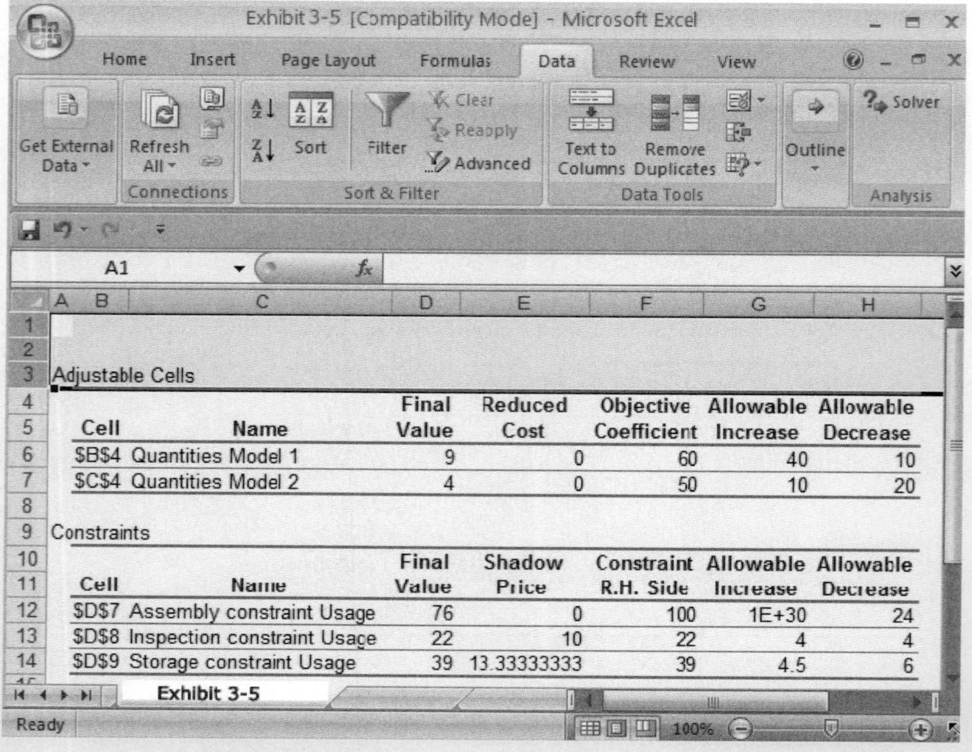

Adjustable Cells

Cell	Name	Final Value	Reduced Cost	Objective Coefficient	Allowable Increase	Allowable Decrease
$B$4	Quantities Model 1	9	0	60	40	10
$C$4	Quantities Model 2	4	0	50	10	20

Constraints

Cell	Name	Final Value	Shadow Price	Constraint R.H. Side	Allowable Increase	Allowable Decrease
$D$7	Assembly constraint Usage	76	0	100	1E+30	24
$D$8	Inspection constraint Usage	22	10	22	4	4
$D$9	Storage constraint Usage	39	13.33333333	39	4.5	6

specifies the optimal value of the model 2 server (4 units). Just to the right of the optimal values of the decision variables in Exhibit 3-5 are reduced costs. A nonzero reduced cost would appear if a decision variable was not in the solution.[1] A nonzero reduced cost would indicate the amount that the variable's objective function coefficient could be increased without that variable coming into the solution. Thus, if a reduced cost was 3.0, that variable's objective function would have to be increased by more than 3.0 for it to be in the solution if the problem was to be reworked with that one change. In other words, a reduced cost of 3.0 shows that variable would not be coming into the solution as long as that variable's objective function would be increased by less than 3.0. In the server problem example, since both of the decision variables are in the optimal solution (both decision variables have nonzero values in the optimal solution), the reduced costs associated with both variables are equal to zero. The column immediately to the right of the reduced costs provides the initial value of the objective function coefficients and the final two columns all the way to the right of the first table in the Sensitivity Report (Exhibit 3-5) display the objective function ranges (range of optimality). The column heading labelled as Allowable Increase shows the amount of increase allowed without changing the optimal mix of the products. In this example, the profit margin of server model 1 could be increased by $40 up to $100 (60 + 40) without changing the optimal product mix. The final column, labelled Allowable

[1] Excel Solver returns a negative reduced cost for a maximization problem or a positive reduced cost for a minimization problem.

Decrease, shows the amount of decrease allowed without changing the optimal mix of the products. In this example, the profit margin of server model 1 could be decreased by \$10 down to \$50 (60 − 10) without changing the optimal product mix. Likewise the Allowable Increase column indicates that the profit margin of server model 2 could be increased by \$10 up to \$60 (50 + 10) without changing the optimal product mix. On the other hand, Allowable Decrease shows that the profit margin of server model 2 could be decreased by \$20 down to \$30 (50 − 20) without changing the optimal product mix.

The second (bottom) portion of the Sensitivity Report given in Exhibit 3-5 begins the constraint analysis. Each row of this portion of the report deals with a separate constraint. The column headings Cell, Name, and Final Value indicate the amount of resource used for each particular constraint. For example, for the assembly constraint, we used 76 of the 100 available hours. Thus, under the column heading Cell, we specify cell D7 (\$D\$7) from Exhibit 3-1; under the column heading Name, we specify the name of the constraint, and under the column heading Final Value, we specify the value of the resource used, which is 76 hours as specified in cell D7 of the input sheet in Exhibit 3-1. The column next to the final value is the shadow price associated with that constraint's slack and/or surplus variables (slack variables for the server problem). In the server problem, the shadow prices are 0, 10, and 13.333 for the three constraints respectively. Since we have slack assembly hours left in the assembly constraint, we would not be willing to pay any additional funds to obtain labour hours in the assembly department because we have some labour hours left over in this department. Therefore, the shadow price associated with the labour hours in the assembly department is equal to zero. However, since we have used up all of the inspection hours and all of the storage space, constraint 2 and constraint 3 would have a nonzero shadow price. The shadow price of \$10 indicates the amount we are willing to pay to obtain one additional labour hour in the inspection department. The shadow price of \$13.33 indicates the amount we are willing to pay to obtain one additional square foot of space for the third constraint. If we decide to use another computer software package, we may see another name in lieu of a shadow price: dual price. The next column to the right of the shadow price specifies the original RHS value of each constraint. In other words, we had 100 labour hours in the assembly department, 22 labour hours in the inspection department, and 39 square feet of storage space. The final two columns of the second (bottom) portion of the Sensitivity Report show the range of feasibility for the RHS ranges. Therefore, the next column to the right of the original RHS value indicates the amount of possible increase and the final column indicates the amount of possible decrease in the original RHS value that will result in the same product mix or the same combination of the variables that are in the solution. In other words the Allowable Increase and the Allowable Decrease show the amounts by which the right-hand side of a constraint can be changed and still be within the range of feasibility. For example, for the storage constraint, the allowable increase is 4.5 and the allowable decrease is 6; therefore, the range of feasibility of the RHS value of the storage constraint is from 39 − 6 = 33 to 39 + 4.5 = 43.5. In other words, the current variables in the optimal solution (x_1 = model 1 and x_2 = model 2) will stay in the optimal solution with the current shadow prices as long as square footage available for storage remains between 33 and 43.5.

3.4 ANALYZING MULTIPLE CHANGES

Ranges of optimality for objective function coefficients and ranges of feasibility for RHS values of constraints were said to be applicable to a change in one parameter only.

In certain instances, the impact of multiple changes (e.g., values of two or more objective function coefficients are changed or values of two or more of the RHS amounts of constraints are changed) can be readily evaluated. It begins with a determination of the ranges of optimality (if objective function changes are involved) or a determination of the ranges of feasibility (if RHS values are involved). That reveals the amount that each parameter is allowed to change (the allowable increase or the allowable decrease) and still be within the range of optimality or the range of feasibility. Next, a set of specific changes is analyzed by computing the percentage of the allowable increase or allowable decrease that each change represents. For instance, suppose we want to evaluate multiple changes that involve two objective function coefficients, and we determine that the first coefficient's change would be 20 percent of its allowable increase and the second coefficient's change would be 40 percent of its allowable increase. As long as the total of these percentages does not exceed 100 percent, the impact of the combined changes will be very similar to the result of a single change that falls within its range of optimality. That is, the original optimal values of all variables with a positive value will remain the same,[2] but the optimal value of the objective function would change, taking into account the new coefficients of the objective function.

Similarly, if, say, three RHS values were to be changed and we determined that the first change would constitute an increase that was 30 percent of the allowable increase for that constraint's RHS, the second was an increases of 30 percent of *its* allowable increase, and the third was 30 percent of *its* allowable *decrease,* the sum of these would be 90 percent (note that the percentage are *added* even though two are for increases and one for a decrease). Because the sum of the percentages does not exceed 100 percent, the changes satisfy the 100 percent requirement. However, the **100 percent rule** does not imply that the optimal solution will change if the sum of the percentage change exceeds 100 percent. When the 100 percent rule is not satisfied, we must re-solve the problem to determine if the optimal solution changes, and if it does, we can easily determine the new optimal values of the decision variables. In the case of RHS changes, this means that the shadow prices remain the same. Consequently, the impact on the optimal value of the objective function can be determined by taking into account the combined effects of RHS changes and the corresponding shadow prices. Similarly, revised Quantity values can be computed using values from the original final solution. The 100 percent rule cannot be applied to changes in both objective function coefficients and right-hand sides simultaneously. To consider simultaneous changes for both RHS and objective function coefficients, the problem must be re-solved.

EXAMPLE 3-3

Let us consider how the solution to the server problem would be affected by multiple changes to *either* its objective function coefficients *or* the RHS values of its constraints. Let's consider these changes:

a. A change in the objective function from maximize $60x_1 + 50x_2$ to maximize $70x_1 + 56x_2$.
b. A change in the RHS of the inspection constraint from 22 to 23 hours and a change in the storage constraint from 39 to 36 cubic feet.

---

[2]If the total percentage *equals* 100 percent, an alternate optimal solution may cause the optimal Quantity values to change.

Solution

(Values for allowable increases and decreases are taken from Exhibit 3-5.)

a. The change in the x_1 coefficient is +10 (i.e., 60 to 70), and the change in the x_2 coefficient is +6 (i.e., 50 to 56). From Exhibit 3-5, the allowable increase for the x_1 coefficient is 40, and the allowable increase for the x_2 coefficient is 10. Thus, we have

Variable	x_1		x_2
Change	+10		+ 6
Allow. inc. or dec.	+40		+10
Percent change	25%	+	60% = 85%

As you can see, the sum of the percentage change does not exceed 100 percent, so it is within the acceptance range for multiple changes. Therefore, we can say that the optimal values of x_1 and x_2 remain the same as in the original problem. However, the optimal value of Z will increase by the sum of the increase in the x_1 coefficient multiplied by the optimal value of x_1 and the increase in the x_2 coefficient multiplied by the optimal value of x_2. Thus, the increase will be $10(9) + 5(4) = 110$; the new value will be $740 + 110 = 850$.

b. For the RHS changes, we have

Constraint	Inspection		Storage
Change	1		−3
Allow. inc. or dec.	4		−6
Percent change	25%	+	50% = 75%

The total change would be 75 percent. Because this does not exceed 100 percent, it is within the range of sensitivity. Consequently, the shadow prices (10.00 and 13.33) do not change. The optimal value of Z will change. The amount of change will be

$$+1(10.00) - 3(13.33) = -30$$

Hence, the optimal value of Z will be $740 - 30 = 710$.

Table 3-1 provides a summary of the impact of a change that falls within the range of optimality or within the range of feasibility.

3.5 INTERPRETATION AND MANAGERIAL USE OF COMPUTER SOLUTION OUTPUTS

The analysis of the shadow prices, the range of optimality, the reduced costs, and the range of optimality enable a manager to cope with a number of important questions without the need of re-solving the problem under study. As stated above, the shadow price is the improvement (increase in a maximization problem or a decrease in a minimization problem) in the optimal value of the objective function per unit increase in the RHS value of a given constraint within the range of feasibility. The values of the shadow prices are related to the **dual prices,** values obtained when solving a dual formulation of every linear programming problem, that

TABLE 3-1 Summary of Results of Changes That Are Within Ranges of Optimality and Feasibility

Objective Function Coefficient Change Within the Range of Optimality	
Factor	**Result**
Variables in solution	Same variables still in solution
Optimal values of solution variables	Don't change
Optimal value of *Z*	Will change
RHS Change Within the Range of Feasibility	
Factor	**Result**
Shadow price	Remains the same
List of variables with positive values	Remains the same
Values of variables with positive values	Changes
Optimal value of *Z*	Changes

is, a kind of a "mirror image" of the original problem, which is also called the primal problem. For a maximization problem, the shadow price is always zero or positive (i.e., nonnegative) for a less-than-or-equal constraint, zero or negative (i.e., non-positive) for a greater-than-or-equal constraint (respectively nonpositive and nonnegative for a minimization problem). The intuitive explanation is that increasing the RHS of a less-than-or-equal constraint by 1 expands the feasible region of the LP model since points are added. This will result in either an improvement or no change of the optimal value of the objective function. Similarly, increasing the RHS of a greater-than-or-equal constraint by 1 will contract the LP feasible region since points are eliminated, resulting in an unchanged or a worse value (lower for a maximization problem or higher for a minimization problem) of the objective function. Formally, let z_{new} be the new optimal objective value, z_{old} the old objective function value as given, and Δb_i the amount of change in the RHS corresponding to the ith constraint. Therefore, $z_{new} = z_{old} + \Delta b_i \times$ (shadow price for the ith constraint). For example, if the ith constraint is a less-than-or-equal constraint, a one unit increase in the RHS, that is 1, will expand the feasible region and $z_{new} \geq z_{old}$ for a maximization problem ($z_{new} \leq z_{old}$ for a minimization problem). This will occur only if the shadow price for the ith constraint is nonnegative (nonpositive for a minimization problem). Similarly, if the ith constraint is a greater-than-or-equal constraint, a one unit increase in the RHS, that is 1, will contract the feasible region and $z_{new} \leq z_{old}$ for a maximization problem ($z_{new} \geq z_{old}$ for a minimization problem). This will occur only if the shadow price for the ith constraint is nonpositive (nonnegative for a minimization problem).

Alternatively, the shadow price associated to a constraint can also be interpreted as the maximum a decision maker is willing to pay for an additional unit of a given resource (or a minimum to accept to give up one unit of a given resource). For example, if a constraint refers to the storage space availability and the corresponding shadow price is \$5, if one unit of storage space is acquired and the new quantity availability remains within the range of feasibility, then the objective function value will be improved (increase for a maximization problem) by \$5. Therefore, the decision maker should not pay more than \$5 for an additional unit of storage space. However, this interpretation of the shadow price holds only if the cost of acquiring the resource does not interfere with how the objective function is determined, that is, the cost of the resource involved is **sunk** or *fixed* and will be incurred regardless of the quantity used. For the storage constraint example, this means the decision maker will have to pay for the full space available even if some remain unused. If the cost of acquiring one unit of the resource is reflected in the determination of the function objective, the cost of such resource is **relevant.** The shadow price would be interpreted as the maximum *premium* above the original unit cost of the resource the decision maker would be willing to pay for one additional unit of the resource. For the storage constraint example, if a storage space already costs \$7 per unit, this means the decision maker should not pay more than \$12 (\$7 + \$5, or storage cost per unit + the shadow price) for an additional unit of storage space.

The **reduced cost** for a variable refers to the value its corresponding objective function coefficient would have to improve at minimum (that is, increase for a maximization problem or decrease for a minimization problem) before that variable could assume a non-zero value in the optimal solution. Generally, in cases other than a **degenerated solution,**[3] the reduced cost for a variable with a positive optimal value would always be zero. The reduced cost for a variable with an optimal value of zero would be a nonzero. In the latter case, the value of the reduced cost in the computer output will be the same as either the allowable increase (for a maximization problem[4]) or the allowable decrease (for a minimization problem).

Let's consider the following examples to illustrate the concepts discussed above about the managerial interpretation of the computer output.

EXAMPLE 3-4

Susan Frank is the operations manager of Arc Manufacturing Inc. She has developed a linear programming model to help her determine the product mix on one of the three production lines for Arc Manufacturing Inc.:

maximize $Z = 15x_1 + 20x_2 + 14x_3$

subject to

$5x_1 + 6x_2 + 4x_3 \leq 210$ pounds per day	(material A constraint)
$10x_1 + 8x_2 + 5x_3 \leq 200$ pounds per day	(material B constraint)
$4x_1 + 2x_2 + 5x_3 \leq 170$ pounds per day	(material C constraint)
$x_1, x_2, x_3 \geq 0$	(nonnegativity constraint)

where x_1, x_2, and x_3 represent production line (product) 1, 2, and 3 respectively.

a. Use Excel to solve the problem for Arc Manufacturing Inc.
b. What is the maximum revenue?
c. How much of each product should be produced each day to achieve the maximum revenue?
d. Are any materials left unused in the solution? If so, how much of each material is unused?

---

[3]Occurs when the number of variables (including slack or surplus) with a positive value is lower than the number of constraints.

[4]The value of the reduced cost is nonpositive in Solver solution output.

e. Explain the amount by which each variable's unit selling price would have to increase for that variable to be profitable enough to produce it.
f. Explain what the shadow prices represent. How are they useful?
g. Determine the range of feasibility for each constraint.
h. What is the meaning of the range of the optimality for the objective function coefficients? What is the range of optimality for the objective function coefficients of product 1, product 2, and product 3?
i. What rule is employed to see if multiple changes in the objective function or the right-hand side of the constraints can be contemplated? Under what conditions does this rule work?

Solution

a. The Excel worksheet and the associated answer sheets are displayed in Exhibits 3-6, 3-7, and 3-8.
b. As displayed in the worksheet of Exhibit 3-6 and also in Exhibit 3-7, the optimal revenue is $Z = \$548$.

EXHIBIT 3-6 Excel Worksheet for Arc Manufacturing Inc.

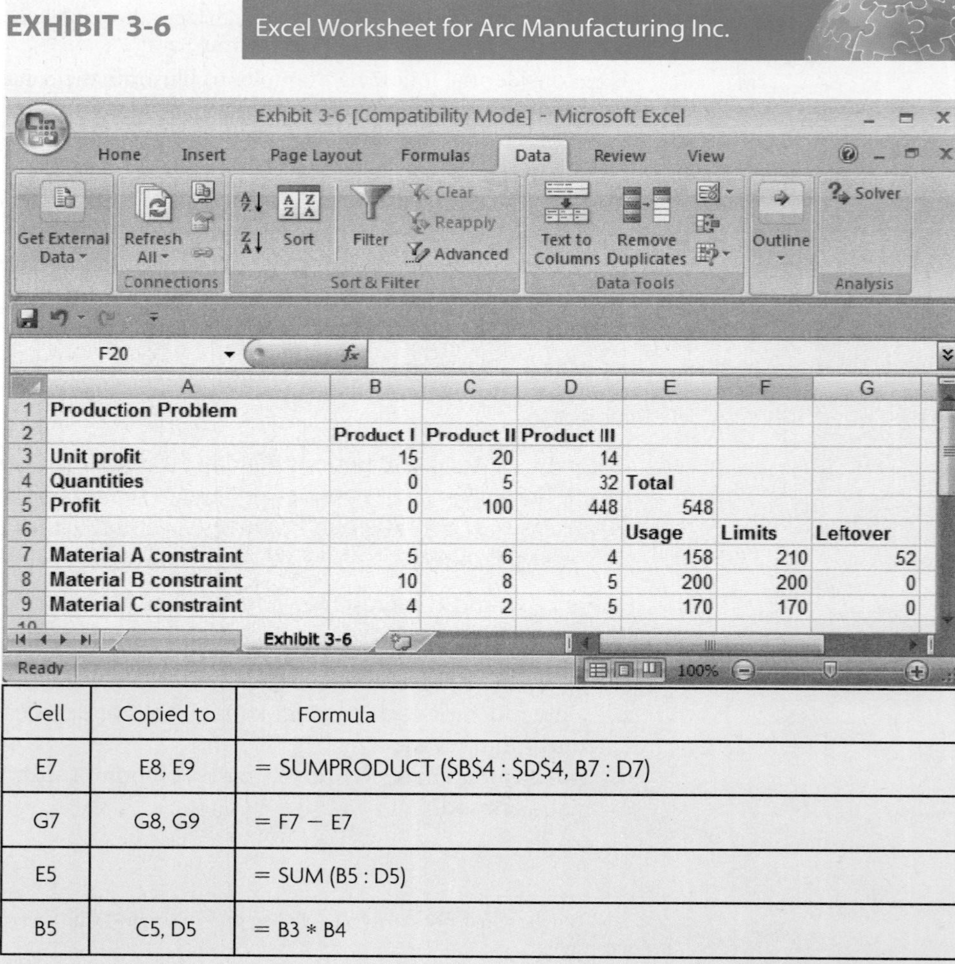

	A	B	C	D	E	F	G
1	Production Problem						
2		Product I	Product II	Product III			
3	Unit profit	15	20	14			
4	Quantities	0	5	32	Total		
5	Profit	0	100	448	548		
6					Usage	Limits	Leftover
7	Material A constraint	5	6	4	158	210	52
8	Material B constraint	10	8	5	200	200	0
9	Material C constraint	4	2	5	170	170	0

Cell	Copied to	Formula
E7	E8, E9	= SUMPRODUCT ($B$4 : $D$4, B7 : D7)
G7	G8, G9	= F7 − E7
E5		= SUM (B5 : D5)
B5	C5, D5	= B3 * B4

EXHIBIT 3-7 Excel Basic Output (Answer) Report for Arc Manufacturing Inc.

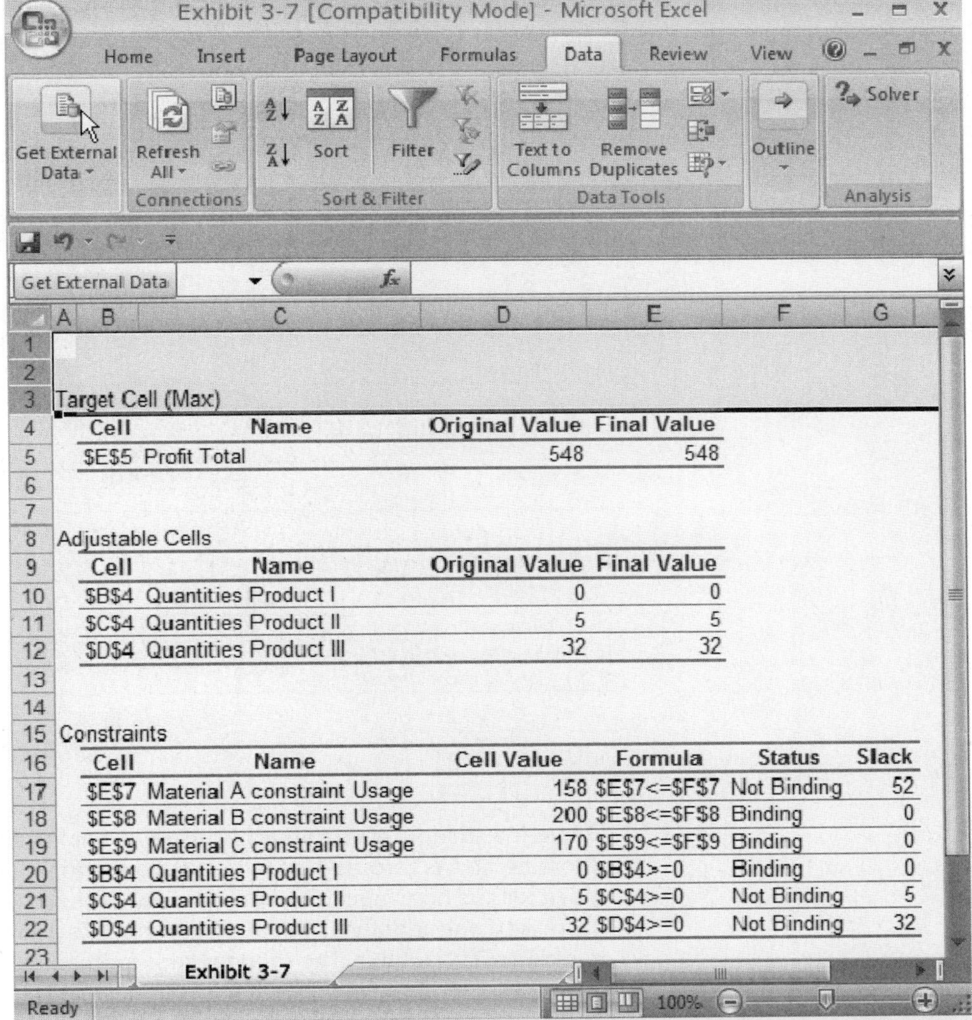

Target Cell (Max)

Cell	Name	Original Value	Final Value
$E$5	Profit Total	548	548

Adjustable Cells

Cell	Name	Original Value	Final Value
$B$4	Quantities Product I	0	0
$C$4	Quantities Product II	5	5
$D$4	Quantities Product III	32	32

Constraints

Cell	Name	Cell Value	Formula	Status	Slack
$E$7	Material A constraint Usage	158	$E$7<=$F$7	Not Binding	52
$E$8	Material B constraint Usage	200	$E$8<=$F$8	Binding	0
$E$9	Material C constraint Usage	170	$E$9<=$F$9	Binding	0
$B$4	Quantities Product I	0	$B$4>=0	Binding	0
$C$4	Quantities Product II	5	$C$4>=0	Not Binding	5
$D$4	Quantities Product III	32	$D$4>=0	Not Binding	32

c. As displayed in the Excel output, in the worksheet of Exhibit 3-6 and also in Exhibit 3-7, $x_1 = 0$, $x_2 = 5$, and $x_3 = 32$

d. We can tell this by looking at the slack column of Exhibit 3-7 of the first row. In this column, in cell G17, there is a value of 52. This indicates that 52 pounds per day of material A will be unused by this solution.

e. This information is given by the reduced cost column in Exhibit 3-8. According to the reduced cost values, the selling price on x_1 would have to increase by at least $10.60 to make it profitable enough to produce it. The other two variables (x_2 and x_3) have reduced costs of 0 because they are already included in the optimal solution.

EXHIBIT 3-8

Excel Sensitivity Analysis for Arc Manufacturing Inc.

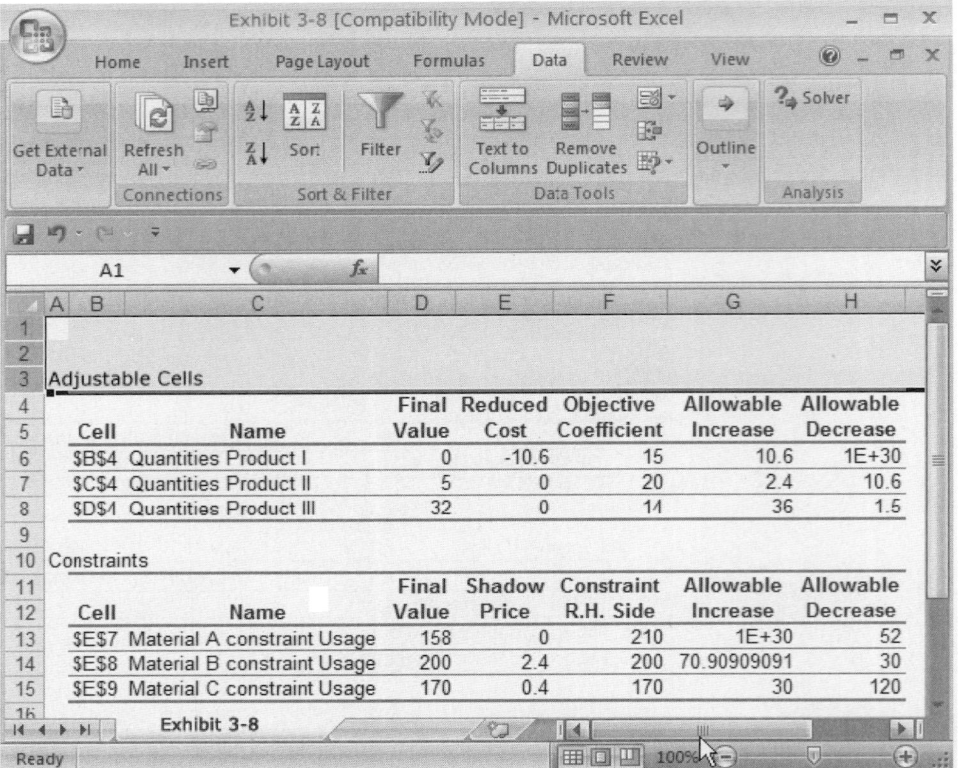

Adjustable Cells

Cell	Name	Final Value	Reduced Cost	Objective Coefficient	Allowable Increase	Allowable Decrease
$B$4	Quantities Product I	0	-10.6	15	10.6	1E+30
$C$4	Quantities Product II	5	0	20	2.4	10.6
$D$4	Quantities Product III	32	0	14	36	1.5

Constraints

Cell	Name	Final Value	Shadow Price	Constraint R.H. Side	Allowable Increase	Allowable Decrease
$E$7	Material A constraint Usage	158	0	210	1E+30	52
$E$8	Material B constraint Usage	200	2.4	200	70.90909091	30
$E$9	Material C constraint Usage	170	0.4	170	30	120

f. There is a shadow price for each constraint. For instance, the shadow price for material A is zero, and material B has a shadow price $2.40. The shadow price tells us how much the optimal value of the objective function would increase if one additional unit of that resource (e.g., one pound of material B per day) was available. The shadow price for material A is zero because the optimal solution leaves some of this resource unused. The shadow price for material B is nonzero ($2.40) because it is a binding constraint. In interpreting this value, the objective function would increase by $2.40 if one additional pound of material B became available. If the cost per pound of material B is less than $2.40, then it is worthwhile to obtain additional pounds of this resource.

g. The range of feasibility for each constraint can be determined from the bottom portion of Exhibit 3-8. The column labelled Constraint R.H. Side indicates the current RHS values that were used to obtain the current solution. The next two columns indicate the amount each of these values can be increased or decreased without exceeding the range of feasibility of the shadow prices. For instance, the right-hand side of material A has no upper limit (Allowable Increase = 1E + 30). Since the allowable decrease is 52, the right-hand side of material A can be decreased to 158 (210 − 52) pounds per day. Similarly, the allowable increase and allowable decrease for material B are 70.91 and 30 pounds respectively. Therefore, material B has a range of feasibility of 200 − 30 = 170 pounds to 200 + 70.91 = 270.91 pounds per day. For material C, the range of feasibility is 170 − 120 = 50 pounds to 170 + 30 = 200 pounds per day.

h. The range of optimality enables us to determine the amount by which one of the objective function coefficients can change without changing the optimal values of x_1, x_2, or x_3. For instance, the coefficient of x_3 can change from its current coefficient value of 14 by as much as the allowable increase of 36 to (14 + 36) = \$50 or decrease by as much as the allowable decrease of 1.5 from 14 to (14 − 1.5) = \$12.5 without causing the current optimal solution to change. The coefficient of x_2 can change from its current coefficient value of 20 by as much as the allowable increase of 2.4 to (2.4 + 20) = \$22.40 or decrease by as much as the allowable decrease of 10.6 from 20 to 9.4 (20 − 10.6) without causing the current optimal solution to change. However, x_1 has a value of zero in the optimal solution. For variables with zero values in the optimal solution, the alternate term is "range of insignificance." The range of x_1 is found by adding the allowable increase to the current objective function coefficient: 15 + 10.6 = \$25.60. since the allowable decrease is ∞ (1E + 30), as long as the profit per unit on x_1 is less than \$25.60, x_1 will have a value of zero in the optimal solution, assuming all other variables remain unchanged.

i. If multiple changes in the objective function or the right-hand side of the constraints are considered, we can use the 100 percent rule provided that certain requirements are met. Basically, there are two requirements. The first requirement is that all changes be of the same type (e.g., all changes involve the right-hand-side values). The second requirement is that each change is measured as a percentage of allowable increase or allowable decrease. The percentages for all changes are added. If their sum does not exceed 100 percent, sensitivity analysis of multiple changes is permissible.

EXAMPLE 3-5

From Example 3-4 assume that material A can be purchased at \$0.60 per pound, material B at \$0.45 per pound, and material C at \$1 per pound. The selling price for each product remains unchanged as well as the quantity of pounds available for each type of material. However, there is a minimum requirement to produce at least 7 units of product 1.

a. Reformulate the Arc Manufacturing Inc. problem to maximize the total profit.
b. How much of each product should be produced each day?
c. Should the company produce product 3 if the corresponding selling price is \$16?
d. If the company is offered the possibility of purchasing 50 additional pounds of material B, what is the maximum amount the company should be willing to pay per pound?
e. What is the impact of decreasing the minimum production requirement of product 1 by 2 units? Increasing the minimum production requirement of product 1 from 7 units to 10 units?

Solution

a. The unit material cost for each product can be obtained as follows:

Product 1 = (5 * \$0.6) + (10 * \$0.45) + (4 * \$1) = \$11.5 per unit
Product 2 = (6 * \$0.6) + (8 * \$0.45) + (2 * \$1) = \$9.25 per unit
Product 3 = (4 * \$0.6) + (5 * \$0.45) + (5 * \$1) = \$9.65 per unit

The function objective is maximize $Z = (15 - 11.5)x_1 + (20 - 9.25)x_2 + (14 - 9.65)x_3 = 3.5x_1 + 10.78x_2 + 4.35x_3$.
Therefore the LP model can be reformulated as:

maximize $Z = 3.5x_1 + 10.78x_2 + 4.35x_3$
subject to

$5x_1 + 6x_2 + 4x_3 \leq 210$ pounds per day (material A availability)
$10x_1 + 8x_2 + 5x_3 \leq 200$ pounds per day (material B availability)
$4x_1 + 2x_2 + 5x_3 \leq 170$ pounds per day (material C availability)
$x_1 \geq 7$ (minimum production requirement for product 1)

$x_1, x_2, x_3 \geq 0$

b. As displayed in the Excel output shown in Table 3-2, $x_1 = 7$, $x_2 = 16.25$, and $x_3 = 0$.

c. As shown in Table 3-3, the unit profit must increase by at least the reduced cost (\$2.4) to produce x_3. The increase of the selling price to \$16 per pound increases the unit profit for product 3 by \$2, that is, \$16 − \$9.65 − \$4.35,

TABLE 3-2 Answer Report

Target Cell (Max)

Cell	Name	Original Value	Final Value
\$E\$6	Profit Total	270	200

Adjustable Cells

Cell	Name	Original Value	Final Value
\$B\$5	Quantities Product I	0	7
\$C\$5	Quantities Product II	25	16.25
\$D\$5	Quantities Product III	0	0

Constraints

Cell	Name	Cell Value	Formula	Status	Slack
\$E\$8	Material A Usage	132.5	\$E\$8 <=\$F\$8	Not Binding	77.5
\$E\$9	Material B Usage	200	\$E\$9 <=\$F\$9	Binding	0
\$E\$10	Material C Usage	60.5	\$E\$10 <=\$F\$10	Not Binding	109.5
\$E\$11	Minimum demand Usage	7	\$E\$11 >=\$F\$11	Binding	0

TABLE 3-3 Sensitivity Analysis Report

Adjustable Cells

Cell	Name	Final Value	Reduced Cost	Objective Coefficient	Allowable Increase	Allowable Decrease
\$B\$5	Quantities Product I	7	0	3.5	10	1E + 30
\$C\$5	Quantities Product II	16.25	0	10.8	1E + 30	3.84
\$D\$5	Quantities Product III	0	−2.4	4.35	2.4	1E + 30

Constraints

Cell	Name	Final Value	Shadow Price	Constraint R.H. Side	Allowable Increase	Allowable Decrease
\$E\$8	Material A Usage	132.5	0	210	1E + 30	77.50000001
\$E\$9	Material B Usage	200	1.35	200	103.33333	130
\$E\$10	Material C Usage	60.5	0	170	1E + 30	109.5
\$E\$11	Minimum demand Usage	7	−10	7	13	7

which is less than the reduced cost. Therefore, the company should not produce x_3. Otherwise, since the revised unit profit for x_3 (\$16 − \$9.65 = \$6.35) will still be within the range of optimality ($-\infty$ to 6.75), the optimal solution shown in part *b* above will remain the same.

d. The shadow price for material B constraint is 1.35 and the range of feasibility is 70 to 303.33 (see Table 3-3). The purchase of 50 pounds of material B will increase the availability to 250 pounds which is within the range of feasibility. Therefore, the shadow price can be used to answer this question. Since the cost of purchasing material B is reflected in the objective function value, it corresponds to a relevant cost. The maximum amount the company should be willing to pay for one additional pound of material B is \$1.80, that is, the sum of the regular material unit cost (\$0.45) and the shadow price (\$1.35).

e. The shadow price for the minimum requirement constraint is -10 as shown in Table 3-3 and it is valid within the range of feasibility of 0 to 20. Therefore, decreasing this minimum by 2 changes the RHS to 5, which is within the range of feasibility. This change will increase the function objective value by \$20 (2 units * \$10 per unit). Alternatively, changing the RHS to 10 remains within the range of feasibility. This change will reduce the objective function value by \$30 (3 units * \$10 per unit).

Summary

Sensitivity analysis enables the decision maker to determine how a change in one of the numerical values of a model will impact the optimal solution and the optimal value of the objective function. The primary purpose of such analysis is to provide the decision maker with greater insight about the sensitivity of the optimal solution to changes in various parameters of a problem. Interest in changes may arise due to improved information relating to a problem or because of the desire to know the potential impact of changes that are contemplated. This chapter begins by describing graphical sensitivity analysis of an optimal solution of a linear programming model, which provides the reader with good intuitive feel for sensitivity analysis. The chapter continues with a discussion of how sensitivity analysis can be done using Excel and the interpretation of the Excel output.

Sensitivity analysis included in this chapter consists of two main parts. First, analysis of a change in the value of an objective function coefficient involves finding the range of objective function values for which the optimal values of the decision variables would not change. This is referred to as the range of optimality for that objective function coefficient. A value of the objective function that falls within the range of optimality will not change the optimal solution, although the optimal value of the objective function will change. Second, analysis of right-hand-side (RHS) changes begins with determination of a constraint's shadow price in the optimal solution. The range of values over which the RHS value can change without causing the shadow price to change is called its range of feasibility. Within this range of feasibility, the same decision variables will remain optimal, although their values and the optimal value of the objective function will change.

Sensitivity analysis and computer solution interpretation of linear programming models provides additional managerial insights in a variety of decision-making situations. The Modern Management Science Application article, "Big Benefits for Big Blue," illustrates how the uses of linear programming and sensitivity analysis enabled IBM Corporation to reengineer some of its manufacturing operations and helped to deliver business value to the company.

A MODERN MANAGEMENT SCIENCE APPLICATION: BIG BENEFITS FOR BIG BLUE

IBM is the world's largest computer hardware, software, and services company with operations worldwide in more than 164 countries including Canada. IBM Canada Ltd. is headquartered in Markham. It operates a semi-conductor plant in Bromont and software development laboratories in Markham, Ottawa, Montreal, and Victoria. There are a variety of projects undertaken where management science techniques such as linear programming have been successfully applied, providing opportunities to answer "what if . . . ?" questions through the use of sensitivity analysis and computer solution interpretation. One project addresses the needs of managers in semi-conductor manufacturing for a decision support system that would assist in identifying the optimal product mix, optimally allocating products to tools, identifying gating tools, and determining a minimum set of tools required to produce for a given demand. IBM Research developed a linear programming model in which the decision variables represent the production volume of each product and the allocation of each product to each tool. The constraints reflect production limits, the required process steps, and the available tool capacity, while the primary objective is to maximize profit. Another project is aimed at solving the allocation of scarce raw materials and capacity in IBM's supply chain through a multi-echelon bill of materials. The core problem was solved using linear programming and greedy heuristics. A key indicator of the decision support system is its ability to identify the production bottlenecks and to indicate how to fix them. It includes modelling constructs to address multi-plant enterprises, semiconductor planning, and component aggregation, as well as a suite of algorithms that provide sensitivity analysis beyond the standard shadow pricing of linear programming.

Source: B. Dietrich, N. Donofrio, G. Lin, and J. Snowdon. "Big Benefits for Big Blue," *OR/MS Today Vol.* 27, no. 3 (June 2000), pp. 52–56. Reprinted with permission.

Glossary

Degenerate Solution A solution where one or more of the basic variables has a value equal to zero.

Dual Price See Shadow Price

100 Percent Rule A rule used to determine whether simultaneous changes for two or more objective function values, or two or more RHS values, are valid.

Range of Feasibility The range in value over which the RHS of a constraint can change without changing its shadow price.

Range of Insignificance The range in value over which an objective function coefficient can change without causing the corresponding decision variable to take on a nonzero value. Applicable only to variables that have a value of zero in the optimal solution.

Range of Optimality The range in value over which an objective function coefficient can change without changing the optimal values of solution variables.

Reduced Cost The value an objective function coefficient of a variable would have to improve before it could be possible for that variable to assume a nonzero value in the optimal solution.

Relevant Cost A cost that is affected by the decision maker. It is reflected in the objective function coefficients.

Right-Hand-Side (RHS) Value The amount of resource available for a $\leq$ constraint or the minimum requirement for some criterion for a $\geq$ constraint.

Sensitivity (Postoptimality) Analysis Analysis of the impact of a change in one of the numerical values of a linear programming model on the optimal solution and the optimal value of the objective function.

Shadow Price The amount of change in the optimal value of the objective function per unit change of the RHS value (e.g., \$2 per pound, \$0.53 per minute) of a constraint.

Sunk Cost A cost that is not affected by the decision maker. Such a cost is not reflected in the objective function coefficients.

Solved Problems

Problem 1

Given this LP model:

$$\text{maximize} \quad Z = 3x_1 + 3x_2$$

subject to

$$\begin{aligned} &\text{A} \quad 6x_1 + 4x_2 \leq 24 \\ &\text{B} \quad 10x_1 + 20x_2 \leq 80 \\ &\quad x_1, x_2 \geq 0 \end{aligned}$$

a. Find the range of optimality, or the range of insignificance, whichever is appropriate, for each objective function coefficient.

b. Find the shadow price and the range of feasibility for the RHS of each constraint.

Solution

Begin by plotting the graph and solving for the optimal solution:

a. We can see that neither decision variable has a value of zero in the optimal solution. Therefore, the range of optimality is appropriate for both of their objective function coefficients. The range of optimality is the amount that an objective function coefficient can change (thereby changing the slope of the objective function line) and still not cause the solution to move to another corner point.

We can determine the range of optimality for each coefficient by determining the value it would need to cause the objective function line to be just parallel to each of the binding constraints. Thus, for the x_1 coefficient, for the objective function line to be parallel to the first constraint, its value would have to be $^6/_4 = 1.5$ times that of the x_2 coefficient, which would make it 4.5. Then, to be parallel to the second constraint, the x_1 coefficient would have to

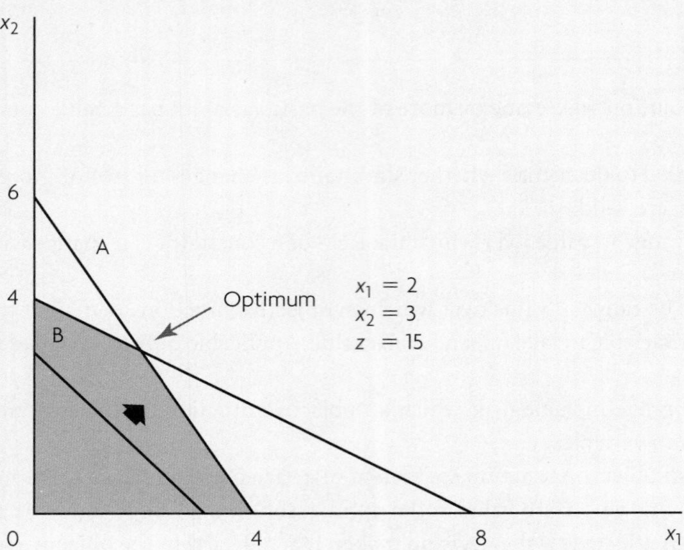

be $^1/_2$ (i.e., $^{10}/_{20} = {}^1/_2$) of the x_2 coefficient, which would make the objective function coefficient of x_1 1.5. Hence, the range of optimality for the x_1 coefficient is 1.5 to 4.5.

Similarly, for the x_2 coefficient, we must find the value that will make the objective function line parallel to the first constraint and then the second constraint. For the first constraint, we know that the ratio of the two coefficients must be $^6/_4 = 1.5$. Given that the x_1 coefficient is 3, the x_2 coefficient would then be 2($^4/_6 * 3$). And, to be parallel to the second constraint, the ratio must be $^{10}/_{20} = {}^1/_2$. So with the x_1 coefficient equal to 3, the x_2 coefficient must be $6 = (2 * 3)$. Hence, the range of optimality for the x_2 coefficient is 2 to 6.

b. To find the shadow price of a constraint that is a binding constraint (both constraints here are binding constraints), increase its RHS by 1 and determine the new optimal values of the decision variables. Then substitute those new values into the objective function to find its new optimal value. Subtract the original Z from the new Z to obtain the shadow price. Note: If a constraint is not binding, its shadow price is 0.

Thus, adding 1 to the RHS of the first constraint and solving for the new intersection with the second constraint, we find $x_1 = 2.25$ and $x_2 = 2.875$. This yields $Z' = 15.375$. The original Z was 15. Therefore, the shadow price is $15.375 - 15 = .375$ for the first constraint.

Similarly, by adding 1 to the RHS of the second constraint (making it 81), and using the original first constraint, we obtain an intersection of $x_1 = 1.95$, $x_2 = 3.075$. Then $Z' = 15.075$, so the shadow price is $15.075 - 15 = .075$ for the second constraint.

Now, to find the range of feasibility for the RHS of a constraint, place a straight edge along the line on the graph. First, hold it parallel to the line while moving away from the origin. Stop when it reaches the last intersection with the other binding constraint in this quadrant. You can see from the graph that the upper limit is at (8, 0). Similarly, moving

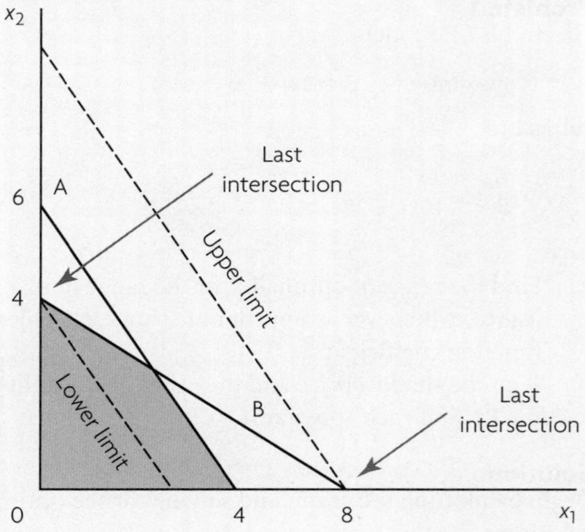

parallel to the first constraint but toward the origin, the lower limit is at (0, 4).

Substituting each of these sets of values into the first constraint will give us our range of feasibility:

8, 0: $6(8) + 4(0) = 48$
0, 4: $6(0) + 4(4) = 16$

Hence, the range of feasibility for the first constraint is 16 to 48.

Similarly, to find the range of feasibility for the second constraint, we hold a straight edge along its graph and move it parallel to the line away from the origin until we reach the last intersection (0, 6) and toward the origin until we reach the last intersection with the other binding constraint (4, 0). Substituting these sets of values into the second constraint, we find

0, 6: $10(0) + 20(6) = 120$
4, 0: $10(4) + 20(0) = 40$

Hence, the range of feasibility for the second constraint is 40 to 120.

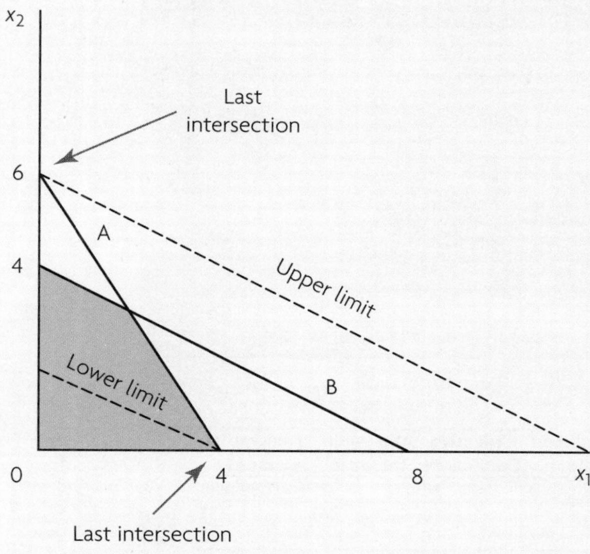

Problem 2

Suppose the objective function in a previous problem had been maximize $Z = 9x_1 + 2.25x_2$. The optimal solution would then have been $x_1 = 4, x_2 = 0$.

Find the range of insignificance for the x_2 coefficient in the objective function.

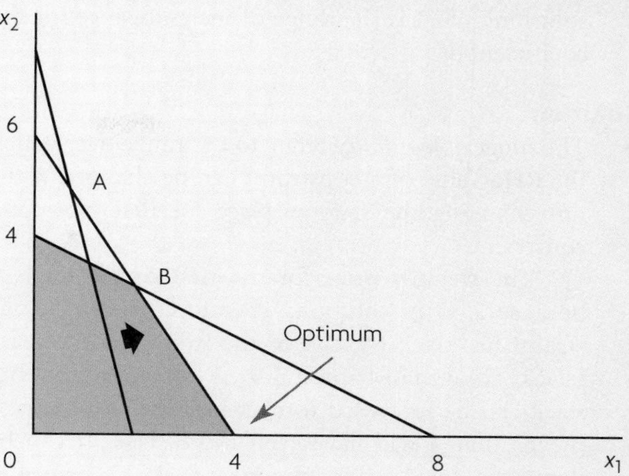

Solution

x_2 will have an optimal value of zero (i.e., it will be insignificant) unless its objective function coefficient becomes large enough for it to make a positive contribution to the objective. This would occur if its value increased to where it caused the objective function line to be at least parallel to the first constraint (constraint A). Thus, the ratio of the x_1 and x_2 coefficients would have to be $^6/_4 = 1.5$. With the x_1 coefficient equal to 9, this would require an x_2 coefficient of at least 6. Hence, the range of insignificance for the x_2 coefficient is a value of less than 6 in the objective function.

Problem 3

Given this LP model

$$\text{maximize} \quad Z = 10x_1 + 6x_2 + 5x_3$$

subject to

$$2x_1 + 3x_2 + 4x_3 \leq 25$$
$$x_1 + 3x_2 + 2x_3 \leq 22$$
$$6x_1 + 3x_2 + 4x_3 \leq 32$$
$$x_1, x_2, x_3 \geq 0$$

where x_1, x_2, and x_3 represent products 1, 2, and 3 and constraints 1, 2, and 3 represent the availability of materials A, B, and C.

a. Use Excel and determine the range of feasibility for each RHS (i.e., original right-hand-side value).
b. Use Excel and determine the range of optimality for the coefficients of the decision variables that are in solution.
c. By how much would the objective function coefficient of x_3 have to increase before it would come into

solution? What is the range of insignificance for the coefficient of x_3?

Solution

a. The *range of feasibility* refers to the range over which the RHS value of a constraint can be changed without changing the shadow price for that particular constraint.

The shadow price for the first constraint is 0 because s_1 is in solution. Therefore, the first constraint has slack ($s_1 = 1$ in the Allowable Decrease (slack) column of Exhibit 3-9). A constraint that has slack can be increased forever because any increase means that it will have even more slack. It can be decreased by 1 (the amount of slack) before it becomes a binding constraint. Hence, its range of feasibility is from 24 (i.e., $25 - 1$) to $+\infty$.

For variables that are not in solution, such as s_2 and s_3, the range of feasibility can be obtained from the Excel Sensitivity Report given in Exhibit 3-9.

For the second constraint, since the Allowable Increase is 1.25 and Allowable Decrease is 16.67, we find

Upper end $= 22 + 1.25 = 23.25$
Lower end $= 22 - 16.67 = 5.33$
Range: 5.33 to 23.25

For the third constraint, since the Allowable Increase is 5 and Allowable Decrease is 10, we find

Upper end $= 32 + 5 = 37$
Lower end $= 32 - 10 = 22$
Range: 22 to 37

Thus, the range of feasibility for each constraint is

Constraint	Current Value	Range of Feasibility
1	25	24 to $+\infty$
2	22	5.33 to 23.25
3	32	22 to 37

b. The ranges of optimality can be obtained from the Excel Sensitivity Report given in Exhibit 3-9. The Allowable Increase and Allowable Decrease columns

EXHIBIT 3-9

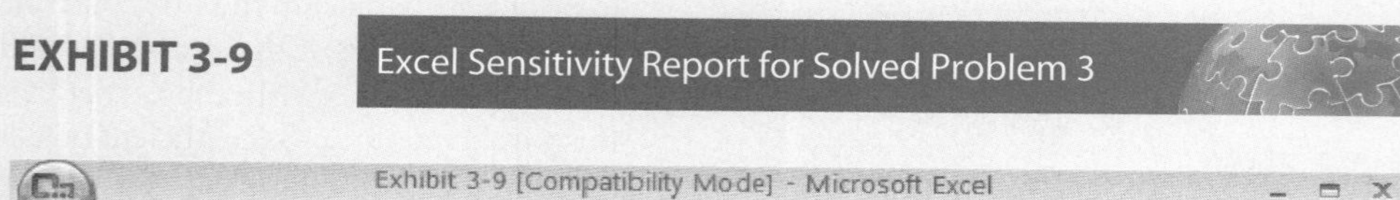

Excel Sensitivity Report for Solved Problem 3

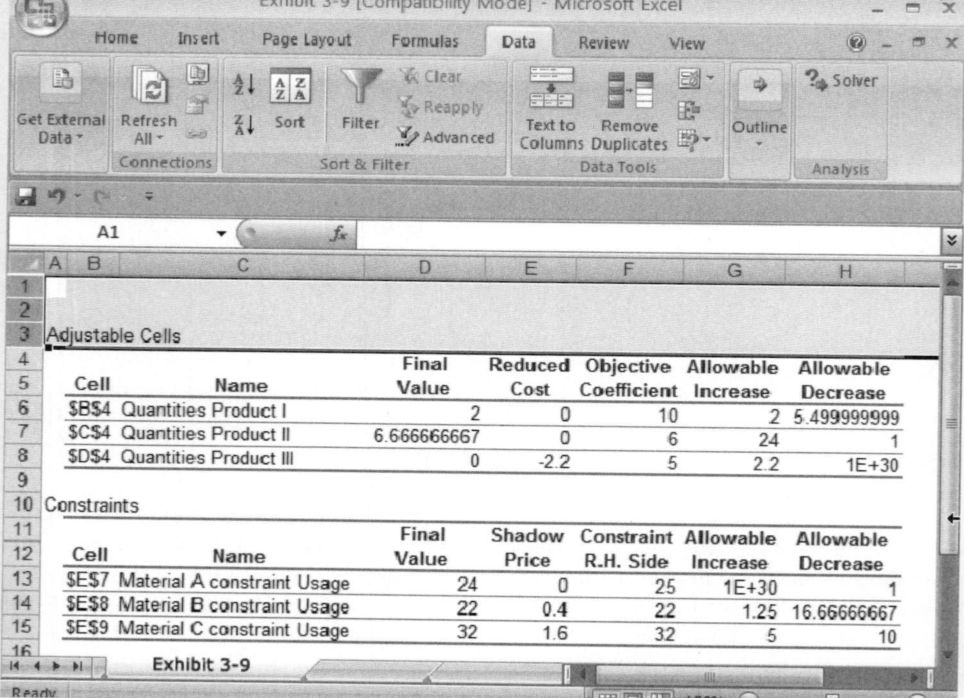

Exhibit 3-9 [Compatibility Mode] - Microsoft Excel

Adjustable Cells

Cell	Name	Final Value	Reduced Cost	Objective Coefficient	Allowable Increase	Allowable Decrease
$B$4	Quantities Product I	2	0	10	2	5.499999999
$C$4	Quantities Product II	6.666666667	0	6	24	1
$D$4	Quantities Product III	0	-2.2	5	2.2	1E+30

Constraints

Cell	Name	Final Value	Shadow Price	Constraint R.H. Side	Allowable Increase	Allowable Decrease
$E$7	Material A constraint Usage	24	0	25	1E+30	1
$E$8	Material B constraint Usage	22	0.4	22	1.25	16.66666667
$E$9	Material C constraint Usage	32	1.6	32	5	10

on the top half of the report in Exhibit 3-9 can be used to obtain the range of optimality for the variables in the solution as follows.

For x_1, the allowable decrease is −5.5 and allowable increase is +2. Therefore, the range of optimality for x_1 is

(10 − 5.5 = 4.5) to (10 + 2 = 12)

For x_2, the allowable decrease is − 1 and the allowable increase is +24. Thus, the x_2 co-efficient of 6 in the objective function can be decreased by as much as 1 or increased by as much as 24. The range of optimality for the x_2 coefficient in the objective function, therefore, is

(6 − 1 = 5) to (6 + 24 = 30)

Thus, the range of optimality for each variable that is in solution is

Variable	Range of Optimality
x_1	4.5 to 12
x_2	5 to 30

c. For variables that are not in solution, such as x_3 in this example, their contribution per unit is too small (in a maximization problem) to cause them to have an optimal value that is nonzero. However, if the objective function coefficient is increased by a sufficient amount, that variable, variable x_3, would come into the solution. Since the allowable increase for variable x_3 is 2.2 in Exhibit 3-9, the objective function coefficient of x_3 must be 2.2 more than the original objective function coefficient for x_3, which is 5 + 2.2, or 7.2, for it to come into solution. Therefore, the range of insignificance for variable x_3 is $-\infty$ to 7.2. In other words, the objective function coefficient for x_3 could be decreased by an unlimited amount and x_3 would not come into the solution. However, if the objective function coefficient of x_3 is increased to 7.2 or more, x_3 would come into the solution as a nonzero value.

Problem 4

(Refer to Solved Problem 3.) Manager Tom Oakley is considering making multiple changes to the original model. For each set of changes, decide if the impact of the changes can be determined without re-solving the entire problem.

a. Increase every RHS value by 1.
b. Increase the objective function coefficient of x_1 by 1 and decrease the objective function coefficient of x_2 by 1.
c. Increase the objective function coefficient of x_1 by .80 and decrease the objective function coefficient of x_2 by .50.
d. Determine the optimal value of the objective function value after the changes in part *c* are incorporated.

Solution

a. Using the feasibility ranges for RHS changes from Solved Problem 3:

Constraint	RHS	Range of Feasibility
1	25	24 to $+\infty$
2	22	5.33 to 23.25
3	32	22 to 37

There is no limit on the first constraint as an upper limit, so we can ignore that increase. (Generally, there would be no benefit in increasing the RHS of a constraint that currently has slack.) The second constraint's increase as a percentage of the allowable increase would be $^1/_{1.25}$ = 80 percent; the third constraint's percentage increase would be $^1/_5$ = 20 percent. (Note: The 5 in the last computation is the difference between the 37 upper limit of the range of feasibility and the current RHS value of 32.) The sum of these two percentages is 100 percent. It just satisfies the requirement that the sum of the percentage changes must not exceed 100 percent. Therefore, the proposed changes are *within* the acceptable range.

b. The ranges of optimality were determined in Solved Problem 3:

Variable	Current Value	Range of Optimality
x_1	10	4.5 to 12
x_2	6	5 to 30

Increasing the x_1 coefficient from 10 to 11 would be an increase of 50 percent of the allowable increase: $^1/_2$ = 50 percent. Decreasing the x_2 coefficient by 1 would be 100 percent of the allowable decrease: $^1/_1$ = 100 percent. The total percentage would be 50 percent + 100 percent = 150 percent; this would exceed the 100 percent limitation. Consequently, these two changes would cause a change in the optimal solution quantities and the optimal solution mix of the variables.

c. Increasing the objective function coefficient of x_1 by .80 would constitute 40 percent of its allowable increase ($^{.8}/_2$) as determined in part *b*. Decreasing the objective function coefficient of x_2 by .50 would constitute 50 percent of its allowable decrease. The total percentage would be 90 percent. Because this total is less than the 100 percent limitation, the optimal values of variables in solution will not change.

d. To find out what the revised profit based on the changes mode in part *c* would be, we can multiply the optimal quantities by their respective objective function changes and then adjust the optimal value of the objective function accordingly. Thus, with $x_1 = 2$ and $x_2 = 6^2/_3$, and ($\Delta c_1 = .80$ and $\Delta c_2 = -.50$), we have

$$\Delta Z = .80(2) - .50(6\ 2/3) = -1.733$$

The revised value of Z is then

$$Z' = 60 - 1.733 = 58.267$$

Problem 5

(Refer to Solved Problem 3.) The manager of the department for which the LP model was formulated would like to know the answers to certain questions:

a. If one additional unit of the third constraint could be obtained at the same cost as the previous units (so that the profits per unit in the objective function did not change), what impact would this have on profit?

b. If one additional unit of the third resource (constraint) could be obtained at a *premium* of $.50, what impact would this have on profit?

c. If 4 units of the third resource were obtained at the original cost per unit, what impact would this have on the optimal value of profit?

Solution

a. The shadow price for the third constraint is $^8/_5$. Therefore, for one additional unit, profit would increase by $^8/_5$, or $1.60.

b. The premium must be deducted from the shadow price. Hence, the net impact would be $1.60 − $0.50 = $1.10 increase in total profit.

c. First, we must check to see if the specified change is within the range of feasibility. An additional 4 units would make the RHS of the third constraint 32 + 4 = 36; the upper end of the range of feasibility for the third constraint is 37 (see Solved Problem 3). Hence, the change is within the range of feasibility.

Since the change is within the range of feasibility and the optimal profit is $60, adding 4 units of the third resource will increase the total profit by 4 × 1.60 = $6.40, where $1.60 is the shadow price associated with the third resource. Therefore, the total profit would be $60 + $6.4 = $66.40.

Discussion and Review Questions

1. Explain how a change in resource availability can affect the optimal solution of a linear programming problem.
2. Explain how we can ensure that the optimal solution to a linear programming problem does not change when we simultaneously change the objective function values of the decision variables.
3. Explain how a change in objective function value of a decision variable can affect the optimal solution of a linear programming problem.
4. Discuss the importance of sensitivity analysis in solving linear programming problems. Compare using sensitivity analysis and solving a problem by changing one of the objective function values from scratch.
5. What is a binding constraint? What is a nonbinding constraint? Discuss the difference between them.
6. What is a shadow price? Explain carefully.
7. Describe how a firm would use the shadow price associated with a given constraint.
8. If the objective function value of a decision variable changes within its allowable change, explain if it will affect the current variable value and the objective function value.
9. Explain the meaning of slack and surplus in a linear programming constraint.
10. Explain the effect of increasing the RHS value of a constraint beyond the allowable increase value shown in the sensitivity report.

Problems

1. Sensitivity analysis can provide a decision maker with additional insights about an optimal solution to an LP model.
   a. Explain in general terms what sensitivity analysis accomplishes.
   b. Why might sensitivity analysis be useful to a decision maker?
   c. List the two types of parameters the discussion of sensitivity analysis the chapter focused on.
2. Briefly define or explain each of these terms.
   a. Shadow price.
   b. Range of feasibility.
   c. Range of optimality.
   d. Range of insignificance.
   e. Binding constraint.
3. Given this LP model and its graph:

maximize $Z = 5x_1 + 9x_2$

subject to

A $2x_1 + 1x_2 \leq 10$
B $1x_1 + 3x_2 \leq 12$
$x_1, x_2 \geq 0$

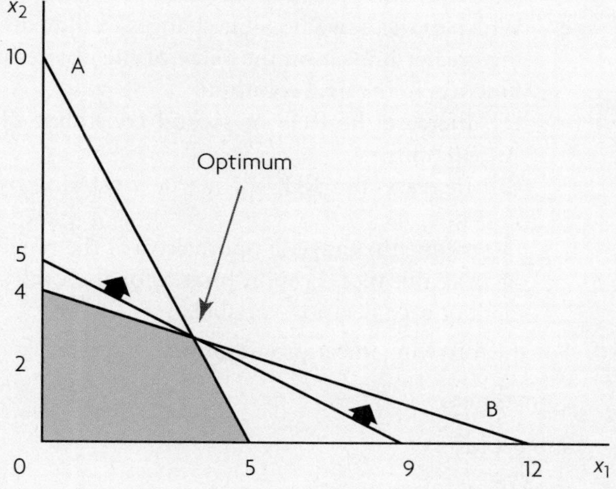

   a. Find the range of optimality for the x_2 coefficient in the objective function.
   b. Find the range of optimality for the x_1 coefficient of the objective function.
   c. Find the shadow price for each constraint's RHS.
   d. Determine the range of feasibility for each constraint's shadow price.
   e. What impact would a change in the objective function coefficient of x_1 from 5 to 4 have on the optimal values of the decision variables? What effect would it have on the optimal value of the objective function?
   f. What effect would a decrease of 1 in the value of the x_2 coefficient of the objective function have on the optimal values of the decision variables? What effect would it have on the optimal value of the objective function? Explain.
4. Given this LP model:

maximize $Z = 8x_1 + 3x_2$

subject to

Labour $5x_1 + 2x_2 \leq 30$ hours
Equipment $1x_1 + 2x_2 \leq 16$ hours
Material $10x_1 + 7x_2 \leq 70$ pounds
$x_1, x_2 \geq 0$

   a. Plot the graph and determine the optimal solution.
   b. Find the range of optimality or insignificance for each objective function coefficient.
   c. Determine the shadow price of each constraint for the optimal solution.
   d. Determine the range of feasibility for the RHS of each constraint.
5. Given this LP model:

minimize $Z = 4x_1 + 8x_2$

subject to

Fibre $5x_1 + 8x_2 \geq 40$
Protein $6x_1 + 4x_2 \geq 24$
$x_1, x_2 \geq 0$

   a. Find the range of optimality or insignificance for each objective function coefficient.
   b. How would a decrease of $1 in the x_1 coefficient of the objective function affect the optimal values of the decision variables? How would it affect the optimal value of the objective function?
   c. What is the shadow price for the fibre constraint's RHS? Over what range of values is it valid?
   d. What is the shadow price for the RHS of the protein constraint? Over what range of values is it valid?

e. What impact on cost would a decrease of 2 units in the RHS of the protein constraint have?

6. The manager of FYZ Incorporated has been presented with the following LP model:

minimize $Z = 30A + 45B$ (cost)

subject to

$$5A + 2B \geq 100$$
$$4A + 8B \geq 240$$
$$B \geq 20$$
$$A \text{ and } B \geq 0$$

The manager would like your assistance in answering her questions:

a. What are the optimal values of A and B? What is the minimum cost?
b. If the cost of B could be reduced to \$42 per unit, how many units of B would be optimal? What would the minimum cost be?
c. What is the shadow price for the RHS of the first constraint? Over what range is it valid?
d. By what amount would the cost change, and in what direction, if the first constraint was changed to 110?

7. The manager of the assembly department of 1KW, Inc., has developed this LP model:

maximize $Z = 12P + 10Q$ (profit)

subject to

Line 1	$11P + 11Q \leq 121$ hours	
Line 2	$8P + 15Q \leq 120$ hours	
Inspection	$3P + 15Q \leq 60$ minutes	
	$P, Q \geq 0$	

a. What are the optimal values of P, Q, and Z?
b. By how much can the profit per unit of P change without changing the optimal values of P and Q?
c. If the amount of time on line 1 could be increased without changing the optimal mix of variables, how much more could be used? What would be the new profit? What would happen if more time than this was added to line 1?
d. If line 2 time was reduced by one hour, what impact would this have on profit?
e. If one additional hour for line 1 could be obtained, how much would profit increase?

8. Sensitivity analysis can provide a decision maker with additional insights about a linear programming solution.

a. List the three types of parameters that sensitivity analysis might focus on. Which two are covered in this chapter?
b. What is an advantage of sensitivity analysis as opposed to solving an LP problem from scratch?
c. Discuss the role of sensitivity analysis in solving LP problem. Under what circumstances is it very useful?

9. For the following LP model

maximize $Z = 20x_1 + 12x_2$

subject to

1	$3x_1 + 2x_2 \leq 180$	(raw material 1)
2	$x_1 \leq 50$	(raw material 2)
3	$x_2 \leq 51$	(raw material 3)
	$x_1, x_2 \geq 0$	

Use Excel in answering the following questions.

a. Identify the shadow prices and indicate the constraint with which each shadow price is associated. Interpret each shadow price.
b. Determine the range of feasibility for raw material 1 and interpret your answer.
c. Determine the range of feasibility for raw material 2 and interpret your answer.
d. Determine the range of feasibility for raw material 3 and interpret your answer.
e. Which of these two possible changes would have the greater impact on the value of the objective function in the final solution?
   (1) Increase the RHS of second constraint by 10 units.
   (2) Increase the RHS of third constraint by 40 units.
f. Determine the range of optimality (or the range of insignificance, if appropriate) for the coefficient of each decision variable.

10. For the following linear programming problem,

maximize $Z = 9x_1 + 6x_2$

subject to

1	$12x_1 + 5x_2 \leq 600$ hours
2	$x_2 \leq 72$ hours
	$x_1, x_2 \geq 0$

Use Excel in answering the following questions:

a. What are the optimal values of x_1, x_2, and Z?
b. Identify the shadow prices and indicate the constraint with which each shadow price is associated. Interpret each shadow price.

c. Determine the range of feasibility for the first constraint and interpret your answer.
d. Determine the range of feasibility for the second constraint and interpret your answer.
e. If the first constraint was revised to 450 hours, what impact would that have on the solution quantities and the value of Z?
f. Determine the range of optimality for each coefficient of the objective function for the original problem.

11. Given the following LP problem, use Excel to complete the sensitivity analysis.

$$\text{maximize} \quad Z = 11x_1 + 10x_2 + 14x_3$$

subject to

$$\begin{aligned} &\text{A} \quad & 4x_2 - 1x_3 &\leq 0 \\ &\text{B} \quad & 5x_1 + 2x_2 + 5x_3 &\leq 72 \\ & & x_1 &\leq 13 \\ & & x_1, x_2, x_3 &\geq 0 \end{aligned}$$

a. Determine the range of insignificance, or the range of optimality (whichever is appropriate), for each of the variables in the objective function.
b. Determine the range of feasibility for each of the constraints and interpret each range.
c. Suppose that the right-hand side of constraint A will be changed to 10. Determine the impact that this change would have on the value of the objective function.

12. (Refer to the preceding problem.) Answer these questions concerning changes in the objective function coefficients:
a. By how much would the contribution of variable x_1 have to change, and in which direction, before x_1 would come into the solution?
b. If the objective function coefficient of variable x_2 were to increase by 5, what impact would this have on the value of the variables and the objective function?
c. If the coefficients of variables x_2 and x_3 were each decreased by 2, would that be within the range of optimality for multiple changes? If so, what would the values of the decision variables be in the optimal solution?
d. Suppose the RHS value of constraint A was 10 and the RHS value of constraint B was 80. Would this be within the range of feasibility for multiple changes? If so, what would be the value of the objective function?

13. The manager of FGH, a small manufacturer of horseback riding accessories, has received a staff report that contains an LP model.

F = quantity of product F
G = quantity of product G
H = quantity of product H

$$\text{maximize} \quad Z = 15F + 20G + 14H$$

subject to

$$\begin{aligned} &\text{A} \quad & 5F + 6G + 4H &\leq 210 \text{ pounds} \\ &\text{B} \quad & 10F + 8G + 5H &\leq 200 \text{ minutes} \\ &\text{C} \quad & 4F + 2G + 5H &\leq 170 \text{ square feet} \\ & & F, G, H &\geq 0 \end{aligned}$$

Use Excel and determine the following:
a. What are the optimal values of F, G, and H? What is the optimal profit?
b. What is the range of optimality for the 20 in the objective function? Interpret your result (i.e., what values of decision variables do not change within this range?)
c. How would the value of the total profit (Z) change if the 20 in the objective function were decreased by 10? Increased by 2?
d. What is the range of feasibility for RHS of constraint A? Interpret your answer.
e. What is the range of feasibility for the RHS of the last constraint?
f. What is the value of the total profit (Z) if the last constraint were increased by 20 units?
g. What is the value of the total profit (Z) if the RHS of the last constraint was 210?

14. The manager of a knitting department has developed the following LP model and the following Excel output in Table 3-4 summarizes the results.

x_1 = units of product 1
x_2 = units of product 2
x_3 = units of product 3

$$\text{maximize } Z = 7x_1 + 3x_2 + 9x_3$$

subject to

$$\begin{aligned} &\text{Labour} \quad & 4x_1 + 5x_2 + 6x_3 &\leq 360 \text{ hours} \\ &\text{Machine} \quad & 2x_1 + 4x_2 + 6x_3 &\leq 300 \text{ hours} \\ &\text{Material} \quad & 9x_1 + 5x_2 + 6x_3 &\leq 600 \text{ pounds} \\ & & x_1, x_2, \text{ and } x_3 &\geq 0 \end{aligned}$$

a. What are the values of x_1, x_2, x_3, and Z in the optimal solution?
b. Why isn't any product 2 called for in the optimal solution? How much would the per-unit profit

TABLE 3-4 Excel Reports for Problem 14

A. Answer Report

Target Cell (Max)

Cell	Name	Original Value	Final Value
$E$5	Profit Total	588	588

Adjustable Cells

Cell	Name	Original Value	Final Value
$B$4	Quantities Product I	48	48
$C$4	Quantities Product II	0	0
$D$4	Quantities Product III	28	28

Constraints

Cell	Name	Cell Value	Formula	Status	Slack
$E$7	Labour Usage	360	$E$7 <= $F$7	Binding	0
$E$8	Machine Usage	264	$E$8 <= $F$8	Not Binding	36
$E$9	Material Usage	600	$E$9 <= $F$9	Binding	0

B. Sensitivity Report

Adjustable Cells

Cell	Name	Final Value	Reduced Cost	Objective Coefficient	Allowable Increase	Allowable Decrease
$B$4	Quantities Product I	48	0	7	6.5	1
$C$4	Quantities Product II	0	−4.500000001	2.999999999	4.500000001	1E + 30
$D$4	Quantities Product III	28	0	9	1.5	4.333333333

Constraints

Cell	Name	Final Value	Shadow Price	Constraint R. H. Side	Allowable Increase	Allowable Decrease
$E$7	Labour Usage	360	1.3	360	25.71428571	93.33333333
$E$8	Machine Usage	264	0	300	1E + 30	36
$E$9	Material Usage	600	0.2	600	210	90

of product 2 have to be for it to enter into the optimal solution mix?

c. What is the range of optimality for the profit per unit of product 1?

d. What would the values in the optimal solution be if the objective coefficient of x_1 were to increase by 3?

e. What is the range of feasibility of the labour constraint?

f. What would the values in the optimal solution be if the amount of labour available decreased by 10 hours?

g. If the manager could obtain additional material, how much more could be used effectively? What would happen if the manager obtained more than this amount?

15. (Refer to the preceding problem.) The manager has some additional questions relative to the optimal solution:

a. If it is possible to obtain an additional amount of *one* of the resources, which one should be obtained, and how much can be effectively used? Explain.

b. If the manager is able to obtain an additional 100 pounds of material at the usual price, what impact would that have on the optimal value of the objective function?

c. If the manager is able to obtain an additional 100 pounds of material but has to pay a premium of 5 cents a pound, what will the net profit be?

d. If knitting machines operate for 10 hours a day, and one of the machines will be out of service for two and a half days, what impact will this have on the optimal value of Z?

16. The A-B-C department of a large company makes three products (A, B, and C). The department is preparing for its final run next week, which is just before the annual two-week vacation during which the entire department shuts down. The manager wants to use up existing stocks of the three raw materials used to fabricate products A, B, and C.

She has formulated the LP model and obtained an optimal solution using Excel, which is displayed in Table 3-5.

A = quantity of product A
B = quantity of product B
C = quantity of product C

maximize $Z = 12A + 15B + 14C$

subject to

Material 1	$3A + 5B + 8C \leq 720$ pounds
Material 2	$2A + 3C \leq 600$ pounds
Material 3	$4A + 6B + 4C \leq 640$ pounds
	$A, B, \text{and } C \geq 0$

As a staff person, the manager has asked you to answer each of the following questions concerning the final solution:

a. Although product B is the most profitable, and product A the least profitable, the solution calls for making none of B but 112 of A. Why?

b. If B's profit per unit could be increased to \$18, how much B would be produced? Explain how you obtained your answer.

c. What is the range of feasibility for the material 3 RHS?

d. By how much would profit increase if an additional 100 pounds of material 3 could be obtained as its usual cost? What if the amount were an additional 400 pounds?

e. Do you see any difficulty in allowing the A-B-C department to take 200 pounds of material 2? Explain.

f. What would be the value of the objective function be if 20 additional pounds of material 1 could be obtained without paying a premium for it?

g. Suppose the manager wants to evaluate the effect of cost changes that would reduce each of the objective function coefficients by 1. Would these changes be within the range of optimality for multiple changes?

h. If the manager can obtain an additional 20 pounds of materials 1 and 3, is that within the range of feasibility?

17. The manager in the server problem discussed in the chapter is considering scheduling overtime in either the assembly or the inspection department.

a. Which department would be the best choice for overtime? Why? (See Exhibits 3-4 and 3-5)

b. Suppose overtime will cost \$7 per hour over the current rate. Does it make sense to schedule overtime? If so, how much overtime, and what effect would there be on total profit by scheduling this overtime?

TABLE 3-5 Excel Reports for Problem 16

A. Answer Report

Target Cell (Max)

Cell	Name	Original Value	Final Value
$E$5	Profit Total	0	2016

Adjustable Cells

Cell	Name	Original Value	Final Value
$B$4	Quantities Product A	0	112
$C$4	Quantities Product B	0	0
$D$4	Quantities Product C	0	48

Constraints

Cell	Name	Cell Value	Formula	Status	Slack
$E$7	Material 1 constraint Usage	720	$E$7<=$F$7	Binding	0
$E$8	Material 2 constraint Usage	368	$E$8<=$F$8	Not Binding	232
$E$9	Material 3 constraint Usage	640	$E$9<=$F$9	Binding	0
$B$4	Quantities Product A	112	$B$4>=0	Not Binding	112
$C$4	Quantities Product B	0	$C$4>=0	Binding	0
$D$4	Quantities Product C	48	$D$4>=0	Not binding	48

B. Sensitivity Report

Adjustable Cells

Cell	Name	Final Value	Reduced Cost	Objective Coefficient	Allowable Increase	Allowable Decrease
$B$4	Quantities Product A	112	0	12	2	2.285714286
$C$4	Quantities Product B	0	−3.2	15	3.2	1E+30
$D$4	Quantities Product C	48	0	14	18	2

Constraints

Cell	Name	Final Value	Shadow Price	Constraint R. H. Side	Allowable Increase	Allowable Decrease
$E$7	Material 1 constraint Usage	720	0.4	720	560	240
$E$8	Material 2 constraint Usage	368	0	600	1E+30	232
$E$9	Material 3 constraint Usage	640	2.7	640	320	280

18. Given this problem and its solution from Excel summarized in Table 3-6:

$$\text{minimize} \quad Z = 10x_1 + 3x_2$$

subject to

$$1 \quad 2x_1 + 1x_2 \geq 80 \quad (A)$$
$$2 \quad 2x_1 + 4x_2 \geq 200 \quad (B)$$

   a. Determine the range of optimality or the range of insignificance (whichever is appropriate) for each decision variable.
   b. Determine the range of feasibility for each of the constraints.

19. Given this problem and the Excel output given in Table 3-7:

$$\text{minimize} \quad Z = 20x_1 + 12x_2 + 18x_3$$

subject to

$$1 \quad x_1 + x_2 + x_3 \geq 25 \quad (A)$$
$$2 \quad 2x_1 + x_2 \leq 52 \quad (B)$$
$$3 \quad x_3 \geq 5 \quad (C)$$
$$x_1, x_2, x_3 \geq 0$$

   a. What are the optimal values of x_1, x_2, x_3, and Z?
   b. What impact on the solution would a decrease of 10 units in the RHS of the first constraint have?
   c. If the first constraint could be decreased by 10 units at a cost per unit of $15, would it be worthwhile to do so? Explain.
   d. What change in the coefficient of x_1 in the objective function would cause it to come into solution?
   e. If the cost coefficient of x_3 decreased by $5, what impact would that have on the quantities and on the value of the objective function in the final solution?

20. The manager of the Happy Dog Company, Sam Smart, has developed this LP model:

x_1 = quantity of regular blend
x_2 = quantity of extra blend
x_3 = quantity of puppy delite

$$\text{maximize} \quad Z = .20x_1 + .18x_2 + .25x_3$$

subject to

$$\text{K9} \quad \tfrac{1}{3}x_1 + \tfrac{1}{2}x_2 \leq 1500 \text{ pounds}$$
$$\text{K8} \quad \tfrac{1}{3}x_1 + \tfrac{1}{4}x_2 + \tfrac{1}{10}x_3 \leq 1000 \text{ pounds}$$
$$\text{K1} \quad \tfrac{1}{3}x_1 + \tfrac{1}{4}x_2 + \tfrac{9}{10}x_3 \leq 1000 \text{ pounds}$$
$$x_1, x_2, x_3 \geq 0$$

The final solution is given in the Excel output in Table 3-8.

   a. What is the marginal value of a pound of K9? Over what range is that value valid?
   b. By how much would profit decrease if there was one less pound of K1 available?
   c. The manager believes it is possible to increase the profit per pound of puppy delite to $0.40. Would that alter the optimal solution? Explain.
   d. If the profit per unit of the extra blend dropped to $0.16 a pound, would the optimal quantities of the variables in solution change? Would the optimal value of the objective function change? If so, would its new value be?
   e. If the unit profits were changed to $0.22 for regular blend, $0.20 for extra blend, and $0.26 for puppy delite, would these changes be within the range of optimality for multiple changes?

21. A firm makes four products. Each product requires material, labour, and machine time. A linear programming model has been developed to describe the situation:

$$\text{maximize} \quad Z = 12x_1 + 10x_2 + 15x_3 + 11x_4 \quad \text{(profit)}$$

subject to

$$\text{Material} \quad 5x_1 + 3x_2 + 4x_3 + 2x_4 \leq 240 \text{ pounds}$$
$$\text{Machine} \quad 6x_1 + 8x_2 + 2x_3 + 3x_4 \leq 240 \text{ hours}$$
$$\text{Labour} \quad 2x_1 + 3x_2 + 3x_3 + 2x_4 \leq 180 \text{ hours}$$
$$x_1, x_2, x_3 \leq 0$$

where

x_1 = quantity of product 1
x_2 = quantity of product 2
x_3 = quantity of product 3
x_4 = quantity of product 4

The optimal solution is given in the Excel output in Table 3-9.

   a. The manager is concerned because none of product 1 is called for in the optimal solution. At what profit per unit would product 1 come into the solution?
   b. What is the marginal value of an hour of machine time? Over what range of machine time is this amount valid?
   c. The manager can secure additional labour hours by the use of overtime. This involves paying a premium of $2 per hour. How much overtime can be effectively used, and what will the *net* total profit be if that amount of overtime is scheduled?

TABLE 3-6 Excel Reports for Problem 18

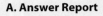

A. Answer Report

Target Cell (Min)

Cell	Name	Original Value	Final Value
$D$5	Cost Total	240	240

Adjustable Cells

Cell	Name	Original Value	Final Value
$B$4	Quantities Product I	0	0
$C$4	Quantities Product II	80	80

Constraints

Cell	Name	Cell Value	Formula	Status	Slack
$D$7	Material A constraint Usage	80	$D$7>=$E$7	Binding	0
$D$8	Material B constraint Usage	320	$D$8>=$E$8	Not Binding	120
$B$4	Quantities Product I	0	$B$4>=0	Binding	0
$C$4	Quantities Product II	80	$C$4>=0	Not Binding	80

B. Sensitivity Report

Adjustable Cells

Cell	Name	Final Value	Reduced Cost	Objective Coefficient	Allowable Increase	Allowable Decrease
$B$4	Quantities Product I	0	4	10	1E + 30	4
$C$4	Quantities Product II	80	0	3	2	3

Constraints

Cell	Name	Final Value	Shadow Price	Constraint R. H. Side	Allowable Increase	Allowable Decrease
$D$7	Material A constraint Usage	80	3	80	1E+30	30
$D$8	Material B constraint Usage	320	0	200	120	1E+30

TABLE 3-7 Excel Reports for Problem 19

A. Answer Report

Target Cell (Min)

Cell	Name	Original Value	Final Value
$E$5	Cost Total	450	330

Adjustable Cells

Cell	Name	Original Value	Final Value
$B$4	Quantities Product x_1	0	0
$C$4	Quantities Product x_2	0	20
$D$4	Quantities Product x_3	25	5

Constraints

Cell	Name	Cell Value	Formula	Status	Slack
$E$7	Material A constraint Usage	25	$E$7 >= $F$7	Binding	0
$E$8	Material B constraint Usage	0	$E$8 <= $F$8	Not Binding	52
$E$9	Material C constraint Usage	5	$E$9 >= $F$9	Binding	0
$B$4	Quantities Product x_1	0	$B$4 >= 0	Binding	0
$C$4	Quantities Product x_2	20	$C$4 >= 0	Not Binding	20
$D$4	Quantities Product x_3	5	$D$4 >= 0	Not Binding	5

B. Sensitivity Report

Cell	Name	Final Value	Reduced Cost	Objective Coefficient	Allowable Increase	Allowable Decrease
$B$4	Quantities Product x_1	0	8.000000001	20	1E + 30	8.000000001
$C$4	Quantities Product x_2	20	0	12	6	12
$D$4	Quantities Product x_3	5	0	18	1E + 30	6

Cell	Name	Final Value	Shadow Price	Constraint R. H. Side	Allowable Increase	Allowable Decrease
$E$7	Material A constraint Usage	25	12	25	1E + 30	20
$E$8	Material B constraint Usage	0	0	52	1E + 30	52
$E$9	Material C constraint Usage	5	6	5	20	5

TABLE 3-8 Excel Reports for Problem 20

A. Answer Report

Target Cell (Max)

Cell	Name	Original Value	Final Value
\$E\$5	Profit Total	660.00003	660.00003

Adjustable Cells

Cell	Name	Original Value	Final Value
\$B\$4	Quantities Regular	1500.00015	1500.00015
\$C\$4	Quantities Extra	2000	2000
\$D\$4	Quantities Puppy delite	0	0

Constraints

Cell	Name	Cell Value	Formula	Status	Slack
\$E\$7	K9 Usage	1500	\$E\$7 <= \$F\$7	Binding	0
\$E\$8	K8 Usage	1000	\$E\$8 <= \$F\$8	Binding	0
\$E\$9	K1 Usage	1000	\$E\$9 <= \$F\$9	Binding	0
\$B\$4	Quantities Regular	1500.00015	\$B\$4 >= 0	Not Binding	1500.00015
\$C\$4	Quantities Extra	2000	\$C\$4 >= 0	Not Binding	2000
\$D\$4	Quantities Puppy delite	0	\$D\$4 >= 0	Binding	0

B. Sensitivity Report

Adjustable Cells

Cell	Name	Final Value	Reduced Cost	Objective Coefficient	Allowable Increase	Allowable Decrease
\$B\$4	Quantities Regular	1500.00015	0	0.2	0.039999976	0.03370372
\$C\$4	Quantities Extra	2000	0	0.18	0.050555586	0.029999985
\$D\$4	Quantities Puppy delite	0	−0.182000108	0.25	0.182000108	1E + 30

Constraints

Cell	Name	Final Value	Shadow Price	Constraint R. H. Side	Allowable Increase	Allowable Decrease
\$E\$7	K9 Usage	1500	0.11999994	1500	500	500
\$E\$8	K8 Usage	1000	0	1000	1E + 30	1.42109E − 13
\$E\$9	K1 Usage	1000	0.48000012	1000	1.42109E − 13	250

TABLE 3-9 Excel Reports for Problem 21

A. Answer Report
Target Cell (Max)

Cell	Name	Original Value	Final Value
$F$5	Profit Total	972	972

Adjustable Cells

Cell	Name	Original Value	Final Value
$B$4	Quantities Product I	1.33227E − 14	0
$C$4	Quantities Product II	0	0
$D$4	Quantities Product III	12	12
$E$4	Quantities Product IV	72	72

Constraints

Cell	Name	Cell Value	Formula	Status	Slack
$F$7	Material Usage	192	$F$7 <= $G$7	Not Binding	48
$F$8	Machine Usage	240	$F$8 <= $G$8	Binding	0
$F$9	Labour Usage	180	$F$9 <= $G$9	Binding	0
$B$4	Quantities Product I	0	$B$4 >= 0	Binding	0
$C$4	Quantities Product II	0	$C$4 >= 0	Binding	0
$D$4	Quantities Product III	12	$D$4 >= 0	Not Binding	12
$E$4	Quantities Product IV	72	$E$4 >= 0	Not Binding	72

B. Sensitivity Report
Adjustable Cells

Cell	Name	Final Value	Reduced Cost	Objective Coefficient	Allowable Increase	Allowable Decrease
$B$4	Quantities Product I	0	−0.8	12	0.8	1E + 30
$C$4	Quantities Product II	0	−8.6	10	8.6	1E + 30
$D$4	Quantities Product III	12	0	15	0.666666667	7.666666667
$E$4	Quantities Product IV	72	0	11	11.5	0.285714286

Constraints

Cell	Name	Final Value	Shadow Price	Constraint R. H. Side	Allowable Increase	Allowable Decrease
$F$7	Material Usage	192	0	240	1E + 30	48
$F$8	Machine Usage	240	0.6	240	30	120
$F$9	Labour Usage	180	4.6	180	30	20

22. A garden store prepares various grades of pine bark for mulch: nuggets (x_1), mini-nuggets (x_2), and chips (x_3). The process requires pine bark, machine time, labour time, and storage space. The following linear programming model has been developed:

maximize $Z = 9x_1 + 9x_2 + 6x_3$ (profit)

subject to

Bark $5x_1 + 6x_2 + 3x_3 \leq 600$ pounds
Machine $2x_1 + 4x_2 + 5x_3 \leq 660$ minutes
Labour $2x_1 + 4x_2 + 3x_3 \leq 480$ hours
Storage $1x_1 + 1x_2 + 1x_3 \leq 150$ bags
$x_1, x_2, x_3 \geq 0$

In addition, the optimal solution is summarized in the Excel output in Table 3-10.

a. What is the marginal value of a pound of pine bark? Over what range is this value valid?
b. What is the maximum price the store would be justified in paying for additional storage space?
c. What is the marginal value of labour? Over what range is this value in effect?
d. The manager obtained additional machine time through better scheduling. How much additional machine time can be effectively used for this operation? Why?
e. If the manager can obtain *either* additional pine bark *or* additional storage space, which one should be chosen and how much should be obtained (assuming additional quantities cost the same as usual)?
f. If a change in the chip operation would increase the profit on chips from \$6 per bag to \$7 per bag, would the optimal quantities change? Would the value of the objective function change? If so, what would the new value(s) be?

23. A firm produces jars of chilled fruit that are sold to restaurants. Three varieties of fruit are sold: California mix (x_1), Florida mix (x_2), and Hawaiian mix (x_3). A linear programming model for the process is

maximize $Z = 4x_1 + 3x_2 + 6x_3$ (profit)

subject to

Oranges $3x_1 + 2x_2 + 1x_3 \leq 920$ pounds
Grapefruit $2x_1 + 2x_2 + 2x_3 \leq 900$ pounds
Pineapple $1x_1 + 2x_2 + 3x_3 \leq 930$ pounds
Peeling/cutting $1.2x_1 + 1.4x_2 + 1.5x_3 \leq 1260$ minutes
Mixing/packaging $1x_1 + 2x_2 + 1x_3 \leq 600$ minutes
$x_1, x_2, x_3 \geq 0$

The optimal solution is summarized in the Excel output in Table 3-11.

a. The equipment used for peeling and cutting must be replaced. The new equipment will have a capacity of only 1200 minutes. What impact will this change have on the optimal values of the decision variables and on profit?
b. What would the unit profit on the Florida mix have to be before it would become profitable to produce?
c. If management had a choice of obtaining more oranges or more pineapples, which one should be chosen? Why?
d. Management has just learned that an additional 50 pounds of pineapples are on hand. What will the new objective function be?
e. Management is considering making changes that will cause the profit on the Hawaiian mix to be \$8 per unit. Would this affect the solution? Will it affect the optimal value of the objective function?
f. Management is considering a change in equipment that would result in increasing the profit on the Hawaiian mix to \$8 per unit but result in decreasing the profit on the California mix by \$1. Would these changes be within the range of optimality? If so, how much would the optimal profit change?

24. Special D, Inc. is a new firm that is engaged in recycling. Its main facility uses a three-step system to process beverage containers. A consultant has developed the following LP model of the process:

maximize $Z = 14Q + 11R + 15T$ (revenue)

subject to

Sorting $2.4Q + 3.0R + 4.0T \leq 960$ minutes
Crushing $2.5Q + 1.8R + 2.4T \leq 607$ minutes
Packing $12Q + 18R + 24T \leq 3600$ minutes
$Q, R, \text{and } T \geq 0$

The consultant has also included an Excel output of sensitivity analysis, shown in Table 3-12.
Answer these questions using the information in Table 3-12:

a. Which decision variables are in the final solution? What are their optimal values?
b. Find the range of optimality for the variables that are in the final solution.
c. Find the range of insignificance for *R*.

TABLE 3-10 Excel Reports for Problem 22

A. Answer Report

Target Cell (Max)

Cell	Name	Original Value	Final Value
$E$5	Profit Total	0	1125

Adjustable Cells

Cell	Name	Original Value	Final Value
$B$4	Quantities Nuggets	0	75
$C$4	Quantities Mini-nuggets	0	0
$D$4	Quantities Chips	0	75

Constraints

Cell	Name	Cell Value	Formula	Status	Slack
$E$7	Bark Usage	600	$E$7 <= $F$7	Binding	0
$E$8	Machine Usage	525	$E$8 <= $F$8	Not Binding	135
$E$9	Labour Usage	375	$E$9 <= $F$9	Not Binding	105
$E$10	Storage Usage	150	$E$10 <= $F$10	Binding	0
$B$4	Quantities Nuggets	75	$B$4 >= 0	Not Binding	75
$C$4	Quantities Mini-nuggets	0	$C$4 >= 0	Binding	0
$D$4	Quantities Chips	75	$D$4 >= 0	Not Binding	75

B. Sensitivity Report

Adjustable Cells

Cell	Name	Final Value	Reduced Cost	Objective Coefficient	Allowable Increase	Allowable Decrease
$B$4	Quantities Nuggets	75	0	9	1	1
$C$4	Quantities Mini-nuggets	0	−1.5	9	1.5	1E + 30
$D$4	Quantities Chips	75	0	6	3	0.6

Constraints

Cell	Name	Final Value	Shadow Price	Constraint R. H. Side	Allowable Increase	Allowable Decrease
$E$7	Bark Usage	600	1.5	600	150	90
$E$8	Machine Usage	525	0	660	1E + 30	135
$E$9	Labour Usage	375	0	480	1E + 30	105
$E$10	Storage Usage	150	1.5	150	14.21052632	30

TABLE 3-11 Excel Reports for Problem 23

A. Answer Report

Target Cell (Max)

Cell	Name	Original Value	Final Value
$E$5	Profit Total	0	2280

Adjustable Cells

Cell	Name	Original Value	Final Value
$B$4	Quantities California mix	0	210
$C$4	Quantities Florida mix	0	0
$D$4	Quantities Hawaiian mix	0	240

Constraints

Cell	Name	Cell Value	Formula	Status	Slack
$E$7	Oranges Usage	870	$E$7 <= $F$7	Not Binding	50
$E$8	Grapefruit Usage	900	$E$8 <= $F$8	Binding	0
$E$9	Pineapple Usage	930	$E$9 <= $F$9	Binding	0
$E$10	Peeling/cutting Usage	612	$E$10 <= $F$10	Not Binding	648
$E$11	Mixing/packaging Usage	450	$E$11 <= $F$11	Not Binding	150
$B$4	Quantities California mix	210	$B$4 >= 0	Not Binding	210
$C$4	Quantities Florida mix	0	$C$4 >= 0	Binding	0
$D$4	Quantities Hawaiian mix	240	$D$4 >= 0	Not Binding	240

B. Sensitivity Report

Adjustable Cells

Cell	Name	Final Value	Reduced Cost	Objective Coefficient	Allowable Increase	Allowable Decrease
$B$4	Quantities California mix	210	0	4	2	2
$C$4	Quantities Florida mix	0	−2	3	2	1E + 30
$D$4	Quantities Hawaiian mix	240	0	6	6	2

Constraints

Cell	Name	Final Value	Shadow Price	Constraint R. H. Side	Allowable Increase	Allowable Decrease
$E$7	Oranges Usage	870	0	920	1E + 30	50
$E$8	Grapefruit Usage	900	1.5	900	25	280
$E$9	Pineapple Usage	930	1	930	420	50
$E$10	Peeling/cutting Usage	612	0	1260	1E + 30	648
$E$11	Mixing/packaging Usage	450	0	600	1E + 30	150

TABLE 3-12 Excel Reports for Problem 24

A. Answer Report

Target Cell (Max)

Cell	Name	Original Value	Final Value
$E$5	Profit Total	0	3485

Adjustable Cells

Cell	Name	Original Value	Final Value
$B$4	Quantities Q	0	190
$C$4	Quantities R	0	0
$D$4	Quantities T	0	55

Constraints

Cell	Name	Cell Value	Formula	Status	Slack
$E$7	Sorting constraint Usage	676	$E$7 <= $F$7	Not Binding	284
$E$8	Crushing constraint Usage	607	$E$8 <= $F$8	Binding	0
$E$9	Packing constraint Usage	3600	$E$9 <= $F$9	Binding	0
$B$4	Quantities Q	190	$B$4 >= 0	Not Binding	190
$C$4	Quantities R	0	$C$4 >= 0	Binding	0
$D$4	Quantities T	55	$D$4 >= 0	Not Binding	55

B. Sensitivity Report

Adjustable Cells

Cell	Name	Final Value	Reduced Cost	Objective Coefficient	Allowable Increase	Allowable Decrease
$B$4	Quantities Q	190	0	14	1.625	6.5
$C$4	Quantities R	0	−0.25	11	0.25	1E + 30
$D$4	Quantities T	55	0	15	13	0.333333333

Constraints

Cell	Name	Final Value	Shadow Price	Constraint R. H. Side	Allowable Increase	Allowable Decrease
$E$7	Sorting constraint Usage	676	0	960	1E + 30	284
$E$8	Crushing constraint Usage	607	5	607	143	247
$E$9	Packing constraint Usage	3600	0.125	3600	2089.811321	686.4

d. Identify the shadow price for each constraint.
e. Determine the range over which each shadow price is valid.
f. By how much would revenue decrease if sorting time was reduced to 900 minutes? How much would revenue increase if sorting time was increased to 1269 minutes?
g. What effect would an increase of $2 in the revenue per unit of *T* have on the optimal value of *T*? On the total revenue?
h. Would an increase of $1 in the revenue per unit of *R* have any impact on the optimal solution? Explain.
i. If you could obtain additional quantities of one resource (either sorting, crushing, or packing) at no additional cost, and your goal was to achieve the greatest increase in revenue, which resource would you add, and how much of it would you add? Explain.

25. Fashion Designs produces four clothing products in one of its factories. The following LP model has been developed and solved using Excel.

x_1 = weekly quantity of slacks
x_2 = weekly quantity of dresses
x_3 = weekly quantity of skirts
x_4 = weekly quantity of blouses

maximize $Z = 15x_1 + 15x_2 + 12x_3 + 16x_4$ (profit)

subject to

Cutting	$x_1 + 2x_2 + 4x_3 + x_4 \le$	800 hours per week
Sewing	$4x_1 + 2x_2 + 3x_4 \le$	700 hours per week
Inspecting	$2x_1 + 2x_2 + x_3 + x_4 \le$	600 minutes per week
Packing	$3x_1 + 2x_2 + 2x_3 \le$	660 minutes per week
	$x_1, x_2, x_3, x_4 \ge 0$	

The results are summarized in Table 3-13.

a. Which departments have capacities that limit output? Explain
b. The plant manager is considering scheduling overtime. Which department or departments should be excluded from consideration? Why?
c. What is the marginal value of overtime scheduled in the cutting department? How much overtime could be effectively used?
d. Overtime costs the company a premium of $3 per hour over regular costs. If one department is scheduled for overtime, which one should be scheduled, and how much overtime can be effectively used? What would the revised optimal value of the objective function be, after an allowance for the premium?
e. If the unit profit on x_3 dropped by 50 percent, how would that affect the optimal values of the decision variables and the optimal value of the objective function?

26. Serious Toys, Unlimited, produces three types of building blocks for preschoolers. Recently, the company underwent a major reorganization of its manufacturing facility and a restructuring of its prices. As a result, a new linear programming model has been formulated to describe the situation:

A = number of advanced sets
B = number of beginner sets
C = number of intermediate sets

maximize $Z = 1.2A + 1.6B + 1.4C$ (profit)

subject to

Plastic	$6A + 5B + 3C \le$	300 pounds
Labour	$9A + 4B + 5C \le$	280 minutes
Machine	$2A + 8B + 4C \le$	320 minutes
B	$B \ge$	18 sets
	$A, B, C \ge 0$	

The model has been processed through Excel. The results are summarized in Table 3-14.

a. How would you interpret the shadow price of 0.2 for labour constraint?
b. What is the range of feasibility for the RHS of the labour constraint?
c. If the amount of labour available were to increase by 60 minutes per hour, would the optimal quantities of the decision variables change? Would the optimal profit change?
d. If machine time increased by 50 minutes, by how much would the profit increase?
e. If machine time increased by 100 minutes, by how much would the profit increase?
f. How much would another 10 pounds of plastic per hour be worth in terms of increased profit? Explain.
g. If the profit per unit on advanced sets increased by 70 percent, would that affect the optimal solution? Explain.

TABLE 3-13 Excel Reports for Problem 25

A. Answer Report

Target Cell (Max)

Cell	Name	Original Value	Final Value
$F$5	Profit Total	0	5508.333333

Adjustable Cells

Cell	Name	Original Value	Final Value
$B$4	Quantities Slacks	0	0
$C$4	Quantities Dresses	0	225
$D$4	Quantities Skirts	0	66.66666667
$E$4	Quantities Blouses	0	83.33333333

Constraints

Cell	Name	Cell Value	Formula	Status	Slack
$F$7	Cutting constraint Usage	800	$F$7 <= $G$7	Binding	0
$F$8	Sewing constraint Usage	700	$F$8 <= $G$8	Binding	0
$F$9	Inspecting constraint Usage	600	$F$9 <= $G$9	Binding	0
$F$10	Packing constraint Usage	583.3333333	$F$10 <= $G$10	Not Binding	76.66666667
$B$4	Quantities Slacks	0	$B$4 >= 0	Binding	0
$C$4	Quantities Dresses	225	$C$4 >= 0	Not Binding	225
$D$4	Quantities Skirts	66.66666667	$D$4 >= 0	Not Binding	66.66666667
$E$4	Quantities Blouses	83.33333333	$E$4 >= 0	Not Binding	83.33333333

B. Sensitivity Report

Adjustable Cells

Cell	Name	Final Value	Reduced Cost	Objective Coefficient	Allowable Increase	Allowable Decrease
$B$4	Quantities Slacks	0	−5.583333333	15	5.583333333	1E + 30
$C$4	Quantities Dresses	225	0	15	11.66666667	0.333333333
$D$4	Quantities Skirts	66.66666667	0	12	1	8.75
$E$4	Quantities Blouses	83.33333333	0	16	0.5	6.7

Constraints

Cell	Name	Final Value	Shadow Price	Constraint R. H. Side	Allowable Increase	Allowable Decrease
$F$7	Cutting constraint Usage	800	2.916666667	800	460	200
$F$8	Sewing constraint Usage	700	4.25	700	900	153.3333333
$F$9	Inspecting constraint Usage	600	0.333333333	600	57.5	225
$F$10	Packing constraint Usage	583.3333333	0	660	1E + 30	76.66666667

TABLE 3-14 Excel Reports for Problem 26

A. Answer Report

Target Cell (Max)

Cell	Name	Original Value	Final Value
$E$5	Profit Total	0	88

Adjustable Cells

Cell	Name	Original Value	Final Value
$B$4	Quantities Advanced Sets	0	0
$C$4	Quantities Beginner sets	0	20
$D$4	Quantities Intermediate sets	0	40

Constraints

Cell	Name	Cell Value	Formula	Status	Slack
$E$7	Plastic Usage	200	$E$7 < = $F$7	Not Binding	80
$E$8	Labour Usage	280	$E$8 < = $F$8	Binding	0
$E$9	Machine Usage	320	$E$9 < = $F$9	Binding	0
$B$4	Quantities Advanced Sets	0	$B$4 > = 0	Binding	0
$C$4	Quantities Beginner Sets	20	$C$4 > = 0	Not Binding	20
$D$4	Quantities Intermediate sets	40	$D$4 > = 0	Not Binding	40

B. Sensitivity Report

Adjustable Cells

Cell	Name	Final Value	Reduced Cost	Objective Coefficient	Allowable Increase	Allowable Decrease
$B$4	Quantities Advanced Sets	0	−0.8	1.2	0.8	1E + 30
$C$4	Quantities Beginner sets	20	0	1.6	0.738461538	0.48
$D$4	Quantities Intermediate sets	40	0	1.4	0.6	0.3

Constraints

Cell	Name	Final Value	Shadow Price	Constraint R. H. Side	Allowable Increase	Allowable Decrease
$E$7	Plastic Usage	220	0	300	1E + 30	80
$E$8	Labour Usage	280	0.2	280	120	120
$E$9	Machine Usage	320	0.1	320	147.6923077	96

27. Dog Daze Manufacturing produces a variety of dog food products. These are made in batches and then kept in inventory that is used to fill orders from kennels and pet stores. The manager has helped to develop a linear programming model of the process for the company's three raw material inputs: x_1, x_2, x_3:

x_1 = bags of raw material 1
x_2 = bags of raw material 2
x_3 = bags of raw material 3

minimize $Z = 38x_1 + 19x_2 + 60x_3$ (cost)

subject to

Protein $2.5x_1 + 4x_2 + 3x_3 \geq 794$ pounds
Fibre $3x_1 + 2x_2 + 4x_3 \geq 908$ pounds
Fat $2x_1 + x_2 + 2x_3 \geq 600$ pounds
$x_1, x_2, x_3 \geq 0$

The manager has obtained the Excel output of sensitivity analysis for the model. The results are summarized in the answers and sensitivity reports given in Table 3-15.

Answer the following questions about the model:

a. Which constraints are binding on the solution? How do you know?
b. What does the reduced cost of 22 indicate?
c. How do you interpret the 608 in the Allowable Increase section of the fibre constraint?
d. Determine the range of optimality for the objective function coefficients of x_1 and x_2.
e. What does the shadow price of 19 reveal?
f. What is the range of feasibility for the fat constraint's RHS?
g. Would a decrease to 575 for the RHS of the fat constraint affect the optimal value of the objective function? If so, by how much?
h. The manager is considering reducing each RHS by 9 percent and asks you to provide information on how that would impact the total cost. What would you need to do? Why?

28. The manager of the server problem analyzed in this chapter wants to reconsider adding a third server model to the product line. After re-evaluating the third server model, the manager now estimates that it will yield a profit of $80 per unit, with resource requirements of 7 hours of assembly time, 3 hours of inspection time, and 5 cubic feet of storage space. Determine if the third model would come into the solution.

29. CanWood Suites is an all-suite, family-based hotel that offers its customers accommodations providing comfort, privacy, and the warmth of home. The suites include spacious studios, one bedroom suites, and two bedroom suites with fully equipped kitchens and numerous other amenities and services. The company offers the general public three rate types at the time of reservation. These are referred to as net direct rate (NDR), length of stay rate (LSR), and market rate (MKR). The profit per night for each rate type and suite category, the number of rooms available in each category of suites, and the management estimates of booking per day in each rate type are shown in Table 3-16.

The following LP model has been developed to determine the number of reservations to accept for each rate types and category of rooms to ensure a maximum daily profit per day.

x_1 = Number of bookings at the net direct rate allocated to studios.
x_2 = Number of bookings at the length of stay rate allocated to studios
x_3 = Number of bookings at the market rate allocated to studios
x_4 = Number of bookings at the net direct rate allocated to one-bedroom suites
x_5 = Number of bookings at the length of stay rate allocated to one-bedroom suites
x_6 = Number of bookings at the market rate allocated to one-bedroom suites
x_7 = Number of bookings at the net direct rate allocated to two-bedroom suites
x_8 = Number of bookings at the length of stay rate allocated to two-bedroom suites
x_9 = Number of bookings at the market rate allocated to two-bedroom suites

maximize $Z = 25x_1 + 27.5x_2 + 30x_3 + 30x_4 + 32.5x_5 + 35x_6 + 36x_7 + 38.5x_8 + 41x_9$

subject to

$x_1 + x_2 + x_3 \leq 100$ (availability of studio suites)
$x_4 + x_5 + x_6 \leq 85$ (availability of one bedroom suites)
$x_7 + x_8 + x_9 \leq 35$ (availability of two bedroom suites)
$x_1 + x_4 + x_7 \leq 100$ (NDR booking estimates)
$x_2 + x_5 + x_8 \leq 60$ (LSR booking estimates)
$x_3 + x_6 + x_9 \leq 80$ (MRK booking estimates)

All variables ≥ 0

TABLE 3-15 Excel Reports for Problem 27

A. Answer Report

Target Cell (Min)

Cell	Name	Original Value	Final Value
$E$5	Cost Total	0	11400

Adjustable Cells

Cell	Name	Original Value	Final Value
$B$4	Quantities Raw Material 1	0	292
$C$4	Quantities Raw Material 2	0	16
$D$4	Quantities Raw Material 3	0	0

Constraints

Cell	Name	Cell Value	Formula	Status	Slack
$E$7	Protein constraint Usage	794	$E$7 >= $F$7	Binding	0
$E$8	Fibre constraint Usage	908	$E$8 > = $F$8	Not Binding	608
$E$9	Fat constraint Usage	600	$E$9 > = $F$9	Binding	0
$B$4	Quantities Raw Material 1	292	$B$4 > = 0	Not Binding	292
$C$4	Quantities Raw Material 2	16	$C$4 > = 0	Not Binding	16
$D$4	Quantities Raw Material 3	0	$D$4 > = 0	Binding	0

B. Sensitivity Report

Adjustable Cells

Cell	Name	Final Value	Reduced Cost	Objective Coefficient	Allowable Increase	Allowable Decrease
$B$4	Quantities Raw Material 1	292	0	38	0	26.125
$C$4	Quantities Raw Material 2	16	0	19	41.8	0
$D$4	Quantities Raw Material 3	0	22	60	1E + 30	22

Constraints

Cell	Name	Final Value	Shadow Price	Constraint R. H. Side	Allowable Increase	Allowable Decrease
$E$7	Protein constraint Usage	794	0	794	1606	44
$E$8	Fibre constraint Usage	908	0	908	608	1E + 30
$E$9	Fat constraint Usage	600	19	600	35.2	401.5

TABLE 3-16 Excel Reports for Problem 29

Room Category	Net Profit per Night per Rate Types			Availability
	Net Direct Rate	Length of Stay Rate	Market Rate	
Studio	25	27.5	30	100
One-bedroom suite	30	32.5	35	85
Two-bedroom suite	36	38.5	41	35
Management demand estimates per day	100	60	80	

Solve the LP model with Excel Solver and use the computer output to answer the following questions.

a. What number of reservations should the company accept for each category of rate types?

b. CanWood Suites is considering offering an in-room movie incentive coupon for up to 10 bookings from customers willing to upgrade from the net direct rate to the market rate. Should the company offer this incentive given it costs $3.75 per coupon per booking? Explain.

c. CanWood Suites is considering reducing the number of rooms available for the general public to make them available to business customers at no additional cost. Would you recommend reducing the number of one-bedroom suites available or the number of two-bedroom suites? Explain.

d. Discuss how this model can be used to develop a plan for 7 successive days.

30. A large Canadian drug company, DrugCo, is considering extending incentive programs to its employees below the senior management ranks to encourage higher levels of performance. The company has devised an incentive plan for four groups of employees (group A, group B, group C, and group D) and has allocated an overall annual budget to this initiative. Management estimates an annual return in performance of 12 percent from employees in group A, 8.5 percent from employees in group B, 6.5 percent from employees in group C, and 11 percent from employees in group D. However, with this initiative, the company also runs the risk of having some employees engaged in questionable behaviour that can have an adverse effect. The company has developed a risk index for each group on a scale of 0 to 1, with a higher value indicating a riskier group. The risk index has been estimated to .6 for employees in group A, .35 for employees in group B, .25 for employees in group C, and .55 for employees in group D. It has been decided that at least 40 percent of the overall incentive program's expenses to be assigned to employees in groups A and C, no more than 35 percent of the overall expenses to be assigned to the total of employees in groups B and D, and an equal proportion of the overall expenses to be invested to employees in groups A and D.

a. Formulate an LP model that can be used to determine the amount of the overall budget to be assigned to each group of employees to minimize the overall risk index while maintaining an expected return in performance of at least 9 percent (HINT: define your decision variables as the proportion of the overall budget to be assigned to each group of employees and add a constraint that restricts their sum to be 1).

b. Would a change to 50 percent of the maximum proportion of the budget assigned to employees in groups B and D have an impact on the overall risk index? Explain.

c. What effect would a change to 10 percent of management's expected return in performance have on the overall risk index? Explain.

31. Assume that in Problem 30 the company seeks to maximize the employee return in performance and has set the overall risk to be less than or equal to 40 percent.

a. Reformulate the LP model and compare both solutions in terms of return in performance and risk.
b. At the current level of the shadow prices, what would the range of risk index of the company be to ensure at least the minimum level of return in performance found in part *a?* What is the maximum return in performance that can be expected in that range?

32. A local cable TV company would like to spend a monthly advertising budget of \$45 000 on a new multicultural TV program. Among its options are phone promotion, newspaper advertising, and promotion through emails. The company incurs a fixed cost of \$3500 to set up a phone promotion, \$8000 in the case of newspaper advertising, and \$1500 in the case of email promotion. The amount of the budget available to spend on phone promotion, excluding the fixed costs, cannot exceed 1.5 times the amount of budget to spend on newspaper advertising and email promotion excluding fixed costs. The management also decided that at least 20 percent of the budget must be spent on each type of promotion media. An index of exposure per dollar of advertising on a scale from 0 to 100 has been developed, with higher values implying a greater exposure. The value of the index is 50 for the newspaper advertising, 65 for phone promotion, and 80 for promotion through email. The company has formulated the following LP model that seeks to allocate the advertising budget among the three promotion vehicles to maximize the overall customer exposure.

x = dollars invested on phone promotion
y = dollars invested on newspaper advertising
z = dollars invested on email promotion

maximize $Z = 65x + 50y + 80z$

subject to

Budget constraint $x + y + z \leq 45\,000$
Maximum on budget to spend on phone promotion
$(x - 3500) \leq 1.5[(y - 8000) + (z - 1500)]$
Minimum budget on phone promotion
$x \geq .20 * 45\,000$
Minimum budget on news paper promotion
$y \geq .20 * 45\,000$
Minimum budget on emails promotion
$z \geq .20 * 45\,000$
$x, y, z \geq 0$

Solve this LP model with Excel Solver and use the computer output to answer the following questions:

a. How many dollars should the company invest in each promotion vehicle?
b. How should the company interpret the shadow price associated with the constraint on the maximum budget to spend on phone promotion?
c. Suppose the minimum budget on newspaper promotion is lowered to 18 percent. Would this change impact the objective function value? Explain.

33. The management of Serious Toys Unlimited is trying to determine the amount of each of the three types of preschooler building blocks to produce weekly to maximize its profits. The unit production of the advanced sets requires 45 minutes of labour time, 18 minutes of machine time, and 6 pounds of plastic. The unit production of the intermediate sets requires 30 minutes of labour time, 21 minutes of machine time, and 3 pounds of plastic. Finally, the unit production of the beginner sets requires 24 minutes of labour time, 33 minutes of machine time, and 5 pounds of plastic. The unit selling price is \$40 for the advanced set, \$35 for the intermediate set, and \$30 for the beginner set. Each week, up to 3500 pounds of plastic can be obtained at a unit cost of \$1.50 per pound, 320 hours of machine time are available, and ten workers work in the production line for 40 hours each. Additional labour time can be obtained by scheduling overtime at the cost of \$30 per hour. A maximum of 12 overtime hours per week can be scheduled per worker. Management estimates that the weekly demand is 200 units for the advanced set, 210 for the intermediate set, and 250 for the beginner set. However, advertising can also be used to stimulate the product demand. A single advertising promotion costs the company \$150 and increases the demand by 5 units for the advanced sets, 7 units for the intermediate sets, and 10 units for the beginner sets. The company is limited to up to 5 advertising promotions per week. Consider the following LP model developed for Serious Toys where:

x_1 = number of advanced sets produced each week
x_2 = number of intermediate sets produced each week
x_3 = number of beginner sets produced each week
T = number of hours of overtime used each week
P = number of pounds of plastic used each week

A = number of advertising promotions undertaken per week

maximize $Z = 40x_1 + 35x_2 + 30x_3 - 30T - 1.5P - 150A$

subject to

Advanced sets demand	$x_1 \le 200 + 5A$
Intermediate sets demand	$x_2 \le 210 + 7A$
Beginner sets demand	$x_3 \le 250 + 10A$
Labour hours available per week	$.75x_1 + .5x_2 + .4x_3 \le 400 + T$

$T \le 120$ hours overtime available per week

$6x_1 + 3x_2 + 5x_3 \le P$ pounds of plastic used per week

$P \le 3500$ pounds of plastic available per week

$A \le 5$ advertising promotion per week

$.3x_1 + .35x_2 + .55x_3 \le 320$ hours machine time available per week

$x_1, x_2, x_3, A, P, T \ge 0$

Solve this LP with Excel Solver and use the computer output to answer the following questions:

a. If each unit of beginner sets is now sold for the same price as a unit of intermediate sets, would the current basis remain optimal? Explain.

b. What should the selling price of an advanced set be for the company to consider producing it?

c. What is the most Serious Toys would be willing to pay for another pound of plastic?

d. How much would Serious Toys be willing to pay for another hour of machine time?

e. If the number of workers available is reduced to eight, what would the company's profits be?

Case 1: Red Brand Canners

On Monday, September 13, Mr. Mitchell Gordon, vice president of operations, asked the controller, the sales manager, and the production manager to meet with him to discuss the amount of tomato products to pack that season. The tomato crop, which had been purchased at planting, was beginning to arrive at the cannery, and packing operations would have to be started by the following Monday. Red Brand Canners was a medium-sized company that canned and distributed a variety of fruit and vegetable products under private brands in the western states.

Mr. William Cooper, the controller, and Mr. Charles Myers, the sales manager, were the first to arrive in Mr. Gordon's office. Dan Tucker, the production manager, came in a few minutes later and said that he had picked up Produce Inspection's latest estimate of the quality of the incoming tomatoes. According to their report, about 20 percent of the crop was Grade A quality, and the remaining portion of the 3-million-pound crop was Grade B.

Gordon asked Myers about the demand for tomato products for the coming year. Myers replied that they could sell all of the whole canned tomatoes they could produce. The expected demand for tomato juice and tomato paste, on the other hand, was limited. The sales manager then passed around the latest demand forecast, which is shown in Table 3-17. He reminded the group that the selling prices had been set in light of the long-term marketing strategy of the company and that the potential sales had been forecast at these prices.

Bill Cooper, after looking at Myers' estimates of demand, said that it looked like the company "should do quite well [on the tomato crop] this year." With the new accounting system that had been set up, he had been able to compute the contribution for each product, and according to his analysis the incremental profit on the whole tomatoes was greater than the incremental profit on any other tomato product. In May, after Red Brand had signed contracts agreeing to purchase the grower's production at an average delivered price of 6 cents per pound, Cooper had computed the tomato products' contributions (see Table 3-18).

Dan Tucker brought to Cooper's attention that although there was ample production capacity, it was impossible to produce all whole tomatoes since too small a portion of the tomato crop was "A" quality. Red Brand used a numerical scale to record the quality of both raw produce and prepared products. This scale ran from 0 to 10, the higher number representing better quality. According to this scale. "A" tomatoes averaged 9 points per pound and "B" tomatoes averaged 5 points per pound. Tucker noted

TABLE 3-17 Demand Forecasts

Product	Selling Price per Case	Demand Forecast (cases)
24—2½ whole tomatoes	$4.00	800 000
24—2½ choice peach halves	5.40	10 000
24—2½ peach nectar	4.60	5000
24—2½ tomato juice	4.50	50 000
24—2½ cooking apples	4.90	15 000
24—2½ tomato paste	3.80	80 000

that the minimum average input quality was 8 points per pound for canned whole tomatoes and 6 points per pound for juice. Paste could be made entirely from "B" grade tomatoes. This meant that whole tomato production was limited to 600 000 pounds.

Gordon stated that this was not a real limitation. He had been recently solicited to purchase 80 000 pounds of grade A tomatoes at 8½ cents per pound and at that time had turned down the offer. He felt, however, that the tomatoes were still available.

Myers, who had been doing some calculations, said that although he agreed that the company "should do quite well this year," it would not be by canning whole tomatoes. It seemed to him that the tomato cost should be allocated on the basis of quality and quantity rather than by quantity only, as Cooper had done. Therefore, he had recomputed the marginal profit on this basis (see Table 3-19), and from his results had concluded that Red Brand should use 2 000 000 pounds of the "B" tomatoes for paste and the remaining 400 000 pounds of "B" tomatoes and all of the "A" tomatoes for juice. If the demand expectations were realized, a contribution of $48 000 would be made on this year's tomato crop.

Discussion Questions

1. Explain why each of these is incorrect:
   a. Bill Cooper's statement to "use the entire crop for whole tomatoes. . . ."
   b. Charles Myer's reasoning, as described in the final paragraph.
2. Formulate the mathematical model that can be used to determine the optimal canning policy for this season's crop. Disregard Mitchell Gordon's idea of purchasing additional tomatoes. Define the decision variables in terms of pounds of tomatoes.
3. Solve your model and interpret the solution.
4. Given the solution to your model, would you recommend the purchase of additional tomatoes (up to 80 000 pounds)? If so, how much should be purchased?
5. Using your answer to the preceding question, reformulate the model, solve the reformulated model, and indicate how the additional tomatoes will be used.
6. (Refer to the model in Question 3.) Suppose Bill Cooper has just learned that the cost of grade B tomatoes should actually be double its current amount (due to an accounting error). Will this change alter the optimal values of the decision variables? Explain. Will it alter the value of the objective function? Explain.

TABLE 3-18 Product Item Profitability

Product	24—2½ Whole Tomatoes	24—2½ Choice Peach Halves	24—2½ Peach Nectar	24—2½ Tomato Juice	24—2½ Cooking Apples	24—2½ Tomato Paste
Selling price	$4.00	$5.40	$4.60	$4.50	$4.90	$3.80
Variable costs						
Direct labour	1.18	1.40	1.27	1.32	0.70	0.54
Variable overhead	0.24	0.32	0.23	0.36	0.22	0.26
Variable selling	0.40	0.30	0.40	0.85	0.28	0.38
Packaging material	0.70	0.56	0.60	0.65	0.70	0.77
Fruit*	1.08	1.80	1.70	1.20	0.90	1.50
Total variable costs	3.60	4.38	4.20	4.38	2.80	3.45
Contribution	0.40	1.02	0.40	0.12	1.10	0.35
Less allocated overhead	0.28	0.70	0.52	0.21	0.75	0.23
Net profit	0.12	0.32	(0.12)	(0.09)	0.35	0.12

*Product usage is as given below:

Product	Pounds per Case
Whole tomatoes	18
Peach halves	18
Peach nectar	17
Tomato juice	20
Cooking apples	27
Tomato paste	25

Case 2: Staffing Nurse Personnel

The dermatology clinic at the Ontario Women's College Hospital offers a wide variety of services and treatments to the community. Some of these include the removal of unwanted marks such as skin lesions or moles, the treatment of general dermatitis, acne, blistering diseases, and alopecia. Patients arrive at the clinic on an appointed schedule and as walk-in patients. Five registered nurses (RNs), three senior registered practical nurses (SRPNs), and five junior registered practical nurses (JRPNs) work in the clinic to move patients through the process in a timely way, as well as to administer care in the form of delivering services and providing instructions. The clinic's administrators are wondering whether they can still provide a high quality service to patients with a lower staffing level. The clinic serves about 100 to 150 patients per year and growth is expected in the foreseeable future. JRPNs are paid $23 000 per year, SRPNs are paid $28 000 per year, and RNs are paid $45 000 per year. To cover the responsibilities of the floor on a weekly basis, it was determined that the clinic required

TABLE 3-19 Marginal Analysis of Tomato Products

Z = cost per pound of Grade A tomatoes in cents

Y = cost per pound of Grade B tomatoes in cents

$$(600\,000 \text{ lb} \times Z) + (2\,400\,000 \text{ lb} \times Y)\ (3\,000\,000 \text{ lb} \times 6) \qquad (1)$$

$$\frac{Z}{9} = \frac{Y}{5} \qquad (2)$$

Z = 9.32 cents per pound

Y = 5.18 cents per pound

Product	Canned Whole Tomatoes	Tomato Juice	Tomato Paste
Selling price	$4.00	$4.50	$3.80
Variable cost (excluding tomato cost)	2.52	3.18	1.95
	$1.48	$1.32	$1.85
Tomato cost	1.49	1.24	1.30
Marginal profit	($0.01)	$0.08	$0.55

134 hours of JRPNs' time, 88 hours of SRPNs' time, and 138 hours of RNs' time. Each nurse works 40 hours per week and is paid for 52 weeks per year. For efficient operations, the clinic has determined that the minimum amount of total nurse time to be covered in a week is 360 hours. Because no other nurse can do an RN's work, the minimum amount of RNs' work per week has been set at 138 hours. It was also determined that the maximum amount of work that RNs can do is 360 hours per week, which theoretically covers all of the nursing work. The maximum amount of work time for JRPNs is 134 hours, because JRPNs cannot do any other nursing duties; and the maximum amount of work time per week for SRPN, is 222 hours, which is the time it takes to theoretically cover weekly SRPN tasks as well as JRPN tasks.

Managerial Report

1. Prepare a report for the senior administrators that would indicate the effective combination of nurses that would allow for all weekly clinic tasks to be covered while providing the lowest possible cost and meeting the operating constraints. Provide your LP model and indicate how many nurses the clinic should staff in each category. Provide a cost analysis of the current situation and the model solution on an hourly, weekly, and yearly basis. What will be the annual savings (or additional costs) in personnel cost if the solution from your model is implemented?
2. Perform a sensitivity analysis to answer the following questions, taken independently.
   a. If one additional SRPN is hired at a salary of $28 000, would the clinic still save money annually?
   b. What saving will result if one RN staff is removed from the payroll?
   c. What saving will result if one SRPN staff is removed from the payroll?
   d. What saving will result if one JRPN staff is added to the payroll?
3. If one wanted to perform such a study in a real-life setting, discuss some of the challenges that might be involved to develop the LP model included in your report and some of the limitations to account for in the study.

Source: Reprinted with permission of Aspen Publishers, Inc. Adapted from Charles H. Matthews, "Using Linear Programming to Minimize the Cost of Nurse Personnel," *Journal of Heath Care Finance,* Vol. 32(1), (2005), pp. 37–49. © 2005.

Case 3: Ottawa Catholic School Board

The Ottawa Catholic School Board has made the decision to close a number of its senior elementary schools (sixth, seventh, and eighth grades) at the end of this school year and reassign all of next year's students to the three remaining senior elementary schools. The school board provides busing for all students who must travel more than approximately a mile (1.6 kilometres). Therefore, the board wants a plan for reassigning the students that will minimize the total busing cost. The annual cost per student for busing from each of the six residential areas of the city to each of the schools is shown in Table 3-20 (along with other basic data for next year), where 0 indicates that busing is not needed and a dash indicates an infeasible assignment.

The school board also has imposed the restriction that each grade must constitute between 30 and 36 percent of each school's population. The Table 3-20 shows the percentage of each area's senior elementary school population for next year that falls into each of the three grades. The school attendance zone boundaries can be drawn so as to split any given area among more than one school, but assume that the percentages shown in the table will continue to hold for any partial assignment of an area to a school. You have been hired as a management science consultant to assist the school board in determining how many students in each area should be assigned to each school. Formulate and solve a linear programming model for this problem. Use your model to develop a managerial report presenting your findings to the following questions.

Managerial Report

Prepare a report to the school board providing answers to the following questions.

a. Determine the number of students assigned to each school, the unused capacity available at each school, the breakdown of each school's population per grade level, the busing costs per school, and the total busing costs.

b. Assume that, due to the ongoing road construction, the busing cost from area 6 would increase by the same percentage for all the schools. How large can this percentage be before the current optimal solution might no longer be optimal?

Assume that the school board has the option of adding temporary classrooms to increase the capacity of one or more of the schools. However, this is a costly move that the board would only consider if it would significantly

TABLE 3-20 Busing Needs

Area	Number of Students	Percentage in 6th Grade	Percentage in 7th Grade	Percentage in 8th Grade	Busing Cost ($/student)		
					School 1	School 2	School 3
1	450	32%	38%	30%	$300	$0	$700
2	600	37%	28%	35%	—	$400	$500
3	550	30%	32%	38%	$600	$300	$200
4	350	28%	40%	32%	$200	$500	—
5	500	39%	34%	27%	$0	—	$400
6	450	34%	28%	38%	$500	$300	$0
School capacity:					900	1100	1000

decrease busing costs. Each temporary classroom holds 20 students and has a leasing cost of $2500 per year. Would it be worthwhile to add a temporary classroom at each school? For each school where it is worthwhile to add any temporary classrooms, how many could be added before the shadow price would no longer be valid (assuming there is only one school receiving portable classrooms)? If it would be worthwhile to add temporary classrooms to more than one school, what are the combinations of the number to add for which the shadow prices would still be valid? Which of these combinations is best in terms of minimizing the total cost of busing students and leasing temporary classrooms?

Source: Based on a case study previously published in F. S. Hillier, M. S. Hillier, *Introduction to Management Science: A Modeling and Case Studies Approach with Spreadsheets*, 3rd ed., (Boston: McGraw-Hill Irwin, 2008).

Applications of Linear Programming

CHAPTER 4

LEARNING OBJECTIVES

After completing this chapter, you should be able to:

1. Formulate linear programming problems with different objectives.
2. Set up constraints that have unique structures.
3. Translate statements into constraint formulas.
4. Utilize Excel to solve a variety of linear programming problems.
5. Make managerial conclusions based on computer (Excel) output.
6. Explain at least two applications of linear programming.

CHAPTER OUTLINE

4.1 INTRODUCTION

There are a wide range of business problems that lend themselves to solution by linear programming techniques. This section briefly describes some of those problem types. The discussion is not meant to be all-inclusive. Rather, its purpose is to give a sense of the importance of LP techniques for managerial decision making and the apparent diversity of situations to which linear programming can be applied. For instance, the Modern Management Science Application, "Workforce Strategic Investment," describes the use of linear programming by human resource managers to cope with the problem of a shortage of skilled workers in the construction industry.

In Chapter 2, we formulated some basic linear programming problems. In this chapter, we will expand our discussion of problem formulation and illustrate a variety of linear programming applications to show that linear programming is a flexible decision-making tool that can assist the decision maker in a wide variety of circumstances. To show the richness and variety of applications involving linear programming problems, we will present applications from marketing, production, agriculture, and finance areas. In our discussion of these applications, first and foremost we emphasize accurate modelling of the real-world problem. Linear programming models always involve simplification of the real-world problem. In formulating a model, some of the assumptions of linear programming (additivity, divisibility, certainty, and proportionality) may be violated. In those cases, it may still be worthwhile to use linear programming provided that we understand the shortcomings of the model, test the model under different circumstances, and perform sensitivity analysis to see how the model reacts to the changes in the value of variables.

A critical question to answer is the degree of simplification in using a linear programming model to solve a real-world problem. In making this decision, we need to weight the potential gains from developing a more complicated model against the potential losses of not including a real-world complication. Although the model should reflect the real-world situation, incorporating every aspect of the problem could add unnecessary complications to the model. On the other hand, if the model is not simplified enough, either it cannot be formulated or it will unnecessarily increase the formulation and/or solution time. The analysts may disagree on how much simplification is necessary. The degree of simplification is generally based on judgment and experience of the analyst. We will start demonstrating the utility of linear programming models by showing a variety of applications. First we will demonstrate a product-mix problem.

4.2 PRODUCT-MIX PROBLEMS

Organizations often produce similar products or offer similar services that use the same resources (for example, labour, equipment, time, materials). Because of limits in the amounts of these resources that are available during any time period, a decision must be made concerning how much of each product to produce, or service to make available, during the time period that will be consistent with the goals of the organization. The basic question that can be answered using linear programming is what mix of output (or service) will maximize profit (revenue, etc.) given the availability of scarce resources?

The server problem presented in Chapter 3 is an example of a **product-mix problem.** In this section, we will give another example of a product-mix problem.

A MODERN MANAGEMENT SCIENCE APPLICATION: WORKFORCE STRATEGIC INVESTMENT

The construction industry in Canada, the United States, and other parts of the world has been facing several challenges, including a shortage of skilled workers. One of the key reasons for this issue is the absence of human resource management strategies for construction workers at project, corporate, regional, or industry levels. This application presents a framework to optimize the investment in, and to make the best use of, the available workforce with the intent to reduce project costs and improve schedule performance. A linear program model, entitled the Optimal Workforce Investment Model, is built to provide an optimization-based framework for matching supply and demand of construction labour more efficiently through training, recruitment, and allocation. Given a project schedule or demand pattern and the available pool of workers, the suggested model provides human resource managers a combined strategy for training the available workers and hiring additional workers. The implementation of the model to a large construction project revealed a benefit-to-cost ratio of 15:1.

Source: I.M. Srour, C.T. Haas, and D.P. Morton, "Linear Programming Approach to Optimize Strategic Investment in the Construction Workforce," *Journal of Construction Engineering and Management* vol. 32, no. 11 (November 2006), pp. 1158–1166.

EXAMPLE 4-1

Product-Mix Example

The Style and Comfort Furniture Manufacturing Company wishes to determine its production schedule for the next quarter. The company produces four types of furniture: sofas, loveseats, recliners, and coffee tables. The profit contribution from selling one sofa is $120, one loveseat is $105, one recliner is $150, and one coffee table is $73. The quarterly production budget is set at $180 000. Each unit of a sofa, loveseat, recliner, and coffee table costs $400, $300, $500, and $150, respectively. The sales forecasts indicate that the potential sales volume is limited to 200 units of sofas, 150 units of loveseats, 100 units of recliners, and 400 units of coffee tables. There are an aggregate of 800 machine hours available and 1200 labour hours available. Table 4-1 summarizes the number of machine hours and the number of labour hours required per unit of each product.

Table 4-1 Per Unit Machine and Labour Hour Required for Each Product

Product	Machine Hours/Unit	Labour Hours/Unit
Sofa	2.0	2.5
Loveseat	1.0	2.0
Recliner	2.2	3.0
Coffee table	.75	1.0

The management also imposed the following policy constraints:

1. At least 40 percent of all production costs must be incurred for the sofas.
2. At least 25 percent of all production costs must be allocated to the recliners.
3. There must be at least 30 loveseats manufactured.

Problem Formulation

In formulating this problem, first we need to define the decision variables. If we define the quantity of the product produced as x_i, we will have the following variable definitions:

$$x_1 = \text{number of sofas produced}$$
$$x_2 = \text{number of loveseats produced}$$
$$x_3 = \text{number of recliners produced}$$
$$x_4 = \text{number of coffee tables produced}$$

After defining the decision variables, we need to state the objective function. Since the amount of profit margin for producing each type of furniture is given, we can establish this as a maximization problem with the profit margin values as the objective function coefficients. Therefore, the objective function can be stated as follows:

$$\text{maximize } Z = 120x_1 + 105x_2 + 150x_3 + 73x_4$$

Once the objective function is determined, then we can determine the constraint equations. For our example, we know that we are constrained by the \$180 000 provided in the budget. Therefore, for the budget limit of \$180 000, we formulate the constraint equation by multiplying each variable by the production cost per unit of each product. For example, since the cost of producing a sofa is \$400, we have $400x_1$ for the sofas. Therefore, the left-hand side of the budget constraint becomes

$$400x_1 + 300x_2 + 500x_3 + 150x_4$$

The sum of the above calculation must be less than or equal to the total production budget; thus, the budget constraint is

$$400x_1 + 300x_2 + 500x_3 + 150x_4 \leq 180\,000 \qquad (1)$$

Note that the above relationship is expressed as an inequality. In other words, it is not a requirement that the entire budget be consumed. Next we will formulate the sales volume limitation constraints. Based on the sales forecast, the production of the products will be limited to the upper bounds given in the problem. Since there is an upper bound for each product, we have the following four sales volume constraints:

$$x_1 \leq 200 \qquad (2)$$
$$x_2 \leq 150 \qquad (3)$$
$$x_3 \leq 100 \qquad (4)$$
$$x_4 \leq 400 \qquad (5)$$

It is typical for the forecasted sales values to represent an upper bound or maximum production quantities to define a range of feasible values.

Next, we need to consider the capacity of the machine hours as well as the capacity of the labour hours. Since there are 800 machine hours available, the value of 800 constitutes the right-hand side of the less than or equal to constraint for the machine hours capacity. The sum of the per unit machine hour requirements multiplied by their respective variable constitutes the left-hand side of the inequality. The resulting inequality is presented below:

$$2x_1 + 1x_2 + 2.2x_3 + .75x_4 \leq 800 \quad \text{(machine hour capacity constraint)} \qquad (6)$$

The labour hour capacity constraint is constructed in a similar fashion:

$$2.5x_1 + 2x_2 + 3x_3 + 1x_4 \leq 1200 \quad \text{(labour hour capacity constraint)} \qquad (7)$$

Finally we will formulate the three management-imposed policy constraints.

Policy 1: At Least 40 Percent of All Production Costs Must Be Incurred for the Sofas In formulating this constraint, we place the sofa variable x_1 multiplied by its unit production cost on the left side of the inequality. The wording "at least" implies a lower bound or a minimum production requirement; therefore, the sign of the inequality is greater than or equal to ($\geq$). On the right-hand side of the constraint, we have 40 percent of total production cost. Since the total production cost is given by $400x_1 + 300x_2 + 500x_3 + 150x_4$, 40 percent of total production costs is given by $.40(400x_1 + 300x_2 + 500x_3 + 150x_4)$. This results in the following inequality:

$$400x_1 \geq .40(400x_1 + 300x_2 + 500x_3 + 150x_4)$$

Note that on the right-hand side of the inequality, 40 percent is not multiplied by the \$180 000 of production budget because not all of the budget will necessarily be spent. Rearranging this inequality to eliminate all of the variables from the right-hand side of the inequality gives us the following inequality:

$$240x_1 - 120x_2 - 200x_3 - 60x_4 \geq 0 \qquad (8)$$

Policy 2: At Least 25 Percent of All Production Costs Must Be Allocated to Recliners Similarly, in formulating this constraint, we place the recliner variable x_3 multiplied by its unit production cost on the left-hand side of the inequality. Again, the wording "at least" implies a lower bound; therefore, the sign on the inequality is greater than or equal to ($\geq$). On the right-hand side of the constraint, we have 25 percent of total production cost. Since the total production cost is given by $400x_1 + 300x_2 + 500x_3 + 150x_4$, 25 percent of total production cost is given by $.25(400x_1 + 300x_2 + 500x_3 + 150x_4)$. This results in the following inequality:

$$500x_3 \geq .25(400x_1 + 300x_2 + 500x_3 + 150x_4)$$

Rearranging this inequality to eliminate all of the variables from the right-hand side of the inequality gives us the following inequality:

$$-100x_1 - 75x_2 + 375x_3 - 37.5x_4 \geq 0 \qquad (9)$$

Policy 3: There Must Be At Least 30 Loveseats Manufactured The minimum production quantity (lower bound) of the loveseats (variable x_2) constraint can be written as follows:

$$x_2 \geq 30 \qquad (10)$$

Since the value of 30 is a minimum production quantity, the sign of the inequality is greater than or equal to.

We have now formulated the entire problem with the exception of nonnegativity constraints. Let's summarize the completed formulation for the Style and Comfort Furniture Manufacturing Company example:

x_1 = number of sofas produced
x_2 = number of loveseats produced
x_3 = number of recliners produced
x_4 = number of coffee tables produced

$$\text{maximize } Z = 120x_1 + 105x_2 + 150x_3 + 73x_4$$

subject to

$$\begin{aligned}
400x_1 + 300x_2 + 500x_3 + 150x_4 &\leq 180\,000 \quad \text{(budget constraint)} && (1)\\
x_1 &\leq 200 && (2)\\
x_2 &\leq 150 && (3)\\
x_3 &\leq 100 \quad \text{(sales volume constraints)} && (4)\\
x_4 &\leq 400 && (5)
\end{aligned}$$

$$2x_1 + 1x_2 + 2.2x_3 + .75x_4 \le 800 \quad \text{(machine hour constraint)} \qquad (6)$$
$$2.5x_1 + 2x_2 + 3x_1 + 1x_4 \le 1200 \quad \text{(labour hour constraint)} \qquad (7)$$
$$240x_1 - 120x_2 - 200x_3 - 60x_4 \ge 0 \quad \text{(sofa production cost)} \qquad (8)$$
$$-100x_1 - 75x_2 + 375x_3 - 37.5x_4 \ge 0 \quad \text{(recliner cost)} \qquad (9)$$
$$x_2 \ge 30 \quad \text{(minimum loveseat production)} \qquad (10)$$
$$x_1, x_2, x_3, x_4 \ge 0 \quad \text{(nonnegativity constraint)}$$

Excel Solution of the Style and Comfort Furniture Company Example

We need to answer two questions to begin the process of utilizing Excel to formulate a linear programming model for this problem:

1. What are the decisions to be made? This question translates into the question of what are the values of the decision variables or the production quantities of each of the products?
2. How do we measure the total performance of the company in regards to this decision? This question can be answered by the total profit per month for all four products.

The Excel spreadsheet associated with this problem is shown in Exhibit 4-1. The variable labels are in cells B3, C3, D3, and E3. Immediately below the variable labels, we have three

EXHIBIT 4-1 Input Screen for the Style and Comfort Furniture Company Problem

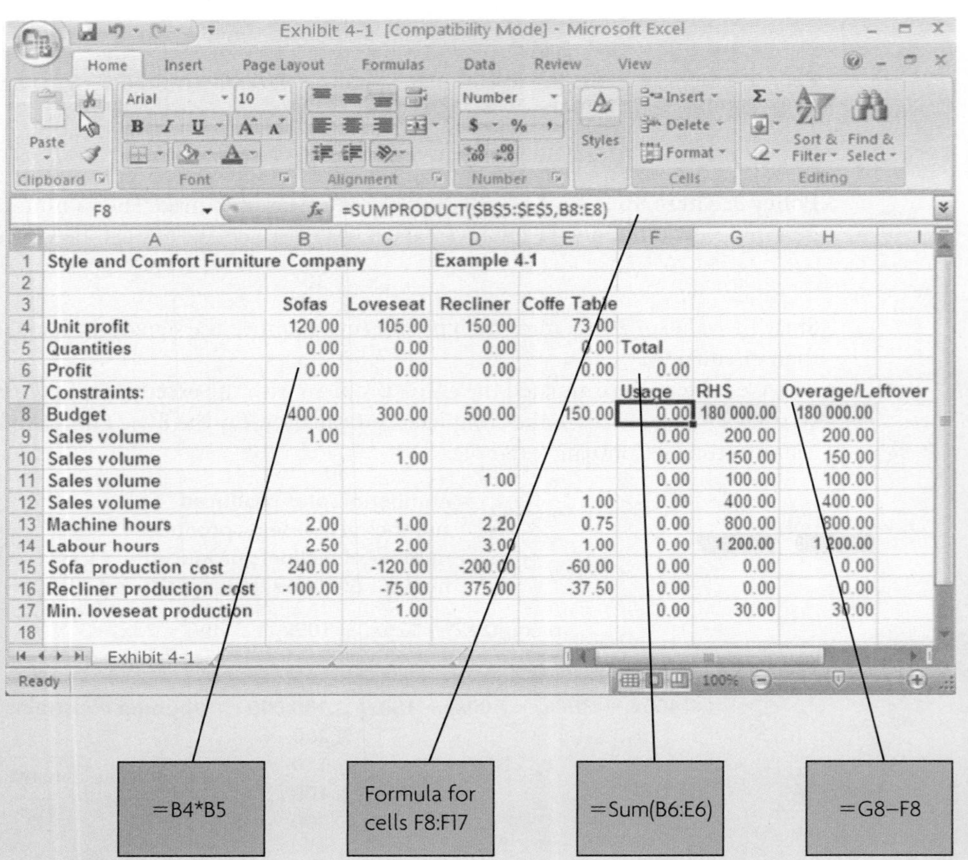

	A	B	C	D	E	F	G	H
1	Style and Comfort Furniture Company			Example 4-1				
2								
3		Sofas	Loveseat	Recliner	Coffe Table			
4	Unit profit	120.00	105.00	150.00	73.00			
5	Quantities	0.00	0.00	0.00	0.00	Total		
6	Profit	0.00	0.00	0.00	0.00	0.00		
7	Constraints:					Usage	RHS	Overage/Leftover
8	Budget	400.00	300.00	500.00	150.00	0.00	180 000.00	180 000.00
9	Sales volume	1.00				0.00	200.00	200.00
10	Sales volume		1.00			0.00	150.00	150.00
11	Sales volume			1.00		0.00	100.00	100.00
12	Sales volume				1.00	0.00	400.00	400.00
13	Machine hours	2.00	1.00	2.20	0.75	0.00	800.00	800.00
14	Labour hours	2.50	2.00	3.00	1.00	0.00	1 200.00	1 200.00
15	Sofa production cost	240.00	-120.00	-200.00	-60.00	0.00	0.00	0.00
16	Recliner production cost	-100.00	-75.00	375.00	-37.50	0.00	0.00	0.00
17	Min. loveseat production		1.00			0.00	30.00	30.00
18								

rows (4, 5, and 6) designated by unit profit, quantity, and profit, respectively. The unit profit values in row 4 are coming from the objective function, while the quantities, called the *output cells*, are the decision variable values that Solver will provide after solving the model. The profit values are obtained by multiplying the unit profit values in row 4 by the quantity values (output cells) in row 5. For example, cell B6 contains the equation = B4*B5, which is the multiplication of the unit profit (B4) by the quantity of the decision variable (B5). The formulas for cells C6, D6, and E6 are very similar to the formula for cell B6. For example, for cell C6, the formula is = C4*C5.

Rows 8 through 17 list the constraints of the model. In listing the model constraints, we need an extra column that will show the value of the left-hand side of each constraint once Solver has determined the values of the decision variables. This column is designated as column F and is labelled as "Usage." In the usage column, we utilize the SUMPRODUCT function, which will sum up the product of each of the individual terms in two different ranges provided that the two ranges have the same number of rows or columns included. For example, for cell F8, we have the equation = SUMPRODUCT ($B$5:$E$5,B8:E8). The values in column G indicate the right-hand-side (RHS) values of each of the constraints. The values in column H represent the difference between the right-hand side and the left-hand side of the inequality or equality sign. For a less-than-or-equal-to resource constraint, column H values are a convenient way of showing the unused resources. Since F8 provides the total for the left-hand side of the equation and G8 is the value of the right-hand side of the constraint equation, = G8–F8 is the correct formula for cell H8.

The overall performance of the model measured by the total profit is stated in cell F6. This total profit value is calculated by summing the values in rows B6 through E6; therefore, the equation in cell F6 is = SUM(B6:E6).

Exhibit 4-2 shows the completed specifications of the Solver dialogue box.

After solving the problem, Solver will change the values of the decision variables (quantities) from blanks to the optimal values, as shown in Exhibit 4-3. According to Exhibit 4-3, the Style and Comfort Manufacturing Company should produce the following: 168.04 sofas (cell B5), 30 loveseats (cell C5), 84.02 recliners (cell D5), and 332.1 coffee tables (cell E5) for a total profit of $60 161.07 (cell F6). Column H, labelled Overage Leftovers, shows the difference between the right- and left-hand side of each constraint. For example, in cell H8 there is a value of 11 958.76. Since row 8 is the row associated with the budget constraint, the interpretation of this value would be that $11 958.76 of the total

EXHIBIT 4-2 Completed Solver Dialogue Box

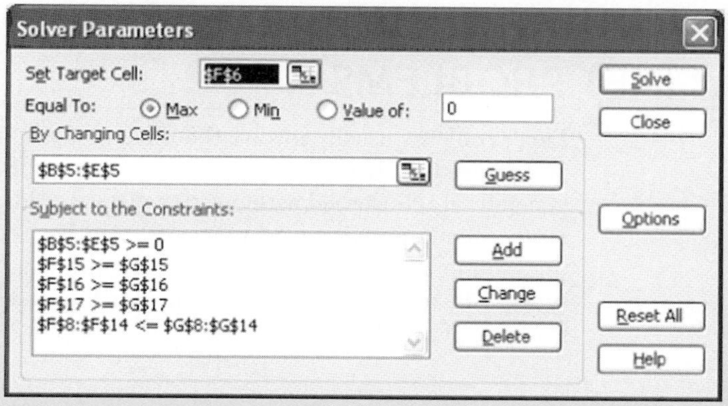

Solver Parameters
Set Target Cell: $F$6
Equal To: Max Min Value of: 0
By Changing Cells:
$B$5:$E$5
Subject to the Constraints:
$B$5:$E$5 >= 0
$F$15 >= $G$15
$F$16 >= $G$16
$F$17 >= $G$17
$F$8:$F$14 <= $G$8:$G$14
Solve Close Guess Options Add Change Delete Reset All Help

EXHIBIT 4-3 Output Screen for the Style and Comfort Furniture Company Problem

Exhibit 4-3 [Compatibility Mode] - Microsoft Excel

F8 =SUMPRODUCT($B$5:$E$5,B8:E8)

	A	B	C	D	E	F	G	H
1	Style and Comfort Furniture Company			Example 4-1				
2								
3		Sofas	Loveseat	Recliner	Coffe Table			
4	Unit profit	120.00	105.00	150.00	73.00			
5	Quantities	168.04	30.00	84.02	332.10	Total		
6	Profit	20 164.95	3 150.00	12 603.09	24 243.02	60 161.07		
7	Constraints:					Usage	RHS	Overage/Leftove
8	Budget	400.00	300.00	500.00	150.00	168 041.24	180 000.00	11 958.76
9	Sales volume	1.00				168.04	200.00	31.96
10	Sales volume		1.00			30.00	150.00	120.00
11	Sales volume			1.00		84.02	100.00	15.98
12	Sales volume				1.00	332.10	400.00	67.90
13	Machine hours	2.00	1.00	2.20	0.75	800.00	800.00	0.00
14	Labour hours	2.50	2.00	3.00	1.00	1 064.25	1 200.00	135.74
15	Sofa production cost	240.00	-120.00	-200.00	-60.00	0.00	0.00	0.00
16	Recliner production cost	-100.00	-75.00	375.00	-37.50	0.00	0.00	0.00
17	Min. loveseat production		1.00			30.00	30.00	0.00
18								

budget has not been spent. At this point, it may be a good idea to change some of the profit or constraint coefficients and run Solver again to see how sensitive the solution is to the changes in the parameters.

If the furniture company routinely makes such production decisions, for example on a daily or weekly basis, a computer code should be written that uses the LP model with an easy-to-use user interface to allow the user to change the model parameters. The code should be able to call Excel Solver to determine the optimal solution. This type of decision support system (DSS) helps the managers who are not experts in management science to easily use such LP models over and over again.

4.3 DIET PROBLEMS

Diet problems usually involve the mixing of raw materials or other ingredients to obtain an end product that has certain characteristics. For instance, food processors and dieticians generally are concerned with meeting dietary needs in food products. There may be specific requirements pertaining to nutrients, calories, sodium content, and so on. The general question to be answered by linear programming is: What mix of inputs (e.g., different food types) will achieve the desired results for the least cost? The following example illustrates this type of problem.

EXAMPLE 4-2

A cereal manufacturer is investigating the possibility of introducing a new cereal. It would be composed of wheat, rice, and corn flakes. The cost per ounce and dietary requirements are shown in Table 4-2.

Table 4-2 Cost per Ounce and Dietary Requirements for Diet Problem

	Wheat	Rice	Corn	Requirements per 12-Ounce Box
Protein (grams per ounce)	4	2	2	At least 27 grams
Carbohydrates (grams per ounce)	20	25	21	At least 240 grams
Calories per ounce	90	110	100	No more than 1260 calories
Cost per ounce	$0.03	0.05	0.02	

Formulate an LP model for this problem that will determine the optimal quantities of wheat, rice, and corn per box that will achieve the requirements at minimum cost.

Solution
Variable definitions

x_1 = ounces of wheat per box
x_2 = ounces of rice per box
x_3 = ounces of corn per box

The decision variables involve the different types of food. Since the data are given in grams per ounce, the decision variables are ounces of food type per box. The objective function for this problem is a minimization type, since we are attempting to minimize cost.

To formulate the constraints for this problem we evaluate the table given above and decide that there should be three constraints: one for protein, one for carbohydrates, and one for calories. The signs of all these three constraints should be greater than or equal to because "requirements" indicate the minimum amount (lower bound) necessary for each constraint. For example, for the protein constraint, each ounce of wheat has 4 grams of protein, each ounce of rice has 2 grams of protein, and each ounce of corn has 2 grams of protein. The total value for protein from all three food types must be at least 27 grams or exceed it. Therefore, we can set this constraint as $4x_1 + 2x_2 + 2x_3 \geq 27$. Utilizing the same logic for the remaining two constraints, the final formulation of this problem is as follows:

minimize $Z = .03x_1 + .05x_2 + .02x_3$

subject to

Protein	$4x_1 + 2x_2 + 2x_3 \geq 27$ grams
Carbohydrates	$20x_1 + 25x_2 + 21x_3 \geq 240$ grams
Calories	$90x_1 + 110x_2 + 100x_3 \leq 1260$ calories
Box size	$x_1 + x_2 + x_3 = 12$ ounces

$x_1, x_2,$ and $x_3 \geq 0$

Note the box size constraint, which is needed to assure that the quantities of inputs per box equal the box size.

Solution to diet problem

$x_1 = 1.5$ (ounces of wheat per box)
$x_3 = 10.5$ (ounces of corn per box)
$z = \$0.26$ (minimum cost per box)

4.4 BLENDING PROBLEMS

Blending problems are very similar to diet problems. In fact, diet and blending problems could be lumped into the same category. Strictly speaking, though, blending problems have an additional requirement: to achieve a mix that has a specific consistency, as illustrated in the next example.

EXAMPLE 4-3

Formulate the appropriate model for the following blending problem: The sugar content of three juices—orange, banana, and pineapple—is 10, 15, and 20 percent, respectively. How many quarts of each must be mixed together to achieve one gallon (four quarts) that has a sugar content of at least 17 percent to minimize cost? The cost per quart is 20 cents for orange juice, 30 cents for banana juice, and 40 cents for pineapple juice.

Solution
Variable definitions

O = quantity of orange juice in quarts
B = quantity of banana juice in quarts
P = quantity of pineapple juice in quarts

In setting up the constraints for this problem, first we need to consider the sugar content of the three juices. Since the sugar content of the juice mix must exceed 17 percent, mixing orange juice with banana juice will not be sufficient because the sugar content of orange juice and banana juice is 10 percent and 15 percent, respectively. Even though it is the most costly, we need to mix pineapple juice (which has a sugar content of 20 percent) to achieve a minimum of 17 percent sugar content. The left-hand side of the sugar content constraint is stated as what the sugar content of each juice is: $.10O + .15B + .20P$. The right-hand side of the constraint provides the minimum sugar content requirement, which is 17 percent. Therefore, the right-hand side of the constraint is $.17(O + B + P)$. The sign of this constraint must be $\geq$ to ensure that we meet the minimum sugar content requirement. This constraint can be written as

$$.10O + .15B + .20P \geq .17\,(O + B + P)$$

Since the profit is stated on a per-quart basis and variables are defined as "quantity of *type of* juice in quarts," the second constraint should indicate the number of quarts mixed. Since the juice has to be exactly 4 quarts, then the constraint is written as $O + B + P = 4$. The final formulation of this problem is summarized below:

minimize $Z = .20O + .30B + .40P$

subject to

Sugar content	$.10O + .15B + .20P \geq .17(O + B + P)$
Total amount	$O + B + P = 4$ quarts

The sugar constraint must be rewritten so that the decision variables are on the left-hand side and the constant is on the right-hand side. Thus, expanding the right-hand-side results in

$$.10O + .15B + .20P \geq .17O + .17B + .17P$$

Then, subtracting the right-hand-side amounts from both sides gives us

$$-.07O - .2B + .03P \geq 0$$

Solution to blending problem

$O = 1.2$ quarts	(quantity of orange juice)
$P = 2.8$ quarts	(quantity of pineapple juice)
$Z = \$1.36$	(minimum total cost of the blended juice per gallon)

Linear programming formulation of blending problems is also commonly used in blending oil or gasoline. This type of application also can be illustrated with the following example.

EXAMPLE 4-4

TUNACO Oil Company produces three grades of gasoline (regular, mid-grade, and premium) by blending three types of crude oil. All three types of crude oil contain two important ingredients (X and Y) required to produce the three gasoline grades. The percentage of these ingredients differs in each type of crude oil. These percentages are given in the following table.

	Crude Oil Type		
	1	**2**	**3**
Ingredient X	40	20	55
Ingredient Y	35	30	60

Cost of each type of crude oil is \$0.82, \$0.75, and \$0.70 per litre for crude oil types 1, 2, and 3, respectively.

Each litre of regular gasoline must contain at least 35 percent of ingredient X. Each litre of mid-grade gasoline can contain at most 45 percent of ingredient Y. Each litre of premium gasoline can contain at most 40 percent of ingredient Y.

Daily demand for regular, mid-grade, and premium grades of gasoline is 1 514 000, 567 750, and 567 750 litres, respectively.

Daily production quantities are 1 324 750 litres for crude oil 1; 946 250 litres for crude oil 2; and 757 000 litres for crude oil 3. How many litres of each type of crude oil should be used in the three grades of gasoline to satisfy demand at minimum cost?

Solution

First, we must define the variables by using a double script notation.

Let X_{ij} = amount of crude oil i used in gasoline type j

where

$i = 1, 2, 3$ 1 = crude oil type 1, 2 = crude oil type 2, 3 = crude oil type 3.
$j = 1, 2, 3$ 1 = regular, 2 = mid-grade, 3 = premium

For example, x_{21} = amount of crude oil 2 used in regular gasoline.

The objective function, which involves the minimization of total cost, can be stated as follows:

$$\text{minimize } Z = .82x_{11} + .82x_{12} + .82x_{13} + .75x_{21} + .75x_{22} + .75x_{23} + .7x_{31} + .7x_{32} + .7x_{33}$$

We can begin to formulate the constraints of this problem by determining the production quantities of each type of crude oil.

$x_{11} + x_{12} + x_{13} \leq 1\,324\,750$ litres (production of crude oil 1)
$x_{21} + x_{22} + x_{23} \leq 946\,250$ litres (production of crude oil 2)
$x_{31} + x_{32} + x_{33} \leq 757\,000$ litres (production of crude oil 3)

Note that in formulating each of the above production constraints, the subscript i remains constant, while the subscript j changes. For example, x_{11}, x_{12}, x_{13} indicates the production of crude oil 1 used in all three types of gasoline. The sign of these production constraints can be set up as $\leq$ or $=$.

The demand quantities for each gasoline type is given by the following constraints:

$x_{11} + x_{21} + x_{31} \geq 1\,514\,000$ litres (demand for regular gasoline)
$x_{12} + x_{22} + x_{32} \geq 567\,750$ litres (demand for mid-grade gasoline)
$x_{13} + x_{23} + x_{33} \geq 567\,750$ litres (demand for premium gasoline)

Note that in formulating each of the above demand constraints, the opposite of the production constraints occurs: the subscript j remains constant, while the subscript i varies. For example, x_{12}, x_{22}, x_{32} indicates the demand for mid-grade gasoline using all three types of crude oil. The sign of these demand constraints can be specified as $\geq$ or $=$. If these constraints were inadvertently specified as $\leq$, the solution quantities of all decision variables would be forced to equal zero since the objective of the problem is to minimize cost.

Now, we must formulate the percentage mix constraints. The constraint that each litre of regular gasoline must contain at least 35 percent of ingredient X can be formulated as follows:

$$0.4x_{11} + 0.2x_{21} + .55x_{31} \geq .35(x_{11} + x_{21} + x_{31}).$$

The left-hand side of the inequality shows the total amount of ingredient X provided by all three types of crude oil in regular gasoline. The right-hand side of the inequality, indicates that the regular gasoline must contain at least (due to the greater-than-or-equal-to sign) 35 percent ingredient X. Rearranging this constraint to move all of the variable values to the left of the inequality so that the right-hand side of the constraint is a numerical value results in the following inequality.

$.05x_{11} - .15x_{21} + .20x_{31} \geq 0$

Likewise, the constraint that each litre of mid-grade gasoline must contain at most 45 percent of ingredient Y can be written as

$.35x_{12} + .30x_{22} + .60x_{32} \leq .45(x_{12} + x_{22} + x_{32})$

The left-hand side of the inequality shows the total amount of ingredient Y in mid-grade gasoline. The right-hand side of the inequality, due to the less-than-or-equal-to sign indicates that mid-grade gasoline must contain at most 45 percent of ingredient Y. Rearranging this constraint to move all of the variable values to the left-hand side of the inequality results in the following:

$-.10x_{12} - .15x_{22} + .15x_{32} \leq 0$

Similarly, the constraint that each litre of premium gasoline can contain at most 40 percent of ingredient Y can be written as follows:

$.35x_{13} + .30x_{23} + .60x_{33} \leq .40(x_{13} + x_{23} + x_{33})$

Rearranging this constraint results in the following:

$-.05x_{13} - .10x_{23} + .20x_{33} \leq 0$

The linear programming formulation of the TUNACO Oil Company problem can be summarized as follows:

x_{ij} = amount of crude oil i used in gasoline type j, where i = crude oil type 1, 2, 3, where j = gasoline type 1, 2, 3 (1 = regular gasoline, 2 = mid-grade gasoline, 3 = premium gasoline)

minimize $Z = .82x_{11} + .82x_{12} + .82x_{13} + .75x_{21} + .75x_{22} + .75x_{23} + .7x_{31} + .7x_{32} + .7x_{33}$

Subject to

$x_{11} + x_{12} + x_{13}$	$\leq$ 1 324 750 litres	(production of crude oil 1)
$x_{21} + x_{22} + x_{23}$	$\leq$ 946 250 litres	(production of crude oil 2)
$x_{31} + x_{32} + x_{33}$	$\leq$ 757 000 litres	(production of crude oil 3)
$x_{11} + x_{21} + x_{31}$	$\geq$ 1 514 000 litres	(demand for regular gasoline)
$x_{12} + x_{22} + x_{32}$	$\geq$ 567 750 litres	(demand for mid-grade gasoline)
$x_{13} + x_{23} + x_{33}$	$\geq$ 567 750 litres	(demand for premium gasoline)

$$\left.\begin{aligned} -.05x_{11} - .15x_{21} + .20x_{31} &\geq 0 \\ -.10x_{12} - .15x_{22} + .15x_{32} &\leq 0 \\ -.05x_{13} - .10x_{23} + .20x_{33} &\leq 0 \end{aligned}\right\} \quad \text{(ingredient constraints)}$$

$x_{ij} \geq 0$ for all i, j combinations

Solution to TUNACO Oil Company problem

x_{11} = 1 324 750	(amount of crude oil 1 used in regular gasoline)
x_{22} = 567 750	(amount of crude oil 2 used in mid-grade gasoline)
x_{23} = 378 500	(amount of crude oil 2 used in premium gasoline)
x_{31} = 567 750	(amount of crude oil 3 used in regular gasoline)
x_{33} = 189 250	(amount of crude oil 3 in premium gasoline)
Z = $2 325 882	(minimum total cost)

A MODERN MANAGEMENT SCIENCE APPLICATION: TELEVISION NETWORKS UP FRONT MARKET SALES PLAN GENERATION

Major television networks in Canada (e.g., CBC, CTV, Global, etc.) or the United States (e.g., ABC, CBS, Fox, NBC, etc.) receive up-front market requests from advertising agencies to purchase time for their clients for the next broadcast year. These requests for advertising slots occur during a brief period shortly after the broadcast networks announce their programming schedules. The problem faced by television networks is to develop a detailed sales plan consisting of the schedule of commercials to be aired to maximize the revenues for the available fixed amount of airtime inventory. To cope with this business problem, NBC television network developed a sales-plan generation system based on management science techniques to improve the sales processes. Between 1996 and 2000, the systems increased revenues by over $200 million, improved sales-force productivity, reduced work by over 80 percent, and improved customer satisfaction. The first version of the system that was developed consisted of a high-level linear programming model directed to provide planning guidelines to a planner by specifying the number of commercial slots that should be allocated to a client by show and by quarter.

Source: Reprinted by permission. Based on S. Bollapragad, H. Cheng, M. Phillips, M. Garbiras, M. Scholes, T. Gibbs, and M. Humphreville, "NBC's Optimization Systems Increase Revenues and Productivity," *Interfaces* vol. 32, no. 1 (January–February 2002), pp. 47–60. Copyright (2002), the Institute for Operations Research and the Management Sciences (INFORMS), 7240 Parkway Drive, Suite 310, Hanover, MD 21076 USA.

4.5 MARKETING APPLICATIONS

There are many applications of linear programming in marketing. These include

1. Media selection (how to allocate an advertising budget among different media of advertising).
2. Determination of the optimal assignment of salespeople that work for the company among the sales territories. In this scenario, there are various territories that need to be covered by a sales force where the sales force have different capabilities.
3. Marketing research study in which the objective is to determine the best number of interviews, mailings, or phone calls, given a number of client-specified constraints and the cost considerations.

The Modern Management Science Application "Television Networks Up Front Market Sales Plan Generation" discusses a marketing application of linear programming at NBC television network.

Media Selection

Media selection problems using linear programming can assist marketing managers in deciding how to allocate a fixed advertising budget among the different media such as television, newspapers, radio, and direct mail. In media selection problems, the objective could be the maximization of profit based on different media usages. However, it is difficult, or somewhat unrealistic, to model a situation to maximize profit based on different media usages because it is very difficult to put dollars and cents to the usage of a certain advertising medium. Therefore, instead of maximizing profit, in media selection problems, the objective is generally to maximize audience exposure. There are generally restrictions on how much each medium can be used. These restrictions are based on overall advertising budget and the cost to utilize a certain medium, company policy, contractual requirements, and so on. The following example demonstrates the use of linear programming in conjunction with the media selection problem.

EXAMPLE 4-5

The Long Last Appliance Sales Company is in the business of selling appliances such as microwave ovens, traditional ovens, refrigerators, dishwashers, washers, dryers, and the like. The company has stores in the greater Toronto area and has a monthly advertising budget of \$90 000. Among its options are radio advertising, advertising on cable TV channels, newspaper advertising, and direct-mail advertising. A 30-second advertising spot on the local cable channel costs \$1800, a 30-second radio ad costs \$350, a half-page ad in the local newspaper costs \$700, and a single mailing of direct-mail insertion for the entire region costs \$1200 per mailing.

The number of potential buying customers reached per advertising medium usage is as follows:

Radio	7000
TV	50 000
Newspaper	18 000
Direct mail	34 000

Due to company restrictions and availability of media, the maximum number of usages of each medium is limited to the following:

Radio	35
TV	25
Newspaper	30
Direct mail	18

The management of the company has met and decided that to ensure a balanced utilization of different types of media and to portray a positive image of the company, at least 10 percent of the advertisements must be on TV. No more than 40 percent of the advertisements can be on radio. The cost of advertising allocated to TV and direct mail cannot exceed 60 percent of the total advertising budget.

What is the optimal allocation of the budget among the four media? What is the total maximum audience contact?

Formulation

Variable definitions

x_1 = Number of radio ads
x_2 = Number of television ads
x_3 = Number of newspaper ads
x_4 = Number of direct-mail ads

The objective function

$$\text{maximize } Z = 7\,000x_1 + 50\,000x_2 + 18\,000x_3 + 34\,000x_4$$

The constraints

$350x_1 + 1800x_2 + 700x_3 + 1200x_4 \leq 90\,000$ (budget constraint) (1)

$\left.\begin{array}{l} x_1 \leq 35 \\ x_2 \leq 25 \\ x_3 \leq 30 \\ x_4 \leq 18 \end{array}\right\}$ (maximum exposure constraints) (2) (3) (4) (5)

$$x_2 \geq .10(x_1 + x_2 + x_3 + x_4) \quad \text{(10\% minimum TV ads)}$$
$$x_1 \leq .40(x_1 + x_2 + x_3 + x_4) \quad \text{(40\% maximum radio ads)}$$

Since the right-hand side of the constraints must be a numeric value, the two constraints given above can be rewritten as follows so that the problem can be solved using Excel:

$$-.10x_1 + .9x_2 - .1x_3 - .1x_4 \geq 0 \quad (6)$$
$$.6x_1 - .4x_2 - .4x_3 - .4x_4 \leq 0 \quad (7)$$

The cost of television and direct-mail ads cannot exceed 67 percent of the total advertising budget. This can be written as

$$1800x_2 + 1200x_4 \leq .67(90\,000) \quad (8)$$
$$x_1, x_2, x_3, x_4 \geq 0 \quad \text{(nonnegativity constraint)}$$

Solution

Solving this problem with Excel results in the following:

$x_1 = 24.86$ (number of radio advertisements)
$x_2 = 21.50$ (number of TV advertisements)
$x_3 = 30$ (number of newspaper advertisements)
$x_4 = 18$ (number of direct-mail advertisements)

$Z = 2\,401\,000$ (total number of potential customers reached)

The results for the Long Last Appliance Sales Company problem are given in Exhibit 4-4. Note that the number of radio and TV advertisements are not integers. We have a couple of options when the number of advertisements results in

EXHIBIT 4-4 Output Screen for the Long Last Appliance Sales Company

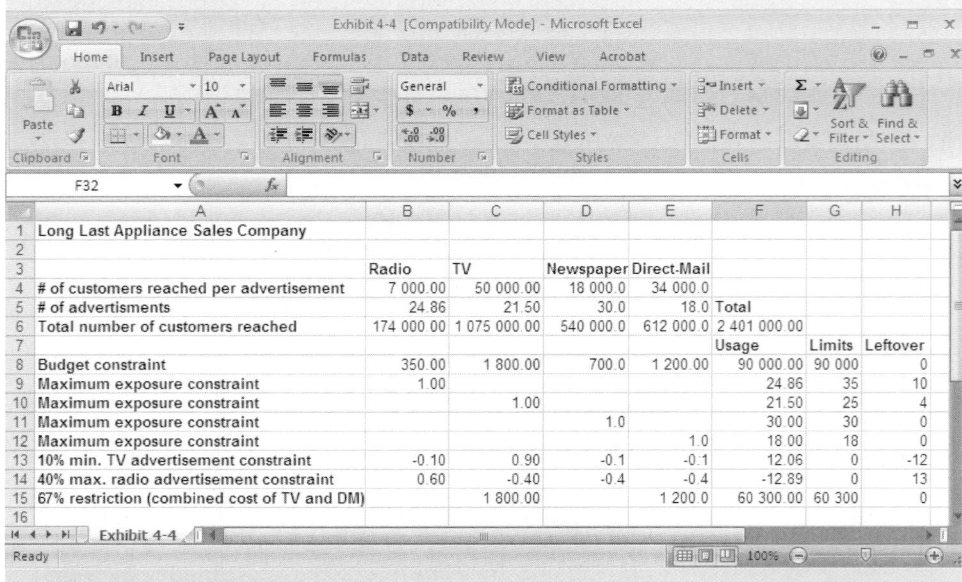

	A	B	C	D	E	F	G	H
1	Long Last Appliance Sales Company							
2								
3		Radio	TV	Newspaper	Direct-Mail			
4	# of customers reached per advertisement	7 000.00	50 000.00	18 000.0	34 000.0			
5	# of advertisments	24.86	21.50	30.0	18.0	Total		
6	Total number of customers reached	174 000.00	1 075 000.00	540 000.0	612 000.0	2 401 000.00		
7						Usage	Limits	Leftover
8	Budget constraint	350.00	1 800.00	700.0	1 200.00	90 000.00	90 000	0
9	Maximum exposure constraint	1.00				24.86	35	10
10	Maximum exposure constraint		1.00			21.50	25	4
11	Maximum exposure constraint			1.0		30.00	30	0
12	Maximum exposure constraint				1.0	18.00	18	0
13	10% min. TV advertisement constraint	-0.10	0.90	-0.1	-0.1	12.06	0	-12
14	40% max. radio advertisement constraint	0.60	-0.40	-0.4	-0.4	-12.89	0	13
15	67% restriction (combined cost of TV and DM)		1 800.00		1 200.0	60 300.00	60 300	0
16								

a noninteger value. First, we could simply round the values down and use 24 for x_1 and 21 for x_2. However, when we round down the noninteger values to integer values, we run the risk that the solution may turn out to be infeasible. The consequences and the magnitude of infeasibility increase as the noninteger value of the decision variable decreases. Second, we could negotiate with the radio station for an ad that is only 86 percent as long as the regular ad at a proportional cost ($x_1 = 24.86$). Likewise with the local television station, we could negotiate an ad that is only 50 percent of the regular 30-second ad ($x_2 = 21.50$). Therefore, instead of a 30-second TV advertisement, an advertisement that is only half as long, or 15 seconds, would be utilized at a proportional cost. Of course another option is to impose an integer restriction on the variables, which we will cover in the integer programming chapter of the book (Chapter 6).

Marketing Research

Companies conduct marketing research to assist with company strategy, product planning, and forecasting product demand by learning about consumer characteristics, spending/ buying tendencies, and consumer preferences toward products. Typically, marketing research firms meet with the client company and determine its needs in consumer buying tendencies and its preferences toward products. Based on the client company's needs, the marketing research firm goes through the following stages of marketing research study development:

1. Design study.
2. Conduct marketing survey.
3. Analyze data and obtain results.
4. Make recommendations based on the results.

In designing the study, the marketing research firm, in consultation with the client company, may establish a target number of respondents to be reached by the market survey being designed. **Marketing research problems** using linear programming occur at this stage and consist of determining the best number of respondents to be reached through various media (for example, interviews, mailings, phone calls, etc.) given a number of client-specified constraints and considerations. After establishing the target number of respondents, the goal of the marketing research company is to conduct a survey to reach the target number of respondents at minimum cost. Let us look at an example.

EXAMPLE 4-6

Market Facts Inc. is a marketing research firm that works with client companies to determine consumer reaction toward various products and services. A client company requested that Market Facts investigate the consumer reaction to a recently developed electronic device. Market Facts and the client company agreed that a combination of telephone interviews and direct-mail questionnaires would be used to obtain the information from different types of households.

The households are divided into six categories:

1. Households containing a single couple under 40 years old and without children under 18 years of age.

2. Households containing a married couple under 40 years old and without children under 18 years of age.
3. Households containing a single couple with children under 18 years of age.
4. Households containing a married couple with children under 18 years of age.
5. Households containing a single couple over 40 years old without children under 18 years of age.
6. Households containing a married couple over 40 years old without children under 18 years of age.

The client company has requested that the total households contacted via direct mail and phone interviews be 50 000. There can be 2000 phone interviews and 48 000 mail-in questionnaires. The cost of a direct-mail questionnaire, including the cost of a self-stamped, mail-back envelope, is \$1.00 for a household without children under 18 years of age and \$1.50 for households with children. The cost of the phone interview also differs depending on whether the household contains children less than 18 years of age and if it contains a married couple. The interview costs more for the households with children because the interviewer has to ask more questions. The cost of a phone interview of a household with a married couple with children is \$15 (\$12 for a single couple). The cost of a phone interview of a household with a married couple under 40 years old and without children is \$11 (for a married couple above 40 years old, it is \$9). For a household with a single couple under 40 years old and without children, the cost is \$10 (for a single couple above 40 years old, it is \$7).

1. At least 60 percent of the phone interviews must be conducted with households with children.
2. At least 50 percent of the direct-mail questionnaires must be mailed to households with children.
3. No more than 30 percent of the phone interviews and mail-in questionnaires can be conducted with households with single people.
4. At least 25 percent of the phone interviews and mail-in questionnaires must be conducted with households that contain married couples.

How many phone interviews will be conducted with different types of households, and how many direct-mail questionnaires will be mailed to different types of households to minimize the total cost of this market survey?

In formulating this problem, we must define the decision variables using the following double subscripted notation:

x_{ij} = number of phone interviews or questionnaires used to reach household type j

where

$i = 1, 2$ 1 = phone interview, 2 = mail-in questionnaire
$j = 1, 2, 3, 4, 5, 6$ (j represents the six household categories defined earlier)

Based on the above definitions of the decision variables, the objective function can be written as

$$\text{minimize } Z = 10x_{11} + 11x_{12} + 12x_{13} + 15x_{14} + 7x_{15} + 9x_{16} + 1x_{21} + 1x_{22} + 1.5x_{23} + 1.5x_{24} + 1x_{25} + 1x_{26}$$

We can begin to write the constraints for this problem by considering the target values of advertising. Since the target number of phone interviews is 2000 and the target number of mail-in questionnaires is 48 000, the two constraints can be written as follows:

$x_{11} + x_{12} + x_{13} + x_{14} + x_{15} + x_{16} = 2000$ (target number of phone interviews)
$x_{21} + x_{22} + x_{23} + x_{24} + x_{25} + x_{26} = 48\,000$ (target number of mail-in questionnaires)

Note that in each of the constraints, the value of subscript i remains constant, while the value of j varies from 1 to 6, representing all six types of households defined earlier. We do not need a constraint that includes the combined phone interview and direct-mail target in one constraint since we accounted for them in separate constraints. In addition, if we erroneously use a less-than-or-equal-to sign instead of an equal to sign, the values of all decision variables will assume zero at the optimal solution.

At least 60 percent of the phone interviews must be conducted with households with children.

$$x_{13} + x_{14} \geq .60(x_{11} + x_{12} + x_{13} + x_{14} + x_{15} + x_{16})$$

The left-hand side of the inequality represents the variables of those phone interviews conducted at households with children, while the right-hand side of the constraint shows the 60 percent of all phone interviews. The above constraint can be put into the form for computer implementation by moving all the variables to the left-hand side of the constraint, leaving only the numerical value of zero on the right-hand side:

$$-.60x_{11} - .60x_{12} + .40x_{13} + .40x_{14} - .60x_{15} - .60x_{16} \geq 0$$

At least 50 percent of the direct-mail questionnaires must be mailed to households with children, a restriction that can be written as follow:

$$x_{23} + x_{24} \geq .50(x_{21} + x_{22} + x_{23} + x_{24} + x_{25} + x_{26})$$

The left-hand side of the inequality includes all of the variables of those mail-in questionnaires sent to households with children, while the right-hand side of the constraint shows the 50 percent of all mail-in questionnaires. This constraint also can be put into computer-implementation-ready form by moving all of the decision variables from the right-hand side of the constraint to the left-hand side. This results in the following inequality:

$$-.50x_{21} - .50x_{22} + .50x_{23} + .50x_{24} - .50x_{25} - .50x_{26} \geq 0$$

No more than 30 percent of the phone interviews and mail-in questionnaires can be conducted with households with single people. There are two separate constraints to be written: one for phone interviews and one for mail-in questionnaires. First we will write the phone interview constraint, then it will be easy to duplicate that for the mail-in questionnaires.

$x_{11} + x_{13} + x_{15} \leq .30(x_{11} + x_{12} + x_{13} + x_{14} + x_{15} + x_{16})$ (30% single people phone interview restriction).

The left-hand side of the inequality indicates the variables of all of the phone interviews conducted with single people, while the right-hand side of the inequality shows 30 percent of all phone interviews. Rewriting this equation results in the following inequality:

$$.70x_{11} - .30x_{12} + .70x_{13} - .30x_{14} + .70x_{15} - .30x_{16} \leq 0$$

Similar logic can be applied to mail-in questionnaires.

$$x_{21} + x_{23} + x_{25} \leq .30(x_{21} + x_{22} + x_{23} + x_{24} + x_{25} + x_{26})$$ (30% single people mail-in questionnaire restriction).

Rewriting this equation results in the following inequality:

$$.70x_{21} - .30x_{22} + .70x_{23} - .30x_{24} + .70x_{25} - .30x_{26} \leq 0$$

At least 25 percent of the phone interviews and mail-in questionnaires must be conducted with households that contain married couples. These are two separate constraints to be written: one for phone interviews and one for mail-in questionnaires. First we will write the phone interview constraint, then it will be easy to duplicate that for the mail-in questionnaires.

$$x_{12} + x_{14} + x_{16} \geq .25(x_{11} + x_{12} + x_{13} + x_{14} + x_{15} + x_{16})$$

Rewriting this equation results in the following inequality:

$$-.25x_{11} + .75x_{12} - .25x_{13} + .75x_{14} - .25x_{15} + .75x_{16} \geq 0$$

Applying the same logic to mail-in questionnaire variables results in the following inequality:

$$x_{22} + x_{24} + x_{26} \geq .25(x_{21} + x_{22} + x_{23} + x_{24} + x_{25} + x_{26})$$

Rewriting this equation results in the following inequality:

$$-.25x_{21} + .75x_{22} - .25x_{23} + .75x_{24} - .25x_{25} + .75x_{26} \geq 0$$

We can summarize the linear programming formulation of this problem as follows:

x_{ij} = number of phone interviews or questionnaires used to reach household type j

where

$i = 1, 2$ 1 = phone interview, 2 = mail-in questionnaire
$j = 1, 2, 3, 4, 5, 6$ (j represents the six household categories defined earlier)

$$\text{minimize } Z = 10x_{11} + 11x_{12} + 12x_{13} + 15x_{14} + 7x_{15} + 9x_{16} + 1x_{21} + 1x_{22} + 1.5x_{23} + 1.5x_{24} + 1x_{25} + 1x_{26}$$

Subject to:

$$x_{11} + x_{12} + x_{13} + x_{14} + x_{15} + x_{16} = 2000$$ (target number of phone interviews)
$$x_{21} + x_{22} + x_{23} + x_{24} + x_{25} + x_{26} = 48\,000$$ (target number of mail-in questionnaires)
$$-.60x_{11} - .60x_{12} + .40x_{13} + .40x_{14} - .60x_{15} - .60x_{16} \geq 0$$
$$-.50x_{21} - .50x_{22} + .50x_{23} + .50x_{24} - .50x_{25} - .50x_{26} \geq 0$$
$$.70x_{11} - .30x_{12} + .70x_{13} - .30x_{14} + .70x_{15} - .30x_{16} \leq 0$$
$$.70x_{21} - .30x_{22} + .70x_{23} - .30x_{24} + .70x_{25} - .30x_{26} \leq 0$$
$$-.25x_{11} + .75x_{12} - .25x_{13} + .75x_{14} - .25x_{15} + .75x_{16} \geq 0$$
$$-.25x_{21} + .75x_{22} - .25x_{23} + .75x_{24} - .25x_{25} + .75x_{26} \geq 0$$
$x_{ij} \geq 0$ for all i, j combinations

Solution

$x_{13} = 600$	(number of phone interviews completed with households containing single parents with children under 18 years of age)
$x_{14} = 600$	(number of phone interviews completed with households containing married families with children under 18 years of age)
$x_{16} = 800$	(number of phone interviews completed with households containing married people over 40 years old without children under 18 years of age)
$x_{22} = 24\ 000$	(number of mail-in questionnaires completed with households containing married people under 40 years old without children under 18 years of age)
$x_{23} = 14\ 400$	(number of mail-in questionnaires completed with households containing single parents with children under 18 years of age)
$x_{24} = 9600$	(number of mail-in questionnaires completed with households containing married families with children under 18 years of age)
$Z = \$83\ 400$	

4.6 FINANCIAL APPLICATIONS

Linear programming has many applications in finance. These applications range from financial planning for banks to portfolio selection. In the next sections, we will first provide an example of how banks can utilize linear programming in planning their finances; then we will illustrate a portfolio selection example.

Financial Planning Problems for Banks

Linear programming can be very beneficial in banking by solving **financial planning problems.** In banking one of the important decisions that bankers make involves how to allocate funds among the various types of loans and investment securities. Decisions are based on maximizing annual rate of return subject to provincial and federal government regulations, and bank policies and restrictions. Consider the following financial planning example.

EXAMPLE 4-7

A Canadian bank issues five types of loans. In addition, to diversify its portfolio, and to minimize risk, the bank invests in risk-free securities. The loans and the risk-free securities with their annual rate of return are given in Table 4-3.

Table 4-3 Rates of Return for Financial Planning Problem

Type of Loan or Security	Annual Rate of Return (%)
Home mortgage (first)	6
Home mortgage (second)	8
Commercial loan	11
Automobile loan	9
Home improvement loan	10
Risk-free securities	4

The bank's objective is to maximize the annual rate of return on investments subject to the following policies, restrictions, and regulations:

1. The bank has $90 million in available funds.
2. Risk-free securities must contain at least 10 percent of the total funds available for investments.
3. Home improvement loans cannot exceed $8 000 000.
4. The investment in mortgage loans must be at least 60 percent of all the funds invested in loans.
5. The investment in first mortgage loans must be at least twice as much as the investment in second mortgage loans.
6. Home improvement loans cannot exceed 40 percent of the funds invested in first mortgage loans.
7. Automobile loans and home improvement loans together may not exceed the commercial loans.
8. Commercial loans cannot exceed 50 percent of the total funds invested in mortgage loans.

First we must define the decision variables:

x_1 = dollars invested in first home mortgage loans
x_2 = dollars invested in second home mortgage loans
x_3 = dollars invested in commercial loans
x_4 = dollars invested in automobile loans
x_5 = dollars invested in home improvement loans
x_6 = dollars invested in risk-free securities

The objective function can be stated as follows:

maximize $Z = .06x_1 + .08x_2 + .11x_3 + .09x_4 + .10x_5 + .04x_6$

This objective function is subject to the following constraints. First we state the budget constraint:

$$x_1 + x_2 + x_3 + x_4 + x_5 + x_6 = 90\,000\,000 \qquad (1)$$

Note that by using the equality sign, we force the entire budget to be spent.

The minimum funds invested in risk-free securities to control risk can be stated as follows:

$$x_6 \geq .10\,(90\,000\,000)$$

or

$$x_6 \geq 9\,000\,000 \qquad (2)$$

The constraint "Home improvement loans cannot exceed \$8 000 000" can be stated as follows:

$$x_5 \le 8\,000\,000 \quad (3)$$

The investment in mortgage loans must be at least 60 percent of all the funds invested in loans.

$$x_1 + x_2 \ge .6(x_1 + x_2 + x_3 + x_4 + x_5)$$

Note that we did not state the right-hand-side of the constraint as 54 000 000 or 60 percent of the total budget value of 90 000 000 because investment in risk-free securities is not included in the restriction.

x_1 and x_2 are decision variables that involve the mortgage loans; x_1 through x_5 are funds invested in all loans. Since investment in mortgage loans must "at least" be equal to 60 percent of the funds invested in all loans, we must utilize the greater than or equal to sign as follows: $x_1 + x_2 \ge .60(x_1 + x_2 + x_3 + x_4 + x_5)$. After converting it into computer-implementation-ready form by moving all of the variable values to the left-hand side of the inequality, the inequality takes the following form:

$$.40x_1 + .40x_2 - .60x_3 - .60x_4 - .60x_5 \ge 0 \quad (4)$$

The investment in first mortgage loans must be at least twice as much as the investment in second mortgage loans. This constraint can be set up so that we must invest at least twice as much funds in the first mortgage loans as we do in the second mortgage loans. This can be stated as $x_1 \ge 2x_2$, and after converting,

$$x_1 - 2x_2 \ge 0 \quad (5)$$

Home improvement loans cannot exceed 40 percent of the funds invested in first mortgage loans. This constraint can be stated as $x_5 \le .40x_1$. The left-hand side of the inequality is the variable home improvement loans and the right side of the inequality is 40 percent of the first home mortgage loans. After converting, the inequality is stated as follows:

$$-.4x_1 + x_5 \le 0 \quad (6)$$

Automobile loans and home improvement loans together may not exceed the commercial loans; this can be stated as $x_4 + x_5 \le x_3$, and after rewriting,

$$-x_3 + x_4 + x_5 \le 0 \quad (7)$$

Commercial loans cannot exceed 50 percent of the total funds invested in mortgage loans: $x_3 \le .50(x_1 + x_2)$, and after rewriting,

$$-.50x_1 - .50x_2 + x_3 \le 0 \quad (8)$$

The linear programming formulation of the bank financial problem can be summarized as follows:

Let

x_1 = dollars invested in first home mortgage loans
x_2 = dollars invested in second home mortgage loans
x_3 = dollars invested in commercial loans
x_4 = dollars invested in automobile loans

x_5 = dollars invested in home improvement loans
x_6 = dollars invested in risk free securities

maximize $Z = .06x_1 + .08x_2 + .11x_3 + .09x_4 + .10x_5 + .04x_6$

subject to:

$$
\begin{array}{lr}
x_1 + x_2 + x_3 + x_4 + x_5 + x_6 = 90\,000\,000 & (1)\\
x_6 \geq 9\,000\,000 & (2)\\
x_5 \leq 8\,000\,000 & (3)\\
.40x_1 + .40x_2 - .60x_3 - .60x_4 - .60x_5 \geq 0 & (4)\\
x_1 - 2x_2 \geq 0 & (5)\\
-.4x_1 + x_5 \leq 0 & (6)\\
-x_3 + x_4 + x_5 \leq 0 & (7)\\
-.50x_1 - .50x_2 + x_3 \leq 0 & (8)
\end{array}
$$

$x_1, x_2, x_3, x_4, x_5, x_6 \geq 0$ (nonnegativity constraint)

Solution

$x_1 = 32\,400\,000$ (dollars invested in first home mortgage loans)
$x_2 = 16\,200\,000$ (dollars invested in second home mortgage loans)
$x_3 = 24\,300\,000$ (dollars invested in commercial loans)
$x_4 = 99\,999.27$ (dollars invested in automobile loans)
$x_5 = 8\,000\,000$ (dollars invested in home improvement loans)
$x_6 = 9\,000\,000$ (dollars invested in risk-free securities)
$Z = \$7\,082\,000.00$ (profit over the investment of $90 000 000)

Portfolio Selection

Portfolio selection problems generally involve allocating a fixed dollar amount (e.g., $100 000) among a variety of investments such as bonds, stocks, real estate, and so on. Usually the goal is to maximize income or total return. The problems take on an added dimension when certain other requirements are specified (for instance, no more than 40 percent of the portfolio can be invested in bonds). The next example illustrates this kind of problem.

EXAMPLE 4-8

A conservative investor has $100 000 to invest. The investor has decided to use three vehicles for generating income: municipal bonds, a certificate of deposit (CD), and a money market account. After reading a financial newsletter, the investor has also identified several additional restrictions on the investments:

1. No more than 40 percent of the investment should be in bonds.
2. The proportion allocated to the money market account should be at least double the amount in the CD.

The annual return will be 8 percent for bonds, 9 percent for the CD, and 7 percent for the money market account. Assume the entire amount will be invested.

Formulate the LP model for this problem, ignoring any transaction costs and the potential for different investment lives. Assume that the investor wants to maximize the total annual return.

Solution

x_1 = amount invested in bonds
x_2 = amount invested in the CD
x_3 = amount invested in the money market account

The annual return from each investment is the product of the rate of return and the amount invested. Thus, the objective function is

maximize $Z = .08x_1 + .09x_2 + .07x_3$

The requirement that no more than 40 percent be in bonds produces this constraint:

$x_1 \leq .40(\$100\ 000)$, which becomes $x_1 \leq \$40\ 000$

The requirement that the proportion invested in the money market account be at least double the amount in the CD leads to: $x_3 \geq 2x_2$. Then, subtracting $2x_2$ from both sides gives us $x_3 - 2x_2 \geq 0$, which can be rearranged so that x_2 comes before x_3: $-2x_2 + x_3 \geq 0$. Finally, the investor must recognize that the amounts invested in bonds, the CD, and the money market account must equal \$100 000. This gives us

$x_1 + x_2 + x_3 = \$100\ 000$ (budget constraint)

In sum, the model is:

maximize $Z = .08x_1 + .09x_2 + .07x_3$

subject to

Amount in bonds	x_1	$\leq \$40\ 000$
Money/CD	$-2x_2 + x_3 \geq$	0
Investment	$x_1 + x_2 + x_3 =$	$\$100\ 000$
	$x_1, x_2, \text{and } x_3 \geq$	0

Solution to portfolio problem

$x_1 = \$40\ 000$ (amount invested in bonds)
$x_2 = \$20\ 000$ (amount invested in CD)
$x_3 = \$40\ 000$ (amount invested in the money market account)
$Z = \$7800$ (profit over the investment of \$100 000)

Note: If the problem had stated that the investor did not necessarily want to invest the entire \$100 000, the investment constraint would have been a less-than-or-equal-to constraint:

$x_1 + x_2 + x_3 \leq \$100\ 000$

In addition, the bond constraint would be affected because the amount in bonds is related to the amount invested. The bond constraint would have been

$x_1 \leq .40(x_1 + x_2 + x_3)$

which would be rearranged to

$.60x_1 - .40x_2 - .40x_3 \leq 0$

Multiperiod Financial Planning Models

The examples discussed in the previous sections and many others in this textbook are concerned with decisions to be made over a single period of time. The models obtained in these examples are called **static models,** since it was assumed that all decisions are taken at one point in time. Various other situations arise where decisions are made at many points in time. The class of models obtained in such situations are called **multiperiod** or **dynamic models,** since future decisions are impacted by decisions made in earlier periods. Example 4-9 provides an illustration of a multiperiod investment problem.

EXAMPLE 4-9

Consider the conservative investor in Example 4-8. We assume that the certificate of deposit (CD) must be locked for three years and yield a total return of 9 percent, the municipal bonds must be locked for two years and yield a total return of 6 percent, and the money market account has an annual return of 4.5 percent. The investor wants to complete his investment strategy for the next four years. The investor has $100 000 available for investment but has set that:

1. No more than $40 000 of the investment should be in bonds at any time.
2. The amount allocated any time to the money market account should be at least double the amount in the CD.
3. At least $45 000 must be available at the beginning of the fifth year to be used for a mortgage renewal.

Formulate a linear program that will help the investor to determine how to invest over the next four years, ignoring any transaction costs. Assume that the investor wants to maximize the total return over the investment planning horizon.

Solution

The conservative investor must decide the amount to invest in each investment type at the beginning of each period. Figure 4-1 illustrates the investment timelines, where for $j = 1,2,3,$ and 4,

x_j = amount invested in the CD at the beginning of year j,
y_j = amount invested in bonds at the beginning of year j,
w_j = amount invested in the money market account at the beginning of year j.

An arrow indicates the length of the investment (e.g., 1 year, 2 years, or 3 years) with the start time and the end time. The arrow head indicates the maturing time of a given investment option. The corresponding amount (the principle) is therefore available for possible re-investment, in addition to the interest earned. For instance, the amounts invested in certificates of deposit at the beginning of the first year (x_1), bonds at the beginning of year 2, and in the money market accounts at the beginning of year 3 will be available at the end of year 3. The return from each investment is the product of the rate of return and the amount invested. Thus, the function objective that defines the total returns over the four years of the investment planning horizon can be stated as follows:

$$\text{maximize} \quad Z = 0.09(x_1 + x_2 + x_3 + x_4) + 0.06(y_1 + y_2 + y_3 + y_4) + 0.045(w_1 + w_2 + w_3 + w_4) \qquad (1)$$

FIGURE 4-1 Investment Timeline Illustration for Example 4-9

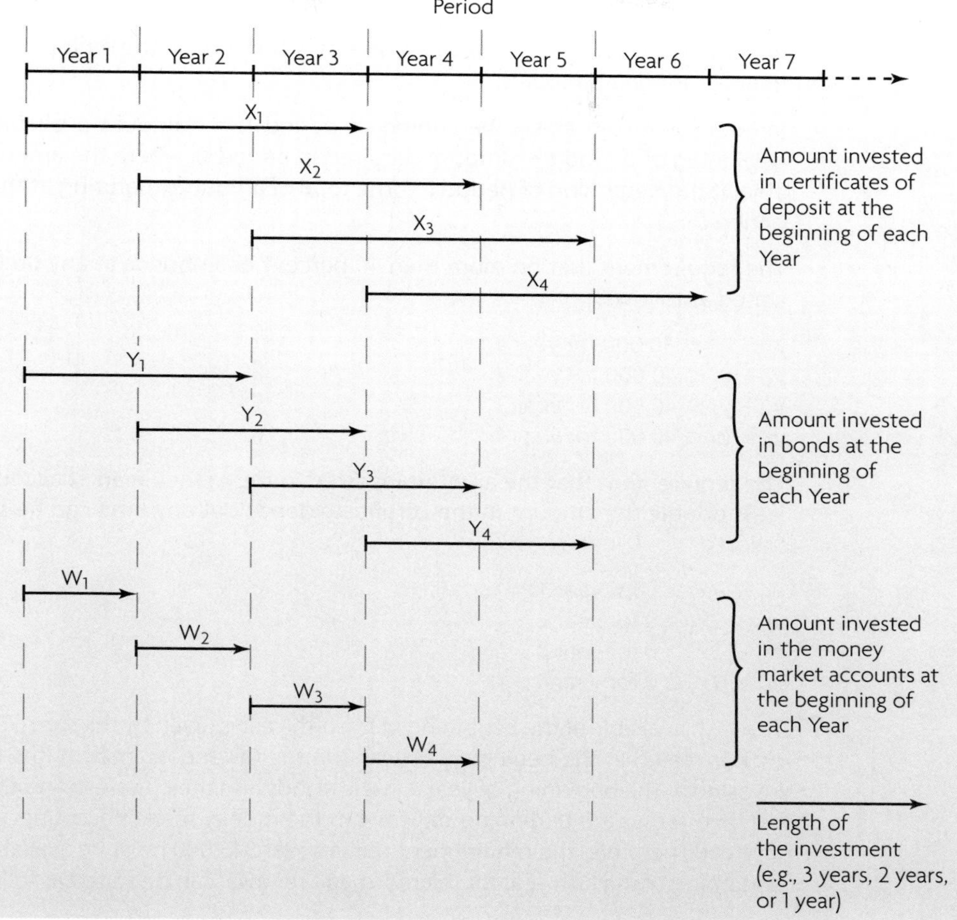

The total investment at the beginning of the first year is limited to \$100 000, the budget available. For the remaining years, the total investment is limited to principal and investment returns from previous years. Therefore, year 1's total investment is limited to \$100 000:

$$x_1 + y_1 + w_1 = 100\,000 \tag{2}$$

Year 2's total investment is limited to principal and interest invested in the money market accounts at the beginning of year 1:

$$x_2 + y_2 + w_2 - 1.045w_1 = 0 \tag{3}$$

Year 3's total investment amount is limited to principal and interest invested in bonds at the beginning of year 1 and in the money market accounts at the beginning of year 2:

$$x_3 + y_3 + w_3 - 1.06y_1 - 1.045w_2 = 0 \tag{4}$$

Year 4's total investment amount is limited to principal and interest invested in the certificate of deposit at the beginning of year 1, in bonds at the beginning of year 2, and in the money market accounts at the beginning of year 3:

$$x_4 + y_4 + w_4 - 1.09x_1 - 1.06y_2 - 1.045w_3 = 0 \quad (5)$$

In general, the following type of constraint is common in the multiperiod financial planning models:

(amount invested at the beginning of period t) = (amount available at the beginning of period t − amount required in period t), where the amount available at the beginning of period t = the total of amounts maturing at the end of period $t - 1$.

The requirement that no more than 40 percent be in bonds at any time can be stated as follows:

$$y_1 \leq 40\,000 \text{ for year 1} \quad (6)$$
$$y_1 + y_2 \leq 40\,000 \text{ for year 2} \quad (7)$$
$$y_2 + y_3 \leq 40\,000 \text{ for year 3} \quad (8)$$
$$y_3 + y_4 \leq 40\,000 \text{ for year 4} \quad (9)$$

The requirement that the amount invested in the money market account be at least double the amount in the certificate deposit at any time can be stated as follows:

$$w_1 - 2x_1 \geq 0 \text{ for year 1} \quad (10)$$
$$w_2 - 2x_2 \geq 0 \text{ for year 2} \quad (11)$$
$$w_3 - 2x_3 \geq 0 \text{ for year 3} \quad (12)$$
$$w_4 - 2x_4 \geq 0 \text{ for year 4} \quad (13)$$

The cash available at the beginning of the fifth year is given by the sum of the principal invested at the beginning of year 2 in the CD and its interest, the principal invested at the beginning of year 3 in the bonds and their interest; and the principal invested at the beginning of year 4 in the money market accounts and their interest. Therefore, the requirement that at least $45 000 must be available at the beginning of the fifth year for the mortgage renewal can be stated as follows:

$$1.09x_2 + 1.06y_3 + 1.045w_4 \geq 45\,000 \quad (14)$$

In summary, combining equations (1) to (14), the model can be stated as:

maximize $Z = 0.09(x_1 + x_2 + x_3 + x_4) + 0.06(y_1 + y_2 + y_3 + y_4) + 0.045 (w_1 + w_2 + w_3 + w_4)$

Subject to

$$x_1 + y_1 + w_1 = 100\,000$$
$$x_2 + y_2 + w_2 - 1.045w_1 = 0$$
$$x_3 + y_3 + w_3 - 1.06y_1 - 1.045w_2 = 0$$
$$x_4 + y_4 + w_4 - 1.09x_1 - 1.06y_2 - 1.045w_3 = 0$$
$$y_1 \leq 40\,000$$
$$y_1 + y_2 \leq 40\,000$$
$$y_2 + y_3 \leq 40\,000$$
$$y_3 + y_4 \leq 40\,000$$

$$w_1 - 2x_1 \geq 0$$
$$w_2 - 2x_2 \geq 0$$
$$w_3 - 2x_3 \geq 0$$
$$w_4 - 2x_4 \geq 0$$
$$1.09x_2 + 1.06y_3 + 1.045w_4 \geq 45\,000$$
$$x_j \geq 0; j = 1,2,3,4$$
$$y_j \geq 0; j = 1,2,3,4$$
$$w_j \geq 0; j = 1,2,3,4$$

The Excel setup of the linear programming model and the solver parameter entries are shown in Exhibit 4-5 and Exhibit 4-6 respectively.

EXHIBIT 4-5 Excel Input Screen for Example 4-9

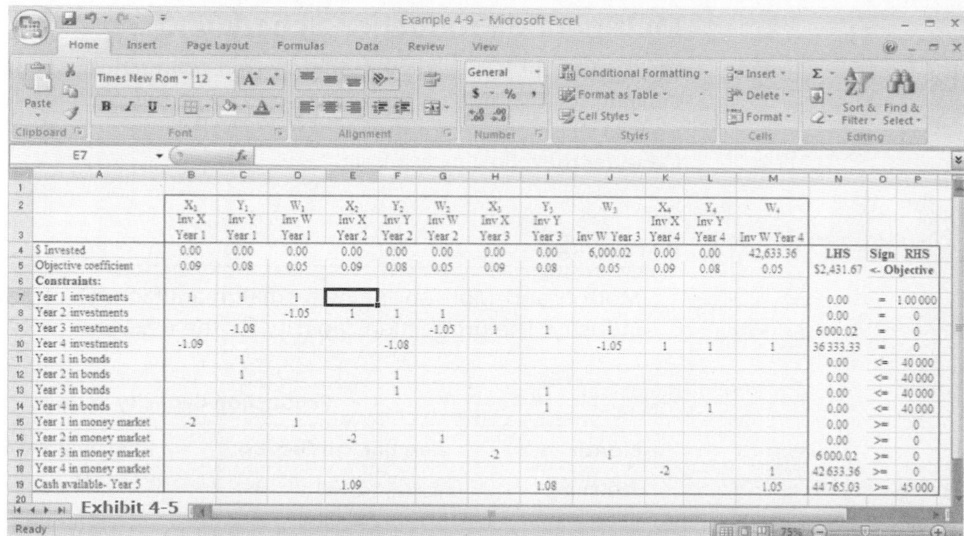

	X_1 Inv X Year 1	Y_1 Inv Y Year 1	W_1 Inv W Year 1	X_2 Inv X Year 2	Y_2 Inv Y Year 2	W_2 Inv W Year 2	X_3 Inv X Year 3	Y_3 Inv Y Year 3	W_3 Inv W Year 3	X_4 Inv X Year 4	Y_4 Inv Y Year 4	W_4 Inv W Year 4			
$ Invested	0.00	0.00	0.00	0.00	0.00	0.00	0.00	0.00	6,000.02	0.00	0.00	42,633.36	**LHS**	**Sign**	**RHS**
Objective coefficient	0.09	0.08	0.05	0.09	0.08	0.05	0.09	0.08	0.05	0.09	0.08	0.05	$2,431.67	**<- Objective**	
Constraints:															
Year 1 investments	1	1	1										0.00	=	1 00 000
Year 2 investments			-1.05	1	1	1							0.00	=	0
Year 3 investments		-1.08				-1.05	1	1	1				6000.02	=	0
Year 4 investments	-1.09				-1.08				-1.05	1	1	1	36 333.33	=	0
Year 1 in bonds		1											0.00	<=	40 000
Year 2 in bonds		1			1								0.00	<=	40 000
Year 3 in bonds					1			1					0.00	<=	40 000
Year 4 in bonds								1			1		0.00	<=	40 000
Year 1 in money market	-2		1										0.00	>=	0
Year 2 in money market				-2		1							0.00	>=	0
Year 3 in money market							-2		1				6000.02	>=	0
Year 4 in money market										-2		1	42 633.36	>=	0
Cash available- Year 5				1.09				1.08				1.05	44 765.03	>=	45 000

EXHIBIT 4-6 Parameters Specification Screen for Example 4-9

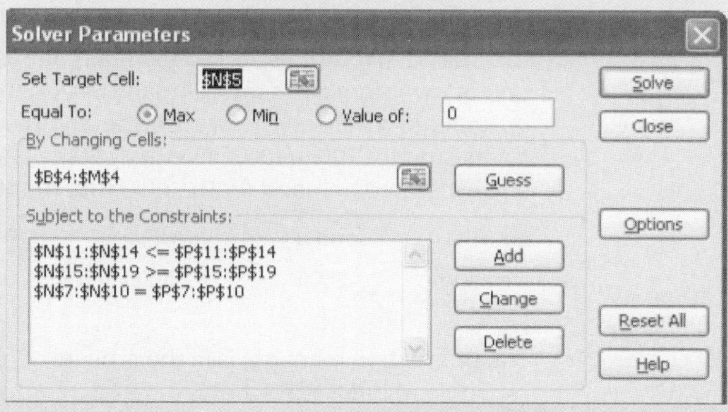

The problem solution requires investing \$100 000 in money market accounts at the beginning of year 1; \$104 500 in money market accounts at the beginning of year 2; \$109 202.50 in money market accounts at the beginning of year 3; and \$38 038.87 in certificates of deposit and \$76 077.74 in money market accounts at the beginning of year 4. The total returns over the investment planning horizon equal \$20 963.61.

4.7 PRODUCTION APPLICATIONS

There are numerous applications of linear programming in production management. This chapter will demonstrate three distinct types of applications that involve manufacturing: production scheduling, workforce scheduling, and make-or-buy decisions.

Multiperiod Production Scheduling

The first of the applications is multiperiod **production scheduling problems.** When the demand for the product varies across different time periods, linear programming can be used to determine a production schedule of a product over several production periods. Consider the following example.

EXAMPLE 4-10

Morton and Monson Inc. is a small manufacturer of parts for the aerospace industry. The production capacity for the next four months is given as follows:

Production Capacity in Units

Month	Regular Production	Overtime Production
January	3000	500
February	2000	400
March	3000	600
April	3500	800

The regular cost of production is \$500 per unit and the cost of overtime production is \$150 per unit in addition to the regular cost of production. The company can utilize inventories to reduce fluctuations in production, but carrying one unit of inventory costs the company \$40 per unit per month. Currently there are no units in inventory. However, the company wants to maintain a minimum safety stock of 100 units of inventory at the end of January, February, and March. The estimated demand for the next four months is as follows:

Month	January	February	March	April
Demand	2800	3000	3500	3000

The production manager is in the process of preparing a four-month production schedule. What is the schedule that minimizes total cost, if the company wants to have 300 units in inventory at the end of April?

First, we define the decision variables as follows:

$i = 1, 2, 3, 4$ $\quad$ 1 = January, 2 = February, 3 = March, 4 = April,
x_i = quantity produced in month i on a regular time basis for $i = 1, 2, 3, 4$
y_i = quantity produced in month i on overtime for $i = 1, 2, 3, 4$
I_i = quantity in inventory at the end of month i for $i = 1, 2, 3, 4$

The objective function and the constraints for this problem can be stated as follows:

$$\text{minimize } Z = 500(x_1 + x_2 + x_3 + x_4) + 650(y_1 + y_2 + y_3 + y_4) + 40(I_1 + I_2 + I_3 + I_4)$$

subject to:

$$\left.\begin{array}{l} x_1 \leq 3000 \\ x_2 \leq 2000 \\ x_3 \leq 3000 \\ x_4 \leq 3500 \end{array}\right\} \text{(regular time production constraint for each month)}$$

$$\left.\begin{array}{l} y_1 \leq 500 \\ y_2 \leq 400 \\ y_3 \leq 600 \\ y_4 \leq 800 \end{array}\right\} \text{(overtime production constraint for each month)}$$

The inventory at the end of the previous period plus the total production (regular + overtime) minus what we carry in inventory must equal the demand for a particular month. These constraints result in the following transition equalities:

$$\begin{array}{l} I_0 + x_1 + y_1 - I_1 = 2800 \\ I_1 + x_2 + y_2 - I_2 = 3000 \\ I_2 + x_3 + y_3 - I_3 = 3500 \\ I_3 + x_4 + y_4 - I_4 = 3000 \end{array}$$

The inventory constraints can be formulated as follows:

$$\begin{array}{l} I_0 = 0 \\ I_1 \geq 100 \\ I_2 \geq 100 \\ I_3 \geq 100 \\ I_4 = 300 \end{array}$$

The addition of the following nonnegativity constraint completes the formulation of this problem.

All $x_i, y_i, I_i \geq 0$ $\quad$ for $i = 1, 2, 3,4$

In summary, the formulation of this problem is as follows:

$$\begin{aligned} \text{minimize } Z = {} & 500x_1 + 500x_2 + 500x_3 + 500x_4 + 650y_1 + 650y_2 + 650y_3 + 650y_4 \\ & 40I_1 + 40I_2 + 40I_3 + 40I_4 \end{aligned}$$

subject to:

$$\left.\begin{array}{l} x_1 \leq 3000 \\ x_2 \leq 2000 \\ x_3 \leq 3000 \\ x_4 \leq 3500 \end{array}\right\} \text{(regular time production constraint for each month)}$$

$$\left.\begin{aligned} y_1 &\le 500 \\ y_2 &\le 400 \\ y_3 &\le 600 \\ y_4 &\le 800 \end{aligned}\right\} \quad \text{(overtime production constraint for each month)}$$

$$\left.\begin{aligned} I_0 + x_1 + y_1 - I_1 &= 2800 \\ I_1 + x_2 + y_2 - I_2 &= 3000 \\ I_2 + x_3 + y_3 - I_3 &= 3500 \\ I_3 + x_4 + y_4 - I_4 &= 3000 \end{aligned}\right\} \quad \text{(transition constraints)}$$

$$\left.\begin{aligned} I_1 &\ge 100 \\ I_2 &\ge 100 \\ I_3 &\ge 100 \end{aligned}\right\} \quad \text{(minimum inventory investment for the first three quarters)}$$

$I_4 = 300$ (ending inventory constraint for the month of April)

All $x_i, y_i, I_i \ge 0$ for $i = 1, 2, 3, 4$

Solution

$x_1 = 3000$ (quantity produced in January on a regular time basis)
$x_2 = 2000$ (quantity produced in February on a regular time basis)
$x_3 = 3000$ (quantity produced in March on a regular time basis)
$x_4 = 3200$ (quantity produced in April on a regular time basis)
$y_1 = 500$ (quantity produced in January on overtime)
$y_2 = 400$ (quantity produced in February on overtime)
$y_3 = 500$ (quantity produced in March on overtime)
$I_1 = 700$ (quantity in inventory at the end of January)
$I_2 = 100$ (quantity in inventory at the end of February)
$I_3 = 100$ (quantity in inventory at the end of March)
$I_4 = 300$ (quantity in inventory at the end of April)
$Z = \$6\,558\,000$

Workforce Scheduling

Linear programming can be extremely helpful in scheduling personnel, that is, **workforce scheduling problems.** Lets consider the following hospital example. Linear programming can be used to determine the best set of assignments of workers subject to demand and company-imposed restrictions to minimize the cost of making those assignments. Let's consider the following example.

EXAMPLE 4-11

Lincoln General Hospital is trying to determine the nursing schedule of the pediatric department. The nursing staff consists of full-time nurses who work eight-hour shifts and part-time nurses who work four-hour shifts. The supervisor of nurses divides the day into six four-hour periods. In each period, a different level of demand (number of cases to be treated) is expected, which requires different numbers of nurses to be hired. The required number of nurses for each time period is given in Table 4-4.

Table 4-4 Staffing Requirements for Workforce Scheduling Problem

i = Time Period Index	Time Period	Required Number of Nurses
1	7–11 a.m.	7
2	11 a.m.–3 p.m.	9
3	3–7 p.m.	12
4	7–11 p.m.	5
5	11 p.m.–3 a.m.	4
6	3–7 a.m.	3

It is also required that there must be at least two full-time nurses at each time period and the number of part-time nurses cannot exceed the number of full-time nurses in any time period. The full-time nurses get paid $160 per shift, while the part-time nurses get paid $50 per shift. The normal shifts can begin at the start of any of the four-hour periods.

The decision variables can be defined as

x_i = number of full-time nurses scheduled during time period i for $i = 1, 2, 3, 4, 5, 6$ as defined in Table 4-4.

y_i = number of part-time nurses scheduled during time period i for $i = 1, 2, 3, 4, 5, 6$ as defined in Table 4-4.

The objective function for this problem can be written as

$$\text{minimize } Z = 160(x_1 + x_2 + x_3 + x_4 + x_5 + x_6) + 50(y_1 + y_2 + y_3 + y_4 + y_5 + y_6)$$

In writing the constraints for this problem, there must be a constraint for each time period, as specified below.

$$\left.\begin{aligned} x_1 + x_6 + y_1 &\geq 7 \\ x_1 + x_2 + y_2 &\geq 9 \\ x_2 + x_3 + y_3 &\geq 12 \\ x_3 + x_4 + y_4 &\geq 5 \\ x_4 + x_5 + y_5 &\geq 4 \\ x_5 + x_6 + y_6 &\geq 3 \end{aligned}\right\} \quad \begin{aligned} &\text{(constraint for nurses starting at 7 a.m.)} \\ &\text{(constraint for nurses starting at 11 a.m.)} \\ &\text{(constraint for nurses starting at 3 p.m.)} \\ &\text{(constraint for nurses starting at 7 p.m.)} \\ &\text{(constraint for nurses starting at 11 p.m.)} \\ &\text{(constraint for nurses starting at 3 a.m.)} \end{aligned}$$

$$\left.\begin{aligned} x_1 + x_6 &\geq 2 \\ x_1 + x_2 &\geq 2 \\ x_2 + x_3 &\geq 2 \\ x_3 + x_4 &\geq 2 \\ x_4 + x_5 &\geq 2 \\ x_5 + x_6 &\geq 2 \end{aligned}\right\} \quad \text{(there must be at least two full-time nurses during any period)}$$

$$\left.\begin{aligned} x_1 + x_6 &\geq y_1 \\ x_1 + x_2 &\geq y_2 \\ x_2 + x_3 &\geq y_3 \\ x_3 + x_4 &\geq y_4 \\ x_4 + x_5 &\geq y_5 \\ x_5 + x_6 &\geq y_6 \end{aligned}\right\} \quad \begin{aligned} &\text{(the number of full-time nurses must be greater than that} \\ &\text{of part-time workers)} \end{aligned}$$

$x_i \geq 0, y_i \geq 0$ for all i (nonnegativity constraint)

Solution

$x_1 = 3.5$	(number of full-time nurses scheduled from 7–11 a.m.)
$x_2 = 1$	(number of full-time nurses scheduled from 11 a.m.–3 p.m.)
$x_3 = 5$	(number of full-time nurses scheduled from 3–7 p.m.)
$x_4 = 0$	(number of full-time nurses scheduled from 7–11 p.m.)
$x_5 = 2$	(number of full-time nurses scheduled from 11 p.m.–3 a.m.)
$x_6 = 0$	(number of full-time nurses scheduled from 3–7 a.m.)
$y_1 = 3.5$	(number of part-time nurses scheduled from 7–11 a.m.)
$y_2 = 4.5$	(number of part-time nurses scheduled from 11 a.m.–3 p.m.)
$y_3 = 6$	(number of part-time nurses scheduled from 3–7 p.m.)
$y_4 = 0$	(number of part-time nurses scheduled from 7–11 p.m.)
$y_5 \geq 2$	(number of part-time nurses scheduled from 11 p.m. –3 a.m.)
$y_6 = 1$	(number of part-time nurses scheduled from 3–7 a.m.)
$Z = \$2690.00$	(total minimum cost associated with scheduling of nurses in pediatrics)

Make-or-Buy Decisions

In production management, production managers are often faced with a **make-or-buy decision,** that is, the decision of either producing a part or purchasing the part from a supplier. Linear programming can be a helpful tool in assisting managers to decide when to produce and when to purchase. Let us consider an example.

EXAMPLE 4-12

The T & L Manufacturing Company produces parts X, Y, and Q. The next month's demand for parts X, Y, and Q are 3000, 5000, and 4000 units, respectively. Even though T & L would like to manufacture all of the units demanded, it is concerned that it does not have the necessary production capacity to make all of the components. Therefore, the company is considering hiring a local supplier of these parts. The production and purchasing cost of parts X, Y, and Q are given in Table 4-5.

Table 4-5 Production and Purchasing Cost of All Parts

Component	Production Cost per Unit	Purchasing Cost per Unit
X	\$2.20	\$3.00
Y	\$1.50	\$2.80
Q	\$1.20	\$2.20

All parts must go through plating and heat-treating processes. The production time requirements per unit of parts X, Y, and Z for the plating and heat-treating processes and capacity are given in Table 4-6.

Table 4-6 Production Time Requirements and Capacity of Process

Processes	Part X	Part Y	Part Q	Total Hours Available
Plating	.2	.3	.10	1500
Heat treating	.1	.2	.05	1000

Determine the optimal production and buying schedule for parts X, Y, and Q.

First we define the decision variables. Since we have to decide between buying and making, we have to define two types of variables: manufacturing variables and purchasing variables.

M_i = number of units of production of product i
P_i = number of units purchased of product i

where

$i = X, Y, Q$

The objective function can be written as

minimize $Z = 2.2M_X + 1.5M_Y + 1.2M_Q + 3P_X + 2.8P_Y + 2.2P_Q$

This objective function is subject to the following constraints. First, we must account for demand for each product.

$$\left.\begin{aligned} M_X + P_X &= 3000 \\ M_Y + P_Y &= 5000 \\ M_Q + P_Q &= 4000 \end{aligned}\right\} \quad \text{(demand constraint for each product)}$$

Now, we need to state the capacity of the plating and heat-treating processes.

$.20M_X + .30M_Y + .10M_Q \leq 1500$ hours (capacity of plating department)
$.10M_X + .20M_Y + .05M_Q \leq 1000$ hours (capacity of heat-treating department)
All M_i and all $P_i \geq 0$ for $i = X, Y, Q$

Solutions

$M_Y = 3667$ (number of units of production of part Y)
$M_Q = 4000$ (number of units of production of part Q)
$P_X = 3000$ (number of units purchased of part X)
$P_Y = 1333$ (number of units purchased of part Y)
$Z = \$23\,033.33$ (maximum profit)

4.8 AGRICULTURE APPLICATIONS

Linear programming has many useful applications in the agriculture sector. The following example demonstrates one such useful application. **Agricultural** applications involve determining the best set of crops to plant on given farmland given demand constraints, land and cultivation, and fertilizer considerations.

EXAMPLE 4-13

A farm owner is interested in determining how to divide the farmland among four different types of crops. The farmer owns two farms in separate locations and has decided to plant the following four types of crops in these farms: corn, wheat, soybeans, and lentils. The first farm consists of 1450 acres of land, while the second farm consists of 850 acres of land. Any of the four crops may be planted on either farm. However, after a survey of the land, based on the characteristics of the farmlands, Table 4-7 shows the maximum acreage restrictions the farmer has placed for each crop.

Table 4-7 Maximum Acreage Restrictions for Agricultural Problem

	Crop			
Farm	**Corn**	**Wheat**	**Soybeans**	**Lentils**
Farm 1	550	450	350	400
Farm 2	250	300	200	350

The profit per acre for each crop is estimated as follows:

Crop	Profit/Acre
Corn	\$500
Wheat	\$400
Soybeans	\$300
Lentils	\$350

In determining the optimal cultivation of land, the farmer has to account for the cost of fertilizer estimated for each acre of land. Due to the different terrain and soil, the two farms have different costs of fertilizers per acre.

Farm	Cost of Fertilizer/Acre
Farm 1	\$100
Farm 2	\$70

Seasonal demand for the four crops is given in Table 4-8.

Table 4-8 Seasonal Demand for the Four Crops

Crop	Seasonal Demand (acres' worth)
Corn	450
Wheat	550
Soybeans	400
Lentils	600

The farmer has a storage facility that can store 100 acres' worth of the excess supply of different types of crops. In addition, the farmer wants to ensure that total wheat and soybean cultivation must be proportionally equal to the maximum acreage restriction of both farms. In other words, the farm owner wants the same proportion of wheat and soybeans on both farms. The farmer's objective is to determine how much of each crop to plant on each farm to maximize profit and satisfy seasonal demand.

First, we can use the double subscripted notation and define variables as follows: Let x_{ij} = number of acres in farm i planted with crop j. In defining the objective function, first we must specify all of the profit values for each crop in each farm and then we must subtract the cost of the fertilizers for each farm. This procedure results in the following:

$$\text{maximize } Z = 500x_{11} + 400x_{12} + 300x_{13} + 350x_{14} + 500x_{21} + 400x_{22} + 300x_{23} + 350x_{24} - 100x_{11} - 100x_{12} - 100x_{13} - 100x_{14} - 70x_{21} - 70x_{22} - 70x_{23} - 70x_{24}$$

After performing the arithmetic operations and collecting the same terms together, the objective function can be rewritten as

$$\text{maximize } Z = 400x_{11} + 300x_{12} + 200x_{13} + 250x_{14} + 430x_{21} + 330x_{22} + 230x_{23} + 280x_{24}$$

We can begin to write the constraints for this problem by considering the maximum acreage available in each farm:

$$x_{11} + x_{12} + x_{13} + x_{14} \leq 1450 \quad \text{(capacity of farm 1)}$$
$$x_{21} + x_{22} + x_{23} + x_{24} \leq 850 \quad \text{(capacity of farm 2)}$$

We can continue writing the constraints by stating the maximum acreage of each farm suitable for a certain type of crop. This requires individual less-than-or-equal-to constraints for each farm–crop combination.

$$\left.\begin{array}{l} x_{11} \leq 550 \\ x_{12} \leq 450 \\ x_{13} \leq 350 \\ x_{14} \leq 400 \\ x_{21} \leq 250 \\ x_{22} \leq 300 \\ x_{23} \leq 200 \\ x_{24} \leq 350 \end{array}\right\} \text{(maximum acreage suitable in each farm for each crop)}$$

Since the farmer can store the excess capacity, we can write the demand constraints as greater than or equal to. The demand constraints can be written as follows:

$$x_{11} + x_{21} \geq 450 \quad \text{(total demand for corn)}$$
$$x_{12} + x_{22} \geq 550 \quad \text{(total demand for wheat)}$$
$$x_{13} + x_{23} \geq 400 \quad \text{(total demand for soybeans)}$$
$$x_{14} + x_{24} \geq 600 \quad \text{(total demand for lentils)}$$

Since we can store 100 acres of crops above the level of demand, we need to add a constraint that restricts the amount of storage. Adding the demand quantities, we get a total acreage of 2000. Since we have the capacity to store up to 100 units of any crop, we add the following constraint:

$$x_{11} + x_{12} + x_{13} + x_{14} + x_{21} + x_{22} + x_{23} + x_{24} \leq 2100$$

In other words, the farmer cannot exceed farming more than 2100 acres (100 more than demanded) total for the crops.

Finally, we need to consider the proportionality constraints. Since the owner wants the same proportion of the maximum acreage for wheat and soybeans cultivated, we need to set up the proportionality constraints as follows. First, in stating the proportion of the maximum acreage cultivated for wheat, it is $(x_{12} + x_{22})/(450 + 300)$, or $(x_{12} + x_{22})/750$.

Stating the proportion of the maximum acreage cultivated for soybeans, it is $(x_{13} + x_{23})/(350 + 200) = (x_{13} + x_{23})/550$. Since the two proportions must be equal, the constraint can be written as follows:

$(x_{12} + x_{22})/750 = (x_{13} + x_{23})/550$

We can rewrite this constraint by multiplying both sides of the equality by (550)(750). The resulting equation is $550(x_{12} + x_{22}) = 750(x_{13} + x_{23})$. Simplifying this equation,

$550x_{12} + 550x_{22} - 750x_{13} - 750x_{23} = 0$

The linear programming formulation of the entire problem is given by

maximize $Z = 400x_{11} + 300x_{12} + 200x_{13} + 250x_{14} + 430x_{21} + 330x_{22} + 230x_{23} + 280x_{24}$

subject to

$x_{11} + x_{12} + x_{13} + x_{14} \leq 1450$ (capacity of farm 1)
$x_{21} + x_{22} + x_{23} + x_{24} \leq 850$ (capacity of farm 2)

$$\left.\begin{array}{l} x_{11} \leq 550 \\ x_{12} \leq 450 \\ x_{13} \leq 350 \\ x_{14} \leq 400 \\ x_{21} \leq 250 \\ x_{22} \leq 300 \\ x_{23} \leq 200 \\ x_{24} \leq 350 \end{array}\right\} \text{(Maximum acreage suitable in each farm for each crop)}$$

$x_{11} + x_{21} \geq 450$ (total demand for corn)
$x_{12} + x_{22} \geq 550$ (total demand for wheat)
$x_{13} + x_{23} \geq 400$ (total demand for soybeans)
$x_{14} + x_{24} \geq 600$ (total demand for lentils)
$x_{11} + x_{12} + x_{13} + x_{14} + x_{21} + x_{22} + x_{23} + x_{24} \leq 2100$
$550x_{12} + 550x_{22} - 750x_{13} - 750x_{23} = 0$ (proportionality constraint)

$x_{ij} \geq 0$ for all i, j combinations, where x_{ij} = number of acreas of crop j cultivated in farm i

Solution

$x_{11} = 296.667$ (acres of corn planted on farm 1)
$x_{12} = 250$ (acres of wheat planted on farm 1)
$x_{13} = 350$ (acres of soybeans planted on farm 1)
$x_{14} = 353.333$ (acres of lentils planted on farm 1)
$x_{21} = 250$ (acres of corn planted on farm 2)
$x_{22} = 300$ (acres of wheat planted on farm 2)
$x_{23} = 53.333$ (acres of soybeans planted on farm 2)
$x_{24} = 246.667$ (acres of lentils planted on farm 2)
$Z = \$639\,833.4$ (total maximum profit)

4.9 DATA ENVELOPMENT ANALYSIS

Managers are often interested in comparing the efficiency of various sections or departments within a company. **Data envelopment analysis (DEA)** is an application of linear programming that is used to make comparisons. DEA is used to measure the relative efficiency of the departments within an organization or relative efficiencies of two different organizations. DEA has been applied in various industries including fast food restaurants, hospitals, schools, and banks. Measuring the efficiency of departments within the same organization is difficult because the departments have multiple input measures (number of workers, cost of labour, cost of machine operations, pay scale for employees, and cost of advertising) and multiple output measures (profit, sales, and market share). In applying DEA, we first have to define the efficiency of a department or an organization so that we can compare the efficiencies of different departments or different organizations.

Let e_i = efficiency of unit i
wo_v = weight v applied to outputs
wi_j = weight j applied to input
O_{iv} = value of department i based on output v
I_{ij} = value of department i based on input j
k = number of output variables
w = number of input variables

Efficiency of unit i can be computed using the following equation.

$$e_i = \frac{\sum_{v=1}^{k} O_{iv}\, wo_v}{\sum_{j=1}^{w} I_{ij}\, wi_j} \tag{4-1}$$

In DEA, executing the linear programming problem will provide us with values of the decision variables, which are the weights wo_j and wi_j.

In DEA we solve a separate linear programming problem for each department, where the objective is to maximize the weighted sum of the units output. In other words, the objective can be stated as follows:

$$\text{Max} \quad \sum_{j=1}^{k} O_{iv} wo_v \tag{4-2}$$

This objective is subject to the constraint that the department's efficiency cannot exceed 100 percent. Therefore, the weighted sum of the department's outputs cannot exceed the weighted sum of the department's inputs. In other words,

$$\sum_{j=1}^{k} O_{iv}\, wo_v - \sum_{j=1}^{w} I_{ij}\, wi_j \le 0 \tag{4-3}$$

To ensure that we have a bounded solution, the sum of the weighted inputs for the department under consideration must equal 1. This requirement is given in equation (4-4).

$$\sum_{j=1}^{W} I_{ij}\, wi_j = 1 \tag{4-4}$$

This constraint also will ensure that the efficiency score for the outputs cannot exceed 1, or 100 percent.

When implementing DEA, the output variables are like profit or sales, where more is better, and the input variables are cost or number of employees, where less is better.

EXAMPLE 4-14

A consumer advocacy group would like to evaluate the efficiency of three airline companies with respect to several criteria that are important to consumers. The three companies are Beta, Unified, and Southeast.

The output measures are identified as average minutes late arriving, number of luggage losses per 10 000 customers, waiting time for check-in, friendliness, and quality of air service (result of a questionnaire that measured this output on a 100-point scale). The input measures were labour cost per day, number of flights per day, and overhead cost per day. Table 4-9 summarizes the results.

Table 4-9 Analysis of Airline Efficiency

	Airline Companies		
	Beta	**Unified**	**Southeast**
Input Measures			
Labour cost per day (i_1)	\$8 000 000	\$10 000 000	\$6 000 000
Overhead cost per day (i_2)	\$2 500 000	\$3 000 000	2 000 000
Number of flights per day (i_3)	300	400	200
Output Measures			
Average minutes late arriving (o_1)	−15	−20	−7
Number of luggage losses per 10 000 (o_2)	−10	−15	−5
Waiting time for check-in (o_3)	−10	−20	−5
Friendliness/quality of air service (o_4)	85	80	95

Note that a minus sign is included for the first three output measures: the higher the value, the better the measure. In other words, if average minutes late are −15, the airplanes are late an average of 15 minutes. Note that positive values for these three measures are impossible.

Use DEA and determine the relative efficiency of the three airline companies.

Solution

First we need to formulate the problem for Beta.

The decision variables are

wo_1 = weight associated with average minutes late arriving
wo_2 = weight associated with the number of luggage lost per 10 000
wo_3 = weight associated with waiting time for check-in
wo_4 = weight associated with friendliness/quality of air service
wi_1 = weight associated with labour cost per day
wi_2 = weight associated with overhead cost per day
wi_3 = weight associated with the number of flights per day

Second, the objective function can be stated as follows:

$$\text{maximize } Z = -15wo_1 - 10wo_2 - 10wo_3 + 85wo_4$$

Third, we need to state the efficiency constraints for each airline company:

$$-15wo_1 - 10wo_2 - 10wo_3 + 85wo_4 - 8\,000\,000wi_1 - 2\,500\,000wi_2 - 300wi_3 \leq 0$$
$$-20wo_1 - 15wo_2 - 20wo_3 + 80wo_4 - 10\,000\,000wi_1 - 3\,000\,000wi_2 - 400wi_3 \leq 0$$
$$-7wo_1 - 5wo_2 - 5wo_3 + 95wo_4 - 6\,000\,000wi_1 - 2\,000\,000wi_2 - 200wi_3 \leq 0$$

Fourth, we need to state the input constraint that the sum of the input weights equals 1.0.

$8\,000\,000wi_1 + 2\,500\,000wi_2 + 300wi_3 = 1$

Finally we need to state the nonnegativity constraint for each variable:

$wo_1, wo_2, wo_3, wo_4, wi_1, wi_2, wi_3 \geq 0$

Solving this using a linear programming software package results in the following: Z = relative efficiency of Beta = 71.4 percent with $wo_4 = .0084$ and the values of the rest of the decision variables equal to zero. Using the same formulation approach but changing the objective function (for instance, the objective function for Unified Airlines is: Maximize $Z = -20wo_1 - 15wo_2 - 20wo_3 + 80wo_4$) and the input constraints to reflect the values of Unified and Southeast, the relative efficiencies of Unified and Southeast are found to be 56.14 percent and 1.0, respectively.

Note that the relative efficiency of 100 percent does not mean that the department or the organization does not have any inefficiencies. It simply means that no linear combination of the other departments' values results in a composite score of 1.0 using the same or less input. More than one department or organization can achieve a relative efficiency of 1.0. The goal of the DEA is to identify departments or organizations that are relatively inefficient. In other words, there exists a linear combination of efficient departments that results in a composite score that yields as much output using the same or less input. However, the results of the DEA is not capable of identifying departments or organizations that are more efficient than others. Once the inefficient departments are identified, we can study the reasons for possible inefficiencies and try to improve the relative efficiency score for a department.

In our example problem, Unified's relative efficiency measure was the lowest at 56.14 percent. Looking at the values of the output measures, on the average, its planes were 20 minutes late, the company lost 15 pieces of luggage per 10 000 customers, the waiting time for check-in was 20 minutes, and the air service quality rating was 80. In all of these output measures, the performance of the company was not as good as its competitors. In addition, the achievement of the current levels of the output measures was possible with higher labour and overhead cost and by scheduling more flights (higher investment in input measures). The company should try to decrease cost or schedule fewer flights while improving its service record in waiting time for check-in, late arrivals, number of luggage lost, and the quality of air service. This may seem like a difficult task to achieve; however, once we begin to study each output measure, we can find ways of improving it without increasing the associated cost.

In summary, the goal of data envelopment analysis (DEA) is to identify the inefficient operating units. However, the goal of DEA is not to identify the relatively efficient operating units. In various DEA studies, it has been found that multiple operating units are classified as inefficient. The challenge of DEA is to understand how each relatively inefficient unit can be improved. One way to analyze the relatively inefficient operating units is to compare the various scores of that inefficient operating unit against the average score or the composite score of given criteria.

A MODERN MANAGEMENT SCIENCE APPLICATION: DEERE AND COMPANY

Deere and Company is a leading producer of equipment for agriculture and forestry with factories in Canada, United States, and other countries worldwide. Deere products are sold through international networks of independently owned dealership and retailer outlets.

Deere's Commercial and Consumer Equipment Division (C&CE) declared a goal of improving its on-time delivery from plants to dealers, while at the same time reducing inventory and maintaining customer service. Most of Deere's C&CE products must be available at the dealerships; otherwise its customers would just purchase from competitors. C&CE serves 2500 dealers, has 100 product families, and utilizes a 26-week planning horizon.

The Canadian division of C&CE is headquartered in Welland, Ontario, and its major products include loaders, rotary cutters, and utility vehicles.

C&CE hired SmartOp to assist with accomplishing this goal. SmartOp used state-of-the-art inventory optimization techniques, which included the use of linear programming. SmartOp developed a multistage inventory planning and optimization (MIPO) system for products that enabled C&CE to set acceptable inventory targets. By implementing MIPO, C&CE changed from a "push" system to a "pull" system, integrating the inventory targets it has set with appropriate dealer incentives to assist in this transformation.

C&CE reduced inventory by $890 million while maintaining service levels and improved its factories' on-time shipment from 63 to 92 percent. The MIPO algorithm that uses linear programming enabled C&CE to offer the dealerships an interest-free financial agreement up to a new recommended stocking level. Reliable inventory targets were a key factor in reducing inventory levels of not only C&CE but also the dealership partners.

Source: Reprinted by permission. L. Troyer, J. Smith, S. Marshall, E. Yaniv, S. Tayur, M. Barkman, A. Kaya, and Y. Liu, "Improving Asset Management and Order Fulfillment at Deere & Company's C&CE Division," *Interfaces* vol. 35, no. 1 (January–February 2005), pp. 76–87. Copyright (2005), the Institute for Operations Research and the Management Sciences (INFORMS), 7240 Parkway Drive, Suite 310, Hanover, MD 21076 USA.

Summary

There are many successful real-world applications of linear programming. Some of these applications are listed in Table 1-2. The Modern Management Science Application box provides another illustration, showing how Deere and Company benefited from the use of linear programming.

In this chapter, we have shown the formulation of 14 applications of linear programming. These applications include product mix, diet, blending, marketing applications in media selection and marketing research, financial applications in financial planning for banks and portfolio selection, production applications in multiperiod production scheduling, make-or-buy decisions, workforce scheduling, agricultural applications, and data envelopment analysis (DEA). The purpose of demonstrating so many different applications of linear programming is twofold. First, this shows the reader a wide variety of areas in which one can utilize linear programming. The second purpose involves the illustration of formulation of problems with different types of decision variables definitions, different types of constraints, and different types of objective functions. In addition, we have shown the Excel-based solutions of most of the linear programming problems discussed in this chapter.

The Modern Management Science Application, "Health Human Resource Planning," discusses an application of linear programming in healthcare.

A MODERN MANAGEMENT SCIENCE APPLICATION: HEALTH HUMAN RESOURCE PLANNING

Many western countries, including Canada, are experiencing a shortage of healthcare professionals that is projected to worsen over the next decade. This shortage of workers is significantly affecting the number of patients that can receive healthcare, the quality and effectiveness of the services provided, workforce attrition rates, and the length of time patients must wait for such care. Thus, effective human resource planning decisions are fundamental in achieving sustainable healthcare systems both in Canada and worldwide To help Canadian decision makers, a team of researchers from the Centre for Health Care Management at the University of British Columbia has developed a multi-period linear programming model for supporting health human resource planning decisions. The model requires multiple inputs that describe the initial characteristics of the health workforce as well as assumptions about attrition rates, demand, and costs. Based on these inputs, the model compares all feasible human resource strategies to identify education, recruitment, and promotion plans that achieve a supply-demand balance at the least cost. Possible outputs of the model include the number of students and health professionals each year in the system, the fraction of recruits from other regions versus professionals that are new to their positions, and key costs incurred. The model allows "what-if" scenario analyses to assess the impact that making changes to the assumptions would have on the solution. Examples of scenarios that could be analyzed with this context include:

- Retaining health professionals on the verge of retirement and providing initiatives aimed at decreasing the attrition rate from the profession.
- Changing assumptions regarding demand for health professionals.
- Addressing the impact that the global shortage of health professionals might have on the entire system.
- Examining changes in skill mix or role changes within a health professional group.
- Analyzing changes in financial costs such as constraining costs or expansions in budgets.
- Changing the duration of educational programs.

The model applies to a wide range of healthcare provider groups. For instance, it has been successfully applied to planning the British Columbia registered nurse workforce, the largest group of healthcare providers in the province, over a 20-year rolling horizon.

Source: M.S. Lavieri, S. Regan, M.L. Paterman, P.A. Ratner, "Applying Operation Research to Health Human Resource Planning: A Case Study of Registered Nurses in British Columbia," working paper, UBC Centre for Healthcare Management. Available online at www.chcm.ubc.ca/documents/ApplyingORtoHHRplanning_rnsinbc.pdf, accessed July 2008.

Glossary

Agricultural Problems Problems that determine the best set of crops to plant on given farmland given demand constraints, land and cultivation, and fertilizer considerations.

Blending Problems Problems that determine the optimal mixing of raw materials or other ingredients to obtain end products that have a specific consistency.

Data Envelopment Analysis (DEA) A linear programming application to measure the relative efficiency of departments or organizations with the same objectives.

Diet Problems Problems that determine the optimal mixing of raw materials or other ingredients to obtain end products that have certain characteristics.

Financial Planning Problems Problems that determine how a bank wants to allocate its funds among the various types of loans and investment securities. Decision is based on maximizing annual rate of return subject to provincial and federal government regulations, and bank policies and restrictions.

Make or Buy Decision Problems Problems that determine when to produce and when to purchase a series of products given certain capacity, cost, and company-imposed restrictions.

Marketing Research Problems Problems that determine the best number of respondents to be reached through various media (for example, interviews, mailings, or phone calls) given a number of client-specified constraints and cost considerations.

Media Selection Problems Problems that determine how to allocate an advertising budget among several different media.

Multiperiod Model Also called a dynamic model. A type of model concerned with decisions to be make at many point in time.

Portfolio Selection Problems Problems that determine the allocation of a fixed dollar amount (budget) among a variety of investments such as bonds, stocks, and real estate such that income or total return is maximized.

Product-Mix Problems Problems that determine the mix of outputs of similar products that utilize similar resources to maximize the profit given the availability of scarce resources.

Production Scheduling Problems Problems that determine a production schedule of a product over several consecutive production periods, when the demand for the product varies across different time periods to maximize profit.

Static Model A type of model concerned with decisions to be make over a single period of time.

Workforce Scheduling Problems Problems that determine the best set of assignments of workers subject to demand and company-imposed restrictions to minimize the cost of making those assignments.

Solved Problems

Problem 1

A soup company wants to determine the optimal ingredients for its vegetable soup. The main ingredients are

- Vegetables:
  - Potatoes
  - Carrots
  - Onions
- Meat
- Water
- Flavourings

The soup must meet these specifications:

a. No more than half of the soup can be vegetables.
b. The ratio of water to meat should be 8:1.
c. The amount of meat should be between 5 and 6 percent of the soup.
d. The flavourings should weigh no more than 1/2 ounce.

The cost per ounce of the ingredients is \$0.02 for potatoes, \$0.03 for carrots, \$0.01 for onions, \$0.05 for the meat, \$0.001 for the water, and \$0.05 for the flavourings.

Formulate an LP model that will determine the optimal amounts of the various ingredients to achieve 15-ounce cans of soup at minimum cost.

Solution

Identify the decision variables:

x_1 = quantity of potatoes in ounces
x_2 = quantity of carrots in ounces
x_3 = quantity of onions in ounces
x_4 = quantity of meat in ounces
x_5 = quantity of water in ounces
x_6 = quantity of flavourings in ounces

Write the objective function:

$$\text{minimize} \quad .02x_1 + .03x_2 + .01x_3 + .05x_4 + .001x_5 + .05x_6$$

Write constraints for each specification:

a. $x_1 + x_2 + x_3 \leq .50(15 \text{ oz.})$. Thus:

$$x_1 + x_2 + x_3 \leq 7.5 \text{ ounces}$$

b. $x_5/x_4 = 8/1$. Cross-multiplying yields $x_5 = 8x_4$. Then, subtracting $8x_4$ from both sides to have all variables on the left-hand side yields

$$-8x_4 + x_5 = 0$$

c. This requires *two* constraints:

$$x_4 \geq .05(15), \text{ which is } x_4 \geq .75 \text{ ounce}$$
$$x_4 \leq .06(15), \text{ which is } x_4 \leq .90 \text{ ounce}$$

d. $x_6 \leq .5$ ounce.

There is one additional constraint: The ingredients must add up to 15 ounces, the weight of a can of soup. Thus:

$$x_1 + x_2 + x_3 + x_4 + x_5 + x_6 = 15 \text{ ounces}$$

Finally, there are the nonnegativity constraints:

$$\text{All variables} \geq 0$$

Discussion and Review Questions

1. List six areas of application of linear programming and discuss the usefulness of LP in three of these areas.
2. Explain the difference in solving diet and blending problems when using linear programming.
3. In formulating many LP problems, we have a budget constraint. Explain the different consequences of using an $=$ sign versus $\leq$ sign in formulating this constraint.
4. Explain the usefulness of double subscript notation in formulating linear programming problems.
5. What is the purpose of data envelopment analysis? How do we apply linear programming in solving data envelopment analysis problems?
6. What does *proportionality constraint* mean? Give an example of setting up a proportionality constraint.
7. When is it useful to formulate a multiperiod production scheduling problem? In multiperiod production scheduling problems described in this chapter, what are the three types of variables?
8. In a multiperiod production scheduling problem, transition constraints are set up. State an example transition constraint involving regular production, overtime production, demand, and inventory.

Problems

1. Sharon Smith is the marketing manager of a large savings and loan association that has branches across Canada. She would like to mail a promotional piece to prospective borrowers. Sharon has selected three regions in which to do a mailing. A marketing agency can supply lists of prospective borrowers in each region, as shown in Table 4-10.

Table 4-10 Data for Problem 1

Region	List Size	Cost per Name
I	10 000	\$0.11
II	20 000	0.12
III	30 000	0.13

Sharon would like to have a pool of 15 000 names and would like the mail to contain at least 10 percent of the people on each list. Also, she doesn't want more than 40 percent of the list to be drawn from any region. Formulate an LP model that will accomplish these requirements for the least cost. Assume that there is no overlap among lists and that any quantity can be ordered from each list.

2. Aviation Electronics produces three types of switching devices. Each type involves a two-step assembly operation. The assembly times are shown in Table 4-11.

Table 4-11 Data for Problem 2

	Assembly Time per Unit (minutes)	
	Station 1	**Station 2**
Model A	2.5	3.0
Model B	1.8	1.6
Model C	2.0	2.2

Each workstation has a daily working time of 7.5 hours. Manager Bob Parkes wants to obtain the greatest possible profit during the next five working days. Model A yields a profit of \$8.25 per unit, Model B a profit of \$7.50 per unit, and Model C a profit of \$7.80 per unit. Assume that the firm can sell all it produces during this time, but it must fill outstanding orders for 20 units of each model type.

Formulate the linear programming model of this problem.

3. A manager of an automobile dealership must decide how many cars to order for the end of the model year. Midsize cars yield an average profit of \$500 each, and compact cars yield an average profit of \$400 each. Either type of car will cost the dealership \$8000 each, and no more than \$720 000 can be invested. The manager wants at least 10 of each type,

but no more than 50 of the midsize cars and no more than 60 of the compact cars. Formulate the linear programming model of this problem.

4. Petfoods makes dog food using a blend of three ingredients: K9, K8, and K1. The company has a regular blend, an extra blend, and puppy delite. The regular blend consists of one-third of each ingredient; the extra blend is 50 percent K9 and 25 percent each of K8 and K1. The puppy delite is 10 percent K8 and the rest K1. The dog food is produced in one-pound cans. There are 1500 pounds of K9 and 1000 pounds of each of the other ingredients available. The regular blend yields a profit of $0.20 per can, the extra blend yields $0.18 per can, and the puppy delite a profit of $0.25 per can. Formulate an LP model that can be used to determine the maximum profit combination of the different types of dog food.
5. A manufacturer of lawn and garden equipment makes two basic types of lawn mowers: a push-type and a self-propelled model. The push-type requires 9 minutes to assemble and 2 minutes to package; the self-propelled mower requires 12 minutes to assemble and 6 minutes to package. Each type has an engine. The company has 12 hours of assembly time available, 75 engines, and 5 hours of packing time. Profits are $70 for the self-propelled model and $45 for the push-type mower, per unit. Formulate a linear programming model that will enable the manager to determine how many mowers of each type to make to maximize total profit.
6. A farm consists of 600 acres of land, of which 500 acres will be planted with corn, soybeans, and wheat, according to these conditions:
   1. At least half of the planted acreage should be in corn.
   2. No more than 200 acres should be soybeans.
   3. The ratio of corn to wheat planted should be 2:1.

   It costs $20 an acre to plant corn, $15 an acre to plant soybeans, and $12 an acre to plant wheat.
   a. Formulate this problem as an LP model that will minimize planting cost while achieving the specified conditions.
   b. How would the model change if the acreage to be planted was *at least* 500?
7. A client has approached a stockbroker with the following request: Invest $100 000 for maximum annual income under these conditions:
   a. Spread the investment over no more than three different stocks.
   b. Put no more than 40 percent of the money into any one stock.
   c. Put a minimum of $10 000 into oil stock.

   The broker has identified three stocks for investing the funds. Their estimated annual returns and price per share are shown in Table 4-12.

Table 4-12 Data for Problem 7

Stock	Price per Share	Estimated Annual Return per Share
Oil	$120	$11
Auto	52	4
Health	18	2

   Formulate an LP model of the problem.
8. A high school dietician is planning menus for the upcoming month. A new item will be spaghetti with sauce. The dietician wants each serving to contain at least 10 grams of protein and at least 40 grams of carbohydrates. Spaghetti contains 5 grams of protein and 32 grams of carbohydrates per cup, and the sauce contains 4 grams of protein and 5 grams of carbohydrates per cup. For aesthetic reasons, the dietician wants the ratio of spaghetti to sauce to be 4:1.

   Spaghetti costs $0.30 per cup to buy and prepare, and sauce costs $0.40 per cup to buy and prepare. The dietician wants to minimize the cost per serving and keep the calories per serving to 330 or less. The sauce contains 100 calories per cup, and the spaghetti contains 160 calories per cup.

   Formulate a linear programming model for this problem.
9. A fuel oil company intends to distribute a new gasoline that has an octane rating of 94 percent. The company has three fuels that can be blended to achieve a range of octanes. The cost per litre and the octane ratings of these fuels are shown in Table 4-13.

Table 4-13 Cost per Litre and Octane Rating of Fuels

Fuel	Cost per Litre	Octane
A10	$0.70	.87
B11	0.75	.90
C12	.82	.98

Due to technical reasons, the ratio of C12 to A10 cannot be more than 3:1.

Prepare an LP model that will achieve the desired octane rating at minimum cost. Assume the octanes mix linearly. *Hint:* See Example 4-4.

10. The trust department of a commercial bank must make frequent decisions on customer portfolios. A typical case might involve a portfolio of $120 000. The bank's policy is to use conservative investments such as treasury notes, municipal bonds, and blue-chip stocks. Treasury notes have an annual return of 9 percent, municipal bonds a return of 8 percent, and blue-chip stocks a return of 10 percent. The bank also has a policy of not placing more of a portfolio into stocks than into treasury notes and bonds combined.

    Formulate an LP model that will yield the largest annual return for the $120 000 portfolio, given the bank's policies. Ignore transaction costs, fees, tax consequences, and so on.

11. A meat packing company makes pork sausage in 2000-pound batches. The sausage is made from pork, beef, and filler. The cost of pork is $2.50 per pound, the cost of beef is $1.80 per pound, and the cost of filler is $1.00 per pound. Each batch must contain the following:
    1. At least 800 pounds of pork.
    2. No more than 30 percent filler.
    3. At least 300 pounds of beef.

    The manager wants to know the mix of ingredients that will minimize cost. Formulate an LP model for this problem.

12. A pharmaceutical company is investigating the possibility of marketing a new dietary supplement that would contain iron, calcium, and phosphorous. The supplement would be made by mixing together three inputs, which the company refers to as T5, N1, and T4. The amounts of the three minerals (mg per ounce) contained in each input, the minimum and maximum levels of each mineral per 12-ounce bottle, and the cost per ounce of the inputs are shown in Table 4-14.

    The manager would like to know what the lowest cost combination of inputs is that would achieve the desired dietary ranges for the three minerals on a per-bottle basis. Formulate this problem as an LP model.

13. A small specialty shop. Nuts-to-You, sells a variety of candy and nuts. The owner is concerned with the problem of how to package nuts. The shop carries four types of nuts, which are sold in one-pound bags. It also sells one-pound bags of its own special mix, which consists of 40 percent peanuts and equal parts of the other three types of nuts. The shop has a limited supply of nuts on hand, and the owner believes that before the next shipment of nuts arrives, the current supply can be sold. However, the owner recognizes that different combinations of nuts (individual bags versus bags of the special mix) will yield different profits. The owner would like to know how much of the current supply to allocate to the mix and how much to each individual type to maximize profits.

    The current supply and cost per pound of each nut type are

Nut	Cost per Pound	Pounds Available
Peanuts(x_2)	$1.00	600
Cashews(x_3)	3.00	360
Walnuts(x_4)	2.50	500
Pecans(x_5)	3.50	400

The selling prices of the packaged nuts are

Package	Price
Mix (x_1)	$4.00
Peanuts (x_2)	1.50
Cashews (x_3)	4.80
Walnuts (x_4)	4.60
Pecans (x_5)	5.00

Assume that mixing costs are negligible.

Formulate this linear programming problem.

Table 4-14 Data for Problem 12

Cost per Ounce:	$0.75	$0.60	$0.55	Minimum	Maximum
Input:	T5	N1	T4	per Bottle	per Bottle
Mineral					
Iron	10	16	12	100 mg	150 mg
Calcium	400	600	800	6000 mg	8000 mg
Phosphorous	800	550	500	6600 mg	8000 mg

14. The AGC Company supplies fruit juice and juice blends to wholesale grocers in the northeast. A list of the firm's products and their revenue per ounce are shown in Table 4-15.

Table 4-15 Revenue per ounce for Different Juices

Product	Revenue per Ounce
Apple juice (x_1)	$0.03
Grape juice (x_2)	0.06
Cranberry juice (x_3)	0.05
Apple-grape juice (x_4)	0.07
Apple-cranberry juice (x_5)	0.08
Apple-cranberry juice—1 qt. (x_6)	0.08
All-in-one juice (x_7)	0.10

The apple-grape juice is 70 percent apple juice and 30 percent grape juice. The apple cranberry juice is 60 percent apple juice and 40 percent cranberry juice, and the all-in-one is 50 percent apple juice, 20 percent grape juice, and the rest cranberry juice.

The company has 200 gallons of apple juice, 100 gallons of grape juice, and 150 gallons of cranberry juice on hand, and the owner wants to know how many containers of each product to prepare to maximize profit. Cost per ounce for apple juice is $0.02; for grape juice, $0.04; and for cranberry juice, $0.03.

All products are sold in 64-ounce (two-quart) containers. The apple-cranberry juice is also sold in a one-quart size. *Hint:* Use quarts rather than ounces.

The company has an order for 10 containers of apple juice and 12 containers of the apple-cranberry one-quart size that must be filled from current supplies.

Formulate the linear programming model of this problem.

15. A small shop located on the edge of a large city sells a variety of dried fruits and nuts. The shop caters to travelers of all types; it sells one-pound boxes of individual items, such as dried bananas, as well as one-pound boxes of mixed fruits and nuts, although its popular trail mix is sold only in the two-pound size.

Because of complaints from customers about long lines at the counters, the manager has decided to prepare boxes ahead of time and place them on shelves for self-service. The manager has specified that 50 percent of current supplies should be prepackaged, and the rest should be unpackaged. The amounts of current supplies are listed in Table 4-16.

Table 4-16 Amount of Supply for Problem 15

Item	Supply (pounds)
Dried bananas	800
Dried apricots	600
Coconut pieces	500
Raisins	700
Walnuts	900

The selling prices of the various types of boxes offered are shown in Table 4-17.

Table 4-17 Prices for Problem 15

Type	Price per Box
Trail mix (x_1)	$7.00
Subway mix (x_2)	3.00
Dried bananas (x_3)	2.80
Dried apricots (x_4)	3.25
Coconut pieces (x_5)	3.60
Raisins (x_6)	3.50
Walnuts (x_7)	5.50

The manager would like to obtain as much revenue as possible from prepackaged sales. The manager has stipulated that no more than 30 percent of the prepackaged stock should be allocated to the mixes. The trail mix consists of equal parts of all individual items, whereas the subway mix consists of two parts walnuts and one part each of dried bananas, raisins, and coconut pieces.

Formulate the linear programming model for this problem.

16. A financial adviser recently received a call from a client who wanted to invest a portion of a $150 000 inheritance. The client wanted to realize an annual income, but also wanted to spend some of the money. After discussing the matter, the client and the adviser agreed that a mutual fund, corporate bonds, and a money market account would make suitable investments. The client was willing to leave allocation of the funds among these investment vehicles to the financial adviser, but with these provisions:

1. At least 20 percent of the amount invested should be in the money market account.
2. The investment must produce at least $12 000 annually.
3. The uninvested portion should be as large as possible.

The annual returns would be 11 percent for the mutual fund, 8 percent for the bonds, and 7 percent for the money market. Formulate an LP model that will achieve the client's requests. Ignore transaction costs, the adviser's fee, and so on. (*Hint:* All terms in the objective function must include a variable.)

17. Wineco produces wine coolers and sells them to retail distributors. One popular blend consists of wine, apple juice, and grape juice. Operators must adhere to certain guidelines when preparing the wine cooler:
    1. At least 10 percent of the mix must be grape juice.
    2. The ratio of apple juice to grape juice must be 2 1/2:1.
    3. The mix must contain between 20 percent and 25 percent wine.

    The company pays $1.20 per gallon for wine, $1.40 per gallon for grape juice, and $0.60 per gallon for apple juice.

    Formulate an LP model that will help the owner to determine how much wine cooler to mix each day if the capacity of the mixing equipment is 200 gallons per day and the wine cooler is sold for $4 a gallon. The owner wants to maximize profits. Ignore mixing and bottling costs.

18. The planning committee of a bank makes monthly decisions on the amount of funds to allocate to loans and to government securities. Some of the loans are secured (backed by collateral such as a home or an automobile), and some are unsecured. A list of the various types of loans and their annual rates of return are shown in Table 4-18.

Table 4-18 Annual Rate of Return for Investments

Type of Investment	Annual Rate of Return
Secured loans	
Residential mortgage (x_1)	11
Commercial mortgage (x_2)	12
Automobile (x_3)	15
Home improvement (x_4)	13
Unsecured loans	
Vacation (x_5)	17
Student (x_6)	10
Government securities (x_7)	9

In making its decision, the planning committee must satisfy certain legal requirements and bank policies. These can be summarized by the following set of conditions:

1. The amount allocated to secured loans must be at least four times the amount allocated to unsecured loans.
2. Auto and home loans should be no more than 20 percent of all secured loans.
3. Student loans should be no more than 30 percent of unsecured loans.
4. The amount allocated to government securities should be at least 10 percent, but no more than 20 percent, of available funds.
5. The amount allocated to vacation loans must not exceed 10 percent of all loans.

The bank has $5 million available for loans and investments in the next month. Formulate a linear programming model that will enable the planning committee to determine the optimal allocation of funds if the objective is to maximize the annual return, given the preceding list of conditions.

19. A classic linear programming problem involves minimizing trim loss. Here is one version of the problem:

    A mill cuts 20-foot pieces of wood into several different lengths: 8-foot, 10-foot, and 12-foot. The mill has a certain amount of 20-foot stock on hand and orders for the various sizes. The objective is to fill the orders with as little waste as possible. For example, if two 8-foot lengths are cut from a 20-foot piece, there will be a loss of 4 feet, the leftover amount.

    Currently, the mill has 350 20-foot pieces of wood on hand and the following orders, which must be filled from stock on hand:

Size in feet	Number Ordered
8	276
10	100
12	250

    a. Formulate an LP model that will enable the mill operator to satisfy the orders with minimum trim loss. (*Hint:* List the different ways the 20-foot pieces could be cut into the desired sizes.)
    b. Using your notation from *a,* write an equation for
        (1) The amount of waste that would result given a solution.
        (2) The number of pieces of each size (8-foot, 10-foot, and 12-foot).

20. This is a multiperiod production scheduling problem. Plastic Molding Manufacturer is planning the production storage and marketing of a product whose demand and selling price vary seasonally.

The company is in the process of developing a manufacturing strategy. According to the formulated strategy, the company wants to manufacture the product in the seasons during which production costs are low, and then store and sell the product when the selling price is high. The manufacturer has obtained the following estimates of the demand, cost, capacity, and expected selling price of the product for each period.

Let:

P_j = Product made (in tons) during period j
I_j = Product left in storage at the end of period j
D_j = Product demanded during period j
Beginning inventory = 500 tons
Desired ending inventory = 300 tons
(Inventory) storage costs = \$2 per ton from one period to the next

Formulate the linear programming problem that provides the optimal production schedule and maximizes the total profit.

21. Use the data envelopment analysis to measure the relative efficiency of the three fast food restaurant franchises located in three different cities in British Columbia operated by the same owner. The owner wants to identify the relatively inefficient operations and try to improve their relative efficiency scores. The relevant information is given in Table 4-20. Use DEA and identify the most efficient and inefficient fast food restaurants.

22. A publisher produces three monthly magazines: *Living Right, Living Today,* and *Living Room.* Printing one copy of a magazine requires the amounts of time and paper shown in Table 4-21, which also includes information on selling prices and demands:

Table 4-19 Data for Problem 20

Period	Production Costs (\$)	Production Capacity (tons)	Demand (tons)	Price (\$)
1	20	1500	1100	180
2	25	2000	1500	180
3	30	2200	1800	250
4	40	3000	1600	270
5	50	2700	2300	300
6	60	2500	2500	320

Table 4-20 Data for Problem 21

	Restaurants		
	Victoria	Whistler	Vancouver
Input Measures			
Weekly hours of operation	84	70	88
Daily number of employees	6	8	7
Daily cost of ingredients	\$2000	\$4000	\$3000
Output Measures			
Weekly profit	4000	\$3000	\$2500
Number of customers served/week	1500	1000	1200
City fast food market share	30%	20%	15%

Table 4-21 Information about Magazine Selling Prices and Demands for Problem 22

Title	Time (min.)	Paper (lb.)	Selling Price (\$)	Maximum Demand/Month
Living Right	1.0	.70	2.25	3000
Living Today	2.0	.90	2.75	2500
Living Room	1.5	.80	2.45	2000

The printer has 150 hours available each month for printing and 5000 pounds of paper. Production cost is a dollar an issue, regardless of which magazines are printed. The manager wants to know how many of each magazine to run each month to maximize profits, given these conditions. Solve using Excel.

23. A business consulting firm is developing a new promotion program for the holiday season for a local company that distributes high quality kitchen and home accessories. The company has recently launched an online shopping service that offers its core customers the opportunity to shop online and create their own gift packages. The company will then package and deliver the customers' orders to individual homes. The marketing campaign will promote the changes made by the company to better serve its customer base. The consulting company wants to develop a promotion plan that comprises two stages. The first stage, three months before the holidays, will target three advertising media: television, magazines, and newspapers. The second stage, one month before the holidays, will target two advertising media: catalogues and online media (e.g. send out emails to customers to offer a discount coupon). Table 4-22 shows the results of marketing research that the consulting company did, and the estimates for the audience, costs, minimum media usage, maximum media usage, and expected audience response rate (the percentage of the audience that will place order).

    a. Formulate the linear programming model that provides the optimal number of advertisements to run in each medium and maximizes the total audience contact. The company has set that magazine advertisements must not exceed 30 percent of the total number of advertisements. The promotional budgets in the first stage and the second stage are limited to \$45 000 and \$18 500 respectively.
    b. How much would adding an extra \$5000 to the promotional budget in the first stage be worth in terms of the audience contact increase? Explain.
    c. How much would adding an extra \$2000 to the promotional budget in the second stage be worth in terms of the audience contact increase? (assuming no change in the promotional budget of the first stage) Explain.
    d. If the promotional budgets are the same as in part *a*, how many commercial messages should be run on each medium to maximize the total response rate?
    e. If each expected audience response can provide \$15 marginal profit contribution for television, \$16 for newspapers, \$38 for magazines, \$23 for catalogues, and \$24 marginal profit contribution for online media, how many commercial messages should be run on each medium to maximize total profits?

24. BH Canada designs and manufactures high-grade plastic based products for industrial, commercial, and residential use. The company is considering leasing a local warehouse to fulfill its needs for additional storage spaces over the next four months, as specified in Table 4-23.

Table 4-22 Marketing Information for Problem 23

	1st Stage			2nd Stage	
	Television	**Magazines**	**Newspapers**	**Catalogue**	**Online Media**
Audience per Advertisement	120 000	25 000	50 000	20 000	50 000
Cost per Advertisement					
Minimum	\$2500	\$800	\$600	\$600	\$800
Usage over all Media					
Retained per Stage (%)	10	20	10	20	50
Maximum media Usage					
over all Retained per Stage (%)	35	60	30	50	75
Expected Audience					
Response Rate (%)	15	50	8	20	50

Table 4-23 Storage Needs for Problem 24

Month	Additional Storage Spaces Required (in square metres $-m^2$)
1	5000
2	3500
3	6500
4	4000

A local warehouse company has offered short-term leasing options that differ in terms of the length of lease, as summarized in Table 4-24.

Table 4-24 Leasing Options for Problem 24

Option	Length of Lease	Cost per Square Metre $-m^2$
1	1 month	1.50
2	2 months	2.10
3	3 months	2.85
4	4 months	3.40

Given that the monthly requirements for additional storage spaces are variable, the company is considering acquiring lease options that differ in terms of length and space size at the beginning of each month.

a. Formulate a linear programming model that can be used by the company to determine the minimum of cost of leasing while meeting the monthly requirement for additional storage space.
b. What is the total cost of the optimal leasing plan?
c. What would be the impact on the total cost of the optimal leasing plan if the requirement for additional storage spaces for month 2 is 4500 square metres?

25. An investment company has targeted small and medium enterprises for a three-year investment program. Candidate companies are classified in two tiers (A, B). Table 4-25 shows, per company in each tier, the amount of cash expenditure required during each of the three years and the expected annual return for each dollar invested. The cash income is paid at the end of each year, whereas the cash expenditure occurs at the beginning. For example, each company classified in tier A requires a cash expenditure of \$75 000 the first year and yield an annual rate of return of 18 percent, \$50 000 the second year with 12 percent annual return, and \$30 000 the third year with 9 percent annual returns. There is a risk of no return of 15 percent of companies in tier A and 30 percent of companies in tier B, indicating the percent of the investment returns that may be lost at the end of each year. The company has \$400 000 available for investment for year 1 and \$300 000 for investment for year 2. The company can also borrow funds up to \$50 000 per year at an annual interest rate of 15 percent. The unused amount is invested in a saving account that yields an annual rate of returns of 5 percent. All returns from investments are paid at the end of each year and can be used, along with the amount of new funds available for investment, to reimburse the loan and interest from the previous period, to pay the cash expenditures, or to place in a saving account.

Formulate and solve a linear program that would determine the optimal number of enterprises in each tier that the investment company should support to maximize its cash value at the end of the three-year investment program.

26. A loading company based in Halifax seeks to develop an employee working schedule for a period of 24 hours. Employees are classified into three skill levels (A, B, and C) with hourly wages of \$40, \$25, and \$15, respectively. There are two types of working shifts: 4 hours for part-time employees and 8 hours for full-time employees. Part-time employees are all classified into skill level C. The

Table 4-25 Cash Expenditure, Rate of Return, and Risk for Problem 25

	Tier A		Tier B	
Year	Cash Expenditures	Rate of Return	Cash Expenditure	Rate of Return
1	\$75 000	18%	\$50 000	25%
2	\$50 000	12%	\$25 000	20%
3	\$30 000	9%	\$15 000	15%
No-return Risk	15%		30%	

expected loading flow for each time period of the day is listed in Table 4-26:

Table 4-26 Loading Flow for Problem 26

Time Periods	Loading Flow (cases)
7:00 – 11:00	400
11:00 – 15:00	200
15:00 – 19:00	250
19:00 – 23:00	300
23:00 – 3:00	600
3:00 – 7:00	200

Each employee with skill level A can load 30 cases per hour, those with skill level B can load 18 cases per hour, and those with skill level C can load 10 cases per hour.

a. Formulate a linear programming model to determine the optimal number of employees required at each time period to minimize the overall costs and meet the loading flow demands. It is recommended that the total number of part-time employees not be over 30 percent of full-time employees. In addition, it is required that at least 25 percent of the total number of employees must be classified as skill level A. How many employees are required in each skill level per time period?

b. If a part-time employee can not work during a morning shift (7:00 – 11:00), what are the changes in the optimal solution found in part *a?*

27. Serious Toys Inc. is a major producer of building blocks for preschoolers located in Regina, Saskatchewan. The bimonthly demand for the advanced sets of building blocks over the next planning horizon is displayed in Table 4-27.

The company has a dedicated production line for the advanced sets of building blocks that works 20 days per month, with a regular shift of eight hours per day. Overtime production may also be used, but is limited to 40 hours per month per employee. The company may also hire or lay off employees at a cost of, respectively, \$450 and \$260 per employee. Employees are paid \$1760 per month and \$16.50 per hour of overtime. Each advanced set of building blocks requires one hour per employee and has an inventory cost of \$5.00 per month. Before the beginning of the planning horizon, the company had 1250 advanced sets of building blocks in inventory and 35 employees. The production line cannot accommodate more than 60 employees per period of time.

a. Develop a linear programming model that can be used to determine the minimum production plan subject to all production requirements and meeting the anticipated demand.

b. Solve the linear programming model with Excel Solver and provide, in addition to the total cost of the production plan, a summary table that shows the number of employees available on a bimonthly basis, the number of employees hired at the beginning of the period, the number of employees laid off at the beginning of the period, the number of advanced sets of building blocks produced in regular time, the number of advanced sets of building blocks produced overtime, and the number in inventory at the end of each period.

28. Cargo Inc. is a leading provider of air cargo transportation services. The company has received the shipment information in Table 4-28 from the Department of National Defense for the next flight. Due to the types of handling processes involved, the profit per tonne varies with the type of cargo.

Table 4-27 Bimonthly Demand for Problem 27

Period	January – February	March – April	May – June	July – August
Demand (units)	12 500	10 000	13 000	9 000

Table 4-28 Shipment Information for Problem 28

Cargo Type	Weight (Tonnes)	Volume (cubic metres/tonne)	Profit (\$/tonne)
CT1	20	500	320
CT2	17	630	365
CT3	25	600	325
CT4	14	410	290
CT5	16	360	300

Table 4-29 Storage Compartment Information for Problem 28

Compartment	Weigh Capacity (Tonnes)	Volume Capacity (cubic metres)
A	15	6500
B	14	8630
C	10	5600

Table 4-30 Cash Requirements for Problem 30

Year	1	2	3	4	5	6
Cash needed ($)	$0	$15 000	$18 000	$22 000	$25 000	$21 000

The scheduled cargo plane is divided in three cargo storing compartments with limits on both weight and space capacities as shown in Table 4-29.
Develop a linear programming model that can be used by the company to determining how much of each cargo type should be accepted and how to distribute each among the compartments so that the total profit for the flight is maximized. It is assumed that each cargo can be split into whatever proportions/fractions necessary and that each cargo can be split between two or more compartments. Furthermore, to ensure load balancing, it is required that the weight of the cargo in the respective compartments must be the same proportion of that compartment's weight capacity.

29. Consider the Aviation Electronics Company in Problem 2, which produces three types of switching devices in a two-step assembly operation. Let's assume that the data in Table 4-11 represents the labour assembly times per unit (in minutes). The company hires five employees in Station 1 and three employees in Station 2. Each station still has a daily working time of 7.5 hours. Model A yields a profit of $8.25 per unit, Model B a profit of $7.50 per unit, Model C a profit of $7.80 per unit. The company can still sell all its weekly production (five working days) but now faces outstanding orders of 40 units for model A, 45 units for model B, and 55 units for model C. To cope with this increase in sales, the company is considering, during the next production week (five working days), the possibility of transferring (at no cost) labour assembly times between both workstations. At most 600 minutes of labour assembly times can be transferred from Station1 to Station 2. Both Stations can also receive labour assembly times transferred from a third Station available in the company, but dedicated to another line of products. The maximum time that can be transferred from the third Station to both Station 1 and Station 2 is limited to 800 minutes during the week. Manager Bob Parkes wants to obtain the greatest possible profit during the next five working days. Formulate the linear programming model of this problem and solve it with Excel Solver.

30. Jean-Louis M. Fuamba, a successful entrepreneur who has recently moved to Canada, seeks to establish an initial investment portfolio to pay for the expenses of some of his family members who still live in his home country. The cash requirements at the beginning of for the next six years are shown in Table 4-30.
Three investment options have been retained, each with a different rate of return and time to maturity, as indicated in Table 4-31.

Table 4-31 Investment Options for Problem 30

Options	Rate (%)	Time to Maturity (years)
A	4	1
B	8.5	2
C	14	3

The businessman wants to determine how much to invest today in each investment alternative to meet the cash requirements for the next five years assuming the following:

a. The amount of cash required per year is due at the beginning of each year.
b. No more than 15 percent of the total investment will be at any time allocated to option C given its relative risk.
c. Each investment option is available at the beginning of each year.

d. The return on investment at the end of each year will be re-invested at the beginning of the next year.
e. No taxes are paid on the returns on investment.

Formulate this problem as a linear programming model and solve it with Excel Solver.

Case 1: Direct Marketing

A direct marketing agency has been asked by a client to do a lead-generation mailing. The purpose of the mailing will be to offer prospective investors long-term notes at preferred rates. Names and addresses for the mailing will be obtained from three lists: CPAs, real estate developers, and personal investors. The cost and response rates for these are shown in Table 4-32:

Table 4-32 Cost and Response Rates

List	Cost per 1000	Expected Response Rate
CPAs	$ 85	2%
Real estate developers	110	3
Personal investors	95	6

The conversion of leads into sales is expected to be 1 in 20. Moreover, the client has stipulated several additional conditions:

1. Between 10 and 20 percent of the mailing should be to CPAs.
2. No fewer than 10 000 pieces should go to real estate developers.

For purposes of analysis, assume that the lists are large enough to support the mailing sizes that will be called for and assume that the amount of duplication in the lists is negligible. However, assume that 5 percent of the names on a list will be unusable because of deaths, changes in address, and so on. Lists can be ordered in any amount.

The account executive in charge of the mailing wants to answer these questions before deciding whether to approve the mailing:

1. What size mailing will be needed?
2. How many names from each list will be needed?
3. What will the list cost be?
4. What is the expected number of responses?
5. What will the cost per lead be?

Required

Prepare a report that addresses the following points:

1. Formulate this as an LP model that will minimize cost assuming the client wants to achieve at least 250 responses.
2. Formulate this as an LP model that will maximize expected responses given a budget of $20 000.
3. For each of the questions posed in the problem, write an equation that can be used to answer the question.

Case 2: Quota Allocation by Linear Programming

VCL Canada Inc. manufactures and markets top-of-the-line central vacuum valves, fittings, and accessories. The adoption by the company of lean manufacturing methodologies in recent years has added pressure to aggregate planners to meet the total customers' demand according to a certain delivery schedule with no late or early deliveries. One problem faced by aggregate planners is that of allocating the production quantities to each sales region over the planning horizon, which has been set to six periods. The company has divided its market in four sales regions. The production capacity available in each period of the planning horizon is respectively 120 000 units for period 1; 200 000 for period 2; 200 000 for period 3; 250 000 for period 4; 200 000 for period 5; and 130 000 for period 6. The total demand for each sales region over the entire planning horizon is estimated to 200 000 units for sales region A; 300 000 for sales region B; 200 000 for sales region C; and 300 000 for sales region D.

Since this demand cannot be delivered all at once, a target demand schedule expressed as a percent of the total demand for a given sales region is determined for each sales region over the planning horizon as shown in

Table 4-33, below. According to this table, for example, for sales region A, 15 percent of the total demand represents the target scheduled for periods 1 and 2 respectively; 20% for period 3; 30 percent for period 4; and 10 percent for periods 5 and 6. However, given the production capacity available per period, while the targeted demand level scheduled for each sales region and period cannot always be met, the demand over the planning horizon must be met. For example, for period 1, the production capacity required over all sales regions is estimated to 130 000 units, whereas the production capacity available is 120 000 units. The cost per unit per period of exceeding the target demand level is evaluated at $5 for sales regions A and B; $5.50 for sales region C; and $4.25 for sales region D. The cost per unit per period of not meeting the target demand level is evaluated at $4.75 for sales regions A and B; $5.75 for sales region C; and $4 for sales region D.

Managerial Report

1. Prepare a linear programming model that can be used by aggregate planners to allocate production quantities to each sales region over the planning horizon, such as the overall cost of deviating from the target demand level scheduled is minimized. Your report should indicate the fraction of the total demand for each sales region allocated to each period of the planning horizon; the fraction by which the targeted demand level for each sales region is exceeded per period; the fraction by which the targeted demand level for each sales region falls short per period; the production capacity used per period; and the total cost incurred.
2. Suppose that the cost of exceeding or not meeting the target demand level is the same for each sales region, and that each period you reformulate your model to determine the allocation that minimizes the maximum deviation from the target demand level. Your report should indicate the maximum fractional deviation over all periods for all sales regions as well as the production capacity used per period.

Source: Adapted from Janny Leung and Alan Yu, "Quota Allocation by LP using a spreadsheet solver," *Asia-Pacific Journal of Operational Research* vol. 19 (2002), pp. 63–70.

Table 4-33 Target Demand Schedule per Period for Case 2 (percent of total demand)

	Period					
	1	2	3	4	5	6
Sales region A	15	15	20	30	10	10
Sales region B	10	15	25	25	15	10
Sales region C	20	20	20	20	10	10
Sales region D	10	10	25	25	15	15

Case 3: Shipping Wood to Market

WDL Canada Inc. is a lumber company that has three sources of wood and five markets to supply. The annual availability of wood at sources 1, 2, and 3 is 15, 20, and 15 million board feet, respectively. The amount that can be sold annually at markets 1, 2, 3, 4, and 5 is 11, 12, 9, 10, and 8 million board feet, respectively. In the past, the company has shipped the wood by train. However, because shipping costs have been increasing, the alternative of using ships to make some of the deliveries is being investigated. This alternative would require the company to invest in some ships. Except for these investment costs, the shipping costs in thousands of dollars per million board feet by rail and by water (when feasible) would be the following for each route (Table 4-34):

Table 4-34 Shipping Unit Cost by Rail and Ship

	Unit Cost by Rail ($1000s to Market)					Unit Cost by Ship ($1000s to Market)				
Source	1	2	3	4	5	1	2	3	4	5
1	61	72	45	55	66	31	38	24	—	35
2	69	78	60	49	56	36	43	28	24	31
3	59	66	63	61	47	—	33	36	32	26

The capital investment (in thousands of dollars) in ships required for each million board feet to be transported annually by ship along each route is given in Table 4-35.

Table 4-35 Capital Investment

	Unit Investment for Ships ($1000s) to Market				
Source	1	2	3	4	5
1	275	303	238	—	285
2	293	318	270	250	265
3	—	283	275	268	240

Considering the expected useful life of the ships and the time value of money, the equivalent uniform annual cost of these investments is one-tenth the amount given in the table. The objective is to determine the overall shipping plan that minimizes the total equivalent uniform annual cost (including shipping costs).

Managerial Report

Prepare a report to the senior administration that provides the shipping plan and the total costs for each of the following three options:

Option 1: Continue shipping exclusively by rail.
Option 2: Switch to shipping exclusively by water (except where only rail is feasible).
Option 3: Ship by either rail or water, depending on which is less expensive for the particular route.

Consider the fact that these results are based on current shipping and investment costs, so that the decision on the option to adopt now should take into account management's projection of how these costs are likely to change in the future. For each option, describe a scenario of future cost changes that would justify adopting that option now.

Source: Based on a case study previously published by F. S. Hillier, M. S. Hillier, *Introduction to Management Science: A modeling and case studies approach with spreadsheets*, 3rd ed., (Boston: McGraw-Hill Irwin, 2008).

Case 4: Workforce Scheduling at ASC

ASC is a cargo handling and shipping company operating from the ports of Halifax and Montreal. Employees of the company are classified into three skill levels (A, B, C). The company has recently signed a short-term contract with the Department of National Defence for handling, processing, and shipping of special materials that require a full assignment of the most skilled employees (level A). The working hours of employees with skill level A required for the next 8 months is shown in Table 4-36.

To meet the monthly demand the company has decided to provide training to employees with skill level B or C. It takes about 50 hours of training for an employee with skill level B and 100 hours of training for an employee with skill level C to develop skills required for level A. All training is provided by employees with skill level A. Each staffperson with skill level A is paid $4500 and works about 200 hours per month. The monthly salary is $3000 and $2000 for an employee with skill level B and skill

Table 4-36 Employee Requirements

Month	1	2	3	4	5	6	7	8
Hours required (1000s)	10	10.5	11	12	12.5	11	10.5	12

level C, respectively. The company has estimated that about 8 percent of employees with skill level A leave to work with a competitor at the end of every month. At the beginning of the first period the company has 55 employees with skill level A. The company has set the number of employees with skill level B in training during every period to be at least 50 percent of the number of employees with skill level C.

Managerial Report

a. Develop a linear programming model to assist the company in determining the work schedule plan for the eight-month period so that the total labour cost is minimized and the demand for employee hours is met. Your report should include a summary table showing, on a monthly basis, the number of employees in each skill level, the associated total salary costs, and the total training costs. What is the total cost of the optimal work schedule plan?
b. Assume that instead of providing training to employees with skill levels B and C, the company is considering the option of transferring employees with skill level A from the port of Montreal to the port of Halifax, under the three options shown in Table 4-37.

Table 4-37 Transfer Options

Option	Minimum Length of Transfer	Additional Cost
1	One month	\$1400
2	Two months	\$2300
3	Three months	\$3500

The length of transfer stipulates the maximum period of employment. For instance, an employee transferred under Option 2 cannot leave before the completion of two months of employment in the port of Halifax. The employee cost will be 2(\$4500) + \$2300) = \$11 300. However, transfers of employees may occur only in periods 1, 4, and 7.

Develop a working plan if this option is retained and compare it with the solution found in part a. Your report should include the number of employees with skill level A transferred each month under each option and the associated costs.

Case 5: Ottawa Catholic School Board (Revisited)

Reconsider the Ottawa Catholic School Board (OCSB) case study at the end of Chapter 3. The OCSB has made the decision to close a number of its senior elementary schools (sixth, seventh, and eighth grades) at the end of this school year and reassign all of next year's students to the three remaining senior elementary schools. Currently, the school board has the policy of providing busing for all students who must travel more than approximately 1.6 kilometres. Therefore, the board wants a plan for reassigning the students that will minimize the total busing cost. The annual cost per student for busing from each of the six residential areas of the city to each of the schools is the same as shown at the end of Chapter 3, and there is no change as well to the percentage of each area's senior elementary school population for next year that falls into each of the three grades. The school board has also imposed the restriction that each grade must constitute between 30 and 36 percent of each school's population. The school board is considering eliminating some busing to reduce costs. Option 1 is to only eliminate busing for students travelling 1.6 to 2.4 kilometres, where the cost per student is given in the table as \$200. Option 2 is to also eliminate busing for students travelling 2.4 to 3.2 kilometres, where the estimated cost per student is \$300. The school board now needs to choose among the three alternative busing plans (the current one or Option 1 or Option 2). One important factor is busing costs. However, the school board also wants to place equal weight on a second factor: the inconvenience and safety problems caused by forcing students to travel by foot or bicycle a substantial distance (more than 1.6 kilometres, and especially more than 2.4 kilometres). Therefore, they want to choose a plan that provides the best trade-off between these two factors.

Managerial Report

Prepare a managerial report for the school board providing the following information:

a. The number of students assigned to each school for each of the three alternatives and the corresponding total busing costs.

b. A summary table of the key information related to the three factors (busing cost, number of students walking between 1.6 and 2.4 kilometres, and number of students walking more than 2.4 kilometres) for each alternative that the school board needs to make the decision.

Source: Based on a case study previously published by F. S. Hillier, M. S. Hillier, Introduction to Management Science: A modeling and case studies approach with spreadsheets, 3rd ed. (Boston: McGraw-Hill Irwin, 2008).

CHAPTER 5

Distribution and Network Flow Models

LEARNING OBJECTIVES

After completing this chapter, you should be able to:

1. State why network models are important tools for problem solving.
2. Describe the nature of transportation, transshipment, and assignment problems.
3. Formulate a transportation problem as a linear programming model.
4. Use the transportation method to solve problems with Excel.
5. Solve maximization transportation problems, unbalanced problems, and problems with prohibited routes.
6. Solve aggregate planning problems using the transportation model.
7. Formulate a transshipment problem as a linear programming model.
8. Solve transshipment problems with Excel.
9. Formulate an assignment problem as a linear programming model.
10. Use the assignment method to solve problems with Excel.
11. Describe the kinds of problems that can be solved using the shortest-route algorithm.
12. Formulate the shortest-route problem as a linear programming problem.
13. Solve the shortest-route problem using Excel.
14. Describe the kinds of problems that can be solved using the maximum flow algorithm.
15. Formulate the maximum flow problem as a linear programming problem.
16. Solve the maximum flow problem using Excel.

CHAPTER OUTLINE

5.1 INTRODUCTION

Certain types of linear programming problems can be best analyzed by means of a network representation. A **Network** model consists of a set of circles, or **nodes,** and lines, which are referred to as either **arcs** or *branches,* which are used to connect some nodes to other nodes. Figure 5-1 illustrates a simple network diagram. This network has four nodes and five branches. Notice that the branches meet only at nodes; the nodes are *intersections* of the branches. For purposes of reference, the nodes are numbered. Moreover, a branch can be referred to by specifying the nodes on each of its ends (e.g., branch 1–2).

This chapter examines five special network models: transportation, transshipment, assignment, shortest route, and maximum flow problems. Model formulation and determining solutions with Excel are covered for each of these classes of problems. Detailed special-purpose procedures to solve some of these models are described in Chapter 16 on the OLC for this textbook, which also includes a procedure to solve the minimum spanning tree problem, another type of network model. These procedures enable practitioners to obtain solutions to these special cases with much less computational burden than the simple solution procedure used to solve linear programming problems.

Many real-world business problems lend themselves to network flow optimization problems. Typical examples of such problems include distribution of goods and services, planning a production system, locating new facilities, assigning sales personnel to sales territories, determining the cheapest route between two locations, determining the maximum flow through a system of pipelines, highways, production system, or through the Web, etc. The following Modern Management Science Application describes how Canada Post benefited from the use of network flow optimization methods.

5.2 TRANSPORTATION PROBLEMS

The **transportation problem** is usually applied to distribution-type problems in which supplies of goods that are held at various locations are to be distributed to other receiving locations. Hence, the solution of a transportation problem will indicate to a manager the quantities to be shipped on various routes and the resulting minimum cost. For example, a company may have 10 warehouses that are used to supply 50 retail stores. Obviously there are many different combinations of warehouse–store supply lines that could be used. Generally, some of these combinations will involve transportation costs that are higher than others. The purpose of using an LP model would be to identify a distribution plan that would minimize

FIGURE 5-1 A Simple Network Diagram

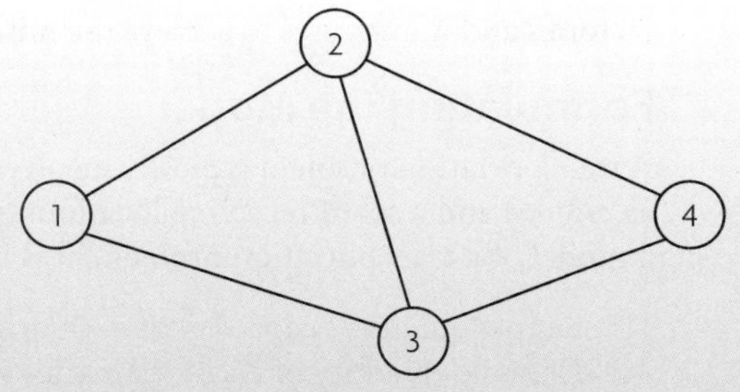

A MODERN MANAGEMENT SCIENCE APPLICATION: OPTIMIZATION OF REUSABLE CONTAINERS AT CANADA POST

Canada Post manages the largest physical distribution network in the country, collecting, sorting, and delivering 40 million pieces of mail a day to over 12 million addresses. The postal network covers all delivery points in Canada every business day, so most of the costs operating the network are high and fixed. The company collects mail from street letterboxes, post offices, and large customers' premises. Seventy-four hundred local post offices ship collected mail to one of the mechanized mail sortation plants or to a distribution centre. After the mail is collected, it is sorted by shape and then by destination. Mail is either for local or regional delivery (local mail) or for delivery beyond a geographic area of a predetermined radius (forward mail). The distribution centres sort mail for their geographic region based on the Canadian alphanumeric postal code and the mechanized plants sort and exchange all the forward mail between the major nodes in the network, that is, between the distribution centres and the other plants.

In any of these facilities Canada Post uses large open cages called monotainers to consolidate mail and transport mail, both within a facility and between facilities. In fact, since its plants' material-handling equipment and facility layouts are configured for monotainers, no other options are left for the company. Therefore, when pre-sorted mail arrives in shrink-wrapped bundles on pallets from large mailing customers they are unwrapped first and containerized in monotainers. Similarly, when mail arrives at a sorting plant in loose mailbags or tubs, they are sorted by destination into monotainers. Most commercial customers presort their mail by type and delivery destination to benefit from Canada Post's incentive discounts. Canada Post can then transfer this presorted mail at the origin dock for transport downstream for final sortation, saving intermediate handling steps and cost. These customers request empty monotainers from Canada Post, which provides them freely.

Given the popularity of monotainers with employees and customers, Canada Post was facing chronic irregular monotainer shortages, especially in plants in the Quebec–Windsor corridor, which were shipping out many more monotainers with mail than they received back from other regions. To solve the non-balanced problem between the shipments out and receipts, a minimum-cost flow problem was developed to plan the distribution of empty monotainers in the postal network, that is, to determine whether enough monotainers were available to meet the demand and whether they were in the right place at the right time. The model saved Canada Post from investing in new monotainers, since it showed that it has enough stock of monotainers to meet an orderly controlled demand.

Source: Reprinted by permission, Based on R. Duhaime, D. Riopel, A. Langevin, "Value Analysis and Optimization of Reusable Containers at Canada Post," Interfaces Vol. 31, no. 3, (May–June 2001), pp. 3–15. Copyright (2001), the Institute for Operations Research and the Management Sciences (INFORMS), 7240 Parkway Drive, Suite 310, Hanover, MD 21076 USA.

the cost of transporting the goods from the warehouses to the retail stores, taking into account warehouse supplies and store demands as well as transportation costs. Other examples of transportation problems include shipments from factories to warehouses, shipments between departments within a company, and production scheduling that includes shipment of goods from a set of departments to another set. Moreover, some companies use the transportation method to compare location alternatives (i.e., to decide where to locate factories and warehouses to achieve the minimum-cost distribution configuration).

Formulating the Model

A transportation problem typically involves a set of sending locations, which are referred to as *origins*, and a set of receiving locations, which are referred to as *destinations*. To develop a model of a transportation problem, it is necessary to have the following information:

1. Supply quantity (capacity) of each origin.
2. Demand quantity of each destination.
3. Unit transportation cost for each origin-destination route.

FIGURE 5-2 Schematic Diagram of a Transportation Problem

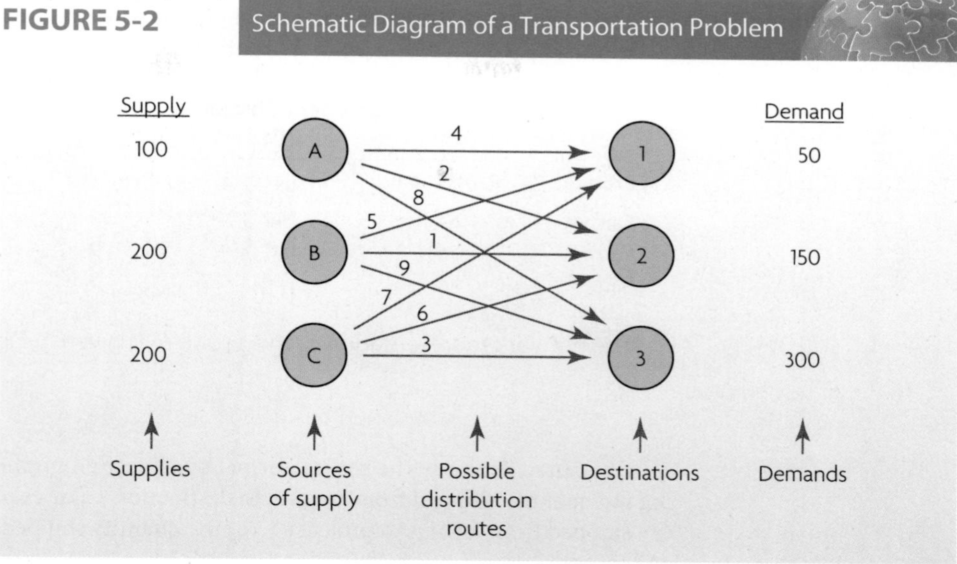

A schematic representation of a transportation problem is shown in Figure 5-2.

In the example given in Figure 5-2, there are 100 units of supply available at source A. There are 50 units demanded at destination 1. The cost of shipping one unit from source A to destination 1 is equal to \$4, and the cost of shipping one unit from source B to destination 3 is \$9. The remaining supply, demand, and per-unit cost values can be interpreted in a similar way.

The transportation problem requires the assumption that all goods be homogeneous, so that any origin is capable of supplying any destination, and the assumption that transportation costs are a direct linear function of the quantity shipped over any route. We shall add one additional requirement that will simplify the problem: The total quantity available for shipment is equal to the total quantity demanded. Later in the chapter we shall see how the problem can be modified to handle cases where this assumption is not met.

EXAMPLE 5-1

Harley's Sand and Gravel Pit has contracted to provide topsoil for three residential housing developments. Topsoil can be supplied from three different "farms" as follows:

Farm	Weekly Capacity (cubic metres)
A	100
B	200
C	200

Demand for the topsoil generated by the construction projects is

Project	Weekly Demand (cubic metres)
1	50
2	150
3	300

The manager of the sand and gravel pit has estimated the cost per cubic metre to ship over each of the possible routes:

	Cost per Cubic Metre To		
From	**Project #1**	**Project #2**	**Project #3**
Farm A	\$4	\$2	\$8
Farm B	5	1	9
Farm C	7	6	3

The network representation of this problem is given in Figure 5-2.

We can write this in the general format of a linear programming model, with x_{ij} denoting the quantity shipped from origin i to destination j. For example, x_{11} denotes the quantity shipped from farm A to project #1, x_{12} the quantity shipped from farm A to project #2, and so on.

In transportation problems, the objective is to minimize the cost of distributing the supplies to the destinations. Therefore, if c_{ij} is the cost per unit to transport units from origin i to destination j, $4x_{11} + 2x_{12} + 8x_{13}$ defines the cost of distributing topsoil from farm A, $5x_{21} + x_{22} + 9x_{23}$ the cost from farm B, and $7x_{31} + 6x_{32} + 3x_{33}$ the cost from farm C. The total transportation cost for Harley's Sand and Gravel is given by the sum of these expressions, i.e.,

$$4x_{11} + 2x_{12} + 8x_{18} + 5x_{21} + x_{22} + 9x_{23} + 7x_{31} + 6x_{32} + 3x_{33}$$

The total supplies from each farm are limited by the quantities available. Therefore, the following relations can be derived:

$$\begin{aligned} x_{11} + x_{12} + x_{13} &= 100 \text{ supply from farm A} \\ x_{21} + x_{22} + x_{23} &= 200 \text{ supply from farm B} \\ x_{31} + x_{32} + x_{33} &= 200 \text{ supply from farm C} \end{aligned}$$

Similarly, the total deliveries to each project are limited to the demand as shown by the following relations:

$$\begin{aligned} x_{11} + x_{21} + x_{31} &= 50 \text{ demand for project \# 1} \\ x_{12} + x_{22} + x_{32} &= 150 \text{ demand for project \# 2} \\ x_{13} + x_{23} + x_{33} &= 300 \text{ demand for project \# 3} \end{aligned}$$

The Hartley problem can be summarized as follows:

$$\text{minimize } Z = 4x_{11} + 2x_{12} + 8x_{13} + 5x_{21} + x_{22} + 9x_{23} + 7x_{31} + 6x_{32} + 3x_{33}$$

subject to

$$\begin{aligned} &\text{Farm A:} && x_{11} + x_{12} + x_{13} = 100 \\ &\text{Farm B:} && x_{21} + x_{22} + x_{23} = 200 \\ &\text{Farm C:} && x_{31} + x_{23} + x_{33} = 200 \end{aligned} \Bigg\} \text{ Supply}$$

$$\begin{aligned} &\text{Project \#1:} && x_{11} + x_{21} + x_{31} = 50 \\ &\text{Project \#2:} && x_{12} + x_{22} + x_{32} = 150 \\ &\text{Project \#3:} && x_{13} + x_{23} + x_{33} = 300 \end{aligned} \Bigg\} \text{ Demand}$$

$$\text{All variables} \geq 0$$

Notice that the unit costs appear only in the objective function, and not in the constraints. Also, because total supply equals total demand, all of the constraints can be written as equalities.

Once we have the problem in this format, we can use Excel to obtain the optimal solution (i.e., the quantities to be shipped from each origin to each destination, some of which will be equal to zero, and the minimal total cost to ship all units.)

Various transportation problems present special cases. Some of these special cases are discussed in the following section.

Special Cases of Transportation Problems

Maximization Problems Some transportation-type problems concern profits or revenues rather than costs. In such cases, the objective is to *maximize* rather than to minimize. Such problems are automatically handled by Excel or other software packages. When the optimal distribution plan has been identified, use the *original cell* (profit per unit) *values* to compute the total profit for that plan.

Unacceptable Routes In some cases, certain origin-destination combinations may be unacceptable. This may be due to weather factors, equipment breakdowns, labour problems, or skill requirements that either prohibit, or make undesirable, certain combinations (routes).

Suppose that in the Harley problem route A–3 was suddenly unavailable because of recent flooding. To prevent that route from appearing in the final solution (as it originally did), the manager could assign a unit cost that was large enough to make that route uneconomical and, hence, prohibit its occurrence. One rule of thumb would be to assign a unit cost of $9999 instead of the original cost of $8 per unit. Then this revised problem could be solved using Excel.

Unequal Supply and Demand Up to this point, examples have involved cases in which supply and demand were equal. As you might guess, there are situations in which the two are not equal. When such a situation is encountered, it is necessary to modify the original problem so that supply and demand are equal. This is accomplished by adding either a dummy origin node if a supply is less than demand or a dummy destination node if demand is less than supply. The capacity of the dummy node is given by the difference in absolute number between the supply and the demand. A unit cost of zero will be assigned to each arc leaving the dummy origin node or entering the dummy destination node. Quantities in dummy routes in the optimal solution are not shipped. Rather, they serve to indicate which supplier will hold the excess supply, and how much, or which destination will not receive its total demand, and how much it will be short.

A General Linear Formulation of a Transportation Problem

The general LP format of a transportation problem with m source (supply) nodes and n destination (demand) nodes can be summarized as follows:

$$\textbf{minimize } Z = \sum_{i=1}^{m}\sum_{j=1}^{n} c_{ij}x_{ij}$$

subject to:

$$\sum_{j=1}^{n} x_{ij} \le S_i \qquad i = 1, 2, ..., m \text{ (supply)}$$

$$\sum_{i=1}^{m} x_{ij} = D_j \qquad j = 1,..., n \text{ (demand)}$$

$$x_{ij} \ge 0 \qquad \text{for all } i \text{ and } j$$

where, as previously defined, c_{ij} is the cost per unit to transport units from source i to destination j, x_{ij} the number of units shipped from source i to destination j, S_i the supply in units available at source i and D_j the demand in units at destination j.

In the next section, we will learn how to solve transportation problems using Excel.

Solving Transportation Problems Using Excel

Since we formulated the transportation problem as a linear programming model, we can solve it using Excel. In this section, we will demonstrate how to solve our topsoil example using Excel spreadsheets. If we use standard Excel, the transportation problem must be formulated and solved as a linear programming problem as we demonstrated in Chapters 2 and 4. Exhibit 5-1 shows how we can set up a spreadsheet formulation of the topsoil problem that was stated earlier in this chapter. In the spreadsheet shown in Exhibit 5-1, the supply locations (farms) are the rows and destinations (projects) are the columns in the upper portion of the worksheet. The right side of the table consists of the supply quantities and the demand quantities are listed at the bottom of the table. A column is inserted on the far right of the spreadsheet with column heading "Topsoil shipped." This column consists of the formulas for each row (or supply location) such that the values of supply stated in the supply column equal the amount shipped from each of the supply locations in each row. For example, supply in farm A must equal 100 cubic metres. Thus, the amount shipped from farm A to project 1, farm A to project 2, and farm A to project 3 must equal a total of 100. To ensure that the above-mentioned constraint is satisfied, the values in cells B5, C5, and D5 add up to 100. The formula for this row is shown in Exhibit 5-1. The topsoil shipped for cell F5 consists of the sum of the values in cells B5, C5, and D5. Likewise we insert a row at the bottom of the table with the row heading "Topsoil shipped." This row includes the formulas for each column (or destination location) such that the values of demand stated in the destination column equal the amount shipped to each of the destination locations. For example, demand for project 2 must equal 150 cubic metres. Thus, the amount shipped from farm A to project 2, farm B to project 2, and farm C to project 2 must equal 150. To ensure that the above-mentioned constraint is satisfied, the values in cells C5, C6, and C7 add up to 150. The topsoil shipped for cell B9 consists of the sum of the values in cells B5, B6, and B7. The formula for this column is also shown in Exhibit 5-1. In Exhibit 5-1, we see the formula for the objective function that is stated in cell B10. This formula utilizes the cell references from the bottom portion of the worksheet labelled "unit cost table." The formula for this cell consists of the cross products of cells associated with the shipping routes (decision variables) as well as the cost of shipping one unit on each of these routes. The formula for cell B10 (the objective function formula for total cost) is as follows:

=B15*B5+C15*C5+D15*D5+B16*B6+C16*C6+D16*D6+B17*B7+C17*C7+D17*D7

The optimal solution to the transportation problem also can be stated in terms of the variables specified in the linear programming formulation of the transportation problem specified earlier. The optimal solution corresponds to the following variable values: $x_{13} = 100, x_{21} = 50, x_{22} = 150$, and $x_{33} = 200$. If we want a more detailed report, we click on the "Answer Report" tab at the bottom of the worksheet. Exhibit 5-2 displays the answer report, which is a more detailed display of the answer than given in the original sheet.

The report displayed in Exhibit 5-2 shows the total cost of the transportation schedule as well as the amounts shipped between various destinations. In addition, the last part of the answer report shows whether the constraints are binding and the amount of slack or surplus associated with each constraint. Of course, in solving this problem the answer report indicates that there is no slack and all of the constraints are binding because all of the constraints have been set up as equalities.

EXHIBIT 5-1 Input and Output Worksheet for the Transportation (topsoil) Problem

Exhibit 5-1 [Read-Only] [Compatibility Mode] - Microsoft Excel

A22 Exhibit 5-1

	A	B	C	D	E	F
1	**Harley's Sand and Gravel Pit**				**Topsoil problem**	
2			**Shipment Table**			
3			**Projects**			
4	**Farms**	Project 1	Project 2	Project 3	Supply	Topsoil shipped
5	Farm A	50	0	50	100	100
6	Farm B	0	150	50	200	200
7	Farm C	0	0	200	200	200
8	Demand	50	150	300		
9	Topsoil shipped	50	150	300		
10	Minimum cost	1 800				
11						
12			**Unit Cost Table**			
13			**Projects**			
14	**Farms**	Project 1	Project 2	Project 3		
15	Farm A	4	2	8		
16	Farm B	9 999	1	9		
17	Farm C	7	6	3		

Exhibit 5-1

Cell	Copied to	Formula
F5	F6 : F7	= B5 + C5 + D5
B9	C9 : D9	= B5 + B6 + B7
B10		= B15 * B5 + C15 * C5 + D15 * D5 + B16 * B6 + C16 * C6 + D16 * D6 + B17 * B7 + C17 * C7 + D17 * D7

Other Applications

There are a number of other situations that can be formulated as transportation problems that do not necessarily involve distributions of products from supply sources to demand destinations. We discuss two applications related to aggregate planning and facility location analysis.

Using the Transportation Problem to Solve Aggregate Planning Problems Aggregate planning involves the long-term production plan of a manufacturing firm. Aggregate planners usually avoid thinking in terms of individual products. The planners are concerned about the quantity and timing of production to meet the expected demand. If the demand is uneven within the planning period, the planners attempt to achieve equality of demand and capacity over the entire planning horizon. Aggregate planners attempt to minimize the production cost over the planning horizon. The transportation method happens to be a

EXHIBIT 5-2 Answer Report for the Topsoil Transportation Problem

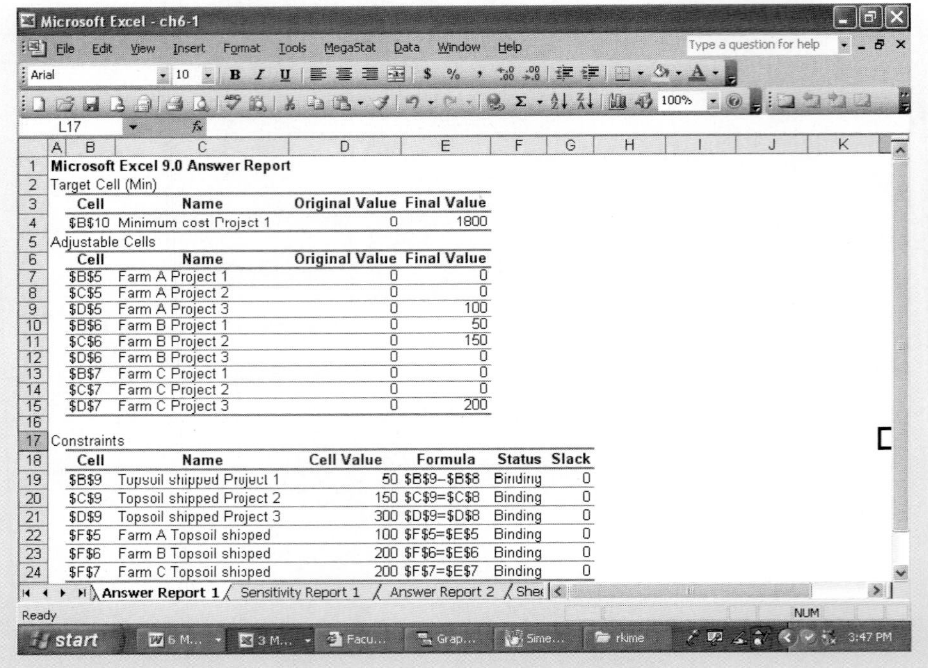

Microsoft Excel 9.0 Answer Report

Target Cell (Min)

Cell	Name	Original Value	Final Value
$B$10	Minimum cost Project 1	0	1800

Adjustable Cells

Cell	Name	Original Value	Final Value
$B$5	Farm A Project 1	0	0
$C$5	Farm A Project 2	0	0
$D$5	Farm A Project 3	0	100
$B$6	Farm B Project 1	0	50
$C$6	Farm B Project 2	0	150
$D$6	Farm B Project 3	0	0
$B$7	Farm C Project 1	0	0
$C$7	Farm C Project 2	0	0
$D$7	Farm C Project 3	0	200

Constraints

Cell	Name	Cell Value	Formula	Status	Slack
$B$9	Topsoil shipped Project 1	50	$B$9=$B$8	Binding	0
$C$9	Topsoil shipped Project 2	150	$C$9=$C$8	Binding	0
$D$9	Topsoil shipped Project 3	300	$D$9=$D$8	Binding	0
$F$5	Farm A Topsoil shipped	100	$F$5=$E$5	Binding	0
$F$6	Farm B Topsoil shipped	200	$F$6=$E$6	Binding	0
$F$7	Farm C Topsoil shipped	200	$F$7=$E$7	Binding	0

good way of tackling some of these issues. To use the transportation problem to solve the aggregate planning problem, the planners first identify the capacity of regular time, overtime subcontracting, and inventory on a period-by-period basis. The most common way to visualize an aggregate planning problem as a transportation problem is to arrange the information into a table as shown in Table 5-1.

Note the systematic way that costs change as you move across a row from left to right. Regular cost, overtime cost, and subcontracting cost are at their lowest when the output is consumed (i.e., delivered, etc.) in the same period it is produced (at the intersection of period 1 row and column for regular cost, at the intersection of period 2 row and column for regular cost, and so on). If goods are made available in one period but carried over to later periods (i.e., moving across a row), holding costs are incurred at the rate of h per period. Thus, holding goods for two periods results in a unit cost of $2h$, whether or not the goods came from regular production, overtime, or subcontracting. Conversely, with back orders, the unit cost increases as you move across a row from right to left, beginning at the intersection of a row and column for the same period (e.g., period 3). For instance, if some goods are produced in period 3 to satisfy backorders from period 2, a unit backorder cost of b is incurred. And if goods in period 3 are used to satisfy back orders two periods earlier (e.g., from period 1), a unit cost of $2b$ is incurred. Unused capacity is generally given a unit cost of 0, although it is certainly possible to insert an actual cost if that is relevant. Finally, beginning inventory is given a unit cost of 0 if it is used to satisfy demand in period 1. However, if it is held over for use in later periods, a holding cost of h per unit is added for each period. If the inventory is to be held for the entire planning horizon, a total unit cost of h times the number of periods, n, will be incurred.

TABLE 5-1 Transportation Table for Aggregate Planning Purposes

Period		Period 1	Period 2	Period 3	...	Ending inventory period n	Unused capacity	Capacity
	Beginning inventory	0	h	$2h$	...	nh	0	I_0
1	Regular time	r	$r+h$	$r+2h$	...	$r+nh$	0	R_1
	Overtime	l	$l+h$	$l+2h$	...	$l+nh$	0	O_1
	Subcontract	s	$s+h$	$s+2h$	...	$s+nh$	0	S_1
2	Regular time	$r+b$	r	$r+h$	...	$r+(n-1)h$	0	R_2
	Overtime	$l+b$	l	$l+h$	...	$l+(n-1)h$	0	O_2
	Subcontract	$s+b$	s	$s+h$	...	$s+(n-1)h$	0	S_2
3	Regular time	$r+2b$	$r+b$	r	...	$r+(n-2)h$	0	R_3
	Overtime	$l+2b$	$l+b$	l	...	$l+(n-2)h$	0	O_3
	Subcontract	$s+2b$	$s+b$	s	...	$s+(n-2)h$	0	S_3
⋮	⋮	⋮	⋮	⋮	⋮	⋮	⋮	⋮
	Regular time	$r+(n-1)b$	$r+(n-2)b$	$r+(n-3)b$	...	$r+(n-(n-1))h$	0	R_n
n	Over time	$l+(n-1)b$	$l+(n-2)b$	$l+(n-3)b$	...	$l+(n-(n-1))h$	0	O_n
	Subcontract	$s+(n-1)b$	$s+(n-2)b$	$s+(n-3)b$	...	$s+(n-(n-1))h$	0	S_n
	Demand	D_1	D_2	D_3	...	D_m		Total

r = Regular production cost per unit

l = Overtime cost per unit

s = Subcontracting cost per unit

h = Holding cost per unit period

b = Backorder cost per unit per period

n = Number of periods in planning horizon

The network representation of the problem can be developed as follows:

1. Define each row in Table 5-1 as a source node with the supply quantity equal to the respective row capacity as indicated in the Capacity column (e.g., I_0, R_1, O_1, etc.).
2. Define each column as a destination node with the demand quantity equal to the respective column demand as indicated in the Demand row (e.g., D_1, D_2, D_3, etc.).
3. Define each entry in the upper-right-hand corner of each cell as the cost of shipping one unit from a source node to a destination node.

Example 5-2 illustrates the setup and final solution of an aggregate planning problem using the transportation model.

EXAMPLE 5-2

Given the following information, set up the problem in a transportation table and solve for the minimum-cost plan:

	Period 1	Period 2	Period 3
Demand	550	700	750
Capacity			
Regular	500	500	500
Overtime	50	50	50
Subcontract	120	120	100
Beginning inventory	100		
Costs			
Regular time		$60 per unit	
Overtime		$80 per unit	
Subcontract		$90 per unit	
Inventory carrying cost		$1 per unit per month	
Backorder cost		$3 per unit per month	

Table 5-2 Transportation Table for the Aggregate Planning Problem of Example 5-2

Period	Supply from	Demand for Period 1	Period 2	Period 3	Unused capacity (dummy)	Total capacity available (supply)
	Beginning inventory	[0] 100	[1]	[2]	[0]	100
1	Regular	[60] 450	[61] 50	[62]	[0]	500
	Overtime	[80]	[81] 50	[82]	[0]	50
	Subcontract	[90]	[91] 30	[92]	[0] 90	120
2	Regular time	[63]	[60] 500	[61]	[0]	500
	Overtime	[83]	[80] 50	[81]	[0]	50
	Subcontract	[93]	[90] 20	[91] 100	[0]	120
3	Regular time	[66]	[63]	[60] 500	[0]	500
	Overtime	[86]	[83]	[80] 50	[0]	50
	Subcontract	[96]	[93]	[90] 100	[0]	100
	Demand	550	700	750	90	2,090

Solution

The transportation table and solution are shown in Table 5-2. Some of the entries require additional explanation:

a. In this example, inventory carrying costs are $1 per unit per period (costs are shown in the upper-right-hand corner of each cell in the table). Hence, units produced in one period and carried over to a later period will incur a holding cost that is a linear function of the length of time held.
b. Linear programming models of this type require that supply (capacity) and demand be equal. A dummy column has been added (unused capacity) to satisfy that requirement. Since it does not "cost" anything extra to not use capacity in this case, cell costs of $0 have been assigned.
c. No backlogs were needed in this example.
d. The quantities (e.g., 100 and 450 in column 1) are the amounts of output or inventory that will be used to meet demand requirements. Thus, the demand of 550 units in period 1 will be met using 100 units from inventory and 450 obtained from regular-time output.

When backlogs are not permitted, the cell costs for the backlog positions can be made prohibitively high so that no backlogs will appear in the solution. The main limitations of LP (transportation) models are the assumptions of linear relationships among variables, the inability to continuously monitor and adjust output rates, and the need to specify a single objective (e.g., minimize costs) instead of using multiple objectives (e.g., minimize cost while stabilizing the workforce).

Using the Transportation Problem to Solve Location Problems Another use of the transportation method is to compare transportation costs for alternative locations. For instance, a company may be preparing to build a new warehouse, and there may be a number of potential locations under consideration. One aspect of the decision may be differences in transportation costs that would result from each alternative.

Suppose that currently the firm has three factories that supply four warehouses, and another warehouse will be added. Suppose that two separate locations for the new warehouse, Windsor and Oshawa, are being studied. The impact of each of the two potential locations can be determined by solving *two* transportation problems, one for each location. In other words, one extra column would be added to the transportation table, representing one of the warehouses, and the problem would be solved for the minimum total cost. That column, then, would be replaced in the table by a column representing the other warehouse, and again the problem would be solved for the minimum cost. This would give decision makers an opportunity to assess the impact of each warehouse location on the total distribution costs for the system. Tables 5-3 and 5-4 summarize the information into a table format as in the case of an aggregate planning problem.

TABLE 5-3 System with Windsor Warehouse

	Warehouse #1	Warehouse #2	Warehouse #3	Warehouse #4	Warehouse Windsor
Factory A					9
Factory B					6
Factory C					5

TABLE 5-4 System with Oshawa Warehouse

	Warehouse #1	Warehouse #2	Warehouse #3	Warehouse #4	Warehouse Oshawa
Factory A					4
Factory B					10
Factory C					7

It should be noted that transportation cost typically would be one of a number of variables that would be taken into account in making such a decision. However, some other factors, such as nearness of the warehouse to a target market, might take precedence over the transportation cost.

5.3 TRANSSHIPMENT PROBLEMS

Certain transportation problems may involve the use of *intermediate* destinations where goods are temporarily stored before being shipped on to their final destinations. Thus, these intermediate points are both destinations and origins. These are called **transshipment problems.** The goal generally is the same as with other transportation problems: to minimize total transportation cost.

Figure 5-3 depicts a transshipment problem. In the figure, the nodes (circles) represent locations where goods are stored or received, and the branches (lines) represent shipping routes. To completely specify a problem, it would be necessary to indicate the quantity available at each source and the demand of each destination as well as the per-unit shipping cost for each route. Also, in some situations, the transshipment points and the routes may have capacity limitations, although we will assume there are no such capacity limitations.

Linear Programming Formulation of the Transshipment Problem

We can easily formulate a linear programming model for this problem. Suppose we define x_{ij} as the quantity shipped from node i to node j. For example, x_{14} would represent the quantity shipped from node 1 to node 4. The supply of each supply node is a constraint

FIGURE 5-3 A Network Diagram of a Transshipment Problem

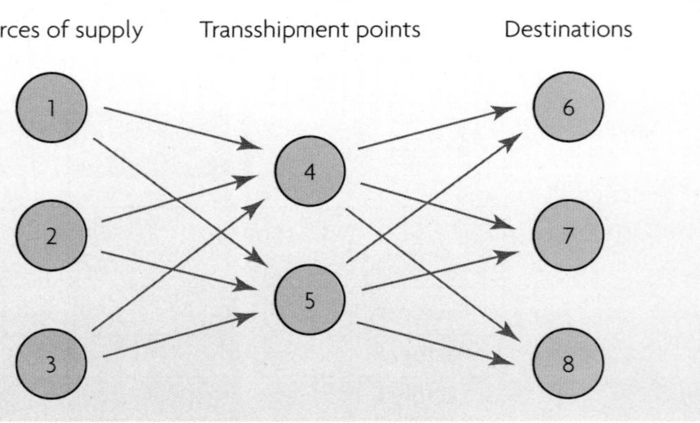

on the quantity that can be shipped from that node. Hence, the model must include a constraint for each supply node. For node 1, this would be

$$x_{14} + x_{15} \leq s_1$$

Similarly, for nodes 2 and 3, the constraints would be

$$\begin{aligned} &\textbf{Node 2:} \quad x_{24} + x_{25} \leq s_2 \\ &\textbf{Node 3:} \quad x_{34} + x_{35} \leq s_3 \end{aligned}$$

S_i represents the supply available at source i.

For the transshipment nodes, if we assume that the incoming and outgoing quantities must be equal, we would have

$$\begin{aligned} &\qquad\qquad\qquad \textbf{(incoming)} \qquad \textbf{(outgoing)} \\ &\textbf{Node 4:} \quad x_{14} + x_{24} + x_{34} = x_{46} + x_{47} + x_{48} \end{aligned}$$

This can be rewritten as

$$x_{14} + x_{24} + x_{34} - x_{46} + x_{47} + x_{48} = 0$$

$$\begin{aligned} &\qquad\qquad\qquad \textbf{(incoming)} \qquad \textbf{(outgoing)} \\ &\textbf{Node 5:} \quad x_{15} + x_{25} + x_{35} = x_{56} + x_{57} + x_{58} \end{aligned}$$

This can be rewritten as

$$x_{15} + x_{25} + x_{35} - x_{56} - x_{57} - x_{58} = 0$$

For the destination nodes, the demands must be satisfied by the shipments from the transshipment points. Thus,

$$\begin{aligned} &\textbf{Node 6:} \quad x_{46} + x_{56} = D_6 \\ &\textbf{Node 7:} \quad x_{47} + x_{57} = D_7 \\ &\textbf{Node 8:} \quad x_{48} + x_{58} = D_8 \end{aligned}$$

D_j represents the demand at destination j.

The objective is to minimize the total cost of shipping. Using c_{ij} to represent the cost per unit to ship from node i to node j, we have

$$\begin{aligned} \textbf{minimize} \quad Z = \; & \textbf{(from sources to transshipment points)} \\ & c_{14}x_{14} + c_{24}x_{24} + c_{34}x_{34} + c_{15}x_{15} + c_{25}x_{25} + c_{35}x_{35} + \\ & \textbf{(from transshipment points to destinations)} \\ & c_{46}x_{46} + c_{47}x_{47} + c_{48}x_{48} + c_{56}x_{56} + c_{57}x_{57} + c_{58}x_{58} \end{aligned}$$

Hence, the model consists of source node constraints, transshipment node constraints, and destination constraints. In its entirety, the model is

$$\begin{aligned} \textbf{minimize} \quad Z = \; & c_{14}x_{14} + c_{24}x_{24} + c_{34}x_{34} + c_{15}x_{15} + c_{25}x_{25} + c_{35}x_{35} + c_{46}x_{46} + \\ & c_{47}x_{47} + c_{48}x_{48} + c_{56}x_{56} + c_{57}x_{57} + c_{58}x_{58} \end{aligned}$$

subject to

$$\begin{aligned} &\textbf{Node 1:} && x_{14} + x_{15} && \leq S_1 \\ &\textbf{Node 2:} && x_{24} + x_{25} && \leq S_2 \quad \textbf{source constraints} \\ &\textbf{Node 3:} && x_{34} + x_{35} && \leq S_3 \\ &\textbf{Node 4:} && x_{14} + x_{24} + x_{34} - x_{46} - x_{47} - x_{48} && = 0 \quad \textbf{transshipment constraints} \\ &\textbf{Node 5:} && x_{15} + x_{25} + x_{35} - x_{56} - x_{57} - x_{58} && = 0 \\ &\textbf{Node 6:} && x_{46} + x_{56} && = D_6 \\ &\textbf{Node 7:} && x_{47} + x_{57} && = D_7 \quad \textbf{destination constraints} \\ &\textbf{Node 8:} && x_{48} + x_{58} && = D_8 \end{aligned}$$

All variables ≥ 0

EXAMPLE 5-3

Transshipment Problem

Suppose the manager of Harley's Sand and Gravel Pit has decided to utilize two intermediate nodes as transshipment points for temporary storage of topsoil. The revised network diagram of the transshipment problem is given in Figure 5-4.

The cost of shipping one unit from the farms to warehouses is given in Table 5-5. The cost of shipping one unit from the warehouses to projects is given in Table 5-6. The unit shipping costs shown in these two tables are also included on the respective arcs in Figure 5-4. For example, we display the number "3" on the arc that connects farm A to warehouse 1.

Table 5-5 Cost of Shipping One Unit from the Farms to Warehouses

From/To	Warehouse 1 (4)	Warehouse 2 (5)
Farm A (1)	3	2
Farm B (2)	4	3
Farm C (3)	2.5	3.5

Table 5-6 Cost of Shipping One Unit from the Warehouses to Projects

From/To	Project 1 (6)	Project 2 (7)	Project 3 (8)
Warehouse 1 (4)	2	1	4
Warehouse 2 (5)	3	2	5

Each source, or farm, is numbered as 1, 2, and 3. The two intermediate nodes (warehouses) are numbered as follows: warehouse 1 = 4, and warehouse 2 = 5. The three destinations (projects 1, 2, and 3) are numbered as 6, 7, and 8 respectively.

FIGURE 5-4 A Network Diagram of Harley's Sand and Gravel Pit Transshipment Example

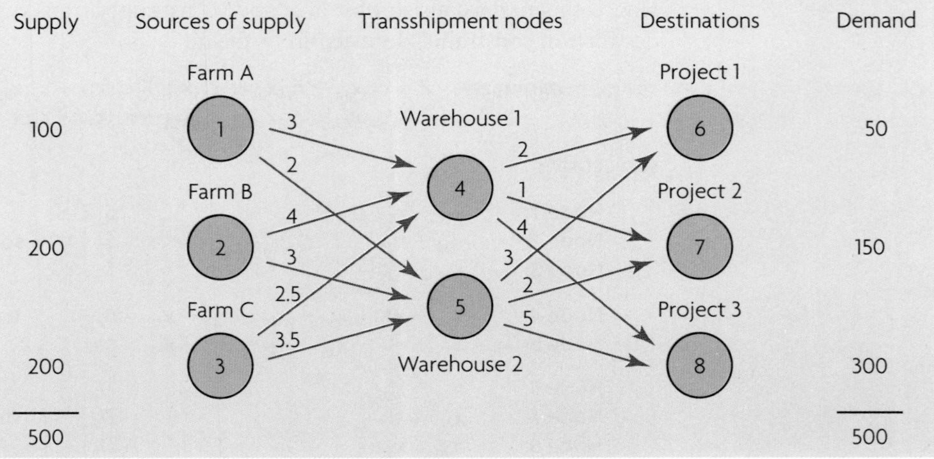

Given the information presented above, we can formulate Harley's topsoil transshipment problem as follows:

Let x_{ij} = amount shipped from source or warehouse *i* to destination or warehouse *j*.

c_{ij} = cost of shipping one unit from source or warehouse *i* to destination or warehouse *j*.

The objective function can be stated as

$$\text{minimize } Z = 3x_{14} + 2x_{15} + 4x_{24} + 3x_{25} + 2.5x_{34} + 3.5x_{35} + 2x_{46} + x_{47} + 4x_{48} + 3x_{56} + 2x_{57} + 5x_{58}$$

Now we are ready to state the constraints of the problem. We can start by stating the supply constraints. The amount shipped from each of the sources (supply nodes) cannot exceed the supply available at each supply node. Therefore, the following supply constraints can be stated:

$x_{14} + x_{15} \leq 100$ (supply constraint associated with farm A)
$x_{24} + x_{25} \leq 200$ (supply constraint associated with farm B)
$x_{34} + x_{35} \leq 200$ (supply constraint associated with farm C)

Next, we need to set up the transshipment constraints for each warehouse (intermediate node). The logic behind transshipment constraints is that what is shipped into a transshipment node must be shipped out. In other words, no units may be left over in a transshipment node. Therefore we can formulate the transshipment constraints for warehouse 1 and warehouse 2 as follows:

$x_{14} + x_{24} + x_{34}$ = $x_{46} + x_{47} + x_{48}$
(units shipped into warehouse 1) (units shipped out of warehouse 1)

$x_{15} + x_{25} + x_{35}$ = $x_{56} + x_{57} + x_{58}$
(units shipped into warehouse 2) (units shipped out of warehouse 2)

The amount shipped from the transshipment (warehouse) nodes to destination nodes must satisfy the demand at each destination node. The demand constraints are set as "equal to" constraints. The three demand constraints are stated as follows:

$x_{46} + x_{56} = 50$ (demand at project 1)
$x_{47} + x_{57} = 150$ (demand at project 2)
$x_{48} + x_{58} = 300$ (demand at project 3)

In summary, the final formulation of Harley's topsoil transshipment problem can be stated as follows:

$$\text{minimize } Z = 3x_{14} + 2x_{15} + 4x_{24} + 3x_{25} + 2.5x_{34} + 3.5x_{35} + 2x_{46} + x_{47} + 4x_{48} + 3x_{56} + 2x_{57} + 5x_{58}$$

subject to

$x_{14} + x_{15} \leq 100$ (supply constraint associated with farm A)
$x_{24} + x_{25} \leq 200$ (supply constraint associated with farm B)
$x_{34} + x_{35} \leq 200$ (supply constraint associated with farm C)
$x_{14} + x_{24} + x_{34} - x_{46} - x_{47} - x_{48} = 0$ (transshipment/warehouse constraint 1)
$x_{15} + x_{25} + x_{35} - x_{56} - x_{57} - x_{58} = 0$ (transshipment/warehouse constraint 2)
$x_{46} + x_{56} = 50$ (demand at project 1)

$x_{47} + x_{57} = 150$ (demand at project 2)
$x_{48} + x_{58} = 300$ (demand at project 3)
$x_{ij} \geq 0$ for all i, j combinations

The general LP format of a transshipment problem with m supply nodes, k transshipment nodes, and n final destination nodes, can be summarized as follows:

$$\text{minimize } Z = \sum_{\text{all arcs}} c_{ij} x_{ij}$$

subject to:

$$\sum_{\text{arcs out}} x_{ij} - \sum_{\text{arcs in}} x_{ji} \leq S_i \qquad i = 1, \ldots, m \text{ (supply nodes)}$$

$$\sum_{\text{arcs out}} x_{ij} - \sum_{\text{arcs in}} x_{ji} = 0 \qquad i = 1, \ldots, k \text{ (transshipment nodes)}$$

$$\sum_{\text{arcs in}} x_{ij} - \sum_{\text{arcs out}} x_{ji} = D_j \qquad j = 1, \ldots, n \text{ (demand nodes)}$$

$$x_{ij} \geq 0 \qquad \text{for all } i \text{ and } j$$

Where c_{ij} refers to the cost per unit to transport units from node i to node j, x_{ij} the number of units shipped from node i to node j, S_i the supply in units available at supply node i, and D_j the demand in units at demand node j.

Solving the Transshipment Problem Using Excel

We prepare the spreadsheet shown in Exhibit 5-3 to solve a transshipment problem using Excel. In preparing the spreadsheet, we divide the sheet into five parts. In part 1, in the upper-left-hand corner, we include the amounts shipped between the farms and warehouses. The Qty Shipped column on the right-hand side of this portion of the sheet is obtained by adding the values shipped from a farm to each warehouse. For example, the quantity shipped from farm A is displayed in cell E5 and can be obtained by using the formula = SUM(B5:C5). This indicates the amount shipped from farm A to warehouse 1 (cell B5) plus the amount shipped from farm A to warehouse 2 (cell C5). Similarly, the total quantity shipped to warehouse 1 is displayed in cell B8 in Exhibit 5-3. The formula for cell B8 is given by = SUM(B5:B7). In this formula, we sum the amount shipped from farm A to warehouse 1 (cell B5), the amount shipped from farm B to warehouse 1 (cell B6), and the amount shipped from farm C to warehouse 1 (cell B7). The quantity-shipped values from farm A, farm B, and farm C to quantity shipped to warehouse 2 are calculated in a similar fashion.

The second part of the table on the lower-left-hand side includes the amounts shipped from warehouses to projects. The Qty Shipped column on the right-hand side of this portion of the sheet shows the total quantity shipped from each warehouse. This value is obtained by adding the values shipped from a warehouse to each project. For example, the quantity shipped from warehouse 1 is displayed in cell E12 and can be obtained by using the formula = SUM(B12:D12) as shown in Exhibit 5-3. This indicates the amount shipped from warehouse 1 to project 1 (cell B12) plus the amount shipped from warehouse 1 to project 2 (cell C12) plus the amount shipped from warehouse 1 to project 3 (cell D12). Similarly, the total quantity shipped to project 1 is displayed in cell B15 in Exhibit 5-3. The formula for cell B15 is given by = SUM(B12:B13). In this formula, we sum the amount shipped from warehouse 1 to project 1 (cell B12) and the amount shipped from warehouse 2 to project 1 (cell B13). The quantity-shipped values from warehouse 1 and warehouse 2 and to project 2 and project 3 are calculated in a similar fashion.

EXHIBIT 5-3 Excel Input and Output Screen for the Transshipment Problem

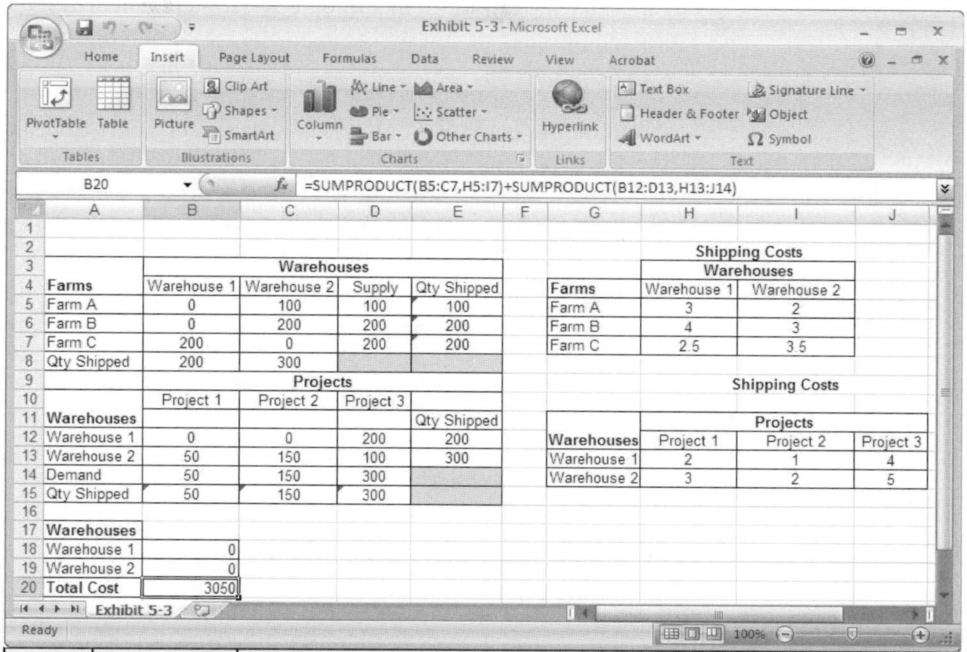

Exhibit 5-3 - Microsoft Excel

B20 f_x =SUMPRODUCT(B5:C7,H5:I7)+SUMPRODUCT(B12:D13,H13:J14)

	Warehouses			
Farms	Warehouse 1	Warehouse 2	Supply	Qty Shipped
Farm A	0	100	100	100
Farm B	0	200	200	200
Farm C	200	0	200	200
Qty Shipped	200	300		

	Projects			
	Project 1	Project 2	Project 3	
Warehouses				Qty Shipped
Warehouse 1	0	0	200	200
Warehouse 2	50	150	100	300
Demand	50	150	300	
Qty Shipped	50	150	300	

Warehouses	
Warehouse 1	0
Warehouse 2	0
Total Cost	3050

Shipping Costs

	Warehouses	
Farms	Warehouse 1	Warehouse 2
Farm A	3	2
Farm B	4	3
Farm C	2.5	3.5

Shipping Costs

	Projects		
Warehouses	Project 1	Project 2	Project 3
Warehouse 1	2	1	4
Warehouse 2	3	2	5

Cell	Copied to	Formula
E5	E6 : E7	= SUM (B5 : C5)
B8	B9	= SUM (B5 : B7)
E12	E13	= SUM (B12 : D12)
B15	C15 : D15	= SUM (B12 : B13)
B18		= B8 − E12
B19		= C8 − E13
B20		= SUMPRODUCT (B5 : C7, H5 : I7) + SUMPRODUCT (B12 : D13, H13 : J14)

The third portion of the table in Exhibit 5-3, on the upper-right-hand side, indicates the unit shipping costs from each of the farms to each of the warehouses. The fourth portion of the table indicates the unit shipping costs from each of the warehouses to each project.

In part 5, which appears at the very bottom of the worksheet, we state the transshipment constraints as well as the objective function. As we discussed earlier, what is shipped in to a warehouse must be shipped out. For warehouse 1, the quantity shipped in is given in cell B8 and the quantity shipped out of warehouse 1 is given in cell E12. Therefore, the formula for cell B18 is = B8 − E12. The formula for warehouse 2 is determined in a similar fashion in cell B19. In setting up the constraints for the transshipment nodes, we will show that we force the values in cell B18 and cell B19 to be equal to zero. The formula for the objective function (total cost) is given in cell B20. This objective function is constructed somewhat differently than the objective function in Exhibit 5-1 for the transportation problem. Instead of entering a single objective function, two cost arrays with SUMPRODUCT functions are developed and added together. For example, the first cost array represented in the first SUMPRODUCT function includes the sum of the cross product of the unit shipping costs from farms to warehouses given in cells H5 through I7 with their respective quantity-shipped values given in cells B5 through C7. The second SUMPRODUCT function includes the sum of the cross products of the unit shipping costs from warehouses to projects given in cells H13 through J14 with their respective quantity-shipped values given in cells B12 through D13. The calculation described above results in the following formula:

= SUMPRODUCT(B5:C7, H5:I7) + SUMPRODUCT(B12: D13, H13:J14)

given in the formula bar at the top of Exhibit 5-3. Stating the objective function with cost arrays as described above is simpler and easier than stating it as a single objective function by entering all the variables and their respective costs.

The results given in Exhibit 5-3 are summarized below:

- Cells B5 to C7 provide the shipment values from supply sources to warehouses. We show the values of the corresponding linear programming variables for each shipment quantity in parentheses.

  Ship 100 units from farm A to warehouse 2 (x_{15} = 100)
  Ship 200 units from farm B to warehouse 2 (x_{25} = 100)
  Ship 200 units from farm C to warehouse 1 (x_{34} = 100)

- Cell B12 to D13 provide the shipment values from warehouses to destinations.

  Ship 200 units from warehouse 1 to project 3 (x_{48} = 100)
  Ship 50 units from warehouse 2 to project 1 (x_{56} = 100)
  Ship 100 units from warehouse 2 to project 3 (x_{58} = 100)
  Ship 150 units from warehouse 2 to project 2 (x_{57} = 100)

- The total cost associated with the transshipment problem is $3,050 and is given in cell B20.

Special Cases of Transshipment Problems

For maximization problems, unacceptable routes, or unequal supply and demand, the approaches devised to handle these special cases for transportation problems can also be applied for transshipment problems.

5.4 ASSIGNMENT PROBLEMS

Assignment problems are characterized by a need to pair items in one group with items in another group in a one-for-one matching. For example, a manager may be faced with the task of assigning four jobs to four machines, one job to a machine. Another manager may be faced with the task of assigning five projects to five staff members, with each staff member responsible for a single project. A marketing manager may be required to assign four salespeople to four territories.

Typically, the time or cost required to complete a job or a project will differ, depending on the machine used for the job or the staff member doing the project. The manager's goal in such cases is to develop a set of assignments that will *minimize* the total time or cost of doing the work. In other cases, the goal may be to minimize distance travelled, scrap, or some other measure of effectiveness. Moreover, some problems involve profit or revenue, and in those cases, the obvious goal would be to develop a set of assignments that would lead to the *maximum* total profit or revenue. Because minimization problems are more common, we begin with a minimization problem.

EXAMPLE 5-4

A manager has prepared a table that shows the cost of performing each of five jobs by each of five employees (see Table 5-7). According to this table, job 1 will cost $15 if done by Al, $20 if it is done by Bill, and so on. The manager has stated that his goal is to develop a set of job assignments that will minimize the total cost of getting all five jobs done. It is further required that the jobs be performed simultaneously, thus requiring one job be assigned to each employee.

Table 5-7 Numerical Example for the Assignment Problem

	Employee				
Job	**Al**	**Bill**	**Cindy**	**David**	**Earl**
1	15	20	18	24	19
2	12	17	16	15	14
3	14	15	19	17	18
4	11	14	12	13	15
5	13	16	17	18	16

In the past, to find the minimum-cost set of assignments, the manager has resorted to listing all of the different possible assignments (i.e., complete enumeration) for small problems such as this one. But for larger problems, the manager simply guesses because there are too many possibilities to try to list them. For example, with a 5×5 table, there are $5! = 120$ different possibilities; but with, say, a 7×7 table, there are $7! = 5040$ possibilities.

Figure 5-5 shows the network representation of the assignment problem described in Example 5-4. The nodes represent either jobs that need to be assigned (sources of supply) or employees to whom jobs can be assigned to (destinations). Arcs represent the cost of performing a given job by an employee. This network is similar to the network of the transportation problem shown in Figure 5-2, except that the supply at each source node or the demand at each destination node is equal to 1. The assignment problem is a special case of a transportation problem in which all supply and demand nodes equal 1.

Linear Programming Formulation of the Assignment Problem

Similar to the formulation of the transportation and transshipment problems, we can easily formulate an assignment problem as a linear programming problem.

FIGURE 5-5 Network Representation of the Personal Assignment Problem Example

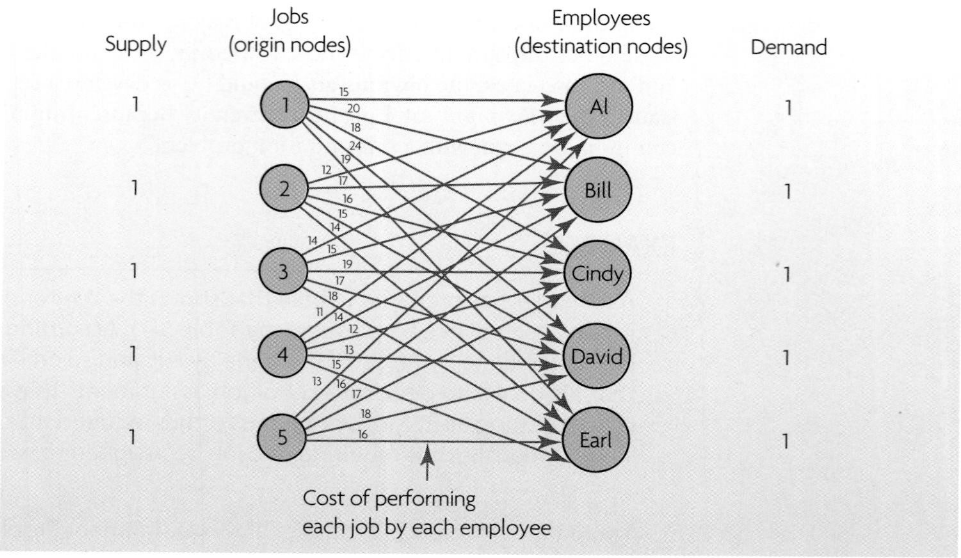

First we will provide a linear programming formulation of this numerical example, then we will provide the Excel solution.

Linear Programming Formulation of the Numerical Example given in Table 5–7 for the Assignment Problem We define $x_{ij} = 1$ if job i assigned to employee j and $x_{ij} = 0$ if job i is not assigned to employee j. The linear programming model can be stated as follows:

$$\text{minimize } Z = 15x_{11} + 20x_{12} + 18x_{13} + 24x_{14} + 19x_{15} + 12x_{21} + 17x_{22} + 16x_{23} + 15x_{24} + 14x_{25} + 14x_{31} + 15x_{32} + 19x_{33} + 17x_{34} + 18x_{35} + 11x_{41} + 14x_{42} + 12x_{43} + 13x_{44} + 15x_{45} + 13x_{51} + 16x_{52} + 17x_{53} + 18x_{54} + 16x_{55}$$

subject to

$$\left.\begin{aligned} x_{11} + x_{12} + x_{13} + x_{14} + x_{15} &= 1 \\ x_{21} + x_{22} + x_{23} + x_{24} + x_{25} &= 1 \\ x_{31} + x_{32} + x_{33} + x_{34} + x_{35} &= 1 \\ x_{41} + x_{42} + x_{43} + x_{44} + x_{45} &= 1 \\ x_{51} + x_{52} + x_{53} + x_{54} + x_{55} &= 1 \end{aligned}\right\}$$

(These are the row constraints. Each job can be assigned to only one employee.)

$$\left.\begin{aligned} x_{11} + x_{21} + x_{31} + x_{41} + x_{51} &= 1 \\ x_{12} + x_{22} + x_{32} + x_{42} + x_{52} &= 1 \\ x_{13} + x_{23} + x_{33} + x_{43} + x_{53} &= 1 \\ x_{14} + x_{24} + x_{34} + x_{44} + x_{54} &= 1 \\ x_{15} + x_{25} + x_{35} + x_{45} + x_{55} &= 1 \end{aligned}\right\}$$

(These are the column constraints. Each employee can only be assigned to one job.)

$$\text{All } x_{ij} \geq 0$$

General Linear Formulation of a Assignment Problem The general LP format of an assignment problem with m source (supply) nodes and n destination (demand) nodes can be summarized as follows:

$$\text{minimize } Z = \sum_{i=1}^{m} \sum_{j=1}^{n} c_{ij} x_{ij}$$

subject to:

$$\sum_{j=1}^{n} x_{ij} \leq 1 \qquad i = 1, 2, ..., m \text{ (job)}$$

$$\sum_{i=1}^{m} x_{ij} = 1 \qquad j = 1, ..., n \text{ (employee)}$$

$$x_{ij} \geq 0 \qquad \text{for all } i \text{ and } j$$

Where, as previously defined, c_{ij} is the cost per unit to transport units from source i to destination j, x_{ij} the number units shipped from source i to destination j, S_i supply in units available at source i and D_j demand in units requested at destination j.

Solving the Assignment Problem Using Excel

In the next few paragraphs, we will demonstrate how to solve the assignment problem using Excel. To do this, we use the numerical example given in Table 5-7. We begin developing the worksheet given in Exhibit 5-4.

The worksheet provided in Exhibit 5-4 consists of two parts. The first part (top portion), labelled "Cost of Each Assignment," is the data input portion where the cost/time/distance of assigning row i to column j is specified. The second part (bottom portion) specifies the optimal values of the decision variables (assignments). Before we run Solver, the values of the decision variables specified at the bottom portion of the worksheet are equal to zero. At the very bottom of the worksheet (in cell C23) is the value of the optimal minimum cost, which is the objective function value for the assignment problem. Again, before we execute Solver, the value of the objective function, or the minimum total cost, is equal to zero. In Exhibit 5-4, the formula bar shows the following formula of the objective function in cell C23: = SUMPRODUCT(C6:G10,C15:G19). This formula is a cross product of the unit cost information provided in the first part of the worksheet (cells C6 through G10) with the decision variables (assignments) provided in the second part of the worksheet (cells C15 through G19). We provide the Jobs Available row and column at the bottom and at the right side of the second part of the worksheet. The Jobs Available section provides the right-hand-side values of all the constraints specified in the linear programming formulation of the assignment problem. Since we have one-to-one assignments, the values of the Jobs Available row and column are equal to one. The far-right-hand-side column and the last row of the second part of the worksheet contain the column and row that are both labelled as "Jobs Assigned." These indicate the number of jobs assigned for that row (job) and column (employee) respectively. The formula for cell I15 is given at the bottom of Exhibit 5-4. This formula, = SUM(C15:G15), represents the total number of assignments for job 1 for all employees. In addition, the formula for cell C21 is given in Exhibit 5-4. This formula, = SUM(C15:C19), shows the number of jobs assigned to Al.

After completing the worksheet given in Exhibit 5-4, we can proceed to solve the problem by choosing **Data|Analysis|Solver|.**

The solution displayed in Exhibit 5-4 shows that job 1 is assigned to Cindy, job 2 to Earle, job 3 to Bill, job 4 to David, and job 5 to Al for a total assignment cost of $73.

Special Cases of Assignment Problems

Since assignment problems are a special case of transportation problems, all approaches devised to handle special cases of maximization problems, unacceptable routes, and unequal supply and demand can also be applied to address similar cases when they occur for assignment problems.

EXHIBIT 5-4 Excel Input and Output Worksheet for the Assignment Problem

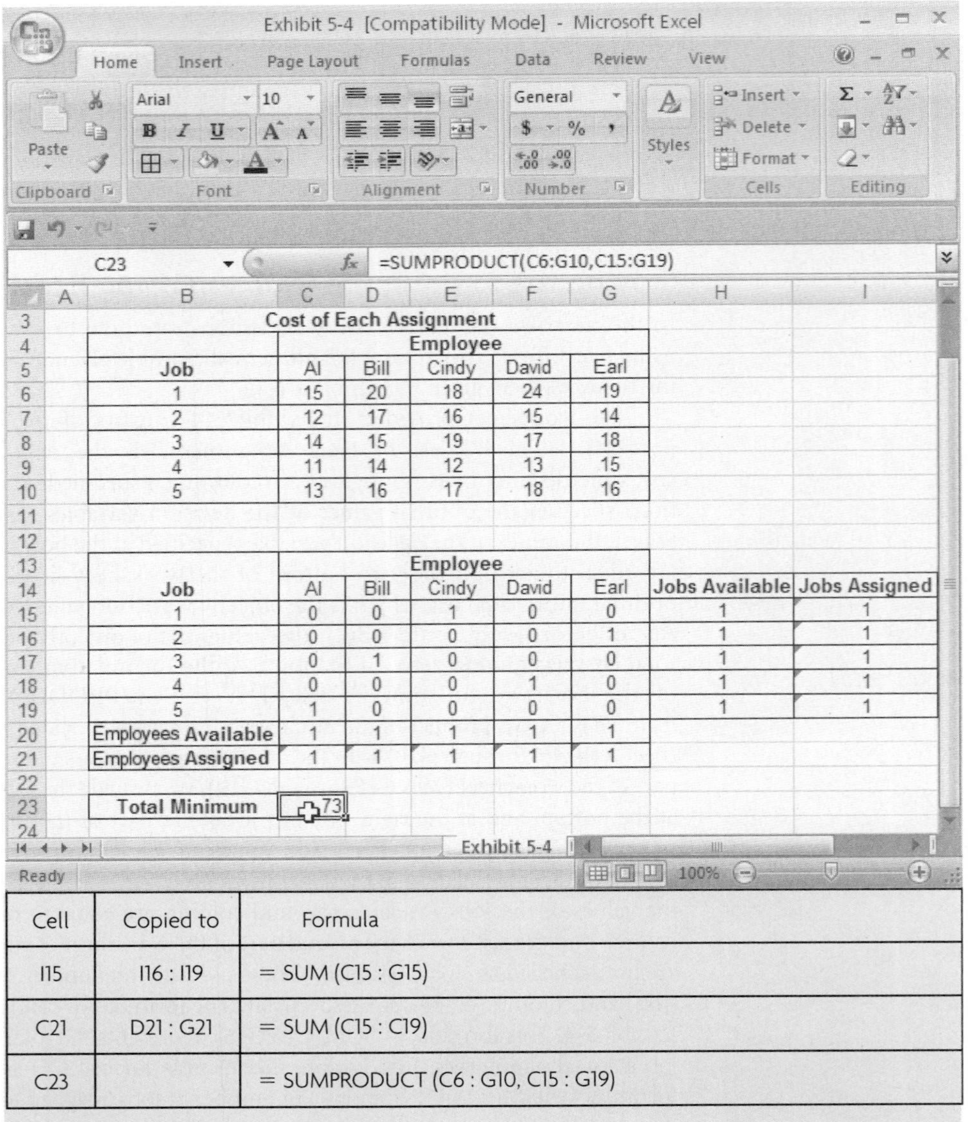

C23 =SUMPRODUCT(C6:G10,C15:G19)

Cost of Each Assignment

Job	Al	Bill	Cindy	David	Earl
	Employee				
1	15	20	18	24	19
2	12	17	16	15	14
3	14	15	19	17	18
4	11	14	12	13	15
5	13	16	17	18	16

Job	Al	Bill	Cindy	David	Earl	Jobs Available	Jobs Assigned
	Employee						
1	0	0	1	0	0	1	1
2	0	0	0	0	1	1	1
3	0	1	0	0	0	1	1
4	0	0	0	1	0	1	1
5	1	0	0	0	0	1	1
Employees Available	1	1	1	1	1		
Employees Assigned	1	1	1	1	1		

Total Minimum	73

Cell	Copied to	Formula
I15	I16 : I19	= SUM (C15 : G15)
C21	D21 : G21	= SUM (C15 : C19)
C23		= SUMPRODUCT (C6 : G10, C15 : G19)

5.5 THE SHORTEST-ROUTE PROBLEM

In the **shortest-route problem,** the objective is to find the shortest distance from one location (origin) to another location (destination) through a network. Very often, the total distance travelled is the measure of effectiveness. Delivery systems and transportation systems are typical examples of where such problems occur. Other measures of effectiveness could be cost or time. Companies are faced with many real-world business applications of the shortest-route problems. The Internet business organization www.mapquest.com provides a typical example of the application of the shortest-route problem.

Linear Programming Formulation of the Shortest-Route Problem

The shortest-route problem also can be solved as a linear programming problem. To demonstrate the linear programming formulation of the shortest-route problem, consider the following example.

EXAMPLE 5-5

The TS Shipping Company transports paint from Cornwall to six other cities located in Ontario and Quebec. Figure 5-6 shows the road network and distances in kilometres between the cities, where node 1 represents the origin city (Cornwall) and node 7 represents the final destination city (Quebec City).

Formulate this problem as a linear program.

Solution

To formulate this problem, we can begin by defining the decision variables as follows:

x_{ij} = the flow from node i to node j

The objective is to minimize the distance between node 1 and each of the remaining 6 nodes. We can express the objective function as follows:

$$\text{minimize } Z = 180x_{12} + 180x_{21} + 200x_{13} + 200x_{31} + 100x_{14} + 100x_{41} + 145x_{24} + 145x_{42} + 300x_{34} + 300x_{43} + 120x_{26} + 120x_{62} + 450x_{35} + 450x_{53} + 215x_{45} + 215x_{54} + 240x_{46} + 240x_{64} + 250x_{47} + 250x_{74} + 225x_{67} + 225x_{76} + 160x_{57} + 160x_{75}$$

The best value for each variable will be either 0 or 1 depending on whether a truck uses the particular route.

There is one constraint for each node. In setting up the constraint for node 1, the right-hand side of the constraint is equal to 1, indicating supply of one at node 1. We assume that one truck leaves node 1 (the origin) and arrives at node 7 (the destination). This is why the right-hand side associated with the node-1 constraint and node-7 constraint will be equal to 1. The left-hand side shows the three possible routes from branch 1: branch 1 to branch 2, branch 1 to branch 3, and branch 1 to branch 4.

$x_{12} + x_{13} + x_{14} = 1$ (supply of one unit at node 1)

The constraint at node 2 involves the concept that whatever comes into node 2 must leave node 2. This type of constraint is similar to the transshipment constraints, discussed earlier in Section 5.3. At node 2, a truck would come from node 1, from node 4, or from node 6. Also, a truck would leave by going to node 1, node 4, or node 6. In other words, what comes into node 2 ($x_{12} + x_{42} + x_{62}$) must leave node 2 ($x_{21} + x_{24} + x_{26}$).

$$x_{12} + x_{42} + x_{62} = x_{21} + x_{24} + x_{26}$$

FIGURE 5-6 Network for TS Shipping Company Shortest-Route Problem

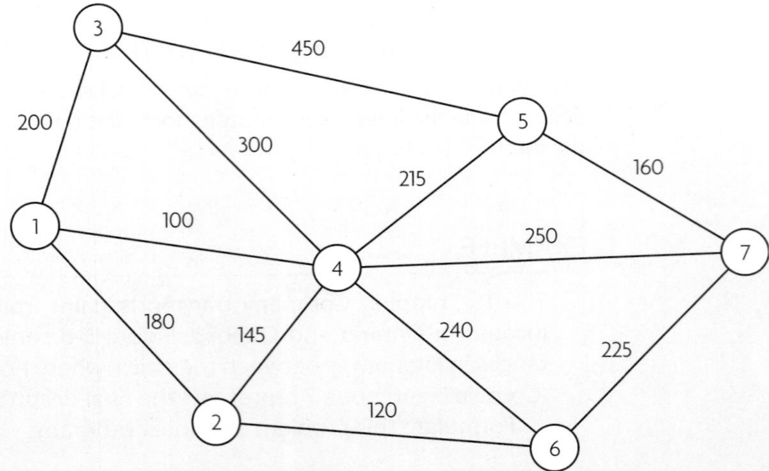

Transferring the outgoing decision variables from the right-hand side to the left-hand side of the equation, we get the following:

$x_{12} + x_{42} + x_{62} - x_{21} - x_{24} - x_{26} = 0$ (transshipment constraint for node 2)

Based on the information given in Figure 5-6, we repeat this process for nodes 3, 4, 5, and 6.

For node 3 we have

$x_{13} + x_{43} + x_{53} = x_{31} + x_{34} + x_{35}$

After moving all of the decision variables to the left side of the inequality, we get

$x_{13} + x_{43} + x_{53} - x_{31} - x_{34} - x_{35} = 0$ (transshipment constraint for node 3)

Repeating this process for nodes 4, 5, and 6, we get the following equations:

$x_{14} + x_{34} + x_{24} + x_{64} + x_{74} + x_{54} - x_{41} - x_{43} - x_{42} - x_{46} - x_{47} - x_{45} = 0$
(transshipment constraint for node 4)

$x_{35} + x_{45} + x_{75} - x_{54} - x_{53} - x_{57} = 0$ (transshipment constraint for node 5)

$x_{26} + x_{46} + x_{76} - x_{62} - x_{64} - x_{67} = 0$ (transshipment constraint for node 6)

To ensure that the route is terminated in Quebec, we only consider the routes or branches going in to node 7 and we will not consider the branches coming out of node 7 (7 to 4, 7 to 5, and 7 to 6). Since this is the ending node, the supply of one that was started at node 1 will end up in node 7. In other words, the right-hand side of the equality constraint for node 7 is equal to 1.

The node 7 constraint can be written as follows:

$x_{47} + x_{57} + x_{67} = 1$ (demand of one unit at node 7).

The complete linear programming formulation of the TS Shipping Company shortest-route linear problem can be stated as follows:

$x_{ij} = 0$ if the route from node i to node j is not selected
$x_{ij} = 1$ if the route from node i to node j is selected

$$\text{minimize } Z = 180x_{12} + 180x_{21} + 200x_{13} + 200x_{31} + 100x_{14} + 100x_{41} + 145x_{24} + 145x_{42} + 300x_{34} + 300x_{43} + 120x_{26} + 120x_{62} + 450x_{35} + 450x_{53} + 215x_{45} + 215x_{54} + 240x_{46} + 240x_{64} + 250x_{47} + 250x_{74} + 225x_{67} + 225x_{76} + 160x_{57} + 160x_{75}$$

subject to

$x_{12} + x_{13} + x_{14} = 1$ (supply of one unit at node 1)

$x_{12} + x_{42} + x_{62} - x_{21} - x_{24} - x_{26} = 0$ (transshipment constraint for node 2)

$x_{13} + x_{43} + x_{53} - x_{31} - x_{34} - x_{35} = 0$ (transshipment constraint for node 3)

$x_{14} + x_{34} + x_{24} + x_{64} + x_{74} + x_{54} - x_{41} - x_{43} - x_{42} - x_{46} - x_{47} - x_{45} = 0$
(transshipment constraint for node 4)

$x_{35} + x_{45} + x_{75} - x_{54} - x_{53} - x_{57} = 0$ (transshipment constraint for node 5)

$x_{26} + x_{46} + x_{76} - x_{62} - x_{64} - x_{67} = 0$ (transshipment constraint for node 6)

$x_{47} + x_{57} + x_{67} = 1$ (demand of one unit at node 7)

$x_{ij} \geq 0$ for all i, j

After formulating the above linear programming problem, we can solve it in a very similar fashion to all of the other linear programming problems we have solved in the previous chapters using Excel.

The shortest route problem formulation corresponds to an integer linear programming model (which is discussed in the next chapter) because of its special structure which ensures that the solution will be integer; however, here it is formulated as a linear programming model.

General Linear Formulation of a Shortest Route Problem The general LP format of a shortest route problem with one origin node, k transshipment nodes, and one destination node can be summarized as follows:

$$\text{minimize } Z = \sum_{\text{all arcs}} c_{ij}x_{ij}$$

subject to

$\sum_{\text{arcs out}} x_{ij} = 1$ **origin node i**

$\sum_{\text{arcs out}} x_{ij} - \sum_{\text{arcs in}} x_{ji} = 0$ **$i = 1, ..., k$ (transshipment nodes)**

$\sum_{\text{arcs in}} x_{ij} = 1$ **destination node j**

$x_{ij} \geq 0$ **for all i and j**

Where, c_{ij} refers to the cost per unit to transport one unit from node i to node j, and x_{ij} the number units shipped from node i to node j.

Solving the Shortest-Route Problem Using Excel

Exhibit 5-5 shows the Excel input worksheet. It consists of three distinct parts. The bottom portion, labelled "Variable Matrix," includes the decision variables. The top portion, labelled "Distance Matrix," includes the distances between the existing routes. If a route is used between location i and location j, then the value of the decision variable in the bottom portion of the matrix will be equal to one; otherwise the value of the decision variable will be equal to zero. In the variable matrix, many of the decision variables do not exist because there

EXHIBIT 5-5 Input Worksheet for the TS Shipping Company Shortest Route Problem (Beginning Node 1, Ending Node 7)

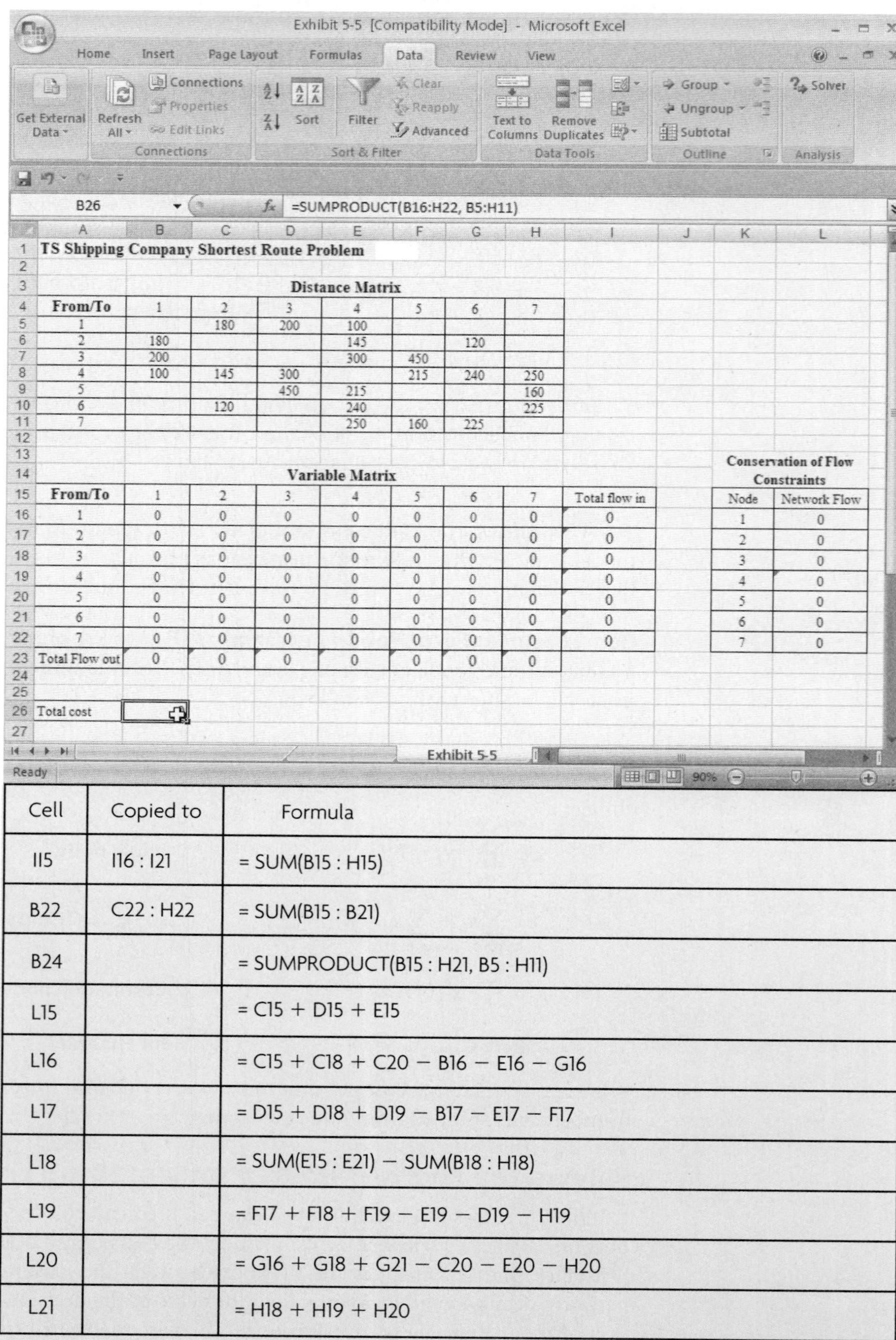

TS Shipping Company Shortest Route Problem

Distance Matrix

From/To	1	2	3	4	5	6	7
1		180	200	100			
2	180			145		120	
3	200			300	450		
4	100	145	300		215	240	250
5			450	215			160
6		120		240			225
7				250	160	225	

Variable Matrix

From/To	1	2	3	4	5	6	7	Total flow in
1	0	0	0	0	0	0	0	0
2	0	0	0	0	0	0	0	0
3	0	0	0	0	0	0	0	0
4	0	0	0	0	0	0	0	0
5	0	0	0	0	0	0	0	0
6	0	0	0	0	0	0	0	0
7	0	0	0	0	0	0	0	0
Total Flow out	0	0	0	0	0	0	0	

Conservation of Flow Constraints

Node	Network Flow
1	0
2	0
3	0
4	0
5	0
6	0
7	0

Total cost

Cell	Copied to	Formula
I15	I16 : I21	= SUM(B15 : H15)
B22	C22 : H22	= SUM(B15 : B21)
B24		= SUMPRODUCT(B15 : H21, B5 : H11)
L15		= C15 + D15 + E15
L16		= C15 + C18 + C20 − B16 − E16 − G16
L17		= D15 + D18 + D19 − B17 − E17 − F17
L18		= SUM(E15 : E21) − SUM(B18 : H18)
L19		= F17 + F18 + F19 − E19 − D19 − H19
L20		= G16 + G18 + G21 − C20 − E20 − H20
L21		= H18 + H19 + H20

is not a direct route between various nodes. To prevent a nonexistent variable from occurring in the solution, we will input "9999" or a very large value so that the corresponding nonexistent decision variable will never come in the solution because the distance is prohibitively large. For instance, there is no direct route between node 1 and node 5 therefore, we will enter "9999" in cell F5. Since this value is unusually large, the corresponding decision variable in the variable matrix will assume a value of zero. Displaying a series of "9999" values in the distance matrix will unnecessarily crowd the distance matrix. Therefore, to prevent the "9999" occurring numerous times in the distance matrix, we will hide these values so that the cell they are in will appear blank even though the number "9999" is actually registered in the cell. To hide these cells, choose **Home|Number|Custom** and enter or choose **;;;.**

The third part of the input worksheet is located on the right-hand side of Exhibit 5-5 and is entitled "Conservation of Flow Constraints." We enter the transshipment, supply, and demand formulas as shown in the linear programming formulation of the shortest route problem. The cell formulas for these cells (L15 through L22) are shown at the bottom of Exhibit 5-5 for the seven nodes. For example, the formula in L15, = C15 + D15 + E15, is equivalent to the left side of the equation for node 1. Cell C15 is x_{12}, cell D15 is x_{13}, and so on. The formula in cell L19 is equivalent to the left side of the equation in node 5: = F13 + F18 + F20 − E14 − D19 − H19. From the variable matrix we can easily ascertain that cell F17 is the variable x_{35}, cell F18 is variable x_{45}, and so forth. Since flow is possible from node 4 to each of the other nodes, and since flow is also possible from each of the other nodes to node 4, we use the SUM command in formulating the equation for node 4 in cell L18. The sum of the values going into node 4, =SUM(E15 : E21), minus the sum of all the values coming out of node 4, = SUM(B18 : H18), must be equal to zero.

The objective function for the problem is stated in cell B24, which is given by the sum of the cross products of the values in the variable matrix and the respective values in the distance matrix. The formula for this cell can be written using the following SUMPRODUCT term: = SUMPRODUCT(B5: H11, B15; H21). In this formula, B15: H21 represents the decision variables in the decision matrix, and B5 : H11 represents the corresponding distance values in the distance matrix. After entering the information given above in the worksheet shown in Exhibit 5-5, we choose **Data|Analysis|Solver.**

Exhibit 5-6 presents the solution summary. The values of 1 in cells E15 and H18 indicate the shortest route from Cornwall (node 1) to Quebec (node 7). Since cell E15 is variable x_{14} and cell H18 is variable x_{47}; the minimum distance solution involves travelling from Cornwall (node 1) to node 4 (variable x_{14}), and then travelling from (node 4) to Quebec (node 7, variable x_{47}). Since the distance from node 1 to node 4 is 100 kilometers and the distance from node 4 to node 7 is 250 kilometers, the total minimum distance is specified in cell B22, which is 100 + 250 = 350. Note that the flow conservation portion of the worksheet now shows that cells L15 and L21 have values equal to 1 based on the way we specified the supply and demand constraints (L15 = Cornwall, L21 = Quebec).

If we need to determine the shortest route from node 1 to node 6 instead of from node 1 to node 7, we need to modify the constraints associated with node 6 and node 7. Node 7's constraint was written as $x_{47} + x_{57} + x_{67} = 1$. However, since we want to determine the shortest route to node 6, we need to change the constraint at node 7 to a transshipment constraint, where whatever comes into node 7 must leave node 7. Therefore, $x_{47} + x_{57} + x_{67} = x_{74} + x_{75} + x_{76}$. Converting this equation so that the problem can be solved using Excel, we move the variables from the right-hand side to the left-hand side of the equation. After this manipulation, we have the following equation: $x_{47} + x_{57} + x_{67} - x_{74} - x_{75} - x_{76} = 0$.

The constraint associated with node 6 was written as a typical transshipment constraint, as stated below, because the ending node was node 7 and not node 6:

$$x_{26} + x_{46} + x_{76} - x_{62} - x_{64} - x_{67} = 0 \qquad \textbf{(transshipment constraint for node 6)}$$

EXHIBIT 5-6 Output Worksheet for the TS Shipping Company Shortest-Route Problem (Beginning Node 1, Ending Node 7)

Exhibit 5-6 [Compatibility Mode] - Microsoft Excel

B24 =SUMPRODUCT(B15:H21, B5:H11)

TS Shipping Company Shortest Route Problem

Distance Matrix

From/To	1	2	3	4	5	6	7
1		180	200	100			
2	180			145		120	
3	200			300	450		
4	100	145	300		215	240	250
5			450	215			160
6		120		240			225
7				250	160	225	

Variable Matrix

From/To	1	2	3	4	5	6	7	Total flow in
1	0	0	0	1	0	0	0	1
2	0	0	0	0	0	0	0	0
3	0	0	0	0	0	0	0	0
4	0	0	0	0	0	0	1	1
5	0	0	0	0	0	0	0	0
6	0	0	0	0	0	0	0	0
7	0	0	0	0	0	0	0	0
Total Flow out	0	0	0	1	0	0	1	

Total cost: 350

Conservation of Flow Constraints

Node	Network Flow
1	1
2	0
3	0
4	0
5	0
6	0
7	1

Exhibit 5-6

Ready

Since we are now trying to determine the shortest route to node 6, there will not be a need to include the $-x_{62} - x_{64} - x_{67}$ portion of the equation because we will not be leaving node 6 to visit any other node since node 6 is now the ending node. Because node 6 is the ending node, the flow or supply of one unit from the constraint associated with node 1 must end up in node 6. Therefore, the right-hand side of the equation for node 6 will be equal to 1. This results in the following equation for node 6 as the ending node: $x_{26} + x_{46} + x_{76} = 1$.

This change requires changing the specification of the formulas in cells L20 (node 6) and L21 (node 7) in Exhibit 5-5. The new solution indicates that the shortest route from node 1 to node 6 is

1. node 1–node 2 (x_{12}).
2. node 2–node 6 (x_{26}).

Since the distance from node 1 to node 2 is 180 kilometers and the distance from node 2 to node 6 is 120 kilometers, the total distance from node 1 to node 6 is 180 + 120 = 300.

We can make other similar changes to modify the beginning node or the ending node. For example, if we want to determine the shortest route from node 3 to node 7, using the original formulation, node 1's constraint is changed as follows because it is no longer the originating node:

$$x_{12} + x_{13} + x_{14} - x_{21} - x_{31} - x_{41} = 0 \quad \text{(transshipment constraint for node 1)}$$

Since node 3 is the new origin, it can be written without the variables going into node 3, and the supply at the origin is equal to 1, which makes the right-hand side of the equation equal to 1. This can be written as

$$x_{31} + x_{34} + x_{35} = 1 \qquad \textbf{(supply of one unit at node 3)}$$

5.6 THE MAXIMUM FLOW PROBLEM

In a **maximum flow problem,** the objective is to maximize flow through a network. For example, a network might represent a system of roads and highways, and the objective might be to maximize the rate of flow of vehicles through the system. Other examples of maximum flow networks can be systems of pipelines that carry natural gas, oil, or water; paperwork systems; airlines routes; production system; and distribution systems.

To determine the maximum flow of a system it is necessary to take into account the *flow capacities* of the various branches of a network. Branch capacities limit the rate of flow through a branch (arc) of the network. Hence, the objective is to determine the amount of flow through each branch that will achieve the maximum possible flow for the system as a whole.

It is assumed that there is a single input node (called a **source**) and a single output node (called a **sink**). It is also assumed that there is *flow conservation,* which means that the flow out of any node is equal to the flow into that node.

As an example of a maximum flow network, consider the network shown in Figure 5-7. As you can see, node 1 is the input node; therefore, all flow entering the system must come through that node. Node 4 is the output node; therefore, all flow leaving the system must go through that node. The numbers of the branches indicate the flow capacity of a branch *in a given direction.* For example, the 10 on branch 1–2 indicates a maximum possible flow rate of 10 coming out of node 1 along that branch. Now some branches permit flow in either direction. However, that is not the case for branch 1–2; the 0 on branch 1–2 indicates that no flow is possible *from* node 2 to node 1. Now consider branch 2–3. We can see that the maximum flow rate along this branch is 2, and that flow can be in *either* direction. However, it is important to recognize that in such a branch flows cannot occur simultaneously in both directions. Consequently, for any branch, flow can occur in one direction only (i.e., it must be *unidirectional*), even though it may be allowable in

FIGURE 5-7 A Flow Network

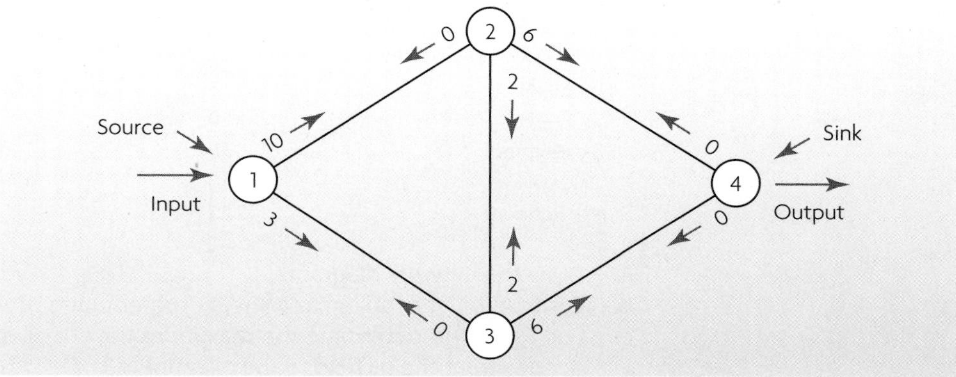

both directions. The determination of which direction, or if there should be any flow at all, is a matter for analysis to resolve.

Linear Programming Formulation of the Maximum Flow Problem

The maximum flow problem also can be solved as a linear programming problem. To demonstrate the linear programming formulation of the maximum flow problem, consider the following example.

EXAMPLE 5-6

Turkmen Oil Ltd. is an oil conglomerate that has a network of pipelines and intermediate oil storage facilities connecting oil fields in Baku, Azerbaijan, and to the newly built oil refinery in Adana, Turkey. Crude oil can be pumped from the oil field to any of the three intermediate storage facilities A, B, and C in Azerbaijan. The maximum flow capacity from the oil field to intermediate storage facilities A, B, and C is 20, 15, and 22 thousand barrels of oil per day respectively. Oil is pumped from these three major intermediate storage facilities to other intermediate processing facilities in Turkey labelled D, E, F, G, and H. The oil is finally pumped from these facilities (D, E, F, G, and H) to the oil refinery in Adana for final processing. The pipeline branches comprising this network and their maximum respective flow capacities are given in Table 5-8.

Table 5-8 Branches of the Network and Flow Capacities of the Branches for the Turkmen Oil Ltd. Maximum Flow Problem

Network Branches	Maximum Flow Capacity
A⟶D	18
A⟶B	20
B⟶A	10
B⟶D	20
B⟶E	13
C⟶B	5
C⟶F	18
D⟶G	14
D⟶E	10
E⟶G	25
E⟶F	5
E⟶H	5
F⟶H	20
G⟶Refinery	30
G⟶H	10
H⟶Refinery	25

a. Draw the network diagram.
b. Formulate this problem as a linear programming problem.
c. Use Excel and determine the maximum flow of oil in thousands of barrels per day from the oil field to the oil refinery.
d. State the amount of flow in thousands of barrels on each branch.

Solution

a. The network diagram for this problem is drawn in Figure 5-8.

b. In formulating this problem as a linear programming problem, we will first define the decision variables. There will be one variable for each unidirectional branch in the problem. There are 19 branches in the network and 18 of the 17 branches flow is in one direction since the capacity of the flow in the opposite direction is equal to zero. However, the branch between node A (2) and node B (3) has a flow capacity in both directions. Therefore, we need two variables for this branch; one of the variables will account for the possible flow from node 2 to node 3 and one variable will account for the flow from node 3 to node 2. Therefore, there will be a total of 18 decision variables.

Let x_{ij} = thousands of barrels of oil that flow from node i to node j
$i = 1, 2, 3, 4, 5, 6, 7, 8, 9, 10$ and $j = 1, 2, 3, 4, 5, 6, 7, 8, 9, 10$
x_{ij} only exists for nodes that are connected in the network.

Since we need to determine the maximum flow in thousands of barrels of oil that originate in the Baku oil field (node 1) and terminate in the oil refinery in Adana (node 10), we need to modify the network by adding a fictitious dummy branch between node 10 and node 1. We need to set the flow capacity to a very high number such as 9999 from node 10 to node 1, and a capacity of zero from node 1 to node 10. This dummy branch is necessary to specify the objective function. After defining the decision variables and establishing the dummy branch (variable), we are ready to determine the objective function. The objective is to maximize the total number of barrels of oil flowing from node 1 (oil field) to node 10 (oil refinery). The flow on the dummy branch from node 10 to node 1 represents the total amount of flow into node 10 from node 1. Thus, the objective is to maximize the flow of the dummy branch. This can be written as

$$\text{maximize} \quad Z = x_{10,1}$$

In formulating the shortest-route problem, we have seen that the intermediate nodes are treated as transshipment nodes. All of the nodes of the maximum flow network also can be shown as transshipment nodes. A unit of flow coming into a node must exit that node. Using this logic, the node 1 transshipment constraint can be written as follows:

$$x_{12} + x_{13} + x_{14} = x_{10,1}$$

FIGURE 5-8 Network Diagram for the Maximum Flow Problem for Turkmen Oil Ltd.

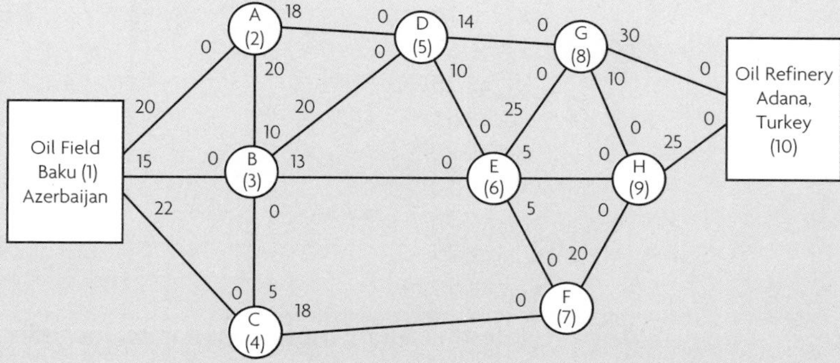

After rearranging the constraint for node 1 so that the right-hand side only consists of numerical values, the net flow constraint for node 1 is as follows:

$x_{12} + x_{13} + x_{14} - x_{10,1} = 0$ (net flow transshipment constraint at node 1)

Using similar logic, the rest of the net flow or transshipment constraints would be written as follows:

$x_{23} + x_{25} - x_{12} - x_{32} = 0$ (net flow transshipment constraint at node 2)

$x_{32} + x_{35} + x_{36} - x_{13} - x_{23} - x_{43} = 0$ (net flow transshipment constraint at node 3)

$x_{43} + x_{47} - x_{14} = 0$ (net flow transshipment constraint at node 4)

$x_{56} + x_{58} - x_{25} - x_{35} = 0$ (net flow transshipment constraint at node 5)

$x_{67} + x_{68} + x_{69} - x_{36} - x_{56} = 0$ (net flow transshipment constraint at node 6)

$x_{79} - x_{47} - x_{67} = 0$ (net flow transshipment constraint at node 7)

$x_{89} + x_{8,10} - x_{58} - x_{68} = 0$ (net flow transshipment constraint at node 8)

$x_{9,10} - x_{69} - x_{79} - x_{89} = 0$ (net flow transshipment constraint at node 9)

$x_{10,1} - x_{8.10} - x_{9,10} = 0$ (net flow transshipment constraint at node 10)

The second type of constraints are the branch capacity constraints and they simply represent the flow capacity of each branch. These constraints can be written as follows:

$x_{12} \leq 20$
$x_{13} \leq 15$
$x_{14} \leq 22$
$x_{23} \leq 20$
$x_{25} \leq 18$
$x_{32} \leq 10$
$x_{35} \leq 20$
$x_{36} \leq 13$
$x_{43} \leq 5$
$x_{47} \leq 18$
$x_{56} \leq 10$
$x_{58} \leq 14$
$x_{67} \leq 5$
$x_{68} \leq 25$
$x_{69} \leq 5$
$x_{79} \leq 20$
$x_{89} \leq 10$
$x_{8,10} \leq 30$
$x_{9,10} \leq 25$
$x_{10,1} \leq 9999$

Note that all of these constraints, including the dummy branch, are less-than-or-equal-to constraints.

The addition of the nonnegativity constraint ($x_{ij} \geq 0$, for all available i, j combinations) completes the linear programming formulation of this maximum flow problem.

c. After formulating the maximum flow problem as a linear programming problem, we can easily solve it using Excel. Exhibit 5-7 shows the input worksheet for the Turkmen Oil Ltd. maximum flow problem. The worksheet illustrated in Exhibit 5-7 is divided into three parts. The bottom part is the matrix that shows the actual flow values of each of the branches. These values, ranging from cell B17 to cell L26 represent the values of the decision variables. The values in column M represent the values of the flow going into each of the nodes and the values in row 27 represent the values of the flow going out of each of the nodes. The top part of the worksheet represents the flow capacities of each node. For example, the value in cell D4 is 20. This value represents the flow capacity of the branch going from the oil fields in Baku (node 1) to node A or 2. Note that the third and final portion of the input worksheet is the Node flow equations, represented next to the actual flow matrix. For example, for node 1, the flow equation is stated as $x_{12} + x_{13} + x_{14} - x_{10,1} = 0$. Since x_{12}, x_{13}, x_{14}, and $x_{10,1}$ are cells D17, E17, F17, and C26 respectively, the left-hand side of the equation for node 1 in cell P17 can be written as D17 + E17 + F17 − C26. Likewise, the equation for node 3 was written as $x_{32} + x_{35} + x_{36} - x_{13} - x_{23} - x_{43} = 0$. Based on this formula, the left-hand side of this formula in cell P19 is = D19 + G19 + H19 − E17 − E18 − E20. The spreadsheet formulas for all 10 nodes are listed at the bottom of Exhibit 5-7. After Exhibit 5-7 is completely prepared, we choose **Data|Analysis|Solver.**

d. The amount of flow in thousands of barrels on each branch is given in Exhibit 5-8. The optimal values of the decision variables, which indicate the flow in thousands of barrels, is summarized in Table 5-9.

Table 5-9 Summary of the Optimal Flow Quantities for Turkmen Old Ltd.

Branch	Decision Variable	Cell	Flow in 1000s of Barrels
Baku to A	x_{12}	C4	20
Baku to B	x_{13}	D4	15
Baku to C	x_{14}	E4	20
A to B	x_{23}	D5	2
A to D	x_{25}	F5	18
B to D	x_{35}	F6	6
B to E	x_{36}	G6	13
C to B	x_{43}	D7	2
C to F	x_{47}	H7	18
D to E	x_{56}	G8	10
D to G	x_{58}	I8	14
E to F	x_{67}	H9	2
E to G	x_{68}	I9	16
E to H	x_{69}	J9	5
F to H	x_{79}	J10	20
G to Adana	$x_{8,10}$	K11	30
H to Adana	$x_{9,10}$	K12	25

EXHIBIT 5-7 Input Worksheet for the Turkmen Oil Ltd. Maximum Flow Problem

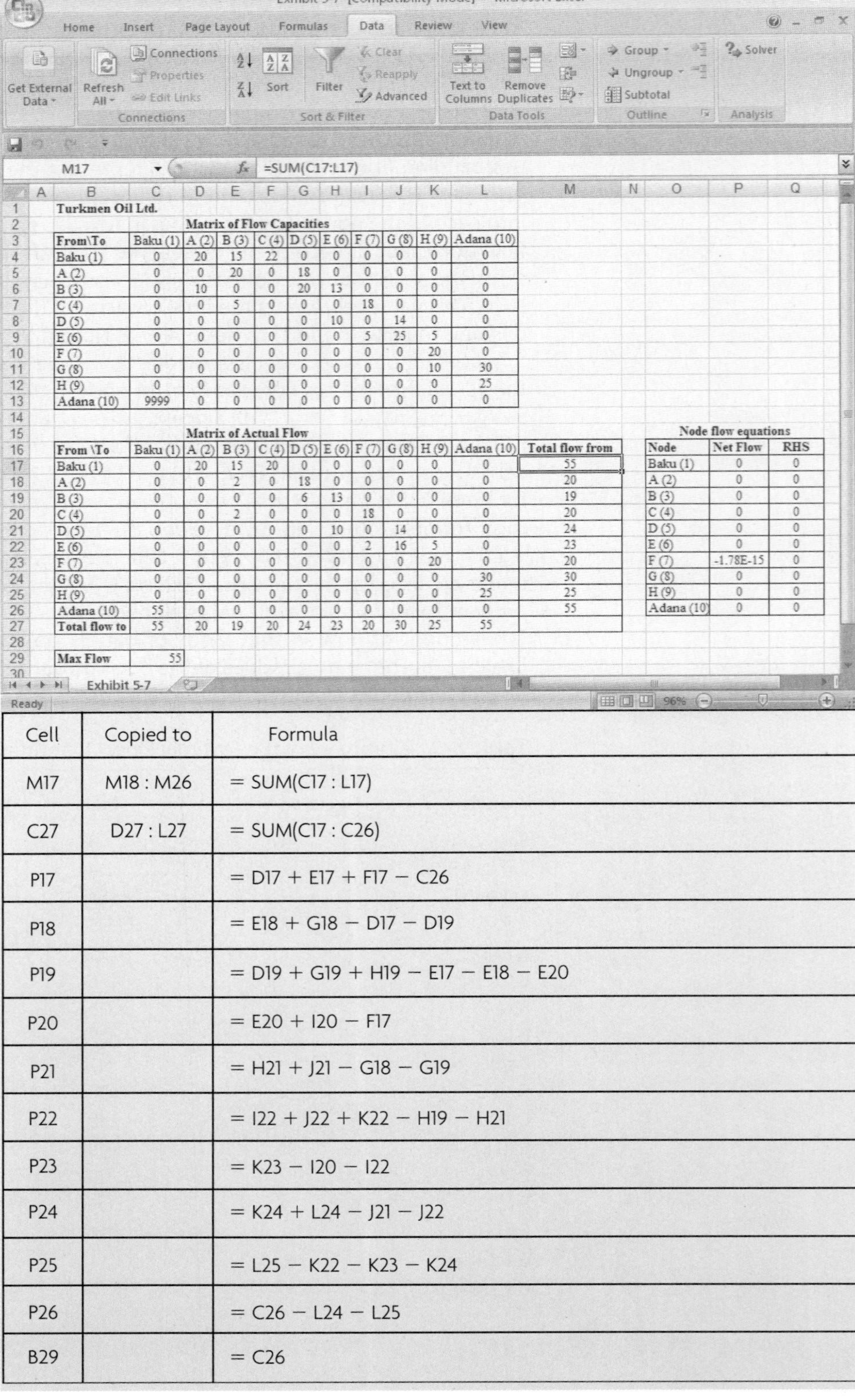

Turkmen Oil Ltd.

Matrix of Flow Capacities

From\To	Baku (1)	A (2)	B (3)	C (4)	D (5)	E (6)	F (7)	G (8)	H (9)	Adana (10)
Baku (1)	0	20	15	22	0	0	0	0	0	0
A (2)	0	0	20	0	18	0	0	0	0	0
B (3)	0	10	0	0	20	13	0	0	0	0
C (4)	0	0	5	0	0	0	18	0	0	0
D (5)	0	0	0	0	0	10	0	14	0	0
E (6)	0	0	0	0	0	0	5	25	5	0
F (7)	0	0	0	0	0	0	0	0	20	0
G (8)	0	0	0	0	0	0	0	0	10	30
H (9)	0	0	0	0	0	0	0	0	0	25
Adana (10)	9999	0	0	0	0	0	0	0	0	0

Matrix of Actual Flow

From \To	Baku (1)	A (2)	B (3)	C (4)	D (5)	E (6)	F (7)	G (8)	H (9)	Adana (10)	Total flow from
Baku (1)	0	20	15	20	0	0	0	0	0	0	55
A (2)	0	0	2	0	18	0	0	0	0	0	20
B (3)	0	0	0	0	6	13	0	0	0	0	19
C (4)	0	0	2	0	0	0	18	0	0	0	20
D (5)	0	0	0	0	0	10	0	14	0	0	24
E (6)	0	0	0	0	0	0	2	16	5	0	23
F (7)	0	0	0	0	0	0	0	0	20	0	20
G (8)	0	0	0	0	0	0	0	0	0	30	30
H (9)	0	0	0	0	0	0	0	0	0	25	25
Adana (10)	55	0	0	0	0	0	0	0	0	0	55
Total flow to	55	20	19	20	24	23	20	30	25	55	

Max Flow	55

Node flow equations

Node	Net Flow	RHS
Baku (1)	0	0
A (2)	0	0
B (3)	0	0
C (4)	0	0
D (5)	0	0
E (6)	0	0
F (7)	-1.78E-15	0
G (8)	0	0
H (9)	0	0
Adana (10)	0	0

Cell	Copied to	Formula
M17	M18 : M26	= SUM(C17 : L17)
C27	D27 : L27	= SUM(C17 : C26)
P17		= D17 + E17 + F17 − C26
P18		= E18 + G18 − D17 − D19
P19		= D19 + G19 + H19 − E17 − E18 − E20
P20		= E20 + I20 − F17
P21		= H21 + J21 − G18 − G19
P22		= I22 + J22 + K22 − H19 − H21
P23		= K23 − I20 − I22
P24		= K24 + L24 − J21 − J22
P25		= L25 − K22 − K23 − K24
P26		= C26 − L24 − L25
B29		= C26

EXHIBIT 5-8 Output Worksheet for the Turkmen Oil Ltd. Maximum Flow Problem

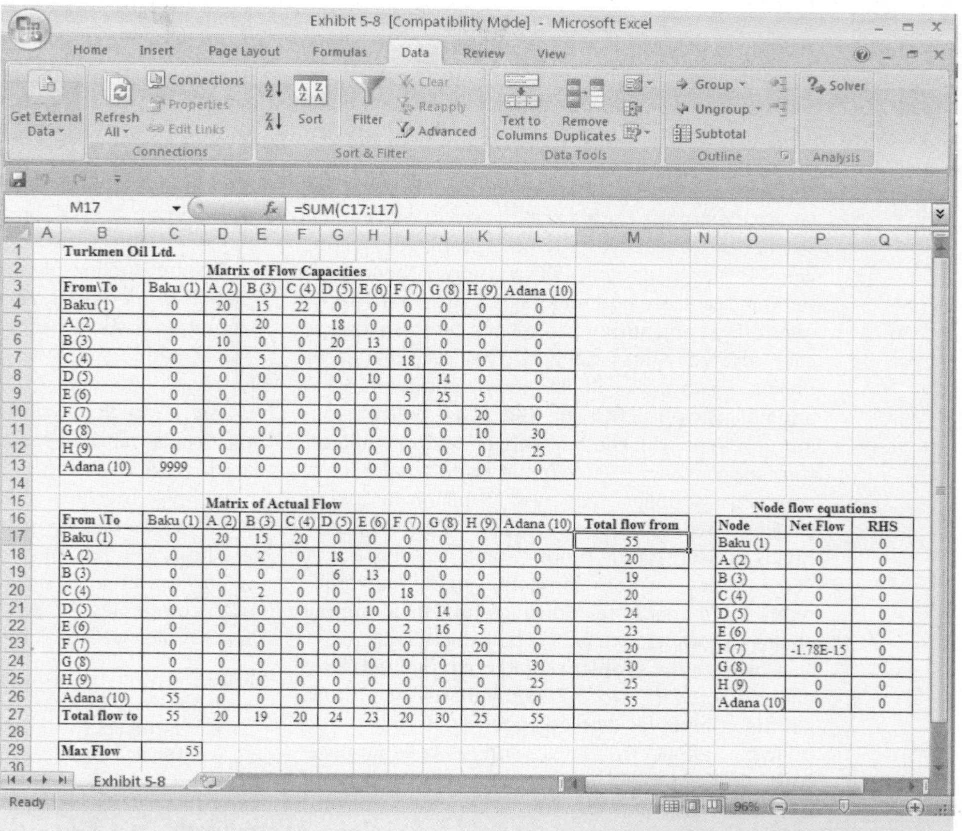

Turkmen Oil Ltd.

Matrix of Flow Capacities

From\To	Baku (1)	A (2)	B (3)	C (4)	D (5)	E (6)	F (7)	G (8)	H (9)	Adana (10)
Baku (1)	0	20	15	22	0	0	0	0	0	0
A (2)	0	0	20	0	18	0	0	0	0	0
B (3)	0	10	0	0	20	13	0	0	0	0
C (4)	0	0	5	0	0	0	18	0	0	0
D (5)	0	0	0	0	0	10	0	14	0	0
E (6)	0	0	0	0	0	0	5	25	5	0
F (7)	0	0	0	0	0	0	0	0	20	0
G (8)	0	0	0	0	0	0	0	0	10	30
H (9)	0	0	0	0	0	0	0	0	0	25
Adana (10)	9999	0	0	0	0	0	0	0	0	0

Matrix of Actual Flow

From \To	Baku (1)	A (2)	B (3)	C (4)	D (5)	E (6)	F (7)	G (8)	H (9)	Adana (10)	Total flow from
Baku (1)	0	20	15	20	0	0	0	0	0	0	55
A (2)	0	0	2	0	18	0	0	0	0	0	20
B (3)	0	0	0	0	6	13	0	0	0	0	19
C (4)	0	0	2	0	0	0	18	0	0	0	20
D (5)	0	0	0	0	0	10	0	14	0	0	24
E (6)	0	0	0	0	0	0	2	16	5	0	23
F (7)	0	0	0	0	0	0	0	0	20	0	20
G (8)	0	0	0	0	0	0	0	0	0	30	30
H (9)	0	0	0	0	0	0	0	0	0	25	25
Adana (10)	55	0	0	0	0	0	0	0	0	0	55
Total flow to	55	20	19	20	24	23	20	30	25	55	

Node flow equations

Node	Net Flow	RHS
Baku (1)	0	0
A (2)	0	0
B (3)	0	0
C (4)	0	0
D (5)	0	0
E (6)	0	0
F (7)	-1.78E-15	0
G (8)	0	0
H (9)	0	0
Adana (10)	0	0

Max Flow	55

General Linear Formulation of a Maximum Flow Problem

The general LP format of a maximum flow problem with k nodes can be summarized as follows:

$$\textbf{maximize } Z = x_{k1}$$

subject to:

$$\sum_{\text{arcs out}} x_{ij} - \sum_{\text{arcs in}} x_{ji} = 0 \qquad i = 1, \ldots, k$$

$$x_{ij} \le v_{ij} \qquad \text{For all } i \text{ and } j$$

$$x_{ij} \ge 0 \qquad \text{For all } i \text{ and } j$$

where x_{ij} is the flow from node i to node j and v_{ij} the maximum flow capacity from node i to node j.

A MODERN MANAGEMENT SCIENCE APPLICATION: PHILIPS ELECTRONICS

The "bullwhip effect" is a phenomenon where the demand variability increases as one moves up a supply chain. In other words, there is less variability in inventory for finished goods than for the individual components that go into those goods.

Philips Electronics Company (PEC) is the 10th largest electronics company in the world with annual sales over $30 billion and 164 000 employees worldwide. Philips Canada, a PEC division, is headquartered in Markham and maintains a large network of sales offices and authorized service centres strategically located across Canada. Two subsidiaries of Philips Electronics—Philips Semiconductors (PS) and Philips Optical Storage (POS)—were experiencing problems with the bullwhip effect in managing their supply chain. PS, one of the world's major semiconductor suppliers, has over $5 billion in annual sales and over 33 000 employees. POS develops and builds optical storage products and has only about 9000 employees. Both companies made a commitment to manage relationships on their supply chains to compensate for the bullwhip effect.

However, this problem could not be solved using existing software. Since POS purchases parts from PS, the companies worked together to reduce the bullwhip effect by developing a collaborative-planning (CP) project to address issues related to the bullwhip effect and the supporting computerized decision support system.

CP used many operations research (management science) techniques to solve the problem faced by the companies, including mathematical programming techniques such as integer programming, and network models to manage multi-echelon inventories. Since PS is a supplier to POS, Philips must manage one level of inventory at PS and a second level of inventory at POS, making it a two-echelon inventory system.

The production planning process involved integration of medium-level planning with short-term planning to avoid miscommunication among the departments. The short-term planning problem is to decide quantities of each "end-item" to release to the shop floor, while medium-term planning involves demand forecasting and overall aggregate production planning. Integrating the short- and medium-term plans is a matter of synchronizing weekly and daily production planning.

This CP project has resulted in savings of up to $5 million annually for PS, but, more importantly, both companies (PS and POS) improved customer and supplier delivery times.

Source: Reprinted by permission, T. de Kok, F. Jansses, J. van Doremlen, E. van Wachem, M. Clerkx, and W. Peeters, "Philips Electronics Synchronizes Its Supply Chain to End the Bullwhip Effect," *Interfaces* Vol. 35, no. 1 (January–February 2005), pp. 37–48. Copyright (2005), the Institute for Operations Research and the Management Sciences (INFORMS), 7240 Parkway Drive, Suite 310, Hanover, MD 21076 USA.

Summary

Network models are an important approach for problem solving. Not only can they be used to model a wide range of problems, they also provide a visual portrayal of a problem. The Modern Management Science Application, "Philips Electronics," is another example of how the company benefited from the use of network flow optimization along with other management science techniques. This chapter describes five types of problems that lend themselves to solutions using linear programming techniques: transportation problems, transshipment problems, assignment problems, shortest-route problems, and maximum flow problems. These problems are part of a larger class of problems known as network flow problems. Transportation-type problems, which include standard transportation problems with multiple sources and multiple destinations, and transshipment problems, which include intermediate nodes in addition to multiple sources and multiple destinations, involve the distribution of goods. The assignment-type problems involve the matching or pairing of two sets of items such as jobs and machines, secretaries and reports, lawyers and cases, and so forth. Transportation problems and transshipments have different costs for different distribution alternatives, while the assignment problems have different costs or time requirements for different pairings. The objective for these types of problems is to identify the transportation or assignment schedule that minimizes total cost or alternatively maximizes profits. Shortest-route problems consist of determining the shortest distance (cost, etc.) from an origin to a destination through a network. Maximum flow problems consist of determining the greatest amount of flow that can be transmitted through a system in which various branches, or connections, have specified flow capacity limitations. The manual solution procedures for all network problems discussed in this chapter are described in Chapter 16, available on the Online Learning Centre, in addition to minimum spanning tree problems, which consist of determining the minimum distance (cost, time) needed to connect a set of locations into a single system. This chapter describes, for each type of problem, how to formulate it as a linear programming problem, how to solve it using Excel, and how to interpret the solution provided by Excel.

Glossary

Arc A branch, or line, in a network.

Assignment Problem A problem that requires pairing two sets of items given a set of paired costs or profits in such a way that the total cost (profit) of the pairings is minimized (maximized).

Maximum Flow Problem Determining the maximum amount of flow that can be obtained for a system of pipes, roads, and so on.

Network A set of nodes and connecting arcs or branches. Can be useful in representing various systems, such as distribution systems, production systems, and transportation systems.

Node A circle in a network. It may represent location or a switching point.

Shortest-Route Problem Determining the shortest path from an origin to a destination through a network.

Sink The one node in a flow network to which all flow is directed; the exit point of a system.

Source The one node in a flow network through which all flow enters the system.

Transportation Problem A distribution-type problem in which supplies of goods that are held at various locations are to be distributed to other receiving locations at minimum cost or maximum profit.

Transshipment Problem A transportation problem in which some locations are used as intermediate shipping points, thereby serving both as origins and as destinations.

Solved Problems

Problem 1

A company ships its products from its two plants to three warehouses. This company wants to minimize total transportation cost of shipment. The cost of shipping one unit from each source (plant) to each destination (warehouse) is given in the following table:

Source	Supply	Destination	Demand
Kingston (1)	61	Toronto (1)	50
Montreal (2)	61	Ottawa (2)	55
		Cornwall (3)	17

	Unit Cost of Shipping		
From\To	Toronto (1)	Ottawa (2)	Cornwall (3)
Kingston (1)	2	3	9
Montreal (2)	7	6	4

Formulate the transportation problem as a linear programming problem given the above and solve it using Excel.

Solution

Let x_{ij} = number of units shipped from source i to destination j.

$$\text{minimize} \quad Z = 2x_{11} + 3x_{12} + 9x_{13} + 7x_{21} + 6x_{22} + 4x_{23}$$

subject to

$$\begin{aligned} x_{11} + x_{12} + x_{13} &\le 61 \\ x_{21} + x_{22} + x_{23} &\le 61 \\ x_{11} + x_{21} &= 50 \\ x_{12} + x_{22} &= 55 \\ x_{13} + x_{23} &= 17 \\ \text{All } x_{ij} &\ge 0 \end{aligned}$$

The Excel solution to this transportation problem is displayed in Exhibit 5-9. The shipment schedule is:

	Units
Kingston to Toronto	50
Kingston to Ottawa	11
Montreal to Ottawa	44
Montreal to Cornwall	17

The total cost for this problem is $465.

Problem 2

Consider the following assignment problem where there are three jobs and three employees and each job has to be performed by one employee and the table values represent the cost of making the particular assignment.

	Employee		
Job	Al(1)	Bob(2)	Cheryl(3)
Job D (1)	6	4	7
Job E (2)	9	5	2
Job F (3)	5	7	1

Solution

Formulate the above problem as a linear programming problem and solve it using Excel. What are the job/employee assignments? What is the total cost of the optimal assignment schedule?

$$\text{minimize} \quad Z = 6x_{11} + 4x_{12} + 7x_{13} + 9x_{21} + 5x_{22} + 2x_{23} + 5x_{31} + 7x_{32} + x_{33}$$

subject to

$$\left.\begin{aligned} x_{11} + x_{12} + x_{13} &= 1 \\ x_{21} + x_{22} + x_{23} &= 1 \\ x_{31} + x_{32} + x_{33} &= 1 \end{aligned}\right\} \text{Each job can only be assigned to one employee. (employee constraints)}$$

$$\left.\begin{aligned} x_{11} + x_{21} + x_{31} &= 1 \\ x_{12} + x_{22} + x_{32} &= 1 \\ x_{13} + x_{23} + x_{33} &= 1 \end{aligned}\right\} \text{Each employee can only be assigned to one job. (job constraints)}$$

$$\text{All } x_{ij} \geq 0$$

Note that there is one constraint for each employee and one constraint for each job. Since the number of employees is equal to the number of jobs, the first three constraints for

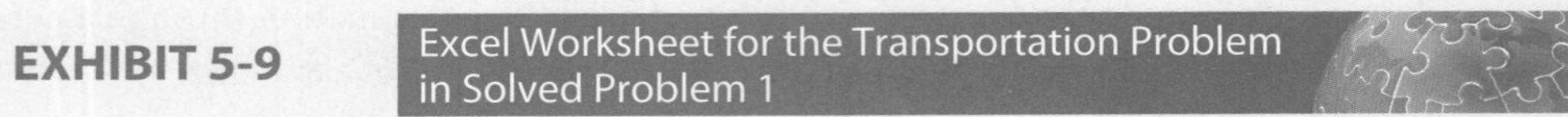

EXHIBIT 5-9 Excel Worksheet for the Transportation Problem in Solved Problem 1

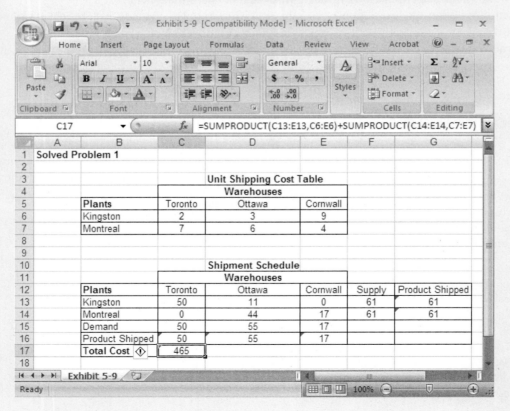

Exhibit 5-9 [Compatibility Mode] - Microsoft Excel

C17 =SUMPRODUCT(C13:E13,C6:E6)+SUMPRODUCT(C14:E14,C7:E7)

Solved Problem 1

Unit Shipping Cost Table

	Warehouses		
Plants	Toronto	Ottawa	Cornwall
Kingston	2	3	9
Montreal	7	6	4

Shipment Schedule

	Warehouses				
Plants	Toronto	Ottawa	Cornwall	Supply	Product Shipped
Kingston	50	11	0	61	61
Montreal	0	44	17	61	61
Demand	50	55	17		
Product Shipped	50	55	17		
Total Cost	465				

EXHIBIT 5-10 Excel Worksheet for the Assignment Problem in Solved Problem 2

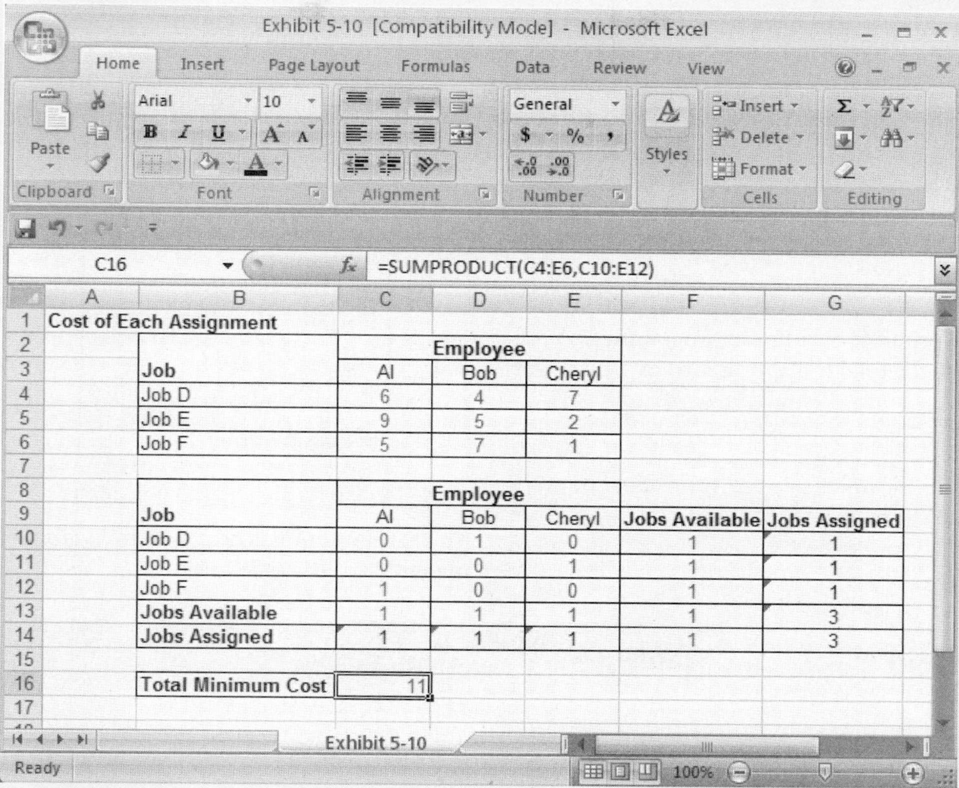

employees are written as equalities. However, if there were more employees than jobs, the first three constraints for employees must be written as less-than-or-equal-to constraints. On the other hand, if there were more jobs than employees, the last three constraints for jobs would have to be written as inequalities.

The Excel solution to this assignment problem is displayed in Exhibit 5-10. The assignment schedule is as follows:

Job D	to	Bob
Job E	to	Cheryl
Job F	to	Al

The total cost for this problem is $11.

Problem 3

Consider the following transshipment problem for a grain manufacturing company.
The supply and demand values are given in tonnes per week.

The unit shipping cost from each source to each warehouse and from each warehouse to each destination is given in the following tables.

Farms: Source Location	Supply	Warehouse Locations	Mills: Destination Locations	Demand
Prince Albert	2000	Chatham	Montreal	2500
Regina	3500	Peterborough	Quebec	2500
Saskatoon	2000		Cornwall	2500

Unit Shipping Cost from the Farms to the Warehouses

From/To	Chatham (4)	Peterborough (5)
Prince Albert (1)	1.00	2.40
Regina (2)	1.50	2.20
Saskatoon (3)	1.20	2.80

Unit Shipping Cost from the Warehouses to the Mills

From\To	Montreal (6)	Quebec (7)	Cornwall (8)
Chatham (4)	1.00	1.10	2.40
Peterborough (5)	2.00	0.90	1.20

Formulate this problem as a linear programming problem to minimize the total transportation cost and solve it using Excel.

Solution

Let x_{ij} = number of units shipped from farm or warehouse i to mill or warehouse j.

$$\text{minimize} \quad Z = x_{14} + 1.5x_{24} + 1.2x_{34} + 2.4x_{15} + 2.2x_{25} + 2.8x_{35} + x_{46} + 1.1x_{47} + 2.4x_{48} + 2x_{56} + .9x_{57} + 1.2x_{58}$$

subject to

$$\left.\begin{aligned} x_{14} + x_{15} &\le 2000 \\ x_{24} + x_{25} &\le 3500 \\ x_{34} + x_{35} &\le 2000 \end{aligned}\right\} \text{(supply constraints)}$$

$$x_{14} + x_{24} + x_{34} = x_{46} + x_{47} + x_{48}$$
$$x_{15} + x_{25} + x_{35} = x_{56} + x_{57} + x_{58}$$

Moving the variables on the right-hand side of the constraint to the left, we get

$$\left.\begin{aligned} x_{14} + x_{24} + x_{34} - x_{46} - x_{47} - x_{48} &= 0 \\ x_{15} + x_{25} + x_{35} - x_{56} - x_{57} - x_{58} &= 0 \end{aligned}\right\} \text{(intermediate node constraints)}$$

$$\left.\begin{aligned} x_{46} + x_{56} &= 2500 \\ x_{47} + x_{57} &= 2500 \\ x_{48} + x_{58} &= 2500 \end{aligned}\right\} \text{(demand constraints)}$$

$x_{ij} \ge 0$ for all i and j combinations

The Excel solution is displayed in Exhibit 5-11. The shipment schedule is as follows:

EXHIBIT 5-11 Excel Worksheet for the Transshipment Problem in Solved Problem 3

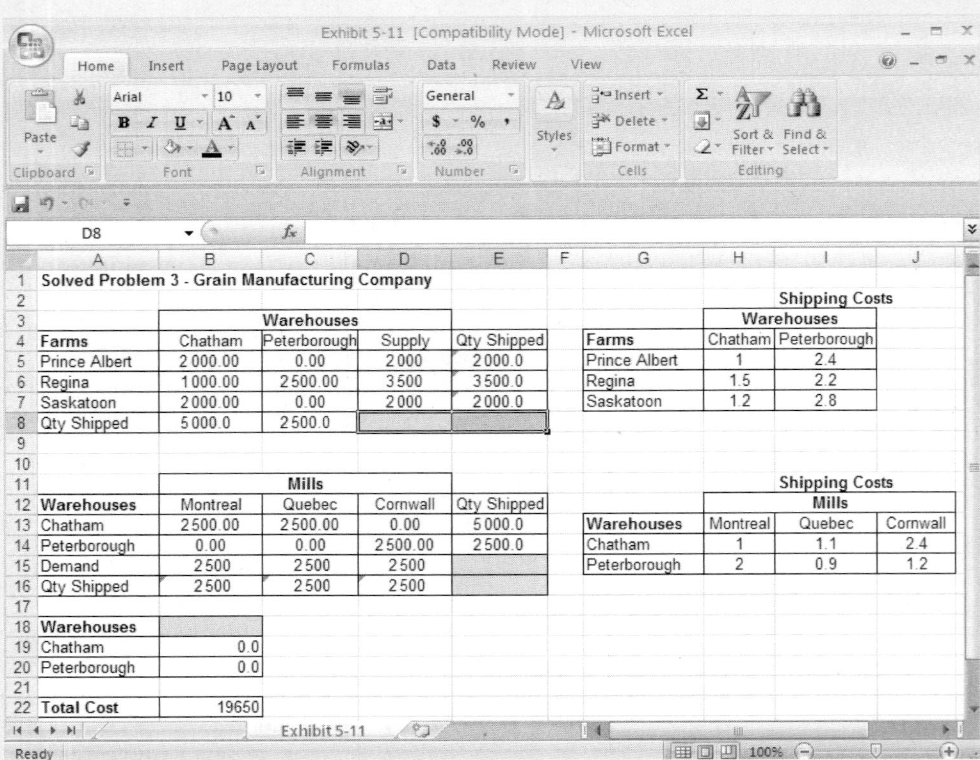

Solved Problem 3 - Grain Manufacturing Company

Farms	Chatham	Peterborough	Supply	Qty Shipped
Prince Albert	2 000.00	0.00	2 000	2 000.0
Regina	1 000.00	2 500.00	3 500	3 500.0
Saskatoon	2 000.00	0.00	2 000	2 000.0
Qty Shipped	5 000.0	2 500.0		

Shipping Costs

Farms	Chatham	Peterborough
Prince Albert	1	2.4
Regina	1.5	2.2
Saskatoon	1.2	2.8

Warehouses	Montreal	Quebec	Cornwall	Qty Shipped
Chatham	2 500.00	2 500.00	0.00	5 000.0
Peterborough	0.00	0.00	2 500.00	2 500.0
Demand	2 500	2 500	2 500	
Qty Shipped	2 500	2 500	2 500	

Shipping Costs

Warehouses	Montreal	Quebec	Cornwall
Chatham	1	1.1	2.4
Peterborough	2	0.9	1.2

Warehouses	
Chatham	0.0
Peterborough	0.0
Total Cost	19650

From	To	Shipment
Prince Albert	Chatham	2000
Regina	Chatham	1000
Regina	Peterborough	2500
Saskatoon	Chatham	2000
Chatham	Montreal	2500
Chatham	Quebec	2500
Peterborough	Cornwall	2500

The total cost for this problem is $19 650.

Problem 4

Shortest route

Given this network, which shows the distance in kilometers between each of five delivery locations, formulate this problem as a linear programming problem.

Use Excel and find the shortest route from the home office (node 1) to delivery location 5 (node 5).

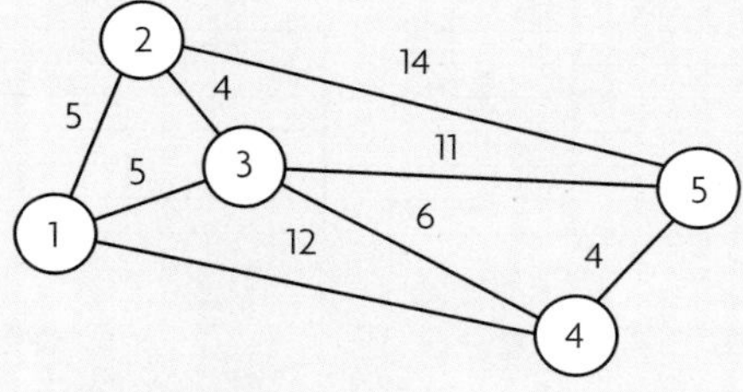

Solution

Here is the linear programming formulation of the shortest-route problem:

$$\text{minimize} \quad Z = 5x_{12} + 5x_{13} + 14x_{25} + 11x_{35} + 6x_{34} + 12x_{14} + 4x_{23} + 4x_{45} + 5x_{21} + 5x_{31} + 14x_{52} + 11x_{53} + 6x_{43} + 12x_{41} + 4x_{32} + 4x_{54}$$

subject to

$x_{12} + x_{13} + x_{14} = 1$ (supply of one unit at node 1)

$x_{32} + x_{52} + x_{12} = x_{25} + x_{23} + x_{21}$

$x_{32} + x_{52} + x_{12} - x_{25} - x_{23} - x_{21} = 0$

(transshipment constraint for node 2)

$x_{23} + x_{13} + x_{53} + x_{43} = x_{31} + x_{32} + x_{35} + x_{34}$

$x_{23} + x_{13} + x_{53} + x_{43} - x_{31} - x_{32} - x_{35} - x_{34} = 0$

(transshipment constraint for node 3)

$x_{14} + x_{34} + x_{54} = x_{41} + x_{43} + x_{45}$

$x_{14} + x_{34} + x_{54} - x_{41} - x_{43} - x_{45} = 0$

(transshipment constraint for node 4)

$x_{25} + x_{35} + x_{45} = 1$ (demand of one unit at node 5)

$x_{ij} = 0$ or 1 for all i, j combinations

The Excel solution is displayed in Exhibit 5-12. The shortest distance from node 1 to node 5 is 15, and, as indicated by 1's in the 0–1 matrix, the shortest route is 1–3–4–5.

Problem 5

Maximum flow

Consider the following network, which represents a system of pipelines. Formulate a linear programming model to determine the maximum flow in the system between node 1 and node 5 and solve it with Excel Solver.

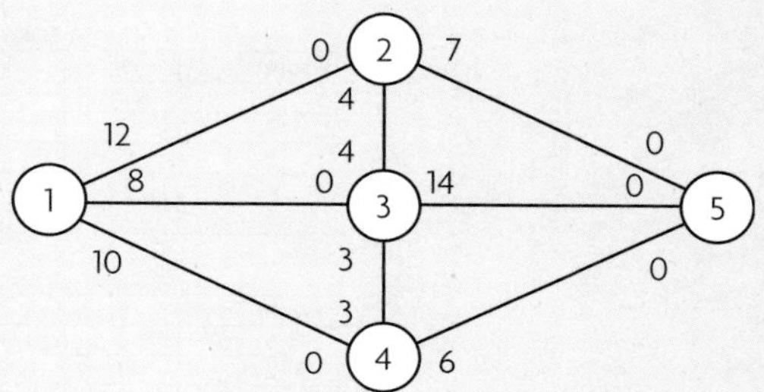

Solution

Here is the linear programming formulation of the maximum flow problem:

$$\text{maximize} \quad Z = x_{51}$$

subject to

$x_{12} + x_{13} + x_{14} = x_{51}$ or,
$x_{12} + x_{13} + x_{14} - x_{51} = 0$ (net flow transshipment constraint at node 1)

$x_{12} + x_{32} = x_{23} + x_{25}$ or,
$x_{12} + x_{32} - x_{23} - x_{25} = 0$ (net flow transshipment constraint at node 2)

$x_{13} + x_{23} + x_{43} = x_{32} + x_{34} + x_{35}$ or,
$x_{13} + x_{23} + x_{43} - x_{32} - x_{34} - x_{35} = 0$ (net flow transshipment constraint at node 3)

$x_{14} + x_{34} = x_{43} + x_{45}$ or,
$x_{14} + x_{34} - x_{43} - x_{45} = 0$ (net flow transshipment constraint at node 4)

$x_{25} + x_{35} + x_{45} = x_{51}$ or,
$x_{25} + x_{35} + x_{45} - x_{51} = 0$ (net flow transshipment constraint at node 5)

The second type of constraints are the branch capacity constraints, which simply represent the flow capacity

EXHIBIT 5-12 Worksheet for Solved Problem 4, the Shortest-Route Problem (Beginning Node 1, Ending Node 5)

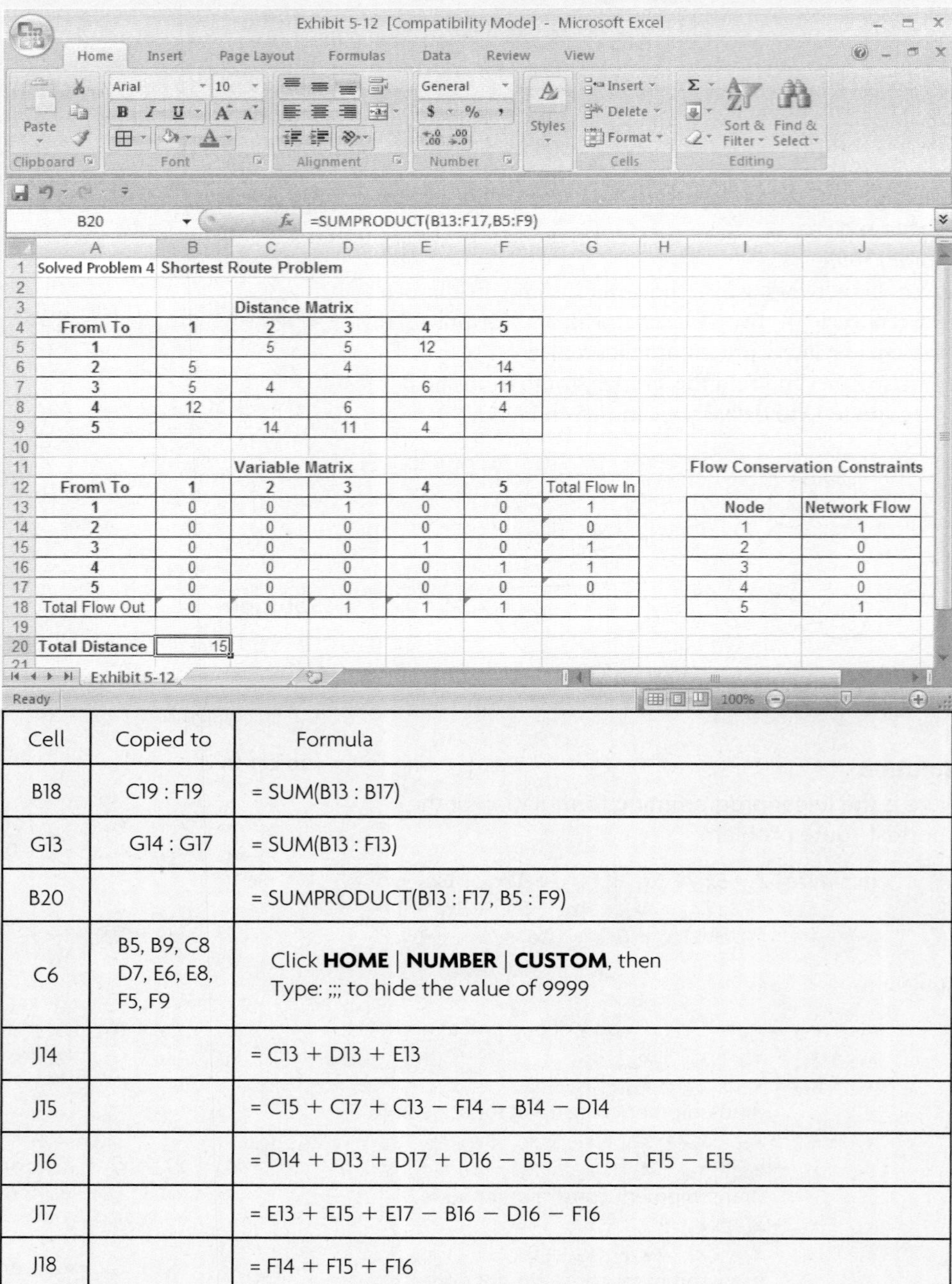

Exhibit 5-12 [Compatibility Mode] - Microsoft Excel

B20 =SUMPRODUCT(B13:F17,B5:F9)

	A	B	C	D	E	F	G	H	I	J
1	Solved Problem 4	Shortest Route Problem								
2										
3			Distance Matrix							
4	From\ To	1	2	3	4	5				
5	1		5	5	12					
6	2	5		4		14				
7	3	5	4		6	11				
8	4	12		6		4				
9	5		14	11	4					
10										
11			Variable Matrix						Flow Conservation Constraints	
12	From\ To	1	2	3	4	5	Total Flow In			
13	1	0	0	1	0	0	1		Node	Network Flow
14	2	0	0	0	0	0	0		1	1
15	3	0	0	0	1	0	1		2	0
16	4	0	0	0	0	1	1		3	0
17	5	0	0	0	0	0	0		4	0
18	Total Flow Out	0	0	1	1	1			5	1
19										
20	Total Distance	15								

Cell	Copied to	Formula
B18	C19 : F19	= SUM(B13 : B17)
G13	G14 : G17	= SUM(B13 : F13)
B20		= SUMPRODUCT(B13 : F17, B5 : F9)
C6	B5, B9, C8 D7, E6, E8, F5, F9	Click **HOME** | **NUMBER** | **CUSTOM**, then Type: ;;; to hide the value of 9999
J14		= C13 + D13 + E13
J15		= C15 + C17 + C13 − F14 − B14 − D14
J16		= D14 + D13 + D17 + D16 − B15 − C15 − F15 − E15
J17		= E13 + E15 + E17 − B16 − D16 − F16
J18		= F14 + F15 + F16

of each branch. These constraints can be written as follows:

$$x_{12} \leq 12$$
$$x_{13} \leq 8$$
$$x_{14} \leq 10$$
$$x_{23} \leq 4$$
$$x_{32} \leq 4$$
$$x_{25} \leq 7$$
$$x_{35} \leq 14$$
$$x_{34} \leq 3$$
$$x_{43} \leq 3$$
$$x_{45} \leq 6$$
$$x_{51} \leq 9999$$
$$\text{All } x_{ij} \geq 0$$

The Excel solution is displayed in Exhibit 5-13. The maximum flow from node 1 to node 5 is 27 and is shown in cell B18, and the matrix of actual flows indicates the flow between various nodes.

EXHIBIT 5-13 Worksheet for Solved Problem 5, the Maximum Flow Problem

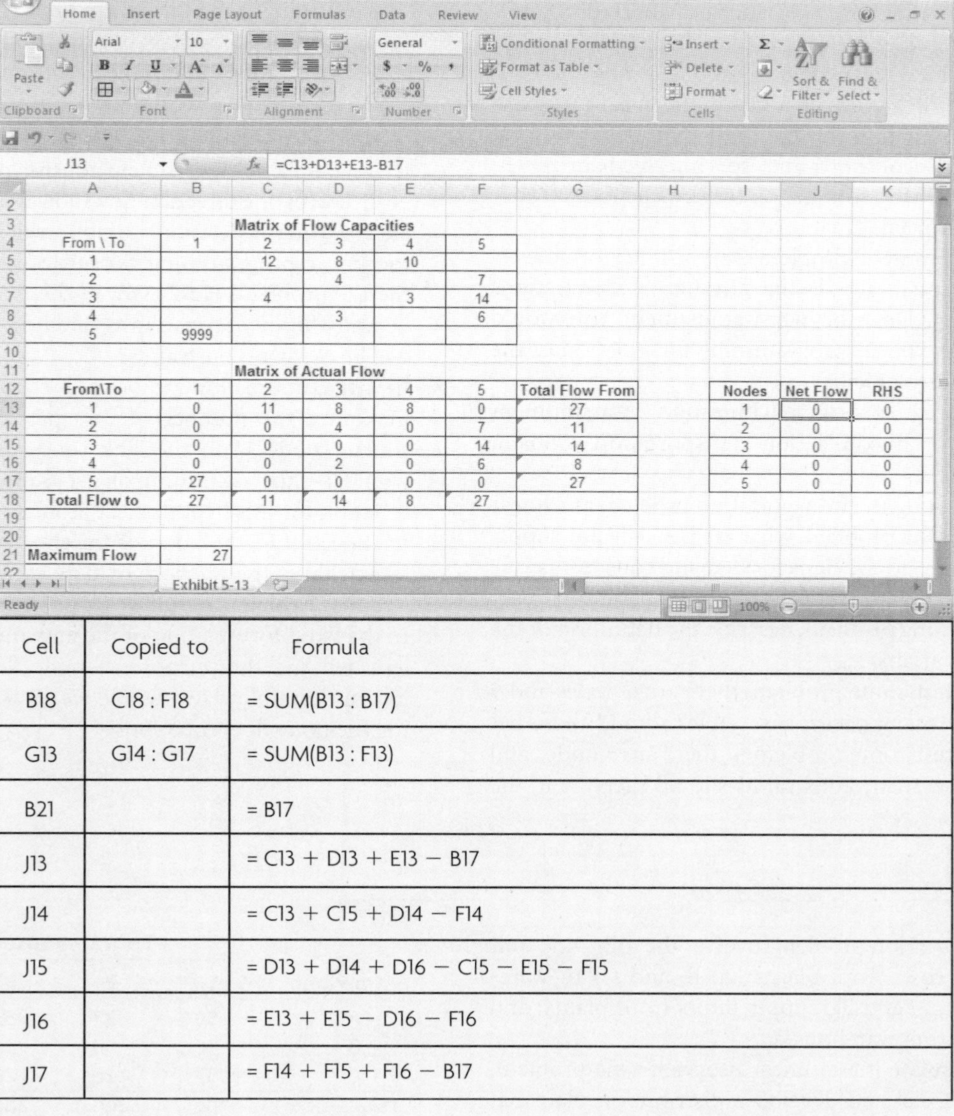

From \ To	1	2	3	4	5
1		12	8	10	
2			4		7
3		4		3	14
4			3		6
5	9999				

From\To	1	2	3	4	5	Total Flow From
1	0	11	8	8	0	27
2	0	0	4	0	7	11
3	0	0	0	0	14	14
4	0	0	2	0	6	8
5	27	0	0	0	0	27
Total Flow to	27	11	14	8	27	

Nodes	Net Flow	RHS
1	0	0
2	0	0
3	0	0
4	0	0
5	0	0

Maximum Flow	27

Cell	Copied to	Formula
B18	C18 : F18	= SUM(B13 : B17)
G13	G14 : G17	= SUM(B13 : F13)
B21		= B17
J13		= C13 + D13 + E13 − B17
J14		= C13 + C15 + D14 − F14
J15		= D13 + D14 + D16 − C15 − E15 − F15
J16		= E13 + E15 − D16 − F16
J17		= F14 + F15 + F16 − B17

Discussion and Review Questions

1. What is the difference between solving a balanced transportation problem and an unbalanced transportation problem?
2. Describe possible applications of an assignment problem.
3. How can a transportation problem be used in making facility location decisions? Describe this application with an example.
4. Describe how a transshipment problem differs from a transportation problem.
5. How can we convert a transshipment problem into a transportation problem?
6. Briefly describe how to balance transportation problems that have more supply than demand.
7. Describe how you would go about setting the constraints for intermediate nodes in the linear programming formulation of the transshipment problem. Formulate two constraints for intermediate nodes, where there are 2 sources, 2 intermediate nodes (warehouses), and 3 destinations.
8. In an assignment problem, the number of sources (assignments) exceeds the number of destinations (assignees). Describe what adjustment you would make to the linear programming formulation of the assignment problem.
9. How can we solve a maximization transshipment problem or maximization transportation problem using Excel?
10. In formulating the transportation problem as a linear programming problem, what are the signs for supply constraints and the signs for demand constraints?
11. In formulating the shortest-route problem as a linear programming problem, describe the definition of the decision variable x_{ij}.
12. In a shortest-route problem, there are 6 nodes and 9 arcs, how many decision variables should there be?
13. In a shortest-route problem, if there are 6 nodes and 9 arcs, how many constraints should there be in the linear programming formulation? If node 1 is the source (starting) node and node 6 is the sink (terminal) node, how many of these constraints will be transshipment constraints? Which of these constraints should be formulated as supply constraints, demand constraints, and transshipment constraints and why? Indicate the signs on the supply, demand, and transshipment constraints.
14. Give two examples of potential applications for the maximum flow problem.
15. a. The linear programming formulation of the maximum flow problem involves which of the following: a maximization objective function or a minimization objective function?
    b. If the starting node of the maximum flow problem is node 1 and the ending node is node 9, set up the objective function for this hypothetical problem.
16. If a maximum flow problem consists of 9 nodes and 16 arcs with one direction flow, how many constraints and how many decision variables will be involved in the linear programming formulation of this hypothetical problem? How many of these constraints will be transshipment constraints, and how many of them will be capacity constraints?
17. In a maximum flow problem, if the objective is to maximize the number of cars per hour from the source (node 1) to the sink (node 10), then what would be the definition of x_{ij}? State the objective function for this hypothetical problem.
18. In the Excel formulation of the shortest-route problem, what is the purpose of flow conservation constraints? Explain carefully.
19. In the Excel formulation of the maximum flow problem, what is the purpose of node flow equations? Explain carefully. How would we go about formulating the node flow equations?

Problems

1. A transportation problem involves the following unit shipping costs from plants (A, B, and C) to warehouses (1, 2, and 3), supply limits from plants, and demand from warehouses.
    a. Formulate it as a linear programming problem.
    b. Use Excel and develop a distribution plan that minimizes total shipping cost.

	To Warehouse (Cost)			
From Plant	1	2	3	Supply
A	50	32	32	700
B	16	30	30	200
C	35	28	28	200
Demand	300	400	400	

c. If route 3–A is unacceptable for some reason, what distribution plan would be optimal? What would its total cost be?

2. Suppose the costs in the previous problem represent unit profits and that all routes are acceptable. Use Excel and determine the distribution plan that would be best in terms of maximizing profits. What would be the total profit for that plan?

3. The owner of Go-Ride, Tom Rider, projects that within three years, demand for riding mowers will exceed supply by approximately 550 units a month. Projected demand and current capacities and unit costs are shown in Table 5-10.
   a. Formulate it as a linear programming problem.
   b. Use Excel and solve this problem to obtain the lowest-cost shipping schedule. What is the minimum shipping cost?

4. A soft drink manufacturer, Sara Soda, Ltd., has recently begun negotiations with brokers in the areas where it intends to distribute its products. Before finalizing the agreements, however, Manager Dave Pepper wants to determine shipping routes and costs. The firm has three plants in Ontario with capacities as shown below:

Plant	Capacity (cases per week)
Newmarket	40 000
London	30 000
Cornwall	25 000

Estimated demands in each of the warehouse localities are

Warehouse	Demand (cases per week)
RS1	24 000
RS2	22 000
RS3	23 000
RS4	16 000
RS5	10 000

The estimated per unit shipping costs per case for the various routes are

From: \ To:	RS1	RS2	RS3	RS4	RS5
Newmarket	.80	.75	.60	.70	.90
London	.75	.80	.85	.70	.85
Cornwall	.70	.75	.70	.80	.80

Use Excel and determine the optimal shipping plan that will minimize total shipping cost under these conditions:
   a. Route London–RS4 is unacceptable.
   b. All routes are acceptable.
   c. What is the additional cost of the London–RS4 route not being acceptable?

5. Solve the following transportation problem formulation using Excel. Find the optimal transportation plan and the minimum cost. Also, decide if there is an alternate solution. If there is one, identify it.

$$\text{minimize} \quad Z = 8x_{11} + 2x_{12} + 5x_{13} + 2x_{21} + x_{22} + 3x_{23} + 7x_{31} + 2x_{32} + 6x_{33}$$

subject to

$$x_{11} + x_{12} + x_{13} = 90$$
$$x_{21} + x_{22} + x_{23} = 105$$
$$x_{31} + x_{32} + x_{33} = 105$$
$$x_{11} + x_{21} + x_{31} = 150$$
$$x_{12} + x_{22} + x_{32} = 75$$
$$x_{13} + x_{23} + x_{33} = 75$$
$$\text{All variables} \geq 0$$

6. Guess Tech is a small plastics company whose products may or may not be biodegradable. Three of its products can be manufactured on either of two machines. Neither machine has the capacity to handle all of the load; therefore, some of the work must be handled by one and the remainder by the other.

Table 5-10 To Warehouse (Cost) for Problem 3

From Plant	1	2	3	4	Supply (mowers per month)
Plant A	10	27	7	14	250
Plant C	12	20	8	30	270
Demand (mowers per month)	340	140	140	450	

The manager of the shop wants to minimize total cost. Cost information is given in the following table:

	Production Cost per Unit	
	Machine 1 (M1)	Machine 2 (M2)
Product A	$1.20	$1.40
Product B	1.50	1.30
Product C	1.60	1.50

Daily capacity of machine 1 is 600 units and daily capacity of machine 2 is 750 units. Production quotas are 400 units of each product per day.

Formulate this problem as a linear programming model, then use Excel and solve for the optimal solution.

7. Use Excel and solve the Harley problem from earlier in this chapter (see Example 5-1), treating the cell values as unit profits instead of unit costs. Determine the optimal distribution plan and the total profit for that plan.
8. The Future Furniture company recently began construction of a new warehouse. During the construction period, several changes have occurred that require development of a new distribution plan. The current figures for supply are

Plant	Capacity (pieces per week)
Burnaby	600
Calgary	800
Prince Rupert	400

Current figures for demand are

Warehouse	Demand (pieces per week)
Prince George	300
Kelowna	400
Lethbridge	200
Edmonton	900

Average shipping costs per unit are shown in Table 5-11.

a. Formulate the problem given above as a linear programming problem.
b. Use Excel and solve to determine the shipping schedule that minimizes the total cost.
c. Use Excel and solve to determine the shipping schedule that minimizes the total cost if Prince Rupert to Prince George is unavailable.

9. Consider the transportation problem of Atlantic Doors Plus, a producer of steel doors for public schools.

Doors are produced at plants in Charlottetown, Edmundston, and Halifax. They are then shipped to three outlets located in Moncton, Sydney, and Saint John. The unit shipping cost from each plant to each outlet, the supply available from each plant, and the demand at each outlet are as follows:

	To (Cost)			
From	Moncton	Sydney	Saint John	Supply
Charlottetown	26	15	22	160
Edmundston	18	12	17	125
Halifax	28	24	20	30
Demand	75	90	150	

a. Formulate this problem as a linear programming problem.
b. Use Excel and determine a distribution plan that will minimize the total cost of shipping.
c. Now suppose that the Charlottetown–Saint John route is temporarily unavailable. Beginning with the solution from part *a*, determine a distribution plan that will avoid this route. How much extra does this plan cost compared to the plan when all routes are possible?

10. Rod Steele, superintendent of Rochester Forging, has developed the following transportation model.

	To (Cost)			
From	Halifax	Victoria	Moncton	Supply
Yellowknife	2	17	12	64
Saskatoon	9	12	6	44
Edmonton	7	5	10	36
Demand	48	48	150	

Use Excel and determine the minimum-cost shipping schedule. What is the total shipping cost?

Table 5-11 Shipping Costs for Problem 8

From: \ To:	Prince George	Kelowna	Lethbridge	Edmonton
Burnaby	$8	$9	$6	$4
Calgary	10	7	2	3
Prince Rupert	5	7	9	12

11. Consider the following transportation problem.

From	Regina	Buffalo	Montreal	Supply (tonnes per day)
	To (Cost)			
Fredericton	14	8	3	40
Toronto	9	5	7	80
Halifax	6	12	4	60
Demand (tonnes per day)	70	60	50	

a. Formulate it as a linear programming problem.
b. Use Excel and determine the minimum-cost shipping schedule. What is the total shipping cost?

12. The manager of Home Office Supplies has just received demand forecasts and capacity (supply) figures for next month. These are summarized along with unit shipping costs in the following table, where D_i refers to demand forecast for region i, $i = 1, 2, 3$, and O_i refers to capacity supply from plant j, $j = 1, 2, 3, 4, 5$.

From	D_1	D_2	D_3	D_4	D_5	Supply
	To (Cost)					
O_1	8	4	12	11	9	220
O_2	7	6	10	5	6	260
O_3	12	13	9	16	9	200
Demand	140	180	150	140	195	

Use Excel and determine the minimum-cost shipping schedule. What is the total shipping cost?

13. Given this LP model of a transportation problem with three sources and three destinations

$$\text{minimize} \quad Z = 5x_{11} + 8x_{12} + 4x_{13} + 5x_{21} + 3x_{22} + 5x_{23} + 9x_{31} + 8x_{32} + 6x_{33}$$

subject to

$$\begin{aligned}
&\text{A: } x_{11} + x_{12} + x_{13} = 35\\
&\text{B: } x_{21} + x_{22} + x_{23} = 45\\
&\text{C: } x_{31} + x_{32} + x_{33} = 60\\
&\text{D: } x_{11} + x_{21} + x_{31} = 50\\
&\text{E: } x_{12} + x_{22} + x_{32} = 50\\
&\text{F: } x_{13} + x_{23} + x_{33} = 40\\
&\quad \text{All variables} \geq 0
\end{aligned}$$

a. Solve for the minimum-cost solution using Excel.
b. What does x_{12} represent in the model?

14. A manager has formulated this LP model for assigning tasks to employees. Solve for the optimal solution using Excel.

$$\text{minimize} \quad Z = 2x_{11} + 5x_{12} + 9x_{13} + 7x_{21} + 4x_{22} + 6x_{23} + 1x_{31} + 7x_{32} + 5x_{33}$$

subject to

$$\begin{aligned}
&\text{Task 1: } x_{11} + x_{12} + x_{13} = 1\\
&\text{Task 2: } x_{21} + x_{22} + x_{23} = 1\\
&\text{Task 3: } x_{31} + x_{32} + x_{33} = 1\\
&\text{Employee 1: } x_{11} + x_{21} + x_{31} = 1\\
&\text{Employee 2: } x_{12} + x_{22} + x_{32} = 1\\
&\text{Employee 3: } x_{13} + x_{23} + x_{33} = 1\\
&\quad \text{All variables} \geq 0
\end{aligned}$$

15. A manager has prepared the following information on a transshipment problem. Locations 1 and 2 are sources, locations 3 and 4 are transshipment points (warehouses), and locations 5 and 6 are destinations.

Unit Shipping Costs to Transshipment Points

From \ To	3	4
1	9	11
2	10	12

Unit Shipping Costs from Transshipment Points

From \ To	5	6
3	8	4
4	6	7

The source supplies and destination demands are shown in the following tables. Assume that there are no restrictions on route quantities or quantities at the transshipment points.

Source	Supply
1	200
2	300

Destination	Demand
5	250
6	250

a. Formulate a linear programming model of this problem.
b. Using Excel, solve for the optimal solution and indicate the quantities to be shipped on each route.

16. The manager of Home Office Supplies has prepared the following information on a transshipment problem. Locations labelled as 1, 2, and 3 are supply points; locations 4 and 5 are intermediate transshipment nodes; and locations 6, 7, and 8 are destinations.

Unit Shipping Costs to Transshipment Points

From \ To	4	5
1	20	15
2	12	14
3	11	12

Unit Shipping Costs from Transshipment Points

From \ To	6	7	8
4	9	7	4
5	8	6	5

The source supplies and destination demands are shown in the following tables. There are no restrictions on quantities at the transshipment points.

Source	Supply
1	200
2	300
3	100

Destination	Demand
6	150
7	400
8	50

a. Draw the network diagram for this problem.
b. Formulate a linear programming model of this problem.
c. Using Excel, solve for the optimal solution and indicate the quantities to be shipped on each route.

17. A firm operates a plant that has a capacity of 650 units per month. The company currently ships to four warehouses with the following demand values: warehouse 1 = 350, warehouse 2 = 200, warehouse 3 = 400, and warehouse 4 = 150 units. The cost of shipping one unit of product from the existing plant to each of the four warehouses is given below in Table 5-12. The firm intends to build a plant with a capacity of 550 units per month, and has narrowed the choices of location to two sites, C1 and C2. Transportation costs for each potential origin (plant) are

C1 to	Unit Cost (in $)	C2 to	Unit Cost (in $)
# 1	13	#1	24
# 2	27	#2	17
# 3	17	#3	15
# 4	25	#4	21

Use Excel and determine the optimal shipping plan and the minimum total cost for each possible location. Which has the lower total cost? What would the annual savings be if the location with the lower cost is selected?

18. A large manufacturing company based in Alberta is trying to optimize its shipping schedule. Currently the monthly manufacturing capacity at three of its plants as is follows:

Plant	Capacity
Grande Prairie	16 000 units
Medicine Hat	10 000 units
Red Deer	26 000 units

The company owns three warehouses—in Edmonton, Burnaby, and Calgary. Demand at these destinations is as follows:

Warehouse	Demand
Edmonton	15 000
Burnaby	12 000
Calgary	18 000

The unit shipping cost from each plant to each warehouse is given in the following table:

From\To	Edmonton	Burnaby	Calgary
Grande Prairie	2.5	3.5	4
Medicine Hat	4.5	1.5	2
Red Deer	2.0	3.2	3

a. Draw the transportation diagram.
b. Formulate this problem as a linear programming problem.
c. Use Excel and determine the optimal transportation schedule for this company.
d. If the route from Grande Prairie to Burnaby is blocked or not feasible, what is the best schedule and how much more does it cost the company to utilize this route?

19. A shop foreman has prepared the following table, which shows the costs for various combinations of job–machine assignments.

	Machine		
Job	A	B	C
1	20	35	22
2	42	18	25
3	8	23	15

a. Use Excel and determine the optimal (minimum-cost) assignment for this problem.
b. What is the total cost for the optimum assignment?

20. The foreman of a machine shop wants to determine a minimum-cost matching for operators and machines. The foreman has determined the hourly cost for each of four operators for the four machines, as shown in the cost table on the next page.

Table 5-12 Unit Cost in Dollars for Problem 17

	Warehouse 1	Warehouse 2	Warehouse 3	Warehouse 4
Plant	20	15	25	18

Operator	Machine A	B	C	D
1	70	80	75	64
2	55	52	58	54
3	58	56	64	68
4	62	60	67	70

a. Formulate the problem stated above as a linear programming problem.
b. Use Excel to determine the minimum-cost assignment for this problem.
c. What is the total cost for the optimal assignment?
d. Is there an alternate optimal assignment? Explain.

21. The approximate travel times for officiating crews for Ontario University Athletics Men's Basketball for four games scheduled for a weekend are shown in the following table:

Crew	Game site City 1	City 2	City 3	City 4
A	1.2*	1.4	0.2	1.5
B	1.0	2.0	0.5	1.0
C	1.2	3.4	2.4	0.5
D	2.1	3.1	1.1	0.8

*Time in hours.

Use Excel to answer the following questions:

a. What set of crew assignments will minimize travel time?
b. What is the total travel time required for the optimal assignment?

22. On Monday morning, the manager of a small print shop, Carri Fonts, finds that four jobs must be handled on a "rush" basis. Fortunately, there are four employees available to work on these jobs, and each will handle one of the jobs. Each employee has a slightly different estimated completion time for each job, as shown in the table below:

Completion time (hours)

Employee	Job A	B	C	D
Tom	4.2	4.1	5.4	5.0
Dick	4.4	4.0	5.2	4.8
Harry	4.3	4.2	5.0	4.9
Jane	4.0	4.1	5.4	5.0

Carri wants to determine how to assign the employees to jobs so that the total completion time is as low as possible.

a. Formulate this as a linear programming model
b. Solve this problem using Excel.

23. The accompanying table shows projected profits for all possible combinations of four workers and jobs awaiting processing.

a. Formulate an LP model of this problem.
b. Use Excel and find the solution that will yield optimal pairings in terms of total profits.

Worker	Job 1	2	3
A	$500	400	450
B	800	300	200
C	700	400	500
D	900	500	799

24. (Refer to Problem 21.) Because of a previous conflict between crew D and one of the teams playing at City 4, crew D cannot be assigned to that location. With this in mind, determine an optimal set of assignments. What effect, if any, does this restriction have on the total travel time for all crews?

25. (Refer to Problem 21.) Suppose that another crew (Crew E) is added to select from. Crew E's travel times to City 1, City 2, City 3, and City 4 are 1.8, .5, .6, and 2.0 hours, respectively. Assume, too, that the D–City 4 assignment is undesirable.

a. Use Excel and determine the set of assignments that will minimize total travel time.
b. Which crew will not be assigned?
c. Is there an alternate optimal solution? Explain.

26. An industrial engineer has prepared a table that shows the costs for each possible combination of job and machine for four jobs and four machines, as shown:

Job	Machine A	B	C	D
1	45	75	80	35
2	55	60	60	65
3	70	65	50	45
4	60	75	70	65

a. Formulate the problem, given the above, as a linear programming problem.
b. Use Excel and determine the set of assignments that will minimize total processing cost.

c. What is total processing cost?
d. Is there an alternate optimal solution? What is it?

27. If the numbers in the previous problem reflected profits rather than costs, what set of assignments would have been optimal?

28. (Refer to Problem 26.) Suppose that job 1 could not be assigned to machine D because of a technical problem.
a. What set of assignments would minimize total cost of the assignments? What additional cost is incurred because of the technical problem?
b. What is the alternate optimal solution?

29. An analyst has kept track of the number of defectives produced by five workers on five different machines. The results are shown below for a run of 400 units per machine:

Worker	Machine A	B	C	D	E
1	9	7	4	6	2
2	7	4	5	2	1
3	3	4	3	2	3
4	9	7	8	6	5
5	0	3	2	4	3

a. Formulate this problem as a linear programming problem.
b. Use Excel and determine a set of assignments that will minimize the total number of errors for a given run size.
c. Is there an alternate optimal solution? Explain.
d. What is the total number of defectives expected for the optimal assignment?

30. In the previous problem, if another machine was available and the number of defectives produced by the five workers for a run of 400 units was 4, 4, 2, 3, and 1 respectively, use Excel and determine the following:
a. What set of assignments that will minimize the total number of expected defectives?
b. Which machine will not be used?
c. Is there an alternate optimal solution? Explain.

31. A manager has four jobs that must be assigned. Estimated processing times for each of four employees are shown in the accompanying table.

Job	Employee Smith (S)	Jones (J)	Green (G)	Mehl (M)
1	6.2*	8.0	5.4	4.8
2	6.0	7.2	5.8	4.4
3	5.5	6.0	6.6	6.8
4	6.3	6.6	7.0	7.3

*Time in hours.

a. Formulate this as an LP problem.
b. Use Excel and determine a set of assignments that will minimize total processing time.
c. What is the total processing time for the optimal assignments?

32. A company has four manufacturing plants and four warehouses. Each of the plants will supply one of the warehouses. Each warehouse has a demand that is equal to a factory's output for a given period. Assume that all capacities and all demands are 300 units per period. The shipping costs for all routes are shown in the table below. The costs are in thousands.

Plant	Warehouse 1	2	3	4
A	2.4	1.8	2.6	1.8
B	2.0	1.9	2.2	2.2
C	1.4	1.7	2.0	1.4
D	1.6	2.1	2.1	1.6

Table 5-13 Data for Problem 33

From	To (Cost) Toronto	Burnaby	Edmonton	Regina	Supply
Sudbury	12	5	7	2	98
Medicine Hat	11	3	6	1	80
Demand	35	50	25	68	

a. Use Excel and determine a set of assignments that will minimize total shipping cost for a period.
b. What is the total shipping cost for your plan?
c. Is there an alternate optimal solution? Explain.
d. Would the optimal solution change if the values represented shipping *time* instead of shipping *cost?* Explain.

33. Consider the transportation problem of Sunbelt Heat Pumps shown in Table 5-13.

a. Formulate it as a linear programming problem.
b. Use Excel and determine the minimum-cost shipping schedule. What is the total shipping cost?

34. Consider the transportation problem of the Calgary Dishwasher Company:

	To (Cost)			
From	**Store 1**	**Store 2**	**Store 3**	**Supply**
Warehouse A	12	20	15	50
Warehouse B	9	11	4	15
Warehouse C	20	14	8	55
Demand	25	50	45	

a. Formulate it as a linear programming problem.
b. Use Excel and determine the minimum-cost shipping schedule. What is the total shipping cost?

35. Consider the previous problem. Treat the values in each cell as revenue per unit instead of cost per unit.

a. Use Excel and determine the total optimal profit.
b. What is the optimal shipment schedule?

36. Refer to Example 5-2. Suppose that an increase in warehousing costs and other costs brings inventory carrying costs to $2 per unit per month. All other costs and quantities remain the same. Determine a revised solution to this transportation problem.

37. Refer to Example 5-2. Suppose that regular-time capacity will be reduced to 440 units in period 3 to accommodate a companywide safety inspection of equipment. What will the additional cost of the optimal plan be as compared to the one shown in Example 5-2? Assume all costs and quantities are the same as given in Example 5-2 except for the regular-time output in period 3.

38. Distances shown on the arcs of the network in Figure 5-9 are in metres. Use Excel and find the shortest route from node 1 to each of the other nodes.

39. Approximate travel times between various customer locations are shown on the accompanying network. Assuming all delivery trucks leave from node 1, use Excel and find the shortest travel time to each customer location. If trucks could make multiple stops and thereby reduce the number of trucks required

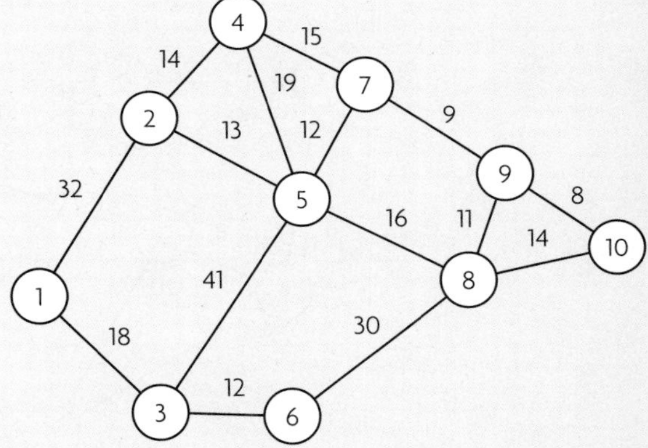

for this system, and assuming truck capacity is not a factor, how many trucks would be needed if the shortest travel times are used?

FIGURE 5-9 Network for Problem 38

40. The following network shows distances in kilometres between villages and towns in a certain area of Saskatoon. A dealer must decide on the route to use to send weekly shipments to a new customer located at node 12. The dealer is located at node 1. Using Excel, find the shortest route and the distance for a round trip.

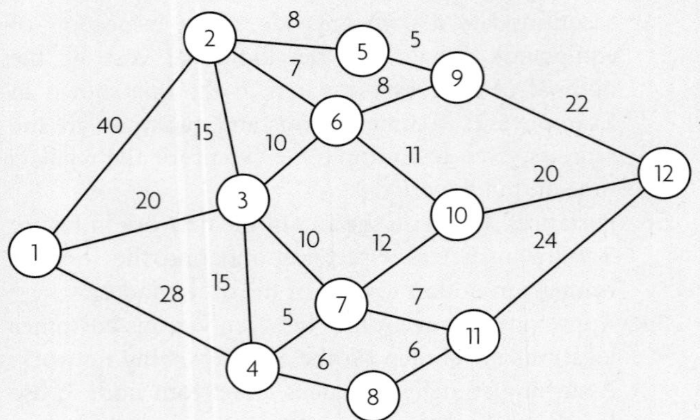

41. Using Excel, determine the maximum flow rate for this system of bicycle paths, given the flow rates shown on the diagram (Figure 5-10). Assume node 1 is the source node and node 13 the sink node.

42. The accompanying network (Figure 5-11) represents a possible design for a system of pipelines for an oil field.

   a. Using Excel, determine the maximum flow of oil based on flow capacities given in the network from the oil field on node 1 to the oil refinery at node 14.

   b. If the capacity of the arc from node 4 to node 6 is increased to 30, what is the maximum flow from node 1 to node 14?

FIGURE 5-10 Network for Problem 41

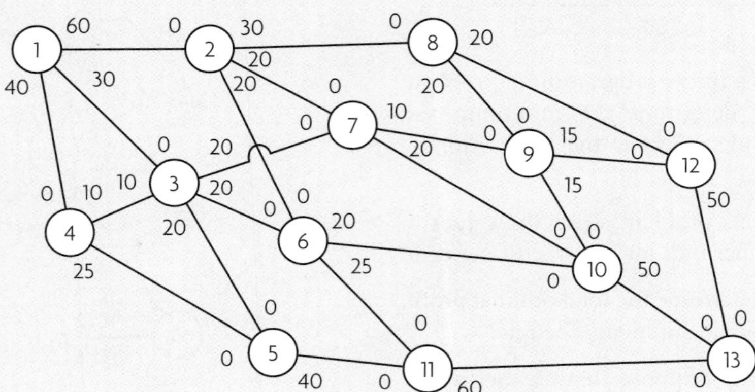

FIGURE 5-11 Network for Problem 42

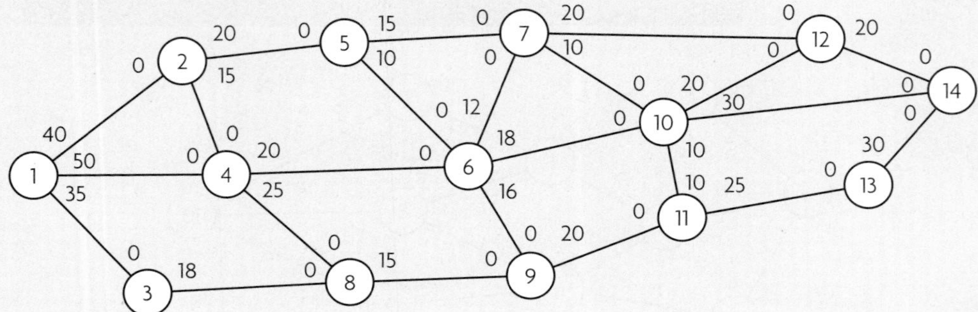

Case 1: Sunshine Tomato Inc.

The Sunshine Tomato Soup Shippers produce tomato soup at three canneries in Toronto, Edmonton, and Thunder Bay. The soup is shipped to four regional warehouses. Due to high demand, the company is considering opening a fourth cannery. The company is considering opening up the fourth cannery either at Windsor, Regina, Sault Ste. Marie, or Saskatoon. The following table shows the cost of shipping a case from each cannery (existing and proposed) to each regional warehouse. The company wishes to ship all of its cannery capacity to the regional warehouses so that monthly transportation cost is minimized.

Discussion Questions

1. What is the total transportation cost if each of the four sites should be selected?
2. Which site should be selected to locate the next cannery? Why?
3. State the shipment schedule associated with the selected site.

Source	Yellow Knife	Sault Ste. Marie	Quebec	Halifax	Maximum Monthly Cannery Capacity
Toronto	$2.80	$0.60	$1.20	$1.50	70 000
Edmonton	$0.50	$1.20	$2.20	$2.90	80 000
Thunder Bay	$1.80	$0.40	$1.80	$2.20	90 000
Sault Ste. Marie	$1.70	$0.75	$1.75	$2.50	110 000
Windsor	$1.80	$0.60	$1.60	$2.60	110 000
Regina	$1.40	$0.70	$2.00	$2.40	110 000
Saskatoon	$1.60	$0.80	$1.80	$2.50	110 000
Monthly warehouse demand	80 000	90 000	70 000	100 000	

Case 2: Furnace County Emergency Response Routes

After several complaints about slow response times to police, fire, and ambulance calls, and hoping to receive federal funds, Furnace County Supervisor, Grant Wise, has decided to seek a plan that will identify travel routes that minimize travel time between the county's police, fire, and ambulance station in Furnace City and every town or village in the county.

Assume you are the consultant Mr. Wise has hired to develop the plan. The accompanying map shows travel distances in kilometres between various Furnace County towns and villages. And because emergency equipment has the right-of-way, travel distances correlate closely with travel times in minutes when multiplied by 1.50, except for travel between Mountain View and Hidden

Valley, and Apresville and Hidden Valley, where travel time in minutes is twice the distance shown due to rough and winding roads. *Note*: The close proximity of the station to Furnace City obviates the need to include the city in the plan.

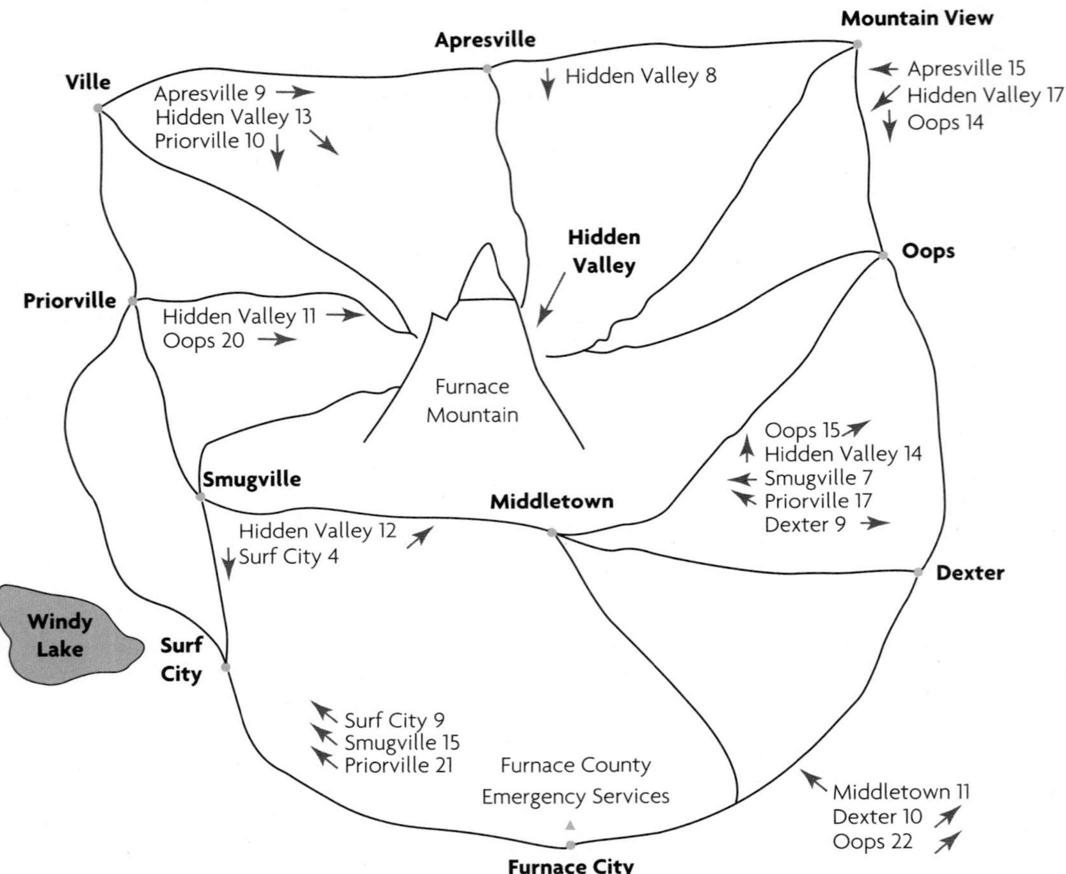

Integer Programming Methods

CHAPTER 6

LEARNING OBJECTIVES

After completing this chapter, you should be able to:

1. Tell how integer programming problems differ from general linear programming problems.
2. Explain the difference among pure, mixed, and 0–1 integer programming problems.
3. Formulate and use Excel to solve integer programming problems.
4. Formulate and use Excel to solve 0–1 integer programming problems.
5. Formulate specialized integer programming problems including knapsack, set covering, fixed charge, and facility location problems.

CHAPTER OUTLINE

6.1 INTRODUCTION TO INTEGER PROGRAMMING

In the preceding chapters, which dealt with linear programming solutions, the issue of non-integer solutions was largely ignored. This was done for a number of reasons. One was that to require integer solutions would have added considerably to the complexity of the models. Another was that numerous applications exist in which integer solutions are not necessary. This is especially true for problems that involve variables that are measured on a *continuous* scale (e.g., volume, weight, length, and time). In other cases, a rounded solution may be acceptable. For example, if a problem involved determining the numbers of various types of nails to produce, an answer of 9200.7 could easily be rounded up to 9201 with little or no consequence. Even if the solution turned out to be infeasible, reality would force a feasible solution (e.g., after making 9200 nails, there might not be enough raw material to make one more nail).

On the other hand, there are important cases in which integer solutions are required. For instance, if a problem concerned the optimal number of cargo ships, apartment houses, or office buildings to build, a noninteger answer would not be acceptable. Similarly, simply rounding to the nearest integer will not necessarily produce an answer that is optimal or near optimal, especially if millions of dollars are involved. Obviously, in cases such as these, it is desirable to identify the optimal, *integer* values of decision variables. This chapter describes methods for doing that. The Modern Management Application, "Société des alcools du Québec," describes how the public corporation of the Province of Quebec responsible for distributing and selling alcohol-based products benefited from the use of integer programming.

When we solve a continuously divisible linear programming problem, where the variables take on fractional values, the solution will travel from corner point to corner point until an optimal solution is reached. However, solving an integer linear programming problem is more difficult because even though we begin by considering all of the corner points, since many of these will not satisfy the integer constraint, we need to consider other integer feasible points. In essence, when we use an integer linear programming problem, the number of feasible points considered is significantly higher compared to a linear programming problem without any integer constraints that considers only the corner points.

6.2 TYPES OF INTEGER PROGRAMMING PROBLEMS

Basically, there are three types of linear programming problems that involve integer solutions: pure-integer problems, mixed-integer problems, and 0–1 problems.

Pure-Integer Problems

Problems requiring that *all* decision variables have integer solutions are referred to as **pure-integer problems.** Examples include the number of each type of plane to produce, the number of each type of large machine to produce, the number of each type of house to construct, and so on.

Mixed-Integer Problems

In **mixed-integer problems,** some, but not all, of the decision variables are required to have integer values in the final solution, whereas others need not have integer values. For example, a landscape design may have a project that requires a decision on what percentage of an area to plant grass (a continuous variable) and how many trees to plant (some integer number).

A MODERN MANAGEMENT SCIENCE APPLICATION: EMPLOYEE SCHEDULING WITH INTEGER PROGRAMMING

The SAQ (in French, Société des alcools du Québec) is a public corporation of the Province of Quebec that is responsible for distributing and selling alcohol-based products in its territory through a large network of more than 400 stores and warehouses. Similar organizations in Canada are the LCBO in Ontario (Liquor Control Board of Ontario), or the Liquor Distribution Branch (LDB) in British Columbia. The SAQ operates different types of stores: some stores offer a large selection of products (for instance, those located in densely populated areas), while others have a limited selection (for example, those located near restaurants where customers can bring their own wine). The stores have various hours of operation depending on the day, but also on their type and location: they open between 9:30 am and 12:00 am, and close between 5:00 pm and 10:00 pm. The warehouses operate overnight. Every week, the SAQ has to schedule more than 3000 employees. Until 2002, it handled this process manually, incurring estimated annual salary expenses of almost $1 000 000. Using the manual process, schedulers made many errors, because they were unable to produce solutions that respected all the complex rules of the union agreement. To deal with complaints that employees filed, the company estimates it paid costs of approximately $300 000 annually. After carefully examining the available computer-based workforce scheduling products, the company realized that none of them could handle its union agreement rules properly. A solution engine, based on an integer programming model and interacting with an in-house web-based database system, was developed to produce the desired employee schedules. The project has contributed to increasing the efficiency of the organization by reducing the costs of producing the schedules and by improving the SAQ's management of human resources. Overall, the SAQ estimates that automated scheduling has saved over $1 000 000 annually.

Source: Reprinted by permission. Based on B. Gendron: "Scheduling Employees in Quebec's Liquor Stores with Integer Programming," *Interfaces* Vol. 35, no. 5, (September–October 2005), pp. 402–410. Copyright (2005), the Institute for Operations Research and the Management Sciences (INFORMS), 7240 Parkway Drive, Suite 310, Hanover, MD 21076 USA.

0–1 Integer Problems

A third kind of problem is where the integer variables require a value of 0 or 1. This type of problem, the **0–1 integer problem**, relates to situations in which decision variables are of the yes-no type. For example, a bank may be considering possible locations for new branch offices. Sites that are chosen would receive a 1, whereas those not chosen would receive a 0. Similarly, in a problem requiring matching, say, of jobs and machines or workers and jobs, the optimal matches would receive a 1 and all others would receive a 0.

This is an important category of integer programming problems that relates to *binary* decisions. Other examples include a manager who may have to decide whether to fund a project (yes) or not (no), whether to hire a person or not, whether to replace an existing machine or not, and so on. Generally, these problems involve multiple variables, such as the need to choose three locations for new convenience stores from a list of 20 potential sites. Even so, a yes-no decision must be made for each potential site (i.e., there are 20 decision variables).

6.3 GRAPHICAL REPRESENTATION OF INTEGER PROGRAMMING PROBLEMS

Integer programming problems can be solved graphically, but only for two-variable problems. With that in mind, let's consider a graphical solution to a very simple problem to better understand the nature of integer programming problems and solutions.

FIGURE 6-1 Graph of an Integer Programming Problem

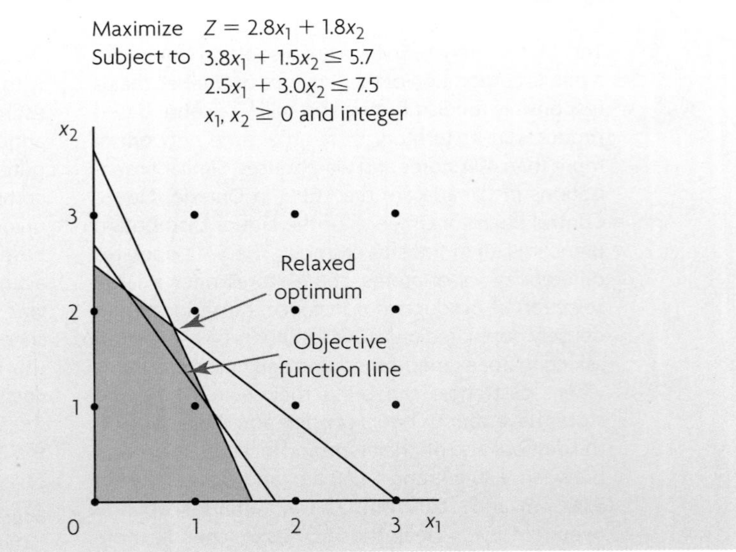

Figure 6-1 shows a simple integer programming problem and a graph of the constraints and the objective function. Note that the feasible solution space consists entirely of positive integers (represented by the dark points) that satisfy the constraints. In an LP problem that did not require an integer solution, the objective function would be plotted, then moved manually away from the origin to determine the optimal intersection. We can see this in Figure 6-1, but we also can see that this is not one of the integer solutions. To obtain a feasible integer solution using the objective function, we must move it (parallel to itself) back toward the origin. Hence, to achieve a feasible integer solution, we must settle for a lower value of the objective function (because moving the objective function toward the origin decreases its value). In moving the line toward the origin, the *first* point we come to will be the optimal integer solution. As you can see in Figure 6-1, that point is 1, 1. Thus, the optimal integer solution is $x_1 = 1, x_2 = 1$.

6.4 SOLVING INTEGER PROGRAMMING PROBLEMS USING EXCEL

We can solve integer programming problems with Excel as well as other computer software packages. In this section, we will demonstrate how to solve a pure-integer programming problem using Excel. Later in the chapter, we will demonstrate how to solve 0–1 integer programming problems using Excel.

Consider the following example.

EXAMPLE 6-1

A producer of pleasure boats wants to maximize profits during the next season. Two types of boats are sold. The first type of boat is a speedboat (x_1), and the second type of boat is a pontoon (x_2). The speedboat sells for \$40 000 and the pontoon sells for \$30 000. The speedboat takes 10 weeks to manufacture, while the pontoon takes 3 weeks to manufacture. One speedboat uses 600 board feet of lumber, while one pontoon uses 1000 board feet of lumber. Each speedboat requires 500 square feet of fibreglass, while each pontoon requires 200 square feet of fibreglass. There are 30 weeks of labour, 3000 board feet of lumber, and 1800 square feet of fibreglass available during the season. Because of the desire to avoid ending up with semicomplete boats, the manager has specified that only integer solutions will be acceptable. Use Excel and determine how many speedboats and how many pontoons the company should manufacture for the next season. What is the optimal profit?

Solution

We can begin the formulation of this problem by defining the variables:

Let x_1 = number of speedboats manufactured
x_2 = number of pontoons manufactured

The objective function involves maximization of profit and can be stated as follows:

maximize $Z = 40\,000x_1 + 30\,000x_2$

There are three constraints for this problem: The first one involves the labour time requirements, the second one involves the lumber usage, and the third one involves the fibreglass consumption. These constraints can be stated as follows:

$10x_1 + 3x_2 \leq 30$ (labour weeks available constraint)
$600x_1 + 1000x_2 \leq 3000$ (board feet of lumber available for production)
$500x_1 + 200x_2 \leq 1800$ (square feet of fibreglass available during season)

Along with the nonnegativity constraint, this information can be entered into the computer as shown in Exhibit 6-1.

After clicking on **Data|Analysis|Solver,** the screen shown in Exhibit 6-2 is displayed. In Exhibits 6-2 and 6-3, we illustrate parameter specification associated with this pure integer programming problem. In Exhibit 6-1, the objective function is specified in cell E6, and we specify this in "Set Target Cell" box in Exhibit 6-2. The decision variables are located in cells C5 and D5 and are specified in the "By Changing Cells" box in Exhibit 6-2. The three constraints are all less-than-or-equal-to types and they are specified in Exhibit 6-2 in aggregate as follows: \$F\$8:\$F\$10<=\$E\$8:\$E\$10. The left-hand side of the inequality (\$F\$8:\$F\$10) is stated in column labelled "Used" and the right-hand side of the inequality (\$E\$8:\$E\$10) is stated under the column labelled "Available" in Exhibit 6-1.

Up to this point, the specification of the problem using Excel was identical to the specification of typical linear programming problems covered in Chapter 2. The integer requirement distinguishes this problem from other noninteger linear programming problems. To solve this problem as a pure integer programming problem using Excel, we need to specify that decision variables may only assume integer values. To do that, we click on "Add" and "Add Constraint," the screen shown in Exhibit 6-3 is displayed. In Exhibit 6-3, on the left side of the screen labelled as "Cell Reference," we simply specify the location of the decision variables in Exhibit 6-1 (\$C\$5:\$D\$5). The middle of Exhibit 6-3 shows the

EXHIBIT 6-1 Input and Output Worksheet for the Boat-Manufacturing Example

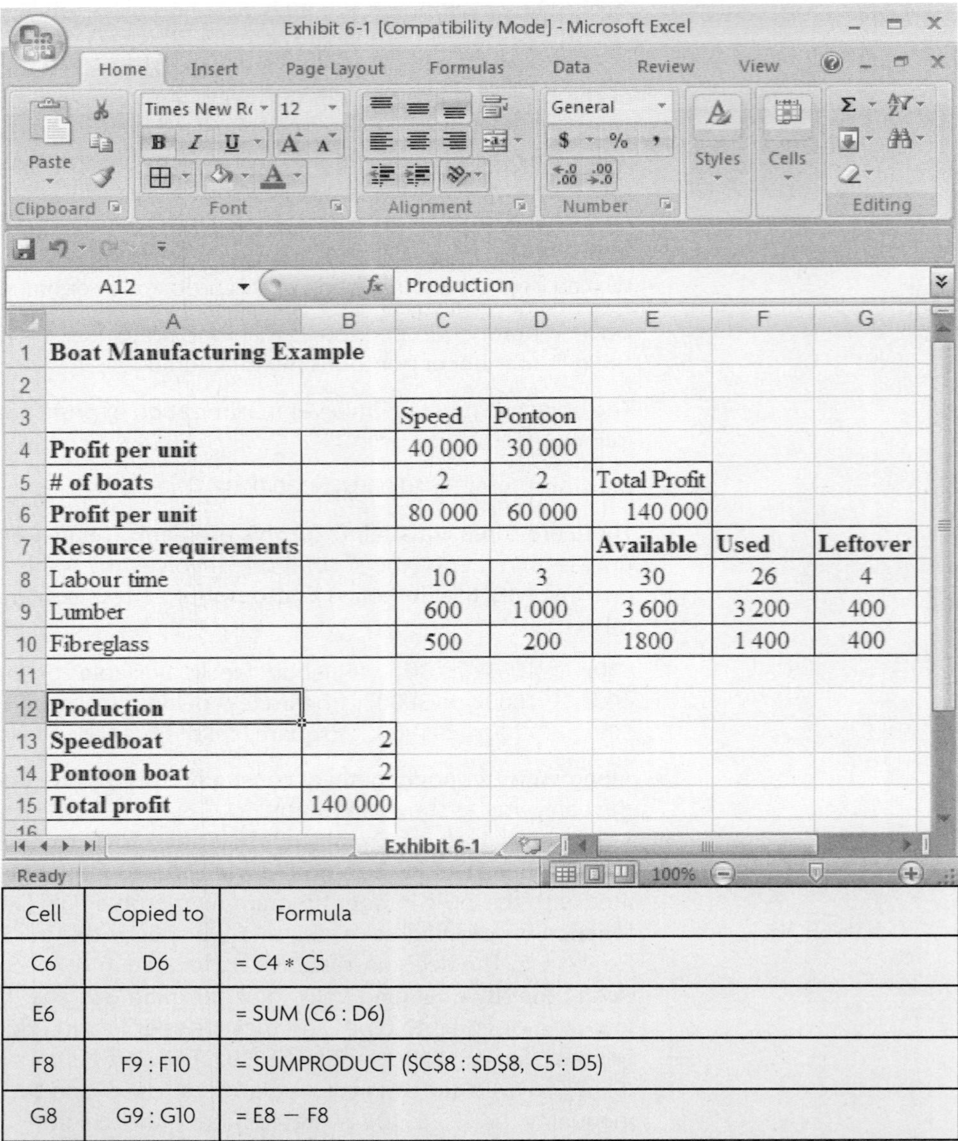

	A	B	C	D	E	F	G
1	**Boat Manufacturing Example**						
2							
3			Speed	Pontoon			
4	**Profit per unit**		40 000	30 000			
5	**# of boats**		2	2	Total Profit		
6	**Profit per unit**		80 000	60 000	140 000		
7	**Resource requirements**				**Available**	**Used**	**Leftover**
8	Labour time		10	3	30	26	4
9	Lumber		600	1 000	3 600	3 200	400
10	Fibreglass		500	200	1800	1 400	400
11							
12	**Production**						
13	**Speedboat**	2					
14	**Pontoon boat**	2					
15	**Total profit**	140 000					

Cell	Copied to	Formula
C6	D6	= C4 * C5
E6		= SUM (C6 : D6)
F8	F9 : F10	= SUMPRODUCT ($C$8 : $D$8, C5 : D5)
G8	G9 : G10	= E8 − F8

sign or the variable type requirements of the constraint. When we click on the down arrow and choose "int," the word "integer" shows up on the left side of the screen in the Constraint box; after we click OK, we see $C$5:$D$5 = integer in the Subject to the Constraints box in Exhibit 6-2. This concludes parameter specification of the boat-manufacturing problem.

EXHIBIT 6-2 Solver Parameters Screen for the Boat-Manufacturing Problem

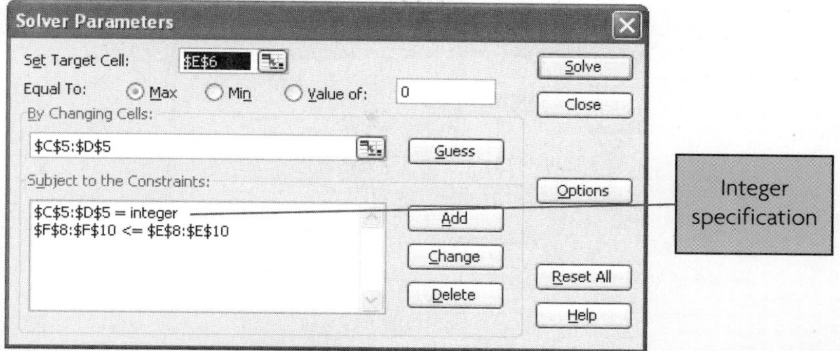

After clicking on the "Solve" button, the solution in Exhibit 6-1 is displayed. Before clicking on the "Solve" button in Exhibit 6-2, the values of the decision variables in Exhibit 6-1 were simply equal to zero. After clicking the "Solve" button, the Solver Results screen shown in Exhibit 6-4 will appear. A more detailed answer report could be obtained by simply clicking on "Answer" in the Reports box on the right side of the "Solver Results" screen.

Based on the results given in Exhibit 6-1, the solution to this problem can be summarized as follows:

$x_1 = 2$ (number of speedboats manufactured)
$x_2 = 2$ (number of pontoon boats manufactured)
$Z = \$140\,000$ (optimal profit associated with the boat production schedule)

Had we solved this problem as a linear programming problem, we would have obtained the following answer:

$x_1 = 2.561$ (number of speedboats manufactured)
$x_2 = 1.4634$ (number of pontoon boats manufactured)
$Z = \$146\,341.46$ (optimal profit associated with the boat production schedule)

As can be observed, rounding down the linear programming solution ($x_1 = 2, x_2 = 1$) is not the same as the optimal integer solution.

EXHIBIT 6-3 Integer Requirement Specification

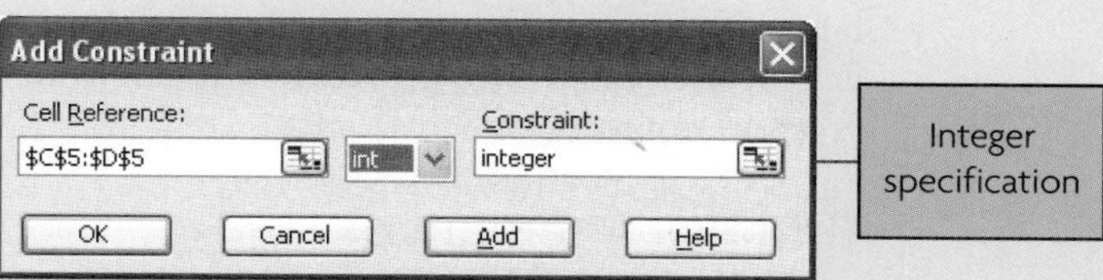

EXHIBIT 6-4 Solver Results Screen

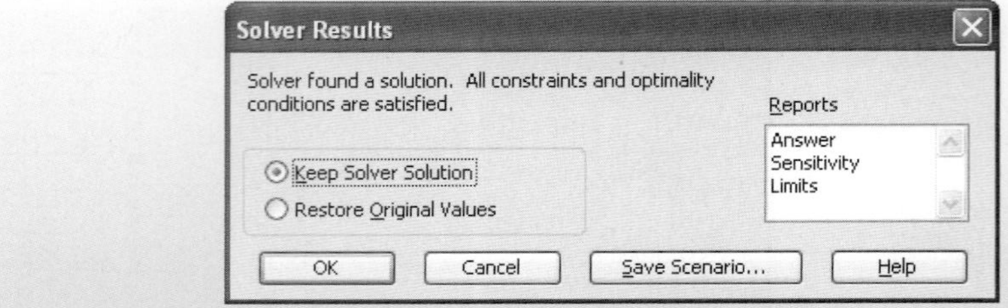

6.5 A COMMENT ABOUT SENSITIVITY

Integer programming problems do not readily lend themselves to the sort of sensitivity analysis that was described in Chapter 3. This stems from the fact that only a relatively few of the infinite solution possibilities in a feasible solution space will meet integer requirements. Unfortunately, there is no easy way to determine the extent to which changes in a right-hand-side quantity will alter the choice of integer alternatives. The only way to accomplish that is to rework the problem with the changes and observe the effect. This is, indeed, unfortunate, because it often happens that relatively small changes in constraints can have large changes on the value of the objective function. If these amounts were known to management, it is highly likely that management would elect to take the necessary action to change the constraints. For this reason, it may make sense to explore a range of constraint quantities to ascertain if the value of the objective function would change materially. In cases in which it would change materially, say, for a slight increase in the right-hand-side value of a constraint, this potential could then be presented to management for consideration.

Similarly, there is no simple way to determine the impact of changes to the objective function coefficients on the solution to a problem. Again, trial-and-error examination of a range of reasonable alternatives involving completely solving each revised problem is required.

6.6 FORMULATING INTEGER PROGRAMMING PROBLEMS WITH 0–1 CONSTRAINTS

Formulating a problem correctly is often the most important phase of decision analysis. In the case of integer programming, problem formulation sometimes requires a fair degree of ingenuity to correctly portray a situation. In this section, a variety of formulations are demonstrated that have proved very useful in setting up commonly encountered integer programming requirements.

Either-Or Alternatives

A manufacturer may need a machine to replace one that recently has failed. Two alternatives, x_1 and x_2, are being considered, but only one will be needed. The constraint that expresses this would be

$$x_1 + x_2 = 1$$

If there is a possibility that neither machine will be acquired, then the constraint would be written as

$$x_1 + x_2 \leq 1$$

In either of these cases, the variables are 0–1 variables.

k-Out-of-*n* Alternatives

In many problems, a decision maker must choose a specified number of alternatives; say, choose two machines from a list of five alternative machines. Or the requirement may be to choose *at least two,* or, perhaps, *no more than two* machines from the list.

The formulation for exactly two machines out of five would be

$$x_1 + x_2 + x_3 + x_4 + x_5 = 2$$

For at least two machines out of five, the formulation would be

$$x_1 + x_2 + x_3 + x_4 + x_5 \geq 2$$

For no more than two out of five machines; the formulation would be

$$x_1 + x_2 + x_3 + x_4 + x_5 \leq 2$$

Sometimes a problem will permit a range of choices. For example, a situation may call for the purchase of anywhere from two to four machines. The problem would then require two constraints, one for the upper bound and the other for the lower bound. Thus, for two to four machines, the constraints would be

$$x_1 + x_2 + x_3 + x_4 + x_5 \geq 2$$
$$x_1 + x_2 + x_3 + x_4 + x_5 \leq 4$$

If-Then Alternatives

It sometimes happens that a decision to take some action necessitates another action that supports the initial decision. For example, the purchase of machine x_2 may necessitate the purchase of another machine, x_1. The formulation would be

$$x_1 \geq x_2$$

Note that this formulation implies that the reverse case is not required: The purchase of x_1 does not require the purchase of x_2. To satisfy the requirement that the right-hand side consist solely of a numerical quantity, this can be rewritten as

$$x_1 - x_2 \geq 0$$

If the purchase of either machine requires the purchase of the other, the appropriate formulation would be

$$x_1 - x_2 = 0$$

Either-Or Constraints

Situations may arise in which a constraint will apply *only if* a particular alternative is chosen. For instance, the choice of a certain machine may necessitate special power requirements. Consequently, it can be useful to be able to "turn on" or "turn off" a constraint as appropriate. This can be accomplished by tying the constraint to the decision variable that will govern its applicability. Suppose the machine in question is choice x_8, which will require the constraint $5x_4 + 3x_5 \geq 100$ if x_8 is chosen. This can be incorporated into the problem by writing the constraint as $5x_4 + 3x_5 \geq 100x_8$, where x_8 is a 0–1 decision variable. Then, if x_8 is selected, $x_8 = 1$, and the constraint will stand. If x_8 is not selected, then $x_8 = 0$, and the constraint will, in effect, drop out. Rearranging terms so that all variables are on the left-hand side and a constant on the right-hand side results in

$$5x_4 + 3x_5 - 100x_8 \geq 0$$

If there are two potential constraints, one of which will apply if a certain choice (say, x_8) is made and the other if that choice is not made, the formulation would be slightly different. For example, suppose the constraints are $5x_4 + 3x_5 \geq 100$ if x_8 is chosen and $5x_4 + 3x_5 \geq 50$ for any other choice (i.e., x_8 is not chosen). This could be expressed as

$$5x_4 + 3x_5 \geq 100x_8 \quad \text{(applies if } x_8 = 1)$$
$$5x_4 + 3x_5 \geq 50(1 - x_8) \quad \text{(applies if } x_8 = 0)$$

These can be written as

$$5x_4 + 3x_5 - 100x_8 \geq 0 \quad \text{and}$$
$$5x_4 + 3x_5 + 50x_8 \geq 50$$

If the constraints relate to *upper limits* (i.e., the constraints are $\leq$), then a slightly different approach should be used. Suppose the constraints are either $4x_1 + 8x_2 \leq 40$, or $2x_1 + x_2 \leq 16$, depending on whether project y_1 is commissioned. Say the first constraint applies if y_1 is not commissioned and the second if it is. This can be handled by writing the constraints in this form:

1 $4x_1 + 8x_2 \leq 40 + My_1$ where M is a very large number
2 $2x_1 + x_2 \leq 16 + M(1 - y_1)$ where

$y_1 = 1$ indicates the project is commissioned
$y_1 = 0$ indicates that the projects is not commissioned

If y_1 is commissioned, then $y_1 = 1$ and the right-hand side of the first constraint becomes so large that it is not binding. Conversely, if $y_1 = 0$, the reverse is true: The first constraint becomes binding, whereas the right-hand side of the second becomes very large and, therefore, not binding.

Variables That Have Minimum Level Requirements

In some cases, a variable either will have to be zero or an amount that exceeds a specified value. For instance, a minimum order size for a purchased part might be required by a vendor. Say the minimum quantity for x_1 is 200 units. This can be expressed using another variable, y_1, that is a 0–1 variable:

$$x_1 - 200y_1 \geq 0$$

where x_1 is integer
$y_1 = 0$ or 1

Then, if $x_1 = 0$, the first constraint would cause y_1 to be zero as well.

MODERN MANAGEMENT SCIENCE APPLICATION:
WASTE MANAGEMENT

We all have to put out garbage approximately once a week to be collected by a garbage collection company. Waste Management (WM) is a private firm that provides comprehensive waste management services in North America. The company manages a network of 293 active landfill disposal sites, 16 waste energy plants, 72 landfill gas-to-energy facilities, 146 recycling plants, 346 transfer stations, and 435 collection depots. WM provides garbage collection and disposal to nearly 20 million residential and 2 million commercial customers throughout the United States and Canada. The company employs over 3400 people in Canada at 116 operating locations in 9 provinces, servicing over 4.5 million residential customers and 170 000 industrial and commercial customers. The company has a large fleet of vehicles that has to be maintained, routed, and dispatched; initially that was done using a decentralized system. WM recognized an opportunity to save a considerable amount of money by improving the routing of its vehicles. WM contracted with the Institute of Information Technology (IIT) to develop a comprehensive route-management system.

The company's garbage collection business consisted of three major areas: (1) residential, (2) commercial; and (3) industrial. Residential customers include people living in individual homes. Commercial customers include strip malls, restaurants, and small office buildings, while industrial customers include rather large businesses. Typically, a commercial container consisted of eight "loose yards," while an industrial container may range from 20 to 40 loose yards.

WM wanted to design a routing system where each route became as profitable as possible. To accomplish this goal, the company invested in a geographical information system (GIS). This system tightly integrates spatial information based on customer addresses. GIS can show the location of the customer on a map along with the surrounding street network. To accomplish the goal, WM and IIT centralized its routing system of 19 600 daily routes and implemented a new scheduling system. The new scheduling system incorporated new variables such as frequency of service based on climate, geography, competition, and the price of service. On one route, a garbage collection truck may serve a small number of customers, while on another route a truck may serve many more customers. However, the first driver may drive a longer distance to serve the smaller number of customers while the second driver has short hops between customers.

The residential and commercial collection problems can be classified as vehicle routing problems (VRP), which is a special case of a travelling salesperson problem. VRPs may have different characteristics (homogeneous versus heterogeneous vehicles, single versus multiple depots). WM's goal was to minimize the number of vehicles and travel time while meeting the following constraints: vehicle capacity, route capacity, routing time limit, disposal trips, and time windows at stops. If the routing capacity exceeds vehicle capacity, the driver will be forced to make multiple disposal stops. On the other hand, if the routing capacity is less than the vehicle capacity, then the driver will make only one disposal stop. WM contracted with IIT to develop a user-friendly, Web-based system to schedule the entire routing for the company. The new routing system resulted in fewer vehicles and, thus, 10 percent fewer drivers were required. WM reduced the number of drivers through regular attrition and did not lay off drivers. The company identified the new routing system (WasteRoute) as one of the key components of its operational excellence.

In less than four years, the company had 984 fewer routes, which translated into savings of \$18 million, with future estimated annual savings expected to reach \$44 million. The improved routing not only resulted in the company cutting costs, but also enabled the company to focus on revenue enhancement. Because of the better efficiency provided by WasteRoute, WM also has a new higher total capacity, and therefore could focus on adding new customers, new routes, and new revenue.

Source: Reprinted by permission, S. Sahoo, S. Kim, B. Kim, B. Kraas, and A. Popov Jr., "Routing Optimization for Waste Management," *Interfaces* Vol. 35, no. 1 (January–February 2005), pp. 24–36. Copyright (2005), the Institute for Operations Research and the Management Sciences (INFORMS), 7240 Parkway Drive, Suite 310, Hanover, MD 21076 USA.

6.7 SPECIALIZED INTEGER PROGRAMMING PROBLEMS

There are special types of business applications that require the decision variables to take on a value of 1 or 0. These include capital budgeting and assignment problems where partial acceptance or rejection of a project, investment alternative, or a job is not acceptable. In such cases, the project, investment, or job is either accepted or rejected.

There are a number of specialized integer programming problems with 0–1 decision variables that deserve discussion in this chapter. These problems are as follows:

1. Fixed-charge problem
2. Set covering problem
3. Knapsack problem
4. Facility location problem
5. Travelling salesperson problem

Fixed-Charge Problem

In the business world, companies face situations that involve fixed costs if a certain activity is undertaken as well as a variable cost, which generally involves the per-unit production cost. In such cases, the objective is to minimize the total cost, which is the sum of the fixed cost plus the variable cost.

It very often happens that the contribution that a variable makes to profit is linear *after* a fixed charge has been deducted. For instance, the profit per unit produced on a machine may be \$20 per unit after a setup cost of \$80 has been allowed for. Suppose the product is x_1. Then without the setup charge, the portion of the objective function with x_1 would be $20x_1$. It might seem that we could simply subtract the fixed charge from the objective function. However, this approach overlooks the possibility that the optimum value of x_1 might be zero, in which case there would be *no* setup charge and, hence, no subtraction from the objective function value. To allow for this, we can introduce another variable, y_1, which can assume values of 0 or 1: 0 if x_1 is 0 and 1 if x_1 is greater than 0.

The portion of the objective function for these two variables is

$$20x_1 - 80y_1$$

In addition, the following constraint will be needed:

$$x_1 \leq My_1 \quad \text{where } M \text{ is a very large number}$$

This constraint will force x_1 to be zero if y_1 is zero. If $y_1 = 1$, there will be no limit on x_1, assuming a very large value has been selected for M. To conform with having a constant on the right-hand side, this constraint can be written as

$$x_1 - My_1 \leq 0$$

Note that this constraint and the portion of the objective function shown would be in addition to any other constraints and other portions of the objective function that may be required by a problem.

Consider the following two examples of **fixed-charge problems.**

EXAMPLE 6-2

A company makes two products, x_1 and x_2. Product x_1 generates a profit of \$20 per unit before a fixed charge of \$80 per batch for setup is allowed for; product x_2 generates a profit of \$30 per unit before a setup charge of \$90 is allowed for. Each product requires two hours of machine time, and 400 hours of machine time are available. Integer values of each product are required for technical reasons. The manager wants to maximize profits. Set up this all-integer linear programming problem.

Solution

x_1 = quantity of product 1
x_2 = quantity of product 2
$y_1 = 1$ if $x_1 > 0$, $y_1 = 0$ if $x_1 = 0$
$y_2 = 1$ if $x_2 > 0$, $y_2 = 0$ if $x_2 = 0$
M = a very large number

maximize $Z = 20x_1 + 30x_2 - 80y_1 - 90y_2$

subject to

Machine time	$2x_1 + 2x_2 \leq 400$ hours
x_1 fixed charge	$x_1 - My_1 \leq 0$
x_2 fixed charge	$x_2 - My_2 \leq 0$
	x_1 and x_2 integer and ≥ 0
	y_1 and y_2 are 0 or 1

Solving,

$x_2 = 200$ (quantity of product 2)
$y_2 = 1$ (set up for product 2)
$Z = \$5910$ (profit)

EXAMPLE 6-3

A company manufactures three different products: A, B, and C. The per-unit profit margins for the three products are \$6, \$10, and \$5. The products could be manufactured using one of two processes. The per-unit production requirements for each product for each process is given in Table 6-1.

Table 6-1 Per-Unit Production Requirements

Process	Product A	Product B	Product C	Total Hours Available
Process 1	4 hours	6 hours	3 hours	2000 hours per week
Process 2	5 hours	7 hours	4 hours	2400 hours per week

The demand for product A is predicted to be between 50 and 100 units per week, demand for product B is predicted to be between 150 and 200 units per week, and demand for product C is predicted to be between 100 and 150 units per week.

If the company decides to use process 1, it will incur a setup cost of \$100 and the setup will take 24 hours. If the company decides to use process 2, it will incur a setup cost of \$80 and the setup will take 18 hours. Determine the production schedule that will maximize the profits for the company and also determine which of the two processes should be utilized.

Solution

We start formulating this problem by defining the decision variables. There are two types of decision variables in this problem. The first type of decision variable is x_{ij} = the number of product i manufactured according to process 1, $i = 1, 2, 3, j = 1, 2$. This is an integer variable, as fractional quantities are not acceptable. The second type of decision variable is $y_i = 0$ or 1. If process 1 is not used in manufacturing the products, then $y_i = 0$, in which case the setup cost associated with process 1 will not be incurred. If process 1 is used in manufacturing the products, then $y_i = 1$, in which case the setup cost associated with process 1 will be incurred. After defining the decision variables, the next step is to prepare the objective function. Since the objective is to maximize profit, the objective function is maximization. In the objective function, the fixed costs can be represented as negative profits.

$$\text{maximize } Z = 6x_{11} + 6x_{12} + 10x_{21} + 10x_{22} + 5x_{31} + 5x_{32} - 100y_1 - 80y_2$$

In setting up the constraints, we not only have to consider and sum the per-unit production hours for each product, but we also need to add the setup time for each product. If the product is not manufactured, the value of the associated y variable is 0 and no setup cost will be incurred. The constraints for each department can be stated as follows:

$$4x_{11} + 6x_{21} + 3x_{31} + 24y_1 \leq 2000y_1 \text{ hours} \quad \text{(constraint for process 1)}$$
$$5x_{12} + 7x_{22} + 4x_{32} + 18y_2 \leq 2400y_2 \text{ hours} \quad \text{(constraint for process 2)}$$

Note that the right-hand side of each constraint for each process contains the y_i variable. If we utilize process 1, y_1 takes on a value of 1; if we do not utilize process 1, $y_1 = 0$. If $y_1 = 0$, the right-hand side of constraint 1 goes to zero, which means that process 1 is not utilized.

Demand constraints are stated below:

$$\left.\begin{aligned} x_{11} + x_{12} &\geq 50 \\ x_{11} + x_{12} &\leq 100 \\ x_{21} + x_{22} &\geq 150 \\ x_{21} + x_{22} &\leq 200 \\ x_{31} + x_{32} &\geq 100 \\ x_{31} + x_{32} &\leq 150 \end{aligned}\right\} \quad \text{(minimum and maximum demand constraints)}$$

Note that there are two demand constraints for each product. One of the two constraints, the greater-than-or-equal-to constraint, is the lower bound (minimum demand); the other, the less-than-or-equal-to constraint, is the upper bound (maximum demand).

The formulation of the above problem can be summarized as follows:

$$\text{maximize } Z = 6x_{11} + 6x_{12} + 10x_{21} + 10x_{22} + 5x_{31} + 5x_{32} - 100y_1 - 80y_2$$

subject to

$$4x_{11} + 6x_{21} + 3x_{31} + 24y_1 \leq 2000y_1 \text{ hours} \quad \text{(constraint for process 1)}$$
$$5x_{12} + 7x_{22} + 4x_{32} + 18y_2 \leq 2400y_2 \text{ hours} \quad \text{(constraint for process 2)}$$

$x_{11} + x_{12} \geq 50$
$x_{11} + x_{12} \leq 100$
$x_{21} + x_{22} \geq 150$
$x_{21} + x_{22} \leq 200$
$x_{31} + x_{32} \geq 100$
$x_{31} + x_{32} \geq 150$
$x_{11}, x_{12}, x_{21}, x_{22}, x_{31}, x_{32} \geq 0$ and integer
$y_1, y_2 = 0$ or 1

The Excel solution and worksheet to this problem are not given to reduce redundancy of Excel worksheets within the chapter, but rather they can be found on the OLC.

$x_{12} = 99$ (# of units of product A scheduled to be manufactured according to process 2)
$x_{22} = 187$ (# of units of product B scheduled to be manufactured according to process 2)
$x_{32} = 127$ (# of units of product C scheduled to be manufactured according to process 2)
$y_1 = 0$ (process 1 is not being utilized)
$y_2 = 1$ (process 2 is being utilized)
$Z = \$3119$ (total maximum profit)

Set Covering Problem

In many business situations, coverage needs to be provided to all areas with minimum cost or time requirements. The **set covering problem** involves deciding on which nodes provide coverage so that all areas are served. In other words, this problem involves deciding which nodes should be used to provide coverage to all areas with minimum cost or time requirements. As the number of locations increases, this can be a difficult problem to solve intuitively.

Consider the following problem from the telecommunication industry.

EXAMPLE 6-4

Vogers Communications Inc. is considering expanding its cable and Internet service operations into a new area. The area is divided into 10 neighbourhoods. The company is considering 7 location nodes to reach all 10 neighbourhoods. Of course, it costs a significant amount of money to open a node or make a node operational. The company would like to minimize total cost but at the same time reach all of the neighbourhoods. The cost of opening a node differs based on the characteristics of the land and the technical aspects of setting up a node.

The costs of opening seven nodes are as follows:

Node 1	Node 2	Node 3	Node 4	Node 5	Node 6	Node 7
125	85	70	60	90	100	110

The seven nodes can reach or provide Internet/cable coverage to the following areas:

Node 1 Neighbourhoods 1, 3, 4, 6, 9, 10
Node 2 Neighbourhoods 2, 4, 6, 8
Node 3 Neighbourhoods 1, 2, 5
Node 4 Neighbourhoods 3, 6, 7, 10
Node 5 Neighbourhoods 2, 3, 7, 9

Node 6 Neighbourhoods 4, 5, 6, 8, 10
Node 7 Neighbourhoods 1, 5, 7, 8, 9

Determine which nodes should be opened to provide coverage to all neighbourhoods at a minimum cost.

Solution

This set covering problem can be formulated as 0–1 integer programming problem. We first start by defining the decision variables:

Let $x_j = 1$ if node j provides service
$x_j = 0$ if node j does not provide service
$c_j =$ cost of opening or setting up node j.

The objective function involves minimization of total cost and can be stated as follows:

$$\text{minimize } Z = 125x_1 + 85x_2 + 70x_3 + 60x_4 + 90x_5 + 100x_6 + 110x_7$$

This objective function is subject to constraints that ensure that Internet and cable service are provided to all areas. Therefore, we need a constraint for each area.

For example, neighbourhood 1 is covered by nodes 1, 3, and 7; therefore, for neighbourhood 1 to be covered, at least one of these three nodes must be operational. Therefore, we can set up the constraint for neighbourhood 1 as a greater-than-or-equal-to 1 constraint: $x_1 + x_3 + x_7 \geq 1$. In other words, at least one of nodes 1, 3, or 7 must be open for neighbourhood 1 to receive coverage. Setting up the constraints using similar logic for the other neighbourhoods results in the following formulation:

$$\text{minimize } Z = 125x_1 + 85x_2 + 70x_3 + 60x_4 + 90x_5 + 100x_6 + 110x_7$$

subject to

$x_1 + x_3 + x_7 \geq 1$ (coverage of neighbourhood 1)
$x_2 + x_3 + x_5 \geq 1$ (coverage of neighbourhood 2)
$x_1 + x_4 + x_5 \geq 1$ (coverage of neighbourhood 3)
$x_1 + x_2 + x_6 \geq 1$ (coverage of neighbourhood 4)
$x_3 + x_6 + x_7 \geq 1$ (coverage of neighbourhood 5)
$x_1 + x_2 + x_6 \geq 1$ (coverage of neighbourhood 6)
$x_4 + x_5 + x_7 \geq 1$ (coverage of neighbourhood 7)
$x_2 + x_6 + x_7 \geq 1$ (coverage of neighbourhood 8)
$x_1 + x_5 + x_7 \geq 1$ (coverage of neighbourhood 9)
$x_1 + x_4 + x_6 \geq 1$ (coverage of neighbourhood 10)
$x_1, x_2, x_3, x_4, x_5, x_6, x_7 = 0$ or 1

Excel Solution of the 0–1 (Set Covering) Problem

The formulation given above can be entered into a worksheet as shown in Exhibit 6-5. In Exhibit 6-5, all of the costs if node i is open are entered into cells C4 thorough I4. Coverage requirements for areas 1 through 10 are listed in rows 7 through 16. In each of these rows, column J, labelled as "Required," provides the right-hand side of the coverage requirement constraints. The Required column for all of these constraints is equal to 1. Column K, labelled as "Used," shows the left-hand side of the coverage requirements constraints. The formula for the left-hand side, shown in Exhibit 6-5, is "=SUMPRODUCT ($C$5:$I$5,C7:I7)," which is the sum of the products of the decision variables and the constraint coefficients on the left-hand side of each constraint. Cell B18 provides the objective function value, which is the minimum total cost for the problem. The formula for the total cost, "= SUMPRODUCT(C4:I4,C5:I5)" in cell B18, is shown in the formula bar in Exhibit 6-5; it is simply the cross-product of the respective decision variable values and the cost of opening the respective nodes. After all the data and the formulas are entered into the computer, choose **Data|Analysis|Solver**; the screen displayed in Exhibit 6-6 appears. In Exhibit 6-6, we illustrate parameter specification associated with this 0–1 integer programming problem. In Exhibit 6-5, the objective function is specified in cell B18; we specify this in the Set Target Cell box in Exhibit 6-6. The decision variables are located in cells C5 through I5 and are specified in the By Changing Cells box in Exhibit 6-6. The 10 coverage constraints are all greater-than-or-equal-to types and are specified in aggregate

EXHIBIT 6-5 Worksheet for the 0–1 Integer Programming Set Covering Problem

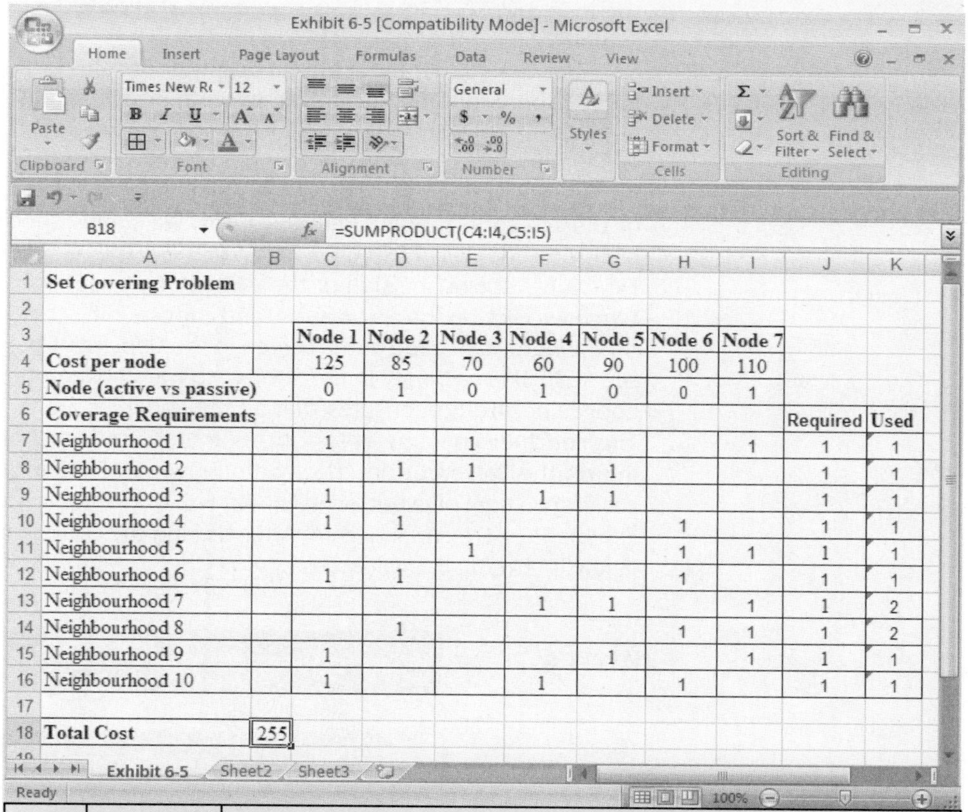

Exhibit 6-5 [Compatibility Mode] - Microsoft Excel

B18 =SUMPRODUCT(C4:I4,C5:I5)

	A	B	C	D	E	F	G	H	I	J	K
1	**Set Covering Problem**										
2											
3			**Node 1**	**Node 2**	**Node 3**	**Node 4**	**Node 5**	**Node 6**	**Node 7**		
4	**Cost per node**		125	85	70	60	90	100	110		
5	**Node (active vs passive)**		0	1	0	1	0	0	1		
6	**Coverage Requirements**									**Required**	**Used**
7	Neighbourhood 1		1		1				1	1	1
8	Neighbourhood 2			1	1		1			1	1
9	Neighbourhood 3		1			1	1			1	1
10	Neighbourhood 4		1	1				1		1	1
11	Neighbourhood 5				1			1	1	1	1
12	Neighbourhood 6		1	1				1		1	1
13	Neighbourhood 7					1	1		1	1	2
14	Neighbourhood 8			1				1	1	1	2
15	Neighbourhood 9		1				1		1	1	1
16	Neighbourhood 10		1			1		1		1	1
17											
18	**Total Cost**	255									

Exhibit 6-5 Sheet2 Sheet3

Cell	Copied to	Formula
B18		= SUMPRODUCT (C4 : I4, C5 : I5)
K7	K8 : K16	= SUMPRODUCT ($C$5 : $I$5, C7 : I7)

EXHIBIT 6-6 Solver Parameters Screen for the Set Covering Problem

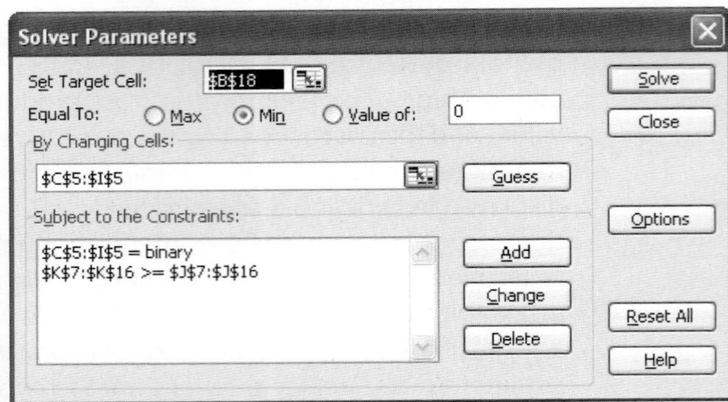

in Exhibit 6-6 as \$K\$7:\$K\$16>= \$J\$7:\$J\$16. The left-hand side of the inequality (\$K\$7:\$K\$16) is stated in the column labelled "Used" and the right-hand side of the inequality (\$J\$7:\$J\$16) is stated under the column labelled "Required" in Exhibit 6-5.

The 0–1 integer requirement distinguishes this problem from other noninteger or pure-integer linear programming problems. To solve this problem as a 0–1 integer programming problem using Excel, we need to specify that decision variables may only assume 0–1 or binary integer values. To do that, we click on Add in Exhibit 6-6; this displays the screen shown in Exhibit 6-7. On the left side of the screen in the Cell Reference box, we simply specify the location of the decision variables in Exhibit 6-5 (\$C\$5:\$1\$5). The middle of screen displayed in Exhibit 6-7 shows the sign or the variable type requirements of the constraint. When we click on the down arrow and choose "bin," the word "binary" shows up on the right-hand side of the screen in the Constraint box; after we click OK, we see \$C\$5:\$I\$5 = binary in the Subject to the Constraints box in Exhibit 6-6. The above specification ensures that all the variables are 0–1, or binary, variables. This concludes parameter specification of the set covering problem. After clicking on the Solve button, the solution given in Exhibit 6-5 is displayed. Before clicking on the Solve button in Exhibit 6-6, the values of the decision variables in Exhibit 6-5 were equal to zero. After clicking the Solve button in Exhibit 6-6, the results of Exhibit 6-5 will appear.

EXHIBIT 6-7 Binary Requirement Specification

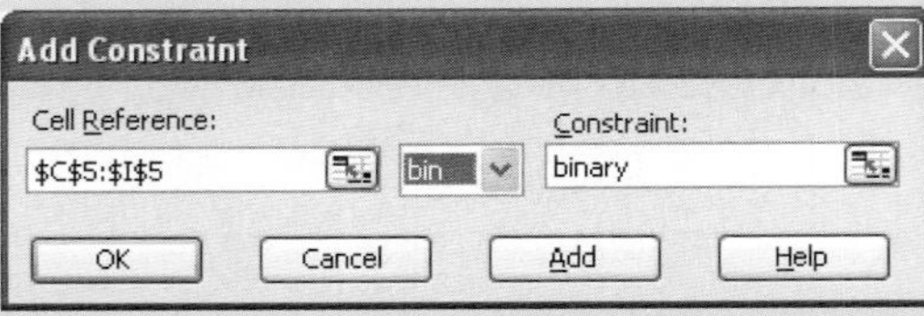

The solution to this set covering problem can be summarized as follows:

$x_2 = 1$ (open Node 2)
$x_4 = 1$ (open Node 4)
$x_7 = 1$ (open Node 7)
$Z = \$255$ (minimum cost to serve the 10 neighbourhoods)

The set covering problem can be expanded to accommodate situations where certain neighbourhoods need additional coverage or coverage by more than one node due to the high volume of business in that neighbourhood. For instance, there might be a need for at least two nodes to provide coverage for neighbourhood 1; therefore, constraint 1 may read as

$$x_1 + x_3 + x_7 \geq 2 \quad \text{(coverage of neighbourhood 1)}$$

Knapsack Problem

The **knapsack problem** is defined as how many units of each different kind of item or product to put in a knapsack with a given capacity to maximize profit. This general basic framework of the knapsack problem is the foundation for many different types of resource allocation problems.

The knapsack problem is a special case of integer linear programming problems where the objective function is a linear maximization function with all positive profit coefficients and a single less-than-or-equal-to linear constraint with all positive constraint coefficients.

Therefore, the general form of the knapsack problem can be stated as

$$\text{maximize: } Z = c_1x_1 + c_2x_2 + \ldots + c_nx_n$$

subject to

$$a_1x_1 + a_2x_2 + \ldots + a_nx_n \leq B$$
$$x_i \geq 0 \text{ and integer, for all } i = 1, 2, 3, \ldots, n$$

where

x_i = number of units of product i
c_i = profit (objective function coefficient) per unit of product i
a_i = weight of one unit of product i
B = total capacity
n = number of different products (product types)

EXAMPLE 6-5

Tri-Province Food Corporation is a food wholesale company that sells various food items to restaurants, hospitals, and the military. One of the superfreezers for this food wholesaler has five tonnes of capacity remaining. Tri-Province has three possible major food items that it wants to store in the superfreezer: beef, poultry, and ice cream. To realize desired quantity discounts, Tri-Province must purchase the food items in batches. One batch (purchase quantity) of poultry weighs two tonnes, one batch of beef weighs three tonnes, and one batch of ice cream weighs one tonne. The batch weights and the average profit value per batch for each food item are summarized in Table 6-2:

Table 6-2 Batch Weights and Profit Per Batch

Food Type	Batch Weight (tonnes)	Profit per Batch ($1000s)
Poultry	2	$90
Beef	3	$150
Ice cream	1	$30

a. Formulate this problem as a knapsack problem.
b. Determine the optimal number of batches of each type of food item that Tri-Province should purchase and store in its superfreezer to maximize total profit using the dynamic programming solution approach.

Solution

a. maximize $Z = 90x_1 + 150x_2 + 30x_3$

subject to

$2x_1 + 3x_2 + x_3 \leq 5$
$x_1, x_2, x_3 \geq 0$ and integer

b. Solving this problem using Excel, we reach the following optimal solution (the Excel solution and worksheet to this problem are not given to reduce redundancy of Excel worksheets within the chapter, but rather they are included on the OLC):

$x_1 = 1$ (number of batches of poultry stored)
$x_2 = 1$ (number of batches of beef stored)
$Z = \$240$ (optimal profit)

The knapsack problem has many applications in the real world. The cargo-loading problem faced by transportation companies is a typical application of the knapsack problem. Even though it may seem easy to solve, the knapsack problem can be computationally burdensome if there are a large number of products involved. The number of possible solutions with n items (products) is 2^n. For instance, a problem with 3 items ($n = 3$) has $2 \times 2 \times 2 = 8$ possible solutions. A problem with 4 items has $2 \times 2 \times 2 \times 2 = 16$ possible solutions. A problem with 8 items has 256 possible solutions. However, a problem with 16 items has 65 536 solutions.

Facility Location Problem

In Chapter 5, we discussed the transportation problem and we learned about how to solve the facility location problem using the transportation method when there were two choices and capacity was not an issue. However, the location problem can be more complicated. Instead of considering just two competing locations, we may have to consider numerous new locations at a given point in time. In addition, we may have to take capacity into consideration. In situations like this, we cannot utilize the transportation method because it does not result in a feasible solution. However, utilizing 0–1 mixed-integer programming problem formulation can assist in finding a feasible and an optimal solution to the multiple **facility location problem.** There are many applications of the 0–1 mixed-integer programming formulation of the multiple facility location problem. They include location of plants, hospitals, health care facilities, fast food restaurants, schools, police, and fire stations.

To better understand this type of problem, let's examine the following example.

EXAMPLE 6-6

Monson and Robinson Manufacturing Company is going through a major expansion. It needs to add a few manufacturing plants. At the present time, it has two plants, one in Windsor, and the other in Montreal. The capacities of these plants are roughly 26 000 units per year in Windsor and 30 000 units per year in Montreal. The company sells exclusively through its retail outlet stores located in Winnipeg, Toronto, Ottawa, and Hamilton. The demand for the product at these retail outlet facilities is as follows:

- Winnipeg: 27 000 units per year
- Toronto: 32 000 units per year
- Ottawa: 23 000 units per year
- Hamilton: 30 000 units per year.

The company is in the process of considering four new manufacturing plant locations. The locations, their capacities, and the cost of purchasing or building the facility are stated in Table 6-3:

Table 6-3 Capacities and Purchase Cost of Proposed Facilities

Manufacturing Facility	Capacity (units per year)	Building/Purchasing Cost
Brandon	30 000	$220 000
Kingston	33 000	$260 000
Regina	26 000	$200 000
Niagara Falls	37 000	$280 000

Even though the unit manufacturing cost in each of these plants is comparable, the unit shipping costs from the existing and the proposed plants to the retail outlets are not, and are given in Table 6-4.

Table 6-4 Per Unit Shipping Costs

Plant\Outlet	Winnipeg (1)	Toronto (2)	Ottawa (3)	Hamilton (4)
Windsor (1)	7	5	4.5	5.5
Montreal (2)	5	7	12	11
Brandon (3)	9	6.5	2	3.5
Kingston (4)	6	3.5	5	3
Regina (5)	8	6	2.5	4
Niagara Falls (6)	6.5	4.5	5	3

The objective of the Monson and Robinson Manufacturing Company is to minimize the total cost, which consists of shipping cost and the building/purchasing cost, such that demand at all retail outlets is satisfied. Determine the optimal shipping schedule that minimizes the total cost. Which locations should be used to build the new plants?

Solution

We will begin formulating this problem by defining the decision variables. There are two types of decision variables. The first type is the type we have utilized in formulating the transportation and transshipment problems in Chapter 5. The definitions associated with that type of variable and the transportation problem presented in Chapter 5 are given below:

Let x_{ij} = number of units shipped from source i to destination j
c_{ij} = cost of shipping one unit from source i to destination j
m = number of sources of supply
k = number of proposed sources of supply
n = number of destinations
S_i = supply available at source i
D_j = demand at destination j

The second type of decision variable is a 0–1 integer variable that will indicate whether a plant is constructed in location i. In other words

Let $y_i = 1$ if a plant is constructed in proposed plant location i
$y_i = 0$ if a plant is not constructed in proposed plant location i

In addition,

Let p_i = cost of constructing or purchasing plant i

The following is the general formulation of the facility location mixed-integer linear programming problem:

$$\text{minimize } Z = \sum_{i=1}^{m+k}\sum_{j=1}^{n} c_{ij}x_{ij} + \sum_{i=1}^{k} p_i y_i$$

subject to

$$\sum_{j=1}^{n} x_{ij} \le S_i \qquad i = 1, 2, \ldots, m$$

$$\sum_{j=1}^{n} x_{ij} \le S_i y_i \qquad i = 1, 2, \ldots, k$$

$$\sum_{i=1}^{m} x_{ij} = D_i \qquad j = 1, 2, \ldots, n$$

$x_{ij} \ge$ for all i and j
$y_i = 0$ or 1

Based on the above notation, the formulation for the Monson and Robinson Manufacturing Company problem is as follows:

$$\begin{aligned}\text{minimize } Z = {} & 7x_{11} + 5x_{12} + 4.5x_{13} + 5.5x_{14} + 5x_{21} + 7x_{22} + 12x_{23} + 11x_{24} + 9x_{31} + \\ & 6.5x_{32} + 2x_{33} + 3.5x_{34} + 6x_{41} + 3.5x_{42} + 5x_{43} + 3x_{44} + 8x_{51} + 6x_{52} + \\ & 2.5x_{53} + 4x_{54} + 6.5x_{61} + 4.5x_{62} + 5x_{63} + 3x_{64} + 220\,000y_1 + \\ & 260\,000y_2 + 200\,000y_3 + 280\,000y_4\end{aligned}$$

subject to

$$\begin{aligned}
x_{11} + x_{12} + x_{13} + x_{14} &\le 26\,000 && (1)\\
x_{21} + x_{22} + x_{23} + x_{24} &\le 30\,000 && (2)\\
x_{31} + x_{32} + x_{33} + x_{34} &\le 30\,000y_1 && (3)\\
x_{41} + x_{42} + x_{43} + x_{44} &\le 33\,000y_2 && (4)\\
x_{51} + x_{52} + x_{53} + x_{44} &\le 26\,000y_3 && (5)\\
x_{61} + x_{62} + x_{63} + x_{64} &\le 37\,000y_4 && (6)\\
x_{11} + x_{21} + x_{31} + x_{41} + x_{51} + x_{61} &= 27\,000 && (7)
\end{aligned}$$

$$x_{12} + x_{22} + x_{32} + x_{42} + x_{52} + x_{62} = 32\,000 \quad (8)$$
$$x_{13} + x_{23} + x_{33} + x_{43} + x_{53} + x_{63} = 23\,000 \quad (9)$$
$$x_{14} + x_{24} + x_{34} + x_{44} + x_{54} + x_{64} = 30\,000 \quad (10)$$
$$x_{ij} \geq \text{ for all } i \text{ and } j$$
$$y_i = 0 \text{ or } 1$$

In the above formulation, the value of $4.5x_{13}$ in the objective function shows that cost of shipping one unit from source 1 (Windsor) to destination 3 (Ottawa) is \$4.50. Note that 0–1 variables (y_i) are included in the objective function. For instance, 220 000y_1 indicates that if $y_1 = 1$, we will build or purchase a plant in Brandon, and the cost of building/purchasing that plant will be \$220 000. However, if the value of y_1 is zero, which means that we will not build/purchase a facility in Brandon, we will not incur the cost of \$220 000 because 220 000 will be multiplied by zero. Constraints 3, 4, 5, and 6 will only become operational if we decide to build a plant in the proposed location. For example, if we decide to build/purchase a plant in Brandon, the value of $y_1 = 1$ and the right-hand side of the inequality will be multiplied by 1, making Brandon's production facility operational. However, if we choose not to build/purchase a facility in Brandon, the value of $y_1 = 0$ and the right-hand side of the third constraint inequality will be multiplied by 0, making Brandon's production facility nonoperational.

The Excel solution and worksheet to this problem are not given to reduce redundancy of Excel worksheets within the chapter, but rather they are included on the OLC.

$x_{12} = 26\,000$ (number of units shipped from Windsor to Toronto)
$x_{21} = 27\,000$ (number of units shipped from Montreal to Winnipeg)
$x_{22} = 3000$ (number of units shipped from Montreal to Toronto)
$x_{34} = 30\,000$ (number of units shipped from Brandon to Hamilton)
$x_{52} = 3000$ (number of units shipped from Regina to Toronto)
$x_{53} = 23\,000$ (number of units shipped from Regina to Ottawa)
$y_1 = 1$ (build a production facility in Brandon)
$y_3 = 1$ (build a production facility in Regina)
$Z = \$886\,500$ (total minimum cost of shipping and building the new facilities)

Travelling Salesperson Problem

In solving the **travelling salesperson problem,** we try to minimize total cost, distance, or time of departing location *i* and returning to the same location *i* in a tour, visiting all locations once. The decision variable is a 0–1 variable and the value of the variable is equal to 1 if we travel from location *i* to location *j*. Otherwise the value of the decision variable is equal to zero. The integer programming formulation of the travelling salesperson problem is similar to the formulation of the transportation problem. However, complete formulation of the travelling salesperson problem is relatively complicated, but we can begin to provide a simplified formulation of this problem in its simplest form.

$$\text{minimize } Z = \sum_{i=1}^{n}\sum_{j=1}^{n} c_{ij}x_{ij}$$

subject to

$$\sum_{j=1}^{n} x_{ij} = 1 \qquad i = 1, 2, \ldots, n, i \neq j \qquad (6\text{-}1)$$

A tour (visiting each city once) must be formed and a tour must start in all cities.

$$\sum_{i=1}^{n} x_{ij} = 1 \qquad j = 1, 2, ..., n, i \neq j \qquad (6\text{-}2)$$

A tour (visiting each city once) must be formed and a tour must arrive at all cities.

$$x_{ij} = 0 \text{ or } 1$$

Let's add another subscript k, which represents the leg of the tour. The subscript k is added to assist in the formulation of the travelling salesperson problem. If there are four locations, then there are four legs of the trip. If node 1 is the home location, one possible routing scheme would involve going from node 1 to node 2 during the first leg, node 2 to node 3 during the second leg, node 3 to node 4 during the third leg, and node 4 to node 1 during the fourth and final leg. In other words, x_{ijk} stands for a trip from location i to location j in leg k. We also can specify the beginning and ending nodes. For example, the beginning node is node 1 on a four-node network, $i = 1$. The following set of constraints will guarantee that not only each node is visited only once, but the tour must start and end at node 1.

$$\sum_{j=2}^{n} x_{1j1} = 1 \qquad i \neq j \qquad (6\text{-}3)$$

The constraint given above ensures that the tour starts in node 1. This results in the following constraint for our four-node example:

$$x_{121} + x_{131} + x_{141} = 1 \qquad \text{(leg 1 visits are limited to 1)}$$

The constraint given below stipulates that the trip must end in node 1 in leg n.

$$\sum_{i=2}^{n} x_{i1n} = 1 \qquad i \neq j \qquad (6\text{-}4)$$

The constraint given above ensures that the tour ends at node 1 at leg n (the last leg of the tour). This results in the following constraint for our four-node example:

$$x_{214} + x_{314} + x_{414} = 1 \qquad \text{(leg 4 visits are limited to 1)}$$

The constraint given in Equations 6-1 and 6-2 can be revised as follows:

$$\sum_{i=2}^{n} \sum_{j=2}^{n} x_{ijk} = 1 \qquad \text{for } k = 2, \ldots, n-1; i \neq j \qquad (6\text{-}5)$$

The constraints given above in Equation 6-5 ensure that we visit each node once in the tour after the first leg. Note that summations start at node 2 in leg 2 and end in node $n - 1$ because travelling from node 1 is already specified in leg 1 in Equation 6-3 and travelling to node 1 in leg n is specified in Equation 6-4. For our four-node example, the constraint given in Equation 6-5 can be stated as follows:

$$x_{232} + x_{242} + x_{322} + x_{342} + x_{422} + x_{432} = 1 \qquad \text{(leg 2 visits are limited to 1)}$$
$$x_{233} + x_{243} + x_{323} + x_{343} + x_{423} + x_{433} = 1 \qquad \text{(leg 3 visits are limited to 1)}$$

$$\sum_{j=1}^{n} \sum_{k=2}^{n} x_{ijk} = 1 \qquad \text{for } i = 2, \ldots, n; i \neq j \qquad (6\text{-}6)$$

if $j = 1, k = n$ or if $k = n, j = 1$

The constraints specified in Equation 6-6 guarantee that there is exactly one departure from each of the nodes. For our four-node example, let's assume that $i = 2$. The constraint in Equation 6-6 would be written as follows:

$$x_{214} + x_{232} + x_{242} + x_{233} + x_{243} = 1 \quad \textbf{(visits from node 2 are limited to 1)}$$

$$\sum_{j=1}^{n} \sum_{k=1}^{n-1} x_{ijk} = 1 \qquad \text{for } j = 2, \ldots, n; i \neq j \qquad (6\text{-}7)$$

if $i = 1, k = 1$ or if $k = 1, i = 1$

The constraints specified in Equation 6-7 guarantee that there is exactly one arrival at each of the nodes. For our four-node example, let's assume that $j = 2$. The constraint in Equation 6-7 would be written as follows:

$$x_{121} + x_{322} + x_{422} + x_{323} + x_{423} = 1 \quad \textbf{(visits to node 2 are limited to 1)}$$

$$x_{1j1} = \sum_{k=2}^{n} x_{ijk} \qquad \text{for } j = 2, \ldots, n; j \neq k \qquad (6\text{-}8)$$

Equation 6-8 ensures that if leg 1 of the trip ends at location j, then leg 2 of the trip starts at location j. For our four-node example, if we assume that $j = 2$, the formula in Equation 6-8 can be written as follows: $x_{121} = x_{232} + x_{242}$.

$$\sum_{i=2}^{n} x_{ijk} = \sum_{l=2}^{n} x_{jm(k+1)} \qquad \text{for } j = 2, \ldots, n; k = 2, i \neq j, j \neq m \qquad (6\text{-}9)$$

Equation 6-9 ensures that if leg k of the trip ends at location j, then leg $k + 1$ of the trip starts at location j. For our four-node example, if we assume that $j = 2$ and $k = 2$, then the formula in Equation 6-9 can be written as follows: $x_{322} + x_{422} = x_{233} + x_{243}$

$$\sum_{k=2}^{n} x_{kj(n-1)} = x_{j1n} \qquad \text{for } j = 2, \ldots, n; j \neq m \qquad (6\text{-}10)$$

Equation 6-10 ensures that if leg $n - 1$ of the trip ends at location j, then the last leg of the trip starts at location j and ends at location 1 to complete the tour. For our four-node example, if we assume that $j = 2$, the formula in Equation 6-10 can be written as follows: $x_{323} + x_{423} = x_{214}$

The constraints 6-8, 6-9, and 6-10 are prepared to prevent subtours from occurring. A subtour is a premature return to the initial city in the tour. For example, in an eight-city problem, if we do not include the constraints 6-8, 6-9, and 6-10, it is possible that two subtours may form. The first subtour may consist of the following sequence of cities: 1–4–3–5–1. The second subtour may consist of the remaining cities in the following sequence: 2–7–6–8–2. The constraints 6-8, 6-9, and 6-10 will prevent these subtours from occurring and force the solution to include only one tour, starting at the home city and ending at the home city while visiting each city once. The travelling salesperson problem has numerous applications in the business world ranging from scheduling vehicles and truck routing to production scheduling.

We have two versions of the travelling salesperson problem. The first version assumes that the travel time from location A to location B is the same as the travel time from location B to location A. This version is referred to as a symmetric travelling salesperson problem. In the second version, travel time from location A to location B is not the same as the travel time from location B to location A. This version is referred to as an asymmetric travelling salesperson problem. Solving the travelling salesperson problem can be extremely computationally burdensome. In the symmetric version, there are $(n - 1)!$ possible routes to consider, where n = number of decision variables. For example if we solve an 11-location travelling salesperson problem, $n = 11$ and there are 10! possible routes (10! = 3 628 800). Of course, if we add one more location, 11! = 39 916 800. In other words, just by adding one more location, the number of possible solutions increases by 36 288 000. Because of the extreme computational burden, using integer linear programming to solve a travelling salesperson problem is not a viable option. There are a number of heuristics developed to deal with the computational burden of the travelling salesperson problem. A simple heuristic is the **nearest-neighbour rule,** where a tour is started at a particular location and we simply go to the nearest location from that location. From there, we go to the nearest location that has not yet been visited. We continue in this fashion until all the locations are visited. However, even though we can reach a solution relatively fast, solution quality of the nearest-neighbour method leaves a lot to be desired.

The Modern Management Application, "Waste Management," provides a business implementation of vehicle routing problems, a special case of a travelling salesperson problem.

Let's consider the following example to demonstrate the formulation of a travelling salesperson problem.

EXAMPLE 6-7

The City of Saskatoon garbage collection team wants to determine the best route for their garbage trucks. There are four sections of the city under consideration. The time of travel (in minutes) between the various sections of the city is given in Table 6-5.

Table 6-5 Travel Time (in minutes) Between Locations

From\To	1	2	3	4
1	0	8	6	5
2	8	0	3	7
3	6	3	0	9
4	5	7	9	0

a. If location 1 is the garage from which garbage trucks leave and to which they return, formulate this problem as a travelling salesperson problem.
b. Solve this problem using Excel.

Solution

The objective function can be stated as follows:

$$\text{minimize } Z = 8x_{121} + 6x_{131} + 5x_{141} + 8x_{214} + 6x_{314} + 5x_{414} + 3x_{232} + 3x_{233} + 7x_{242} + 7x_{243} + 9x_{342} + 9x_{343} + 7x_{422} + 7x_{423} + 9x_{432} + 9x_{433} + 3x_{322} + 3x_{323}$$

subject to

$x_{121} + x_{131} + x_{141} = 1$ (starting node is node 1)
$x_{214} + x_{314} + x_{414} = 1$ (ending node is node 1)

$$x_{232} + x_{242} + x_{342} + x_{422} + x_{322} + x_{432} = 1 \quad \text{(leg 2 visits limited to 1)}$$
$$x_{233} + x_{243} + x_{343} + x_{423} + x_{323} + x_{433} = 1 \quad \text{(leg 3 visits limited to 1)}$$

$$\left.\begin{aligned} x_{214} + x_{232} + x_{242} + x_{233} + x_{243} &= 1 \\ x_{314} + x_{322} + x_{323} + x_{342} + x_{343} &= 1 \\ x_{414} + x_{422} + x_{432} + x_{423} + x_{433} &= 1 \end{aligned}\right\} \text{(visits from nodes 2, 3, and 4 are limited to 1)}$$

$$\left.\begin{aligned} x_{121} + x_{322} + x_{422} + x_{323} + x_{423} &= 1 \\ x_{131} + x_{232} + x_{233} + x_{432} + x_{433} &= 1 \\ x_{141} + x_{242} + x_{243} + x_{342} + x_{343} &= 1 \end{aligned}\right\} \text{(visits to nodes 2, 3, and 4 are limited to 1)}$$

$$\left.\begin{aligned} x_{121} &= x_{232} + x_{242} \\ x_{131} &= x_{322} + x_{342} \\ x_{141} &= x_{422} + x_{432} \end{aligned}\right\} \text{(leg 1 of the tour ends and leg 2 of the tour starts where leg 1 of the tour ends)}$$

$$\left.\begin{aligned} x_{322} + x_{422} &= x_{233} + x_{243} \\ x_{232} + x_{432} &= x_{323} + x_{343} \\ x_{242} + x_{342} &= x_{423} + x_{433} \end{aligned}\right\}$$
(if leg 2 of the trip ends at location 2, 3, or 4, leg 3 of the trip must start at node 2, 3, or 4, respectively; the first equation is for node 2, the second equation is for node 3, and the third equation is for node 4)

$$\left.\begin{aligned} x_{323} + x_{423} &= x_{214} \\ x_{233} + x_{433} &= x_{314} \\ x_{243} + x_{343} &= x_{414} \end{aligned}\right\} \text{(last leg of the trip must end at location 1)}$$

All $x_{ijk} = 0$ or 1

There are two optimal solutions.

1. $x_{141} = 1, x_{422} = 1, x_{233} = 1, x_{314} = 1, z = 21$ minutes
   An optimal sequence is 1–4–2–3–1 or
2. $x_{131} = 1, x_{322} = 1, x_{243} = 1, x_{414} = 1, z = 21$ minutes
   An optimal sequence is 1–3–2–4–1

Solving a Travelling Salesperson Problem Using Excel

Although it is cumbersome, the travelling salesperson problem can be solved using Excel. Exhibit 6-8 shows the worksheet for the travelling salesperson problem of Example 6-7. In row 2 of the worksheet, all of the decision variables are defined. In row 3 the appropriate distances are specified. Row 4 displays the values associated with all of the decision variables. Row 5 is simply the multiplication of row 3 (distances) and row 4 (value of the decision variable, either zero or one). We are trying to minimize the value of cell T5 subject to all of the constraints listed in rows 7 through 25. Column T represents the left-hand side of the constraints, and column U represents the right-hand side of the constraints.

6.8 DIFFICULTIES IN SOLVING INTEGER PROGRAMMING PROBLEMS

From our previous discussion of integer programming problems and linear programming problems, the integer programming problems may seem easy to solve. As was discussed in earlier chapters, the simplex method is very efficient in solving linear programming problems

EXHIBIT 6-8 Excel Worksheet for Example 6-7 (Travelling Salesperson Problem)

Exhibit 6-8 [Compatibility Mode] - Microsoft Excel

T5 f_x =SUM(B5:S5)

	A	B	C	D	E	F	G	H	I	J	K	L	M	N	O	P	Q	R	S	T	U
1	Elmhurst Garbage Collection Travelling Salesman Problem																				
2		x121	x131	x141	x214	x314	x414	x232	x233	x242	x243	x342	x343	x422	x423	x432	x433	x322	x323		
3	Travel Time	8	6	5	8	6	5	3	3	7	7	9	9	7	7	9	9	3	3		
4	Route Travelled	0	0	1	0	1	0	0	1	0	0	0	0	1	0	0	0	0	0	Total	
5	Travel Time	0	0	5	0	6	0	0	3	0	0	0	0	7	0	0	0	0	0	21	
6		x121	x131	x141	x214	x314	x414	x232	x233	x242	x243	x342	x343	x422	x423	x432	x433	x322	x323	Usage	Limits
7	Starting Node 1	1	1	1																1	1
8	Ending Node 1				1	1	1													1	1
9	Leg 2 visits limit = 1							1		1		1		1		1		1		1	1
10	Leg 3 visits limit = 1								1		1		1		1		1		1	1	1
11	Visits from Node 2 limit = 1				1			1	1	1	1									1	1
12	Visits from Node 3 limit = 1					1						1	1					1	1	1	1
13	Visits from Node 4 limit = 1						1							1	1	1	1			1	1
14	Visits to Node 2 limited to 1	1												1	1			1	1	1	1
15	Visits to Node 3 limited to 1		1					1	1							1	1			1	1
16	Visits to Node 4 limited to 1			1						1	1	1	1							1	1
17	End of Leg 1 = Start of Leg 2	1						-1		-1										0	0
18	End of Leg 1 = Start of Leg 2		1									-1						-1		0	0
19	End of Leg 1 = Start of Leg 2			1										-1		-1				0	0
20	End of Leg 2 = Start of Leg 3								-1		-1			1				1		0	0
21	End of Leg 2 = Start of Leg 3							1					-1			1			-1	0	0
22	End of Leg 2 = Start of Leg 3									1		1			-1		-1			0	0
23	Last Leg ends at Location 1				-1										1				1	0	0
24	Last Leg ends at Location 1					-1			1								1			0	0
25	Last Leg ends at Location 1						-1				1		1							0	0
26																					

Exhibit 6-8

Ready

Cell	Copied to	Formula
B5	C5 : S5	= B3 ∗ B4
T5		= SUM (B5 : S5)
T7	T8 : T25	= SUMPRODUCT ($B$4 : $S$4, B7 : S7)

because we have relatively few extreme points to consider. In solving integer programming problems, we consider a finite number of integer solutions. We consider more feasible points in solving an integer linear programming problem compared to solving linear programming problems using the simplex method. However, while we consider a finite number of feasible solutions to an integer programming problem, as the number of variables increases, the numbers of possible solutions increase at an exponential rate. For instance, in solving 0–1 integer programming problems, if the number of decision variables is equal to n, we need to consider 2^n solutions. For a small-size problem with $n = 10$, there are $2^{10} = 1024$ possible solutions. However, if $n = 20$, there are $2^{20} = 1\,048\,576$ solutions. Even with the advances in computer technology and the increasing speed of computer processing, the complete enumeration of all possible solutions is problematic for large 0–1 integer

A MODERN MANAGEMENT SCIENCE APPLICATION: GENERAL MOTORS

General Motors (GM) designs and develops vehicles that meet corporate engineering standards and government regulations. To achieve attractive designs that meet the standards and regulations, GM tests samples of its completed vehicles under a wide range of conditions. One of the tests involving cold weather is done at the GM Cold Weather Development Center in Kapuskasing, Ontario. Vehicles that perform well in Kapuskasing will perform well anywhere since Kapuskasing is the coldest available environment available for testing. Testing takes place from November though April in the coldest temperatures Kapuskasing has to offer. During the testing season, the facility performs full vehicle road (durability) tests. Vehicles are evaluated over different distances as well as different road conditions, and data are collected about oil pressure, coolant temperatures, and battery condition. Engineers use this information to identify and resolve design issues. Since the testing season is limited and the severity of winter weather varies, it is important to maximize and even improve "throughput" (the number of vehicles tested) in this system.

The GM management at the facility schedules and executes all vehicle tests. Since the daily temperature determines what tests are possible, the staff develops a master testing schedule each day. In preparing the master schedule, variables the schedulers consider include vehicle test limits, soaking requirements, grouping policies, and driver break policies. Vehicle test limits are such that the facility can perform a maximum of three tests on any single vehicle per day. "Soaking requirements" is the time that a vehicle must be inactive for cooling off between tests. Vehicle grouping policy involves testing a group of vehicles together. Driver break policies means that the drivers must be provided with two short breaks and a lunch break per shift. The objective in scheduling is to take all these variables and constraints into account and then maximize the overall efficiency. This turns out to be a special case of the resource constrained project scheduling problem (RCPSP). GM developed a multipass heuristic and a decision support tool to implement the heuristic. The decision support tool consisted of a front-end-user interface and the scheduling module.

As a result of implementing this new scheduling approach, which involves an integer programming model, GM realized reduction in operation risk, improvement in throughput, a reduction in warranty costs, and improvement in employee relationships. GM significantly reduced the time required to generate the master schedule. The company was able improve information accuracy by 192 percent and reduced waste test mileage by 96 percent. The improved scheduling resulted in 129 percent improvement in the total vehicle completion rate (percentage of vehicles that complete the required testing during the winter season). GM also realized 25 percent improvement in total test completion rate. It is estimated that the company saved millions of dollars in warranty costs as a result of timely correction of design issues revealed through the testing. The successful implementation of this system also helped worker–management relations as employee enthusiasm improved by 23 percent (as measured by employee surveys). In implementing this system, it is important to point out that there was significant support from GM top management, which helped to successfully execute the system.

Source: Reprinted by permission, C. Hsu, Y. de Blois, and M. Pyle, "General Motors Optimizes Its Scheduling of Cold-Weather Tests," *Interfaces* Vol. 34, no. 5 (September–October 2004), pp. 334–41. Copyright (2004), the Institute for Operations Research and the Managements Science (INFORMS), 7240 Parkway Drive, Suite 310, Hanover, MD 21076 USA.

programming problems. Of course, the difficulty is compounded when we solve pure-integer programming problems that can take on any integer value as opposed to being restricted to the values of 0 and 1.

The second problem stems from the fact that integer linear programming problems do not have one set of extreme points to visit. For instance, if we use the branch and bound method (see Chapter 17 on the OLC), we need to visit a set of extreme points at each node. The set of extreme points visited at node 1 is different than the set of extreme points visited at node 2. Because of this characteristic, the computational requirements and solution of a linear programming problem are much easier than solving integer linear programming problems. Therefore the basic Excel Solver is suitable only for problems with a small number of integer variables. Larger-sized problems may be handled by other general-purpose computer packages, such as Frontline Systems' Premium Solver Platform (www.solver.com/about.htm) or CPLEX, offered by ILOG, Inc (www.ilog.com/products/cplex/).

Summary

Problems that lend themselves to a linear programming formulation are frequently encountered in practice. In many instances, some or all of the decision variables may also be required to be integer. In such cases, the goal is to identify the best solution that will meet the integer requirements. In general, the simplex method cannot be used to directly obtain integer solutions. Instead, an intelligent search procedure usually must be employed to identify an optimal solution. This involves the use of the branch and bound method. The branch and bound method creates subproblems to be solved. The subproblems are solved by successive application of the simplex method until an optimal solution is found.

An important class of integer programming problems involves situations in which decision variables can take on values of only 0 to 1, often synonymous with yes-no decisions. Large 0–1 integer programming problems are solved using the branch and bound method and small 0–1 integer programming problems can be solved using enumeration. The manual solution of the branch and bound and the enumeration methods are illustrated in Chapter 17 on the OLC. The formulations of the 0–1 problems that involve either-or alternatives, *k*-Out-of-*n* alternatives, if-then alternatives are discussed and the formulation of the constraints for each situation is provided.

Using 0–1 integer programming, we can solve many specialized problems. These include: fixed charge problems, set covering problems, knapsack problems, facility location problems, travelling salesperson problems, as well as others. We utilize examples to illustrate the formulation of the aforementioned problems. The Modern Management Application, "General Motors," provides another example of a successfully use of integer programming. However, the difficulty is not in the formulation of the model, but in finding an efficient solution to the model. Even with fast computers available today, many large-size integer programming problems are difficult to solve by integer programming methods such as branch and bound. We hope that continued research would provide faster solution methods to solve integer programming problems.

Glossary

Facility Location Problem This mixed-integer programming problem involves providing service to multiple market areas by deciding on multiple facility locations. Demand is known at various markets and transportation costs are known from potential facilities to destinations. The location variable is a 0–1 variable. The value of the location variable is 1 if a certain location is selected, 0 if the location is not utilized.

Fixed-Charge Problem A 0–1 mixed-integer programming problem that involves fixed costs (0–1 variable) if a certain activity is undertaken as well as a variable cost.

Knapsack Problem This problem is defined as how many units of each different kind of item or product to put in a knapsack with a given capacity to maximize profit.

Mixed-Integer Problem A problem that requires that some, but not all, decision variables will have integer or binary values.

Nearest-Neighbour Rule A method of the travelling salesperson problem where a tour is started at a particular location and then goes to the nearest location. It then goes to the nearest location not yet visited, continuing until all locations have been visited.

Pure-Integer Problem An integer programming problem requiring that all decision variables have integer values.
Set Covering Problem It involves a number of nodes and a number of areas, where nodes provide coverage to the areas. This problem involves deciding which nodes should be used to provide coverage to all areas with minimum cost or time requirements.
Travelling Salesperson Problem In solving this problem, we try to minimize total cost, distance, or time of departing location i and returning to the same location i in a tour, visiting all locations once. The decision variable is a 0–1 variable and the value of the variable is equal to 1 if we travel from location i to location j, and zero otherwise.
Zero–One (0–1) Integer Programming Problem An integer programming problem requiring that all decision variables have a value of either zero (0) or one (1).

Solved Problems

Problem 1

PPRS Construction Company has an opportunity to build five shopping malls during the next year. The expected net profit and expected cost for each of the shopping malls are shown in Table 6-6.

Table 6-6 The Expected Net Profit and Expected Net Cost

Shopping Mall	Expected Net Profit ($000)	Expected Cost ($000)
1	200	150
2	150	90
3	140	50
4	125	80
5	180	100

The company has budgeted $300 000 for the construction of shopping malls during the next year. Also, due to various legal restrictions and marketing considerations, the following relationships among the projects must be met.

1. Exactly one of three shopping malls 1, 2, or 5 must be constructed.
2. At most one of the two shopping malls 1 or 4 may be constructed.
3. If shopping mall 5 is constructed, then shopping mall 4 must also be constructed.

a. Formulate this problem as an integer programming model and use Excel to determine the best set of shopping malls that PPRS Construction Company should build to maximize total net profit.
b. Assume that the top management for PPRS Construction Company has cut the budget for the shopping mall construction project to $225 000. Show the change in the formulation and use Excel to determine the best set of shopping malls that PPRS Construction Company should build to maximize total net profit.

Solution

a. Let $x_i = 1$ if shopping mall i is selected
$x_i = 0$ if shopping mall i is not selected

maximize $Z = 200x_1 + 150x_2 + 140x_3 + 125x_4 + 180x_5$

subject to

$150x_1 + 90x_2 + 50x_3 + 80x_4 + 100x_5 \leq 300$ (1) (budget constraint)
$x_1 + x_2 + x_5 = 1$ (2)
$x_1 + x_4 \leq 1$ (3)
$x_4 \geq x_5$ or $x_4 - x_5 \geq 0$ (4)
$x_i = 0$ or 1 (5)

The Excel solution to this problem is depicted in Exhibit 6-9. The company should invest in malls 3, 4, and 5 for a total net profit of $445 000.

b. Let $x_i = 1$ if shopping mall i is selected
$x_i = 0$ if shopping mall i is not selected

maximize $Z = 200x_1 + 150x_2 + 140x_3 + 125x_4 + 180x_5$

subject to

$150x_1 + 90x_2 + 50x_3 + 80x_4 + 100x_5 \leq 225$ (1) (budget constraint)
$x_1 + x_2 + x_5 = 1$ (2)
$x_1 + x_4 \leq 1$ (3)
$x_4 \geq x_5$ or $x_4 - x_5 \geq 0$ (4)
$x_i = 0$ or 1 (5)

After updating the problem by changing the right-hand side of the budget constraint, we obtain the following result, displayed in Exhibit 6-10. The company should invest in malls 2, 3, and 4 for a total net profit of $415 000.

EXHIBIT 6-9 Excel Worksheet for Solved Problem 1, Part *a* (Shopping Mall Problem)

Exhibit 6-9 [Compatibility Mode] - Microsoft Excel

	A	B	C	D	E	F	G	H	I
1	Variables	X_1	X_2	X_3	X_4	X_5	Shopping Mall Problem		
2		0	0	1	1	1			
3		X_1	X_2	X_3	X_4	X_5			
4	Objective Function	200	150	140	125	180	445		
5	Constraints						Used	Available	Leftover
6	Budget	150	90	50	80	100	230	300	70
7	One Mall of 1, 2, 5	1	1			1	1	1	0
8	At Most One of 1 & 4	1			1		1	1	0
9	If 4 then 5				1	-1	0	0	0

Cell	Copied to	Formula
G4		= SUMPRODUCT (B4 : F4, B2 : F2)
G6	G7 : G9	= SUMPRODUCT ($B$2 : $F$2, B6 : F6)
I6	I7 : I9	= H6 − G6

EXHIBIT 6-10 Excel Worksheet for Solved Problem 1, Part *b* (Shopping Mall Problem)

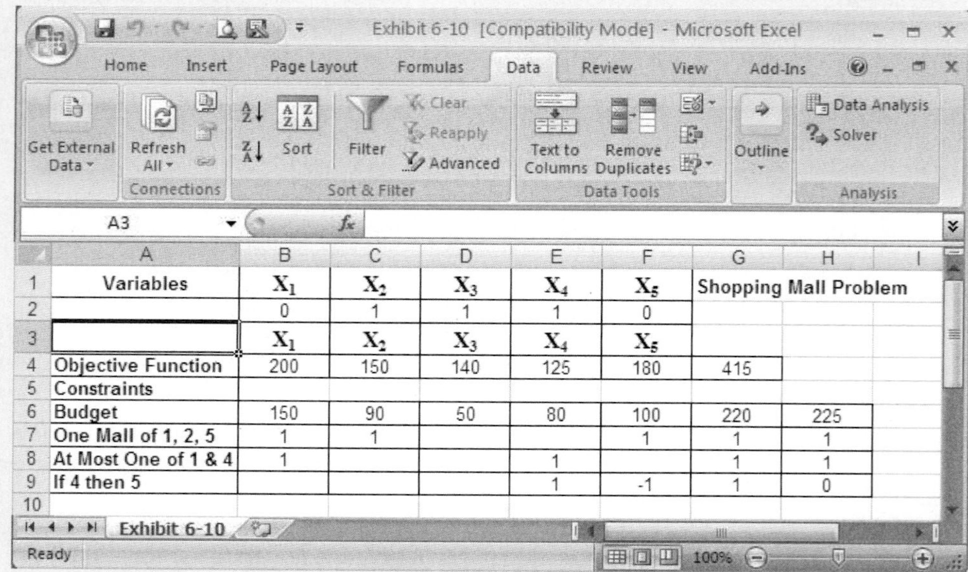

Exhibit 6-10 [Compatibility Mode] - Microsoft Excel

	A	B	C	D	E	F	G	H
1	Variables	X_1	X_2	X_3	X_4	X_5	Shopping Mall Problem	
2		0	1	1	1	0		
3		X_1	X_2	X_3	X_4	X_5		
4	Objective Function	200	150	140	125	180	415	
5	Constraints							
6	Budget	150	90	50	80	100	220	225
7	One Mall of 1, 2, 5	1	1			1	1	1
8	At Most One of 1 & 4	1			1		1	1
9	If 4 then 5				1	-1	1	0

Problem 2

A cargo plane is contracted to transport heavy machinery from Toronto to Los Angeles. The plane has a cargo capacity of 8.5 tonnes. The company that contracted this cargo plane wants to transport four types of machinery. The weights and values of the four types of machinery are given in Table 6-7.

Table 6-7 Weights and Profit Values of Machines

Machine Type	Weight	Value ($1000s)
A	2	65
B	3	90
C	1.5	40
D	1	28

a. Formulate the above problem as an integer programming problem. The cargo company wants to determine how many of each machine to ship on the cargo plane to maximize the total value of the products shipped.

b. Use Excel and solve the above problem to determine how many of each machine to ship on the cargo plane from Toronto to Los Angeles.

Solution

a. Let x_i = number of machine i shipped

$$\text{maximize } Z = 65x_1 + 90x_2 + 40x_3 + 28x_4$$

subject to

$$2x_1 + 3x_2 + 1.5x_3 + 1x_4 \leq 8.5 \quad (1)$$
$$x_i \geq 0 \text{ and integer} \quad (2)$$

b. The Excel solution to this problem is shown in Exhibit 6-11. The most profitable option for the company is to ship three units of machine 1, one unit of machine 3, and one unit of machine 4, for a total profit of $263 000.

EXHIBIT 6-11 Excel Worksheet for Solved Problem 2 (Cargo Plane Problem)

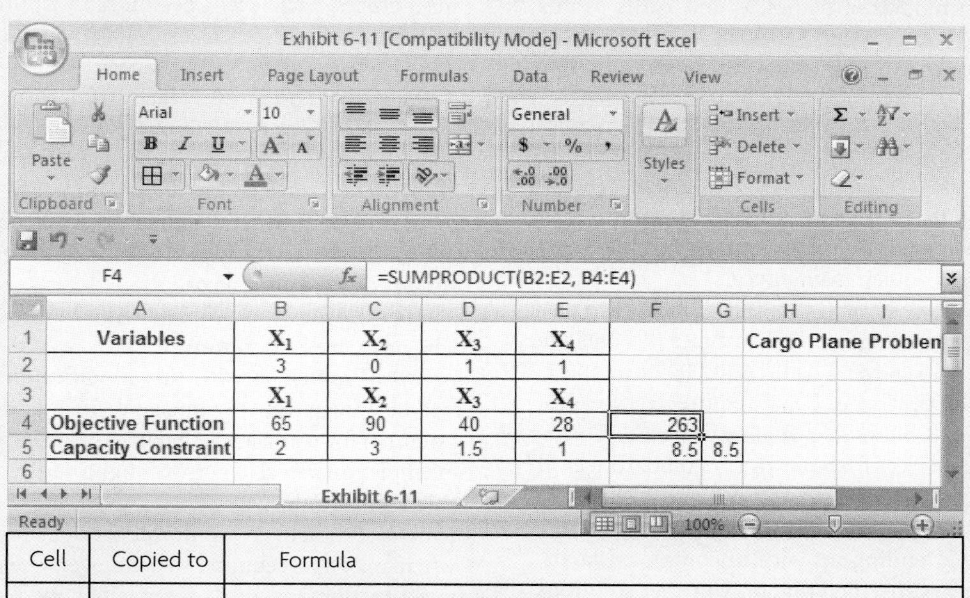

Cell	Copied to	Formula
F4		= SUMPRODUCT (B2 : E2, B4 : E4)
F5		= SUMPRODUCT (B2 : E2, B5 : E5)

Discussion and Review Questions

1. Discuss the computational difficulties associated with solving integer linear programming problems.
2. Explain why it is computationally easier to solve linear programming problems as compared to integer linear programming problems.
3. Explain the difference between pure-integer programming, mixed-integer programming, and 0–1 integer programming problems.
4. Describe why a facility location problem is formulated as a mixed-integer programming problem. What are the continuous variables and what are the 0–1 integer variables?
5. What assumption of linear programming has to be violated for being prompted to solve a problem using integer programming? Explain.
6. If a problem requires an integer solution, under what circumstances is it appropriate to use a linear programming problem instead of integer programming? Under what circumstances is it required that we use integer programming?
7. Explain the difficulties involved in solving large travelling salesperson problems.
8. Why is it difficult to perform sensitivity analysis when we use integer programming?
9. Describe an example of a set covering problem.
10. Define a knapsack problem and describe an example of a knapsack problem.
11. Explain the difficulties involved in solving large integer programming problems.

Problems

1. A manufacturer of executive jet aircraft is concerned with its profit picture over the short run. It produces two different models of planes, x_1 and x_2. Its profits are \$30 000 for each x_1 and \$20 000 for each x_2. There are two major constraints on production:

   Labour $4x_1 + 2x_2 \leq 17$ weeks
   Materials $5x_1 + 4x_2 \leq 21$ tonnes
   $x_1, x_2 \geq 0$ and integer

   Also, assume that no more than 4 x_2's can be produced due to a prior union agreement.

   Solve this problem using Excel.
2. A producer of pleasure boats wants to maximize revenue during the next month. Two types of boats are sold, x_1 and x_2. Type x_1 sells for \$40 000 and type x_2 sells for \$30 000. The x_1 boats require 10 weeks of labour and 600 board feet of lumber each. The x_2 boats need 3 weeks of labour and 1000 board feet of lumber. There are 30 weeks of labour and 3000 board feet of lumber available this season. Because of the desire to avoid ending up with uncompleted boats, the manager has specified that only integer solutions will be accepted. Use Excel to obtain the optimal solution.
3. A janitorial service, Mother's Helpers, provides workers to clean office buildings during late evening hours using workers with two skill levels, 1 and 2. Each level 1 person is paid \$12 per hour and each level 2 person is paid \$8 per hour. The workers wash floors and vacuum offices. Each level 1 person can vacuum 9 offices per hour, whereas each level 2 person can vacuum only 2 offices per hour. Each level 1 person can wash 2 floors per hour and each level 2 person can wash 3 floors per hour. To complete a new job in the allotted time, 18 offices must be vacuumed per hour and 12 floors must be washed per hour. Use Excel and determine the number of each type of person that will be needed to complete the job within the allotted time and at minimum cost.
4. Answer the previous problem with this modification: The objective is to minimize $5x_1 + 7x_2$.
5. Answer Problem 4 with this modification: x_1 need not be integer, but x_2 must be. This is due to the potential for using level 1 people on a nearby job. For example, one level 1 person might be used for one-third time on this job.
6. Answer Problem 3 (janitorial service) for the case where only x_1 is required to be integer. Use the objective function $6x_1 + 4x_2$. Explain how x_2 could be noninteger.
7. Solve the following 0–1 problem for the optimal integer solution using Excel.

   maximize $Z = 70x_1 + 40x_2 + 60x_3 + 80x_4$

subject to

$$5x_1 + 6x_2 + 8x_3 + 10x_4 \leq 20$$
$$4x_1 + 2x_2 + 2x_3 + 5x_4 \leq 6$$

All variables 0 or 1

8. All Electronics Manufacturer produces a toy robot that suddenly is in great demand. The firm can produce three versions of the robot. One version yields a contribution to profit of $22 per unit; the second, a contribution to profit of $18 per unit; and the third, a contribution to profit of $25 per unit. The firm can produce and sell any of the versions, subject to these limitations for each hour: 40 pounds of raw material are available, four assembly workers are available, and there are two inspectors who work exclusively on this plus another who works 40 percent of the time on this. Each version 1 robot requires 4 pounds of raw material, 12 minutes for assembly, and 12 minutes for inspection; whereas each version 2 requires 8 pounds of raw material, 24 minutes for assembly, and 6 minutes of inspection; and each version 3 requires 3 pounds of raw material, 18 minutes for assembly, and 12 minutes for inspection. Assuming that only integer values will be acceptable because the robots are packaged and shipped hourly, use Excel and determine the quantity of each type that will maximize total hourly contribution to profits.
9. A direct marketing manager wants to select prototypes of letters to send out to the company's customers. There are four prototypes to choose from. In previous trials, type 1 had a response rate of 30 percent, type 2 a response rate of 25 percent, type 3 a response rate of 35 percent, and type 4 a response rate of 40 percent. No more than three types will be chosen, however, due to other considerations. Type 1 will mean a cost of $6000, type 2 a cost of $4000, type 3 a cost of $5000, and type 4 a cost of $7000. The manager has $18 000 to spend. If the goal is to maximize total responses, which version of the letter should be sent out? Use Excel to determine the optimal solution.
10. A franchise operation that sells frozen custard intends to open one or more new stores in a medium-sized metropolitan area. Three sites are under consideration. Each site has a somewhat different projected profit contribution and different supervision requirements. The first site has an estimated daily profit of $200 and a weekly supervision requirement of 48 hours; the second site has a projected profit of $100 per day a weekly supervision requirement of 30 hours; and the third site has a projected profit of $150 per day and a weekly supervision requirement of 20 hours. The firm will have 65 hours available per week for supervision. Use Excel to determine which site or sites should be selected to obtain the highest projected daily profit. What projected daily profit will your solution produce?
11. A vice president of finance of a bank holding company recently faced this problem. Proposals for four projects were submitted to her. Project A had an estimated total return to the company of $210 000, project B had an estimated return of $180 000, project C a return of $160 000, and project D a return of $175 000. In weighing these proposals, the vice president had to take into account the cash requirements of the projects and the available cash for the time periods involved. This information is summarized below.

	Cash Needs			
Project	Period 1	Period 2	Period 3	Period 4
A	$8000	$8000	$10 000	$10 000
B	7000	9000	9000	11 000
C	5000	7000	9000	11 000
D	9000	8000	7000	6000

Cash availability is $22 000 for period 1, $25 000 for period 2, $38 000 for period 3, and $30 000 for period 4. Using Excel, determine which projects to fund and the amount of cash that will be needed per period to maximize the total estimated return.
12. The operations manager of a power company must design a set of crew assignments for cleanup duties after a severe windstorm, which knocked out power in various spots throughout the county. At least 40 workers and 20 supervisors must be assigned. The operations manager is particularly determined to minimize the cost of operating the trucks assigned for cleanup. Three types of trucks are suitable: type 1, with an hourly operating cost of $60; type 2, with an hourly operating cost of $30; and type 3, with an hourly operating cost of $80. The type 1 trucks have a crew of two workers and one supervisor; the type 2 trucks have one worker and two supervisors; and the type 3 trucks have four workers and one supervisor. Use Excel and determine the number of each truck type that should be used to both minimize the total hourly operating cost and satisfy the worker and supervisor requirements. Assume only integer solutions are acceptable. Also, determine the total cost of your solution.

13. East Jet Airlines is planning to expand its fleet of aircraft. Four different models are under consideration: A, B, C, and D. The estimated annual contribution to profits of these models is \$4.5 million, \$6 million, \$6.5 million, and \$5 million respectively. Two important factors that must be taken into account are the fuel requirements and the maintenance requirements for each model. The monthly fuel requirements (in thousands of gallons) are 18, 25, 28, and 20, respectively, and the monthly maintenance requirements (in hours) are 20, 18, 28, and 30, respectively. Fuel availability will be 710 000 gallons per month and maintenance capacity is 900 worker-hours per month. Use Excel and determine the number of aircraft of each model that the company should purchase if its goal is to achieve the greatest contribution to annual profits. Assume that only integer solutions are acceptable.
14. An investor must decide how to invest \$70 000. After considerable research, the investor has narrowed the investment alternatives to four possibilities: Invest \$25 000 in a real estate plan, invest \$20 000 in a new product, invest \$30 000 in a certificate of deposit, and invest \$35 000 in a certain stock. The first three investments, if selected, must be in the exact amounts listed, although the last can be in any amount up to \$35 000. The expected returns for each dollar invested are \$0.30 for the real estate, \$0.20 for the new product, \$0.40 for the CD, and \$2.50 for the stock. Assume that stock amounts must be in multiples of \$7000. Solve for the optimum solution using Excel.
15. Solve the following problem using Excel:

maximize $Z = 5x_1 + 8x_2 + 4x_3$

subject to

1 $\quad 1.5x_1 + 2x_2 + 1.6x_3 \leq 10$

2 $\quad 25x_1 + 50x_2 + 20x_3 \leq 160$

$x_1, x_2,$ and $x_3 \geq 0$ and integer

16. The Rubber Blanket Company has recently undergone a reorganization. It must now decide on quantity levels for these products: x_1, x_2, and x_3. Their respective contributions to profits are estimated to be \$10, \$15, and \$18 per unit, in thousands. The products are subject to the following constraints:

$$4x_1 + 6x_2 + 3x_3 \leq 70$$
$$90x_1 + 80x_2 + 100x_3 \leq 1200$$

The variables (quantities of x_1, x_2, and x_3) do not need to be integer. In addition, there is a one-time cost associated with the production of each product. For x_1 the cost would be \$3000, for x_2 the cost would be \$4000, and for x_3 the cost would be \$6000.
   a. Formulate the problem.
   b. Use Excel and determine the optimal values for the decision variables and the maximum profit.
17. Manager Cheryl Carver is faced with this problem: A product can be made on either one of two machines: x_1 or x_2. However, the machines have different processing requirements and different profit and cost structures. These differences are summarized in the following table:

Machine	Profit per Unit	Setup Cost	Raw Material #1 per unit	Raw Material #2 per unit
x_1	\$50	\$250	2 pounds	4 quarts
x_2	40	210	3 pounds	2 quarts

Cheryl wants to determine whether all of the output should be produced on one of the machines (if so, which machine) or whether the output should be split between these two machines. The goal is to maximize the contribution to profit. Thirty pounds of raw material #1 and thirty-six quarts of raw material #2 will be available for this production run.
   a. Set up (formulate) her problem in a format suitable for integer programming.
   b. Assuming that an integer solution is required, determine the optimal solution to Cheryl's problem.
18. (Refer to Problem 17.) Treat the unit profits in the previous problem as unit costs. In addition, suppose that the firm has an order for 10 units of the product.
   a. Formulate this problem in an integer programming format.
   b. Use Excel and solve for the optimal integer solution. Interpret your answer.
19. The product manager at a trust company must have a large mailing printed and sent out to customers. A previous mailing was delayed due to a problem at the printer's shop, and the product manager wants to reduce that risk by giving no more than 3/4 of the job to one printer. The total job will consist of 400 pieces. The product manager has obtained cost quotations from the four local shops that she feels can handle the job and meet quality specifications. This information is summarized in the following table:

Printer	Cost per Piece	Base Fee
A	$0.50	$300
B	0.40	350
C	0.45	380
D	0.47	320

Assume that the goal is to minimize the total cost of printing the mailing pieces. Use Excel and determine the integer solution that will yield the lowest possible total cost.

20. The new manager of a plastics division must make a decision on shipping containers that will be used to ship products by truck. The main issue is to decide how many of each type container to use. Three types are available: A, B, and C. Type A has a loaded weight of 60 pounds and a volume of 16 cubic feet, type B has a weight of 64 pounds and a volume of 20 cubic feet, and type C has a weight of 48 pounds and a volume of 14 cubic feet. Each truck has a volume of 1200 cubic feet and a weight limit of 2000 pounds. The containers have profit contributions of $200 for each A, $220 for each B, and $240 for each C. Use Excel and determine how many of each container should be allocated per truck to maximize the total contribution to profit.

21. The owner of a new Edmonton-based cab company wants to determine locations for cab waiting points. He has gathered the following information:

Location	Can Serve Areas	Cost per Day
1	A, E	$400
2	A, C, D	500
3	B, C, E	450
4	B, D	440
5	D, E	430

The owner wants to be sure that all areas can be served, yet he wants this done for as little cost as possible. Use Excel and determine the choice of locations that will accomplish this goal.

22. A group of investors is contemplating opening a number of restaurants in the city of Calgary. Some of these will offer full service and some take-out service only. The group has identified five potential locations for take-out restaurants, of which it will select at least three, and it has identified six potential locations for full-service restaurants, of which it will select at least two. Operating costs will be $15 000 per month for take-out service only and $25 000 per month for full-service restaurants. The group has a monthly budget of $195 000 for operating costs. Estimated profits are $5000 per month for take-out service and $7000 a month for full-service restaurants. The group needs to know how many of each type restaurant to select and the profit that will be generated.
   a. Formulate a model for this problem.
   b. Solve for the optimal solution using Excel.
   c. How much of the operating budget will be unused?

23. Solve this all-integer problem for the optimal solution using Excel:

$$\text{maximize } Z = 13x_1 + 26x_2 + 14x_3$$

subject to

$$16x_1 + 9x_2 + 4x_3 \leq 44$$
$$6x_2 + 10x_3 \leq 20$$
$$x_1, x_2, \text{ and } x_3 \geq 0 \text{ and integer}$$

24. Find the optimal solution to this problem using Excel:

$$\text{maximize } Z = 9x_1 + 5x_2 + 5x_3$$

subject to

$$20x_1 + 14x_2 + 19x_3 \leq 100$$
$$8x_1 + 4x_2 \leq 18$$
$$x_1, x_2, \text{ and } x_3 \geq 0 \text{ and integer}$$

25. The manager of a stamping department is getting ready to begin a new operation. A single product is to be produced. It can be produced on any of three machines. Information concerning the machines is contained in the following table:

Machine	Setup Cost	Profit per Unit	Daily Capacity
A	$300	$10	500
B	250	12	450
C	325	13	450

Each machine requires an operator, and two operators are available. The profit per unit excludes setup cost, and setups must be done at the start of each new day.
   a. Formulate this profit maximization problem.
   b. Use Excel and solve for the optimal quantities to produce per day on each machine.

26. A department has three machines available, and the new department manager must select one of the machines to assign to a new product line. The product line will consist of three slightly different

products, A, B, and C. Production requirements, machine capacities, and setup costs are given in the following table:

Machine	Setup Cost	Production Time per Pound A	B	C	Capacity (hours)
1	$150	4	3	5	1000
2	120	3	2	4	800
3	110	2	4	2	700

The profit per pound on the three products is listed in the following table:

Product	Profit
A	$13
B	10
C	12

a. Formulate this problem taking into account an additional factor: At least 40 pounds of each product must be made.
b. Solve for the optimal solution and profit using Excel.

27. Find the optimal solution to this problem using Excel.

$$\text{maximize } Z = 12x_1 + 18x_2 + 14x_3$$

subject to

$$6x_1 + 5x_2 + 5x_3 \le 48$$
$$x_1, x_2, \text{ and } x_3 \ge 0 \text{ and integer}$$

28. Find the optimal solution to this problem using Excel. If there are multiple optimal solutions, identify each one.

$$\text{maximize } Z = 5x_1 + 6x_2 + 5x_3 + 4x_4$$

subject to

$$10x_1 + 11x_2 + 9x_3 + 7x_4 \le 39$$
$$2x_1 + 3x_2 + 3x_3 + 2x_4 \le 13$$
$$\text{All variables} \ge 0 \text{ and integer}$$

29. Find the optimal solution to this problem using Excel.

$$\text{minimize } Z = x_1 + x_2 + 2x_3 + x_4$$

subject to

$$3x_1 + 2x_2 + 4x_3 + x_4 \ge 41$$
$$\text{All variables} \ge 0 \text{ and integer}$$

30. Determine the optimal solution to this all-integer problem using Excel.

$$\text{minimize } Z = 10x_1 + 11x_2 + 12x_3$$

subject to

$$8x_1 + 9x_2 + 10x_3 \ge 20$$
$$3x_1 + 4x_2 + 3x_3 \ge 13$$
$$\text{All variables} \ge 0 \text{ and integer}$$

31. A cargo plane is flying from Chicago to Vancouver. The plane has a remaining capacity of five tonnes. Joe's machinery company wants to ship two types of large machinery on the plane. The weights and dollar profit values of each type of machinery are given in the following table:

Machinery	Weight (tonnes)	Profit ($1000s)
Lathe	1	$13
Punch press	2	$27

a. State the integer programming formulation of this problem.
b. Using Excel determine the optimal number of each type of machinery to ship on the cargo plane to maximize total profit.

32. Waste Canada Inc. is interested in minimizing total travel time of its trucks for garbage collection. There are five neighbourhoods that trucks serve. Location 1 serves as the home location from which trucks leave and to which they must return. The company is interested in minimizing total travel time starting at the home location, visiting each of the neighbourhoods once, and then returning to the home location.

Let $x_{ijk} = 1$ if a truck travels from node i to node j during leg k of the trip
$x_{ijk} = 0$ if a truck does not travel from node i to node j during leg k of the trip

Prepare the following constraints for this problem:

a. The constraint that ensures that if leg 3 of the trip ends at location 2, then leg 4 of the trip starts at location 2.
b. The constraint that ensures that if leg 3 of the trip starts at location 2, then the fourth leg of the trip ends at location 14.
c. The constraint that ensures that the tour starts in node 1.
d. The constraint that stipulates that the trip must end in node 1 in leg 5.
e. The constraint that specifies that there is exactly one arrival at node 3.
f. The constraint that specifies that there is exactly one departure from node 2.
g. The constraint that ensures that we visit any node once in the second leg of the trip.

33. The Meadow Cutting and Tooling Manufacturing Company is experiencing a large increase in demand. The production at the current manufacturing facilities is not able to satisfy demand. The company needs to add new manufacturing plants. At the present time it has two plants, one in Chatham, and the other in Arnprior. The capacities of these plants are roughly 23 000 units per year in Chatham and 27 000 units per year in Arnprior. The company sells through its retail outlet stores located in Montreal, Windsor, Ottawa, and Toronto. The demand for the product at these retail outlet facilities is as follows:

- Montreal: 28 000 units per year
- Windsor: 30 000 units per year
- Ottawa: 24 000 units per year
- Toronto: 32 000 units per year

The company is in the process of considering five new manufacturing plant locations. The locations, their capacities, and the cost of purchasing or building the facility are stated in the following table:

Manufacturing Facility	Capacity (units per year)	Building/ Purchasing Cost
Cornwall (y_1)	28 000	\$210 000
Welland (y_2)	30 000	\$240 000
Huntsville (y_3)	25 000	\$200 000
Peterborough (y_4)	27 000	\$205 000
Quebec (y_5)	24 000	\$185 000

While the unit manufacturing cost in each of these plants is comparable, the unit shipping cost from the existing and the proposed plants to the retail outlets is given in Table 6-8.

The objective of the Meadow Cutting and Tooling Manufacturing Company is to minimize the total cost, which consists of the shipping cost and the building/purchasing cost, such that demand at all retail outlets is satisfied.

a. Use the numbers given next to each city in Table 6-8 and formulate this problem as a 0–1 mixed-integer linear programming problem.

b. Use Excel and determine the optimal shipping schedule that minimizes the total cost. Which locations should be used to build the new plants?

34. The matrix in Table 6-9 represents the changeover times (in minutes) of 10 products for a cable manufacturer.

a. Use the nearest-neighbour method and determine the sequence of jobs.

b. How long will it take to do the changeovers among the 10 products? You can begin production with any of the 10 products.

35. Determine the number of possible solutions for a 0–1 integer programming problem with the following number of decision variables:

a. 5 decision variables

b. 10 decision variables

Table 6-8 Per-Unit Shipping Costs for Problem 33

Plant\Outlet	Montreal (1)	Windsor (2)	Ottawa (3)	Toronto (4)
Chatham (1)	7	3	3.5	7.5
Arnprior (2)	2	4	2.5	4
Cornwall (3)	3.5	3	4.5	8
Welland (4)	7.5	4.5	5	6.5
Huntsville (5)	2.5	5	5.5	6
Peterborough (6)	4	5	3	5
Quebec (7)	5.5	8	4	2

Table 6-9 Changeover Matrix (times in minutes) To Product for Problem 34

From Product	1	2	3	4	5	6	7	8	9	10
1	0	58	48	44	67	2	34	28	16	51
2	17	0	31	24	4	44	74	4	68	99
3	44	38	0	5.1	8	32	20	81	74	88
4	10	.5	53	0	24	1	4	46	36	8
5	41	15	77	12	0	11	4	41	70	38
6	37	71	95	15	34	0	44	75	82	72
7	98	47	3	39	12	28	0	50	51	20
8	36	61	100	62	95	79	57	0	40	43
9	52	25	60	48	32	6	84	26	0	11
10	74	72	19	21	31	63	11	13	41	0

c. 15 decision variables
d. 18 decision variables

36. Consider a symmetric travelling salesperson problem. Determine the number of possible routes, if there are
   a. 7 locations
   b. 9 locations
   c. 11 locations
   d. 14 locations
   e. Based on the answers you have obtained in parts *a* through *d*, comment on the potential problems in solving travelling salesperson problems.

37. HOL, the second-largest municipal electricity distribution company in the province of Ontario, needs an efficient schedule for their meter readers. The are five neighbourhoods to be served. The headquarters is located in neighbourhood 1. The time estimates (in minutes) of travelling between the neighbourhoods in given in the following table.

From\To	1	2	3	4	5
1	0	3	7.5	6.6	2.5
2	3	0	2	8	7.7
3	7.5	2	0	3	8.5
4	6.6	8	3	0	3.5
5	2.5	7.7	8.5	3.5	0

   a. Formulate this problem as a travelling salesperson problem.
   b. Use the formulation from part *a* and Excel and determine the schedule that minimizes the total transportation time of a meter reader starting in neighbourhood 1 and ending in neighbourhood 1.

38. A big computer company is planning to redesign its reverse logistic network for repackaging, recycling, and remanufacturing purposes. The company has three collection centres (A, B, C) in Ontario and plans to open up to two others (D, E) to meet the increasing demand in its portfolio of products. The costs of opening each planned collection centre are \$50 000 and \$75 000, respectively. Products collected at these collection centres (existing and planned) are shipped to three warehouses owned by the company. The warehouse located in region 1 has an average demand of 7000 remanufactured computers per month and serves the North and Central Ontario market. The warehouse located in region 2 has an average demand of 9000 remanufactured computers per month and serves the East Ontario market. The warehouse located in region three has an average demand of 6200 remanufactured computers per month and serves the West Ontario market. Collection centres D and E can handle each up to 6500 units per month.

   The costs of shipping a remanufactured computer from one collection centre to a warehouse are as follows:

	Collection Centre				
Warehouse	**A**	**B**	**C**	**D**	**E**
North & Central Ontario (R1)	\$100	\$110	\$50	—	\$65
East Ontario (R2)	\$60	—	\$80	\$90	\$45
West Ontario (R3)	\$90	\$45	\$100	\$75	—

   If the company expects an increase in the average demand per month in the coming year of 30% from warehouse R1, 30% from warehouse R2, and 40% from warehouse R3, develop an integer programming model that can be used to determine if the new collection centres should be opened or not and how many units of returned products should be handled at each collection centre to meet the demand level required at each warehouse at the minimum cost. What is the optimal shipment plan?

39. Consider the big computer company described in Question 38. How will the optimal solution change if in addition the following restrictions are to be considered:
   a. At least 30% of the returned products out of collection centre A are shipped to warehouse R1 and at most 80% of the returned products out of collection centres D and E are shipped to warehouse R2.
   b. Each collection centre can handle up to 8000 units per month.

40. A famous winery located in the Niagara Peninsula makes three types of products: ice wine, regular wine, and concentrated grape juice. The winery has its own grape farms, which produce class A and class B grapes. Ice wine is made with class A grapes, regular wine can be made from the mix of class A and class B grapes, and concentrated grape juice is made with class B grapes. Due to the increasing demand for ice wine, the winery is short of class A grapes. The company is considering two options to cope with this increase: either to buy class A grapes from two outside suppliers or to invest in its own farms to increase the internal production. The costs and profits of products and raw materials are listed as follows, where 1 case = 12 bottles and 1 bottle = 250ml.

The cost to grow the class A grapes used in the production of ice wine is much higher because the grapes for ice wine are left on the vine past the time when grapes are picked for regular wine. The grapes lose a portion of their moisture and thus there is a reduction in the amount of juice that can be extracted from them.

	Ice wine (per bottle)	Regular wine (per bottle)	Concentrated grape juice (per case)
Production Cost	$20	$12	$60
Shipment Cost	$5	$5	$10
Revenue	$80	$30	$120
Demand during last Christmas season	20 000	30 000	1000
Forecast demand increases	20%	5%	−5%

Develop in each of the following cases an integer programming model and solve it with Excel Solver to assist the company to evaluate its course of actions:

a. If none of the options to get more grapes is considered, how many bottles of ice wine, regular wine, and concentrated juice should the company produce to maximize its overall profit?

b. If only the option of purchasing additional class A and class B grapes from outside suppliers is considered, how many bottles of ice wine, regular wine, and concentrated juice should the company produce from in-house grapes and grapes purchased from suppliers to maximize the overall profit?

c. If both purchasing and additional investment on capacity are considered, how many of each type of grapes should the company purchase from outside suppliers to meet the demand and minimize the total costs, assuming that the company has determined that at least 40% of the demand should be met from in-house production of grapes?

Raw material	Ice wine (per bottle)	Regular wine (per bottle)	Concentrated grape juice (per case*)
Class A usage	90%*	50%	—
Class B usage	—	40%	90%

	Class A grapes		Class B grapes
	Ice wine	Regular wine	
Cost to grow grapes (per 250 ml)	$3	$1	$0.5
Capacity available per year		500 000 ml	600 000 ml
Fixed investment needed to increase capacity		$300 000	$300 000
Cost of purchases (per 250 ml) from other suppliers		$5	$3

*90% means 90% per bottle of wine are from the grapes.

Case 1: Suburban Kelowna

The Suburban Kelowna Corporation manufactures a line of high-priced outdoor furniture consisting of a picnic table, a bench, an armchair, and a chaise lounge. The picnic table is sold in a set with two of the benches; the benches may also be sold separately. Below is information on pieces and resource availability for next month.

Redwood costs $8 per board foot; cedar costs $6 per board foot; 12-inch fittings cost $2.50; 8-inch fittings cost $1.50; bolts cost $.50. The hourly wage rate and fringe benefits of the workers average $9.00 per hour.

Because of prior orders, at least 50 (separate) benches and at least 40 chaise lounges must be produced.

Discussion Question

Determine the quantity of each product to be produced next month. Assume partial units are unacceptable.

Source: Written by Professor Paul Van Ness, College of Business, Rochester Institute of Technology. Reprinted by permission.

	Picnic Table (set)	Bench (separate)	Armchair	Chaise Lounge	Available
Price	\$725	\$225	\$275	\$300	
Redwood (board ft.)	22	6	7	8	4500
Cedar (board ft.)	12	4	4	0	3600
12-inch fittings (number)	18	4	0	2	2250
8-inch fittings (number)	12	4	6	6	2075
Bolts (number)	48	12	12	20	5925
Labour (hours)	20	5	8	12	4800

Case 2: City Hall of Ottawa (CHO)

Each winter season, the City Hall of Ottawa (CHO) subcontracts private contractors to haul the snow cleared from roads and sidewalks to snow disposal facilities. The purpose is to keep streets safe and passable by reducing the hazards caused by snow and ice accumulation. Thus, very high quality standards have been set, defined by the time to clear snow accumulation for each road maintenance class (e.g., high priority roads, arterials, major collectors, minor collectors, and residential roads and lanes) or each sidewalk/pathway maintenance class (class 1, class 2, and class 3) as well as the standard type of treatment required (e.g., bare pavement, center bare, bare surface, or snow packed). For management purposes, the CHO has divided the town in j areas and has determined the number of trucks n_j required by each area j to meet its requirements of snow clearing per season. To be considered by the CHO, each private contractor is required to put in a tender at the beginning of each year, which includes the quote price per truck for the season's work and the total number of trucks that can be supplied. Given the nature of work that needs to be done per area, the CHO pays a fixed price per truck per season regardless of the number of trips made carrying snow. Therefore, each contractor price varies per area in which the work needs to be done. A contractor cannot supply more than the number of trucks available and must be prepared to send its trucks to any areas tendered and at any time when required. All contractors are required to use trucks that meet the fixed cargo capacity determined in the policy of the CHO (20 feet). Once a year, the CHO has to decide how many trucks to allocate to each area from each private contractor to minimize the costs for maintenance of roads and streets. The demand for trucks per area needs to be met and no contractor supplies more trucks than what is available. To prevent overdependence on single contractors, the CHO has also determined that each area be serviced by a minimum number of contractors.

Managerial Report

1. Prepare a mixed integer programming model that can be used once a year to allocate areas to private contractors such that the allocation costs are minimized and all requirements are met. Let's assume that I contractors tendered, t_i is the number of trucks available from contractor i, c_{ij} is the quote price per season from contractor i to provide services area j, and m_j is the minimum number of contractors required in area j.
2. Suppose that the town is divided into 5 areas and 7 contractors have tendered. The following table provides quote prices per season per contractor per area, the number of trucks available from each contractor, the number of trucks required per area, and the minimum number of contractors required per area. Use the model defined in the previous question to determine the minimum-cost allocation of contractors to areas. In addition to the total cost in percent from each contractor, your report must also include the number of trucks allocated to each area from each contractor and the total number of contractors assigned to each area.

Contractor	Costs per season per truck per area (thousand)					Number of trucks available from each contractor
	1	2	3	4	5	
1	25	29	35	20	X	30
2	35	27	28	X	26	22
3	X	30	30	24	X	25
4	28	X	32	22	27	30
5	30	26	X	21	25	28
6	27	30	29	23	24	25
7	X	X	28	22	28	25
Number of trucks required per area	30	35	40	30	35	
Minimum number of contractors required per area	2	2	2	2	2	

Case 3: Ottawa Catholic School Board (Revisited)

Reconsider the Ottawa Catholic School Board (OCSB) case study at the end of Chapter 3. The OCSB has made the decision to close a number of its senior elementary schools (sixth, seventh, and eighth grades) at the end of this school year and reassign all of next year's students to the three remaining senior elementary schools. Currently, the school board has the policy of providing busing for all students who must travel more than approximately one mile (1.6 kilometre). Therefore, the board wants a plan for reassigning the students that will minimize the total busing cost. The annual cost per student for busing from each of the six residential areas of the city to each of the schools is shown in the following table (along with other basic data for next year), where 0 indicates that busing is not needed and a dash indicates an infeasible assignment. The table also shows the percentage of each area's senior elementary school population for next year that falls into each of the three grades as well as the number of current students in each area.

					Busing Cost ($/student)		
Area	Number of Students	Percentage In 6th Grade	Percentage In 7th Grade	Percentage in 8th Grade	School 1	School 2	School 3
1	450	32%	38%	30%	$300	$0	$700
2	600	37%	28%	35%	—	$400	$500
3	550	30%	32%	38%	$600	$300	$200
4	350	28%	40%	32%	$200	$500	—
5	500	39%	34%	27%	$0	—	$400
6	450	34%	28%	38%	$500	$300	$0
School capacity:					900	1100	1000

The school board also has imposed the restriction that each grade must constitute between 30 and 36 percent of each school's population. Assume now the school board has made the decision to prohibit the splitting of residential areas among multiple schools. Thus, each of the six areas must be assigned to a single school.

Managerial Report

Formulate and solve an integer programming model under the current policy. Determine the number of students in each school and the total busing cost.

The school board is considering eliminating some busing to reduce costs. Option 1 is to only eliminate busing for students traveling 1.6 to 2.4 kilometres, where the cost per student is given in the table as $200. Option 2 is to also eliminate busing for students traveling 2.4 to 3.2 kilometres, where the estimated cost per student is $300. The school board now needs to choose among the three alternative busing plans (the current one or Option 1 or Option 2). Provide the board with an analysis that summarizes for each option the total busing cost and the total number of students in each school.

Source: Based on a case study previously published by F. S. Hillier, M. S. Hillier, *Introduction to Management Science: A modeling and case studies approach with spreadsheets*, 3rd ed., (Boston: McGraw-Hill Irwin, 2008), 602 pages.

Nonlinear Programming

CHAPTER 7

LEARNING OBJECTIVES

After completing this chapter, you should be able to:

1. Explain the difference between optimization problems that can be solved using linear programming methods and those that require nonlinear programming or calculus-based methods.
2. Find the optimal values of the decision variable and the objective function in problems that involve one decision variable (unconstrained and constrained).
3. Solve one-decision variable problems with a nonlinear objective function using Excel (unconstrained or constrained).
4. Find the optimal values of the decision variables and the objective function in unconstrained problems that involve two decision variables.
5. Solve one-decision-variable unconstrained problems with a nonlinear objective function using Excel.
6. Use the Lagrange multiplier to find the optimal values of two decision variables and the objective function in problems that involve equality constraints.
7. Solve two-decision-variable problems with a nonlinear objective function and an equality constraint using Excel.
8. Find the optimal values of the decision variables and the objective function in problems that involve two decision variables and one inequality constraint.
9. Solve two-decision-variable problems with a nonlinear objective function and multiple constraints using Excel.

CHAPTER OUTLINE

Many of the chapters in this book describe models that involve only linear relationships. The widespread use of linear models in practice necessitates devoting substantial coverage to linear models. However, an important class of problems involves nonlinear relationships. Examples of such relationships include, among others, the demand or the price of a product, returns or interest rate, firms' growth opportunities or profitability, or payroll costs as estimated by hours worked and wage rates. This chapter illustrates methods that can be used to find optimal solutions for simple models that involve nonlinear relationships.

7.1 INTRODUCTION

The models described in this chapter are in some ways similar to the *linear programming* models described in Chapters 2 through 6. For example, all of the models have an objective function that is to be maximized or minimized. Some also have one or more constraints, but others involve only an objective function. However, all of the models in this chapter involve one or more *nonlinear relationships.*

There are many real-life examples of problems that involve nonlinear relationships. For instance, the inventory EOQ model's objective is to minimize the cost function:

$$TC = \frac{Q}{2}H + \frac{D}{Q}S$$

where

TC = total annual cost
Q = order quantity
H = annual holding cost per unit
D = annual demand
S = ordering cost

A graph of this U-shaped cost function is illustrated in Figure 7-1. Similar U-shaped cost curves can be used to describe other inventory cost functions as well as costs in forecasting

FIGURE 7-1 A U-Shaped Cost Function

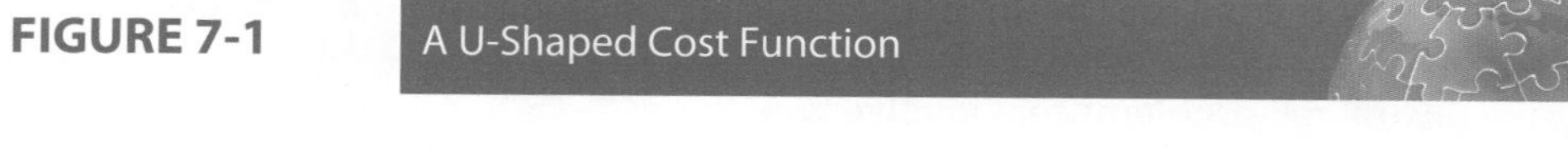

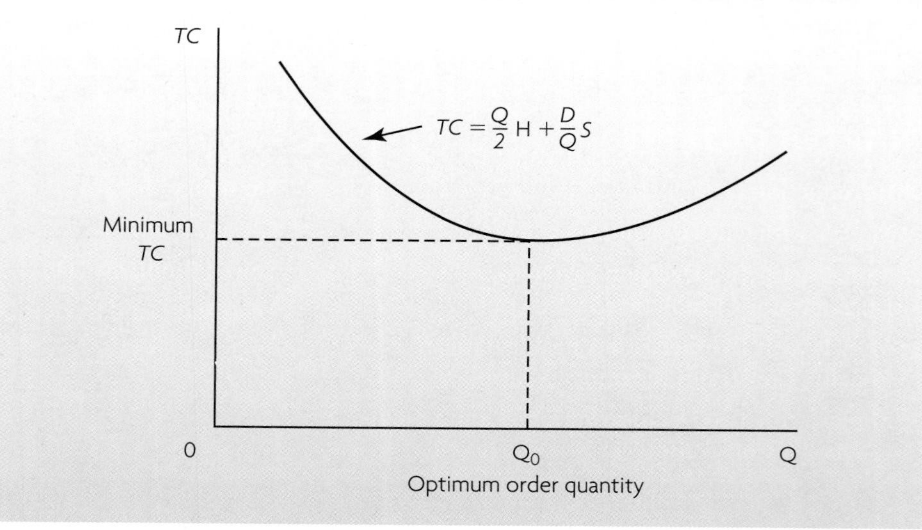

models, waiting-line models, and quality control. Moreover, cost-profit-volume models may also involve nonlinear relationships. The Modern Management Application on Bombardier Flexjet later in the chapter illustrates a practical application of nonlinear programming optimization methods for assigning aircraft and crews to flights, a business problem faced by Flexjet, a leader company in fractional aircraft ownership wholly owned by Bombardier Aerospace.

Nonlinear relationships occur because one or more of the causes of linearity are absent. For example, there may be a nonproportional relationship between two variables (such as price and quantity demanded; the relationship may only be linear over a limited range of price), or the relationship may be nonadditive (if you add one cup of sugar to one cup of water, the resulting volume will be less than two cups).

The difficulty with nonlinear models in general is that they can be significantly harder to solve than linear models. Moreover, linear models often provide reasonably good approximations to nonlinear models. Thus, the efficiency of solution techniques for linear models and the fact that they perform well as approximations in many cases that involve nonlinear relationships explain the popularity of linear models. Nonetheless, there are many instances for which linear approximations are not acceptable. Judgment and experience on the part of the decision maker are necessary to determine when linear approximations are suitable and when they are not. For those cases that are deemed unsuitable for linear models, the methods described in this chapter may be of use if the model is fairly simple.

The chapter begins with a discussion of models that have one decision variable, including both unconstrained models (i.e., models that have only an objective function) and constrained models. It then moves on to a discussion of unconstrained models with two decision variables. For the special case of equality-constrained models, the use of *Lagrange multipliers* is demonstrated.

7.2 MODELS WITH ONE DECISION VARIABLE

In this section, the use of first and second derivatives for identifying maximum and minimum values of a mathematical function is illustrated. The section is presented in two parts. The first part illustrates the procedure for an *unconstrained function,* while the second part illustrates the procedure for a *constrained function.*

Unconstrained Problem with One Decision Variable

EXAMPLE 7-1

Consider the case of Larry Brown, manager of a small manufacturing company. Larry has ordered a new machine that will increase the productivity of an existing machine. Larry must now select a location for the new machine. He knows that the closer the new machine is to the existing machine, the lower the cost of transporting work in process between the two machines. On the other hand, the closer the two machines are, the greater the cost to remodel the area to accommodate the new machine.

With the help of the accounting department, Larry developed a model that expressed the combined cost of remodelling and transporting work on a per-unit basis:

Cost per piece $= 1.5(\text{Distance})^2 - 42(\text{Distance}) + 300$

In mathematical terms, this can be expressed as

$$Z = 1.5x^2 - 42x + 300$$

where

Z = cost per unit
x = distance between the two machines in feet

Larry's problem is to determine the value of x that will minimize this cost function. He can do this by using differential calculus.[1] By taking the first derivative of the cost function and setting that equal to zero, he can solve for the value(s) of x for which the function reaches a local maximum or a local minimum. Then, by finding the second derivative of the function, he will be able to determine that at that value of x the function is a minimum. Let's see how this is accomplished.

There are two conditions that must be satisfied:

Condition 1 (necessary): The first derivative of a function must equal zero at every point that is a local maximum or a local minimum.

Condition 2 (sufficient): If the first condition is satisfied at a point, then it can be concluded that

1. The point will be a local minimum *if* the sign of the second derivative is positive.
2. The point will be a local maximum *if* the sign of the second derivative is negative.

The term **local minimum** means that the function reaches a minimum value *relative* to nearby values. Similarly, a **local maximum** occurs when a function reaches a value that is higher than its value at nearby points. If that local maximum (or minimum) is the highest (lowest) value reached by the function for any value of x, then that value is also a **global maximum** (or **minimum**).

Consider the functions shown in Figure 7-2. In 7-2a, we see a function that is convex; it has a single minimum, so the local minimum is also the global minimum. Similarly, in 7-2b, we see a function that is strictly concave, with a single maximum that is a global maximum. Figure 7-2c shows a more complex function; it has a number of turns. The function has two minimum points and one maximum. The lower of the two minimum points is both a local minimum and a global minimum (assuming that these three turning points are the only ones the function has). Similarly, if the maximum is the only maximum point for the function, then it is also the global maximum. In the case of a function with more turning points, there would be an even greater number of local maxima and local minima.

It is generally not practical to plot the graph of a function to determine the point(s) at which it achieves a local maximum or local minimum. Instead, the procedure involves finding the first derivative of the function and setting it equal to zero. Condition 1—necessary condition—requires that the first derivative equal zero at a local maximum or a local minimum. The solution (or solutions, if there are more than one) that makes the first derivative equal to zero is the point that must be evaluated to determine if it is a local maximum or a local minimum. That is accomplished by taking the second derivative of the function

[1] OLC Chapter 18 illustrates rules that can be used to differentiate frequently encountered simple mathematical expressions.

FIGURE 7-2 Illustrations of Local Maximum and Local Minimum Points

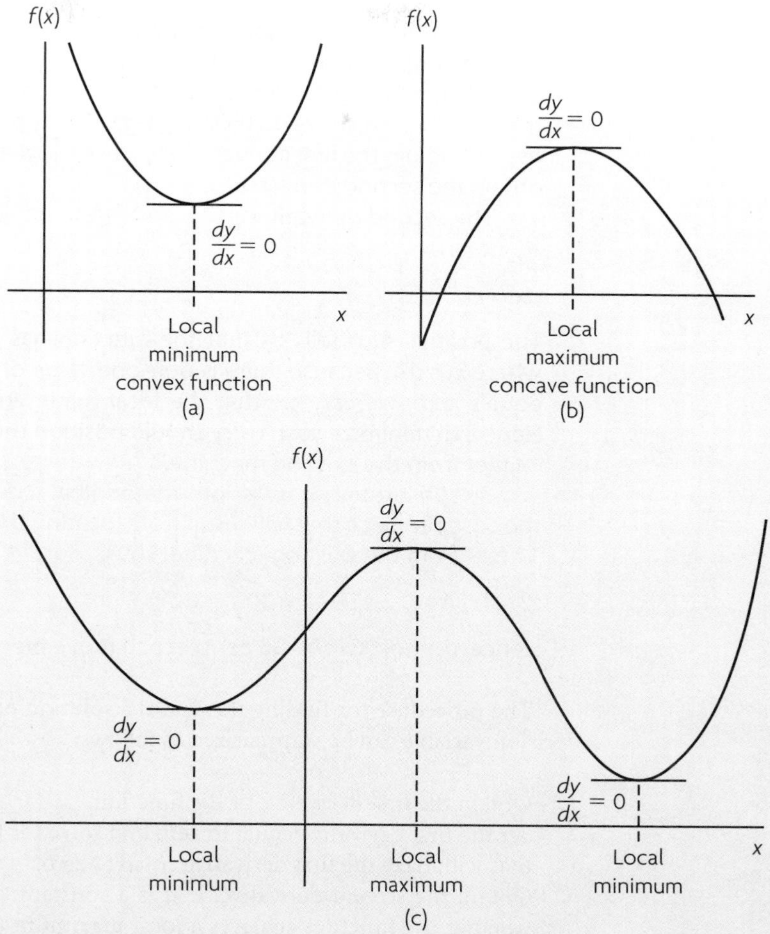

and noting its sign (Condition 2—sufficient condition); a plus sign indicates a local minimum and a minus sign indicates a local maximum. Note that if there are multiple solutions for the first derivative (e.g., $x = 2$, $x = -2$), each of these would be substituted into the second derivative to obtain the sign of the second derivative.

Now let's see how we can use calculus and the two conditions mentioned previously to determine the solution to Larry's problem. Recall that the cost function was

$$Z = 1.5x^2 - 42x + 300$$

The first derivative of this function is

$$\frac{dz}{dx} = 3x - 42$$

Setting this equal to zero (Condition 1) and solving for x, we find

$$3x - 42 = 0$$
$$x = 14$$

This indicates that the slope of the function (i.e., the first derivative) is zero at only one point, where $x = 14$. We must now determine whether this one point is a maximum or a minimum. To do this, we must obtain the second derivative of the function, which we do by applying to the first derivative the same procedure used to obtain the first derivative (i.e., take the derivative of the first derivative to obtain the second derivative).

The second derivative is

$$\frac{d^2z}{dx^2} = +3$$

The positive sign tells us that the function has a local minimum at the point where $x = 14$. Because there is only one value of x for which the first derivative equals zero, we can say that the local minimum is also the *global* minimum. Hence, to minimize cost. Larry should position the new machine at a distance of 14 feet from the existing machine.

By substituting $x = 14$ into the original (cost) function, we can determine the cost per piece that will result from locating the new machine at a distance of 14 feet from the existing machine. Thus:

$$Z = 1.5(14)^2 - 42(14) + 300 = 6$$

Hence, the cost will be \$6 per piece to move pieces between the two machines.

The procedure for finding the optimal solution of an unconstrained model with one decision variable can be summarized as follows:

1. Obtain the first derivative of the function.
2. Set the first derivative equal to zero and solve for the value(s) of the decision variable that will make the first derivative equal to zero.
3. Obtain the second derivative. If it is a constant (e.g., +5, −2), its sign will indicate whether the function achieves a local maximum (the sign of the second derivative is negative) or a local minimum (the sign of the second derivative is positive). If the second derivative includes the decision variable (e.g., $4x$, $x + 6$), substitute the value(s) found in step 2 and note the resulting sign(s) to determine if the function achieves a local max (−) or a local min (+) at each value.

EXAMPLE 7-2

Given this function:

$$Z = \frac{1}{3}x^3 - 5x^2 + 21x + 100$$

a. Determine the value of x for which the function is a maximum.
b. Compute the value of the function at its maximum.
c. Determine the value of x for which the function is a minimum.
d. Compute the value of the function at its minimum.

Solution

a. 1. Obtain the first derivative of the function:

$$\frac{dz}{dx} = x^2 - 10x + 21$$

2. Set the first derivative equal to zero and solve for x:

$$x^2 - 10x + 21 = 0$$

This can be factored into

$$(x - 3)(x - 7) = 0$$

Solving, $x = +3$ or $x = +7$, for this to equal zero.

3. The second derivative is

$$\frac{d^2z}{dx^2} = 2x - 10$$

At $x = +3$, this is $2(3) - 10 = -4$
At $x = +7$, this is $2(7) - 10 = +4$

The *negative* result (-4) indicates a local maximum; the positive result ($+4$) indicates a local minimum. Hence, the function reaches a local maximum at $x = +3$.

b. To find the value of the function at its maximum, substitute the value of *x* for which it is a maximum into the original function and solve. Thus:

$$Z = \frac{1}{3}(3)^3 - 5(3)^2 + 21(3) + 100 = 127$$

c. The function reaches a local minimum at $x = +7$ because at that point, the second derivative of the original function is positive ($+4$).

d. To find the value of the function at its minimum, substitute the value of *x* for which it is a minimum into the original function and solve. Therefore:

$$Z = \left(\frac{1}{3}\right)(7)^3 - 5(7)^2 + 21(7) + 100$$

$$Z = 114.33 - 245 + 147 + 100 = 116.33$$

Solution of One-Decision-Variable, Unconstrained Problem with Excel

To demonstrate the solution of an unconstrained nonlinear programming problem with a single decision variable, consider the following example.

EXAMPLE 7-3

X-Tech Inc. produces specialized bolts for the aerospace industry. The operating cost of producing a single bolt is \$2.00. The company sells the bolts for \$6.00 per unit. Each time the company arranges to sell a batch, it incurs a fixed cost of \$20. This fixed cost mainly includes administrative expenses. The volume of sales is primarily dependent on the price of the product. The manager has come up with the following relationship between volume and price:

Volume = 500 − 25(Price)

a. Draw the volume–price relationship diagram.
b. Draw the profit function as it relates to the price.
c. Determine the optimal price and the optimal volume that will result in the maximum profit.

Solution

a. Figure 7-3 represents a schematic diagram of the relationship between volume and price. On one extreme, if the company decides not to charge anything for the specialty bolt, it could sell or give away 500 units. However, a rational businessperson would not choose this option. On the other extreme, if the company charges \$20 (500/25) or more, X-Tech would not be able to sell any units. Even though this relationship is good to know, the company is interested in estimating the profit. The profit function is given by the following basic equation:

Profit = Revenue − Cost
Profit = Revenue − (Variable cost + Fixed cost)

Revenue = Price × Volume
Variable cost = Volume × Operating cost
Volume = 500 − 25(Price)

Therefore,

Profit = Price[Volume] − (Volume × Operating cost) − Fixed cost
Profit = Price[500 − 25(Price)] − (Volume × 2) − 20
Profit = Price[500 − 25(Price)] − [500 − 25(Price)] × 2) − 20

FIGURE 7-3 Volume–Price Relationship for the X-Tech Inc. Problem

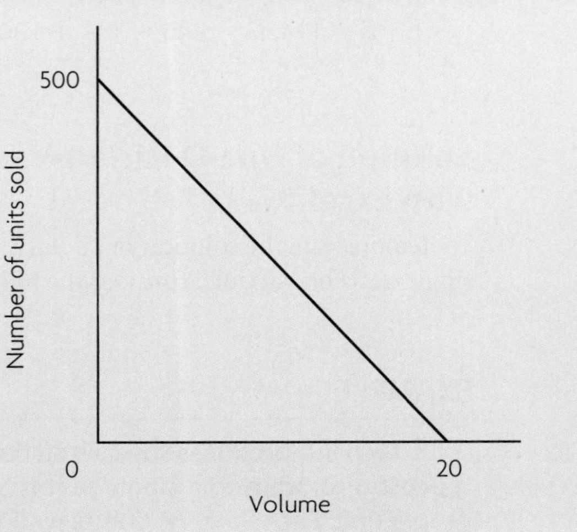

Simplifying the above equation results in the following:

$$\text{Profit} = 500(\text{Price}) - 25(\text{Price})^2 - 1000 + 50(\text{Price}) - 20$$
$$\text{Profit} = -25(\text{Price})^2 + 550(\text{Price}) - 1020 \qquad \textbf{(7-1)}$$

b. The graph of this relationship can be seen in Figure 7-4.

c. The first derivative of this function is

$$\frac{d(\text{Profit})}{d(\text{Price})} = -50(\text{Price}) + 550$$

Setting this equal to zero and solving for price results in the following:

$$-50(\text{Price}) + 550 = 0$$

$$\text{Price} = \frac{550}{50} = 11$$

This indicates that the slope of a tangent line at this point on this function is equal to zero only where Price equals \$11. Next, we have to determine if this one point is a minimum or a maximum. To do this, we take the second derivative of the profit function with respect to price. The second derivative is

$$\frac{d^2(\text{Profit})}{d(\text{Price})^2} = -50$$

Because the second derivative is a negative number, the profit function has a local maximum at this point. In addition, because there is only one value of price for which the first derivative is equal to zero, we can conclude that the local maximum is also the global maximum. By substituting 11 into the profit

FIGURE 7-4 The Graph of the Profit Function for the X-Tech Inc. Problem

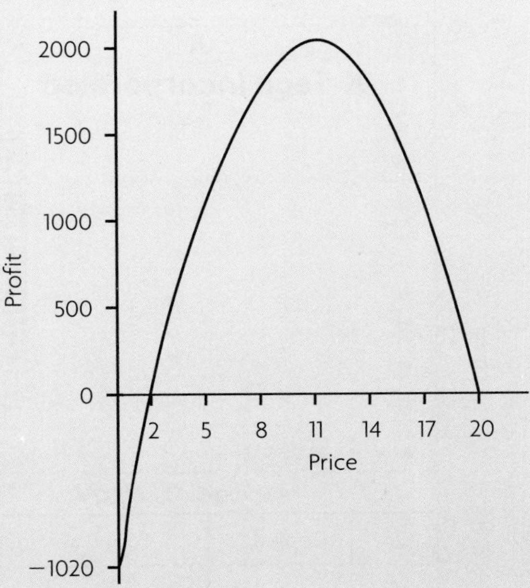

function formula, we can calculate the value of the profit at the optimal price. Therefore:

$$\text{Profit} = -25(11)^2 + 550(11) - 1020 = \$2005$$

Substituting 11 into the volume formula can determine the volume, or the number of specialty bolts to be sold:

$$\text{Volume} = 500 - 25(\text{Price})$$
$$\text{Volume} = 500 - 25(11)$$
$$\text{Volume} = 225$$

From Figure 7-4, the profit increases as price increases up to \$11. However, any further increase in price beyond \$11 results in the decline of profits. At the maximum price of \$20, the expected profit is −\$20.

Exhibit 7-1 shows the Excel worksheet for this problem. The formula for the profit function is contained in cell C7.

EXHIBIT 7-1 Worksheet for the One-Decision-Variable, Unconstrained Problem (X-Tech Inc., Example 7-3)

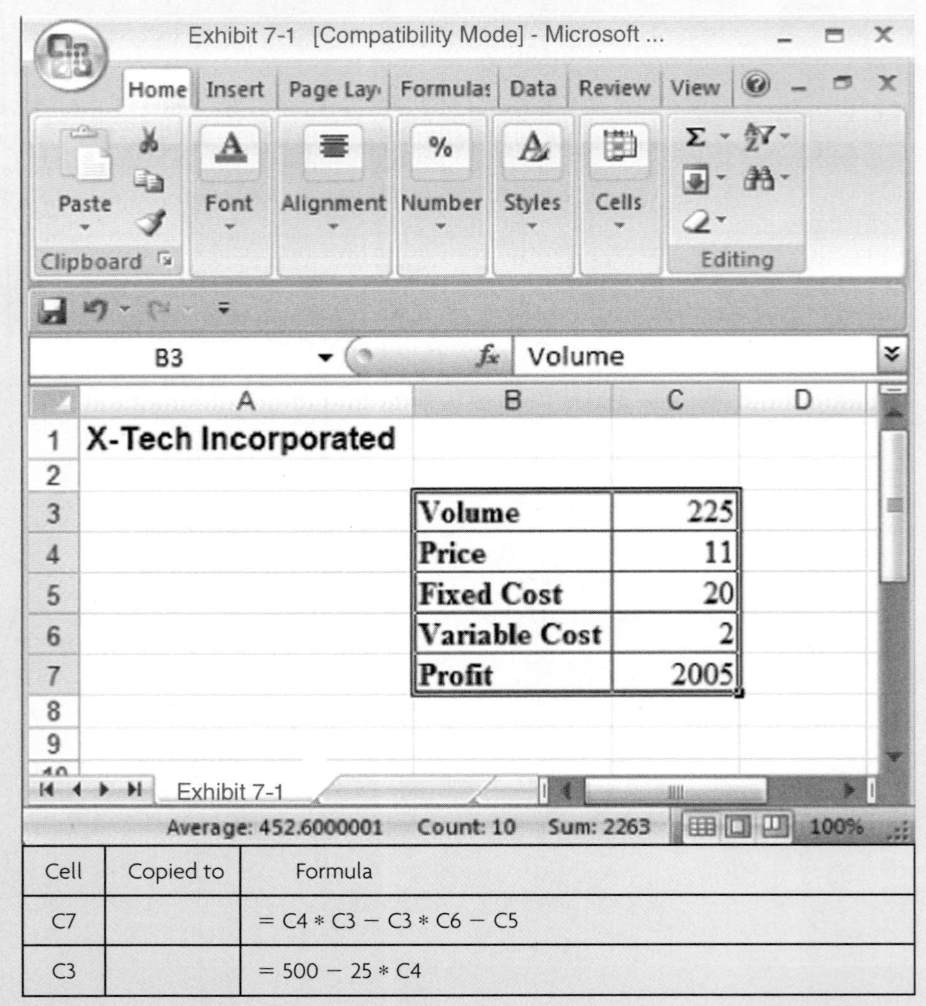

Cell	Copied to	Formula
C7		= C4 * C3 − C3 * C6 − C5
C3		= 500 − 25 * C4

EXHIBIT 7-2 Parameter Specification Screen for the One-Decision-Variable, Unconstrained Problem (X-Tech Inc., Example 7-3)

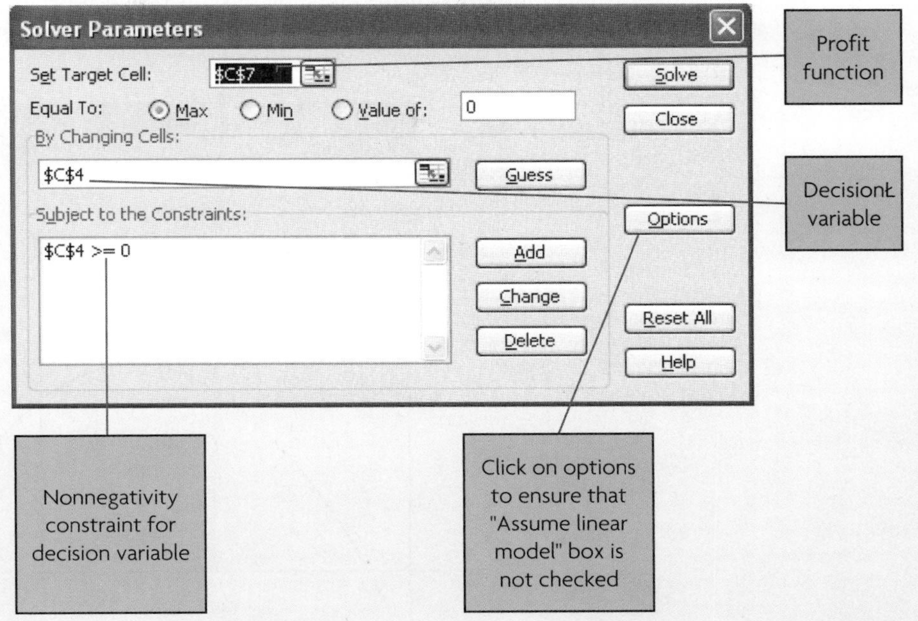

This formula looks a little different than Equation 7-1, because there is a separate equation for the volume in cell C3, = 500 − 25 × C4. Thus, if we substitute 500 − 25 × C4 into the equation given in cell C7 and simplify, then we will obtain the equivalent of Equation 7-1. After choosing **Data|Analysis|Solver,** we will get the Solver Parameters screen shown in Exhibit 7-2. On this screen, for the "Set Target Cell" box, we choose the profit function specified in cell C7. In the "Equal To" portion, we click on "Max." In the "By Changing Cells" box, we include the input variable Price, which is given in C4. In the constraints section, we simply specify that the value of the input variable (Price) has to be a nonnegative value (i.e., $C$4 ≥ 0). Since this is a nonlinear model, to ensure that a linear model is not utilized, we click on "Options" and make sure that the "Assume linear model" box is *not* checked. After clicking on "Solve" we obtain the solution given in Exhibit 7-1. We could determine the effect of changing the price on volume and on profits. For example, if we decide to price the specialty bolt at $15, we can expect to sell 125 units for a total profit of $1605.

Constrained Problem with One Decision Variable

The procedure for finding the optimal value of a constrained decision variable is very similar to the procedure for an unconstrained decision variable. The key difference between the two is that the existence of a constraint means that there is a *feasible solution space* that must be taken into account. The feasible solution space may or may not include the optimum that would be indicated if the function were not constrained. To understand the consequences of this, consider the two cases depicted in Figure 7-5.

Figure 7-5a illustrates a case where the function attains its optimum *within* the feasible solution space. In Figure 7-5b, the function attains its optimum *outside* of the feasible solution space. In the first case, the optimum is unaffected by the constraint; in the second case, the optimum is determined by the constraint. It occurs at the point where the decision variable equals the constraint. Note, too, an important difference between nonlinear

FIGURE 7-5A The Optimal Point Lies Within the Feasible Solution Space

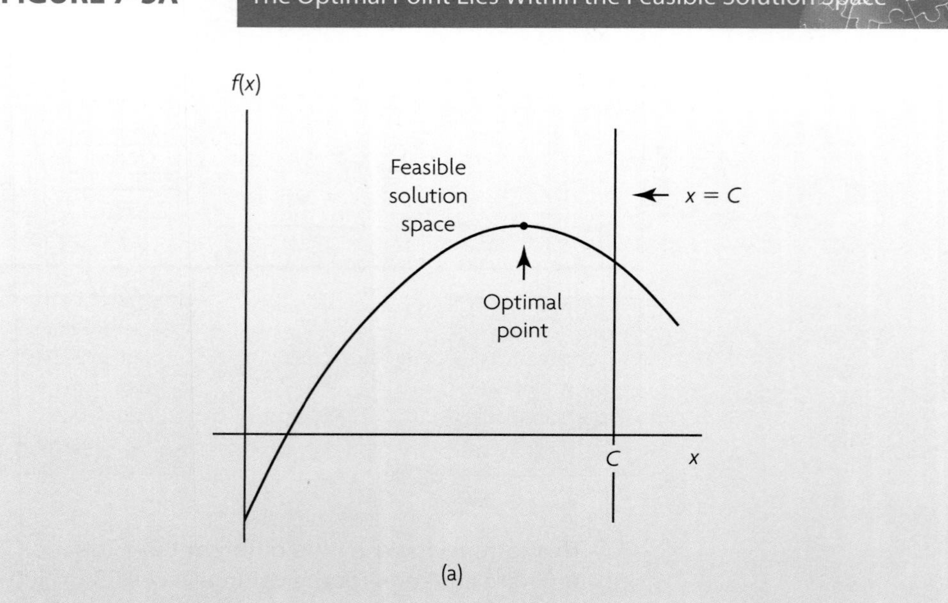

FIGURE 7-5B The Optimal Point is on the Boundary of the Feasible Solution Space

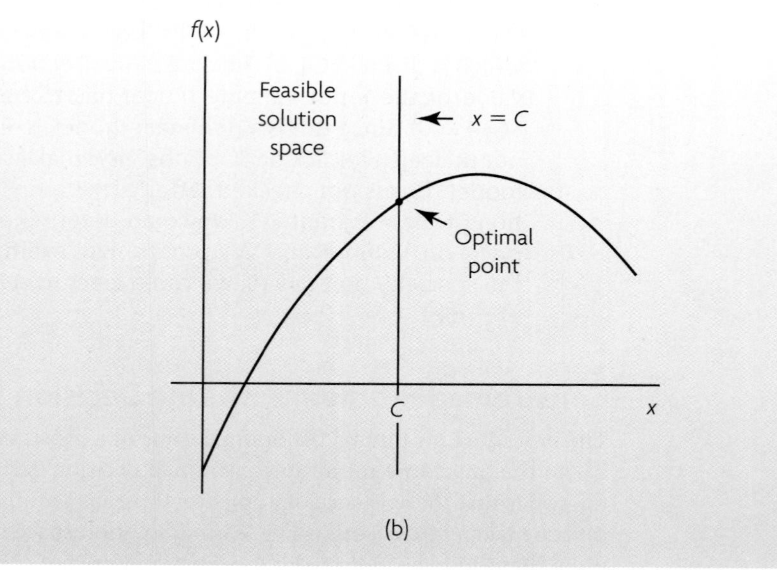

FIGURE 7-6 The Global Maximum Can Be at the Point Where $x = C$

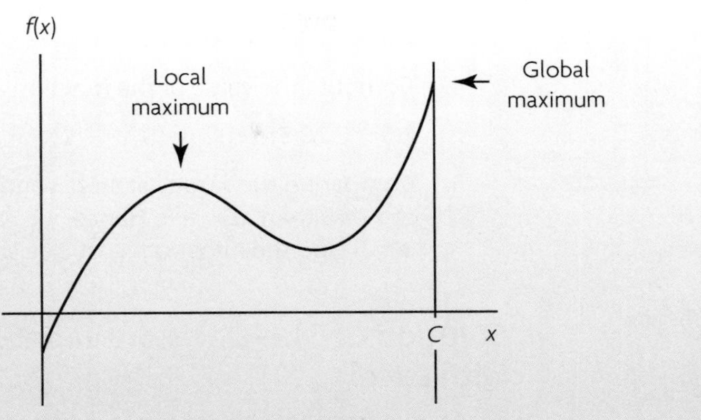

models and linear models: The optimal solution is not always on the boundary of the feasible solution space, although it may be.

The procedure for constrained optimization is to proceed as in the case of unconstrained optimization to identify local maximum and local minimum points. Then, check to see if the solution satisfies the constraint. For instance, suppose you find $x = 5$, and the constraint is that $x \leq 7$. Obviously, the solution satisfies the constraint, so $x = 5$ *may be* the optimal solution. The other possibility is that the value of x equal to the constraint (e.g., $x = 7$) may yield a better solution. To complete the analysis, substitute that value ($x = 7$) into the objective function and compare the result to the value of the objective function with the apparent optimum (e.g., $x = 5$) to see which actually gives the better solution. Figure 7-6 illustrates a case for which the constraint provides a better solution than the apparent (local) optimum.

EXAMPLE 7-4

Determine the minimum cost for this model:

minimize $Z = 2x^2 - 20x + 60$

subject to

$x \leq 8$

Solution

1. Obtain the first derivative and set it equal to zero:

$$\frac{dy}{dx} = 4x - 20 = 0$$

Solving, $x = 5$. Note that this value *satisfies* the constraint $x \leq 8$.

2. Obtain the second derivative and note its sign:

$$\frac{d^2y}{dx^2} = +4$$

The plus sign indicates that at $x = 5$, the function $2x^2 - 20x + 60$ reaches a local minimum.

3. Compute the value of the function at $x = 8$ (the constraint):

   $2(8)^2 - 20(8) + 60 = 28$

4. Compute the value of the function at its local minimum, $x = 5$:

   $2(5)^2 - 20(5) + 60 = 10$

5. Comparing the results at step 3 and 4, we can see that the function is lower at $x = 5$ than at $x = 8$. Hence, we can say that the function is minimized at $x = 5$, and the minimum cost (see step 4) is 10.

Solution of One-Decision-Variable, Constrained Problem with Excel

To demonstrate how to solve a constrained single-decision-variable problem, we will slightly modify Example 7-3.

EXAMPLE 7-5

X-Tech Inc. produces specialized bolts for the aerospace industry. The operating cost of producing a single bolt is \$2.00. The company sells the bolts for \$6.00 per unit. Each time the company arranges to sell a batch, it incurs a fixed cost of \$20. This fixed cost mainly includes administrative expenses. The volume of sales is mainly dependent on the price of the product. The manager has come up with the following relationship between volume and price:

$$\text{Volume} = 500 - 25(\text{Price})$$

However, due to marketing and competitive considerations, X-Tech decided to limit its price to \$8.

a. State the nonlinear programming formulation of this problem.
b. Draw the profit function and the feasible solution space.
c. Determine the optimal price and optimal volume that will result in the maximum profit.
d. Repeat parts *a, b,* and *c,* by changing the restriction on price from a maximum of \$8 to a maximum of \$14.

Solution

a. maximize $\text{Profit} = Z = -25(\text{Price})^2 + 550(\text{Price}) - 1020$

   subject to

   $\text{Price} \leq 8$
   $\text{Price} \geq 0$

b. The drawing of the profit function and the feasible solution space is given in Figure 7-7.

FIGURE 7-7

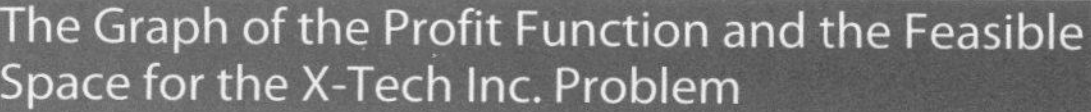
The Graph of the Profit Function and the Feasible Space for the X-Tech Inc. Problem

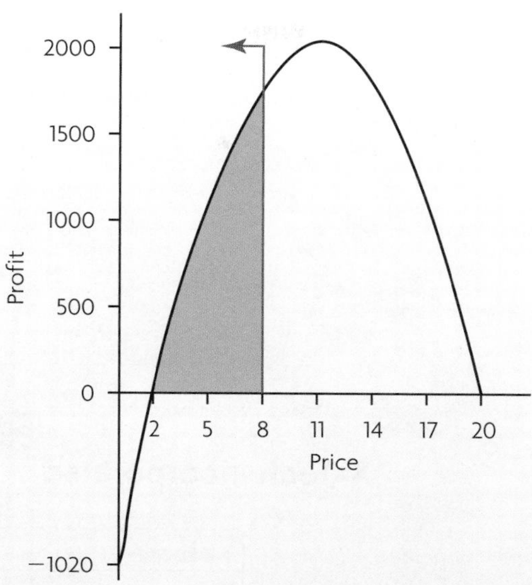

c. In observing Figure 7-7, we see that the feasible region does not include the optimal price of \$11. Furthermore, the price that results in the highest profit is \$8. To verify this answer, we utilize Excel. The preparation of the worksheet is identical to the preparation of the worksheet in Exhibit 7-1. The only difference in the preparation of this version of the problem is the specification of the Price $\leq$ 8 constraint in the Solver Parameters screen. The solution to this problem is given in Exhibit 7-3. As expected, the optimal solution has a price of \$8 per unit, with a volume of 300 units, resulting in a total profit of \$1780.

Exhibit 7-4 shows the parameter specification screen. The only difference between the contents of this screen in Exhibit 7-4 and the contents of Exhibit 7-2 is the specification of the new constraint (Price $\leq$ 8, specified as \$C\$4 $\leq$ 8).

d. Maximize Profit $= Z = -25(\text{Price})^2 + 550(\text{Price}) - 1020$

subject to

Price $\leq$ 14
Price $\geq$ 0

The drawing of the profit function and the feasible solution space is given in Figure 7-8. As we mentioned earlier, the optimal solution to a constrained nonlinear programming problem may or may not occur at a corner point. As we can see from Figure 7-8, since the maximum point of the function is feasible, the corner point A provides a lower profit than the peak of the function (point B). Therefore, the optimal solution occurs at a price of \$11 (point B), which results in a volume of 225 units and an optimal profit of \$2005.

EXHIBIT 7-3 Worksheet for the One-Decision-Variable, Constrained Problem (X-Tech Inc., Example 7-5)

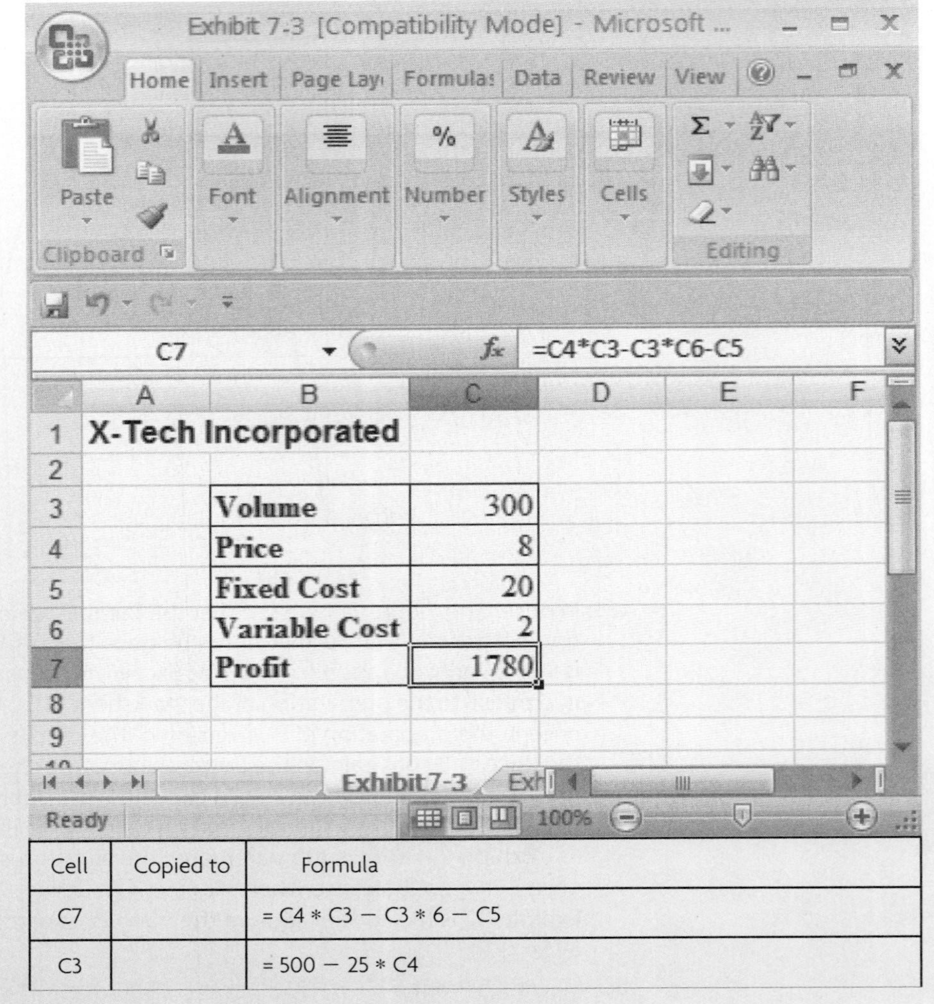

Cell	Copied to	Formula
C7		= C4 * C3 − C3 * 6 − C5
C3		= 500 − 25 * C4

7.3 MODELS WITH TWO DECISION VARIABLES, UNCONSTRAINED PROBLEM

Solution of models that involve two decision variables parallels the procedure used for models with one decision variable, except that the analysis is a bit more complicated, owing to the presence of a second decision variable. It becomes necessary to obtain the **partial derivative** of a function (i.e., the derivative of the function with respect to one variable, treating the other variable as a *constant*), as well as the second partial derivative of

EXHIBIT 7-4 Parameter Specification Screen for the One-Decision-Variable, Constrained Problem (X-Tech Inc. Example 7-5)

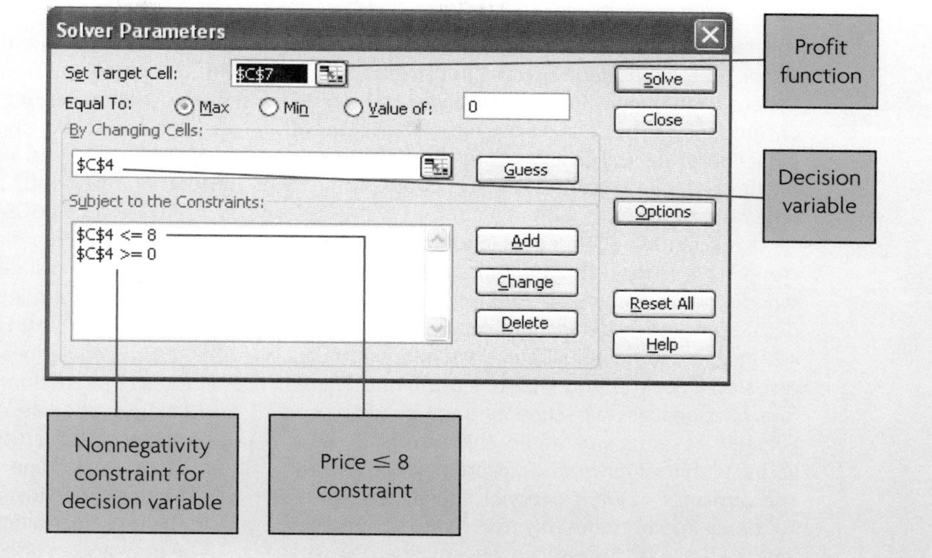

FIGURE 7-8 The Graph of the Profit Function and the Feasible Space for the X-Tech Inc. Problem (X-Tech Inc. Example 7-5)

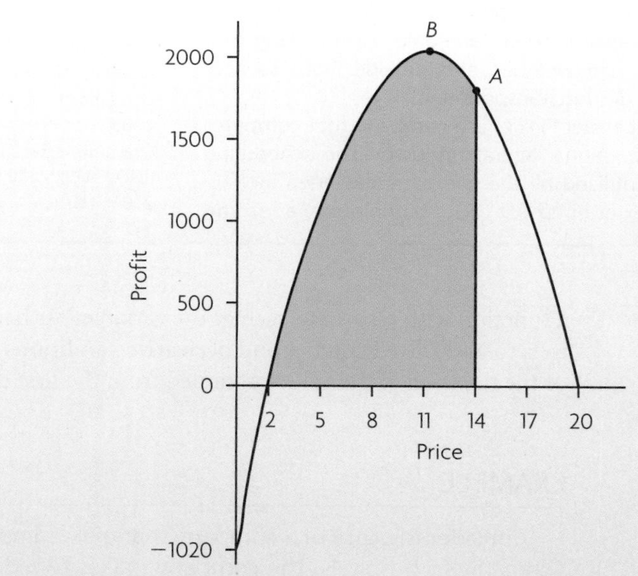

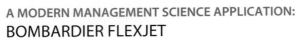

A MODERN MANAGEMENT SCIENCE APPLICATION: BOMBARDIER FLEXJET

The fractional aircraft market is the fastest-developing sector of the business aircraft industry. The fractional aircraft ownership program allows individuals or companies to buy a share of a business airplane at a fraction of the full cost of ownership. The cost to the buyer depends on the number of hours of flight time per year.

The scheduling of flights and the associated crews in a fractional aircraft market is different than scheduling commercial flights. Major airlines decide the flight schedule of their aircraft months in advance, while fractional aircraft scheduling takes place only several hours before the flight. Therefore, fractional aircraft scheduling can be very complicated as firms guarantee the buyers 24-hour access within a four-hour decision-making window. The airplanes in the fractional aircraft market fly 10 times more frequently than the commercial flights. These airplanes can fly anywhere in the world with as little as 48 hours' notice.

The fractional aircraft owners have to pay monthly management and usage fees. Operators of these aircraft must manage maintenance, crews, fuel, and insurance on behalf of the fractional owners. Operators also must meet owners' demand for flight schedules at the requested times, schedule crew members, perform maintenance, schedule flights taking into account bad weather, and provide flight services (such as ground transportation).

Bombardier Flexjet is a company that competes in the fractional aircraft industry. The scheduling system utilized by the company has been ineffective. Flexjet hired AD-OPT Technologies, a leading management consulting company. AD-OPT, along with the personnel from Flexjet, were responsible for maximizing Flexjet's aircraft, crew, and facilities planning and scheduling.

AD-OPT uses TOSCA (The Optimizer for Scheduling Corporate Aircraft) to schedule the flights and crews for Flexjet. TOSCA decides the type of aircraft to schedule for each flight request and when and where to perform maintenance and swap crews. The scheduling is determined for a one- to three-day period by considering Federal Aviation Administration (FAA) regulations, company-enforced constraints, aircraft performance limits, and required maintenance schedule. AD-OPT Technologies developed three modules using the GENCOL optimizer. This software package decomposes a large-scale, mixed-integer, nonlinear programming problem to assist the implementation of TOSCA.

The new system also uses crews more efficiently by performing effective crew swaps, reducing crew members by 20 percent. The new integrated system improved operational efficiency considerably at Flexjet, saving the company $27 million annually, and reducing the aircraft fleet by 40 percent.

Source: Reprinted by permission, R. Hicks, R. Madrid, C. Milligan, R. Pruneau, M. Kanaley, Y. Dumas, B. Lacroix, J. Desrosiers, and F. Soumis, "Bombardier Flexjet Significantly Improves Its Fractional Aircraft Ownership Operations," *Interfaces* Vol. 35, no. 1 (January–February 2005), pp. 59–60. Copyright (2005), the Institute for Operations Research and the Management Sciences (INFORMS), 7240 Parkway Drive, Suite 310, Hanover, MD 21076 USA.

a function with respect to each of the variables. As before, the first derivatives are set equal to zero and solved, and second derivative conditions are checked to determine the nature of the function at the values obtained from the first derivative results.

EXAMPLE 7-6

Consider the case of a company that makes imaging equipment that it sells primarily to hospitals. The company makes two different models. Suppose we let x_1 = the quantity of model 1 and x_2 = the quantity of model 2. Model 1 sells for \$64 000 and model 2 sells for \$72 000. The fixed cost of producing model 1 equipment is \$500 000 and the fixed cost of producing model 2 is \$600 000. The variable cost to produce each model (c_1, c_2) is complex and dependent on the quantity of each model that is produced and can be expressed as follows:

$c_1 = .4x_1 + .2x_2$ (in thousands of dollars)
$c_2 = .3x_2 + .2x_1$ (in thousands of dollars)

The manager of the company wants to determine the values of x_1 and x_2 that will maximize profit.

Solution

Variable costs can be calculated as follows:

$$x_1c_1 = .4x_1^2 + .2x_1x_2$$
$$x_2c_2 = .3x_2^2 + .2x_1x_2$$

The formula for the total profit is

$$\begin{aligned} Z &= \text{Total revenue} - (\text{Variable cost} - \text{Fixed cost}) \\ &= 64x_1 + 72x_2 - [x_1c_1 + x_2c_2 - (500 + 600)] \\ &= 64x_1 + 72x_2 - .4x_1^2 - .2x_1x_2 - .3x_2^2 - .2x_1x_2 - 1100 \end{aligned}$$

Combining the two x_1x_2 terms, we have

$$Z = 64x_1 + 72x_2 - .4x_1^2 - .4x_1x_2 - .3x_2^2 - 1100$$

To solve problems of this type, it is necessary to obtain the partial derivative of the function (i.e., *P*) with respect to each of the decision variables, and then set these equal to zero.

Condition 3 (*necessary*): The partial derivatives of an unconstrained function of two variables must both equal zero at a local maximum or a local minimum of the function.

Finding the partial derivatives and setting them equal to zero, we obtain

$$\frac{\partial Z}{\partial x_1} = 64 - .8x_1 - .4x_2 = 0$$

$$\frac{\partial Z}{\partial x_2} = 72 - .4x_1 - .6x_2 = 0$$

Rearranging terms, we can write

$$\frac{\partial Z}{\partial x_1}: = .8x_1 + .4x_2 = 64$$

$$\frac{\partial Z}{\partial x_1}: = .4x_1 + .6x_2 = 72$$

We can solve this by multiplying the second equation by 2 and then subtracting the first equation from the revised second equation. Thus:

$$\begin{aligned} .8x_1 + 1.2x_2 &= 144 \\ -(.8x_1 + .4x_2 &= 64) \\ \hline .8x_2 &= 80, \quad x_2 = 100 \end{aligned}$$

Substituting this value into either equation and solving for x_1, we obtain $x_1 = 30$. Hence, the optimal values *appear* to be $x_1 = 30$ and $x_2 = 100$.

Once these values have been obtained, we can check the second-order conditions to determine what sort of point they represent.

First, compute D, where

$$D = \left(\frac{\partial^2 Z}{\partial x_1^2}\right)\left(\frac{\partial^2 Z}{\partial x_2^2}\right) - \left(\frac{\partial^2 Z}{\partial x_1 \partial x_2}\right)^2$$

Then check the second-order conditions:

Condition 4 (*sufficient*). If Condition 3 is satisfied, and:

a. $D > 0$

   1. The point is a local minimum if $\frac{\partial^2 Z}{\partial x_1^2} > 0$
   2. The point is a local maximum if $\frac{\partial^2 Z}{\partial x_1^2} < 0$

b. $D < 0$

   The point is neither a local minimum nor a local maximum. Instead, it is a **saddle point,** which means one of the variables reaches a local maximum at the same point that the other variable reaches a local minimum.

In this example, the second partials and the mixed partial are

$$\frac{\partial^2 Z}{\partial x_1^2} = -.8, \qquad \frac{\partial^2 Z}{\partial x_2^2} = -.6, \qquad \text{and} \qquad \frac{\partial^2 Z}{\partial x_1 \partial x_2} = -.4,$$

Hence, $D = (-.8)(-.6) - (.4)^2 = +.32$. Because $D > 0$ and $\frac{\partial^2 Z}{\partial x_1^2} < 0$ this point ($x_1 = 30, x_2 = 100$) is a local maximum (see Condition 4).

By substituting the optimal values into the original profit function, we also can determine the maximum profit:

$$Z = 64(30) + 72(100) - .4(30^2) - .4(30)(100) - .3(100^2) - 1100$$
$$Z = 3460, \text{ or } \$3\,460\,000$$

Solution of Unconstrained Problems with Two Decision Variables Using Excel

To see how an unconstrained nonlinear programming model with two decision variables may be solved using Excel, we will consider Example 7-6. In Example 7-6, the goal was to maximize the following profit equation:

$$\mathbf{Z = 64x_1 + 72x_2 - .4x_1^2 - .4x_1x_2 - .3x_2^2 - 1100}$$

In maximizing this profit equation, we prepare the worksheet shown in Exhibit 7-5. In preparing this worksheet, we begin by defining the variables in cells B5 and C5. Row 7 shows the headings used for the revenue and variable cost terms. Row 8 actually defines these in terms of Excel variables. For example, we set the values in cell B8 and C8 equal to the value of the decision variables in cells B5 and C5. The formula for cell D8 is the product

EXHIBIT 7-5 Worksheet for the Two-Decision-Variable, Unconstrained Problem (Example 7-6, Imaging Equipment)

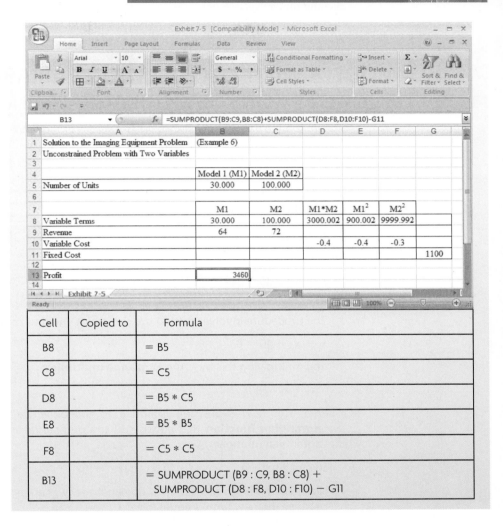

Exhibit 7-5 [Compatibility Mode] - Microsoft Excel

B13 f_x =SUMPRODUCT(B9:C9,B8:C8)+SUMPRODUCT(D8:F8,D10:F10)-G11

	A	B	C	D	E	F	G
1	Solution to the Imaging Equipment Problem	(Example 6)					
2	Unconstrained Problem with Two Variables						
3							
4		Model 1 (M1)	Model 2 (M2)				
5	Number of Units	30.000	100.000				
6							
7		M1	M2	M1*M2	M1^2	M2^2	
8	Variable Terms	30.000	100.000	3000.002	900.002	9999.992	
9	Revenue	64	72				
10	Variable Cost			-0.4	-0.4	-0.3	
11	Fixed Cost						1100
12							
13	Profit	3460					
14							

Cell	Copied to	Formula
B8		= B5
C8		= C5
D8		= B5 * C5
E8		= B5 * B5
F8		= C5 * C5
B13		= SUMPRODUCT (B9 : C9, B8 : C8) + SUMPRODUCT (D8 : F8, D10 : F10) − G11

of the two decision variables; x_1x_2, represented as B5 × C5. The formulas for the squared decision variable terms x_1^2 and x_2^2 in cells E8 and F8 are given in Exhibit 7-5. In the revenue, variable cost, and the fixed cost rows (rows 9, 10, and 11), we simply enter the appropriate revenue or cost coefficient from the profit equation given above. The profit is calculated by the profit equation given in cell B13 of Exhibit 7-5. This equation is shown in the formula bar at the bottom of Exhibit 7-5 and repeated here: =SUMPRODUCT (B9 : C9, B8 : C8) + SUMPRODUCT (D8 : F8, D10 : F10) − G11. In this equation, the first SUMPRODUCT term includes the calculation of the revenue. Cells B9 : C9 represent the revenue coefficient of the decision variables and cells B8 : C8 represent the decision variables. The second SUMPRODUCT term consists of the calculation of the variable cost. Cells D8 : F8 are the nonlinear terms involving the variable cost and cells D10 : F10 are the appropriate coefficients for the variable cost. Finally, the value in cell G11 represents the fixed cost. After preparing the worksheet in Exhibit 7-5, we click **Data|Analysis|Solver**.

Because this is a nonlinear model, to ensure that a linear model is not utilized, we click on "Options" and make sure that the "Assume Linear Model" box is *not* checked. After clicking on "Solve," we obtain the solution given in Exhibit 7-5. Based on the results, we should produce 30 units of model 1 and 100 units of model 2 for a total profit of \$3460.

7.4 MODELS WITH TWO DECISION VARIABLES AND AN EQUALITY CONSTRAINT (LAGRANGE MULTIPLIERS)

The solution to a problem that involves two variables and one or more equality constraints when either the function or the constraints (or both) are nonlinear can be handled using the *Lagrangian method*. For an illustration, consider the following example.

EXAMPLE 7-7

maximize $Z = -2.5x_1^2 - x_2^2 + 3x_1x_2 + 18x_1 + 6x_2 + 100$

subject to

$x_1 + x_2 = 40$

Solution

The procedure involves setting the constraint equal to zero:

$x_1 + x_2 - 40 = 0$

and multiplying this by λ, the **Lagrange multiplier:**

$\lambda(x_1 + x_2 - 40)$

Then this new expression is added to the objective function to obtain a **Lagrangian function** that consists of the original decision variables and the Lagrangian multiplier, λ:

$L(x_1, x_2, \lambda) = -2.5x_1^2 - x_2^2 + 3x_1x_2 + 18x_1 + 6x_2 + 100 + \lambda(x_1 + x_2 - 40)$

Note that adding this new term does not really change the objective function because the new term is equal to zero.

Once we have obtained the Lagrangian function, we can analyze the problem in a way that is very similar to the procedure described in the preceding section for two-variable, unconstrained models. The only difference is that we now have a third variable to deal with.

As before, we obtain the partial derivative of the objective function with respect to each of the variables (x_1, x_2, and λ):

$$\frac{\partial L}{\partial x_1} = -5x_1 + 3x_2 + 18 + \lambda = 0$$

$$\frac{\partial L}{\partial x_2} = -2x_2 + 3x_1 + 6 + \lambda = 0$$

$$\frac{\partial L}{\partial \lambda} = x_1 + x_2 - 40 = 0$$

We can solve this system of equations for the values of x_1, x_2, and λ by first eliminating λ from the first two equations (e.g., subtract the first equation from the second). The result is

$$(-2x_2 + 3x_1 + 6 + \lambda) - (-5x_1 + 3x_2 + 18 + \lambda) = 0$$
$$(5x_1 + 3x_1) + (-3x_2 - 2x_2) + (-18 + 6) + (-\lambda + \lambda) = 0$$
$$8x_1 \quad -5x_2 \quad -12 \quad = 0$$

Then, using this new equation and the third partial derivative, we have

$$\begin{array}{ll} \text{(new)} & 8x_1 - 5x_2 - 12 = 0 \\ \text{(third)} & x_1 + x_2 - 40 = 0 \end{array}$$

Solving these equations simultaneously, we get

$$x_1 = 16.307$$

and substituting this into the (third) equation, we find that $x_2 = 23.693$.

We can now determine the value of λ, using $x_1 = 16.307$ and $x_2 = 23.693$, and either of the first two partial derivative equations. For example, using the first partial derivative equation, we find

$$-5(16.307) + 3(23.693) + 18 + \lambda = 0$$

Solving, $\lambda = -7.544$.

At this point, we have found what appear to be optimal values of x_1 and x_2. However, instead of *maximizing* the original function, it may be that they actually *minimize* the function. Or they may constitute a *saddle point*. The same conditions that applied in the previous section apply here. To check them, we must first substitute the value of $\lambda = -7.544$ into the first partial derivatives of L with respect to x_1 and x_2. Thus:

$$\frac{\partial L}{\partial x_1} = -5x_1 + 3x_2 + 18 - 7.544$$

$$\frac{\partial L}{\partial x_2} = -2x_2 + 3x_1 + 6 - 7.544$$

The second partials and the mixed partial are

$$\frac{\partial^2 L}{\partial x_1^2} = -5. \qquad \frac{\partial^2 L}{\partial x_2^2} = -2, \qquad \text{and} \qquad \frac{\partial^2 L}{\partial x_1 \partial x_2} = +3$$

As before, we compute the value of D:

$$D = \left(\frac{\partial^2 L}{\partial x_1^2}\right)\left(\frac{\partial^2 L}{\partial x_2^2}\right) - \left(\frac{\partial^2 L}{\partial x_1 \partial x_2}\right)^2 = (-5)(-2) - (3)^2 = 10 - 9 = 1$$

Because $D > 0$ and $\frac{\partial^2 L}{\partial x_1^2} < 0$, we do, in fact, have a local maximum. We can determine the value of the function at its local maximum by substituting the values we found for x_1 and x_2 into the original function, Thus:

$$Z = -2.5(16.307)^2 - (23.693)^2 + 3(16.307)(23.693) + 18(16.307) + 6(23.693) + 100 = 468.61$$

Let's take a moment to recap the Lagrange procedure:

1. Form the Lagrange function. Do this by making the constraint equal to zero, multiplying it by λ, and adding the result to the original objective function.
2. Obtain the partial derivative of the Lagrange function with respect to each of the decision variables and to λ. Set these equal to zero.
3. Find the solution(s) for the decision variables. Do this by eliminating λ from the partials of x_1 and x_2, and then using the partial of the Lagrange multiplier. Then find the value of λ.
4. Treating the value of λ as fixed, find the second partials of x_1, x_2, and the mixed partial.
5. Determine if the solution(s) is (are) a local maximum, local minimum, or a saddle point, according to Condition 4 that was described in the previous section.

Interpreting λ

The Lagrange multiplier, λ, has an important economic interpretation, analogous to dual variables in linear programming. Its value indicates the (sometimes approximate) amount that the objective function will change for a one-unit change in the right-hand-side value of the constraint. For instance, in the preceding example, we found $\lambda = -7.544$. This means that if the right-hand-side value of the constraint were to be increased by one unit (from 40 to 41) the resulting optimal value of the objective function would increase by 7.544. Conversely, if the right-hand-side value of the constraint were to be decreased by one unit, the optimal value of the objective function would decrease by 7.544. Moreover, if the sign of λ had been positive (say, +22), the opposite would have been true: A one-unit decrease in the right-hand-side value of the constraint would have caused an *increase* of 22 in the optimal value of the objective function, and a one-unit increase in the right-hand-side value of the constraint would have caused a *decrease* of 22 in the end optimal value of the objective function.

Solution of Problems with Two Decision Variables and a Single Equality Constraint Using Excel

To see how a nonlinear programming model with two decision variables may be solved using Excel, we will consider the following example.

EXAMPLE 7-8

The Daisy-Fresh Company produces two types of deodorants. Let x_1 be equal to the quantity of roll-on deodorant and let x_2 be equal to the quantity of stick deodorant. The profit contribution for the roll-on deodorant is estimated as $3.2x_1 - .02x_1^2$. In interpreting this equation, the expected revenue is \$3.20 for each roll-on deodorant. However, the variable cost of production is a nonlinear function of the number of units produced. In other words, the total units of roll-on deodorant (x_1) being produced by Daisy-Fresh Company cost Daisy-Fresh $\$0.02x_1^2$ in production costs. Likewise, the profit contribution for the stick deodorant is estimated as $4x_2 - .03x_2^2$. The estimated revenue per unit of stick deodorant is \$4, and the total variable cost is $.03x_2^2$. The hourly fixed cost of producing both products together is estimated as \$150. Each unit of roll-on deodorant takes 20 seconds to manufacture on a machine, while each unit of stick deodorant takes 30 seconds to manufacture on a machine. A machine has 60 minutes of productive capacity in an hour before minor maintenance has to be performed.

a. Formulate this problem as a single constrained nonlinear programming problem.
b. Use Excel and determine the hourly number of units of each deodorant type to produce.
c. What is the optimal profit?

Solution

a. Formulation:

x_1 = quantity of roll-on deodorant
x_2 = quantity of stick deodorant

maximize $Z = 3.2x_1 - .02x_1^2 + 4x_2 - .03x_2^2 - 150$

subject to

$20x_1 + 30x_2 = 3600$ seconds
$x_1, x_2 \geq 0$

b. As a starting point, we prepare the worksheet shown in Exhibit 7-6. In preparing this worksheet, first we begin by defining the variables in cells B5 and C5. Row 7 shows the headings used for the revenue and variable cost terms. Row 8 actually defines these items in terms of Excel variables. For example, we set the values in cell B8 and C8 equal to the value of the decision variables in cells B5 and C5. The formulas for the squared decision variable terms x_1^2 and x_2^2 in cells D8 and E8 are given in Exhibit 7-6. Cell D8 contains B5 * B5, and cell E8 contains C5 * C5. In the revenue, variable cost, and fixed-cost rows (rows 9, 10, and 11), we simply enter the appropriate revenue or cost coefficient from the profit equation given in the objective function of this problem. The profit is calculated by the profit equation given in cell B13 of Exhibit 7-6. This equation is shown in the formula bar of Exhibit 7-6 and is repeated here: = SUMPRODUCT(B9 : C9, B8 : C8) + SUMPRODUCT(D8 : E8, D10 : E10) − F11. In this equation, the first SUMPRODUCT term includes the calculation of the revenue. Cells B9 : C9 represent the revenue coefficient of the decision variables, and cells B8 : C8 represent the decision variables. The second SUMPRODUCT term consists of the calculation of the variable cost. The cells D8 : E8 are the nonlinear terms involving the variable cost and the cells D10 : E10 are the appropriate coefficients for the variable cost. Finally, the value in cell F11 represents the fixed cost. The machine time constraint is specified in row 12. In this row, we first specify the amount of time it takes to produce each unit in cells B12 (20 seconds to produce one unit of roll-on deodorant) and C12 (30 seconds to produce one unit of stick deodorant). The right-hand side of the constraint is entered in the Time Available column in cell H12. The sum of the left-hand side of the constraint is calculated by cross-multiplying the decision variable values with the amount of time it takes to produce one unit. This is accomplished by the following formula: = SUMPRODUCT(B12 : C12, B5 : C5). In this formula, cells B12 : C12

EXHIBIT 7-6 Worksheet for the Problem with Two Decision Variables and a Single Equality Constraint (Example 7-8, Daisy-Fresh Company Deodorant Problem)

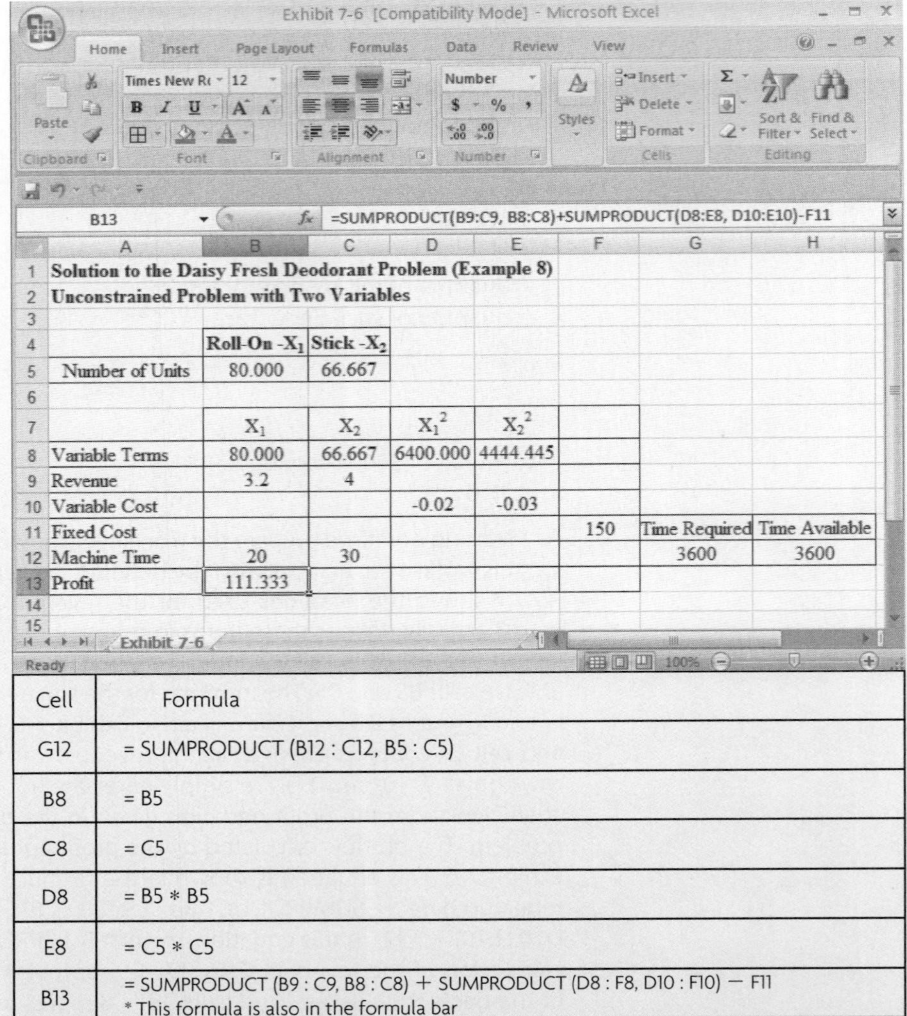

B13 =SUMPRODUCT(B9:C9, B8:C8)+SUMPRODUCT(D8:E8, D10:E10)-F11

	A	B	C	D	E	F	G	H
1	**Solution to the Daisy Fresh Deodorant Problem (Example 8)**							
2	**Unconstrained Problem with Two Variables**							
3								
4		**Roll-On -X_1**	**Stick -X_2**					
5	Number of Units	80.000	66.667					
6								
7		X_1	X_2	X_1^2	X_2^2			
8	Variable Terms	80.000	66.667	6400.000	4444.445			
9	Revenue	3.2	4					
10	Variable Cost			-0.02	-0.03			
11	Fixed Cost					150	Time Required	Time Available
12	Machine Time	20	30				3600	3600
13	Profit	111.333						

Cell	Formula
G12	= SUMPRODUCT (B12 : C12, B5 : C5)
B8	= B5
C8	= C5
D8	= B5 * B5
E8	= C5 * C5
B13	= SUMPRODUCT (B9 : C9, B8 : C8) + SUMPRODUCT (D8 : F8, D10 : F10) − F11 * This formula is also in the formula bar

represent the production time per unit, and cells B5 : C5 are the values of decision variables x_1 and x_2.

After preparing the worksheet in Exhibit 7-6, we click **Data|Analysis|Solver**. Since this is a nonlinear model, to ensure that a linear model is not utilized, we click on "Options" and make sure that the "Assume Linear Model" box is *not* checked. After clicking on "Solve", we obtain the solution given in Exhibit 7-6. Based on the results, the Daisy-Fresh Company should produce 80 units of roll-on deodorant and 66.67 units of stick deodorant.

c. Total optimal profit associated with this production schedule is specified in cell B13 and it is $111.33 per hour, per machine.

7.5 MODELS WITH TWO DECISION VARIABLES AND A SINGLE INEQUALITY CONSTRAINT

The procedure described in the previous section can be modified a little if we have a problem that involves two variables and a single inequality constraint. In demonstrating how to solve this type of problem, let's consider Example 7-7 from the last section. We will switch the constraint from = to ≤.

EXAMPLE 7-9

Let

x_1 = number of units of product 1 manufactured
x_2 = number of units of product 2 manufactured

maximize $z = -2.5x_1^2 - x_2^2 + 3x_1x_2 + 18x_1 + 6x_2 + 100$

subject to

$x_1 + x_2 \leq 40$ (labour hours constraint)

There are two possibilities with respect to the constraint. The first one involves the possibility that the constraint is binding. If it is a binding constraint, then the left-hand side of the constraint must equal the right-hand side of the constraint. Since it becomes an "equal to" constraint, it can be solved by the method described in answering Example 7-7. However, if $x_1 + x_2 < 40$, then the constraint is not binding. In this case, we will ignore the constraint and solve it as an unconstrained problem. This solution procedure can be summarized as follows:

1. Assume the constraint is not binding and solve it as an unconstrained problem. In solving it this way, we are attempting to determine if a global maximum exists. We can determine if a given point is a global maximum by applying the necessary and sufficient conditions test from the previous section. If we establish that the point is indeed the global maximum, then we need to test it to see if it satisfies the constraint. If the global maximum satisfies the constraint, we stop and the global maximum found is the optimal solution to this problem. Based on the necessary and sufficient conditions test, if the point is not a global maximum, then we will simply maintain any local maximum that satisfies the constraints in our records and go to step 2.
2. We assume that the constraint is binding and apply the solution procedure utilized with a single equality constraint utilized in solving Example 7-7. If a local maximum is found in step 1, we compare the results from step 2 with the local maximum results from step 1. The global maximum is given by the solution that gives the largest profit among these values.

In other words, if the constraint is not satisfied in step 1, we go to step 2. If the constraint is satisfied but necessary and sufficient conditions for global optimality are not satisfied, the values of the decision variables at the local maximum are recorded and step 2 is executed.

Solution

1. *(Necessary conditions)* Take the partial derivative with respect to each variable and set the resulting equations equal to zero.

$$\frac{\partial Z}{\partial x_1} = -5x_1 + 3x_2 + 18 = 0$$

Rearranging the terms:

$$5x_1 - 3x_2 = 18$$

$$\frac{\partial Z}{\partial x_2} = 3x_1 - 2x_2 + 6 = 0$$

Rearranging the terms:

$$-3x_1 + 2x_2 = 6$$

We can solve the two rearranged equations simultaneously.

$$(2)(5x_1 - 3x_2) = (2)18 \quad \text{or}$$
$$10x - 6x_2 = 36$$
$$(3)(-3x_1 + 2x_2) = (3)6 \quad \text{or}$$
$$-9x_1 + 6x_2 = 18$$

$$\begin{array}{l} 10x_1 - 6x_2 = 36 \\ \underline{+ - 9x_1 + 6x_2 = 18} \\ x_1 = 54 \end{array}$$

$$\begin{aligned} 5(54) - 3x_2 &= 18 \\ -3x_2 &= -252 \\ x_2 &= 84 \end{aligned}$$

Once these values have been obtained, we can check the second-order conditions.

Sufficient Conditions In this example, second partial derivatives and mixed partial derivatives are as follows:

$$\frac{\partial^2 Z}{\partial x_1^2} = -5$$

$$\frac{\partial^2 Z}{\partial x_2^2} = -2$$

$$\frac{\partial^2 Z}{\partial x_1 \partial x_2} = -3$$

$$D = \left(\frac{\partial^2 Z}{\partial x_1^2}\right)\left(\frac{\partial^2 Z}{\partial x_2^2}\right) - \left(\frac{\partial^2 Z}{\partial x_1 \partial x_2}\right)^2 = (-5)(-2) - (-3)^2$$

$$D = 10 - 9 = 1$$

Since D > 0 and $\frac{\partial^2 Z}{\partial x_1^2} < 0$, this point ($x_1 = 54, x_2 = 84$) is an optimal solution to the unconstrained problem. However, since $x_1 + x_2 = 54 + 84 = 138 > 40$, the constraint is not satisfied. Therefore, we go to step 2.

2. Since we have already utilized the solution procedure for step 2 in solving Example 7-7, the optimal solution to this problem is

   $x_1 = 16.307 \qquad x_2 = 23.693 \qquad \text{and} \qquad Z = 468.61$

   Had the constraint been satisfied as the end of step 1, then the solution found in step 1 would have been the optimal solution to Example 7-9. The constraint represents the availability of weekly labour hours. There are 40 labour hours available each week and each unit of product 1 and product 2 takes 1 hour to manufacture respectively. Solving the unconstrained problem resulted in production of 54 units of product 1 and 84 units of product 2. However, producing these values will exceed the labour hours available and violate the constraint. That is why we utilize the method involving the Lagrange multiplier because the Lagrange multiplier method assumes that the constraint is binding and solves for the optimal values of x_1 and x_2. Had we found a local optimal point that satisfies the constraint but does not satisfy the necessary and sufficient conditions for global optimality, we would have recorded that solution and compared it to the solution found in step 2 and then chosen the solution with the larger profit.

The solution procedure we have described in this section cannot be applied to problems that involve multiple constraints. In many real-world problems, there are multiple constraints. In solving these problems, we utilize Excel or other software packages. The solution procedures that solve these problems are iterative and complex; therefore, we do not provide the steps or detailed description of these algorithms. However, in the next section, we will provide an example with multiple constraints and solve it using Excel.

Solution of Problems with Two Decision Variables and Multiple Constraints Using Excel

We can use Excel to solve nonlinear programming problems with two decision variables and multiple constraints. Let's consider the following example for demonstration purposes.

EXAMPLE 7-10

East-West Computer Storage produces CDs, DVDs, and diskettes. The company earns a profit of \$5 for each CD and \$2.80 for each diskette. However, in producing the DVDs, we take advantage of fixed overhead costs. The more DVDs produced, the higher the profit. Let's define the variables as CD = CD, Diskette = DI, and DVD = DV. The profits on the DVDs can be expressed as $1DV + .02DV^2$. East-West Computer Storage Company's nonlinear objective function can be stated as follows:

maximize $\quad Z = 5CD + 2.8DI + 1DV + .02DV^2$

This objective function is subject to the following labour and machine constraints. East-West Computer Storage Company has 40 hours of labour available per week and 36.66 machine hours available per week. Each unit of CD, Diskette, and DVD requires the following number of labour and machine hours:

	CD	Diskette	DVD
Labour hours per unit (minutes)	4	2	8
Machine hours per unit (minutes)	3	2.5	6.5

Based on marketing considerations, the minimum production requirement of DVDs is 100 units.

Formulate the nonlinear program for this problem and use Excel to determine the optimal production schedule of these three products. What is the maximum profit?

Solution

The nonlinear programming formulation of this problem is as follows:

maximize $Z = 5CD + 2.8DI + 1DV + .02DV^2$

subject to

$4CD + 2DI + 8DV \leq 2400$ minutes (labour time available)

$3CD + 2.5DI + 6.5DV \leq 2200$ minutes (machine time available)

$DV \geq 100$ (minimum DVD production requirement)

$CD, DI, DV \geq 0$

The Excel worksheet shown in Exhibit 7-7 includes the input as well as the output from this model. In preparing this worksheet, we begin by defining the location of the three decision variables CD, Diskette (DI), and DVD (DV) in cells B5, C5, and D5 respectively. Variable terms are defined in cells B8, C8, D8, and E8. Cells B8, C8, and D8 are simply the values of the decision variables in cells B5, C5, and D5. However, we define the formula in cell E8 (D5 × D5) as the square of the DVD variable in cell D5. Row 9 shows the revenue values from the objective function, while rows 10 and 11 indicate the labour and machine constraints. Cell F10, labour minutes used, represents the left-hand side of the labour constraint. Cell F11, machine minutes used, represents the left-hand side of the machine constraint. Cells G10 and G11 represent the right-hand side of the labour and machine constraints respectively. In developing the formula for cell F10, we use the following: =SUMPRODUCT (B10 : D10, B5 : D5). In this equation, B10 : D10 are the coefficients of the labour constraints (amount of labour time required to produce one unit of each product). B5 : D5 represent the values of the decision variables. The formula for cell F11 is developed in a similar fashion for the machine time constraint. Column H provides the values of slack associated with labour and machine time constraints. The formula for profit, = SUMPRODUCT (B9 : E9, B8 : E8), is shown in the formula bar of Exhibit 7-7. This formula is the cross-product of the decision variables with the profit margin for each variable. B9 : E9 represent the profit margin for each product as well as the squared DVD term. B8 : D8 includes the values of the decision variables. Finally, in cell E8 the number of DVDs is squared to reflect

EXHIBIT 7-7 Worksheet for a Two-Decision-Variable, Multiple-Constraint Problem (Example 7-10, East-West Company Computer Storage Problem)

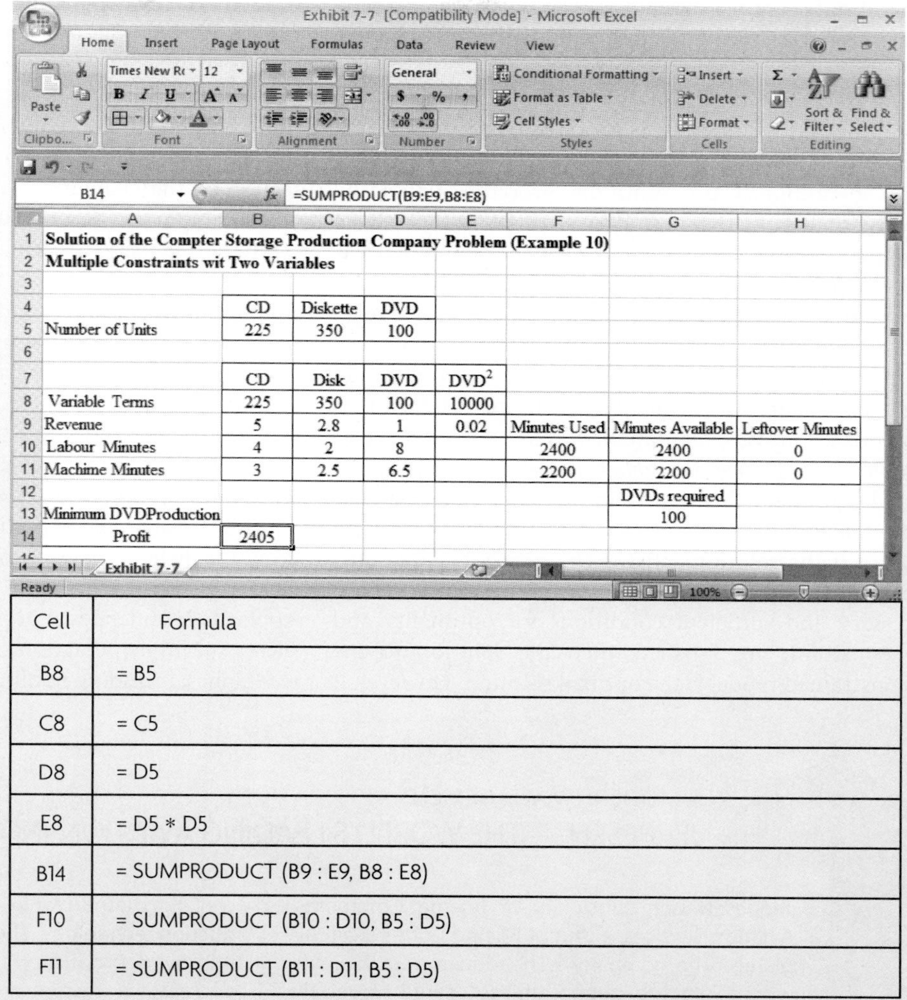

	A	B	C	D	E	F	G	H
1	**Solution of the Compter Storage Production Company Problem (Example 10)**							
2	**Multiple Constraints wit Two Variables**							
3								
4		CD	Diskette	DVD				
5	Number of Units	225	350	100				
6								
7		CD	Disk	DVD	DVD^2			
8	Variable Terms	225	350	100	10000			
9	Revenue	5	2.8	1	0.02	Minutes Used	Minutes Available	Leftover Minutes
10	Labour Minutes	4	2	8		2400	2400	0
11	Machime Minutes	3	2.5	6.5		2200	2200	0
12							DVDs required	
13	Minimum DVDProduction						100	
14	Profit	2405						

Cell	Formula
B8	= B5
C8	= C5
D8	= D5
E8	= D5 * D5
B14	= SUMPRODUCT (B9 : E9, B8 : E8)
F10	= SUMPRODUCT (B10 : D10, B5 : D5)
F11	= SUMPRODUCT (B11 : D11, B5 : D5)

the DV2 term in the objective function. The formulas used to prepare the worksheet shown in Exhibit 7-7 are stated at the bottom of the worksheet.

After entering the values and the formulas shown at the bottom of Exhibit 7-7, we proceed to choose **Data|Analysis|Solver.** Since this is a nonlinear model, to ensure that a linear model is not utilized, we click on "Options" and make sure that the "Assume Linear Model" box is *not* checked. After clicking on "Solve," we obtain the solution given in Exhibit 7-7. Based on these results, East-West Computer Storage Company should produce 225 CDs, 350 Diskettes, and 100 DVDs. Total optimal profit associated with this production schedule is specified in cell B14 as $2405.

Summary

The models presented in this chapter are similar to the linear programming models presented in earlier chapters. The essential difference is that the models in this chapter have one or more *nonlinear* components. These models generally cannot be handled using conventional linear programming techniques. Instead, nonlinear programming procedures must be used.

The nonlinear programming procedures typically involve obtaining the first derivative of the objective function, finding all solutions for which the first derivative is equal to zero, and then checking second derivative conditions to ascertain the nature of the zero points (e.g., a local maximum or a local minimum). If two or more decision variables are involved, partial derivatives are used. If equality or inequality constraints and two or more decision variables are involved, a method that involves a *Lagrange multiplier* is used. If the model includes an inequality constraint and two or more decision variables, first we solve the model as unconstrained and see if the solution satisfies the necessary and sufficient conditions and also satisfies the constraint. If the necessary and sufficient conditions for optimality and the constraint are satisfied, then the solution to the unconstrained model is the optimal solution. However, if the constraint is violated, we go to the next step (step 2). In the next step, we assume that the constraint is binding and use the Lagrange multiplier method that we employed when we solved the problem with a single equality constraint.

Throughout the chapter, we show the Excel solution to various nonlinear programming problems. In the last section of the chapter, we demonstrate how a problem with multiple decision variables and multiple constraints can be solved using Excel.

The models presented in this chapter are relatively simple. More complex models are more challenging to deal with. Some lend themselves to computer solution. Unfortunately most management science computer packages including Excel are not equipped to handle these sorts of more complicated problems. These problems require the use of more specialized software. Formulating and solving nonlinear programming problems may require considerable expertise and some such problems do not truly lend themselves to solution, even with a specialized computer software. The Modern Management Application on Jeppesen provides another illustration of a successful implementation of some management science techniques, including nonlinear optimization methods.

A MODERN MANAGEMENT APPLICATION: JEPPESEN — THE WORLD'S LEADING AVIATION-INFORMATION COMPANY

Jeppesen is a subsidiary of Boeing Commercial Aviation Services, a unit of Boeing Commercial Airplanes. The company is headquartered in Englewood, Colorado, but has offices located around the world. Its Canadian office is located in Montreal, Quebec. Among its portfolio of products and services, Jeppesen maintains, manufactures, and distributes flight manuals containing safety information for over 300 000 pilots and 400 airlines from over 80 countries. Jeppesen has been very innovative, but in 1997, its growing product line overwhelmed what had been an efficient production system. It could not maintain its once stellar service and was threatened with losing a major customer. To cope with this threat, a suite of optimization-based decision support tools were developed to improve the company's production planning as well as a method for evaluating investments in production technology. The work reduced lateness and improved production processes, which led to a decrease in customer complaints, a reduction in costs of nearly 10 percent, and an increase in profit of 24 percent. Models used in decision support tools included, among others, linear programming, mixed integer linear programming, nonlinear mixed integer programming, stochastic programming, and simulation.

Source: Reprinted by permission, E. Katok, W. Tarantino, and R. Tiedeman: "Improving Performance and Flexibility at Jeppesen: The World's Leading Aviation-Information Company," *Interfaces* Vol. 31, no 1, (January–February 2001), pp. 7–29. Copyright (2001), the Institute for Operations Research and the Management Sciences (INFORMS), 7240 Parkway Drive, Suite 310, Hanover, MD 21076 USA.

Glossary

Global Maximum The highest value attained by a function over its entire range.

Global Minimum The lowest value attained by a function over its entire range.

Lagrange Multiplier, λ An additional variable used to incorporate the constraint(s) into the objective function in a model that has equality constraints.

Lagrangian Function In models that have equality constraints, a modified objective function that incorporates the constraint(s) as part of the objective function.

Local Maximum The highest point of a function relative to nearby values. It may or may not be the highest point overall.

Local Minimum The lowest point of a function relative to nearby values. It may or may not be the lowest point overall.

Necessary Conditions For the solution to be a candidate for the optimal solution, these conditions require first derivatives to be set equal to zero. However, satisfying these conditions does not guarantee optimality.

Partial Derivative When a function has more than one decision variable, a derivative of the function with respect to one of the decision variables with all other variables treated as constants.

Saddle Point A point that is neither a maximum nor a minimum; with two variables, the function attains a maximum with respect to one variable while attaining a minimum with respect to the other variable.

Sufficient Conditions Assist in determining whether a solution is associated with a maximum, minimum, or no solution. They involve taking the second partial derivative of the objective function and observing the signs of the second partial derivatives and the sign of D

where $D = \left(\frac{\partial^2 Z}{\partial x_1^2}\right)\left(\frac{\partial^2 Z}{\partial x_2^2}\right) - \left(\frac{\partial^2 Z}{\partial x_1 \partial x_2}\right)^2$.

Solved Problems

Problem 1

One variable, unconstrained. Given the following function:

$$y = \frac{1}{3}x^3 - 6x^2 + 27x$$

a. Determine the value of x for which the function reaches (1) a local maximum and (2) a local minimum.

b. Determine the value of the function at the local maximum and local minimum.

c. Use Excel to solve the above problem. What is the maximum value of the function and the optimum value of x?

Solution

a. 1. Obtain the first derivative of the function:

$$\frac{dy}{dx} = x^2 - 12x + 27$$

2. Set the first derivative equal to zero and solve for x:

$$x^2 - 12x - 27 = 0$$

Factoring, we obtain

$$(x - 3)(x - 9) = 0$$

Hence, the roots are $x = +3$ and $x = +9$.

3. Obtain the second derivative:

$$\frac{d^2y}{dx^2} = 2x - 12$$

Substitute the roots obtained in step 2 into the second derivative:

At $x = +3$, the second derivative equals -6
At $x = +9$, the second derivative equals $+6$

We can conclude that the function reaches a local maximum at $x = 3$ because the sign of the second derivative is negative for $x = +3$: and we can conclude that the function reaches a local minimum at $x = 9$ because the sign of the second derivative is positive for that value of x.

b. Substituting $x = 3$ and $x = 9$ into the original function, we find

At $x = 3$, the value of the function y equals 36
At $x = 9$, the value of the function y equals 0

c. The Excel spreadsheet along with all of the necessary formulas is given in Exhibits 7-8.

Problem 2

Constrained optimization with one variable.

a. Manually find the optimal profit for the model, and the value of the decision variable that will produce the optimal profit for the following model.

$$\text{maximize} \quad Z = -10x^2 + 5x + 1000$$

subject to

$$x \leq 12$$

b. Use Excel and solve the problem given above.

EXHIBIT 7-8 Worksheet for Solved Problem 1: One-Decision-Variable, Unconstrained Problem

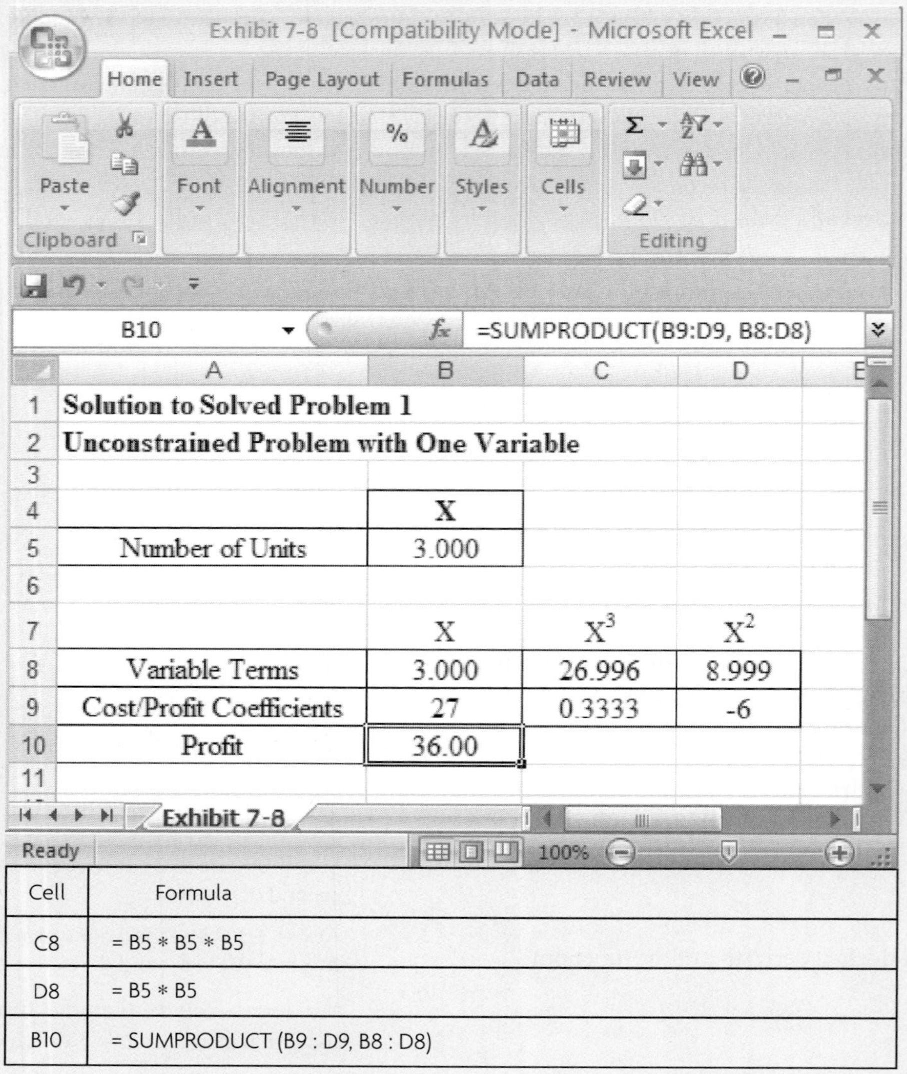

	A	B	C	D
1	**Solution to Solved Problem 1**			
2	**Unconstrained Problem with One Variable**			
3				
4		X		
5	Number of Units	3.000		
6				
7		X	X^3	X^2
8	Variable Terms	3.000	26.996	8.999
9	Cost/Profit Coefficients	27	0.3333	-6
10	Profit	36.00		
11				

Cell	Formula
C8	= B5 * B5 * B5
D8	= B5 * B5
B10	= SUMPRODUCT (B9 : D9, B8 : D8)

Solution

a. 1. Obtain the first derivative of the function, set it equal to zero, and solve for x:

$$\frac{dy}{dx} = -20x + 5 = 0$$

Solving, $x = {}^{1}/_{4}$. Note that this value *satisfies* the constraint $x \leq 12$.

2. Obtain the second derivative and note its sign:

$$\frac{d^2y}{dx^2} = -20$$

EXHIBIT 7-9 Worksheet for Solved Problem 2: One-Decision-Variable Constrained Problem

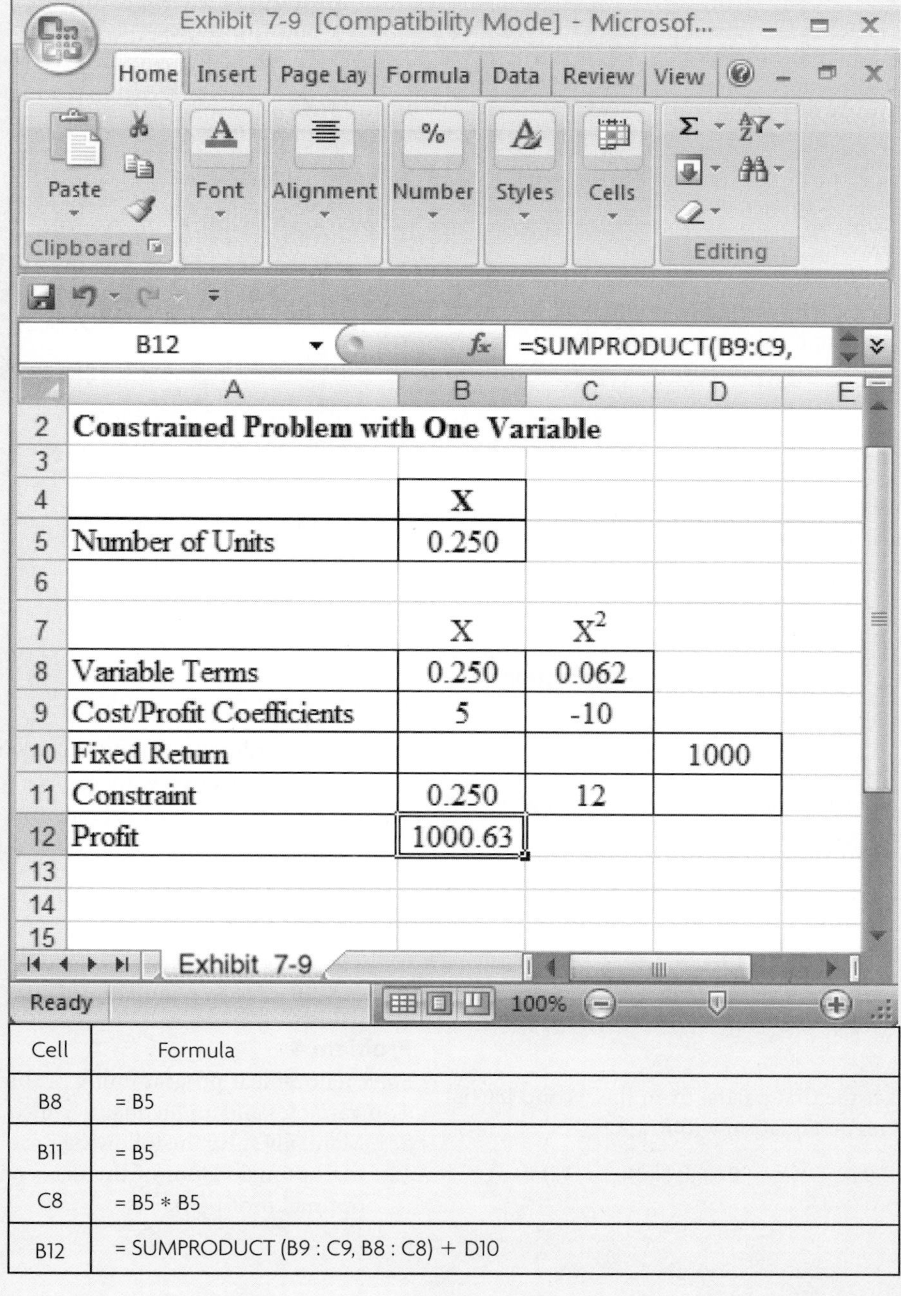

Cell	Formula
B8	= B5
B11	= B5
C8	= B5 * B5
B12	= SUMPRODUCT (B9 : C9, B8 : C8) + D10

The negative sign indicates that the function reaches a local maximum at $x = {}^1/_4$.

3. Compute the value of the function at the local maximization point and compare the result to the result to the result obtained when $x = 12$ (the constraint):

$$\text{At } x = {}^1/_4, f(x) = -10({}^1/_4)^2 + 5({}^1/_4) + 1000 = 1000.625$$
$$\text{At } x = 12, f(x) = -10(12)^2 + 5(12) + 1000 = -380$$

The value of the function at $x = {}^1/_4$ is greater than the value of the function at $x = 12$. Hence, the maximum value of the function (the optimal profit) is 1000.625, where the optimal value of $x = {}^1/_4$.

b. The Excel spreadsheet along with all of the necessary formulas is given in Exhibit 7-9.

Problem 3

Equality constraints: Lagrange multiplier.

a. Manually solve the problem given below for the optimal values of the decision variables and determine if the optimal values produce a point that is a local maximum, a local minimum, or a saddle point.

$$Z = -6x_1^2 - 4x_2^2 - 9x_1x_2 + 18.5x_1 + 12x_2$$

subject to

$$x_1 + x_2 = 3$$

b. Use Excel to find the maximum profit and the optimal values of x_1 and x_2.

Solution

a. 1. Let $\lambda = x_1 + x_2 - 3$.

2. Form a Lagrangian function incorporating λ:

$$L(x_1, x_2, \lambda) = -6x_1^2 - 4x_2^2 - 9x_1x_2 + 18.5x_1 + 12x_2 + \lambda\,(x_1 + x_2 - 3)$$

3. Obtain partial derivatives for x_1, x_2, and λ and set each equal to zero:

$$\frac{\partial L}{\partial x_1} = -12x_1 - 9x_2 + 18.5 + \lambda = 0$$

$$\frac{\partial L}{\partial x_2} = -8x_2 - 9x_1 + 12 + \lambda = 0$$

$$\frac{\partial L}{\partial \lambda} = x_1 + x_2 - 3 = 0$$

4. Subtract the first partial from the second partial to obtain an equation without λ:

$$(12x_1 - 9x_1) + (9x_2 - 8x_2) + (-18.5 + 12) + (-\lambda + \lambda) = 0$$

$$= 3x_1 + x_2 + (-6.5) = 0$$

5. Use the third partial equation and this new equation to solve for x_1 and x_2. Subtract the third partial from the new equation:

$$\begin{array}{ll} \text{(new)} & 3x_1 + x_2 - 6.5 = 0 \\ \text{(third)} & -(x_1 + x_2 - \ \ 3 = 0) \\ \hline & 2x_1 \qquad\ \ - 3.5 = 0 \end{array}$$

Solving, $x_1 = 1.75$. By substituting this into the (third) equation, we obtain $x_2 = 1.25$.

6. Substituting $x_1 = 1.75$ and $x_2 = 1.25$ into either of the first two partial derivative equations, we can solve for λ. Using the first equation, we find

$$-12(1.75) - 9(1.25) + 18.5 + \lambda = 0$$

Solving, $\lambda = 13.75$.

7. With λ fixed at 13.75, the first partial derivatives of x_1 and x_2 become

$$\frac{\partial L}{\partial x_1} = -12x_1 - 9x_2 + 18.5 + 13.75 \quad \text{or} \quad -12x_1 - 9x_2 + 32.25$$

$$\frac{\partial L}{\partial x_1} = -8x_1 - 9x_2 + 12 + 13.75 \quad \text{or} \quad -8x_2 - 9x_1 + 25.75$$

8. The second partials and the mixed partial are

$$\frac{\partial^2 L}{\partial x_1^2} = -12, \quad \frac{\partial^2 L}{\partial x_2^2} = -8, \quad \frac{\partial^2 L}{\partial x_1 \partial x_2} = -9$$

9. Computing D, we find

$$D = \left(\frac{\partial^2 L}{\partial x_1^2}\right)\left(\frac{\partial^2 L}{\partial x_2^2}\right) - \left(\frac{\partial^2 L}{\partial x_1 \partial x_2}\right)^2$$

$$= (-12)(-8) - (-9^2) = +15$$

10. According to Condition 4, with the second partial derivative with respect to x_1 negative, and $D > 0$, this is a local maximum.

$$Z = -6(1.75)^2 - 4(1.25)^2 - 9(1.75)(1.25) + 18.5(1.75) + 12(1.25)$$
$$Z = 3.0625$$

b. The Excel spreadsheet along with all of the necessary formulas is given in Exhibit 7-10.

Problem 4

Solve a nonlinear programming problem with two decision variables and an inequality constraint:

a. Manually solve the following problem and determine the optimal values of the decision variables and the optimal profit (Z).

EXHIBIT 7-10 Worksheet for Solved Problem 3: Two Decision Variables and a Single Equality Constraint

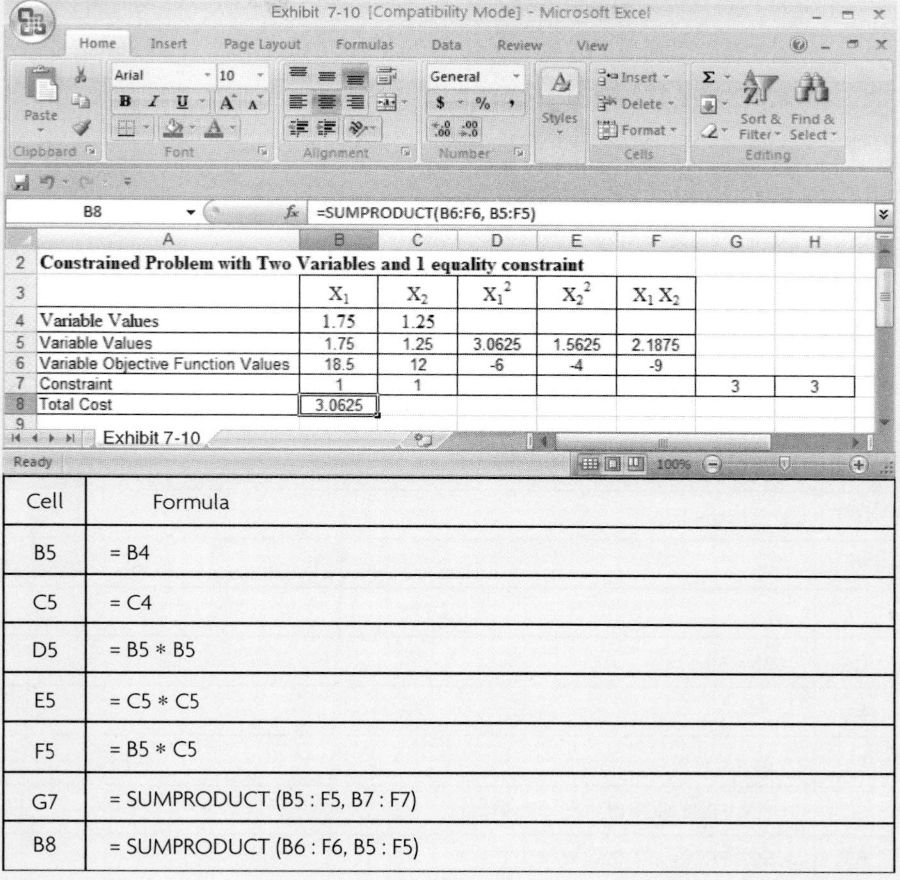

B8 =SUMPRODUCT(B6:F6, B5:F5)

	A	B	C	D	E	F	G	H
2	**Constrained Problem with Two Variables and 1 equality constraint**							
3		X_1	X_2	X_1^2	X_2^2	$X_1 X_2$		
4	Variable Values	1.75	1.25					
5	Variable Values	1.75	1.25	3.0625	1.5625	2.1875		
6	Variable Objective Function Values	18.5	12	-6	-4	-9		
7	Constraint	1	1				3	3
8	Total Cost	3.0625						

Cell	Formula
B5	= B4
C5	= C4
D5	= B5 * B5
E5	= C5 * C5
F5	= B5 * C5
G7	= SUMPRODUCT (B5 : F5, B7 : F7)
B8	= SUMPRODUCT (B6 : F6, B5 : F5)

b. Solve the problem below using Excel and find the maximum profit and the optimal values of the decision variables.

Let x_1 = number of units of product 1 manufactured
x_2 = number of units of product 2 manufactured

maximize $Z = -4x_1^2 - 3x_2^2 + 2x_1x_2 + 14x_1 + 24x_2$

subject to

$4x_1 + 3x_2 \leq 28$ (daily machine hours constraint)

Solution

a. First, we assume that the constraint is not binding and solve it as an unconstrained problem. In solving it as an unconstrained problem, we take the first derivative of the objective function with respect to x_1 and take the first derivative of the objective function with respect x_2.

1. *Necessary conditions.* Take the partial derivative with respect to each variable and set the resulting equations equal to zero.

$$\frac{\partial Z}{\partial x_1} = -8x_1 + 2x_2 + 14 = 0$$

Rearranging the terms:

$$8x_1 - 2x_2 = 14$$

$$\frac{\partial Z}{\partial x_1} = 2x_1 - 6x_2 + 24 = 0$$

Rearranging the terms:

$$-2x_1 + 6x_2 = 24$$

We can solve the two rearranged equations simultaneously.

EXHIBIT 7-11 Worksheet for Solved Problem 4: Two Decision Variables and a Single Inequality Constraint

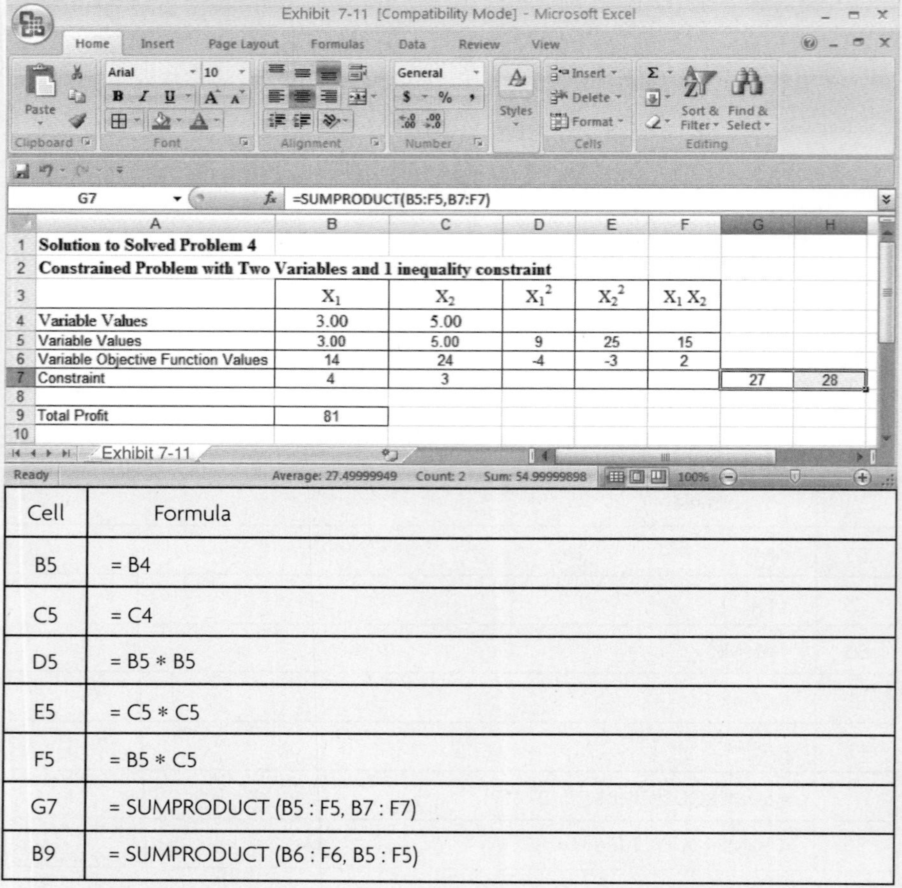

Exhibit 7-11 [Compatibility Mode] - Microsoft Excel

G7 =SUMPRODUCT(B5:F5,B7:F7)

	A	B	C	D	E	F	G	H
1	**Solution to Solved Problem 4**							
2	**Constrained Problem with Two Variables and 1 inequality constraint**							
3		X_1	X_2	X_1^2	X_2^2	$X_1 X_2$		
4	Variable Values	3.00	5.00					
5	Variable Values	3.00	5.00	9	25	15		
6	Variable Objective Function Values	14	24	-4	-3	2		
7	Constraint	4	3				27	28
8								
9	Total Profit	81						
10								

Ready Average: 27.49999949 Count: 2 Sum: 54.99999898

Cell	Formula
B5	= B4
C5	= C4
D5	= B5 * B5
E5	= C5 * C5
F5	= B5 * C5
G7	= SUMPRODUCT (B5 : F5, B7 : F7)
B9	= SUMPRODUCT (B6 : F6, B5 : F5)

$$(3)(8x_1 - 2x_2) = 3(14) \quad \text{or}$$

$$\begin{aligned} 24x_1 - 6x_2 &= 42 \quad \text{(rearranged equation 1)} \\ -2x_1 + 6x_2 &= 24 \quad \text{(rearranged equation 2)} \\ 22x_1 &= 66 \\ x_1 &= 3 \end{aligned}$$

Substituting $x_1 = 3$, into the first equation

$$\begin{aligned} 8x_1 - 2x_2 &= 14 \\ 8(3) - 2x_2 &= 14 \\ -2x_2 &= -10 \\ x_2 &= 5 \end{aligned}$$

Once these values have been obtained, we can check the second-order conditions.

2. *Sufficient conditions.* In this example, second partial derivatives and mixed partial derivatives are as follows:

$$\frac{\partial^2 Z}{\partial x_1^2} = -8$$

$$\frac{\partial^2 Z}{\partial x_2^2} = -6$$

$$\frac{\partial^2 Z}{\partial x_1 \partial x_2} = -2$$

$$D = \left(\frac{\partial^2 Z}{\partial x_1^2}\right)\left(\frac{\partial^2 Z}{\partial x_2^2}\right) - \left(\frac{\partial^2 Z}{\partial x_1 \partial x_2}\right)^2$$

$$= (-8)(-6) - (-2)^2$$

$$D = 48 - 4 = 44$$

Since $D > 0$ and $\frac{\partial^2 Z}{\partial x_1^2} < 0$, this point $(x_1 = 3, x_2 = 5)$ is an optimal solution to the unconstraint problem.

Next, we substitute these optimal values for x_1 and x_2 into the inequality constraint. Since $4x_1 + 3x_2 = 4(3) + 3(5) = 27 < 28$, the constraint is satisfied. Therefore, we do not need to go to step 2. $x_1 = 3, x_2 = 5$ is the optimal solution to our original problem.

Substituting these values into the objective function, we get

$$Z = -4x_1^2 - 3x_2^2 - 2x_1x_2 - 14x_1 - 24x_2$$
$$Z = -4(3)^2 - 3(5)^2 + 2(3)(5) + 14(3) + 24(5)$$
$$Z = -36 - 75 + 30 + 42 + 120$$
$$Z = 81$$

Therefore, the optimal solution to this problem is $x_1 = 3, x_2 = 5$, and $Z = 81$.

b. The Excel spreadsheet along with all of the necessary formulas is given in Exhibit 7-11.

Discussion and Review Questions

1. Describe the difference between satisfying the necessary and sufficient conditions for an unconstrained problem with one decision variable with satisfying the necessary and sufficient conditions for a problem with two decision variables.
2. What is the difference between local maximum and global maximum? Explain briefly.
3. When is it appropriate to use the Lagrange multiplier approach? How can we use the Lagrange multiplier approach to solve nonlinear programming problems?
4. For a given problem with one decision variable with a single constraint, the value of $\lambda = 8.5$. What is the general economic interpretation of this value?
5. What do we have to do differently in running Excel to solve a nonlinear programming problem rather than a linear programming problem? Explain carefully.
6. What is a saddle point?
7. Does the optimal solution to a constrained nonlinear programming problem occur at a corner point? Why?
8. When there are multiple decision variables, briefly list and explain the steps of how to solve unconstrained nonlinear programming problems with two decision variables.
9. Briefly explain what *partial derivative* means?
10. List and discuss the steps briefly in solving a nonlinear programming problem with two decision variables with an equality constraint. How do we know whether we have reached a local maximum, a local minimum, or a saddle point?
11. Compare the methods to solve a nonlinear programming problem with two decision variables with an equality constraint and an unconstrained nonlinear programming problem with two decision variables.
12. Explain how partial derivatives are used to solve nonlinear programming problems.

Problems

1. Find the minimum of this function and then answer the following questions:

   $$Z = 4x^2 - 30x + 40$$

   a. At what value of x does the function have its minimum?
   b. How do you know that this is a minimum rather than a maximum?

2. For the function, given below, answer the following questions.

   $$Z = -5x^2 + 4x + 2$$

   a. Find the maximum value of Z.
   b. At what value of the decision variable does the function attain its maximum value?
   c. How can you be sure that the value you have found is a maximum?

3. The manager of a small plastics company has developed the following cost function and determined its minimum value to be 68. Explain why you agree or disagree with this finding.

   $$Z = \frac{1}{2}x^2 - 8x + 90$$

4. For the following function, determine the value of x at which it attains a local maximum value, the value

of x at which it attains a local minimum value, and the value of the function at each of those points.

$$Z = \frac{1}{3}x^3 - 4.5x^2 + 18x + 10$$

5. Determine the point at which the following function attains its local maximum, its local minimum, and the value of the function at each of those points.

$$Z = x^3 - 12x^2 + 36x + 3$$

6. A manager has developed the following cost function:

$$Z = \frac{1}{3}x^3 - 3x^2 + 70$$

where

x = amount spent on preventive maintenance of equipment (in thousands of dollars)

Find the optimal amount of preventive maintenance in thousands of dollars

7. Find the local maximum and local minimum points of this function:

$$Z = 2x^3 - 18x^2 + 48x$$

8. Find the optimal solution to this problem:

maximize $Z = -2x^2 + 20x + 15$

subject to

$x \leq 4.$

9. Find the optimal solution to this problem:

minimize $Z = 5x^2 - 20x + 18$

subject to

$x \geq 4$

10. Find the optimal solution to this problem:

maximize $Z = -10x^2 + 40x - 1$

subject to

$x \geq 3$

11. Given this model:

minimize $Z = 2x_1^2 + 6x_2^2 - 10x_1 - 10x_2 + 3x_1x_2 + 8$

Find the optimal values of the decision variables and the value of the objective function.

12. Given the following model, find the optimal values of x_1 and x_2 and determine if the result is a local maximum, local minimum, or saddle point:

$$f(x_1,x_2) = 5x_1^2 + 4x_2^2 - 8x_1x_2 - 6x_1 - 8x_2 + 7$$

where

x_1 = setting on machine control 1
x_2 = setting on machine control 2

13. For the following model, find the optimal values of the decision variables and determine whether those values refer to a local maximum, a local minimum, or a saddle point.

$$f(x_1,x_2) = -10x_1^2 - 6x_2^2 + 50x_1 + 40x_2 - x_1x_2 + 100$$

14. The cost to produce each of two products is dependent on the quantity of each product (x_1, x_2) that is produced:

$c_1 = x_1 + x_2$ (in thousands of dollars)
$c_2 = 2x_2 + x_1$ (in thousands of dollars)

The manager of the department wants to determine the quantity of each product to produce to maximize profits. Product 1 sells for $10 000 a unit, and product 2 sells for $12 000 a unit. Fixed cost is $2000 for each product. Find the optimal quantity of each product and the maximum profit.

15. For the following model, find the optimal values of x_1 and x_2, and determine the solution that provides the maximum objective function value.

maximize $Z = -4x_1^2 - 2x_2^2 - 6x_1x_2 + 33x_1 + 22x_2 + 40$

subject to

$x_1 + 2x_2 = 8$

16. Find the values of the decision variables that will minimize the value of this function:

minimize $Z = 3x_1^2 + 3x_2^2 - 20x_1 - 20x_2 + 2x_1x_2 - 100$

subject to

$x_1 + x_2 = 5$

17. Given this model, find the minimum value of the function:

minimize $Z = -2x_1^2 - 2x_2^2 + 3x_1x_2 + 10x_1 + 10x_2$

subject to

$x_1 + x_2 = 7$

18. Given this model:

$$Z = x_1^2 + 3x_2^2 + 2x_1x_2 - 6x_1 - 14x_2 + 2$$

subject to

$x_1 + x_2 = 12$

a. Find the minimum value of the function and the optimal values of x_1 and x_2.
b. How much would you expect the optimal value to change if the constraint was changed from 12 to 13?

19. Consider problem 10. Use Excel and find the optimal solution (optimal value of decision variable x and the objective function).
20. Consider problem 6. Set up the nonlinear programming model using Excel and find the optimal amount of preventive maintenance in thousands of dollars.
21. Consider problem 9. Set up the Excel worksheet. Based on the worksheet, find the optimal solution.
22. Consider problem 14. Using Excel, determine the optimal quantity of each product to maximize the profits.
23. Use Excel and solve problem 15.
24. Use Excel and solve problem 16.
25. Use Excel and solve problem 17.
26. Use Excel and solve problem 18.
27. A computer manufacturing company manufactures and sells two types of computers (model 1 and model 2). Let m_1 denote the number of model 1's produced and let m_2 denote the number of model 2's produced respectively. The firm earns a profit of \$30 for each unit of model 1 produced and \$18 for each unit of model 2 produced. However, due to being able to spread fixed overhead cost, as more units of model 2 are produced, the company earns an additional profit total of $.1m_2^2$.

Thus, the company's objective function is nonlinear. The firm's profit is subject to four constraints. The first two constraints are the minimum production constraints as specified by the marketing department. The company wishes to produce at least 50 units of computer model 1 and 40 units of computer model 2. In addition, the company has 40 machine hours and 50 labour hours available per week. The production time requirements for machines and labour are given in the following table.

	Model 1	Model 2
Machine hours required per unit	.30	.50
Labour hours required per unit	.40	.40

a. Formulate this problem as a nonlinear programming problem.
b. Use Excel and solve this problem. How many units of each model should the company produce? What is the optimal profit?

28. Set up and solve the following nonlinear programming problem with Excel:

$$\text{maximize } Z = 3x_1 + 2x_2 + x_1x_2 + x_3 + .2x_3^2$$

subject to

$$\begin{aligned} 3x_1 + 2x_2 + x_3 &\le 100 \\ 2x_1 + x_2 + 1.5x_3 &\le 60 \\ 2.5x_1 + 1.5x_2 + 3x_3 &\le 110 \\ x_3 &\ge 5 \\ x_1, x_2, x_3 &\ge 0 \end{aligned}$$

Case 1: Koch International Incorporated

Koch International Incorporated assembles two products: laptop computers and flat-screen televisions. The company believes that the price of the product is related to the demand for these products. The company would like to develop a model to plan production within the capacity constraints. Koch has three types of machines to produce these products: (1) assembly, (2) drilling, and (3) cutting. Total number of hours per week and the number of hours it takes to process each unit of laptops and TVs for all of these three machines are given in the following table.

	Departments		
Products	**Assembly**	**Drilling**	**Cutting**
Laptop computers	3*	2	1.5
Flat-screen TVs	4**	1	2
Department capacity	1600†	600‡	750

*Three hours are required to produce one unit of laptop computer.
**Four hours are required to produce one unit of flat-screen TVs.
†There are 1600 hours available per week in the assembly department.
‡There are 600 hours available per week in the drilling department.

The board of directors of the company has met and made certain decisions. The management expressed concerns about one product dominating the sales of the company. The objective of the company is to maximize revenue given the following constraints in addition to the capacity constraints:

1. The maximum number of laptop computers cannot exceed 60 percent of all units produced for both products.
2. The minimum number of laptop computers cannot be less than 30 percent of all units produced for both products.

If the company produces a total of 10 units for both products, then it cannot produce more than 6 computers or less than 3 computers.

Demand is a function of price for each product. The higher the price, the lower the demand where:

x_1 = demand for laptop computers
p_1 = price of a laptop computer
x_2 = demand for flat-screen TVs
p_2 = price of a flat-screen TV

The demand function for each product is defined as

Laptop computer: $x_1 = 5000 - 7p_1$
Flat-screen TV: $x_2 = 1000 - 10p_2$

Discussion Question

Develop and solve a nonlinear programming model for Koch International Incorporated and determine the price and the demand for both products that will maximize the total revenue for the company.

Project Scheduling: PERT/CPM

CHAPTER 8

LEARNING OBJECTIVES

After completing this chapter, you should be able to:

1. Describe the role and application of PERT/CPM for project scheduling.
2. Define a project in terms of activities such that a network representation can be developed.
3. Develop a complete project schedule.
4. Compute the critical path, the project completion time and its variance.
5. Convert optimistic, most likely, and pessimistic time estimates into expected activity time estimates.
6. Compute the probability of the project being completed by a specific time.
7. Compute the project completion time given a certain level of probability.
8. Find the least expensive way to shorten the duration of a project to meet a target completion date.
9. Formulate the crashing problem as a linear programming model.
10. Formulate project scheduling as a linear programming model.
11. Know some of the specialised software available in the market for scheduling and tracking project activities.

CHAPTER OUTLINE

8.1 INTRODUCTION

Project scheduling is at the heart of many decision problems that are, in nature, non-repetitive, unique, and clearly defined in terms of scope, objectives, and time frame. These decisions are referred to as a **project;** an interrelated set of activities directed towards the accomplishment of a unique, often major outcome and that have a definite starting and ending point. Every organization may be involved at any time in a project of any size, duration, and complexity level. Examples of typical projects are setting up of a stage for a rock concert, the construction of a new plant or facility, the design and the marketing of a new product or service, the redesign of a business process, the construction (or repair) of a bridge, the development of a new drug, and the acquisition and installation of an enterprise planning system. All these projects consist of several activities that have to be completed and some of them are interdependent, that is, they cannot start before the completion of some other activities. In many situations, managers face the challenges of planning, coordinating, and monitoring these activities so that the project of interests is completed on time and within the allocated budget. Project management provides a number of approaches to cope with these challenges.

This chapter introduces the **critical path method (CPM)** and the **program evaluation review technique (PERT),** two management science techniques developed in the late 1950s to plan, schedule, and control large, complex projects with many activities. These approaches differ primarily on how the duration and the cost of activities are processed. In the case of CPM, it is assumed that details about these inputs are known with certainty, whereas for PERT, these details are not known with certainty. Both approaches use a network representation (see Chapter 5) to display the relationships between project activities and to help managers to address questions such as:

1. What is the total time required to complete the project (the expected total time for PERT)?
2. What are the start and the completion times for individual activities?
3. Which critical activities must be completed as scheduled to meet the estimated project completion time?
4. How much delay can be tolerated for non-critical activities without incurring a delay in the estimated project completion time?
5. What is the least expensive way to speed up a project to meet a targeted completion time?

PERT also provides answers to the following additional questions:

6. What is the probability of completing a project within a given time frame?
7. What is the variability in the project completion time?

We will first introduce a project example that will be used in the chapter to illustrate the project graphical representation and to discuss both approaches, CPM and PERT. The chapter ends with a discussion on time–cost trade-offs in project acceleration and on the use of linear programming in project acceleration as well as in project scheduling. It is worthwhile to note that project scheduling, the focus of this chapter, is only one of the major phases involved in the management of a project. Project planning and project control processes, as well as their related challenges, are two other phases, not discussed in this chapter, that are required to ensure the effective use of resources to deliver the project objectives on time and within cost constraints. Other management variables that also matter include the senior managers' support, a clear definition of roles and responsibilities, the communication systems, and the human resource management practices.

8.2 A PROJECT EXAMPLE: REPLACEMENT OF AN AIRPORT GATE-MANAGEMENT SYSTEM

AC Inc. is a full-service, major airline company in the international market. It relies on a user-friendly gate management software system at its hub airport to decide how to assign aircrafts to gates. Based on a flight schedule and various business criteria, the system serves for long-, medium-, and short-term planning of gate requirements. It also serves for real-time allocation of gates during the day of operation. The company faces the challenge of replacing its current system because its hardware platform is obsolete and no longer supported. As well, a considerable increase of activities at its hub facility is making the current environment less suitable. The company is concerned with the overall cost involved if a manual process would have to take place in case of a breakdown of the current system. Therefore, a project has been set-up with a mandate of acquiring and implementing a new gate management system to replace the current system. Soad El-Taji is project manager at AC Inc., and has many years of experience. Her exemplary performance in similar projects in the past has earned her the confidence of senior management. It was with unanimity that she was called once again to manage this acquisition project to ensure that it was successfully completed on time. As in the past, she resorted to PERT/CPM approaches. The first step she completed was to accurately establish a list of **activities** that needed to be undertaken, their precedence relationships and the time estimates for each activity. Table 8-1 shows the list of activities. The **immediate predecessors** of an activity refer to those activities that must be completed prior to the starting time of a given activity. Similarly, **immediate successors** of an activity refer to those that follow the completion of a given activity. The "—" in this table indicates an activity without a predecessor.

After the completion of the project activities, Soad El-Taji wants to know how to better visualize these activities and how to develop answers to questions listed at the end of the previous section.

8.3 PROJECT NETWORK REPRESENTATION

A **project network** representation is used to depict the project activities and their relationships. As discussed in Chapter 5, a network consists of a set of circles referred to as nodes and lines connecting nodes together referred to as arcs. The two common approaches of a project network representation are **activity on node (AON)** or **activity on arc (AOA).** In the first approach, the nodes of the network represent the project activities and the arcs show their precedence relationships. In the second approach, the project activities are reported on arcs and nodes represent the starting or the completion of activities. We focus in this textbook solely on the activity on node representation, given its large adoption in many software packages. It is common in this approach to add one dummy source activity node (referred to as Start) and connect it to all activities nodes with no immediate predecessors as well as one dummy destination activity node (referred to as Finish) and connect it to the project network with arcs from activities with no immediate successors. This ensures that there is one starting point and one finish point in the project network. Figure 8-1 shows the network representation of the airport gate management system acquisition project example. Note that a dummy Finish node is added to ensure that the project network has one starting node and one finish node. Since there is only one node without a predecessor (A), no dummy Start node is added in this network.

TABLE 8-1 List of Activities for the Airport Gate Management System (AGMS) Acquisition Project

Activity	Description	Immediate Predecessors	Estimated Time (weeks)
A	Set up the project acquisition team	—	2
B	Write down the software requirements	A	2
C	Develop a contractor evaluation grid that will be used to evalute proposals	B	1
D	Identify and select potential contractors	A	1
E	Develop and send out a request for proposal to potential contractors	B, D	4
F	Audit candidate contractors, select one contractor, negotiate and sign an agreement contract with the selected contractor	C, E	2
G	Prepare the definition of functional specifications	F	5
H	Develop a software testing plan	G	2
I	Software customization phase I	G	12
J	Purchase and install the hardware	G	2
K	Test the first release	H, I, J	1
L	Develop a training plan for key users	K	1
O	Train key users	L, N	2
M	Software customization phase II	K	6
N	Test the second release	M	1
P	Software customization phase III	N	3
Q	Test the final release	P	2
R	Software deployment and project sign-off	Q	4

For a small project network, one convenient way to determine its duration and critical activities (questions 1 and 3 above) is through the enumeration of all the different paths in the network. A **path** is a sequence of connected nodes in the network from the start node to the finish node. The **length of the path** is given by the sum of the durations of the activities on the path. For the network shown in Figure 8-1, the corresponding paths are shown in Table 8-2. In this list, path # 1 is the longest, while paths # 23 and # 24 are the shortest. Path # 1 is critical, because any delay in the duration of an activity located in this path will delay the entire project. For instance, increasing the duration of activity A by 2 weeks will increase the length of path # 1 by 2 weeks for a total duration of 46 weeks. Whereas, for path # 23 and # 24, the length will only increase to 20 weeks, respectively. Hence, in any project network, the path with the longest duration is called a **critical path** and the corresponding activities are called **critical activities** in that they must be completed as scheduled to meet the scheduled project completion time. The estimated duration of the project is

FIGURE 8-1 Network Representation for the AGMS Acquisition Project

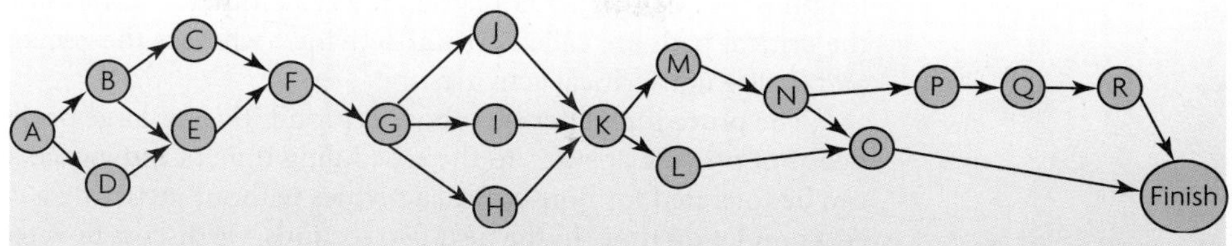

TABLE 8-2 List of Paths for the AGMS Acquisition Project

Path #	Sequence of Nodes	Length (total time in weeks)
1	A-B-E-F-G-I-K-M-N-P-Q-R-Final	44
2	A-B-E-F-G-J-K-M-N-P-Q-R-Final	34
3	A-B-E-F-G-H-K-M-N-P-Q-R-Final	34
4	A-B-C-F-G-I-K-M-N-P-Q-R-Final	41
5	A-B-C-F-G-J-K-M-N-P-Q-R-Final	31
6	A-B-C-F-G-H-K-M-N-P-Q-R-Final	31
7	A-D-E-F-G-I-K-M-N-P-Q-R-Final	43
8	A-D-E-F-G-J-K-M-N-P-Q-R-Final	33
9	A-D-E-F-G-H-K-M-N-P-Q-R-Final	33
10	A-B-E-F-G-I-K-M-N-O-Final	37
11	A-B-E-F-G-J-K-M-N-O-Final	27
12	A-B-E-F-G-H-K-M-N-O-Final	27
13	A-B-C-F-G-I-K-M-N-O-Final	34
14	A-B-C-F-G-J-K-M-N-O-Final	24
15	A-B-C-F-G-H-K-M-N-O-Final	24
16	A-D-E-F-G-I-K-M-N-O-Final	36
17	A-D-E-F-G-J-K-M-N-O-Final	26
18	A-D-E-F-G-H-K-M-N-O-Final	26
19	A-B-E-F-G-I-K-L-O-Final	31
20	A-B-E-F-G-J-K-L-O-Final	21
21	A-B-E-F-G-H-K-L-O-Final	21
22	A-B-C-F-G-I-K-L-O-Final	28
23	A-B-C-F-G-J-K-L-O-Final	18
24	A-B-C-F-G-H-K-L-O-Final	18
25	A-D-E-F-G-I-K-L-O-Final	30
26	A-D-E-F-G-J-K-L-O-Final	20
27	A-D-E-F-G-H-K-L-O-Final	20

therefore given by the length of the critical path. It is possible to find more than one critical path in a network project, but all critical paths will have the same length. For the network shown in Figure 8-1, the critical path is A-B-E-F-G-I-K-M-N-P-Q-R and its corresponding length is 44 weeks. Therefore, the project's estimated duration is 44 weeks. All activities in the critical path are called critical activities, whereas the remaining activities (C, D, H, L, and O) are non-critical activities.

The procedure described above is prohibitive for large project networks. In addition, it does not provide answers to the scheduling time of individual activities and the delay that can be tolerated for non-critical activities without incurring a delay in the scheduled project completion time. In the next two sections, we discuss how techniques such as CPM and PERT help managers to address these questions.

8.4 PROJECT SCHEDULING WITH DETERMINISTIC ACTIVITY DURATIONS

For larger project networks, CPM provides a most efficient approach for project scheduling when the duration of activities are known with certainty. The approach consists of finding the earliest and the latest schedules to avoid delays in project completion. Therefore, for all activities in the network the following information is computed:

1. The **earliest start time (EST):** the earliest time at which an activity can start if no delays occur in the project;
2. The **earliest finish time (EFT):** The earliest time at which an activity can finish if no delays occur in the project;
3. The **latest start time (LST):** The latest time at which an activity can start without delaying the completion of the project;
4. The **latest finish time (LFT):** The latest time at which an activity can finish without delaying the completion of the project.

A **forward pass** (from the starting node to the finish node) is used to compute the EST and EFT, whereas a **backward pass** (from the finish node to the starting node) is used for the LST and LFT. To determine the critical path and the project schedule, the approach consists of calculating, respectively, the starting time and the completion time for each activity as well as identifying the corresponding slack.

The basis of the forward pass is the EST rule that states that all immediate predecessors must be completed before an activity can begin. Let t be the duration (estimated) of an activity. If no delay occurs anywhere in the project, the earliest finish time for an activity is

$$EFT = EST + t \tag{8-1}$$

It results from the EST rule that the earliest start time for each activity is equal to the largest earliest finish times of the immediate predecessors.

For example, consider the network shown in Figure 8-1. The project-starting activity A has no predecessor. Therefore, it can start as soon as the project starts, which we assume to be time 0. The earliest finish time of activity A can now be computed as $0 + 2 = 2$. Activities B and D have activity A as their immediate predecessor. The EST for B is 2 and the EFT is $2 + 2 = 4$. The EST for D is 2 and EFT is $2 + 1 = 3$. Activity B is the only immediate predecessor of activity C and its EFT is known. Therefore, the EST for C is 4 and the EFT is $4 + 1 = 5$. Activity E has two predecessor activities, B and D, with known EFT (4 and 3).

FIGURE 8-2 Nodes Notation

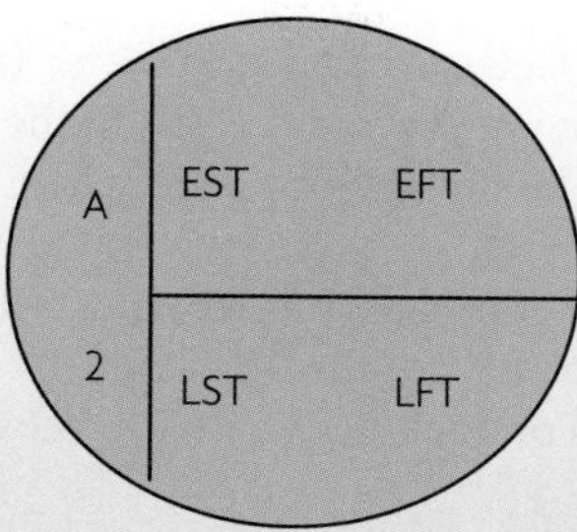

The EST for D is 4, or the maximum between 4 and 3. The EFT of activity D is $4 + 4 = 8$. If we continue this forward pass, the EST and the EFT for all activities can be computed as summarized in Figure 8-3, in which the node is expanded to include additional information (as shown in Figure 8-2). We show in the top left side of the node, the activity name (e.g., A); in the bottom left side, the activity duration; and in the top right side, the activity's EST and EFT. Later in our discussion we will place the activity's LST and LFT on the bottom right of the node.

The forward pass to obtain the EST and the EFT can be summarized as follows:

1. For each activity with no predecessor, set EST = 0.
2. For each activity with known EST, calculate EFT using Equation 8-1, that is, $EFT = EST + t$.
3. For each new activity where all immediate predecessors have known EFT values, apply the EST rule to obtain the EST and step 2 to calculate EFT.
4. Repeat step 3 until EST and EFT have been obtained for all activities.

The basis of the backward pass is the LFT rule which states that an activity can start at the latest time if and only if all its immediate predecessors are completed. Hence, the latest finish time for each activity is equal to the smallest latest start times of the immediate successors'

FIGURE 8-3 EST and EFT Computation for the AGMS Acquisition Project

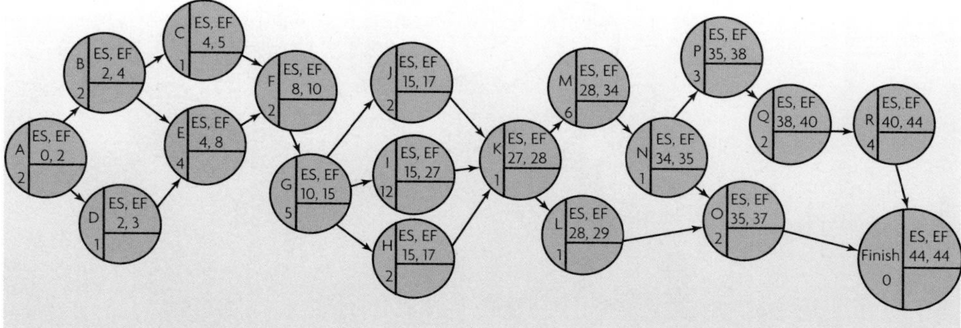

activities. Therefore, if no delay occurs anywhere in the project, the latest start time for an activity that will result on not delaying the completion of the project is:

$$LST = LFT - t \tag{8-2}$$

The backward pass starts by setting up the LFT of all activities without successors (including the finish node) equal to the maximum EFT and then works backward from the finish node to the starting node. The procedure can be summarized as follows:

1. For each of the activities without successors (including the finish node), set LFT equal to EFT of the finish node.
2. For each activity with known LFT value, calculate LST using Equation 8-2, that is, $LST = LFT - t$.
3. For each new activity where immediate successors have known LST values, apply, respectively, the LFT rule to obtain the corresponding LFT and step 2 to calculate LST.
4. Repeat step 3 until LFT and LST have been obtained for all activities.

For the network shown in Figure 8-4, we set the LFT and the LST of the finish node equal to its EFT = 44 weeks. The immediate successor of activities R and O is the finish node. Hence, the LFT is 44 weeks and LST = 44 − 4 = 40 weeks for activity R. For activity O, LFT is 44 weeks and LST = 44 − 2 = 42 weeks. Activity R is the immediate successor for activities Q. Hence the corresponding LFT for activity Q is 40 weeks, whereas the LST = 40 − 2 = 38 weeks. Activity Q is the immediate successor for activity P. The LFT = 38 for activity P and the LST = 38 − 3 = 35 weeks. Activity P and O are immediate successors for activity N. Hence, LFT = minimum (35, 42) = 35 weeks for activity N. If we proceed backward until the starting node, the LFT and the LST for all activities can be computed as summarized in Figure 8-4. For example, Activity G has activities J, I, and H as immediate successors. Its corresponding LFT = min (25, 15, 25) = 15 weeks and LST = 15 − 5 = 10 weeks.

The **slack time** for an activity refers to the length of time that can be tolerated without incurring a delay in the scheduled project completion time. The slack time per activity needs to be calculated first to identify the critical path(s), by considering either the start times or the finish times. Hence, for each of the activities in the project network, the slack time can be calculated as follows:

$$Slack = LST - EST \text{ or } LFT - EFT \tag{8-3}$$

FIGURE 8-4 LST and LFT Computation for the AGMS Acquisition Project

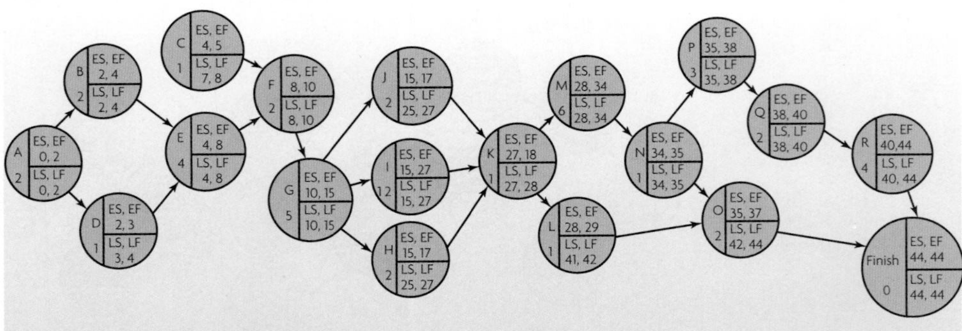

Table 8-3 summarizes the activities' slack times for the airport gate management system acquisition project example. Activities A, B, E, F, G, I, K, M, N, P, Q, and R have zero or no slack, meaning that these activities cannot be delayed without delaying the entire project. Alternately, a reduction in the duration of one these activities will result in the reduction of the entire project's length. They are called critical activities and belong to the critical path(s). The remaining activities (C, D, H, J, L, and O) are non-critical activities since they provide managers with some degree of freedom about when to start or complete them without delaying the entire project. Therefore, Table 8-3 provides the project manager with answers to some of the questions raised at the end of the introduction section.

For the airport gate management system acquisition project example, the critical path is A-B-E-F-G-I-K-M-N-P-Q-R-Finish, the estimated project completion time is 44 weeks, and each activity has to be completed according to the schedule shown in Table 8-3. As stated earlier, note that it is possible for a project to have multiple critical path(s). The slack times provide valuable information for the overall management of the project. For example, an activity with smaller slack time (e.g., activity D with 1 week) will need tighter control than an activity with a larger slack time (e.g. activities H and J with 10 weeks).

TABLE 8-3 Summary of Activities' Start, Finish, and Slack Times

Activity	EST	EFT	LST	LFT	Slack	Critical Activity
A	0	2	0	2	0	Yes
B	2	4	2	4	0	Yes
C	4	5	7	8	3	
D	2	3	3	4	1	
E	4	8	4	8	0	Yes
F	8	10	8	10	0	Yes
G	10	15	10	15	0	Yes
H	15	17	25	27	10	
I	15	27	15	27	0	Yes
J	15	17	25	27	10	
K	27	28	27	28	0	Yes
L	28	29	41	42	13	
M	28	34	28	34	0	Yes
N	34	35	34	35	0	Yes
O	35	37	42	44	7	
P	35	38	35	38	0	Yes
Q	38	40	38	40	0	Yes
R	40	44	40	44	0	Yes
Finish	44	44	44	44	0	Yes

8.5 PROJECT SCHEDULING WITH PROBABILISTIC ACTIVITY DURATIONS

The CPM approach assumes that the duration of activities are known with certainty and the actual duration will turn out to be exactly as estimated. However, in practice this is not always possible and many projects involve variability in activity times due to factors such as lack of prior experience, equipment breakdown, unpredictable weather conditions, late delivery of supplies, and others. PERT analysis is used when the duration of activities are not known with certainty. It involves three types of estimates of the duration of an activity instead of one single value as in the case of CPM:

1. The optimistic duration a = the time an activity will take under the most favourable conditions.
2. The pessimistic duration b = the time an activity will take under the most unfavourable conditions.
3. The most likely duration m = the most realistic time an activity will require to be completed, that is, the time an activity will take under normal conditions.

The duration of an activity is therefore assumed to have a **beta probability distribution** in PERT analysis. Following this distribution, the expected activity time, t_e, and the variance of the activity completion time, σ^2 can be obtained as follows:

$$t_e = \frac{a + 4m + b}{6} \qquad (8\text{-}4)$$

$$\sigma^2 = \left(\frac{b - a}{6}\right)^2 \qquad (8\text{-}5)$$

Figure 8-5 illustrates the shape of the beta distribution, where at the two extremes we have the two estimates a and b with a very small probability, whereas the third estimate m provides the highest point (mode) of the probability distribution.

In PERT analysis, the project completion time is computed in a similar manner as in the CPM approach, but by substituting the three estimates of the activity duration with the expected activity time, t_e, as obtained according to Equation 8-4, and by the variance of the activity completion time, σ^2, as obtained according to Equation 8-5. Therefore, the expected completion time of the project (μ_p) can be derived as well as the variability in the project completion time (σ_p), as follows:

$$\mu_p = \max(\text{EFT}) = \max(\text{LFT}) \qquad (8\text{-}6)$$
$$= \text{sum of the expected duration for the activities in the critical path}$$

$$\sigma_P = \sqrt{(\text{sum of the variances of the duration for the activities in the critical path})} \qquad (8\text{-}7)$$

Assume that, due to variability in activity times, the three estimates of activities duration for the airport gate management system acquisition project example are as shown in Table 8-4. (see columns 2–4). Therefore, by applying Equations 8-4 and 8-5 the mean and the variance of the activity duration shown in the last two columns of Table 8-4 can be computed.

The estimated start and finish times for all activities according to the forward pass and the backward pass were summarized in Figure 8-4. The critical path is A-B-E-F-G-I-K-M-N-P-Q-R-Finish. The expected project completion time (μ_p) is 44 weeks (given by the

FIGURE 8-5 Illustration of the Shape of the Beta Probability Distribution

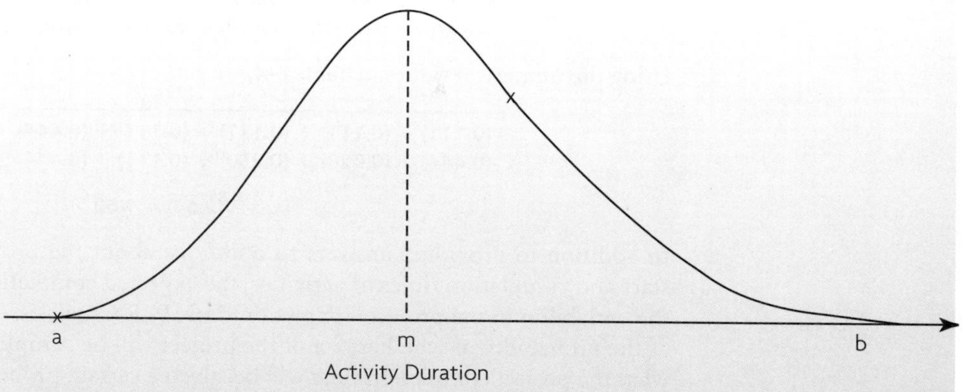

TABLE 8-4 Activities Expected Times and Variances for the AGMS Acquisition Project

ACTIVITY	a	m	b	Mean, $t_e = \frac{a + 4m + b}{6}$	Variance, $\sigma^2 = \left(\frac{b - a}{6}\right)^2$
A	1	2	3	2	0.111
B	1	2	3	2	0.111
C	0.5	1	1.5	1	0.028
D	0.5	1	1.5	1	0.028
E	3	4	5	4	0.111
F	1	2	3	2	0.111
G	3	5	7	5	0.444
H	1	2	3	2	0.111
I	10	12	14	12	0.444
J	1	2	3	2	0.111
K	0.5	1	1.5	1	0.028
L	0.5	1	1.5	1	0.028
M	4	6	8	6	0.444
N	0.5	1	1.5	1	0.028
O	1	2	3	2	0.111
P	1.5	3	4.5	3	0.250
Q	1	2	3	2	0.111
R	2	4	6	4	0.444

maximum EFT or LFT). Given the data in Figure 8-4, the standard deviation for the project equals 1.62 weeks, computed as follows:

$$\sigma_p = \sqrt{\begin{array}{l}(\text{var(A)} + \text{var(B)} + \text{var(E)} + \text{var(F)} + \text{var(G)} + \text{var(I)} + \text{var(K)} + \\ \text{var(M)} + \text{var(N)} + \text{var(P)} + \text{var(Q)} + \text{var(R)}\end{array}}$$

Using the numerical values in Table 8-4, we get:

$$\sigma_p = \sqrt{\begin{array}{l}(0.111) + (0.111) + (0.111) + (0.111) + (0.444) + (0.444) + (0.028) + \\ (0.444) + (0.028) + (0.250) + (0.111) + (0.444)\end{array}}$$

$$\sigma_p = \sqrt{(2.64)} = 1.62$$

In addition to providing answers to questions about the project's critical activities, the start and completion times of activities, the expected completion time of the project, and the variability in the project completion time, PERT analysis also answers questions such as the probability of whether or not the project will be completed on time or, conversely, what the project completion time will be, given a certain probability.

Probability of Whether a Project Can Be Completed or Not by a Specific Deadline

Let *c* and *d* denote the possible project specified deadlines (assuming $c < d$) and X the total time required to complete the project. Due to the central limit theorem, which indicates that the sum of independent random variables can be approximately represented by a normal distribution as the number of random variables becomes larger, the project completion is approximated by a normal distribution with mean μ_p and standard deviation σ_p. Without loss of generality, the three possible situations of interests are illustrated in Figure 8-6 and refer, respectively, to the probability that the project duration (X):

- does not exceed the deadline *b*, i.e., $P(X \leq d)$;
- does exceed the deadline *b*, i.e., $P(X \geq d)$;
- falls between *c* and *d*, i.e., $P(c \leq X \leq d)$.

The approach consists of converting X into a standard normal distribution and determining the area under the normal curve using Table A in Appendix B. To that end the *z* value is computed as follows,

$$z = \frac{x - \mu_p}{\sigma_p} \tag{8-8}$$

where

$$x = c \text{ or } d$$

For the airport gate management system acquisition project, what is the probability of completing the project within 46 weeks? The *Z* value for the normal probability distribution at $x = 46$ is

$z = \dfrac{46-44}{1.62} = 1.23$. Therefore from Table A in Appendix B,

$P(X \leq 1.23) = 0.50 + 0.3907 = 0.8907$ or 89.07%. Hence, there is about 89% probability that the project will be completed on time. Alternatively the Excel function NORMSDIST(z) can be used to seek the probability corresponding to the *z* value.

What is the probability that the project lasts more than 46 weeks?

$P(X > 46) = 1 - P(X \leq 46) = 1 - P(X \leq 46) = 1 - 0.8907 = 0.1093$ or 10.93%. There is a 11% probability that the project will not be completed on time.

FIGURE 8-6 Illustration of Possible Situations of Interest for Probability Computation

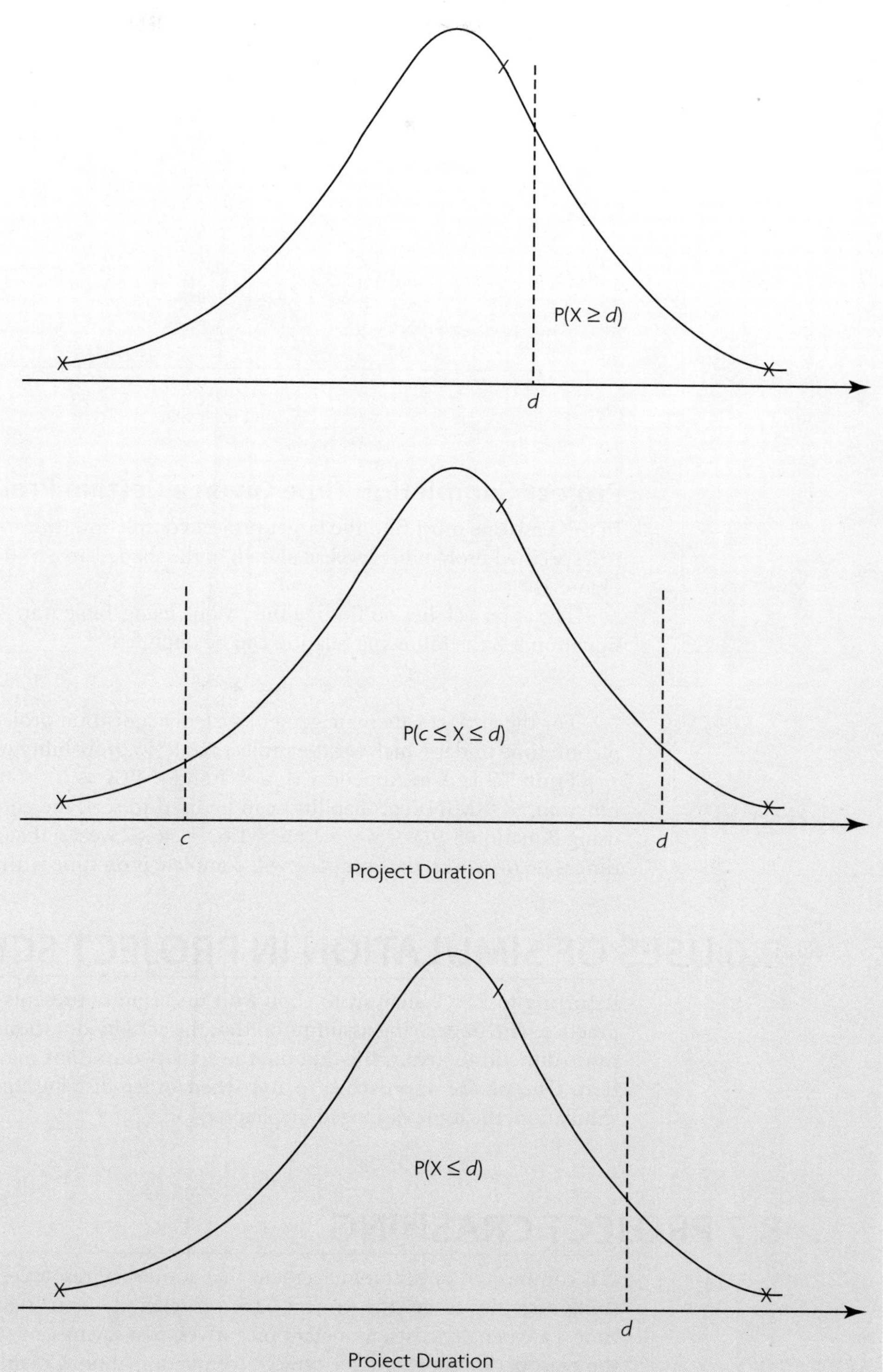

FIGURE 8-7 Project Completion Time Given a Certain Probability

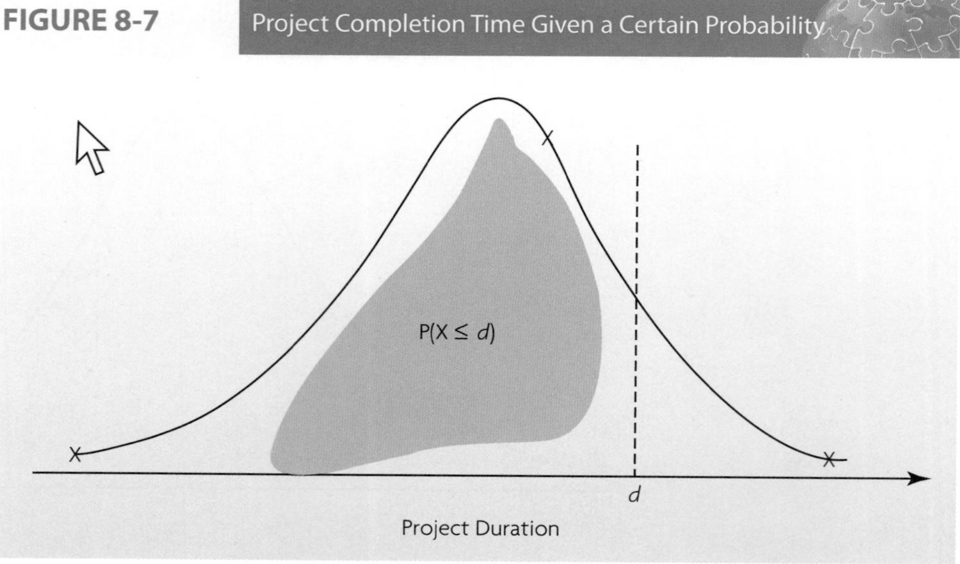

Project Completion Time Given a Certain Probability

In this case one must find the target project completion time (value of d) that corresponds to a specified probability level, as shown in the shaded area of the standard normal curve in Figure 8-7.

The approach lies on finding the z value using Table A in Appendix B. Therefore from Equation 8-8 the following relation can be obtained:

$$x = \mu_p + z \times \sigma_p \qquad (8\text{-}9)$$

For the airport gate management system acquisition project, what would be the completion time under which for the project has 95% probability of completing?

From Table A in Appendix B, $z = 1.65$ for $P(X \leq b) = 0.95$. Alternatively, the Excel function NORMINV(probability) can be used to seek the corresponding z value. Hence, using Equation 8-9, $x = 44 + 1.65 \times 1.62 = 46.67$ weeks, that is, if the project completion time is 46.67 weeks, the company will complete it on time with a 95% probability.

8.6 USES OF SIMULATION IN PROJECT SCHEDULING

Resorting to PERT analysis to cope with uncertainty presents a number of difficulties in practice. The underlying assumption that the activity durations are independents is sometimes difficult to justify. In addition, the activity durations may not follow a beta distribution. One of the approaches to use when other distribution functions are involved is simulation, the topic discussed in Chapter 13.

8.7 PROJECT CRASHING

It is common in project management that additional resources are used to either speed up some activities to get the project back on schedule or to reduce the project completion time. Late penalty costs, monetary incentives, cost savings, or strategic benefits are some of the reasons for shortening a project completion time. **Crashing** an activity refers to the speeding up or shortening of the duration of an activity by using additional resources. These include overtime, hiring temporary staff, renting more efficient equipment, and other measures. **Project crashing** refers to the process of shortening the duration of the project by crashing the duration of a number of activities. Since it generally results in an increase of the overall project costs, the challenge faced by the project manager is to identify the activities to crash and the duration reduction for each activity such that as the project crashing is done in the least expensive manner possible. This section discusses a procedure that can be used for small-sized projects. We also discuss how linear programming (Chapter 3) can be used to investigate project crashing decisions, especially for larger size projects. Figure 8-8 illustrates the activity costs and activity duration relationships, where the **normal time** refers to the estimated activity duration used with CPM or PERT in the computation of earliest (latest) start or finish times. The **normal cost** refers to the activity cost under the normal activity time. The **crash time** refers to the shortest possible time to complete an activity with additional resources. The **crashing cost** refers to the activity cost under the crashing activity time.

This relationship is assumed to be linear. Hence, for each activity a crash cost per period (e.g., per week) can be derived as follows:

$$\textbf{crash cost per period} = \frac{\textbf{(Crash cost} - \textbf{Normal Cost)}}{\textbf{(Normal time} - \textbf{Crash time)}} \quad (8\text{-}10)$$

FIGURE 8-8 Activity Cost and Activity Time Relationship

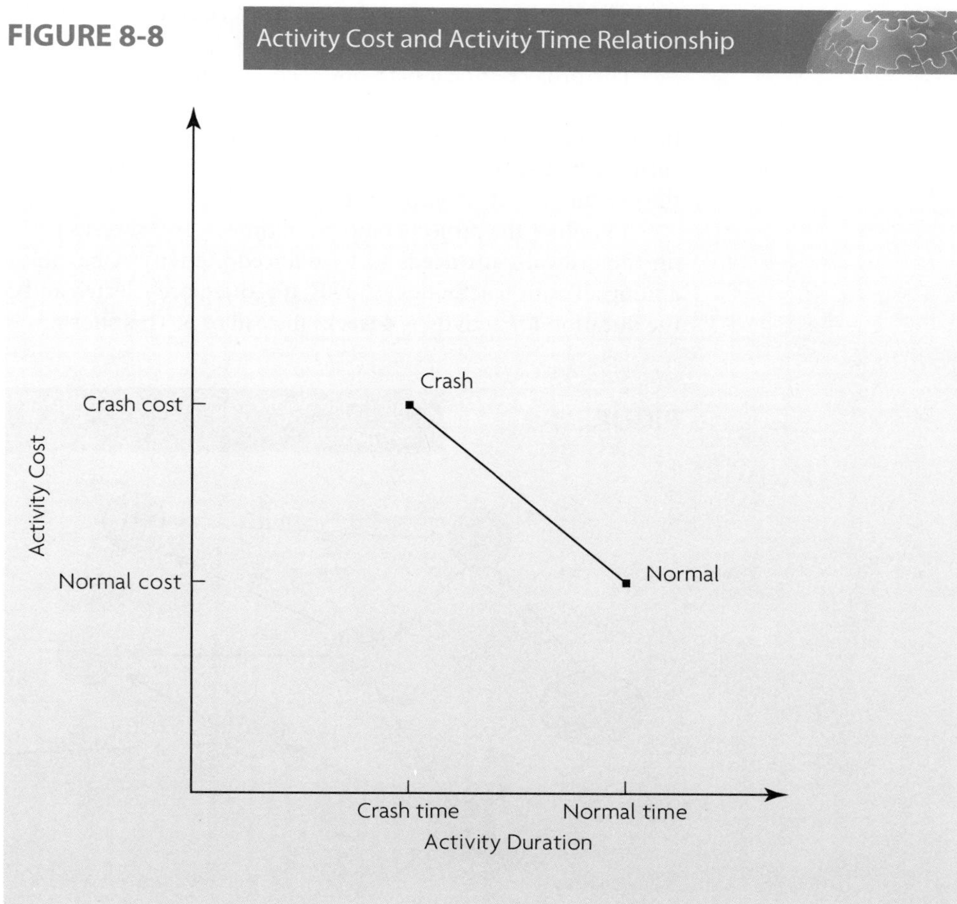

The general procedure for project crashing involves the following four steps:

1. Compute the crash cost per period for all activities using Equation 8-10.
2. Find critical path(s) in the project network using the normal times and identify critical activities.
3. Select a critical activity with the smallest crash cost per week that can still be crashed, in the case that there exists only one critical path. Otherwise, select one activity from each critical path that can be still crashed and yield the smallest total crash cost per period (including a common activity among critical paths). Crash the selected activity or activities by one period. Update the length of paths.
4. Stop the procedure if the completion deadline is reached. Otherwise, check to ensure current critical path(s) are still critical and find the new ones, if any. Return to Step 3.

To illustrate the procedure above, consider the network shown in Figure 8-9, which shows the activities for a new product development project and their precedence relationships. Start is a dummy activity with zero duration added to ensure that all activities have one starting node.

Table 8-5 provides the information about the activities normal times and costs, crash times and costs, the maximum crashing reduction in time as obtained by the difference between the normal time and the crash time, and the crash cost per week as obtained using Equation 8-10. For example, the normal time for activity C is 10 weeks and its cost is $45 000. It can be shortened by up to 4 weeks at an additional cost of $36 000 or $9000 per week of reduction.

The project critical path obtained by using normal times is Start-A-C-E-H. The estimated project completion time is 28 weeks. Suppose that management wants to shorten the project to 24 weeks to beat competition. Which activities should be crashed, and for each crashed activity provide the total number of weeks crashed and the total cost. What is the overall project crashing cost?

To reduce the project completion time from 28 weeks to 27 weeks, one of the activities on the critical path needs to be reduced. Activity A has the lowest crash cost per week among all critical activities ($3000). It is therefore selected and crashed by one week, that is, the duration for activity is 4 weeks instead of 5. This shortens the project completion time

FIGURE 8-9 Project Network for the New Product Development Example

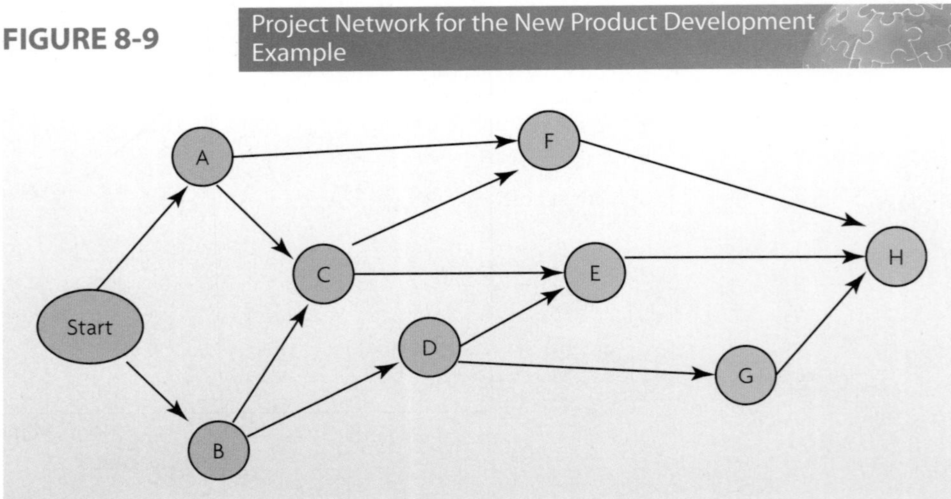

TABLE 8-5 Time and Cost Information for the New Product Development Project

Activity	Time (weeks)		Cost ($)		Maximum Reduction in Time (weeks)	Crash Cost per Week
	Normal	Crash	Normal	Crash		
A	5	2	25 000	34 000	3	3000
B	4	2	30 000	40 000	2	5000
C	10	6	45 000	81 000	4	9000
D	5	3	30 000	38 000	2	4000
E	7	6	30 000	37 000	1	7000
F	5	3	20 000	26 000	2	3000
G	4	2	35 000	44 000	2	4500
H	6	3	35 000	65 000	3	10 000

to 27 weeks and Start-A-C-E-H is still the single critical path. To shorten the project completion to 26 weeks, activity A is once again selected, given that it can still be crashed and it has the lowest crash cost per week among all critical activities ($3000). The project completion time is now 26 weeks. Start-A-C-E-H is still a critical path but another path, Start-B-C-E-H, has also become critical. To reduce the entire project to 25 weeks, one activity from each critical path needs to be crashed. One option is to choose activity A and B, respectively, but the total cost would be $8000 ($3000 + $5000). Activity E is common to both critical paths, has a crash cost per week of $7000, which is lower than $8000 (if A and B are crashed), and will reduce both path simultaneously if selected. We crash activity E by one week to reduce the project completion time to 25 weeks.

At this stage, we have 3 critical paths: Start-A-C-E-H, Start-B-C-E-H, and Start-B-C-F-H. Activity E cannot be crashed further. To reduce the project completion time to 24 weeks, Activities A and B will be crashed for a total cost of $8000 ($3000 + $5000), any other combination being more costly. Note that the option of shortening A and F is cheaper, but it does not reduce the length of the critical path Start-B-C-E-H.

In conclusion, to shorten the completion project duration to 24 weeks, activity A should be crashed by 3 weeks at a cost of $9000 (3 × $3000), activity E by 1 week at a cost of $7000, and activity B by one week at a cost of $5000. The total project crashing cost is $21 000 ($9000 + $7000 + $5000). Table 8-6 provides a summary of the procedure after 4 weeks of project crashing, where * indicates a critical path.

Using Linear Programming to Make Crashing Decisions

The manual procedure described above is suitable for projects involving a small number of activities. For large-scale projects, linear programming can be used to make crashing decisions. The problem consists of minimizing the total cost of the project (including the extra cost of crashing activities), subject to the constraint that project duration must be less than or equal to the desired deadline. The decision variables are the start time of each activity, the reduction in the duration of each activity due to crashing, and the finish time of the project. The constraints are that the maximum reduction in time for each activity cannot be exceeded, the project finish time must be less or equal to the desired finish time; and the precedence relationships of all activities must be respected.

TABLE 8-6 Summary Output from the Crashing Procedure

	Length After Crashing x Weeks				
Paths	**0**	**1**	**2**	**3**	**4**
Start-A-F-H	15	14	13	13	12
Start-A-C-E-H	28*	27*	26*	25*	24
Start-A-C-F-H	21	20	19	19	18
Start-B-C-F-H	25	25	25	25*	24
Start-B-C-E-H	26	26	26*	25*	24
Start-B-D-E-H	22	22	22	21	20
Start-B-D-G-H	19	19	19	19	18
Activity crashed		A	A	E	A,B
Crashing cost		\$3000	\$3000	\$7000	\$8000

For the new product development project, the linear programming will be formulated as follows, where X_j = starting time for activity j and Y_j = number of weeks by which activity i is crashed.

The cost for completing the project using normal times is fixed. Hence, the objective function is formulated as minimizing the project crashing:

$$\text{minimize } Z = 3000Y_A + 5000Y_B + 9000Y_C + 4000Y_D + 7000Y_E + 3000Y_F + 4500Y_G + 10\,000Y_H$$

Precedence Relationship Constraints To express the precedence relationships between activities, the following three relations are used for each activity: (1) Earliest start time ≥ Finish time of preceding activity(ies); (2) Finish time = Earliest start time + activity duration; and (3) Activity duration = Normal activity time − number of weeks by which an activity is crashed. Therefore, the following constraints are developed:

$X_A = 0$ (Earliest starting time for activity A)
$X_B = 0$ (Earliest starting time for activity B)
$X_C \geq X_A + 5 - Y_A$ (C cannot start earlier than the completion of activity A)
$X_C \geq X_B + 4 - Y_B$ (C cannot start earlier than the completion of activity B)
$X_D \geq X_B + 4 - Y_B$ (D cannot start earlier than the completion of activity B)
$X_E \geq X_C + 10 - Y_C$ (E cannot start earlier than the completion of activity C)
$X_E \geq X_D + 5 - Y_D$ (E cannot start earlier than the completion of activity D)
$X_F \geq X_A + 5 - Y_A$ (F cannot start earlier than the completion of activity A)
$X_F \geq X_C + 10 - Y_C$ (F cannot start earlier than the completion of activity C)
$X_G \geq X_D + 5 - Y_D$ (G cannot start earlier than the completion of activity D)
$X_H \geq X_E + 7 - Y_E$ (H cannot start earlier than the completion of activity E)
$X_H \geq X_F + 5 - Y_F$ (H cannot start earlier than the completion of activity F)
$X_H \geq X_G + 4 - Y_G$ (H cannot start earlier than the completion of activity G)

Maximum Reduction Constraints This set of constraints refers to the limits by which each activity can be crashed.

$Y_A \leq 3$ **(activity A can be crashed up to 3 weeks)**
$Y_B \leq 2$ **(activity B can be crashed up to 2 weeks)**
$Y_C \leq 4$ **(activity C can be crashed up to 4 weeks)**
$Y_D \leq 2$ **(activity D can be crashed up to 2 weeks)**
$Y_E \leq 1$ **(activity E can be crashed up to 1 week)**
$Y_F \leq 2$ **(activity F can be crashed up to 2 weeks)**
$Y_G \leq 2$ **(activity G can be crashed up to 2 weeks)**
$Y_H \leq 3$ **(activity H can be crashed up to 3 weeks)**

Project Completion Deadline Since H is the finish activity of the project, its finishing time must be no longer than the project deadline, that is, $X_H + 6 - Y_H \leq 24$ weeks.

Non-negativity Constraints This set of constraints stipulates that all variables must be non-negative, that is, all X_j and $Y_j \geq 0, j =$ A, B, C, D, E, F, G, H.

Exhibit 8-1 shows the Excel Solver layout for the new product development crashing project. The Excel's function SUMPRODUCT is used in the LHS column as well as in the Z value cell. The solution is shown in the bottom section of the Exhibit. It shows that activity A should be crashed by 2.5 weeks and activity C should be crashed by 1.5 week for a total crashing cost of $21 000. Note that the Solver's solution has the same objective function as the manual procedure, but with a different solution. This indicates that the problem has multiple solutions.

EXHIBIT 8-1 Excel Solver Output for the Crashing Example

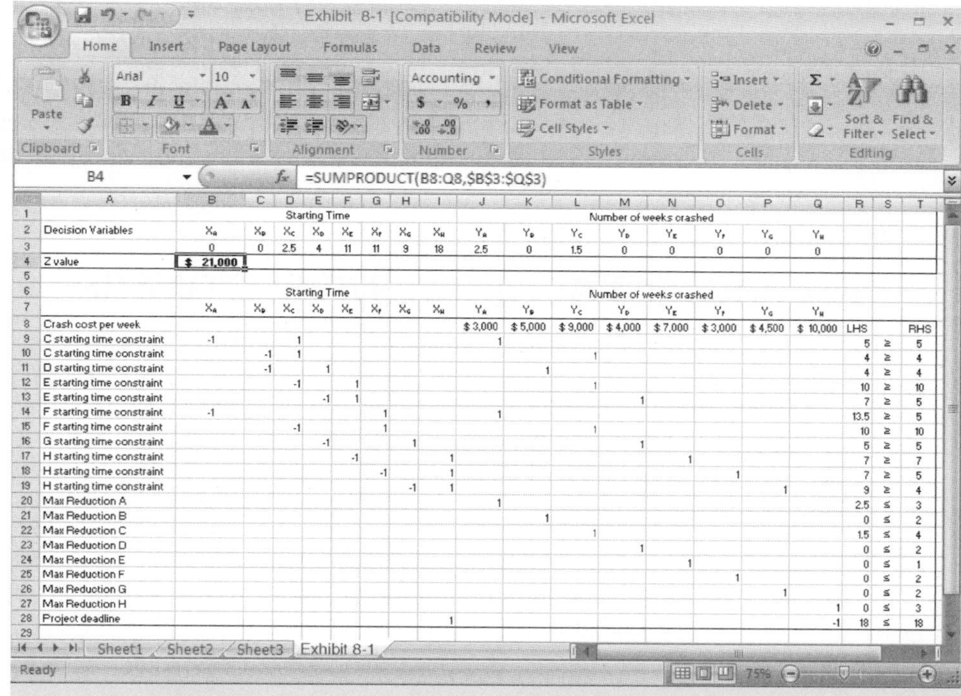

B4 =SUMPRODUCT(B8:Q8,$B$3:$Q$3)

	A	B	C	D	E	F	G	H	I	J	K	L	M	N	O	P	Q	R	S	T
1				Starting Time								Number of weeks crashed								
2	Decision Variables	X_A	X_B	X_C	X_D	X_E	X_F	X_G	X_H	Y_A	Y_B	Y_C	Y_D	Y_E	Y_F	Y_G	Y_H			
3		0	0	2.5	4	11	11	9	18	2.5	0	1.5	0	0	0	0	0			
4	Z value	$ 21,000																		
5																				
6				Starting Time								Number of weeks crashed								
7		X_A	X_B	X_C	X_D	X_E	X_F	X_G	X_H	Y_A	Y_B	Y_C	Y_D	Y_E	Y_F	Y_G	Y_H			
8	Crash cost per week									$ 3,000	$ 5,000	$ 9,000	$ 4,000	$ 7,000	$ 3,000	$ 4,500	$ 10,000	LHS		RHS
9	C starting time constraint	-1		1						1								5	≥	5
10	C starting time constraint		-1	1								1						4	≥	4
11	D starting time constraint		-1		1						1							4	≥	4
12	E starting time constraint			-1		1						1						10	≥	10
13	E starting time constraint				-1	1							1					7	≥	5
14	F starting time constraint	-1					1			1								13.5	≥	5
15	F starting time constraint			-1			1					1						10	≥	10
16	G starting time constraint				-1			1					1					5	≥	5
17	H starting time constraint					-1			1					1				7	≥	7
18	H starting time constraint						-1		1						1			7	≥	5
19	H starting time constraint							-1	1							1		9	≥	4
20	Max Reduction A									1								2.5	≤	3
21	Max Reduction B										1							0	≤	2
22	Max Reduction C											1						1.5	≤	4
23	Max Reduction D												1					0	≤	2
24	Max Reduction E													1				0	≤	1
25	Max Reduction F														1			0	≤	2
26	Max Reduction G															1		0	≤	2
27	Max Reduction H																1	0	≤	3
28	Project deadline								1								-1	18	≤	18
29																				

8.8 USING LINEAR PROGRAMMING IN PROJECT SCHEDULING

The project scheduling problem can also be formulated as a linear programming problem that seeks to determine the project completion time subject to meeting the precedence relationships between activities. To determine the EST and the EFT for activities the following model can be developed. Let X_j = earliest start time for activity j, t_j = the duration for activity j, and $P(j)$ = set of immediate predecessors of activity j. Therefore, the linear programming model consists of:

$$\text{minimize } Z = \sum_j X_j \tag{8-11}$$

Subject to

$$X_j \geq X_i + t_i, \text{ for all } j, \text{ for all } i \in P(j) \tag{8-12}$$

$$X_j \geq 0, \text{ for all } j \tag{8-13}$$

The objective function minimizes the sum of earliest start times of activities. Its value is only to ensure that each activity starts at the earliest time. Constraint 8-12 states that an activity cannot start unless all its immediate predecessors are completed. Constraint 8-13 is the non-negativity constraint.

To determine the LST and LFT for activities, the linear programming model can be written as follows, where W_j = latest start time for activity j:

$$\text{maximize } Z = \sum_j W_j \tag{8-14}$$

Subject to

$$W_j \geq W_i + t_i, \text{ for all } j, \text{ for all } i \in P(j) \tag{8-15}$$

$$W_j + t_j = EFT_j, \quad j = \text{finish activity} \tag{8-16}$$

$$W_j \geq 0, \text{ for all } j \tag{8-17}$$

The objective function to maximize the sum of all activity start times to ensure the latest activity start times. Constraint 8-15 defines the activity precedence relationships. Constraint 8-16 states the completion time of the finish activity in the project network.

8.9 PROJECT SCHEDULING SOFTWARE

For efficient management of large scale projects, many specialized project management software packages have been developed for scheduling and tracking project activities. Examples include Microsoft Project (www.microsoft.com/office/project), Primavera (http://www.primavera.com/products/p6/index.asp), and Artemis Project (http://www.aisc.com/). Microsoft Project, a project management software program developed and sold by Microsoft, is one of the most-used products of this type in the market. It allows users to draw the project network, develop the project schedule, assign resources, track the project's progress, manage the budget, and analyze the project workload. As the focus of this chapter is how to develop a basic project schedule, the capabilities of these software packages will not be discussed further.

Summary

This chapter introduced the critical path method (CPM) and the program evaluation review technique (PERT), two management science techniques developed in the late 1950s to plan, schedule, and control large, complex projects with many activities. We showed when and how these approaches can be used to help managers address questions such as what is the expected total time required to complete a project; what are the start and the completion times for individual activities; which critical activities must be completed as scheduled; how much delay can be tolerated for non-critical activities; what is the least expensive way to speed up a project; and in the case where the durations of activities are not known with certainty, the probability to complete a project according to a given time frame and the variability in the project completion time. The chapter also showed how the network representation can be used to depict the project activities and their relationships, how to handle crashing decisions heuristically or using a linear programming model, and how the project scheduling problem can be formulated as a linear programming problem that seeks to determine the project completion time subject to meeting the precedence relationships between activities. Finally, a brief list was provided of specialized project management software packages that have been developed for scheduling and tracking project activities.

Glossary

Activity A task that needs to be completed within a project and consumes both time and resources.

Activity on arc (AOA) A project network representation in which the project activities are reported on arcs and the nodes represent the starting or the completion of activities.

Activity on node (AON) A project network representation in which the project activities are reported on nodes and the arcs represent their precedence relationships.

Backward pass The process used to determine the latest start time and the latest finish time of an activity, which consists of moving backward through the project network from the finish node to the starting node.

Beta probability distribution A form of distribution used to represent the duration of an activity in PERT analysis.

Critical path method (CPM) An analysis approach used in project scheduling when the project inputs (e.g., activities duration and costs) are assumed to be known with certainty.

Crashing Speeding up or shortening the duration of an activity by using additional resources.

Crash time The shortest possible time to complete an activity with additional resources.

Crash cost The cost to crash an activity.

Critical path(s) The path(s) with the longest length in the project network.

Critical activities Activities in the critical path. These activities must be completed as scheduled to prevent delaying the project completion.

Earliest start time (EST) The earliest time at which an activity can start if no delays occur in the project.

Earliest finish time (EFT) The earliest time at which an activity can finish if no delays occur in the project.

Forward pass A process used to determine the earliest start time and the earliest finish time of an activity, which consists of moving forward through the project network from the starting node to the finish node.

Immediate predecessors Activities that must be completed prior to the starting time of a given activity.

Immediate successors Activities that follow the completion of a given activity.

Latest start time (LST) The latest time at which an activity can start without delaying the completion of the project.

Latest finish time (LFT) The latest time at which an activity can finish without delaying the completion of the project.

Length of path The sum of the durations of the activities on the path.

Normal time The estimated activity duration used with CPM or PERT in the computation of earliest (latest) start or finish times.

Normal cost The activity cost under the normal activity time.

Path A sequence of connected nodes in the network from the start node to the finish node.

Program evaluation review technique (PERT) An analysis approach used in project scheduling when some of the project inputs (e.g., activities duration and costs) are not known with certainty

Project A set of activities interrelated by their precedence relationships that need to be undertaken in the accomplishment of a unique, often major outcome.

Project crashing The process of shortening the duration of a project by crashing the duration of a number of activities.

Project network A representation used to depict the project activities.

Slack time The length of time that can be tolerated for an activity without incurring a delay in the estimated project completion time.

Solved Problems

Problem 1

Expected durations (in weeks) and variances for the major activities of an R&D project are depicted in the precedence network diagram chart. Determine the probability that project completion time in Figure 8-10 will be

a. Less than 50 weeks.
b. More than 50 weeks.

Solution

Because S and End have zero durations, we can ignore them in the following calculations. The mean and standard deviation for each path are shown in Table 8-7. Path S-1-5-8-End is the critical path. Therefore, the project expected completion time is 51 weeks and the corresponding variance is 1.488 weeks.

a. The z value for the normal distribution at $x = 50$ is

$$z = \frac{50 - t_{S1}}{1.22} = -.82. \text{ Hence, } P(x \leq 50) = .2061.$$

b. $P(x > 50) = 1 - P(x \leq 50) = .7939.$

FIGURE 8-10 Precedence Network Diagram Chart for Problem 1

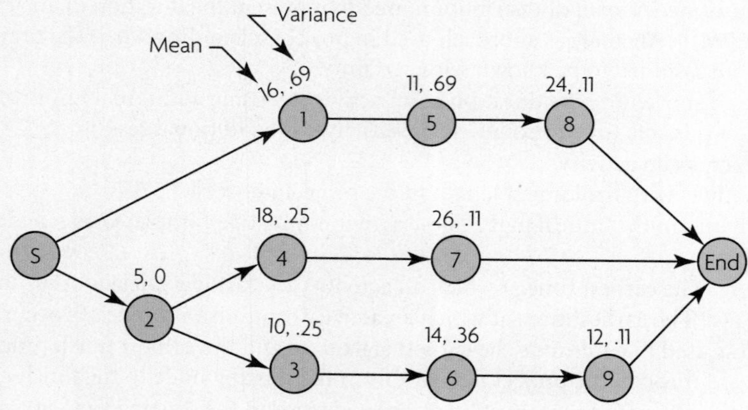

Table 8-7 Probabilities for Problem 1

Path	Expected Time (weeks)	Standard Deviation (weeks)
S-1-5-8-End	$16 + 11 + 24 = 51$	$\sqrt{.69 + .69 + .11} = 1.22$
S-2-4-7-End	$5 + 18 + 26 = 49$	$\sqrt{.00 + .25 + .11} = .60$
S-2-3-6-9-End	$5 + 10 + 14 + 12 = 41$	$\sqrt{.00 + .25 + .36 + .11} = .85$

Problem 2

Table 8-8 shows the information related to a project that involves the merger of two marketing firms (in days).

Table 8-8 Data for Solved Problem 2

Activity	Immediate predecessor(s)	Estimated duration(days)
A	—	10
B	—	15
C	A	5
D	B	12
E	C, D	14
F	B	8
G	D, F	15
H	E	10
I	E, G	6
J	F, I	9

a. Draw the project network.
b. Develop the project schedule (EST, EFT, LST, LFT).
c. What are the critical activities?
d. What is the project completion duration?
e. If there is an option to delay one activity without delaying the entire merge project, which activity would you delay and why?
f. Formulate the LP model that would determine the earliest start times of activities.

Solution

a. The project network is shown in Figure 8-11.
b. The project schedule is as follows:

Activity	Earliest Start	Latest Start	Earliest Finish	Latest Finish	Slack
Start	0	0	0	0	0
A	0	13	10	23	13
B	0	0	15	15	0
C	10	23	15	28	13
D	15	15	27	27	0
E	27	28	41	42	1
F	15	19	23	27	4
G	27	27	42	42	0
H	41	47	51	57	6
I	42	42	48	48	0
J	48	48	57	57	0
Finish	57	57	57	57	0

c. The critical activities are: B-D-G-I-J
d. The project completion duration is 57 days.
e. Activity A or C since they have the largest slack times.
f. The LP formulation of the model is as follows, where X_j = earliest start time for activity j = A, B, C, D, E, F, G, H, I, and J.

$$\text{minimize } Z = X_A + X_B + X_C + X_D + X_E + X_F + X_G + X_H + X_I + X_J$$

FIGURE 8-11 Network for Solved Problem 2

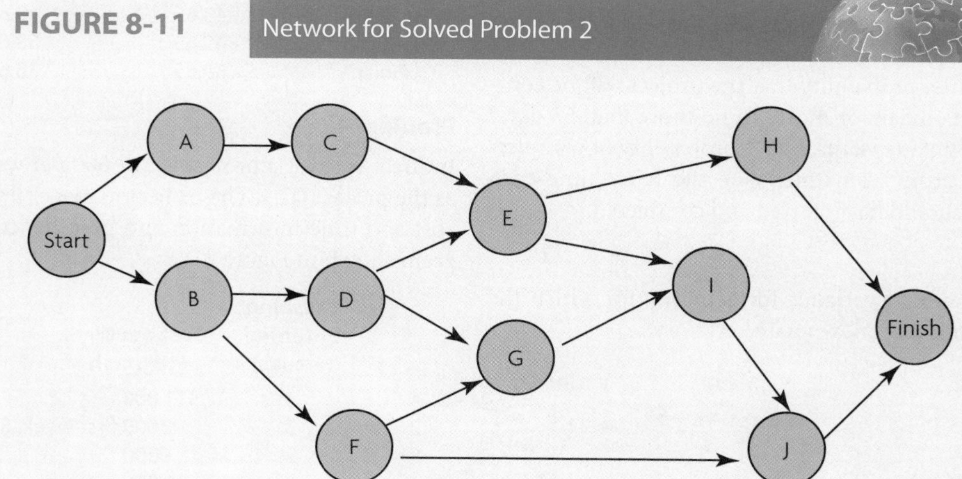

subject to

$X_C \geq X_A + 10$
$X_D \geq X_B + 15$
$X_E \geq X_C + 5$
$X_E \geq X_D + 12$
$X_F \geq X_B + 15$
$X_G \geq X_D + 12$
$X_G \geq X_F + 8$
$X_H \geq X_E + 14$
$X_I \geq X_E + 14$
$X_I \geq X_G + 15$
$X_J \geq X_F + 8$
$X_J \geq X_I + 6$
$X_A = X_B = 0$

All variables ≥ 0

Problem 3

Consider the network information shown in the previous problem (Problem 2) and assume that the duration of some activities is not known with certainty. The estimates of these activities are shown below, assuming that the duration for the other activities remains unchanged.

Activity	Optimistic	Most Likely	Pessimistic
A	8	10	12
C	3	5	7
D	10	12	14
G	13	15	17
H	8	10	12

a. What is the critical path?
b. What is the project's expected completion time and its variance?
c. What is the probability that the project will be completed in 60 days or more? In no more than 55 days?
d. If the company wants a 96% probability of completing the project on time, state the latest time each activity should have started and completed.

Solution

a. The mean and variance for activities for which the duration is not known with certainty:

Activity	a	m	b	Mean, $t_e = \frac{a+4m+b}{6}$	Variance, $\sigma^2 = \left(\frac{b-a}{6}\right)^2$
A	8	10	12	10	0.44
C	3	5	7	5	0.44
D	10	12	14	12	0.44
G	13	15	17	15	0.44
H	8	10	12	10	0.44

The critical path is Start – B – D – G – I – J – Finish.

b. The expected project completion time is 57 days and its variance is .44 + .44 = .88.

c. The probability that the project will be completed in 60 days or more: $P(X \geq 60) = P(X \geq z)$, where

$z = \frac{60-57}{\sqrt{0.88}} = 3.198$. Therefore from Table A in Appendix B, $P(X \geq 3.198) = 0.5 - 0.4990 = 0.001$ or 0.1 percent.

The probability that the project will be completed in 55 days or less: $P(X \leq 50) = P(X \leq z)$, where

$z = \frac{55-57}{\sqrt{0.88}} - 2.13$. Therefore from Table A in Appendix B, $P(X \geq -2.13) = 0.5 - .4788 = .0212$ or 2.12 percent.

d. $z_{0.96} = 1.76$. Using Equation 8-9, the project completion time $X = 57 + 1.76 \times .938 = 58.65$ days. Therefore to meet this completion time, the latest start and finish times for each activity should be as follows:

Activity	Latest Start	Latest Finish
Start	1.65	1.65
A	14.65	24.65
B	1.65	16.65
C	24.65	29.65
D	16.65	28.65
E	29.65	43.65
F	20.65	28.65
G	28.65	43.65
H	48.65	58.65
I	43.65	49.65
J	49.65	58.65
Finish	58.65	58.65

Problem 4

Indirect cost for a project is \$12 000 per week for as long as the project lasts. The project manager has supplied the cost and time information and precedence network diagram shown in Figure 8-12.

Activity	Crashing Potential (weeks)	Cost per Week to Crash
A	3	\$11 000
B	3	3000 first week, \$4000 after that
C	2	6000
D	1	1000
E	3	6000
F	1	2000

Use the information to:

a. Determine an optimum crashing plan.
b. Graph the total costs for the plan.

FIGURE 8-12 Network Diagram for Solved Problem 4

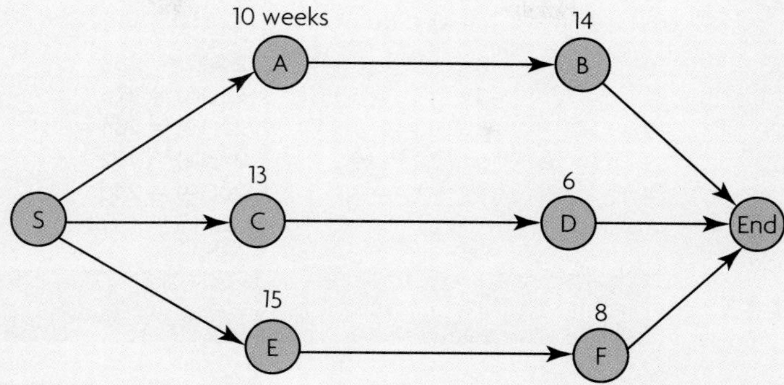

Solution

a. 1. Calculate path lengths and identify the critical path:

Path	Duration (weeks)
S-A-B-End	24 (critical path)
S-C-D-End	19
S-E-F-End	23

2. Rank critical activities according to crash costs:

Activity	Cost per Week to Crash
B.............	$3000 first week, $4000 after that
A.............	11 000

Activity B should be shortened one week since it has the lower crashing cost per week. This would reduce indirect costs by $12 000 at a cost of $3000, for a net savings of $9000. At this point, paths S-A-B-End and S-E-F-End would both have a length of 23 weeks, so both would be critical.

3. Rank activities by crashing cost on the two critical paths:

Path	Activity	Cost per Week to Crash
S-A-B-End	B	$4000
....	A	11 000
S-E-F-End	F	2000
....	E	6000

Choose one activity (the least costly) on each path to crash: B on S-A-B-End and F on S-E-F-End, for a total cost of $4000 + $2000 = $6000 and a net savings of $12 000 − $6000 = $6000.

Note: There is no activity common to the two critical paths.

4. Check to see which path(s) might be critical: S-A-B-End and S-E-F-End would be 22 weeks in length, and S-C-D-End would still be 19 weeks.

5. Rank activities on the critical paths:

Path	Activity	Cost per Week to Crash
A-B	B	$4000
....	A	11 000
E-F	E	6000
....	F	(no further crashing possible)

Crash B on path S-A-B-End and E on S-E-F-End for a cost of $4000 + $6000 = $10 000, for a net savings of $12 000 − $10 000 = $2000.

6. At this point, no further reduction is cost-effective: paths S-A-B-End and S-E-F-End would be 21 weeks in length, and one activity from each path would have to be shortened. This would mean activity A at $11 000 and E at $6000 for a total of $17 000, which exceeds the $12 000 potential savings in indirect costs. Note that no further crashing for activity B is possible.

b. The following table summarizes the results, showing the length of the project after crashing n weeks:

Path	n = 0	1	2	3
S-A-B-End	24	23	22	21
S-C-D-End	19	19	19	19
S-E-F-End....................	23	23	22	21
Activity crashed		B	B,F	B,E
Crashing costs ($000)		3	6	10

A summary of costs for the preceding schedule would look like Table 8-9.

The graph of total cost is shown in Figure 8-13.

Table 8-9 Summary of Costs for Solved Problem 4

Project Length	Cumulative Weeks Shortened	Cumulative Crashing Costs ($000)	Indirect Costs($000)	Total Costs ($000)
24	0	0	24(12) = 288	288
23	1	3	23(12) = 276	279
22	2	3 + 6 = 9	22(12) = 264	273
21	3	9 + 10 = 19	21(12) = 252	271
20	4	19 + 17 = 36	20(12) = 240	276

FIGURE 8-13 Total Cost for Solved Problem 4

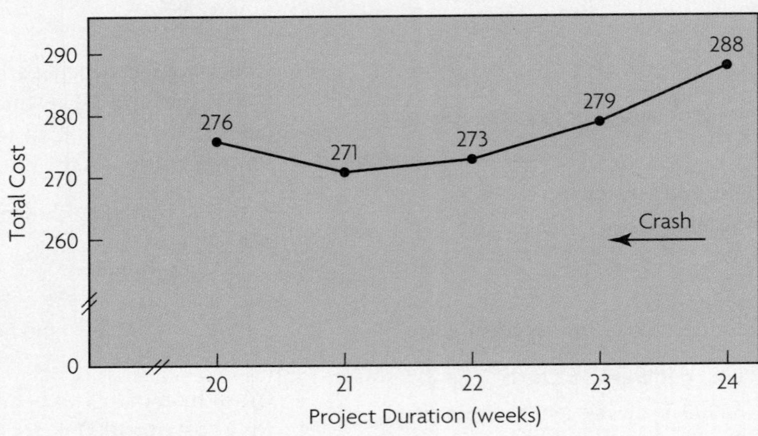

Discussion and Review Questions

1. Explain differences and similarities between CPM and PERT.
2. What are the different types of information that need to be gathered to depict a project network?
3. Explain briefly two approaches that can be used to determine the project critical path(s) and when each is the most suitable.
4. What is the meaning of activity slack times and how are they computed?
5. Explain why the project manager should monitor the progress of activities with small slack times.
6. Why is it important in project management to identify and monitor the critical activities?
7. When is simulation approach the most appropriate in project scheduling?
8. Why must all immediate predecessor activities be considered when determining the activity's earliest start time?
9. Why must all immediate successor activities be considered when finding the activity's latest finish time?
10. What is project crashing and how can it be done manually?
11. Provide some of the reasons for a company to consider project crashing.
12. What constraints are involved in formulating the project crashing problem as a linear programming model?
13. What constraints are involved in formulating the project scheduling problem as a linear programming model?

Problems

1. For the precedence network diagram in Figure 8-14, determine both the critical path and the project duration by determining the length of each path. The numbers above the nodes represent activity duration in days.
2. Using the data in Table 8-10 construct a precedence network diagram. The project is completed when activities H, I, and J are all finished.
3. Using the data in Table 8-11 construct a precedence network diagram. The project is completed when activities D, F, J, and K are all finished.
4. ET+ is an entertainment group that specializes in the management of band tours around the world. The company is considering placing a bid for the management of the next 2-day concert of a very popular rock band in the city of Toronto. As part of the planning process, the company has determined that the list of activities in Table 8-12 would need to be performed to carry out the project.
Construct the precedence network diagram that can be used in the scheduling of these activities.

FIGURE 8-14 Network Diagram for Problem 1

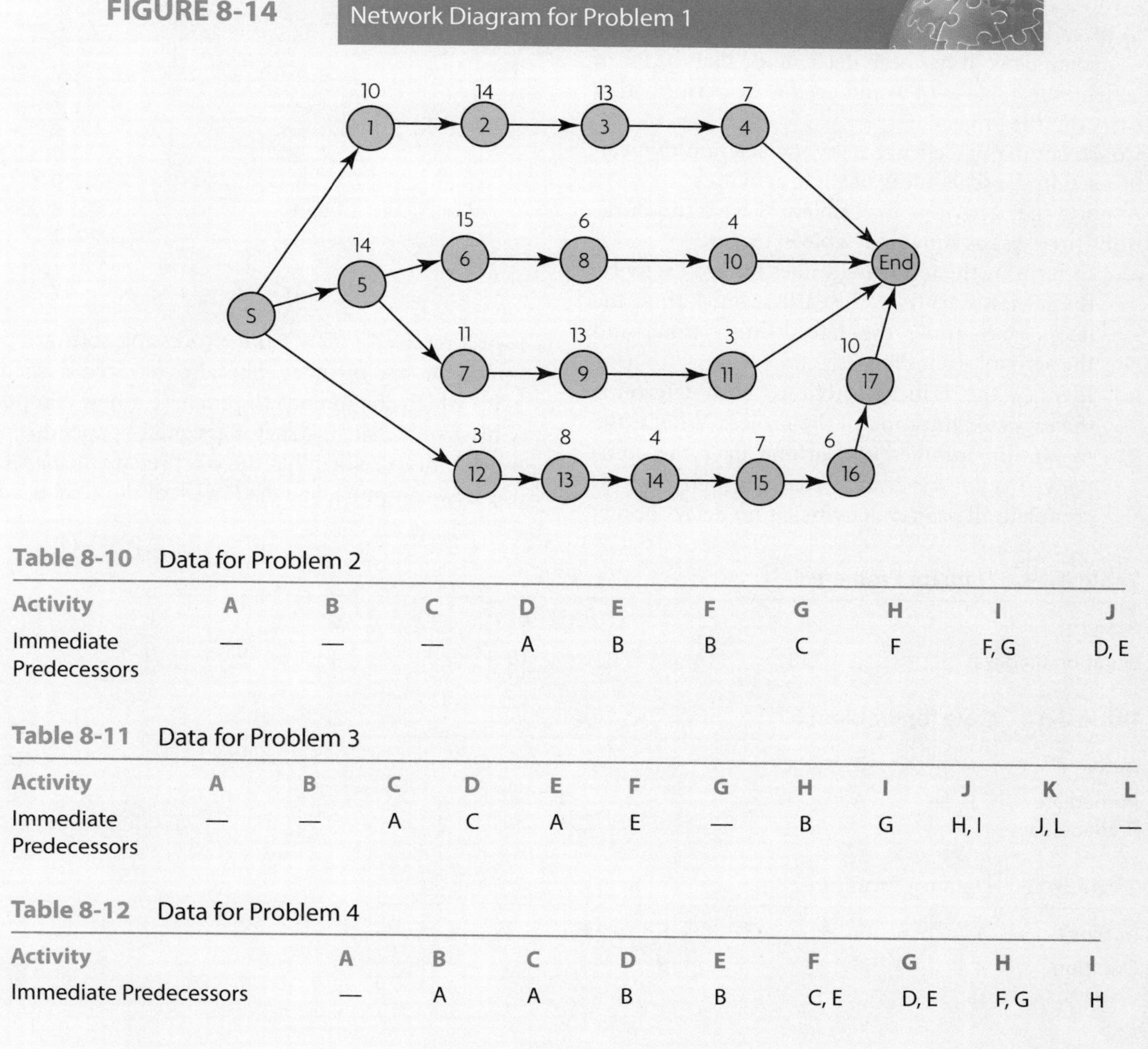

Table 8-10 Data for Problem 2

Activity	A	B	C	D	E	F	G	H	I	J
Immediate Predecessors	—	—	—	A	B	B	C	F	F, G	D, E

Table 8-11 Data for Problem 3

Activity	A	B	C	D	E	F	G	H	I	J	K	L
Immediate Predecessors	—	—	A	C	A	E	—	B	G	H, I	J, L	—

Table 8-12 Data for Problem 4

Activity	A	B	C	D	E	F	G	H	I
Immediate Predecessors	—	A	A	B	B	C, E	D, E	F, G	H

5. Assume that the activities in Problem 4 have the duration (in days) as shown in Table 8-13.
   a. What is the maximum number of working days the company would have to write in their bid to complete all activities of this project if no delays occur?
   b. What are the critical activities?
   c. When would each activity have to start and finish at the earliest to complete this project on time?
   d. When would each activity have to start and finish at the latest to complete this project on time?
6. Softbank is a consulting company that specializes in the customization of software in the banking industry. The company has been hired to serve on a project that involves the replacement of the user interface currently in place for online banking in the website of a large Canadian bank. It has been determined that the list of activities in Table 8-14 would need to be performed to carry out the project.
   Construct the precedence network diagram that can be used in the scheduling of these activities.
7. Assume that activities in Problem 6 have the durations (in days) as shown in Table 8-15.
   a. Determine the following values for each activity: the earliest start time, the earliest finish time, the latest start time, the latest finish time, and the activity slack time.
   b. Identify the critical activities, and determine the expected duration of the project. What is the maximum number of working days the company would have to write in their bid to complete all project activities if no delays occur?
8. Reconsider the list of activities in Problem 6 and their corresponding durations in Problem 7. Suppose that after 12 days, activities A, B, and I have been finished, activity E is 75 percent finished, and activity J is half finished. How many days after the original start time would the project finish?
9. The following table contains information related to the major activities of a research project. Use the information to do the following:
   a. Draw a precedence network diagram.
   b. Find the critical path by identifying all the start to end paths and calculating their lengths.
   c. What is the expected duration of the project?

Activity	Immediate Predecessor(s)	Expected Duration (days)
A	—	5
C	A	8
D	C	2
B	A	7
E	—	3
F	E	6
I	B, D	10
M	F	8
G	—	1
H	G	2
K	H	17

10. Chris received a new word-processing software program for her birthday. She also received a cheque, with which she intends to purchase a new computer. Chris's university instructor assigned a paper due next week. Chris decided that she will prepare the paper on the new computer. She made a list of the activities and

Table 8-13 Data for Problem 5

Activity	A	B	C	D	E	F	G	H	I
Duration (in days)	5	18	13	3	10	11	4	9	2

Table 8-14 Data for Problem 6

Activity	A	B	C	D	E	F	G	H	I	J	K	L	M
Immediate Predecessors	—	A	B	C	A	E	F	D, G	—	I	J	K	L

Table 8-15 Data for Problem 7

Activity	A	B	C	D	E	F	G	H	I	J	K	L	M
Duration (in days)	4	9	5	2	8	7	2	3	10	6	4	5	6

their estimated durations. Chris's friend has offered to shop for, select and purchase a computer, and install the software.

a. Arrange the activities into two logical sequences.
b. Construct a precedence network diagram.
c. Determine the critical path and its expected duration.
d. What are some possible reasons for the project to take longer than the expected duration?

Estimated Time (hours)	Activity (abbreviation)
.8	Install software (Install)
.4	Outline the paper (Outline)
.2	Submit paper to instructor (Submit)
.6	Choose a topic (Choose)
.5	Use grammar-checking routine and make corrections (Check)
3.0	Write the paper using the word-processing software (Write)
2.0	Shop for a new computer (Shop)
1.0	Select and purchase computer (Select)
2.0	Library research on chosen topic (Library)

11. The information in the following table pertains to a project that is about to commence.

Activity	Immediate Predecessor(s)	Estimated Duration (days)
A	—	15
B	A	12
C	B	6
D	B	5
E	C	3
F	—	8
G	F	8
H	F	9
I	G	7
J	H	14
K	J	6

a. As the project manager, which activities would you be concerned with in terms of timely project completion? Explain.
b. Determine the following values for each activity: the earliest start time, the earliest finish time, the latest start time, the latest finish time, and the activity slack time.

12. Three recent university graduates have formed a partnership and have opened an advertising firm. Their first project consists of activities listed in the following table.

a. Draw the precedence network diagram.
b. What is the probability that the project can be completed in 24 days or less? In 21 days or less?
c. Suppose it is now the end of the seventh day and that activities A and B have been completed while activity D is 50 percent completed. Optimistic, most likely, and pessimistic estimates for the completion of activity D are now 5, 6, and 7 days. Activities C and H are ready to begin. Determine the probability of finishing the project by day 24 and the probability of finishing by day 21.

Activity	Immediate Predecessor(s)	DURATION IN DAYS Optimistic	Most Likely	Pessimistic
A	—	5	6	7
B	—	8	8	11
C	A	6	8	11
D	—	9	12	15
E	C	5	6	9
F	D	5	6	7
G	F	2	3	7
H	B	4	4	5
I	H	5	7	8

13. The new director of special events at a large university has decided to completely revamp graduation ceremonies. Toward that end, a precedence network diagram of the major activities has been developed. The chart has five paths with expected durations and variances as shown in the following table. Graduation day is 16 full weeks from now. Assuming that the project begins now, what is the probability that the project will be completed before:

a. Graduation time?
b. The end of week 15?
c. The end of week 13?

Path	Expected Duration (weeks)	Variance
A	10	1.21
B	8	2.00
C	12	1.00
D	15	2.89
E	14	1.44

14. What is the probability that the following project will take more than 10 weeks to complete if the precedence network diagram, activity means, and

standard deviations (both in weeks) are as shown below?

Activity	Mean	Standard Deviation
A	5	1.3
B	4	1.0
C	8	1.6

15. The project described in the following table and precedence network diagram has just begun. It is scheduled to be completed in 11 weeks.
    a. If you were the manager of this project, would you be concerned? Explain.
    b. If there is a penalty of $5000 a week for each week the project is late, what is the probability of incurring a penalty of at least $5000?

Activity	Expected Duration (weeks)	Standard Deviation (weeks)
A	4	.70
B	6	.90
C	3	.62
D	9	1.90

16. The precedence network diagram in Figure 8-15 reflects optimistic, most likely, and pessimistic estimates for each activity. Determine:
    a. The expected completion time for each path and its variance.
    b. The probability that the project will require more than 49 weeks.
    c. The probability that the project can be completed in 46 weeks or fewer.

17. A project manager has compiled a list of major activities that will be required to install a computer information system in her company. The list includes three estimates of durations (optimistic, most likely, pessimistic) for activities and precedence relationships.

Activity	Precedes	3-Point Estimates (weeks)
A	—	2-4-6
D	A	6-8-10
E	D	7-9-12
H	E	2-3-5
F	A	3-4-8
G	F	5-7-9
B	—	2-2-3
I	B	2-3-6
J	I	3-4-5
K	J	4-5-8
C	—	5-8-12
M	C	1-1-1
N	M	6-7-11
O	N	8-9-13

If the project is finished within 26 weeks of its start, the project manager will receive a bonus of $1000; and if the project is finished within 27 weeks of its start, the bonus will be $500. Find the probability of each bonus.

FIGURE 8-15 Precedence Network Diagram for Problem 16

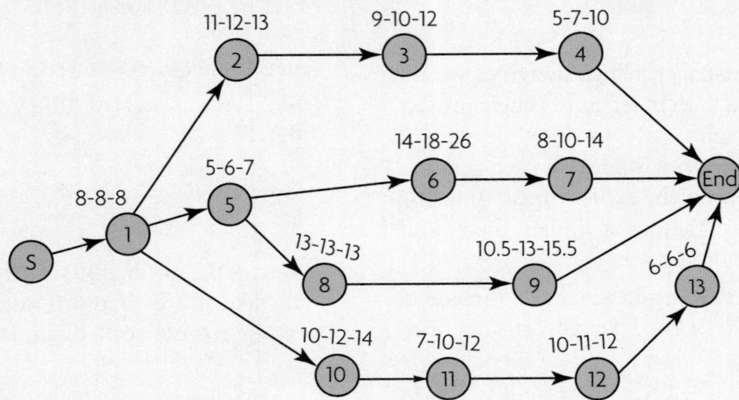

18. The project manager of a task force planning the construction of a domed stadium had hoped to be able to complete construction prior to the start of the next season. After reviewing construction duration estimates, it now appears that a certain amount of crashing will be needed to ensure project completion before the season opener. Given the following information, determine a minimum-cost crashing schedule that will shave five weeks off the project length.

Activity	Precedes	Normal Duration (weeks)	CRASHING COSTS First Week	Second Week
A	—	12	$15 000	$20 000
B	A	14	10 000	10 000
C	—	10	5000	5000
D	C	17	20 000	21 000
E	C	18	16 000	18 000
F	C	12	12 000	15 000
G	D	15	24 000	24 000
H	E	8	—	—
I	F	7	30 000	—
J	I	12	25 000	25 000
K	B	9	10 000	10 000
M	G	3	—	—
N	H	11	40 000	—
P	H, J	8	20 000	20 000

19. A construction project has indirect costs totalling $40 000 per week. Major activities in the project and their expected durations are shown in the precedence network diagram in Figure 8-16:

Crashing costs for each activity are:

Activity	CRASHING COSTS ($000) First Week	Second Week	Third Week
1	$18	$22	$—
2	24	25	25
3	30	30	35
4	15	20	—
9	30	33	36
5	12	24	26
6	—	—	—
8	40	40	40
7	3	10	12
10	2	7	10
15	26	—	—
11	10	15	25
12	8	13	—
13	5	12	—
14	14	15	—

a. Determine a minimum-cost crashing plan that will take off six weeks from the project duration.

b. Plot the total-cost curve from part *a* against project duration. What is the optimum number of weeks to crash?

20. Chuck's Custom Boats (CCB) builds luxury yachts to customer order. CCB has landed a contract with a Vancouver businessman (Mr. P). Relevant data are shown below. The complication is that Mr. P wants delivery in 32 weeks or he will impose a penalty of $375 for each week his yacht is late.

FIGURE 8-16 Precedence Network Diagram for Problem 19

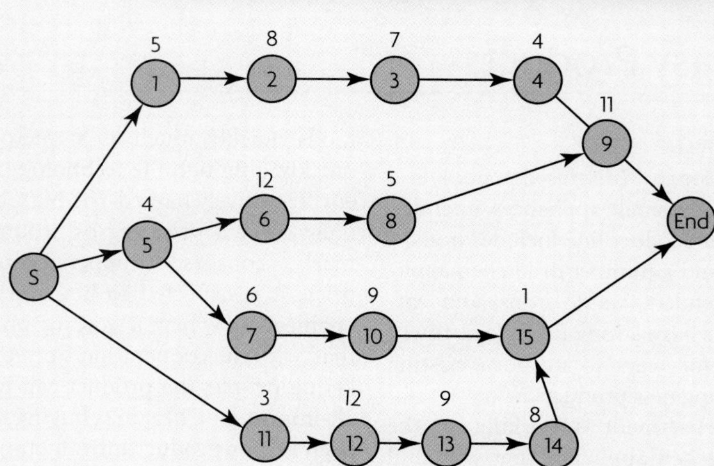

Activity	Immediate Predecessor(s)	Normal Duration (weeks)	CRASHING COSTS 1st Week	2nd Week
K	—	9	$410	$415
L	K	7	125	—
N	K	5	45	45
M	L	4	300	350
J	N	6	50	—
Q	M, J	5	200	225
P	Q	8	—	—
Y	Q	7	85	90
Z	P	6	90	—

Develop a minimum cost crashing schedule.

21. Table 8-16 is a list of activities and their expected duration, used by a component supplier to automobile manufacturers, to plan for QS9000 (the auto industry version of ISO9000) certification (registration).
    a. Draw the precedence network diagram.
    b. Determine the earliest and latest times, and identify the critical activities and the project duration.

Table 8-16 Data for Problem 21

A List of Activities in a QS-9000 Registration Project

Activity	Description	Immediate Predecessor(s)	Estimated time*
A	Appointment of QS-9000 taskforce	none	1 week
B	Preparation of a feasible plan	A	1 week
C	Delegation of authority responsibilities	B	1 week
D	Searching for a QS-9000 registrar	C	1 week
E	Preparation of three levels of documentation	C	12 weeks
F	QS-9000 awareness training	C	6 weeks
G	QS-9000 training of auditors and quality personnel	F	6 weeks
H	Preparing the plant for QS-9000 registrar	C	24 weeks
I	Conference with lead auditor	D	1 week
J	Examination of documentation	E, I	3 weeks
K	Internal audit of plant sections	G, H, J	12 weeks
L	Corrective actions of plant sections	K	12 weeks
M	Lead auditor and audit team audit plant	L	1 week
N	Audit conference and corrective action plan	M	2 weeks
O	Implementation of corrective action plans	N	12 weeks
P	Lead auditor re-audit corrective actions	O	2 weeks
Q	Lead auditor's recommendation	P	1 week

*These are estimates of time and may vary based upon situation, company, and registrar.

Case 1: Fantasy Products

Company Background

The Fantasy Products Company (disguised name) is a manufacturer of high-quality small appliances intended for home use. Their current product line includes irons, a small hand-held vacuum, and a number of kitchen appliances such as toasters, blenders, waffle irons, and coffeemakers. Fantasy Products has a strong R&D department that continually searches for ways to improve existing products as well as developing new products.

Currently, the R&D department is working on the development of a new kitchen appliance that will chill foods quickly much as a microwave oven heats them quickly, although the technology involved is quite different. Tentatively named The Big Chill, the product will initially carry a price tag of around $125, and the target market consists of upper-income consumers. At this price, it is expected to be a very profitable item. R&D engineers now have a working prototype and are satisfied that, with the cooperation from the production and marketing people, the product can be ready in time for the all-important Christmas buying season. A target date has been set for product introduction that is 24 weeks away.

Current Problem

Fantasy Products' Marketing Vice-President Vera Sloan has recently learned from reliable sources that a competitor is also in the process of developing a similar product, which it intends to bring out at almost the same time. In addition, her source indicated that the competitor plans to sell its product, which will be smaller than The Big Chill, for $99 in the hope of appealing to more customers. Vera, with the help of several of her key people who are to be involved in marketing The Big Chill, has decided that to compete, the selling price for The Big Chill will have to be lowered to within $10 of the competitor's price. At this price level it will still be profitable, although not nearly as profitable as originally anticipated.

However, Vera is wondering whether it would be possible to expedite the usual product introduction process to beat the competition to the market. If possible, she would like to get a six-week jump on the competition; this would put the product introduction date only 18 weeks away. During this initial period, Fantasy Products could sell The Big Chill for $125, reducing the selling price to $109 when the competitor's product actually enters the market. Since forecasts based on market research show that sales during the first six weeks will be about 400 per week, there is an opportunity for $25 per unit profit if the early introduction can be accomplished. In addition, there is a certain amount of prestige involved in being first to the market. This should help enhance The Big Chill's image during the anticipated battle for market share.

Data Collection

Since Fantasy Products has been through the product-introduction process a number of times, Vera has developed a list of the tasks that must be accomplished and the order in which they must be completed. Although the duration and costs vary depending on the particular product, the basic process does not. The list of activities involved and their precedence relationships are presented in Table 8-17. Duration and cost estimates for the introduction of The Big Chill are presented in Table 8-18. Note that some of the activities can be completed on a crash basis, with an associated increase in cost. For example, activity B can be crashed from 8 weeks to 6 weeks at an additional cost of $3000 (i.e., $12 000–$9000). Assume that if B is crashed to 7 weeks, the additional cost will be $1500 (i.e., $3000/2).

TABLE 8-17 List of Activities and Precedence Relationships

Activity	Description	Immediate Predecessor(s)
A	Select and order equipment	—
B	Receive equipment from supplier	A
C	Install and set up equipment	B
D	Finalize bill of materials	—
E	Order component parts	D
F	Receive component parts	E
G	First production run	C, F
H	Finalize marketing plan	—
I	Produce magazine ads	H
J	Script for TV ads	H
K	Produce TV ads	J
L	Begin ad campaign	I, K
M	Ship product to consumers	G, L

TABLE 8-18 Duration and Cost Estimates

Activity	Normal Duration (weeks)	Normal Cost	Crash Duration (weeks)	Normal & Crash Cost
A	3	$2000	2	$4400
B	8	9000	6	12 000
C	4	2000	2	7000
D	2	1000	1	2000
E	2	2000	1	3000
F	5	0	5	0
G	6	12 000	3	24 000
H	4	3500	2	8000
I	4	5000	3	8000
J	3	8000	2	15000
K	4	50 000	3	70 000
L	6	10 000	6	10 000
M	1	5000	1	5000

Managerial Report

Fantasy Products needs to decide whether to bring The Big Chill to market 18 weeks from now as Vera Sloan is recommending. As the project management specialist in the R&D department, you have been asked to answer the following questions:

1. When would the project be completed using normal durations?
2. Is it possible to complete the project in 18 weeks? What would the associated additional cost be? Which activities would need to be completed on a crash basis?
3. Is there some time frame shorter than the 18 weeks Vera has recommended that would make more sense in terms of profits?

Source: Adapted from an original case by Robert J. Thieraus, Margaret Cunningham, and Melanie Blackwell, Xavier University, Cincinnati, Ohio.

Multicriteria Decision-Making Models

CHAPTER 9

LEARNING OBJECTIVES

After completing this chapter, you should be able to:

1. Describe the type of problems that goal programming is designed to handle.
2. Describe the similarities and differences between goal programming and linear programming models.
3. Formulate goal programming models.
4. Solve goal programming models that have two decision variables using a graphical approach.
5. Solve goal programming models using Excel and interpret solutions of goal programming models.
6. Describe the type of problems that the analytical hierarchy process (AHP) is designed to handle.
7. Describe how to determine pairwise comparisons.
8. Describe what a consistency check is and calculate a consistency ratio, priority percentage, and priority score for each alternative using AHP.
9. Use Excel to solve analytical hierarchy process problems.
10. Describe and solve scoring model multicriteria decision-making problems.

CHAPTER OUTLINE

9.1 INTRODUCTION

Linear programming (LP) is a powerful analytical tool that can be applied to a wide range of problems. However, its use is limited to problems that can be expressed in terms of a single objective (e.g., maximize profits). There are many instances in which a single objective is appropriate. Nonetheless, there also are many instances in which multiple objectives are appropriate. For example, a manager may have quality, productivity, *and* profit objectives. But unless these can be reduced to a common unit of measure, such as dollars of profit, standard linear programming models cannot be used. One alternative is to use goal programming.

Goal programming is a variation of linear programming that can be used for problems that involve multiple objectives. Goal programming (GP) models are quite similar to LP models. Both are formulated under the same requirements and assumptions (e.g., linearity, nonnegativity, certainty). Moreover, graphical methods can be used to illustrate the basic concepts of goal programming, just as they were used to illustrate linear programming concepts, and computers (Excel) can be used to handle problems that do not lend themselves to graphical solution.

When it was first introduced in the 1960s, goal programming was designed to handle linear problems. Since then, it has been extended to integer and nonlinear problems. However, the discussion here will focus exclusively on linear problems.

The following section introduces the basic concepts of goal programming. It begins with a discussion of how GP differs from LP, then goes on to formulation and solution of GP models.

The second and third sections of the chapter cover two other multicriteria decision-making methods. In the second section of the chapter, we cover the analytical hierarchy process (AHP). While goal programming answers the question of "how much" for each decision variable, the AHP addresses the issue of "which" alternative to select based on multiple criteria. In the third section of the chapter, the scoring model is discussed; this simplistic, subjective method also answers the question of "which" alternative to select based on multiple criteria. The scoring model is easier to understand than AHP, but it is more subjective.

9.2 GOAL PROGRAMMING MODELS

Goal programming models differ from the previously described linear programming models in two key ways. One relates to constraints and the other to model objectives.

In the context of goal programming, multiple objectives are referred to as **goals.** Each goal relates to a target level of performance. For instance, a problem may involve a goal for *labour* utilization: The performance target may be to use 100 hours of labour on a job. Another goal may relate to an advertising budget: The target may be an expenditure of $25 000 on advertising.

In goal programming models, goals are expressed as *constraints.* However, **goal constraints** are somewhat different than the ones encountered in previous chapters. Recall that in linear programming models, a solution would not be considered feasible if it violated any of the constraints. Because of the absolute requirement that constraints be satisfied, you might think of those constraints as **hard constraints.** In contrast, goal constraints specify desirable levels of performance. These are treated as approximate rather than absolute amounts that should be achieved to the extent possible. Therefore, you might think of a goal constraint as a **soft constraint.**

Goal programming models may consist entirely of soft (goal) constraints or they may consist of a combination of soft and hard (nongoal) constraints. The solution to a goal programming model must satisfy any hard constraints, although it may not necessarily achieve the target levels of the goal (soft) constraints. When one or more goals are not achieved by a solution, it is because there are conflicts either between goals or between goals and hard constraints. For example, one constraint might specify that x_1 should be 10 units, whereas another constraint might specify that x_1 should be at least 20 units. Because these two cannot both be satisfied by a single solution, we say that they conflict. In linear programming terms, we would say that such a problem has no feasible solution space. However, this is the sort of problem goal programming is designed to handle. *Deviations* from goals are permitted if they are needed to obtain a solution. Thus, in goal programming, the objective is to satisfy the hard constraints (if any) and achieve reasonably *acceptable levels* for the goal constraints. This is referred to as **satisficing.**

To obtain a solution that provides acceptable levels of satisfaction of goals when there are conflicts, it becomes necessary to make *trade-offs:* satisfying hard constraints and achieving higher levels of certain goals at the expense of other goals. When goal programming was originally introduced, the approach used was to treat goals as equally important in terms of searching for an acceptable solution. Thus, a deviation from one goal was just as acceptable as a deviation from another goal. Later versions permitted weighting of deviations so that differences in importance in goals could be taken into account. However, this required decision makers to come up with a set of weights that truly reflected differences in importance. Some decision makers found this process to be difficult and somewhat artificial. More recently, interest has centered on **prioritized goal programming models,** wherein decision makers are merely required to *rank* deviations from the various goals in their order of importance. That approach seems to hold considerable promise. It is the one we shall focus on. However, we also will present the goal programming approach involving weights called goal programming with weighted goals.

Deviation Variables

To account for possible deviation from a goal, **deviation variables** are incorporated into each goal to represent the differences between actual performance and target performance. There are two possible kinds of deviations from a target: being under the targeted amount (*underachievement*) and being over the targeted amount (*overachievement*). Deviation variables are included in each goal constraint: u_i for underachievement and v_i for overachievement, where i is the number of the constraint ($i = 1, 2, 3, \ldots$). Adding these two deviation variables to a goal constraint creates an equality because the deviation variables account for any discrepancy between actual and target. We can readily see this by considering a goal constraint.

Suppose a manager has formulated a goal for labour hours. The mathematical expression of the goal constraint might look like this:

$$4x_1 + 2x_2 + u_1 - v_1 = 100 \text{ hours}$$

Variables x_1 and x_2 represent decision variables, whereas u_1 stands for the amount of underutilization of labour and v_1 stands for overtime hours. The subscripts for u and v indicate that this is the first constraint (in a list of goal constraints).

The right-hand side of the equation indicates the target (goal) amount. In this case, it is 100 hours. The left-hand side of the equation contains both the decision variables and the deviation variables. The fact that both underachievement and overachievement variables are included in the goal indicates that a deviation in either direction is permissible (although not necessarily desirable). If a deviation is not permissible, it would not appear in the goal equation. For example, if overachievement were not permissible in the labour constraint, then v_1 would be omitted from the constraint.

Note the signs of the deviational variables and consider that the purpose of these variables is to indicate the amount of any discrepancy between the target level and the amount actually achieved by a particular solution. In effect, the deviation variables are equivalent to slack (amount of underachievement) and surplus (amount of overachievement). Hence, u is added and v is subtracted in a goal constraint. For instance, suppose that the quantity $4x_1 + 2x_2$ is equal to 80 hours, which is 20 hours less than the goal of 100 hours. Thus, utilization is *under* by 20 hours: $u_1 = 20$. Conversely, suppose the quantity $4x_1 + 2x_2$ is equal to 110. This is *over* the goal of 100 hours by 10 hours. Therefore, $v_1 = 10$. Now notice that in each of these cases, the other deviation variable would equal zero because it would be physically impossible to be over and under a goal simultaneously. Of course, if the quantity $4x_1 + 2x_2$ is exactly equal to 100, then both of the deviation variables would equal zero. Thus, at least one of the two deviation variables in each goal must equal zero in any solution.

The Modern Management Application, "Vehicle Park Management," illustrates a practical application of goal programming methods to a business problem faced by the Quebec's Transport Ministry in managing its fleet of vehicles and equipment. The goals (soft constraints) are reducing the fleet of vehicles by 20 percent during the next year, respecting the budget, and meeting the customer requirements.

Model Formulation

A goal programming model consists of an objective function and a set of constraints. The constraints may be goal constraints or they may be a mix of goal and nongoal constraints. In addition, there is the nonnegativity requirement that all variables (decision variables and deviation variables) must be nonnegative.

In priority models, the **objective function** indicates which deviation variables will be minimized and their order of importance. Thus, it seeks to minimize specified deviations from certain goals according to priority.

Consider this goal programming model:

$$\text{minimize} \quad P_1u_1, P_2v_1, P_3u_2$$

subject to

A	$4x_1 + 2x_2 \le 40$	Nongoal (hard)
B	$2x_1 + 6x_2 \le 60$	
1	$3x_1 + 3x_2 + u_1 - v_1 = 75$	Goal (soft)
2	$x_1 + 2x_2 + u_2 - v_2 = 50$	
	All variables ≥ 0	

There are three deviation variables specified in the objective function: u_1, v_1, and u_2. Their subscripts indicate the goal to which they pertain. The *P*'s represent priorities, and their subscripts indicate order of importance, with 1 being the highest priority. Hence, we can see in the objective function that the highest priority is to minimize being under on the first goal. (Note that u_1 appears only in that goal.) The next highest priority is to minimize being over on the first goal, and the last priority is to minimize being under on the second goal. Note that not every deviational variable is specified in the objective function. The second deviation variable in the second constraint, v_2, is not included in the objective function. Evidently, the decision maker does not want to minimize being over on the second goal. If, for example, that second goal relates to profit, we could understand why a decision maker would not want to minimize being over on that goal.

MODERN MANAGEMENT SCIENCE APPLICATION: VEHICLE PARK MANAGEMENT

The Ministère des Transports du Québec owns a fleet of equipment for maintenance of the road network of the province of Quebec. The management of the fleet is the responsibility of a new agency, the Centre de Gestion de l'Équipement Roulant, which was mandated to ensure the availability of vehicles and related equipment for customers and maintenance of vehicles to keep them in good operating condition. In 2001, the equipment park of the Ministry was composed of 1450 light vehicles, 650 trucks, 1000 motorized pieces of equipment, and almost 5000 other pieces of equipment. The agency was assuming almost all the costs associated with the park management, such as preventive maintenance, both minor and major. The greatest challenge faced by the agency was, within a budgetary restriction, to find a way of managing the park at a low cost while offering good service to its customers. The agency had to decide whether a piece of equipment in the park should be sold, replaced, or maintained. Several factors, sometimes conflicting, came into play in the decision-making process. These included reducing the fleet by 20 percent, respecting the budget, meeting customer requirements, and maintaining and renovating certain aspects of the equipment. A management tool, based on a goal programming model, was developed and implemented. It took into account the government's budgetary constraints, the customers' needs, and the managers' preferences. It helped managers to define their best compromise fleet and provided useful managerial insights on a number of practical issues.

Source: Reprinted by permission, H. Goghrod, J. M. Martel and B. Aouni, "Vehicle Park Management Through the Goal Programming Model," *INFORMS*, vol. 41, no. 1, (February 2003) pp. 93–104. Copyright 2003, the Institute for Operations Research and the Management Sciences (INFORMS), 7240 Parkway Drive, Suite 310, Hanover, MD 21076 USA.

To differentiate goal and *nongoal* constraints, the nongoal constraints have been assigned capital letters, whereas the goal constraints have been assigned numbers. Note that only the goal constraints have deviation variables and all goal constraints are expressed as equalities.

Having now examined the goal model, let's turn our attention to formulating such a model. One approach would be as follows:

1. Identify the decision variables.
2. Identify the constraints and determine which ones are goal constraints.
3. Formulate the nongoal (hard) constraints (if any).
4. Formulate the goal (soft) constraints.
5. Formulate the objective function.
6. Add the nonnegativity requirement statement.

The next example illustrates this process.

EXAMPLE 9-1

A company manufactures three products: x_1, x_2, and x_3. Material and labour requirements per unit are

Product	x_1	x_2	x_3	Availability
Material (lb./unit)	2	4	3	600 pounds
Assembly (min./unit)	9	8	7	900 minutes
Packing (min./unit)	1	2	3	300 minutes

The manager has listed the following objectives in order of priority:

1. Minimize overtime in the assembly department.
2. Minimize undertime in the assembly department.
3. Minimize both undertime and overtime in the packaging department.

Solution

Apparently, there are three constraints: material, assembly time, and packing time. Moreover, assembly and packing constraints should be expressed as goals because they are included in the priority list. Material is not included so it should be a nongoal constraint. The constraints are

Material	$2x_1 + 4x_2 + 3x_3$	≤ 600 pounds
Assembly	$9x_1 + 8x_2 + 7x_3 + u_1 - v_1$	$= 900$ minutes
Packing	$1x_1 + 2x_2 + 3x_3 + u_2 - v_2$	$= 300$ minutes
	All variables	≥ 0

The objective function is based on the listing and the deviation variables as defined in the constraints. It is

minimize $P_1v_1, P_2u_1, P_3(u_2 + v_2)$

The third priority, P_3, expresses the fact that minimizing both under and over on the second goal are equally important. Thus, the complete model is

minimize $P_1v_1, P_2u_1, P_3(u_2 + v_2)$

subject to

A	$2x_1 + 4x_2 + 3x_3$	≤ 600 pounds
1	$9x_1 + 8x_2 + 7x_3 + u_1 - v_1$	$= 900$ minutes
2	$1x_1 + 2x_2 + 3x_3 + u_2 - v_2$	$= 300$ minutes
	All variables	≥ 0

Graphical Solutions

Graphical solutions are limited to goal problems that have two decision variables. As you might suspect, many real problems involve more than two decision variables. Nonetheless, the graphical approach provides a visual illustration of certain goal programming concepts. For that reason, it is invaluable in terms of the insight it can produce.

The graphical approach involves plotting all of the constraints, both hard and soft. To plot a goal constraint, ignore the deviation variables and simply plot it as a constraint that has no deviation variables. Thus, the goal constraint

$$x_1 + x_2 + u_1 - v_1 = 60$$

would be plotted as if it were

$$x_1 + x_2 = 60$$

The deviation variables do not appear on the graph; instead their values are determined algebraically at the end of the analysis along with the optimal values of the decision variables. However, over- and underdeviations correspond to the regions on either side of the line, as illustrated in Figure 9-1.

FIGURE 9-1 A Plot of a Goal Constraint

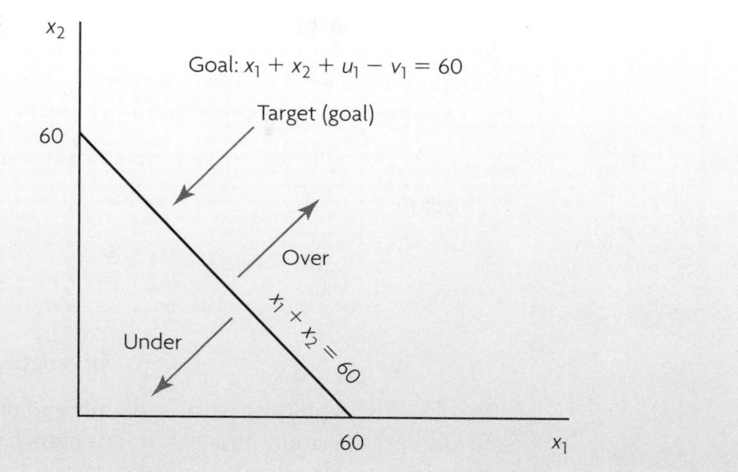

After plotting a goal constraint, indicate the direction that will satisfy the objective, as illustrated in Figure 9-2. Notice that the region that will satisfy the objective (minimize P_1u_1) is the line itself plus the area *opposite* the deviation specified. In other words, we minimize being under by being *on or over* the goal.

Taken as a whole, the graphical approach to goal programming involves plotting all the nongoal constraints (if any), just as in LP, and identifying the feasible solution space. However, unlike LP, the objective is not plotted. Instead, the goals are plotted one at a time, according to the priorities given by the objective. After each is plotted, the best solution to that point is found. However, as successive goals are plotted, only solutions that do not

FIGURE 9-2 Designating Priority and Direction

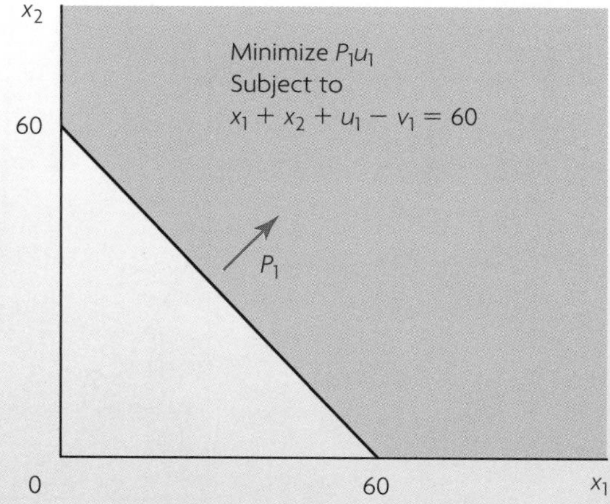

require additional deviations from the higher-level goals already plotted are considered. In effect, minimizing the deviation with the highest priority is treated as infinitely more desirable than minimizing the deviation with the next highest priority, and minimizing the next highest priority is treated as infinitely more important than minimizing the deviation for the next highest priority, and so on, as each additional goal is added to the graph. This solution procedure will become more apparent as we work through a number of examples.

Consider this goal programming model:

$$\text{minimize} \quad P_1u_1, P_2u_2, P_3u_3$$

subject to

$$\begin{aligned} 5x_1 + 3x_2 \qquad\qquad\quad &\le 150 \qquad (A) \\ 2x_1 + 5x_2 + u_1 - v_1 &= 100 \qquad (1) \\ 3x_1 + 3x_2 + u_2 - v_2 &= 180 \qquad (2) \\ x_1 \qquad\quad + u_3 - v_3 &= \;\;40 \qquad (3) \\ \text{All variables} &\ge 0 \end{aligned}$$

To solve this graphically, we first identify and plot any hard constraints: the constraints that do not have deviation variables. In this model, only the first is the hard type. It is plotted in Figure 9-3, and the feasible solution space is shaded in.

Next, we see in the objective that the highest priority is to minimize being under on the first goal constraint. So, we plot the first goal constraint (second constraint overall) and indicate that the desirable region is on the line and above it. (See Figure 9-4.) Now we can see that a portion of the feasible solution space also includes some of the desirable region. At this stage, any point in the overlap area would be acceptable.

Next, we see that the second highest priority relates to the second goal constraint (i.e., the subscript of u_2 tells us this). Hence, we plot the second goal constraint (third constraint overall) and indicate its area of desirability, which is on and above the line (see Figure 9-5). This region does not overlap the acceptable region as previously determined. However, we must not sacrifice a higher-level priority for a lower one. Therefore, there will be some underdeviation on the second goal. By inspecting

FIGURE 9-3 Plot of the Hard Constraint and the Feasible Solution Space

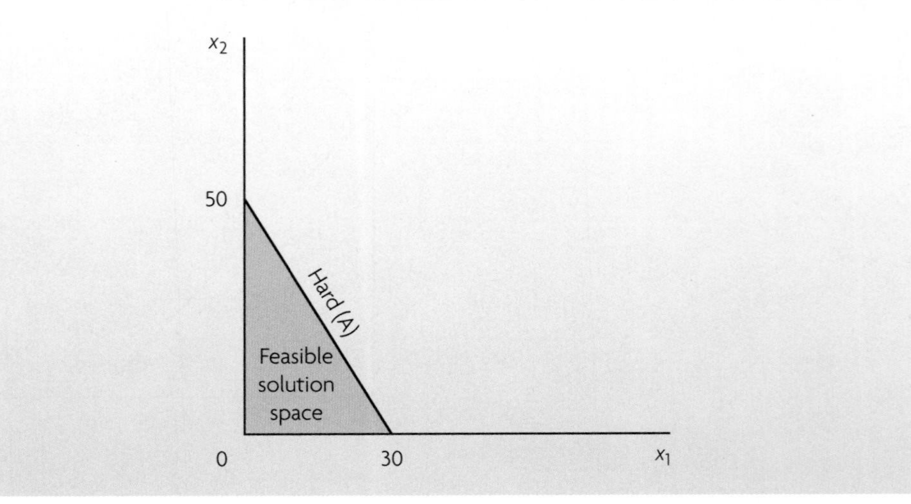

FIGURE 9-4 The Acceptable Region After Adding the First Goal Constraint

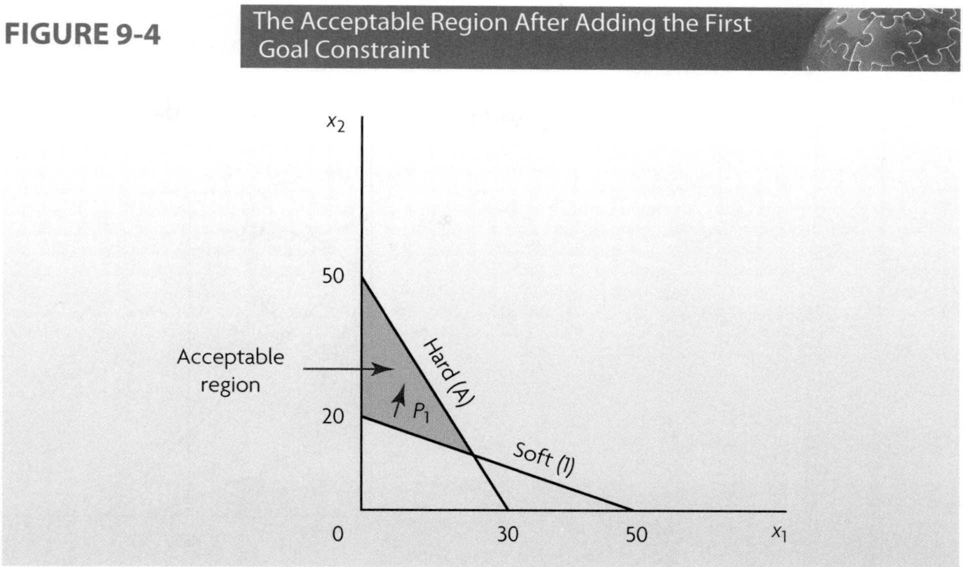

FIGURE 9-5 The Second Goal Is Added to the Graph

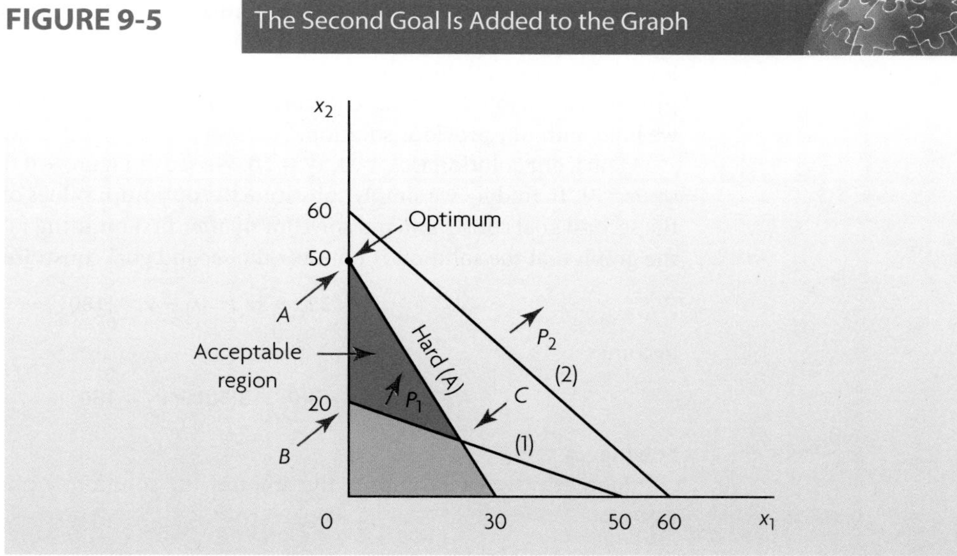

Figure 9-5, we will find that the closest portion of the acceptable region to the second goal is the point $x_1 = 0, x_2 = 50$. This is the best point because it satisfies the first two constraints while minimizing the amount of underdeviation from the third (i.e., second goal) constraint.

Finally, we see in the objective that the last priority is to minimize being under on the third goal. Hence, we add the third goal to the graph (see Figure 9-6). The third goal does not overlap the acceptable region either. As with the second goal, we must not sacrifice a higher-level priority (i.e., u_1) for a lower one (i.e., u_3). Therefore, adding the third goal does not change the previous solution because that solution satisfies the hard constraint and the

FIGURE 9-6 The Third Goal Is Added

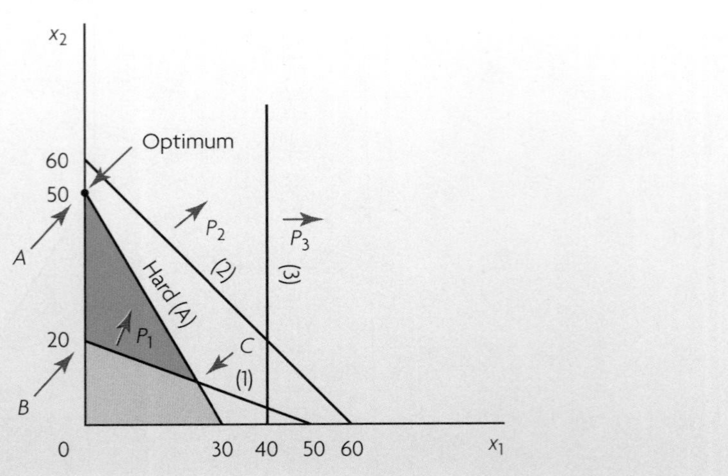

highest priority (i.e., $u_1 = 0$) and it minimizes the amount of underdeviation (u_2) on the second goal. Even though another point in the acceptable region (point C) would yield a lower value for u_3, this would be at the expense of increasing u_2. Because higher-level priorities are treated as infinitely more valuable than lower-level priorities (i.e., P_2 and P_3), we hold with our previous solution.

Thus, our solution is $x_1 = 0, x_2 = 50$. We see in Figure 9-6 that the solution satisfies P_1, so $u_1 = 0$. To find u_2, we simply substitute the optimum values of the decision variables into the second goal constraint and solve for u_2 after first omitting v_2 because it is apparent from the graph that the solution is not over the second goal constraint. Thus:

$$3x_1 + 3x_2 + u_2 - v_2 = 180$$

becomes

$$3(0) + 3(50) + u_2 = 180$$

Solving, $u_2 = 30$.

Similarly, we can compute the amount the solution is under on the third goal constraint:

$$x_1 + u_3 - v_3 = 40$$

becomes

$$0 + u_3 = 40$$

Hence, $u_3 = 40$.

It is important to note that deviations generally cannot be read directly from the graph but, instead, must be computed using the appropriate goal constraints and the optimal values of the decision variables.

The next example illustrates a case in which there are no hard constraints, only goal constraints.

EXAMPLE 9-2

Solve this goal programming model for the optimal values of the decision variables using the graphical approach, then determine the optimal values of each deviation variable specified in the objective function.

minimize P_1v_1, P_2u_2, P_3v_3

subject to

Material	$5x_1 + 4x_2 + u_1 - v_1 = 200$ pounds	(1)
Profit	$2x_1 + x_2 + u_2 - v_2 = 40$ (\$000)	(2)
Machine	$2x_1 + 2x_2 + u_3 - v_3 = 30$ minutes	(3)

All variables ≥ 0

Solution

Because there are no hard constraints, we begin by noting that the highest priority is to minimize being over on the first goal constraint. Hence, we plot the first constraint and indicate the acceptable region (see Figure 9-7a).

The second highest priority is to minimize being under the second goal constraint, so we plot the second goal and indicate the region that will satisfy both the first and second goals (see Figure 9-7b).

The third priority refers to the third goal, so we plot and see that it does not have any points in common with the acceptable region. Consequently, some amount of overdeviation on the third goal constraint will be unavoidable. We can see on the graph that this deviation can be minimized by the point $x_1 = 20, x_2 = 0$ (point D, see Figure 9-7c), since this point is closest to the third goal.

Now we can determine the values of the deviation variables specified in the objective. By inspection of the graph, we can see that the solution satisfies the first two priorities. Therefore, $v_1 = 0$ and $u_2 = 0$. We also can see that the

FIGURE 9-7 Plot of Goal Constraints

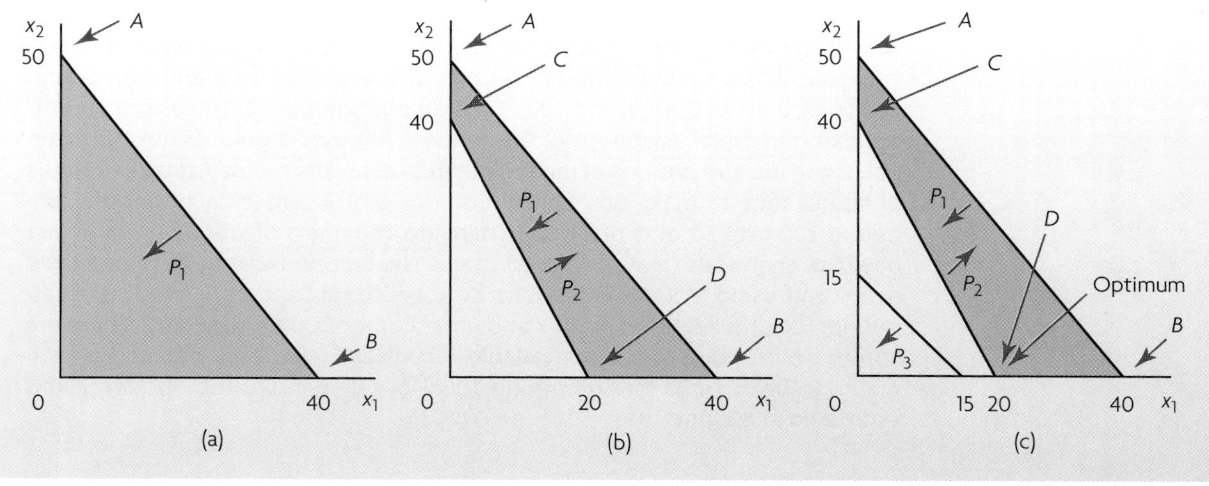

solution is over on the third goal. We can determine this amount by substituting the optimal values of x_1 and x_2 into the third constraint and solving for v_3 (u_3 is omitted because we can see on the graph that the solution is not under on the third goal):

$2(20) + 2(0) - v_3 = 30$
Solving, $v_3 = 10$.

Solving Goal Programming Problems Using Excel

Goal programming problems can be solved using Excel. The approach is conceptually similar to the graphical solution, except that more than two decision variables can be handled when utilizing the computer and Excel. When we utilize Excel, goals are handled one at a time, starting with the highest priority goal. Once the first priority goal is satisfied, then try to solve to satisfy the second priority, while ensuring that the first priority goal is still satisfied. Using Excel to solve goal programming problems differs from the graphical approach in three important ways. The first difference is that the visual benefit of a graph is absent for problems that involve three or more decision variables. The second difference relates to the objective function. When using Excel, the objective function changes and the goals are added sequentially. As new priority goals are satisfied, lower priority goals are added, whereas, when utilizing the graphical approach, the objective function includes all priority goals. The third difference is that when using Excel, the results of each sequential solution may be used to modify a goal before proceeding to the next stage in the sequence.

The process begins by solving a model that includes any nongoal (hard) constraints and all goal constraints. We need to set up the Solver so that only the highest priority goal is considered. The goal constraint that contains the deviation variable has the highest priority from the objective function. The solution for that model fixes the value of that deviation variable for the remainder of the analysis. This process is repeated using the remaining deviation variable that has the highest priority, and so on, until all priorities have been considered. The following example illustrates the process.

EXAMPLE 9-3

Robinson Chemical Manufacturing company produces two types of chemical compounds: Compound 100 (x_1 = units of Compound 100) and Compound 200 (x_2 = units of Compound 200). Each unit of Compound 100 uses 5 pounds of mixing material. Each unit of Compound 200 uses 3 pounds mixing material. There are 150 pounds of mixing material available per day. It takes 2 hours of labour time to make one unit of Compound 100, while each unit of Compound 200 uses 5 hours of labour. There are 100 hours of labour available per day. The chemicals (materials used to mix the compounds) have to be mixed and cured using Mixer 5000. It takes 3 hours to mix and cure a unit of Compound 100 and 3.6 hours to mix and cure a unit of Compound 200. There are 180 machine hours per day available for Mixer 5000. Daily demand is estimated to be 40 units for Compound 100. Daily demand for Compound 200 is estimated at 50 units.

The company identified the following four priority goals for this problem:

1. Minimize being under the labour hours constraint.
2. Minimize being under the machine hours constraint.
3. Minimize being under the demand constraint for Compound 200.
4. Minimize being under the demand constraint for Compound 100.
5. Minimize labour overtime.

As you can see this problem involves five prioritized goals.
Formulate the problem described in Example 9-3 as a goal programming problem and solve it using Excel.

Solution

In formulating this problem, we begin to formulate the objective function as follows:

$$\text{minimize} \quad P_1u_1, P_2u_2, P_3u_4, P_4u_3, P_5v_1$$

Note that the company has five different priority goals. These goals are subject to the following constraints:

$5x_1 + 3x_2$	≤ 150	(mixing material, nongoal constraint)
$2x_1 + 5x_2 + u_1 - v_1$	$= 100$	(labour hours, goal constraint)
$3x_1 + 3.6x_2 + u_2 - v_2$	$= 180$	(machine hours, goal constraint)
$x_1 + u_3 - v_3$	$= 40$	(demand "goal" constraint for Compound 100)
$x_2 + u_4 - v_4$	$= 50$	(demand "goal" constraint for Compound 200)
All variables	≥ 0	

Solving a goal programming model with prioritized goals requires us to solve a series of linear programming problems. In solving the first model, we only consider the highest priority (P_1) goal and we do not consider any of the other goals (P_2 through P_5). Therefore, the objective is to minimize the deviation variable associated with priority 1. In other words, the objective function reduces to the following:

$$\text{minimize} \quad P_1u_1$$

subject to the same constraints listed above.

In solving this goal programming problem, we prepare the Excel worksheet shown in Exhibit 9-1. After preparing the worksheet shown in Exhibit 9-1, from the Excel menu, we choose **Data|Analysis|Solver** and obtain the Solver Parameters screen shown in Exhibit 9-2. On this screen, we first specify the objective function in the "Set Target Cell" box by choosing cell B5, since our first priority goal is to minimize the labour underutilization goal (u_1). The formula for cell B5, simply minimizes the labour underutilization goal (u_1), which is = D9 * D4. We proceed by choosing minimization (Min) as our objective, and specify the variables in the "By Changing Cells" box. Our variables include the two decision variables as well as all of the deviational variables. These variables are stated in cells B4 through K4. Next, we specify the constraints in the Subject to the Constraints area. In specifying the constraints, we first state the nongoal constraints. In our problem involving the Robinson Chemical Company, we have just one nongoal constraint (constraint 1, specified in row 11). Note that in Exhibit 9-1, the L column represents the total from the left-hand side of each constraint.

EXHIBIT 9-1 Excel Worksheet for Robinson Chemical Company Goal Programming Problem, Considering Only Priority 1 (Minimizing Labour Underutilization) Goal

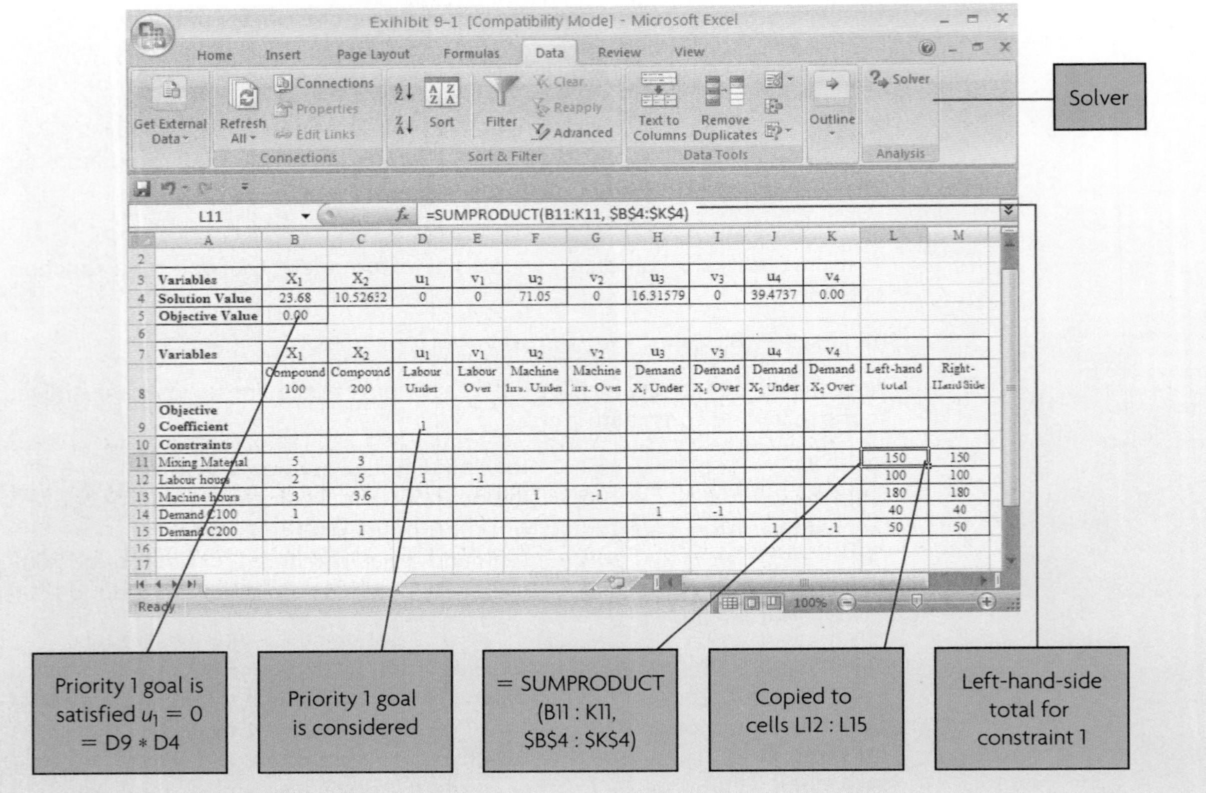

Row	A	B	C	D	E	F	G	H	I	J	K	L	M
3	Variables	X_1	X_2	u_1	v_1	u_2	v_2	u_3	v_3	u_4	v_4		
4	Solution Value	23.68	10.52632	0	0	71.05	0	16.31579	0	39.4737	0.00		
5	Objective Value	0.00											
7	Variables	X_1	X_2	u_1	v_1	u_2	v_2	u_3	v_3	u_4	v_4		
8		Compound 100	Compound 200	Labour Under	Labour Over	Machine hrs. Under	Machine hrs. Over	Demand X_1 Under	Demand X_1 Over	Demand X_2 Under	Demand X_2 Over	Left-hand total	Right-Hand Side
9	Objective Coefficient			1									
10	Constraints												
11	Mixing Material	5	3									150	150
12	Labour hours	2	5	1	-1							100	100
13	Machine hours	3	3.6			1	-1					180	180
14	Demand C100	1						1	-1			40	40
15	Demand C200		1							1	-1	50	50

To get the total of the left-hand side of the equation, the SUMPRODUCT function is utilized to calculate the total value obtained by multiplying the constraint coefficients on the left-hand side of the constraint with the values of the decision variables and then summing the cross-products. For example, to calculate the left-hand side of the mixing material constraint, we first multiply the constraint coefficients in cells B11 and C11 with the values of decision variables in cells B4 and C4 respectively. Summing the cross-products ($5 \times 23.68 + 3 \times 10.526$), results in the total left-hand-side value of 150. In Exhibit 9-1, the goal constraints are stated in rows 12 through 15. These goal constraints are specified in Exhibit 9-2 as follows: $L$12:$L$15 = $M$12:$M$15. The left-hand-side of the constraint equations is specified by stating $L$12:$L$15 and the right-hand side of the constraint equations is specified by stating $M$12:$M$15. Since all four of these equations are goal constraints, the sign of all of these constraints is equality. After specifying the constraints, in Exhibit 9-2 we click "Options," and in the Options dialogue screen, we check the boxes "Assume Linear Model" and "Assume Nonnegativity". We proceed by clicking on "OK" to close the Options dialogue screen. Next, click on "Solve" in Exhibit 9-2 and obtain the solution given in Exhibit 9-1. In other words, we should produce 23.68 units of

EXHIBIT 9-2 Excel Solver Parameters Screen for Robinson Chemical Company Goal Programming Problem Considering Only Priority 1 (Minimizing Labour Underutilization) Goal

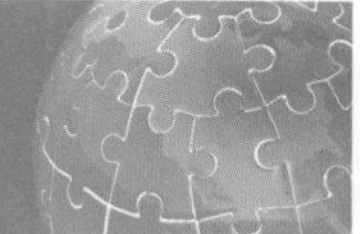

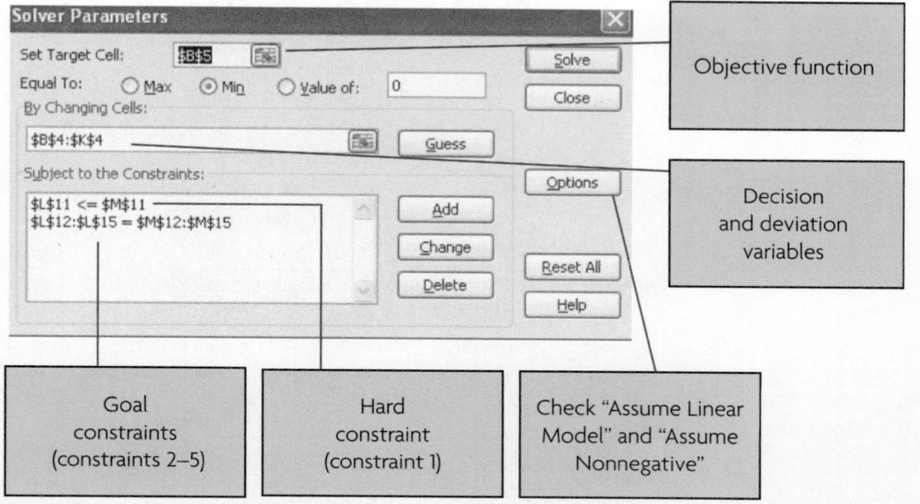

Compound 100 ($x_1 = 23.68$) and 10.526 units of Compound 200 ($x_2 = 10.53$) and we will be 71.05 ($u_2 = 71.05$) hours under the machine hours available. Since the demand for Compound 100 is 40 units, $u_3 = 16.32$, or $(40 - 23.68)$, meaning that the company is not supplying enough units of Compound 100 to satisfy the market demand of 40 units. Therefore, the company has a shortage of 16.32 units of Compound 100.

Likewise, the company also is not supplying enough units of Compound 200 to satisfy the market demand of 50 units. Since the demand for Compound 200 is 50 units, $u_4 = 39.47$, calculated as $(50 - 10.53)$. The shortage for Compound 200 is 39.47 units.

Since the first priority goal is satisfied, we solve the same goal programming problem with the objective of satisfying the second priority goal. In other words, the objective function reduces to the following:

minimize $\quad P_2u_2$

subject to the same constraints listed above.

The new Excel worksheet shown in Exhibit 9-3 shows the problem being solved at the second stage. Note that the objective coefficient is no longer 1 for u_1 (labour underutilization). The objective coefficient is now equal to 1 for u_2 (machine hours underutilization). Also change the formula for the objective function located in cell B5 from minimizing u_1 to minimizing u_2. In other words, the formula in cell B5 is changed from = D9 * D4 to = F9 * F4.

In addition, we now have to make sure that the first priority goal is not sacrificed at the expense of the second priority goal. To ensure that the first priority goal is still satisfied, we add a constraint equation that indicates that $u_1 = 0$. This

EXHIBIT 9-3 Excel Worksheet for Robinson Chemical Company Goal Programming Problem, Considering Priority 1 (Minimizing Labour Underutilization) and Priority 2 (Minimizing Machine Hour Underutilization) Goals

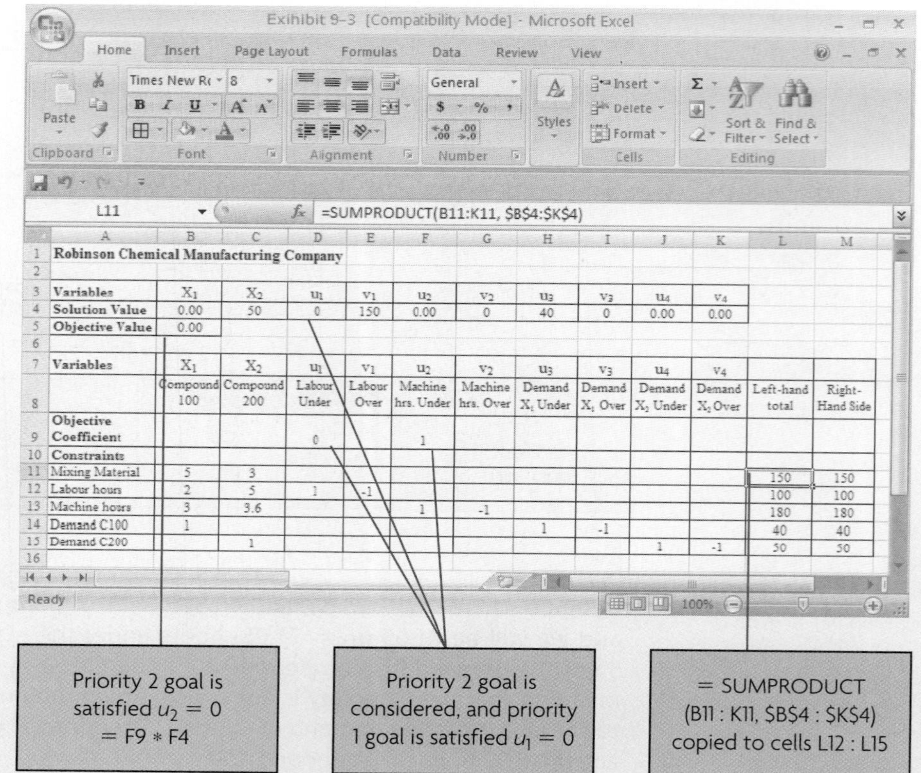

Variables	X1	X2	u1	v1	u2	v2	u3	v3	u4	v4
Solution Value	0.00	50	0	150	0.00	0	40	0	0.00	0.00
Objective Value	0.00									

Variables	X1 Compound 100	X2 Compound 200	u1 Labour Under	v1 Labour Over	u2 Machine hrs. Under	v2 Machine hrs. Over	u3 Demand X_1 Under	v3 Demand X_1 Over	u4 Demand X_2 Under	v4 Demand X_2 Over	Left-hand total	Right-Hand Side
Objective Coefficient			0		1							
Constraints												
Mixing Material	5	3									150	150
Labour hours	2	5	1	-1							100	100
Machine hours	3	3.6			1	-1					180	180
Demand C100	1						1	-1			40	40
Demand C200		1							1	-1	50	50

new constraint is shown in the Solver Parameters screen shown in Exhibit 9-4. Exhibit 9-4 is identical to Exhibit 9-2 except that we have added the constraint that $D$4 = 0 ($u_1 = 0$).

The solution values for this problem are given in row 4 of Exhibit 9-3; these solution values are summarized below:

$x_1 = 0$, $x_2 = 50$, $u_3 = 40$, $v_1 = 150$, and all of the rest of the deviational variables are equal to zero

Since the priority 1 and priority 2 goals have been met, we proceed to solve the same goal programming problem with the objective of satisfying the priority 3 goal. In other words, the objective function reduces to the following:

minimize $P_3 u_4$

subject to all of the original constraints.

The objective coefficient is no longer 1 for u_2 (underutilization of machine hours). The objective coefficient is now equal to 1 for u_4 (unsatisfied demand for Compound 200). We also have changed the formula for the objective function

EXHIBIT 9-4 Excel Solver Parameters Screen for Robinson Chemical Company Goal Programming Problem, Considering Priority 2 (Minimizing Machine Hours Underutilization) Goal While Ensuring that Priority 1 Goal Is Satisfied

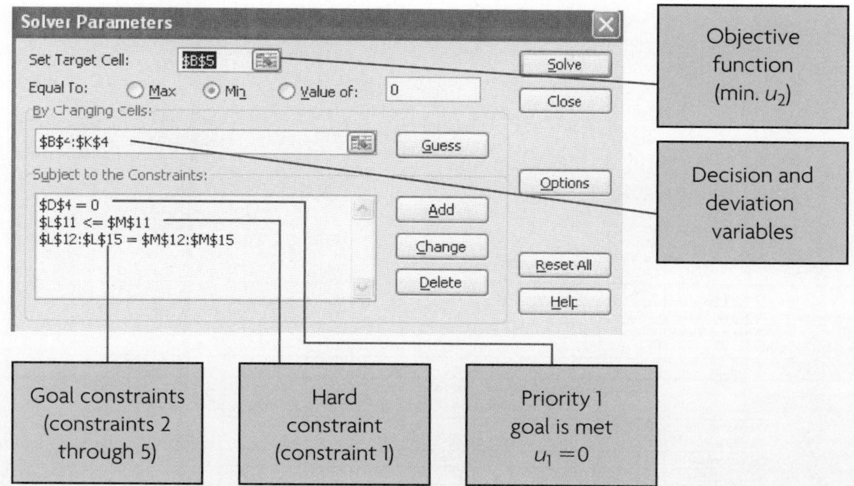

located in cell B5 from minimizing u_2 to minimizing u_4. In other words, the formula in cell B5 is changed from =F9 * F4 to =J9 * J4. The result of this iteration is identical to the result of the previous iteration. The Solver Parameters screen includes two new constraints ($u_1 = u_2 = 0$) to ensure that the priority 1 goal ($D$4 = 0) and priority 2 goal ($F$4 = 0) are still satisfied.

Since the priority 1, priority 2, and priority 3 goals have been met, we proceed to solve the same goal programming problem with the objective of satisfying the priority 4 goal. In other words, the objective function reduces to the following:

minimize $\quad P_4 u_3$

subject to all of the original constraints.

In solving this goal programming problem, the objective coefficient is no longer 1 for u_4 (unsatisfied demand for Compound 200). The objective coefficient is now equal to 1 for u_3 (unsatisfied demand for Compound 100). We also have changed the formula for the objective function located in cell B5 from minimizing u_4 to minimize u_3. In other words, the formula in cell B5 is now = H9 * H4. The Solver Parameters screen includes new constraints ($u_1 = u_2 = u_4 = 0$) to ensure that the priority 1 goal ($D$4 = 0), priority 2 goal ($F$4 = 0), and priority 3 goal ($J$4 = 0) are still satisfied.

As can be observed from Exhibit 9-5, the fourth priority goal is not satisfied, because the objective function value in cell B5 is 40. In other words, since we are not producing any units of Compound 100, and since the demand for Compound 100 is 40, the company is underutilizing the demand for Compound 100 by 40 units. At this point, we can try to see how much of the fifth goal (minimizing overtime) we can meet without sacrificing any of the higher priority goals.

EXHIBIT 9-5 Excel Worksheet for Robinson Chemical Company Goal Programming Problem, Considering Priority 4 Goal (Minimizing Unsatisfied Demand for Compound 200) While Ensuring that Priority 1 (Minimizing Labour Underutilization), Priority 2 (Minimizing Machine Hour Underutilization), and Priority 3 (Unsatisfied Demand for Compound 200) Goals Are Satisfied

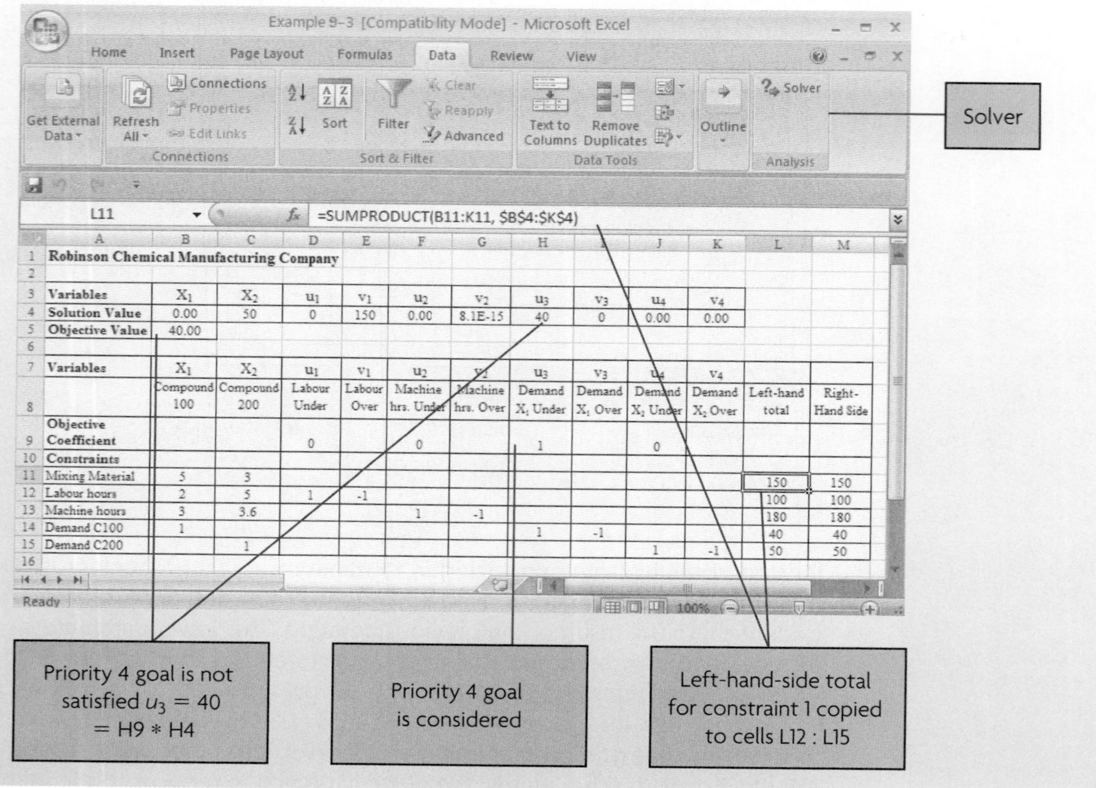
Example 9-3 [Compatibility Mode] - Microsoft Excel
L11
=SUMPRODUCT(B11:K11, $B$4:$K$4)
Solver
Priority 4 goal is not satisfied $u_3 = 40$ = H9 * H4
Priority 4 goal is considered
Left-hand-side total for constraint 1 copied to cells L12 : L15

	A	B	C	D	E	F	G	H	I	J	K	L	M
1	Robinson Chemical Manufacturing Company												
2													
3	Variables	X_1	X_2	u_1	v_1	u_2	v_2	u_3	v_3	u_4	v_4		
4	Solution Value	0.00	50	0	150	0.00	8.1E-15	40	0	0.00	0.00		
5	Objective Value	40.00											
6													
7	Variables	X_1	X_2	u_1	v_1	u_2	v_2	u_3	v_3	u_4	v_4		
8		Compound 100	Compound 200	Labour Under	Labour Over	Machine hrs. Under	Machine hrs. Over	Demand X_1 Under	Demand X_1 Over	Demand X_2 Under	Demand X_2 Over	Left-hand total	Right-Hand Side
9	Objective Coefficient			0		0		1		0			
10	Constraints												
11	Mixing Material	5	3									150	150
12	Labour hours	2	5	1	-1							100	100
13	Machine hours	3	3.6			1	-1					180	180
14	Demand C100	1						1	-1			40	40
15	Demand C200		1							1	-1	50	50
16													

In other words, the objective function reduces to the following:

minimize $\quad P_5 v_1$

subject to all of the original constraints.

In solving this goal programming problem, we have to make certain changes in the Excel worksheet given in Exhibit 9-5. The objective coefficient is not 1 for v_1 and the objective function located in B5 now involves the minimization of v_1. In other words, the formula in cell B5 is now = E9 * E4.

Since the first three goals are satisfied, in completing the Solver Parameters screen we need to continue setting the deviation variables associated with the first three priority goals equal to zero. In other words, $u_1 = u_2 = u_4 = 0$ are added to ensure that the priority 1 goal ($D$9 = 0), priority 2 goal ($F$9 = 0), and priority 3 goal ($J$9 = 0) are still satisfied. However, we need to also ensure that the priority 4 goal is not sacrificed from its current level. Even though the fourth priority goal is not satisfied, we do not want to see an increase in its deviation variable at the expense of satisfying the fifth priority goal. Therefore, in the Solver Parameters screen we add another constraint, indicating that

$u_3 \leq 40$, or \$H\$4 ≤ 40. In this example, since u_3 is at its maximum value of 40, it is impossible to increase it any further. Since the optimal solution to this problem is identical to the optimal solution to the problem involving priority goal 4, we did not show the results associated with solving the goal programming problem involving priority goal 5. In other words, the optimal values of the decision variables as well as the deviation variables remain the same, that is, $x_1 = 0$, $x_2 = 50$, $u_3 = 40$, $v_1 = 150$, and the rest of the deviation variables are equal to zero. Note that the solution to the priority 5 goal problem did not result in the improvement of the deviational variable v_1 (minimizing overtime ($v_1 = 150$)).

However, in solving other problems, the deviation variable at a given priority level may not be satisfied, and its value may be between 0 and its maximum value. Therefore, in solving the problem to improve a lower-level priority goal, we need to ensure that the current priority goal is not diminished, or the deviation variable associated with it does not increase. To ensure this, we simply include a less-than-or-equal-to constraint where the right-hand-side value of the constraint is the current value of the deviation variable at the current solution.

For example, let's assume that for a given goal programming problem, the second priority is to minimize the value of the deviation variable u_2. Also assume the priority 1 goal (minimizing u_1) is completely satisfied and suppose that the maximum possible value of u_2 is 40. In solving the goal programming at the priority level 2, the goal is to minimize the deviation variable u_2. In solving this problem, we obtain a value of 20 for u_2. In other words, the second priority goal is not met. We can now proceed to solve the third priority goal, but we need to ensure that the second priority goal does not deteriorate. When solving the priority 3 goal programming problem, to ensure that u_1 and u_2 do not increase from their current levels, we include the following constraints: $u_1 = 0$ and $u_2 \leq 20$. These constraints will ensure that the priority 1 goal is still met and u_2 does not increase above 20, while trying to minimize the third priority goal.

Weighted Goals

Instead of prioritizing the goals, we can assign weights to the goals to distinguish the importance of various goals. The weights are utilized as the objective function coefficients for the goal programming problem.

Let's demonstrate an example with weighted goals by modifying Example 9-3. The company had five prioritized goals to satisfy. Now, we will ask the Robinson Chemical Company manager, Michelle Robinson, to assign weights to the five goals. To make it easier for Michelle, we use the following allocation approach and we simply ask her to assign 100 points to the five goals. Michelle assigns the following weights to the five goals:

Goal	Weight
1. Minimize being under the labour hours constraint (u_1)	35
2. Minimize being under the machine hours constraint (u_2)	25
3. Minimize being under the demand constraint for Compound 200 (u_4)	20
4. Minimize being under the demand constraint for Compound 100 (u_3)	15
5. Minimize labour overtime (v_1)	5
Total	100

To provide some meaning to the goals, we can take the first goal (minimizing being under the labour hours constraint) and compare it against other goals based on the weights:

- Fully utilizing the desired labour hours is 1.4 times (35/25) as important as the goal of fully utilizing the desired machine hours.
- Fully utilizing the desired labour hours is 1.75 times (35/20) as important as the goal of meeting the demand for Compound 200.
- Fully utilizing the desired labour hours is 2.33 times (35/15) as important as the goal of meeting the demand for Compound 100.
- Fully utilizing the desired labour hours is 7 times (35/5) as important as the goal of minimizing overtime.

We also can compare other goals in terms of their weights against each other. For example, meeting the demand for Compound 200 is 4 times (20/5) as important as the goal of minimization of overtime.

However, assigning weights to the various goals introduces an element of subjectivity to the problem. Therefore, if the weights can be derived naturally from the process, the weighted goal programming problem becomes a more effective solution methodology. Since Example 9-3 doesn't lend itself to the natural derivation or statement of the weights, the procedure for assigning weights involves subjectivity. We can eliminate the subjectivity if the goals and the associated deviation variables involve the same unit of measurement. For example, if all of the deviation variables are measured in dollars, it becomes much easier to assign weights to the deviation variables. If each goal is measured in dollars, we can assign weights to the deviation variables based on per-unit cost of production, per-unit profit margin, and so forth. However, in solving Example 9-3, it is not possible to assign weights using the same units. Therefore, the weights are assigned by the allocation method described earlier. If the management of the company feels that the allocation method introduces too much subjectivity, then the company can use the priority goal programming problem described in the previous section.

Solution of the Weighted Goal Programming Problem The advantage of solving a weighted goal programming problem over solving the prioritized goal programming problem is that the weighted goal programming problem can be solved in one step because the **weighted goal programming model** is treated as a linear programming problem with a single objective function. The objective function minimizes the sum of the weighted deviation variables. As we demonstrated in the previous section, in utilizing the prioritized goal programming model, we needed to solve a sequence of goal programming problems. Therefore, preparing the Excel worksheet and solving the weighted goal programming problem is a relatively simple task compared to solving the prioritized goal programming problem since the prioritized goal programming problem involves multiple steps, where the same problem is solved using different objective function values in multiple iterations.

For the weighted goal programming problem example we stated earlier, the objective function and the constraints can be stated as follows:

$$\text{minimize weighted deviation variables} \quad 35u_1 + 25u_2 + 20u_4 + 15u_3 + 5v_1$$

subject to

$$\begin{aligned}
5x_1 + 3x_2 &\le 150 && \text{(mixing material, nongoal constraint)}\\
2x_1 + 5x_2 + u_1 - v_1 &= 100 && \text{(labour hours, goal constraint)}\\
3x_1 + 3.6x_2 + u_2 - v_2 &= 180 && \text{(machine hours, goal constraint)}\\
x_1 + u_3 - v_3 &= 40 && \text{(demand "goal" constraint for Compound 100)}\\
x_2 + u_4 - v_4 &= 50 && \text{(demand "goal" constraint for Compound 200)}\\
\text{All variables} &\ge 0
\end{aligned}$$

EXHIBIT 9-6 Excel Worksheet for Robinson Chemical Company Weighted Goal Programming Problem

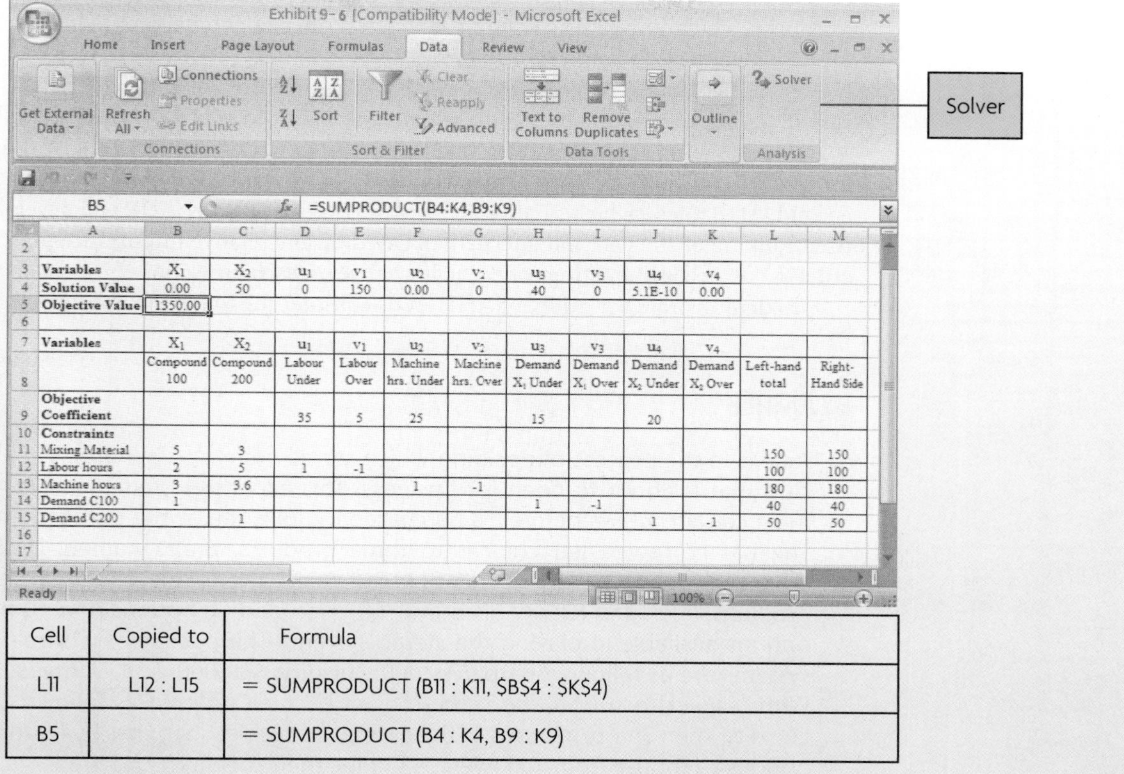

	A	B	C	D	E	F	G	H	I	J	K	L	M
3	Variables	X_1	X_2	u_1	v_1	u_2	v_2	u_3	v_3	u_4	v_4		
4	Solution Value	0.00	50	0	150	0.00	0	40	0	5.1E-10	0.00		
5	Objective Value	1350.00											
7	Variables	X_1	X_2	u_1	v_1	u_2	v_2	u_3	v_3	u_4	v_4		
8		Compound 100	Compound 200	Labour Under	Labour Over	Machine hrs. Under	Machine hrs. Over	Demand X_1 Under	Demand X_1 Over	Demand X_2 Under	Demand X_2 Over	Left-hand total	Right-Hand Side
9	Objective Coefficient			35	5	25		15		20			
10	Constraints												
11	Mixing Material	5	3									150	150
12	Labour hours	2	5	1	-1							100	100
13	Machine hours	3	3.6			1	-1					180	180
14	Demand C100	1						1	-1			40	40
15	Demand C200		1							1	-1	50	50

Cell	Copied to	Formula
L11	L12 : L15	= SUMPRODUCT (B11 : K11, $B$4 : $K$4)
B5		= SUMPRODUCT (B4 : K4, B9 : K9)

The Excel worksheet to solve this problem is shown in Exhibit 9-6. This worksheet is very similar to the worksheets used to solve the prioritized goal programming problem. The only difference is in the objective function, which is stated in cell B5. The formula for cell B5 is shown at the bottom of Exhibit 9-6. This formula =SUMPRODUCT(B4:K4,B9:K9) involves the sum of the multiplication of the weights and the resulting values of the deviation variables. The statement of the Solver Parameters screen is identical to the Solver Parameters screen displayed in Exhibit 9-2. Note that since the weights of the goals are consistent with the prioritized goals of the earlier section, the solution to the problem displayed in Exhibit 9-6 is identical to the solution to the goal programming problem with prioritized weights, that is, $x_1 = 0, x_2 = 50, v_1 = 150, u_3 = 40$, and the rest of the deviation variables are equal to zero. However, it is possible to obtain different results using prioritized goals versus weighted goals. The resulting objective function value of 1350 is not a meaningful value because it is a function of the weights assigned to the different deviation variables, where the deviation variables are stated in different unit terms.

9.3 ANALYTICAL HIERARCHY PROCESS

In addition to goal programming, the **analytical hierarchy process (AHP)** is another multicriteria decision-making method. If we are deciding the quantity of each decision variable, then the goal programming model provides the right solution procedure since it generates the quantity of decision variables while taking priorities into account. On the other hand, if we want to decide the rank order of decision alternatives or select an alternative from a set of alternatives based on multiple criteria, then AHP can be utilized. AHP can be very useful when a decision maker is determining which type of car to buy, which major to choose, which university to attend, which job offer to choose, or at which site to locate the new plant based on several different criteria.

While the goal programming answers the question of "how much" for each decision variable, AHP addresses the issue of "which" alternative to select based on multiple criteria.

In developing an AHP model, first the decision maker provides weighted preferences for the criteria that are used to determine the preferences for the decision alternatives. Second, AHP rates each alternative using each criterion. Finally, AHP will develop a prioritized ranking of the decision alternatives based on the relative importance placed on each criterion as well as the ratings of each alternative on each criterion.

To demonstrate the utility of AHP, let us consider the following example.

EXAMPLE 9-4

Julie is in the process of deciding which stereo system to purchase for a night club that is about to open for business. This expensive stereo system has to meet certain criteria before it's purchased by Julie, the owner of the night club. She has narrowed her choices to three products, brand named, (1) Sharp, (2) Lucidity, and (3) Clarity. She will utilize three criteria to evaluate these three products: (1) sound (clarity of sound), (2) price, and (3) options (the number of options available in playing the stereo system). The prices of the three stereo systems are as follows: Sharp, \$15 000; Lucidity, \$30 000; and Clarity, \$22 500. With respect to sound, the products can be rank ordered as follows: Clarity, Lucidity, then Sharp. In terms of the options available, Sharp has by far the most options to choose from, followed by Clarity, then Lucidity.

Note that in this problem, some of the criteria, such as price and options available, are fairly objective, whereas sound is a subjective criterion. However, even for an objective criterion such as price, there could be a fair amount of subjectivity involved. For example, let us consider the price of Lucidity versus the price of Sharp. Clearly, Lucidity is the more expensive of the two products. However, different customers may have a completely different view of the price differential. If a customer is in a good financial situation, then the difference in price may not amount to much of a difference, while it might mean a significant difference for a person or a company that is in financial difficulty. The ability of the decision maker to include his or her subjective judgments makes AHP a very attractive multicriteria decision-making tool.

Solution

To clearly understand the hierarchical relationships between criteria and the decision alternatives, we first develop a graphical representation of the problem. The importance of the graph is that it clearly depicts the hierarchies in the specification of the criteria for the problem. Figure 9-8 shows the graphical representation of the stereo system problem.

In Figure 9-8, the first level of **hierarchy diagram** is the achievement of the overall objective, which is to buy a stereo system that fits the preferences of Julie. The second level of the graph includes the three criteria utilized by Julie.

FIGURE 9-8 Graphical Representation of the Hierarchies for the Stereo System-Selection Problem

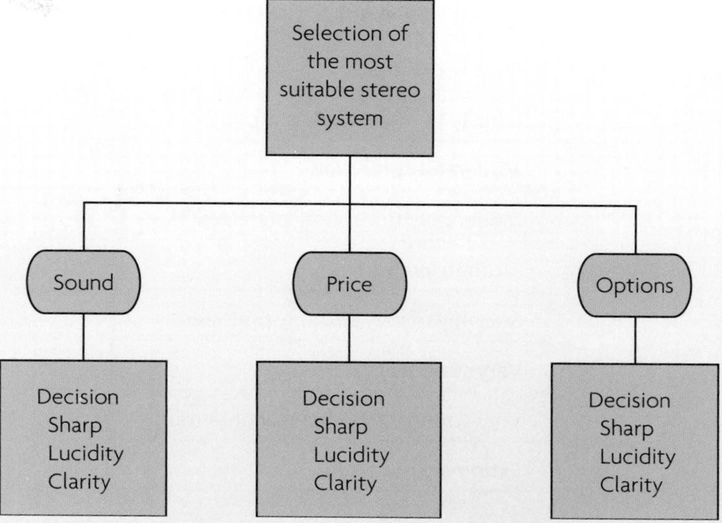

The third level includes the decision alternatives. In the next section, we will develop and explain the AHP procedure utilizing the stereo system example.

In this example, we first compare the three criteria in terms of importance to Julie; then we rate the three brands of stereo systems with respect to each criterion. To do these comparisons, we need to use pairwise comparisons.

Pairwise Comparisons

Pairwise comparisons are the foundation of AHP, and with the assistance of these pairwise comparisons we can effectively compare criteria and the decision alternative with respect to each criterion. We begin the pairwise comparison procedure by comparing the criteria in pairs. Since we have three criteria, we need three basic pairwise comparisons: price versus sound; price versus options; and sound versus options. To compare these criteria, the preference scale provided in Table 9-1 is used. This is a nine-point preference scale. Numerical values and the associated verbal statement of the preference are also stated.

Julie felt that price was moderately preferred to sound, price was moderately to strongly preferred to options, and sound was moderately preferred to options.

Based on Julie's preferences, we formulate the pairwise comparison matrix shown in Table 9-2. The diagonal values are 1, because we are comparing the criterion against itself. The price-sound preference rating is 3 because Julie indicated that price was moderately preferred to sound. From Table 9-1, a moderately preferred rating is 3. On the other hand, we observe that the sound-price preference rating is 1/3. Since the price-sound preference rating was 3, we utilize the reciprocal rating approach and indicate that the sound-price preference rating is 1/3. Similarly, the price-option preference rating is 4 because Julie indicated that price was moderately to strongly preferred to options. Likewise, we observe that the options-price preference rating is 1/4. Since the price-options preference rating was 4, the reciprocal rating approach is utilized to obtain the options-price preference rating of 1/4.

TABLE 9-1 Preference Scale for the Pairwise Comparisons

Verbal Statement of the Preference	Numerical Value
Equally preferred	1
Equally to moderately preferred	2
Moderately preferred	3
Moderately to strongly preferred	4
Strongly preferred	5
Strongly to very strongly preferred	6
Very strongly preferred	7
Very strongly to extremely preferred	8
Extremely preferred	9

TABLE 9-2 Pairwise Comparison Table for the Stereo-System Selection Problem

Criterion	Price	Sound	Options
Price	1	3	4
Sound	1/3	1	3
Options	1/4	1/3	1
Totals	1.5833	4.333	8

Normalized Pairwise Comparison Matrix

Dividing each value by its column total normalizes the values in the pairwise comparison matrix shown in Table 9-2. The **normalized pairwise comparison** matrix is given in Table 9-3. The row averages given in the far right column of Table 9-3 represent Julie's priority for each criterion. Thus, price with a priority of .6079 is the most important criterion while options, with .1199, is the least important criterion.

Consistency Check for Criteria

Since the analytical hierarchy process primarily depends on the pairwise comparisons provided by the decision maker, and since these comparisons are subjective, the preference indicated for a pairwise comparison has to be consistent with a different, but related, pairwise comparison. For example, if the preference score for the pairwise comparison A-B is 2 and B-C is 4, then the preference score A-C should be 8. If the decision maker scores the

TABLE 9-3 Normalized Pairwise Comparison Table for the Stereo-System Selection Problem

Criterion	Price	Sound	Options	Average %
Price	.6316	.6923	.500	.6079
Sound	.2105	.2308	.375	.2721
Options	.1579	.0769	.125	.1199
Totals	1.0	1.0	1.0	1.0

A-C preference rating as 6, then a certain amount of inconsistency exists in her preferences. This type of inconsistency increases as the number of pairwise comparisons increases. A certain level of inconsistency is expected; however, if the amount of inconsistency gets to be too high, then the results of AHP become questionable. In an AHP study, the inconsistencies are measured using a consistency index, or **consistency ratio.** If the consistency index is 0, then the decision maker has perfect consistency in his or her preferences. The consistency ratio (CR) is calculated as the ratio of the consistency index (CI) to the random index (RI). RI is the consistency index of a randomly generated pairwise comparison matrix. In other words, CR = CI/RI. If the consistency ratio exceeds .10, then there may be serious inconsistencies in the pairwise comparisons and the results provided by AHP may be questionable.

Multiplying the pairwise comparison matrix by the criteria percentages given in the last column of Table 9-3 results in the following matrix.

$$\begin{bmatrix} 1 & 3 & 4 \\ 1/3 & 1 & 3 \\ 1/4 & 1/3 & 1 \end{bmatrix} \begin{bmatrix} .608 \\ .2721 \\ .1199 \end{bmatrix} = \begin{bmatrix} 1.904 \\ .8345 \\ .3626 \end{bmatrix} \begin{pmatrix} \text{Price} \\ \text{Sound} \\ \text{Options} \end{pmatrix}$$

Dividing the weighted sums obtained above by the priority percentages results in the weighted sum priority values displayed in Table 9-4.

The weighted sum priority values displayed in Table 9-4 are averaged below to determine the average ratio, or λ_A.

$$\lambda_A = \text{average ratio} = \frac{3.13136 + 3.0663 + 3.0242}{3} = 3.0742$$

TABLE 9-4 Calculation of the Weighted Priorities for the Criteria

Criterion (1)	Weighted Sum (2)	Priority (3)	Weighted Sum Priority (4) = (2)/(3)
Price	1.9040	.608	3.13134
Sound	.8345	.2721	3.0669
Options	.3626	.1199	3.0242

Using the value of λ_A calculated above, we calculate the consistency index formula using the following equation. In this equation, $n = 3$, which is the number of criteria being compared.

$$\text{CI} = \frac{\lambda_A - n}{n - 1} = \frac{3.0742 - 3}{2} = \frac{.0742}{2} = .0371$$

Using the consistency index value, we proceed to calculate the consistency ratio as follows. In calculating the consistency ratio, we divide the consistency index calculated above by the random index value, which is the value of the consistency index if each pairwise comparison is randomly generated. The random index values are given in Table 9-5. Since we have three criteria, $n = 3$, and the value of RI is .58.

$$\text{CI} = \frac{\text{CI}}{\text{RI}} = \frac{.0371}{.58^*} = .064$$

As we discussed earlier, a consistency ratio greater than .10 will affect the results of AHP. However, in this study, since the consistency ratio is less than .10, the level of **consistency** is at an acceptable level; that is, $.064 < .10$.

Next we need to determine three pairwise comparison matrices, one for each criterion comparing the three products. The pairwise comparison matrix given in Table 9-6 includes the pairwise comparisons of the three products in relation to the price criterion. As before, diagonal values of this matrix are equal to 1 since we are comparing the same products. However, the pairwise comparison value of Sharp to Lucidity is equal to 4. This implies that the price of the Sharp product is moderately to strongly preferred to the price of the Lucidity product. In addition, the price of the Sharp product is equally to moderately preferred to the price of the Clarity product

*From Table 9-5.

TABLE 9-5 Random Index Values for the Comparison of *n* items

n	2	3	4	5	6	7	8	9	10
RI	0	.58	.90	1.12	1.24	1.32	1.41	1.45	1.51

TABLE 9-6 Pairwise Comparison Matrix Price

Product	Sharp	Lucidity	Clarity
Sharp	1	4	2
Lucidity	1/4	1	1/3
Clarity	1/2	3	1
Σ	1.75	8	3.333

TABLE 9-7 Proportion Percentage Matrix for Price

Product	Sharp	Lucidity	Clarity
Sharp	.5714	.5	.60
Lucidity	.1429	.125	.10
Clarity	.2857	.375	.30
Σ	1.0	1.0	1.0

TABLE 9-8 Priority Percentage for Price

Product	Percentage
Sharp	.5571*
Lucidity	.1226
Clarity	.3202
Σ	1.0

*(.5714 + .50 + .60)/3 = .5571

which is equal to 2. Applying the reciprocal rule, we obtain the preference of Lucidity to Sharp as 1/4 and the preference of Clarity to Sharp as 1/2. Addition of the column values results in the column totals. The smallest column total indicates that the product is the most preferred, while the largest column total indicates that the product is the least preferred. In our example, the column for the Sharp product has the smallest total, while the column Lucidity has the largest total. Therefore, the Sharp product is the most preferred in terms of the price criterion, while the Lucidity product is the least preferred in terms of price.

The information captured in the pairwise comparison matrix can be converted into percentages by simply dividing the cell value by the column total. For example, the pairwise comparison value of cell Sharp to Lucidity is 4 and the column total for Lucidity is 8; thus the proportion matrix value of Sharp to Lucidity is, 4/8 = .5. The proportion matrix in Table 9-7 shows the percentage (proportion) value for each cell for the pairwise comparison matrix for price.

Averaging the proportions for each row, we determine the priority percentage for price exhibited in Table 9-8. In other words, the Sharp product captures 55.71 percent of the value and the Lucidity product captures only 12.26 percent of the value in terms of price.

The pairwise comparison matrix, the proportion matrix, and the priority percentages for sound and options are computed in the same way as the computations for the price criterion as shown below.

Pairwise Comparison Matrix for Sound

Product	Sharp	Lucidity	Clarity
Sharp	1	1/2	1/4
Lucidity	2	1	1/3
Clarity	4	3	1
Σ	7	4.5	1.5833

Proportion Matrix for Sound

Product	Sharp	Lucidity	Clarity	Priority Percentage
Sharp	.1429	.1111	.1579	.1373
Lucidity	.2857	.2222	.2105	.2395
Clarity	.5714	.6667	.6316	.6232
Σ	1.0	1.0	1.0	1.0

Pairwise Comparison Matrix for Options

Product	Sharp	Lucidity	Clarity
Sharp	1	4	2
Lucidity	1/4	1	1
Clarity	1/2	1	1
Σ	1.75	6	4

Proportion Matrix for Options

Product	Sharp	Lucidity	Clarity	Priority Percentage
Sharp	.5714	.6667	.50	.5794
Lucidity	.1429	.1667	.25	.1865
Clarity	.2857	.1667	.25	.2341
Σ	1.0	1.0	1.0	1.0

After the computation of the average priority percentages, we can develop the overall priority rankings for each product as follows. For instance, in calculating the weighted score for the Sharp product, we multiply the criteria weights for price, sound, and options with their respective priority percentage scores. The average priority percentage for the Sharp product is .5571 for price, .1373 for sound, and .5794 for options. In other words, according to Julie, the Sharp product is viewed favourably with respect to price and options and unfavourably with respect to sound. The weights used for the criteria by Julie indicate that price is by far the most important criterion (weight of .608), and options, with a weight of .1199, is the least important criterion. Summing the products of each criterion weight percentage and average priority percentage results in the **weighted product scores** for each decision alternative. Table 9-9 shows the calculation of the weighted product score for each decision alternative. The sum of the weighted scores for the three products sum to one (.4456 + .1621 + .3924 = 1.0).

TABLE 9-9 Determination of the Overall Priority

Sharp			
Criterion	**Weight % (1)**	**Priority % (2)**	**(1) * (2)**
Price	.608	.5571	.3387
Sound	.2721	.1373	.0374
Options	.1199	.5794	.0695
Weighted score for Sharp			.4456
Lucidity			
Criterion	**Weight % (1)**	**Priority % (2)**	**(1) * (2)**
Price	.608	.1226	.0745
Sound	.2721	.2395	.0652
Options	.1199	.1865	.0224
Weighted score for Lucidity			.1621
Clarity			
Criterion	**Weight % (1)**	**Priority % (2)**	**(1) * (2)**
Price	.608	.3202	.1947
Sound	.2721	.6232	.1696
Options	.1199	.2341	.0281
Weighted score for Clarity			.3924

In our example, it appears that Julie favours Sharp to Clarity and also favours Clarity to Lucidity. In other words, since .4456 > .3924 > .1621, Julie should choose Sharp.

Analytical Hierarchy Process Using Excel

Excel can be a handy tool to perform the analytical hierarchy process (AHP). The following AHP process is shown in Exhibit 9-7.

1. We first state the pairwise comparison matrix comparing the criteria (B2:D4). In stating this matrix, we only specify the values in the upper diagonal (cells B2, C2, D2, C3, D3, and D4). The lower diagonal values (B3, B4, and C4 are obtained using the reciprocal rating formulas. For instance, the formula for cell B4 is the reciprocal value of cell B2; therefore, the formula for cell B4 is =1/B2.
2. We then normalize the pairwise comparisons by simply taking the ratio of each comparison value divided by the total for each column. For instance, the normalized value for cell B2 is specified in cell F2 and the formula for cell F2 is B2/B$5. In other

EXHIBIT 9-7 Analytical Hierarchy Process for the Stereo System Selection Example

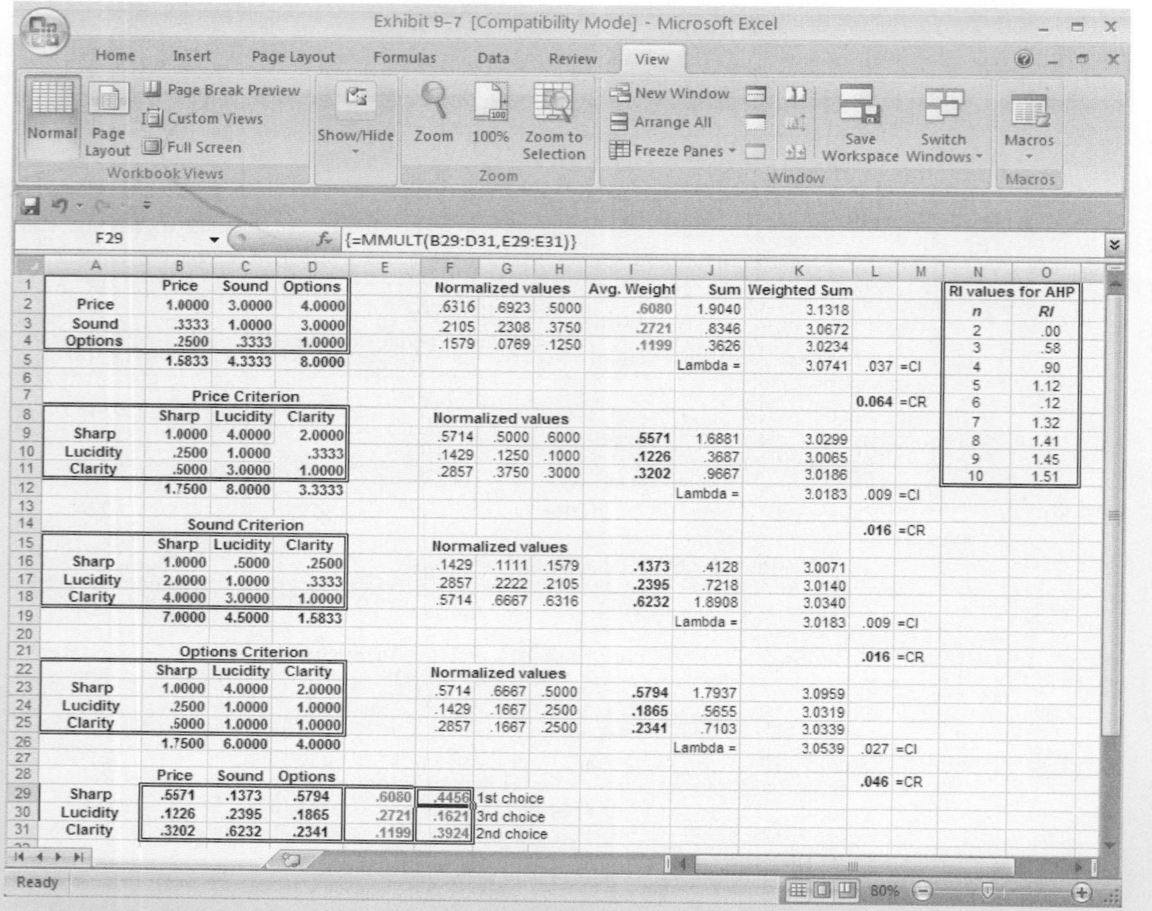

words, 1/1.583 gives us the normalized value for this cell. We calculate the rest of the normalized matrix in a similar fashion.

3. Next, we determine the average percentage for each row of the normalized matrix. The average weight for the first row of the normalized matrix is given in cell I2 under the heading "Avg. Weight." Therefore, the formula for cell I2 is =AVERAGE(F2:H2); in other words, (.6316 + .6923 + .5000)/3 = .608.
4. After obtaining the average percentages for each criterion, multiply the pairwise comparison matrix with the average criteria percentage (labelled as "Avg. Weight" in Exhibit 9-7). Since this involves multiplication of two matrices, we utilize the matrix multiplication command in Excel. The command =MMULT(B2:D4, $I$2:$I$4) multiplies the pairwise comparison matrix for criteria with the average criteria percentage. In this formula, B2:D4 represents the pairwise comparison matrix, and $I$2:$I$4 represents the average percentage for each criterion. After specifying the formula, we highlight the cells in which we want the answer to be displayed (cells J2, J3, and J4) in column J of Exhibit 9-7, labelled as column "Sum." We proceed by highlighting the

formula we just typed in the formula bar and hit Ctrl-Shift-Enter. The results of 1.9040, .8346, and .3626 are displayed in cells J2, J3, and J4 respectively.

5. We calculate the weighted priorities for the criteria using the ratio of the weighted sum priorities and average criteria percentage. For instance, the weighted sum priority for the criterion price is calculated in cell K2 by the formula = J2/I2. In other words, the weighted sum priority for the price criterion is calculated by 1.904/.608 = 3.1318.
6. After the calculation of the weighted priorities, we proceed to the calculation of the consistency index. The formula for the consistency index is determined in two steps. First, we calculate the average of the weighted sum priorities in cell K5 by using the formula = AVERAGE(K2:K4). In the second step, the consistency index for criteria is calculated by using the following formula = (K5−COUNT(K2:K4))/((COUNT(K2:K4))–1). In other words, we subtract the average weighted priority by *n*, which is equal to the number of observations used to calculate the average. This result is divided by the number of observations minus 1. The COUNT command simply counts the number of observations used to calculate the weighted priorities. Once the consistency index is calculated, it is very easy to calculate the consistency ratio. The consistency ratio is the consistency index divided by the random index. The random index values are given in a table in cells N3:O11. The random index value is chosen with the help of the following VLOOKUP command: = VLOOKUP(COUNT(K2:K4),N3:O11,2). In executing this command, Excel counts the number of observations used to calculate the weighted priorities, COUNT (K2:K4), then goes to a lookup table consisting of cells N3:O11 and chooses the value of the random index in the second column of the VLOOKUP table based on the count. In our example, since the count is three, the Excel program goes to the third value in the second column of the VLOOKUP table and chooses the appropriate entry, .58. Therefore, the consistency ratio for criteria is calculated in cell L7 by taking consistency index value and dividing by the random index value (cells L5/O4 = .037/.58 = .064).
7. We state the pairwise comparison matrix, one for each criterion comparing the three products (Sharp, Lucidity, and Clarity) . Exhibit 9-7 shows the outcome in relation to the price criterion (see cells B9:D11), the sound criterion (see cells B16:D18), and the options criterion (B23:D25). For these pairwise comparison matrices, we calculate the proportion matrices (normalized matrices) by taking the ratio of the pairwise comparison value in each column and dividing it by the column total, similar to the calculation of the normalized values for the criteria as described above. Exhibit 9-7 also shows the values of the priority percentage for each criterion. Cells I9:I11 display the priority percentage for price, cells I16:I18 display the priority percentage for sound, and cells I22:I24 display the priority percentage values for options. These priority percentages are calculated by simply averaging the respective rows for the proportion (normalized) matrices. The consistency index and the consistency ratio for the products are calculated in the same way that they were calculated for the comparison of criteria. All of the relevant formulas are listed in Table 9-10.
8. The last step in the analytical hierarchy process is the calculation of the weighted score and the overall priority for each product. The weighted scores are calculated in Exhibit 9-7 in cells F29 through F31. In determining the weighted scores, we multiply the average criteria percentage calculated for each criterion (weight) with the average priority percentage for each product-criterion combination. In other words, we have to calculate another matrix multiplication similar to the matrix multiplication calculation described in the multiplication of the pairwise comparison matrix for criteria with the average criteria percentage described earlier. In this matrix multiplication, simply multiply the average priority percentage matrix (cells B29:D31) with the average criteria

TABLE 9-10 Excel Formulas for the AHP Worksheet in Exhibit 9-7

Cell	Copied to	Formula
B5	C5:D5	=SUM(B2:B4)
B3		=1/C2
B4		=1/D2
C4		=1/D3
F2	F3:F4	=B2/B$5
G2	G3:G4	=C2/C$5
H2	H3:H4	=D2/D$5
I2	I3:I4	=AVERAGE(F2:H2)
J2	J3:J4	=MMULT(B2;D4,I2:I4)
K2	K3:K4	=J2/I2
K5		=AVERAGE(K2:K5)
L5		=(K5 − COUNT(K2:K4))/((COUNT(K2:K4)) − 1)
L6		=L5/VLOOKUP(COUNT(K2:K4),$N$3:$O$11,2)
F29	F30:F31	=MMULT(B29:D31,E29:E31)
B23	B24	=I8
C23	C24	=I13
D23	D24	=I18
E23	E24:E25	=I2

percentage matrix (cells E29:E31) to obtain the overall priority percentage given in cells F29 through F31. Another name for overall priority percentage is the weighted criteria scores. The priority percentage values are given in cells F29:F31 in Exhibit 9-7.

The results are consistent with the manual calculation results provided earlier; it appears that Julie favours Sharp to Clarity and also favours Clarity to Lucidity. In other words, since .4456 > .3924 > .1621, Julie should choose Sharp.

Although Excel has the potential to implement the analytical hierarchy process, it requires a setup that might need further training. The software package Expert Choice (www.expertchoice.com) offers an alternative for implementing the analytical hierarchy process (AHP) on personal computers. It provides users with appropriate tools, structure, and a process to conduct the steps involved in an AHP study. It helps decision makers to arrive at the decision without the cumbersome use of Excel and provides a clear rationale for that decision.

9.4 SCORING MODELS

The **scoring model** is a subjective multicriteria method that enables the decision maker to assign weights to each criterion that describes the importance of the criterion and then assign a rating for each decision alternative on each criterion. The outcome is the sum of the products of the criteria weight with the respective ratings of criteria for that decision alternative. This simplistic selection procedure has many areas of application. The three most common areas of application are (1) facility location, (2) product selection, and (3) job selection.

The scoring model is a very flexible method that considers both tangible and intangible factors. It has the capability to consider multiple decision criteria simultaneously.

The Steps for the Scoring Model

1. Develop a list of (factors) criteria to be considered. The decision maker should consider these factors important in evaluating each decision alternative.
2. Assign a weight to each factor that describes the factor's relative importance.

   Let w_i = the weight for factor i, where $i = 1, 2, \ldots F$
   F = the number of factors considered

   The higher the weight, the more important the criterion.
   We will use a five-point scale to establish the relative importance of the factors considered. The following table provides an interpretation of the weight scale:

   Factor Weight Interpretation Table

Importance	Weight
Very important	5
Somewhat important	4
Average importance	3
Somewhat unimportant	2
Very unimportant	1

   For example, if a factor has a weight of 4, it is somewhat more important than the average factor. If a factor has weight of 1, relative to the other factors being considered, the factor in question is very unimportant.
3. Determine a list of decision alternatives. Let d_j = decision alternative j and assign a rating for each factor/decision alternative combination.

   Let r_{ij} = the rating for factor i and decision alternative j

   where

   $j = 1, 2, \ldots D$
   D = number of decision alternatives considered

   For the purposes of rating each decision alternative/factor combination, we use the following nine-point scale.

Decision Alternative Rating Interpretation Table

Level of Satisfaction	Rating
Extremely high	9
Very high	8
High	7
Slightly high	6
Average	5
Slightly low	4
Low	3
Very low	2
Extremely low	1

For example, a score of 7 for a given decision alternative would indicate that the decision maker (manager) rates this decision alternative (location) high with respect to a given factor (availability of qualified labour).

4. Compute the factor score for each decision alternative. Let S_j = factor score for decision alternative j.

$$S_j = \sum_{i}^{F} W_i r_{ij}$$

5. Sequence the decision alternatives from the highest score to the lowest score. The decision alternative with the highest factor score is the recommended decision alternative. The decision alternative with the second highest factor score is the second-choice decision alternative, and so on.

Product selection and facility location are company-related problems, while job selection is an individualized problem. An example for the product selection problem follows.

EXAMPLE 9-5

Product Selection

An appliance manufacturing company is considering expanding its product line. It has sufficient capital to introduce only one of the three following products:

1. Microwave ovens
2. Refrigerators
3. Stoves

The management thinks the following decision criteria should be used in selecting the product:

1. Manufacturing capability/cost
2. Market demand
3. Profit margin
4. Long-term profitability/growth
5. Transportation costs
6. Useful life

The company has determined the following weights for the decision criteria:

Factors	
Criterion	**Weight**
Manufacturing capability/cost	4
Market demand	5
Unit profit margin	3
Long-term profitability/growth	5
Transportation costs	2
Useful life	1

The decision factor ratings for each criterion are given in the following table:

	Decision Factor Ratings		
Factor	**Microwave**	**Refrigerator**	**Stove**
1	4	3	8
2	8	4	2
3	6	9	5
4	3	6	7
5	9	2	4
6	1	5	6

Based on the information provided, determine the factor scores for all three products. What is the best choice for the appliance manufacturing company? What is the second-best choice?

Solution

$$S_{\text{micro}} = 4(4) + 5(8) + 3(6) + 5(3) + 2(9) + 1(1) = 108$$
$$S_{\text{refrigerator}} = 4(3) + 5(4) + 3(9) + 5(6) + 2(2) + 1(5) = 98$$
$$S_{\text{stove}} = 4(8) + 5(2) + 3(5) + 5(7) + 2(4) + 1(6) = 106$$

Therefore, the first choice is the microwave oven and the second choice is the stove.

Summary

This chapter utilizes three multicriteria decision-making models: goal programming, the analytical hierarchy process (AHP), and the scoring model. Goal programming is a variation of linear programming that can be used to handle problems that have multiple objectives. AHP is designed to solve complex multicriteria decision-making problems. If we are deciding the quantity of each decision variable, then the goal programming model provides the right solution procedure because it provides the quantity of each decision variable, while taking priorities into account. However, if the goal of the decision maker is to select an alternative from a set of alternatives based on multiple criteria, then AHP or the scoring model are the more appropriate methods.

In goal programming, the objectives (goals) are expressed as soft constraints that reflect target levels to be achieved. In addition, some goal programming models also have constraints that specify upper and lower bounds rather than target levels specified in soft constraints. These are referred to as hard constraints and are identical to the constraints of the linear programming models of the previous chapters. This chapter illustrates the

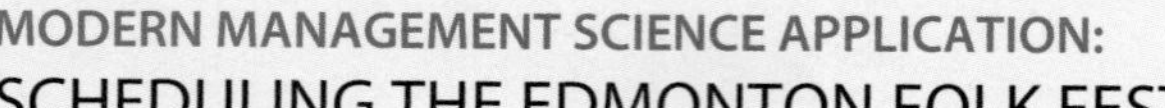

MODERN MANAGEMENT SCIENCE APPLICATION: SCHEDULING THE EDMONTON FOLK FESTIVAL

The Edmonton Folk Festival is a four-day event, where over 15 000 people attend the various functions of the event. Approximately 1800 volunteers make the Edmonton Folk Festival successful, working over 50 000 hours. In return for their services these volunteers receive free admission, T-shirts, and meals. Edmonton has a population of over 670 000 people and the city is known as "City of Festivals" because it hosts four festivals and a major sporting event over the summer months. Therefore the competition for attracting volunteers is severe.

In past years, the coordinators served as manual schedulers for all volunteers based on given constraints. However manually scheduling the volunteers to the festival activities was very time consuming and making changes to the schedule was very difficult. Even minor changes took considerable time. To reduce the burden on the event coordinators and make this scheduling system as efficient as possible, faculty from the University of Alberta School of Business were asked to develop an efficient volunteer scheduling system that met most of the constraints presented. Integer programming was used to develop an initial schedule that satisfied the constraints that were easy to state. A goal programming model was used to minimize the imbalance between the numbers of shifts scheduled at different functions of the festival. Examples of constraints considered in the study included meeting the number of volunteers needed during each shift, ensuring that each person worked exactly 20 hours, that no-one was scheduled to work back to back shifts or late-night, early-morning combinations, and that the minimum number of experienced people working on each shift was always met.

This was a successful application of management science because not only was the consulting team successful in using optimization tools such as integer and goal programming, but they also integrated what if features, and developed a successful user interface using Excel and VBA.

Source: L. Gordon, E. Erkut "Improving Volunteer Scheduling for the Edmonton Folk Festival" Interfaces 34, no. 5, (September– October 2004) pp. 367–76.

---

formulation of the various constraints and the associated goal programming models. In a prioritized goal programming model, the focus is on minimizing deviations from the various goals according to a priority ranking established by the decision maker. In the analysis of a goal programming model, the deviation with the highest priority is minimized while disregarding the other goals. After achieving priority goal 1, the deviation with the second highest priority is minimized as long as it does not require any increase or sacrifice in the highest priority deviation. This process continues until all priorities have been attended to.

In a weighted goal programming model, instead of rank-ordering the goals, the decision maker assigns numerical weights to each goal. If a goal has twice the numerical value of another goal, then it is considered to be twice as important as the other goal. The advantage of solving weighted goal programming models using Excel as opposed to solving prioritized goal programming models using Excel is that the weighted goal programming model can be solved in one step, similar to a simple linear programming model with a single objective function. In solving the prioritized goal programming model with Excel, we need to solve a sequence of goal programming problems.

Three solution approaches are demonstrated in the chapter: (1) a graphical approach similar to graphical linear programming (2) use of Excel for the solution of prioritized goal programming problems, and (3) use of Excel for the solution of weighted goal programming problems.

The Modern Management Application, "Scheduling the Edmonton Folk Festival," illustrates a problem faced by this organization and the successful use of goal programming to minimize the imbalance between the numbers of shifts scheduled at different functions of the festival.

In presenting the AHP model, the chapter demonstrates how judgments concerning the relative importance of criteria or decision alternatives are converted into pairwise comparisons. A consistency ratio is computed to determine the consistency of the pairwise comparisons provided by the decision maker. The solution procedure for AHP is described and finally the priority levels for each decision alternative are multiplied by the criteria weights reflecting the importance of the criteria. The sum of the products of the criteria weights and priority levels provides the overall priority level for each decision alternative.

The chapter concludes with a discussion and demonstration of scoring models. The objective of the scoring model is very similar to AHP. The scoring model is very simplistic and tends to be subjective. The scoring model is a multicriteria method that enables the decision maker to assign weights to each criterion and then assign a rating for each alternative on each criterion.

Glossary

Analytical Hierarchy Process (AHP) An approach to multicriteria decision making based on pairwise comparisons.

Consistency A concept that compares the quality of pairwise comparisons made by the decision maker. It measures how consistent the decision maker is regarding the values he or she assigns to the pairwise comparisons.

Consistency Ratio A numerical measure of the consistency of pairwise comparisons made by the decision maker. A ratio of less than .10 is considered acceptable.

Deviation Variable A variable used to account for the amount by which a solution to a goal programming problem overachieves or underachieves a goal.

Goal A target level of performance (e.g., a profit of $30 000).

Goal Constraint A constraint equation whose right-hand-side value is the target for the goal; the left-hand side of the equation represents the decision and the deviation variables and the level of the goal achieved.

Goal Programming A variation of linear programming that allows multiple objectives.

Hard Constraint A nongoal constraint; equal-to, less-than-or-equal-to, or greater-than-or-equal-to constraint that does not involve deviation variables. Specifies upper and lower bounds that cannot be exceeded, or an equality that must be exactly met.

Hierarchy Diagram A diagram that shows the level of hierarchies in AHP problems in terms of the overall objective, the decision criteria, and the decision alternatives.

Normalized Pairwise Comparisons Numerical values obtained by dividing each pairwise comparison value by its column total. The normalized pairwise comparisons are also referred to as proportions.

Objective Function In priority and goal programming models, this indicates which deviation variables will be minimized and their order of importance.

Pairwise Comparisons A paired, relative comparison of the criteria or decision alternatives that consist of preference of relative importance.

Prioritized Goal Programming Model A goal programming model that ranks the deviation variables according to their relative importance based on the decision maker's judgment.

Satisficing An analytical process in which trade-offs are made to find a satisfactory solution.

Scoring Model A subjective multicriteria method that enables the decision maker to assign weights to each criterion that describes the importance of the criterion and then assign a rating for each decision alternative on each criterion. The outcome is a score for each decision alternative.

Soft Constraint A goal constraint that involves the deviation variables.

Weighted Goal Programming Model A goal programming model that assigns weights to the deviation variables according to their relative importance based on the decision maker's judgment. These weights serve as the objective function coefficients for the associated goal programming problem.

Weighted Product Score In AHP for each decision alternative, the sum of the products of priority percentage values and the criteria weight percentages.

Solved Problems

Problem 1

a. Formulate a goal programming model and solve it graphically, given the following information:

The manager of a company that makes quilted material that is sold by the metre wants to determine the mix of products to make during a week shortened by a holiday. Material supplies are plentiful, but labour is not. There are 24 hours of labour available; each metre of Colonial quilt requires 2 hours of labour and each metre of Southern Comfort quilt requires 3 hours of labour.

The manager's priorities, in order of importance, are

1. Minimize the underutilization of labour.
2. If there is any overtime, try to keep it to 12 hours or less.
3. Try to avoid making less than 10 metres of Southern Comfort.
4. Avoid using any overtime, if possible.

b. Solve the problem you formulated in part a using Excel.

Solution

a. Start by identifying the decision variables:

x_1 = amount of Colonial quilt to produce
x_2 = amount of Southern Comfort quilt to produce

Begin formulation by listing the *names* of the constraints or goals. Thus, the constraints relate to

1. Labour.
2. Overtime.
3. Amount of Southern Comfort.
4. Overtime (same as 2).

This suggests that there are three constraints.

For the labour constraint, apparently, it is possible to be either under ("minimize underutilization") or over ("avoid overtime if possible"). Hence, the labour constraint is a goal constraint:

$$2x_1 + 3x_2 + u_1 - v_1 = 24 \text{ hours}$$

The overtime constraint is a bit unusual because it pertains only to a deviation variable (being over on the labour goal). The overtime goal is

$$v_1 + u_2 - v_2 = 12 \text{ hours}$$

The manager has listed as the third priority to try to avoid making less than 10 metres of Southern Comfort; it would seem that deviations in either direction are possible. That goal constraint is

$$x_2 + u_3 - v_3 = 10 \text{ metres}$$

Next, the priorities can be arranged into the objective function:

$$P_1u_1, P_2v_2, P_3u_3, P_4v_1$$

where

u_1 = amount of underutilization of labour
v_2 = amount of overtime above 12 hours of overtime
u_3 = amount of Southern Comfort under 10 metres
v_1 = amount of overtime

In summary, the model is

minimize $P_1u_1, P_2v_2, P_3u_3, P_4v_1$

subject to

Labour	$2x_1 + 3x_2 + u_1 - v_1 = 24$ hours
Overtime	$v_1 + u_2 - v_2 = 12$ hours
Southern	$x_2 + u_3 - v_3 = 10$ metres
	All variables ≥ 0

To solve this graphically, because there are no hard constraints, begin by plotting the goal constraint that contains the deviation variable with the highest priority (u_1) and indicate the direction of the priority (see Figure 9-9).

FIGURE 9-9 Identifying the Feasible Solution Space for Solved Problem 1

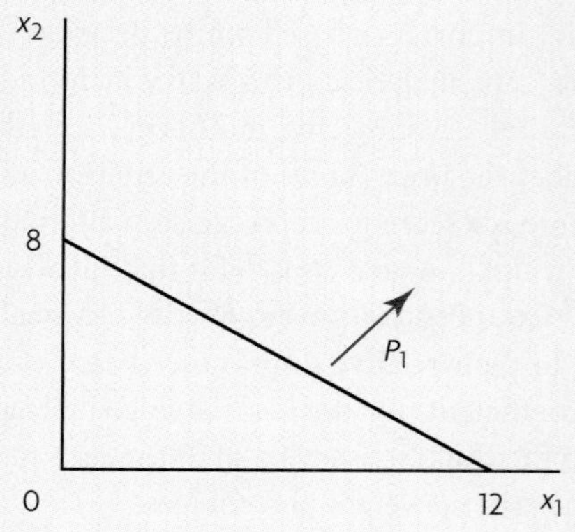

Next, add the goal constraint containing the deviation variable (v_2) that has the second highest priority and indicate the direction of the priority (see Figure 9-10). To plot a deviation goal, set $v_1 = 12$, then add the amount of overtime to the right-hand-side of the labour constraint (because v_1 is in that constraint). The result is

$$2x_1 + 3x_2 + u_1 = 36 \text{ hours}$$

Plotting this line produces the dashed line in Figure 9-10. The dashes differentiate this *deviation constraint* from the other constraints.

FIGURE 9-10 Identifying the Feasible Solution Space for Solved Problem 1

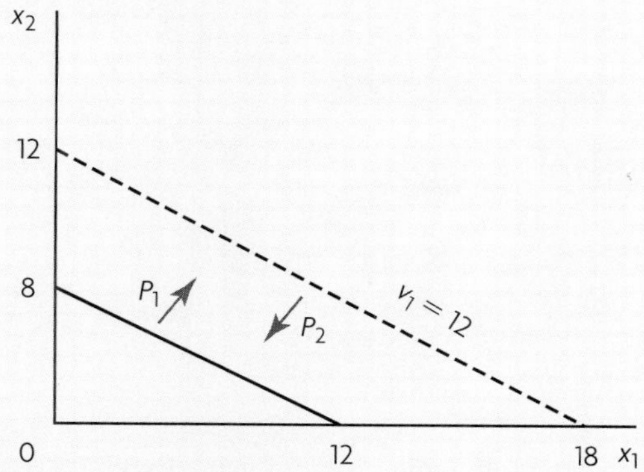

At this point, any combination of x_1 and x_2 that lies on or between the two goal constraints would be acceptable.

The third priority refers to u_3. Hence, we add the third goal constraint to the plot (see Figure 9-11). The shaded region indicates the area of acceptability.

The fourth priority refers to v_1 and, thus, to the first goal constraint, which is already on the graph. Therefore, the only addition is an indication of the direction of P_4 (see Figure 9-12). This makes the optimum point the point that is in the acceptable area that is closest to the first goal constraint (i.e., $x_2 = 10$).

In terms of the deviations, we see in Figure 9-12 that the optimum point lies in the area that is acceptable for the first three priorities. Hence, only the fourth will be nonzero. We can determine its value by submitting the optimal values of the decision variables (i.e., $x_1 = 0, x_2 = 10$) into the labour goal, omitting the deviation variables:

$$2(0) + 3(10) = 30$$

FIGURE 9-11 Identifying the Feasible Solution Space for Solved Problem 1

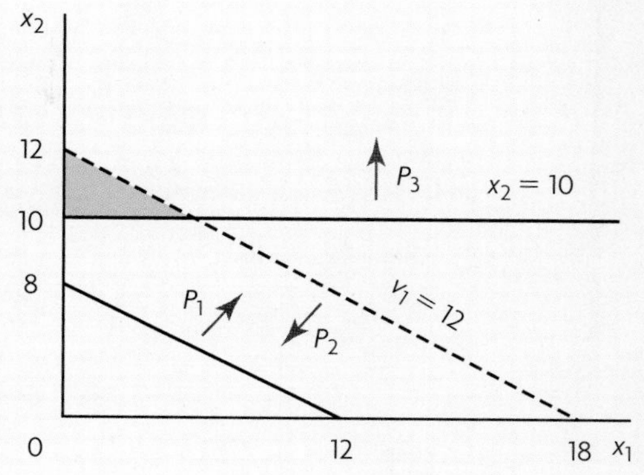

FIGURE 9-12 Identifying the Feasible Solution Space for Solved Problem 1

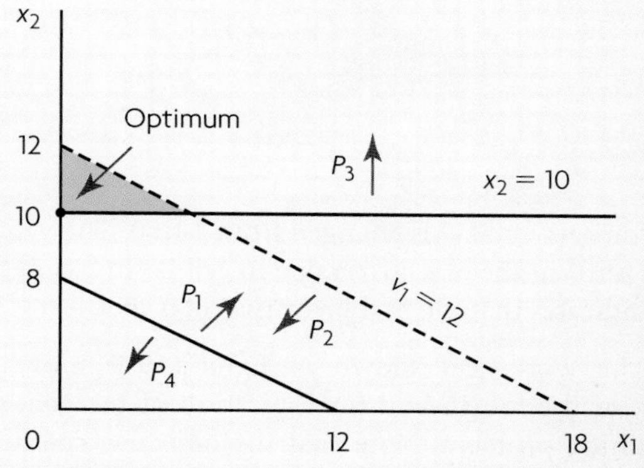

This is 6 above the original 24; hence, $v_1 = 6$.

b. The worksheet shown in Exhibit 9-8 shows the result of the first iteration of the goal programming problem. The worksheets for iterations 2 and 3, which involve the objective of meeting priority goals 2 and 3, are identical to the worksheet shown in Exhibit 9-8, except in iteration 2, the objective function coefficient for v_2 in cell G9 becomes 1 while the objective function coefficient for u_1 in cell D9 is changed from 1 to 0. Likewise in iteration 3, the objective coefficient for u_3 in cell H9 becomes 1 while the objective function coefficient for u_1 in cell D9 remains at 0 and the objective function coefficient

EXHIBIT 9-8 Excel Worksheet for Solved Problem 1, Goal Programming Problem, Considering Only Priority 1 (Minimizing Labour Underutilization) Goal

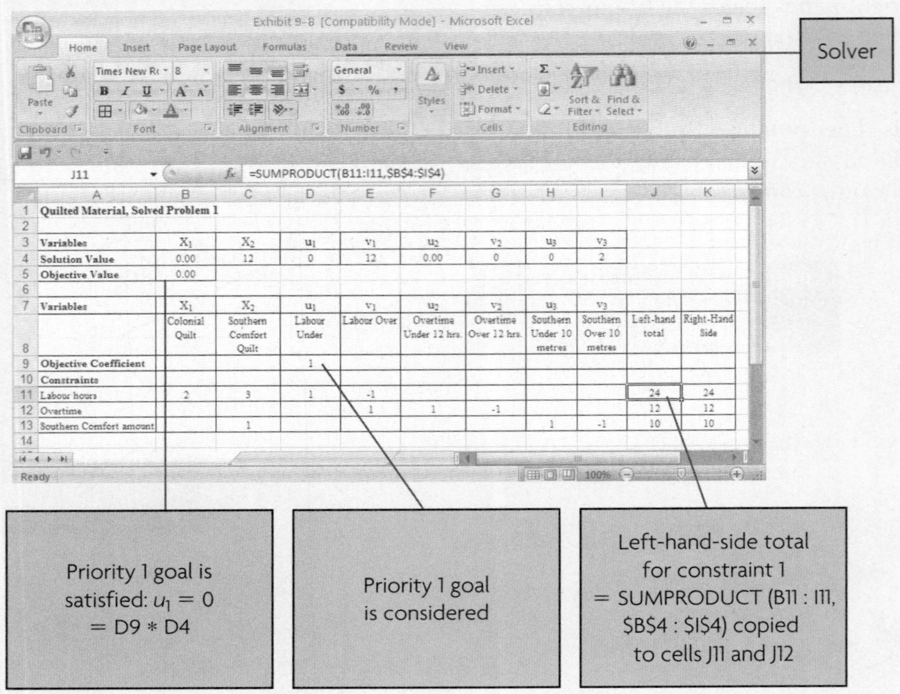

Solver
J11 =SUMPRODUCT(B11:I11,$B$4:$I$4)
Priority 1 goal is satisfied: $u_1 = 0$ = D9 * D4
Priority 1 goal is considered
Left-hand-side total for constraint 1 = SUMPRODUCT (B11 : I11, $B$4 : $I$4) copied to cells J11 and J12

	A	B	C	D	E	F	G	H	I	J	K
1	Quilted Material, Solved Problem 1										
2											
3	Variables	X1	X2	u1	v1	u2	v2	u3	v3		
4	Solution Value	0.00	12	0	12	0.00	0	0	2		
5	Objective Value	0.00									
6											
7	Variables	X1	X2	u1	v1	u2	v2	u3	v3		
8		Colonial Quilt	Southern Comfort Quilt	Labour Under	Labour Over	Overtime Under 12 hrs.	Overtime Over 12 hrs.	Southern Under 10 metres	Southern Over 10 metres	Left-hand total	Right-Hand Side
9	Objective Coefficient			1							
10	Constraints										
11	Labour hours	2	3	1	-1					24	24
12	Overtime				1	1	-1			12	12
13	Southern Comfort amount		1					1	-1	10	10
14											

for v_2 in cell G9 is changed from 1 to 0. The value of "zero" in the objective value in cell B5 in Exhibit 9-8 indicates that the first priority goal is met.

The worksheet shown in Exhibit 9-9 shows the result of the fourth and final iteration of the goal programming problem. Note that the objective coefficient for v_1 in cell E9 is equal to one, indicating that we are solving the fourth iteration of the goal programming problem.

The same solution as indicated by the graphical solution is obtained, where $x_2 = 10$, $v_1 = 6$, and $u_2 = 6$. This indicates that we were not able to satisfy the fourth priority goal ($v_1 = 6, v_1 \neq 0$)

Problem 2

a. Graphically solve the following goal programming model for the optimal values of the decision variables and determine the optimal values of the deviation variables that are specified in the objective function.

b. Solve the following problem using Excel.

$$\text{minimize} \quad P_1u_1, P_2u_2$$

subject to

$$\begin{aligned} 4x_1 + x_2 &\leq 40 \quad (1)\\ x_1 + 2x_2 &\leq 24 \quad (2)\\ x_1 + 2x_2 + u_1 - v_1 &= 30 \quad (3)\\ x_1 \quad + u_2 - v_2 &= 15 \quad (4) \end{aligned}$$

$$\text{All variables} \geq 0$$

Solution

a. We first note which ones are hard constraints: the first two because they do not have any deviation variables. These are plotted, and the feasible solution space is identified (see Figure 9-13a).

Next, we see that the highest priority is to minimize being under on the first goal. We add this to the graph and see that some amount of underdeviation is unavoidable because the goal

EXHIBIT 9-9

Excel Worksheet for Solved Problem 1, Goal Programming Problem, Considering Priority 4 (Minimizing Labour Overutilization) Goal Given that Priority 1, 2, and 3 Goals Have Been Met

Exhibit 9-9 [Compatibility Mode] - Microsoft Excel

J11 =SUMPRODUCT(B11:I11,$B$4:$I$4)

	A	B	C	D	E	F	G	H	I	J	K
1	**Quilted Material, Solved Problem 1**										
2											
3	**Variables**	X_1	X_2	u_1	v_1	u_2	v_2	u_3	v_3		
4	**Solution Value**	0.00	10	0	6	6.00	0	0	0		
5	**Objective Value**	6.00									
6											
7	**Variables**	X_1	X_2	u_1	v_1	u_2	v_2	u_3	v_3		
8		Colonial Quilt	Southern Comfort Quilt	Labour Under	Labour Over	Overtime Under 12 hrs.	Overtime Over 12 hrs.	Southern Under 10 meters	Southern Over 10 meters	Left-hand total	Right-Hand Side
9	**Objective Coefficient**				1						
10	**Constraints**										
11	Labour hours	2	3	1	-1					24	24
12	Overtime				1	1	-1			12	12
13	Southern Comfort		1					1	-1	10	10
14											

Solver

Priority 4 goal is not satisfied $v_i = 6 = D9 * D4$

Priority 4 goal is considered

Left-hand-side total for constraint 1 = SUMPRODUCT (B11 : I11, $B$4 : $I$4) copied to cells J12 and J13

does not have any points in common with the feasible solution space. In addition, note that the goal constraint is *parallel* to one of the hard constraints. Therefore, the portion of the feasible solution space that minimizes the underdeviation on the first goal is the line segment indicated in Figure 9-13b.

The other priority is to minimize being under on the second goal. Adding that goal to the graph (see Figure 9-13c) reveals that the best part of the line segment from Figure 9-13b is the point where the two hard constraints intersect (point A). Hence, point A is the optimum. Solving for point A using simultaneous equations as follows:

$$4x_1 + x_2 = 40$$
$$-\tfrac{1}{2}(x_1 + 2x_2 = 24)$$

$$4x_1 + x_2 = 40$$
$$-\tfrac{1}{2}x_1 - x_2 = -12$$
$$\tfrac{7}{2}x_1 = 28, x_1 = 8$$

This yields $x_1 = 8$, $x_2 = 8$

Substituting these values into the first goal constraint (omitting v_1 because it is obviously zero) and solving for u_1 yields

$$x_1 + 2x_2 + u_1 = 30$$

and becomes

$$8 + 2(8) + u_1 = 30$$

Thus, $u_1 = 6$.

Doing the same for the second constraint yields

$$x_1 + u_2 = 15$$

FIGURE 9-13 Identifying the Feasible Solution Space for Solved Problem 2

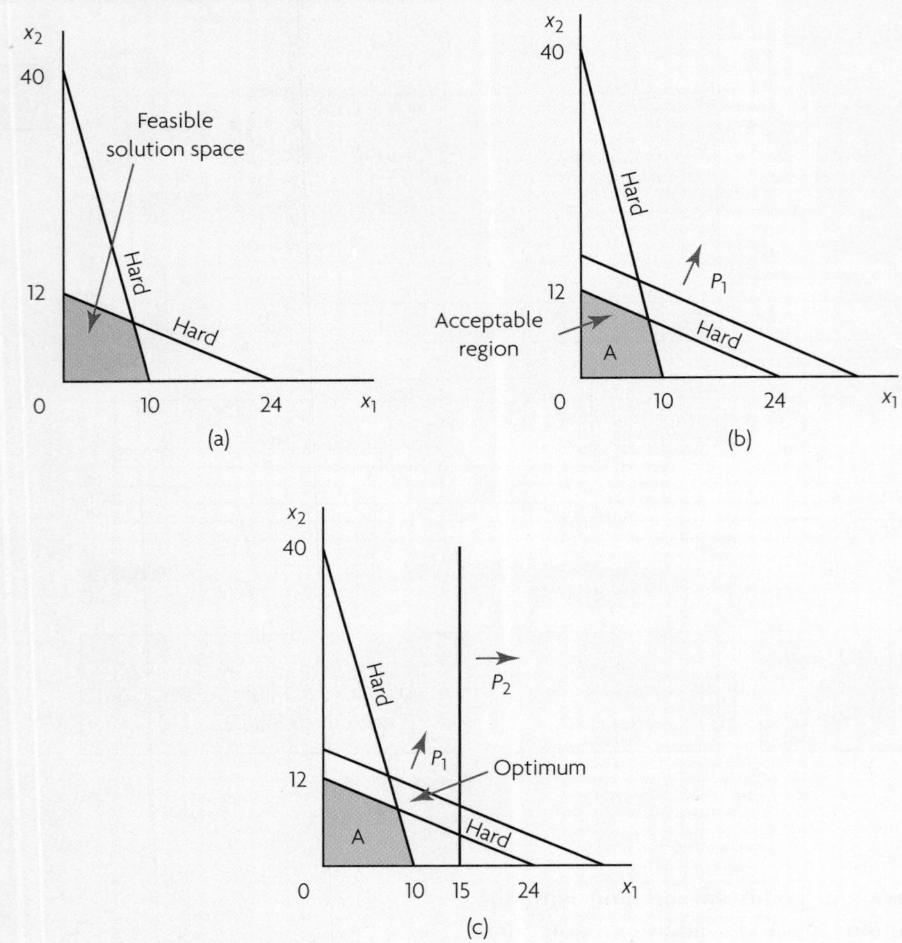

and becomes

$$8 + u_2 = 15$$

Thus, $u_2 = 7$.

b. The worksheet shown in Exhibit 9-10 shows the result of the first iteration of the goal programming problem. The value of 6 in the objective function value in cell B5 in Exhibit 9-10 indicates that the result of the first priority goal is $u_1 = 6$ and $u_1 \neq 0$. Therefore, the first priority goal has not been met.

The worksheet shown in Exhibit 9-11 shows the result of the second and final iteration of the goal programming problem. Note the objective function coefficient for u_2 in cell F7 is equal to one, indicating that we are solving the second iteration of the goal programming problem. The same solution indicated by the graphical solution is obtained, where $x_1 = 8, x_2 = 8, u_1 = 6$, and $u_2 = 7$. This indicates that we were not able to satisfy either the first or the second priority goal ($u_1 = 6, u_1 \neq 0, u_2 = 7, u_2 \neq 0$).

Problem 3

Carleton University is in the process of searching for a head coach for its men's basketball program. It has narrowed the field of candidates to two: (1) Byron Duclos and (2) Eric Meyer. The search committee is split as to

EXHIBIT 9-10 Excel Worksheet for Solved Problem 2, Goal Programming Problem, Considering Only Priority 1 (Minimizing u_1) Goal

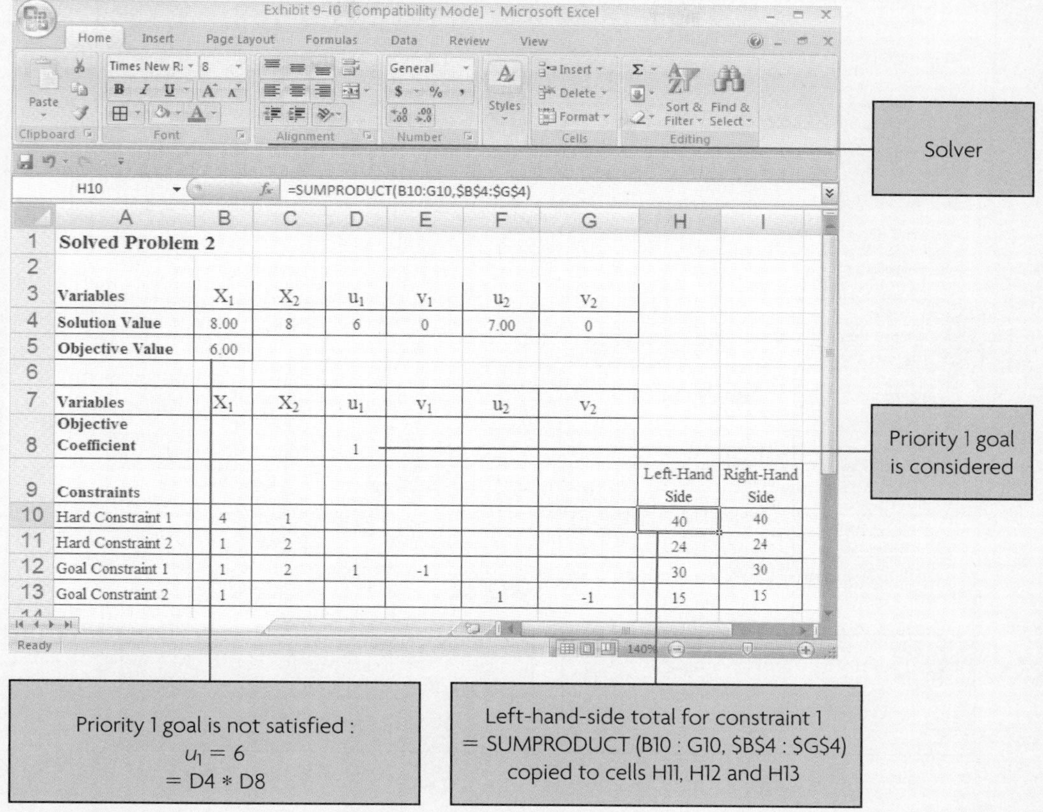

	A	B	C	D	E	F	G	H	I
1	Solved Problem 2								
2									
3	Variables	X_1	X_2	u_1	v_1	u_2	v_2		
4	Solution Value	8.00	8	6	0	7.00	0		
5	Objective Value	6.00							
6									
7	Variables	X_1	X_2	u_1	v_1	u_2	v_2		
8	Objective Coefficient			1					
9	Constraints							Left-Hand Side	Right-Hand Side
10	Hard Constraint 1	4	1					40	40
11	Hard Constraint 2	1	2					24	24
12	Goal Constraint 1	1	2	1	-1			30	30
13	Goal Constraint 2	1				1	-1	15	15

whom to select for the position. The committee has been recommended to use AHP to assist in the selection process. The committee feels that the following three factors are the most important qualities needed from a basketball coach: (1) coaching experience (preferably head coaching experience) at the University level; (2) coaching ability and interpersonal skills: and (3) recruiting skills and potential.

The search committee is asked to perform pairwise comparisons of the criteria and the pairwise comparison of each candidate relative to each criterion. The following results are obtained:

Criteria Pairwise Comparisons

	Experience	Ability	Recruiting
Experience	1	3	5
Ability	1/3	1	2
Recruiting	1/5	1/2	1
Σ	1.53333	4.5	8

Pairwise Comparisons—Experience

	Duclos	Meyer
Duclos	1	2
Meyer	1/2	1
Σ	1.5	3

Pairwise Comparisons—Ability

	Duclos	Meyer
Duclos	1	1/6
Meyer	6	1
Σ	7	1.16667

Pairwise Comparisons—Recruiting

	Duclos	Meyer
Duclos	1	1/3
Meyer	3	1
Σ	4	1.3333

EXHIBIT 9-11 Excel Worksheet for Solved Problem 2, Goal Programming Problem, Considering Priority 2 (Minimizing u_2) Goal Given That Priority 1 Goal Has Not Been Met: $u_1 = 6$

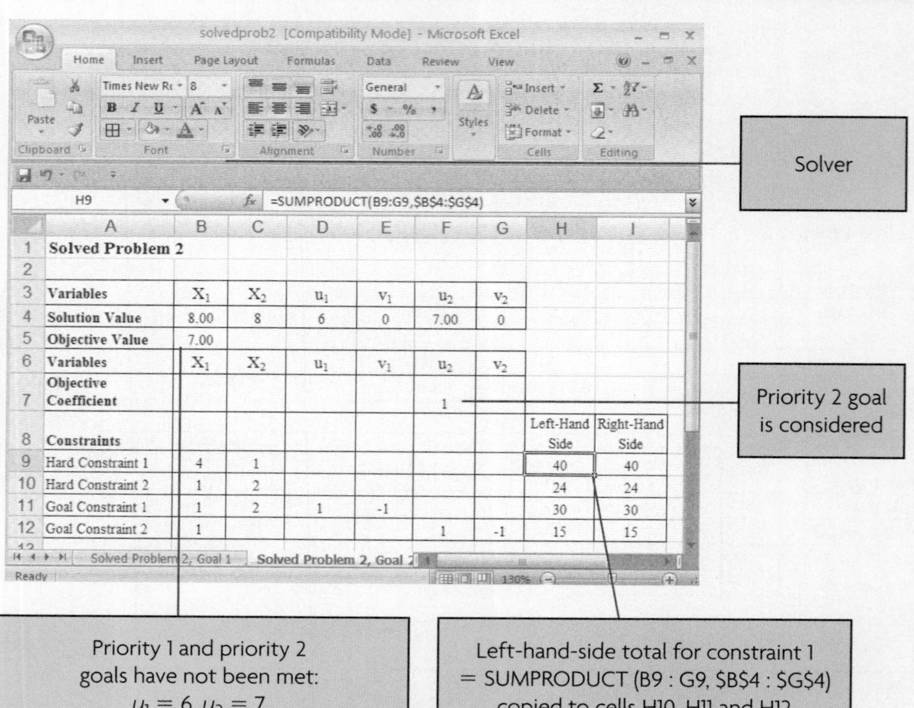

a. Determine if the criteria pairwise comparisons established by the search committee are acceptable.
b. Calculate the priority percentage for each candidate on each criterion.
c. Determine the overall priority for each candidate.
d. Solve this problem using Excel to decide which coach should be hired.

Solution

a. To determine if the criteria pairwise comparisons are acceptable, first, normalize the pairwise comparisons by dividing each pairwise comparison value by its column total.

Normalized Criteria Pairwise Comparisons

	Experience	Ability	Recruiting
Experience	0.6521753	.66667	0.625
Ability	0.2173892	.22222	0.250
Recruiting	0.1304348	.11111	0.125
Σ	1.0	1.0	1.0

Average criteria percentages for the three factors are calculated by averaging the normalized criteria priority percentages for each row:

Experience:

$$(0.6521753 + .66667 + 0.625)/3 = .6479474$$

Ability:

$$(0.2173892 + .22222 + 0.25)/3 = .22986973$$

Recruiting:

$$(0.1304348 + .11111 + 0.125)/3 = .122182$$

Then multiply the pairwise comparison matrix by the average criteria percentages calculated above to obtain the weighted sums for each criterion.

$$\begin{bmatrix} 1 & 3 & 5 \\ 1/3 & 1 & 2 \\ 1/5 & 1/2 & 1 \end{bmatrix} \begin{bmatrix} .6479474 \\ .22986973 \\ .122182 \end{bmatrix} = \begin{bmatrix} 1.9484625 \\ 0.6902162 \\ 0.36671 \end{bmatrix}$$

The weighted-sum values are divided by their respective priority percentages for each criterion to obtain the weighted sum percentages.

Criterion (1)	Weighted Sum (2)	Priority % (3)	Weighted Sum (4) = (2) * (3)
Experience	1.9484625	.6479474	3.00713067
Ability	0.6902162	.22986973	3.00264067
Recruiting	0.36671	.122182	3.00134226

These weighted-sum values displayed in the above table are averaged to obtain λ_A (average ratio).

$$\lambda_A = \frac{3.00713067 + 3.00264067 + 3.00134226}{3} = 3.0037045$$

Using the value of λ_A calculated above, we calculate the value of the consistency index (CI).

$$CI = \frac{\lambda_A - 3}{n - 1} = \frac{3.0037045 - 3}{3 - 1} = .00185227$$

In the CI equation, $n = 3$ because there are three criteria being compared. Using the CI value, we proceed to calculate the consistency ratio (CR) using the following equation: $CR = CI/RI$. In this equation, RI = random index (value of the consistency index if each pairwise comparison is randomly generated. The RI values are displayed in Table 9-5. Since $n = 3$, RI = .58; therefore, CR = (0.00185227)/.58 = 0.0031936.

Since the CR value of 0.0031936 < .10, the consistency of the pairwise comparison of the criteria is at an acceptable level.

b. The totals for the pairwise comparisons of each candidate on each criterion are given in the problem. We simply normalize these pairwise comparisons by dividing each pairwise comparison by its column total to obtain the proportion matrices in the next column.

Proportion Matrix—Experience

	Duclos	Meyer	Average
Duclos	.66667	.66667	.66667
Meyer	.33333	.33333	.33333
Σ	1	1	1

Proportion Matrix—Ability

	Duclos	Meyer	Average
Duclos	.14285714	.14285714	.14285714
Meyer	.85714286	.85714286	.85714286
Σ	1.0	1.0	1.0

Proportion Matrix—Recruiting

	Duclos	Meyer	Average
Duclos	.25	.25	.25
Meyer	.75	.75	.75
Σ	1.0	1.0	1.0

The average priority percentage for each criterion, for each candidate, is shown in the rightmost column of each proportion matrix.

c. The overall priority for each candidate is calculated by multiplying the criteria weights (percentages) by the average priority percentage for each candidate on each criterion. The resulting values are called the weighted scores for each candidate. These weighted scores are calculated in the table below.

Calculation of the Overall Priority (Weighted Scores)

Byron Duclos

Criterion (1)	Weight (%) (2)	Priority % (3)	(2) * (3)
Experience	.6479474	.66667	.43196495
Ability	.22986973	.14285714	.03283853
Recruiting	.122182	.25	.0305455
Weighted score for Mr. Duclos			.49535

Eric Meyer

Criterion (1)	Weight (%) (2)	Priority % (3)	(2) * (3)
Experience	.6479474	.33333	.21598245
Ability	.22986973	.85714286	.19571766
Recruiting	.122182	.75	.0916365
Weighted score for Mr. Meyer			.504651

EXHIBIT 9-12 Analytical Hierarchy Process for Solved Problem 3 (Selection of the Head Coaching Job)

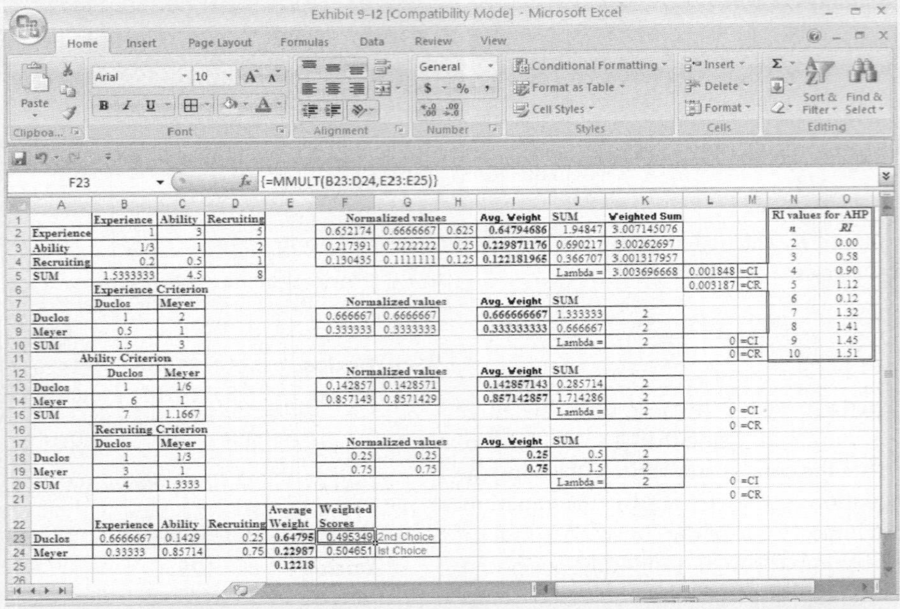

Exhibit 9-12 [Compatibility Mode] - Microsoft Excel

F23 f_x {=MMULT(B23:D24,E23:E25)}

	A	B	C	D	E	F	G	H	I	J	K	L	M	N	O
1		Experience	Ability	Recruiting		Normalized values			Avg. Weight	SUM	Weighted Sum			RI values for AHP	
2	Experience	1	3	5		0.652174	0.6666667	0.625	0.64794686	1.94847	3.007145076			*n*	*RI*
3	Ability	1/3	1	2		0.217391	0.2222222	0.25	0.229871176	0.690217	3.00262697			2	0.00
4	Recruiting	0.2	0.5	1		0.130435	0.1111111	0.125	0.122181965	0.366707	3.001317957			3	0.58
5	SUM	1.5333333	4.5	8						Lambda =	3.003696668	0.001848	=CI	4	0.90
6		Experience Criterion										0.003187	=CR	5	1.12
7		Duclos	Meyer			Normalized values			Avg. Weight	SUM				6	0.12
8	Duclos	1	2			0.666667	0.6666667		0.666666667	1.333333	2			7	1.32
9	Meyer	0.5	1			0.333333	0.3333333		0.333333333	0.666667	2			8	1.41
10	SUM	1.5	3							Lambda =	2	0	=CI	9	1.45
11	Ability Criterion											0	=CR	10	1.51
12		Duclos	Meyer			Normalized values			Avg. Weight	SUM					
13	Duclos	1	1/6			0.142857	0.1428571		0.142857143	0.285714	2				
14	Meyer	6	1			0.857143	0.8571429		0.857142857	1.714286	2				
15	SUM	7	1.1667							Lambda =	2	0	=CI		
16		Recruiting Criterion										0	=CR		
17		Duclos	Meyer			Normalized values			Avg. Weight	SUM					
18	Duclos	1	1/3			0.25	0.25		0.25	0.5	2				
19	Meyer	3	1			0.75	0.75		0.75	1.5	2				
20	SUM	4	1.3333							Lambda =	2	0	=CI		
21												0	=CR		
22		Experience	Ability	Recruiting	Average Weight	Weighted Scores									
23	Duclos	0.6666667	0.1429	0.25	0.64795	0.495349	2nd Choice								
24	Meyer	0.33333	0.85714	0.75	0.22987	0.504651	Ist Choice								
25					0.12218										
26															

Since .49535 < .5033366, the committee should recommend to offer the Carleton University's men's basketball head coaching job to Mr. Eric Meyer.

d. When solving this problem using Excel, we prepare the worksheet shown in Exhibit 9-12. The formulas for this worksheet are shown in Table 9-11 on pg 439. As can be seen from this worksheet, the same results are obtained as in parts a, b, and c of this problem and the committee should offer the Carleton University's men's basketball head coaching job to Mr. Eric Meyer.

Discussion and Review Questions

1. Describe how goal programming differs from linear programming.
2. Discuss what the deviation variable u_i means and how we would go about formulating a goal constraint when we have two products: x_1 and x_2 and the total demand for both products equals 200 units.
3. The per-unit profit margin for product 1 is 5 and the per-unit profit margin for product 2 is 8. The company's goal is to earn a profit of $2000 per day. Assume that this is the first of a few goal constraints. Formulate a goal constraint utilizing the deviation variable u_1 only. Indicate why it would not be necessary to utilize v_1.
4. When solving a goal programming problem, we try to reach a satisficing solution. When solving a linear programming problem, we attempt to find an optimal solution. Explain the difference between optimizing and satisficing.
5. In solving a goal programming problem, we can use one of two approaches. In utilizing the first approach, we can assign weights to goals, and in utilizing the second approach, we can rank the goals in order of importance. Explain the difference between these two approaches.
6. What are the differences between goal programming and the analytical hierarchy process?
7. Explain the circumstances in which the pairwise comparisons have to be utilized.
8. Explain how the numerical values are assigned in making pairwise comparisons. Describe the scale.
9. Explain the meaning of the reciprocal rating approach with an example.
10. In AHP, why is it important to use the consistency ratios?

TABLE 9-11 Excel Formulas for the AHP Worksheet in Exhibit 9-12

Cell	Copied to	Formula
B5	C5:D5	=SUM(B2:B4)
B3		=1/C2
B4		=1/D2
C4		=1/D3
F2	F3:F4	=B2/B$5
G2	G3:G4	=C2/C$5
H2	H3:H4	=D2/D$5
I2	I3:I4	=AVERAGE(F2:H2)
J2	J3:J4	=MMULT(B2;D4,I2:I4)
K2	K3:K4	=J2/I2
K5		=AVERAGE(K2:K5)
L5		=((K5 − COUNT(K2:K4)))/((COUNT(K2:K4)) − 1)
L6		=L5/VLOOKUP(COUNT(K2:K4),$N$3:$O$11,2)
F23	F24	=MMULT(B23:D24,E23:E25)

11. In calculating the consistency ratio, explain the calculation of the weighted sum and weighted sum priority.
12. What is the procedure for computing the proportion matrix from the pairwise comparison matrix?
13. Once we calculate the proportion matrix for a given criterion, explain the procedure for calculating the priority percentage.
14. Explain the procedure for calculating the weighted scores (overall priority) for each option considered.

Problems

1. Manager Barney Bidwell has formulated the following LP model:

   x_1 = amount of Product 1
   x_2 = amount of Product 2
   x_3 = amount of Product 3

   maximize $Z = 4x_1 + 2x_2 + 3x_3$

   subject to

   Labour $2x_1 + x_2 + 4x_3 \leq 160$ hours
   Storage $x_1 + 2x_2 + 3x_3 \leq 150$ square feet
   Product 1 $x_1 \geq 10$ units
   $x_1, x_2, x_3 \geq 0$

After discussions with several colleagues, Barney now believes that a goal programming model would be more appropriate. Accordingly, the manager has decided on these priorities, which are listed in order of importance.

a. Minimize the underutilization of labour.
b. Achieve a satisfactory profit level of $300.
c. Try to avoid making less than 10 units of x_1.

Reformulate this as a goal programming model.

2. For the preceding problem, incorporate one additional priority:

d. If overtime is used, try to avoid using more than 10 hours. Indicate how the model of the previous problem would *change.*

3. Given this goal programming model:

minimize P_1u_2, P_2v_1

subject to

Labour	$10x_1 + 10x_2 + u_1 - v_1 = 600$ hours
Product 1	$x_1 + u_2 - v_2 = 80$ units
	All variables ≥ 0

a. Is the first constraint a hard or a soft constraint? How do you know?
b. What is the highest priority in this model?
c. Solve the problem graphically for the optimal solution. What are the optimal values of the decision variables? What are the optimal values of the deviation variables u_2 and v_1?
d. Suppose that the objective had been P_1v_1, P_2u_2. What would your answers to the question posed in part *c* be?

4. Given this goal programming problem:

minimize P_1u_1, P_2v_2, P_3u3

subject to

Newspaper advertising	$8x_1 + 15x_2 + u_1 - v_1 = 120$ lines
Budget	$2x_1 + 3x_2 + u_2 - v_2 = 12$ ($000)
Direct marketing	$6x_1 + 18x_2 + u_3 - v_3 = 54$ hours
	All variables ≥ 0

a. Plot the first constraint and indicate the direction that will satisfy the highest priority.
b. Plot the second constraint and indicate the direction that will satisfy the second highest priority.
c. What is the optimal solution at this point?
d. Add the third constraint and indicate the direction that will satisfy the third priority. Does the addition of the third constraint and the third priority alter the solution? Why? Would changing the third priority to P_3v_3 alter the solution? Why?
e. Compute the values of the deviation variables u_1, v_2, and u_3 for the optimal solution.

5. Find the values of the decision variables that will minimize the objective function for the following goal programming model and also find the resulting values of each of the deviation variables that are listed in the objective function:

minimize $P_1v_1, P_2v_3, P_3u_2, P_4u_4$

subject to

Plastic	$2x_1 + 4x_2 + u_1 - v_1 = 80$ kgs
Cloth	$3x_1 + 6x_2 + u_2 - v_2 = 180$ square metres
Product 1	$x_1 + u_3 - v_3 = 30$ units
Painting	$5x_1 + u_4 - v_4 = 250$ minutes
	All variables ≥ 0

6. Given the following goal programming model:

minimize P_1v_1, P_2u_2, P_3u_3

subject to

Budget	$2A + 4B + u_1 - v_1 = 80$	($000)
Profit	$2A + 4B + u_2 - v_2 = 120$	($000)
Product A	$A + u_3 - v_3 = 30$ barrels	
	All variables ≥ 0	

a. Find the values of the decision variables that minimize the objective function.
b. Determine the values of the deviation variables that are in the objective function that will result from your solution.

7. Given this goal programming model:

minimize $P_1u_1, P_2u_2, P_3(u_3 + v_3)$

subject to

Sodium	$8N + 6L \leq 48$ grams
Carbohydrate	$N + 6L + u_1 - v_1 = 24$ grams
Protein	$5N + L + u_2 - v_3 = 10$ grams
Input L	$L + u_3 - v_3 = 3$ cubic centimetres
	All variables ≥ 0

a. Find the best values of the decision variables.
b. Find the values of all deviation variables that are listed in the objective function.

8. Given this goal programming model:

minimize P_1v_1, P_2u_2

subject to

Product A	$A \leq 30$ units	
Budget	$3A + 5B + u_1 - v_1 = 300$	(\$)
Revenue	$9A + 10B + u_2 - v_2 = 900$	(\$)
	All variables ≥ 0	

a. Determine the optimal values of the decision variables and the resulting values of v_1 and u_2.
b. How would your answers change if the first constraint was $A \geq 30$?

9. Solve this goal programming problem for the optimal solution.

minimize $P_1v_1, P_2u_2, P_3u_3, P_4u_4$

subject to

Profit	$9S + 5T \geq 45$	(\$000)
Budget	$8S + 9T + u_1 - v_1 = 72$	(\$000)
Material	$S + 5T + u_2 - v_2 = 5$	
T	$T + u_3 - v_3 = 10$	
S	$S + u_4 - v_4 = 9$	
	All variables ≥ 0	

Then, indicate the optimal values of the decision variables *and* the values of each of the deviation variables that are listed in the objective. Solve using the graphical method.

10. Given this goal programming model, determine the optimal values of the decision variables and the resulting values of the deviation variables that are listed in the objective function:

minimize $P_1v_1, P_2v_2, P_3u_2, P_4v_3, P_5u_3$

subject to

Product 1	$x_1 \leq 100$ units
Storage	$x_1 + x_2 + u_1 - v_1 = 80$ square metres
Product 1	$x_1 + u_2 - v_2 = 40$ units
Material	$2x_1 + 4x_2 + u_3 - v_3 = 320$ kgs
	All variables ≥ 0

11. Solve this goal programming problem for the optimal solution using Excel:

minimize P_1v_1, P_2u_2, P_3v_3

subject to

Material	$5x_1 + 4x_2 + u_1 - v_1 = 200$ kgs
Profit	$2x_1 + x_2 + u_2 - v_2 = \$40\,000$
Machine	$2x_1 + 2x_2 + u_3 - v_3 = 30$ minutes
	All variables ≥ 0

(This problem was solved in the chapter (Example 9-2) using the graphical approach. It would be helpful to compare the Excel solution and the graphical solution.)

12. Solve Problem 6 using Excel.
13. Solve Problem 9 using Excel.
14. Solve Problem 7 using Excel.
15. Solve Problem 10 using Excel.
16. A plastics manufacturer is experiencing sustained increase in the demand for its products. The demand has been substantially exceeding capacity. The company has decided to build a new manufacturing facility. The committee responsible for the new facility has narrowed its choices to three locations: (1) Ottawa; (2) Toronto, and (3) Windsor. The management has decided to utilize AHP to decide where the facility should be located. The management feels that there are three dominating factors in making this decision: (1) construction and land costs, (2) proximity to suppliers and customers, and (3) labour relations/availability of qualified labour in the region.

The management has provided the following pairwise comparisons for the criteria and for the locations on each criterion. These matrices are presented below:

Criteria Pairwise Comparisons

	Construction/Land Cost	Transportation Cost	Labour
Construction/Land Cost	1	1/3	2
Transportation Cost	3	1	6
Labour	1/2	1/6	1
Σ	4.5	1.5	9

Pairwise Comparisons—Construction/Land Cost

	Ottawa	Toronto	Windsor
Ottawa	1	3	6
Toronto	1/3	1	2
Windsor	1/6	1/2	1
Σ	1.5	4.5	9

Pairwise Comparisons—Transportation Cost

	Ottawa	Toronto	Windsor
Ottawa	1	1/4	2
Toronto	4	1	7
Windsor	1/2	1/7	1
Σ	5.5	1.393	10

Pairwise Comparisons—Labour

	Ottawa	Toronto	Windsor
Ottawa	1	4	1/2
Toronto	1/4	1	1/8
Windsor	2	8	1
Σ	3.25	13	1.625

a. Determine if the criteria pairwise comparisons established by the search committee are acceptable.
b. Calculate the priority percentage for each location on each criterion.
c. Determine the overall priority for each location.

17. Solve Problem 16 using Excel.
18. A manufacturer of cleaning products (Top-to-Bottom-Clean) is interested in knowing the market response towards one of the laundry detergents it manufactures. To assess the effectiveness of this laundry detergent, the company has selected a number of volunteers to participate in a market study. In this study, each participant is given a small bottle of this detergent (Brand A) and, further, they are asked to wash a similar load of laundry with brand A, brand B, and brand C. Brand A is manufactured by Top-to-Bottom-Clean, while brand B and brand C are manufactured by the competition. There are three criteria to evaluate these detergents: (1) cleanliness, (2) brightness, and (3) price.

Regarding the cleanliness criterion, the first respondent stated the following:

- Brand A is moderately preferred to brand B.
- Brand A is strongly preferred to brand C.
- Brand B is equally to moderately preferred to brand C.

Regarding the brightness criterion, the first respondent stated the following:

- Brand B is moderately preferred to brand A.
- Brand A is moderately preferred to brand C.
- Brand B is strongly preferred to brand C.

Regarding the price criterion, the first respondent stated the following:

- Brand A is very strongly preferred to brand B.
- Brand A is moderately preferred to brand C.
- Brand C is equally to moderately preferred to brand B.

The respondent also provided the following pairwise ratings in comparing the criteria:

- Price is strongly to very strongly preferred to brightness.
- Price is moderately preferred to cleanliness.
- Cleanliness is equally to moderately preferred to brightness.

a. Set up the cleanliness pairwise comparison matrix for this respondent.
b. Set up the brightness pairwise comparison matrix for this respondent.
c. Set up the price pairwise comparison matrix for this respondent.
d. Use Excel and determine if the cleanliness, brightness, and price pairwise comparisons established by the respondent are consistent.
e. Set up the criteria pairwise comparison matrix for this respondent.
f. Use Excel and determine if the criteria pairwise comparisons established by the respondent are consistent.
g. Use Excel and calculate the priority percentage for each brand of detergent on each criterion.
h. Use Excel and determine the overall priority for each brand of detergent.
i. Which detergent does the respondent prefer?

19. In the upcoming election, there are three candidates running for the provincial premier's position (Mr. Leach, Ms. Borck, and Mr. Thompson). Provincial taxes happen to be an important issue for the election. Each candidate has his or her own tax proposal. Individuals are asked to compare the fairness and effectiveness of the three tax proposals. A potential voter provides the following pairwise comparisons of the three tax proposals.

- Mr. Thompson's plan is extremely preferred to Mr. Leach's plan.
- Mr. Thompson's plan is equally to moderately preferred to Ms. Borck's plan.
- Ms. Borck's plan is moderately preferred to Mr. Leach's plan.

a. Prepare the pairwise comparison matrix for this voter.
b. Are his pairwise comparisons consistent?

20. An individual is interested in investing his money in one of two stocks; stock 1, ALO; stock 2: PHI stock. ALO stock has higher expected returns but is also more risky. The investor cannot decide which stock to invest in. The stockbroker has decided to utilize AHP in the decision-making process. There are two relevant criteria: risk and return. The investor is risk averse and therefore, views return moderately preferred to risk.

In addition, the stockbroker provides the following additional information:

- In terms of risk, PHI is strongly to very strongly preferred to ALO.
- In terms of return, ALO is moderately preferred to PHI.

a. Determine the values of all the pairwise comparison matrices.
b. Determine the overall priority for the two stocks. Which investment should the investor undertake?

21. Complete the following partially completed pairwise comparisons matrix and normalize the pairwise comparisons.

	Criterion A	Criterion B	Criterion C
Criterion A		5	4
Criterion B			3
Criterion C			

22. Compute the proportion (normalized) matrix from the following pairwise comparison matrix.

	Option A	Option B	Option C
Option A	1	5	3
Option B	1/5	1	1/2
Option C	1/3	2	1

23. Use the following proportion matrix for a given criterion and calculate the priority percentage for options A, B, and C.

	Option A	Option B	Option C
Option A	.6	.5	.4
Option B	.3	.3	.3
Option C	.1	.2	.3

24. The weight percentages for criteria X,Y, and Z are .55, .25, and .20 respectively. The priority percentages for options A, B, and C on criteria X, Y, and Z are given in the following table:

	Criterion X	Criterion Y	Criterion Z
Option A	.5	.60	.55
Option B	.3	.25	.20
Option C	.2	.15	.25

Calculate the overall priority of each option.

25. A company is in the process of deciding among three different advertising media: (1) television, (2) radio, and (3) newspaper. The company feels that three criteria are very important in making this decision: (1) cost, (2) audience exposure, and (3) flexibility (ability to cancel or change contracts quickly and without penalty). The associated pairwise comparison matrices are given below.

Criteria Pairwise Comparisons

	Cost	Audience Exposure	Flexibility
Cost	1	1/2	4
Audience Exposure	2	1	7
Flexibility	1/4	1/7	1

Pairwise Comparisons—Cost

	Television	Radio	Newspaper
Television	1	1/5	1/8
Radio	5	1	1/3
Newspaper	8	3	1

Pairwise Comparisons—Audience Exposure

	Television	Radio	Newspaper
Television	1	5	7
Radio	1/5	1	3
Newspaper	1/7	1/3	1

Pairwise Comparisons—Flexibility

	Television	Radio	Newspaper
Television	1	1/5	1/8
Radio	5	1	2
Newspaper	8	1/2	1

a. Use Excel and determine if the criteria pairwise comparisons established by management are acceptable.

b. Calculate the priority percentage for each medium, or each criterion.

c. Determine the overall priority for each medium. Which medium should the company select?

26. Due to a significant sustained increase in demand, the ITM fastener manufacturing company has decided to build a new plant. After an initial study, it has narrowed its choices to four locations: (1) Regina; (2) Calgary; (3) Winnipeg, and (4) Victoria.

ITM also identified the following as being important factors in terms of the facility location decision:

a. Transportation costs
b. Construction/land costs
c. Labour climate
d. Availability of qualified labour
e. Production costs

On a five-point scale, the company has determined the following weights for these factors:

Factor Weights

Factor	Weight
Transportation costs	5
Construction/land costs	3
Labour climate	1
Availability of qualified labour	2
Production costs	4

The decision factor ratings for each criterion are given in the following table:

Decision Factor Ratings

Factor	Regina	Calgary	Winnipeg	Victoria
1	3	8	6	1
2	5	4	7	8
3	3	5	2	9
4	8	7	6	2
5	4	5	6	7

Determine the factor scores for all four locations. What is the recommended site? If the first site is not available, what is the second choice?

27. Assume that you are a senior student majoring in marketing. You have been involved in the job search process for the last few months. At this time you have three job offers from three different firms. Your potential job titles and the locations of the jobs are presented below:

a. Pharmaceutical sales—Toronto
b. Marketing research—Edmonton
c. Advertising promotions—Vancouver

The salaries of the jobs are as follows:

a. Toronto, $37 000
b. Edmonton, $30 000
c. Vancouver, $40 000

The following table provides additional information about each job and company:

Company/Job Characteristics

Characteristic	Toronto	Edmonton	Vancouver
Culture	Formal	Mix	Informal
Job Security	High	Medium	Low
Future earnings and advancement potential	Limited	Medium	High
Job expectations	Reasonable	Medium	Very high

a. Determine the weights for all the listed factors (5 being very important and 1 being very unimportant) and rate the importance of the factors from one to five.

Factor #	Factor	Weight
1	Salary and benefits	
2	Type of job	
3	Location: social/cultural	
4	Location: climate	
5	Location: proximity to family and friends	
6	Type of company	
7	Opportunities for advancement	

b. Complete the following table indicating your decision factor ratings for each criterion.

Factor	Toronto	Edmonton	Vancouver
1			
2			
3			
4			
5			
6			
7			

c. Determine the factor score for each location.

d. Based on your answer to part c, indicate the best choice and the second best choice.

28. X-Tech Inc. is interested in determining the best location of a new plant it plans to open up in a year. After a detailed analysis, the company was able to come up with three choices. Three final choices are Ottawa, Oshawa, and Windsor. The facility location project team studied these three sites and rated them with respect to six criteria. The following table indicates those ratings on a 9-point scale as well as the criteria importance weights on a 5-point scale. Use a scoring model and select the best location of the new plant for X-Tech Inc.

Criterion	Weight	Ottawa	Oshawa	Windsor
Labour cost	4	6	7	8
Labour availability	3	7	6	8
Labour climate	2	5	8	4
Land cost	5	7	9	3
Transportation—outbound	4	8	6	4
Transportation—inbound	5	5	8	7
Construction cost	3	7	8	6

Case 1: Hi-Tech Incorporated

Hi-Tech Incorporated is a small company that produces three products daily: (1) CD players, (2) cell phones, and (3) photograph cameras. The company has a limited amount of resources used in the production of these products. The limited resources are labour, machine hours, and inventory space allocated to all products. Hi-Tech has 1560 labour hours per day, 1900 machine hours per day, and 1400 square feet of storage space capacity availability to store the three different products each day. In addition, the management policies of the company dictate the following:

- The minimum number of cell phones produced needs to be at least 20 percent of all units produced for all three products.
- The minimum number of CD players produced needs to be at least 40 percent of all units produced for all three products.

Given the above production requirements, Hi-Tech Incorporated has resource requirements for production and profit for each product being produced as shown in the table below.

a. If Hi-Tech's goal is to maximize the profit, what would be the production quantity of each product and the total profit?
b. Instead of a single objective of maximizing profit, the company has listed the following objectives in order of importance:

1. The owner of Hi-Tech, Donald Schroeder, wants to be able to provide a stable environment for his employees. To accomplish his goal of having a stable workforce, he does not want to use fewer than 1560 hours of labour per day.
2. Hi-Tech would like to achieve a satisfactory daily profit level of $32 000.
3. Donald Schroeder also is concerned about the machine utilization at his company. He wants to be able to effectively utilize the machine hours. To reach his goal of high machine utilization, he would like a utilization of at least 1900 machine hours.
4. Hi-Tech does not want to utilize more than 1400 square feet of inventory space available.
5. Because Mr. Schroeder has to pay overtime, and due to high overhead costs when the plant is kept open past the normal operating hours, he wants to minimize the amount of overtime by its employees.
6. Due to warehouse space regulations, the company cannot produce more than 180 cell phones per day.
7. If the company can meet the restrictions on manufacturing cell phones specified in objective 6, the company also would like to limit the production of cameras in the following way: Due to warehouse space regulations, the company wants to limit the production of photograph cameras to 220 units per day.

Formulate and solve the goal programming problem and comment on the goals achieved and the goals not achieved.

c. Mr. Schroeder has accepted the fact that some overtime may be unavoidable. He revised the fifth priority goal such that overtime may be limited to 20 hours per day. How will the formulation in part b change? Solve the resulting goal programming problem. How is the solution different than the solution in part b?

Resource Requirements

Product	Labour Hours	Machine Hours	Storage Space (square metres)	Profit per Unit
CD players	1	1.25	.5	27
Cell phones	5	5.00	4.5	55
Photograph cameras	3	3.50	2.5	80

PART 3

Probabilistic Decision Models

PART OUTLINE

Part II studied deterministic models, where the assumption is made that the parameters and variable values are known with certainty. However, in the real world, organizations and individuals face many uncertainties, which make the use of deterministic models unrealistic and unsuitable.

Part III discusses probabilistic decision models, which, unlike deterministic models, can be used when the value of the variable(s) are uncertain. Probabilities must be incorporated into the models to account for randomness. The solutions to probabilistic models take the form of expected values, which can be thought of as an approximate average.

Chapter 10 will investigate the decision theory models. Decision theory models require a decision maker to choose one alternative from a list of alternatives. In making that choice, he or she will consider the uncertainty using probabilities, then choose the alternative that will result in the best outcome.

Chapter 11 discusses Markov analysis, which studies the evolution of a system over repeated time periods. Markov analysis is often used to model probabilistic changeover behaviours in "systems" or cases such as brand switching, machine breakdown, or accounts receivable over time. Steady-state probabilities (long-term average probabilities) are determined by using Markov analysis, which helps decision makers understand how the system behaves over time.

Chapter 12 studies waiting-line models, which are a common occurrence at services such as gas stations, fast food restaurants, post offices, banks, as well in manufacturing and supply chain systems. Waiting-line models can be particularly useful in making capacity decisions, such as how many machines or employees to utilize at a given time. These models must take into account the trade-off between the cost of waiting and the cost and speed of service.

Chapter 13 considers simulation models, which are frequently used when other models cannot deal with the complicated nature of the real world. Simulation models represent a system and can be used to determine the effect that variables, conditions, or changes in parameters would have on that system. An advantage of simulation models is that they do not require the decision maker to experiment with the real world. Simulation models are used to study system outcomes, often with the goal of exploring the "what if . . .?" that affects the behaviour of variables.

Decision Analysis

CHAPTER 10

LEARNING OBJECTIVES

After completing this chapter, you should be able to:

1. Outline the characteristics of a decision theory approach to decision making.
2. Describe and give examples of decisions under certainty, risk, and complete uncertainty.
3. Make decisions using maximin, maximax, minimax regret, Hurwicz, equally likely, and expected value criteria and use Excel to solve problems involving these techniques.
4. Use Excel to solve decision-making problems under risk using the expected value criterion.
5. Develop decision trees that consist of a combination of decision alternatives and events.
6. Use TreePlan to develop decision trees with Excel.
7. Determine if acquiring additional information in a decision problem will be worth the cost.
8. Calculate revised probabilities manually and with Excel.
9. Analyze the sensitivity of decisions to probability estimates.
10. Describe how utilities can be used in lieu of monetary value in making decisions.

CHAPTER OUTLINE

Most decision makers are called on to make a variety of decisions. Very often they encounter situations in which they must choose one alternative from a list of alternatives. For instance, the president of a small manufacturing firm may have to select a site for a new warehouse from a list of potential sites. Similarly, a marketing manager may have to select a pricing strategy from a list of strategies.

Let's take a young couple in the process of buying their first home. In the meantime, they must make a decision about buying a car without knowing what house they will end up with. The alternatives are the possible new and used cars they can buy now and future conditions are the house payments for the house they will eventually buy. Alternatives and future conditions are among the characteristics and components discussed in the next section.

Decision theory is important in decisions such as the ones mentioned above because it provides decision makers with a rational way of making a selection: it provides a logical framework for analyzing the situation and coming up with a selection. Unlike optimizing approaches, such as linear programming, decision theory does not guarantee an "optimal" decision. This is because the type of problems that lend themselves to linear programming solutions involve complete *certainty*. Decision theory problems, on the other hand, are characterized by at least some uncertainty, and very often, by a considerable amount of uncertainty. But even though decision theory cannot provide optimal solutions, it can indicate to the decision maker which alternative on a list is most suited to the decision maker's own philosophy, be it optimistic, pessimistic, or somewhere in between.

Applications of decision theory are widespread. They include selection of investment portfolios, oil and gas exploration (to drill or not to drill), contracting (to bid or not to bid), agriculture (which crops to plant, how much acreage, whether to use pest control), manufacturing (which technology to invest in, which machines, how much capacity, maintenance schedules), marketing (introduction of new products, advertising/trade promotion/couponing strategies), home buying (selection of mortgage type—conventional fixed or adjustable rate), retailing (strategies for buying, pricing, and inventories), and so on. The Modern Management Application, "Early Detection of High-risk Claims," describes the application of decision theory for identifying high-risk claims at the Worker's Compensation Board of British Columbia.

This chapter introduces the general approach of decision theory and two important tools of analysis: payoff tables and decision trees. These provide structure for organizing relevant information in a format conducive to rational decision making. The chapter begins with a description of the components of a decision model. Later, a variety of methods are illustrated, ranging from situations in which there is complete uncertainty as to how likely the various conditions are, to partial uncertainty, where some assessment of the likelihood of the various conditions is possible. Tabular and graphical methods are illustrated for analyzing decision problems and selecting appropriate alternatives.

10.1 INTRODUCTION

Decision theory problems are characterized by the following:

1. A list of alternatives.
2. A list of possible future states of nature.

MODERN MANAGEMENT SCIENCE APPLICATION: EARLY DETECTION OF HIGH-RISK CLAIMS

The Workers' Compensation Board of British Columbia (WCB) is a statutory agency responsible for the occupational health and safety, rehabilitation, and compensation interests of British Columbia's workers and employers. Created in 1917, the WCB's main objective is to help workers and employers to create and maintain safe workforces and to ensure injured workers secure income and a safe return to work. The WCB obtains the funds to make compensation payments and meet its other financial obligations from assessments levied on employers. In return, employers receive protection from lawsuits arising from work-related injuries and diseases. For waiving the right to sue, injured workers receive the right to benefits on a no-fault basis. In 2002, the WCB served more than 165 000 employers who employed about 1.8 million workers in British Columbia, and spent over $1 billion on compensation and rehabilitation. The WCB processes two types of claims for compensation from an injured worker for any injury or illness sustained at work. Whenever a claim corresponding to an injury or illness resulting from a person's employment causes temporary absence from work, the claim is referred to as a *short-term disability claim* or an *STD claim.* For STD claims, the WCB provides wage-loss payments for the workdays lost and pays for the cost of hospitalization, treatment, prescription drugs, and necessary medical appliances. The vast majority (96 percent) of injured workers with STD claims recover from their injuries and return to work within a few months. Whenever a worker fails to recover completely from a work-related injury or illness and is left with a permanent partial disability or permanent total disability, the STD claim is reclassified as *long-term disability claim* or *LTD claim.*

The claims of this second type, also called high-risk claims, are extremely costly to the WCB. For the approximately 321 000 short-term disability claims with injury dates between 1989 and 1992, high-risk claims accounted for $1.2 billion (64 percent) of the total payment of $1.8 billion, even though they constituted only 4.2 percent of the claims. The WCB determined that early detection of such claims and subsequent intervention was likely to reduce their eventual cost and to speed up worker rehabilitation. A methodology based on a decision analysis was developed and implemented to assist WCB managers to classify claims as high risk or low risk. This approach of early detection of high-risk claims has considerably improved the practice of claims management at the WCB. Savings in the order of $4.7 million annually have been reported.

Source: Reprinted by permission, E. Urbanovich, E. E. Young, M. L. Puterman, S. O. Fattedad: "Early Detection of High-Risk Claims the Workers' Compensation Board of British Columbia", *Interfaces* vol. 33, no. 4 (July–August 2003), pp. 15–26. Copyright 2003, the Institute for Operations Research and the Management Sciences (INFORMS), 7240 Parkway Drive, Suite 310, Hanover, MD 21076 USA.

3. Payoffs associated with each alternative/state of nature combination.
4. An assessment of the degree of certainty of possible future events.
5. A decision criterion.

Let's examine each of these.

List of Alternatives

The list of alternatives must be a set of mutually exclusive and collectively exhaustive decisions that are available to the decision maker. (Sometimes, but not always, one of these alternatives will be to "do nothing.")

Suppose that a real estate developer must decide on a plan for developing a certain piece of property. After careful consideration, the developer has ruled out "do nothing" and is left with the following list of acceptable alternatives:

1. Residential proposal.
2. Commercial proposal #1.
3. Commercial proposal #2.

States of Nature

States of nature refer to a set of possible future conditions, or *events,* beyond the control of the decision maker that will be the primary determinants of the eventual consequence of the decision. The states of nature, like the list of alternatives, must be mutually exclusive and collectively exhaustive. Suppose, in the case of the real estate developer, the main factor that will influence the profitability of the development is whether or not a shopping centre is built, and the size of the shopping centre, if one is built. Suppose that the developer views the possibilities as:

1. No shopping centre.
2. Medium-sized shopping centre.
3. Large shopping centre.

Payoffs

For a decision maker to be able to rationally approach a decision problem, it is necessary to have some idea of the payoffs that would be associated with each decision alternative and the various states of nature. The payoffs might be profits, revenues, costs, or other measure of value. Usually the measures are financial. They may be weekly, monthly, or annual amounts, or they might represent *present values* of future cash flows.[1] Usually, payoffs are estimated values. The more accurate these estimates, the more useful they will be for decision-making purposes and the more likely it is that the decision maker will choose an appropriate alternative.

The number of payoffs depends on the number of alternative/state of nature combinations. In the case of the real estate developer, there are three alternatives and three states of nature, so there are $3 \times 3 = 9$ possible payoffs that must be determined.

Degree of Certainty

The approach used by a decision maker often depends on the degree of certainty that exists. There can be different degrees of certainty. One extreme is complete **certainty** and the other is complete **uncertainty.** The latter exists when the likelihood of the various states of nature are unknown. Between these two extremes is **risk,** a term that implies that probabilities are known for the states of nature.

Knowledge of the likelihood of each of the states of nature can play an important role in selecting a course of action. Thus, if a decision maker feels that a particular state of nature is highly likely, this will mean that the payoffs associated with that state of nature are also highly likely. This enables the decision maker to focus more closely on probable results of a decision. Consequently, probability estimates for the various states of nature can serve an important function *if they can be obtained.* Of course, in some situations, accurate estimates of probabilities may not be available, in which case the decision maker may have to find a way to estimate the probabilities or select a course of action without the benefit of probabilities.

Decision Criterion

The process of selecting one alternative from a list of alternatives is governed by a **decision criterion,** which embodies the decision maker's attitudes toward the decision as well as the degree of certainty that surrounds a decision. For instance, some decision makers tend to

[1]A *present value* is a lump-sum payment that is the current equivalent of one or a set of future cash amounts using an assumed interest rate.

be optimistic, whereas others tend to be pessimistic. Moreover, some want to maximize gains, whereas others are more concerned with protecting against large losses.

One example of a decision criterion is "Maximize the expected payoff." Another example is "Minimize opportunity cost." A variety of the most popular decision criteria are presented in the remainder of this chapter.

10.2 THE PAYOFF TABLE

A **payoff table** is a device a decision maker can use to summarize and organize information relevant to a particular decision. It includes a list of the alternatives, the possible future states of nature, and the payoffs associated with each of the alternative/state-of-nature combinations. If probabilities for the states of nature are available, these also can be listed. The general format of a payoff table is illustrated in Table 10-1.

A payoff table for the real estate developer's decision is shown in Table 10-2. The three alternatives under consideration are listed down the left side of the table and the three possible states of nature are listed across the top of the table. The payoffs that are associated with each of the alternative/state-of-nature combinations are shown in the body of the table. Suppose that those values represent profits. Hence, if the residential proposal is chosen and no shopping centre is built, the developer will realize a profit of $400 000. Similarly, if the second commercial proposal is selected and no centre is built, the developer will lose $100 000.

TABLE 10-1 General Format of a Payoff Table

	State of Nature		
Alternative	s_1	s_2	s_3
a_1	V_{11}	V_{12}	V_{13}
a_2	V_{21}	V_{22}	V_{23}
a_3	V_{31}	V_{32}	V_{33}

where

a_i = the ith alternative
s_j = the jth state of nature (event)
V_{ij} = the value of payoff that will be realized if alternative i is chosen and event j occurs

TABLE 10-2 Payoff Table for Real Estate Developer

	State of Nature		
Alternative	**No centre**	**Medium centre**	**Large centre**
Residential	$400 000	$1 600 000	$1 200 000
Commercial #1	$600 000	$500 000	$1 400 000
Commercial #2	−$100 000	$400 000	$1 500 000

10.3 DECISION MAKING UNDER CERTAINTY

The simplest of all circumstances occurs when decision making takes place in an environment of complete certainty. For example, in the case of the real estate problem, an unexpected early announcement concerning the building of the shopping centre could reduce the problem to a situation of certainty.

Thus, if there is an announcement that no shopping centre will be built, the developer then can focus on the first column of the payoff table (see Table 10-3). Because the Commercial #1 proposal has the highest payoff in that column ($600 000), it would be selected. Similarly, if the announcement indicated that a medium-sized shopping centre is planned, only the middle column of the table would be relevant, and the residential alternative would be selected because its estimated payoff of $1 600 000 is the highest of the three payoffs for a medium-sized shopping centre; whereas if a large centre is planned, the developer could focus on the last column, selecting the Commercial #2 proposal because it has the highest estimated payoff of $1 500 000 in that column.

In summary, when a decision is made under conditions of complete certainty, the attention of the decision maker is focused on the column in the payoff table that corresponds to the state of nature that will occur. The decision maker then selects the alternative that will yield the best payoff, given that state of nature.

10.4 DECISION MAKING UNDER COMPLETE UNCERTAINTY

Under complete uncertainty, the decision maker either is unable to estimate the probabilities for the occurrence of the different states of nature, or else he or she lacks confidence in available estimates of probabilities, and for that reason, probabilities are not included in the analysis. Still another possibility is that the decision is a one-shot case, with an overriding goal that needs to be satisfied (e.g., a firm may be on the verge of bankruptcy and this might be the last chance to turn things around).

Decisions made under these circumstances are at the opposite end of the spectrum from the certainty case just mentioned. We shall consider five approaches to decision making under complete uncertainty:

1. Maximin
2. Maximax
3. Minimax regret
4. Hurwicz
5. Equal likelihood

TABLE 10-3 If It Is Known That No Shopping Centre Will Be Built, Only the First Column Payoffs Would Be Relevant

	State of Nature		
Alternative	No centre	Medium centre	Large centre
Residential	$400 000	$1 600 000	$1 200 000
Commercial #1	$600 000	$500 000	$1 400 000
Commercial #2	−$100 000	$400 000	$1 500 000

TABLE 10-4 Maximin Solution for Real Estate Problem

Alternative		State of Nature No centre	Medium centre	Large centre	Worst payoff	
Residential		$400 000	$1 600 000	$1 200 000	$400 000	
Commercial	#1	$600 000	$500 000	$1 400 000	$500 000	← Maximum of the worst payoffs
Commercial	#2	−$100 000	$400 000	$1 500 000	−$100 000	

Maximin

The **maximin** strategy is a conservative approach; it consists of identifying the worst (minimum) payoff for each alternative and then selecting the alternative that has the best (maximum) of the worst payoffs. In effect, the decision maker is setting a floor for the potential payoff; the actual payoff cannot be less than this amount.

For the real estate problem, the maximin solution is to choose the second alternative, Commercial #1, as illustrated in Table 10-4.

Many people view the maximin criterion as pessimistic because they believe that the decision maker must assume that the worst will occur. In fact, if the minimum payoffs are all negative, this view is accurate. Others view the maximin strategy in the same light as a decision to buy insurance: Protect against the worst possible events, even though you neither expect them nor want them to occur.

Maximax

The **maximax** approach is the opposite of the previous one: The best payoff for each alternative is identified, and the alternative with the maximum of these is the designated decision.

For the real estate problem, the maximax solution is to choose the residential alternative, as shown in Table 10-5.

Just as the maximin strategy can be viewed as pessimistic, the maximax strategy can be considered optimistic: that is, choosing the alternative that could result in the maximum payoff.

Minimax Regret

Both the maximax and maximin strategies can be criticized because they focus only on a single, extreme payoff and exclude the other payoffs. Thus, the maximax strategy ignores the possibility that an alternative with a slightly smaller payoff might offer a

TABLE 10-5 Maximax Solution for Real Estate Problem

Alternative		State of Nature No centre	Medium centre	Large centre	Best payoff	
Residential		$400 000	$1 600 000	$1 200 000	$1 600 000	← Maximum
Commercial	#1	$600 000	$500 000	$1 400 000	$1 400 000	
Commercial	#2	−$100 000	$400 000	$1 500 000	$1 500 000	

TABLE 10-6 Payoff Table with Similar Maximum Payoffs

Alternative	State of Nature s_1	s_2	s_3
a_1	−$500 000	$1 600 000	−$1 000 000
a_2	$1 500 000	$1 500 000	$1 500 000
a_3	$1 500 000	$1 500 000	$1 500 000

better overall choice. For example, consider the payoff given in Table 10-6. The maximax criterion would lead to selecting alternative a_1, even though two out of the three possible states of nature will result in negative payoffs. Moreover, both other alternatives will produce a payoff that is nearly the same as the maximum, regardless of the state of nature.

A similar example could be constructed to demonstrate comparable weakness of the maximin criterion, which is also due to the failure to consider all payoffs.

An approach that does take all payoffs into account is **minimax regret.** To use this approach, it is necessary to develop an *opportunity loss or regret* table. The **opportunity loss or regret** reflects the difference between each payoff and the best possible payoff in a column (i.e., given a state of nature). Hence, opportunity loss amounts are found by identifying the best payoff in a column and then subtracting each of the other values in the column from that payoff. For the real estate problem, the conversion of the original payoffs into an opportunity loss table is shown in Table 10-7.

TABLE 10-7 Opportunity Loss or Regret Table for Real Estate Problem

Original Payoff Table

Alternative	No centre	State of Nature Medium centre	Large centre
Residential	$400 000	$1 600 000	$1 200 000
Commercial #1	$600 000	$500 000	$1 400 000
Commercial #2	−$100 000	$400 000	$1 500 000
Best Payoff in column	$600 000	$1 600 000	$1 500 000

Opportunity Loss Table

Alternative	No centre	State of Nature Medium centre	Large centre
Residential	$200 000	0	$300 000
Commercial #1	0	$1 100 000	$100 000
Commercial #2	$700 000	$1 200 000	0

Hence, in column 1, the best payoff is \$600 000; therefore, all payoffs are subtracted from \$600 000 to determine the amount of payoff the decision maker would miss by not having chosen the alternative that would have yielded the best payoff *if that state of nature* (no centre) *occurs.* Of course, there is no guarantee that it will occur. Similarly, the best payoff in column 2 is \$1 600 000, and all payoffs are subtracted from that number to reflect the opportunity losses that would occur if a decision other than Residential was selected *and* a medium-sized shopping centre turned out to be the state of nature that comes to pass. And, for column 3, the opportunity costs evolve by subtracting each payoff from \$1 500 000. Note that for every column, this results in a value of zero in the opportunity loss table in the same position as the best payoff for each column. For example, the best payoff in the last column of the payoff table is \$1 500 000, and the corresponding position in the last column of the opportunity loss table is 0.

The values in an opportunity loss table can be viewed as potential **regrets** that might be suffered as the result of choosing various alternatives. A decision maker could select an alternative in such a way as to minimize the maximum possible regret. This requires identifying the maximum opportunity loss in each row and then choosing the alternative that would yield the best (minimum) of those regrets. As illustrated in Table 10-8, for the real estate problem, this leads to selection of the residential alternative.

Although this approach has resulted in the same choice as the maximax strategy, the reasons are completely different; therefore, it is merely coincidence that the two methods yielded the same result. Under different circumstances, each can lead to selection of a different alternative.

This approach makes use of more information than either maximin or maximax. However, it still ignores some information and, therefore, can lead to a poor decision. Consider, for example, the opportunity loss table illustrated in Table 10-9. Using minimax regret, a decision maker would be indifferent between alternatives a_2 and a_3, although a_1 would be a better choice because for all but one of the states of nature there would be *no* opportunity loss, and in the worst case, a_1 would result in an opportunity loss that exceeded the other worst cases by \$1.

In summary, the opportunity loss or regret is represented by the following expression:

$$r_{ij} = |V_j^* - V_{ij}| \tag{10-1}$$

where

r_{ij} = the regret associated with the decision alternative a_i and state of nature s_j

V_{ij} = the value of payoff corresponding to the decision alternative a_i and state of nature s_j

V_j^* = value of payoff corresponding to the best alternative decisions for state of nature s_j (the highest value for a maximization problem or the smallest value for a minimization problem)

TABLE 10-8 Identifying the Minimax Regret Alternative

Opportunity Losses

	State of Nature				
Alternative	**No centre**	**Medium centre**	**Large centre**	**Maximum loss**	
Residential	\$200 000	0	\$300 000	\$300 000	← Minimum
Commercial #1	0	\$1 100 000	\$100 000	\$1 100 000	
Commercial #2	\$700 000	\$1 200 000	0	\$1 200 000	

TABLE 10-9 Minimax Regret Can Lead in a Poor Decision

Opportunity Loss Table

Alternative	State of Nature s_1	s_2	s_3	s_4	s_5	Worst in Row
a_1	0	0	0	0	24	24
a_2	23	23	23	23	0	23 ← Minimum regret
a_3	23	23	23	23	0	23 ← Minimum regret

Now, let r_i^* be the maximum regret corresponding to the decision alternative a_i, therefore the minimax regret approach consists of selecting the decision alternative a_i with the smallest r_i^*.

The Hurwicz (Realism) Criterion

Still another approach is to use the **Hurwicz criterion,** also referred to as weighted average or realism criterion, which offers the decision maker a compromise between the maximax and the maximin criteria. This approach requires the decision maker to specify a degree of optimism, in the form of a **coefficient of optimism,** α. Possible values of α range from 0 to 1.00. The closer the selected value of α is to 1.00, the more optimistic the decision maker is, and the closer the value of α is to 0, the more pessimistic the decision maker is. Note that a value of 1.00 would be equivalent to using the maximax criterion, while a value of 0 would be equivalent to using the maximin criterion.

To use the Hurwicz criterion, for each alternative, the best payoff is multiplied by α and the worst payoff is multiplied by $1 - \alpha$, and the results are added. The totals for all alternatives are then compared, and the alternative that has the best overall result (maximum payoff for a maximization problem or minimum payoff for a minimization problem) is selected.

For instance, suppose the decision maker in the real estate example elects to use the Hurwicz criterion. And suppose the decision maker feels somewhat pessimistic and chooses a coefficient of optimism equal to .30 (hence, $1 - \alpha = .70$). Using the following format,

$$\alpha \text{ (Best payoff)} + (1 - \alpha) \text{ (Worst payoff)}$$

the decision maker would choose Commercial #1:

Alternative:	Best payoff ↓ + Worst payoff ↓		
Residental	.30($1 600 000) + .70($400 000)	= $760 000	
Commercial #1	.30($1 400 000) + .70($500 000)	= $770 000	(best)
Commercial #2	.30($1 500 000) + .70(−$100 000)	= $380 000	

Equal Likelihood Criterion

The minimax regret criterion weakness is the inability to factor row differences. Hence, sometimes the minimax regret strategy will lead to a poor decision because it ignores certain information.

The **equal likelihood criterion** offers a method that incorporates more of the information. It treats the states of nature as if each were equally likely, and it focuses on the average payoff for each row, selecting the alternative that has the highest row average.

TABLE 10-10 Equal Likelihood Criterion

	Payoff Table State of Nature						
Alternative	s_1	s_2	s_3	s_4	s_5	**Row Average**	
a_1	28	28	28	28	4	23.2	← Minimum
a_2	5	5	5	5	28	9.6	
a_3	5	5	5	5	28	9.6	

The payoff table from which the opportunity losses of Table 10-9 were computed is shown in Table 10-10, along with the row averages. Note how a_1 now stands out compared to the others. In fact, we could have obtained a similar result by finding the row averages for the opportunity loss table and then choosing the alternative that had the lowest average. Thus, the row averages for the opportunity losses presented in Table 10-9 are

Alternative	Row Average	
α_1	24/5 = 4.8	← Minimum
α_2	92/5 = 18.4	
α_3	92/5 = 18.4	

Note that in both cases, the difference between the average of a_1 and the average of the other two is the same ($23.2 - 9.6 = 13.6$ or $18.4 - 4.8 = 13.6$). Hence, we could obtain the same result from *either* the payoff table *or* the opportunity loss table; they will both always lead to the same decision.

The basis for the equal likelihood criterion is that under complete uncertainty, the decision maker should not focus on either high or low payoffs, but should treat all payoffs (actually, all states of nature) as if they were *equally likely.* Averaging row payoffs accomplishes this.

Table 10-11 provides a summarization of methods used in decision making under complete uncertainty.

TABLE 10-11 Summary of Methods for Decision Making Under Complete Uncertainty

Method	Description of the Decision-Making Criteria
Maximax	Choose the maximum of the largest payoffs from the payoff table (optimistic).
Maximin	Choose the maximum of the smallest payoffs from the payoff table (pessimistic).
Minimax regret	Choose the minimum of the maximum losses from the opportunity loss table (loss oriented).
Hurwicz	Weighted-average approach where the largest payoff for an alternative is weighted with the coefficient of optimism (α) and the smallest payoff is weighted with $1 - \alpha$, and the largest weighted average is chosen.
Equal likelihood	Weighted-average approach where each decision alternative is weighted equally and the largest average is chosen.

Using Excel for Decision Making Under Complete Uncertainty

In the previous section, we demonstrated how to use five different types of criteria for decision making under complete uncertainty. Excel worksheets also can be prepared to solve decision-making problems given complete uncertainty. Exhibit 10-1 shows the Excel worksheet that includes all five criteria using the real estate example that was discussed earlier in the chapter. Note that the values in Exhibit 10-1 are truncated by 100 000 to make the exhibit fit into one screen.

The upper-right-hand side of the worksheet shows the payoff table for this problem. Next to the payoff table, on the left side, are the calculations and the results of the maximax and the maximin approaches. The equations associated with both approaches are given at the bottom of Exhibit 10-1. In cells E4 through E6, we simply record the maximum payoff for each row or decision alternative. For example, the maximum value for the residential alternative is given in cell E4 by specifying the equation = MAX(B4:D4). In cell F4, under the column heading Criterion Choice, the following IF statement is provided:

=IF(E4 = MAX(E$4 : E$6), "Select", " ")

In this IF statement, we simply state that if E4 is the maximum value of the cells E4, E5, and E6, then we select the residential decision alternative. However, if E4 is not the maximum value of the cells E4, E5, and E6, then we include two quotation marks to prevent the cell returning a FALSE answer. If the condition is not met, and the two quotation marks are not included at the end of the IF statement, then the cell would include a FALSE statement. The equation from cell E4 is copied to cells E5 and E6, and likewise the equation from cell F4 is copied to cells F5 and F6 to complete the maximax rule for the Commercial #1 and Commercial #2 options. In completing the section of the worksheet in Exhibit 10-1 concerning the maximin method (cells G2:H6), in cells G4 through G6, we simply record the minimum payoff for each row or decision alternative. For example, the minimum value for the Residential alternative is given in cell G4 by specifying the equation = MIN(B4:D4). In cell H4, under the column heading Criterion Choice, the following IF statement is provided:

=IF(G4 = MAX(G$4 : G$6), "Select", " ")

We can interpret this IF statement as follows: If G4 is the maximum value of the minimum values given in cells G4, G5, and G6, then we select the residential decision alternative. In completing the maximin rule for the Commercial #1 and Commercial #2 options, we copy the equation from cell G4 to cells G5 and G6, and likewise the equation from cell H4 is copied to cells H5 and H6.

The payoff table is repeated in cells A9:D12 to simplify the formulas that will need to be prepared to demonstrate the equal likelihood and Hurwicz criteria. The equal likelihood criterion is displayed in cells E8:F12. The formulas for the equal likelihood criterion in cells E10:E12 and F10:F12 are shown at the bottom of Exhibit 10-1. Note that using the equal likelihood criterion we choose the residential alternative. The Hurwicz criterion is displayed in cells G8:H13 in Exhibit 10-1. The formulas for the Hurwicz criterion in cells G10:G12 and H10:H12 are shown at the bottom of Exhibit 10-1. In using the Hurwicz criterion, we need to utilize the coefficient of optimism (α), which is displayed in cell H13. In cell G10 we utilize the following equation:

=$H$13*MAX(B10 : D10) + (1 − $H$13)*MIN(B10 : D10)

EXHIBIT 10-1 Using Excel to Make Decisions Under Complete Uncertainty

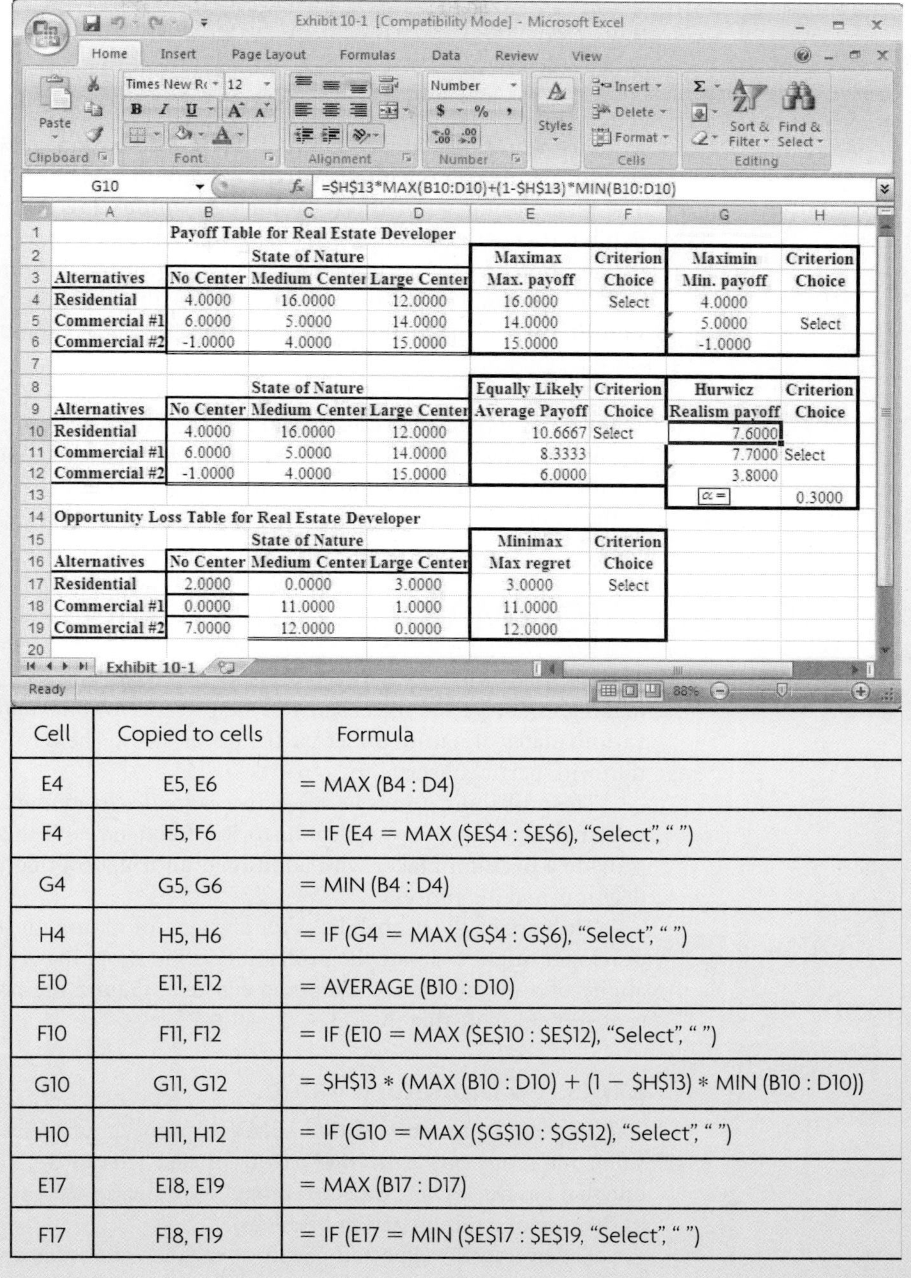

G10 =$H$13*MAX(B10:D10)+(1-$H$13)*MIN(B10:D10)

Payoff Table for Real Estate Developer

	State of Nature			Maximax	Criterion	Maximin	Criterion
Alternatives	No Center	Medium Center	Large Center	Max. payoff	Choice	Min. payoff	Choice
Residential	4.0000	16.0000	12.0000	16.0000	Select	4.0000	
Commercial #1	6.0000	5.0000	14.0000	14.0000		5.0000	Select
Commercial #2	-1.0000	4.0000	15.0000	15.0000		-1.0000	

	State of Nature			Equally Likely	Criterion	Hurwicz	Criterion
Alternatives	No Center	Medium Center	Large Center	Average Payoff	Choice	Realism payoff	Choice
Residential	4.0000	16.0000	12.0000	10.6667	Select	7.6000	
Commercial #1	6.0000	5.0000	14.0000	8.3333		7.7000	Select
Commercial #2	-1.0000	4.0000	15.0000	6.0000		3.8000	
						α =	0.3000

Opportunity Loss Table for Real Estate Developer

	State of Nature			Minimax	Criterion
Alternatives	No Center	Medium Center	Large Center	Max regret	Choice
Residential	2.0000	0.0000	3.0000	3.0000	Select
Commercial #1	0.0000	11.0000	1.0000	11.0000	
Commercial #2	7.0000	12.0000	0.0000	12.0000	

Cell	Copied to cells	Formula
E4	E5, E6	= MAX (B4 : D4)
F4	F5, F6	= IF (E4 = MAX ($E$4 : $E$6), "Select", " ")
G4	G5, G6	= MIN (B4 : D4)
H4	H5, H6	= IF (G4 = MAX (G$4 : G$6), "Select", " ")
E10	E11, E12	= AVERAGE (B10 : D10)
F10	F11, F12	= IF (E10 = MAX ($E$10 : $E$12), "Select", " ")
G10	G11, G12	= $H$13 * (MAX (B10 : D10) + (1 − $H$13) * MIN (B10 : D10))
H10	H11, H12	= IF (G10 = MAX ($G$10 : $G$12), "Select", " ")
E17	E18, E19	= MAX (B17 : D17)
F17	F18, F19	= IF (E17 = MIN ($E$17 : $E$19, "Select", " ")

In interpreting this equation, we multiply the coefficient of optimism specified in cell H13 by the maximum payoff for the residential row (B10:D10) and add to it

[1 − α or (H13)] multiplied by the minimum payoff for the residential row (B10 : D10).

At the bottom of Exhibit 10-1, we show how to use the minimax regret criterion with Excel. In using the minimax regret criterion, first we need to develop the opportunity loss table from the payoff table. In determining the opportunity loss table given in cells B17:D19 in Exhibit 10-1, we subtract each cell value from the maximum value in given column. For example, in determining the opportunity loss for the residential alternative and no centre, we use the following formula:

=MAX($B$10 : $B$12) − B10

In other words, we simply subtract the payoff associated with this decision alternative/state-of-nature combination from the maximum payoff for that column, or state of nature. The formulas for selected cells in the opportunity loss matrix are given at the bottom of Exhibit 10-1. After determining the opportunity loss matrix, we proceed to calculate the maximum regret (opportunity loss) values by simply choosing the maximum opportunity loss in each row. For instance, in determining the maximum regret for the residential decision alternative, the following Excel formula in cell E17 is used:

=MAX(B17 : D17)

This formula is copied to cells E18 and E19. We simply select the minimum of the maximum regrets, as shown in the formulas for cells F17:F19 at the bottom of Exhibit 10-1. Most of the formulas used to develop the worksheet shown in Exhibit 10-1 are given at the bottom of the exhibit.

10.5 DECISION MAKING UNDER RISK

The essential difference between decision making under complete uncertainty and decision making under partial uncertainty is the presence of *probabilities* for the occurrence of the various states of nature under partial uncertainty. The term *risk* is often used in conjunction with partial uncertainty.

The probabilities may be subjective estimates from managers or from experts in a particular field, or they may reflect historical frequencies. If they are reasonably correct, they provide a decision maker with additional information that can dramatically improve the decision-making process.

The sum of the probabilities for all states of nature must be 1.00. Thus, the real estate developer might estimate the probability of no shopping centre being built at .2, the probability of a medium-sized shopping centre at .5, and the probability of a large shopping centre at .3. (Note that .2 + .5 + .3 = 1.0.)

Expected Monetary Value

The **expected monetary value (EMV)** approach provides the decision maker with a value that represents an *average* payoff for each alternative. The best alternative is, then, the one that has the highest expected monetary value (or the smallest expected monetary value in the case of a minimization problem).

The average or expected payoff of each alternative is a weighted average: the state of nature probabilities are used to weight the respective payoffs. Thus, the expected monetary value for each alternative is

$$\text{EMV}_i = \sum_{j=1}^{k} P_j V_{ij} \quad (10\text{-}2)$$

TABLE 10-12 Real Estate Payoff Table with Probabilities

		State of Nature			
Probabilities	.2	.5	.3		
Alternative	**No centre**	**Medium centre**	**Large centre**	**Expected payoff**	
Residential	\$400 000	\$1 600 000	\$1 200 000	\$1 240 000	← Maximum
Commercial #1	\$600 000	\$500 000	\$1 400 000	790 000	
Commercial #2	−\$100 000	\$400 000	\$1 500 000	630 000	

where

$$\text{EMV}_i = \text{the expected monetary value for the } i^{\text{th}} \text{ alternative}$$
$$P_j = \text{the probability of the } j^{\text{th}} \text{ state of nature}$$
$$V_{ij} = \text{the estimated payoff for alternative } i \text{ under state of nature } j$$

For example, using the figures in Table 10-12, we can compute the expected payoffs for the real estate developer's alternatives. The expected monetary value of the residential alternative is

$$\text{EMV}_R = .2(\$400\,000) + .5(\$1\,600\,000) + .3(\$1\,200\,000) = \$1\,240\,000$$

Similarly, the expected monetary values of the other alternatives are

$$\text{EMV}_{C1} = .2(\$600\,000) \quad + .5(\$500\,000) + .3(\$1\,400\,000) = \$790\,000$$
$$\text{EMV}_{C1} = .2(-\$100\,000) + .5(\$400\,000) + .3(\$1\,500\,000) = \$630\,000$$

Because the residential alternative has the largest expected monetary value, it would be selected using this criterion.

Note that it does *not* necessarily follow that the developer will actually realize a payoff equal to the expected monetary value of a chosen alternative. For example, note that the possible payoffs for the residential proposal are \$400 000, \$1 600 000, and \$1 200 000, whereas the expected payoff is \$1 240 000, which is not equal to any of the payoffs. Similarly, the expected payoffs for either of the other alternatives do not equal any of the payoffs in those rows. What, then, is the interpretation of the expected payoff? It is simply a long-run average amount; the approximate average amount one could reasonably anticipate for a large number of identical situations.

In contrast to the strategies outlined for decision making under complete uncertainty, which are realistically best used for one-time major decisions, the expected value approach is more suited to an ongoing decision strategy. Over the long run, taking probabilities into account will yield the highest payoff, even though in the short run actual payoffs will tend to be higher or lower than the expected amounts. Conversely, over the long run, a strategy that failed to take probabilities into account would tend to yield lower payoffs than one that does take the probabilities into account.

Expected Opportunity Loss

An alternate method for incorporating probabilities into the decision-making process is to use **expected opportunity loss (EOL).** The approach is nearly identical to the EMV approach, except that a table of opportunity losses is used rather than a table of payoffs.

Hence, the opportunity losses for each alternative are weighted by the probabilities of their respective states of nature to compute a long-run average opportunity loss, and the alternative with the *smallest* expected loss is selected as the best choice.

For the real estate problem, the expected opportunity losses based on the values given in Table 10-8 can be calculated as follows:

$$\text{EOL}_R = .2(\$200\,000) + .5(0) + .3(\$300\,000) = \$130\,000 \leftarrow \text{Minimum}$$
$$\text{EOL}_{C1} = .2(0) + .5(\$1\,100\,000) + .3(\$100\,000) = \$580\,000$$
$$\text{EOL}_{C1} = .2(\$700\,000) + .5(\$1\,200\,000) + .3(0) = \$740\,000$$

Note that the EOL approach resulted in the same alternative as the EMV approach. This is more than coincidence; the two methods will always result in the same choice because they are equivalent ways of combining the values; maximizing the payoffs is equivalent to minimizing the opportunity losses.

Expected Value of Perfect Information

It can sometimes be useful for a decision maker to determine the potential benefit of knowing for certain which state of nature is going to prevail. For instance, a decision maker might have the option of delaying a decision until it is evident which state of nature is going to materialize. The obvious benefit of waiting would be to move the decision into the realm of certainty, thereby allowing the decision maker to obtain the maximum possible payoff. Such delays typically will involve a cost of some sort (e.g., higher prices, the cost of an option, storage costs). Hence, the question is whether the cost of waiting outweighs the potential benefits that could be realized by waiting. Or the decision maker might wonder if it would be worth the cost to refine or eliminate the probabilities of the states of nature (e.g., using marketing research or a better forecasting technique). Although such techniques may not completely eliminate uncertainty, the decision maker often can benefit from knowledge of the upper limit of the potential gain that perfect information would permit.

The **expected value of perfect information** (**EVPI**) is a measure of the difference between the certain payoff that could be realized under a condition of certainty and the expected payoff under a condition involving risk.

Consider the payoff that the real estate developer could expect under certainty. If the developer knew that no centre would be built, the Commercial #1 proposal would be chosen with a payoff of \$600 000; if the developer knew a medium-sized shopping centre would be built, the residential alternative would be chosen for a payoff of \$1 600 000; and if the developer knew that a large centre would be built, the Commercial #2 proposal would be chosen for a payoff of \$1 500 000. Hence, if it were possible to remove the uncertainty surrounding the states of nature, the decision maker could capitalize on the knowledge. Obviously, before investing time or money in eliminating the possibilities, it is impossible for the decision maker to say which state of nature will turn out to be the one that will occur. However, what can be said is that the probability that perfect information will indicate that no centre will be built is .2, that the probability that perfect information will indicate a medium centre will be built is .5, and the probability of perfect information indicating a large centre is .3. Thus, these probabilities, which are the original state-of-nature probabilities, can be used to weight the best payoffs, one of which will occur under certainty. This is called the **expected payoff under certainty** (**EPC**), and is computed in the following way for the real estate problem:

$$\text{EPC} = .2(\$600\,000) + .5(\$1\,600\,000) + .3(\$1\,500\,000) = \$1\,370\,000$$

The difference between this figure and the expected payoff under risk (i.e., the EMV) is the expected value of perfect information. Thus:

$$\text{EVPI} = \text{EPC} - \text{EMV} \tag{10-3}$$

For the real estate problem, with EPC = \$1 370 000 and EMV = \$1 240 000, we find

$$\text{EVPI} = \$1\ 370\ 000 - \$1\ 240\ 000 = \$130\ 000$$

The EVPI represents an *upper bound* on the amount of money the real estate developer would be justified in spending to obtain perfect information. Thus, the real estate developer would be justified in spending up to \$130 000 to find out for certain which state of nature will prevail. Of course, it is not always possible to completely remove uncertainty. In such cases, the decision maker must weigh the cost to reduce the uncertainty (i.e., obtain better estimates of the probabilities) against the expected benefits that would yield.

Note that the EVPI is exactly equal to the previously computed EOL. In fact, these two quantities will always be equal. The EOL indicates the expected *opportunity loss* due to imperfect information, which is another way of saying the expected *payoff* that could be achieved by having perfect information. Hence, there are two equivalent ways to determine the expected value of perfect information: subtract the EMV from the expected payoff under certainty or compute the EOL.

The expected value (EMV) approach is particularly useful for decision making when a number of similar decisions must be made; it is a "long-run" approach. For one-shot decisions, where none of the alternatives have very high or very low (extreme) payoffs, the EMV approach may still be preferred to other methods. However, when there are extreme payoffs and/or the decision maker does not have confidence in probabilities, then other methods (perhaps maximax or maximin) may be preferable. In addition, nonmonetary factors, although not included in a payoff table, may be of considerable importance. Unfortunately, there is no convenient way to include them in an expected value analysis.

Using Excel for Decision Making Under Risk

Excel can easily be utilized to calculate expected monetary values (EMV), expected opportunity losses (EOL), and the expected value of perfect information (EVPI). Exhibit 10-2 demonstrates how a worksheet is used to calculate EMVs, EOLs, and EVPI.

First we copy the payoff table from Exhibit 10-1 to Exhibit 10-2. EMV values are computed on the right-hand side of the payoff table in cells E4 through E6. For example, the expected monetary value for the residential alternative in cell E4 is calculated by using the following formula: = SUMPRODUCT(B4:D4, $B$7:$D$7). In this formula, first we multiply cells B4:D4 (residential net returns for each state of nature) by the respective cells B7:D7 (probabilities of each state-of-nature occurrence) and then sum the products. We repeat this calculation for the Commercial #1 and Commercial #2 options in cells E5 and E6 respectively. In cells F4 through F6, we simply have Excel specify the largest of the values in cells E4, E5, and E6. The following formula is used in cell F4 to determine if the largest value among cells E4, E5, and E6 is in cell E4:

=IF(E4 = MAX($E$4 : $E$6), "Select", " ")

Since the largest EMV is for the residential option, cell F4 indicates "Select".

EXHIBIT 10-2 Using Excel to Make Decisions Under Risk

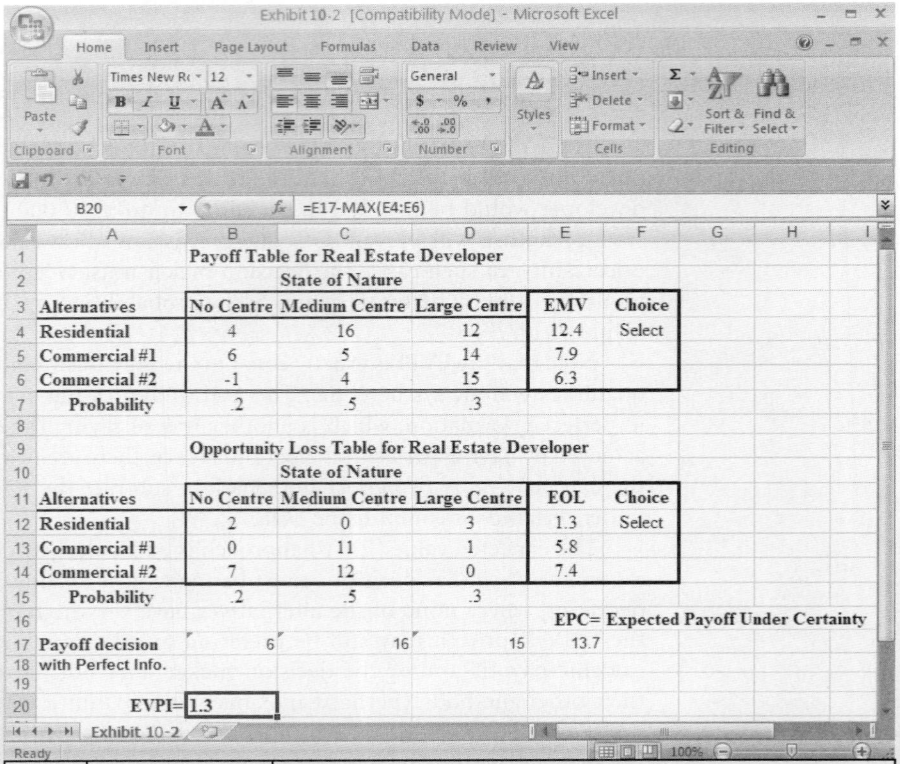

Exhibit 10-2 [Compatibility Mode] - Microsoft Excel

B20 =E17-MAX(E4:E6)

Payoff Table for Real Estate Developer

	State of Nature				
Alternatives	**No Centre**	**Medium Centre**	**Large Centre**	**EMV**	**Choice**
Residential	4	16	12	12.4	Select
Commercial #1	6	5	14	7.9	
Commercial #2	-1	4	15	6.3	
Probability	.2	.5	.3		

Opportunity Loss Table for Real Estate Developer

	State of Nature				
Alternatives	**No Centre**	**Medium Centre**	**Large Centre**	**EOL**	**Choice**
Residential	2	0	3	1.3	Select
Commercial #1	0	11	1	5.8	
Commercial #2	7	12	0	7.4	
Probability	.2	.5	.3		

EPC= Expected Payoff Under Certainty

Payoff decision with Perfect Info.	6	16	15	13.7

EVPI= 1.3

Cells	Copied to cells	Formula
E4	E5 : E6	= SUMPRODUCT (B4 : D4, $B$7 : $D$7)
F4	F5 : F6	= IF (E4 = MAX ($E$4 : $E$6), "Select", " ")
B12	B13 : B14	= MAX ($B$4 : $B$6) − B4
C12	C13 : C14	= MAX ($C$4 : $C$6) − C4
D12	D13 : D4	= MAX ($D$4 : $D$6) − D4
E12	E13 : E14	= SUMPRODUCT (B12 : D12, $B$7 : $D$7)
F12	F13 : F14	= IF (E12 = MIN ($E$12 : $E$14), "Select", " ")
E17		= SUMPRODUCT (B7 : D7, B17 : D17)
B20		= E17 − MAX (E4 : E6)

The bottom portion of Exhibit 10-2 contains the opportunity loss matrix used in conjunction with the minimax regret criterion. As you recall, we displayed the opportunity loss table and the minimax regret criterion in Exhibit 10-1. The reason for copying the opportunity loss table from Exhibit 10-1 to Exhibit 10-2 is that in Exhibit 10-2 we demonstrate the calculation of the expected opportunity loss (EOL) values for each decision alternative. As you recall, the calculation of the EOL values requires the use of the opportunity loss table. The expected opportunity loss value for the residential alternative in cell E12 is calculated by using the following formula:

=SUMPRODUCT(B12 : D12, $B$7 : $D$7)

In this formula, first we multiply cells B12:D12 (opportunity loss for each state of nature for the residential alternative) by the respective cells B7:D7 (probabilities of each state-of-nature occurrence), and then sum the products. We repeat this calculation for the Commercial #1 and Commercial #2 options in cells E13 and E14 respectively. In cells F12:F14, we simply have Excel specify the smallest of the values in cells E12, E13, and E14. For instance, for cell F12, we use the following formula:

=IF(E12 = MIN($E$12 : $E$14), "Select", " ")

Since the smallest EOL is for the residential option, cell F12 (residential) indicates "Select".

After the computation of the EMV and EOL values in Exhibit 10-2, we compute the expected value of perfect information (EVPI). This calculation is shown at the bottom of Exhibit 10-2. First we compute the expected payoff under certainty (EPC) by using the following formula: =SUMPRODUCT(B7:D7, B17:D17). In this formula, we calculate the sum of the cross products of the probabilities in each state of nature (B7:D7) with the maximum payoff for each state of nature (B17:D17). Finally we compute EVPI in cell B20 using the following formula: =E17 − MAX(E4:E6). As you recall from our earlier discussion, the EVPI represents the difference between the EPC value in cell E17 and the maximum of the EMV values in cells E4, E5, and E6. Most of the formulas used to develop the worksheet shown in Exhibit 10-2 are stated at the bottom of the exhibit.

10.6 DECISION TREES

Decision trees sometimes are used by decision makers to obtain a visual portrayal of decision alternatives and their possible consequences. The term gets its name from the treelike appearance of the diagram (see Figure 10-1).

A tree is composed of squares, circles, and lines. The squares indicate decision points or decision nodes while the circles represent chance events or chance nodes. The lines or "branches" that emanate from a square represent alternatives, while the branches that emanate from a circle represent states of nature. The tree is read from right to left.

Decision trees are fairly simple to construct. The decision tree for the real estate developer's problem is shown in Figure 10-2. The dollar amounts alongside each chance node (circle) indicate the expected payoff of the alternative that leads into that particular chance node. The expected payoffs are computed in the same manner as previously described, and, as before, the decision maker will select the alternative with the largest expected payoff if maximizing expected payoff is the decision criterion (or the smallest expected monetary value in the case of a minimization problem).

It should be noted that although decision trees represent an alternative approach to payoff tables, they are not commonly used for problems that involve a single decision. Rather, their greatest benefit lies in portraying **sequential decisions** (i.e., a series of chronological decisions). In the case of a single decision, constructing a tree can be

FIGURE 10-1 Decision Tree Format

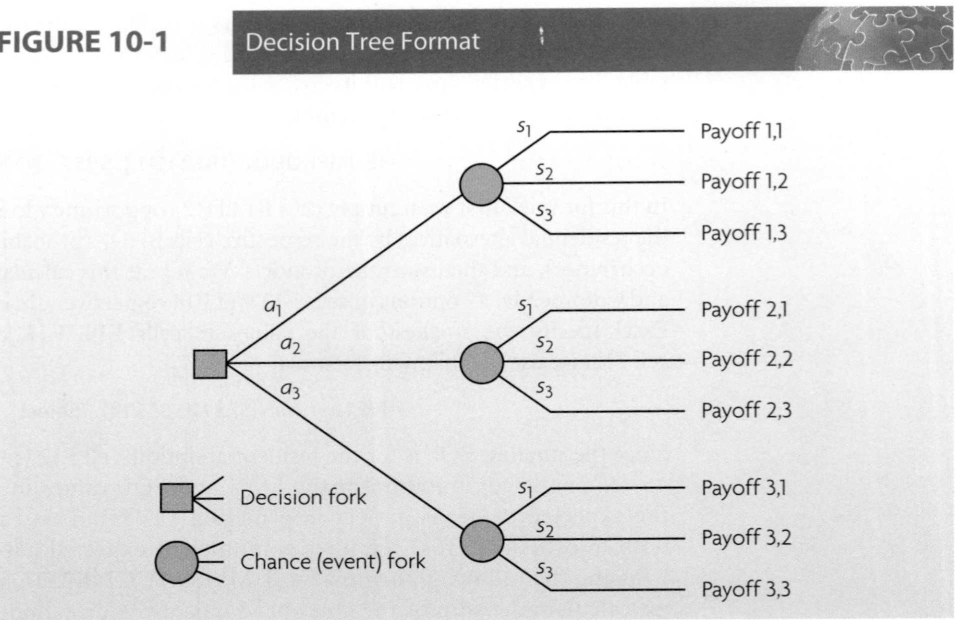

FIGURE 10-2 Decision Tree for Real Estate Developer Problem

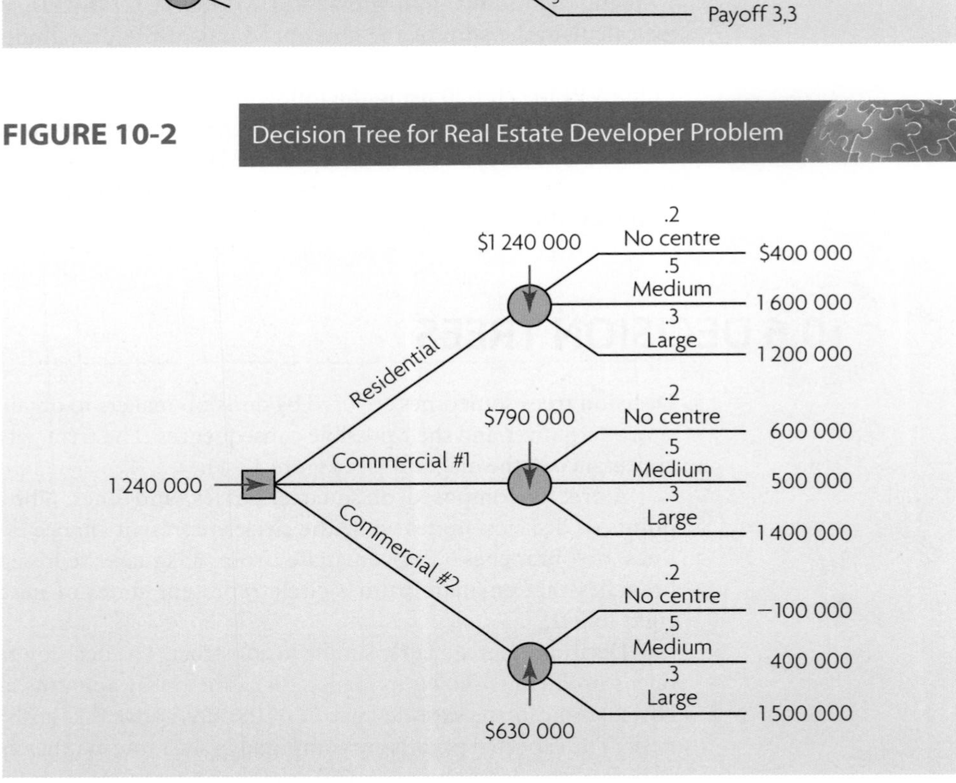

cumbersome and time-consuming. For example, imagine the decision tree that would be necessary to portray a decision with 7 alternatives and 10 states of nature; there would be 70 payoffs, and, hence, 70 branch-ends on the right side of the tree. Conversely, situations that involve sequential decisions are difficult to represent in payoff tables.

As an example of a sequential decision, suppose that the real estate developer has several options that might be considered after the initial decision. For instance, regardless of which of the three alternatives he chooses, the worst payoff will result if no shopping centre is built. Hence, it might be prudent for the developer to plan for that contingency. Thus, the developer might consider certain options. Suppose the developer states that he would consider these additional alternatives in the event that no centre is built:

1. Do nothing.
2. Develop a small shopping centre.
3. Develop a park.

The tree diagram of Figure 10-2 has been modified to include these additional options, along with their estimated payoffs as supplied by the real estate developer, and it is shown in Figure 10-3. Note that the payoffs for Do nothing are the same as in the original tree for the event no centre is built.

FIGURE 10-3 Real Estate Problem with a Second Possible Decision

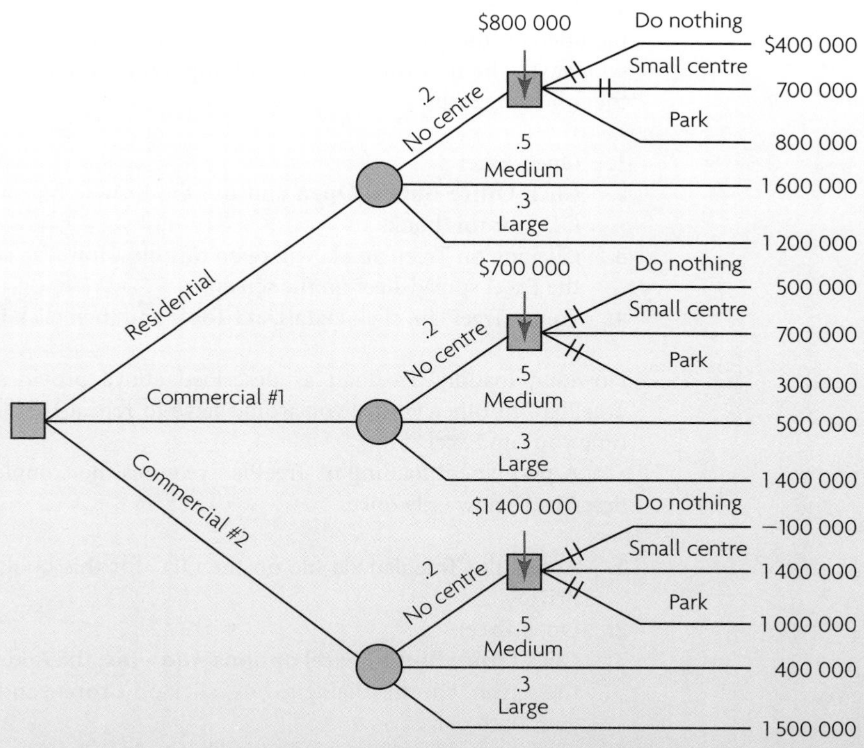

Note: Double line "II" for the last decision indicates the choices that are eliminated (pruned).

To analyze this modified tree (i.e., to make a choice among the alternatives residential, Commercial #1, and Commercial #2), the branches for each possible second decision must be reduced in each instance to a single branch. This is easily accomplished by recognizing that at each of those points, a rational decision maker would simply choose the alternative with the largest payoff. Hence, if residential were chosen initially and no centre was built, a park would be selected because it would have the largest payoff. Similarly, if Commercial #1 was chosen and no centre was built, the small centre option would be chosen because it offers the largest payoff, and if Commercial #2 were initially chosen and no centre was built, the developer would choose the option of building a small centre because its payoff is greater than either Do nothing or Park. Thus, in each case, the tree is pruned by cutting the undesirable options and keeping the one best option. This also is illustrated in Figure 10-3. Note that the payoff for the best option for each alternative, then, becomes the payoff for each no centre branch. The tree would then be analyzed as previously.

Using TreePlan to Develop Decision Trees with Excel

We can use an Excel add-in program called TreePlan to develop and solve decision tree problems. Even though we can write the formulas to develop decision trees without TreePlan, it is a very complicated and cumbersome process. TreePlan provides us with a template that significantly simplifies the process of developing decision trees using Excel since it operates in an Excel environment. The first step in using TreePlan is to load TreePlan. The TreePlan program consists of an Excel file, TreePlan.xla. This file is included on the OLC for this textbook. Loading TreePlan can be accomplished in one of two ways. The first way, which is a temporary manual loading, can be accomplished by the following steps:

1. Open Excel
2. Click **Office Button|Open** and use the Browse button to locate TreePlan.xla on the OLC for this book.
3. Clicking on Treeplan.xla will open this file. However, opening this file will not change the Excel spreadsheet on the screen.
4. To use TreePlan, click **Data|Data Tools** and then click **Decision Tree.**

However, loading TreePlan as described above provides only a temporary access to TreePlan. In other words, you would have to repeat the procedure described above each time you run Excel.

A permanent loading of TreePlan requires the completion of the loading procedure described below only once.

1. Access the Treeplan.xla file on the OLC for this book and copy this file to the hard drive.
2. Open Excel.
3. Click **Office Button|Excel options|Add - Ins;** the Add-in dialogue box will appear on the screen. On this dialogue box, click on B**rowse** and locate the TreePlan.xla file on your hard drive.
4. Click on the TreePlan.xla file. Scroll down the options on the Add-in dialogue box, and toward the end of the Add-in options you will see TreePlan. Make sure the box next to

EXHIBIT 10-3 Initial TreePlan Dialogue Box

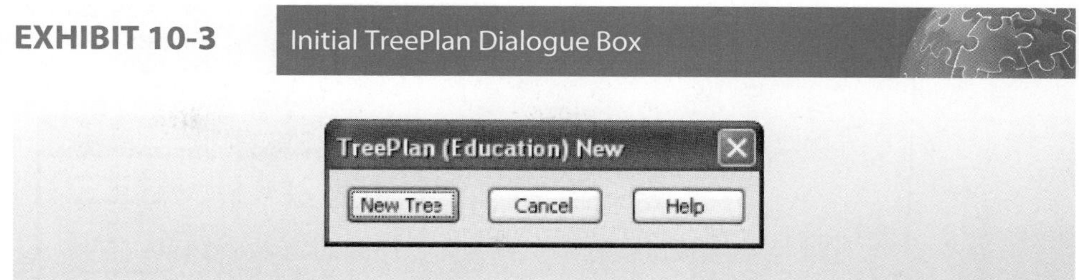

TreePlan is checked. If you want to remove Treeplan, simply click **Office Button|Excel Options|Add - Ins** and uncheck the Treeplan box.

5. To use TreePlan, click **Data|Data Tools** and then **Decision Tree.**

Once we load TreePlan, we can utilize it to prepare and solve decision tree problems. Let us consider the real estate example that we have used earlier in the chapter. The decision tree for this real estate developer example is given in Figure 10-2. Now we will develop and solve the same decision tree problem using TreePlan.

We begin utilizing TreePlan by choosing **Data|Data Tools|Decision Tree,** which brings up the initial TreePlan dialogue box shown in Exhibit 10-3. On this initial TreePlan dialogue value box, if we click on "New Tree," TreePlan will display the initial decision tree shown in Exhibit 10-4.

EXHIBIT 10-4 Decision Tree Initially Developed by TreePlan

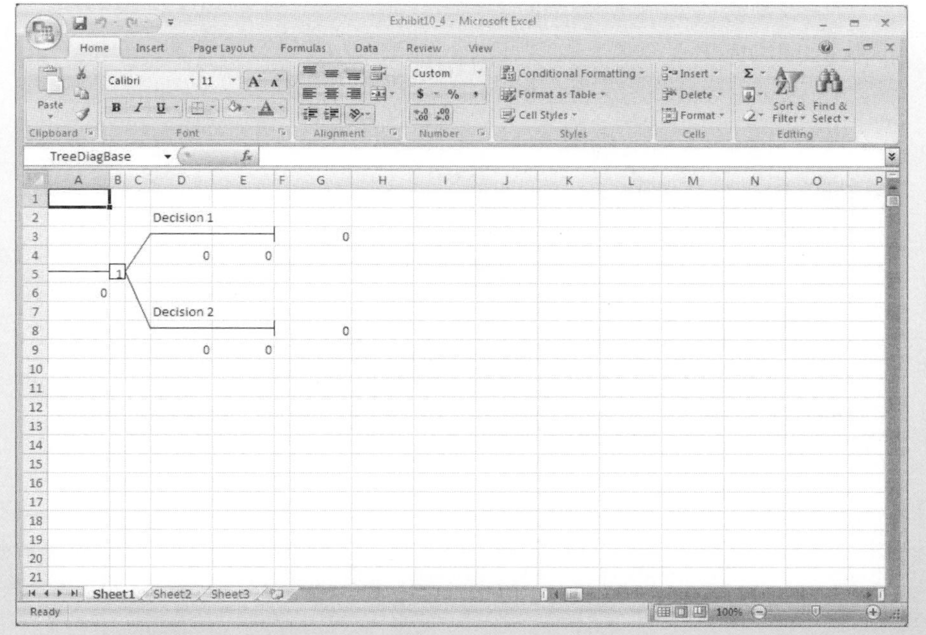

EXHIBIT 10-5 TreePlan Dialogue Box to Add Branches, Decision Nodes, or Events

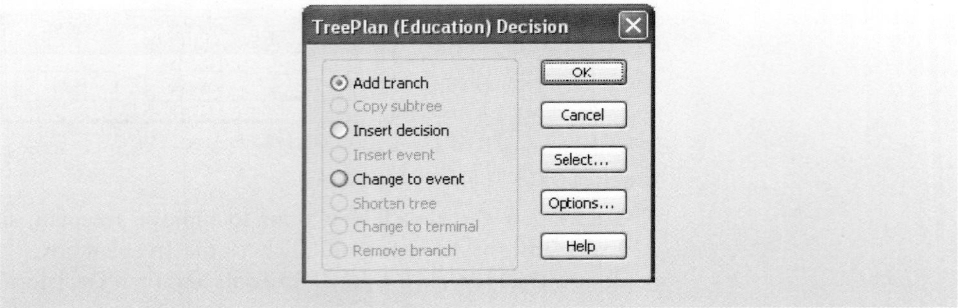

TreePlan (Education) Decision

- Add branch
- Copy subtree
- Insert decision
- Insert event
- Change to event
- Shorten tree
- Change to terminal
- Remove branch

OK | Cancel | Select... | Options... | Help

If we put the cursor on the initial decision node and click on **Data|Data Tools| Decision Tree**, TreePlan will bring up the dialogue box shown in Exhibit 10-5. In the real estate problem, since there are three choices (Residential, Commercial #1, Commercial #2), a new branch needs to be added. After clicking on the Add branch option and clicking OK, the decision tree will be modified from the initial tree with two branches to the modified tree with three branches, as shown in Exhibit 10-6.

EXHIBIT 10-6 Modified Decision Tree with Three Branches

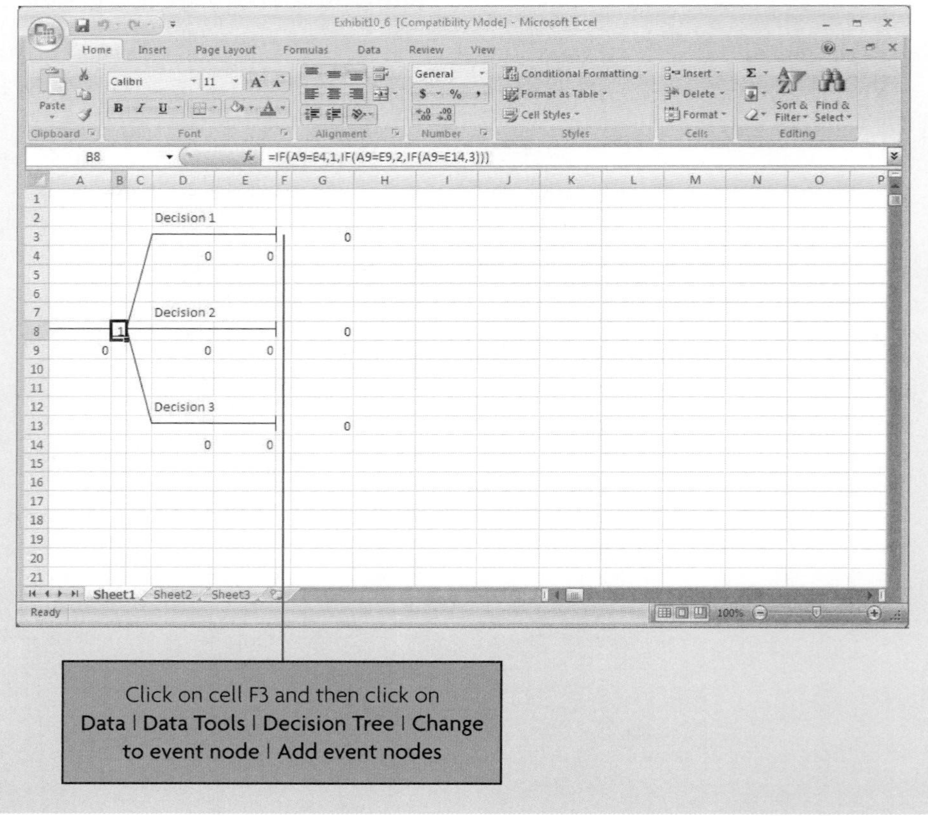

EXHIBIT 10-7 TreePlan Dialogue Box to Add or Change Decision Nodes for Events

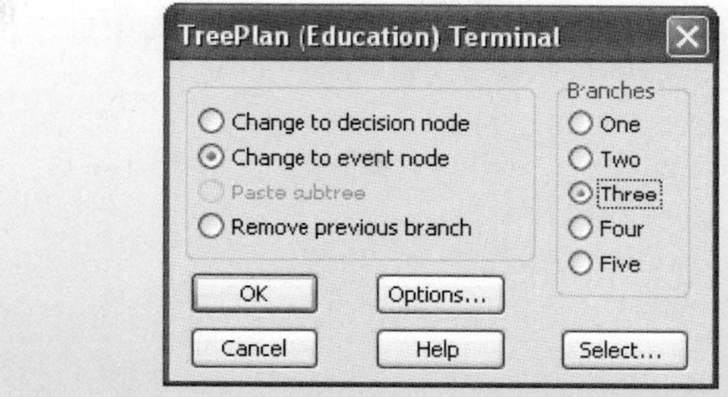

After obtaining the tree shown in Exhibit 10-6, we put the cursor at the end of the first branch on cell F3 and click on **Data|Data Tools|Decision Tree,** and TreePlan will bring up the dialogue box shown in Exhibit 10-7. At this stage, we can choose to add another decision node or to add an event (chance) node. In the real estate problem, at this stage the tree contains event nodes; therefore, we click on "Change to event node." On the right side of Exhibit 10-7, the dialogue box gives us the option to choose the number of branches emanating from the chance node. Since there are three chance events (no centre, medium, and large), click on "Three branches" and click OK. This will result in the partially completed decision tree shown in Exhibit 10-8. Note that since there are three branches coming out of the event node, the default probability on each branch is .3333. Based on Figure 10-2, the other two decisions also have event nodes following them. Therefore, on Exhibit 10-8, we repeat the same process for cell F18 and cell F23 (before we add the event node on cell F18).

After adding the event nodes, we need to change the labels and probabilities on the decision tree. The labels are edited the same way we would edit any label on any spreadsheet. The final step is to add the numerical data at the end of each branch. The revised decision tree is shown in Exhibit 10-9. The numerical values (payoffs for each branch) are changed from 0 to their respective values in Figure 10-2 as shown in cells K3, K7, K11, K15, K19, K23, K27, K31, and K35. The first label in cell D6 was Decision 1. We click on cell D6 and simply relabel it as "Residential". The rest of the numerical values shown as "zeros" in column E and column I in the decision tree represent the formulas for TreePlan. Do not type in these cells. Note that the expected monetary value for the three decision alternatives (Residential, Commercial #1, Commercial #2) are calculated by TreePlan and shown in cells E8, E20, and E32. Since the residential alternative results in the largest expected monetary value, the value of 1 240 000 (12.4–EMV associated with the residential option) in cell E8 is repeated in cell A20. The following example illustrates another sequential decision-making problem.

EXAMPLE 10-1

Unicom Inc. is adding a new product. To accommodate the anticipated capacity needs of the new product, the firm believes that a new plant must be built. The firm has to make a decision to build a large plant or a small plant. In either case, demand will be either favourable or unfavourable with probabilities of 0.55 and 0.45 respectively. If a large plant is built and demand is favourable, the net present value of returns is estimated at $1 500 000. If demand is unfavourable, the net loss with the large plant is estimated to be $50 000.

EXHIBIT 10-8 Modified Decision Tree with Three Branches and the Added Event Node with Three Nodes

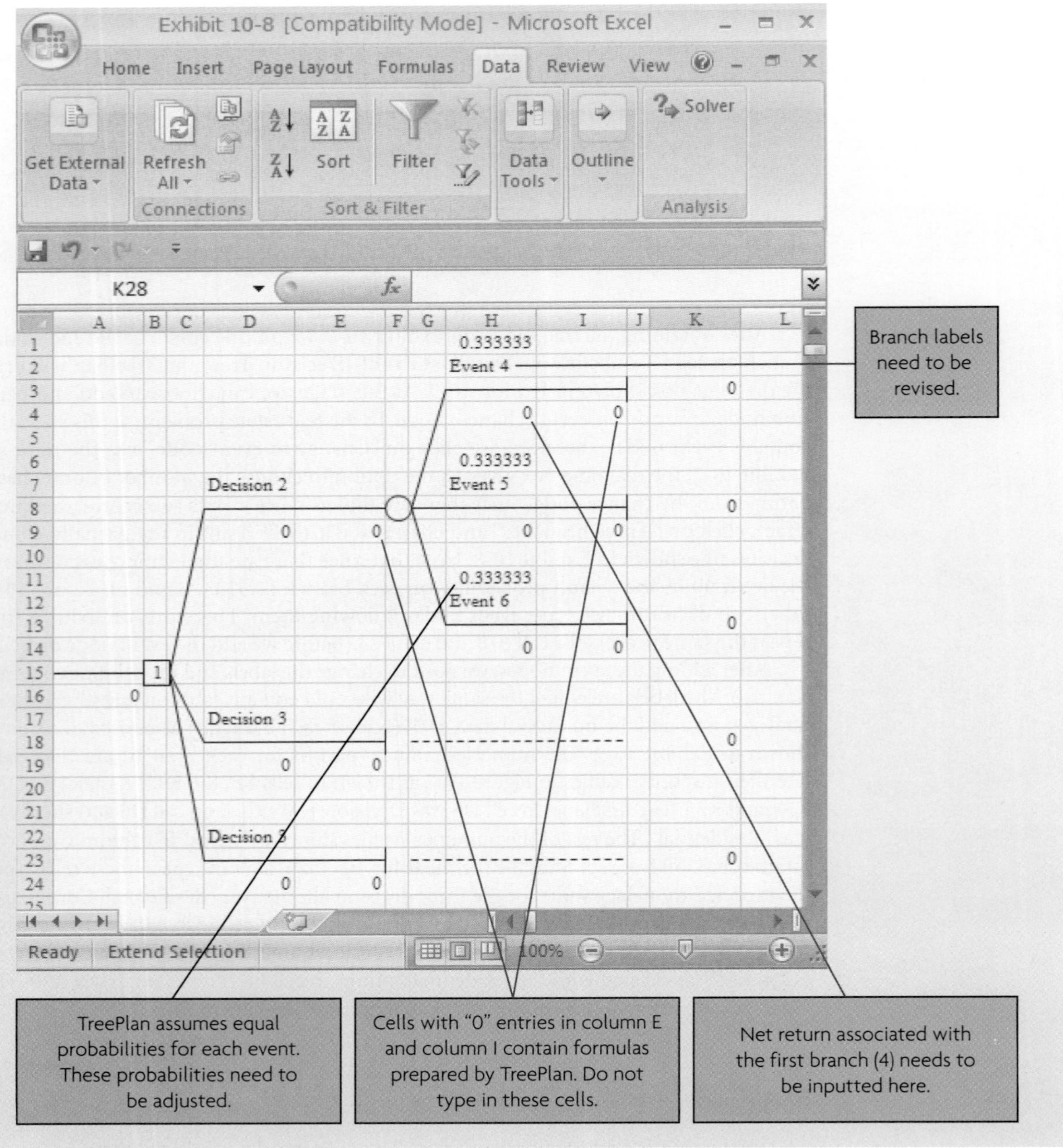

Exhibit 10-8 [Compatibility Mode] - Microsoft Excel
Branch labels need to be revised.
TreePlan assumes equal probabilities for each event. These probabilities need to be adjusted.
Cells with "0" entries in column E and column I contain formulas prepared by TreePlan. Do not type in these cells.
Net return associated with the first branch (4) needs to be inputted here.

If a small plant is built and demand is unfavourable, the net present value is $700 000. If demand proves to be favourable, the firm can either maintain the small plant or expand it. Maintaining the small plant has a net present value of $950 000. If the firm decides to expand, the firm can expect a high return or a low return. There is a 40 percent change of earning a net present

EXHIBIT 10-9 Excel Solution to the Real Estate Developer Decision Tree Problem

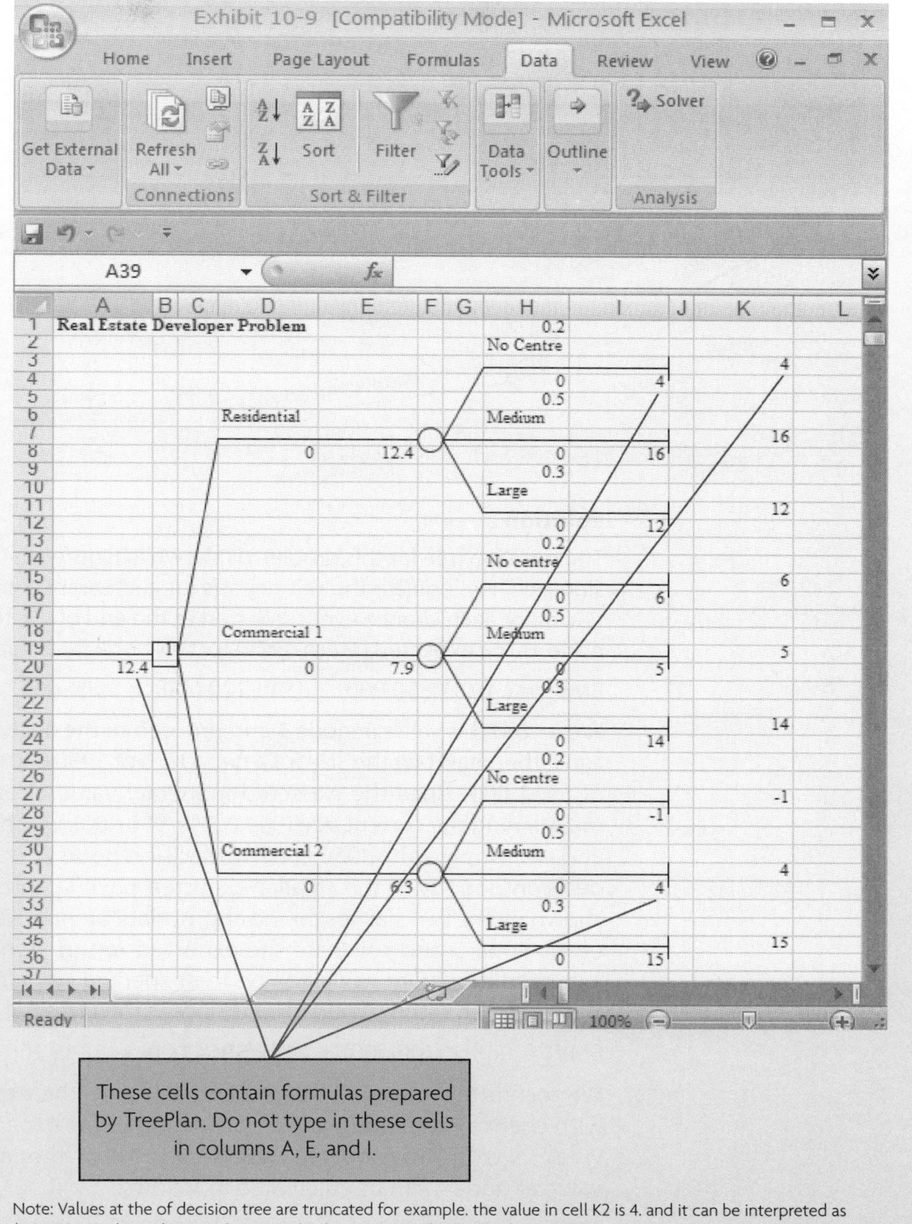

Note: Values at the of decision tree are truncated for example. the value in cell K2 is 4. and it can be interpreted as \$400 000. Each number in column I and column K are multiplied by \$100 000.

value of \$1 330 000 (high return) and a 60 percent chance of earning \$720 000 (low return).

a. Draw a decision tree for this problem
b. Calculate all of the necessary expected values and determine the best course of action for management.

FIGURE 10-4 Sequential Decision Tree for Unicom Inc. (Example 10-1, part a)

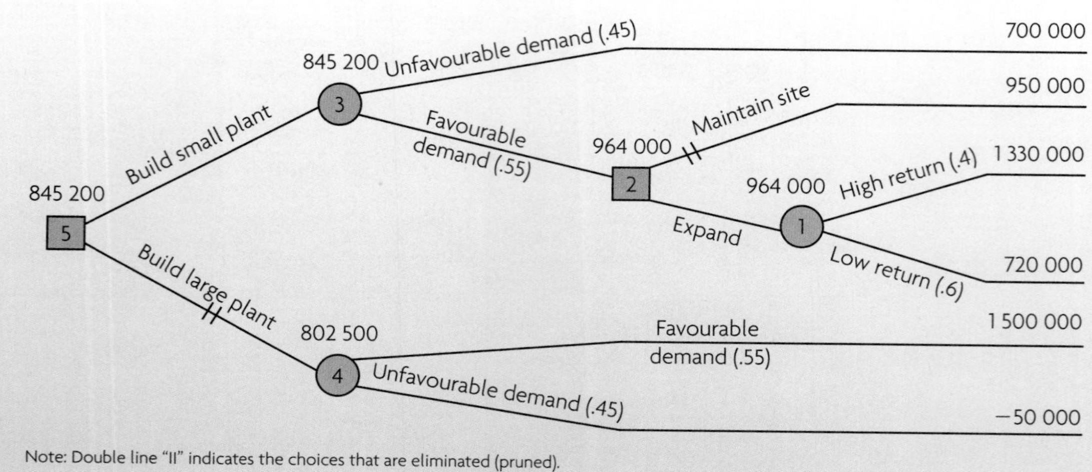

Note: Double line "II" indicates the choices that are eliminated (pruned).

Solution

The decision tree for this problem is shown in Figure 10-4. After setting up the decision tree, we indicate the net payoffs for each branch and calculate the expected return for each chance event. We start at the end of the tree with the chance event node 1. The expected return (EMV) for this node is calculated as follows:

$EMV_1 = (.4)(\$1\,330\,000) + (.6)(\$720\,000) = \$964\,000$

We record this value at node 1 and proceed to the decision node 2. At node 2, we can either maintain the size for a net return of $950 000 or expand for a net return of $964 000. Since the expected monetary value of expanding is greater than maintaining the current size (964 000 > 950 000), we choose to expand the plant and we simply write "964 000" on decision node 2. The branch at each ending decision node with the smaller expected payoff can be "cut" or eliminated, as shown by the two slashes on the appropriate branch. Next we proceed to chance event node 3 and calculate the expected return associated with node 3. This expected monetary value will be the expected value of building a small plant. The expected return (EMV) for this node is calculated as follows:

$EMV_3 = (.45)(\$700\,000) + (.55)(\$964\,000) = \$845\,200$

We record this value on node 3 and calculate the expected return associated with chance event node 4. The calculation of the expected value at node 4 provides us with the expected monetary value of the large plant. The expected value at node 4 can be calculated as follows:

$EMV_4 = (.55)(\$1\,500\,000) + (.45)(-\$50\,000) = \$802\,500$

We record this value on node 4 and at decision node 5, we compare the expected values of nodes 3 and 4. Since the expected value of node 3 is greater than the expected value of node 4 (845 200 > 802 500), we record "845 200" on node 5.

We can summarize the results associated with this sequential decision tree as follows: Unicom Inc. should choose to build a small plant, and if the demand is favourable, the company should choose to expand. The overall expected net return for the company is $845 200.

In the previous section we have already demonstrated in detail how we can use TreePlan to develop and solve a single decision problem. In Exhibit 10-10, we show the decision tree using TreePlan for the sequential decision tree example that we have solved above.

Even though this particular decision tree, shown in Exhibit 10-10, is a little more complicated than the decision tree we developed using TreePlan in the previous section, the decision tree displayed in Exhibit 10-10 was developed in the same way as the decision tree shown in Exhibit 10-9. Therefore, we will not spend any time explaining the development and solution of the decision tree in Exhibit 10-10.

10.7 DECISION MAKING WITH ADDITIONAL INFORMATION

Decision makers can sometimes improve decision making by bringing additional information into the process. The additional information can come from a variety of sources. For example, either a market survey might be used to acquire additional information or a forecasting technique might be employed. In certain situations, it may be possible to delay a decision; the passage of time often allows a decision maker to obtain a clearer picture of the future because it shortens the time horizon the decision maker must deal with. Whatever the source of information, the benefit is that *estimates of probabilities* of possible future events tend to become more accurate.

EXHIBIT 10-10 Excel Solution to the Unicom Inc. Sequential Decision Tree Problem

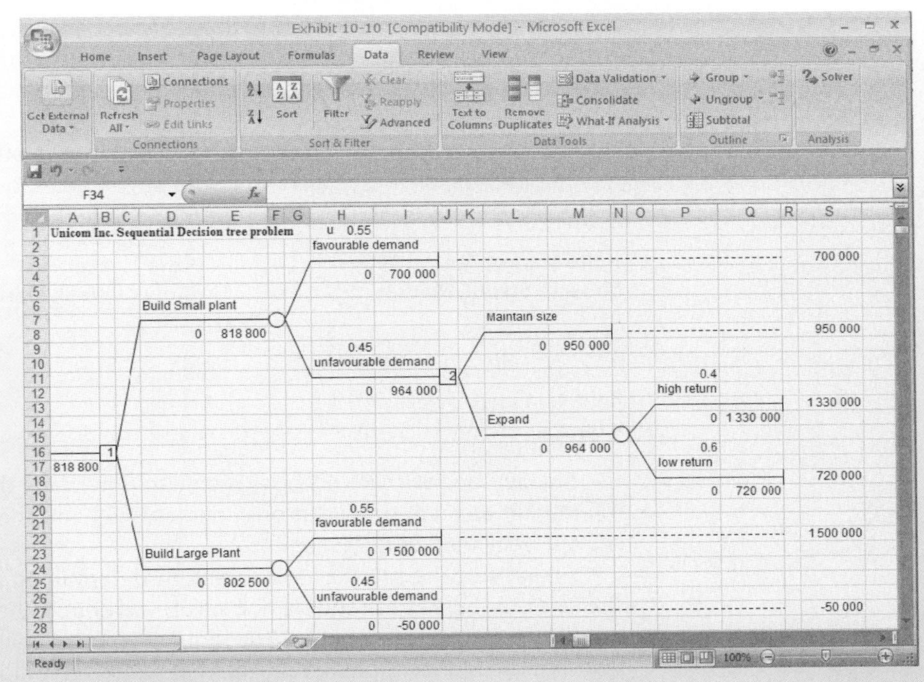

In general, obtaining additional (sample) information includes an associated cost. Consequently, a key question for a decision maker in such circumstances is whether the value of additional information is worth the cost of obtaining that information. The analysis of that type of problem is the subject of this section.

Let's take a look at an example.

EXAMPLE 10-2

Suppose an advertising manager is trying to decide which of two advertising proposals to use for an upcoming promotion. The manager has developed the following payoff table:

	Market	
	.70	.30
Alternative	**Strong**	**Weak**
Print Media	40*	20
Video media	50	10

*($000)

At this point, the manager simply could make a decision using the expected value criterion with the information given. However, suppose that the manager has the option of testing the market, and this testing will provide *additional information* in the form of revised probabilities on whether the market will be strong or weak. If the manager chooses to test the market, it will cost $1000; the manager, therefore, must decide whether the expected benefit from the test will offset the cost required to conduct the test.

If the manager conducts the test, this will undoubtedly alter the probabilities of a strong and weak market that were originally estimated. In fact, an integral part of the analysis in assessing the value of this sample information involves computing revised conditional probabilities. However, to home in on what we are trying to accomplish, let's suppose that the revised probabilities have been calculated, and consider how the decision maker could use that new information to make a decision.

The market test can show one of two things: a strong market or a weak market. Each result would pertain to the payoff table, but with different probabilities for the states of nature. Suppose these are the two possible results:

If the Market Test Shows a Strong Market

	.95	.05
	Strong	**Weak**
Print	40	20
Video	50	10

If the Market Test Shows a Weak Market

	.34	.66
	Strong	**Weak**
Print	40	20
Video	50	10

Finally, suppose the manager is able to determine that the probability that the market test will show a strong market is .59 and the probability that it will show a weak market is .41.

Analysis of the problem will result in determining an expected payoff for the two branches at the square node. This will enable the manager to select the branch (i.e., alternative) that has the higher expected payoff. Thus, if "Use market test" has the higher expected payoff, the manager would select that alternative, assuming the difference between its payoff and the payoff for "Don't use market test" is enough to cover the cost ($1000) of the market test. Of course, if "Don't use market test" has the higher expected payoff, the manager would select that alternative because it would not require the cost of the market test.

The overall problem is shown in the tree diagram of Figure 10-5.

FIGURE 10-5 Decision Tree of the Market Test Example

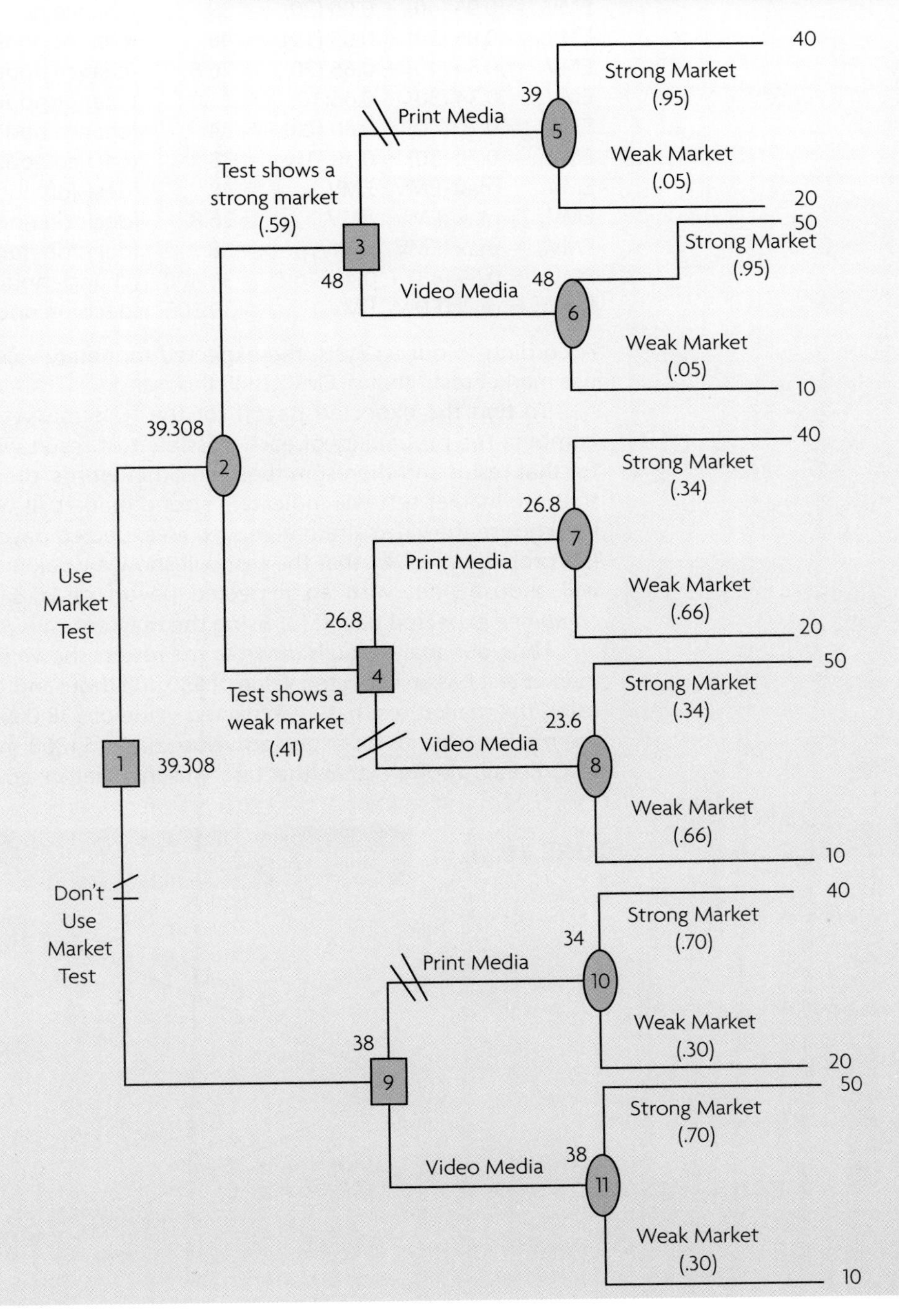

As in the previous example, to derive the course of actions we start the analysis at the end of the decision tree and work backwards from right to left until we reach decision node 1. At each chance event (node), the expected monetary value (EMV) is computed using Equation 10-2. At each decision node the alternative with the largest EMV is selected.

Therefore, starting from node 5 and working backwards, the analysis provides the following results (also shown in the decision tree in Figure 10-5):

EMV_5	$= 0.95\ (40) + 0.05\ (20)$	$= 39$	(chance node 5)
EMV_6	$= 0.95\ (50) + 0.05\ (10)$	$= 48$	(chance node 6)
EMV_7	$= 0.34\ (40) + 0.66\ (20)$	$= 26.8$	(chance node 7)
EMV_8	$= 0.34\ (50) + 0.66(10)$	$= 23.6$	(chance node 8)
EMV_{10}	$= 0.70\ (40) + 0.30\ (20)$	$= 34$	(chance node 10)
EMV_{11}	$= 0.70\ (50) + 0.30\ (10)$	$= 38$	(chance node 11)
EMV_3	$= \max\ (EMV_5, EMV_6)$	$= 48$	(decision node 3)
EMV_4	$= \max\ (EMV_7, EMV_8)$	$= 26.8$	(decision node 4)
EMV_9	$= \max\ (EMV_{10}, EMV_{11})$	$= 38$	(decision node 9)
EMV_2	$= 0.59\ (48) + 0.41\ (26.8)$	$= 39.308$	(chance node 2)
EMV_1	$= \max\ (EMV_2, EMV_9)$	$= 39.308$	(decision node 1)

According to our analysis, the expected monetary value of the branch "Don't use market test," that is, EMV_9, is 38 thousand.

To find the expected payoff for the "Use market test" branch, we must combine the probability of each possible test result with the expected payoff for that result and then sum these. In other words, there is a probability of .59 that the market test will indicate a strong market, in which case the manager will choose the *video* alternative with an expected payoff of 48. Likewise, there is a probability of .41 that the test will show a weak market, and the manager will choose *print* with an expected payoff of 26.8. Hence, the overall or *combined* expected payoff for using the market test is 39.308.

Thus, our analysis boils down to the results shown in Figure 10-6. Using the market test has an expected value of $39.308 thousand, or $39 308, whereas not using the market test has an expected value of $38 000. We can see that using the market test has an expected value that is $1308 more than not using the test. Recall, though, that the test will involve an additional cost of $1000.

FIGURE 10-6 Summary of Analysis of Market Test Example

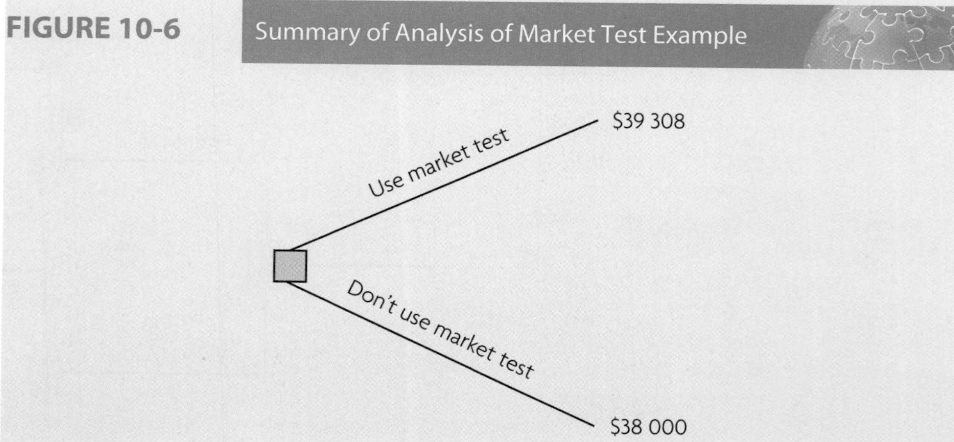

It would be prudent to spend $1000 if the additional expected payoff is $1308. Hence, the manager should use the market test because to do so would lead to an expected gain of $308:

$1308 − $1000 = $308

The decision strategy can be summarized as follows: the advertising manager should use the market test first. If the test shows a strong market, the decision should be to use print media for the upcoming promotion. However, if the test shows a weak market, the decision should be to use video media for the upcoming promotion.

The preceding analysis illustrates how a manager can assess the value of additional (sample) information when such information is available. In this instance, we found that the expected gain that would result from using the additional information outweighed the cost that would be needed to acquire that additional information.

In sum, we can compute the **expected value of sample** (additional) **information,** or **EVSI,** as

$$\text{EVSI} = \begin{matrix}\textbf{Expected value}\\ \textbf{\textit{with} sample}\\ \textbf{information}\end{matrix} - \begin{matrix}\textbf{Expected value}\\ \textbf{\textit{without} sample}\\ \textbf{informaton}\end{matrix} \qquad (10\text{-}4)$$

Then, if the *cost* of obtaining the additional information is less than this amount, it would seem reasonable to spend the money to obtain the information. But if the cost equals or exceeds the expected value of the information, it would seem reasonable to *not* spend the additional money needed to obtain the information.

To complete our discussion of decision making using additional information, we need to see how the revised probabilities are computed and how the probabilities for the test results are computed. Before doing that, let's take a brief look at a measure that sometimes is used to express the degree of increase in information from a sample (e.g., test results) relative to perfect information.

Efficiency of Sample Information

One way to judge how much information is generated by a sample is to compute the ratio of EVSI to EVPI. This is known as the *efficiency of sample information.* Thus:

$$\begin{matrix}\textbf{Efficiency of}\\ \textbf{Sample information}\end{matrix} = \frac{\textbf{EVSI}}{\textbf{EVPI}} \qquad (10\text{-}5)$$

For the preceding example, the probabilities *without* additional information were .70 and .30, and the payoff table was

	Market	
	.70 Strong	**.30 Weak**
Print	40	20
Video	50	10

The expected monetary value was 38 (i.e., $38 000). The expected profit (EPC) is

$$.70(50) + .30(20) = 41, \text{ or } \$41\ 000$$

(To compute EPC, multiply the best payoff in each column by the column probability and sum the products.)

EVPI is the difference between EPC and EMV. Thus:

$$\text{EVPI} = \$41\,000 - \$38\,000 = \$3000$$

In the preceding example, it was determined that the EVSI = \$1308. Hence, the efficiency of the sample information is

$$\frac{1308}{3000} = .436$$

This number is interpreted as follows: The number can range from 0 to 1.00. The closer the number is to 1.00, the closer the sample information is to being perfect; the closer the number is to 0, the less information there is in the sample. Thus, a value such as .436 is mid-range, meaning that relative to perfect information, the information that could be gained from the market test is moderate.

Computing the Probabilities

Two sets of probabilities were used in the analysis of sample information: the probabilities of the test results (.59 and .41) and the revised probabilities for the states of nature (i.e., strong and weak markets) given the test results (i.e., .95, .05 and .34, .66). We now turn our attention to the calculation of those values by applying **Bayesian analysis**.

A basic piece of information that is necessary to the procedure is the reliability of the source of sample information (in this case, the market test). In assessing this reliability, the manager might make use of historical data on test results versus actual results, expert opinion, or his or her personal judgment of the probabilities. Let's suppose that in this case, the manager was able to obtain the reliability information from past records. The reliability information pertains to every possible combination of test result and actual result. The reliability figures for the preceding example are shown in Table 10-13, where F refers to a market test that shows a strong market, U to a market test that shows a weak market, s_1 to the state of nature corresponding to strong market, and s_2 to the state of nature corresponding to weak market.

The figures indicate that in past cases when the market actually was strong, the market test correctly indicated this information 80 percent of the time and incorrectly indicated a weak market 20 percent of the time, that is, $P(F/s_1) = 0.80$ and $P(U/s_1) = 0.2$, respectively. Moreover, when a weak market existed, the market test incorrectly indicated a strong market 10 percent of the time, while it correctly indicated a weak market 90 percent of the time, that is, $P(F/s_2) = 0.10$ and $P(U/s_2) = 0.90$, respectively. (Note that the probabilities in each *column* add to 1.00.) These probabilities are known as *conditional* probabilities because they express the reliability of the sampling device (e.g., market test) *given* the condition of actual market type.

To calculate the desired probabilities, we must combine these conditional probabilities with the original **(*prior*) probabilities** (.70 and .30) that were associated with the original payoff table. We must do this for each of the possible test results.

For a strong market test result, the calculations are shown in Table 10-14.

The first column of the table lists the two possible actual market conditions: strong and weak. The next column shows the probability of a market test that will show a strong

TABLE 10-13 Reliability of Market Test

	Actual State of Nature	
Results of Market Test	**Strong Market (s_1)**	**Weak Market (s_2)**
Shows strong market (F)	$P(F/s_1) = .80$	$P(F/s_2) = .10$
Shows weak market (U)	$P(U/s_1) = .2$	$P(U/s_2) = .90$

TABLE 10-14 Calculation of the Revised Probabilities for the Market Test Example

Actual Market	Prior Probabilities $P(s_j)$		Conditional Probabilities $P(F/s_j)$		Joint Probabilities $P(F \cap s_j)$	Posterior Probabilities $P(s_j/F)$
Strong (s_1)	.70	×	.80	=	.56	.56/.59 = .95
Weak (s_2)	.30	×	.10	=	.03	.03/.59 = .05
Marginal probability showing a strong market				=	.59	

market, given each possible actual market condition. The **prior probabilities** are the initial estimates of each type of market condition. Multiplying the prior probabilities by the conditional probabilities yields the *joint* probability of each market condition. The sum of these (e.g., .59) is the marginal probability that a test result will show a strong market, that is, $P(F) = .59$. (Note that it is one of the two types of probabilities we set out to compute.) The last column of the table illustrates the computation of the **revised posterior probabilities,** given a market test that shows a strong market. The computation involves obtaining the ratio of the joint probability of each market condition to the marginal probability (in this case, .59). The resulting values are .95 and .05, that is, $P(s_1/F) = .95$ and $P(s_2/F) = .05$. (Note that these are two of the revised probabilities we set out to compute.)

Probabilities for a market test that shows a weak market are computed in a similar way. These are illustrated in Table 10-15. As in the preceding table, the sum of the joint probabilities indicates the marginal probability of this test result (weak market, that is, $P(U) = .41$), and the ratios in the last column are the revised probabilities, that is, $P(s_1/U) = .34$ and $P(s_2/U) = .66$.

In summary, assuming J states of nature and K possible outcomes from research or a study for additional information, the marginal probabilities and the revised (posterior) probabilities can be developed as follows:

For each possible outcome O_i, $i = 1, \ldots, K$,

1. Compute the joint probability for each state of nature s_j, $j = 1, \ldots J$ as $P(O_i \cap s_j) = P(O_i / s_j) \times P(s_j)$;
2. Compute the marginal probability as $P(O_i) = \sum_{j=1}^{J} P(O_i \cap s_j)$;
3. Compute the revised probability for each state of nature s_j as

$$P(s_j / O_i) = \frac{P(O_i \cap s_j)}{P(O_j)}.$$

TABLE 10-15 Probability Calculations Given the Market Test Indicates a Weak Market

Actual Market	Prior Probabilities $P(s_j)$		Conditional Probabilities $P(U/s_j)$		Joint Probabilities $P(U \cap s_j)$	Posterior Probabilities $P(s_j/U)$
Strong (s_1)	.70	×	.20	=	.14	.14/.41 = .34
Weak (s_2)	.30	×	.90	=	.27	.27/.41 = .66
Marginal probability of showing a weak market				=	.41	

EXHIBIT 10-11 Calculation of the Revised Probabilities for the Market Test Example

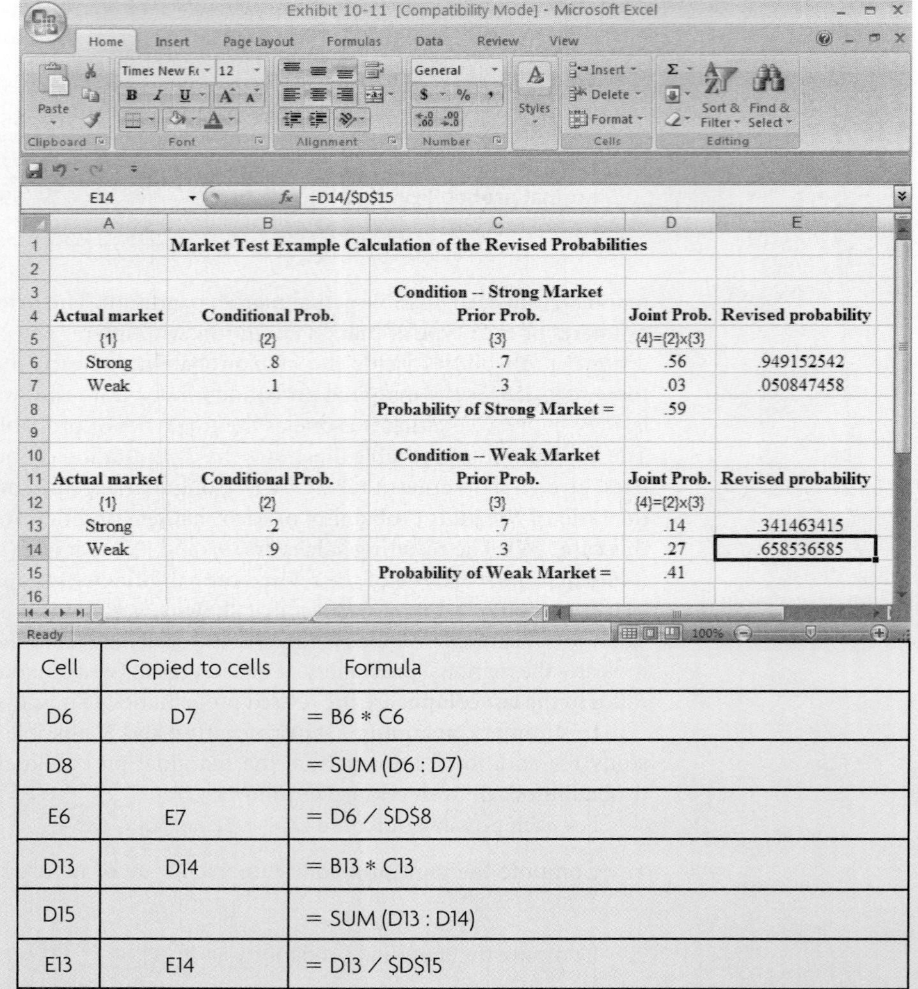

	A	B	C	D	E
1		Market Test Example Calculation of the Revised Probabilities			
2					
3			Condition -- Strong Market		
4	Actual market	Conditional Prob.	Prior Prob.	Joint Prob.	Revised probability
5	{1}	{2}	{3}	{4}={2}x{3}	
6	Strong	.8	.7	.56	.949152542
7	Weak	.1	.3	.03	.050847458
8			Probability of Strong Market =	.59	
9					
10			Condition -- Weak Market		
11	Actual market	Conditional Prob.	Prior Prob.	Joint Prob.	Revised probability
12	{1}	{2}	{3}	{4}={2}x{3}	
13	Strong	.2	.7	.14	.341463415
14	Weak	.9	.3	.27	.658536585
15			Probability of Weak Market =	.41	
16					

Cell	Copied to cells	Formula
D6	D7	= B6 * C6
D8		= SUM (D6 : D7)
E6	E7	= D6 / $D$8
D13	D14	= B13 * C13
D15		= SUM (D13 : D14)
E13	E14	= D13 / $D$15

Computing Revised Probabilities with Excel

The revised probabilities calculated in Tables 10-14 and 10-15 also can be obtained using Excel. The calculation of the revised probabilities is repeated in Exhibit 10-11. The formulas used to calculate the revised probabilities are reported at the bottom of Exhibit 10-11.

10.8 SENSITIVITY ANALYSIS

Analyzing decisions under risk requires working with estimated values: Both the payoffs and the probabilities for the states of nature are typically estimated values. Inaccuracies in these estimates can have an impact on choice of an alternative, and, ultimately, on the outcome of a decision. Given such possibilities, it is easy to see that a decision maker could benefit from an analysis of the *sensitivity* of a decision to possible errors in estimation. If it turns out that a certain decision will be deemed optimal over a wide range of values, the

FIGURE 10-7 Format of Graph for Sensitivity Analysis

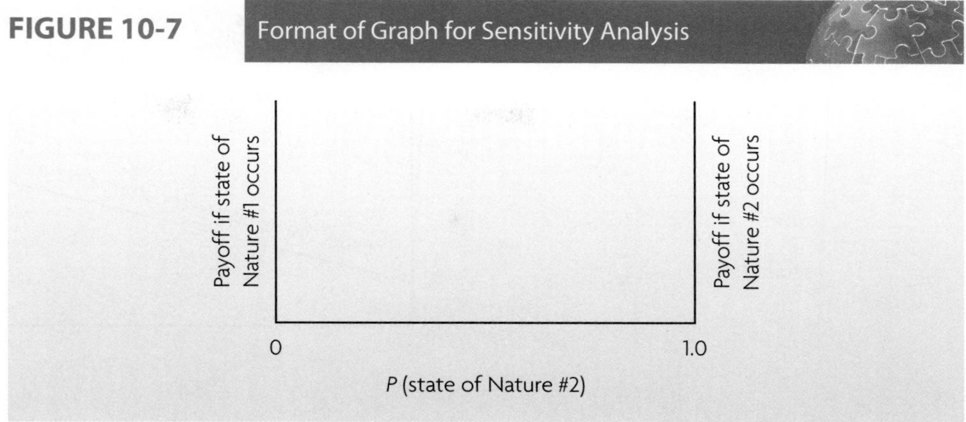

decision maker can proceed with relative confidence. Conversely, if analysis indicates a low tolerance for errors in estimation, additional efforts to pin down values may be needed.

In this section, sensitivity to *probability* estimates is examined. Sensitivity to payoff estimates is not covered; that topic is beyond the scope of this text.

Probability estimates are particularly interesting because it is not unusual to find instances in which managers are reluctant to attempt to pinpoint probabilities. This may stem from a desire to avoid having to justify those estimates, or it may be that certain managers are uncomfortable with making such estimates. The approach described here enables decision makers to identify a *range* of probabilities over which a particular alternative would be optimal. In other words, the manager or decision maker is presented with ranges of probabilities for various alternatives, and he or she need only decide if a probability is within a range, rather than decide on a specific value for the probabilities of a state of nature.

Let's consider an example that has two states of nature. Because only two states of nature can occur, this permits us to use *graphical analysis.* Suppose a decision maker has prepared this profit payoff table:

	State of Nature	
Alternative	**#1**	**#2**
a	3	9
b	12	1
c	9	6

The analysis is designed to provide ranges for the probability of state of nature #2, merely because it is convenient to do so. Nonetheless, these ranges can easily be converted into ranges for state of nature #1, as you will see. We will use a graph that has two vertical axes and one horizontal axis, as shown in Figure 10-7. The left vertical axis pertains to payoffs if state of nature #1 occurs, whereas the right vertical axis pertains to payoffs if state of nature #2 occurs. The horizontal axis represents the probability of state of nature #2, *P*(#2). Each alternative can be represented on the graph by plotting its payoff for state of nature #1 on the left side and its payoff for state of nature #2 on the right side and then connecting those two points with a straight line. This is illustrated for alternative *a* in Figure 10-8. The line represents the expected value of alternative *a* for the entire range of *P*(#2). Thus, for any value of *P*(#2), the expected value of alternative *a* can be found by running a vertical line from the value of *P*(#2) on the horizontal axis up to the point where it intersects the line. By running a horizontal line to either axis from that intersection, the expected value for that probability can be determined. An example is illustrated in Figure 10-9.

FIGURE 10-8 The Expected Value Line for Alternative *a*.

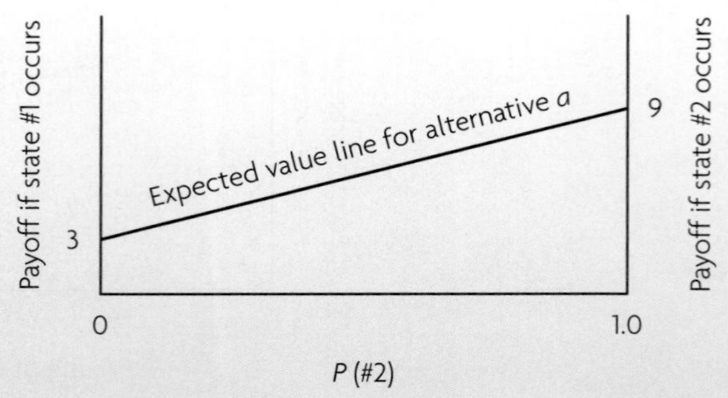

FIGURE 10-9 Example of Finding the Expected Value for Alternative *a* when *P*(#2) Is .50

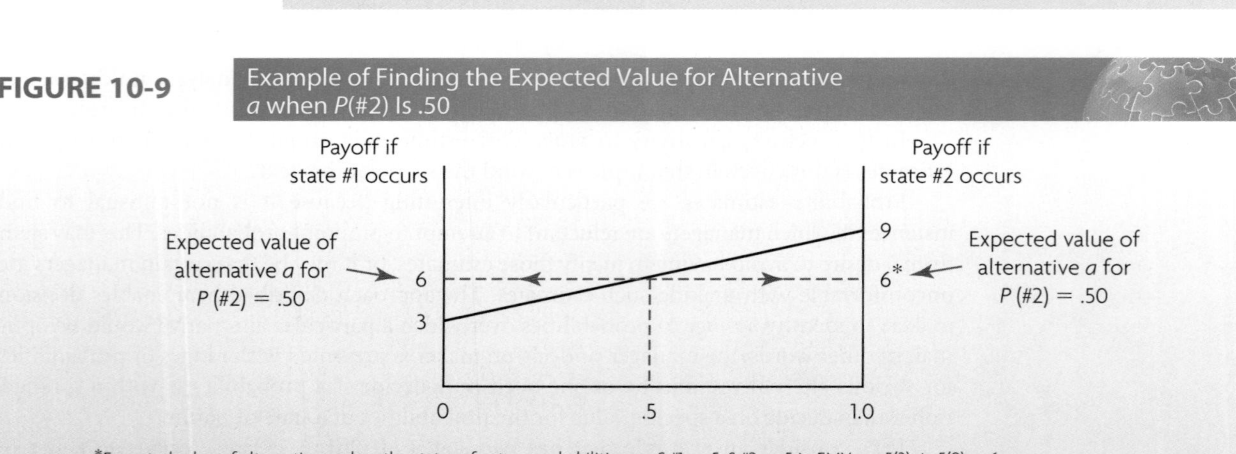

*Expected value of alternative a when the states of nature probabilities are S #1 = .5, S #2 = .5 is: $EMV_a = .5(3) + .5(9) = 6$

FIGURE 10-10 All Three Alternatives Are Plotted on a Single Graph

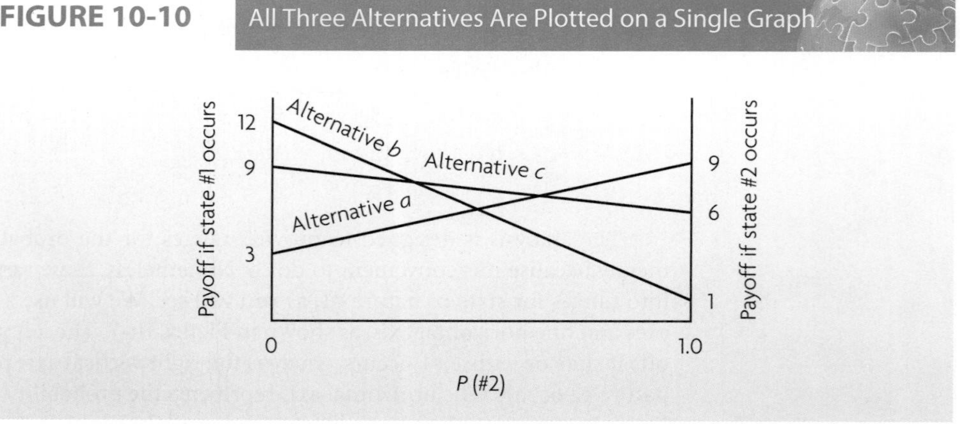

Of course, different values of $P(\#2)$ would produce different expected values. In general, you should be able to see from the graph that the nearer $P(\#2)$ is to 0, the closer the expected value of alternative *a* will be to the payoff for state of nature #1, whereas the nearer $P(\#2)$ is to 1.0, the closer the expected value will be to the payoff for state of nature #2.

Our analysis of sensitivity requires that all the alternatives be plotted on the same graph. Adding the other two alternatives produces the graph shown in Figure 10-10. You

FIGURE 10-11 The Line with the Highest Expected Profit Is Optimal for a Given Value of $P(\#2)$

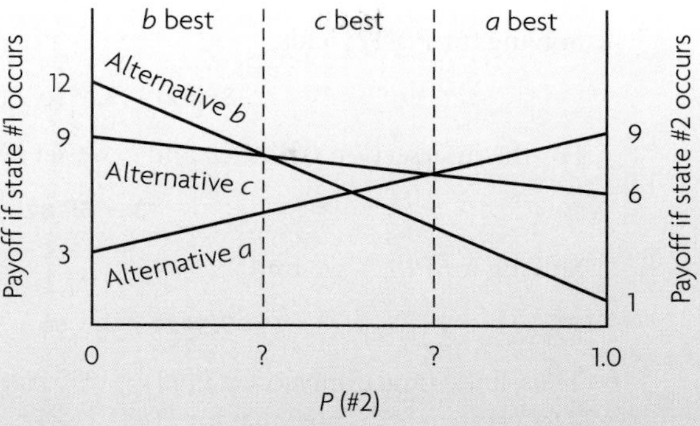

will recall that plotting the line for an alternative involves connecting its payoff for #1 (left axis) and its payoff for #2 (right axis.)

Because higher expected profits are more desirable than lower expected profits, the highest line for any given value of $P(\#2)$ represents the optimal alternative for that probability. Thus, referring to Figure 10-10, for low values of $P(\#2)$, alternative b would give higher expected profits than either alternative a or c. However, for values of $P(\#2)$ close to 1.0, alternative a would have higher expected profits than either b or c, whereas for values of $P(\#2)$ somewhere in the middle, alternative c would yield the highest expected profits. What we want to determine is the *range* of $P(\#2)$ for which each alternative is the best.

We can see in Figure 10-11 that alternative b is best up to the point (probability) where lines b and c intersect because the b line is highest from $P(\#2) = 0$ up to that probability. Then, line c is highest from that point until it intersects with line a; after that, line a is highest all the way to $P(\#2) = 1.0$. Hence, the values of $P(\#2)$ at these intersections are the key values in our analysis because they represent the end points of the ranges. These concepts are illustrated in Figure 10-11.

To be able to determine the $P(\#2)$ values at the line intersections, it is necessary to first develop equations of the lines in terms of $P(\#2)$. Typically, the expected value (EV) is computed in the following way:

$$\text{EV} = P(\#1) \times \text{Payoff } \#1 + P(\#2) \times \text{Payoff } \#2$$

Because $P(\#1) + P(\#2) = 1$, $P(\#1) = 1 - P(\#2)$. Substituting $1 - P(\#2)$ in the expected value formula, we can eliminate $P(\#1)$ from the expression:

$$\text{EV} = (1 - P(\#2)) \times \text{Payoff } \#1 + P(\#2) \times \text{Payoff } \#2$$

Expanding the first term, and then rearranging terms, we obtain

$$\text{EV} = \text{Payoff } \#1 + (\text{Payoff } \#2 - \text{Payoff } \#1)P(\#2) \tag{10-5}$$

Thus, for alternative a, the equation is

$$\text{EV}_a = 3 + (9 - 3)P(\#2), \quad \text{which is } \text{EV}_a = 3 + 6P(\#2)$$

Similarly, for b and c we have

$$\text{EV}_b = 12 + (1 - 12)P(\#2), \quad \text{which is } \text{EV}_b = 12 - 11P(\#2)$$
$$\text{EV}_c = 9 + (6 - 9)P(\#2), \quad \text{which is } \text{EV}_c = 9 - 3P(\#2)$$

Now, to find the values of $P(\#2)$ at the intersections, we can set two equations equal to each other and solve for $P(\#2)$. Thus, for the intersection of lines *b* and *c*, we have

$$12 - 11P(\#2) = 9 - 3P(\#2)$$

Solving for $P(\#2)$ yields

$$8P(\#2) = 3, \quad \text{so} \quad P(\#2) = 3/8, \quad \text{or } .375$$

For the intersection of lines *a* and *c*, we set $EV_a = EV_c$:

$$3 + 6P(\#2) = 9 - 3P(\#2)$$

Solving for $P(\#2)$, we find

$$9P(\#2) = 6, \quad \text{so} \quad P(\#2) = 6/9, \quad \text{or } .67$$

Thus, lines *b* and *c* intersect at $P(\#2) = .375$. So, alternative *b* is best over the range of $P(\#2)$ from 0 to less than .375 (note that for $P(\#2) = .375$, *b* and *c* are equivalent). Similarly, alternative *c* is best from $P(\#2) > .375$ to $P(\#2) < .67$, and from there up to $P(\#2) = 1.0$, alternative *a* is best.

In sum, the range of $P(\#2)$ over which each alternative is best is

$$\begin{aligned} &\text{For alternative } a\text{:} \quad .67 < P(\#2) \leq 1.0 \\ &\text{For alternative } b\text{:} \quad 0 \leq P(\#2) < .375 \\ &\text{For alternative } c\text{:} \quad .375 < P(\#2) < .67 \end{aligned}$$

These ranges give the decision maker important insight on probability estimates. For example, a decision maker may be reluctant to specify an exact probability for state of nature #2. However, with this information, the decision maker merely has to identify the most appropriate *range* for $P(\#2)$. Thus, if the decision maker believes that $P(\#2)$ is somewhere in the range of, say, .80 to .90, according to the preceding calculations, alternative *a* would be best. Or, if the decision maker believes that $P(\#2)$ lies close to .50, then alternative *c* would be best.

A similar analysis can be performed if the payoffs are costs or other values that are to be minimized rather than maximized. In such cases, the *lowest* line for a given value of $P(\#2)$ would be most desirable. An example of this is illustrated in the Solved Problems section at the end of this chapter.

One final comment regarding the use of $P(\#2)$. It was mentioned previously that $P(\#2)$ is used for convenience. It happens that the equations of the lines are a bit easier to develop using $P(\#2)$ rather than $P(\#1)$. However, should a problem refer to $P(\#1)$ ranges rather than $P(\#2)$, you can proceed by finding the ranges in terms of $P(\#2)$ and then converting these into $P(\#1)$ ranges as the final step. This merely involves recognizing that $P(\#1)$ and $P(\#2)$ are complements. For example, if $P(\#2) = 0$, then $P(\#1) = 1.0$; if $P(\#2) = .40$, then $P(\#1) = .60$; and so on. Hence, if alternative *a* is optimal for the range $0 \leq P(\#2) < .40$, then in terms of $P(\#1)$, alternative *a* is optimal for the range $.60 < P(\#1) \leq 1.00$. $P(\#1)$ line drawn at the bottom of Figure 10-12 further illustrates this concept using the previous example.

10.9 UTILITY

Throughout this chapter, decision criteria have been illustrated that use monetary value as the basis of choosing among alternatives. Although monetary value is a common basis for decision making, it is not the only basis, even for business decisions. In certain instances, decision makers use *multiple criteria,* one of which is the potential *satisfaction* or *dissatisfaction* associated with possible payoffs.

For example, many people participate in lotteries. However, the fact is lotteries have a *negative* expected value: the *expected* return is less than the cost of the lottery. If it were not,

FIGURE 10-12 Converting $P(\#2)$ Ranges into $P(\#1)$ Ranges

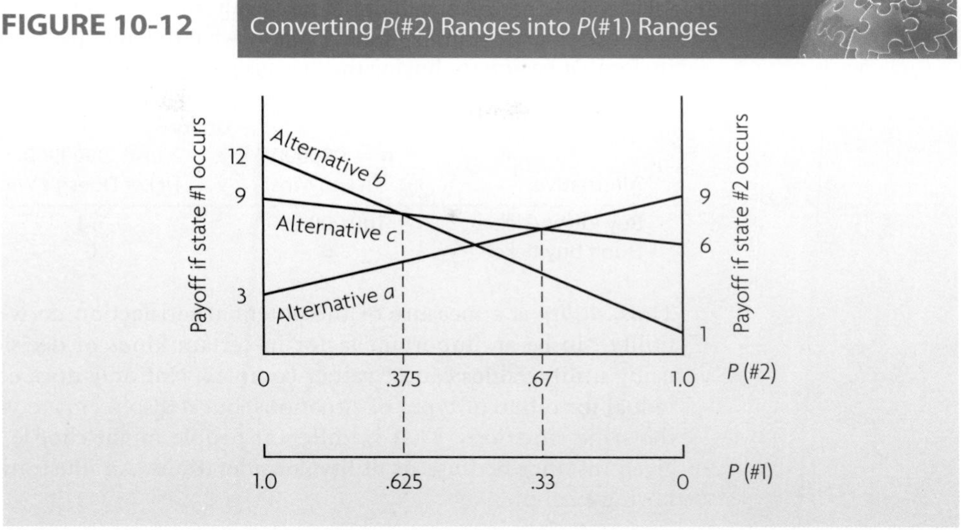

the lottery corporations would lose money by running lotteries. Why do people play lotteries, then? The answer is that they are hoping to win a large amount of money, and they are willing to sacrifice a relatively small amount of money to have that chance. In other words, even though their chances of winning are close to zero, they have a greater **utility** for the potential winnings, despite a negative expected value, than for the amount of money they have to give up (pay) to participate in the lottery. Similar arguments can be made for other forms of wagering. People who behave in this fashion, whether for purposes of wagering or in other forms of decision making, are sometimes referred to as **risk takers.**

Just the opposite happens when a person buys insurance, giving up a fixed dollar amount to insure against an event (e.g., a fire) that has very little chance of occurring. Even so, if a fire or other insured event did occur, the consequences would be so catastrophic that an individual would not want to be exposed to that degree of risk. Thus, even though buying insurance carries a negative monetary value, most individuals recognize the merit of doing so. We refer to such individuals as **risk averters.** Of course, some individuals exhibit both forms of behaviour in their decision making; they are risk takers for certain kinds of decisions but risk averters for others. A lottery player who owns a life insurance policy would be an example of this.

To get an idea of how a decision maker might use utilities in making a decision, consider a person who buys a lottery ticket. Suppose that each ticket costs \$1 and that the chance of winning the \$1 000 000 jackpot is 1/10 million. The payoff table would look like this:

	Dollar Value		
	$p = .0000001$	$p = .9999999$	Expected
Alternative	Ticket Wins	Ticket Doesn't Win	Payoff
Buy lottery ticket	\$999 999	−\$1	−\$.90
Don't buy ticket	0	0	0

Note that the expected payoff from buying a lottery ticket is negative, raising the question of why a person would buy a ticket at all. However, suppose we were to ask such a person his or her subjective assessment of the utilities of the various payoffs. We might discover that winning the lottery would have a disproportionately high utility relative to the cost of a ticket.

Hence, if we replace the dollar payoffs with some measure of the utility of that payoff, and then compute the expected *utility*, a somewhat different picture emerges. The expected utility for that person for buying the ticket is *positive:*

	Utility		
	$p = .0000001$	$p = .9999999$	Expected
Alternative	Ticket Wins	Ticket Doesn't Win	Utility
Buy lottery ticket	100 000 000	−1	90
Don't buy ticket	0	0	0

Thus, *utility* is a measure of the potential satisfaction derived from money. Although utility can be an important factor in certain kinds of decision making, assessing and using utility values can be rather complex. Not only does utility vary within an individual for different types of situations, but it also seems to vary among individuals for the same situations. That is, different people might choose different alternatives in a given instance because of utility considerations. An illustration is provided in the following example.

EXAMPLE 10-6

Medev Inc. is a small business company that specializes on the design and manufacture of a wide variety of electronic medical devices. The company is about to introduce a new product, an endoscope leaking detection system, in the market. The senior management has to decide yet about the start-up model size that will be used to test the market during the next eighteen months. The following payoff table (Table 10-16) shows the projected profit (in thousands of dollars) for each of three model sizes based upon three possible levels of demand. The probabilities for the states of nature are .30, .35, and .35 respectively.

Table 10-16 Payoff Table for the Medev Inc. Example

	Market Demand		
Model Size	**Good (s_1)**	**Fair (s_2)**	**Poor (s_3)**
Small (d_1)	\$250	\$125	(\$100)
Medium (d_2)	\$480	\$275	(\$600)
Large (d_3)	\$650	\$325	(\$850)
Probability	.30	.35	.35

The three members in the board of directors diverge on the model size to choose, due to their differences about the utility for money. Karl Apollon, one of the decision makers, is risk-neutral. The two other decision makers, Tony Beaupre and Guy Daigle, are respectively a risk avoider and a risk taker. Let's assume the following utility for money for these two decision makers, where x is the amount, $u_1(x)$ is the utility value corresponding to the amount x for Tony Beaupre, and $u_2(x)$ is the utility value corresponding to the amount x for Guy Daigle.

Table 10-17 Utility Values for the Decision Makers in the Medev Inc. Example

x	$u_1(x)$	$u_2(x)$
$650	1	1
$450	.95	.55
$325	.9	.5
$275	.85	.4
$250	.7	.35
$125	.6	.3
($200)	.5	.2
($600)	.3	.1
($850)	0	0

a. Determine the best decision for each decision maker that maximizes his expected utility.
b. What is the value of this decision problem to Tony Beaupre?
c. What is the value of this decision problem to Guy Daigle?

Solution

a. Since Karl Apollon is risk-neutral, the expected monetary value approach is applicable. Equation 10-2 yields the following results:

	Market Demand			
Model Size	**Good (s_1)**	**Fair (s_2)**	**Poor (s_3)**	**Expected Payoff**
Small (d_1)	$250	$125	($200)	$48.75
Medium (d_2)	$450	$275	($600)	$21.25
Large (d_3)	$650	$325	($850)	$11.25
Probabilities	.3	.35	.35	

Karl Apollon's decision is to produce the small size model.
For Guy Daigle and Tony Beaupre, the approach consists of first substituting out the payoff values in Table 10-16 with the corresponding utility values in Table 10-17. Then, use Equation 10-2 to compute the expected utility for each decision maker. The following table is obtained for Tony Beaupre. The decision is to produce the medium size model.

	Market Demand			
Model Size	**Good (s_1)**	**Fair (s_2)**	**Poor (s_3)**	**Expected Payoff**
Small (d_1)	.7	.6	.5	0.595
Medium (d_2)	.95	.85	.3	0.687
Large (d_3)	1	.9	0	0.615

In regards to Guy Daigle, the following table is obtained. The decision is to select the large size model.

	Market Demand			
Model Size	**Good (s_1)**	**Fair (s_2)**	**Poor (s_3)**	**Expected Payoff**
Small (d_1)	.35	.3	.2	.280
Medium (d_2)	.55	.4	.1	.340
Large (d_3)	1	.5	0	.475

b. The decision maker Tony Beaupre assigns a utility of .95 to a payoff of $450 and a utility of .6 to $125. Therefore, linearly interpolating in this range yields a payoff of $206.25 for a utility of .6875. Therefore, the value of the decision problem is worth $206 250 to this decision maker.

c. The decision maker Guy Daigle assigns a utility of .5 to a payoff of $325 and a utility of .4 to $275. Therefore, linearly interpolating in this range yields a payoff of $312.5 for a utility of .475. Therefore, the value of the decision problem worth $312 500 to this decision maker.

MODERN MANAGEMENT SCIENCE APPLICATION: DECISION ANALYSIS TO EVALUATE A NEW DRUG CANDIDATE

Johnson & Johnson Pharmaceutical Research & Development (J&J PRD) is one of the fastest-growing global pharmaceutical research and development companies and part of the world's largest health-care company, Johnson & Johnson. In Canada, the Johnson & Johnson's family of companies are located in the provinces of British Columbia (Burnaby), Ontario (Don Mills, Mississauga, Markham, and Guelph), and Quebec (Montreal). J&J PRD was facing the issue of determining the best testing strategy to pursue for a new drug candidate, which had successfully passed human safety trials (Phase 1), and was being considered for a full development program (Phases 2b and 3), with a projected investment of the order of $200 million over five years. Before committing to full development, management wanted to consider further testing via proof-of-principle (POP), or Phase 2a, clinical trials, which are designed to provide information to aid in major development decisions at a relatively low cost (roughly $10–$20 million). Management decisions included (1) whether or not to conduct a POP trial and, if so, what type of POP trial to conduct, and (2) whether or not to include an "active comparator arm" in the trial. The decision analysis department within J&J PRD was asked to provide assistance in choosing a clinical development strategy. The team used decision trees, including Bayesian updating of probabilities, to represent and analyze the various sequential strategies, and find the best strategy with respect to net present value (NPV). The model developed included four clinical trial alternatives for the POP trial. Design A involved four arms—one placebo arm, two trial arms with different dosing levels, and a possible active comparator arm. Design B was similar to Design A but with only one trial arm, that is, only one dosing level. Design C was essentially equivalent to replicating Design B (that is, performing two separate trials based on Design B). Design D was similar to Design B but with a bigger sample size for the trial arm. The states of nature included (a) the underlying effectiveness of the drug candidate at four levels, not effective at any level, effective at lower dose, effective at higher dose, and effective at both doses; and (b) the different levels of placebo response, strong, typical, and weak. To get the necessary probability data, the team combined judgmental assessments, using standard decision analysis procedures with Bayesian posterior analysis. Working with an expert panel consisting of three clinicians, a biostatistician, and a project manager, the team developed an influence diagram to describe the relationships among effectiveness, the placebo effect, and the trial results. This diagram was then used to guide the probability assessment process and subsequent calculations. Based on expected NPV, the analysis showed that it was optimal to conduct the POP trial and use Design A, which had an expected NPV $9 million greater than that of Design B, the next best alternative. It also showed that including a comparator arm does not add any information value for decision making in this specific situation. Management benefited from this study in several ways: (a) a confirmation was obtained that doing the POP trial will help it make a better decision resulting in higher expected NPV; (b) an objective assessment was provided to help in the selection of the best trial design, which it could implement immediately; and (c) the analysis helped to rethink the need for an active comparator arm and ensure that it is included for the right reasons.

Source: Reprinted by permission, V. Viswanathan, R. Bayney: "Decision Analysis to Evaluate Proof-of-Principle Trial Design for a New Drug Candidate," *Interfaces,* vol. 34, no. 3, (May–June 2004), pp. 206–207. Copyright 2004, the Institute for Operations Research and the Management Sciences (INFORMS), 7240 Parkway Drive, Suite 310, Hanover, MD 21076 USA.

Summary

Decision theory is a general approach to decision making. It is very useful for a decision maker who must choose from a list of alternatives, knowing that one of a number of possible future states of nature will occur and that this will have an impact on the payoff realized by a particular alternative.

Decision models can be categorized according to the degree of uncertainty that is assigned to the occurrence of the states of nature. This can range from complete knowledge about which state will occur, to partial knowledge (probabilities), to no knowledge (no probabilities, or complete uncertainty). When complete uncertainty exists, the approach a decision maker takes in choosing among alternatives depends on how optimistic or pessimistic he or she is, and it also depends on other circumstances related to the eventual outcome or payoff. Under complete certainty, decisions are relatively straightforward. Under partial uncertainty, expected values often are used to evaluate alternatives. An extension of the use of expected values enables decision makers to assess the value of improved or perfect information about which state of nature will occur.

Problems that involve a single decision are usually best handled through payoff tables, whereas problems that involve a sequence, or possible sequence, of decisions are usually best handled using tree diagrams because payoff tables are difficult to utilize if there are multiple stages to be considered.

Sometimes decision makers can improve the decision process by taking into account additional (sample) information, which enables them to modify state-of-nature probabilities. Because there is almost always an additional cost associated with obtaining that sample information, the decision maker must decide whether the expected value of that information is worth the cost necessary to obtain it.

Sensitivity analysis can sometimes be useful to decision makers, particularly for situations in which they find it difficult to accurately assess the probabilities of the various states of nature. Sensitivity analysis can help by providing ranges of probabilities for which a given alternative would be chosen, using expected monetary value as the criterion. Hence, the problem of specifying probabilities is reduced to deciding whether a probability merely falls within a range of values.

Although expected monetary value is a widely used approach to decision making, certain individuals and certain situations may require consideration of utilities, which reflect how decision makers view the satisfaction associated with different monetary payoffs.

The Modern Management Application, "Decision Analysis to Evaluate a New Drug Candidate," describes how the uses of some of the principles presented in this chapter enabled Johnson & Johnson Pharmaceutical Research & Development to determine the best testing strategy to pursue for a new drug candidate.

Glossary

Bayesian Analysis An analysis that enables the use of sample information to revise prior probabilities.

Certainty Refers to a decision problem in which probabilities of occurrence for the various states of nature are known.

Coefficient of Optimism, α Used with Hurwicz criterion; ranges from 0 (pessimistic) to 1. 0 (optimistic).

Decision Criterion A standard or rule for choosing among alternatives (e.g., choose the alternative with the highest expected profit).

Decision Tree A schematic representation of a decision problem that involves the use of branches and nodes.

Equal Likelihood Criterion A decision criterion that seeks the alternative with the best average payoff, assuming all states of nature are equally likely to occur.

Expected Monetary Value (EMV) For an alternative, the sum of the products of each possible payoff and the probability of that payoff.

Expected Opportunity Loss (EOL) For an alternative, the sum of the products of each possible regret and the probability of that regret.

Expected Payoff Under Certainty (EPC) For a set of alternatives, the sum of the products of the best payoff for each state of nature and that state's probability.

Expected Regret See **Expected Opportunity Loss.**

Expected Value of Perfect Information (EVPI) The maximum additional benefit attainable if a problem involving risk could be reduced to a problem in which it was certain which state of nature would occur. Equal to the minimum expected regret. Also equal to EPC minus best EMV.
Expected Value of Sample Information (EVSI) The expected benefit of acquiring sample information. Equal to the difference between the best EMV without information and the best EMV with information.
Hurwicz Criterion A decision criterion that allows the decision maker to incorporate his/her degree of optimism in choosing an alternative.
Maximax A decision criterion that specifies choosing the alternative with the best overall payoff. When costs or times are involved, the term *minimin* is used.
Maximin A decision criterion that specifies choosing the alternative with the best of the worst payoffs for all alternatives. When costs or times are involved, the term *minimax* is used.
Minimax Regret A decision criterion that specifies choosing the alternative that has the lowest regret (opportunity loss).
Opportunity Loss For an alternative given a state of nature, the difference between that alternative's payoff and the best possible payoff for that state of nature.
Payoff Table A table that shows the payoff for each alternative for each state of nature.
Posterior Probabilities Probabilities of the state of nature obtained after the revision of prior probabilities based on sample information.
Prior Probabilities Probabilities of the state of nature prior to obtaining sample information.
Regret See **Opportunity Loss.**
Risk A decision problem in which the states of nature have probabilities associated with their occurrence.
Risk Averters Individuals that avoid taking risks. The decision maker has less utility for greater risk.
Risk Takers Individuals that like taking risks and that have a greater utility for the potential winnings even though their chances of winning are very low.
Sequential Decisions Decisions where the outcome of one decision affects other decisions.
State of Nature Possible future events.
Uncertainty Refers to a decision problem in which probabilities of occurrence for the various states of nature are unknown.
Utility Of a payoff, a measure of the personal satisfaction associated with a payoff.

Solved Problems

Problem 1

Given this *profit* payoff table:

Alternative	State of Nature #1	#2	#3
a	12	18	15
b	17	10	14
c	22	16	10
d	14	14	14

Determine which alternative would be chosen using each of these decision criteria:

a. Maximax
b. Maximin
c. Minimax regret
d. Equal likelihood
e. The Hurwicz criterion with $\alpha = .40$
f. Repeat part *a* through part *e* using Excel

Solution

a. The maximax approach seeks the alternative that has the best overall payoff. Because these are profits, the best payoff would be the largest value, which is the payoff 22 (row *c*, column #1). Thus, to have a chance at that payoff, the decision maker should choose alternative *c*.
b. The maximin approach is to choose the alternative that will provide the best of the worst possible

payoffs. To find this, first identify the worst profit possible for each alternative:

Alternative	Worst Payoff	
a	12	
b	10	
c	10	
d	14	(best)

Because alternative *d* has the best of the worst payoffs, it would be chosen using maximin.

c. To find the minimax regret decision, we must first obtain the opportunity loss, or regret, table. This is a two-step process. First, identify the best payoff in each *column.* Then subtract every payoff in each column from the best payoff in the column. Hence, the best payoffs are: 22 in column #1, 18 in column #2, and 15 in column #3. The resulting regret (opportunity loss) table is

Opportunity Loss Table

	State of Nature			
Alternative	**#1**	**#2**	**#3**	**Worst Regret**
a	10	0	0	10
b	5	8	1	8
c	0	2	5	5 (minimum) (regret)
d	8	4	1	8

(Notice that none of the regrets is negative. This will *always* be the case.) Because alternative *c* has the lowest of the worst regrets, it would be chosen.

d. Using the equal likelihood criterion, we must determine the average payoff for each alternative. We do this by summing the payoffs for each and then dividing by the number of payoffs (three). The resulting averages are

Alternative	Average Payoff
a	15 = (12 + 18 + 15)/3
b	13.67 = (17 + 10 + 14)/3
c	16 (best) = (22 + 16 + 10)/3
d	14 = (14 + 14 + 14)/3

Because alternative *c* yields the highest average profit using the equal likelihood criterion, it would be chosen.

e. For the Hurwicz criterion, identify the best and worst payoffs for each alternative. Then, multiply the best payoff by the coefficient of optimism, α, and the worst payoff by $(1 - \alpha)$ and sum the results. The alternative that has the highest sum (if profits or a similar type payoff is involved would be chosen. For costs, the alternative with the lowest sum would be chosen. Thus,

Alternative *a*	.40(18) + .60(12) = 14.40	
Alternative *b*	.40(17) + .60(10) = 12.80	
Alternative *c*	.40(22) + .60(10) = 14.80	(best)
Alternative *d*	.40(14) + .60(14) = 14.00	

f. Exhibit 10-12 shows how to solve Solved Problem 1 using Excel. The necessary formulas are exhibited at the bottom of Exhibit 10-12.

Problem 2

Suppose the payoffs in the preceding problem had been *costs* rather than profits. Determine which alternative would be chosen, using these decision criteria:

a. Minimin
b. Minimax
c. Minimax regret
d. Equal likelihood
e. Hurwicz criterion with $\alpha = .4$
f. Use Excel and solve part *a* through part *e*

Solution

a. The minimin approach seeks the lowest overall cost. Hence, the smallest value is the best. The smallest value in the table given in Solved Problem 1 is 10. It appears both as a possible cost for alternative *b* and for alternative *c*. Hence, using minimin, the decision maker would be indifferent between those two alternatives.

b. For minimax, we must determine the worst cost for each alternative. Because the values are now *costs,* the *largest* value for each alternative is listed:

Alternative	Worst Cost	
a	18	
b	17	
c	22	
d	14	(lowest cost)

Because alternative *d* has the best of the worst costs, it would be chosen.

c. To obtain the regret table, we must identify the best cost for each column. Because costs are involved, we want the lowest cost in each column. For column #1, 12 is the lowest; for column #2, 10 is the lowest; and for column #3, 10 is the lowest. When costs are involved, the regrets are obtained by subtracting the lowest cost

EXHIBIT 10-12 Solved Problem 1: Decision Making Under Complete Uncertainty—A Profit Maximization Problem (Part I)

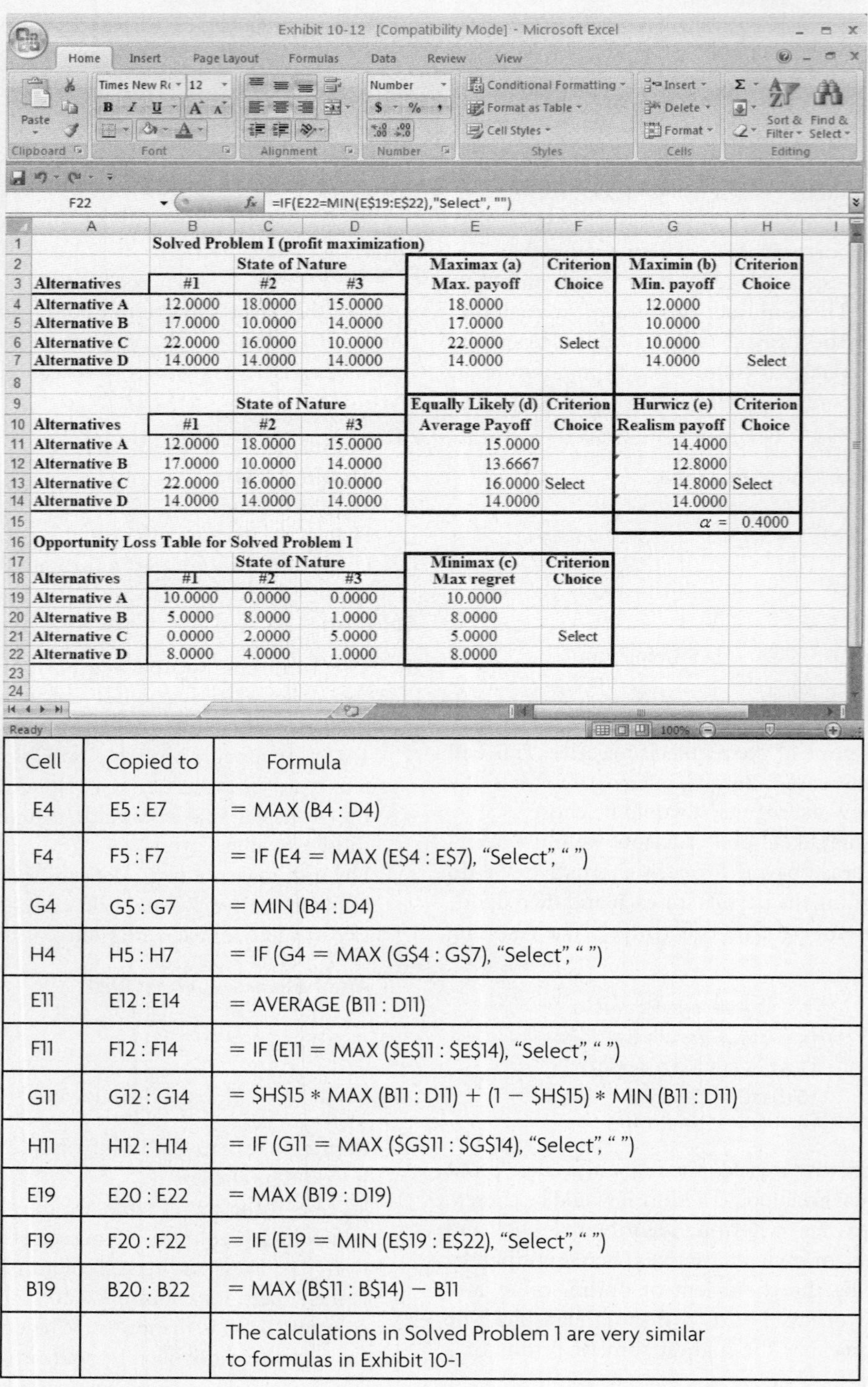

Exhibit 10-12 [Compatibility Mode] - Microsoft Excel

F22 =IF(E22=MIN(E$19:E$22),"Select", "")

	A	B	C	D	E	F	G	H
1		Solved Problem I (profit maximization)						
2			State of Nature		Maximax (a)	Criterion	Maximin (b)	Criterion
3	Alternatives	#1	#2	#3	Max. payoff	Choice	Min. payoff	Choice
4	Alternative A	12.0000	18.0000	15.0000	18.0000		12.0000	
5	Alternative B	17.0000	10.0000	14.0000	17.0000		10.0000	
6	Alternative C	22.0000	16.0000	10.0000	22.0000	Select	10.0000	
7	Alternative D	14.0000	14.0000	14.0000	14.0000		14.0000	Select
8								
9			State of Nature		Equally Likely (d)	Criterion	Hurwicz (e)	Criterion
10	Alternatives	#1	#2	#3	Average Payoff	Choice	Realism payoff	Choice
11	Alternative A	12.0000	18.0000	15.0000	15.0000		14.4000	
12	Alternative B	17.0000	10.0000	14.0000	13.6667		12.8000	
13	Alternative C	22.0000	16.0000	10.0000	16.0000	Select	14.8000	Select
14	Alternative D	14.0000	14.0000	14.0000	14.0000		14.0000	
15							α =	0.4000
16	Opportunity Loss Table for Solved Problem 1							
17			State of Nature		Minimax (c)	Criterion		
18	Alternatives	#1	#2	#3	Max regret	Choice		
19	Alternative A	10.0000	0.0000	0.0000	10.0000			
20	Alternative B	5.0000	8.0000	1.0000	8.0000			
21	Alternative C	0.0000	2.0000	5.0000	5.0000	Select		
22	Alternative D	8.0000	4.0000	1.0000	8.0000			

Cell	Copied to	Formula
E4	E5 : E7	= MAX (B4 : D4)
F4	F5 : F7	= IF (E4 = MAX (E$4 : E$7), "Select", " ")
G4	G5 : G7	= MIN (B4 : D4)
H4	H5 : H7	= IF (G4 = MAX (G$4 : G$7), "Select", " ")
E11	E12 : E14	= AVERAGE (B11 : D11)
F11	F12 : F14	= IF (E11 = MAX ($E$11 : $E$14), "Select", " ")
G11	G12 : G14	= $H$15 * MAX (B11 : D11) + (1 − $H$15) * MIN (B11 : D11)
H11	H12 : H14	= IF (G11 = MAX ($G$11 : $G$14), "Select", " ")
E19	E20 : E22	= MAX (B19 : D19)
F19	F20 : F22	= IF (E19 = MIN (E$19 : E$22), "Select", " ")
B19	B20 : B22	= MAX (B$11 : B$14) − B11
		The calculations in Solved Problem 1 are very similar to formulas in Exhibit 10-1

in the column *from* all of the costs in the column. Again, this results in all positive and zero regrets:

Opportunity Loss Table

Alternative	State of Nature #1	#2	#3	Worst Regret
a	0	8	5	8
b	5	0	4	5
c	10	6	0	10
d	2	4	4	4 (minimum regret)

Because alternative *d* had the lowest of the worst regrets, it would be chosen.

d. Using the equal likelihood criterion, we find the average cost for each alternative. These averages are the same as determined in the preceding problem:

Alternative	Average Cost	
a	15	
b	13.67	(best)
c	16	
d	14	

Because alternative b has the lowest average cost, it would be chosen.

e. Hurwicz criterion

Alternative *a* .4(12) + .6(18) = 15.6
Alternative *b* .4(10) + .6(17) = 14.2
Alternative *c* .4(10) + .6(22) = 17.2
Alternative *d* .4(14) + .6(14) = 14 (select)

Using the Hurwicz criterion, the best and worst cost would be selected for each alternative. The best (lowest) cost would be multiplied by $\alpha = .4$ and the the worst (highest) cost would be multiplied by $(1 - \alpha)$. The sum of these two cross products would be the total cost for each alternative using the Hurwicz Criterion. For example, for alternative *a*, the lowest cost is 12 and the highest cost is 18. Therefore, (.4)(12) + (.6)(18) = 15.6.

f. Exhibit 10-13 shows how to solve Solved Problem 2 using Excel. The necessary formulas are displayed at the bottom of Exhibit 10-13. Note that the approach is very similar to solving Solved Problem 1. However, instead of maximizing profit, the objective is to minimize cost.

Problem 3

For the payoff table given in Solved Problem 1, suppose the manager has assigned probabilities of .2 to the occurrence of state #1, .5 to the occurrence of state #2, and .3 to the occurrence of state #3.

a. Which alternative would be chosen using maximum expected value as the criterion, treating the payoffs as profits?
b. Calculate the expected value of perfect information using (1) the expected payoff under certainty approach and (2) the expected regret approach.
c. Repeat parts *a* and *b* using Excel.

Solution

a. Compute the expected value of each alternative:

EV_a: .2(12) + .5(18) + .3(15) = 15.9 (best)
EV_b: .2(17) + .5(10) + .3(14) = 12.6
EV_c: .2(22) + .5(16) + .3(10) = 15.4
EV_d: .2(14) + .5(14) + .3(14) = 14.0

Because alternative *a* has the largest expected profit, it would be selected using expected monetary value as the decision criterion.

b. (1) The expected payoff under certainty approach is

EVPI = Expected payoff under certainty − Expected monetary value

The expected payoff under certainty is found by taking the best payoff in each column, multiplying that by the column probability, and summing the results for all columns. Thus:

EPC: .2(22) + .5(18) + .3(15) = 17.9

Then:

EVPI: 17.9 − 15.9 = 2.0

(2) Using the regret approach, find the expected regret for each alternative: Using the opportunity loss table obtained in Solved Problem 1*c*, we have

Alternative	Expected Regret	
a	.2(10) + .5(0) + .3(0) = 2.0	(lowest)
b	.2(5) + .5(8) + .3(1) = 5.3	
c	.2(0) + .5(2) + .3(5) = 2.5	
d	.2(8) + .5(4) + .3(1) = 3.9	

The lowest expected regret is equal to 2.0. This amount is the expected value of perfect information, EVPI. Note that this agrees with the answer obtained in 1*b*.

c. For Solved Problem 3, Excel is used to calculate the expected value and EVPI. The bottom of Exhibit 10-14 shows all of the necessary formulas.

EXHIBIT 10-13 Solved Problem 2: Decision Making Under Complete Uncertainty—A Cost Minimization Problem (part *f*)

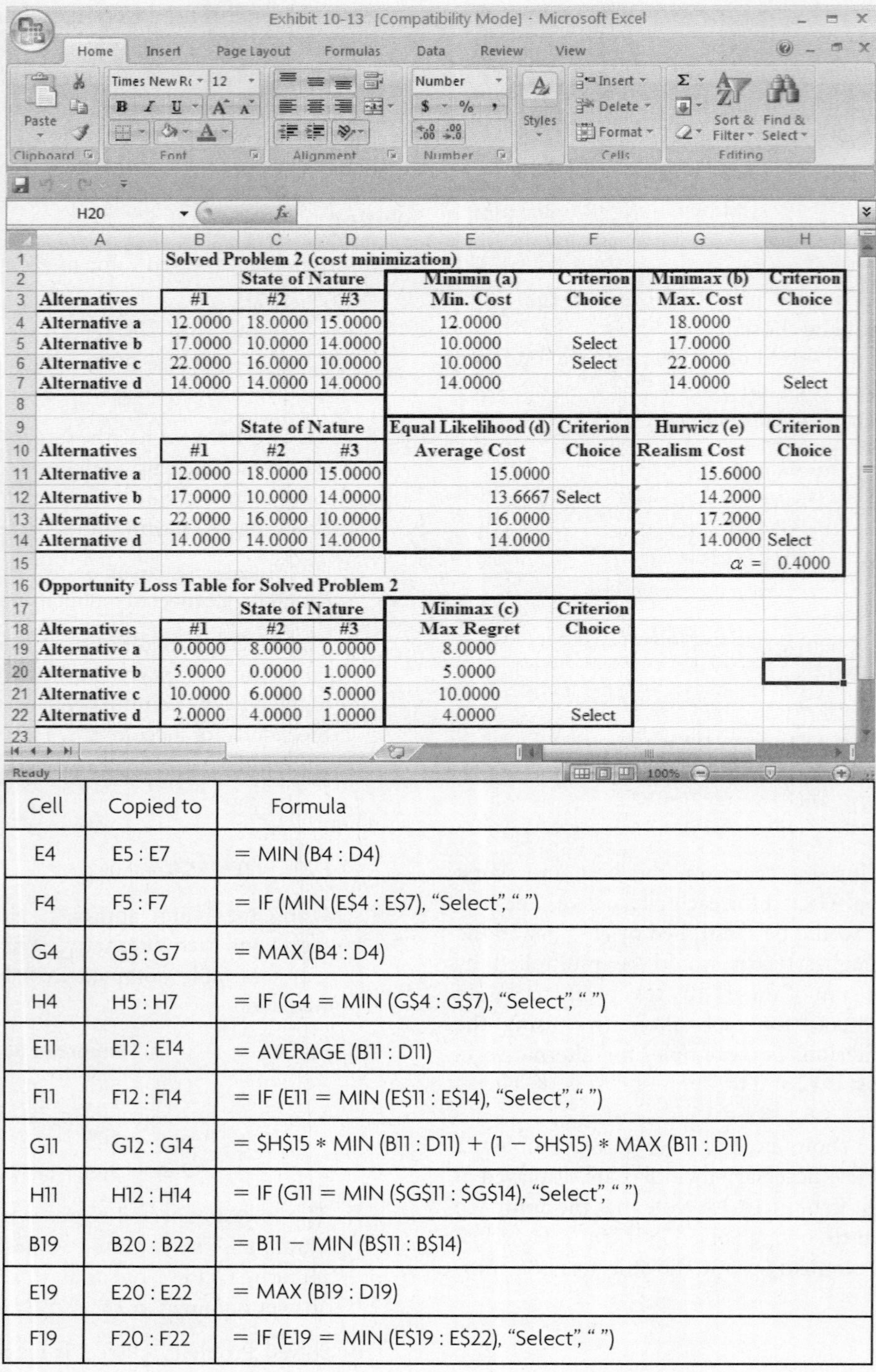

	A	B	C	D	E	F	G	H
1		Solved Problem 2 (cost minimization)						
2			State of Nature		Minimin (a)	Criterion	Minimax (b)	Criterion
3	Alternatives	#1	#2	#3	Min. Cost	Choice	Max. Cost	Choice
4	Alternative a	12.0000	18.0000	15.0000	12.0000		18.0000	
5	Alternative b	17.0000	10.0000	14.0000	10.0000	Select	17.0000	
6	Alternative c	22.0000	16.0000	10.0000	10.0000	Select	22.0000	
7	Alternative d	14.0000	14.0000	14.0000	14.0000		14.0000	Select
8								
9			State of Nature		Equal Likelihood (d)	Criterion	Hurwicz (e)	Criterion
10	Alternatives	#1	#2	#3	Average Cost	Choice	Realism Cost	Choice
11	Alternative a	12.0000	18.0000	15.0000	15.0000		15.6000	
12	Alternative b	17.0000	10.0000	14.0000	13.6667	Select	14.2000	
13	Alternative c	22.0000	16.0000	10.0000	16.0000		17.2000	
14	Alternative d	14.0000	14.0000	14.0000	14.0000		14.0000	Select
15							α =	0.4000
16	Opportunity Loss Table for Solved Problem 2							
17			State of Nature		Minimax (c)	Criterion		
18	Alternatives	#1	#2	#3	Max Regret	Choice		
19	Alternative a	0.0000	8.0000	0.0000	8.0000			
20	Alternative b	5.0000	0.0000	1.0000	5.0000			
21	Alternative c	10.0000	6.0000	5.0000	10.0000			
22	Alternative d	2.0000	4.0000	1.0000	4.0000	Select		

Cell	Copied to	Formula
E4	E5 : E7	= MIN (B4 : D4)
F4	F5 : F7	= IF (MIN (E$4 : E$7), "Select", " ")
G4	G5 : G7	= MAX (B4 : D4)
H4	H5 : H7	= IF (G4 = MIN (G$4 : G$7), "Select", " ")
E11	E12 : E14	= AVERAGE (B11 : D11)
F11	F12 : F14	= IF (E11 = MIN (E$11 : E$14), "Select", " ")
G11	G12 : G14	= $H$15 * MIN (B11 : D11) + (1 − $H$15) * MAX (B11 : D11)
H11	H12 : H14	= IF (G11 = MIN ($G$11 : $G$14), "Select", " ")
B19	B20 : B22	= B11 − MIN (B$11 : B$14)
E19	E20 : E22	= MAX (B19 : D19)
F19	F20 : F22	= IF (E19 = MIN (E$19 : E$22), "Select", " ")

EXHIBIT 10-14 Calculation of the Revised Probabilities and Expected Value of Perfect Information for Solved Problem 3 (part c)

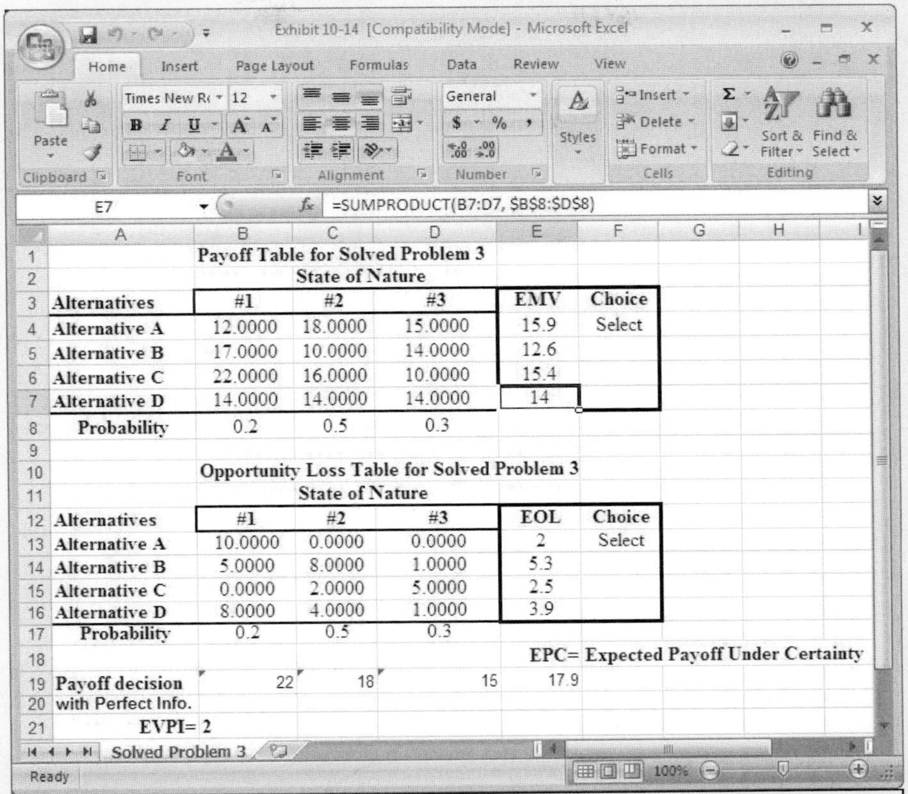

Exhibit 10-14 [Compatibility Mode] - Microsoft Excel

E7 =SUMPRODUCT(B7:D7, $B$8:$D$8)

	A	B	C	D	E	F
1		Payoff Table for Solved Problem 3				
2			State of Nature			
3	**Alternatives**	#1	#2	#3	EMV	Choice
4	**Alternative A**	12.0000	18.0000	15.0000	15.9	Select
5	**Alternative B**	17.0000	10.0000	14.0000	12.6	
6	**Alternative C**	22.0000	16.0000	10.0000	15.4	
7	**Alternative D**	14.0000	14.0000	14.0000	14	
8	**Probability**	0.2	0.5	0.3		
9						
10		Opportunity Loss Table for Solved Problem 3				
11			State of Nature			
12	**Alternatives**	#1	#2	#3	EOL	Choice
13	**Alternative A**	10.0000	0.0000	0.0000	2	Select
14	**Alternative B**	5.0000	8.0000	1.0000	5.3	
15	**Alternative C**	0.0000	2.0000	5.0000	2.5	
16	**Alternative D**	8.0000	4.0000	1.0000	3.9	
17	**Probability**	0.2	0.5	0.3		
18					EPC= Expected Payoff Under Certainty	
19	**Payoff decision**	22	18	15	17.9	
20	with Perfect Info.					
21	EVPI= 2					

Solved Problem 3

Ready

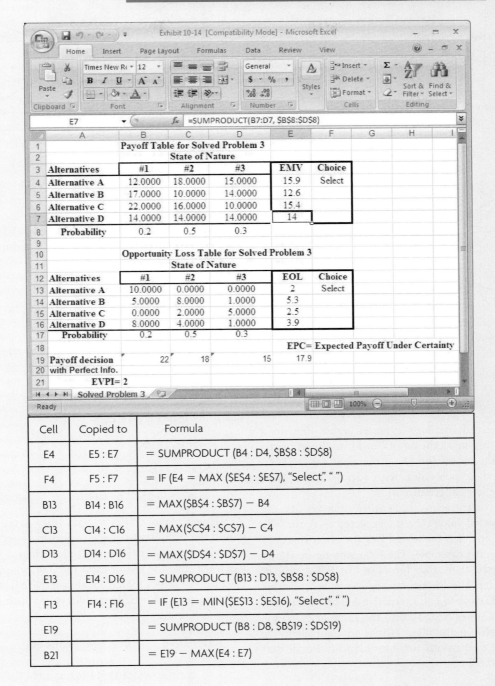

Cell	Copied to	Formula
E4	E5 : E7	= SUMPRODUCT (B4 : D4, $B$8 : $D$8)
F4	F5 : F7	= IF (E4 = MAX ($E$4 : $E$7), "Select", " ")
B13	B14 : B16	= MAX($B$4 : $B$7) − B4
C13	C14 : C16	= MAX($C$4 : $C$7) − C4
D13	D14 : D16	= MAX($D$4 : $D$7) − D4
E13	E14 : D16	= SUMPRODUCT (B13 : D13, $B$8 : $D$8)
F13	F14 : F16	= IF (E13 = MIN($E$13 : $E$16), "Select", " ")
E19		= SUMPRODUCT (B8 : D8, $B$19 : $D$19)
B21		= E19 − MAX(E4 : E7)

Problem 4

Given this table of estimated *costs:*

Alternative	State of Nature #1	#2
a	10	1
b	2	8
c	7	6

Find the range of $P(\#2)$ for which each alternative has the best expected value.

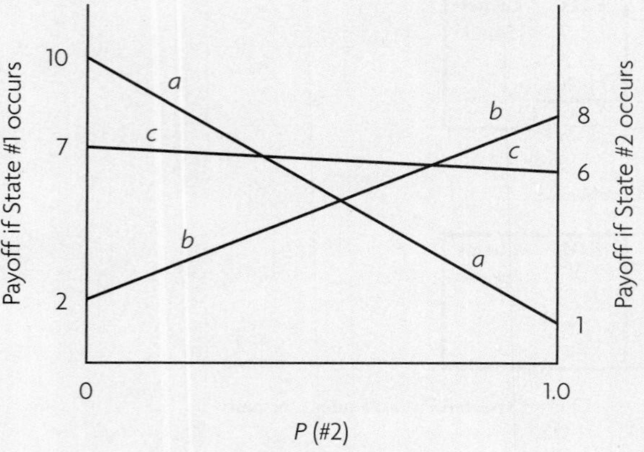

Solution

First, plot each alternative's expected value line on a graph. To do this, mark the payoff for #1 on the left vertical axis and the payoff for #2 on the right vertical axis, then connect these two points with a straight line. Then label each line (e.g., alternative *a*).

Because costs are involved rather than profits, the *lower* the expected value (i.e., the expected *cost*), the better. Consequently, it is the lowest line for given values of $P(\#2)$ that is most desirable. The following figure shows this. We can see, then, that for values of $P(\#2)$ near 0, alternative *b* has the lowest expected cost, whereas for values of $P(\#2)$ close to 1.0, alternative *a* is best. Note that alternative *c* is never best. To find the value of $P(\#2)$ for which Alternative *b* and alternative *a* are equivalent, we must formulate equations for lines *a* and *b*. Recall that each line has the form:

$$EV = \text{Payoff } \#1 + (\text{Payoff } \#2 - \text{Payoff } \#1) \times P(\#2)$$

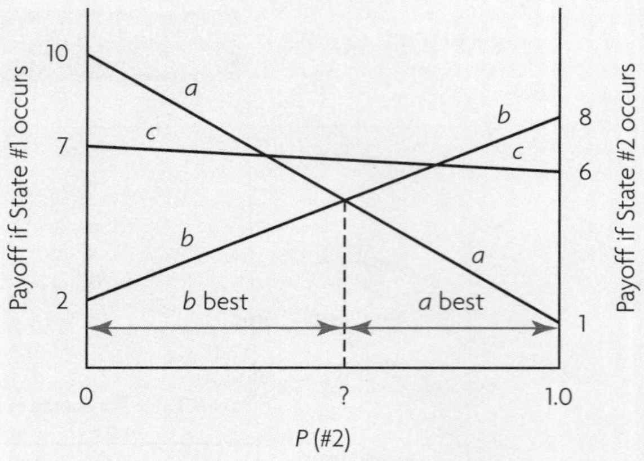

Thus, for line *a* we have

$$EV_a = 10 + (1 - 10)P(\#2), \quad \text{which reduces to}$$
$$EV_a = 10 - 9P(\#2)$$

For line *b*, we have

$$EV_b = 2 + (8 - 2)P(\#2), \quad \text{which reduces to}$$
$$EV_b = 2 + 6P(\#2)$$

Setting these equal to each other and solving for $P(\#2)$ gives us

$$10 - 9P(\#2) = 2 + 6P(\#2)$$

Rearranging terms produces

$$15P(\#2) = 8$$

Solving for $P(\#2)$:

$$P(\#2) = 8/15 \quad \text{or } .533$$

Thus, when $P(\#2) = .533$, the decision maker would be indifferent between choosing alternative *a* or *b*. For values of $P(\#2)$ from 0 to less than .533, alternative *b* will give the lowest expected cost, whereas for values of $P(\#2)$ larger than .533, alternative *a* has the lowest expected cost. Hence, the ranges over which each alternative is best are

Alternative	Best over Range of
b	$0 \le P(\#2) < .533$
a	$.533 < P(\#2) \le 1.0$
c	Never

Problem 5

Decision making with sample information A manager has developed a table that shows payoffs ($000) for a future store. The payoffs depend on the size of the store and the strength of demand:

	Payoff Table States of Nature Demand		
	Alternative	Low	High
	Small	30	50
Store Size	Large	10	80

The manager estimates that the probability of low demand is .50, and the probability of high demand is .50.

The manager could request that a local research firm conduct a survey (cost: $2000) that would better indicate whether demand will be low or high. In discussions with the research firm, the manager has learned the following about the reliability of surveys conducted by the firm:

	Actual Result Was	
Survey Showed	Low	High
Low	.90	.30
High	.10	.70

a. If the manager should decide to use the survey, what would the revised probabilities be for demand, and what probabilities should be used for survey results (i.e., survey shows Low and survey shows High demand)?
b. Construct a tree diagram for this problem.
c. Determine the EVSI.
d. Would you recommend that the manager use the survey? Explain.

Solution

a. Table 10-18 shows revised probabilities if the survey shows Low demand.

Table 10-19 shows revised probabilities if survey shows High demand.

Hence, the revised probabilities are $P(\text{Low}) = .75$ and $P(\text{High}) = .25$ if the survey shows Low demand; and $P(\text{Low}) = .125$ and $P(\text{High}) = .875$ if the survey shows High demand. Further, the probability that the survey will show Low demand is .60 (the sum of joint probabilities) and the probability the survey will show High demand is .40.

TABLE 10-18 Problem 5: Revised Probabilities if the Survey Shows Low Demand

Actual Demand	Conditional Probability		Prior Probability		Joint Probability	Revised Probability
Low	.90	×	.50	=	.45	.45/.60 = .75
High	.30	×	.50	=	.15	.15/.60 = .25
Marginal probabilty of low demand				=	.60	1.00

TABLE 10-19 Problem 5: Revised Probabilities if the Survey Shows High Demand

Actual Demand	Conditional Probability		Prior Probability		Joint Probability	Revised Probability
Low	.10	×	.50	=	.05	.05/.40 = .125
High	.70	×	.50	=	.35	.35/.40 = .875
Marginal probabilty of low demand				=	.40	1.000

b.

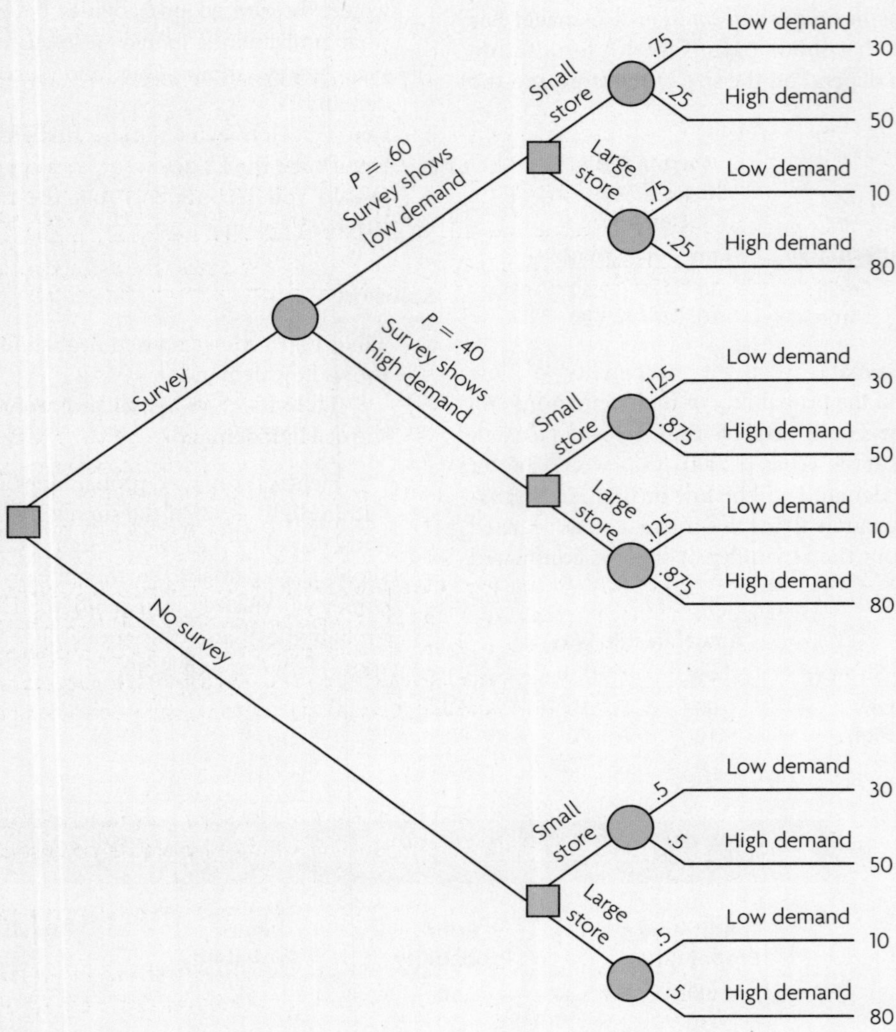

c. To find EVSI, first find the expected payoffs for store size for each of the following: Survey shows low demand, Survey shows high demand, and No survey. Thus:

Survey shows low demand:

Small store	.75(30) + .25(50) = 35.00
Large store	.75(10) + .25(80) = 27.50

Survey shows high demand:

Small store	.125(30) + .875(50) = 47.50
Large store	.125(10) + .875(80) = 71.25

No Survey:

Small store	.50(30) + .50(50) = 40.00
Large store	.50(10) + .50(80) = 45.00

These then can be placed on a tree diagram as expected payoffs for store size decisions:
Next, the branch at each ending decision node with the smaller expected payoff can be "cut" or eliminated, as shown by the two slashes on appropriate branches.

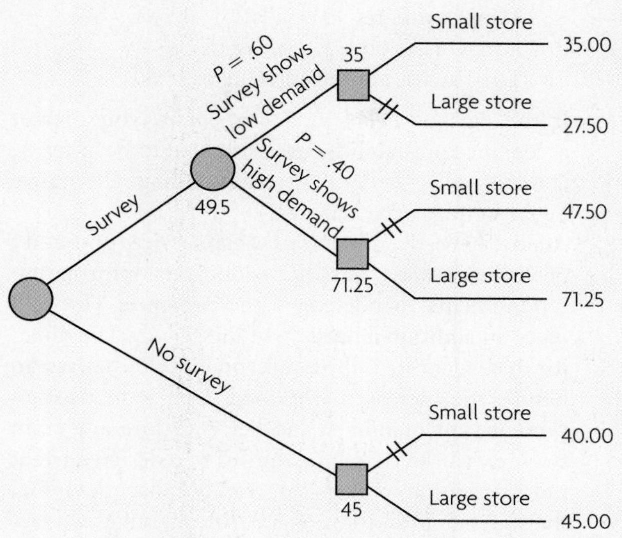

Then, the expected payoff for using the survey can be computed using the remaining branches and their expected payoffs. Thus:

$$.60(35.00) + .40(71.25) = 49.50$$

The expected payoff for No survey is shown on the tree. It is 45.00.

The expected value of sample information is the difference between these two. Thus:

$$\text{EVSI} = 49.50 - 45.00 = 4.50 \text{ thousand, or } \$4500$$

e. Because the EVSI is $4500, whereas the cost of the survey is $2000, it would seem reasonable for the manager to use the survey; the expected gain would be $2500 ($4500 − $2000)

Discussion and Review Questions

1. Describe the difference between a state of nature and decision alternative.
2. Describe the difference between prior and posterior probabilities.
3. Explain maximax and maximin criteria and describe the difference between them.
4. Explain Hurwicz criterion and the relationship between Hurwicz criterion and maximax and maximin criteria.
5. Describe the difference among decision making under certainty, decision making under uncertainty, and decision making under risk.
6. Describe the meaning of Expected Monetary Value (EMV).
7. Describe the meaning of Expected Value of Perfect Information (EVPI).
8. Describe the meaning of a circle and a square in developing a decision tree. What is the difference between a single decision and a sequential decision? Describe when it is most useful to utilize the decision tree approach.
9. Describe the difference between risk averters and risk takers by giving examples of both types of behaviour from real world.
10. What is utility theory and how does it differ from making decisions based on monetary value?
11. Describe why is it important to perform sensitivity analysis when decisions are made under risk.
12. Describe how to determine the opportunity loss table from the payoff table and the meaning of the minimax regret approach.
13. How does Equally Likely criterion differ from Hurwicz criterion?

Problems

1. Consider the following payoff table (profits in $100 000):

	State of Nature			
Alternative	s_1	s_2	s_3	s_4
a_1	7	14	13	10
a_2	3	6	12	15
a_3	−8	−1	11	22

Which alternative would be chosen for each of the following decision criteria?

a. Maximin
b. Maximax
c. Minimax regret
d. Equal likelihood
e. The Hurwicz criterion with $\alpha = .70$

2. Suppose that probabilities were available for the states of nature in the previous problem. Which alternative would maximize expected payoff if the probabilities were $P(s_1) = .2$, $P(s_2) = .1$, $P(s_3) = .4$, and $P(s_4) = .3$?
3. Farah Fashion, an assistant buyer of a sportswear department, must decide on clothes orders for the winter season. Two new styles of coats were introduced at a recent show. The styles are quite different, and the assistant buyer must decide whether to fill the entire order with one of the styles or to split the order between the two. The profits for various states of nature have been estimated by the head buyer, and are shown in the following payoff table:

	Market Acceptance		
Alternative	**Style A**	**Style B**	**Split**
Style A	80	30	45
Style B	20	90	55
Split	60	70	96

Use Excel and determine which alternative would be selected for each of these decision criteria:

a. Maximin
b. Maximax
c. Minimax regret
d. Equal likelihood
e. The Hurwicz criterion using $\alpha = .60$

4. Suppose that the assistant buyer in the preceding problem is able to estimate that the probability for market acceptance of Style A is .30, the probability for market acceptance of Style B is .20, and the probability of a market split is .50.

a. Which alternative would maximize the expected profit?
b. Determine the expected value of perfect information using the expected payoff under certainty approach.
c. Verify that using the opportunity loss table results in the same expected value of perfect information found in part *b*.
d. Construct a decision tree. Indicate expected branch profits.

5. Suppose that the amounts given in the payoff table of Problem 3 were costs rather than profits. Use Excel and determine the appropriate decision for each of the following criteria:

a. Minimax
b. Minimin
c. Minimax regret
d. Equal likelihood
e. The Hurwicz criterion using $\alpha = .60$

6. If the data in Problem 3 were costs, and market acceptance probabilities are estimated to be .3 for A, .2 for B, and .5 for split, determine which alternative will minimize expected cost.
7. Anabelle Lee, the director of social services of the city of Regina, has just learned of additional information requirements mandated by the province. This will place an additional burden on the agency. The director has identified three acceptable alternatives to handle the increased workload. One is to reassign present staff members, another is to hire and train two new workers, and the third is to redesign current practice so that workers can readily collect the information with little additional effort. An unknown factor is the caseload for the coming year, during which time the new data will be collected on a trial basis. The estimated costs for various options and caseloads are shown in the table that follows:

Cost Table

	Caseload		
	Moderate	**High**	**Very high**
Reassign staff	\$50*	60	85
New staff	60	60	60
Redesign collection	40	50	90

*Cost in thousands.

Assuming that probabilities of various caseloads are unreliable, based on past experience, what decision would be appropriate using each of the following criteria?

a. Minimax
b. Minimin
c. Minimax regret
d. Equal likelihood
e. The Hurwicz criterion using $\alpha = .20$

8. After contemplating the caseload question, Annabelle (see Problem 7) has decided that reasonable caseload probabilities are .10 for moderate, .30 for high, and .60 for very high.

a. Which alternative will yield the minimum expected cost?
b. Construct a decision tree for this problem. Indicate the expected costs for the three decision branches.
c. Determine the expected value of perfect information using an opportunity loss table.

9. Suppose the director of social services will have the option of hiring an additional staff member if one staff member is hired initially and the caseload turns out to be high or very high. Under that plan, the first entry in row 2 of the cost table (see Problem 7) will be 40 instead of 60, the second entry will be 75 instead of 60, and the last entry will be 80 instead of 60. Assume the caseload probabilities as noted in Problem 8. Construct a decision tree that shows the sequential nature of this decision, and determine which alternative will minimize expected cost.
10. The owner of a small business is considering three options: buying a computer, leasing a computer, or getting along without a computer. Based on the information obtained from the firm's accountant, the following payoff table was developed.

	State of Nature	
Alternative	s_1	s_2
Do nothing	4	2
Buy	8	1
Lease	5	3

The owner would like to use the expected value criterion to make a decision, but she is hesitant because her probability estimates are quite rough.

a. Eliminate the alternative that is dominated by another alternative.
b. Determine $P(s_1)$ and $P(s_2)$ such that the owner would be indifferent between the two remaining alternatives.
c. For what range of probability would Lease have a higher expected payoff than the other alternative?
d. If probabilities are ignored, which alternative would offer the more conservative choice in this situation? Why?
e. Which alternative would the owner choose using the Hurwicz criterion if her degree of optimism is .6?

11. Given the payoff table that follows, determine the value of $P(\text{low})$ and $P(\text{moderate})$ that would make a decision maker indifferent between London and Tokyo.

	State of Nature	
Alternative	**Low**	**Moderate**
London	10	8
Tokyo	6	12

12. The owner of the Danish Pastry Baking Company, Fred Butterfield, recently submitted two bids, one to the city of Calgary to supply baked goods to various city buildings for two years, and the other to supply baked goods to the city's Catholic school board, again for two years. The owner estimates the probabilities of receiving the contracts as follows:

Outcome	Probability
No contracts	.20
City only	.20
Catholic school board only	.50
City and Catholic school board	.10

Fred has just learned that a competing bakery is about to close, and that two delivery trucks will be for sale. These trucks can be bought for a very reasonable price compared to the cost of new trucks, but Fred is unsure of whether to buy one truck, two trucks, or no trucks.

If Fred does not buy any trucks and no contracts are awarded, the net profit will be zero. If the city of Calgary contract alone is awarded, a profit of \$14 000 will be realized even without any trucks because the firm has some excess capacity at present. If the Catholic school board contract alone is awarded, the profit will be only \$10 000. If both contracts are awarded, Fred can buy either one truck, two trucks, or no trucks. The estimated profits considering salvage and depreciation are \$12 000 for one truck, \$15 000 for two trucks, and a loss of \$2000 for no trucks.

If one of the used delivery trucks is purchased, the estimated profits are −\$3000 for No contract, \$8000 for city only, \$6000 for Catholic school board only, and \$11 000 for city and Catholic school board. However, in the event that both contracts are awarded to the bakery, Fred has the option of buying another truck and realizing a net profit of \$16 000.

If two used trucks are initially bought, the estimated profits are −\$7000 for No contract, \$9000 for city only, \$5000 for the Catholic school board only, and \$25 000 for both. If No contract is awarded, the owner has the option of selling one or both trucks. For one truck, the net profit would be \$3000, whereas if two are sold, the net profit would be \$6000. If Fred uses maximum expected profits as the decision criterion, use Excel and determine which alternative should be chosen. Explain your reasoning.
13. Use Excel and analyze the tree diagram shown in Figure 10-3 using expected monetary value as the decision criterion. What alternative is recommended?
14. A manufacturer produces and sells chilled, ready-to-eat pasta salad in round lots of 50 serving units each. These items have a very limited shelf life; therefore, if

items are made but not sold, they have no value. Conversely, if demand exceeds supply during the week (regular production runs are made on Friday of each week for sales the following week), an extra production run can be made. The cost per unit for a regular run is $5 per unit, whereas the cost of an extra production run is $7 per unit. All items are sold for $10 per unit regardless of production cost. Historically, demand has been for 50, 100, or 150 units each week, so the company makes one of those run sizes. In the past, the manager of the department has made 100 units per week for regular production.

a. Prepare a payoff table showing profits for each of the lot sizes.
b. If probability of demand for 50 units is .40, probability of demand of 100 units is .50, and probability of demand for 150 units is .10, what lot size would you recommend if the goal is to maximize expected profit?
c. What is the EVPI?
d. Answer parts *a*, *b*, and *c* given this additional consideration: Suppose that disposal cost for unsold items is $1 per unit.

15. For Solved Problem 5, determine the EVSI, and decide if you would recommend using the survey if the reliability of surveys conducted by the firm was *changed* to the following:

	Actual Result Was	
Survey Showed	**Low**	**High**
Low	.75	.15
High	.25	.85

Assume that all other information remains unchanged. What is the efficiency of sample information in this instance?

16. A lawyer is preparing a case for trial. In an attempt to decide whether to follow an aggressive approach or a conservative approach in presenting his client's case, the lawyer has developed this payoff table:

	Case	
Approach	**Win**	**Lose**
Aggressive	$40 000	−10 000
Conservative	20 000	−6000

The lawyer believes there is a probability of .30 that he can win the case. However, for a fee of $2000, he can consult with an expert who is familiar with this type of case and can provide another opinion on whether the case will be won. Previous experience with using that expert can be summarized by the following table:

	Outcome	
Expert predicted	**Won**	**Lost**
Win	.85	.05
Lose	.15	.95

Is the expected value of the expert's advice worth the fee? Illustrate your analysis using a decision tree.

17. Barry Greene, the manager of a commercial loan department of a bank, must decide how to allocate loans among various loan proposals. The manager has the following payoff table, which shows profits for various loan strategies and economic scenarios:

	State of Nature Economy	
Alternative	**Stable**	**Changing**
Strategy A	$50 000	20 000
Strategy B	10 000	80 000

Barry believes that a stable economy is four times as likely as a changing economy. However, the manager is somewhat uncomfortable with this personal assessment and would like to take advantage of a governmental research agency's services regarding the probability of each type of economy.

According to the agency, its reliability for such forecasts in the past has been

	Actual	
Forecast	**Stable**	**Changing**
Stable	.88	.08
Changing	.12	.92

a. Using the criterion of maximizing expected payoff, what strategy would Barry select without using the agency?
b. If Barry decides to use the agency, what would be the revised probabilities for the economy for each forecast possibility?
c. Prepare a tree diagram that illustrates the problem.
d. Determine the EVSI.
e. If the agency fee is $3000, would you recommend using the agency? Explain. What is the efficiency of sample information?

18. Annabelle Lee, the director of social services (see Problems 7 and 8), has just learned about a consulting firm that has worked with similar departments throughout the country in making similar

assessments. After discussing the matter with a representative of the firm, the following table was produced to summarize the firm's reliability in terms of this problem:

	Actual Caseload		
Predicted Caseload	**Moderate**	**High**	**Very high**
Moderate	.80	0	0
High	.10	.90	.10
Very high	.10	.10	.90

The firm's fee to handle this prediction problem would be $8000.

a. Determine the EVSI and the efficiency of sample information.
b. Do you recommend that the consulting firm be used? Explain.

19. Given this payoff table:

	Demand low	Demand high
Build small	20	20
Build large	10	40

a. Suppose the values in the table are profits. In terms of the probability that demand will be high, over what range of probability will each alternative action be best?
b. Now suppose that the values in the payoff table are costs. Over what range of values for *P*(Demand high) will each alternative be best?

20. Manager Sara Stern has compiled estimated profits for various alternative courses of action, but she is reluctant to assign probabilities to the states of nature. The payoff table is

	State of Nature	
Alternative	**#1**	**#2**
A	20	140
B	120	80
C	100	40

a. Plot the expected value lines on a graph.
b. Is there any alternative that would never be appropriate in terms of maximizing expected profit? Explain on the basis of your graph.
c. For what range of *P*(#2) would alternative B be the best choice if the goal is to maximize expected profit?
d. For what range of *P*(#1) would alternative B be the best choice if the goal is to maximize expected profit?

21. Repeat all parts of the preceding question assuming the values in the payoff tables are estimated *costs* and the goal is to minimize expected cost.

22. The research staff of a marketing agency has assembled the following payoff table of estimated profits:

Proposal	Receive contract	Not receive contract
#1	10	−2
#2	8	3
#3	5	5
#4	0	7

Relative to the probability of not receiving the contract, determine the range of probability for which each of the proposals would maximize expected profit.

23. Although he has prepared a payoff table for a decision problem, manager John Burns is reluctant to assign probabilities to the two states of nature he has determined will occur (i.e., one of these two will definitely occur). Given his payoff table and his feeling that the probability of receiving the job is between .45 and .50, which alternative should John choose if it is his intention to maximize expected profits?

Alternative	Receive job	Do not receive job
A	90	30
B	40	70
C	10	80

24. Given this payoff table:

	State of Nature	
Alternative	**#1**	**#2**
A	120	20
B	60	40
C	10	110
D	90	90

a. Determine the range of *P*(#1) for which each alternative would be best, treating the payoffs as profits.
b. Answer part *a* treating the payoffs as costs.

25. A manager must decide how many machines of a certain type to buy. The manager has narrowed the decision to two alternatives: (1) buy one machine or (2) buy two machines. If only one machine is purchased and demand is more than the company can handle, then a second machine will be purchased at a

later date. However, the cost per machine would be lower if the two machines were to be purchased at the same time. The initial purchase of two machines has a net value of $75 000 if demand is low and $140 000 if demand is high. The probability of low demand is .45. The initial purchase of one machine has a net value of $85 000 if demand is low. If demand is high, and the company decides to purchase one machine initially, the manager has three options. The first option is to do nothing with a net value of $85 000. The second option is to subcontract. If the firm decides to subcontract, there is a 65 percent chance of using vendor X with a net return of $100 000. There is a 35 percent chance of using vendor Y with a net return of $135 000. The third option is to purchase a second machine with a net value of $115 000. How many machines should the firm purchase initially and why? Use a decision tree to analyze the problem.

26. Given the following payoff table:

Alternative	State of Nature #1	#2
A	3	8
B	10	2

a. Plot each alternative's expected value line on a graph. Label the left vertical axis as "Payoff if state #1 occurs"; the right axis as "Payoff state #2 occurs"; and the horizontal axis as $P(\#2)$.

b. Determine the range of $P(\#2)$ for which each alternative would be best

c. Plot each alternative's expected value line on a graph. Label the left vertical axis as "Payoff if state #2 occurs"; the right axis as "Payoff if state #1 occurs"; and the horizontal axis as $P(\#1)$.

d. Determine the range of $P(\#1)$ for which each alternative would be best.

e. Answer part *b* treating the payoffs as costs.

f. Answer part *d* treating the payoffs as costs.

27. Jo-Jo Inc. is a manufacturing firm that produces soap. The company is owned by two brothers, Donald and David Schroeder, and has one plant. The company has experienced significant growth in demand, and the current plant does not appear to have sufficient capacity to meet demand. The company has decided to build a new plant to meet the additional capacity. However, the brothers must decide whether to construct a small, medium, or large plant. The brothers hired a forecasting consultant to predict demand. The consultant's report indicates that there is a 25 percent chance that the demand will be low and a 75 percent chance that the demand will be high. If Jo-Jo Inc. builds a small facility and the demand indeed turns out to be low, the consultant expects net profit of $40 million. If the firm builds a small plant and the demand turns out to be high, then the firm has two options: (1) subcontract or (2) expand the facility. If Jo-Jo Inc. decides to subcontract, the expected net return will be $44 million. If the firm expands the new facility, there is a 40 percent chance that the net return will be $42 million and a 60 percent chance that the net return will be $48 million. If the medium-size facility is constructed and the demand turns out to be low, the net return is estimated at $28 million. However, if the medium-size facility is built and the demand turns out to be high, Jo-Jo Inc. has two options: (1) do nothing, for an expected net return of $48 million, or (2) expand. If the firm decides to expand, there is a 35 percent chance that it will earn a net return of $44 million and a 65 percent chance that it will earn a net return of $54 million. If the firm decides to build a large facility and demand turns out to be low, the net return will be $10 million. However, if the firm decides to build a large plant and the demand turns out to be high, the expected net return is $58 million. Use decision tree analysis and determine the best option for Jo-Jo Inc.

Case 1: MKGP Construction Company

MKGP has just introduced a new product line. It is considering three options regarding its new product line: (1) subcontract, (2) expand existing facility, or (3) build a new facility. A consultant's report indicates a 30 percent probability that the demand will be low, a 50 percent probability that the demand will be medium, and a 20 percent probability that the demand will be high.

If MKGP decides to subcontract and demand turns out to be low, the net present value of the returns will be $550 000. If the firm decides to subcontract and demand turns out to be medium, the firm has two options available. (1) do nothing, with a net present value of $660 000; or (2) expand its operations. If the firm decides to expand its operations, there is a 35 percent chance of earning a net return of $620 000 and a 65 percent chance of earning a net return of $740 000. If the firm decides to subcontract and demand turns out to be high, then the firm has three options available. (1) do nothing, with a net present value of $620 000; (2) expand, with a net present value of $810 000; or (3) build a new facility, with a net present value of $890 000.

If MKGP decides to expand and the demand turns out to be low, then the company has two choices: (1) do nothing, with an expected net present return of $360 000, or (2) use the expansion for other purposes. Depending on the result of negotiations regarding facilities, there is a 65 percent chance that the firm uses the expansion for manufacturing another product and a 35 percent chance that it will use it for the purposes of warehousing and storage. The net present value of using the expansion for other manufacturing purposes is $700 000, and the net present value of using the expansion as a storage facility is $400 000.

If MKGP decides to expand and the demand is medium, then the expected net return is $510 000. If the firm decides to expand and the demand is high, then the company has the following options available: (1) do nothing (net return of $810 000), (2) subcontract (net return of $740 000), or (3) build a new facility (net return of $840 000).

If MKGP decides to build a new facility and the demand is low, then the company has two choices: (1) do nothing, with an expected net present return of $340 000, or (2) use the new facility for other purposes. Depending on the result of negotiations regarding facilities, there is a 42 percent chance that the firm uses the new building for manufacturing another product and a 58 percent chance that it will use it for the purposes of warehousing and storage. The net present value of using the new building for manufacturing another product is $670 000 and the net present value of using the new building as a storage facility is $490 000. If the firm decides to build a new facility and the demand is medium, then the company has a 35 percent chance of earning a net return of $600 000 and a 65 percent chance of earning a net return of $730 000. If the firm decides to build a new facility and the demand is high, the net present value of the return is $1 200 000. Using decision tree analysis, make a recommendation for MKGP.

Case 2: Cerebrosoft Inc.*

Cerebrosoft, a small company located in Ottawa, develops PC-based software for the multimedia sector and sells it over the World Wide Web. Two of its products generate 80 percent of the company's revenues: Audiatur and Vidcatur. Customers can download a trial version of the software, test it, and if they are satisfied with what they see, they can purchase the product (by using a password that enables them to disable the time counter in the trial version). Both products are priced at $75.95. For Cerebrosoft, selling software over the Web eliminates many of the traditional cost factors of consumer products: packaging, storage, distribution, sales force, and so on. Instead, potential customers can download a trial version take a look at it (that is, use the product) before its trial period expires, and then decide whether to buy it. Furthermore, Cerebrosoft can always make the most recent files available to the customer, avoiding the problem of having outdated software in the distribution pipeline. The company is contemplating launching a new product, Brainet. However, Raphael Alexandre, CEO, major shareholder and founder of the company, is concerned about the risk involved. In effect, in this competitive market, marketing Brainet also could lead to substantial losses. Should the company go ahead anyway and start the marketing campaign? Or should it just abandon the product? Or perhaps it should buy additional marketing research information from a local market research company before deciding whether to launch the product? According to the information available, four main factors are relevant to the success of this project: competition, units sold, cost, and pricing. The marketing department is considering three pricing alternatives: selling for $50.00 and trying to maximize revenue, selling for $30.00 and trying to maximize market share, or selling for $40.00 and trying to do well in both revenue and market share. With respect to costs, the company has basically amortized the development costs incurred for Brainet. So far $800 000 has been spent and the company expects to spend another $50 000 per year for support and shipping the CDs to those who want a hard copy on top of their downloaded software. The company has also gathered some data on the industry showing the corresponding probability of various amounts of sales for each pricing alternative given the level of competition (severe, moderate, or weak) that develops from other companies. The information gathered is summarized in the following three tables. From the company's past experience, the likelihood of facing severe competition has been estimated at 20 percent, 70 percent for moderate competition, and 10 percent for weak competition.

TABLE 10-20 Probability Distribution of Unit Sales Given a High Price ($50)

	Level of Competition		
Sales	**Severe**	**Moderate**	**Weak**
50 000 units	0.20	0.25	0.30
30 000 units	0.25	0.30	0.35
20 000 units	0.55	0.45	0.35

TABLE 10-21 Probability Distribution of Unit Sales Given a Medium Price ($40)

	Level of Competition		
Sales	**Severe**	**Moderate**	**Weak**
50 000 units	0.25	0.30	0.40
30 000 units	0.35	0.40	0.50
20 000 units	0.40	0.30	0.10

TABLE 10-22 Probability Distribution of Unit Sales Given a Low Price ($30)

	Level of Competition		
Sales	**Severe**	**Moderate**	**Weak**
50 000 units	0.35	0.40	0.50
30 000 units	0.40	0.50	0.45
20 000 units	0.25	0.10	0.05

If the company would like to consider gathering additional marketing research information before deciding to launch the new product and at what price, the cost would be $10 000. The study of past records of the marketing research firm that the company might consider to hire shows very good predictions in other similar projects. Given that the competition turned out to be severe, the firm predicted it correctly 80 percent of the time, while 15 percent of the time a moderate competition was predicted in that setting. Given that the competition turned out to be moderate, the firm predicted severe competition 15 percent of the time and moderate competition 80 percent of the time. Finally, for the case of weak competition, the numbers were 90 percent of the time a correct prediction, 7 percent of the time a "moderate" prediction and 3 percent of the time a "severe" prediction.

Managerial Report

a. For the initial analysis, ignore the opportunity of obtaining more information by hiring the marketing research company. Identify the decision alternatives and the states of nature. Construct the payoff table. Then formulate the decision problem in a decision tree. Clearly distinguish between decision and event nodes and include all the relevant data.
b. What should Raphael Alexandre's decision be if the expected monetary value rule is used?
c. Now consider the possibility of doing the market research. Develop the corresponding decision tree. Calculate the relevant probabilities and analyze the decision tree. Should Cerebrosoft pay the $10 000 for the marketing research? What is the overall optimal policy? What is the efficiency of the information?

Source: Used with permission from Hillier & Hillier, *Introduction to Management Science*, 2nd ed. (Boston: McGraw-Hill Irwin, 2003).

CHAPTER 11

Markov Analysis

LEARNING OBJECTIVES

After completing this chapter, you should be able to:

1. Give examples of systems that may lend themselves to be analyzed by a Markov model.
2. Explain the meaning of transition probabilities.
3. Describe the kinds of system behaviours that Markov analysis pertains to.
4. Use a tree diagram to analyze system behaviour.
5. Use matrix multiplication to analyze system behaviour.
6. Use an algebraic method to solve for steady-state probabilities.
7. Analyze absorbing states, namely accounts receivable, using a Markov model.
8. List the assumptions of a Markov model.
9. Use Excel to solve various problems pertaining to a Markov model.

CHAPTER OUTLINE

11.1 INTRODUCTION

This chapter describes the analysis of *Markov* systems. Markov systems are very useful in studying the development of a system over repeated trials. Repeated trials often involve successive time periods where the state of the system in any particular time period is unknown. Therefore, we are interested in determining the probability of a system being in a particular state at a given time period (trial). A Markov system has these characteristics:

1. It will operate or exist for a number of periods (trials).
2. In each period, the system can assume one of a number of states or conditions.
3. The states are both mutually exclusive and collectively exhaustive.
4. System changes between states from period to period can be described by *transition probabilities,* which remain constant.
5. The probability of the system being in a given state in a particular period depends only on its state in the preceding period and the transition probabilities. It is independent of all earlier periods.

Table 11-1 gives some illustrations of systems that may lead themselves to Markov analysis.[1]

The use of Markov analysis on such systems can help decision makers understand how the systems behave over time. This sort of knowledge can be useful for *short-term* decisions such as scheduling a workforce, stocking inventory, and budgeting, and for *long-term* decisions such as determining locations for new facilities and capacity planning. These decisions may simply involve dealing with expected system behaviours or they may involve strategies for favourably altering the system (e.g., through price changes, advertising, and so on). For instance, the Modern Management Science Application, "Airline Meal Provisioning," describes the application of Markov analysis to the meal ordering process in the airline industry as an attempt to identify better ordering policies.

TABLE 11-1 Examples of Systems That May Be Described as Markov

System	Possible System States	Transition Probabilities
Brand switching	Proportion of customers who buy Brand A, Brand B, Brand C, etc.	Probability that a customer will switch from Brand A to Brand B, etc.
TV market share	Proportion of viewers who watch Channel 8, Channel 10, etc.	Probability that a viewer who watched Channel 8 news will switch to Channel 10 news, etc.
Rental returns	Proportion of renters who return rentals to various locations.	Probability that a renter will return item to a different location than the one it was rented from.
Machine breakdowns	Proportion of machines running, proportion not running.	Probability that a machine's condition—running/not running—will change in the next period.

[1]For a system to be considered Markov, it must satisfy certain assumptions that are described later in the chapter.

MODERN MANAGEMENT SCIENCE APPLICATION: AIRLINE MEAL PROVISIONING

The passenger airline industry operates on low profit margins with many competitors. To sustain profitability, some airline carriers are attempting to generate savings through efficiency improvements in their periphery operations. In-flight meal provisioning is one such area worthy of pursuit as it involves high volumes, significant costs, and has a direct impact on customer service. This service is typical for long duration flights and involves producing meals in an airport kitchen by a caterer and delivering them to a plane for eventual in-flight passenger service. A fundamental question is how to determine the number of meals to be prepared so as to ensure a high level of passenger service while keeping costs as low as possible. Excess costs are incurred when the meal quantity on the aircraft exceeds the passenger load. Furthermore, customer service costs are incurred when the meal quantity is lower than the passenger load. The caterer seeks to provide a meal quantity that closely matches the passenger load at departure. The process of meal ordering is challenging for two basic reasons. Firstly, significant lead time is required to produce a meal order. Meal provisioning involves preparation, cooking, assembling, chilling, and transporting the meal order, and in some airports, large flights depart within minutes of each other. Secondly, the passenger load may vary considerably within the lead time. Last minute ticket purchases, missed flights, stand-by passengers, and upgrade coupons all contribute to variability in passenger load. A Markov decision process model was developed and applied to the meal ordering process on a flight-by-flight basis in an attempt to identify better ordering policies. Applied to data from a Canadian airline company, improvements in overage and shortage were achieved. Overall, the model outperforms current practice on 52.5 percent of the flights, and closely matches the performance of actual practice in 20 percent of the flights. Applying the optimal policies at a level of service comparable to current practice yields cost savings of 17% in the long-duration flights.

Source: J. H. Goto, M. E. Lewis, M. L. Puterman: "Coffee, Tea, or . . .?: A Markov Decision Process Model," *Transportation Science* vol. 38, no. 1, (February 2004), pp. 107–118.

The chapter begins with an illustration of transition probabilities, which are the foundation of a Markov analysis. Then, three methods of analysis are illustrated: graphical and matrix, which are useful for describing short-term behaviour; and the algebraic method, which is useful for describing long-term behaviour patterns.

11.2 TRANSITION PROBABILITIES

A system whose behaviour can be described as a **Markov process** can be summarized by a set of conditional, or **transition probabilities,** which indicate the tendencies of the system to change from one period to the next. An example will help to clarify this important concept.

EXAMPLE 11-1

Consider a car rental agency that has offices at each of a city's two airports. Customers are allowed to return a rented car to either airport, regardless of which airport they rented from. (It is assumed that this is a closed system: All cars must be returned to one of the two airports.) If some cars will be used for one-way rentals to another city, or if some cars are dropped off from other cities, they can be excluded from the system and treated separately. In addition, it is assumed that all rentals will be for only one day, and that at the end of the day, every car will be returned to one of the two rental offices. Suppose that the manager of the rental agency has made a study of return behaviour and has found the following information: 70 percent of the cars rented from Airport A tend to be returned to that airport, and 30 percent of the Airport A cars tend to be returned to Airport B; 10 percent of the cars rented from Airport B are returned to Airport A, and 90 percent of the cars are returned to Airport B.

Prepare the transition matrix.

Solution

This information is summarized in the **transition matrix** illustrated in Table 11-2.

Because it is assumed that all of the rentals will be returned to one of the two airports, the *row* totals are 1.00, or 100 percent. The same does not apply to the column totals, because these *conditional* probabilities are stated in terms of *renting* locations rather than return locations. That is, the first value in the table, .70, represents the proportion of cars that can be expected to be returned to Airport A, *given* that they were rented at Airport A. Similarly, the .30 represents the proportion of cars expected to be returned to Airport B, *given* that they were rented at Airport A.

Table 11-2 Transition Probabilities for Car Rental Example

		Returned to		
		Airport A	**Airport B**	
Rented from	Airport A	.70	.30	1.00
	Airport B	.10	.90	1.00

In general, managers may be interested in either the short-run or the long-run behaviour of a system, or in both. The following section gives an overview of these two behaviours.

11.3 SYSTEM BEHAVIOUR

Both the long-term behaviour and the short-term behaviour of a system are completely determined by the system's transition probabilities. Short-term behaviour is solely dependent on the system's state in the current period and the transition probabilities. Thus, in the case of the car rental system, it can be seen from the transition matrix that 70 percent of the cars rented at Airport A are expected to be returned to Airport A and that 30 percent are expected to be returned to Airport B. Likewise, 10 percent of the cars rented from Airport B are expected to be returned to Airport A and 90 percent to Airport B. These proportions are expected to remain in effect. Consequently, the *number* of cars returned to each location in any given period is simply a function of the transition probabilities and the number rented from each location in the preceding period. Knowledge of the number of cars at each location at a given point in time can be used to track the short-term behaviour of the system. Moreover, the number of cars at each location in the preceding period is normally a significant factor that affects the number of cars at each location in the next several periods. However, the long-term behaviour of the system will be unaffected by the initial number of cars at each location; the proportion of cars returned to each location over the long run will be the same, regardless of initial conditions (the number of cars). The long-run proportions are referred to as the **steady-state** proportions, or probabilities, of the system. Not every system has a tendency to stabilize, though. Some tend to cycle back and forth, and some tend to converge on a single state called an *absorbing state.* More will be said about these cases later. Because such systems are less common than steady-state systems, the discussion here will emphasize steady-state systems.

These short-term and long-term tendencies of steady-state systems can be seen in Figure 11-1, which shows the proportion of returns to Airport A as a function of where they were rented in Period 0. Notice that in the first few periods, the original starting point (Airport A or Airport B) has a marked effect on the proportions, but that effect becomes less and less as time goes by, and that after about 10 periods, the original (Period 0) renting location is immaterial. As shown in Figure 11-1, the long-run proportion of those Period 0 rentals ending up at Airport A is 25 percent. A similar graph could be constructed showing the proportion of original rentals from each location returned to Airport B. It would show a long-run proportion of 75 percent of those Period 0 rentals ending up at Airport B.

11.4 METHODS OF ANALYSIS

As previously noted, a manager's interest in system behaviour can be related to either short-term considerations or long-term considerations, and often it is related to both. Methods for analyzing system behaviours relate to either the short term or the long term. Short-term behaviour can be described using either a tree diagram or matrix multiplication. Long-term behaviour could theoretically be analyzed by either of those approaches, but for practical reasons related to the amount of effort that would be involved, an algebraic method is used.

Each of these methods is presented below, beginning with a tree diagram for describing short-term system behaviour.

FIGURE 11-1 Expected Proportion of Period 0 Rentals Returned to Airport A

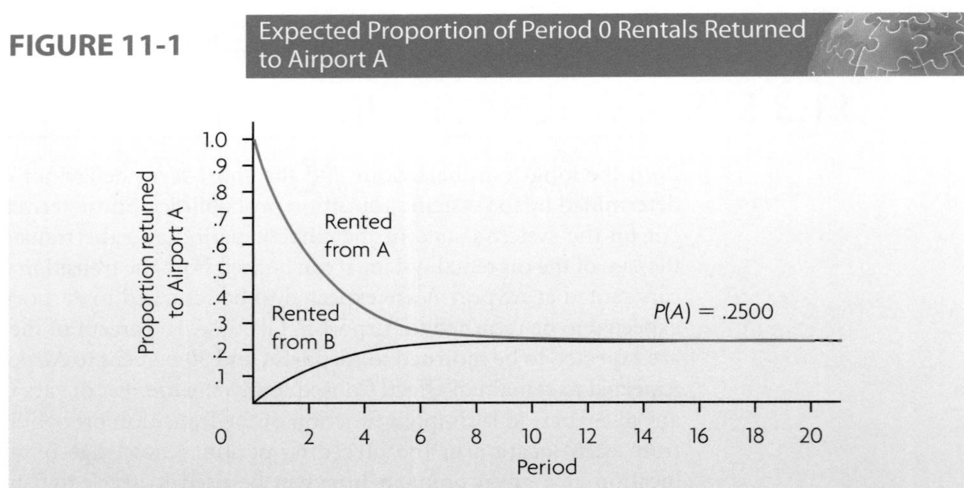

Tree Diagram

A **tree diagram** is a visual portrayal of a system's transitions. It is composed of a series of branches, which represent the possible choices at each stage (period) and the conditional probabilities of each choice being selected. For example, a car rented from Airport A can be returned to either Airport A or Airport B. Thus, there are two choices, the first with a probability of .70 and the second with a probability of .30. Similarly, a car rented at Airport B has two possible return locations, Airport A with a probability of .10 and Airport B with a probability of .90. Hence, each possible starting point (rental location) has two possible return locations. Moreover, we can represent the choices for each with separate tree diagrams. The two diagrams are illustrated in Figure 11-2.

If two or more periods are involved, the tree becomes more involved, but it is also more informative, particularly if the *joint* probabilities are shown for each branch. These reflect the proportion of members of the system (e.g., rental cars) that can be expected to follow a certain path (series of branches) through the tree diagram. The next example illustrates this.

EXAMPLE 11-2

Consider the car rental agency example discussed in Example 11-1. Prepare a tree diagram that shows the choices for two periods using the information contained in Table 11-2. Then, compute joint probabilities and use them to determine *how many* cars will be at Location A if A originally has 100 cars and Location B has 80 cars. That is, what proportion of cars will be returned to each airport in the short run (e.g., over the next several days)? This information will help the manager in scheduling counter staff for each location.

FIGURE 11-2 Tree Diagrams for the Car Rental Example for One Period

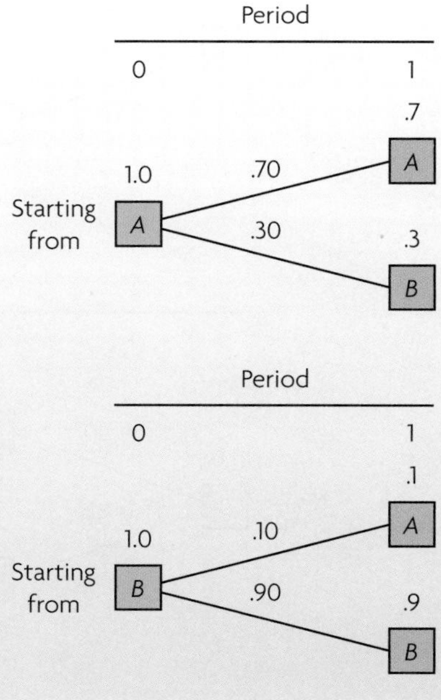

Solution

The two tree diagrams (one for a car rented from Airport A and the other for a car rented from Airport B) are shown in Figure 11-3. The joint probabilities are computed by multiplying the probabilities along each particular branch. Therefore, the proportion of cars rented from A in Period 0 that can be expected to be returned to A in Period 1 and then rented out and returned a second time to A is .70 × .70 = .49. Similarly, the proportion of cars first rented from A in Period 0, then returned to B in Period 1, and finally rented from B in Period 1 and returned to A in Period 2 is .30 × .10 = .03. Then, the total proportion of cars rented from A in Period 0 and expected back at A in Period 2 is .49 + .03 = .52, as shown. The other joint probabilities have a similar interpretation.

In effect, the joint probabilities reveal that 52 percent of the cars originally rented from A in Period 0 and 16 percent of the cars originally rented from B in Period 0 will end up at A in Period 2. Multiplying these probabilities by the number of cars originally at each location will yield the *expected number* of cars at Airport A at the end of Period 2. Because Airport A had 100 cars in Period 0 and Airport B had 80 cars, we find:

$$\underset{A}{100(.52)} + \underset{B}{80(.16)} = 64.8 \text{ cars}$$

FIGURE 11-3 Two-Period Tree Diagrams for Car Rental Example

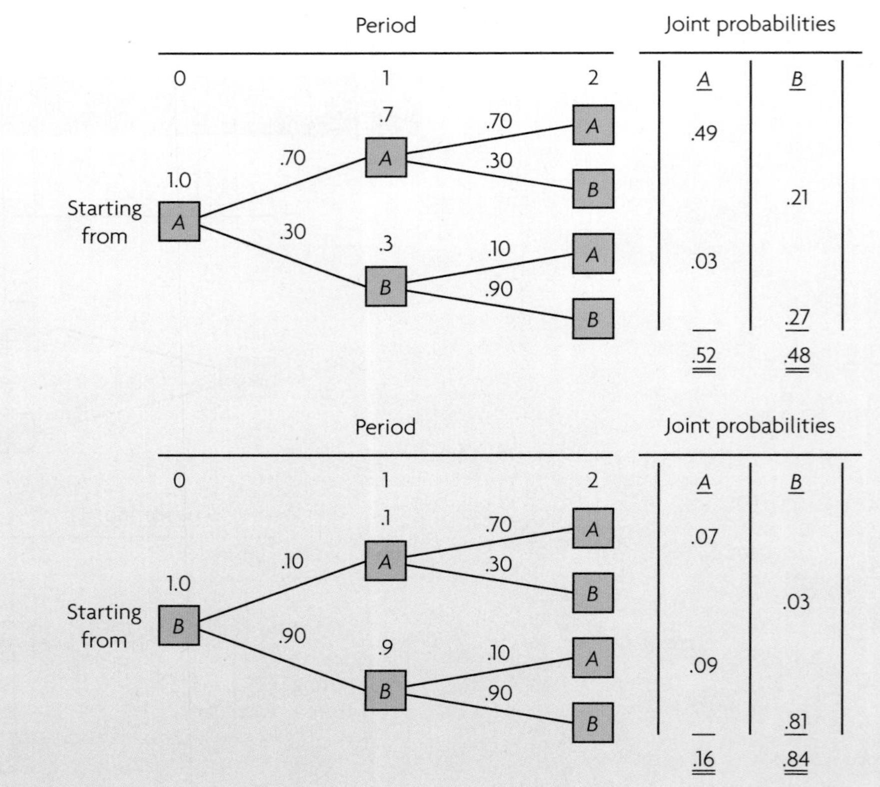

The fractional value of .8 does not imply that one of the cars may be returned with a missing door or bumper. The 64.8 represents an *average* number of cars. The actual number of cars would be an *integer* value. For repeated period, the number of cars returned to airport A will average 64.8.

Advantages of a tree diagram are that it is simple to construct and it provides us with a visual model that illustrates how the transition probabilities combine to determine system behaviour over the short run. However, as the number of periods covered by a tree increases beyond two or three, the number of branch ends tends to become large, making this method impractical. For example, to portray 5 periods would require 32 branch ends, and 6 periods would require 64 branch ends.

A more compact method for generating the short-term probabilities involves the use of matrix multiplication, which is covered in the next section.

Matrix Multiplication

A fairly simple method for obtaining expected state proportions over the short run is to use **matrix multiplication.** It is based on state proportions for any period being equal to the product of the proportions in the preceding period multiplied by the matrix of transition probabilities. Because the proportions, at any time, can be expressed in matrix form, this approach involves the multiplication of the "current" proportions, which is referred to as a *probability vector,* by the transition matrix. The vector has one row and the same number of columns as the transition matrix. For instance, the initial "current" vector for a case with two possible states of nature, and starting from State A, would be [1 0]. For the car rentals, this would mean all cars are at Airport A at the start. Conversely, starting in Period 0 from State B would be represented by [0 1]. For the car rentals, this would mean that all cars are at Airport B at the start. If there were three states of nature in the car rentals example (let's assume that Airport C is added), Period 0 would be expressed in the following way, depending on the starting state:

Starting from	Current Matrix
A	[1 0 0]
B	[0 1 0]
C	[0 0 1]

Matrix multiplication requires that the elements of the row of the first (current) matrix be matched with (multiplied by) the elements of the first column of the transition matrix and summed to obtain the first state proportion for the next period. Then, the elements of the row of the current matrix are matched with the elements of the second column and summed to obtain the second state proportion, and so on. The number of columns for the first matrix must be equal to the number of rows for the second matrix. The multiplication of two matrices, where the first matrix is of the order K^*M and the second matrix is of the order M^*N, will result in the following:

$$(K^*M)(M^*N) = (K^*N)$$

For example, we can calculate the state proportions for Period 1 for the car rental example for State (airport) A as follows:

$$[1 \quad 0]\begin{bmatrix} .70 & .30 \\ .10 & .90 \end{bmatrix} = \begin{array}{r} 1(.70) \\ +\ 0(.10) \\ \hline .70 \end{array} \qquad \begin{array}{r} 1(.30) \\ +\ 0(.90) \\ \hline .30 \end{array}$$

These values are, of course, simply the elements of the first row of the transition matrix. This is because the transition matrix describes the proportion of system members that are expected to end up in each state in Period 1, given State A start (the first row) and given State B start (the second row). The main point, here, though, is how to complete the matrix multiplication to obtain those values, so that values for subsequent periods can be calculated. You might find it helpful to think of the initial matrix as *vertical* rather than horizontal. That is:

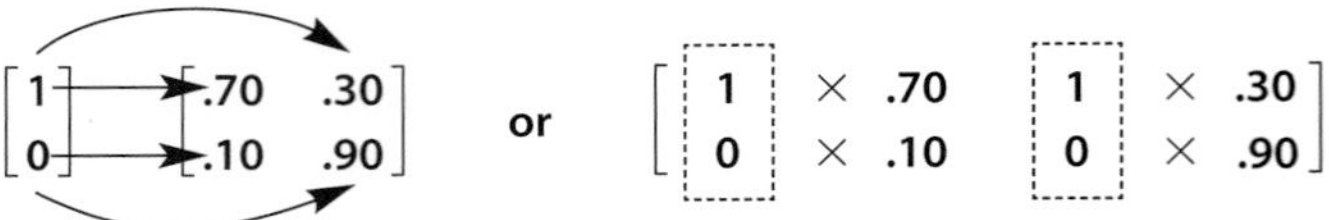

EXAMPLE 11-3

Consider the car rental agency example discussed in Example 11-1. Use matrix multiplication to find the state proportions for Periods 2 and 3, assuming State A start.

Solution

Because Period 1 proportions are .70 and .30, for Period 2 we have:

$$[.70 \quad .30]\begin{bmatrix} .70 & .30 \\ .10 & .90 \end{bmatrix} = \begin{matrix} .70(.70) = .49 & .70(.30) = .21 \\ .30(.10) = \underline{.03} & .30(.90) = \underline{.27} \\ .52 & .48 \end{matrix}$$

Thus, the Period 2 matrix is [.52 .48], which means that 52 percent are expected to be in State A and 48 percent are expected to be in State B. Now, we can calculate the proportions for Period 3:

$$[.52 \quad .48]\begin{bmatrix} .70 & .30 \\ .10 & .90 \end{bmatrix} = \begin{matrix} .52(.70) = .364 & .52(.30) = .156 \\ .48(.10) = \underline{.048} & .48(.90) = \underline{.432} \\ .412 & .588 \end{matrix}$$

Note that in each period, the state proportions sum to 1.00, and that the calculation for any period using this approach requires the proportions from the preceding period.

If we continued this sequential multiplication of each period's matrix and the transition matrix, we would discover that after a time the state proportions would not change significantly. That is, multiplying the state proportions by the transition matrix would result in the same state proportions. This condition is referred to as the *steady-state,* and the proportions indicate the expected percentage of system members in each state over the long run. Moreover, these steady-state values will be the same irrespective of which starting state is used, although the number of periods required to reach the steady-state may vary, depending on which state is used as a starting point. Table 11-3 illustrates the results of matrix multiplications from each starting point and the eventual steady-state proportions for each state. Thus, starting from State A, the steady-state values were obtained in approximately 19 periods, while starting from State B, the steady-state proportions were obtained in approximately 17 periods.

As you can surmise, considerable effort would be required to obtain these values manually. A computer could remove this burden. However, the primary concern is with

TABLE 11-3 Period-by-Period Proportions for the Rental Example, and the Steady-State Proportions Based on Matrix Multiplications

	Starting from A		Starting from B	
Period	$P(A)$	$P(B)$	$P(A)$	$P(B)$
0	1.0	0.0	0.0	1.0
1	.70	.30	.10	.90
2	.52	.48	.16	.84
3	.412	.588	.196	.804
4	.3472	.6528	.2176	.7824
5	.3083	.6917	.2306	.7694
6	.2850	.7150	.2384	.7616
7	.2710	.7290	.2430	.7570
8	.2626	.7374	.2458	.7542
9	.2576	.7424	.2475	.7525
10	.2546	.7454	.2485	.7515
11	.2528	.7472	.2491	.7509
12	.2517	.7483	.2495	.7505
13	.2510	.7490	.2497	.7503
14	.2506	.7494	.2498	.7502
15	.2504	.7496	.2499	.7501
16	.2502	.7498	.2499	.7501
17	.2501	.7499	.2500	.7500
18	.2501	.7499		
19	.2500	.7500		

the *values* at steady-state, rather than with how many periods would be required to obtain the values. And for that purpose, there is a much simpler method for deriving these steady-state proportions, which is described in the next section.

Algebraic Solution

An **algebraic approach** provides the most efficient method for obtaining the steady-state probabilities. The basis for an algebraic solution is a set of equations developed from the transition matrix. Moreover, because the states are mutually exclusive and collectively exhaustive, the sum of the state probabilities must be 1.00, and another equation can be developed from this requirement. The result is a set of equations that can be used to solve for the steady-state probabilities.

We will now develop the equations needed for an algebraic solution to the steady-state of a Markov process and then use the equations to determine the steady-state probabilities.

The steady-state equations for the car rental example can be developed in the following manner. Because the ending states are represented by the *columns* of the transition matrix, the *probabilities in each column* supply the necessary information for that state's long-term probabilities. Thus, the equation for Airport A is

$$P(A) = .70P(A) + .10P(B)$$

where

$$P(A) = \text{proportion of cars at Airport A}$$
$$P(B) = \text{proportion of cars at Airport B}$$

In effect, it expresses that the expected proportion of system members (or, equivalently, the proportion of time the system is expected to be in that state) is comprised of 70 percent from *A* and 10 percent from *B*. Similarly, the equation for Airport B is

$$P(B) = .3P(A) + .90P(B)$$

This equation is derived from the fact that the expected proportion in *B* is 30 percent of *A*'s "output" and 90 percent of *B*'s "output." Still a third equation can be developed since the total of the two probabilities must be 1.00:

$$P(A) + P(B) = 1$$

The development of these equations is illustrated in Figure 11-4.

Another way of developing the equations needed for algebraic solution is illustrated below.

In general, from the calculations shown in Table 11-3, we can state that

$$[P(A_{n+1}) \quad P(B_{n+1})] = [P(A_n) \quad P(B_n)] \underbrace{\begin{bmatrix} P_{11} & P_{12} \\ P_{21} & P_{22} \end{bmatrix}}_{\text{Transition Matrix}}$$

where n = period number.

However, as shown in Table 11-3, as n gets larger, the difference between $P(A_{n+1})$ and $P(A)$ and the difference between $P(B_{n+1})$ and $P(B)$ become negligible.

After a large number of periods, $P(A_{n+1}) = P(A)$ and $P(B_{n+1}) = P(B)$. Therefore, we can state that:

$$[P(A) \quad P(B)] = [P(A) \quad P(B)] \begin{bmatrix} P_{11} & P_{12} \\ P_{21} & P_{22} \end{bmatrix}$$

FIGURE 11-4 Development of Algebraic Equations

		To:	
		A	*B*
From:	*A*	.70	.30 → $P(A) = .7P(A) + .10\,P(B)$
	B	.10	.90 → $P(B) = .3P(A) + .90\,P(B)$
			$P(A) + P(B) = 1$

or by substituting the transition probabilities, we get

$$[P(A) \quad P(B)] = [P(A) \quad P(B)] \begin{bmatrix} .7 & .3 \\ .1 & .9 \end{bmatrix}$$

After performing matrix multiplication of the right-hand side, we get

$$[P(A) \quad P(B)] = [.70P(A) + .10P(B); .30P(A) + .90P(B)]$$

We can write these equations as

$$P(A) = .70P(A) + .10P(B)$$
$$P(B) = .30P(A) + .90P(B)$$

In addition to these equations we have the following equation that specifies the two probabilities for A and B must sum to 1.

$$P(A) + P(B) = 1$$

Because there are two unknowns and three equations, one of the equations is superfluous and can be eliminated. As a general rule, it will be most efficient to eliminate either of the state equations while retaining the other state equation as well as the last equation. Suppose that we arbitrarily eliminate the equation for B. We are then left with these two equations:

$$P(A) = .70P(A) + .1P(B)$$
$$P(A) + P(B) = 1$$

From the second equation, we can express B in terms of A:

$$P(B) = 1 - P(A)$$

We can then substitute this for B in the equation for A and solve for A:

$$P(A) = .70P(A) + .10[1 - P(A)]$$
$$P(A) = .70P(A) + .10 - .10P(A)$$
$$P(A) = .60P(A) + .10$$

Collecting terms yields:

$$P(A) - .60P(A) = .10$$
$$.40P(A) = .10$$
$$P(A) = \frac{.10}{.40} = .25$$

Since $P(B) = 1 - P(A)$,

$$P(B) = 1 - .25 = .75$$

Therefore, the proportion of cars that will be returned to each location over the long run is respectively .25 for Airport A and .75 for Airport B. Taking the example one step further, if there were initially 400 cars at Airport A and 300 at Airport B, we can determine the expected number of cars at each airport once the system has reached steady-state. Assume that all cars remain in the system, no new cars are added, and there is no transporting of cars between locations. The expected number for each airport is the product of the *total* number of cars (i.e., 700) and the steady-state probability of that airport. Thus, for A we have $700(.25) = 175$ cars, and for B we have $700(.75) = 525$ cars. This information will be helpful, for example, in deciding which of the two locations should be chosen for construction of a facility to service and repair cars.

11.5 USING EXCEL FOR MARKOV ANALYSIS

In demonstrating how Excel can be utilized to perform Markov analysis, consider the following example.

EXAMPLE 11-4

Joe's machine shop is developing a machine maintenance management program. Joe believes that the functioning of a major machine can be explained based on a transition matrix and Markov analysis can be used to analyze it.

Let State 1 (O = Operation) = machine is in operation
State 2 (B = Broken) = machine is down and/or is being repaired

p_{ij} = probability of making a transition from state i to state j in the next period (day)
P = transition probability matrix

Joe has determined that when the machine was in operation on a given day, it was also in operation on the following day 90 percent of the time. When the machine was in operation on a given day, it was broken on the next day 10 percent of the time. Joe also has estimated that when the machine was down on a given day, it was operational on the following day 70 percent of the time. When the machine was broken on a given day, it remained broken on the next day 30 percent of the time.

a. Determine the transition matrix P.
b. Use Excel and determine the probability that the machine is broken two days from today (the second day) given that the machine is in operation today (day zero).
c. Use Excel and determine the probability that the machine is functioning two days from today (the second day) given that the machine is in operation today (day zero).
d. Draw the tree diagram associated with parts *b* and *c*.
e. Use Excel and determine the probability that the machine is broken two days from today (the second day) given that the machine is down (broken) today (day zero).
f. Use Excel and determine the probability that the machine is operating two days from today (the second day) given that the machine is down (broken) today (day zero).
g. Draw the tree diagram associated with parts *e* and *f*.
h. Use Excel and determine the steady-state probabilities.

Solution

a. Transition probabilities for the machine maintenance example are given in Table 11-4.

Table 11-4 Transition Probabilities for the Machine Maintenance Example

From: \ To:	State 1 (Operating)	State 2 (Broken)
State 1 (Operating)	.90	.10
State 2 (Broken)	.70	.30

We will answer parts *b, c, e, f,* and *h* utilizing Excel. Exhibit 11-1 includes the Excel worksheet that contains the calculations necessary to answer parts *b, c, e, f,* and *h*. In preparing the worksheet shown in Exhibit 11-1, first we enter the transition matrix and current state matrix in the top portion of the worksheet. The portion labelled as "Daily Probabilities" illustrates the calculation of the probabilities of being in different states based on a given starting state. For example, if the machine is initially operating (during day zero), the probability of it operating and the probability of it being broken during day 1 can be calculated using matrix multiplication. The Excel function MMULT can be utilized to multiply two matrices. In multiplying two matrices, it is required that the number of columns in the first matrix be equal to the number of rows in the second matrix. If the first matrix has an order *M*N,* then the second matrix must be of the order *N*Q,* the resulting matrix will be of the order *M*Q*. In determining the probability of the machine operating and broken on day 1 given that it is currently operating (day 0), we need to multiply the first row of the current state matrix by the probability transition matrix. Multiplication of these two matrices can be accomplished by typing in the following formula in the formula bar: =MMULT(D3:E3, $B$3:$C$4). In this formula, D3:E3 represents the first row of the current state matrix (machine currently operating) and $B$3:$C$4 represents the probability transition matrix.

After specifying the formula, we highlight the cells in which we want the answer to be displayed (cells B7 and C7). We proceed by highlighting the formula we just typed in the formula bar and press Ctrl-Shift-Enter. The results of .9 and .1 are displayed in cells B7 and C7 respectively. These probabilities represent the machine operating and machine broken, respectively, on day 1.

We proceed in a similar fashion and calculate the probability of the machine operating or broken on day 1 given that it is currently broken. This time, we need to multiply the second row of the current state matrix by the probability transition matrix. Multiplication of these two matrices can be accomplished by typing in the following formula in the formula bar: =MMULT(D4:E4, $B$3:$C$4). In this formula, D4:E4 represents the second row of the current state matrix (machine currently broken) and $B$3 : $C$4 represents the probability transition matrix.

b. The answer to part *b* is given in row 9 of Exhibit 11-1. In answering this part of the problem, we need to determine the probability that the machine is broken two days from today (the second day) given that the machine is in operation today (day zero). We need to multiply matrices again. However, instead of multiplying the part of the current state matrix by the probability transition matrix, we multiply the results we have obtained above in row 7 (B7:C7) by the transition matrix. We multiply the transition matrix by the row matrix given in B7 : C7 because B7 : C7 contain the probabilities of the two states on day 1 given that the machine is operating on day zero. This can be accomplished by using the following formula: =MMULT(B7:C7, $B$3:$C$4). After specifying the formula, we highlight the cells in which we want the answer to be displayed (cells B9 and C9). We proceed by highlighting the formula we just typed in the formula bar and pressing Ctrl-Shift-Enter. The results (.88 and .12) are displayed in cells B9 and C9 respectively. The answer to part *b* is 12 percent and is given in cell C9. In other words, if the machine is operating on day zero, the probability that it is broken on day 2 is 12 percent.

EXHIBIT 11-1 Worksheet for the Markov Analysis of the Machine Maintenance Problem

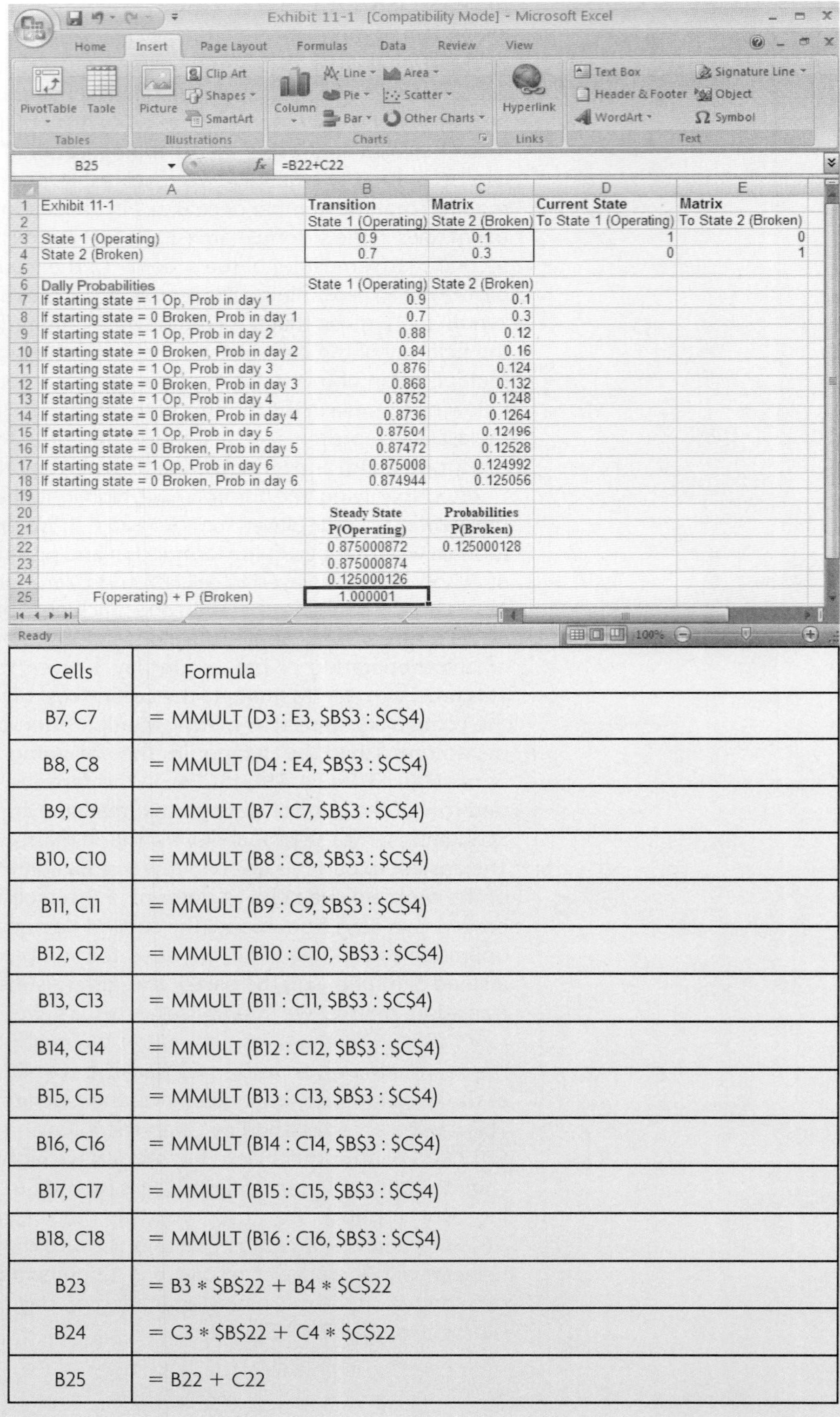

	A	B	C	D	E
1	Exhibit 11-1	Transition	Matrix	Current State	Matrix
2		State 1 (Operating)	State 2 (Broken)	To State 1 (Operating)	To State 2 (Broken)
3	State 1 (Operating)	0.9	0.1	1	0
4	State 2 (Broken)	0.7	0.3	0	1
5					
6	Daily Probabilities	State 1 (Operating)	State 2 (Broken)		
7	If starting state = 1 Op, Prob in day 1	0.9	0.1		
8	If starting state = 0 Broken, Prob in day 1	0.7	0.3		
9	If starting state = 1 Op, Prob in day 2	0.88	0.12		
10	If starting state = 0 Broken, Prob in day 2	0.84	0.16		
11	If starting state = 1 Op, Prob in day 3	0.876	0.124		
12	If starting state = 0 Broken, Prob in day 3	0.868	0.132		
13	If starting state = 1 Op, Prob in day 4	0.8752	0.1248		
14	If starting state = 0 Broken, Prob in day 4	0.8736	0.1264		
15	If starting state = 1 Op, Prob in day 5	0.87504	0.12496		
16	If starting state = 0 Broken, Prob in day 5	0.87472	0.12528		
17	If starting state = 1 Op, Prob in day 6	0.875008	0.124992		
18	If starting state = 0 Broken, Prob in day 6	0.874944	0.125056		
19					
20		Steady State	Probabilities		
21		P(Operating)	P(Broken)		
22		0.875000872	0.125000128		
23		0.875000874			
24		0.125000126			
25	F(operating) + P (Broken)	1.000001			

Cells	Formula
B7, C7	= MMULT (D3 : E3, \$B\$3 : \$C\$4)
B8, C8	= MMULT (D4 : E4, \$B\$3 : \$C\$4)
B9, C9	= MMULT (B7 : C7, \$B\$3 : \$C\$4)
B10, C10	= MMULT (B8 : C8, \$B\$3 : \$C\$4)
B11, C11	= MMULT (B9 : C9, \$B\$3 : \$C\$4)
B12, C12	= MMULT (B10 : C10, \$B\$3 : \$C\$4)
B13, C13	= MMULT (B11 : C11, \$B\$3 : \$C\$4)
B14, C14	= MMULT (B12 : C12, \$B\$3 : \$C\$4)
B15, C15	= MMULT (B13 : C13, \$B\$3 : \$C\$4)
B16, C16	= MMULT (B14 : C14, \$B\$3 : \$C\$4)
B17, C17	= MMULT (B15 : C15, \$B\$3 : \$C\$4)
B18, C18	= MMULT (B16 : C16, \$B\$3 : \$C\$4)
B23	= B3 * \$B\$22 + B4 * \$C\$22
B24	= C3 * \$B\$22 + C4 * \$C\$22
B25	= B22 + C22

FIGURE 11-5 Decision Tree Representation of the Machine Maintenance Problem: Initial State = Operation

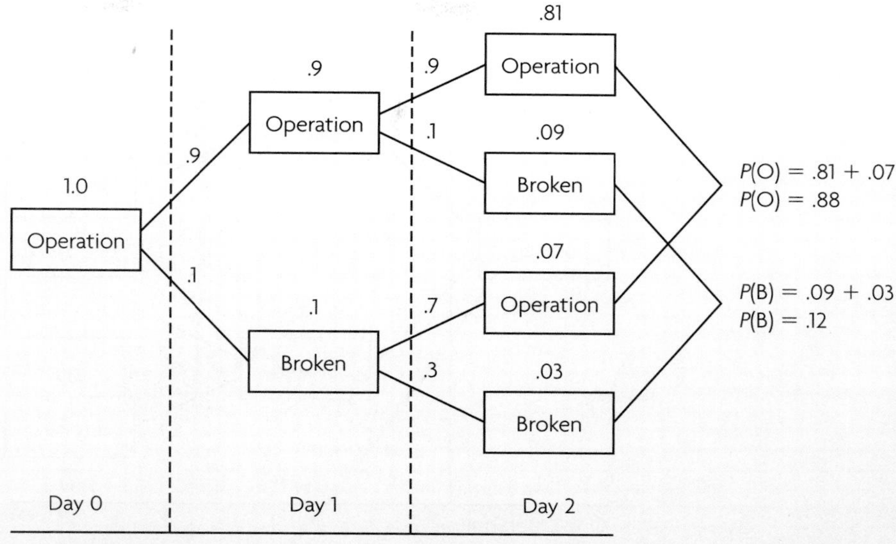

c. The answer to part *c* as given in cell B9 is 88 percent. Interpretation of this value is as follows: If the machine is operating on day zero, the probability that it is operating on day 2 is 88 percent.

d. The decision tree of the machine maintenance problem when the machine is currently operating is given in Figure 11-5.

e. The answer to this part is given in row 10 of Exhibit 11-1. In answering this part of the problem, we need to determine the probability that the machine is broken two days from today (the second day) given that the machine is broken today (day zero). The answer to this part is found in a similar fashion to the solutions to parts *b* and *c*. The main difference from parts *b* and *c* is that the initial state of the machine is broken. Since the machine is initially broken, we multiply the probabilities from row 8 in cells B8 (Probability of Operating = .70 given that the machine is currently broken) and C8 (Probability of Broken = .30 given that the machine is currently broken) by the transition matrix. This can be accomplished by using the following formula: =MMULT(B8:C8, $B$3:$C$4). In this formula B8:C8 represents the probability of State 1 and State 2 as discussed above and $B$3:$C$4 is the transition matrix. After specifying the formula, we highlight the cells where we want the answer to be displayed (cells B10 and C10). We proceed by highlighting the formula we just typed in the formula bar and pressing Ctrl-Shift-Enter. The results (.84 and .16) are displayed in cells B10 and C10 respectively. Thus, if the machine is broken on day zero, the probability that it is broken on day 2 is 16 percent.

f. The answer to part *f*, given in cell B10, is interpreted as follows: If the machine is broken on day zero, the probability that it is operating on day 2 is 84 percent.

g. The decision tree of the machine maintenance problem when the machine is currently broken is given in Figure 11-6.

FIGURE 11-6 Decision Tree Representation of the Machine Maintenance Problem Initial State = Broken

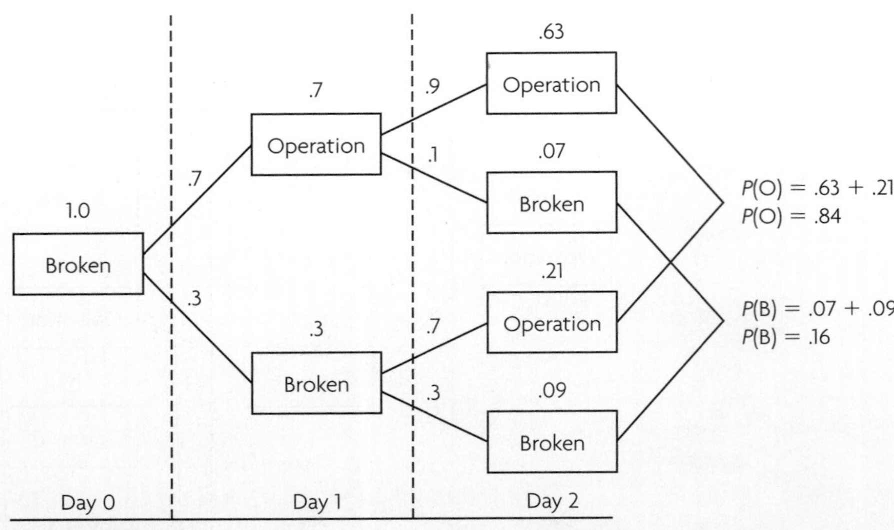

h. The steady-state probabilities are calculated at the bottom of the worksheet in Exhibit 11-1. Cells B21 and C21 are set up as the steady-state probabilities for which we will solve. Cells B22, B23, and B24 contain the equations utilized in algebraically solving for steady-state probabilities. These three equations are

$P(O) = .9P(O) + .7P(B)$ (The right-hand side of the equation is contained in cell B22)

$P(B) = .1P(O) + .3P(B)$ (The right-hand side of the equation is contained in cell B23)

$P(A) + P(B) = 1$ (The left-hand side of the equation is contained in cell B24)

The Excel versions of the formulas for these three equations are shown at the bottom of Exhibit 11-1. After entering these three formulas and arbitrary values of 0 for the decision variables, we choose **Data | Data Analysis | Solver** and obtain the Solver parameters screen shown in Exhibit 11-2.

After specifying the constraints, we simply click on "Options" and check the "Assume Nonnegative" box. Finally we select "Solve" and the Solver provides the values of the steady-state probabilities in cells B22 and C22 in Exhibit 11-1. As can be observed, the steady-state probability for operating is .875 and the steady state probability for broken is .125.

Steady-State Probabilities

$P(O) = .875$
$P(B) = .125$

The remaining entries in rows 11 through 18 continue the short-term calculations for days 5 through 11. In cells A11 through A18 are the descriptions of

EXHIBIT 11-2 Solver Parameters Specification Screen of the Machine Maintenance Problem

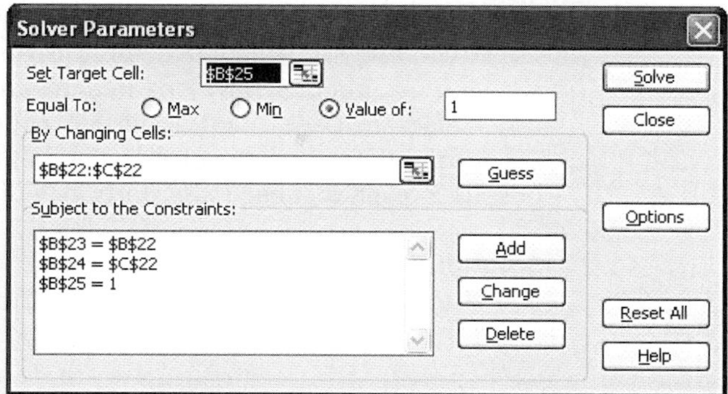

the probabilities for the respective rows, cells B11 through B18 contain the probability of operating, and cells C11 through C18 contain the probability of broken. The probabilities in cells B11 through C18 are calculated by the matrix multiplication procedure described earlier. The formulas for the various matrix multiplications are given at the bottom of Exhibit 11-1. Note that if the starting (current) state is 1, or operating, the state probability for operating in column B decreases toward the steady-state probability of .875, while the state probability for broken in column C increases toward the steady-state probability of .125.

However, if the starting (current) state is 2, or broken, the state probability for operating in column B increases towards the steady-state probability of .875, while the state probability for broken in column C decreases towards the steady-state probability of .125.

11.6 ANALYSIS OF A 3 × 3 MATRIX

The same methods that were used to analyze a transition matrix with two states can be readily adapted to handle larger problems. The following examples illustrate this. Examples 11-5, 11-6, and 11-7 refer to the transition matrix shown in Table 11-5.

TABLE 11-5 Transition Matrix for Examples 11-5, 11-6, and 11-7

		To:		
		X	*Y*	*Z*
	X	.70	.20	.10
From:	*Y*	.40	.50	.10
	Z	.30	.10	.60

Tree Diagram

EXAMPLE 11-5

Construct two tree diagrams for the transition matrix in Table 11-5, each showing two periods. Have one tree diagram show a starting state of *X* and the other diagram begin with a starting state of *Y*. In both cases, use the tree diagram to determine the probability that the system will be in state *X*, state *Y*, or state *Z* given that each tree starts in Period 0.

Solution

See the two tree diagrams and the desired probabilities in Figures 11-7 and 11-8.

FIGURE 11-7 Tree Diagram for Example 11-5, Starting from *X* (Initial State = *X*)

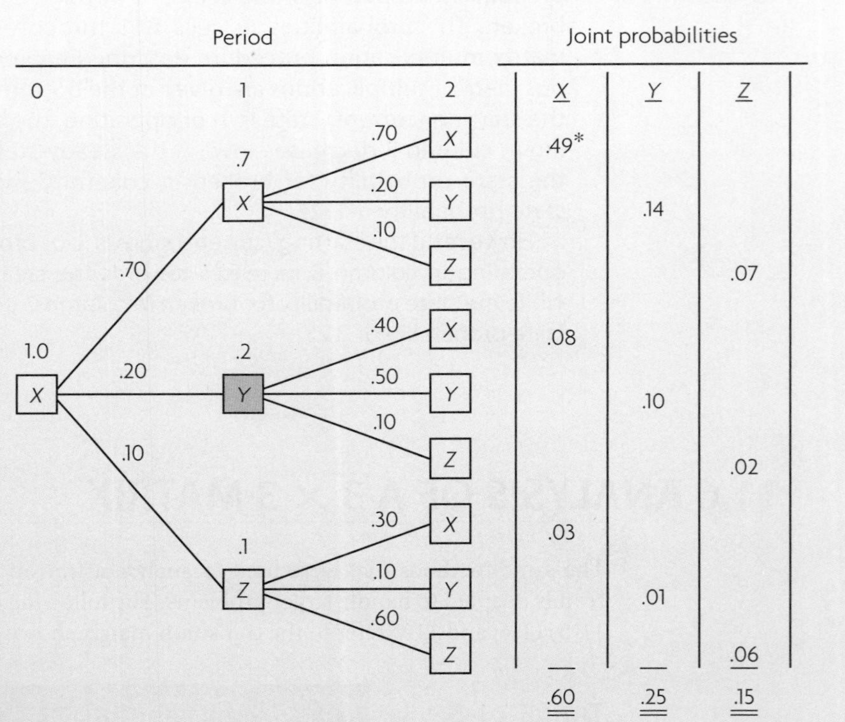

*This value is calculated by multiplying .7 (on the arc between x and x, from period 0 to 1 by the arc between x and x from period 1 to 2.

FIGURE 11-8 Tree Diagram for Example 11-5, Starting from *Y* (Initial State = *Y*)

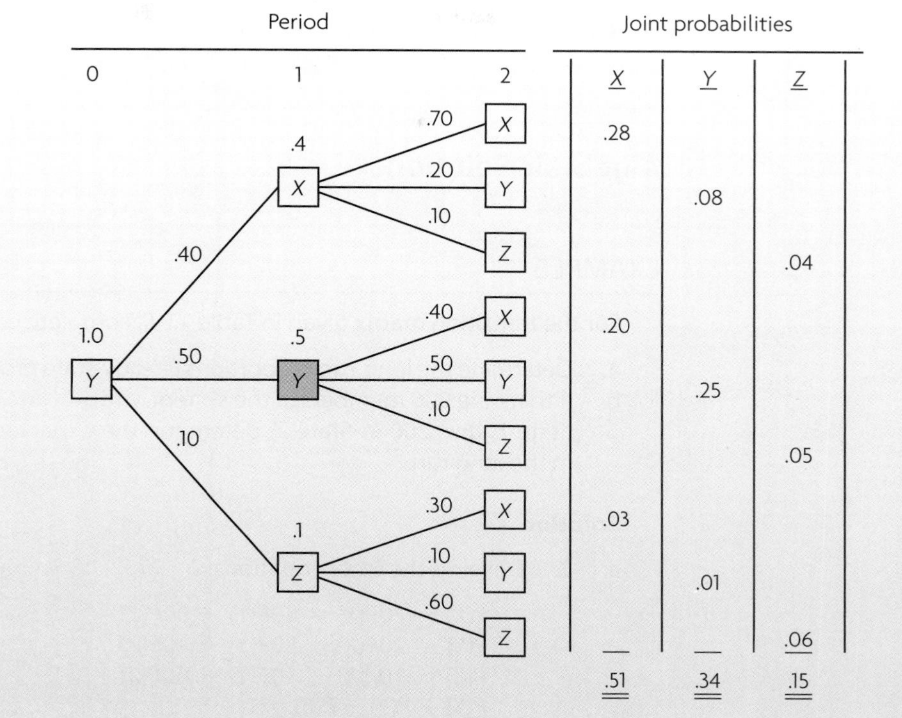

Matrix Multiplication

EXAMPLE 11-6

Use matrix multiplication to determine the probability that the system described in Table 11-5 will be in each of the various possible states (*X, Y,* and *Z*) for Periods 0, 1, 2, and 3, given that the initial state is *X* in Period 0.

Solution

Period

0 $\quad [1 \quad 0 \quad 0]$

1 $$[1 \quad 0 \quad 0]\begin{bmatrix} .70 & .20 & .10 \\ .40 & .50 & .10 \\ .30 & .10 & .60 \end{bmatrix} = \begin{matrix} 1(.70) & 1(.20) & 1(.10) \\ 0(.40) & 0(.50) & 0(.10) \\ 0(.30) & 0(.10) & 0(.60) \\ \hline [.70 & .20 & .10] \end{matrix}$$

2 $$[.70 \quad .20 \quad .10]\begin{bmatrix} .70 & .20 & .10 \\ .40 & .50 & .10 \\ .30 & .10 & .60 \end{bmatrix} = \begin{matrix} .70(.70) & .70(.20) & .70(.10) \\ .20(.40) & .20(.50) & .20(.10) \\ .10(.30) & .10(.10) & .10(.60) \\ \hline [.60 & .25 & .15] \end{matrix}$$

(Note that this agrees with the answer for an X start in the preceding example.)

3 $$[.60 \quad .25 \quad .15]\begin{bmatrix} .70 & .20 & .10 \\ .40 & .50 & .10 \\ .30 & .10 & .60 \end{bmatrix} = \begin{array}{ccc} .60(.70) & .60(.20) & .60(.10) \\ .25(.40) & .25(.50) & .25(.10) \\ .15(.30) & .15(.10) & .15(.60) \\ \hline [.565 & .260 & .175] \end{array}$$

Algebraic Solution

EXAMPLE 11-7

For the transition matrix given in Table 11-5, complete each of the following:

a. Determine the long-run proportions (steady-state probabilities) for each state.
b. If there are 900 members in the system, with 400 in State X in Period 0, 300 in State Y, and 200 in State Z, determine the expected number in each state in the long run.

Solution

a. 1. Develop the state equations:

$$P(X) = .70P(X) + .40P(Y) + .30P(Z)$$
$$P(Y) = .20P(X) + .50P(Y) + .10P(Z)$$
$$P(Z) = .10P(X) + .10P(Y) + .60P(Z)$$
$$P(X) + P(Y) + P(Z) = 1$$

2. Eliminate one of the equations arbitrarily, but not the last one. Suppose the third equation is eliminated. Because it is the state equation for Z, solve for Z in the last equation:

$$P(Z) = 1 - P(X) - P(Y)$$

3. Substitute for Z in the first and second equations:

$$P(X) = .70P(X) + .40P(Y) + .30[1 - P(X) - P(Y)]$$
$$P(Y) = .20P(X) + .50P(Y) + .10[1 - P(X) - P(Y)]$$

4. Simplify each equation with the constant term on the right:

$$.60P(X) - .10P(Y) = .30$$
$$-.10P(X) + .60P(Y) = .10$$

5. Solving, we find

$$P(X) = .543,\ P(Y) = .257$$

Using $P(Z) = 1 - P(X) - P(Y)$ and these values of $P(X)$ and $P(Y)$, we find

$$P(Z) = .200$$

b. Using the answers from part *a*, we find the expected number in each state at steady-state, given 900 system members:

$$X = 900(.543) = 488.7$$
$$Y = 900(.257) = 231.3$$
$$Z = 900(.200) = \underline{180.0}$$
$$900.0$$

(It should be noted that the results are independent of the initial conditions.)

Excel is also a valuable tool to solve three-state problems. Since the principal ideas for setting up and using Excel to solve three-state problems are essentially the same as in the case of two-state problems, we do not provide an example that demonstrates how a 3 × 3 Markov analysis problem can be solved with Excel. The set of problems provided at the end of this chapter include some exercises that require a 3 × 3 Markov analysis with Excel.

11.7 CYCLICAL, TRANSIENT, AND ABSORBING SYSTEMS

Cyclical, transient, and absorbing systems offer a contrast to the ones described so far in this chapter. **Cyclical systems** are those that have a tendency to move from state to state in a definite pattern or cycle. An example of a cyclical system is presented in the transition matrix in Table 11-6.

Let's see why this is a cyclical system. Suppose the system begins in state *A*. Because of the transition probability of 1 for *A* to *B*, the system will be in state *B* in the following period. Then in the next period, it will move from *B* to *C* and then back to *A* and so on. Consequently, we can say with certainty which state the system will be in at any future period (e.g., Period 42) if we know its state in any earlier period (e.g., Period 1).

A **transient system** is a system in which there is at least one state—the transient state—where once a system leaves it, the system will never return to it. In Table 11-7,

TABLE 11-6 An Example of a Cyclical System

		To:		
		A	*B*	*C*
	A	0	1	0
From:	*B*	0	0	1
	C	1	0	0

TABLE 11-7 An Example of System with a Transient State

		To:		
		A	*B*	*C*
	A	.4	0	.6
From:	*B*	0	.65	.35
	C	0	.80	.20

TABLE 11-8 An Example of a System with Absorbing States

		To:			
		A	*B*	*C*	*D*
	A	.5	.2	.1	.2
From:	*B*	.3	.2	.1	.4
	C	0	0	1.0	0
	D	0	0	0	1.0

state *A* is considered a transient state because if the system is in state *A* in period 1, the system has a 40 percent chance of returning to state *A* in period 2. However, if the system leaves state *A*, the probability of going to state *A* from state *B* is zero and the probability of going to state *A* from state *C* is zero. Therefore, once the system leaves state *A* by going to state *C*, because state *A* has a 60 percent chance of going to state *C* and has zero percent chance of going from state *C* and state *B* to state *A*. The system will not be able to return to state *A* again.

An **absorbing system** is one in which the system gravitates to one or more states. In effect, once a member of such a system enters one of the absorbing states, it becomes trapped and can never exit that state. An example of a transition matrix for an absorbing system is shown in Table 11-8.

States *C* and *D* are absorbing states. We can readily observe this by noting that probabilities for exiting to other states from either of these states are equal to zero, whereas the probability of remaining in the state is 1.0, or 100 percent. Note that even though a system may begin with members in nonabsorbing states such as *A* or *B*, eventually the system will be reduced to members only in the absorbing states.

The transition matrices displayed in Tables 11-6, 11-7, and 11-8 also can be displayed as **probability transition diagrams.** Showing the transition probabilities in the form of a diagram with nodes that represent states and directed branches that show the probability of going from state *i* to state *j* helps in determining whether the transition matrix contains an absorbing or transient state or if the matrix contains a cycle. The probability transition diagrams associated with Tables 11-6, 11-7, and 11-8 are given in Figure 11-9.

Analysis of Accounts Receivable

One example of absorbing states occurs when using Markov analysis for accounts receivable. The states of interest are possible classifications of accounts such as paid, one month overdue, two months overdue, and bad debt. The states paid and bad debt are absorbing states because once an account achieves either status, the passage of time will not change its classification; a paid bill will not become unpaid and a bad debt will be turned over to a collection agency. Even though the bad debt eventually may be collected, the costs associated with collecting it may offset all or a good part of the amount collected. Therefore, it would be misleading to label the bill as "paid" in the sense we are talking about here. Analysis of accounts receivable can provide management with an estimate of the proportion of current accounts receivable that will end up in each of the two absorbing states: *paid* and *bad debt.*

Consider the following example.

FIGURE 11-9 Probability Transition Diagrams for the Transition Matrices Given in Tables 11-6, 11-7, and 11-8

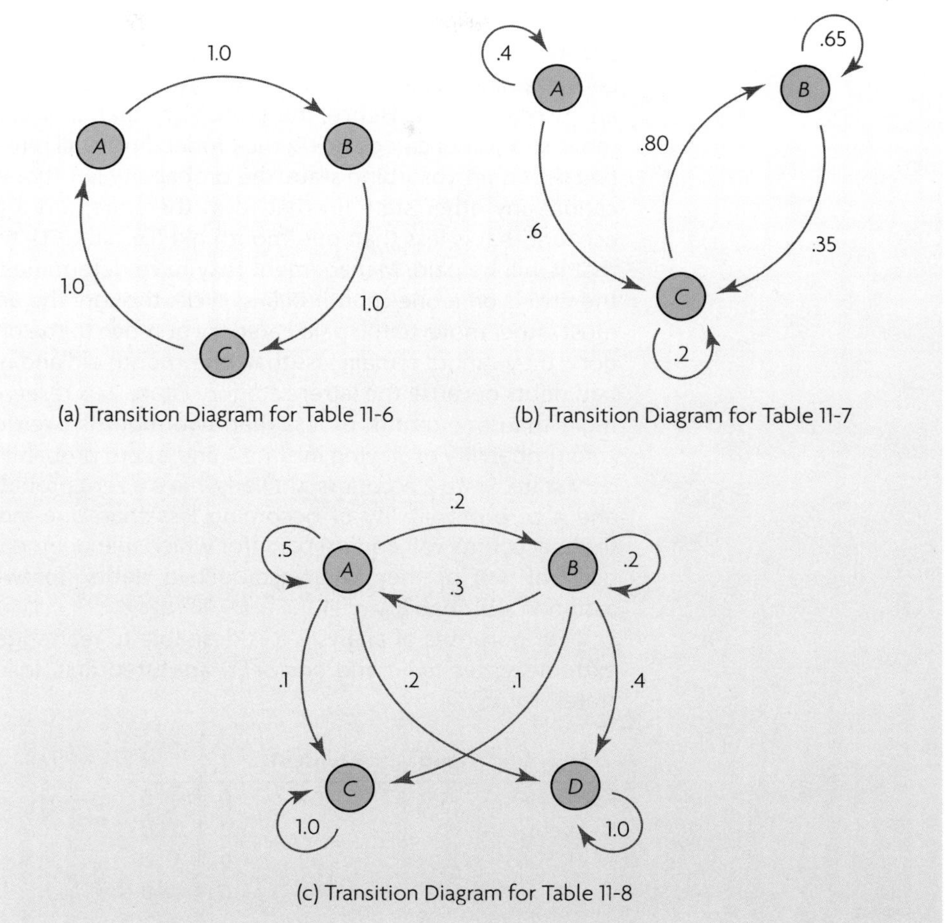

(a) Transition Diagram for Table 11-6

(b) Transition Diagram for Table 11-7

(c) Transition Diagram for Table 11-8

EXAMPLE 11-8

A firm has a one-month billing cycle. At the end of each month, outstanding bills are classified into one of the following categories: paid, less than one-month old, more than one-month and less than two-months old, and bad debt. Now, suppose that a transition matrix has been developed that contains probabilities for the accounts:

		Next state			
		Paid	**1**	**2**	**Bad debt**
	Paid	1	0	0	0
Current	1	.80	0	.20	0
state	2	.60	0	0	.40
	Bad debt	0	0	0	1

If there is $30 000 in one-month-old receivables and $45 000 in two-month-old receivables, determine the total amount that will be paid and the total amount that will become a bad debt.

Solution

Let's examine the logic of this matrix. As previously noted, the paid category is an absorbing state. Hence, the probability that an account in this category will move to another category is 0; the probability it will remain as paid is 1. Similarly, *bad debt* is an absorbing state; the probability is 1 that it will retain that classification; any other state (in that row), therefore, has a probability of 0. For an account that is less than one-month old (i.e., state 1), there is some probability that it will be paid. Management may have determined this to be .80. Because the firm is on a one-month billing cycle, though, the accounts in this category must either move to the paid category or move to the one and two-month category; they cannot remain less than one-month old and neither can they become bad debts because the latter category (state 2) is reserved for accounts that are more than one month or less than two months overdue. Therefore, there is a zero probability of staying in state 1 and a zero probability of moving to the *bad debt* state. State 2 accounts, similarly, have a zero probability of remaining there and a zero probability of becoming less than one-month old. Instead either these accounts will end up paid (for which management has assigned a probability of .60) or they will become bad debts (for which management has assigned a probability of .40).

For purposes of analysis, it is desirable to rearrange the matrix so that the extreme states (*paid* and *bad debt*) are listed first, followed by the other two states. Thus:

	Paid	Bad debt	1	2
Paid	1	0	0	0
Bad debt	0	1	0	0
1	.80	0	0	.20
2	.60	.40	0	0

Next, we partition this transition matrix into four parts:

	Paid	Bad debt	1	2
Paid	1	0	0	0
Bad debt	0	1	0	0
1	.80	0	0	.20
2	.60	.40	0	0

We, then, label the parts as follows:

	Paid	Bad debt	1	2
Paid Bad debt	I		O	
1 2	R		Q	

In this way, we can see that

$$I = \begin{array}{r} \\ \\ \text{paid} \\ \text{Bad debt} \end{array} \begin{array}{c} & \text{Bad} \\ \text{paid} & \text{debt} \\ \left[\begin{array}{cc} 1 & 0 \\ 0 & 1 \end{array}\right] \end{array}$$

$$O = \begin{array}{r} \\ \text{paid} \\ \text{Bad debt} \end{array} \begin{array}{c} 1 \quad 2 \\ \left[\begin{array}{cc} 0 & 0 \\ 0 & 0 \end{array}\right] \end{array}$$

$$R = \begin{array}{r} \\ \\ 1 \\ 2 \end{array} \begin{array}{c} & \text{Bad} \\ \text{paid} & \text{debt} \\ \left[\begin{array}{cc} .80 & 0 \\ .60 & .40 \end{array}\right] \end{array}$$

$$Q = \begin{array}{r} \\ 1 \\ 2 \end{array} \begin{array}{c} 1 \quad 2 \\ \left[\begin{array}{cc} 0 & .20 \\ 0 & 0 \end{array}\right] \end{array}$$

Matrix I is an *identity matrix:* It has 1s on the diagonal and 0s everywhere else. Matrix O is simply a matrix of all 0s. Matrix R contains the transition probabilities of absorptions in the next period, and matrix Q contains the transition probabilities of movement between nonabsorbing states.

Partitioning the matrix in this way allows us to compute the **fundamental matrix,** N:

$$N = (I - Q)^{-1} \tag{11-1}$$

The -1 refers to the *inverse* of a matrix. Hence, to obtain the fundamental matrix, we must subtract matrix Q from matrix I, then find the inverse of the result. Therefore, we subtract Q from I:

$$(I - Q) = \begin{bmatrix} 1 & 0 \\ 0 & 1 \end{bmatrix} - \begin{bmatrix} 0 & .20 \\ 0 & 0 \end{bmatrix}$$

$$= \begin{bmatrix} 1 & -.20 \\ 0 & 1 \end{bmatrix}$$

Then, we find the inverse of this matrix.

In general, the inverse of a matrix is found in the following way. If matrix M is defined as

$$M = \begin{bmatrix} m_{11} & m_{12} \\ m_{21} & m_{22} \end{bmatrix} \tag{11-2}$$

then its inverse is

$$M^{-1} = \begin{bmatrix} m_{22}/d & -m_{12}/d \\ -m_{21}/d & m_{11}/d \end{bmatrix} \tag{11-3}$$

where d is the determinant of a matrix. The determinant of a matrix is calculated in Equation 11-4:

$$d = m_{11}m_{22} - m_{21}m_{12} \tag{11-4}$$

For our accounts receivable problem, the inverse of the matrix (I − Q) is found in the following way:

$$(I - Q) = \begin{bmatrix} 1 & -.20 \\ 0 & 1 \end{bmatrix}$$

Using Equation 11-4, $d = 1(1) - 0(-.20) = 1$. Then

$$N = (I - Q)^{-1} = \begin{bmatrix} 1/1 & -(-.20)/1 \\ -0/1 & 1/1 \end{bmatrix} = \begin{bmatrix} 1 & .20 \\ 0 & 1 \end{bmatrix}$$

Thus, the fundamental matrix, N is

$$N = \begin{matrix} & \begin{matrix} 1 & 2 \end{matrix} \\ \begin{matrix} 1 \\ 2 \end{matrix} & \begin{bmatrix} 1 & .20 \\ 0 & 1 \end{bmatrix} \end{matrix}$$

The fundamental matrix indicates the expected probability that the system will be in any of the nonabsorbing states before absorption occurs. Hence, if an account is in state 1, the expected probability that the customer would move to state 2 is .20.

The fundamental matrix can be used to determine the probability that an account eventually will move to the various absorbing states (i.e., paid or bad debt). This can be accomplished by multiplying matrix R by the fundamental matrix. The result in our example is

$$NR = \begin{matrix} & \begin{matrix} 1 & 2 \end{matrix} \\ \begin{matrix} 1 \\ 2 \end{matrix} & \begin{bmatrix} 1 & .20 \\ 0 & 1 \end{bmatrix} \end{matrix} \times \begin{matrix} & \begin{matrix} \text{Paid} & \text{Bad debt} \end{matrix} \\ \begin{matrix} 1 \\ 2 \end{matrix} & \begin{bmatrix} .80 & 0 \\ .60 & .40 \end{bmatrix} \end{matrix}$$

$$= \begin{matrix} & \begin{matrix} \text{Paid} & \text{Bad debt} \end{matrix} \\ \begin{matrix} 1 \\ 2 \end{matrix} & \begin{bmatrix} .92 & .08 \\ .60 & .40 \end{bmatrix} \end{matrix}$$

The interpretation of this matrix is that if an account is currently less than one-month overdue (i.e., in state 1), the probability is .92 that it will end up being paid and .08 that it will end up a bad debt. Similarly, if an account is currently in state 2 (more than one month overdue, but less than two months overdue), there is a probability of .60 that it will be paid and a probability of .40 that it will end up a bad debt.

If we know the value of the accounts in each state, we can use the NR matrix to determine the expected amount that will be paid and the expected amount of bad debt. Since the amount owed for accounts in state 1 is currently $30 000 and the amount owed for accounts in state 2 is currently \$45 000, if B = amount-owed matrix, then the expected paid and bad debt amounts can be calculated by multiplying B and NR:

$$B^*NR = \begin{bmatrix} \overset{1}{30\,000} & \overset{2}{45\,000} \end{bmatrix} \begin{matrix} 1 \\ 2 \end{matrix} \begin{bmatrix} \overset{\text{Paid}}{.92} & \overset{\text{Bad debt}}{.08} \\ .60 & .40 \end{bmatrix} = \begin{bmatrix} \overset{\text{Paid}}{54\,600} & \overset{\text{Bad debt}}{20\,400} \end{bmatrix}$$

11.8 ANALYSIS OF ABSORBING STATES USING EXCEL

The absorbing states also can be analyzed using Excel. Let's consider the following example.

EXAMPLE 11-9

Acorn General Hospital is well known for its practice of accepting patients regardless of their ability to pay the medical bills. However, as a result of this practice, the hospital is experiencing accounts receivable problems.

The hospital's accounting department has established the following four categories for all medical accounts.

1. Fully paid.
2. Bad debt, written off.
3. Current and due within 30 days.
4. Delinquent, 31 days to 120 days old.

The above-listed categories will be treated as the states in our Markov analysis. The accounting department has analyzed the past data and came up with the following transition probability matrix, where

p_{ij} = probability of a dollar in a given week in state i moving to state j in the next week.

$$P = \begin{matrix} 1 \\ 2 \\ 3 \\ 4 \end{matrix} \begin{bmatrix} 1 & 0 & 0 & 0 \\ 0 & 1 & 0 & 0 \\ .6 & 0 & .2 & .2 \\ .4 & .2 & 0 & .4 \end{bmatrix}$$

Use Excel to answer the following questions:

a. What is the probability that the delinquent accounts (dollars) will be paid?
b. What is the probability that the current accounts (dollars) will be paid?
c. What is the probability that the delinquent accounts (dollars) will be written off?
d. What is the probability that the current accounts (dollars) will be written off?

e. Currently, Acorn General Hospital has a total of \$200 000 in total accounts receivable. As was described earlier, the accounts receivable is further classified as either current or delinquent. Of the \$200 000 total accounts receivable, \$150 000 is in current accounts receivable and \$50 000 is delinquent accounts receivable. Determine the amount of the \$200 000 accounts receivable that the hospital can expect to be paid.

f. Determine the amount (of the \$200 000 accounts receivable) that is expected to turn into bad debts.

Solution

In solving this problem using Excel, we prepare the worksheet shown in Exhibit 11-3. The top portion of the exhibit, in cells B2 through E5, contains the transition matrix. As you may recall in our earlier discussion, we divided the transition matrix into four sub matrices (I, O, R, and Q). Three of the four submatrices are displayed in Exhibit 11-3.

Submatrix I is shown in cells B8 through C9, submatrix Q is shown in cells E8 through F9, and submatrix R is shown in cells B16 through C17. First we subtract the matrix Q from matrix I in cells A12 through B13. Second we find the determinant and the inverse of this matrix. Calculation of the determinant is not necessary because in calculating the inverse, Excel automatically calculates the determinant. However, the calculation of the determinant by Excel is included since we have shown the manual calculation of the determinant in our previous discussion. The value of the determinant is displayed in cell C12 of Exhibit 11-3 and is calculated by the following formula: =MDETERM(A12:B13). The inverse of the I–Q matrix is shown in cells E12 through F13. This inverse is calculated by entering the following formula in cell E12, =MINVERSE(A12:B13), and highlighting cells E12 through F13. To ensure that the entire inverse appears in cells E12 through F13, we need to highlight the formula we just entered in the formula bar for cell E12 and hit Ctrl-Shift-Enter. The resulting matrix is the matrix N (the fundamental matrix).

Next we multiply matrix N and matrix R. In multiplying these two matrices, first we enter the matrix multiplication formula in cell E16 as =MMULT(E12:F13, B16:C17). After specifying the formula, we highlight the cells where we want the answer to be displayed (cells E16 through F17). We proceed by highlighting the formula we just typed in the formula bar and pressing Ctrl-Shift-Enter. In this formula, cells E12:F13 represent the fundamental matrix N, while cells B16 through C17 represent the submatrix R. Multiplication of these two matrices results in the answer given in cells E16, E17, F16, and F17 of Exhibit 11-3.

After finding the N*R matrix, we multiply the B, or "amount-owed," matrix by the N*R matrix. We enter the following formula in cells E21 and F21: =MMULT(B21:C21, E16:F17). In this formula, cells B21:C21 represent the amount-owed matrix B, while cells E16 through F17 represent the N*R matrix. The resulting matrix, given in cells E21 and F21, shows the amount of money that is expected to be eventually paid and the amount of money that has to be written off as bad debt. The formulas for various cells are stated at the bottom of Exhibit 11-7. The answer to the questions in part *a* through part *f* can easily be obtained from Exhibit 11-3. Table 11-9 summarizes the answers along with the cells the answers are displayed in.

EXHIBIT 11-3 Excel Worksheet for Example11-9: The Acorn Hospital Absorbing State Problem

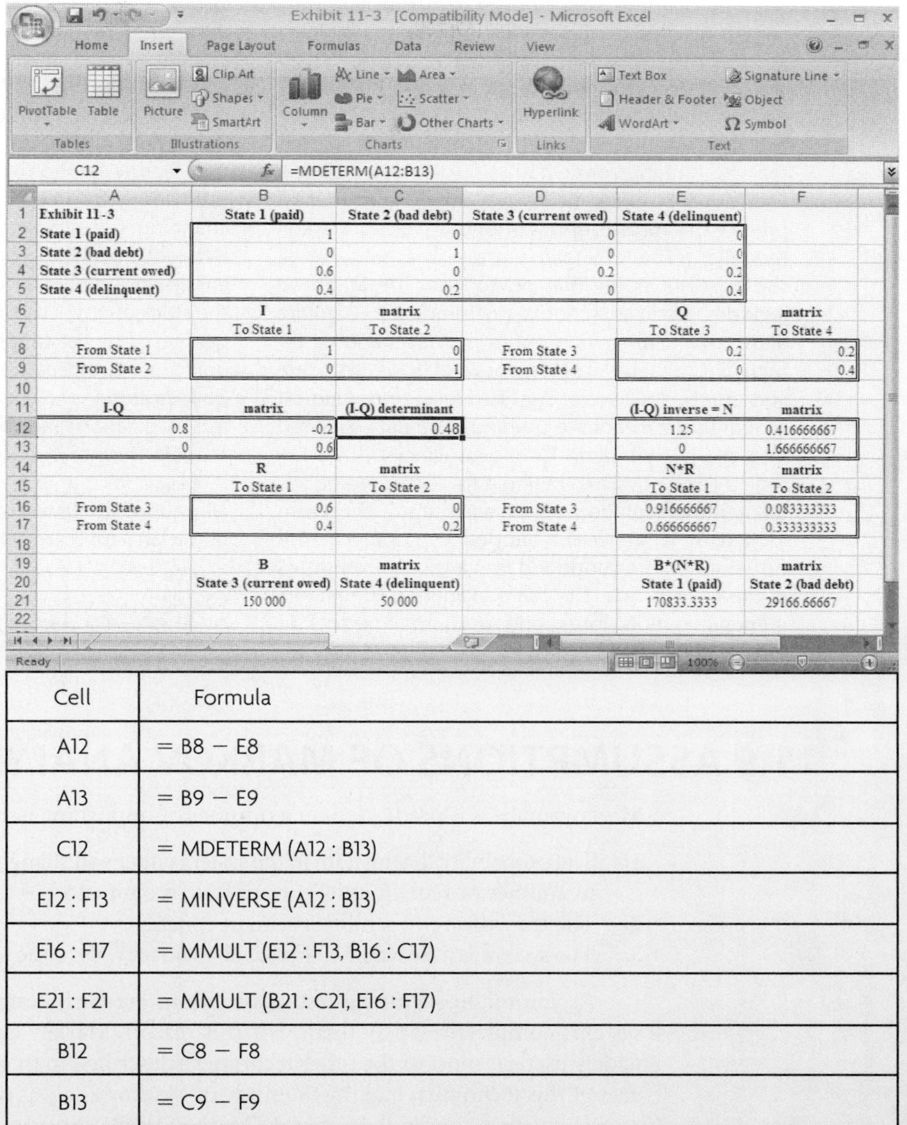

	A	B	C	D	E	F
1	Exhibit 11-3	State 1 (paid)	State 2 (bad debt)	State 3 (current owed)	State 4 (delinquent)	
2	State 1 (paid)	1	0	0	0	
3	State 2 (bad debt)	0	1	0	0	
4	State 3 (current owed)	0.6	0	0.2	0.2	
5	State 4 (delinquent)	0.4	0.2	0	0.4	
6		I	matrix		Q	matrix
7		To State 1	To State 2		To State 3	To State 4
8	From State 1	1	0	From State 3	0.2	0.2
9	From State 2	0	1	From State 4	0	0.4
10						
11	I-Q	matrix	(I-Q) determinant		(I-Q) inverse = N	matrix
12	0.8	-0.2	0.48		1.25	0.416666667
13	0	0.6			0	1.666666667
14		R	matrix		N*R	matrix
15		To State 1	To State 2		To State 1	To State 2
16	From State 3	0.6	0	From State 3	0.916666667	0.083333333
17	From State 4	0.4	0.2	From State 4	0.666666667	0.333333333
18						
19		B	matrix		B*(N*R)	matrix
20		State 3 (current owed)	State 4 (delinquent)		State 1 (paid)	State 2 (bad debt)
21		150 000	50 000		170833.3333	29166.66667

Cell	Formula
A12	= B8 − E8
A13	= B9 − E9
C12	= MDETERM (A12 : B13)
E12 : F13	= MINVERSE (A12 : B13)
E16 : F17	= MMULT (E12 : F13, B16 : C17)
E21 : F21	= MMULT (B21 : C21, E16 : F17)
B12	= C8 − F8
B13	= C9 − F9

Table 11-9 Answers to Example 11-3, Parts 1 *a* through *f*

Part	Cell in Exhibit 11-3 Where Answer Is Displayed	Answer
a	E17	.6667
b	E16	.9167
c	F17	.3333
d	F16	.0833
e	E21	$170 833.33
f	F21	$29 166.67

A MODERN MANAGEMENT SCIENCE APPLICATION: ENSURING PHYSICIANS SUPPLY IN ONTARIO

During the last three decades in Canada, physician supply lurched back and forth between surplus and shortage. The challenge of anticipating how many doctors a province will need in 5, 10, or even 20 years has long confounded system planners and decision makers. A team from Ontario's Institute for Clinical Evaluative Sciences (ICES) developed a model to predict the future supply of doctors using Markov modelling. The ICES team started by identifying all the possible states that doctors can be in. These include medical school, postgraduate training, active practice, moving out of province, and retirement. From there, all of the possible "flows" from one state to the next were identified (e.g., from medical school to postgraduate training). The data they fed into the model came from a provincial physician registry and physician billing. After determining initial numbers of doctors in each state, the team looked at what would happen to supply in the future if doctors continued moving between states at the current rate. The team examined the factors influencing flow rates, and used their model to determine the impact of trends in these rates, such as more women entering medical school. The tool also enabled the ICES team to assess the impact of predictable changes, such as the impact of population aging on different specialties. The most important feature of the tool, however, was its ability to estimate what impact different policies—such as changing the allocation of residency positions to different specialties or increasing medical school enrolment—would have on flow rates and ultimately, the stock of physicians in the future. The information generated by the model was instrumental in developing a consensus about health human resource policies among the health ministry, the Ontario Medical Association, and the deans of Ontario's medical schools. Despite opposing viewpoints initially, these three groups ultimately agreed to increase residency allocations to family medicine to stabilize family physician supply over the next two decades.

Source: *QReview*. A publication of the Health Quality Council of Saskatchewan, Summer 2005 Issue, 16 pages (available online January 30, 2008, at www.hqc.sk.ca.

11.9 ASSUMPTIONS OF MARKOV ANALYSIS

Markov analysis is predicated on a number of important assumptions. These are

1. The probability that an item in the system either will change from one state (e.g., Airport A) to another or remain in its current state is a function of the transition probabilities only.
2. The transition probabilities remain constant.
3. The system is a closed one; there will be no arrivals to the system or exits from the system.

As you might surmise, these assumptions are fairly restrictive; not very many real-life systems completely satisfy them. For this reason, Markov analysis is not as useful, nor as widely used, as most of the other techniques described in this book. Even so, there are some uses of this technique, making the study of Markov analysis worthwhile. Moreover, analysis of systems that can be described in Markov terms can provide some insight into system behaviours, and this knowledge can be generalized to other systems.

Summary

Markov analysis can be useful for describing the behaviour of a certain class of systems that change from state to state on a period-by-period basis according to known transition probabilities. Consumer buying patterns, market shares, sporting events, and equipment breakdowns sometimes lend themselves to description in Markov terms. The Modern Management Science Application, "Ensuring Physicians Supply in Ontario," describes how a team from Ontario's Institute for Clinical Evaluative Sciences (ICES) developed a Markov-based model to predict the future supply of physicians in the province of Ontario.

Markov analysis uses tree diagrams, matrix multiplication, and an algebraic approach. The first two approaches are especially useful for describing short-term system behaviour, whereas the third approach is more appropriate for describing long-term behaviour.

We analyzed absorbing, transient, and cyclical states and provided the accounts receivable example to show an application of two absorbing states, titled as "paid" and "bad debt" categories. The analysis shows how to estimate the dollars in accounts receivable that would be absorbed by each of these two states.

The primary objective of Markov analysis is to estimate the probability of each state after a large number of transitions.

Glossary

Absorbing System A system in which members gravitate to one or a few states; eventually all members end up in those states.

Algebraic Approach Solving the equations developed from the transition matrix simultaneously to obtain the steady-state probabilities.

Cyclical System A system that moves from state to state in a repetitive pattern.

Fundamental Matrix (matrix $N = (I - Q)^{-1}$) A matrix calculated to determine the probabilities associated with problems that have two absorbing states of a Markov process.

Markov Process A closed system that changes from state to state according to stable transition probabilities.

Matrix Multiplication A method of obtaining the short-term state probabilities. It is based on state probabilities being equal to the product of the probabilities in the preceding period multiplied by the matrix of transition probabilities.

Probability Transition Diagrams Showing the transition probabilities in the form of a diagram with nodes that represent states and directed branches that show the probability of going from state i to state j.

State of the System One of a set of mutually exclusive and collectively exhaustive conditions a system can assume.

Steady-State Long-term tendencies of a Markov system to be in its various states.

Transient System A system in which there is at least one state where once a system leaves this particular state, there is no return possible to that state.

Transition Matrix A matrix that shows the probability of a Markov system changing from its current state to each possible state in the next period.

Transition Probability Given that a system is in state i during a given period, the transition probability p_{ij} is the probability that the system will be in state j in the next period. p_{ij} remains constant from period to period.

Tree Diagram A visual portrayal of a system's transitions. It is composed of a series of nodes and branches. The branches represent the possible choices at each stage (period).

Solved Problems

Problem 1

Tree diagram Given this transition matrix, find the probabilities of the system being in state 1 and state 2 in period 3 if the system begins in state 1 in period 0:

		To: 1	2
From:	1	.80	.20
	2	.40	.60

Solution

For each branch end, multiply the probabilities of the branches that lead to it, separating by 1 or 2, then add the results as shown. Thus, the probability is .688 that the system will be in state 1 and .312 that it will be in state 2.

Problem 2

Matrix multiplication For the transition matrix of the previous problem, use matrix multiplication to find the probabilities that the system will be in state 1 and state 2 in period 3 if the system beings in state 1 at period 0.

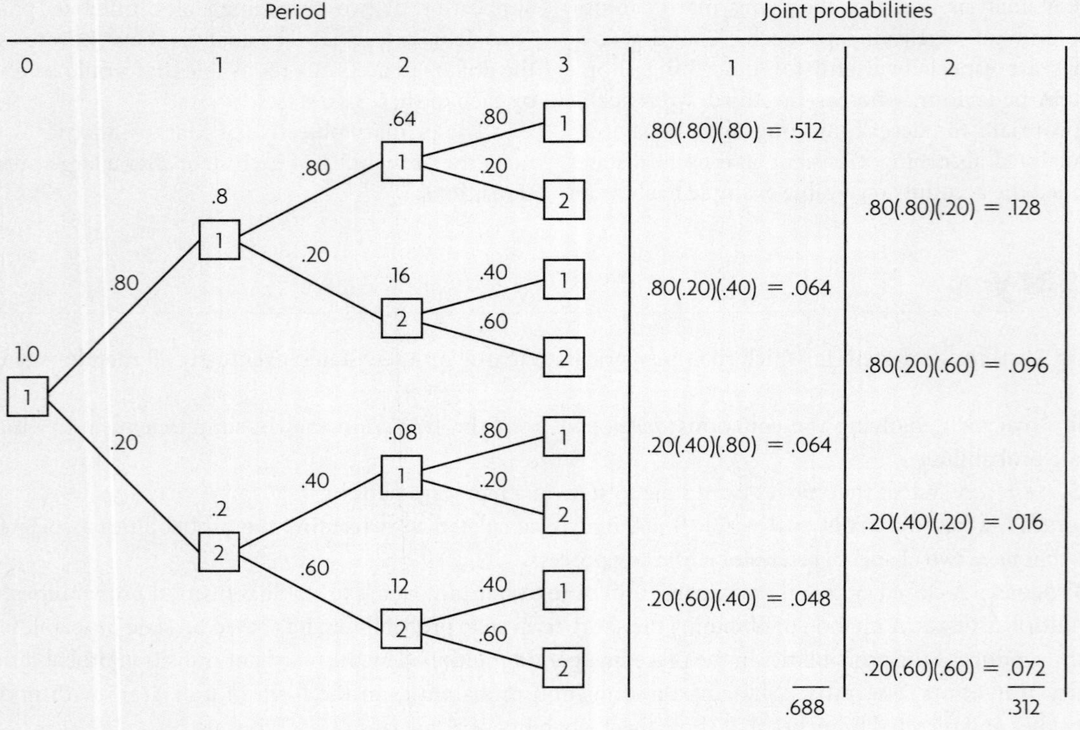

Solution

Period		P(state 1) = 1	P(state 2) = 0
1	$[1 \quad 0]\begin{bmatrix} .80 & .20 \\ .40 & .60 \end{bmatrix}$	1(.80) = .80 0(.40) = .00 .80	1(.20) = .20 0(.60) = .00 .20
2	$[.80 \quad .20]\begin{bmatrix} .80 & .20 \\ .40 & .60 \end{bmatrix}$	.80(.80) = .64 .20(.40) = .08 .72	.80(.20) = .16 .20(.60) = .12 .28
3	$[.72 \quad .28]\begin{bmatrix} .80 & .20 \\ .40 & .60 \end{bmatrix}$	.72(.80) = .576 .28(.40) = .112 .688	.72(.20) = .144 .28(.60) = .168 .312

Based on the calculations given in the above table, the probabilities in period 3 are *P* (state 1) = .688, *P*(state 2) = .312.

Problem 3

Matrix multiplication and steady-state probabilities

a. Given the transition matrix of the previous problem, use matrix multiplication to find the probabilities that the system will be in state 1 and state 2 in period 3 if the system begins in state 2 in period 0.

b. Find the steady-state probabilities for the transition matrix of the previous problem.

Solution

a.

Period		P(state 1) = 0	P(state 2) = 1
1	$[1 \quad 0]\begin{bmatrix} .8 & .2 \\ .4 & .6 \end{bmatrix}$	0(.8) = 0 1(.4) = .4 .4	0(.2) = 0 1(.6) = .6 .6
2	$[4. \quad .6]\begin{bmatrix} .8 & .2 \\ .4 & .6 \end{bmatrix}$	.4(.8) = .32 .6(.4) = .24 .56	.4(.2) = .08 .6(.6) = .36 .44
3	$[.56 \quad .44]\begin{bmatrix} .8 & .2 \\ .4 & .6 \end{bmatrix}$	.56(.8) = .448 .44(.4) = .176 .624	.56(.2) = .112 .44(.6) = .264 .376

Based on the calculations given above, if the system begins in state 2 in period 0, the probabilities in period 3 are *P*(state 1) = .624 and *P*(state 2) = .376.

b. Calculation of steady-state probabilities:

$$[P(\text{state} = 1)\ P(\text{state} = 2)] = [P(\text{state} = 1)\ P(\text{state} = 2)]\begin{bmatrix} .8 & .2 \\ .4 & .6 \end{bmatrix}$$

After performing matrix multiplication of the right-hand side, we get

$$[P(\text{state} = 1)] = [.80P(\text{state} = 1) + .40P(\text{state} = 2)]$$
$$[P(\text{state} = 2)] = [.20P(\text{state} = 1) + .60P(\text{state} = 2)]$$

In addition to these equations, we have the following equation that specifies the two probabilities for state 1 and state 2 must sum to 1.

$$P(\text{state} = 1) + P(\text{state} = 2) = 1$$

In other words, $P(\text{state} = 2) = 1 - P(\text{state} = 1)$

Substituting $P(\text{state} = 2) = 1 - P(\text{state} = 1)$ in equation 1:

$$P(\text{state} = 1) = .80P(\text{state} = 1) + .40(1 - P(\text{state} = 1)$$

Solving for $P(\text{state} = 1)$:

$$P(\text{state} = 1) = .80P(\text{state} = 1) + .40 - .40P(\text{state} = 1)$$
$$.60P(\text{state} = 1) = .40$$
$$P(\text{state} = 1) = 2/3$$

Since $P(\text{state} = 1) + P(\text{state} = 2) = 1$:

$$2/3 + P(\text{state} = 2) = 1$$
$$P(\text{state} = 2) = 1/3$$

Problem 4

Use Excel and provide the solution for Solved Problems 1, 2, and 3.

Exhibit 11-4 shows the Excel solution to Solved Problems 1, 2, and 3. The necessary formulas for the Excel worksheet are given at the bottom of Exhibit 11-4.

Problem 5

Steady-state equations

a. Manually find the steady-state probabilities for this transition matrix.
b. Use Excel and find the steady-state probabilities for this problem.

		To:		
		A	*B*	*C*
	A	.5	.4	.1
From:	*B*	.2	.5	.3
	C	.3	.1	.6

Solution

a. The steady-state equations are derived from *column* probabilities of each state. Thus, we have

$$P(A) = .5P(A) + .2P(B) + .3P(C)$$
$$P(B) = .4P(A) + .5P(B) + .1P(C)$$
$$P(C) = .1P(A) + .3P(B) + .6P(C)$$

In addition, we know that the three probabilities must sum to 1.00:

$$P(A) + P(B) + P(C) = 1$$

We can use this to solve for one of the three probabilities in terms of the other two. For convenience, let's choose C. Then we have

$$P(C) = 1 - P(A) - P(B)$$

With three unknowns, we need only three equations. We can eliminate a steady-state equation for C shown above this paragraph, and then substitute this last equation for C in the first two steady-state equations. That is:

$$P(A) = .5P(A) + .2P(B) + .3[1 - P(A) - P(B)]$$
$$P(B) = .4P(A) + .5P(B) + .1[1 - P(A) - P(B)]$$

Expanding the first of these yields

$$P(A) = .5P(A) + .2P(B) + .3 - .3P(A) - .3P(B)$$

Combining terms and moving the variables to the left side of the equation for A yields

$$.8P(A) + .1P(B) = .3$$

Expanding the steady-state equation for B yields

$$P(B) = .4P(A) + .5P(B) + .1 - .1P(A) - .1P(B)$$

Combining terms and moving the variables to the left side of the equation yields

$$-.3P(A) + .6P(B) = .1$$

Thus, the two resulting equations are

$$.8P(A) + .1P(B) = .3$$
$$-.3P(A) + .6P(B) = .1$$

Solving simultaneously, we find

$$P(A) = .333$$
$$P(B) = .333$$

Given these values and that $P(A) + P(B) + P(C) = 1$, we can determine that

$$P(C) = .333$$

b. The Excel worksheet for Solved Problem 5 is given in Exhibit 11-5. The necessary formulas for this problem are given at the bottom of Exhibit 11-5.

EXHIBIT 11-4 Worksheet for the Markov Analysis of Solved Problem 4

Exhibit 11-4 [Compatibility Mode]

B21 =B18+C18

	A	B	C
1	**Solved Problem 4**	**Transition**	**Matrix**
2		State 1	State 2
3	State 1	0.8	0.2
4	State 2	0.4	0.6
5			
6	Current state = 1	1	0
7	Current state = 2	0	1
8		State 1	State 2
9	If starting state = 1, Prob in period 1	0.8	0.2
10	If starting state = 0, Prob in period 1	0.4	0.6
11	If starting state = 1, Prob in period 2	0.72	0.28
12	If starting state = 0, Prob in period 2	0.56	0.44
13	If starting state = 1, Prob in period 3	0.688	0.312
14	If starting state = 0, Prob in day 3	0.624	0.376
15			
16		**Steady State**	**Probabilities**
17		**P(state 1)**	**P(state 2)**
18		0.6667	0.3333
19	P(state 1)=	0.6667	
20	P(state 2)=	0.3333	
21	P(state 1) + P (state 2) = 1	1.0000	

Cell	Copied to	Formula
B9	C9	= MMULT (B6 : C6, $B$3 : $C$4)
B10	C10	= MMULT (B7 : C7, $B$3 : $C$4)
B11	C11	= MMULT (B9 : C9, $B$3 : $C$4)
B12	C12	= MMULT (B10 : C10, $B$3 : $C$4)
B13	C13	= MMULT (B11 : C11, $B$3 : $C$4)
B14	C14	= MMULT (B12 : C12, $B$3 : $C$4)
B19		= B3 * B18 + B4 * C18
B20		= C3 * C18 + C4 * C18
B21		= B18 + C18

EXHIBIT 11-5 Worksheet for the Steady-State Calculations of Solved Problem 5

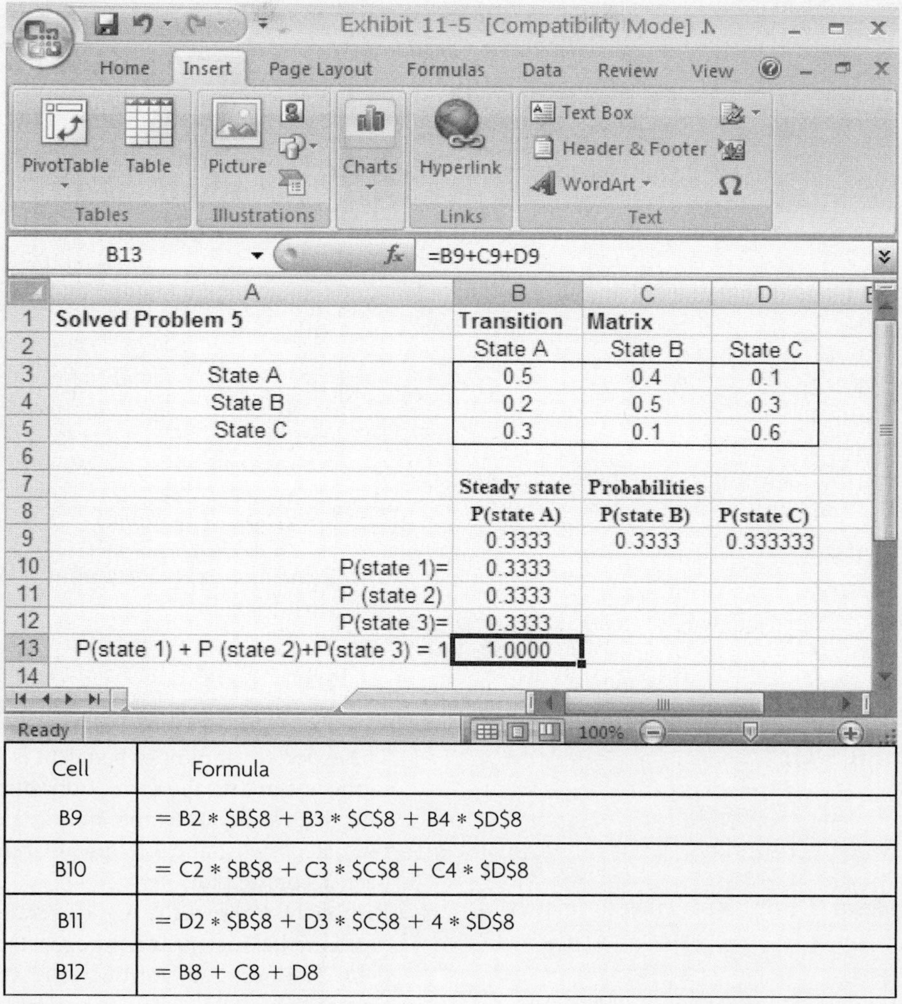

	A	B	C	D
1	**Solved Problem 5**	**Transition**	**Matrix**	
2		State A	State B	State C
3	State A	0.5	0.4	0.1
4	State B	0.2	0.5	0.3
5	State C	0.3	0.1	0.6
6				
7		**Steady state**	**Probabilities**	
8		**P(state A)**	**P(state B)**	**P(state C)**
9		0.3333	0.3333	0.333333
10	P(state 1)=	0.3333		
11	P (state 2)	0.3333		
12	P(state 3)=	0.3333		
13	P(state 1) + P (state 2)+P(state 3) = 1	1.0000		
14				

Cell	Formula
B9	= B2 * $B$8 + B3 * $C$8 + B4 * $D$8
B10	= C2 * $B$8 + C3 * $C$8 + C4 * $D$8
B11	= D2 * $B$8 + D3 * $C$8 + 4 * $D$8
B12	= B8 + C8 + D8

Problems 6

Accounts receivable A manager has developed the following transition matrix for a firm's accounts receivable:

$$\begin{array}{c} \\ p \\ 1 \\ 2 \\ b \end{array}\begin{array}{c} \begin{array}{cccc} p & 1 & 2 & b \end{array} \\ \begin{bmatrix} 1 & 0 & 0 & 0 \\ .5 & .3 & .2 & 0 \\ .3 & 0 & .4 & .3 \\ 0 & 0 & 0 & 1 \end{bmatrix} \end{array}$$

where

p = paid
1 = 1 to 30 days overdue
2 = 31 to 60 days overdue
b = bad debt

(*Note:* Accounts are billed weekly but classified in terms of months overdue. Consequently, it is possible for an account to remain in either the 1 or 2 category for several periods. Therefore, there is a nonzero probability of remaining in either 1 or 2.)

a. Obtain the fundamental matrix.
b. If there is currently $10 000 in accounts in the 1 category and $6000 in the 2 category, determine the expected amount of bad debt.
c. Repeat parts *a* and *b* using Excel.

Solution

a. Begin by rearranging the transition matrix so that the two absorbing states (*p* and *b*) are listed first, followed by the two nonabsorbing states. This yields the matrix

$$\begin{array}{c} \\ p \\ b \\ 2 \\ 1 \end{array}\begin{array}{c} \begin{array}{cccc} p & b & 1 & 2 \end{array} \\ \begin{bmatrix} 1 & 0 & 0 & 0 \\ 0 & 1 & 0 & 0 \\ .5 & 0 & .3 & .2 \\ .3 & .3 & 0 & .4 \end{bmatrix} \end{array}$$

Then, partition the matrix into four parts that are defined as I, O, R, and Q:

$$\begin{array}{c} \\ p \\ b \\ 1 \\ 2 \end{array}\begin{array}{c} \begin{array}{cc:cc} p & b & 1 & 2 \end{array} \\ \left[\begin{array}{cc:cc} 1 & 0 & 0 & 0 \\ 0 & 1 & 0 & 0 \\ \hdashline .5 & 0 & .3 & .2 \\ .3 & .3 & 0 & .4 \end{array}\right] \end{array} \quad \text{where} \quad \begin{array}{c} \\ p \\ b \\ 1 \\ 2 \end{array}\begin{array}{c} \begin{array}{cccc} p & b & 1 & 2 \end{array} \\ \left[\begin{array}{c:c} \text{I} & \text{O} \\ \hdashline \text{R} & \text{Q} \end{array}\right] \end{array}$$

Next, compute (I − Q):

$$\begin{bmatrix} 1 & 0 \\ 0 & 1 \end{bmatrix} - \begin{bmatrix} .3 & .2 \\ 0 & .4 \end{bmatrix} = \begin{bmatrix} .7 & -.2 \\ 0 & .6 \end{bmatrix}$$

Find the inverse of (I − Q). Recall that for matrix M, where M is

$$\begin{bmatrix} m_{11} & m_{12} \\ m_{21} & m_{22} \end{bmatrix}$$

the inverse is

$$\begin{bmatrix} m_{22}/d & -m_{12}/d \\ -m_{21}/d & m_{11}/d \end{bmatrix}$$

where

$$\begin{aligned} d &= m_{11}m_{22} - m_{12}m_{21} \\ &= .7(.6) - 0(-.2) = .42 \end{aligned}$$

Thus:

$$(\text{I} - \text{Q})^{-1} = \begin{bmatrix} .6/.42 & .2/.42 \\ -0/.42 & .7/.42 \end{bmatrix} = \begin{bmatrix} 1.429 & .476 \\ 0 & 1.667 \end{bmatrix}$$

This is the fundamental matrix, N.

b. First, multiply matrix R by the fundamental matrix:

$$\text{NR} = \begin{array}{c} \\ 1 \\ 2 \end{array}\begin{array}{c} \begin{array}{cc} 1 & 2 \end{array} \\ \begin{bmatrix} 1.429 & .476 \\ 0 & 1.667 \end{bmatrix} \end{array} \begin{array}{c} \\ 1 \\ 2 \end{array}\begin{array}{c} \begin{array}{cc} p & b \end{array} \\ \begin{bmatrix} .5 & 0 \\ .3 & .3 \end{bmatrix} \end{array}$$

$$\text{NR} = \begin{array}{c} \\ 1 \\ 2 \end{array}\begin{array}{c} \begin{array}{cc} p & b \end{array} \\ \begin{bmatrix} .857 & .143 \\ .500 & .500 \end{bmatrix} \end{array}$$

Then, find the expected amounts of *paid* and *bad debt* categories:

$$\begin{array}{c} \begin{array}{cc} 1 & 2 \end{array} \\ \begin{bmatrix} 10\,000 & 6000 \end{bmatrix} \end{array} \begin{array}{c} \\ 1 \\ 2 \end{array}\begin{array}{c} \begin{array}{cc} p & b \end{array} \\ \begin{bmatrix} .857 & .143 \\ .500 & .500 \end{bmatrix} \end{array} = \begin{array}{c} \begin{array}{cc} p & b \end{array} \\ \begin{bmatrix} 11\,570 & 4430 \end{bmatrix} \end{array}$$

The expected amount of bad debt is $4430. Note that in the last matrix the sum of the amounts in the two categories is equal to the amounts currently in the two categories, 1 and 2. Thus, all of the amounts have been accounted for.

c. Exhibit 11-6 shows the worksheet that calculates the fundamental matrix and the expected amount of bad debt. The necessary formulas are stated at the bottom of Exhibit 11-6. The variation from the manual calculation is due to rounding.

Discussion and Review Questions

1. What are the characteristics of Markov systems?
2. Explain the meaning of transition probabilities.
3. Provide two examples of the Markov systems. Explain the possible system states and the possible transition probabilities.
4. Explain the meaning of an absorbing state.
5. Explain the meaning of a transient state.
6. Explain the meaning of cyclical system.
7. What are steady-state proportions?
8. Explain how the tree diagram is structured in solving a Markov analysis problem.
9. Explain the difference between the matrix multiplication approach and the algebraic solution.

EXHIBIT 11-6 Excel Worksheet for Solved Problem 6: Accounts Receivable—Absorbing State Problem

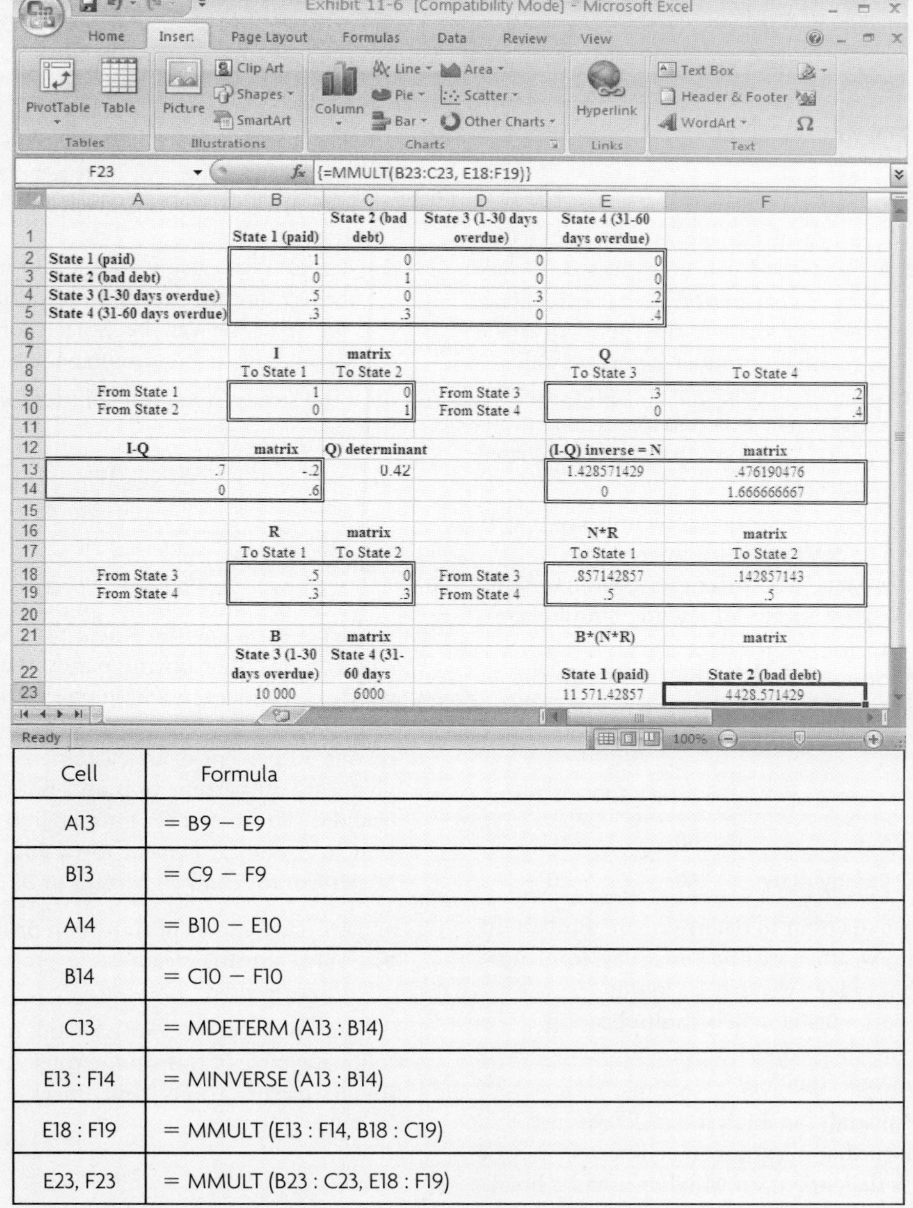

	A	B	C	D	E	F
1		State 1 (paid)	State 2 (bad debt)	State 3 (1-30 days overdue)	State 4 (31-60 days overdue)	
2	State 1 (paid)	1	0	0	0	
3	State 2 (bad debt)	0	1	0	0	
4	State 3 (1-30 days overdue)	.5	0	.3	.2	
5	State 4 (31-60 days overdue)	.3	.3	0	.4	
6						
7		I	matrix		Q	
8		To State 1	To State 2		To State 3	To State 4
9	From State 1	1	0	From State 3	.3	.2
10	From State 2	0	1	From State 4	0	.4
11						
12	I-Q	matrix	Q) determinant		(I-Q) inverse = N	matrix
13	.7	-.2	0.42		1.428571429	.476190476
14	0	.6			0	1.666666667
15						
16		R	matrix		N*R	matrix
17		To State 1	To State 2		To State 1	To State 2
18	From State 3	.5	0	From State 3	.857142857	.142857143
19	From State 4	.3	.3	From State 4	.5	.5
20						
21		B	matrix		B*(N*R)	matrix
22		State 3 (1-30 days overdue)	State 4 (31-60 days		State 1 (paid)	State 2 (bad debt)
23		10 000	6000		11 571.42857	4428.571429

Cell	Formula
A13	= B9 − E9
B13	= C9 − F9
A14	= B10 − E10
B14	= C10 − F10
C13	= MDETERM (A13 : B14)
E13 : F14	= MINVERSE (A13 : B14)
E18 : F19	= MMULT (E13 : F14, B18 : C19)
E23, F23	= MMULT (B23 : C23, E18 : F19)

10. In the analysis of accounts receivable example, the absorbing states are (1) paid and (2) bad debt. If we formulate a similar problem dealing with a life-threatening hospital surgery, where the ultimate goal is full recovery of the patients and the concern is for the health of the patients, what are the two absorbing states?
11. As the matrix multiplication is performed stage after stage, explain what happens to probabilities of states in comparison to steady-state probabilities.

Problems

1. The following table contains transition probabilities for two products, A and B:

		Next period	
		A	B
This	A	.70	.30
period	B	.20	.80

   a. What percentage of customers who purchased product A this period can be expected to purchase product A next period? What percentage who purchased product A this period can be expected to purchase product B next period?
   b. Use a tree diagram to determine the proportion of customers who can be expected to purchase product A in period 2, given that they purchased product B in period 0.

2. Repeat part *b* of the previous problem using matrix multiplication to determine the answer.
3. Find the steady-state proportions for products A and B in Problem 1 by means of solving simultaneous equations.
4. The weather on an island in the Caribbean can be described by the following transition probabilities:

		Tomorrow	
		Sunny	Cloudy/rainy
Today	Sunny	.90	.10
	Cloudy/rainy	.80	.20

   a. Use a tree diagram to determine the probability of sunny weather on the third day from now, given that today's weather is cloudy.
   b. Repeat part *a* using matrix multiplication.
   c. Determine the proportion of sunny days using simultaneous equations.

5. After a careful study, an analyst has determined that the probability that a certain machine will have a breakdown is dependent on whether it had a breakdown on the previous day and was repaired. The relevant probabilities are

		Tomorrow	
		No breakdown	Breakdown
Today	No breakdown	.88	.12
	Breakdown	.96	.04

   a. Given that the machine has a breakdown today, what is the probability that it will also experience a breakdown tomorrow?
   b. What is the probability that the machine will experience a breakdown two days in a row?
   c. Use a tree diagram to determine the probability that a machine will have a breakdown on the day after tomorrow, given that no breakdown occurs today.
   d. Repeat part *c* using matrix multiplication.
   e. Determine the steady-state proportion of days the machine can be expected to experience a breakdown using simultaneous equations.

6. Find the steady-state probabilities for this transition matrix:

		To:	
		1	2
From:	1	.75	.25
	2	.40	.60

7. A market researcher for Know Your Market, Inc., has studied consumer buying patterns in a situation in which consumers purchase one of three competing brands each week. The researcher found that Brand A retains 50 percent of its customers each week while giving up 30 percent to brand B and 20 percent to brand C. The researcher found that B gave up 50 percent to A and 20 percent to C, and that C gave up 50 percent to A and 30 percent to B.

   a. Develop a table of transition probabilities.
   b. What are the steady-state probabilities for the three brands?

8. A bank manager at Country Bank has compiled the following table of transition probabilities for the customers' use of various bank offices:

		Next period		
	Office	Main	East	South
	Main	.60	.10	.30
This period	East	.20	.70	.10
	South	.25	.15	.60

   a. Which office tends to have the highest "loyalty"? Why?
   b. What proportion of customers who banked at the Main office this time can be expected to

bank at the East office two periods later? Solve using a tree diagram.

c. Repeat the previous part using matrix multiplication.

9. Determine the steady-state probabilities for the previous problem.

10. If the transition probabilities for the South office in Problem 8 change from .25, .15, and .60 to .20 for Main, .10 for East, and .70 for South, what impact will this have on the steady-state probabilities for each office?

11. After studying a brand-switching problem, an analyst concluded that brand A loses 20 percent of its customers each period to brand B and 10 percent to brand C; brand B loses 10 percent of its customers each period to brand A and 30 percent to brand C; and brand C loses 30 percent to brand A and 20 percent to brand B.

a. Develop a table of transition probabilities for this situation.

b. If brand A initially has 400 customers, brand B has 250 customers, and brand C has 350, what average number of customers will each brand have in the long run?

12. A small, rural town has two movie theatres. Transition probabilities for weekly attendance for Sunday matinees are shown in the following table:

		Next week	
		Cameo	Strand
This week	Cameo	.60	.40
	Strand	.40	.60

a. Determine the steady-state probability of theatregoers for each theatre.

b. A group of local investors plans to open a new theatre. A consultant has projected transition probabilities for the three theatres for Sunday matinees as follows:

	Next week		
	Cameo	Strand	Cine
Cameo	.50	.30	.20
Strand	.30	.60	.10
Cine	.25	.25	.50

Use Excel and determine the steady-state probability of customers for each theatre.

c. Which original theatre, the Cameo or the Strand, stands to suffer the greater loss of customers based on the projected probabilities?

13. Residents of Halifax buy their Christmas trees from one of three local dealers. The following switching probabilities have been determined:

		This year		
		A	B	C
Last year	A	.65	.25	.10
	B	.35	.60	.05
	C	.40	.30	.30

a. Use Excel and determine the steady-state probability of customers for each dealer.

b. Suppose that dealer C is now considering advertising as a means of increasing his market share, since each customer represents a profit of \$4. The dealer projects the following transition probabilities:

		This year		
		A	B	C
Last year	A	.60	.20	.20
	B	.30	.50	.20
	C	.30	.20	.50

If the cost of advertising will be \$375, would you recommend that dealer C advertise? Explain, assuming that there are 800 customers in the "system."

14. A firm that rents video equipment has three stores. Customers are allowed to return rental equipment to any of the stores, regardless of which store they rented the equipment from. A study of rental returns has produced the following probabilities.

		Returned to		
		A	B	C
Rented at	A	.84	.09	.07
	B	.20	.70	.10
	C	.14	.06	.80

a. Determine the steady-state probability for the stores.

b. Using Excel and matrix multiplication, determine the expected proportion of customers returning equipment to each store for the next three periods, assuming a rental at store B in the initial period.

15. The following table gives a breakdown of customers staying and switching brands for two periods:

		This period		
		Brand A	Brand B	Brand C
	A	350	80	70
Last period	B	240	480	80
	C	210	140	350

Assume that these figures accurately reflect period-to-period behaviours of brand switching.

a. Find the transition probabilities.
b. Determine the steady-state probabilities for each brand using Excel.

16. A serviceperson is responsible for handling breakdowns of three robots at Global Manufacturing. Management is concerned about the number of robots waiting for repair, and the service manager has developed the following table that describes recent experience:

		Number waiting next period		
		0	1	2
Number waiting this period	0	.50	.50	0
	1	.25	.50	.25
	2	0	.50	.50

a. What is the probability that 1 robot will be waiting for repair next period, given 2 are waiting this period?
b. What is the probability that 1 robot will be waiting for repair in Period 3, given none are waiting this period (Period 0)?
c. What proportion of time will there be a waiting line in this system?

17. A machine breaks down and is repaired according to the following transition matrix:

		Next day	
		Operating	Down
Current	Operating	.85	.15
	Down	.35	.65

The cost for machine downtime is $800 per day. The manager has been presented with a proposal for preventive maintenance that will alter operating transition probabilities from .85 and .15 to .95 and .05. The other probabilities will remain the same. The cost of the preventive maintenance program would be $500 per day. Is the improvement in the steady-state probability of operating enough to justify the cost of the program? Explain.

18. (Refer to Problem 17.) Suppose the manager has a second proposal that relates to repair time. This proposal would change down probabilities from .35 and .65 to .45 and .55, while not affecting the operating probabilities. The cost of this proposal would be $700 per day. If the manager could choose only one proposal, which should it be?

19. Find the determinant and inverse of each matrix.

a. $\begin{bmatrix} .6 & -.2 \\ -.3 & .8 \end{bmatrix}$

b. $\begin{bmatrix} .7 & -.1 \\ 0 & 5 \end{bmatrix}$

c. $\begin{bmatrix} .8 & -.1 \\ 0 & .4 \end{bmatrix}$

20. Given this transition matrix for accounts receivable for GGM, Inc.:

		Next period			
		p	1	2	*b*
Current	*p*	1	0	0	0
	1	.7	0	.3	0
	2	.8	0	0	.2
	b	0	0	0	1

where

p = paid
1 = 1 to 30 days late
2 = 31 to 60 days late
b = bad debt

a. Interpret each of the values in row 1.
b. Rearrange the matrix so the row and column headings follow the sequence $p\ b\ 1\ 2$.
c. Partition the new matrix into I, O, R, and Q matrices, and identify each.
d. Obtain the matrix (I − Q) and then find its inverse.
e. What is the fundamental matrix in this problem?

f. Determine the proportion of current accounts receivable that will end up as bad debt.

g. If there is currently \$5000 in category 1 and \$8000 in category 2, what is the expected account that will end up as bad debt? What is the expected amount that will end up as paid?

21. A manager has prepared this transition matrix for the accounts receivable of a firm. However, some of the values are missing.

		Next period			
		p	1	2	*b*
Current	*p*	1			
	1	.8	0		0
	2	.8		0	
	b				1

where

p = paid
1 = 1 to 30 days late
2 = 31 to 60 days late
b = bad debt

a. Fill in the missing values.
b. Use Excel and obtain the fundamental matrix.
c. Use Excel and determine the proportion of accounts that will end up as paid.
d. There is currently \$50 000 in accounts that are 1 to 30 days late and double that amount that are 31 to 60 days late. Use Excel and determine the expected amount that will end up as paid.

22. Suppose the following transition matrix pertains to a food brokerage that has \$40 000 in accounts receivable that are 1 to 30 days overdue and \$20 000 in accounts receivable that are 31 to 60 days overdue. How much should be allowed for bad debt? (*Note:* Accounts are billed weekly.)

		Next period			
		p	1	2	*b*
Current	*p*	1	0	0	0
	1	.6	.3	.1	0
	2	.7	0	.2	.1
	b	0	0	0	1

where

p = paid
1 = 1 to 30 days overdue
2 = 31 to 60 days overdue
b = bad debt

23. A manager has developed the following transition matrix for accounts receivable:

		Next period			
		p	1	2	*b*
Current	*p*	1	0	0	0
	1	.6	.2	.2	0
	2	.5	.2	.1	.2
	b	0	0	0	1

where

p = paid
1 = 1 to 30 days overdue
2 = 31 to 60 days overdue
b = bad debt

A typical situation is to have approximately \$30 000 in accounts receivable that are 1 to 30 days overdue and \$10 000 in accounts receivable that are 31 to 60 days overdue. The manager has received a proposal from the marketing department for increasing the collection rate. Estimated probabilities under the proposal for Row 1 are .7, .2, .1, and 0 and for Row 2, .6, .2, .1, and .1. It will cost \$1000 per period to maintain this new system. Can the proposal be justified on a cost basis? Explain.

24. The local department store's accounting department is trying to determine how much of the accounts receivable will be paid and how much of it will become bad debt. If an account is not paid, it will become delinquent. The manager is trying to predict how much of the outstanding debts will be paid. To estimate this correctly, the manager of the store decided to use Markov analysis and classified the results into one of four states:

1. Paid
2. Not paid (bad debt)
3. Regular accounts receivable
4. Delinquent accounts receivable

The manager has determined the following probabilities for the transition matrix.

		To:			
		1	2	3	4
Current	1	1	0	0	0
	2	0	1	0	0
	3	.70	0	.17	.13
	4	.30	.40	0	.30

Currently there \$300 000 in the regular accounts receivable and \$120 000 in the delinquent accounts receivable. How much of the accounts receivable funds (regular and delinquent) will be paid?

25. Draw the probability transition diagrams for the following transition matrices. Then identify the probability transition matrices as

- cyclical;
- transient; or
- absorbing.

Explain the rationale for your classification.

a. $\begin{bmatrix} .3 & .6 & .1 \\ .4 & .3 & .3 \\ 0 & 0 & 1 \end{bmatrix}$

b. $\begin{bmatrix} .25 & .60 & .15 \\ 0 & 1 & 0 \\ .30 & .45 & .25 \end{bmatrix}$

c. $\begin{bmatrix} .2 & .3 & .4 & .1 \\ 0 & 0 & 0 & 1 \\ .5 & .2 & .2 & .1 \\ 0 & 1 & 0 & 0 \end{bmatrix}$

d. $\begin{bmatrix} .4 & .6 & 0 \\ .7 & .3 & 0 \\ .4 & .4 & .2 \end{bmatrix}$

e. $\begin{bmatrix} 0 & 0 & 1 \\ .2 & .5 & .3 \\ 0 & 0 & 1 \end{bmatrix}$

f. $\begin{bmatrix} 0 & 0 & 1 \\ .3 & .4 & .3 \\ 1 & 0 & 0 \end{bmatrix}$

g. $\begin{bmatrix} 0 & 0 & 1 \\ .4 & .2 & .4 \\ .5 & 0 & .5 \end{bmatrix}$

26. At Carleton University students change among the three faculties according to Table 11-10.
P_{ij} = probability of switching from faculty i to faculty j in the next period (year)
At the beginning of the 2005–2006 academic year, the number of students in each of the three faculties for the incoming freshman class at Carleton University was as follows:

Social Sciences:	8000 students
Engineering:	4000 students
Business:	3000 students

Use Excel to complete parts *a* through *d*.

a. Forecast the number of students in each faculty at the end of the 2006–2007 academic year.
b. Forecast the number of students in each faculty at the end of the 2007–2008 academic year.
c. Determine the steady-state probabilities.
d. Forecast the number of students in each faculty in the long run.

Table 11-10 Transition Matrix for Problem 26

		To:		
		Social Sciences	**Engineering**	**Business**
	Social Sciences	.75	.10	.15
From:	Engineering	.15	.65	.20
	Business	.05	.10	.85

Case1: Montreal Heart Institute

The Montreal Heart Institute (MHI) is the leading hospital specializing in cardiology in Canada and one of the largest such hospitals in the world. The bypass surgery physicians are very well respected. The director of the heart unit, Dr. Joe Weiss, wants to study the mortality rate of the patients that go through a bypass operation. He just hired Dr. Sandra Strasser as a consultant to analyze the mortality rate of the bypass surgery patients. As a first step, Dr. Strasser decided to use the Markov process and fundamental matrix analysis. To implement this method, she classified the patients into four groups (states):

Group 1: Patient dies as a result of the surgery
Group 2: Patient is in the intensive care unit or in surgery
Group 3: Patient is in the heart care/rehabilitation unit
Group 4: Patient is released from the hospital

States 1 and 4 are considered to be absorbing states. Based on analysis of records and discussions with physicians, Dr. Strasser determined the following probabilities for moving between the four states. (The time period for moving from one state to another is one day.) There is a 10 percent chance that a patient in intensive care will die due to various complications. There is a 50 percent chance that a patient in intensive care will remain in intensive care and a 40 percent chance that the patient will be moved from intensive care to the heart care/heart rehabilitation unit. There is a 2 percent chance that a patient in the heart care/heart rehabilitation unit will die. There is a 10 percent chance that a patient in the heart care unit will become critically ill and will have to be placed in intensive care. There is a 65 percent chance that a patient in the heart care department will remain in the heart care department. There is a 23 percent chance that a patient in the heart care department will be released from the hospital.

Annually, MHI performs an average of 800 bypass surgeries. On the average, at any point in time, 10 percent of the heart patients are in intensive care and 90 percent of them are in the heart care unit. Dr. Weiss wants to know the number of patients expected to die and the number of patients expected to survive annually. Determine the expected mortality rate and the annual expected number of patients surviving/ dying as a result of the bypass surgery.

CHAPTER 12

Waiting-Line Models

LEARNING OBJECTIVES

After completing this chapter, you should be able to:

1. Explain why waiting lines can occur in service systems.
2. Identify typical goals for designing service systems with respect to waiting.
3. Read the description of the queuing problem and identify the appropriate queuing model needed to solve the problem.
4. Manually solve typical problems using the formulas and tables provided in this chapter.
5. Use Excel to solve typical queuing problems associated with this chapter.
6. Use Excel and perform sensitivity analysis and what-if analysis with the results of various queuing models.
7. Outline the psychological aspects of waiting lines.
8. Explain the value of studying waiting-line models to those who are concerned with service systems.

CHAPTER OUTLINE

12.1 INTRODUCTION

An important problem faced by many organizations in private and public sectors is that of managing waiting lines. Examples abound that involve situations where waiting lines occur. Waiting lines are experienced in transportation systems, such as planes circling an airport awaiting clearance from the control tower, trucks waiting to load or unload cargo, buses backed up waiting to enter a terminal, cabs queuing up at airports, passengers queuing up waiting for cabs, and ferrys queuing up waiting to off-load passengers and autos. Frequently, there are waiting lines at banks, post offices, and other personal-service operations such as a hospital facility (e.g., an emergency room, an operating room), a public service centre (e.g., a passport office, licensing office, or Service Canada Centre). In factories, jobs queue up awaiting processing, orders need to be filled, machines need repairs or need to be loaded after a job, and employees wait to punch the time clock or to eat in the cafeteria. Waiting time for access to health care is one of the major complaints about the Canadian health care system. Therefore, the federal government has committed itself to set benchmarks for appropriate waits in key areas and many provincial governments have built centralized waiting times reporting systems.

Most of these systems are characterized by highly variable arrival and service rates. Consequently, even though overall system capacity exceeds processing requirements, lines tend to form from time to time because of temporary system overloads caused by this variability. At other times, the reverse is true; variability in demand for service results in idle servers or idle service facilities because of a temporary absence of customers.

A number of management science models have been developed to provide very valuable insights to decision makers who must make capacity decisions to improve processes or services. This chapter provides an overview of some of these models.

12.2 GOALS OF QUEUING SYSTEM DESIGN

Waiting-line models are *predictive* models of the expected behaviour of a system in which waiting lines form, that is, a **queuing system.** Such a system might be one that is in existence but is not performing satisfactorily. In this case, the emphasis is on deciding how to modify the system so that it does perform in a satisfactory manner. Also, the system might be in the design stage, in which case the emphasis would be placed on achieving a design that will produce the desired system performance.

A very common goal in designing a queuing system is to attempt to balance the cost of providing service capacity with the cost of customers waiting for service. These two costs are in direct conflict: a decrease in customer waiting cost can be achieved by increasing the amount of capacity (either by increasing the *number* of servers or by increasing the service rate). However, increasing the service capacity means an increase in the cost of the service. The combined cost of service capacity and customer waiting cost is U-shaped because of this trade-off relationship, as depicted in Figure 12-1. The total cost is minimized at the lowest point of the total cost curve. Finding the minimum point often involves successively incrementing service capacity until there are no further decreases. Because increments of service capacity often are discrete (e.g., one server, two servers, etc.), it may be more realistic to represent the cost of service capacity through a series of steps, rather than through a straight line, and, therefore, the total cost curve would not be as smooth as the one shown. Nonetheless, the purpose of the graph is merely to illustrate the general nature of the cost-minimization goal in system design.

MODERN MANAGEMENT SCIENCE APPLICATION:
BELL CANADA'S BUSINESS OFFICE

Bell Canada's Business Office (BO) acts as a coordinator between customers and other Bell Canada offices. A customer contacts a BO for services or billing information (such as reporting poor transmission, a move to a new address, or a billing error) by calling a designated number. There are two types of customers serviced by a BO: residential customers and business customers. The BO satisfies the customer directly if the request is within the BO's jurisdiction, otherwise the BO has to contact the appropriate office to schedule the required activities. The company's service objective was to answer x fraction of the calls in t seconds (for example, answer 90 percent of the calls in 10 seconds). Calls to a BO are answered by Service Representatives (SR). There are two types of SR—the scheduled SR and the standby SR. Scheduled SRs are those scheduled to be available for incoming calls. Standby SR are staff that are scheduled to perform other call-related activities. They do not usually answer a call. However, when the number of calls waiting to be answered has reached the queue-size threshold, a standby SR will immediately join the system and answer a call. Upon the completion of the call, this SR will stay in the system if the queue-size threshold is still reached or exceeded. Otherwise, this SR will leave the system. Because of changes in operational environment and service requirements, a flexible staffing model is required. A queuing model was developed to efficiently determine the number of scheduled SR and standby SR required in Bell Canada's Business Office (BO) to meet, in a cost-effective manner, the service objective defined in terms of the average call waiting time.

Source: S. K. Mok, J. G. Shanthikumar, "A transient queuing model for Business Office with standby servers," *European Journal of Operational Research* 28, no. 1, (February 1987), pp. 158–174.

Another approach, sometimes called for in designing or redesigning queuing systems, is to satisfy desired specifications. For example, a bank manager may request that the average number of customers kept waiting in line should be below seven. In this case, the question would involve determining the number of tellers needed to satisfy that objective. Similarly, the manager of a new restaurant may want to know what size waiting area will be needed to accommodate customers who are waiting to be seated.

The Modern Management Science Application, "Bell Canada's Business Office," describes Bell Canada's use of a queuing model to efficiently determine the number of scheduled and standby staff required in Bell Canada's Business Office to effectively achieve the designated service objective cost.

FIGURE 12-1 The Total Cost Curve Is U-Shaped

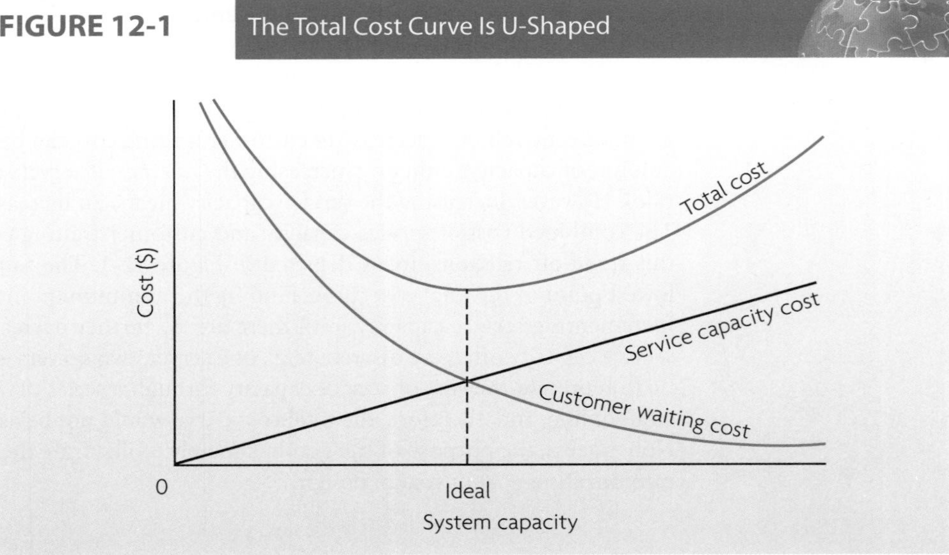

12.3 ELEMENTS AND CHARACTERISTICS OF WAITING-LINE SYSTEMS

Waiting-line systems can be differentiated by certain characteristics, such as the number of servers or whether access to the system is unrestricted or limited. Knowledge of such characteristics can help an analyst first to model the system and then to select an appropriate method for analyzing the system.

For illustration purposes, let's consider the information desk at Carleton University, which provides students, prospective students, faculty, staff, alumni, and visitors to the university the information, referrals, and access to the resources they need. The major elements of its queuing system and all waiting-line systems are outlined in Figure 12-2. Each of the elements is discussed briefly in this section.

Calling Population

The **calling population** refers to the pool of potential arrivals to the system. In queuing terminology, it is often called the *customer source.* If the source is large enough that the probability of an arrival is not significantly influenced by the fact that some of the customers are waiting in line, we say that the calling population is **infinite**. Examples of such systems are those open to the general public (gas stations, theatres, restaurants, supermarkets, banks, post offices, ticket counters, and so on). For Carleton University's information desk example, the customer source comprises students, prospective students, faculty, staff, alumni and visitors to the university. Although none of these populations is truly infinite, the fact that some customers are waiting in line does not diminish the potential of others in the population entering the system. On the other hand, there are systems that have limited access for service. For example, a machine operator may be responsible for loading and unloading five presses in a factory. Therefore, there is a limit to the number of presses waiting to be loaded or unloaded. Similarly, a repairman may be responsible for emergency calls to fix a limited number of machines, a sales rep may handle a limited number of customers, and usually, a secretary works for a limited number of people. If the number of jobs that require service or the number of customers waiting for services causes the probability of another arrival to decrease (because the percentage in the population is substantially reduced), the calling population, or population source, is described as **finite** or *limited.*

FIGURE 12-2 Major Elements of Waiting-Line Systems

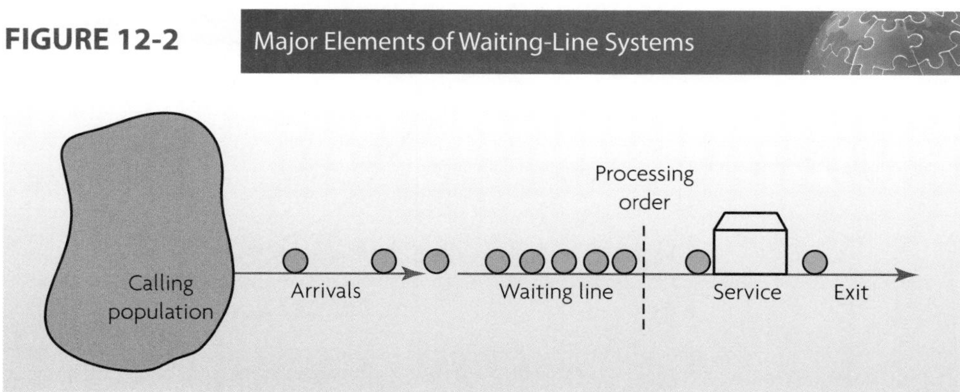

FIGURE 12-3 A Poisson Distribution Is Usually Used to Describe the Variability in Arrival Rate

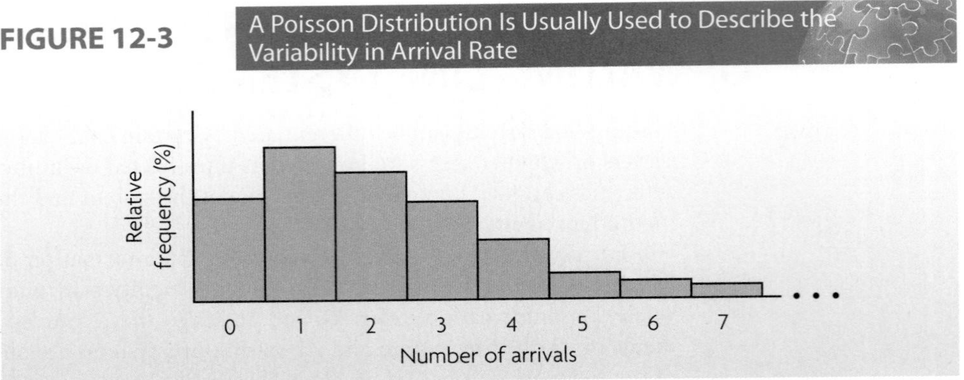

Customer Arrivals

Customers are considered units that request or require service. In some systems the customers are people, and in others they are not. Examples of nonpeople systems include automobiles arriving at intersections, trucks arriving at a loading dock, machines awaiting repair, orders waiting to be filled, planes waiting to land, animals waiting for veterinarian attention, telephone calls waiting to be answered, and so on.

One key question is whether customers arrive at the system in single units (i.e., one at a time) or whether they arrive in batches. For instance, cars usually arrive at a car wash singly, whereas an entire busload of customers may arrive at a fast-food restaurant. Some situations might be called borderline cases: Theatre patrons sometimes arrive in groups of two or more, as do diners at restaurants. For cases in which some arrivals are single units and others are small groups, we often treat them as single-unit arrivals for convenience. In fact, all of the models described in this chapter assume single unit arrivals. For Carleton University's information desk example, customers are likely people arriving in single units.

A second key question relates to the distribution of customer arrivals. Generally, the models require that the arrival *rate* variability follow a *Poisson* distribution. A typical distribution is illustrated in Figure 12-3. An equivalent distribution that describes the **interarrival time** (i.e., the average time between arrivals) when the arrival rate is Poisson is the *negative exponential* distribution. A typical distribution is illustrated in Figure 12-4. Note that the Poisson distribution describes a *discrete* random variable, which is the number of customers

FIGURE 12-4 If the Arrival Rate Is Poisson, the Interarrival Time Is a Negative Exponential

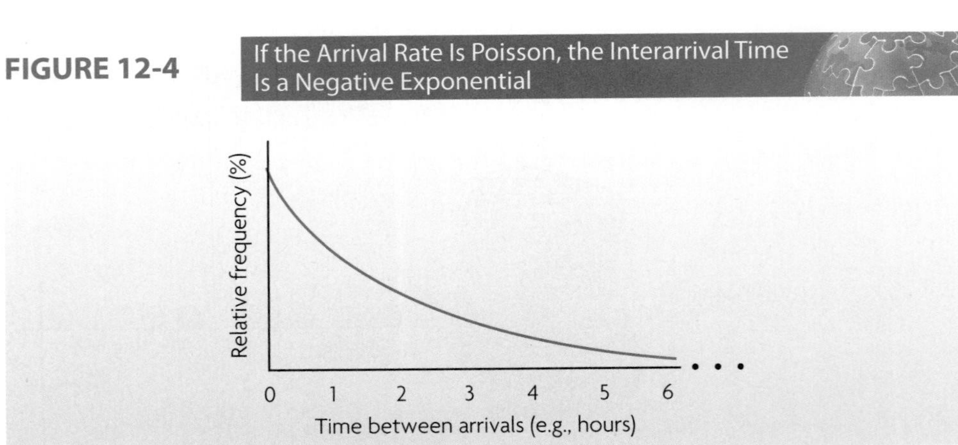

per unit of time, whereas the exponential distribution describes a *continuous* random variable, which is the time between arrivals. Perhaps the relationship between these two distributions can be understood better through an example. Suppose that the mean arrival rate of customers (people) at Carleton University's information desk is four people per hour and this arrival rate can be described by a Poisson distribution. Therefore, the mean time between arrivals is 15 minutes (i.e., the *reciprocal* of the arrival rate of four per hour, which is 1/4 hour), and this can be described by a negative exponential distribution.

Poisson arrival rates are commonly used in practice, and all of the models described in this chapter assume a Poisson distribution for the arrival rate. In practice, it may be necessary to determine if this assumption is true by using a Chi-square goodness-of-fit test.[1] For cases in which the assumption of a Poisson distribution does not hold, simulation (see the next chapter) may be the most reasonable alternative.

In the next section, we will describe the Poisson distribution in more detail, discuss its assumptions, and demonstrate how to find probabilities using this distribution.

Poisson Distribution

The Poisson distribution enables us to describe the number of times an event (arrival) occurs within an interval of time or space.

The assumptions for using the Poisson distribution are:

1. The probability of occurrence of an event (arrival) in a given interval does not affect the probability of occurrence of an event in another nonoverlapping interval.
2. The expected number of occurrences of an event in an interval is proportional to the size of the interval.
3. The probability of occurrence of an event in one interval is equal to the probability of occurrence of the event in another equal-size interval.

If the variable of interest (x) is the number of occurrences of an event within a given interval, then the probability that the event will occur x times within a given interval is specified by the following probability function.

$$P(x) = \frac{e^{-\lambda}\lambda^{x}}{x!} \qquad \textbf{(12-1a)}$$

where

λ = **expected (mean) number of occurrences within a given interval**
e = **base of the natural logarithms**

Similarly, the probability that event x will occur less than a times, more than a times, or between a and b times, are obtained by the following cumulative probability functions, respectively:

$$p(x \leq a) = \sum_{y=0}^{a} p(y) \qquad \textbf{(12-1b)}$$

$$p(x > a) = 1 - p(x \leq a) \qquad \textbf{(12-1c)}$$

$$p(a \leq x \leq b) = \sum_{y=a}^{b} p(y) \qquad \textbf{(12-1d)}$$

[1]Although beyond the scope of this text, Chi-square tests are commonly described in most basic statistics textbooks.

The mean number of occurrence within a given interval is called the arrival rate. The value of the arrival rate must always also be consistent with the time frame. Therefore, it may need to be adjusted according to the time interval of interest. For instance, let's consider that the arrival rate at Carleton University's information desk is 4 people per 15-minute period. If the time interval of interest is an hour, since there are an average of four arrivals per 15-minute period, then there are sixteen arrivals per hour, or $\lambda = 16$ per hour.

EXAMPLE 12-1

Machines in need of repair arrive for service at the maintenance and repair shop of the Miller Machine shop at the rate of three per 20-minute period.

a. What is the probability that there will be six machines arriving in a 20-minute period in need of repair?
b. What is the probability that there will be 12 machines arriving needing service in one hour?
c. What is the probability that there will be less than three machines arriving for service in a 20-minute period?

Solution

a. The parameter associated with the Poisson distribution in this problem is $\lambda = 3$ per 20-minute period. Using Equation 12-1a, the probability of six arrivals in a 20-minute period is

$$P(x = 6) = \frac{e^{-3}3^6}{6!} = \frac{(.049787)(729)}{720} = .05041$$

b. In doing this problem, we have to use a value of λ consistent with the time frame. Since there are an average of three arrivals for 20 minutes, then there are nine arrivals in an hour, or $\lambda = 9$ per hour. Therefore, the probability of 12 arrivals in an hour can be calculated as follows:

$$P(x = 9) = \frac{e^{-9}9^{12}}{12!} = \frac{(.00012341)(282\ 429\ 500\ 000)}{479\ 001\ 600} = .07276516$$

c. Since $\lambda = 3$ per 20 minutes,

$$p(x \leq 2) = p(x = 0) + p(x = 1) + p(x = 2)$$

The following probability calculations are based on Equation 12-1a:

$$P(x = 0) = \frac{e^{-3}3^0}{0!} = \frac{(.049787)(1)}{1} = .049787$$

$$P(x = 1) = \frac{e^{-3}3^1}{1!} = \frac{(.049787)(3)}{1} = .149361$$

$$P(x = 2) = \frac{e^{-3}3^2}{2!} = \frac{(.049787)(9)}{2} = .2240415$$

$$p(x \leq 2) = .049787 + .149361 + .2240415 = .4231895$$

As can be observed in the previous example, the calculation of probabilities using the Poisson distribution can be very cumbersome. Tables have been developed to calculate the probabilities using Poisson distribution.

Using Tables to Calculate Poisson Probabilities The cumulative Poisson probability table is included in Table B in Appendix B.

1. For instance, to obtain the answer to Example 12-1, part *a*, we first locate the mean number of arrivals (λ) on the left column of Table B, labelled as λ/x. Since this is a cumulative table and $\lambda = 3$, we find the probability for $x \leq 6$, which is .966, and then we find the probability that $x \leq 5$ (.916). Subtracting $P(x \leq 5)$ from $P(x \leq 6)$, we obtain $P(x = 6) = .966 - .916 = .05$.
2. Since $\lambda = 9$, in the row $\lambda = 9$, we find the probability of $x \leq 12$, which is .876; we also find the probability that $x \leq 11$ (.803). Subtracting $P(x \leq 11)$ from $P(x \leq 12)$, we obtain $P(x = 12) = .876 - .803 = .073$.
3. We locate $P(x \leq 2)$ in the row $\lambda = 3$. Therefore, $P(x \leq 2) = .423$.

Calculation of Poisson Probability Using Excel

It is very easy to calculate a Poisson probability using Excel. First, click on Excel's function wizard labelled as f_x on the worksheet. This will bring up the selection dialogue box shown in Exhibit 12-1. At this point, you can either type Poisson on the first line of that dialogue box or select the "All" or "Statistical" category and select Poisson distribution from the list by scrolling down.

When you click on Poisson distribution, the dialogue screen shown in Exhibit 12-2 will appear.

We will illustrate the use of this Poisson function using Excel by redoing Example 12-1, part *a*. In this example, $x = 6$ arrivals in 20 minutes and $\lambda = 3$ arrivals per 20 minutes.

EXHIBIT 12-1 Selection of a Specified Function from the Function Wizard

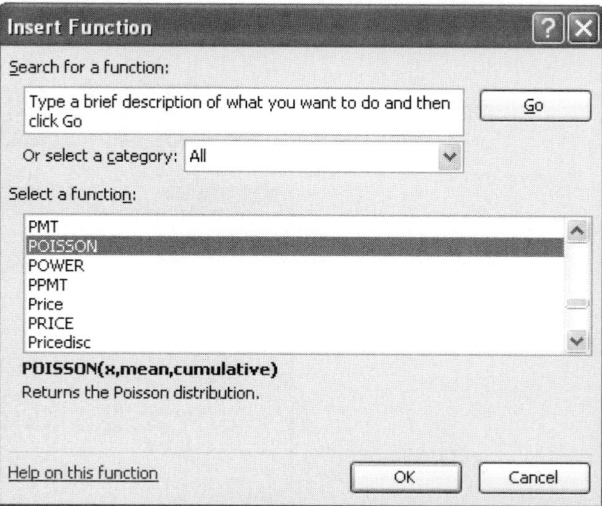

EXHIBIT 12-2 Calculation of a Probability Using the Poisson Distribution

Function Arguments

POISSON

X 6 = 6

Mean 3 = 3

Cumulative False = FALSE

= 0.050409407

Returns the Poisson distribution.

Cumulative is a logical value: for the cumulative Poisson probability, use TRUE; for the Poisson probability mass function, use FALSE.

Formula result = 0.050409407

Help on this function OK Cancel

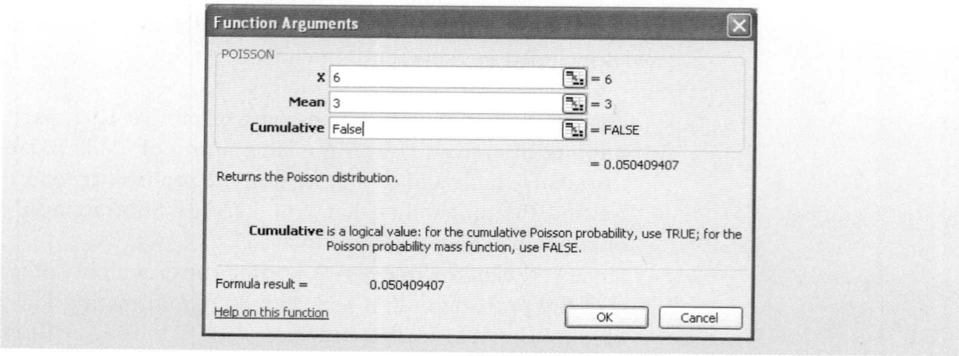

Therefore in Exhibit 12-2, enter 6 for *x* and 3 for Mean. Since this is not a calculation of a cumulative probability, indicate False in the Cumulative box and then click OK. The Poisson probability of .05041 that we had obtained in answering part *a* of Example 12-1 will appear both in the dialogue box and on the worksheet.

Cumulative probabilities can be calculated as well. When there is a need to calculate a cumulative Poisson probability, simply change the response to the Cumulative box to True.

To illustrate how we might obtain cumulative probabilities with Excel, we obtain the solution to Example 12-1, part *c*. First we enter 2 for *x* and 3 for Mean. Since this is a calculation of a cumulative probability, indicate TRUE in the Cumulative box and then click OK. The cumulative Poisson probability of .423190 will appear in the dialogue box as well as on the worksheet. This solution is displayed on the dialogue box in Exhibit 12-3.

In summary, the Poisson distribution is obtained in Excel with the following function: POISSON(*x, Mean, Cumulative*), where *x* is the number of occurrences, *Mean* is the arrival rate or the mean number of occurrences, and *Cumulative* is a logical value that determines the form of the probability distribution returned. If Cumulative is TRUE, POISSON returns the cumulative Poisson probability that the number of random events occurring will be between zero and *x* inclusive; if FALSE, it returns the Poisson probability mass function that the number of events occurring will be exactly *x*.

EXHIBIT 12-3 Calculation of a Cumulative Probability Using the Poisson Distribution

Function Arguments

POISSON

X 2 = 2

Mean 3 = 3

Cumulative TRUE = TRUE

= 0.423190081

Returns the Poisson distribution.

Cumulative is a logical value: for the cumulative Poisson probability, use TRUE; for the Poisson probability mass function, use FALSE.

Formula result = 0.423190081

Help on this function OK Cancel

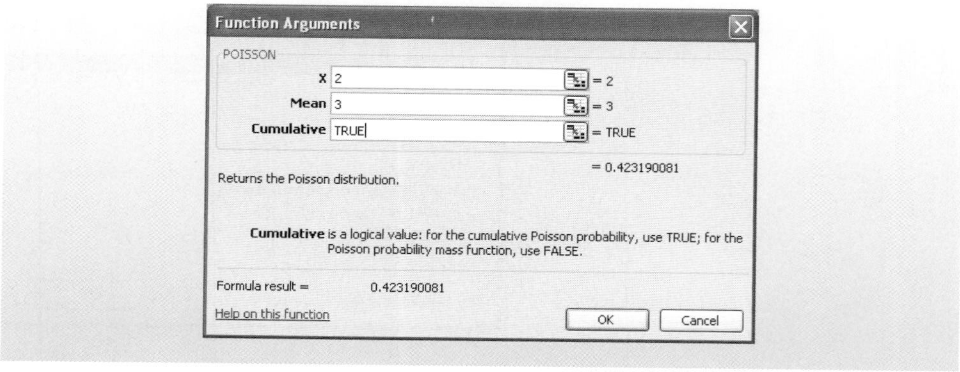

The Waiting Line

The waiting line consists of customers who have been admitted to the system and are awaiting service. In the Carleton University's information desk illustration, the waiting line would consist of customers (people) lined up and waiting for service. Some key issues are whether arriving customers may refuse to enter the system (**balking**), say, because of a long waiting line; whether customers may arrive, wait for a while, but then leave without being served (**reneging**); or whether customers may switch lines (e.g., checkout lines at supermarkets) in an attempt to lessen waiting time (**jockeying**). The models in this chapter do not deal with these interesting, but somewhat complex, situations. Instead, all models assume that once customers enter the queue, they remain there until they have been served. Moreover, a single waiting line is assumed in which customers are directed to the next available server.

Processing Order

A commonly encountered **queue discipline** (processing order) rule is *first-come, first-served.* When people are involved, this rule is widely perceived as "fair." In some instances, customers take a number when they enter the line (e.g., at a bakery, at a delicatessen take-out counter, or at a catalogue sales desk in a department store); in other instances, customers actually wait in a single line (e.g., at many banks and post offices). Another approach is to assign arriving customers a **priority** classification, and process waiting customers according to those priorities. A hospital emergency room is an example of such a system; seriously ill or injured persons are treated before those with lesser illnesses or injuries. Similarly, time-sharing computer systems usually have priority classifications for jobs (e.g., the shortest job first), factories may process rush jobs ahead of routine jobs, and at many firms, orders of important customers may be processed ahead of orders of less important customers.

Both priority and first-come, first-served (FCFS) systems are presented in this chapter; however, most models use the first-come, first-served rule.

Service

The key issues for service concern the number of servers, the number of steps in the service process, and the distribution of service time.

A service centre can have one server (**single channel**) or more than one server (**multiple channel**). Unless otherwise specified, we will assume that servers work *independently,* so that if a system has three servers, for example, this implies that as many as three customers could be handled simultaneously. Conversely, if you are told that the three servers work together as a crew, they would be treated as a single-channel system. Both single-channel and multiple-channel models are described in this chapter.

Service may consist of one or a few steps that are handled together (e.g., a banking transaction that consists of making a deposit and cashing a cheque, or simply making a deposit). This is called **single phase**. Conversely, some systems involve a series of steps (e.g., multiple-step manufacturing processes, registration at a university where students move through a sequence of checkpoints, loan processing that requires multiple steps before final approval or rejection). Such service systems are called **multiple phase**. All models in this chapter assume single-phase systems. In the Carleton University's information desk illustration, a single channel or multiple channel may be used and the service consists of a single phase.

A comparison of single- and multiple-channel, and single- and multiple-phase systems is presented in Figure 12-5. The waiting lines may constitute multiple lines. However, in this chapter, we will only discuss models with single lines.

FIGURE 12-5 Comparison of Single- and Multiple-Channel Queuing Systems and Comparison of Single and Multiple Phase Sytems

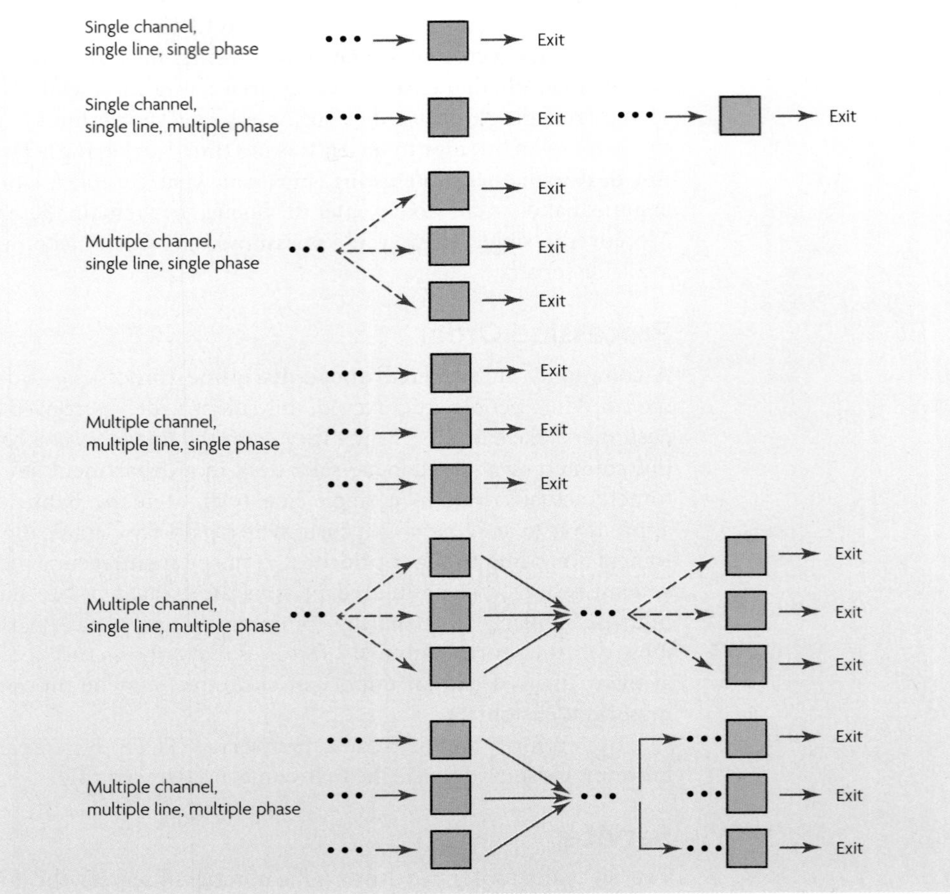

The third important issue is the *distribution* of processing or service time. The most common assumption is that service time can be described by a negative exponential distribution[2] (see Figure 12-6). The implication of this sort of distribution is that most customers require short service times, a small proportion require moderate service times, and a few may require relatively long service times. In practice, exponential service times seem less pervasive than Poisson arrival rates. However, for simplicity, most of the models described in this chapter assume an exponential service time distribution.

Again, testing the assumption of a distribution would involve the use of a Chi-square goodness-of-fit test. If the assumption does not hold, either another queuing model that does not require this assumption should be used, or simulation could be used.

In the following section, we will discuss the exponential distribution and the calculation of probabilities using the exponential distribution.

[2]Exponentially distributed service *times* are equivalent to Poisson-distributed service rates. So, if the service rate is Poisson with mean μ, then the service time is exponential with mean $1/\mu$, and vice versa.

FIGURE 12-6 An Exponential Service-Time Distribution

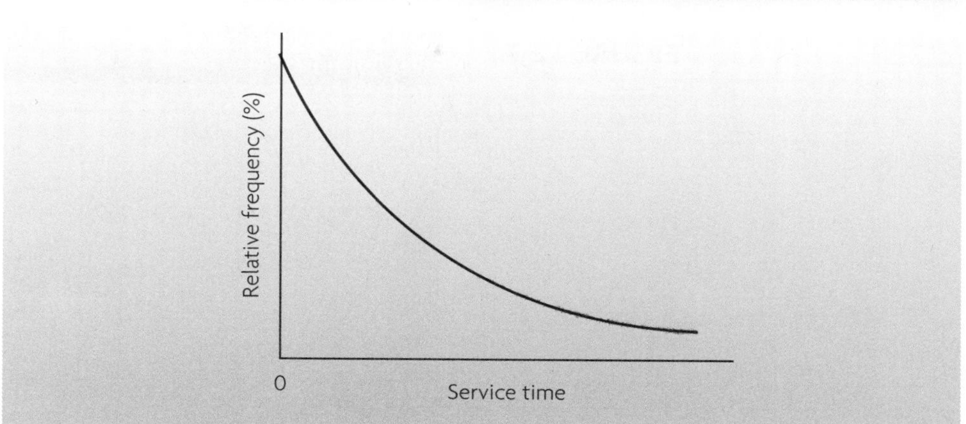

Exponential Distribution

In this section we will discuss the exponential distribution in relation to the Poisson distribution. As we discussed earlier, if the Poisson distribution represents the arrival of customers, then the exponential distribution represents the time elapsed between successive customers arriving. Therefore, the exponential distribution is a continuous distribution and is a function of time. It is often used for inter-arrival times, as well as service times.

The probability density function of the exponential distribution can be written as follows:

$$f(t) = \begin{cases} \lambda e^{-\lambda t} & \text{for } t, \lambda \geq 0 \\ 0 & \text{elsewhere} \end{cases} \qquad (12\text{-}2)$$

where

λ = **mean number of occurrences of a particular event per time unit**

The meaning of λ in equation 12-2 is different than the one used earlier for the Poisson distribution in Equation 12-1a.

Therefore, for an exponential distribution, the mean and standard deviation are

$$\mu_t = \sigma_t = \frac{1}{\lambda}$$

Integrating this probability density function, it can be shown that

$$P(t \leq a) = 1 - e^{-\lambda a} \qquad (12\text{-}3)$$

This is the probability of t being at most a. Graphically, this probability can be depicted as the shaded area in Figure 12-7a.

$$P(t \geq b) = e^{-\lambda b} \qquad (12\text{-}4)$$

This is the probability of t being at least b. Graphically, this probability can be depicted as the shaded area in Figure 12-7b.

Based on the above probability formulas, we can also show that

$$P(a \leq t \leq b) = e^{-\lambda a} - e^{-\lambda b} \qquad (12\text{-}5)$$

This is the probability of t being between a and b. Graphically, this probability can be depicted as the shaded area in Figure 12-7c.

FIGURE 12-7 Graphical Depiction of Probabilities Using the Exponential Distribution

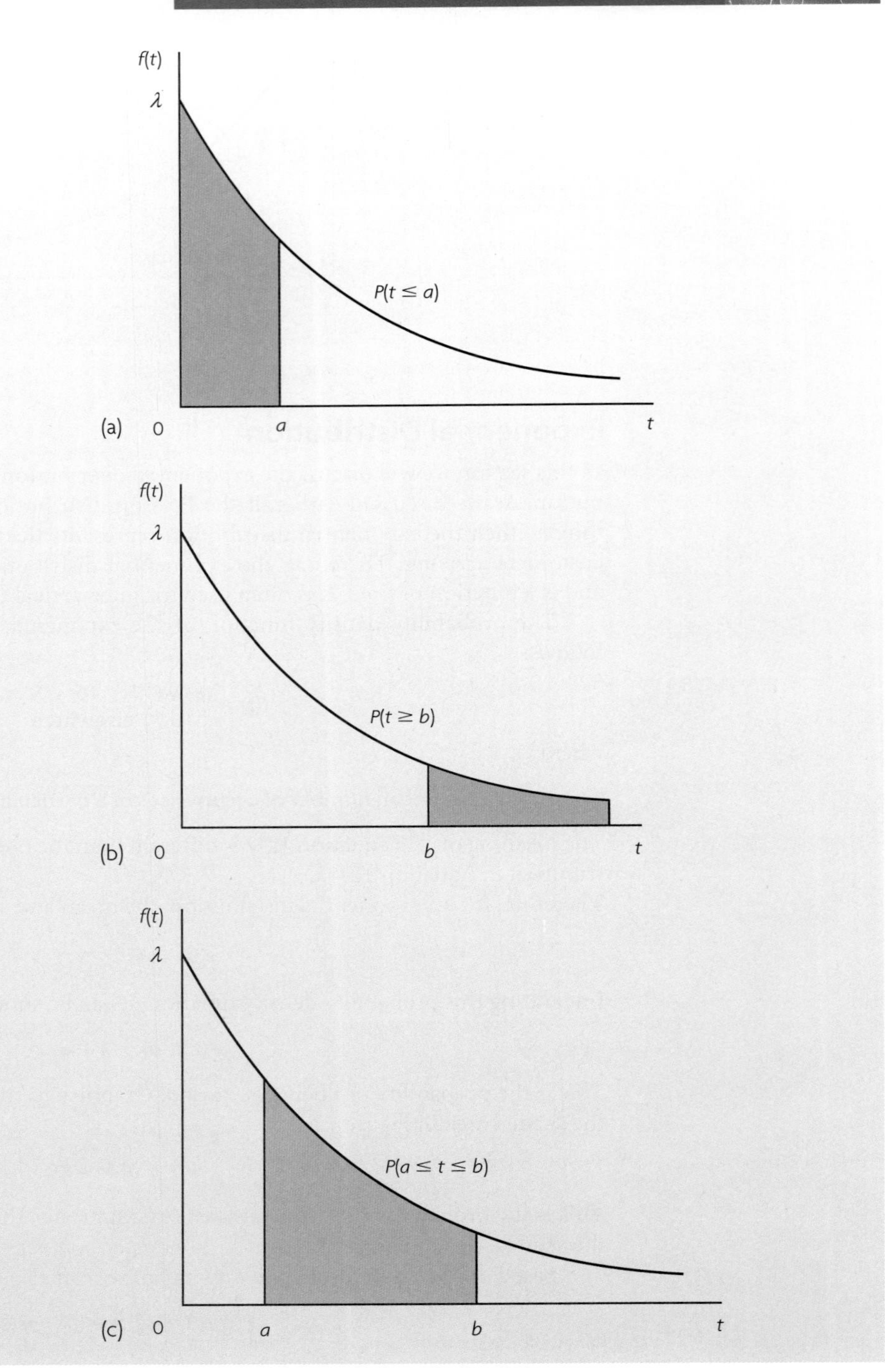

EXAMPLE 12-2

At the Tip-Top grocery store, time between arrivals is distributed according to the exponential distribution. On the average two customers arrive every four minutes. In addition, the service time is distributed according to the exponential distribution as well, with a mean service rate of 40 customers per hour.

a. What is the probability that no more than four minutes elapse between successive arrivals of customers?
b. What is the probability that more than six minutes elapse between successive arrivals of customers?
c. What is the probability that between four minutes and six minutes elapse between successive arrivals of customers?
d. What is the expected time between successive arrivals of customers? What is the standard deviation of time between arrivals of customers?
e. What is the expected service time? What is the standard deviation of service time?
f. What is the probability that service time is one minute or less?
g. What is the probability that the service time is more than two minutes?
h. What is the probability that the service time is between one minute and two minutes?

Solution

Since the question involves a time period of minutes, first we convert λ into number of arrivals per minute. $\lambda = 2/4 = .5$ arrivals per minute.

a. The probability that no more than four minutes elapse between successive arrivals of customers can be computed using Equation 12-3:

$$P(t \leq 4) = 1 - e^{(-.5)(4)} = 1 - e^{-2} = 1 - (.13534) = .86466$$

b. The probability that more than six minutes elapse between successive arrivals of customers can be computed using Equation 12-4:

$$P(t \geq 6) = e^{(-.5)(6)} = e^{-3} = .049787$$

c. The probability that between four minutes and six minutes elapse between successive arrivals of customers can be computed using Equation 12-5:

$$P(4 \leq t \leq 6) = e^{(-.5)(4)} - e^{(-.5)(6)} = .13534 - 0.49787 = 0.85553$$

d. The mean time between successive arrivals of customers and standard deviation of time.

$$\mu_t = \sigma_t = \frac{1}{\lambda} = \frac{1}{.5} = 2$$

In other words, we can say that the mean time between successive arrivals is equal to two minutes, and the standard deviation is also two minutes.

e. The mean service time and standard deviation of service time can be calculated as follows:

$$\lambda = \frac{40}{60} = .6667$$

$$\mu_t = \sigma_t = \frac{1}{\lambda} = \frac{1}{.6667} = 1.5 \text{ minutes}$$

In other words, we can say that the mean service time is equal to 1.5 minutes, and the standard deviation of service time is also 1.5 minutes.

f. $P(t \leq 1) = 1 - e^{(-.6667)(1)} = 1 - e^{-.6667} = 1 - .5134 = .486$

g. $P(t \geq 2) = e^{(-.667)(2)} = e^{-1.3334} = .2636$

h. $P(1 \leq t \leq 2) = e^{(-.6667)(1)} - e^{(-.6667)(2)} = .5134 - .2636 = .2498$

Calculation of Exponential Probability Using Excel

Calculation of exponential probability is very similar to the calculation of Poisson probability using Excel. First, click on Excel's function wizard labelled as f_x on the worksheet. This will bring up the selection dialogue box shown in Exhibit 12-1. At this point, you can either type Exponential on the first line of that dialogue box or select "All" or "Statistical" category and select Exponential distribution from the list by scrolling down. When you click on Exponential distribution on the dialogue screen in Exhibit 12-1, another dialogue screen, shown in Exhibit 12-4, will appear.

We will illustrate the calculation of exponential probability using Excel by redoing Example 12-2, part *a*. In this example, on the dialogue screen shown Exhibit 12-4, enter 4 (minutes) for *x*, .5 (arrivals per minute) for Lambda, and TRUE in the Cumulative box. Entering "true" in the Cumulative box ensures that a less-than-or-equal-to probability is calculated, as required to answer Example 12-2, part *a*. To answer Example 12-2, part *b*, we would obtain another cumulative probability in the same way as for part *a* and subtract the answer obtained from 1. Therefore, 1 − .950213 = .049787. In other words, all greater-than-or-equal-to probabilities are calculated by subtracting the result obtained using Excel (less-than-or-equal-to, or cumulative, probability) from one. Always respond to the Cumulative box as "true" to obtain an exponential probability. Answering Cumulative as "false" will calculate the probability density function (height of the curve in Figure 12-7) associated with particular values of x and λ, and will not calculate cumulative probabilities.

In summary, the exponential distribution is obtained in Excel with the following function: EXPONDIST(*x*, *Lambda*, *Cumulative*), where *x* is the number of occurrences, *Lambda* is the arrival rate or the mean number of occurrences, and *Cumulative* is a logical value that determines the form of the probability distribution returned. If cumulative

EXHIBIT 12-4 Calculation of a Probability Using the Exponential Distribution

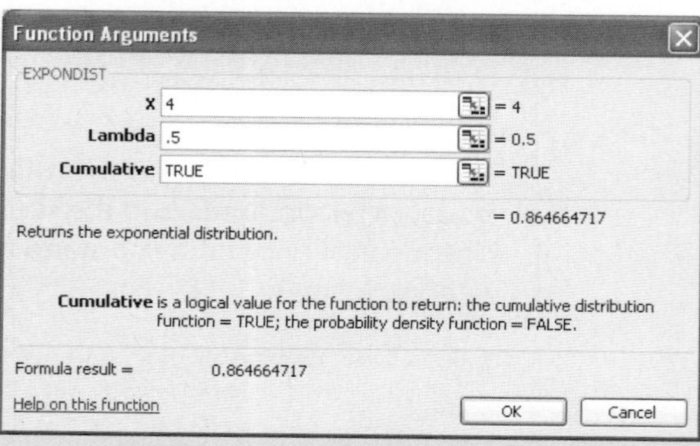

is TRUE, EXPONDIST returns the cumulative exponential probability that the number of random events occurring will be between zero and x inclusive; if FALSE, it returns the exponential probability density function value at x (which is the curve height).

Exit

The final consideration is what customers do after leaving the system. For them, possible choices include rejoining the source pool immediately, rejoining the source pool after a delayed interval (e.g., hospital patients recovering at home, car wash customers not immediately returning for another wash, and so on), and permanent departure from the pool (e.g., patients who develop a permanent immunity to a disease). The models presented here assume either an immediate return to the pool (especially with limited calling populations) or a population that is large enough so that delayed returns or permanent departures have almost no impact on the arrival rate. In the Carleton University's information desk illustration, it is assumed that customers rejoin the source pool immediately.

12.4 MEASURES OF SYSTEM PERFORMANCE

A number of different performance measures can be computed that summarize waiting line behaviour given the customer arrival rate, the number of servers, the service rate, and certain other information. Among the most commonly used measures, referred to as operating characteristics, are the following:

L_q = the average number waiting for service
L = the average number in the system (i.e., waiting for service or being served)
P_0 = the probability of zero units in the system
ρ = the system utilization (percentage of time servers are busy serving customers)
W_q = the average time customers must wait for service
W = the average time customers spend in the system (i.e., waiting for service and service time)
M = the expected maximum number waiting for service for a given level of confidence

One additional measure is the total cost of the system, which is generally based on the cost of customer waiting time and the cost of server time.

For example, the future owner of a proposed car wash may want to know the following:

1. On the average, how many cars/customers will be waiting for a wash?
2. How long, on the average, will a customer have to wait in line?
3. What proportion of the time will no customers be in the system?
4. What will be the upper limit on the number of cars waiting that will not be exceeded, say, 99 percent of the time?
5. How sensitive are the performance measures to changes in either the number of servers or the service rate? How sensitive is the system to changes in the arrival rate?
6. What level of capacity will minimize the sum of capacity costs and customer waiting costs?

Two key parameters in any waiting line system are the mean arrival rate, which is represented by the Greek letter λ (lambda), and the mean service rate, which is represented by the Greek letter μ (mu). Table 12-1 presents the symbols for number waiting and time waiting in an easy-to-remember format. Note the difference in the definition of λ in Table 12-1 in comparison to relations (12-1a) and (12-2).

TABLE 12-1 Line and Service Symbols for Average Number Waiting, and Average Waiting and Service Times

	System		
	In the waiting line	Being served	In the system
Average number	L_q	$\frac{\lambda}{\mu}$	$L = L_q + \frac{\lambda}{\mu}$
Average time	$W_q = \frac{L_q}{\lambda}$	$\frac{1}{\mu}$	$W = W_q + \frac{1}{\mu}$

where

λ = mean arrival rate

μ = mean service rate

In the following pages, models are presented that provide formulas and tables enabling one to determine values for various measures of system performance. All of these formulas and table values pertain to a system that is in a *steady state.* In a steady state, various measures, such as the average number waiting in line, or the average waiting time, are *independent* of a particular time. That is not always the case, though. Very often, when a system begins operating after a period of inactivity (e.g., a bank opens in the morning, repair crews arrive for work after a long weekend, and so on), a system goes through a transient state before it settles down. For instance, there may already be a line of customers waiting outside the bank before it opens. Then, too, when human servers are involved, they often go through a warmup period before they reach their usual operating efficiency. Once the system moves into its normal operating pattern, it is usually considered to be in a steady state, and that condition is the one to which the various models apply.

Basic Relationships

There are certain fundamental relationships that hold for all infinite-source models. These relationships can be valuable for converting performance measures from *number* waiting to *time* waiting, and vice versa. The most useful of these relationships are

1. System utilization (percentage of time server is busy) for a single channel system or the average number being served:

$$\rho = \frac{\lambda}{\mu} \tag{12-6}$$

where

λ = **customer arrival rate**
μ = **service rate**

2. The average number in the system:

$$L = L_q + \rho \tag{12-7}$$

where

L = **average number in the system**
L_q = **average number in line**

3. The average time in line (Little's Law):

$$W_q = \frac{L_q}{\lambda} \tag{12-8}$$

4. The average time in the system, including service:

$$W = W_q + \frac{1}{\mu} \tag{12-9}$$

5. System utilization (proportion of time servers are busy) for multiple channel systems:

$$\rho = \frac{\lambda}{s\mu} \tag{12-10}$$

where

s = number of channels or servers

For a system to be feasible (i.e., underloaded), system utilization must be less than 1.00.

The equation (12-8) is referred to as Little's Law. It shows the relationship between the average number waiting for service (L_q) and the average time customers must wait for service (W_q).

EXAMPLE 12-3

The owner of a car wash franchise intends to construct another car wash in a suburban location. Based on experience, the owner estimates that the arrival rate for the proposed facility will be 20 cars per hour and the service rate will be 25 cars per hour. (Let's assume, for the sake of illustration, that the arrival rate is Poisson and the service time is exponential). Service time will be variable because all cars are washed by hand rather than by machine. Cars will be processed one at a time (hence, this is a single-channel, or one-server system). Determine the following:

1. The average number of cars being washed.
2. The average number of cars in the system (i.e., either being washed or waiting to be washed), for a case where the average number waiting in line is 3.2.
3. The average time in line (i.e., the average time cars wait to get washed).
4. The average time cars spend in the system (i.e., waiting in line and being washed).
5. The system utilization.

Solution

Arrival rate, λ, = 20 cars per hour
Service rate, μ, = 25 cars per hour
Number of servers, s, = 1
$L_q = 3.2$

1. $\rho = \frac{\lambda}{\mu} = \frac{20}{25} = .80$ car being served

2. $L = L_q + \rho$

   $= 3.2 + .8 = 4.0$ cars

3. $W_q = \frac{L_q}{\lambda}$

$$= \frac{3.2}{20 \text{ cars per hour}} = .16 \text{ hour. which is } .16 \text{ hour} \times 60 \text{ minutes/hour}$$

$$= 9.6 \text{ minutes}$$

4. $W = W_q + \frac{1}{\mu}$

$$= .16 \text{ hour} + \frac{1}{25} \text{ hour} = .20 \text{ hour, which is } .20 \text{ hour} \times 60 \text{ minutes/hour}$$

$$= 12 \text{ minutes}$$

5. $\rho = \frac{\lambda}{s\mu} = \frac{20 \text{ cars per hour}}{(1)(25 \text{ cars/per hour}) =} = .80, \text{ or } 80 \text{ percent}$

12.5 QUEUING MODELS

In this section, the following queuing models are described:

1. Basic single-channel
2. Multiple-channel

Basic Single-Channel (M/M/1) Model

This model pertains to situations in which there is one channel or server that processes all customers. Note that if a group of servers works as a single team, that situation would be considered a single-channel system.

A single-channel (M/M/1) model is appropriate when these conditions exist:

1. One server or channel
2. A Poisson arrival rate
3. A negative exponential service time
4. First-come, first-served processing order
5. An infinite calling population
6. No limit on queue length

M/M/1 stands for **M**arkovian (Poisson) arrivals, **M**arkovian (negative exponential) service, and **1** (single) server.

The necessary formulas for the single-server model are presented in Table 12-2. The formulas enable us to compute various measures of system performance. For the most part, the meaning of each measure is readily apparent. One exception may be the last measure: average waiting time for an arrival that is not immediatley served.

Let us consider that measure somewhat further. Suppose we observe a system for a period of time, and that during time, five customers arrive. Suppose, further, that their waiting times (in minutes) are 2.1, 0, 1.4, 0, and .8. We can determine their average waiting time by summing their waiting imes and dividing by 5. This would be analogous to W_q. Now suppose we focus on just those who actually waited (the 0 times mean that those customers went directly into service; they did not have to wait in line). Hence, the average time for those who had to wait would be the three nonzero times divided by 3. Note that in both cases, the numerator (the sum of times) would be the same. By eliminating those who did not wait, we obtain a higher average waiting time that we did with all arrivals included.

TABLE 12-2 Formulas for Basic Single Server (M/M/1) Model

Performance Measure	Formula	Formula Number
System utilization	$\rho = \frac{\lambda}{\mu}$	(12-11)
Average number in line	$L_q = \frac{\lambda^2}{\mu(\mu-\lambda)}$	(12-12)
Average number in system	$L = L_q + \frac{\lambda}{\mu}$	(12-13)
Average time in line	$W_q = \frac{L_q}{\lambda}$	(12-14)
Average time in system	$W = W_q + \frac{1}{\mu}$	(12-15)
Probability of zero units in the system	$P_0 = 1 - \left(\frac{\lambda}{\mu}\right)$	(12-16)
Probability of *n* units in the system	$P_n = P_o\left(\frac{\lambda}{\mu}\right)^n$	(12-17)
Probability the waiting line won't exceed *k* units	$P_{n\le k} = 1 - \left(\frac{\lambda}{\mu}\right)^{k+1}$	(12-18)
Average waiting time for an arrival not served immediately	$W_a = \frac{1}{\mu-\lambda}$	(12-19)

Hence, if we are truly concerned with the waiting times of those who actually wait, we should then focus on W_a rather than on W_q.

With that in mind, let us take a moment to see how the formula for W_a can be derived. We have just seen that W_q is made up of two parts: actual waiting and nonwaiting. In fact, W_q is the *weighted average* of W_a and 0. That is, the proportion of customers that don't wait is $1-(\lambda/\mu)$ (i.e., P_0), and the proportion that do wait is λ/μ. Therefore, W_a is equal to the proportion that wait multiplied by W_a plus the proportion that don't wait multiplied by 0, divided by the sum of the weights:

$$W_q = \frac{\frac{\lambda}{\mu}W_a + \left(1 - \frac{\lambda}{\mu}\right)0}{\frac{\lambda}{\mu} + \left(1 - \frac{\lambda}{\mu}\right) = 1} = \frac{\lambda}{\mu}W_a$$

Now refer to Table 13-2 for the equation for W_q. You can see that it is L_q divided by λ. Referring to Equation 13-11, we can see that $W_q = \lambda/(\mu(\mu - \lambda))$. We just found that $W_q = (\lambda/\mu)W_a$.

Substituting the equation for W_q here, we can solve for W_a:

$$W_q = \frac{\lambda}{\mu(\mu - \lambda)} = \frac{\lambda}{\mu}W_a \quad \text{so} \quad W_a = \frac{\frac{\lambda}{\mu(\mu - \lambda)}}{\lambda/\mu} = \frac{1}{\mu - \lambda}$$

EXAMPLE 12-4

The mean arrival rate of customers at a ticket counter with one server is 3 per minute, and the mean service rate is 4 customers per minute. Calculate each of the performance measures listed in Table 12-2. Suppose that $n = 2$ and $k = 5$, where n = number of customers in the system, and k = maximum length of the line.

Solution

1. $\rho = \frac{3}{4} = .75$ or 75 percent.
2. $L_q = \frac{3^2}{4(4-3)} = 2.25$ customers.
3. $L = 2.25 + \frac{3}{4} = 3.00$ customers.
4. $W_q = \frac{2.25}{3} = .75$ minute.
5. $W = .75 + \frac{1}{4} = 1.00$ minute.
6. $P_0 = 1 - \frac{3}{4} = .25$. This means that the probability is 25 percent that an arriving unit will not have to wait for service. Hence, the probability that an arrival *will* have to wait for service is 75 percent.
7. Suppose $n = 2$. $P_2 = .25\left(\frac{3}{4}\right)^2 = .1406$.
8. Suppose $k = 2$. $P_5 = 1-\left(\frac{3}{4}\right)^{5+1} = .822$. In other words, there is an 82.2 percent chance that the waiting line won't exceed five customers.
9. $W_a = \frac{1}{4-3} = 1.0$ minute.

Basic Single-Channel Model with Poisson Arrival and Exponential Service Rate (M/M/1 Model) with Excel

Excel spreadsheets can be used to determine the operating characteristics associated with queuing models. The only disadvantage of developing waiting-line models using Excel spreadsheets is that some of the formulas for various operating characteristics can be somewhat complex. However, once the appropriate formulas are entered and the Excel spreadsheet is prepared to model a waiting-line problem, Excel provides tremendous flexibility to do the various calculations. For instance, arrival rate or service rate or other model parameters can be changed to analyze different what-if scenarios. To demonstrate preparation of an Excel worksheet for the basic single-server model, we will use Example 12-3.

The Excel worksheet for this model is presented in Exhibit 12-5. The arrival rate is specified in cell D1 and the service rate is specified in cell D2. The basic single-server model formulas specified in the previous section are entered in cells C4 through C12. The Excel formulas for these cells can be observed at the bottom of Exhibit 12-5. For example, cell C9 includes the formula for L_q, which is also displayed on the formula bar at the top of the spreadsheet.

An important characteristic of queuing systems with variable arrival and service rates can be illustrated by noting what happens to the average number waiting for service as the utilization ratio increases. Table 12-3 lists values of L_q for a sequence of increases in **system utilization.**

EXHIBIT 12-5 Basic Single-Channel Model with Poisson Arrival and Exponential Service Rate (M/M/1 Model)

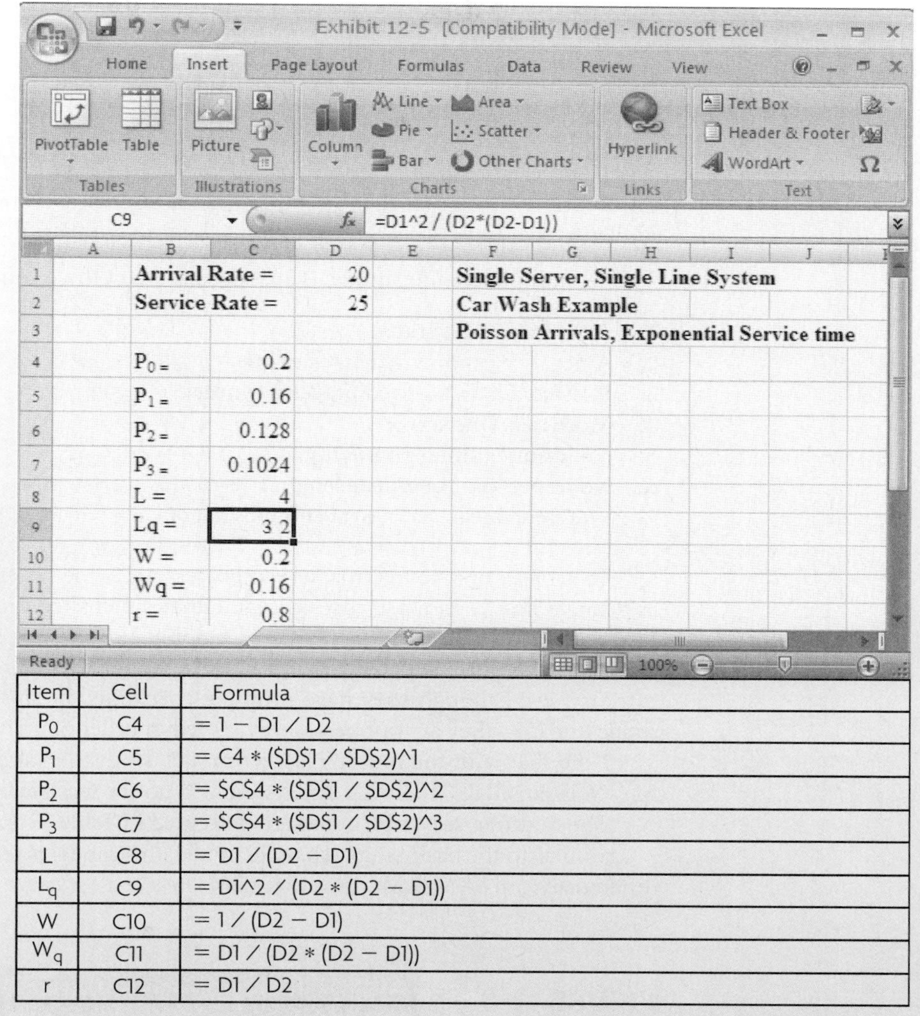

Item	Cell	Formula
P_0	C4	= 1 − D1 / D2
P_1	C5	= C4 * ($D$1 / $D$2)^1
P_2	C6	= $C$4 * ($D$1 / $D$2)^2
P_3	C7	= $C$4 * ($D$1 / $D$2)^3
L	C8	= D1 / (D2 − D1)
L_q	C9	= D1^2 / (D2 * (D2 − D1))
W	C10	= 1 / (D2 − D1)
W_q	C11	= D1 / (D2 * (D2 − D1))
r	C12	= D1 / D2

TABLE 12-3 Average Number Waiting for Services as the Utilization Ratio Increases

λ	μ	λ / μ	L_q Using Formula 12-12
3.00	5	.60	.900
3.50	5	.70	1.633
4.00	5	.80	3.200
4.50	5	.90	8.100
4.75	5	.95	18.050

You can see that as utilization increases, the average number waiting in line increases. Note, too, that as the utilization ratio gets closer and closer to the maximum of 100 percent, the average line length increases rapidly, as illustrated in Figure 12-8. The moral is obvious: heavily loaded systems will tend to have a disproportionate amount of waiting time. By the same token, when a system is heavily loaded, a disproportionate reduction in both the average number waiting and the time they wait can be achieved by modest reductions in the utilization (say, by increasing the service rate or, reducing the arrival rate, or diverting the arrivals through other options).

Multiple-Channel Model (M/M/s)

The multiple-server model, or multiple-channel model, as it is sometimes referred to, is very similar to the single-server model, except that the number of servers is not limited to one.

The multiple-channel model is appropriate when these conditions exist:

1. A Poisson arrival rate
2. A negative exponential service time
3. First-come, first-served processing order
4. More than one server
5. An infinite calling population
6. No upper limit on queue length
7. The same mean service rate for all servers

To achieve first-come, first-served processing, some systems may have customers wait in a single line (e.g., most post offices). Other systems record order of arrival (e.g., busy restaurants) or have customers take a number on arrival (e.g., some bakeries and deli counters). Usually, supermarket checkouts would not fall into the multiple-channel category, even though they have multiple checkouts, because customers do not form a single line (i.e., they are not necessarily served in order of arrival at the checkout area).

Note that with the multiple-server model, s must be large enough that the condition $s\mu > \lambda$ is satisfied. Otherwise, the system will not be feasible because it is overloaded.

The multiple-server formulas are presented in Table 12-4.

Similar to the basic single-channel model, this model is referred to as M/M/s. The only difference from M/M/1 Model is that there are $s > 1$ servers.

FIGURE 12-8 As Utilization Approaches 100 percent, L_q and W_q Rapidly Increase

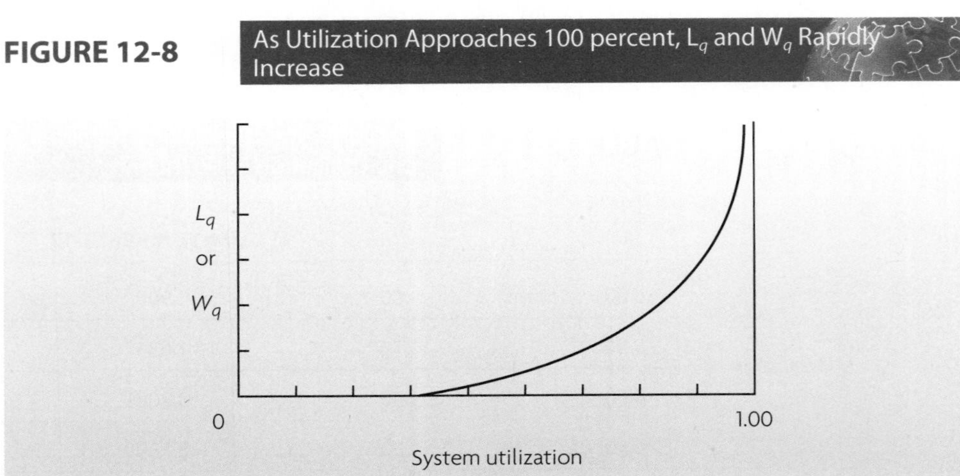

TABLE 12-4 Multiple-Channel Formulas

Performance Measure	Formula	Formula Number
System utilization	$\rho = \frac{\lambda}{s\mu}$	(12-20)
Average number in line	$L_q = \frac{\lambda\mu(\lambda/\mu)^s}{(s-1)!(s\mu-\lambda)^2} P_0$	(12-21)
Average number in the system	$L = L_q + \frac{\lambda}{\mu}$	(12-22)
Average time in line	$W_q = \frac{L_q}{\lambda}$	(12-23)
Average time in the system	$W = W_q + \frac{1}{\mu}$	(12-24)
Probability of zero units in the system	$P_o = \left[\sum_{n=0}^{s-1} \frac{(\lambda/\mu)^n}{n!} + \frac{(\lambda/\mu)^s}{s!(1-(\lambda/s\mu))}\right]^{-1}$	(12-25)
Probability of n units in the system, where $n \leq s$	$P_n = P_0 \frac{(\lambda/\mu)^n}{n!}$	(12-26)
Probability of n units in the system, where $n > s$	$P_n = \frac{P_0(\lambda/\mu)^n}{s!(s^{n-s})}$	(12-27)
Average waiting time for an arrival not immediately served	$W_a = \frac{1}{s\mu - \lambda}$	(12-28)
Probability that an arrival will have to wait for service	$P_w = (\lambda/\mu)^s \frac{P_0}{s!(1-(\lambda/s\mu))}$	(12-29)

s = number of servers or channels.

EXAMPLE 12-5

The management of a grocery chain plans to open a new store. The store will have a bakery counter with a projected mean arrival rate during the evening hours of 1.2 customers per minute. Three clerks will be employed, and each will have an average service rate of one customer per minute. Compute each of the performance measures listed in Table 12-4 using the formulas. Additional information will be given where necessary to illustrate the solution.

Solution

$\lambda = 1.2$ customers per minute
$\mu = 1.0$ customer per minute
$s = 3$ servers

1. $\rho = \frac{1.2}{3(1.0)} = .40$

2. $L_q = \frac{1.2(1.0)(1.2/1.0)^3}{(3-1)!(3(1.0)-1.2)^2} P_0$

$= .32P_0$

$$P_0 = \frac{1}{\left[\frac{(1.2/1.0)^0}{0!} + \frac{(1.2/1.0)^1}{1!} + \frac{(1.2/1.0)^2}{2!}\right] + \frac{(1.2/1.0)^3}{3!(1-(1.2/3(1.0)))}} = .294$$

$L_q = .32(.294) = .094$ customers

3. $L = .094 + \frac{1.2}{1.0} = 1.294.$

4. $W_q = \frac{.094}{1.2} = .078$ minute.

5. $W = .078 + \frac{1}{1.0} = 1.078$ minutes.

6. P_0 (see part 2 above).

7. Suppose $n = 2$.

$$P_2 = \frac{.294(1.2/1.0)^2}{2!} = .212$$

8. Suppose $n = 4$.

$$P_4 = \frac{.294(1.2/1.0)^4}{3!(3^{4-3})} = \frac{.60964}{18} = .034$$

9. $W_a = \frac{1}{3(1.0) - 1.2} = .556$ minute.

10. $P_w = \left(\frac{1.2}{1.0}\right)^3 \frac{.294}{3!(1-(1.2/3(1.0)))} = .141$

The computations for some of the multiple-server performance measures can be quite formidable, particularly for large values of s. Fortunately, there is an easier method for obtaining values for two key performance measures, L_q and P_0. Table C in Appendix B contains those values for selected values of λ/μ. The advantage of having a table that can provide values of L_q and P_0 can be seen from these two lists of performance measures that can be computed from them:

L_q: L, W, and W_q
P_0: P_n and P_w

The remaining measures do not involve the computational burden that the listed measures do. Thus, obtaining performance measures for many multiple-channel problems is, indeed, simplified. The exception would be for situations in which the ratio λ/μ is not listed in the table, although, even then, rounding to a listed value is often reasonable.

To use the table, determine the value of λ/μ and read L_q and P_0 for s. For instance, in the preceding example with $\lambda/\mu = 1.2$, we found the value of L_q to be .094 after considerable effort. That same value can be read from Table C (see Appendix B). At the same time, we can read the value $P_0 = .294$, which agrees with the previous calculated value. We can further appreciate the value of having this table by considering this question: What are the values of L_q when $\lambda/\mu = 1.2$ for $s = 2, 3, 4$, and 5? We can quickly read all of the values from the table. Thus, we find $L_q = .675$ for $s = 2$, .094 for $s = 3$, and .016 for $s = 4$.

The table also allows us to gain some insights into how sensitive a waiting line system is to change in the utilization. For example, suppose $\lambda/\mu = 2.9/1 = 2.9$. With three servers, the utilization is $2.9/3 = .967$, a fairly high load. This results in a high average number waiting (27.193). Adding one server reduces the utilization to $2.9/4 = .725$, and the average waiting line is reduced to 1.234. Thus, modest changes to a heavily loaded system can produce rather sizeable improvements in such performance measures as the average number waiting in line and in the system, and the associated average waiting times in line and system. For lighter system loads, the improvements become less and less: Adding a fifth server yields a reduction of about 1.0 in the average number waiting, and adding a sixth server yields a reduction of only about .20.

Finally, note that the single-channel model is a special case of the more general multiple-channel model. Therefore, single-channel problems also can be handled using Table C provided in Appendix B.

Multiple-Channel Model with Poisson Arrival and Exponential Service Rate (M/M/s Model) with Excel

It is difficult to use Excel to formulate the multiple-channel waiting-line model because the formulas are somewhat cumbersome to prepare. Exhibit 12-6 shows the Excel worksheet for the multiple-channel waiting line model with Poisson arrivals and exponential service times based on Example 12-5. The formulas for this model are given below Exhibit 12-6. As can be observed, some of these formulas can be very complicated. For example, the formula for P_0 in cell B7 is long and complex. The summation terms are directly entered into the formula. Thus, if a problem involved a larger number of servers, additional summation terms would have to be added to the formula in cell B7. As you notice, we have utilized the FACT() term in our formulas. FACT() takes the factorial of a number. For example, the term FACT(4) is $4! = 4 \times 3 \times 2 \times 1 = 24$. Therefore, even though it is difficult to perform sensitivity analysis by changing the number of servers, it is fairly easy to perform what-if analysis assuming different arrival or service rates.

Determining Maximum Length of Waiting Lines

An important issue in waiting line system design relates to the amount of space that will be needed to accommodate waiting customers. This, naturally, is a function of the maximum expected length of the waiting line. Theoretically, for infinite-source systems, the line can be infinitely long. However, in practical terms, it is possible to determine a figure for the number of customers waiting that will not be exceeded a specified percentage of time. For example, we could determine the line length that probably will not be exceeded 95 percent of the time or 99 percent of the time.

An approximate line length that will satisfy any stated probability can be determined by solving the following equation for *n:*

$$\rho^n = K \tag{12-30}$$

where

$$K = \frac{1 - \text{Probability}}{L_q(1-\rho)}$$

and L_q is from Table C in Appendix B.

The equation can be readily solved using logarithms (either to the base 10 or to the base *e*):

$$n = \frac{\log K}{\log \rho} \quad \text{or} \quad \frac{\ln K}{\ln \rho} \tag{12-31}$$

The resulting value of n usually will not be an integer. In general, *round up* to the next higher integer and use that value as n_{max}.

EXHIBIT 12-6 Multiple-Channel Model with Poisson Arrival and Exponential Service Rate (M/M/s Model)

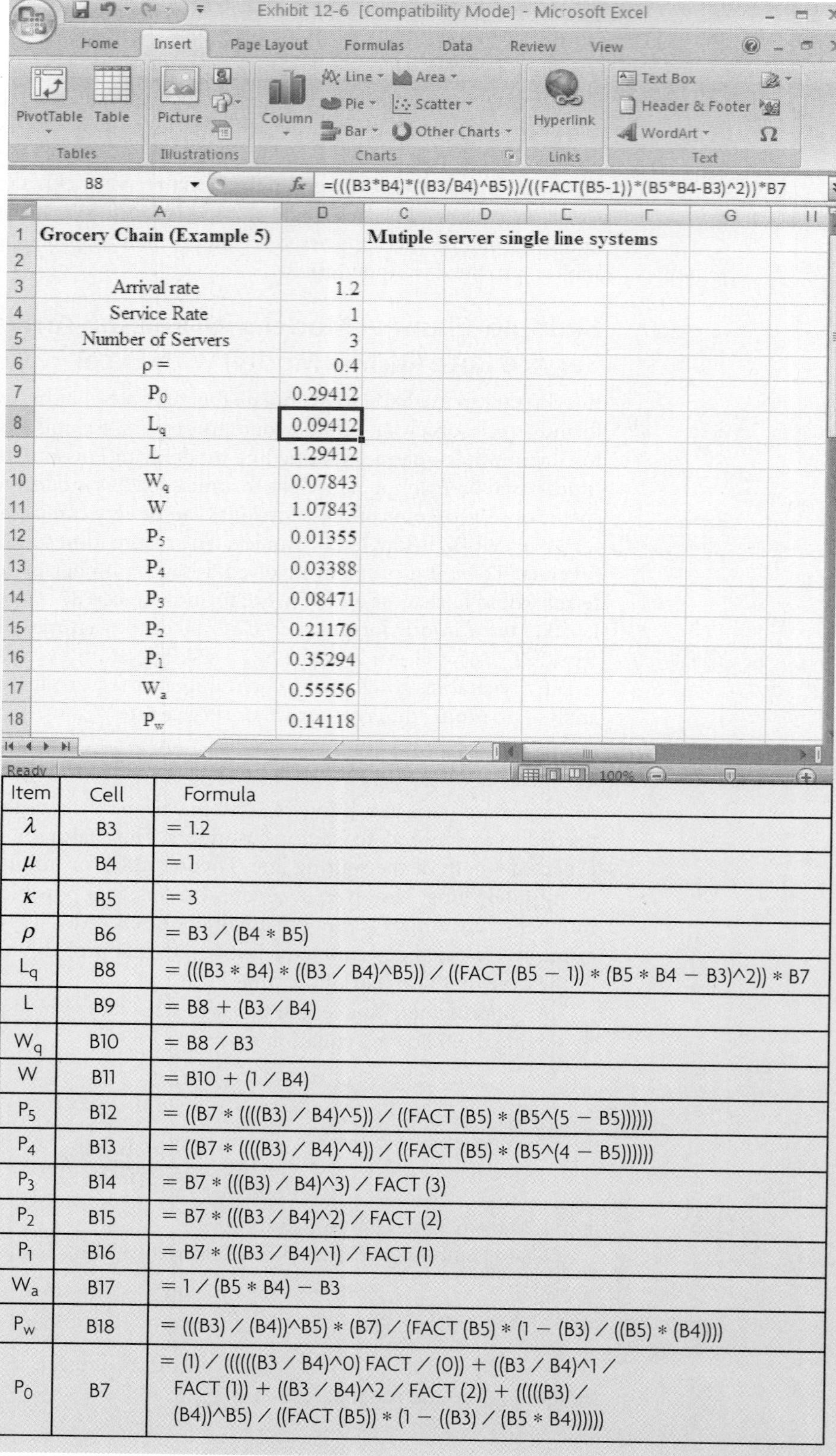

	A	B
1	**Grocery Chain (Example 5)**	**Mutiple server single line systems**
2		
3	Arrival rate	1.2
4	Service Rate	1
5	Number of Servers	3
6	ρ =	0.4
7	P_0	0.29412
8	L_q	0.09412
9	L	1.29412
10	W_q	0.07843
11	W	1.07843
12	P_5	0.01355
13	P_4	0.03388
14	P_3	0.08471
15	P_2	0.21176
16	P_1	0.35294
17	W_a	0.55556
18	P_w	0.14118

Item	Cell	Formula
λ	B3	= 1.2
μ	B4	= 1
κ	B5	= 3
ρ	B6	= B3 / (B4 * B5)
L_q	B8	= (((B3 * B4) * ((B3 / B4)^B5)) / ((FACT (B5 − 1)) * (B5 * B4 − B3)^2)) * B7
L	B9	= B8 + (B3 / B4)
W_q	B10	= B8 / B3
W	B11	= B10 + (1 / B4)
P_5	B12	= ((B7 * ((((B3) / B4)^5)) / ((FACT (B5) * (B5^(5 − B5))))))
P_4	B13	= ((B7 * ((((B3) / B4)^4)) / ((FACT (B5) * (B5^(4 − B5))))))
P_3	B14	= B7 * (((B3) / B4)^3) / FACT (3)
P_2	B15	= B7 * (((B3 / B4)^2) / FACT (2)
P_1	B16	= B7 * (((B3 / B4)^1) / FACT (1)
W_a	B17	= 1 / (B5 * B4) − B3
P_w	B18	= (((B3) / (B4))^B5) * (B7) / (FACT (B5) * (1 − (B3) / ((B5) * (B4))))
P_0	B7	= (1) / (((((B3 / B4)^0) FACT / (0)) + ((B3 / B4)^1 / FACT (1)) + ((B3 / B4)^2 / FACT (2)) + (((((B3) / (B4))^B5) / ((FACT (B5)) * (1 − ((B3) / (B5 * B4))))))

EXAMPLE 12-6

Determine the maximum number of customers waiting in line for probabilities of both 95 percent and 99 percent for this situation:

$s = 1$
$\lambda = 4$ per hour
$\mu = 5$ per hour

Solution

$$\rho = \frac{\lambda}{s\mu} = \frac{4}{1(5)} = .80 \quad \text{and} \quad \frac{\lambda}{\mu} = \frac{4}{5} = .80$$

From Table C in Appendix B with $\lambda/\mu = .80$ and $s = 1$, $L_q = 3.2$.

$$\text{For 95 percent, } K = \frac{1 - .95}{3.2(1 - .80)} = .078$$

$$n = \frac{\log .078}{\log .80} = 11.43 \quad \text{Hence, } n_{\text{max}} = 12$$

$$\text{For 99 percent, } K = \frac{1 - .99}{3.2(1 - .80)} = .0156$$

$$n = \frac{\log .0156}{\log .80} = 18.64 \quad \text{Hence, } n_{\text{max}} = 19$$

In some instances, the solution to Equation 12-31 will yield a negative value for n. If that happens, round up to zero. That happens when a system is only very lightly loaded and, in effect, most of the time there will not be a waiting line; hence, the zero.

A related question of interest is the number of channels needed to achieve a specified n_{max}. For example, the platform manager of a commercial bank may want to know how many tellers will be needed to hold the maximum number of waiting customers to 7. The solution to this question requires successively solving Equation 12-31, incrementing s each time, until the desired n_{max} is achieved.

EXAMPLE 12-7

Suppose that during a noon hour at a bank, the arrival rate is 8 customers per minute and the service rate is 2 customers per minute. This produces λ/μ of $8/2 = 4.0$. Using Table C in Appendix B, we obtain the following:

s	L_q
5	2.216
6	.570
7	.180
8	.059

Using Equation 12-31 with appropriate values of ρ (as shown), n_{max} for, say, 95 percent and 99 percent can be determined:

s	ρ	$n_{.95}$	$n_{.99}$
5	.80	10	17
6	.67	4	8
7	.57	1	4
8	.50	0	2

Therefore, 6 servers would achieve a probability of at least 95 percent that the number of waiting customers would not exceed 4, while 7 servers would achieve a probability of at least 99 percent that the line would not exceed 4 waiting customers.

12.6 COST CONSIDERATIONS

The design of a service system often reflects the desire of management to balance the cost of capacity with the expected cost of customers waiting in the system. For example, in designing loading docks for a warehouse, the cost of docks plus loading crews must be balanced against the cost of trucks and drivers that will be in the system, both while waiting to be unloaded and while actually being unloaded. Similarly, the cost of having a mechanic wait for tools at a tool crib must be balanced against the cost of servers at the crib.

The optimal capacity (usually in terms of number of channels) is that which minimizes the sum of customer waiting costs and capacity or server costs. Thus, the goal would be

Minimize Total cost = Customer waiting cost + Capacity (service) cost

The simplest approach to a cost analysis involves computing *system* costs; that is, computing costs for customers in the system and total capacity cost.

To identify the capacity size that will minimize total costs, an iterative process is used: Capacity is incremented one unit at a time (e.g., increase the number of channels by one) and the total cost is computed at each increment. Because the total cost curve is U-shaped (see Figure 12-1), usually the total cost will initially decrease as capacity is increased and then it will eventually begin to rise. Once it begins to rise, additional increases in capacity will cause it to continue to rise. Hence, once that occurs, the optimal capacity size can be readily identified.

The computation of customer waiting costs is based on the average *number* of customers in the *system*. This is, perhaps, not intuitively obvious; beginners usually feel that customer waiting *time* in the system would be more appropriate. However, that approach would pertain to only *one* customer—it would not convey information concerning *how many* customers would wait that long. Obviously, an average of 5 customers waiting would involve a lower waiting cost than an average of, say, 10 customers waiting. Therefore, it is necessary to focus on the number waiting. Moreover, if, say, an average of 2 customers are in the system, this is equivalent to having *exactly* two customers in the system at all times, even though in reality there will be times when there are 0, 1, 2, 3, or more customers in the system.

Therefore, the customer waiting cost (CWC) is the product of the average number in the system (L) and the waiting cost per time period of each unit (c_w), that is, $CWC = L \times c_w$. The computation of the capacity cost (CC) is based on the cost per unit (c_u) and the capacity size or the number of servers (s), that is, $CC = s \times c_u$.

Hence, the total cost (z) is given by the following relation:

$$z = CWC + CC = L \times c_w + s \times c_u$$

For illustration purposes, let's consider Example 12-8.

EXAMPLE 12-8

Trucks arrive at a warehouse at a rate of 15 per hour during business hours. Crews can unload the trucks at a rate of 5 per hour. The high unloading rate is due to cargo being containerized. Recent changes in wage rates have caused the warehouse manager to reexamine the question of how many crews to use. The new rates for crew and dock cost is \$100 per hour; truck and driver cost is \$120 per hour.

Solution

(L_q values are from Table C in Appendix B using $\lambda/\mu = 15/5 = 3.0$.)

Note that in Table 12-5, because the total cost will continue to increase once the minimum is reached, it is not really necessary to compute total costs for crew sizes larger than 6, because total cost increased as the crew size was increased from 5 to 6, indicating that a crew size of 5 is optimal.

Table 12-5 Total Cost Computation for Example 12-8

Crew Size	Service Cost: Crew/Dock Cost	$L = L_q + (\lambda/\mu)$ Average Number in System	Waiting Cost: Driver/Truck Cost @\$120 per Hour	Total Cost = Service Cost + Waiting Cost
4	\$400	1.528 + 3.0 = 4.528	\$543.36	\$943.36
5	500	.354 + 3.0 = 3.354	402.48	902.48 (minimum)
6	600	.099 + 3.0 = 3.099	371.88	971.88
7	700	.028 + 3.0 = 3.028	363.36	1063.36

One additional point should be made concerning cost analysis. Because both customer waiting costs and capacity costs often reflect estimated amounts, the apparent optimal solution may not, in fact, represent the true optimum. One ramification of this is that when computations are shown to the nearest penny, or even the nearest dollar, the total cost figures may seem to imply a higher degree of precision than is really justified by the cost estimates. This is compounded by the fact that arrival and service rates may either be approximations or not be exactly represented by the Poisson/exponential distributions. Another ramification is that if cost estimates can be obtained as *ranges* (e.g., customer waiting cost is estimated to range between \$40 and \$50 per hour), total costs should be computed using both ends of the range to see if the optimal solution is affected by this. If it is, management must decide whether additional effort should be expanded to obtain more precise cost estimates or else choose one of the two indicated optimal solutions. For instance, the latter strategy would most likely be employed if there were little disparity between total costs of various capacity levels close to the indicated optimal solutions.

The \$40–\$50 range of waiting cost is not an out-of-pocket cost. It is a dollar amount to reflect that the revenues and profits will suffer as a result of customer waiting time. Certain customers will choose not to wait and, as a consequence, the company will lose sales revenue and the associated profit. By adding another service line, we can reduce the waiting time (cost) at the expense of higher service cost. The key is to determine the lowest total cost that will minimize the cost of waiting plus cost of service.

12.7 OTHER QUEUING MODELS

The two previously described models (the single-channel and the multiple-channel, infinite-source queuing models) represent what might be thought of as the "mainstream" queuing models. This stems partly from the conceptual understanding of waiting-line systems that they convey and partly from the ease with which system performance measures can be obtained. However, the field of queuing contains a rich variety of models. This section is designed to illustrate some of that richness, and to enhance your appreciation for modelling waiting-line systems.

Each of the models presented in this section offers a slight variation in the assumptions that underlie the two basic models. For example, the first model allows for any service time distribution; the second pertains to constant service time; the third has Poisson arrivals and exponential service times but limits the potential length of the waiting line; the fourth has Poisson arrivals and exponential service but a finite calling population; and the fifth has priority service instead of first-come, first-served. Each of these models is presented briefly. Note that all of the models except the priority service one pertain to a single-server situation. The principal ideas for setting up and using Excel to solve each of the models discussed in this section are essentially the same as in the case of basic models. Therefore, we do not provide an example that demonstrates how to solve each model with Excel.

Model Variation I: Poisson Arrival Rate with Any Service Distribution (M/G/1)

The assumptions of this model are identical to the basic single-server model, except that service time need not be exponential. The service times can be of any distribution. This is indicated by the letter "G" for general in the abbreviated statement of the model. To use this model, however, it is necessary to have an estimate of the variance, σ^2, of the service time distribution. Some key formulas are presented in Table 12-6.

TABLE 12-6 Formulas for Poisson Arrivals, Any Service Distribution

Performance Measure	Formula	Formula Number
Average number waiting in line	$L_q = \frac{(\lambda/\mu)^2 + \lambda^2\sigma^2}{2(1 - \lambda/\mu)}$	(12-32)
Average number in the system	$L = L_q + \frac{\lambda}{\mu}$	(12-33)
Average time waiting in line	$W_q = \frac{L_q}{\lambda}$	(12-34)
Average time in the system	$W = W_q + \frac{1}{\mu}$	(12-35)
System utilization	$\rho = \frac{\lambda}{s\mu}$	(12-36)

EXAMPLE 12-9

Joe's Tailor Shop is a one-man operation, and owner Fred White does all of the work. The customer arrival rate is Poisson with a mean of .25 per minute. Service time has a mean of 2.0 minutes and a standard deviation of 0.9 minute. Compute each of the performance measures listed in Table 12-6.

Solution

$\lambda = .25$ per minute
$\mu = .50$ per minute
$\sigma = 0.9$ minute

1. $L_q = \dfrac{(.25/.50)^2 + .25^2(0.9)^2}{2(1-(.25/.50))} = .301$ customer.
2. $L = .301 + (.25/.50) = .801$ customer.
3. $W_q = .301/.25 = 1.203$ minutes.
4. $W = 1.203 + 2.0 = 3.203$ minutes.
5. $\rho = \dfrac{.25}{.50} = .50.$

Model Variation II: Poisson Arrival Rate, Constant Service Time (M/D/1)

The assumptions of this model are identical to those of the basic single-server model (and the preceding model), except that the service time is constant. This waiting line is described by the M/D/1 model, where D indicates that service times are deterministic.

$$L_q = \frac{(\lambda/\mu)^2}{2(1-(\lambda/\mu))} = \frac{\lambda^2}{2\mu(\mu-\lambda)} \qquad (12\text{-}37)$$

The basis for this formula can be seen by referring to the formula for L_q with any service distribution (see Table 12-6). Because the service time is constant, $\sigma^2 = 0$; thus, the second term in the numerator drops out, reducing to the above formula. The formulas for performance measures other than L_q are the same as those shown in Table 12-6.

EXAMPLE 12-10

A video arcade game is designed to operate for exactly three minutes, during which time a player attempts to capture as many purple monkeys as possible. Customer player arrivals can be described by a Poisson distribution with a mean arrival rate of 12 per hour. Compute each of the performance measures listed in Table 12-6.

Solution

$\lambda = 12$ per hour
$\mu = 20$ per hour

1. $L_q = \dfrac{12^2}{2(20)(20-12)} = .45$ customer.

2. $L = .45 + \frac{12}{20} = 1.05$ customers.

3. $W_q = \frac{.45}{12} = .0375$ hour or $.0375 \times 60 = 2.25$ minutes.

4. $W = 2.25 + 3.00 = 5.25$ minutes.

5. $\rho = \frac{12}{20} = .60.$

Model Variation III: Finite Queue Length

This model incorporates all of the assumptions of the basic single-server model. In addition, it allows for a limit on the maximum length of the line. The implication is that once the line reaches its maximum length, no additional customers will be allowed to join the line. New customers will not be allowed on a space-available basis. For instance the drive-through pick-up window at a local fast-food store may exhibit this model, where the number of cars in the waiting line is limited by the size of the parking lot and also the access from the street. The necessary formulas are shown in Table 12-7.

EXAMPLE 12-11

A single-bay car wash waiting line has a driveway that can only hold 4 cars. Because the car wash is on a busy highway, when there are 5 cars in the system, no additional cars can enter. The arrival and service rates are Poisson, the mean arrival rate is 9 per hour, and the mean service rate is 15 per hour. Compute each of the performance measures listed in Table 12-7.

Solution

$\lambda = 9$ per hour
$\mu = 15$ per hour
$m = 5$

1. $\rho = \frac{9}{15} = .60.$

2. $P_0 = \frac{1 - .6}{1 - .6^{5+1}} = .420.$

3. $P_5 = .420(.6^5) = .033.$

4. $L = \frac{.6}{1 - .6} - \frac{(5 + 1)(.6^{5+1})}{1 - .6^{5+1}} = 1.5 - .294 = 1.206$ cars.

5. $L_q = 1.206 - (1 - .420) = .626$ car.

6. $W = \frac{.626}{9(1 - .033)} + \frac{1}{15} = .139$ hour.

7. $W_q = .139 - \frac{1}{15} = .072$ hour.

TABLE 12-7 Single-Server, Finite Queue Length Formulas

Performance Measure	Formula	Formula Number
System utilization	$\rho = \frac{\lambda}{s\mu}$	(12-38)
Probability of zero units in the system	$P_0 = \frac{1-\rho}{1-\rho^{m+1}}$	(12-39)
Probability of n units in the system	$P_n = P_0\rho^n$	(12-40)
Average number of units in the system	$L = \frac{\rho}{1-\rho} - \frac{(m+1)\rho^{m+1}}{1-\rho^{m+1}}$	(12-41)
Average number of units waiting in line	$L_q = L - (1 - P_0)$	(12-42)
Average time in system	$W = \frac{L_q}{\lambda(1-P_n)} + \frac{1}{\mu}$	(12-43)
Average time waiting in line	$W_q = W - \frac{1}{\mu}$	(12-44)

m = maximum number permitted in the system.

The physical space may only permit five cars to be lined up in the parking lot; the sixth car is not permitted to enter the system because we simply ran out of space in the parking lot and, if allowed, the sixth car would have to wait on a busy street. We can easily modify the basic single-channel system to accommodate a finite queue. It should be noted that for the finite queue model, the service rate does not have to exceed the arrival rate.

Specific assumptions of the model with a finite queue length are presented below:

1. The arrivals are distributed according to the Poisson distribution and the service time distribution is negative exponential. However, the service time distribution assumption can be relaxed to allow any distribution.
2. The system has s servers and the service rate is the same for each server.
3. An arrival that occurs when all the servers are busy and the waiting line is full (maximum number of cars in the waiting line) is denied service and is not permitted to enter the system.

Model Variation IV: Finite Calling Population

This model has the same assumptions as the basic single-server model except that there is a limited calling population. A typical example of such a waiting line system would be a machine operator who is responsible for loading and unloading five machines. Hence, the calling population is five.

Some appropriate formulas are listed in Table 12-8. Note that λ is defined as the mean arrival rate *per unit.*

TABLE 12-8 Finite Calling Population Formulas

Performance Measure	Formula	Formula Number
Probability of no units in the system	$P_0 = \dfrac{1}{\sum_{i=0}^{N} (\lambda/\mu)^i \left[\dfrac{N!}{(N-i)!}\right]}$	(12-45)
Probability of n units in the system	$P_n = \dfrac{N!}{(N-n)!}\left(\dfrac{\lambda}{\mu}\right)^n P_0$	(12-46)
Average number waiting in line	$L_q = N - \dfrac{\lambda + \mu}{\lambda}(1 - P_0)$	(12-47)
Average number in the system	$L = L_q + (1 - P_0)$	(12-48)
Average waiting time in line	$W_q = \dfrac{L_q}{\lambda(N - L)}$	(12-49)
Average time in the system	$W = W_q + \dfrac{1}{\mu}$	(12-50)

N = number in calling population.

λ = mean arrival rate *per unit* in the population.

EXAMPLE 12-12

One person handles adjustments for four machines. The machines run an average of 60 minutes before adjustments are needed, and the average adjustment time is 15 minutes. Service time can be described by a negative exponential distribution, and the call rate for each machine can be described by a Poisson distribution. Compute each of the performance measures listed in Table 12-8.

Solution

λ = 1 call per hour per machine

μ = 4 machines per hour

$N = 4$

$$\frac{\lambda}{\mu} = \frac{1}{4} = .25$$

1. $$P_0 = \frac{1}{.25^0\frac{4!}{(4-0)!} + .25^1\frac{4!}{(4-1)!} + .25^2\frac{4!}{(4-2)!} + .25^3\frac{4!}{(4-3)!} + .25^4\frac{4!}{(4-4)!}}$$
$$= \frac{1}{3.219} = .311$$

2. (Suppose $n = 4$): $P_4 = \dfrac{4!}{(4-4)!}.25^4(.31068) = .02913$

Therefore, it is highly unlikely that no machines will be running (i.e., that all will be awaiting adjustments).

3. $L_q = 4 - \dfrac{1+4}{1}(1 - .311) = .555$ machine.

4. $L = .555 + (1 - .311) = 1.244$ machines.

5. $W_q = \dfrac{.555}{1(4 - 1.244)} = .2014$ hour.

6. $W = .2014 + .25 = .4514$ hour.

Model Variation V: Multiple-Server, Priority Servicing Model

This model incorporates all of the assumptions of the basic multiple-server model except that priority serving is used rather than first-come, first-served. Arrivals to the system are assigned a priority as they arrive (e.g., highest priority = 1, next priority class = 2, next priority class = 3, and so on). An existing queue might look something like this:

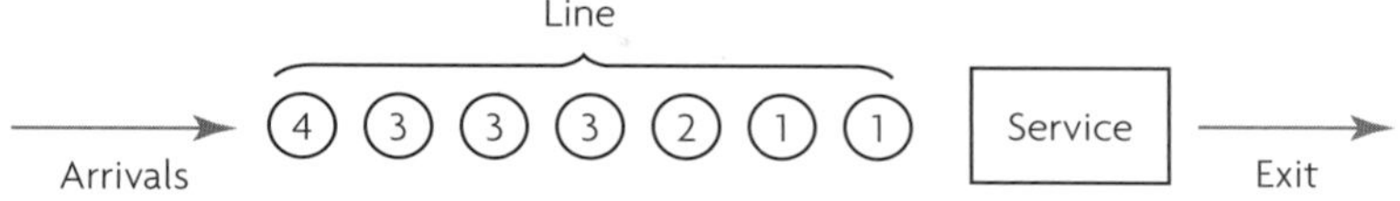

Within each class, waiting units are processed in the order they arrived (i.e., first-come, first-served). Thus, in this sequence, the first #1 would be processed as soon as a server was available. Then, the second #1 would be processed when that server, or another one, became available. If, in the interim, another #1 arrived, it would be next in line *ahead of the first #2.* If there were no new arrivals, the only #2 would be processed by the next available server. At that point, if a new #1 arrived, it would be processed ahead of the #3s and the #4. Similarly, a new #2 would be processed ahead of the #3s and the #4. Conversely, if a new #4 arrived, it would take its place at the end of the line.

Obviously, a unit with a low priority could conceivably wait a rather long time for processing. In some cases, units that have waited more than some specified time are reassigned a higher priority.

This model assumes that service is not **preemptive.** This means that service on a low priority unit is not interrupted even though a higher-priority unit arrives after service has begun.

The appropriate formulas for this multiple-channel, priority service model are given in Table 12-9.

TABLE 12-9 Multiple-Server, Priority Service Model

Performance Measure	Formula	Formula Number
System utilization	$\rho = \frac{\lambda}{s\mu}$	(12-51)
Intermediate values: (L_q from Table C in Appendix B)	$A = \frac{\lambda}{(1-\rho)L_q}$	(12-52)
	$B_k = 1 - \sum_{c=1}^{k} \frac{\lambda_c}{s\mu}$ ($B_0 = 1$)	(12-53)
Average waiting time in line for units in k^{th} priority class	$W_k = \frac{1}{A(B_{k-1})(B_k)}$	(12-54)
Average time in the system for units in the kth priority class	$W = W_k + \frac{1}{\mu}$	(12-55)
Average number waiting in line for units in the kth priority class	$L_k = \lambda_k \times W_k$	(12-56)

EXAMPLE 12-13

A machine shop handles tool repairs in a large company. Each job is assigned a priority when it arrives in the shop that is based on the urgency for that tool. Requests for repair can be described by a Poisson distribution. Arrival rates are $\lambda_1 = 2$ per hour, $\lambda_2 = 2$ per hour, and $\lambda_3 = 1$ per hour. The service rate is one tool per hour for each server, and there are six servers in the shop. Determine the following information:

1. The system utilization
2. The average time a tool in each of the priority classes will wait for service
3. The average time a tool spends in the system for each priority class
4. The average number of tools waiting for repair in each class

Solution

$\lambda = \Sigma\lambda_k = 2 + 2 + 1 = 5$ per hour

$s = 6$ servers

$\mu = 1$ customer per hour

1. $\rho = \dfrac{\lambda}{s\mu} = \dfrac{5}{6(1)} = .833$

2. Intermediate values: $\lambda/\mu = 5/1 = 5$; from Table C in Appendix B, $L_q = 2.938$

$$A = \frac{5}{(1 - .833)2.938} = 10.19$$

$$B_0 = 1$$

$$B_1 = 1 - \frac{2}{6(1)} = \frac{2}{3} = .667$$

$$B_2 = 1 - \frac{2 + 2}{6(1)} = \frac{1}{3} = .333$$

$$B_3 = 1 - \frac{2 + 2 + 1}{6(1)} = \frac{1}{6} = .167$$

$$W_1 = \frac{1}{A(B_0)(B_1)} = \frac{1}{10.19(1)(.667)} = .147 \text{ hour}$$

$$W_2 = \frac{1}{A(B_1)(B_2)} = \frac{1}{10.19(.667)(.333)} = .442 \text{ hour}$$

$$W_3 = \frac{1}{A(B_2)(B_3)} = \frac{1}{10.19(.333)(.167)} = 1.765 \text{ hours}$$

3. Average time in system $= W_k + 1/\mu$. In this case, $1/\mu = 1/1 = 1$. Thus, we have

Class	$W_k + 1 = W$ (hours)
1	.147 + 1 = 1.147
2	.442 + 1 = 1.442
3	1.765 + 1 = 2.765

4. The average number of units waiting in each class is $L_k = \lambda_k \times W_k$. Thus, we have

Class	$\lambda_k \times W_k = L_k$ (units)
1	2(.147) = .294
2	2(.442) = .884
3	1(1.765) = 1.765

Revising Priorities

If any of the waiting times computed in the preceding example are deemed as too long by management (e.g., a waiting time of .147 hour for tools in the first class might be too long), there are several options. One would be to increase the number of servers. Another would be to attempt to increase the service rate, say, by introducing new methods. If such options are not feasible, another approach would be to reexamine the membership of each of the priority classifications. The reason for this is that if some repair requests, say, in the first priority class can be reassigned to the second priority class, this will tend to decrease the average waiting times for repair jobs that retain the highest priority classification simply because the arrival rate of those items will be lower. The repair requests reassigned from the first priority class to the second priority class may be subject to longer waiting times.

EXAMPLE 12-14

Suppose the manager of the repair shop, after consulting with the managers of the departments that use the shop's services, has been able to revise the list of tools that are given the highest priorities. This would be reflected by revised arrival rates. Suppose that the revised rates are $\lambda_1 = 1.5$, $\lambda_2 = 2.5$, and λ_3 remains unchanged at 1.0. Determine the following information:

1. The system utilization
2. The average waiting time for units in each priority class

Solution

$\lambda = \Sigma\lambda_k = 1.5 + 2.5 + 1.0 = 5.0$
(Note that in the previous problem (12–13), $\lambda_1 + \lambda_2 = 2 + 2 = 4$ and in this problem $\lambda_1 + \lambda_2 = 1.5 + 2.5 = 4$. Therefore, the total arrival rate is unchanged since $\lambda_3 = 1$ in both problems.

$s = 6$
$\mu = 1$

(Note that these values are the same as in the previous example.)

1. $\rho = 5.0/6(1) = .833$, which is the same as in the previous example.
2. The value of A, since it is a function of s, μ, and λ, is the same as in the preceding example because these values are the same. Therefore, $A = 10.19$. and

$B_0 = 1$ (always)

$$B_1 = 1 - \frac{1.5}{6(1)} = .75$$

$$B_2 = 1 - \frac{1.5 + 2.5}{6(1)} = .333$$

$$B_3 = 1 - \frac{1.5 + 2.5 + 1.0}{6(1)} = .167$$

Then:

$$W_1 = \frac{1}{10.19(1)(.75)} = .131 \text{ hour}$$

$$W_2 = \frac{1}{10.19(.75)(.333)} = .393 \text{ hour}$$

$$W_3 = \frac{1}{10.19(.333)(.167)} = 1.765 \text{ hours}$$

Here, we find several interesting results. One is that by reducing the arrival rate of the highest priority class, the average waiting time for units in that priority class decreased. Hence, removing some members of the highest class and placing them into the next lower priority class reduced the average waiting time for units that remained in the highest class. Note, though, that the average waiting time for the *second* priority class also was reduced, even though units were added to that class. Although this may appear counterintuitive, it is necessary to recognize that the *total* waiting time (when all arrivals are taken into account) will remain unchanged. We can see this by noting that the average *number* waiting in Example 12-13 (see part 4) was .294 + .884 + 1.765 = 2.943. In this example, using the average waiting times just computed, the average number waiting in all three classes is

$$\sum_{k=1}^{3} \lambda_k W_k = 1.5(.131) + 2.5(.393) + 1.0(1.765) = 2.944$$

Aside from a slight difference due to rounding, the totals are the same.

Another interesting observation is that the average waiting time for customers in the third priority class did not change from the preceding example. The reason for this is that the *total* arrival rate for the two higher priority classes did not change, and its own average arrival rate did not change. Hence, units assigned to that lowest class must still contend with a combined arrival rate of 4 for the two higher priority classes.

Utilization of Excel's Goal Seek Function

The goal seek function can be a very useful function to determine the value of a queuing parameter to achieve a specific goal. Let's consider the single-channel car wash example given in Example 12-3. In this problem, assume that the owner of the car wash wants the average customer waiting time not to exceed 6 minutes, or .10 hour. Currently, a customer has to wait an average of .16 hour, or 9.6 minutes, before he or she is served. The owner of the car wash wants to know how much would he have to accelerate the service to reduce the average waiting time from 9.6 minutes to 6 minutes. In the worksheet shown in Exhibit 12-5, we can simply try different values for the service rate and keep track of the W_q value. We can stop the trial-and-error process when the value of W_q falls slightly below .10. However, the trial-and-error approach could be time consuming. An alternative approach that most managers would prefer involves the utilization of Excel's goal seek function. We utilize this function by selecting **Data | Data Analysis | Goal Seek** from Excel's main tool bar. The window

EXHIBIT 12-7 Goal Seek Input Window

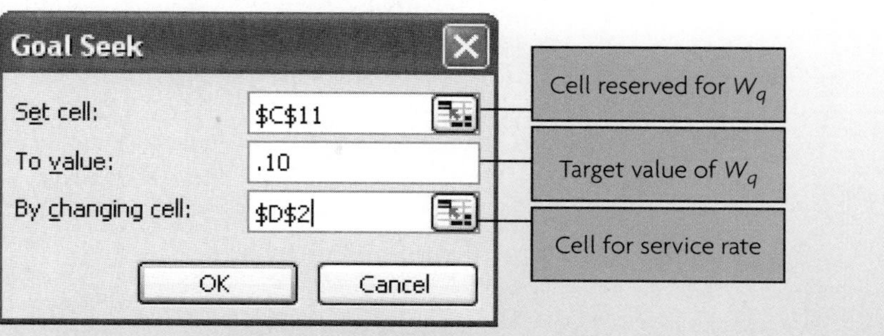

shown in Exhibit 12-7 shows how we can utilize the goal seek function for Example 12-3 (car wash problem) so that the maximum waiting time is limited to 6 minutes, or .10 hour. The goal seek procedure tries to find the value of the changing cell that will allow the target cell to achieve its desired value. As shown in Exhibit 12-7, in this problem the "Set Cell", or target cell, is $C$11 and its desired value is specified in the "To value" box as .10 hour (6 minutes). The value to be manipulated to achieve the target cell value of .10 hour is the service rate specified in the "By changing cell" box as $D$2.

After clicking OK, the goal seek output window indicating whether the desired goal was achieved is shown in Exhibit 12-8. In addition, the values in the worksheet are updated and the results displaying the updated values are shown in Exhibit 12-9. These results can be interpreted as follows: Instead of .16 hour (9.6 minutes) of waiting time based on a service rate of 25 cars, we can achieve a waiting time of .10 hour (6 minutes) with a service rate of 27.30 cars shown in cell D2 of Exhibit 12-9. In other words, instead of washing a car in 2 minutes and 24 second (60/25), we need to be able to reduce the average time to wash a car to 60/27.301 = 2 minutes and 12 seconds. The manager of the car wash can try to figure out how to improve the system to wash a car on the average 12 seconds faster. This can be accomplished in a number of different ways. The least costly way of reducing the service time is by improving the service process without changing the service system. Improving the speed at which the car is washed, faster entry to the system, or faster departure from the system, and so forth, might improve the system or reduce the service time. If reduction in service time cannot be achieved by improving the process, the other alternative is to change the car wash system to improve the service rate, which generally involves higher cost.

EXHIBIT 12-8 Goal Seek Output Window

Goal Seek Status

Goal Seeking with Cell C11 found a solution.

Target value: 0.1
Current value: 0.10033646

OK
Cancel
Step
Pause

Statement indicating targeted value of W_q was achieved

Showing the target value of W_q and the achieved value of W_q

EXHIBIT 12-9 Worksheet Showing the Results of Goal Seek for Example 12-3 (Car Wash Problem)

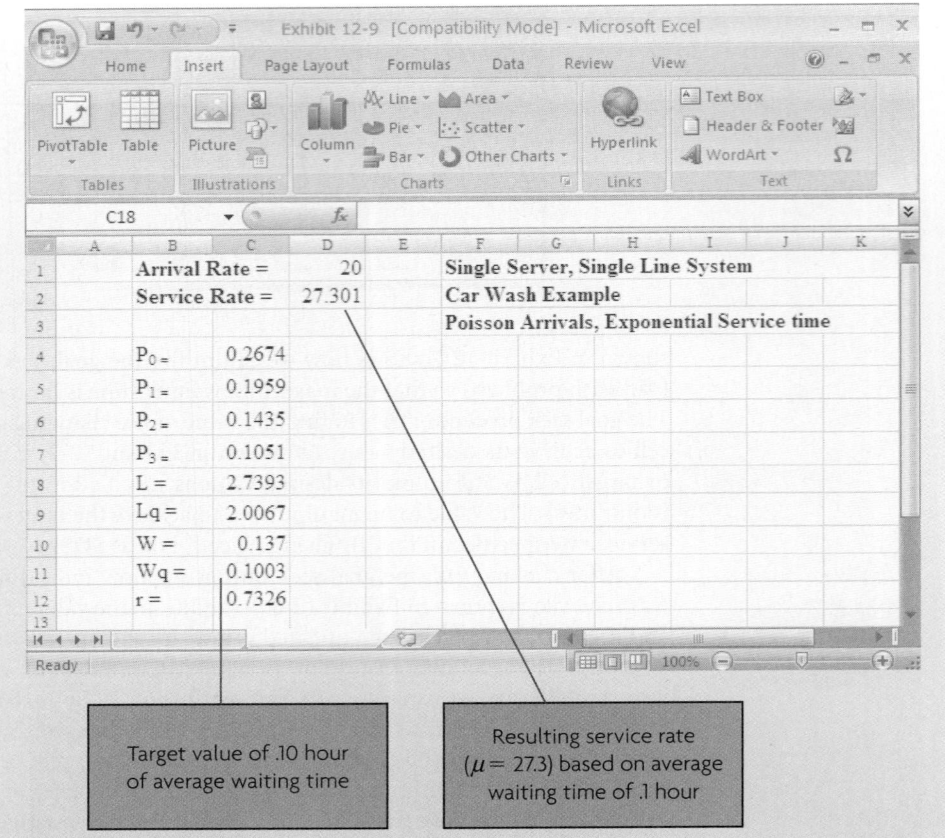

12.8 THE PSYCHOLOGY OF WAITING-LINE MODELS

The emphasis in this chapter has been on mathematical analysis of systems in which waiting lines tend to form. The underlying theme was predicting performance characteristics to make decisions relating to system capacity. In certain instances, especially those in which a system is currently in operation and capacity changes would be either difficult or impossible, reduction of waiting times may not be feasible. Nonetheless, in many instances it is possible to diminish the *effects* of waiting, even though the length of a wait cannot be shortened. Some of these approaches are described in this section.

Two costs are generally associated with waiting lines. One is an economic cost, related to factors such as the cost of space that must be provided for potential waiting customers; the cost of employee time spent waiting (e.g., for tools, for repairs); the cost of machines waiting for service (e.g., loading/unloading, repairs); and the cost of idle servers and service capacity. These costs usually can be estimated with a fair degree of accuracy. Another economic cost is related to the potential for lost business due to customers failing to join a line that they perceive as too long. Other customers may wait in line for a while, then leave. In either case, customers may return to the line at a later time, may decide to forgo the service, or may go elsewhere for it. If the customer returns, the impact on profits may be negligible; but if the customer does not return, the loss can be more significant, particularly if potential profit on *additional* products or services the customer may have bought also is taken into account. In other words, the question is: Does the company lose future sales and/or goodwill as a result of missing the current sale? However, estimating such additional lost sales or profits may be difficult at best. Consequently, taking such costs into account may be problematic.

A cost that is closely related to customers leaving a line is the *psychological* cost associated with the waiting customer's perception of the waiting time. For example, if customers believe that their time could be better spent elsewhere, they are apt to resent waiting, especially if they feel that management could remedy the length of wait (e.g., simply by adding additional servers). Conversely, if customers are occupied during the waiting period, either in a constructive way or through some form of distraction, they are less likely to resent the waiting experience. Examples of situations in which the psychological aspects of waiting are attended to include doctors' and dentists' offices providing magazines to help patients pass the time; airlines providing music or in-flight movies on long flights; and asking people to fill out forms while waiting (e.g., unemployment office, doctor, dentist), thus making the wait somewhat constructive.

Oddly enough, in certain retail situations, a moderate amount of waiting time is desirable. For instance, supermarkets place an array of impulse-purchase items at checkouts (e.g., candy, gum, cigarettes, magazines, batteries). Waiting customers may add these to their other purchases; the waiting period provides the opportunity for them to consider additional spending.

12.9 THE VALUE OF WAITING-LINE MODELS

Waiting line analysis is sometimes criticized on the grounds that the assumptions required by the models are not satisfied in many real-life situations. Among the more common complaints are the following:

1. Often, service times are not negative exponential.
2. The system is not in steady-state, but tends to be dynamic.
3. "Service" is difficult to define because service requirements can vary considerably from customer to customer.

To be sure, it is important that the assumptions of arrival and service distributions be reasonably satisfied. A Chi-square goodness-of-fit test should be used for that purpose. Note that one of the special-purpose models described in this chapter allows *any* service distribution.

The second criticism is true in many cases. For example, the customer arrival rates at banks, supermarkets, and post offices, and highway and telephone traffic intensities vary by time of day and day of week. In some of these situations, it may be possible to restrict the analysis to a narrow time interval for which the system is stable (e.g., for the lunch hour, the morning rush hour, and so on).

The last criticism may or may not be as important. Even if service requirements vary, taken as a whole, those times may exhibit an exponential distribution. Conversely, the times may be so disparate (e.g., some jobs require a few minutes and some a day or more) that two or more distributions are represented. In such cases, more elaborate modelling may be called for.

In any case in which the assumptions of the basic models are not met, the analyst must decide whether to search for, or develop, a more complex model, whether to use simulation, or whether to simply rely on intuition and experience. The choice will depend on time and cost considerations as well as on the abilities of the analyst.

Certainly the pervasiveness of waiting lines justifies some formal study of queuing systems and their characteristics. The basic models presented here, along with the several tables and Excel models, enable beginners to grasp the important concepts associated with such systems without the need to deal with the fairly complex mathematics that are generally associated with queuing models. Thus, performance measures could be readily calculated, and the sensitivity of those measures to changes in system parameters (arrival and service rates, number of servers) also could be readily assessed.

Summary

Waiting lines are commonly found in a wide range of production and service systems that encounter variable arrival rates and service times. This chapter presents a number of management science models that have been developed to provide valuable insights to decision makers on how to improve processes or services. Questions such as how to design systems that minimize the combined costs of providing capacity and customer waiting or that attain specific performance criteria (for example, that keep the average waiting time to under five minutes) can be addressed with the use of these models. The chapter also provides some examples of the performance measures available to decision makers as well as the important characteristics of a queuing system in terms of modelling. Performance measures for queuing systems include the average number of customers waiting in line, the average waiting time, system utilization, and the maximum number waiting in line. The important characteristics of queuing systems include the calling population, the arrival distribution, line features, the order of selection for processing, and the service distribution. In general, the models presented in this chapter assume that there is an infinite calling population; that an arrival rate can be adequately described by a Poisson distribution; that customers arrive individually rather than in batches; that customers funnel into a single waiting line when more than one server is used; that service is on a first-come, first-served basis; and that service time can be adequately described by a negative exponential distribution. The chapter also analyzed models with a finite calling population and service based on priorities rather than first-come-first-serve basis. The models described in this chapter and some of their main features are summarized in Table 12-9. It is important to stress that the models described in this chapter cannot substitute for good judgment and the use of common sense in decision-making in practical contexts. This is illustrated in the Modern Management Science Application, "Alberta Bone & Joint Health Institute (ABJHI)," an organization dedicated to the transformation in the way orthopaedic health care is provided in Alberta, where dramatic improvement on waiting times were achieved in hip and knee replacement services in three health regions in Alberta within a period of one year.

TABLE 12-10 Summary of Queuing Models Described in This Chapter

Model	Number of Servers	Calling Population	Arrival Distribution	Service Distribution	Maximum Queue	Processing Order	Necessary Formulas
Single-channel	1	∞	Poisson	Exponential	∞	FCFS	See Table 12-2
Multiple-channel	s	∞	Poisson	Exponential	∞	FCFS	See Table 12-4
Any service	1	∞	Poisson	Any	∞	FCFS	See Table 12-6
Constant service	1	∞	Poisson	Constant	∞	FCFS	See Table 12-6 and (12-37)
Finite queue	1	∞	Poisson	Exponential	m	FCFS	See Table 12-7
Priority discipline	s	∞	Poisson	Exponential	∞	FCFS by priority	See Table 12-9
Limited population	1	N	Poisson	Exponential	N	FCFS	See Table 12-8

MODERN MANAGEMENT SCIENCE APPLICATION: ALBERTA BONE & JOINT HEALTH INSTITUTE

Canadians place high value on their public health care system but are concerned about lengthy waits for services, such as wait times for specialist consultations and wait times for hip and knee joint replacement surgery. In Alberta, the Department of Health and Wellness, Alberta Orthopaedic Society, health regions, and Alberta Bone and Joint Health Institute launched a collaborative effort in 2004 to improve the quality and efficiency of and access to hip and knee joint replacements, an area of rising need.

A new clinical care path for hip and knee joint replacements was developed that standardized the entire pathway from primary care through surgery, recovery, and rehabilitation. Tools and processes for standardization included a consultation referral template, patient contracts, customized treatment plans, a patient optimization program, evidence-based clinical practices and procedures, and scheduled patient follow-up.

All aspects of the new care path were based on informed decision-making using a combination of the best available evidence and standards of care. Fully integrated patient care delivered by a multidisciplinary team was a critical feature of the new care path, as was a single intake process. The multidisciplinary team approach was designed to provide assessment, diagnosis, and non-surgical treatment in single-purpose hip and knee joint replacement clinics. The role of case manager was designed for assignment to each patient who needed surgery in order to facilitate each patient's progress through the new care path.

A pilot was launched in April 2005 to test the new care path using a randomized control trial approach. It involved 1125 patients who followed the new care path and 513 who followed the conventional approach. Patients in the new care path had greater improvement in general health and less pain after surgery. Reductions in wait time to see an orthopedic specialist, wait time for surgery, and length of hospital stay were achieved within the protected research environment. Patients and care providers reported greater satisfaction.

The new care path had several benefits for patients and providers, related to improved management and greater certainty about when and how services will be provided. These benefits were due to a collaborative approach to care delivery with a greater focus on care standards, use of case management, and the centralization of patient intake, assessment, and measurement of outcomes.

The pilot demonstrated the potential for improvement in the critical areas of quality, efficiency, and access when services are standardized, evidence-based, and integrated. Although the new care path is currently being implemented as the standard of care for hip and knee joint replacements in Alberta, results approaching those of the controlled study will be more difficult and take longer to achieve in the normal day-to-day operating environment of public health care.

Source: The Alberta Hip and Knee Joint Replacement Project Partners: Alberta Health and Wellness, Calgary Health Region, Capital Health, David Thompson Health Region, Alberta Orthopaedic Society, Alberta's physicians, and Alberta Bone and Joint Health Institute.

Finally, many queuing systems that exist in practice do not always lend themselves to any of the specific models discussed in this chapter. In many cases, computer simulation, the topic discussed in the next chapter, provides a better and unique approach of study.

Glossary

Balking Potential customers refuse to enter a waiting line, usually because they feel the line is too long.

Calling Population Pool of potential customers.

Finite Calling Population A system in which the pool of potential customers is limited in size.

Infinite Calling Population A system in which the pool of potential customers is relatively large or unlimited.

Interarrival Time Length of time between customer arrivals.

Jockeying In systems that have multiple waiting lines, when waiting customers switch from one waiting line to another.

Multiple-Channel System A queuing system with more than one server or service facility.

Multiple-Phase System A system with multiple processing steps.

Preemptive Service In a priority service model, this exists if service can be interrupted to handle a customer who has a higher priority than the one who is being served.

Priority Servicing Model Arriving customers are assigned to a priority class according to a predetermined rule and then they are serviced in order of priority class, using first-come, first-served within each class.

Queue Discipline (Processing Order) Order in which waiting customers are served. Usually by order of arrival (first-come-first-serve), except for priority servicing models.

Queuing System System in which waiting lines tend to develop.

Reneging Occurs when a customer, after a period of waiting in line, leaves the waiting line before being serviced.

Single-Channel System A system with one server or one service facility.

Single-Phase System A system with one processing step.

System A waiting line system consists of a waiting line and a service facility.

System Utilization The proportion of time that servers are busy (i.e., serving customers).

Solved Problem

Note: This chapter covers a wide range of queuing models. Rather than attempt to illustrate all of those models and variations, which would merely duplicate the examples presented in the chapter, this section is devoted to emphasizing a few of the basic concepts that underlie applying the queuing models presented in this chapter.

Problem 1

Customers arrive at the checkout area of a large supermarket during the early afternoon hours at the rate of four per minute. Checkout time averages two minutes per customer. There are six cashiers on duty. Assume that the arrival and checkout rates can be modelled by Poisson distributions. After arriving at the checkout area, customers select one of the six checkout lanes by choosing the one that appears to have the shortest line, and they wait in that line.

Answer these questions about this queuing system:

a. What is the significance of the phrase "during the early afternoon hours"?
b. What is the service rate, and why is it necessary to know it?
c. Is the system underloaded? Why is it important for a system to be underloaded?
d. We are told to assume the service rate can be modelled by a Poisson distribution. Is this any different than being told that the service time can be modelled by an exponential distribution?
e. How important is it to be able to assume either that the arrival and service rates are Poisson or that inter-arrival and service times are exponential? How could these be checked in practice?
f. What requirement of the waiting-line models presented in this chapter is violated if customers can select their own checkout lines? For the system to satisfy this requirement, what change would have to be made to the system?

Solution

a. In many waiting-line systems, the average customer arrival rate tends to vary by time of day. For example, lunch-hour demand is higher in restaurants, banks, shops near office buildings, and the like, than during, say, the midmorning hours. Thus, performance measures will differ depending on the time of day. Consequently, performance measures should be related to specific time and/or day intervals.
b. The service rate is the reciprocal of the service time. Here, the service time is 2 minutes. Therefore, the service rate is.

$$\frac{1 \text{ customer}}{2 \text{ minutes}} = .5 \text{ customer per minute}$$

It is important to know the service rate because many of the formulas in the chapter require the service rate rather than the service time.

c. This question involves the concept of system utilization, which can be calculated as follows:

$$\rho = \frac{\lambda}{s\mu} = \frac{4 \text{ per minutes}}{6(.5 \text{ per minutes})} = 1.33$$

An underloaded system is one in which the system utilization is less than 1.00. In this case, the system is overloaded. The majority of queuing models require that the system be underloaded. If a system is overloaded, waiting lines will tend to grow longer and longer. Thus, overloaded systems are somewhat unrealistic. The exception would be a finite source system because the arrival rate would decrease as a larger and larger percentage of the population waited in line.

d. No, a Poisson *rate* is equivalent to an exponential *time.*
e. The majority of the models require these assumptions. Hence, if the assumptions are not valid, strictly speaking, the models will not provide results that will be realized (i.e., the calculated values will not reflect reality). Obtaining data (if possible) and using a Chi-square goodness-of-fit test would be a good way to test this.
f. The models require that service be done on a first-come, first-served basis (with the exception of the multiple-priority model). To achieve this, customers either could be asked to wait in a single line, as is often done in banks and post offices, or could be given numbers when they arrive and serviced in that order. In this example both would seem to be impractical; some other queuing model (or simulation) would be needed to handle this situation.

Discussion and Review Questions

1. What are the basic characteristics (elements) of a queuing system?
2. What are the basic measures of system performance?
3. First-come, first-served waiting line discipline is assumed in the queuing systems studied in this chapter. Describe two circumstances (business situations) where first-come, first-served discipline is not applicable.
4. In this chapter, one of the waiting line models studied involved a limited or finite waiting line. Provide examples of two situations with finite waiting lines.
5. In studying the basic single-channel waiting line model (M/M/1), what assumptions must be met?
6. What does the three-letter designation for a queuing model stand for? Describe what each position of the three positions such as (M/M/1) entails.
7. In the single-server waiting line models we have studied, the service rate is greater than the arrival rate. Why must this assumption hold for a single-server queuing system?
8. In the study of queuing systems, it is difficult to estimate the cost of waiting. The cost of waiting is generally divided into two components: (1) economic costs and (2) psychological costs. Describe both of these types of waiting costs.
9. One of the main criticisms of waiting line models is that the service times are not distributed according to the negative exponential distribution. In this chapter, we have studied three types of service distributions including the negative exponential distribution. List and briefly describe each type of service distribution that is described in this chapter. Explain when it is appropriate to use the three different service distributions.
10. Provide two examples of when the finite calling population model is applicable.
11. In this chapter, we have studied two versions of multiple-channel waiting line models. The first version involves first-come, first-served service type and the second one involves priority servicing. Explain how the two types of service differ and describe how the priority servicing system works. Explain the statement that in a priority system, service is not preemptive.
12. In a waiting line system, the total cost is made up of two components: (1) waiting cost and (2) service cost. Discuss these costs in the context of a realistic business example. Which of the two costs is more difficult to estimate? Why?
13. In a waiting line system designed for a grocery store, what is the objective that a grocery store manager is trying to achieve? What specific costs is he/she trying to balance?
14. Certain waiting line systems involve multiple phases. How does a single-phase system compare to a multiple-phase system? Provide a realistic example of a multiple-phase waiting line system.

Problems

1. Relative to waiting line models:
   a. What is meant by the terms *single-channel system* and *multiple-channel system?* If a crew of four workers operates as a team in servicing a customer, how many channels does the system have?
   b. Contrast the terms *service time* and *service rate.* Explain how one can convert from time to rate. Why is this important?
   c. Explain the terms *calling population, infinite source,* and *finite source.*

d. How does the phrase *first-come, first-served* apply in waiting line? Which models described in the chapter assume this?
e. What does the phrase *the number in the system* refer to?
f. Why do waiting lines form in systems that are underloaded?
g. Which of these are assumptions of most or all of the models presented in this chapter?
   (1) Underloaded system.
   (2) Variable arrival rate.
   (3) Variable service rate.
   (4) Processing is first-come, first-served.
h. What are the major elements of a waiting line system?

2. An infinite source queuing system has an arrival rate of 45 customers per hour and an average service time of 2 minutes per customer. The arrival rate can be described as Poisson, and the service time distribution can be described as negative exponential. Suppose it has been determined that the average number of customers waiting for service is 1.929. There are two servers. Determine (*hint:* see Example 12-3):
   a. The average number of customers being served.
   b. The average number of customers in the system.
   c. The average time customers wait in line before being served.
   d. The average time customers spend in the system.
   e. System utilization.
   f. What is the probability that there will be less than six customers arriving in three minutes?
   g. What is the probability that there will be two or more customers arriving in three minutes?
   h. What is the probability of no more than three minutes elapsing between successive arrivals of customers?
   i. What is the probability that the service time is less than 3 minutes?
   j. What is the probability that the service time is more than 2.5 minutes?
   k. What is the probability that the service time is between 2.5 and 3 minutes?

3. One clerk is on duty during evening hours at the customer service desk of a supermarket. The clerk can process customer requests in an average time of 3 minutes, and this can be described by a negative exponential distribution that has a mean of 3. Customers arrive at a rate of 15 per hour (Poisson). Find:
   a. The expected number of customers waiting to be served.
   b. The average time customers spend waiting in line for service.
   c. The proportion of time that the clerk is not busy with customers.
   d. What is the probability that there will be less than seven customers arriving in a 20-minute period?
   e. What is the probability that there will be three or more customers arriving in a 20-minute interval?
   f. What is the probability that the service time is less than two minutes?
   g. What is the probability that the service time exceeds four minutes?
   h. What is the probability that the service time is between two and four minutes?

4. For the preceding question, determine:
   a. The probability of no customers in the system.
   b. The probability of two customers at the service counter.
   c. The probability that a customer will have to wait for service.

5. Customers in a cafeteria line during lunch on weekdays arrive at the cashier's booth at a mean rate of 2.6 per minute. The cashier can process 4 customers per minute. Arrival rate is Poisson and service time is described by one exponential distribution. Compute each of the performance measures listed in Table 12-2 for this system. For Equation 12-17, use $n = 2$, and for Equation 12-18, use $k = 3$.

6. A lawn mower repair service employs one repairperson, who takes an average of one hour to service a lawn mower. A mower is brought in for service on the average of one every 90 minutes. Assume that arrival rate and service time can be described by Poisson distributions. Determine the following:
   a. The average number of mowers awaiting service.
   b. The average time a mower waits for service.
   c. The probability that the number waiting for service will exceed 4 mowers.
   d. The probability that the repairperson will be without a mower to service.

7. Customers at a bank wait in a single line for the next available teller. Customer arrivals can be modelled by a Poisson distribution that has a mean of 70 per hour during the midmorning hours. A teller can process an average of 100 customers per hour, which also can

be modelled by a Poisson distribution. If there is one teller on duty, determine:

a. The average time a customer must wait in line for the teller.
b. The average number of customers waiting in line.
c. Average service time.
d. System utilization.
e. The probability of no customers waiting in line.

8. What values would be appropriate for the performance measures listed in the preceding problem for the case in which two tellers are available?
9. A supermarket deli counter has a ticket dispenser from which customers take tickets that maintain first-come, first-served processing. The mean arrival rate during the morning hours is 84 per hour. Each server can handle an average of 30 customers per hour. Arrival rate and service time can be reasonably well described by Poisson and exponential distributions respectively. Assume that three clerks are on duty. Compute each of the performance measures for this system using the equations listed in Table 12-4. For Equation 12-26, use $n = 2$, and for Equation 12-27, use $n = 4$.
10. For the preceding problem, answer the following questions.
    a. What is the probability that there will be less than seven customers arriving in a five-minute period?
    b. What is the probability that there will be three or more customers arriving in a five-minute interval?
    c. What is the probability that the service time exceeds three minutes?
    d. What is the probability that the service time is less than two minutes?
    e. What is the probability that the service time is between two and three minutes?
11. For Problem 9, how many clerks would be necessary to keep the average time customers spend waiting *in line* to no more than 2.5 minutes? How many clerks would be needed to keep the average time customers spend *in the system* to under 2.5 minutes?
12. The owner of a bakery is thinking about installing a system of poles and chain links that will make customers wait in a single waiting line, instead of having them mill about the store waiting to be served. During evening hours, there are two clerks on duty, and the mean customer arrival rate is .8 per minute. Service time averages 2.375 minutes per customer, and this can be reasonably described by an exponential distribution. The arrival rate can be described by a Poisson distribution. Compute each of the performance measures in Table 12-4, beginning with Equation 12-22, but omitting Equation 12-25. Find L_q and P_0. For Equation 12-26, assume $n = 2$, and for Equation 12-27, assume $n = 6$.
13. Answer these additional questions concerning the previous problem:
    a. For the information given, what line length will not be exceeded with a probability of 95 percent?
    b. How many servers would be needed to keep the maximum line length to under five with a probability of 95 percent?
    c. How many servers would be needed to keep the average number waiting to be served (line only) to under three?
14. Library users request assistance in locating items at an information desk at a mean rate of 13.8 requests per hour. Each assistant librarian can handle a request in an average of 10 minutes. Suppose that students from a nearby college have studied this system and found arrival rate to be Poisson and service time to be exponential.
    a. How many assistants would be needed to keep the average time in the system to 16 minutes or less?
    b. Determine the maximum number of persons waiting to submit a request for probabilities of 95 percent and 99 percent if five assistants will be used.
    c. How many assistants would be needed to have a probability of 95 percent that line length would not exceed seven persons?
15. In a large plant, a centralized tool crib is used to dispense tools to mechanics on a per-need basis. Mechanics request tools at a mean rate of 40 per hour (Poisson). Clerks can handle requests in a mean time of 4.5 minutes each, including the paperwork that is involved. Service time can be described by an exponential distribution. Mechanics represent a cost of \$25 per hour each, and clerks represent a cost of \$15 per hour each. Determine the number of clerks that will be needed to minimize the total cost of mechanics and clerks in the system.
16. In the parts department of a large automobile dealership, there is a counter that is used exclusively for mechanics' requests for parts. It has been determined

that such requests occur once every five minutes, on the average, and the time between the requests can be modelled by a negative exponential distribution that has a mean of five minutes. A clerk can handle requests at a rate of 15 per hour, and this can be modelled by a Poisson distribution that has a mean of 15. Suppose there are two clerks at the counter.

a. On the average, how many mechanics would be at the counter, including those being served?
b. What is the probability that a mechanic would have to wait for service?
c. If a mechanic has to wait, how long, on the average, would the wait be?
d. If clerks represent a cost of $20 per hour and mechanics represent a cost of $30 per hour, what number of clerks would be optimal in terms of minimizing cost?
e. What is the probability that there will be less than four requests occurring in a 20-minute period?
f. What is the probability that there will be two or more requests occurring in a 20-minute interval?
g. What is the probability that the service time exceeds three minutes?
h. What is the probability that the service time is less than one minute?
i. What is the probability that the service time is between one and three minutes?

17. During the daytime hours, calls for paramedics come into an emergency switchboard at the rate of two per hour. The operations chief can schedule two, three, or four crews to work this shift. The average time required to complete a trip and return to base is 40 minutes. Arrival rate is Poisson and service time is exponential.
    a. If the chief wants to maintain an average time of no more than 20 minutes between the time a call comes in and the time a crew is dispatched, how many crews should be scheduled?
    b. Suppose that two crews are used. What would the average time to dispatch be? What would the system utilization be?
    c. Suppose three crews are used. What would the average time to dispatch be? What would the system utilization be?

18. One aspect of designing an industrial plant concerns the number of loading docks to include in the design. Driver and truck cost will be $200 per hour, while equivalent dock cost will be $140 per hour. Average loading time is expected to be three hours, and trucks will arrive randomly at a rate of one truck every two hours. Arrival rates can be assumed to be Poisson distributed and service times are distributed according to exponential distribution. Determine the number of loading docks that will minimize dock and truck/driver costs.

19. Certain automated equipment needs part replacement on a random basis. This can be described by a Poisson distribution that has a mean of one part every other hour. When a break occurs, a technician diagnoses the problem, then goes to the parts counter to obtain the appropriate part. The average time for a clerk to obtain the part is 30 minutes because of the need to check various parts catalogues and retrieve the part from storage. Assume service times are exponential. Clerk time represents a cost of $30 per hour per clerk. Equipment downtime and technician time represent $400 per hour.
    a. If two clerks are used, what would be the average number of machines (i.e., automated equipment) waiting for parts? Assume there are a large number of machines in service (i.e., treat as infinite source calling population)
    b. What number of clerks would be optimal for minimizing cost?

20. A clerk in the children's shoes department of a large store waits on customers in the order that they arrive. Each customer signs in when entering the department. A recent study shows that the customer arrival rate on Wednesday mornings can be represented adequately by a Poisson distribution with a mean of 8 per hour. The clerk can handle customers at a mean rate of 12 per hour. Determine the mean number of customers in the system, and the mean time they spend in the system, under each of the following conditions:
    a. The service rate is exponential.
    b. The service rate is constant.
    c. The service time is neither exponential nor constant, but it is known that service time has a standard deviation of 3.5 minutes per customer.

21. A vending machine dispenses apples at a constant rate of 4 per minute. Apple eaters arrive to purchase apples at a mean rate of 3.4 per minute during breaks from classes held in the same building. Arrival rates are distributed according to Poisson distribution.

a. Compute the mean number of persons waiting to buy an apple.
b. Compute each of the remaining performance measures using the formulas in Table 12-6.
c. What is the probability that the service time exceeds 30 seconds?
d. What is the probability that the service time is less than 20 seconds?
e. What is the probability that the service time is less than 15 seconds?
f. What is the probability that the service time exceeds 45 seconds?
g. What is the probability that more than four apple eaters arrive in one minute?
h. What is the probability that the number of apple eaters arriving in half a minute will not exceed two?
i. What is the probability that the number of apple eaters arriving in a minute will not exceed two?

22. If the apple machine in the previous problem was temporarily out of order and apples were sold by one server who had the same 15-second service time but with a standard deviation of 2 seconds, what values would each of the performance measures in Table 12-6 have?
23. Calls come into the reservations desk of a resort motel during the morning hours (weekdays only) at a rate of 15 per hour (Poisson distribution). In this telephone system, as many as two calls can be automatically placed on hold if the reservations clerk is busy with another call. Compute each of the performance measures in Table 12-7 with $\mu = 25$ per hour (exponential distribution).
24. One librarian is on duty at the reference desk of a branch of the public library during the morning hours. The librarian gets a request for assistance approximately once every four minutes. The time between requests can be modelled using a negative exponential distribution with a mean of four minutes. Each request requires an average of three minutes of the librarian's time. This can be modelled using a normal distribution with a mean of three minutes and a standard deviation of one minute. Determine each of the following performance measures:
    a. The average number of people waiting for the librarian, not including the person being helped.
    b. The average time needed for a person to make a request and to be helped.
    c. The proportion of time the librarian is not working on requests.
25. Many of a bank's customers use its automatic teller machine to transact business after normal banking hours. During the early evening hours in the summer months, it has been determined that customers arrive at a certain location at the rate of one every other minute. This can be modelled using a Poisson distribution. Each customer spends an average of 90 seconds completing his or her transactions. This time has a standard deviation of 20 seconds. Determine
    a. The average time customers spend at the machine, either waiting in line or completing transactions.
    b. The probability that a customer will not have to wait upon arriving at the automatic teller machine.
    c. The average number waiting to use the machine.
26. In an automatic car wash, it takes four minutes to wash each car. Suppose cars arrive at the car wash at the rate of 12 per hour (Poisson). Hint: Because the carwash uses automatic equipment, it always takes four minutes to wash a car. Determine the following:
    a. The average number of cars waiting to be washed.
    b. The average time between the car's arriving and leaving.
    c. The probability that a car will not have to wait in line.
27. The service department of an automobile dealership can handle only six transmission repair jobs per day. Customers who need transmission repairs come in at the rate of one per hour during the morning and early afternoon. Repair time averages 50 minutes. The arrival rate can be modelled by Poisson distribution and service time is distributed according to exponential distribution. One repair person handles all transmission work. Compute each of the performance measures listed in Table 12-7.
28. A telephone reservation system can accept a maximum of two calls waiting. The reservationist processes calls in an average of four minutes. Average time between calls is five minutes. Service time can be modelled by exponential distribution and arrival rate can be modelled using Poisson distribution. Determine each of the following measures:
    a. The average number of calls waiting.
    b. The probability of two or more calls waiting.
    c. The probability that a caller will not have to wait for the reservationist.

29. An operator handles loading/unloading a group of three machines. The machines operate an average of 30 minutes per job, and loading/unloading time averages 5 minutes. Service time can be modelled by exponential distribution and the arrivals are distributed according to Poisson distribution. Compute each of the performance measures listed in Table 12-8. Use $n = 3$ for Equation 12-46.
30. A repair crew handles equipment breakdowns of construction equipment. There is one piece of equipment at each of five construction sites. When a request for repair comes in, the crew travels to the site, repairs the equipment, and returns to its base. Travel and repair time can be described by an exponential distribution with a mean of 3.5 hours. Equipment breakdowns occur at the rate of one every five hours (Poisson distribution).
    a. What is the probability that at any given instant, none of the equipment is being serviced due to breakdowns?
    b. On the average, how long does it take from the time a call comes in until the crew leaves to repair that piece of equipment?
    c. On the average, how many machines are out of service?
    d. What is the probability that the crew will be idle?
    e. What is the probability of no more than one breakdown in 2.5 hours?
    f. What is the probability that the number of breakdowns will exceed one in a five-hour period?
    g. What is the probability of no breakdowns in an hour?
    h. What is the probability that the service time will exceed four hours?
    i. What is the probability that the service time will be no more than two hours?
    j. What is the probability that the service time will be between two and four hours?
31. Customers arriving at a service centre are assigned to one of three categories (1, 2, or 3, with Category 1 given the highest priority) for servicing. Records indicate that an average of nine customers arrive per hour, and that one-third are assigned to each category. There are two servers, and each can process customers at the rate of five per hour. Arrival rate can be described by Poisson distributions and service time is distributed according to exponential distribution.
    a. What is the utilization rate for this system?
    b. Determine the average waiting time for units in each class.
    c. Find the average number of customers in each class that are waiting for service.
32. A manager must determine requirements for waiting space for customers. A priority system is used to process customers who are assigned to one of two classes when they enter the processing centre. The highest priority class has an arrival rate of four per hour, while the other class has an arrival rate of two per hour. Both can be described as Poisson distributed. There are two servers, and each can process customers in an average of six minutes. Service rate is distributed according to exponential distribution.
    a. What is the system utilization?
    b. Determine the number of customers of each class that are waiting for service.
    c. Determine the average waiting time for each class.
    d. If the manager was able to alter the assignment rules so that arrival rates of the two classes were equal (3 per hour for each priority class), what would be the revised average waiting times for each priority class?
33. A priority waiting system assigns arriving customers to one of four classes. Arrival rates (Poisson) of the classes are shown in the following table:

Class	Arrivals per hour
1	2
2	4
3	3
4	2

    Five servers process the customers, and each can handle three customers per hour. Service rate is distributed according to exponential distribution.
    a. What is the system utilization?
    b. On the average, how long do customers in the various classes wait for service? On the average how many are waiting in each class?
    c. If the arrival rate of the second priority class could be reduced to three units per hour by shifting some arrivals into the third priority class, how would your answers to part *b* change?
    d. What observations can you make based on your answers to part *c*?
34. Referring to the preceding problem, suppose that each server could handle four customers per hour. Answer the questions posed in the preceding problem. Explain why the impact of reassigning customers is much less than in the preceding problem.
35. An immigration agent at Pearson Airport in Toronto could process 120 entrants on average during an

eight-hour duty if the agent was busy all the time Assume that time to process each entrant is a random variable with an exponential distribution. On average, an entrant arrives at the agent's station once every six minutes. The number of arrivals is based on a Poisson distribution.

a. What is the mean service time?
b. What is the mean service rate?
c. What is the mean arrival rate?
d. What is the probability that the service time is more than five minutes?
e. What is the probability that the service time is between three and five minutes?
f. Delay problems are expected to occur if more than two entrants arrive during any 10-minute period. What is the probability that a delay problem will occur?
g. What is the expected number in the system?
h. What is the expected number in the waiting line?
i. Determine the amount of time an entrant spends in the system?
j. What is the expected waiting time in the queue?

36. Solve Problem 4 using Excel.
37. Solve Problem 7 using Excel.
38. Solve Problem 12 using Excel.
39. Solve Problem 14 using Excel.
40. Solve Problem 15 using Excel.
41. Solve Problem 17 using Excel.
42. Solve Problem 18 using Excel.
43. Solve Problem 19 using Excel.
44. Solve Problem 20 using Excel.
45. Solve Problem 25 using Excel.
46. Solve Problem 27 using Excel.
47. Solve Problem 30 using Excel.
48. Solve Problem 35 using Excel.

Case 1: Big Bank

The operations manager of a soon-to-open branch of a large bank is in the process of configuring teller operations. Currently some branches have a separate teller line for customers who have a single transaction, while other branches don't have separate lines. The manager wants to avoid complaints about long waits that have been received at some branches. Because the demographics differ from location to location, a system that works at one branch won't necessarily work at another.

The manager has obtained data on processing times from the bank's home office, and is ready to explore different options for configuring operations. (Fortunately she has her textbook from when she took management science course at a nearby university.)

One time that will get special attention is the noon hour on Friday. The plan is to have five tellers available. Under consideration are the following options:

1. Have one waiting line and have the first person in line go to the next available teller.
2. Have two waiting lines: one teller for customers who have a single transaction and four tellers who would handle customers who have multiple transactions.

Processing Information

An average of 80 customers are processed during the noon hour. The average processing time for customers with a single transaction is 90 seconds, while the processing time for customers with multiple transactions is 4 minutes. Sixty percent of the customers are expected to have multiple transactions.

Questions

If you were the manager, which option would you select? Why? Explain the disparity between the results for the two options. What assumptions did you make in your analysis?

Case 2: Adjusting Centralized Appointment Scheduling at the Ottawa General Hospital

When walk-in clinics referred their patients for various services (such as x-rays) to the Ottawa General Hospital, their staff had tough time getting through to the hospital's centralized appointment office. Most of the time, the line was busy. The installation of a call waiting system did not improve the situation, because callers were put on hold for indefinite lengths of time. The poor service resulted in numerous complaints. One of the managers at the Hospital was put in charge of finding a solution, and a goal of answering at least 90 percent of calls without delay was set. Ottawa General Hospital was willing to employ more staff to receive calls. The manager studied this queuing problem by collecting data for 21 workdays during which additional staff were used to answer calls and no call received a busy signal or was put on hold. The number of calls per day ranged between 220 and 350, with no day-of-the week seasonality. Most days, the number of calls was between 250 and 300. The average number of calls arriving during each 15-minutes interval peaked at about 10 calls during 9:00–11 :30 a.m. and 2:00–3:45 p.m. The 944 service durations had a distribution similar to exponential with a mean of 3.11 minutes. The manager also found out that the 6.5 full-time-equivalent employees usually spent half their time doing other tasks and turned off their phones when they were busy. Using the multiple-servers queuing model and a service goal of at least 90 percent probability of not having to wait, the manager determined the staff required for each 15 minutes interval. When the original staffing levels were compared with the model-determined ones, it was discovered that more staff were required earlier in the day and later in the afternoon, and fewer were needed around noon. The problem was solved by rearranging work shifts. The manager is charge of the study has left the organization and the hospital's senior management is concerned about the decrease of the service level due to the increase of the average service times from 3:11 minutes to 5 minutes.

Managerial Report

Provide senior management with a report that determines the minimum number of staff needed during the busy periods (9:00 a.m. – 11:30 a.m. and 2:00 p.m. – 3:45 p.m.), assuming that the central office receives 40 calls per hour, each call takes an average of 5 minutes to serve, and it is desired that at least 90 percent of calls be received without waiting. Your findings will then be compared with current figures.

Source: W. J. Stevenson and M. Hojati, *Operations Management*, 3rd Canadian Edition, (Toronto: McGraw-Hill Ryerson, 2007).

Simulation

CHAPTER 13

LEARNING OBJECTIVES

After completing this chapter, you should be able to:

1. Explain what the term *simulation* means and how simulation differs from analytical techniques.
2. Explain the difference between discrete and continuous simulations, between fixed-interval and next-event simulations, and between discrete and probabilistic simulations.
3. List and briefly describe the steps in simulation.
4. Use the Monte Carlo method to generate random numbers.
5. Conduct manual simulations using various distributions.
6. Conduct simulation with Excel using various distributions.
7. Conduct simple waiting-line simulation using Excel.
8. Conduct inventory management simulation using Excel.
9. Conduct capital budgeting simulation using Excel.
10. Conduct simulation with Crystal Ball.
11. Conduct capital budgeting simulation using Crystal Ball.
12. List the advantages and limitations of simulations.

CHAPTER OUTLINE

13.1 INTRODUCTION

Simulation represents a marked departure from the other tools of analysis described in this book, such as linear programming, decision analysis, and waiting-line models. All of those other techniques were directed toward helping decision makers to identify an *optimal solution* to a problem. This is not the case with simulation; it is not an optimizing tool. Instead, its purpose is to enable a manager or analyst to *experiment* with a system—to **simulate**—in order to better understand its behaviour, and as a result, to make better decisions with regard to the system.

Simulation involves the use of a model that exhibits the important behavioural characteristics of a real system. Studying the behaviour of the model under various conditions can lead to tremendous insights with broad applications. Consider these examples:

1. Medical researchers use various animals to *simulate* the effects of certain drugs on human beings.
2. Aircraft designers use wind tunnels to *simulate* the effect of air turbulence on wings and other structural parts of an airplane.
3. NASA trains astronauts in environments that *simulate* the conditions they are likely to encounter on future space missions.
4. Football teams conduct contact drills to prepare their members for upcoming games by *simulating* playing conditions.
5. Training programs for commercial pilots put trainees through a relatively large number of *simulated* takeoffs and landings on the ground before exposing them to the reality of performing actual takeoffs and landings.
6. Automotive safety experts crash test cars to *simulate* accidents.

In each of these examples, an important benefit of simulation is the ability to *experiment* with a situation under *controlled conditions*. Thus, simulation is used to answer "What if . . . ?" questions. For example: What if the drug dosage is increased by a factor of two? What if the curvature of the wing is changed slightly? What would happen if a new pass defence is used by the other team? Decision makers can use simulation not only to obtain answers to such questions, but also to redesign a system that will perform in a more desirable way. The redesigned system, then, can be simulated to test its behaviour under realistic conditions. The models involved in these examples are called *physical* simulations.

Another important class of simulation models, especially in business, is *mathematical* simulations. These involve modelling the key aspects of *events* (e.g., use of spare parts, demand for a product, machine breakdowns) in mathematical terms. Then, the model can be studied and modified in roughly the same manner as physical simulations. Because they are mathematical, such simulations lend themselves to computerization. This is important because many simulations are fairly complex and require numerous calculations, and computers offer the only feasible approach to handling such problems.

The simulations that we shall study are mathematical. They can be applied to a wide range of business problems. However, although most real-life simulations tend to be fairly complex, the discussion here will be limited to situations that are not very complex. In fact, many of the problems presented in this chapter lend themselves to *analytical* solutions rather than repeated *simulation runs,* which yield only approximate results. Nonetheless, there are several important reasons for limiting our study to fairly simple problems. One is that such problems lend themselves to *manual* procedures, which will produce identical results across the board. This means that everyone who tries a certain problem will come up with the same result, and this allows for discussion of that result. More important, the simple problems permit illustrating the basic concepts of simulation without being obscured by unnecessary, albeit realistic, complexity.

The discussion begins with an outline of the different types of simulation, followed by a description of how to actually do a simulation. The remainder of the chapter includes a broader discussion of simulation techniques, validation of simulation models, computer simulation using Excel, computer simulation with Crystal Ball, and the advantages and limitations of simulation as a management tool.

13.2 TYPES OF SIMULATION

There are various ways of classifying simulation types. Some of those ways are presented in this section. The purpose in contrasting the approaches to simulation is to help you gain some additional perspective on simulation.

Simulations can be classified as discrete or continuous, fixed-interval or next-event, deterministic or probabilistic, and static or dynamic. Let's take a look at each of these contrasting pairs, beginning with discrete versus continuous simulations.

Discrete Versus Continuous Simulations

A discrete simulation is one in which the variable of interest is discrete, that is, it takes an integer value. There are many similar situations that involve discrete variables. For the most part, such situations can be described by a *count* of the *number of occurrences* (e.g., number of cars serviced, number of items sold, number of complaints received, and so on).

In certain instances, the variable of interest is *continuous:* It can assume both integer and noninteger values over a range of values. Recall that quantities that are *measured* rather than counted have this characteristic, such as time, weight, distance, and length. The distinction between discrete and continuous variables is important for simulation design. Both cases are illustrated in the following pages.

Fixed-Interval Versus Next-Event Simulations

In certain instances, an analyst will be interested in simulating the value of a variable over a given or *fixed interval.* For example, the situation may involve sales of a product, and the analyst may want to simulate the number of units sold *per day,* or *per week.* Hence, the analyst would design the simulation to indicate the sales over one of these intervals. Although time intervals are the most typical intervals, distance and area are two other possible intervals. For instance, a problem may involve the number of defects *per mile* of roadway, or the number of breaks *per square yard* of cloth. In such cases, interest usually centres on *how many* occurrences there are rather than the *where* or *when* of an occurrence. Hence, a manager of an automobile dealership will be mainly concerned with *how many* cars were sold on a particular day rather than whether a car was sold at 1:30 p.m. or 1:40 p.m. Similarly, the superintendent of a mill will often be more concerned with keeping track of the number of defects in cloth that the mill produces rather than exactly where defects occurred; his or her main interest will be deciding if there is a major problem, and the number of defects would be an indicator of a potential problem.

When interest centres on the accumulated value of a variable over a length of time or other interval, we say that the simulation is a **fixed-interval simulation,** and we design the simulation to generate results that correspond to the interval of interest (e.g., sales per day).

Another type of simulation focuses on *when* something happens, or *how much time* is required to perform a task. For instance, a simulation of machine breakdowns may involve information on how long a machine operated before a breakdown and, perhaps, on how much time was required to repair the machine. This sort of information can be very useful for choosing among alternative machines, for deciding how many machines will be needed to meet production quotas, and for scheduling maintenance and repair crews.

When interest centres on *an occurrence* of an event (e.g., a breakdown, a fire alarm, an accident) and, perhaps, how much time or effort is required for the event (e.g., repair time, response time), we refer to the simulation of these situations as **next-event simulations.** Both types of simulations are illustrated in this chapter.

Deterministic Versus Probabilistic Simulations

Another important aspect of a simulation is whether it involves a deterministic or a probabilistic situation. The former pertains to cases in which a specific outcome is *certain,* given a set of inputs; the latter pertains to cases that involve *random* variables and, therefore, the exact outcome cannot be predicted with certainty, given a set of inputs.

Consider a case in which an employer is contemplating changes in pay rates and working times for his employees. Although there may be many employees that would be affected, given the pay rates and projected hours of work, the total payroll can be determined right down to the penny. That would not be the case for, say, projecting the amount of time required to repair a complex piece of equipment that has malfunctioned. Because each case would differ somewhat from other cases, the time would be more appropriately modelled as a random variable. The resulting simulation would then have to be *probabilistic* to incorporate that feature. This chapter focuses exclusively on probabilistic simulations, which both tend to have broad application and are commonly encountered in managerial environments. This is not to say that deterministic cases are not encountered, but rather that they typically do not involve the level of insight or understanding that probabilistic simulations require.

All probabilistic simulations have a certain feature in common: They incorporate some mechanism for mimicking random behaviour in one or more variables.

Static Versus Dynamic Simulations

Static simulations are used to represent a system in which time plays no role or a system at a particular time. Such simulations operate by randomly sampling the variables of interest in the model according to some pre-defined probability functions. Equations or rules are then used to transform these variables into the characteristics under study. By repeating this process many times, a set of independent and identically distributed observations can be produced and be used to gather the performance measures of interest. This chapter focuses on static simulations since basic models can be easily developed in spreadsheets.

Dynamic simulations, on the other hand, are used to represent a system that evolves over time. Such simulations are time-dependant and operate by explicitly mimicking the sequences of events that occur over time in the system under study. Although spreadsheets can be valuable tools, their capabilities are too limited to handle dynamic simulations properly. Over the years, a number of simulation languages have been developed that make the task of writing dynamic simulation programs less cumbersome. ARENA® (www.arenasimulation.com) is one of these packages, which has been successfully used to develop simulation models with applications in health care, manufacturing, call centres, and business process re-engineering (see more discussion on simulation languages later in this chapter).

A MODERN MANAGEMENT SCIENCE APPLICATION: AIR CARGO OPERATIONS EVALUATION AND ANALYSIS THROUGH SIMULATION

Air Canada is the largest full-service airline in the Canadian market. Witnessing an impressive growth of its air cargo operations, the airline company built a state-of-the art cargo facility at Toronto's Pearson International Airport, Canada's busiest airport. It was equipped with some of the latest in modern material handling systems, such as a small-package handling system, flexible build-up and break-down workstations, unmanned elevating transfer vehicles, manned and unmanned transfer vehicles, scissor lifts, turntables and right angle decks, powered conveyors, vertical conveyors, an automated storage and retrieval system (AS/RS), and a computer-based inventory control system that tracks movement of units throughout the terminal and interfaces with all aspects of cargo operations. One of the challenges faced by the company is that of redesigning the cargo handling processes to ensure that products and services are aligned with customers' needs in terms of speed, quality, service, and cost. Air Canada turns to simulation to quantitatively evaluate and compare different policies, business practices, and procedures within a given set of operational and business constraints. The use of simulation provides practical insights to a number of issues, such as the effects of an increase of cargo volume, changing the product service standard, changing the shipment storage policy at the export level or import level, processing time changes, or certain equipment components being out of order.

Source: A. L. Nsakanda, M. Turcotte, M. Diaby, "Air cargo operations evaluation and analysis through simulation," *Proceedings of the 2004 Winter Simulation Conference*, R .G. Ingalls, M. D. Rossetti, J. S. Smith, and B. A. Peters, eds.

The Modern Management Science Application, "Air Cargo Operations Evaluation and Analysis Through Simulation," reports the uses of this class of simulation models by Air Canada to investigate the effects of various operational scenarios, without having to risk the costs associated with experimenting with real-life system.

13.3 STEPS IN SIMULATION

In designing a simulation, an analyst is typically guided by this basic principle: Of necessity, the simulation model will be a simplification of reality. However, it must be realistic enough to provide meaningful results so that it will be useful for problem-solving and decision making.

Now that we have considered some of the different types of simulations, let us turn our attention to how to conduct a simulation.

Simulation typically involves these steps:

1. Defining the problem and setting objectives
2. Developing the model
3. Gathering data
4. Validating the model
5. Designing experiments
6. Performing simulation runs
7. Analyzing and interpreting the results

These steps are illustrated in Figure 13-1.

Let's take a brief look at each of these steps.

Defining the Problem and Setting Objectives

The first step in simulation is to clearly define the problem that is to be studied. This involves a determination of what is to be accomplished (i.e., objectives of the simulation) and the reasons for using simulation. Once the objectives have been established, a means of

FIGURE 13-1 Steps in Simulation

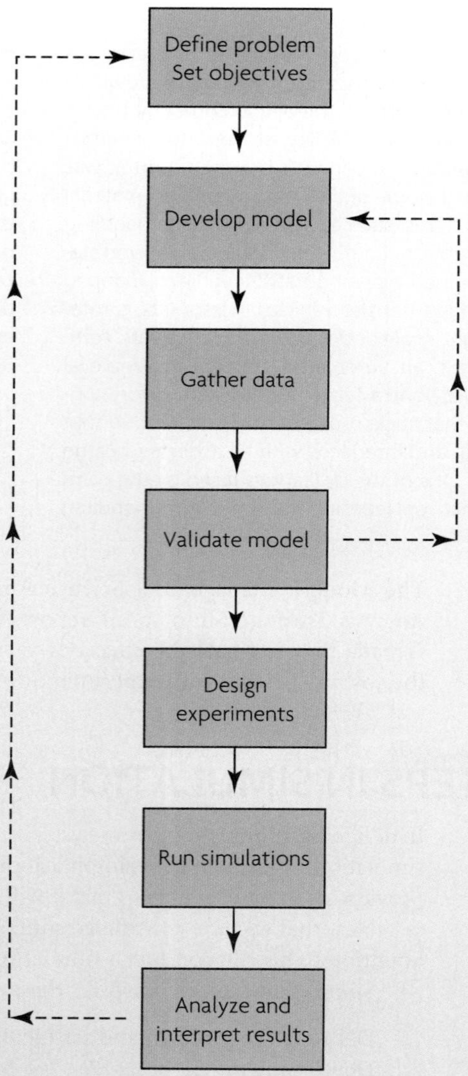

measuring the degree to which objectives are met by the simulation study must be established. Unless the objectives are determined at the outset, there is the danger that the results of the study will be used to determine them. In general, the goal of a simulation study is to ascertain how a system will behave under certain conditions. However, it is important to specify in as much detail as possible what information is desired. This will help in evaluating the success of the simulation, and it also will provide guidance for model development and the design of simulation experiments.

In the problem definition phase, the *scope* of the study and the *level of detail* that is needed to obtain desired results also must be decided. For example, if a simulation study is to be made of a bus system's passenger ridership patterns, will its scope encompass all routes and all times of the day, or just certain routes and/or certain hours? Will its scope cover all days of the week, or just certain peak days? Will it extend to different seasons, holiday travel, and so on? Will the level of detail include such factors as weather conditions, road conditions, traffic patterns, vehicle breakdowns, department store sales, community events, accidents, and the like? Moreover, will demographic information on riders (e.g., age, income, and occupation) be included? These questions are important because they have a bearing on model design and development, as well as the cost and time needed to accomplish this phase of the simulation.

Developing a Model

The second step in simulation is to develop a model that will accomplish the intended results. Usually, this involves determining the structure of the model, then using computer software such as Excel that will actually perform the simulations. Because manual simulations are employed in the text examples and accompanying chapter problems, using a computer software such as Excel will not be necessary to learn the concepts. Nevertheless, most practical applications of simulation do have that requirement. The structure of the model refers to the elements of a problem that are to be included in the model as well as their interrelationships. As in data gathering, capturing those interrelationships is an important aspect of model design, because unless they are realistically portrayed in the model, the results probably will not adequately reflect reality.

Finally, the model must be designed so that it will enable key decision alternatives to be tested. For instance, if bus size or maneuverability have alternatives with related consequences, the model must allow for those possibilities.

Gathering Data

The amount and type of data needed are a function of the scope of the simulation and the level of detail that was decided on in the problem definition stage. The data will be needed both for model development and for evaluating and testing the model. Data may come from direct observation of a system, or they may come from existing historical records. In either case, it is important that the data capture the essence of the system being simulated so they will provide a realistic representation for modelling purposes. Thus, it is usually prudent to verify that this is the case before proceeding with model development. This may involve observation and/or checking with individuals who are knowledgeable about the system.

Validating the Model

This phase of simulation is closely related to model development. The purpose of **validation** is to check to determine if the model adequately reflects the real system performance. There are two aspects of the validation procedure. The first is to compare the results of the model with known system performance under identical circumstances. Ideally, the model should generate the same results as the real system. Discrepancies should be noted, and the model should be revised as needed to achieve this goal. Naturally, this assumes that there is an existing system that can be used for this purpose. If this is not the case, validation must rely on a second aspect: a test of reasonableness.

The test of reasonableness refers to testing the performance of the model under conditions that relate to questions that are to be answered by the simulation. For instance, in the bus simulation, the question of the impact of different size buses may be important. Presumably, historical data on this are not available, because if they were, there would be no reason to employ simulation. Even though there has been no experience with certain conditions, it should be possible for individuals who are closely associated with the real system, or similar systems, to make meaningful assessments about the reasonableness of simulation results under such modified conditions.

Another aspect of this phase involves careful checking of both the assumptions that underlie the model and the values of the parameters used in the model. The judgment of those who will be using the results of the simulation is a key factor. Not only are those persons apt to be very knowledgeable about such matters, but by being asked for their inputs, they also become an integral part of model design. If those people are not consulted, there is a real possibility that the value of the simulation results will suffer. Either the users will not understand the model and, therefore, will not "buy into" the results, or they will resent having been left out of the development of something that they will be expected to make work.

Notice the feedback loop between validation and model development. The validation phase often uncovers deficiencies in the model that must be corrected, and the ensuing results must then be validated. In fact, it is not unusual to go around this loop a number of times before the final model is obtained.

Designing Experiments

The fifth step in simulation is designing experiments. The experiments are the heart of a simulation study. They are intended to answer the "what if . . .?" questions posed to the model. It is through this process of exploring the model's response to issues of concern that the manager or analyst learns about system behaviour. The person who is designing the experiments must look to the objectives of the simulation for guidance. Hence, the more completely those objectives have been spelled out, the better the chances will be for designing experiments that will provide the desired answers to management's questions.

While further study of experimental design is beyond the scope of this book, Douglas Montgomery's *Design and Analysis of Experiments*[1] provides an excellent insight in understanding this material.

Running Simulations

The sixth step in the simulation process is actually "running" or performing the simulations. If a simulation is deterministic, runs that are made under identical sets of conditions will produce exactly the same result. Consequently, only one run is required for each set of conditions in a deterministic simulation. Probabilistic simulations, on the other hand, tend to produce different results with successive runs, even though the set of conditions under which the simulations are run are unchanged. Therefore, a probabilistic simulation will require a number of runs—perhaps a large number—to "average out" the variability that is inherent in such a simulation.

Probabilistic simulation amounts to a form of sampling, and each run represents one observation. Therefore, the same concepts used in random sampling to determine how large a sample to take, apply to deciding how many simulation runs to make. In general, the higher the amount of variation observed in values of variables of primary interest in repeated runs, the greater the number of runs needed to estimate the expected values of those variables. The higher variability among certain variables will be the main determinant of the number of runs needed. Further, the greater the variability obtained during simulation for a particular variable, the greater the likelihood that the behaviour exhibited by the real system will differ from the expected value developed from the simulation study. If the observed variability is deemed excessive, management may want to devote some effort to redesigning the system to reduce the

[1]Douglas C. Montgomery, *Design and Analysis of Experiments,* 5th ed., (New York: John Wiley & Sons, 2003).

variability to a more acceptable level or, perhaps, to better cope with the variability. For example, flexible systems due to multipurpose equipment and/or personnel that are capable of performing different tasks can offset some of the effects of variability in demand for services. Flexible scheduling and selective pricing policies are also possible solutions.

Analyzing and Interpreting the Results

The final step in the simulation process is to analyze and interpret the results. Probabilistic simulations tend to require more effort in this phase than deterministic simulations. Due to the presence of random variability, one can never be completely sure that the observed results are completely representative. Statistical analysis of probabilistic simulations provides the key for dealing with random variability; expected values, confidence intervals, and tests of significance are vital tools of analysis. Thus, analysis of simulation results should provide the decision maker with both an expected value for a given variable and a range of values in which the actual value may fall. Moreover, significance tests can be used to help decide whether observed differences among alternatives are indicative of real, or simply chance, factors.

Interpreting simulation results depends to a certain extent on the degree to which the simulation model correctly portrays the real system. Obviously, if the simulation model is a crude approximation of the system, for whatever reason, applying those results to the real system will present a greater challenge, and greater risk, than if the model is a close approximation of reality. Hence, it is essential to take the degree of closeness between the model and the real system into account when interpreting the results.

13.4 THE MONTE CARLO SIMULATION METHOD

The central feature of probabilistic simulations is the incorporation of *random behaviour* for the variable or variables of interest. Random behaviour is exemplified by many games of chance, such as drawing cards from a well-shuffled deck, rolling dice, and spinning roulette wheels. In each case, the outcome of a particular draw, or roll, or spin has a *numerical value.* And while the probability of the occurrence of any particular value can be readily computed, it is impossible to predict precisely which value will occur next.

These same characteristics are exhibited in a wide range of situations that are of interest to decision makers, such as the occurrence of accidents, fires, equipment breakdowns, the rate of demand for products and services, and service times. It is convenient to use an approach based on the type of random behaviour that games of chance exhibit to *simulate* behaviour of variables in these other situations because of the ease and simplicity with which randomness can be generated.

A commonly used approach for achieving randomness is **Monte Carlo Simulation,** which derives its name from its similarity to games of chance. Conceptually, this approach is analogous to placing consecutively numbered chips (0, 1, 2, . . .) in a large bowl, mixing the chips, and then drawing a chip from the bowl and recording that number. By returning the chip to the bowl and repeating the process, a series of randomly generated numbers could be obtained. However, the process would be tedious and inefficient. Moreover, there are much better ways of obtaining random numbers. For manual simulation of the sort described in this chapter, a **random number table** is very useful. Computer simulations generally rely on internally generated random numbers.

TABLE 13-1 Random Numbers

	1	2	3	4	5	6	7	8	9	10	11	12
1	18	20	84	29	91	73	64	33	15	67	54	07
2	25	19	05	64	26	41	20	09	88	40	73	34
3	73	57	80	35	04	52	81	48	57	61	29	35
4	12	48	37	09	17	63	94	08	28	78	51	23
5	54	92	27	61	58	39	25	16	10	46	87	17
6	96	40	65	75	16	49	03	82	38	33	51	20
7	23	55	93	83	02	19	67	89	80	44	99	72
8	31	96	81	65	60	93	75	64	26	90	18	59
9	45	49	70	10	13	79	32	17	98	63	30	05
10	01	78	32	17	24	54	52	44	28	50	27	68
11	41	62	57	31	90	18	24	15	43	85	31	97
12	22	07	38	72	69	66	14	85	36	71	41	58

Table 13-1 is the table of random numbers that we will use for many of the problems and examples in this chapter. It has been constructed to conform to the following characteristics when numbers are read in any order (e.g., across rows, up or down columns):

1. All numbers are equally likely
2. No patterns appear in *sequences* of numbers

The numbers are grouped in sets of two for convenience. However, they can be read in sets of one, two, three, or more as needed. The first characteristic—that the numbers are equally likely—means that if one-digit numbers are read, each number has a probability of one-tenth (there are 10 one-digit numbers, 0 through 9) of occurring at any point. Therefore, knowing that a 3 has just been read has no relevance on predicting the next number; the probability of a 3 or any other number occurring next is still 1 in 10. Similarly, the probability for any two-digit number is one-hundredth because there are one hundred two-digit numbers (00, 01, 02, . . . , 99), and the probability is one-thousandth for any three-digit number.

When we say that no patterns will appear, this means, for example, that high values won't have a tendency to follow high values or low values won't have a tendency to follow high values. In other words, it will not be possible to predict which values will occur next in a sequence of values read from the table on the basis of previous values.

The obvious question at this point is: How can random numbers be used to simulate the behaviour of a random variable? The answer lies in the way in which the random numbers are interpreted. How the numbers are interpreted is largely a function of the nature of the variable whose behaviour is to be simulated.

The essence of using random numbers is to establish a set of rules that can be used to convert the random numbers to simulated results. In general, problems will involve either *theoretical distributions* or *empirical distributions.* Hence, there will be the need to assign random numbers to outcomes that relate to a specified distribution for the random variable in question.

Simulation Using Empirical Distributions

A simulation involves the uses of empirical distributions when the values of a variable of interest are derived directly from the historical data themselves. Example 13-1 provides an illustration for a replacement parts example.

EXAMPLE 13-1

The manager of a repair shop in a large manufacturing firm had recently been informed that a new type of processing equipment would soon be installed in the plant. The manager was concerned about what level of replacement parts would be needed to maintain one vital part requiring frequent replacement. If the part was overstocked, the shop would be needlessly tying up funds and space that could be better used for other purposes. Conversely, understocking the item would have serious consequences in terms of equipment downtime while replacement parts were rush-ordered. Moreover, rush-ordered parts tend to be more costly than those that are not rush-ordered. To better understand the demands this new equipment would put on the shop's inventory, the manager decided to do a simulation analysis of potential usage for a 10-day period. Because the equipment was new, there was no historical data on usage. Nonetheless, on the basis of usage of replacement parts for a similar piece of equipment plus discussions with engineers who were familiar with the new equipment, the manager developed the following distribution for demand frequency:

Parts per Day, x	$f(x)$
0	.60
1	.25
2	.10
3	.04
4	.01
	1.00

To assign random numbers to this distribution, it is convenient to first develop the cumulative distribution. Thus:

Parts per Day, x	$f(x)$	Cumulative $f(x)$
0	.60	.60
1	.25	.85
2	.10	.95
3	.04	.99
4	.01	1.00

Because the cumulative probabilities are two-digit, it made sense to assign two-digit random number ranges because then there could be exact correspondence between the cumulative frequencies and the random numbers. The assignments for the random numbers are shown in Table 13-2. Note that the assignments begin at the low end of the distribution (i.e., demand of 0), with the smallest possible random number at that end. It will be helpful to note that after the first class, the left (lower) end of each range is equal to 1 more than the cumulative frequency (ignoring the decimal point) of the preceding class, whereas the right (upper) end of each range is equal to the cumulative probability for its class. For

TABLE 13-2 Assigning Random Numbers for the Replacement Parts Example

Demand per Day, *x*	Cumulative *f* (*x*)	Random Ranges
0	.60	01 to 60
1	.85	61 to 85
2	.95	86 to 95
3	.99	96 to 99
4	1.00	00

instance, for the second class (i.e., demand = 1), the range of two-digit random numbers that will correspond to that class is 61 to 85. Other ranges are similarly determined.

Now, daily usage of replacement parts can be simulated by obtaining a series of random numbers from Table 13-1 and, by noting in which range each random number falls, translating the numbers into number of parts demanded per simulated day. This is illustrated in Table 13-3 using two-digit random numbers from column 10 of Table 13-1.

Thus, simulated usage was 1 part on day 1, no parts on day 2, 1 part on day 3, and so on. From this, the manager could see that daily usage of spares was typically 0 or 1. Also, a simple computation would show that average daily usage was 0.60 part.

This example has a relatively small number of simulated days. As a practical matter, the number is too small to enable the manager to gain much insight into the situation. However, the purpose of the example was to illustrate the kind of results one might obtain from a simulation. Had the number of observations been larger, the manager could have learned a number of things about potential usage of replacement parts. For instance, suppose that 10 days constitutes an order cycle. The manager could have run many 10-day simulations. The resulting values could have indicated such information as the average number of parts used over a 10-day cycle as well as information on the *sequence* of daily usage (e.g., the strings of days with no usage, the occurrence of heavy usage on sequential days, and so on). This information would be helpful for establishing a reorder policy and setting stocking levels.

Moreover, we have seen how a random number table can be used in conjunction with a frequency distribution to simulate the behaviour of a random variable.

TABLE 13-3 Simulation of Replacement Parts Usage

Demand per Day, *x*	Random Number Range	Day Random Number	1 67	2 40	3 61	4 78	5 46	6 33	7 44	8 90	9 63	10 50
0	01 to 60	⟶		0			0	0	0			0
1	61 to 85	⟶	1		1	1					1	
2	86 to 95	⟶								2		
3	96 to 99											
4	00											

Although Monte Carlo simulation is relatively simple to understand and to use, it provides the manager or analyst with a powerful tool by enabling that person to study the behaviour of random variables over any desired number of periods, in a very short "real" time frame. Thus, experience can be quickly built up on paper using simulation, as opposed to going through the process of waiting that would be required if the experience were to come from observing reality.

Simulation Using a Theoretical Distribution

We have seen how frequency distributions based on historical data can be used to conduct a simulation. It is also possible to employ a theoretical distribution, such as a Poisson distribution, exponential distribution, or a normal distribution, for a simulation. In this section, use of a Poisson distribution is demonstrated; in the following section, the use of a normal distribution, an exponential distribution, and a uniform distribution are demonstrated.

EXAMPLE 13-2

Distress calls are received at a coast guard station at a rate that can be modelled using a Poisson distribution with a mean of .50 call per hour during weekends. Simulate three hours of experience.

Solution

We must first obtain cumulative Poisson probabilities for the stated mean of .50 from Appendix B Table B. Those probabilities must then be used to develop ranges for random number interpretation. Thus:

x	**Cumulative Probability**	**Number Ranges**
0	.607	001–607
1	.910	608–910
2	.986	911–986
3	.998	987–998
4	1.000	999–000

Note that the number ranges are expressed to three digits. This will make it easier to use the Poisson table, which also is expressed in three-digit numbers. Suppose we want to use numbers from columns 1 and 2 of Table 13-1. We can use the two digits from column 1 plus the first digit from column 2 to obtain a three-digit random number. Thus, reading down the top of columns 1 and 2, we would obtain these three-digit numbers:

182
251
735
124
.
.
.

To simulate three hours of calls, we can use the first three numbers. The first number, 182, falls in the range 001 to 607, so it corresponds to no calls in the first hour. Similarly, the second number, 251, falls in the same range, so it corresponds to no calls in the second hour. The third number, 735, falls in the range 608 to 910, so it corresponds to one call in the third hour. These results can be summarized as follows:

Hour	Random Number	Simulated Number of Calls
1	182	0
2	251	0
3	735	1

In each of the preceding examples, the random variable of interest was discrete: Only certain distinct values were possible. In many cases, the random variable is continuous rather than discrete: It can assume *any* value, integer or noninteger, over some range. Service time would be an example of such a variable. For example, the time to repair a piece of equipment could be 53.28 minutes.

Simulations that involve continuous variables typically are next-event simulations, or they are otherwise concerned with *how much* value (time, distance, area, etc.) a random variable assumes.

Three distributions that are commonly encountered in such simulations are the uniform distribution, the exponential distribution, and the normal distribution. The generation of random numbers based on each of these distributions is described in the following sections, beginning with the uniform distribution.

The Uniform Distribution

In the case of a continuous uniform distribution, a random variable can assume any value over a certain specified range, and all values in that range have an equal probability of being selected. For instance, suppose that service time for a particular process varies uniformly between 2 and 3 minutes. This means that any value in this range is possible, and no value is any more likely than any other.

To simulate values of such a random variable, use the following procedure:

1. Obtain a two-digit random number (RN) from Table 13-1. Place a decimal in front of it (.RN).
2. Treat the lower end of the range as *a* and the upper end of the range as *b*. Compute the simulated value using the equation:

   Simulated value $= a + .\text{RN}(b - a)$ (13-1)

3. For each simulated value, repeat steps 1 and 2.

Figure 13-2 illustrates this concept.

FIGURE 13-2 Conversion of a Random Number to a Uniform Distribution

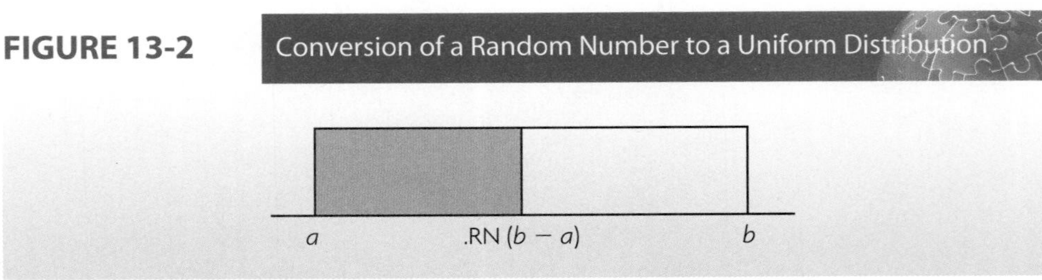

EXAMPLE 13-3

The time needed to process a job order can be modelled using a uniform distribution with endpoints of $a = 2$ minutes and $b = 5$ minutes. Simulate two processing times. Use random numbers from Table 13-1, row 3.

Solution

The random numbers are 73 and 57. The simulated times are

For 73: $2 + .73(5 - 2) = 4.19$ minutes
For 57: $2 + .57(5 - 2) = 3.71$ minutes

The Exponential Distribution

In the negative exponential distribution, the probability is relatively high that the variable will assume a small value. Moreover, the probability decreases as the value in question increases. The probability that a random variable will take on a value greater than T given that the variable can be described by an exponential distribution with mean equal to $1/\lambda$ is given by the equation

$$P(t > T) = e^{-\lambda T} \tag{13-2}$$

To simulate exponential values, we let the random number serve as this probability, $P(t > T)$, and then solve the equation for T. The result will be a simulated value from the exponential distribution with the given mean, λ. We can obtain an expression for T by taking the natural logarithm (ln) of both sides of the equation. Thus, with $P(t > T) = .\text{RN}$, we have

$$\ln(.\text{RN}) = \ln(e^{-\lambda T}) = -\lambda T$$

$$\text{Then } T = -\frac{1}{\lambda}\ln(.\text{RN}) \tag{13-3}$$

The effect of Equation 13-3 is that small random numbers produce large time values. This concept is illustrated in Figure 13-3.

FIGURE 13-3

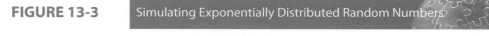

Simulating Exponentially Distributed Random Numbers

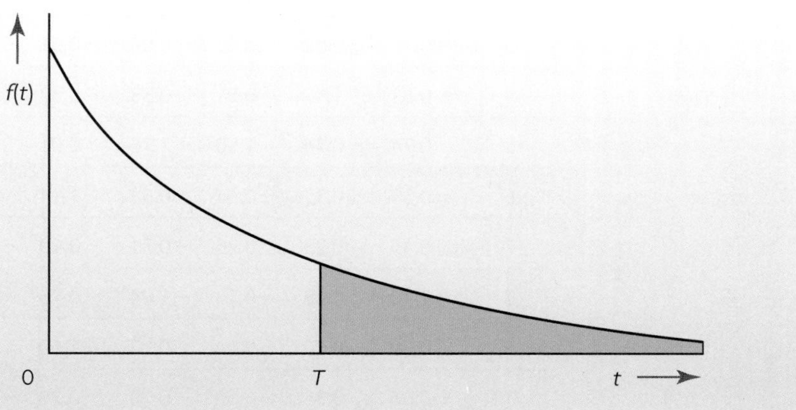

EXAMPLE 13-4

An analyst has found that the length of time needed to repair a certain type of equipment when it fails can be described by a negative exponential distribution with a mean of four hours. Simulate two repair times for this type of equipment.

Solution

$\frac{1}{\lambda} = 4$ **hours**

Suppose the two random numbers are 45 and 81. Using Equation 13-3, the simulated repair times are,

For 45: $T = -4 \ln(.45) = 3.194$ hours
For 81: $T = -4 \ln(.81) = .843$ hour

The Normal Distribution

It is not unusual to find simulation problems that involve the normal distribution. In fact, the normal distribution is probably the most frequently encountered distribution in practice. This is due, in part, not only to the fact that many natural phenomena can be well-represented by a normal distribution, but also to the fact that the normal distribution is an important theoretical distribution in statistical sampling.

There are a number of different ways to achieve random numbers that are normally distributed. For instance, such random numbers can be easily generated by computers. For hand simulations, an extremely simple approach is to use a special table of normally distributed random numbers. This approach will be demonstrated here.

Table 13-4 contains normally distributed random numbers. Numbers can be obtained from this table in essentially the same manner that we obtained random numbers from Table 13-1. Thus, numbers can be read one by one, in either rows or columns. The numbers represent z, which measures the number of standard deviations an observation is from the

TABLE 13-4 Normally Distributed Random Numbers

	1	2	3	4	5	6	7	8	9	10
1	1.46	0.09	−0.59	0.19	−0.52	−1.82	0.53	−1.12	1.36	−0.44
2	−1.05	0.58	−0.67	−0.16	1.39	−1.21	0.45	−0.62	−0.95	0.27
3	0.15	−0.02	0.41	−0.09	−0.61	−0.18	−0.63	−1.20	0.27	−0.50
4	0.81	1.87	0.51	0.33	−0.32	1.19	2.18	−2.17	1.10	0.70
5	0.74	−0.44	1.53	−1.76	0.01	0.47	0.07	0.22	−0.59	−1.03
6	−0.39	0.35	−0.37	−0.52	−1.14	0.27	−1.78	0.43	1.15	−0.31
7	0.45	0.23	0.26	−0.31	−0.19	−0.03	−0.92	0.38	−0.04	0.16
8	2.40	0.38	−0.15	−1.04	−0.76	1.12	−0.37	−0.71	−1.11	0.25
9	0.59	−0.70	−0.04	0.12	1.60	0.34	−0.05	−0.26	0.41	0.80
10	−0.06	0.83	−1.60	−0.28	0.28	−0.15	0.73	−0.13	−0.75	−1.49

FIGURE 13-4 Simulation Using Normally Distributed Random Numbers

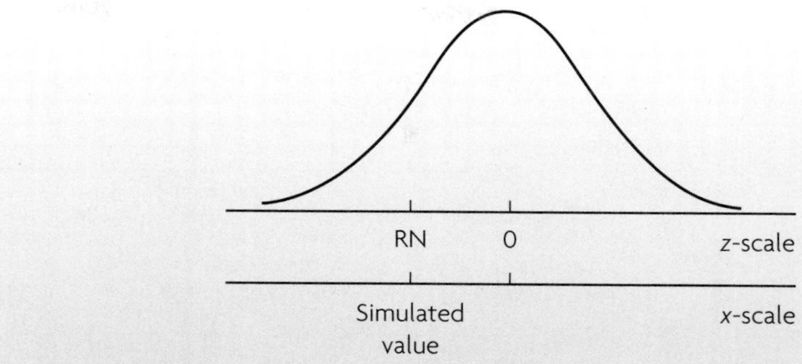

mean of the normal distribution. For example, a value of −2.13 would indicate a simulated value that is 2.13 standard deviations *below* the distribution mean. This concept is illustrated in Figure 13-4.

To determine the value of the observation, the following formula can be applied:

$$\textbf{Simulated value} = \textbf{Mean} + \textbf{RN} \times \textbf{Standard deviation} \quad (13\text{-}4)$$

EXAMPLE **13-5**

Simulate two values from a normal distribution that has a mean of 200 and a standard deviation of 10. Use the first two random numbers in column 5 of Table 13-4.

Solution

The random numbers are −0.52 and 1.39. Using Equation 13-4, the simulated values are

For −0.52: 200 − 0.52(10) = 194.8
For 1.39: 200 + 1.39(10) = 213.9

13.5 MULTIPLE-VARIABLE SIMULATIONS

The preceding examples illustrate situations in which the behaviour of a single variable is being simulated, such as the usage of parts per day, or the length of the repair time. To simulate the occurrence of an event, or the experience of one period of time (e.g., a day), in a single-variable problem, one random number is required. Single-variable examples are useful for illustrating important simulation concepts. Moreover, there are many applications of single-variable problems in real life. Nevertheless, there also are many cases in real life that involve *multiple* variables, and we now turn our attention to that class of simulations.

A multiple-variable problem has at least two variables. For example, we might want to simulate a situation in which there are a number of machines that need a variety of services

FIGURE 13-5 Two Common Types of Multiple-Variable Simulations

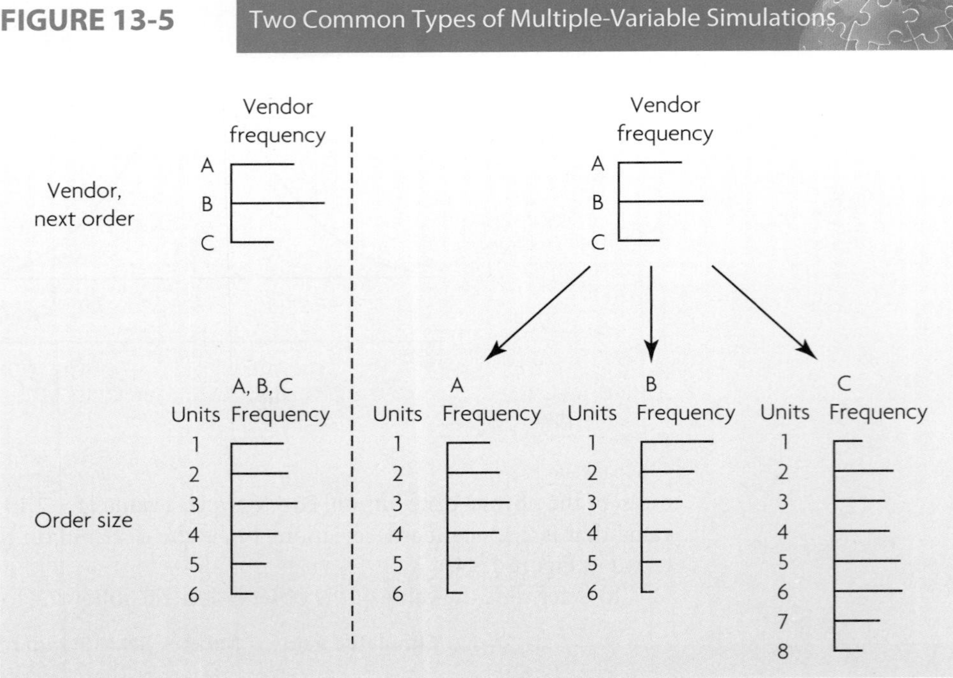

from time to time. The simulation might involve these phases: which machine needs service, what service is needed, and how much time is required to perform the service. Hence, *three* variables are involved, and *three* sets of random numbers will be needed, one to simulate each of the variables. Another example of a multiple-variable situation would be a case in which the first variable of interest was the type of job to be processed and the second was length of processing time. One set of random numbers would be needed to simulate the type of job and a second set for processing time. Such a simulation may involve two distributions, the first for the type of job and the second for length of processing time. However, if different jobs had processing times that were described by *different* frequency distributions, then simulation of the processing time would depend on which type of job was generated by the simulation of job type.

A similar situation might involve order sizes that were dependent on which vendor was ordering. Figure 13-5 presents a comparison of these two types of multiple-variable simulations.

EXAMPLE 13-6

An analyst wants to simulate ordering stock from each of three departments, A, B, and C. The percentage of orders by department is shown in the following distribution:

Department	Frequency
A	.35
B	.25
C	.40

The order sizes for these departments can be described by these frequency distributions:

A:	Order Size	Frequency	B:	Order Size	Frequency	C:	Order Size	Frequency
	10	.15		20	.20		15	.25
	15	.45		25	.25		20	.55
	20	.25		30	.30		25	.15
	25	.15		35	.15		30	.05
				40	.10			

Simulate four orders. For each order, indicate which department has placed the order and the size of the order. Read two-digit numbers from Table 13–1, column 2 for department and two-digit numbers from column 4 of the same table for order size.

Solution

The first step is to develop ranges for random number interpretations using the frequency distributions. Thus, for department we have

Department	Frequency	Cumulative Frequency	Number Range
A	.35	.35	01–35
B	.25	.60	36–60
C	.40	1.00	61–00

For order size, each department has its individual distribution,

A:	Order Size	Frequency	Cumulative Frequency	Number Range	B:	Order Size	Frequency	Cumulative Frequency	Number Range
	10	.15	.15	01–15		20	.20	.20	01–20
	15	.45	.60	16–60		25	.25	.45	21–45
	20	.25	.85	61–85		30	.30	.75	46–75
	25	.15	1.00	86–00		35	.15	.90	76–90
						40	.10	1.00	91–00

C:	Order Size	Frequency	Cumulative Frequency	Number Range
	15	.25	.25	01–25
	20	.55	.80	26–80
	25	.15	.95	81–95
	30	.05	1.00	96–00

Next, we obtain random numbers from the specified columns of Table 13-1. Using numbers from column 2 for *departments* and numbers from column 4 for *order size*, we have the following:

Order Number	RN	Simulated Department	RN	Simulated Order Size	
1	20	A	29	15	(Using Department A distribution)
2	19	A	64	20	(Using Department A distribution)
3	57	B	35	25	(Using Department B distribution)
4	48	B	09	20	(Using Department B distribution)

Thus, the first random number in column 2 is 20. Referring to the frequency distribution for departments, this corresponds to Department A. Next, the order size is found by selecting the first random number from column 4 and referring to *Department A's* frequency distribution. Hence, the interpretation of the order size random number is dependent on the department, so we must first determine (simulate) the department and then determine (simulate) order size.

Up to this point, the emphasis in this chapter has been on manual simulation. The primary reason for this is to focus on understanding the *concepts* of simulation, and a "hands on" approach is usually the best way to accomplish that goal. Nevertheless, most real-life applications of simulation involve the use of computers. To get meaningful results, a large number of runs may have to be made. Sometimes, the required number of runs can be very large, say in the hundreds. This alone would be a reason not to use manual simulation. Beyond that, however, is the fact that many applications involve a great deal of complexity because of the need to simulate the interactions of multiple stages and numerous variables. Again, this is a reason to use computer simulation. In the next sections, we will utilize Excel and Crystal Ball to demonstrate how simulations can be conducted using the computer.

13.6 COMPUTER SIMULATION USING EXCEL

The manual simulation performed in answering Example 13-6 was manageable because there were not many repetitions as there were only four orders. However, if one were to perform the same simulation for 2000 orders, the task would quickly become unmanageable. In addition, the simulation performed in Example 13-6 was relatively simple. As simulations get more complex, and as the number of runs increases, it becomes necessary to utilize the computer. In addition, for the simulation results to be valid and accepted, it is necessary that we perform many (hundreds or thousands) of repetitions. Since spreadsheets have the ability to generate random numbers from various probability distributions, they provide a convenient tool to develop spreadsheet models.

When starting to develop a simulation model, a random number generator can be used to generate random numbers. Excel uses the **RAND()** function to generate **random numbers.**

We can generate random numbers in a cell when we enter the formula = RAND(). To demonstrate this, 60 random numbers are generated in Exhibit 13-1. To do this, enter the formula = RAND() in cell A3 and copy this cell using the right mouse button to cells A3:F12. The 60 random numbers are provided in Exhibit 13-1. The function RAND() gives results in the range of 0 − 0.9999 (it never reaches 1).

However, if we attempt to duplicate the table given in Exhibit 13-1, a different set of random numbers would be generated. In fact, any changes made to the spreadsheet will result in the recalculation of the random numbers over and over again. Considering the random numbers in Exhibit 13-1, by hitting F9, one can see that all of the 60 random numbers change. Each time F9 is hit, the random number generator generates a different set of random numbers. However, if it is important to maintain the same set of random numbers, we can freeze the random numbers generated by first highlighting the range of cells to freeze, then hitting the commands **Home|Paste|Paste Special**. Clicking on Paste Special brings up another screen with various options. On this screen choosing "Values" and clicking OK in essence freezes the random numbers already generated in their

EXHIBIT 13-1 60 Random Numbers Generated by the RAND() Function

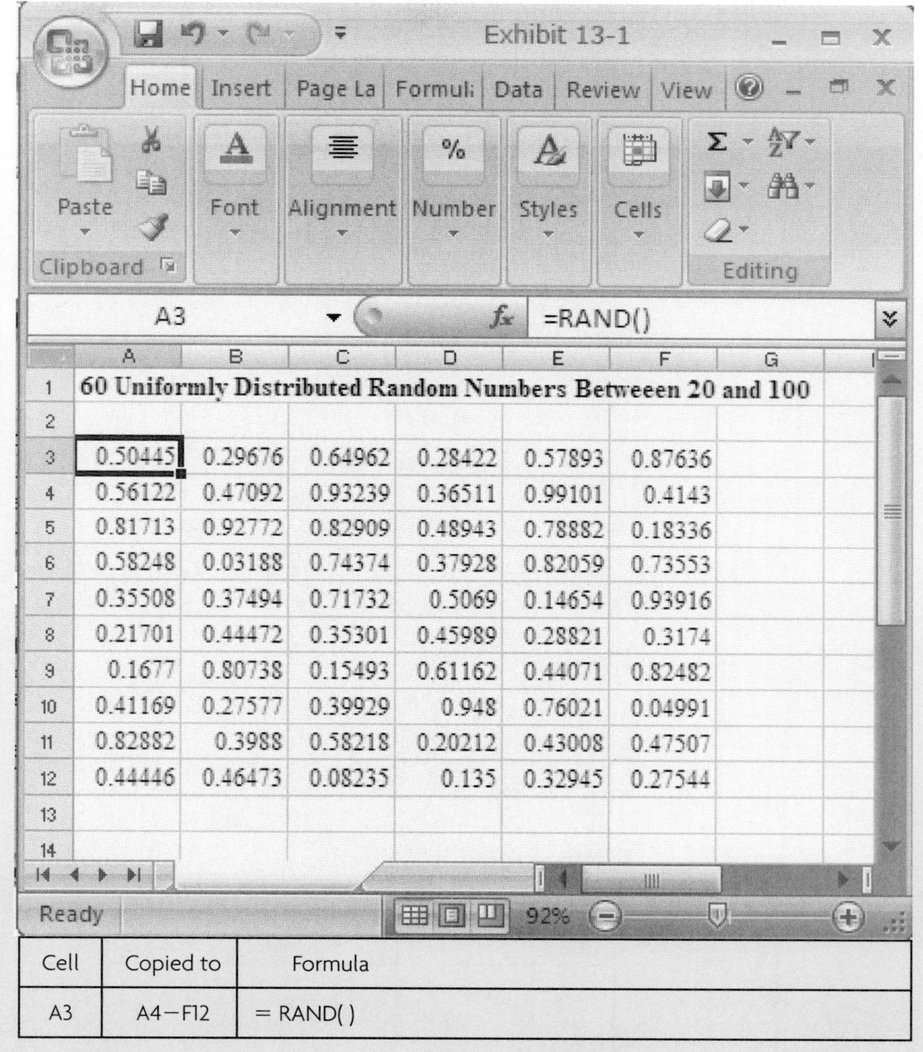

	A	B	C	D	E	F	G
1	60 Uniformly Distributed Random Numbers Betweeen 20 and 100						
2							
3	0.50445	0.29676	0.64962	0.28422	0.57893	0.87636	
4	0.56122	0.47092	0.93239	0.36511	0.99101	0.4143	
5	0.81713	0.92772	0.82909	0.48943	0.78882	0.18336	
6	0.58248	0.03188	0.74374	0.37928	0.82059	0.73553	
7	0.35508	0.37494	0.71732	0.5069	0.14654	0.93916	
8	0.21701	0.44472	0.35301	0.45989	0.28821	0.3174	
9	0.1677	0.80738	0.15493	0.61162	0.44071	0.82482	
10	0.41169	0.27577	0.39929	0.948	0.76021	0.04991	
11	0.82882	0.3988	0.58218	0.20212	0.43008	0.47507	
12	0.44446	0.46473	0.08235	0.135	0.32945	0.27544	
13							
14							

Cell	Copied to	Formula
A3	A4−F12	= RAND( )

respective cells. At this point, nothing happens to the random numbers when we hit F9 because they are frozen. Note that in Exhibit 13-1, all of the random numbers are between 0 and 1. Even though it is perfectly okay to utilize random numbers between 0 and 1, if the random numbers need to be converted to values between 0 and 100, simply use the following formula: 100*RAND(). Exhibit 13-2 demonstrates how to generate random numbers between 0 and 100. By entering the formula = 100*RAND() in cell A2 and copying this cell using the right mouse button to cells A2 : J21, the 200 random numbers between 0 and 100 in Exhibit 13.2 are generated.

For a simulation study to provide valid results, the random numbers generated must be distributed according to the uniform distribution, and the sequence of numbers cannot represent any patterns or trends.

EXHIBIT 13-2 200 Random Numbers Generated Between 0 and 100

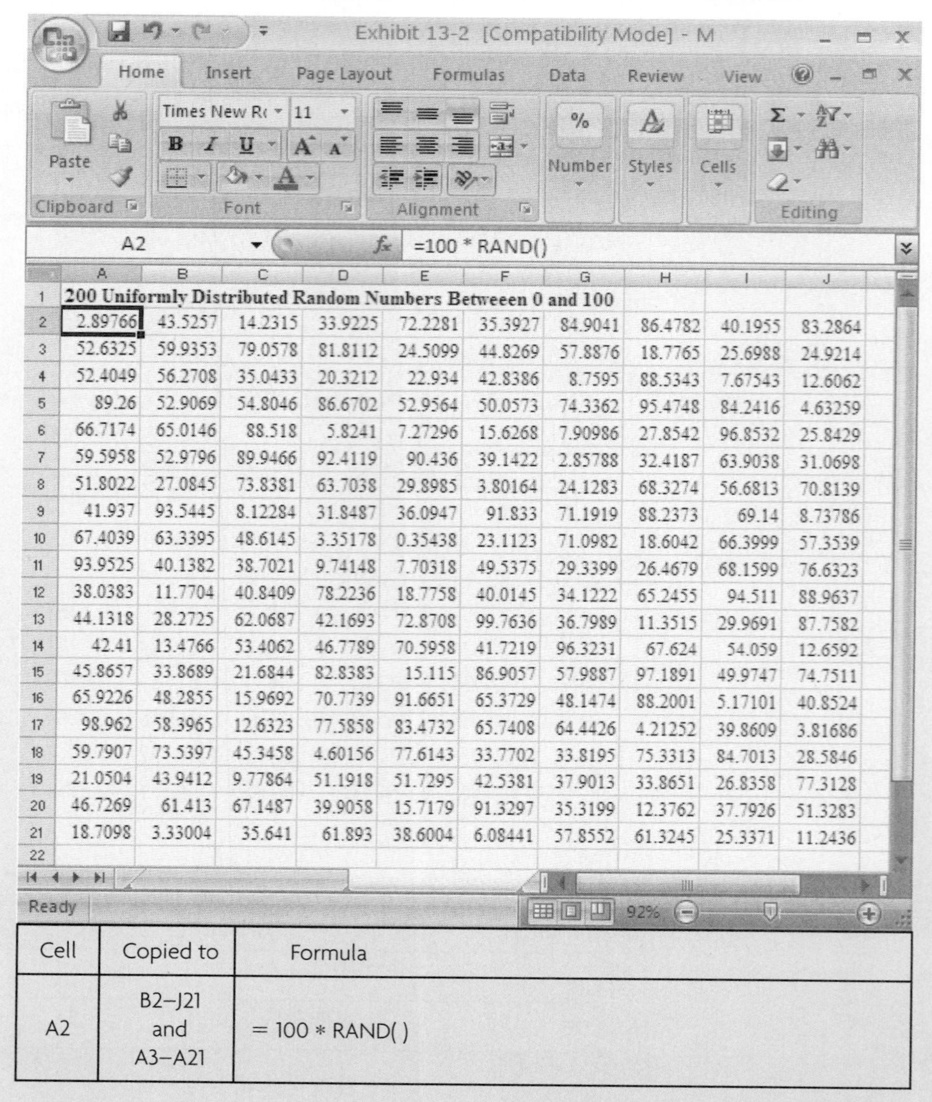

A2 | =100 * RAND()

	A	B	C	D	E	F	G	H	I	J
1	200 Uniformly Distributed Random Numbers Betweeen 0 and 100									
2	2.89766	43.5257	14.2315	33.9225	72.2281	35.3927	84.9041	86.4782	40.1955	83.2864
3	52.6325	59.9353	79.0578	81.8112	24.5099	44.8269	57.8876	18.7765	25.6988	24.9214
4	52.4049	56.2708	35.0433	20.3212	22.934	42.8386	8.7595	88.5343	7.67543	12.6062
5	89.26	52.9069	54.8046	86.6702	52.9564	50.0573	74.3362	95.4748	84.2416	4.63259
6	66.7174	65.0146	88.518	5.8241	7.27296	15.6268	7.90986	27.8542	96.8532	25.8429
7	59.5958	52.9796	89.9466	92.4119	90.436	39.1422	2.85788	32.4187	63.9038	31.0698
8	51.8022	27.0845	73.8381	63.7038	29.8985	3.80164	24.1283	68.3274	56.6813	70.8139
9	41.937	93.5445	8.12284	31.8487	36.0947	91.833	71.1919	88.2373	69.14	8.73786
10	67.4039	63.3395	48.6145	3.35178	0.35438	23.1123	71.0982	18.6042	66.3999	57.3539
11	93.9525	40.1382	38.7021	9.74148	7.70318	49.5375	29.3399	26.4679	68.1599	76.6323
12	38.0383	11.7704	40.8409	78.2236	18.7758	40.0145	34.1222	65.2455	94.511	88.9637
13	44.1318	28.2725	62.0687	42.1693	72.8708	99.7636	36.7989	11.3515	29.9691	87.7582
14	42.41	13.4766	53.4062	46.7789	70.5958	41.7219	96.3231	67.624	54.059	12.6592
15	45.8657	33.8689	21.6844	82.8383	15.115	86.9057	57.9887	97.1891	49.9747	74.7511
16	65.9226	48.2855	15.9692	70.7739	91.6651	65.3729	48.1474	88.2001	5.17101	40.8524
17	98.962	58.3965	12.6323	77.5858	83.4732	65.7408	64.4426	4.21252	39.8609	3.81686
18	59.7907	73.5397	45.3458	4.60156	77.6143	33.7702	33.8195	75.3313	84.7013	28.5846
19	21.0504	43.9412	9.77864	51.1918	51.7295	42.5381	37.9013	33.8651	26.8358	77.3128
20	46.7269	61.413	67.1487	39.9058	15.7179	91.3297	35.3199	12.3762	37.7926	51.3283
21	18.7098	3.33004	35.641	61.893	38.6004	6.08441	57.8552	61.3245	25.3371	11.2436
22										

Cell	Copied to	Formula
A2	B2–J21 and A3–A21	= 100 * RAND( )

Random Number Generation with Probability Distributions Using Excel

Uniform Distribution There are two types of uniform distributions: continuous and discrete. The formula for a variable distributed according to a continuous uniform distribution is $=c+(d-c)$*RAND(). According to this formula, the continuous uniform distribution is defined between c, the lower limit, and d, the upper limit. For example, if $c=20$ and $d=100$, the formula = 20 + (100 − 20) * RAND() will generate random numbers between 20 and 100.

The following built-in formula using Excel's **RANDBETWEEN** function is utilized for the discrete uniform distribution: =RANDBETWEEN(c,d). In other words, if $c = 20$ and $d = 100$, entering the following formula =RANDBETWEEN(20, 100) will generate discrete random numbers between 20 and 100. The outcome associated with generating these random numbers is provided in Exhibit 13-3.

To demonstrate that the values in Exhibit 13-3 indeed come from a uniform distribution, we prepare the histogram shown in Exhibit 13-5. In charting this histogram, in Exhibit 13-3 write the values of 30, 40, 50, 60, 70, 80, 90, and 100 in column L labelled "Bin," and then click on **Data|Data Analysis|Histogram.** The histogram specification screen displayed in Exhibit 13.4 will appear. On this screen, click on the Input Range and highlight all of the 200 values in cells A2 : J21. Then proceed to click on the Bin Range and highlight the values in cells L2 : L9. For example, the value in cell L2 represents all the values that are less than or equal to 30. Cell L3 will include values greater than 30 and less than or equal to 40. In terms of output options, click on "New Worksheet Ply" and "Chart Output" and click OK.

Clicking OK will show the worksheet displayed in Exhibit 13-5. The cells A2 : B9 show the frequency table where 30, 40, 50, 60, 70, 80, 90, and 100 serve as the class limits. In this

EXHIBIT 13-3 200 Uniform Discrete Random Numbers Generated Between 20 and 100

Exhibit 13-3 [Compatibility Mode] - Microsoft Excel

A2 f_x 95

	A	B	C	D	E	F	G	H	I	J	K	L
1	200 Uniformly Distributed Random Numbers Betweeen 20 and 100											Bin
2	95	55	69	35	22	34	73	27	76	39		30
3	31	23	49	35	34	67	33	37	85	34		40
4	64	71	34	65	77	25	94	80	81	29		50
5	55	54	61	55	39	47	44	46	48	44		60
6	71	77	52	93	32	41	50	69	35	27		70
7	63	29	57	89	21	74	67	67	78	46		80
8	38	35	94	98	24	58	60	31	71	32		90
9	72	73	75	55	53	40	28	75	63	52		100
10	51	23	23	41	99	44	100	77	73	25		
11	82	36	20	22	96	89	58	90	47	26		
12	88	59	85	91	32	38	27	52	93	35		
13	58	93	37	52	86	21	60	38	84	64		
14	38	39	30	60	66	87	42	26	90	40		
15	87	26	93	28	53	27	92	56	39	96		
16	27	80	53	91	96	71	63	79	24	66		
17	34	36	100	74	83	52	27	95	46	66		
18	44	51	51	93	43	88	35	33	98	51		
19	45	95	72	27	77	72	61	74	91	34		
20	87	61	49	31	50	68	46	70	52	63		
21	24	74	56	41	100	46	44	46	24	27		
22												

Exhibit 13-3

Cell	Copied to	Formula
A2	B2 J21 and A3 A21	= RANDBETWEEN (20, 100)

EXHIBIT 13-4 Histogram Specification Screen

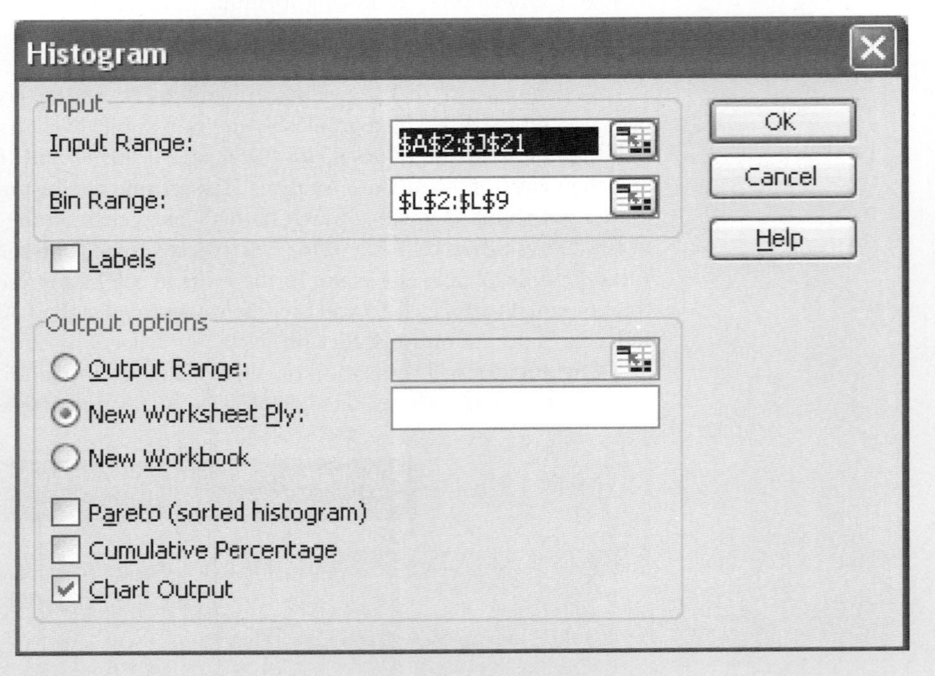

EXHIBIT 13-5 Histogram of the Values in Exhibit 13-3

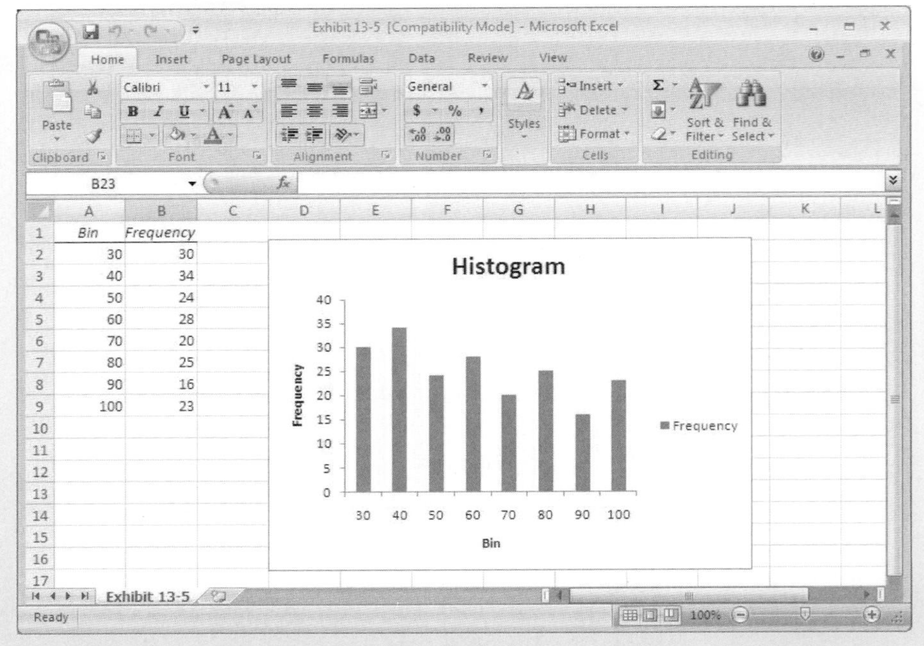

particular problem, 27 (cell B2 in Exhibit 13-5) of the 200 values fall in the range between 20 and 30. The histogram chart shown in Exhibit 13-5 verifies that the numbers in Exhibit 13-3 do come from a uniform distribution because the bars have approximately equal heights. The variation in the frequencies is as a result of random variation in the data. Collecting a larger sample will eliminate the random variation. Histograms also can be graphed to see if other distribution assumptions hold in a simulation study.

Normal Distribution The normal distribution is frequently used in simulation studies. To simulate a normally distributed random variable with two parameters, μ (mean) and σ (standard deviation), Excel's **NORMINV** function is used with the following formula: =NORMINV(RAND(), μ, σ).

If $\mu = 100$ and $\sigma = 10$, then =NORMINV(RAND(),100, 10) will generate a normally distributed random variable with a mean of 100 and a standard deviation of 10.

Exponential Distribution As illustrated in Chapter 12, the exponential distribution is commonly used in analyzing waiting lines. To generate random numbers based on an exponential distribution, one can use the following formula: $= -\mu *$ LN(RAND()), where μ the mean of the exponentially distributed random variable.

A Discrete Distribution with Two Outcomes

One can utilize Excel's IF function to separate two distinct outcomes. Consider the following example where 35 percent of the items produced need to be heat treated and 65 percent of the items do not need to be heat treated. The IF function can be utilized in one of the two following ways:

IF(RAND() <0.35,"heat treat", "no heat treat")

IF(RAND() <0.65,"no heat treat", "heat treat")

A Discrete Distribution with More Than Two Outcomes

If the number of outcomes is more than two, then a nested IF statement can be utilized. However, setting up IF statements when there are more than two outcomes is much more complicated. In this case, instead of using IF statements, we should utilize the VLOOKUP function.

EXAMPLE 13-7

The number of cars arriving at Andersen Quick Oil and Lube during the last 200 hours of operations, which uses a single waiting line, is observed to be the following:

Number of Cars Arriving	Frequency
3 or less	0
4	30
5	40
6	50
7	40
8	40
9 or more	0

Estimated revenue for car arrivals is given in the following table:

Number of Cars Arriving	Revenue
3 or less	0
4	100
5	125
6	150
7	175
8	200
9 or more	0

a. Determine the probability distribution of car arrivals.
b. Use Excel and simulate 10 hours of car arrivals and compute the average number of arrivals per hour.
c. Based on the simulated 10 hours of car arrivals, determine the estimated average revenue for the Andersen Quick Oil and Lube.

The information given in Example 13-7 is repeated in the top portion of Exhibit 13-6. The bottom portion of Exhibit 13-6 provides the simulation of 10 hours of car arrivals. In cells B10 through B19, random numbers are generated, using the RAND() command. To control the random numbers generated, one can have the random numbers generated manually. To generate the numbers manually, choose **Excel Options| Formulas| Calculation Options** and click on Manual rather than Automated. Remember, to regenerate the random numbers, one must now hit F9. If the calculation option is left on automated, then it will recalculate a new set of random numbers any time a change is made to the worksheet. Using these random numbers, utilize the **VLOOKUP** command in cells C10 through C19 to determine the number of cars arriving. To generate the number of arrivals in cells C10 through C19, do the following: First indicate the cumulative probabilities and the associated number of arrivals in cells E3 through F7. In creating the VLOOKUP formula, first state the cell where the number of arrivals will be specified, then specify the range of columns used to look up the particular value of arrivals ($E$3:$F$7). In this range, column E contains the cumulative probabilities (input column) and column F contains the number of arrivals (output column). The final statement can be stated as follows: =VLOOKUP(B10, $E$3:$F$7, 2). In this statement, the probability value in cell B10 will be compared against the cumulative probabilities in cell E3 through E7. The output value in the second column, specified as 2, will indicate the number of arrivals in the first hour. Since the first random number in cell B10 is .140, which is less than .15 in the cumulative probability column, 4 car arrivals are chosen by the VLOOKUP function. Once all of the car arrivals in cells B10:B19 are determined, we utilize the VLOOKUP function once again to determine the revenue associated with the number of arrivals. Again in this new VLOOKUP statement, the random number value in cell B10 will be compared against the cumulative probabilities in cell E3 through E7. However, instead of the output values being the number of car arrivals, the output value is the estimated revenue based on arrivals. Therefore in cells D10:D19, the revenue based on the number of car arrivals has been estimated. The statement is as follows: =VLOOKUP(B10, $E$3:$G$7, 3). Note that compared to the VLOOKUP statement written for cells C10:C19, this statement has two major differences:

EXHIBIT 13-6 Excel Worksheet and the Results Associated with the Andersen Quick Oil and Lube Example

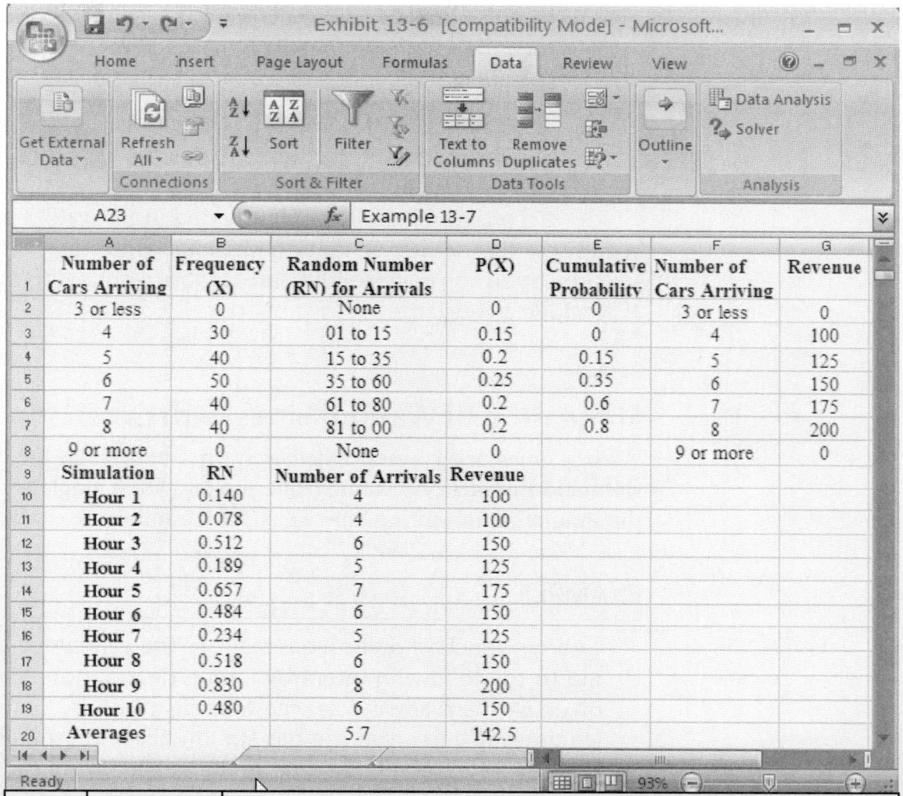

Exhibit 13-6 [Compatibility Mode] - Microsoft...

A23 Example 13-7

	A	B	C	D	E	F	G
1	Number of Cars Arriving	Frequency (X)	Random Number (RN) for Arrivals	P(X)	Cumulative Probability	Number of Cars Arriving	Revenue
2	3 or less	0	None	0	0	3 or less	0
3	4	30	01 to 15	0.15	0	4	100
4	5	40	15 to 35	0.2	0.15	5	125
5	6	50	35 to 60	0.25	0.35	6	150
6	7	40	61 to 80	0.2	0.6	7	175
7	8	40	81 to 00	0.2	0.8	8	200
8	9 or more	0	None	0		9 or more	0
9	Simulation	RN	Number of Arrivals	Revenue			
10	Hour 1	0.140	4	100			
11	Hour 2	0.078	4	100			
12	Hour 3	0.512	6	150			
13	Hour 4	0.189	5	125			
14	Hour 5	0.657	7	175			
15	Hour 6	0.484	6	150			
16	Hour 7	0.234	5	125			
17	Hour 8	0.518	6	150			
18	Hour 9	0.830	8	200			
19	Hour 10	0.480	6	150			
20	Averages		5.7	142.5			

Cell	Copied to	Formula
D2	D3 : D8	= B2 / SUM ($B$2 : $B$8)
E2		= D2
E3	E4 : E7	= D2 + E2
B10	B11 : B19	= RAND( )
C10	C11 : C19	= VLOOKUP (B10, $E$3 : $F$7, 2)
D10	D11 : D19	= VLOOKUP (B10, $E$3 : $G$7, 3)
C20		= AVERAGE (C10 : C19)
D20		= AVERAGE (D10 : D19)

1. The range of values specified is \$E\$3:\$G\$7, and not \$E\$3:\$F\$7. In other words, the additional cells G3 through G7 are specified.
2. The last observation in the statement is a value 3 instead of 2. This indicates that the output column is the third column (column G), consisting of the revenue values, instead of the second column (number of car arrivals) specified in the range of columns.

The first random number in cell B10 is .140, which is less than .15 in the cumulative probability column. Therefore, based on 4 car arrivals, a revenue value of \$100 is chosen by the VLOOKUP function.

According to the results provided in Exhibit 13-6, the average number of arrivals per hour is 5.7 and the estimated average revenue is \$142.50. For the simulation to provide valid and reliable results, this simulation study needs to include a very large number of hours.

Simulation of Waiting Lines with Excel

Waiting lines are covered extensively in Chapter 12. In this section of the chapter, a simulation model of a waiting-line model with a single server will be built. To illustrate the simulation of waiting lines, consider the following example.

EXAMPLE 13-8

George Nanchoff owns a gas station. The cars arrive at the gas station according to the following interarrival-time distribution. The time to service a car is given by the following service-time distribution. Simulate the arrival and service times of 11 cars at the gas station. Estimate the average customer waiting time, average server idle time, and average time a car spends in the system.

Interarrival Time (Minutes)	P(X)	Service Time (Minutes)	P(X)
4	.35	2	.30
7	.25	4	.40
10	.30	6	.20
20	.10	8	.10

Exhibit 13-7 demonstrates how a discrete event simulation for the waiting-line problem described in Example 13-8 can be shown. The top part of Exhibit 13-7 repeats the input information given in Example 13-8, while the bottom part of Exhibit 13-7 shows the simulation of the waiting line at the gas station. Cells A8 through D18 show the simulation of the arrivals at the gas station. Cells A8 through A18 indicate the number of people served, while cells B8 through B18 indicate the value of the random number generated using the RAND() command. Based on the random number values in cells B8:B18, use the = VLOOKUP(B8, \$C\$2:\$D\$5, 2) command. This command uses the random number value in cell B8 and looks up the value of the arrival time based on the random number in cell B8 and the cumulative probability values of interarrival times in cells C2 through C5. It assigns an interarrival time based on the cumulative probability distribution of interarrival times. For example, the value in cell B8 is .451; therefore, from the cumulative probability distribution, this value is

EXHIBIT 13-7 The Excel Worksheet for the Simulation of the Gas Station Waiting-Line Problem

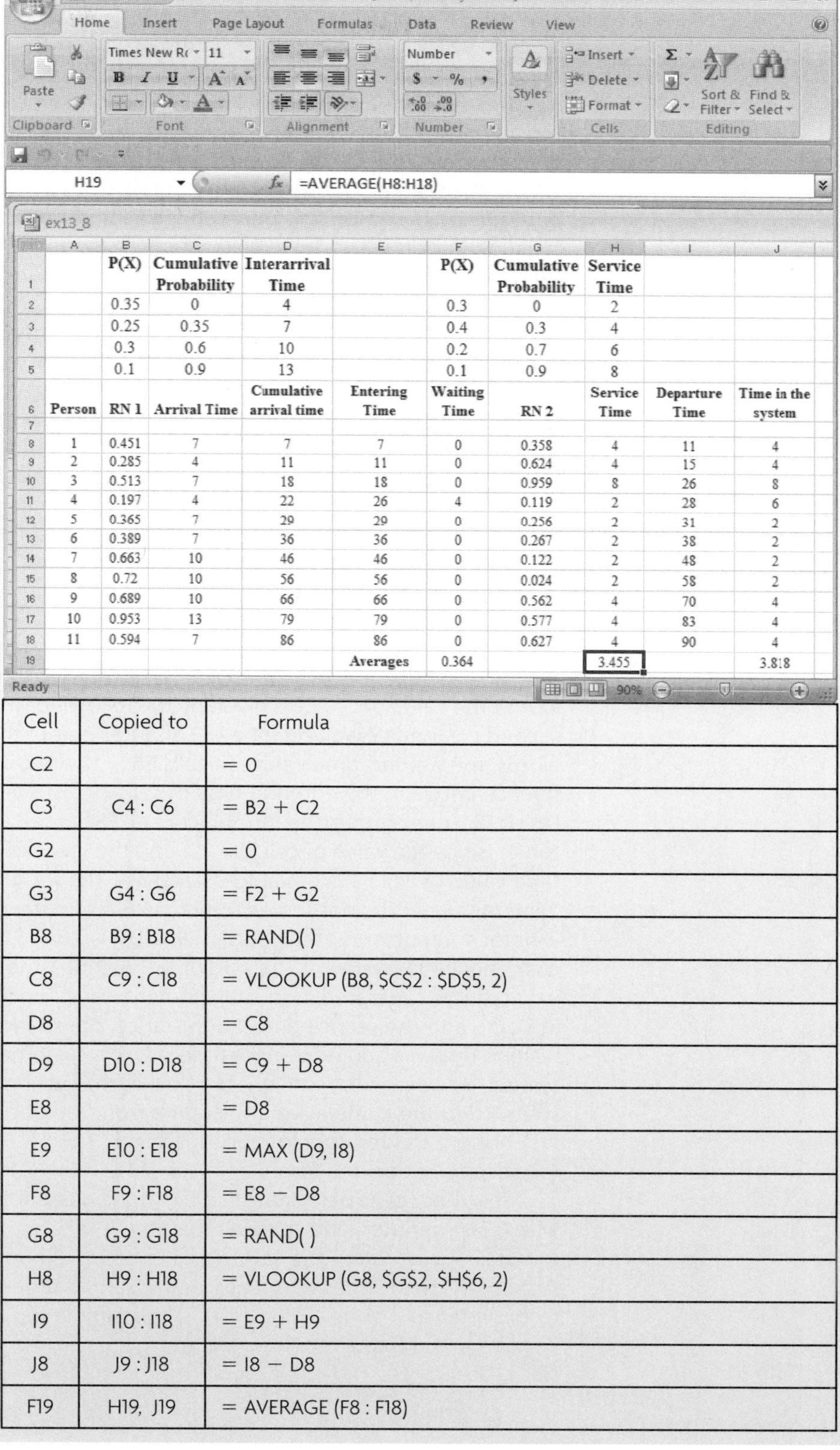

Exhibit 13-7 [Compatibility Mode] - Microsoft Excel

H19 =AVERAGE(H8:H18)

ex13_8

	A	B	C	D	E	F	G	H	I	J
1		P(X)	Cumulative Probability	Interarrival Time		P(X)	Cumulative Probability	Service Time		
2		0.35	0	4		0.3	0	2		
3		0.25	0.35	7		0.4	0.3	4		
4		0.3	0.6	10		0.2	0.7	6		
5		0.1	0.9	13		0.1	0.9	8		
6	Person	RN 1	Arrival Time	Cumulative arrival time	Entering Time	Waiting Time	RN 2	Service Time	Departure Time	Time in the system
7										
8	1	0.451	7	7	7	0	0.358	4	11	4
9	2	0.285	4	11	11	0	0.624	4	15	4
10	3	0.513	7	18	18	0	0.959	8	26	8
11	4	0.197	4	22	26	4	0.119	2	28	6
12	5	0.365	7	29	29	0	0.256	2	31	2
13	6	0.389	7	36	36	0	0.267	2	38	2
14	7	0.663	10	46	46	0	0.122	2	48	2
15	8	0.72	10	56	56	0	0.024	2	58	2
16	9	0.689	10	66	66	0	0.562	4	70	4
17	10	0.953	13	79	79	0	0.577	4	83	4
18	11	0.594	7	86	86	0	0.627	4	90	4
19					Averages	0.364		3.455		3.818

Cell	Copied to	Formula
C2		= 0
C3	C4 : C6	= B2 + C2
G2		= 0
G3	G4 : G6	= F2 + G2
B8	B9 : B18	= RAND( )
C8	C9 : C18	= VLOOKUP (B8, $C$2 : $D$5, 2)
D8		= C8
D9	D10 : D18	= C9 + D8
E8		= D8
E9	E10 : E18	= MAX (D9, I8)
F8	F9 : F18	= E8 − D8
G8	G9 : G18	= RAND( )
H8	H9 : H18	= VLOOKUP (G8, $G$2, $H$6, 2)
I9	I10 : I18	= E9 + H9
J8	J9 : J18	= I8 − D8
F19	H19, J19	= AVERAGE (F8 : F18)

greater than the cutoff value for the class whose cumulative probability values start with .35. This corresponds to an interarrival time of 7 minutes. The arrival time of each person is shown in cells D8 : D18. For example, since the first person arrived 7 minutes after the store opened up, the second person's arrival time is given in cell D9. The arrival time of the second customer is calculated by the formula = C9 + D8.

The columns E through J demonstrate the simulation of service based on the arrivals and the associated arrival times. For example, column E determines when the customer actually enters the system to be served. To determine the values in column E, we need to determine the service time. The service time is determined based on the generation of random numbers using the RAND() function in cells G8 : G18. In cells H8 : H18, the following VLOOKUP function is utilized: =VLOOKUP(G8,$G$2 : $H$5,2). This command looks up the value of the service time based on the random number in cell G8 and the cumulative probability values for service in cells G2 through G5. Then, it assigns a service time based on the cumulative probability distribution of service times. Since the VLOOKUP function designates H2 : H5 as the output column values, the remainder of the service times are looked up from the values shown in cells H2:H5. The departure times in cells I8 : I18 are calculated by adding the service times determined in cells H8 : H18 to the entering time given in cells E8 : E18. The entry time for the first customer is simply the cumulative arrival time given in cell D8. Thus, the formula for cell E8 is = D8. The departure time of the first customer in cell I8 is simply the sum of the arrival time for the first customer in cell E8 and the service time of the first customer in cell H8. Thus, the formula for the departure time of the first customer in cell I8 is = E8 + H8, or 7 + 4 = 11. The acceptance of the arrival of the second customer is the maximum value of the arrival time of the second customer and the departure time of the first customer. In other words, the value of cell E9 is given by the following formula: = MAX(D9, I8). The second customer's waiting time is 0 minutes before the service begins. In other words, the waiting-time values in cells F8 : F18 are calculated by taking the difference between the entering time in cells E8 : E18 and the arrival time in cells D8 : D18. For example, the formula for cell F8 is = E8 − D8. For the second customer, since the value of cell E9 is 11 and the value of cell D9 is 11, the waiting-time value of cell F9 is equal to 0. Likewise, the fourth customer arrives on the 22nd minute and is not served until the 26th minute; thus, this customer had to wait for 4 minutes. In other words, E9 − D9 = 26 − 22 = 4. The time spent by a customer in the system is the sum of the waiting time and the service time. This value can be calculated in several different ways. The first way is to add the waiting time and the service time. For instance, observing customer four, since the waiting time is 4 and the service time is 2, this customer spends 6 minutes in the system. However, alternatively, the time in the system also can be calculated by subtracting the cumulative arrival time from the departure time. If we use the first option, the formula for cell J11 is = F11 + H11, or 4 + 2 = 6. If we use the second option, the formula for cell J11 is I11 − D11, or 28 − 22 = 6.

Row 19 depicts basic statistics about the gas station. On average customers wait 0.364 minutes, and the average time it takes to serve a customer is 3.455 minutes. A customer (or a car) takes about 3.818 minutes (.364 + 3.455) in the system, which includes waiting as well as service times. Again, for the simulation to provide valid and reliable results, this simulation study needs to include a very large number of repetitions or a large number of customers.

Simulation of Inventory Systems with Excel

When studying inventory management, an analyst is concerned with answering two questions, (1) when to reorder and (2) how much to order. However, in traditional inventory analysis, most of the time, it is assumed that the models are deterministic. In other words, assume that demand is known with certainty and the lead time (time between placing an order and receiving that order) is fixed and known. In some circumstances, it is assumed that the demand and lead time are not known with certainty, but the demand distribution can be defined by a theoretical probability distribution. If there is no theoretical distribution (i.e., normal) that can be used to define the probability distribution of demand or lead time, simulation can be used. Even if the demand can be defined based on a theoretical probability distribution, the analysis can be very complicated and the analyst may choose to utilize simulation. The following example is used to illustrate a problem where demand is a random variable defined by the empirical probability distribution and the lead time is also a random variable defined by a discrete uniform distribution.

EXAMPLE 13-9

Golden Eagle Plumbing Company installs plumbing for new constructions and existing buildings. Over the past 400 days, the company has observed the following demand pattern for the PVC Couplings.

Daily Demand for PVC Couplings	Frequency	Probability
0	20	20/400 = .05
1	50	50/400 = .125
3	80	80/400 = .20
5	100	100/400 = .25
7	60	60/400 = .15
9	60	60/400 = .15
11	30	30/400 = .075
Totals	400	1.0

In addition, the company also observed that the lead time is distributed according to the uniform distribution, where the maximum lead time is 3 days and the minimum lead time is 1 day. The management of Golden Eagle Plumbing Company wants to identify the reorder point (ROP) and the fixed order quantity (*Q*) that will result in low monthly total cost.

The total cost has three components:

1. Cost of carrying inventory ($.50 per unit per day).
2. Cost of stockout ($15 per unit).
3. Cost of ordering ($25 per order).

Currently the company has 6 units of PVC couplings in its inventory. To get a feel for which combination of reorder point and order quantity will result in a lower cost, we simply try different combinations of order quantity and reorder points. Exhibit 13-8 illustrates the Excel worksheet that employs an order quantity of 12 and reorder point of 5 units.

The Excel worksheet in Exhibit 13-8 shows the layout for the Golden Eagle Plumbing Company inventory problem. The demand distribution is given in cells A3:C9. Other relevant information includes order quantity (cell H1), reorder point

EXHIBIT 13-8 Excel Worksheet and the Results for the Golden Eagle Plumbing Company Inventory Problem Where Quantity = 12, ROP = 5

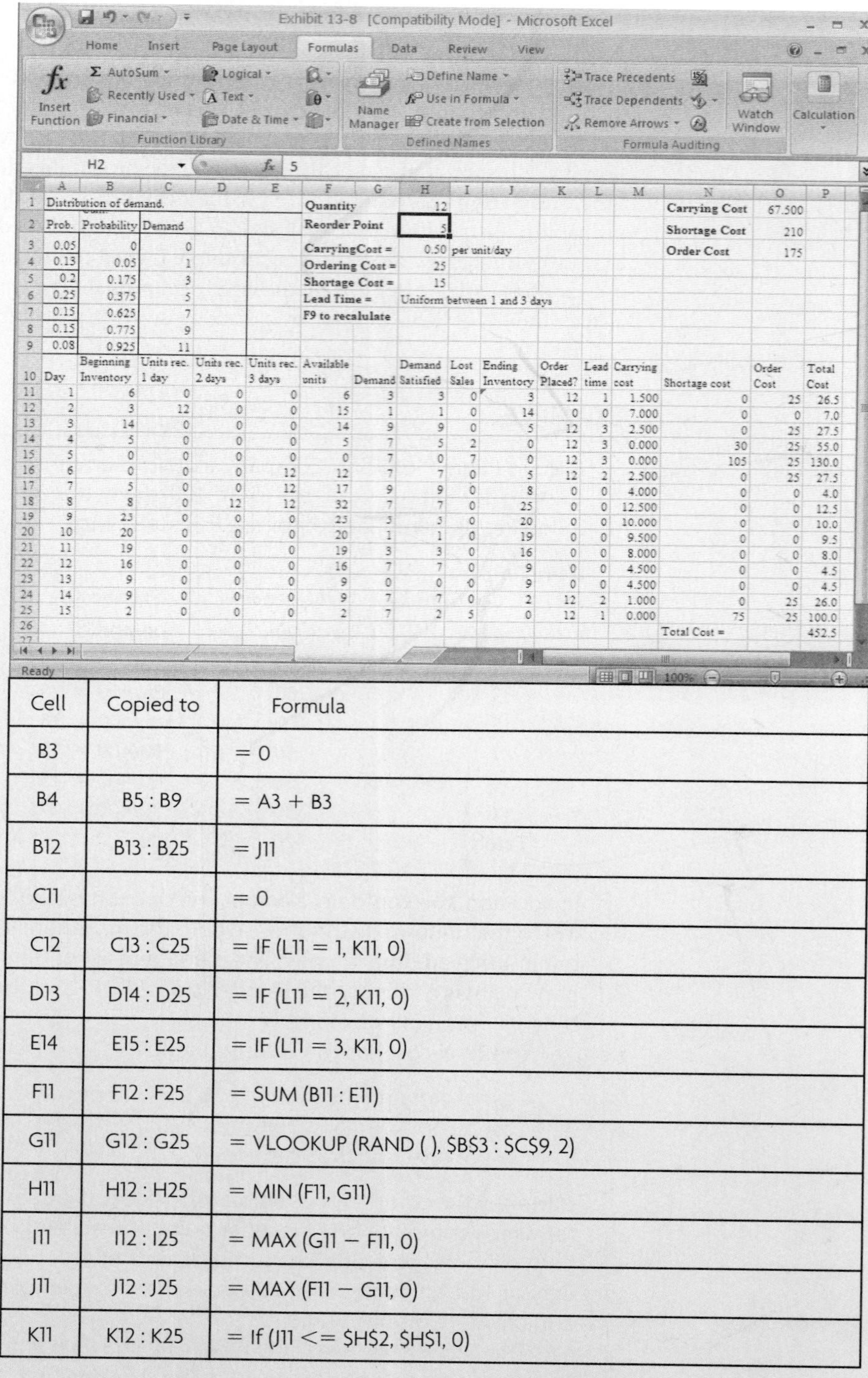

	A	B	C	D	E	F	G	H	I	J	K	L	M	N	O	P
1	Distribution of demand.					Quantity		12						Carrying Cost	67.500	
2	Prob.	Cum. Probability	Demand			Reorder Point		5						Shortage Cost	210	
3	0.05	0	0			CarryingCost =		0.50	per unit/day					Order Cost	175	
4	0.13	0.05	1			Ordering Cost =		25								
5	0.2	0.175	3			Shortage Cost =		15								
6	0.25	0.375	5			Lead Time =		Uniform between 1 and 3 days								
7	0.15	0.625	7			F9 to recalulate										
8	0.15	0.775	9													
9	0.08	0.925	11													
10	Day	Beginning Inventory	Units rec. 1 day	Units rec. 2 days	Units rec. 3 days	Available units	Demand	Demand Satisfied	Lost Sales	Ending Inventory	Order Placed?	Lead time	Carrying cost	Shortage cost	Order Cost	Total Cost
11	1	6	0	0	0	6	3	3	0	3	12	1	1.500	0	25	26.5
12	2	3	12	0	0	15	1	1	0	14	0	0	7.000	0	0	7.0
13	3	14	0	0	0	14	9	9	0	5	12	3	2.500	0	25	27.5
14	4	5	0	0	0	5	7	5	2	0	12	3	0.000	30	25	55.0
15	5	0	0	0	0	0	7	0	7	0	12	3	0.000	105	25	130.0
16	6	0	0	0	12	12	7	7	0	5	12	2	2.500	0	25	27.5
17	7	5	0	0	12	17	9	9	0	8	0	0	4.000	0	0	4.0
18	8	8	0	12	12	32	7	7	0	25	0	0	12.500	0	0	12.5
19	9	25	0	0	0	25	5	5	0	20	0	0	10.000	0	0	10.0
20	10	20	0	0	0	20	1	1	0	19	0	0	9.500	0	0	9.5
21	11	19	0	0	0	19	3	3	0	16	0	0	8.000	0	0	8.0
22	12	16	0	0	0	16	7	7	0	9	0	0	4.500	0	0	4.5
23	13	9	0	0	0	9	0	0	0	9	0	0	4.500	0	0	4.5
24	14	9	0	0	0	9	7	7	0	2	12	2	1.000	0	25	26.0
25	15	2	0	0	0	2	7	2	5	0	12	1	0.000	75	25	100.0
26														Total Cost =		452.5

Cell	Copied to	Formula
B3		= 0
B4	B5 : B9	= A3 + B3
B12	B13 : B25	= J11
C11		= 0
C12	C13 : C25	= IF (L11 = 1, K11, 0)
D13	D14 : D25	= IF (L11 = 2, K11, 0)
E14	E15 : E25	= IF (L11 = 3, K11, 0)
F11	F12 : F25	= SUM (B11 : E11)
G11	G12 : G25	= VLOOKUP (RAND ( ), $B$3 : $C$9, 2)
H11	H12 : H25	= MIN (F11, G11)
I11	I12 : I25	= MAX (G11 − F11, 0)
J11	J12 : J25	= MAX (F11 − G11, 0)
K11	K12 : K25	= If (J11 <= $H$2, $H$1, 0)

(cell H2), carrying cost per unit per year (cell H3), ordering cost (cell H4), and shortage cost per unit (cell H5). Hence, as can be observed from Exhibit 13-8, all input parameters of this model (order quantity, reorder point, carrying cost per unit per year, etc.) are stated in separate cells. All of the formulas in this simulation model utilize these cell references rather than the values associated with these parameters. To perform what-if analysis by changing the values of some of the parameters, we don't need to change the equations that involve those parameters; instead, just change the cell references stated in cells H1:H5.

In the bottom portion of Exhibit 13-8 we perform the simulation for the inventory example involving Golden Eagle Plumbing Company. Column A indicates the number for the day simulated. Column B shows the beginning inventory. In other words, the beginning inventory is the inventory at the beginning of the day. On day 1, the beginning inventory value is given. For the rest of the days, the beginning inventory is equal to the ending inventory from the day before. For example, the beginning inventory in day 2 is the ending inventory of day 1. Therefore, if the ending inventory of day 1 is 1 unit (cell J11), then the beginning inventory of day 2 is 1 unit. The equation for the beginning inventory in day 2 in cell B12 is =J11. Column C (C11:C25), column D (D11:D25), and column E (E11:E25) are dedicated to the units received. Column C is used if the lead time is one day. Column D is used if the lead time is two days. Column E is used if the lead time is three days. The lead time distribution specified in column L (L11 : L25) is as follows: = IF(K11 > 0, RANDBETWEEN(1, 3), 0). In other words, if there is an order (an order quantity value appears in column K), then use the discrete uniform distribution via the RANDBETWEEN command to generate lead time values between one day and three days. However, if the order is not present, then we simply use a lead time of 0 days. In cells C12 : C25, if the lead time is one day, then an order quantity was received from the previous day. Therefore, the formula for cell C12 is = IF(L11 = 1, K11, 0): If the lead time is one day, choose the quantity specified in cell K11. Cells K11:K25 represent the values of order quantities. However, if the lead time is not one or two or three, then no orders are received in column C. Similarly, cells D13 : D25 involve receiving orders when the lead time is two days. In cells D13 : D25, receive an order quantity from two days ago. Therefore, the formula for cell D13 is = IF(L11 = 2, K11, 0): If the lead time is two days, choose the quantity specified in K11. However, if the lead time is not two, simply do not receive any orders in column D. Repeat a similar procedure for cells E14 : E25, where these cells are dedicated to receiving orders with a lead time of three days. Therefore, the formula for cell E14 is = IF(L11 = 3, K11, 0): If the lead time is three days, choose the quantity specified in K11. However, if the lead time is not three, do not receive any orders in column E. The values in cells F11 : F25 represent the available units. The calculation of the available units is relatively easy. It involves the summation of the beginning inventory and three possible receipts: the first one for a lead time of one day, the second one for a lead time of two days, and the third one for a lead time of three days. For example, we can calculate the available units on day seven in Exhibit 13-8 as follows: =SUM(B17 : E17). Since the beginning inventory in day seven is five units and three-day lead time receipt is 12 units, the available units for day seven are calculated as follows: 5 + 0 + 0 + 12 = 17.

Column G shows the demand for each day. The demand values are generated from a general discrete probability distribution specified in cells A3 through C9. A3:A9 indicate the probability of various demand values. B3:B9 display the cumulative probabilities, and C3:C9 show the demand values. The values in cells G11 through G25 are generated using a VLOOKUP function. This function for cell G11 is as follows: = VLOOKUP(RAND(), $B$3 : $C$9 ,2). Based on the random number generated and the cumulative probabilities given in cells B3 : B9, demand values in cells G11 : G25 are generated. After determining the demand value, the next task is to determine if demand specified in cells G11:G25 are satisfied. To determine if the demand is satisfied, compare the value of demand against the value of the available units calculated in cells F11:F25. The minimum of these two values is the amount of demand satisfied. Therefore, the formula for demand satisfied in cell H11 is = MIN(F11, G11). Since the value of available inventory in cell F14 is 5 and the value of demand in cell G14 is 7, the minimum of these values is 5; therefore, five units of demand are satisfied and two units of demand are shown as a lost sale. In cases where the value of demand is greater than the value of available units, the company experiences lost sales. The lost sales are shown in cells I11:I25. The formula for lost sales in cell I11 is given by = MAX(G11 − F11, 0). In other words, the company experiences lost sales equal to the difference between demand and available units when the demand is greater than the available units. However, if the demand is less than or equal to the available units, the company does not experience any lost sales, based on the 0 at the end of the MAX statement. Finally, calculate the ending inventory value in cell J11 and copy it to cells J12:J25 as follows: = MAX(F11 − G11, 0). In determining the ending inventory value, take the difference between the available units and the demand. If the difference is negative, choose 0 (the last value in the MAX statement) as the ending inventory value. This is because when the available units are less than demand, the company actually experiences lost sales.

The formulas for the cost calculations as well as the lead time also are given at the bottom of Exhibit 13-8. The inventory carrying cost is calculated in cells M11:M25 by multiplying the inventory carrying cost per unit specified in cell H3 by the value of ending inventory in cells J11:J25. The carrying cost formula for the first day in cell M11 is = $H$3 * J11. In this formula, use absolute references for carrying cost per unit per day so that the formula can be copied to cells M12:M25. The shortage cost values are displayed in cells N11:N25. These values are calculated by multiplying the per-unit shortage cost with the lost sales values for each day. The shortage cost formula for cell N11 is = $H$5 * I11. Note that cells I11:I25 contain the number of units of lost sales and H5 is the shortage cost per unit. Again, the absolute reference values are used to enable us to copy the formula to other cells. Cells O11:O25 display the order cost values. The order cost is a fixed cost; however, it only occurs if there is an order placed during that period.

The total carrying costs, total order costs, and total shortage costs are given in cells O1, O2, and O3, respectively, as SUM functions. Overall total cost is also given in cell P26 as a SUM function. Hence, using an order quantity of 12 and a reorder point of 5 resulted in a total cost of $452.50.

We can try different combinations of order quantities and reorder points to determine which combination of order quantity and reorder point provides the lowest cost. However, due to space restrictions in Exhibit 13-8, only 15 days are simulated. To get a much better feel for the problem, it is very important to simulate many more days. For example, simulation of 360 days would give more validity and confidence regarding the results, in comparison to simulating only 15 days. Nevertheless, based on 15 days of simulation using an order quantity of 10 in cell H1 instead of 12 and a reorder point of 7 in cell H2 instead of 5 will result in a lower overall total cost of $369.50 in cell P26. Therefore, based on the limited information, an order quantity of 10 and a reorder point of 7 is preferred to an order quantity of 12 with a reorder points of 5. The question still remains as to what the best combination of order quantity and reorder point is. To answer this question, many more combinations of order quantity and reorder point must be attempted, and many more days of simulation should be used. However, one may also want to try different shortage, carrying, and ordering cost values to see how sensitive the solution is to these changes.

Simulation of Financial Applications with Excel

There are many financial applications that lend themselves to simulation because of the uncertainty of their future outcomes. Examples of applications for simulation include cash budgeting, estimating stock prices and options, investing for retirement, capital budgeting, computing rate of return of investments (e.g., acquiring a new company, building a new plant, etc.). A capital budgeting application is used in the following example to illustrate simulation with Excel.

EXAMPLE 13-10

Cerebrosoft, a small company located in Ottawa (Ontario), develops PC-based software for the multimedia sector and sells them over the World Wide Web. Two of its products generate 60 percent of the company's revenues: Audiatur and Vidcatur. Customers can download a trial version of the software, test it, and if they are satisfied with what they see, they can purchase the product (by using a password that enables them to disable the time counter in the trial version). The company is contemplating launching a new product: Brainet. The cost of developing the new product is estimated to be normally distributed with mean $95 000 and standard deviation $5000. This cost will be incurred before the startup production of the new product. In the first year of the product production, the company has estimated a fixed cost of $18 500 and a variable production cost of $10 per unit sold. For every subsequent year, these costs are adjusted by an inflation factor that is assumed to be normally distributed with mean 1.04 and standard deviation 0.002. The company has estimated the yearly demand of the product to follow a normal distribution with mean 10 000 units and standard deviation 2000 units. The initial selling price of the product has been set at $35.00 and will be increased every subsequent year by the same inflation factor. The company cost of capital is 10 percent and the tax rate is 28 percent. The company wants to develop a simulation model that can be used to evaluate the net present value of the new product development project over a period of 5 years. Raphael Alexandre, CEO, major shareholder, and founder of the company, is seeking answers to the following questions:

a. What are the mean and variance of the net present value?
b. What is the range of the possible net present values that could occur?
c. What is the 95 percent net present value confidence interval?

The Excel worksheet in Exhibit 13-9 shows the layout of the Cerebrosoft new product development problem. The input parameters of the problem are specified in cells A2:C10. The setup of the simulation model is shown in the middle portion, in rows 13–26. It corresponds to a single 5-year simulation model. The demand values in cells C13 through G13 are generated using the formula INT (NORMINV (RAND(),$B$8,$C$8)) for a normal distribution function. The inflation

EXHIBIT 13-9 Results for the Cerebrosoft New Product Development Problem

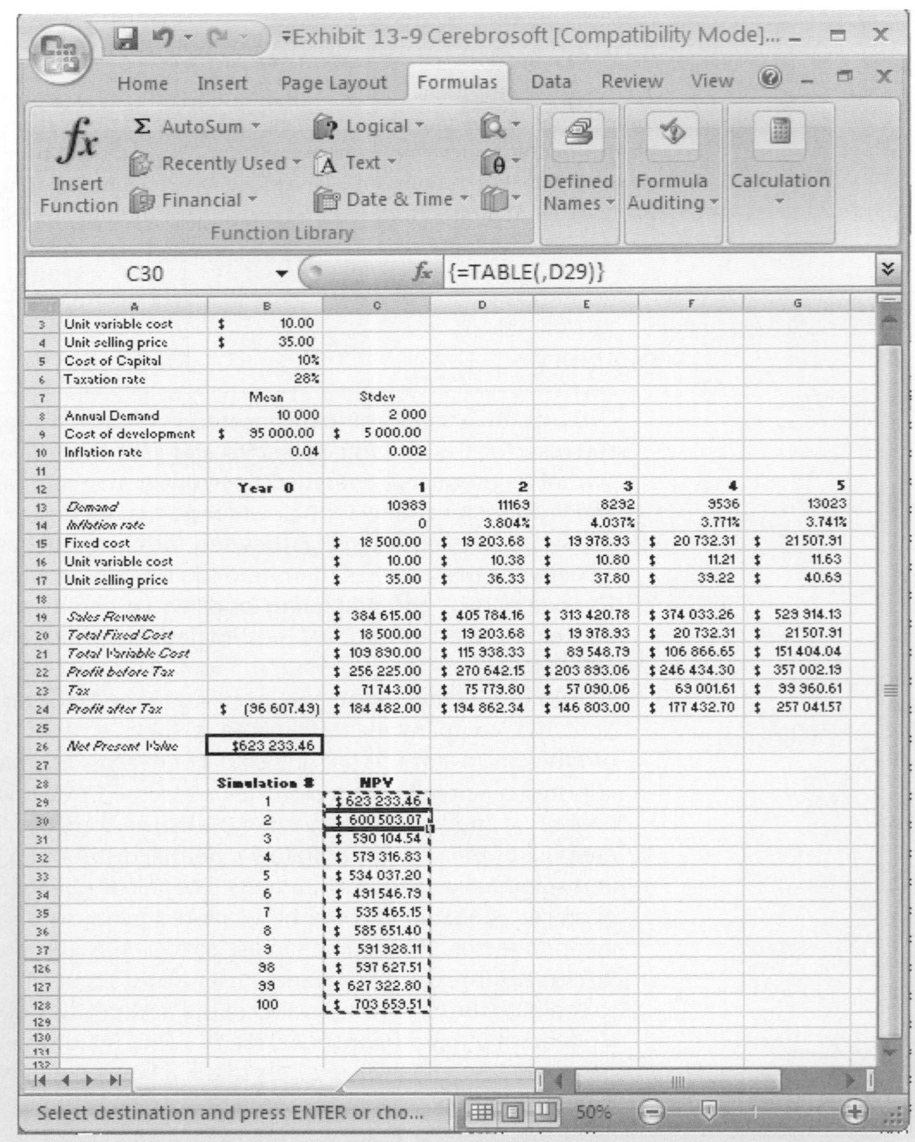

C30 {=TABLE(,D29)}

	A	B	C	D	E	F	G
3	Unit variable cost	$ 10.00					
4	Unit selling price	$ 35.00					
5	Cost of Capital	10%					
6	Taxation rate	28%					
7		Mean	Stdev				
8	Annual Demand	10 000	2 000				
9	Cost of development	$ 95 000.00	$ 5 000.00				
10	Inflation rate	0.04	0.002				
11							
12		**Year 0**	**1**	**2**	**3**	**4**	**5**
13	*Demand*		10989	11169	8292	9536	13023
14	*Inflation rate*		0	3.804%	4.037%	3.771%	3.741%
15	Fixed cost		$ 18 500.00	$ 19 203.68	$ 19 978.93	$ 20 732.31	$ 21 507.91
16	Unit variable cost		$ 10.00	$ 10.38	$ 10.80	$ 11.21	$ 11.63
17	Unit selling price		$ 35.00	$ 36.33	$ 37.80	$ 39.22	$ 40.69
18							
19	*Sales Revenue*		$ 384 615.00	$ 405 784.16	$ 313 420.78	$ 374 033.26	$ 529 914.13
20	*Total Fixed Cost*		$ 18 500.00	$ 19 203.68	$ 19 978.93	$ 20 732.31	$ 21 507.91
21	*Total Variable Cost*		$ 109 890.00	$ 115 938.33	$ 89 548.79	$ 106 866.65	$ 151 404.04
22	*Profit before Tax*		$ 256 225.00	$ 270 642.15	$ 203 893.06	$ 246 434.30	$ 357 002.19
23	*Tax*		$ 71 743.00	$ 75 779.80	$ 57 090.06	$ 69 001.61	$ 99 960.61
24	*Profit after Tax*	$ (96 607.49)	$ 184 482.00	$ 194 862.34	$ 146 803.00	$ 177 432.70	$ 257 041.57
25							
26	*Net Present Value*	$623 233.46					
27							
28		**Simulation #**	**NPV**				
29		1	$ 623 233.46				
30		2	$ 600 503.07				
31		3	$ 590 104.54				
32		4	$ 579 316.83				
33		5	$ 534 037.20				
34		6	$ 491 546.79				
35		7	$ 535 465.15				
36		8	$ 585 651.40				
37		9	$ 591 928.11				
126		98	$ 597 627.51				
127		99	$ 627 322.80				
128		100	$ 703 659.51				
129							
130							
131							
132							

Select destination and press ENTER or cho...

rate in cell C14 is initialized to 0 since this is the first year. For cells D14 through G14, the inflation rate values are generated using the NORMINV (RAND(),$B$10,$C$10) function. In the first year, the fixed cost (cell C15), the unit variable cost (cell C16), and the unit selling price (in C17), are set to their respective initial values as defined in the input parameters section. Therefore, the formula = B2 is entered in cell C15, = B3 in cell C16, and = B4 in cell C17. For the remaining years, the formula = C15 * D14 is entered in cell D15 and copied across the row to get the fixed cost values, the formula = C16 * D14 is entered in cell D16 and copied across the row to get the unit variable cost values, and the formula = C17 * D14 is entered in cell D17 and copied across the row to get the unit selling price values. The sales revenue for year 1 (in cell C19) is calculated with the formula = C13 * C17 and copied to the rest of row 19 to get the sales revenue for other years. The total fixed costs for year 1 (in C20) are calculated with the formula = C15 and copied to the rest of row 20 to get the total fixed costs for other years. The total variable costs for year 1 (in cell C21) are calculated with the formula = C13 * C16 and copied to the rest of row 21 to get the total variable costs for other years. The profit before tax for year 1 (in C22) is obtained with the formula = C19 − C20 − C21 and copied to the rest of row 22 to get the profit before tax for other years. The tax amount for year 1 (in C23) is obtained with the formula = C22 * $B$6 and copied to the rest of row 23 to get the tax amounts for other years. The profit after tax for year 1 (in C24) is obtained with the formula = C22 − C23 and copied to the rest of row 24 to get the profit after tax for other years. The cost of development in cell B24 is obtained with the formula =NORMINV (RAND (), $B$9,$C$9). The Net Present Value (NPV) in cell B26 is obtained with the formula = NPV ($B$5, C24:G24) + B24. To provide answers to the CEO's questions, we need to run the 5-year simulation model a number of times. Cells B29:C128 display the simulation results for 100 runs (some rows are hidden). The Data Table command is used as follows: (a) enter the formula =B26 in cell C29; (b) select B29:C128 and Table in the Excel Data menu; (c) enter cell D29 or any other empty cell in the column input cell box and click OK. Cells (B29–B128) contain new values representing the NPV for 100 runs.

Note that the NORMINV function, as defined above, has the RAND () function as one parameter, so the NPV values in these cells will be recalculated and new values will be obtained each time a change is made in the simulation model. To perform the problem analysis, the content of cells B29–B128 is first converted from formulas to values using in the Excel Edit menu, the Copy, Paste Special, and Values commands. This allows focusing the analysis on 100 specific NPV values, as shown in Exhibit 13-10. The uses of the built-in data analysis tool available in Excel (see **Data | Analysis**) provides some of the descriptive statistics shown in Exhibit 13-10. The estimated mean NPV is $583 019.57 and the standard deviation is $67 899.74. The range of possible NPV that could occur is between $433 107.68 and $778 068.40. How much confidence should the CEO have in the simulation outcomes? The CEO can have 95% confidence that the true mean NPV will fall between $569 711.22 and $596 327.92.

Scenario Manager

Scenario manager can be used with any spreadsheet model to compare the affect of several different combinations of parameters (scenarios) on results. The analyst can select from the menu **Data|Data Tools|What-if Analysis|Scenario Manager** to define scenarios. For instance, refer to Example 13-9.

EXHIBIT 13-10 Statistics Summary for the Cerebrosoft New Product Development Problem

Exhibit 13-10 Cerebrosoft [Compatibility Mode]

B6 f_x 623233.461801405

	A	B	C	D	E
2				*SUMMARY STATISTICS*	
3					
4				Mean	$ 585 132.39
5	**Simulation #**	**NPV**		Standard Deviation	$ 66 640.37
6	1	$ 623 233.46		Standard Error	$ 6 664.04
7	2	$ 600 503.07		Range	$ 339 864.75
8	3	$ 590 104.54		Minimum	$ 415 937.44
9	4	$ 579 316.83		Maximum	$ 755 802.18
10	5	$ 534 037.20		Count	100
11	6	$ 491 546.79			
12	7	$ 535 465.15		95% Confidence Interval	
13	8	$ 585 651.40		Lower Bound	$ 572 070.88
14	9	$ 591 928.11		Upper Bound	$ 598 193.90
103	98	$ 597 627.51			
104	99	$ 627 322.80			
105	100	$ 703 659.51			
106					

Average: $588,366.36 Count: 12 Sum: $7,060,396.37

We choose cell H1 (order quantity) and cell H2 (reorder point) as scenarios in the "changing cells" box, then we choose the appropriate names: order quantity and reorder point for cell H1 and H2 respectively. Exhibit 13-11 provides the dialogue box that shows the specification of scenarios. In this exhibit, we only show the specification of H2 (reorder point), but preparation of the scenario dialogue box for order quantity (Q) is done in a very similar way.

Since we are trying to estimate the most appropriate values of quantity and reorder point, we can try various values of Q and ROP and chose the values of ROP and Q that gives the smallest total cost (sum of the costs in cells O1, O2, and O3). Scenario Manager provides a convenient way for Excel to try different values of input parameters. For example, we can try Q = 11 and ROP = 6 in the Scenario Values screen shown in Exhibit 13-12. For both of the parameters to be considered simultaneously, we need to specify multiple cells (H1 and H2) in the Add Scenario "Changing Cells" box. Finally, from the scenario dialogue box, we click on "Summary," and then we indicate the cells that contain Q and ROP (input parameter cells of H1 and H2) and specify the cells that contain the costs as output in cell O1 (carrying cost), cell O2 (shortage cost), and cell O3 (order cost) and click OK. The model will run the simulation and generate the summary table shown in Exhibit 13-13. This summary sheet provides a simple way to easily compare different scenarios with different values given to input parameters.

EXHIBIT 13-11 
Add Scenario Dialogue Box

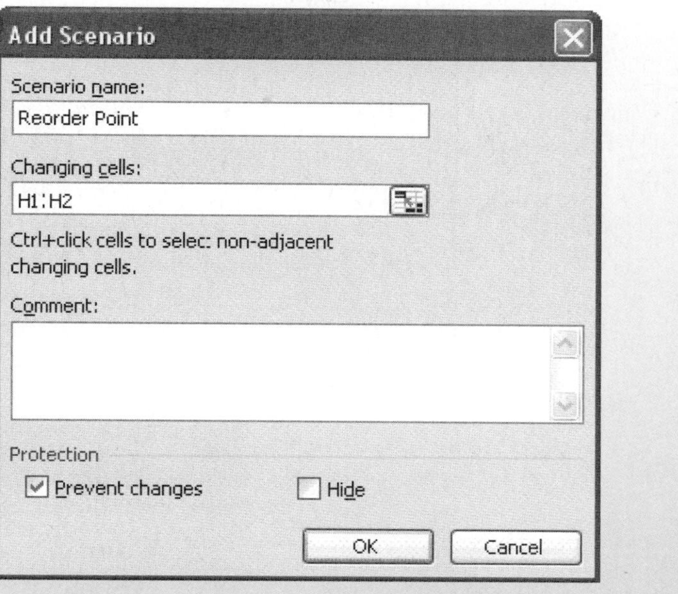

13.7 COMPUTER SIMULATION USING CRYSTAL BALL

Crystal Ball (www.crystalball.com) is an Excel add-in software package used to analyze the uncertainties in spreadsheet models. It provides many features that make its use in simulation modelling more attractive and more convenient than setting up simulation models using Excel's built-in functions. Some of the features of the software package are the variety of different probability distribution functions included; the capabilities offered to perform multiple replications of a simulation model; the ability to collect, present, and display the simulation output measures; and the capability to perform sensitivity analysis. The purpose of this section is to illustrate the uses of Crystal Ball in the Cerebrosoft new product development problem described in Example 13-10. We assume that the software has

EXHIBIT 13-12 Scenario Values

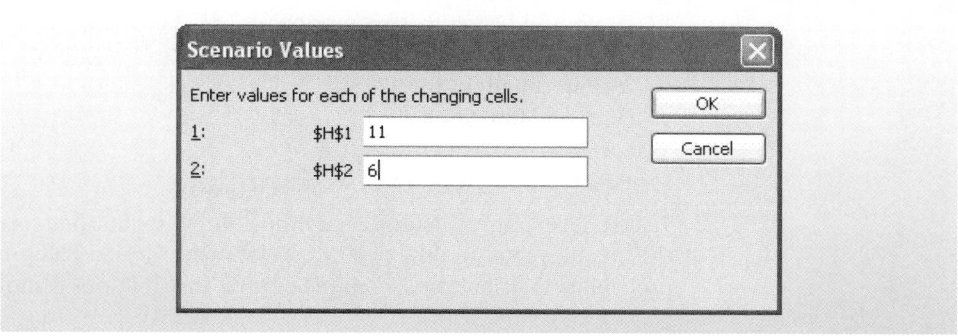

Scenario Values

Enter values for each of the changing cells.

1: $H$1 11

2: $H$2 6

OK

Cancel

EXHIBIT 13-13 Scenario Summary Table

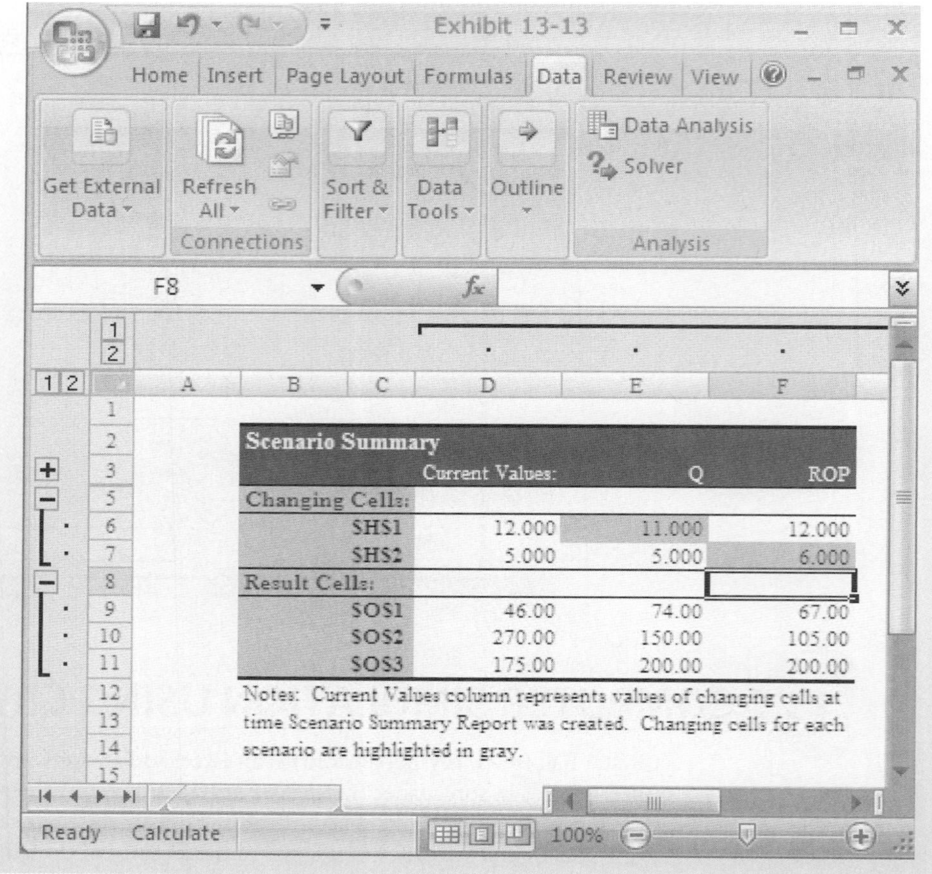

already been successfully installed and Crystal Ball is loaded in Excel. At this stage, as shown in Exhibit 13-14, the Crystal Ball toolbar and three additional menus (Define, Run, and Analyze) should be displayed in the Excel main menu bar.

The Excel worksheet in Exhibit 13-14 shows the layout of the Cerebrosoft new product development problem. The input parameters of the problem are specified in cells A2:C10. To use Crystal Ball, the following basic steps are required:

1. Define and enter the assumptions
2. Define forecasts
3. Set up run preferences
4. Run the simulation

Define and Enter the Assumptions

This step consists of defining the probability distributions corresponding to the demand, the inflation rate, and the cost of development. Crystal Ball provides a variety of 21 built-probability distributions. A sample of these distributions is shown in Exhibit 13-15.

EXHIBIT 13-14 Excel Main Menu Bar and Toolbar with Crystal Ball

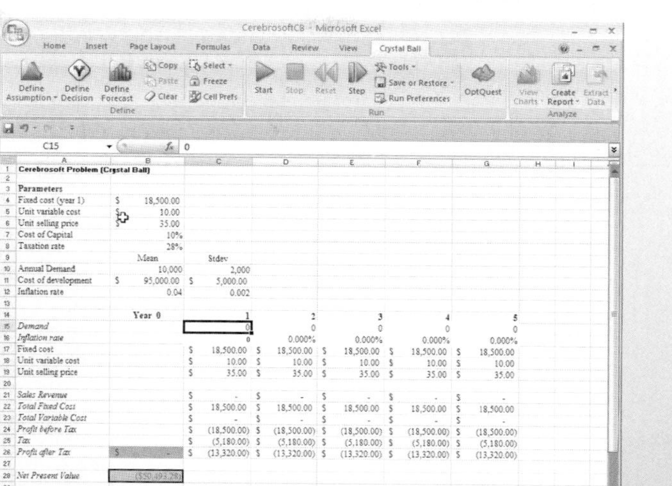

EXHIBIT 13-15 Crystal Ball Probability Distribution Gallery

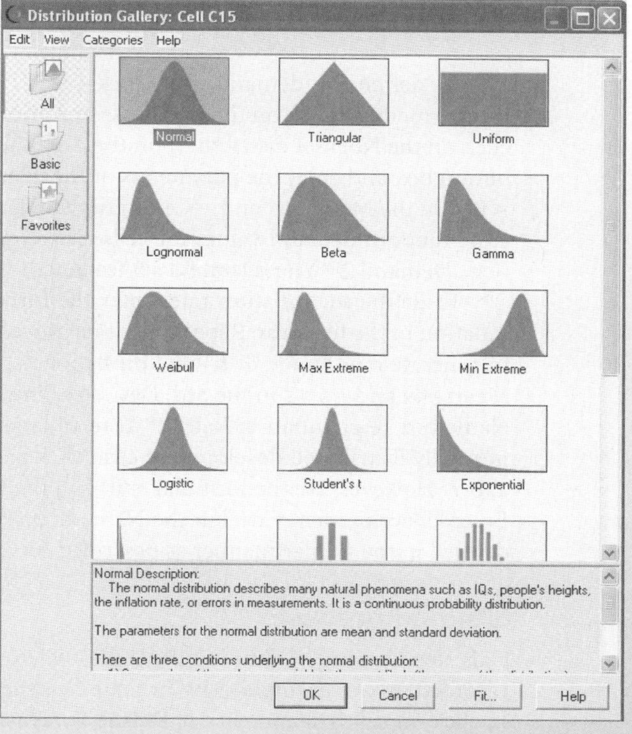

EXHIBIT 13-16 Crystal Ball Normal Distribution Box

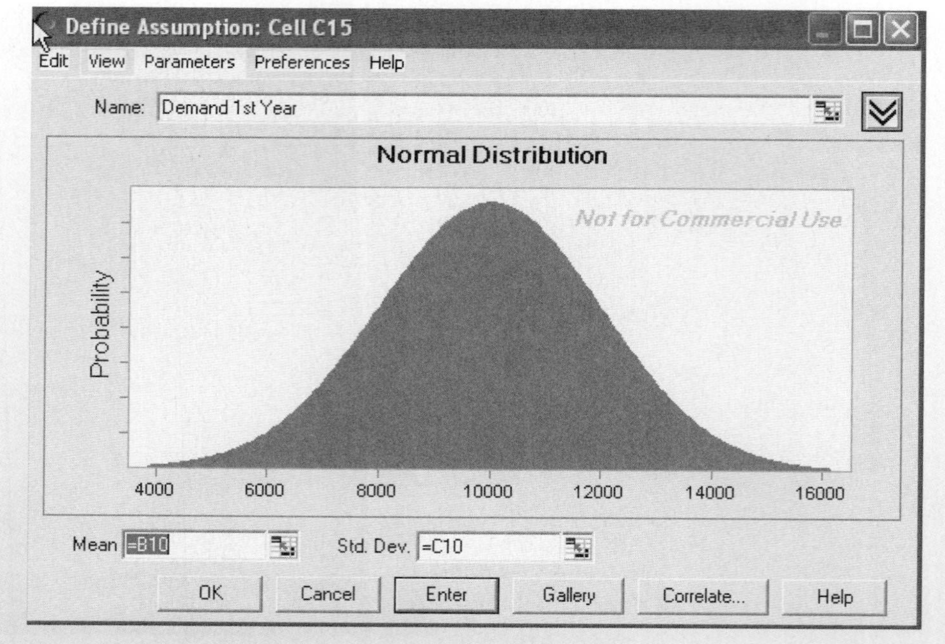

To define the demand, first click cell C15 and choose **Define Assumption** in the **Define** menu or click on the **Define Assumption** button of the CrystalBall toolbar. Double click on the **Normal** distribution in the distribution gallery to bring up the Normal distribution box and enter the parameters of the distribution as shown in Exhibit 13-16, that is, =B10 in the **Mean** box and =C10 in the **Std. Dev.** box. Repeat the same procedure to generate random demand values for cells C16–C19, but use different titles in the **Name** box (e.g., Demand 2nd Year, Demand 3rd Year, etc.).

To define the inflation rate, enter the formula 0 in cell C15 to state that there is no inflation in the first year. Repeat the same procedure described above from cells D16 to D19 to generate a normally distributed inflation rate. However, use the formulas =B12 in the **Mean** box and =C12 in the **Std. Dev.** box. The appropriate title needs to be entered in the **Name** box (e.g., Inflation Rate 2nd Year, Inflation Rate 3rd Year, etc.). Finally, to generate a normally distributed development cost, click on cell B26 and repeat the same procedure as above. However, use the formulas =B11 in the **Mean** box and = C11 in the **Std. Dev.** box. Enter "Development Cost" in the **Name** box. All the remaining cells in the worksheet are defined in the similar manner as described earlier in Example 13-9.

Define Forecast

This step consists of defining the cell(s) where the simulation output measure(s) is (are) recorded. In our example, NPV in cell B28 is the sole output measure considered. To define it, click on cell B28 and choose **Define Forecast** in the Excel **Define** menu bar or click on the **Define Forecast button** of the Crystal Ball toolbar. A dialogue box shown in Exhibit 13-17 will be opened. Enter the formula =B28 in the Units box.

EXHIBIT 13-17 Crystal Ball Define Forecast Dialogue Box

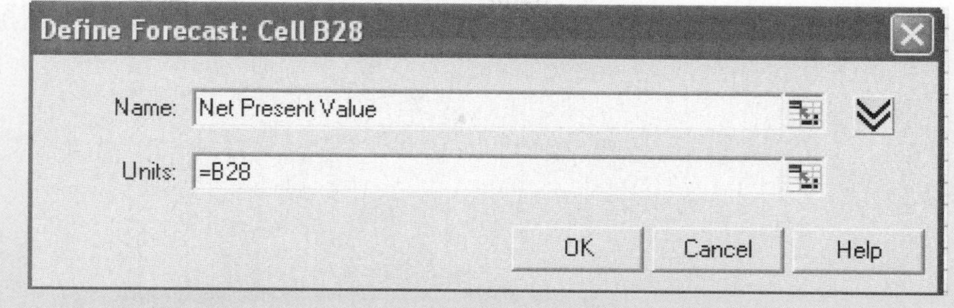

Set the Run Preferences

This step consists of defining the simulation specifications. The dialogue box shown in Exhibit 13-18 is opened when **Run Preferences** in the **Run** Excel menu bar or the Crystal Ball toolbar is selected. It contains six tabs that can be used to specify simulation preferences, such as the number of replications, the simulation speed, the sequence of random number, etc. To specify the number of simulation runs, click on the Trials tab and enter 500 in the "Number of trials to run" box.

Run the Simulation

To run the simulation, choose **Start Simulation** in the Excel Run menu bar or in the Crystal Ball toolbar. Crystal Ball provides various displays of the simulation outputs.

EXHIBIT 13-18 Crystal Ball Run Preferences Dialogue Box

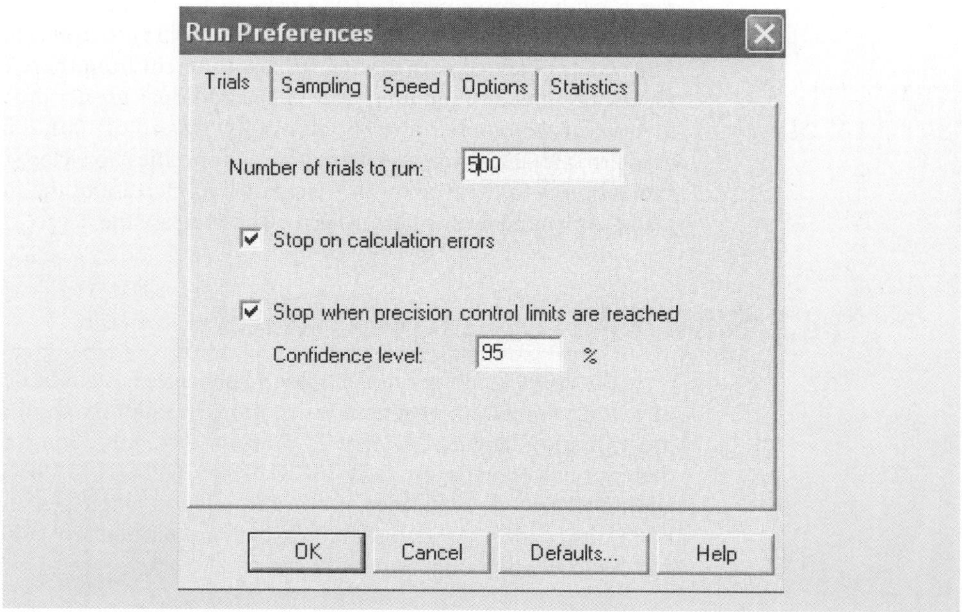

Run Preferences

Trials | Sampling | Speed | Options | Statistics

Number of trials to run: 500

Stop on calculation errors

Stop when precision control limits are reached

Confidence level: 95 %

OK Cancel Defaults... Help

EXHIBIT 13-19 Crystal Ball Sample Output Reports

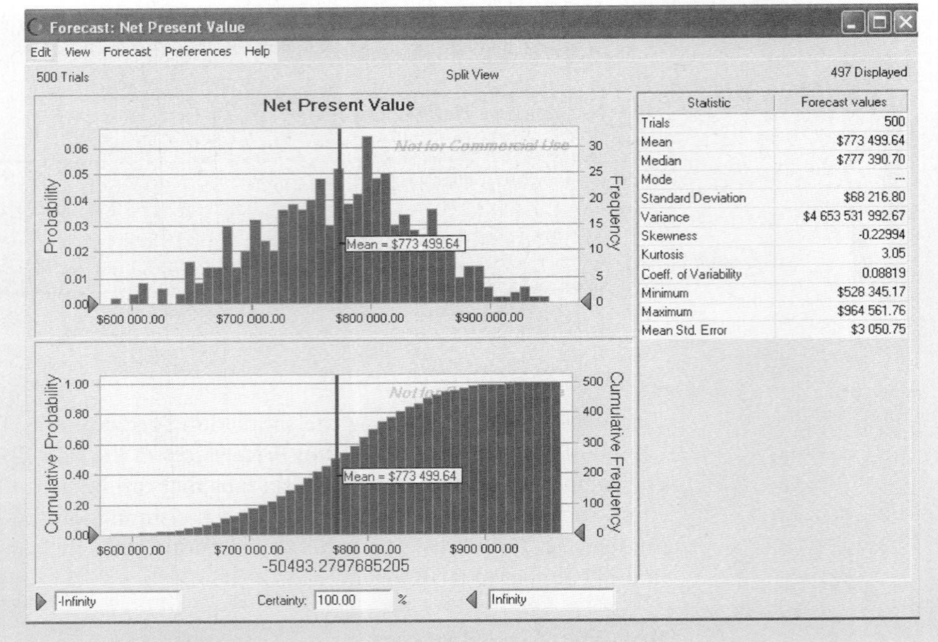

Exhibit 13-19 shows the NPV, the frequency distribution, the cumulative frequency distribution, and a summary of descriptive statistics, based on the selection in the **View** Menu of **Frequency, Cumulative Frequency, Statistics,** and **Split View.**

The estimated mean NPV is $773 499.64 and the standard deviation is $68 216.80. The range of possible NPV that could occur is between $528 345.17 and $964 561.76. How much confidence should the CEO have in the simulation outcomes? The CEO can have 95 percent confidence that the true NPV mean will fall between $767 520.17 and $779 479.11. The results obtained with Crystal Ball are different from those from Example 13-10 due to the use of different random numbers. In addition, a greater precision is obtained due to the increase of the number of replications (500 instead of 100) as indicated by the mean standard error (3050.75 versus 6399.63), which specifies how close the mean obtained with the simulation is to the true mean. Therefore, an increase in the number of trials would normally reduce the mean standard error and increase the degree of precision of the outcome.

13.8 SIMULATION LANGUAGES

Over the years, a number of simulation languages have been developed that make the task of writing simulation programs much more straightforward than working with a standard programming language such as FORTRAN or C++ . Some of the most widely used of these specialty languages are SIMSCRIPT II.5, GPSS/H, GASP, SLAM II, and DYNAMO. In addition, there are a number of other simulation languages such as ARENA, Micro Saint, Build Sim, and ProModel, some of which are particularly suited to a narrow application such as simulation of queuing systems or networks.

Most of the simulation packages have certain features in common. In general, they provide capabilities for random number generation from different statistical distributions, collection and tabulation of simulation results, time keeping, and printouts of results.

Some managers prefer to write their own simulations, or have their staff do so, using one of the standard programming languages such as FORTRAN, Pascal, or C++ rather than a simulation language. In cases where simulation is used infrequently, this approach may be practical; it may not be worth the time and effort to learn how to use a special simulation language. Conversely, if simulation is used fairly regularly to analyze problems, use of a simulation language is the expedient choice.

13.9 PSEUDO-RANDOM NUMBERS

Although computers could be programmed to read random numbers from a table of numbers that has been put into memory, such an approach would not be an efficient use of computer storage. Instead, computer codes usually incorporate a random number generator based on an algorithm that produces a string of digits that exhibit the characteristics of randomness. The resulting numbers, for all practical purposes, can be regarded as random numbers. However, they are referred to as **pseudo-random numbers** because the "next" number at any point in the series can be determined by using the same algorithm used by the computer. In that sense, the numbers are not truly random. Nevertheless, this condition does not impair the usefulness of computer-generated random numbers.

13.10 ADVANTAGES AND LIMITATIONS OF SIMULATION

Simulation has proven to be a valuable tool for exploring complex problems. Among the major advantages of simulation are the following:

1. It is particularly well-suited for problems that are difficult or impossible to solve mathematically.
2. It allows an analyst or decision maker to experiment with system behaviour in a controlled environment instead of in a real-life setting that has inherent risks.
3. It enables a decision maker to compress time to evaluate the long-term effects of various alternatives.
4. It can serve as a mode for training decision makers by enabling them to observe the behaviour of a system under different conditions.

Despite the obvious benefits of simulation, decision makers must exercise a certain amount of care in deciding when to use a simulation approach. The reasons for this are varied. Among the main reasons are the following:

1. Probabilistic simulation results are *approximations,* rather than optimal solutions.
2. Good simulations can be costly and time-consuming to develop properly; they also can be time-consuming to run, especially in cases in which a large number of trials are indicated.
3. A certain amount of expertise is required to design a good simulation, and this may not be readily available.
4. Analytical techniques may be available that can provide better answers to problems.

13.11 WHEN TO USE SIMULATION

Because of the time, effort, and cost associated with simulation studies, and because probabilistic simulations only provide approximate answers to "What if . . .?" questions, simulation is generally not the first choice of a decision maker who is faced with a problem. Instead, other approaches must first be examined; simulation may be used if other approaches are deemed inappropriate. In most instances, an intuitive solution to a problem based on judgment and experience should be considered. If that does not provide a satisfactory solution, suitable analytical techniques should be considered. If none are suitable, simulation may be a reasonable alternative. The decision maker must still weigh the costs and benefits of simulation before using that route, and be fully cognizant that simulation will not guarantee an optimal decision to a problem.

Summary

Simulation can be an important tool for managerial decision making. Unlike analytical techniques such as linear programming, simulation is not an optimizing technique. Instead, simulation is a *descriptive* tool. The goal in simulation is to create a model that will reflect the behaviour of some real-life system to be able to observe how it may behave when certain inputs or parameters are changed.

The chapter focuses on manual simulations using Monte Carlo simulation. Simulations are illustrated for both fixed-interval and next-event simulations, using a variety of discrete and continuous distributions. In addition, single-variable and multiple-variable simulations are described.

Simulation is useful for problems that are too complex to be handled by either intuitive approaches or analytical models. Simulation models enable decision makers to compress time and to observe system behaviours under a variety of different circumstances (i.e., to answer "What if . . .?" questions). However, simulations sometimes

A MODERN MANAGEMENT SCIENCE APPLICATION: LOGISTICS PLANNING AT THE DEPARTMENT OF NATIONAL DEFENCE (DND) OF CANADA

The Department of National Defence (DND) of Canada sometimes outsources mission-support services to private contractors to help alleviate strain on the Canadian Forces (CF) in areas where military expertise is less crucial. The challenge for Canadian military planners is to decide upon those missions in which to utilize private contractors, to what extent and in which capacities. A simulation model was built by Syllogix, a Montreal-based management science consulting firm, to support the logistics planning effort of the Canadian Forces. Starting with the current state of CF resources and based on historical and live operational mission data, the model simulates how the current mission requirements might evolve over time and how this, combined with future mission requests, would impact the CF's need to use private contractors to support its desired international engagements. Implemented in a commercial simulation package, and wrapped with attractive and easy-to-use input/output modalities in a spreadsheet format, the Syllogix solution comprises a complete decision-support tool that requires little-to-no modelling expertise to understand and interact with. By running a number of scenarios with different starting assumptions and analyzing the results, CF logistics planners can now answer a number of what-if questions. For instance, the planning model could be used to study how expanding the Forces over time, combined with accepting a growing mission load, might affect the use contractors over a 5-year planning horizon.

Source: "International Logistics Planning," http://www.syllogix.ca/en/Our%20Services/projects.html (February 25, 2008).

yield only approximate results, they can be costly and/or time-consuming, and they often require considerable expertise to achieve satisfactory models.

The Modern Management Science Application, "Logistic Planning at the Department of National Defence of Canada," reports a use of simulation by the Canadian Forces to analyze how its mission requirements might evolve over time and how this would impact its need for private contractors.

Glossary

Fixed-Interval Simulation A simulation in which the value of a variable is counted at the end of an interval.
Monte Carlo Simulation A method for generating random numbers that duplicates chance variability.
Next-Event Simulation A simulation in which the time or distance between event occurrences is simulated.
NORMINV An Excel function used to generate values from a normal probability distribution.
Pseudo-Random Number A random number generated by a computer based on an algorithm.
RAND() An Excel function that generates random numbers ranging from 0 to 1 from a uniform distribution.
RANDBETWEEN An Excel function that generates values between two specified values from a discrete uniform distribution.
Random Number A number typically between 0 and 1 whose value is selected at random.
Random Number Table A table of randomly distributed digits used in Monte Carlo simulations.
Simulate Use a model to obtain observations that represent the behaviour of a system.
Simulation A study of the behaviour of a system under various conditions.
Validation Checking the output of a simulation model to determine if it approximates the known or expected behaviour of its real-life counterpart.
VLOOKUP An Excel function that "looks up" values from a different location on a worksheet.

Solved Problems

Problem 1

a. Simulate the number of calls per day to a fire station for a five-day interval, given the following information that was obtained from station records. Read two-digit numbers across row 11 of Table 13-1.

Calls	Number of Days
0	21
1	15
2	12
3	9
4	3
	60

b. Use Excel to simulate the number of calls per day for a 10-day interval given the information above.

a. If the frequency (number of days) is in actual counts rather than relative frequencies (i.e., relative frequencies would add to 1.00), the frequencies must be converted to relative frequencies. To do this, divide each count by the total (e.g., 21/60 = .35, 15/60 = .25, etc.). Next, obtain the cumulative relative frequencies by successively summing the relative frequencies (see the third and fourth columns below). Then, obtain the random number range for each cumulative frequency (see the fifth column below). For example, the first range is 01 to 35. The second range is from 36 to 60, and so on.

Calls	Number of Days	Relative Frequency	Cumulative Relative Frequency	Random Number Range
0	21	.35	.35	01 to 35
1	15	.25	.60	36 to 60
2	12	.20	.80	61 to 80
3	9	.15	.95	81 to 95
4	3	.05	1.00	96 to 00
	60	1.00		

Note: If you look at the numbers on the right-hand side of the Random Number Range column, you will see that they are exactly the same as the numbers in the Cumulative Relative Frequency column (ignoring the decimal points). Therefore, it is entirely possible to omit the Random Number Range column and work directly with the cumulative frequencies when doing a simulation. For instance, looking at the Cumulative Relative Frequency column, it is easy to see that a random number such as 55 falls between 35 and 60, and so would be interpreted as one call. Similarly, the random number 62 would be interpreted as two calls.

The first random number in row 11 of Table 13-1 is 41. Comparing this to the random number ranges, we can see that it falls in the second range, which corresponds to one call. Hence, the simulated number of calls on the first day is one. The second random number is 62, which falls in the range 61 to 80. This corresponds to two calls on day 2. The third random number is 57. It falls in the range 36 to 60, which corresponds to one call on day 3. The fourth number is 31, which falls in the range 01 to 35. This corresponds to zero calls on day 4. Lastly, the fifth number is 90, which corresponds to three calls on day 5. These results can be summarized as follows:

Day	1	2	3	4	5
Random number	41	62	57	31	90
Simulated number of calls	1	2	1	0	3

b. Exhibit 13-20 shows the Excel worksheet and the associated formulas for Solved Problem 1.

Problem 2

a. Travel time to fire calls can be modelled by a normal distribution that has a mean of 6 minutes and a standard deviation of 2 minutes. Simulate travel time for three calls using values from row 2 of Table 13-1.

b. Use Excel to determine the average travel time for 10 calls.

Solution

a. The random numbers are −1.05, 0.56, and −0.67, Using Equation 13-4 shown at the bottom of Exhibit 13-21 for cells B2 : B11 we obtain the following:

Call	Random Number	Calculation		Simulated Travel Time
1	−1.05	6 − 1.05(2)	=	3.90 minutes
2	0.58	6 + 0.56(2)	=	7.12
3	−0.67	6 − 0.67(2)	=	4.66

b. Exhibit 13-21 shows the Excel worksheet and the associated formulas for Solved Problem 2. It demonstrates a problem where service times are normally distributed.

Problem 3

Multi-event Telephone company repair trucks require emergency repairs on a random basis. The company has three different types of emergencies, which it has classified as A, B, and C. They occur with these frequencies:

Type	Frequency
A	.35
B	.45
C	.20

Repair times tend to be *uniformly* distributed within these ranges:

Type	Repair Time
A	20 to 40 minutes
B	30 to 60 minutes
C	10 to 50 minutes

a. Simulate repair for five emergencies. Read two-digit numbers across row 2 of Table 13-1 for type of emergency and two-digit numbers across row 3 for repair time.

b. Use Excel to simulate 12 repairs and find the average repair time.

Solution

a. Prepare a cumulative distribution for type of emergency and establish ranges:

Type	Frequency	Cumulative Frequency	Random Number Ranges
A	.35	.35	01 to 35
B	.45	.80	36 to 80
C	.20	1.00	81 to 00
	1.00		

As specified in the question, obtain random numbers from row 2 for type of emergency and random numbers from row 3 for repair time. These result in Table 13-5.

Table 13-5 Data for Solved Problem 3

Emergency	Row 2 Random Number	Simulated Type	Row 3 Random Number	Calculation		Simulated Repair Time
1	25	A	73	20 + .73(40 − 20)	=	34.6
2	19	A	57	20 + .57(40 − 20)	=	31.4
3	05	A	80	20 + .80(40 − 20)	=	36.0
4	64	B	35	30 + .35(60 − 30)	=	40.5
5	26	A	04	20 + .04(40 − 20)	=	20.8

EXHIBIT 13-20 Excel Worksheet and the Results Associated with Solved Problem 1 (Fire Station)

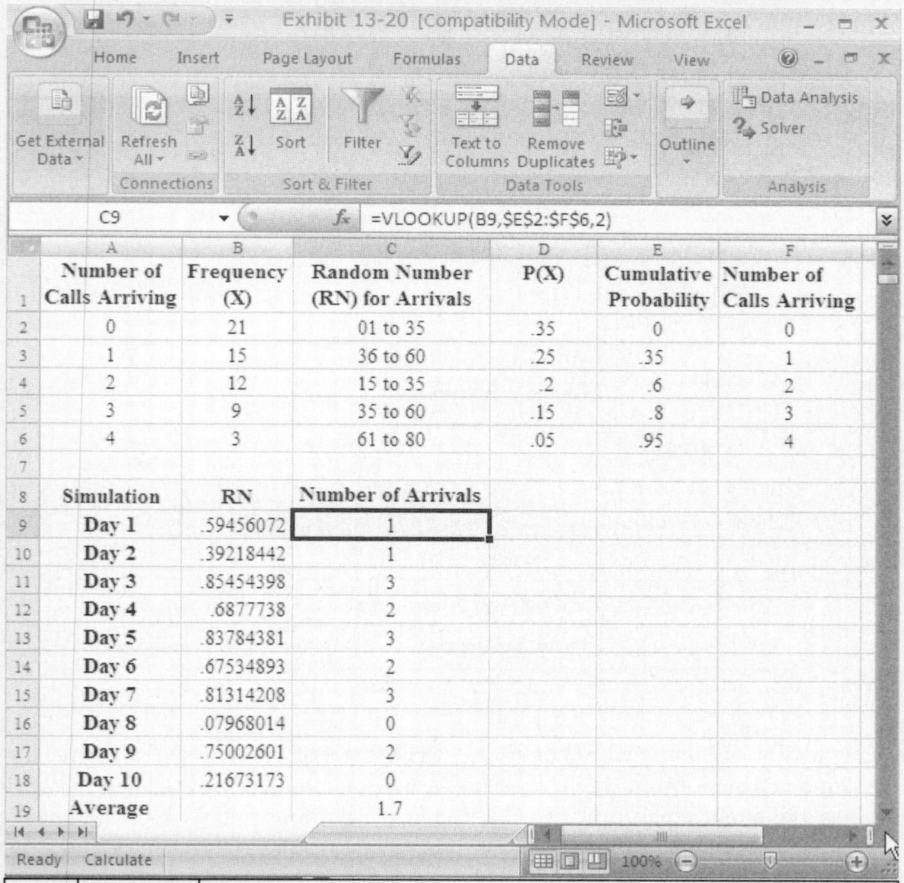

Exhibit 13-20 [Compatibility Mode] - Microsoft Excel

C9 =VLOOKUP(B9,$E$2:$F$6,2)

	A	B	C	D	E	F
1	Number of Calls Arriving	Frequency (X)	Random Number (RN) for Arrivals	P(X)	Cumulative Probability	Number of Calls Arriving
2	0	21	01 to 35	.35	0	0
3	1	15	36 to 60	.25	.35	1
4	2	12	15 to 35	.2	.6	2
5	3	9	35 to 60	.15	.8	3
6	4	3	61 to 80	.05	.95	4
7						
8	Simulation	RN	Number of Arrivals			
9	Day 1	.59456072	1			
10	Day 2	.39218442	1			
11	Day 3	.85454398	3			
12	Day 4	.6877738	2			
13	Day 5	.83784381	3			
14	Day 6	.67534893	2			
15	Day 7	.81314208	3			
16	Day 8	.07968014	0			
17	Day 9	.75002601	2			
18	Day 10	.21673173	0			
19	Average		1.7			

Cell	Copied to	Formula
E3		= D2
E4		= D3 + E3
E5		= D4 + E4
E6		= D5 + E5
D2	D3 : D6	= B2 / SUM ($B$2 : $B$6)
B9	B10 : B18	= RAND( )
C9	C10 : C18	= VLOOKUP (B9, $E$2 : $F$6, 2)
C19		= AVERAGE (C9 : C18)

EXHIBIT 13-21 Excel Worksheet and the Results Associated with Solved Problem 2

B11 f_x =NORMINV(

	A	B	C	D
1	Call Number	TRAVEL TIME		
2	Call 1	11.663		
3	Call 2	5.730		
4	Call 3	2.806		
5	Call 4	7.198		
6	Call 5	5.515		
7	Call 6	5.167		
8	Call 7	4.307		
9	Call 8	5.349		
10	Call 9	5.952		
11	Call 10	6.364		
12	Average	6.005		

Cell	Copied to	Formula
B2	B3 : B11	= NORMINV (RAND( ), 6, 2)
B12	–	= AVERAGE (B2 : B11)

Note that the calculation of simulated repair time *depends* on the simulated type of emergency; each emergency type has a different repair time distribution. In this instance, the first three simulated emergencies involved Type A, the fourth involved Type B, and the fifth involved Type A again. The A calculations are based on a uniform distribution of 20 to 40 minutes, whereas the B calculation is based on its uniform repair distribution of 30 to 60 minutes. And it happened that no Cs occurred, due to the small number of observations.

b. Exhibit 13-22 shows the Excel worksheet and the associated formulas for Solved Problem 3. This demonstrates a problem where there are multiple events. Note the nested "IF" statement in cells D6:D7.

Problem 4

A manager could use simulated repair times to schedule repair personnel and to assess the need to have backup trucks available. A consultant for a regional planning commission has developed a model for the purpose of studying population growth in a certain community. As part of the investigation, the consultant intends to simulate population growth to assess community demand for energy. The model to be used is the following:

$$P = 200\,000 + 100t + 30e$$

where

P = total population
t = year t
e = error term

EXHIBIT 13-22 Excel Worksheet and the Results Associated with Solved Problem 3 (Emergency Repairs)

Exhibit 13-22 [Compatibility ...

Home | Insert | Page Layout | Formulas | Data | Review | View

Get External Data | Refresh All | Connections | Sort & Filter | Data Tools | Outline | Data Analysis | Solver | Analysis

Get External Data | f_x =AVERAGE(D6:D17)

	A	B	C	D	E
1	Type	P(X)	Cumulative Probability	Emergency Type	
2	A	.35	0	A	
3	B	.45	.35	B	
4	C	.2	.8	C	
5	Emergency	RN 1	Emergency Type	Repair Time (uniform distr.)	
6	1	.067	A	38	
7	2	.628	B	42	
8	3	.884	C	42	
9	4	.817	C	50	
10	5	.792	B	52	
11	6	.958	C	14	
12	7	.543	B	37	
13	8	.256	A	24	
14	9	.314	A	34	
15	10	.592	B	51	
16	11	.278	A	28	
17	12	.149	A	36	
18			Average Repair Time	37.333	

Ready 100%

Cell	Copied to	Formula
C3		= B2 + C2
C4		= B3 + C3
B6	B7 : B17	= RAND( )
C6	C7 : C17	= VLOOKUP (B6, \$C\$2 : \$D\$4, 2)

D6	D7 : D17	= IF (C6 = "A," RANDBETWEEN (20, 40),
		IF (C6 = "B," RANDBETWEEN (30, 60),
		IF (C6 = "C," RANDBETWEEN (10, 50))))

D18		= AVERAGE (D6 : D17)

The error term, e, is expected to be normally distributed with a mean of zero and a standard deviation of 40. Simulate population totals for years $t = 3$ to $t = 5$, using values from column 2 of Table 13-4, reading down.

Solution

The values from Table 13-4 are

.09
.56
−.02

The first value corresponds to e to $t = 3$, the second corresponds to e for $t = 4$, and the third for e with $t = 5$. Therefore, the simulated population totals are

$$P_{t=3} = 200\,000 + 100(3) + 30[40(.09)] = 200\,408$$
$$P_{t=4} = 200\,000 + 100(4) + 30[40(.56)] = 201\,072$$
$$P_{t=5} = 200\,000 + 100(5) + 30[40(-.02)] = 200\,476$$

The planning commission could use the simulated values to project energy needs for the years covered by this study.

Problem 5

The time between mechanics' requests for tools in a large plant is normally distributed with a mean of 10 minutes and a standard deviation of 1 minute. The time to fill requests is also normal with a mean of 9 minutes per request and a standard deviation of 1 minute. Mechanics' waiting time represents a cost of \$2 per minute, and servers represent a cost of \$1 per minute.

a. Simulate arrivals for the first nine mechanic requests and their service times, and determine the mechanics' waiting time, assuming one server. Would it be economical to add another server? Explain. Use Table 13-4, column 8 for requests and column 9 for service.

b. Repeat the same analysis for 10 requests using Excel.

Solution

a. 1. Obtain random numbers and convert to times (see columns a and b in Table 13-6 for requests and columns f, g, and h for service).
2. Determine arrival times (column c) by successive adding to times between arrivals in column b.
3. Use arrival times for service start *unless service is still in progress on a previous request*. In that case, determine how long the arrival must wait (column e − column c). Column e values are the sum of starting time and service time (column g), which is the time service ends (column h). Thus, service on each new request begins (column e) at the same time that service on the previous request ends (column h).
4. The simulation and resulting waiting times for the first nine arrivals are shown in the table. Total waiting time is 8.26 minutes.
5. The total cost for the 93.64 minutes (end of service on the ninth request) of the simulation is

Waiting cost	8.26 minutes at \$2 per minute =	\$16.52
Server cost	93.64 minutes at \$1 per minute =	93.64
		\$110.16

6. Usually, a second simulation with two servers would be needed (but with the same arrival times so that the results would be comparable). However, in this case it is apparent that a second server would increase server cost by about \$93 but could not eliminate more than \$16.52 of waiting cost. Hence, the second server would not be justified.

Table 13-6 Data for Solved Problem 5

	Customer Arrivals				Service			
	(a)	(b)	(c)	(d)	(e)	(f)	(g)	(h)
Customer	Random → Number	Time between Arrivals	Cumulative Arrivals Time	(e − c) Customer Waiting Time	Service Begins	Random → Number	Service Time	(e + g) Service Ends
1	−1.12	8.88	8.88	0.00	8.88	1.36	10.36	19.24
2	−0.62	9.38	18.26	0.98	19.24	−0.05	9.05	28.29
3	−1.20	8.80	27.06	1.23	28.29	0.27	9.27	37.56
4	−2.17	7.83	34.89	2.67	37.56	1.10	10.10	47.66
5	0.22	10.22	45.11	2.55	47.66	−0.59	8.41	56.07
6	0.43	10.43	55.54	0.53	56.07	1.15	10.15	66.22
7	0.38	10.38	65.92	0.30	66.22	−0.04	8.96	75.18
8	−0.71	9.39	75.31	0.00	75.31	−1.11	7.89	83.20
9	−0.26	9.74	85.05	0.00	85.05	−0.41	8.59	93.64
				8.26				

Waiting cost (2.47 minutes) × ($2 per minute) = $4.94
Server cost (117.3 minutes) × ($1 per minute) = $117.30

Since 117.3 > 4.94, the second server is not justified.

b. Exhibit 13-23 shows the Excel worksheet and the associated formulas for Solved Problem 5. This illustrates a problem where there are multiple events that are normally distributed.

EXHIBIT 13-23 Excel Worksheet and the Results Associated with Solved Problem 5 (Mechanic)

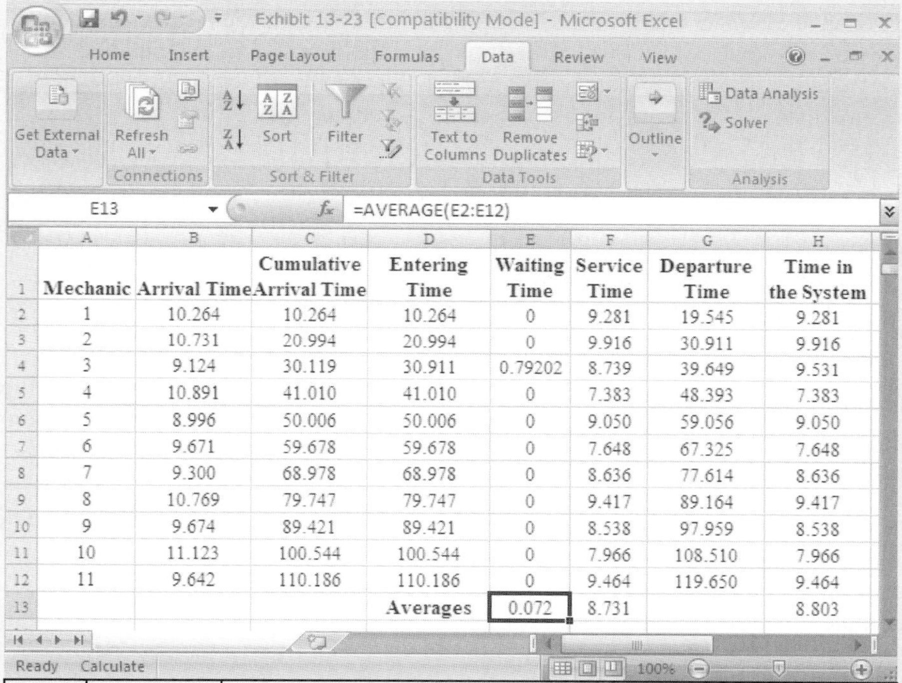

Exhibit 13-23 [Compatibility Mode] - Microsoft Excel

E13 =AVERAGE(E2:E12)

	A	B	C	D	E	F	G	H
1	Mechanic	Arrival Time	Cumulative Arrival Time	Entering Time	Waiting Time	Service Time	Departure Time	Time in the System
2	1	10.264	10.264	10.264	0	9.281	19.545	9.281
3	2	10.731	20.994	20.994	0	9.916	30.911	9.916
4	3	9.124	30.119	30.911	0.79202	8.739	39.649	9.531
5	4	10.891	41.010	41.010	0	7.383	48.393	7.383
6	5	8.996	50.006	50.006	0	9.050	59.056	9.050
7	6	9.671	59.678	59.678	0	7.648	67.325	7.648
8	7	9.300	68.978	68.978	0	8.636	77.614	8.636
9	8	10.769	79.747	79.747	0	9.417	89.164	9.417
10	9	9.674	89.421	89.421	0	8.538	97.959	8.538
11	10	11.123	100.544	100.544	0	7.966	108.510	7.966
12	11	9.642	110.186	110.186	0	9.464	119.650	9.464
13				Averages	0.072	8.731		8.803

Cell	Copied to	Formula
B2	B3 : B12	= NORMINV (RAND( ), 10, 1)
C2		= B2
C3	C4 : C12	= B3 + C2
D2		= C2
D3	D4 : D12	= MAX (C3, G2)
E2	E3 : E12	= D2 − C2
F2	F3 : F12	= NORMINV (RAND( ), 9, 1)
G2		= C2 + F2
G3	G4 : G12	= D3 + F3
H2	H3 : H12	= G2 − C2
E13	F13	= AVERAGE (E2 : E12)
H13		= AVERAGE (H2 : H12)

Discussion and Review Questions

1. What are the advantages and limitations of simulation models?
2. Describe the difference between probabilistic and deterministic simulation.
3. List two applications of simulation.
4. Describe what is meant by discrete event simulation.
5. Why is the utilization of computer software such as Excel to run a medium to large simulation study essential?
6. List the steps involved in performing simulation.
7. What are the two main characteristics of random numbers?
8. List the theoretical distributions used in simulation studies in this chapter.
9. Explain when it is appropriate to use simulation.
10. What is Monte Carlo simulation? In using the Monte Carlo approach, how is randomness achieved?
11. The final step in a simulation study is "analyzing and interpreting the results." Explain this step carefully.
12. The first step in a simulation study is "defining the problem and setting the objectives." Explain this step carefully.

Problems

(Unless otherwise specified, read random numbers *down* columns and from left to right *across* rows.)

1. Simulation has proven to be a valuable tool for decision makers over a wide range of problems.
   a. Explain what the term *simulation* means as employed in this chapter.
   b. Explain why simulation usually is the approach of last resort.
   c. What main characteristic did each of the simulation examples in this chapter possess?
2. The cumulative frequency distribution for the number of birthday cakes ordered per day at a bakery is as follows:

Number of Cakes	Cumulative Frequency
0	.01
1	.08
2	.18
3	.32
4	.51
5	.73
6	.89
7	.97
8	1.00

   a. Establish random number ranges for each possible order size.
   b. Using two-digit random numbers reading down column 9 of Table 13-1 simulate orders for a six-day period. What is the average number of orders?
   c. Simulate a second six-day period, continuing in column 9. What is the average number of orders? How different are these results than those of part *b?* Why are the results different? What is the implication of this?
3. The number of wide-screen television sets sold per day at a department store can be described by this frequency distribution:

Number of Sets	Frequency
0	.16
1	.24
2	.22
3	.15
4	.10
5	.08
6	.05

   a. Indicate how random numbers could be assigned to this distribution.
   b. Simulate the number of sets sold for a five-day period. Use random numbers from Table 13-1, row 2, and determine the average number of sets sold in five days.
   c. Repeat part *b* continuing in row 2 of the random number table.
   d. Why do the weekly averages vary? How do the totals compare to expected sales?
4. The number of typographical errors in letters typed by a certain secretary can be described by this frequency distribution:

Number of Errors per Page	Frequency
0	.75
1	.18
2	.05
3	.02

a. Indicate how random numbers could be assigned to this distribution.

b. Simulate the number of errors in four two-page letters, reading two-digit numbers from row 7 of Table 13-1. What is the average number of errors per page?

c. Based on the results of part *b*, compute the average number of errors per letter.

5. The manager of an auto service centre has compiled data on the number of cars per day that need transmission work. The numbers are repeated here:

Number of Cars	Frequency
0	6
1	14
2	18
3	10
4	2

a. Indicate how random numbers could be assigned to this distribution.

b. Simulate experience for a five-day period. Read two-digit numbers going down column 8, Table 13-1. What is the average number of cars?

6. The number of days beyond the promised date that customers leave their dry cleaning at a certain store can be summarized by these data, which were obtained from the store's records:

Days Beyond Date Promised	Frequency
0	104
1	46
2	16
3	6
4	14
5	10
6	0
7	4

Simulate the days beyond the promised date that the next seven customers leave their clothes. Use two-digit numbers from column 6 of Table 13-1, reading down. Compute the average number of days clothes are left beyond the promised date for the simulation.

7. The night manager of a resort hotel has asked the telephone operator to keep track of the nature of all calls received from outside of the hotel. The results for 100 calls are shown below:

Nature of Call	Number of Calls
R: Make a reservation	42
C: Confirm/cancel	27
A: Check availability	14
P: Price inquiry	7
O: Other	10

The manager knows that the amount of time spent by the operator in responding to the calls differs depending on the nature of the call. The manager is, therefore, particularly interested in getting an idea of the sequence of calls, to gain insight into how the operator's time might be spent with the calls. To do this, the manager wants to simulate 10 calls.

a. Keeping the list of call types in the order shown, indicate how random numbers would be assigned to each call type.

b. Reading two-digit numbers from row 8 of Table 13-1, simulate the 10 calls. What proportion of calls involve confirming or cancelling?

c. What proportion of calls involve making a reservation? Does this proportion seem reasonable? Explain why it is different than the data collected by the telephone operator.

d. Repeat parts *b* and *c* reading two-digit numbers from row 9 of Table 13-1.

8. A company that sells canoes fills orders from independent retailers from a single warehouse. The manager of the warehouse has collected data on the number of canoes sold per day. The distribution is

Number Sold	Frequency
1	.02
2	.13
3	.20
4	.25
5	.15
6	.10
7	.10
8	.05
	1.0

The same distribution holds for each day. The warehouse is open five days a week. The manager wants to simulate daily demand for four five-day periods to test the merits of beginning each week with 20 canoes on hand. Canoes are received from the factory once a week.

a. Read two-digit numbers from row 4 and then from row 5 of Table 13-1 to simulate daily demand for the four weeks. Use this format to record your results:

	Day		1	2	3	4	5
	1	RN					
		Demand					
	2	RN					
Week		Demand					
	3	RN					
		Demand					
	4	RN					
		Demand					

b. Estimate the proportion of weeks that demand will exceed supply if supply equals 20 canoes.

c. Comment on how accurate you believe your estimate is and why.

9. The managing partner of a construction firm has determined from company records that a certain piece of heavy equipment has a breakdown frequency that can be described by a Poisson distribution with a mean of 2 per month.

   a. Simulate one year of breakdown experience for this equipment. Read three-digit numbers from columns 2 and 3 of Table 13-1 (e.g., 208, 190, . . .). What is the average number of breakdowns per year?

   b. How many months experienced no breakdowns? Does this result seem reasonable? Explain.

   c. There are no instances where there were two months in a row without a breakdown. How plausible is this? Explain.

10. The fire chief in a certain city has been told by a consultant that the occurrence of three-alarm fires can be described by a Poisson distribution that has a mean of .4 fires per day. The chief is concerned because it requires approximately two days after fighting a major fire to return equipment to good working order, and she wonders if additional equipment should be requested from the planning board. The consultant has suggested a simulation study of the problem.

    a. Simulate 24 days of experience using columns 10 and 11 of Table 13-1 (e.g., 675, 407. . . .) for the first 12 days and columns 11 and 12 (e.g., 540, 733, . . .) for the second 12 days. What is the average number of fires in 24 days?

    b. For each fire, determine if there was adequate time to prepare the equipment for the next fire.

    c. Determine the proportion of fires for which there was not sufficient time to prepare for the next fire.

11. Demand for pineapple juice at a theme park can be described by a uniform distribution that ranges between 50 and 130 gallons per day. Simulate daily demand for pineapple juice for 10 consecutive days. Read two-digit random numbers from column 5 of Table 13-1. For what proportion of days is simulated demand greater than expected demand? Does this seem reasonable? Explain.

12. The amount of insecticide dispensed by a crop duster has been found to vary uniformly between 60 and 80 gallons per run. Simulate 12 runs reading two-digit random numbers from row 6 of Table 13-1. Determine the average gallons of insecticide for the 12 runs.

13. A design engineer has estimated that the time to perform a service using state-of-the-art equipment will vary uniformly between five and seven minutes. Simulate service times for eight requests using two-digit random numbers from column 9 of Table 13-1. What is the average time to perform the service for the eight requests?

14. After reviewing processing times, the manager of a computer service agrees that computer processing times for a certain class of jobs can be described by a negative exponential distribution with a mean of 1.2 minutes of CPU. Using two-digit numbers from row 3 of Table 13-1, simulate the processing times for the next 10 jobs. Then, compute the mean processing time for the simulated jobs. Explain why it does not equal the distribution mean.

15. The manager of a shop that repairs telephone equipment has determined that repair time can be modelled by a negative exponential distribution with a mean repair time of one hour. Simulate repair times for a sequence of seven jobs, using two-digit numbers from column 4 of Table 13-1. Then, compute the mean repair time for the simulated jobs.

16. In a study of the length of telephone calls, an analyst found that account representatives in a stockbroker's office spent an average of five minutes per call, and that

call length could be modelled using a negative exponential distribution with that mean. Using Table 13-1, row 6, simulate the time for 12 calls. Compute the mean simulated time and compare it to the theoretical mean. Does the difference seem reasonable?

17. A consultant found that the time a doctor spent with a patient who was recovering from major surgery could be modelled by a normal distribution with a mean of 7 minutes and a standard deviation of 2 minutes. Simulate the times doctors might spend with a sequence of five patients using random numbers from row 2 of Table 13-4. Then compute the mean time a doctor spends with a patient.

18. The time it takes a typist to type a letter in a certain office can be modelled by a normal distribution that has a mean of 4 minutes and a standard deviation of 1 minute. Using values from column 2 of Table 13-4, simulate the times for six letters and then determine the total time required to type those six letters.

19. After careful study of operating room procedures, an analyst concluded that the amount of time required to perform a certain type of surgery could be modelled using a normal distribution with a mean of 120 minutes and a standard deviation of 10 minutes. The analyst wants to simulate times for nine operations. Using random numbers for column 4 of Table 13-4, simulate the times for the nine operations. Compare the average simulated time with the model average. How do they compare?

20. On the basis of historical data, a manager concluded that the length of time between failures for a certain piece of food-processing equipment could be modelled by an exponential distribution that has a mean of 8 hours. In addition, the manager found that repair times could be modelled by a normal distribution with a mean of 4 hours and a standard deviation of 1.1 hours. For the next five breakdowns, simulate the length of time between breakdowns and the time needed for repairs. Then, find the waiting time for each breakdown (i.e., the length of time equipment waited for repair because the repairperson was busy working on a previous breakdown). Read values from Table 13-1, row 3 for breakdowns and values from Table 13-4, column 6 for repair times. For each breakdown, indicate operating time before breakdown, waiting time, and repair time. What are the average waiting time and repair time for the simulated five breakdowns?

21. A small supplier receives orders from three different companies for a certain piece of electrical equipment. Forty-five percent of the orders come from firm A, 35 percent from firm B, and the remainder from firm C. Order sizes vary, depending on the firm involved. In the past, orders were as follows:

	Relative Frequency		
Order Size	**A**	**B**	**C**
4	.15	.05	.25
8	.30	.25	.35
12	.40	.35	.25
16	.13	.25	.12
20	.02	.10	.03

Using two-digit numbers from rows 5 and 6 of Table 13-1, simulate the next six orders: For each order, determine which firm ordered (row 5), then the size of the order (row 6). How many of the six simulated orders come from each firm? What is the average order size for time six simulated orders?

22. A firm that replaces windshields receives from 0 to 4 calls per day for a midsized windshield that fits GM cars. The manager of the firm has compiled a frequency distribution for such calls and a distribution of replacement times. The daughter of a friend is currently enrolled in a business program. She examined the replacement time distribution and concluded that a normal distribution with a mean of 1.30 hours and a standard deviation of .20 hour would adequately describe the situation. The distribution of calls for the windshields is

Calls	Frequency
0	7
1	10
2	15
3	10
4	8

Simulate four days' worth of experience. Read two-digit numbers from Table 13-1, column 4 for calls, and values from Table 13-4, column 4 for times for each call. Determine the average time per day for replacements of this type.

23. A recent graduate of a prominent university's business school encounters six traffic lights on the way to work in the morning. The traffic lights have a two-minute cycle: red for one minute and yellow/green for one minute. This person stops only for a red light. Assume the lights operate independently of each other.

    a. What is the probability that any particular light will be red when the motorist in this problem approaches it?

b. What probability distribution—normal, exponential, or uniform—would best describe the length of time the motorist would have to wait for a red light? What are the parameters of the distribution?
c. Simulate four trips for this motorist. For each light's colour, use two-digit numbers from Table 13-1, columns 5 and 6. If a light is red (01–50), determine the length of wait the motorist has before the light turns green using two-digit numbers from Table 13-1, column 8. For each light, indicate its condition. For red lights, indicate the amount of waiting time.
d. Based on the results of part c, compute an estimate of the average amount of time per trip the motorist waits at red lights.

24. The motorist in the preceding problem wonders if an alternate route would result in a shorter waiting time. The alternate route has only two stoplights with the same two-minute cycle previously described. It also has two stop signs. The number of cars waiting at each stoplight can be described by a Poisson distribution with a mean of 2.0. The wait at a stop sign is approximately 30 seconds, if no cars are waiting. For each car that is waiting, an additional 30 seconds is added to the waiting time of the motorist.
a. Simulate four trips on the alternate route. For each light, read a two-digit number from Table 13-1, column 7. For light waiting time, read a two-digit number from column 10 of Table 13-1. For stop signs, read a three-digit number from Table 13-1, columns 5 and 6, to determine the number of cars waiting.
b. Compute the waiting time for each trip, then the average waiting time. How does this compare to the results of the preceding problem? Which route seems to offer the shorter waiting time? Is that necessarily the better route? Explain.

25. The owner of a firm that installs blacktop driveways wants to simulate weekly revenues. He notes that 70 percent of the jobs the firm receives are for residential work and the rest are for commercial work. The revenue for residential work tends to be uniformly distributed between $400 and $1000. The revenue for commercial work tends to be normally distributed with a mean of $1800 and a standard deviation of $500. The number of jobs per week can be modelled by a Poisson distribution with a mean of 2. Simulate total revenue for four weeks using random numbers as follows: For number of jobs per week, read a two-digit random number from Table 13-1, column 7; for type of work, read a two-digit number from Table 13-1, column 8; for residential income, read a two-digit number from row 4 of Table 13-1; and for commercial income, read a number from row 3 of Table 13-4. Indicate the total revenue from each type of work and the total combined weekly revenue.

26. A service department in a manufacturing firm handles requests for service from a machine centre that has five machines. The service requests can be for cleaning/adjustment, minor repair, or major repair. Records indicate that 25 percent of the requests are for machine 1, 15 percent for machine 2, 30 percent for machine 3, 10 percent for machine 4, and 20 percent for machine 5. The nature of the requests is summarized in the following table:

	Machine				
Service	**1**	**2**	**3**	**4**	**5**
Cleaning/adjustment	.20	.30	.25	.40	.50
Minor repair	.45	.55	.35	.25	.28
Major repair	.35	.15	.40	.35	.22

Cleaning and adjustment time is uniformly distributed between 20 minutes and 40 minutes for all machines. Minor repair times are exponential with a mean of 30 minutes for all machines, and major repair times are normal with a mean of 5 hours and a standard deviation of 1 hour for all machines. Use random number tables in this way: two-digit numbers from Table 13-1, column 5 for machine, two-digit numbers from Table 13-1, column 7 for type of service, two-digit numbers from Table 13-1, column 8 for cleaning and adjustment or minor repair service times, and random numbers from Table 13-4, row 1, for major repair service time. Simulate five requests for service. For each request indicate (*a*) which machine, (*b*) what service is requested, and (*c*) the service time required. Read random numbers from the appropriate tables in order, and simulate each request completely before moving on to the next request. What is the average service time for cleaning/ adjustment? Minor repairs? Major repairs?

27. The manager of a building supply company has constructed a model that portrays monthly demand for exterior plywood. The model is

$$\text{Total Demand for } 4 \times 8 \text{ sheets} = 2000 + 20t + e$$

where

e = forecast error
t = period number

The manager is reasonably comfortable with a forecast error that is normally distributed with a mean of zero and a standard deviation of 100. Using values from Table 13-4, column 5, simulate demand for periods 10 through 15. What is the average simulated demand?

28. The owner of a fruit farm sells peaches at two roadside stands. Based on past experience and the aid of a retired professor, the owner has developed two models that portray weekly revenue generated by each of the two locations. The models are

Hillside location	$4500 + 80t - 10t^2 + e$
Farmdale location	$3000 + 90t - 10t^2 + e$

For the Hillside location, e is normally distributed with a mean of zero and a standard deviation of 100; for the Farmdale location, e is uniformly distributed with endpoints of −50 and +50. Simulate the revenue generated at each location for weeks $t = 2$ through $t = 9$. For the Hillside simulation, use values from Table 13-4, column 2, reading down. For the Farmdale location, read two-digit numbers from Table 13-1, column 4, reading up from the bottom. What is the average simulated demand for the Hillside location? What is the mean simulated demand for the Farmdale location?

29. John Stewart designs video games for a toy manufacturer. He has recently been working on a video pinball game and has established a set of probabilities for the movements of the "ball" during a game. The player receives points depending on the positions the ball strikes during a game. These are shown below, along with probabilities for ball paths. Simulate the paths for three balls, and determine the number of points received for each ball. Use row 1 of Table 13-1 for ball 1, row 9 for ball 2, and row 3 for ball 3. Read from left to right.

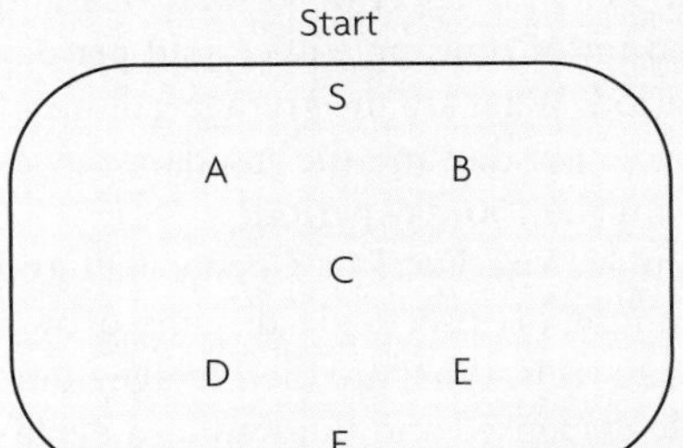

Start

S

A B

C

D E

F

Position	Points
A	500
B	400
C	300
D	200
E	100
F	50

Path	Probability	Path	Probability
S to A	.30	C to A	.10
B	.30	B	.15
C	.25	C	.20
D	.10	D	.10
E	.04	E	.30
F	.01	F	.15

Path	Probability	Path	Probability
A to A	.25	D to A	.10
B	.25	B	.05
C	.25	C	.25
D	.10	D	.15
E	.10	E	.30
F	.05	F	.15
B to A	.30	E to A	.05
B	.20	B	.10
C	.20	C	.15
D	.15	D	.15
E	.10	E	.20
F	.05	F	.35

What are the total simulated points of ball 1, ball 2, and ball 3?

30. A distributor supplies pool chemicals to three firms that handle swimming pool maintenance. The distributor maintains an inventory of sodium bisulfate for the three firms. The distributor wants to limit the amount of supplies on hand due to storage problems. Nevertheless, the distributor would like to have a probability of at least 90 percent of not running out of stock during the week. Stocks are replenished every Monday and then picked up during the week by the three firms as needed. The chemicals are sold in multiples of five bags. Historical demand distributions for these firms are

	Relative Frequency		
Weekly Demand	Firm A	Firm B	Firm C
5	.10	.15	.20
10	.20	.25	.30
15	.20	.30	.25
20	.20	.20	.20
25	.30	.10	.05

Simulate demand for 10 weeks. Use row 1 of Table 13-1 for firm A, row 2 for firm B, and row 3 for firm C. Based on your results, how many bags of sodium bisulfate should the distributor plan to have on hand at the beginning of each week to have a probability of 90 percent of satisfying weekly demand? Explain how you arrived at your answer.

31. Jobs are delivered to a workstation at random intervals. The time between job arrivals tends to be normally distributed with a mean of 15 minutes and a standard deviation of 1 minute. Job processing time is also normally distributed with a mean of 14 minutes per job and a standard deviation of 2 minutes.

a. Using Table 13-4, simulate the arrival and processing of five jobs. Use column 4 of the table for job arrival times and column 3 for processing times. *Start each column at row 4.* Find the total times jobs wait for processing.

b. The company is considering the use of new equipment that would result in processing time that is normal with a mean of 13 minutes and a standard deviation of 1 minute. Job waiting represents a cost of $3 per minute, and the new equipment would represent an additional cost of $0.50 per minute. Would the equipment be cost justified? (*Note:* Use the same arrival times and the same random numbers for processing times.

32. Customers arrive randomly at a catalogue department of a large store. The time between arrivals varies uniformly between 10 and 20 minutes. Service time is normal with a mean of 15 minutes and a standard deviation of 2 minutes.

a. Simulate processing and waiting times for nine customers. Read three-digit numbers going down columns 9 and 10 of Table 13-1 for arrivals (e.g., 156, 884, 576). Use column 8, Table 13-4 for processing time. What are the total waiting time and the average service time?

b. If management can reduce the range of arrival times to between 13 and 17 minutes, what would the impact be on customer waiting times? (Use the same service times and the same random numbers for arrival times from part *a.*) Round arrival times to two decimal places. What is the total waiting time?

33. Suppose a manager is concerned about complaints from customers about being out of stock on a certain item. The current policy is to reorder the item when there are four units in stock.

The manager has determined that the time it takes to receive an order (lead time) is from one to three days, with frequencies as shown in the following table:

Lead Time (days)	Relative Frequency
1	.33
2	.45
3	.22

The manager also has determined that daily demand can be modelled using a Poisson distribution that has a mean of 1.9 units per day.

Simulate 10 order cycles (i.e., simulate the number of days needed to receive an order, and the demand for each day during that time, for each cycle). Use random numbers from Table 13-1: For lead times, read two-digit numbers from column 6; for daily demands, read three-digit numbers, starting with the second number of column 2 and both numbers of column 3 (e.g., 084, 905, 780, etc.) and then the first two numbers of columns 4 and the first number of column 5 (e.g., 299, 642, 350, etc.). Then answer these questions:

a. Assuming there were four units on hand at order time, what percentage of cycles would demand have exceeded stock on hand?

b. If the manager wants to reduce the stockout percentage to 10 percent, based on this (limited) simulation, how many items should be in stock when new stock is ordered?

34. Refer to Problem 2. Use Excel or Crystal Ball and simulate the number of cake orders for 360 days. What is the average number of cakes for this problem? What is the difference in the averages between Problem 2 and this problem?

35. Refer to Problem 3. Use Excel or Crystal Ball and simulate the number of TV sets sold per day for a 150-day period. What are the average sales and the standard deviation of the sales for the 150-day period?

36. Refer to Problem 4. Use Excel or Crystal Ball and simulate the number of errors per page for a 180-page book. What is the total number of errors in the book? What is the average number of errors in the book?

37. Refer to Problem 8. Use Excel or Crystal Ball and simulate the number of canoes sold per day for a 150-day period. What are the average number of canoes sold and the standard deviation of the sales for the 150-day period?

38. Refer to Problem 11. Use Excel or Crystal Ball and simulate the amount of pineapple juice sold per day for a 150-day period. What are the average gallons of pineapple juice sold per day and the standard deviation of the sales for the 150-day period?

39. Refer to Problem 12. Use Excel or Crystal Ball and simulate the amount of insecticide dispensed by a crop duster for 120 runs. What are the average number of insecticide dispensed and the standard deviation of the insecticide dispensed for 120 runs?

40. Refer to Problem 15. Use Excel or Crystal Ball and simulate repair times for 130 jobs. What are the average repair time and the standard deviation of repair times?

41. Refer to Problem 16. Use Excel or Crystal Ball and simulate the length of telephone calls for 150 telephone calls. What is the average length of time of a phone call?

42. Refer to Problem 17. Use Excel or Crystal Ball and simulate the amount of time a doctor spends with patients recovering from major surgery based on 140 surgeries. Based on the simulated results of the 140 surgeries, what is the average time a doctor spends with a patient recovering from a major surgery?
43. Refer to Problem 18. If there were 120 letters to type, use Excel or Crystal Ball and simulate the amount of time it takes to type the letters. What is the total estimated typing time for the 120 letters?
44. Refer to Problem 19. Assume that a hospital performs 100 surgeries per day and use Excel or Crystal Ball to simulate the amount of time it takes to perform 100 surgeries. What is the total estimated time to perform 100 surgeries?
45. Refer to Problem 20. The company wants to simulate the breakdown of the next 100 pieces of equipment. Based on the simulated results of the breakdown of the next 100 pieces of equipment, calculate the time between breakdowns. Assuming there is one repairperson, calculate the average waiting time for repairs and the average time needed for repairs.
46. Repeat the simulation conducted in Problem 31, parts *a* and *b*, for 120 jobs.
47. Refer to Problem 32, part *a*. Simulate the arrival, processing, and waiting times for 120 customers. What is the total waiting time? What is the average processing time?
48. Refer to Problem 32, part *b*. Simulate the arrival, processing, and waiting times for 120 customers. What is the total waiting time? What is the average processing time?
49. The manager of a bank is concerned about the waiting lines forming in front of the two tellers. The bank consists of a single-line system with two servers. Based on historical data, the empirical distributions on time between arrivals and time to serve the bank customers have been observed as shown in Table 13-7. Assume that the second teller serves as a backup teller. In other words, the customers are always assigned to the first teller unless he or she is occupied with another customer. The second teller has other responsibilities; however, if the teller is needed by a customer, he or she will stop and assist the customer.
    a. Simulate the arrival and service of 11 customers. Calculate the average waiting time for the customers, average idle time for the tellers, and average time a customer spends in the bank. Use random numbers from column 3 of Table 13-1 for arrivals (e.g., 84, 05, 80, etc.) and from column 4 of Table 13-1 for service (e.g., 29, 64, 35, etc.).
    b. Use Excel or Crystal Ball and simulate the arrival and service of 100 customers. Calculate the average waiting time and average time a customer spends in the bank.

Table 13-7 Data for Problem 49

Time Between Arrivals (minutes)	Probability of Arrivals	Service Time (minutes)	Probability of Service Time
.50	.30	.5	.25
1.0	.20	1.0	.20
1.5	.15	2.0	.25
2.0	.13	3.0	.15
3.0	.14	4.0	.10
4.0	.08	5.0	.05

Case 1: Krohler Supermarkets

The management of Krohler Supermarkets, a national chain, has become aware of decreasing profit margins from its stores during the previous year. Three factors contributed to this earnings decline: (1) rapidly increasing labour costs, (2) increasing costs of wholesale merchandise and inability to increase retail prices because of governmental controls and consumer resistance, and (3) increasing price competition from their major national competitors. Even though earnings have declined significantly, sales volume has been increasing from year to year, but at a lower rate in the immediate past year than in previous years.

Merchandise typically accounted for the largest proportion of a store's operating costs (roughly 80 percent), with the inventory control and stocking functions being critical to this aspect of managing operations. Inventory was ordered each week from a central warehouse by means of a fixed-interval system. Stocking consisted primarily of placing the commodities on display, pricing each item, controlling pilferage, and removing damaged goods.

Labour costs were the second largest factor in supermarket operations (roughly 10 percent). More than 40 percent of the store's wages went to people manning the "front end," which include cashiers and baggers. About 33 percent of the wages went to the stockers, and the balance went to people in the meat, produce, bakery, or deli departments or to the store supervisors. Krohler management personnel felt that a prime area in which to reduce overall operating costs would be the labour requirements, but they were unwilling to reduce their service level to the consumer because of the negative effect it would have on their competitive stance in the supermarket industry.

Krohler's small industrial engineering department had recommended to the management that an investigation be made of the potential savings associated with implementing automatic point-of-sale (APOS) systems at the checkout counters. These APOS systems combined electronic cash registers and optical scanning devices that interact with an in-store minicomputer, and they could substantially boost labour productivity and provide greater control over inventory levels and ordering requirements. Since almost every commodity Krohler carried was labelled with a unique manufacturing code (called the Universal Product Code), the system functioned by having a checker pull an item across the optical scanner so the code could be read. The price of the item would be obtained immediately from the mini-computer's memory, displayed on the register, and tallied into the customer's bill. At the same time, the computer would compute any applicable sales tax and note the sale of all items in its inventory control program for later summarization of daily stock levels and order requirements. If a particular item did not have the code attached to it (for example, a bag of apples, deli specialties, or nonuniform packages of meats), the cashier would enter the price and an item code manually into the register. In addition to the time savings anticipated in checking out individual customers, the industrial engineering department pointed out that a significant amount of time would be saved in closing out a register (counting the cash and reconciling opening and closing balances with the intervening sales) and also in not having to price each item on the shelves.

With the existing manual system in place, the basic functions of front-end personnel, including cashiers and baggers, were (1) enter the merchandise cost into the register, (2) enter applicable sales taxes, (3) total the cost of purchases and taxes, (4) receive payment (cash, cheque, food stamps, discount coupons, etc.) and make change, (5) bag the items purchased, and (6) assist a customer in removing the bag(s) from the store. Miscellaneous tasks also included cheque cashing, looking up prices on unmarked items, weighing and pricing produce, and responding to any customer questions.

In a typical Krohler Supermarket, there would be 10 checkout counters placed in a row at the store front, with one designated as an "express" lane to serve customers with 10 items or less. However, because sales fluctuated greatly by day and by hour, management tried very hard to match the number of counters open with expected demand so that both a high level of customer service and a high level of checkout-counter productivity would be maintained. Customer-service level was defined as the percentage of time that more than a certain number of customers were either being served or waiting in line to be checked out. A general rule of thumb used by Krohler management was that the percentage of time that more than three customers waited in line (including the person being served) should be held to 5 percent or less. Checkout-counter productivity was measured on the basis of sales dollars per manned checkout-counter hour.

As one means of examining the possible savings associated with an APOS system versus the existing manual system, Krohler's industrial engineering department was given the task of simulating the store operations with two systems. Assume you are part of the study team and develop responses to the following questions:

1. What specific questions should a simulation of the two different systems address?
2. What data must be collected before a simulation could be performed?

Discussion Question

Given your responses to the above questions, develop a flowchart of a simulation model that could be used to study the operation of an APOS system at a typical Krohler Supermarket.

Source: James A. Fitzsimmons and Robert S. Sullivan, *Service Operations Management* (New York: McGraw-Hill, 1982).

Case 2: CerebroTech Inc.

CerebroTech Inc. manufacturers and distributes a line of metal pads that wirelessly recharges mobile phones, BlackBerries, iPods, and other electronic devices laid on top of them, thereby eliminating the annoyance of charger cables. The company is seeking to establish the budgeted cash flow for the next four quarters. The budgeted sales in units for the next four quarters are normally distributed with a mean of 12 000 units and a standard deviation of 2500 units for quarters 1 and 3; a mean of 16 000 units and a standard deviation of 4500 for quarters 2 and 4. Sales are collected as follows: 40 percent of sales in the quarter that are made, but this figure has been as low as 30 percent and as high as 52 percent, according to a triangular distribution. The remainder of the sales are collected in the following quarter, but carry 2.5 percent interest. The company incurs a per-unit variable cost ranging between $30 and $45, according to a uniform distribution. This cost includes direct material and labour costs, variable manufacturing overhead costs, and variable selling and administrative costs. In addition, the company incurs a monthly fixed cost of $62 000 (including salaries, advertising, utilities, depreciation, rent, insurance, and general administrative expenses), a tax installment of $40 000 in quarter 2, and a capital expenditure of $45 000 in quarter 4. The cash balance available at the beginning of quarter 1 is $65 000, and the company's policy is to maintain a minimum balance of $50 000 all times. Therefore, if required, the company will take out a short-term loan to ensure that the minimum balance is achieved, but it must be fully paid back with interest in the following quarter. The loan interest rate has been set to prime + 2 percent. Any cash balance available at the end of each quarter is carried forward to the following quarter and yields savings interest, which has been set to prime − 2 percent. The prime interest rate at the beginning of the first quarter is 4 percent but for each of the next quarters, the company has estimated that there is 60 percent probability that it will be unchanged, 25 percent probability that it will increase by $^1/_4$ percent, and 15 percent probability that it will decrease by $^1/_4$ percent. The interests on loans and saving are paid at the end of each quarter. The unit selling price of the product is $62. There are no sales remaining to be collected at the beginning of quarter 1.

Management Report

Develop a simulation model that shows the company cash balance at the end of each quarter. Run 1000 trials and perform the appropriate analysis to provide managers practical insights to the following questions:

1. What is the probability that the cash balance will exceed the minimum requirement, that is, that no loan is required?
2. What is the probability that the company will have to borrow more than $75 000 during the year?
3. What is the size (minimum, maximum, and average) of short-term loan that might be needed during the entire year as well as each quarter? What is the range in which the true size of the yearly short-term loan will fall in at 95 percent of confidence level?
4. What is the amount of credit line the company would need to secure during the entire year?

Appendix

Tables

TABLE A Areas Under the Normal Curve, 0 to z

z	.00	.01	.02	.03	.04	.05	.06	.07	.08	.09
0.0	.0000	.0040	.0080	.0120	.0160	.0199	.0239	.0279	.0319	.0359
0.1	.0398	.0438	.0478	.0517	.0557	.0596	.0636	.0675	.0714	.0753
0.2	.0793	.0832	.0871	.0910	.0948	.0987	.1026	.1064	.1103	.1141
0.3	.1179	.1217	.1255	.1293	.1331	.1388	.1406	.1443	.1480	.1517
0.4	.1554	.1591	.1828	.1664	.1700	.1736	.1772	.1808	.1844	.1879
0.5	.1915	.1950	.1985	.2019	.2054	.2088	.2123	.2157	.2190	.2224
0.6	.2257	.2291	.2324	.2357	.2389	.2422	.2454	.2486	.2517	.2549
0.7	.2580	.2611	.2642	.2673	.2703	.2734	.2784	.2794	.2823	.2852
0.8	.2881	.2910	.2939	.2967	.2995	.3023	.3051	.3078	.3106	.3133
0.9	.3159	.3186	.3212	.3238	.3264	.3289	.3315	.3340	.3365	.3389
1.0	.3413	.3438	.3461	.3485	.3508	.3531	.3554	.3577	.3599	.3621
1.1	.3643	.3665	.3686	.3708	.3729	.3749	.3770	.3790	.3810	.3830
1.2	.3849	.3869	.3888	.3907	.3925	.3944	.3962	.3980	.3997	.4015
1.3	.4032	.4049	.4066	.4082	.4099	.4115	.4131	.4147	.4162	.4177
1.4	.4192	.4207	.4222	.4236	.4251	.4265	.4279	.4292	.4306	.4319
1.5	.4332	.4345	.4357	.4370	.4382	.4394	.4405	.4418	.4429	.4441
1.6	.4452	.4463	.4474	.4484	.4495	.4505	.4515	.4525	.4535	.4545
1.7	.4554	.4564	.4573	.4582	.4591	.4599	.4608	.4516	.4625	.4633
1.8	.4641	.4649	.4656	.4664	.4671	.4678	.4686	.4693	.4699	.4706
1.9	.4713	.4719	.4726	.4732	.4738	.4744	.4750	.4756	.4761	.4767

(continued)

z	.00	.01	.02	.03	.04	.05	.06	.07	.08	.09
2.0	.4772	.4778	.4783	.4788	.4793	.4798	.4803	.4808	.4812	.4817
2.1	.4821	.4826	.4830	.4834	.4838	.4842	.4846	.4850	.4854	.4857
2.2	.4861	.4864	.4868	.4871	.4875	.4878	.4881	.4884	.4887	.4890
2.3	.4893	.4896	.4898	.4901	.4904	.4906	.4909	.4911	.4913	.4916
2.4	.4918	.4920	.4922	.4925	.4927	.4929	.4931	.4932	.4934	.4936
2.5	.4938	.4940	.4941	.4943	.4945	.4946	.4948	.4949	.4951	.4952
2.6	.4953	.4955	.4956	.4957	.4959	.4960	.4961	.4962	.4963	.4964
2.7	.4965	.4966	.4967	.4968	.4969	.4970	.4971	.4972	.4973	.4974
2.8	.4974	.4975	.4976	.4977	.4977	.4978	.4979	.4979	.4980	.4981
2.9	.4981	.4982	.4982	.4983	.4984	.4984	.4985	.4985	.4986	.4986
3.0	.4987	.4987	.4987	.4988	.4988	.4989	.4989	.4989	.4990	.4990

TABLE B Cumulative Poisson Probabilities

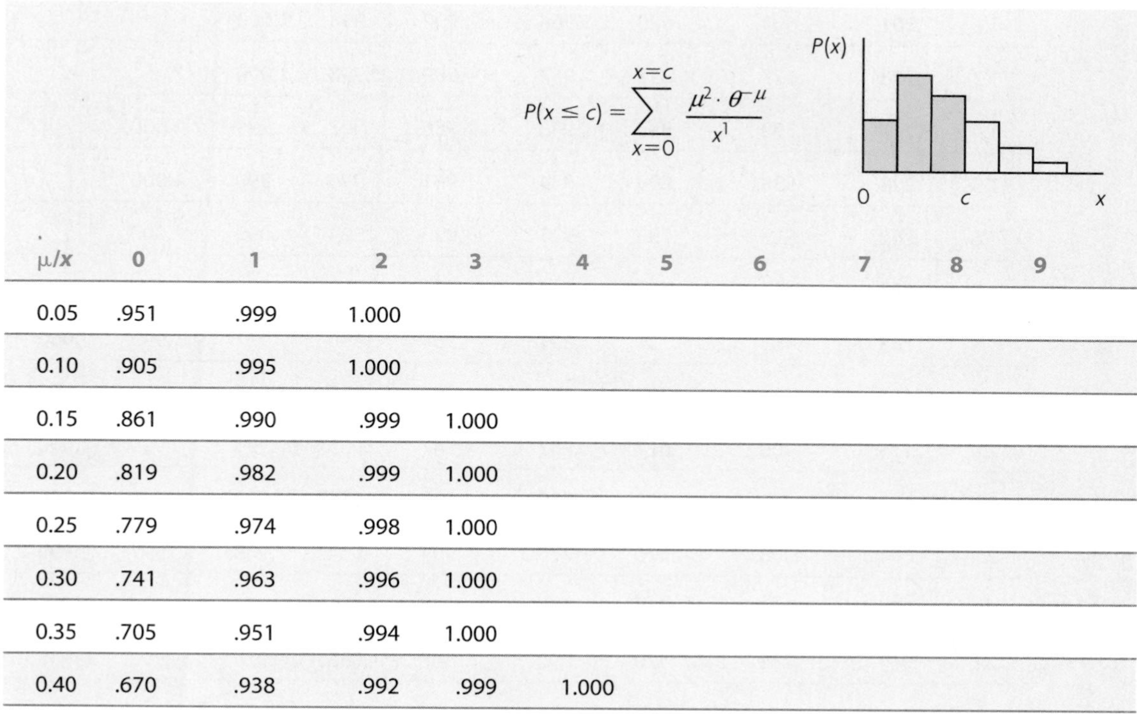

$$P(x \le c) = \sum_{x=0}^{x=c} \frac{\mu^2 \cdot \theta^{-\mu}}{x^1}$$

μ/x	0	1	2	3	4	5	6	7	8	9
0.05	.951	.999	1.000							
0.10	.905	.995	1.000							
0.15	.861	.990	.999	1.000						
0.20	.819	.982	.999	1.000						
0.25	.779	.974	.998	1.000						
0.30	.741	.963	.996	1.000						
0.35	.705	.951	.994	1.000						
0.40	.670	.938	.992	.999	1.000					

TABLE B Cumulative Poisson Probabilities (*continued*)

μ/x	0	1	2	3	4	5	6	7	8	9
0.45	.638	.925	.989	.999	1.000					
0.50	.607	.910	.986	.998	1.000					
0.55	.577	.894	.982	.998	1.000					
0.60	.549	.878	.977	.997	1.000					
0.65	.522	.861	.972	.996	.999	1.000				
0.70	.497	.844	.966	.994	.999	1.000				
0.75	.472	.827	.960	.993	.999	1.000				
0.80	.449	.809	.953	.991	.999	1.000				
0.85	.427	.791	.945	.989	.998	1.000				
0.90	.407	.772	.937	.987	.998	1.000				
0.95	.387	.754	.929	.984	.997	1.000				
1.0	.368	.736	.920	.981	.996	.999	1.000			
1.1	.333	.699	.900	.974	.995	.999	1.000			
1.2	.301	.663	.880	.966	.992	.998	1.000			
1.3	.273	.627	.857	.957	.989	.998	1.000			
1.4	.247	.592	.833	.946	.986	.997	.999	1.000		
1.5	.223	.558	.809	.934	.981	.996	.999	1.000		
1.6	.202	.525	.783	.921	.976	.994	.999	1.000		
1.7	.183	.493	.757	.907	.970	.992	.998	1.000		
1.8	.165	.463	.731	.891	.964	.990	.997	.999	1.000	
1.9	.150	.434	.704	.875	.956	.987	.997	.999	1.000	
2.0	.135	.406	.677	.857	.947	.983	.995	.999	1.000	
2.2	.111	.355	.623	.819	.928	.975	.993	.998	1.000	
2.4	.091	.308	.570	.779	.904	.964	.988	.997	.999	1.000
2.6	.074	.267	.518	.736	.877	.951	.983	.995	.999	1.000
2.8	.061	.231	.470	.692	.848	.935	.976	.992	.998	.999

TABLE B Cumulative Poisson Probabilities (*continued*)

μ/x	0	1	2	3	4	5	6	7	8	9	10	11	12	13	14	15	16	17	18	19	20
3.0	.050	.199	.423	.647	.815	.916	.966	.988	.996	.999	1.000										
3.2	.041	.171	.380	.603	.781	.895	.955	.983	.994	.998	1.000										
3.4	.033	.147	.340	.558	.744	.871	.942	.977	.992	.997	.999	1.000									
3.6	.027	.126	.303	.515	.706	.844	.927	.969	.988	.996	.999	1.000									
3.8	.022	.107	.269	.474	.668	.816	.909	.960	.984	.994	.998	.999	1.000								
4.0	.018	.092	.238	.433	.629	.785	.889	.949	.979	.992	.997	.999	1.000								
4.2	.015	.078	.210	.395	.590	.753	.868	.936	.972	.989	.996	.999	1.000								
4.4	.012	.066	.185	.359	.551	.720	.844	.921	.964	.985	.994	.998	.999	1.000							
4.6	.010	.056	.163	.326	.513	.686	.818	.905	.955	.980	.992	.997	.999	1.000							
4.8	.008	.048	.143	.294	.476	.651	.791	.887	.944	.975	.990	.996	.999	1.000							
5.0	.007	.040	.125	.265	.441	.616	.762	.867	.932	.968	.986	.995	.998	.999	1.000						
5.2	.006	.034	.109	.238	.406	.581	.732	.845	.918	.960	.982	.993	.997	.999	1.000						
5.4	.005	.029	.095	.213	.373	.546	.702	.822	.903	.951	.978	.990	.996	.999	1.000						
5.6	.004	.024	.082	.191	.342	.512	.670	.797	.886	.941	.972	.988	.995	.998	.999	1.000					
5.8	.003	.021	.072	.170	.313	.478	.638	.771	.867	.929	.965	.984	.993	.997	.999	1.000					

TABLE B Cumulative Poisson Probabilities (*continued*)

μ/x	0	1	2	3	4	5	6	7	8	9	10	11	12	13	14	15	16	17	18	19	20
6.0	.003	.017	.062	.151	.285	.446	.606	.744	.847	.916	.957	.980	.991	.996	.999	.999	1.000				
6.2	.002	.015	.054	.134	.259	.414	.574	.716	.826	.902	.949	.975	.989	.995	.998	.999	1.000				
6.4	.002	.012	.046	.119	.235	.384	.542	.687	.803	.886	.939	.969	.986	.994	.997	.999	1.000				
6.6	.001	.010	.040	.105	.213	.355	.511	.658	.780	.869	.927	.963	.982	.992	.997	.999	.999	1.000			
6.8	.001	.007	.030	.082	.173	.301	.450	.599	.729	.830	.915	.955	.978	.990	.996	.998	.999	1.000			
7.0	.001	.007	.030	.082	.173	.301	.450	.599	.729	.830	.901	.947	.973	.987	.994	.998	.999	1.000			
7.2	.001	.006	.025	.072	.156	.276	.420	.569	.703	.810	.887	.937	.967	.984	.993	.997	.999	.999	1.000		
7.4	.001	.005	.022	.063	.140	.253	.392	.539	.676	.788	.871	.926	.961	.980	.991	.996	.998	.999	1.000		
7.6	.001	.004	.019	.055	.125	.231	.365	.510	.648	.765	.854	.915	.954	.976	.989	.995	.998	.999	1.000		
7.8	.000	.004	.016	.048	.112	.210	.338	.481	.620	.741	.835	.902	.945	.971	.986	.993	.997	.999	1.000		
8.0	.000	.003	.014	.042	.100	.191	.313	.453	.593	.717	.816	.888	.936	.966	.983	.992	.996	.998	.999	1.000	
8.2	.000	.003	.012	.037	.089	.174	.290	.425	.566	.692	.796	.873	.926	.960	.979	.990	.995	.998	.999	1.000	
8.4	.000	.002	.010	.032	.079	.157	.267	.400	.537	.666	.774	.857	.915	.952	.975	.987	.994	.997	.999	1.000	
8.6	.000	.002	.009	.030	.074	.150	.256	.386	.523	.653	.763	.849	.909	.949	.973	.986	.993	.997	.999	1.000	
8.8	.000	.002	.007	.024	.062	.128	.226	.348	.482	.614	.729	.822	.889	.935	.964	.981	.990	.995	.998	.999	1.000
9.0	.000	.001	.006	.021	.055	.116	.207	.324	.456	.587	.706	.803	.876	.926	.959	.978	.989	.995	.998	.999	1.000
9.5	.000	.001	.004	.015	.040	.089	.165	.269	.392	.522	.645	.752	.836	.898	.940	.967	.982	.991	.996	.998	.999

TABLE C Infinite Source Values P_0 Given λ/μ and s

λ/μ	s	P_0
.15	1	.850
	2	.860
.20	1	.800
	2	.818
.25	1	.750
	2	.778
.30	1	.700
	2	.739
.35	1	.650
	2	.702
.40	1	.600
	2	.667
.45	1	.550
	2	.633
	3	.637
.50	1	.500
	2	.600
	3	.606
.55	1	.450
	2	.569
	3	.576
.60	1	.400
	2	.538
	3	.548
.65	1	.350
	2	.509
	3	.521
.70	1	.300
	2	.481
	3	.495
.75	1	.250
	2	.455
	3	.471
.80	1	
	2	.429
	3	.447
.85	1	.150
	2	.404
	3	.425
	4	.427
.90	1	.100
	2	.379
	3	.403
	4	.406
.95	1	.050
	2	.356
	3	.383
	4	.386
1.0	2	.333
	3	.364
	4	.367
1.1	2	.290
	3	.327
	4	.367
1.2	2	.250
	3	.294
	4	.300
	5	.301
1.3	2	.212
	3	.264
	4	.271
	5	.272
1.4	2	.176
	3	.236
	4	.245
	5	.246
1.5	2	.143
	3	.211
	4	.221
	5	.223
1.6	2	.111
	3	.187
	4	.199
	5	.201
1.7	2	.081
	3	.156
	4	.180
	5	.182
1.8	2	.053
	3	.146
	4	.162
	5	.165
1.9	2	.026
	3	.128
	4	.145
	5	.149
	6	.149
2.0	3	.111
	4	.130
	5	.134
	6	.135
2.1	3	.096
	4	.117
	5	.121
	6	.122
2.2	3	.081
	4	.105
	5	.109
	6	.111
2.3	3	.068
	4	.093
	5	.099
	6	.100
2.4	3	.056
	4	.083
	5	.089
	6	.090
	7	.091

(continued)

TABLE C Infinite Source Values P_0 Given λ/μ and s (*continued*)

λ/μ	s	P_0
2.5	3	.045
	4	.074
	5	.080
	6	.082
	7	.082
2.6	3	.035
	4	.065
	5	.072
	6	.074
	7	.074
2.7	3	.025
	4	.057
	5	.065
	6	.067
	7	.067
2.8	3	.016
	4	.050
	5	.058
	6	.060
	7	.061
2.9	3	.008
	4	.044
	5	.052
	6	.054
	7	.055
3.0	4	.038
	5	.047
	6	.049
	7	.050
	8	.050
3.1	4	.032
	5	.042
	6	.044
	7	.045
	8	.045

λ/μ	s	P_0
3.2	4	.027
	5	.037
	6	.040
	7	.040
	8	.041
3.3	4	.023
	5	.033
	6	.036
	7	.037
	8	.037
3.4	4	.019
	5	.029
	6	.032
	7	.033
	8	.033
3.5	4	.015
	5	.026
	6	.029
	7	.030
	8	.030
	9	.030
3.6	4	.011
	5	.023
	6	.026
	7	.027
	8	.027
	9	.027
3.7	4	.008
	5	.020
	6	.023
	7	.024
	8	.025
	9	.025
3.8	4	.005
	5	.017

λ/μ	s	P_0
	6	.021
	7	.022
	8	.022
	9	.022
3.9	4	.002
	5	.015
	6	.019
	7	.020
	8	.020
	9	.020
4.0	5	.013
	6	.017
	7	.018
	8	.018
	9	.018
4.1	5	.011
	6	.015
	7	.016
	8	.016
	9	.017
4.2	5	.009
	6	.013
	7	.014
	8	.015
	9	.015
	10	.015
4.3	5	.008
	6	.012
	7	.130
	8	.013
	9	.014
	10	.014
4.4	5	.006
	6	.010
	7	.012

TABLE C Infinite Source Values P_0 Given λ/μ and s (*continued*)

λ/μ	s	P_0
	8	.012
	9	.012
	10	.012
4.5	5	.005
	6	.009
	7	.010
	8	.011
	9	.011
	10	.011
4.6	5	.004
	6	.008
	7	.009
	8	.010
	9	.010
	10	.010
4.7	5	.003
	6	.007
	7	.008
	8	.008
	9	.009
	10	.009
4.8	5	.002
	6	.006
	7	.008
	8	.008
	9	.008
	10	.008
4.9	5	.001
	6	.005
	7	.007
	8	.007
	9	.007
	10	.007
	11	.077
5.0	6	.005
	7	.006

λ/μ	s	P_0
	8	.006
	9	.007
	10	.007
	11	.007
5.1	6	.004
	7	.005
	8	.006
	9	.006
	10	.006
	11	.006
5.2	6	.003
	7	.005
	8	.005
	9	.005
	10	.005
	11	.006
5.3	6	.003
	7	.004
	8	.005
	9	.005
	10	.005
	11	.005
	12	.005
5.4	6	.002
	7	.004
	8	.004
	9	.004
	10	.004
	11	.005
	12	.005
5.5	6	.002
	7	.003
	8	.004
	9	.004
	10	.004

λ/μ	s	P_0
	11	.004
	12	.004
5.6	6	.001
	7	.003
	8	.003
	9	.004
	10	.004
	11	.004
	12	.004
5.7	6	.001
	7	.002
	8	.003
	9	.003
	10	.003
	11	.003
	12	.003
5.8	6	.001
	7	.002
	8	.003
	9	.003
	10	.003
	11	.003
	12	.003
5.9	6	.000
	7	.002
	8	.002
	9	.003
	10	.003
	11	.003
	12	.003
6.0	7	.001
	8	.002
	9	.002

(*continued*)

TABLE C Infinite Source Values P_0 Given λ/μ and s (*continued*)

λ/μ	s	P_0
	10	.002
	11	.002
	12	.002
6.1	7	.001
	8	.002
	9	.002
	10	.002
	11	.002
	12	.002
6.2	7	.001
	8	.002
	9	.002
	10	.002
	11	.002
	12	.002
6.3	7	.001
	8	.001
	9	.002
	10	.002
	11	.002
	12	.002
6.4	7	.001
	8	.001
	9	.002
	10	.002
	11	.002
	12	.002
6.5	7	.001
	8	.001
	9	.001
	10	.001
	11	.001
	12	.001
6.6	7	.000
	8	.001
	9	.001
	10	.001
	11	.001
	12	.001
6.7	7	.000
	8	.001
	9	.001
	10	.001
	11	.001
	12	.001
6.8	7	.000
	8	.001
	9	.001
	10	.001
	11	.001
	12	.001
6.9	7	.000
	8	.001
	9	.001
	10	.001
	11	.001
	12	.001
7.0	8	.001
	9	.001
	10	.001
	11	.001
	12	.001
7.1	8	.000
	9	.001
	10	.001
	11	.001
	12	.001
7.2	8	.000
	9	.001
	10	.001
	11	.001
	12	.001
7.3	8	.0003
	9	.0005
	10	.0006
	11	.0007
	12	.0007
7.4	8	.0003
	9	.0005
	10	.0006
	11	.0006
	12	.0006
7.5	8	.0002
	9	.0004
	10	.0005
	11	.0005
	12	.0005
7.6	8	.0002
	9	.0004
	10	.0004
	11	.0005
	12	.0005
7.7	8	.0001
	9	.0003
	10	.0004

TABLE C Infinite Source Values P_0 Given λ/μ and s (*continued*)

λ/μ	s	P_0	λ/μ	s	P_0	λ/μ	s	P_0
	11	.0004	8.0	9	.00020	8.3	9	.00011
	12	.0004		10	.00028		10	.00019
				11	.00031		11	.00022
7.8	8	.0001		12	.00033		12	.00024
	9	.0002						
	10	.0004	8.1	9	.00017	8.4	9	.00009
	11	.0004		10	.00025		10	.00017
	12	.0004		11	.00028		11	.00020
7.9	8	.00003		12	.00029		12	.00021
	9	.00023	8.2	9	.00014	8.5	9	.00007
	10	.00031		10	.00022		10	.00015
	11	.00035		11	.00025		11	.00018
	12	.00036		12	.00026		12	.00019

Index

B

C

E

F

M

P

T

U

V

W